STRATEGIC MANAGEMENT

Competitiveness & Globalization

Concepts and Cases

13e

Michael A. Hitt
Texas A&M University
and
Texas Christian University

R. Duane Ireland
Texas A&M University

Robert E. Hoskisson
Rice University

Australia • Brazil • Mexico • Singapore • United Kingdom • United States

***Strategic Management: Competitiveness & Globalization: Concepts and Cases,* 13th Edition**

Michael A. Hitt, R. Duane Ireland, and Robert E. Hoskisson

Senior Vice President, Higher Ed Product, Content, and Market Development: Erin Joyner

Product Director: Bryan Gambrel

Senior Product Manager: Michael Giffen

Content Manager: Amanda White

Product Assistant: Nick Perez

Marketing Manager: Audrey Wyrick

Marketing Coordinator: Rachel Treinen

Production Service: MPS Limited

Senior Art Director: Bethany Bourgeois

Text Designer: Tippy McIntosh

Cover Designer: Bethany Bourgeois

Cover Image: iStock.com/DNY59

Strategic Focus: © RomanOkopny/Getty Images

Watercolor Opener: © BerSonnE/Getty Images

Intellectual Property Analyst: Diane Garrity

Intellectual Property Project Manager: Betsy Hathaway

For product information and technology assistance, contact us at **Cengage Customer & Sales Support, 1-800-354-9706** or **support.cengage.com.**

For permission to use material from this text or product, submit all requests online at **www.cengage.com/permissions.**

Library of Congress Control Number: 2018959064

Soft Cover Edition ISBN: 978-0-357-03383-8
Loose-Leaf Edition ISBN: 978-1-337-91682-0

Cengage
200 Pier 4 Boulevard
Boston, MA 02210
USA

Cengage is a leading provider of customized learning solutions with employees residing in nearly 40 different countries and sales in more than 125 countries around the world. Find your local representative at **www.cengage.com.**

Cengage products are represented in Canada by Nelson Education, Ltd.

To learn more about Cengage platforms and services, register or access your online learning solution, or purchase materials for your course, visit **www.cengage.com.**

Printed at CLDPC, USA, 02-20

To Frankie:

You are my partner in life. I love you and look forward to our future together.

—**MICHAEL**

To Mary Ann:

We have reached that place we want to go and we will now walk in the sun. I love you.

—**DUANE**

To Kathy:

You are the best and my love for you is eternal. Thanks for all the support and love you've given me and our children throughout our life together.

—**ROBERT**

Brief Contents

Contents

6: Corporate-Level Strategy 176

7: Merger and Acquisition Strategies 208

Part 3: Strategic Actions: Strategy Implementation 310

10: Corporate Governance 310

13: Strategic Entrepreneurship 416

Part 4: Case Studies C-1

Preface

Our goal in writing each edition of this book is to present a new, up-to-date standard for explaining the strategic management process. To reach this goal with the 13th edition of our market-leading text, we again present you with an intellectually rich yet thoroughly practical analysis of strategic management.

With each new edition, we work hard to achieve the goal of maintaining our standard of presenting strategic management knowledge in a readable style. To prepare for each new edition, we carefully study the most recent academic research to ensure that the content about strategic management we present to you is up to date and accurate. In addition, we continuously read articles appearing in many different business publications (e.g., *Wall Street Journal*, *Bloomberg Businessweek*, *Fortune*, *Financial Times*, *Fast Company*, and *Forbes*, to name a few). We also study postings through social media (such as blogs) given their increasing use as channels of information distribution. By studying a wide array of sources, we are able to identify valuable examples of how companies across the world are using (or not using) the strategic management process. Though many of the hundreds of companies that we discuss in the book will be quite familiar, some will likely be new to you. One reason for this is that we use examples of companies from around the world to demonstrate the globalized nature of business operations. Some of these firms are quite large and known to many while others are small and known primarily to the customers they serve. To maximize your opportunities to learn as you read and think about how actual companies use strategic management tools, techniques, and concepts (based on the most current research), we emphasize a lively and user-friendly writing style. To facilitate learning, we use an Analysis–Strategy–Performance framework; we explain this framework in Chapter 1 and reference it throughout the book.

Several *characteristics* of this 13th edition of our book are designed to enhance your learning experience:

- First, we are pleased to note that this book presents you with the most comprehensive and thorough coverage of strategic management that is available in the market.
- We draw the research used in this book from the "classics" as well as the most recent contributions to the strategic management literature. The historically significant "classic" research provides the foundation for much of what we know about strategic management, while the most recent contributions reveal insights about how to use strategic management effectively in the complex, global business environment in which firms now compete. Our book also presents you with a large number of up-to-date examples of how firms use the strategic management tools, techniques, and concepts that prominent researchers and business practitioners have developed. Indeed, although the relevant theory and current research are the foundation for this book, it also is strongly application oriented and presents you, our readers, with a large number of examples and applications of strategic management concepts, techniques, and tools. In this edition, for example, we examine more than 600 companies to describe

the use of strategic management. Collectively, no other strategic management book presents you with the *combination* of useful and insightful *research* and *applications* in the variety of organizations as does this text.

Company examples you will find in this edition include large U.S.-based firms such as Apple, Amazon.com, McDonald's, FedEx, Starbucks, Walmart, Walt Disney, General Electric, Intel, American Express, Coca-Cola, Netflix, Google, Tesla, Target, UPS, Kellogg, 3M, DuPont, and Marriott. In addition, we examine firms based in countries other than the United States such as AXA, Airbus, Deutche Bank, LafargeHolcim, Sony, Softbank, Kering, Anbang Insurance, Teva, ChemChina, Bayer, Tokyo Electric Power Company, Nestlé, Mahindra, Air France-KLM, Toyota, Aldi, Honda, Ahold, Tata Consultancy, Alibaba, IKEA, Lenova, Volkswagen, and Samsung. As these lists suggest, the firms examined in this book compete in a wide range of industries and produce a diverse set of goods and services.

- We use the ideas of many prominent scholars (e.g., Ron Adner, Rajshree Agarwal, Ruth Aguilera, Gautam Ahuja, Raffi Amit, Africa Arino, Jay Barney, Paul Beamish, Peter Buckley, Alfred Chandler, Ming-Jer Chen, Russ Coff, Brian Connelly, Rich D'Aveni, Kathy Eisenhardt, Nicolas Foss, Gerry George, Javier Gimeno, Luis Gomez-Mejia, Melissa Graebner, Ranjay Gulati, Don Hambrick, Connie Helfat, Amy Hillman, Tomas Hult, Dave Ketchen, Ryan Krause, Dovev Lavie, Haiyang Li, Yadong Luo, Shige Makino, Costas Markides, Anita McGahan, Danny Miller, Will Mitchell, Margie Peteraf, Michael Porter, Nandini Rajagopalan, Jeff Reuer, Joan Ricart, Richard Rumelt, Wei Shi, David Sirmon, Ken Smith, Steve Tallman, David Teece, Rosalie Tung, Michael Tushman, Eero Vaara, Margarethe Wiersema, Oliver Williamson, Mike Wright, Anthea Zhang, Shaker Zahara, and Ed Zajac among others) to shape the discussion of *what* strategic management is. We describe the practices of prominent executives and practitioners (e.g., Thomas Buberl, Tim Cook, Brian Cornell, James Dyson, Steve Easterbrook, Reed Hastings, Jan Jenisch, Jack Ma, Elon Musk, James Park, Chuck Robbins, Howard Schultz, Hock Tan, Meg Whitman, and many others) to help us describe *how* strategic management is used in many types of organizations.

The authors of this book are also active scholars. We conduct research on a number of strategic management topics. Our interest in doing so is to contribute to the strategic management literature and to enhance our understanding of how to apply strategic management tools, techniques, and concepts effectively as a means of increasing organizational performance. Thus, we integrate our own research in the appropriate chapters along with the research of numerous other scholars, some of whom we list above.

In addition to our book's *characteristics*, there are some specific *features* and *revisions* that we have made in this 13th edition that we are pleased to highlight for you:

- **New Opening Cases and Strategic Focus Segments** We continue our tradition of providing virtually all-new Opening Cases and Strategic Focus segments! Almost all of these features are new to this edition; we updated completely the few remaining from the 12th edition because of their continuing relevance and importance. Many of these application-oriented features deal with companies located outside North America. In addition, all of the *company-specific examples* included in each chapter are either new or substantially updated. Through all of these venues, we present you with a wealth of examples of how actual organizations, most of which compete internationally as well as in their home markets, use the strategic management process for the purpose of outperforming rivals and increasing their performance.
- **Twenty Cases** are included in this edition. Offering an effective mix of organizations headquartered or based in North America and a number of other countries as well, the cases deal with contemporary and highly important topics. Many of the cases have

full financial data (the analyses of which are in the Case Notes that are available to instructors). These timely cases present active learners with opportunities to apply the strategic management process and understand organizational conditions and contexts and to make appropriate recommendations to deal with critical concerns. These cases also appear in MindTap.

- **New Mini-Cases** appear at the end of each chapter. In these cases, we describe how companies deal with major issues highlighted in the text. There are 13 of these cases, one for each chapter, although some of them can overlap with other chapter content. Students will like their conciseness, but they likewise provide rich content that can serve as a catalyst for individual or group analysis and class discussion. A set of questions, which guide analysis and discussion, follows each Mini-Case.
- **More than 1,200 new references** from 2017 and 2018 appear in the chapters' endnotes. We used the materials associated with these references to support new material added or current strategic management concepts that are included in this edition. In addition to demonstrating the classic and recent research from which we draw our material, the large number of references supporting the book's contents allow us to integrate cutting-edge research and thinking into a presentation of strategic management tools, techniques, and concepts.
- **New content** appears in several chapters. Examples include: (1) the discussion of digitalization and its link with the forming and execution of strategies in Chapter 1; (2) a description of the changing competitive landscape due to new technology development, changing government policies (political landscape), and global competition in Chapter 2; (3) the importance and use of big data analytics and artificial intelligence in Chapter 3; (4) the analysis of digital strategies in Chapter 4's Opening Case; (5) the description of business models and their relationship with business-level strategies in Chapter 4; and (6) our discussion and analysis of the emergence and competitive significance of Amazon's acquisition of Whole Foods in several chapters.
- **Updated information** appears in several chapters. Examples include updates about the rapid pace of technology diffusion (Chapter 1), all new and current demographic data (e.g., ethnic mix, geographic distribution) that describe the economic environment (Chapter 2), the general partner strategies of private equity firms (Chapter 7), information from the *World Economic Forum Competitiveness Report* regarding political risks of international investments (Chapter 8), updates about corporate governance practices being used in different countries (Chapter 10), updated data about the number of internal and external CEO selections occurring in companies today (Chapter 12), a ranking of countries by the amount of their entrepreneurial activities (Chapter 13), and a ranking of companies on their total innovation output (Chapter 13).
- **An Exceptional Balance** between current research and up-to-date applications of that research in actual organizations located throughout the world. The content has not only the best research documentation but also the largest number of effective real-world examples to help active learners understand the different types of strategies organizations use to achieve their vision and mission and to outperform rivals.

Supplements to Accompany This Text

MindTap. MindTap is the digital learning solution that helps instructors engage students and helps students become tomorrow's strategic leaders. All activities are designed to teach students to problem-solve and think like leaders. Through these activities and real-time course analytics, and an accessible reader, MindTap helps you turn cookie cutter into cutting edge, apathy into engagement, and memorizers into higher-level thinkers.

Customized to the specific needs of this course, activities are built to facilitate mastery of chapter content. We've addressed case analysis from cornerstone to capstone with a functional area diagnostic of prior knowledge, guided cases, branching activities, multimedia presentations of real-world companies facing strategic decisions, and a collaborative environment in which students can complete group case analysis projects together synchronously.

Instructor Website. Access important teaching resources on this companion website. For your convenience, you can download electronic versions of the instructor supplements from the password-protected section of the site, including Instructor's Resource Manual, Comprehensive Case Notes, Cognero Testing, and PowerPoint® slides. To access these additional course materials and companion resources, please visit www.cengage.com.

- **Instructor's Resource Manual.** The Instructor's Resource Manual, organized around each chapter's knowledge objectives, includes teaching ideas for each chapter and how to reinforce essential principles with extra examples. This support product includes lecture outlines and detailed guides to integrating the MindTap activities into your course with instructions for using each chapter's experiential exercises, branching, and directed cases. Finally, we provide outlines and guidance to help you customize the collaborative work environment and case analysis project to incorporate your approach to case analysis, including creative ideas for using this feature throughout your course for the most powerful learning experience for your class.
- **Case Notes.** These notes include directed assignments, financial analyses, and thorough discussion and exposition of issues in the case. Select cases also have assessment rubrics tied to National Standards (AACSB outcomes) that can be used for grading each case. The Case Notes provide consistent and thorough support for instructors, following the method espoused by the author team for preparing an effective case analysis.
- **Cognero Test Bank.** This program is easy-to-use test-creation software that is compatible with Microsoft Windows. Instructors can add or edit questions, instructions, and answers, and select questions by previewing them on the screen, selecting them randomly, or selecting them by number. Instructors can also create and administer quizzes online, whether over the Internet, a local area network (LAN), or a wide area network (WAN). Thoroughly revised and enhanced, test bank questions are linked to each chapter's knowledge objectives and are ranked by difficulty and question type. We provide an ample number of application questions throughout, and we have also retained scenario-based questions as a means of adding in-depth problem-solving questions. The questions are also tagged to National Standards (AACSB outcomes), Bloom's Taxonomy, and the Dierdorff/Rubin metrics.
- **PowerPoints®.** An updated PowerPoint presentation provides support for lectures, emphasizing key concepts, key terms, and instructive graphics.

Acknowledgments

We express our appreciation for the excellent support received from our editorial and production team at Cengage Learning. We especially wish to thank Michael Giffen, Senior Product Manager; Bryan Gambrel, Product Director; Audrey Wyrick, Marketing

Manager; and Amanda White, our Content Manager. We are grateful for their dedication, commitment, and outstanding contributions to the development and publication of this book and its package of support materials.

We are highly indebted to all of the reviewers of past editions. Their comments have provided a great deal of insight in the preparation of this current edition:

Jay Azriel
York College of Pennsylvania

Lana Belousova
Suffolk University

Ruben Boling
North Georgia University

Matthias Bollmus
Carroll University

Erich Brockmann
University of New Orleans

David Cadden
Quinnipiac University

Ken Chadwick
Nicholls State University

Bruce H. Charnov
Hofstra University

Jay Chok
Keck Graduate Institute, Claremont Colleges

Peter Clement
State University of New York–Delhi

Terry Coalter
Northwest Missouri University

James Cordeiro
SUNY Brockport

Deborah de Lange
Suffolk University

Irem Demirkan
Northeastern University

Dev Dutta
University of New Hampshire

Scott Elston
Iowa State University

Harold Fraser
California State University–Fullerton

Robert Goldberg
Northeastern University

Monica Gordillo
Iowa State University

George Griffin
Spring Arbor University

Susan Hansen
University of Wisconsin–Platteville

Glenn Hoetker
Arizona State University

James Hoyt
Troy University

Miriam Huddleston
Harford Community College

Carol Jacobson
Purdue University

James Katzenstein
California State University, Dominguez Hills

Robert Keidel
Drexel University

Nancy E. Landrum
University of Arkansas at Little Rock

Mina Lee
Xavier University

Patrice Luoma
Quinnipiac University

Mzamo Mangaliso
University of Massachusetts–Amherst

Michele K. Masterfano
Drexel University

James McClain
California State University–Fullerton

Jean McGuire
Louisiana State University

John McIntyre
Georgia Tech

Rick McPherson
University of Washington

Karen Middleton
Texas A&M–Corpus Christi

Raza Mir
William Paterson University

Martina Musteen
San Diego State University

Louise Nemanich
Arizona State University

Frank Novakowski
Davenport University

Consuelo M. Ramirez
University of Texas at San Antonio

Barbara Ribbens
Western Illinois University

Jason Ridge
Clemson University

William Roering
Michigan State University

Manjula S. Salimath
University of North Texas

Deepak Sethi
Old Dominion University

Manisha Singal
Virginia Tech

Warren Stone
University of Arkansas at Little Rock

Elisabeth Teal
University of N. Georgia

Jill Thomas Jorgensen
Lewis and Clark State College

Len J. Trevino
Washington State University

Edward Ward
Saint Cloud State University

Marta Szabo White
Georgia State University

Michael L. Williams
Michigan State University

Diana J. Wong-MingJi
Eastern Michigan University

Patricia A. Worsham
California State Polytechnic University, Pomona

William J. Worthington
Baylor University

Wilson Zehr
Concordia University

Michael A. Hitt
R. Duane Ireland
Robert E. Hoskisson

About the Authors

Michael A. Hitt

Michael A. Hitt is a University Distinguished Professor Emeritus at Texas A&M University and a Distinguished Research Fellow at Texas Christian University. Dr. Hitt received his Ph.D. from the University of Colorado. He has co-authored or co-edited 27 books and authored or co-authored many journal articles. A recent article listed him as one of the 10 most cited authors in management over a 25-year period. The *Times Higher Education 2010* listed him among the top scholars in economics, finance, and management based on the number of highly cited articles he has authored. A recent article in the *Academy of Management Perspectives* lists him as one of the top two management scholars in terms of the combined impact of his work both inside (i.e., citations in scholarly journals) and outside of academia. And, a recent article in the *Academy of Management Learning and Education* lists him as the highest cited author in strategic management textbooks. He has served on the editorial review boards of multiple journals and is a former editor of the *Academy of Management Journal* and a former co-editor of the *Strategic Entrepreneurship Journal*. He is a fellow in the Academy of Management, the Strategic Management Society, and the Academy of International Business. He has received honorary doctorates (Doctor Honoris Causa) from the Universidad Carlos III de Madrid and from Jonkoping University. He is a former president of both the Academy of Management and the Strategic Management Society. He received awards for the best article published in the *Academy of Management Executive* (1999), *Academy of Management Journal* (2000), *Journal of Management* (2006), and *Family Business Review* (2012). In 2001, he received the Irwin Outstanding Educator Award and the Career Achievement Award for Distinguished Service from the Academy of Management. In 2004, Dr. Hitt was awarded the Best Paper Prize by the Strategic Management Society. In 2006, he received the Falcone Distinguished Entrepreneurship Scholar Award from Syracuse University. In 2017, he received the Career Achievement Award for Distinguished Educator from the Academy of Management. He received Distinguished Alumnus Awards from Texas Tech University and from the University of Colorado in 2018. In 2014–2018, Dr. Hitt was listed as a Thomson Reuters Highly Cited Researcher (a listing of the world's most influential researchers).

R. Duane Ireland

R. Duane Ireland is a University Distinguished Professor, holder of the Benton Cocanougher Chair in Business, and the Executive Associate Dean in Mays Business School, Texas A&M University. Dr. Ireland teaches strategic management courses at all levels. He has more than 200 publications, including approximately 25 books. His research, which focuses on diversification, innovation, corporate entrepreneurship, strategic entrepreneurship, and the informal economy, appears in an array of journals. He has served as a member of multiple editorial review boards and is a former editor (and a former associate editor) of the *Academy of Management Journal.* He has been a guest editor for 12 special issues of journals. He is a past president of the Academy of Management. Dr. Ireland is a fellow of the Academy of Management, a fellow of the Strategic Management Society, and a research fellow in the Global Consortium of Entrepreneurship Centers. A recent article in the *Academy of Management Learning and Education* lists him as among the most highly cited authors in strategic management textbooks. He received awards for the best article published in *Academy of Management Executive* (1999), the *Academy of Management Journal* (2000), and the *Journal of Applied Management and Entrepreneurship* (2010). He received an Association of Former Students Distinguished Achievement Award for Research from Texas A&M University (2012). In 2014, 2015, and 2018, Thomson Reuters identified Dr. Ireland as a Thomson Reuters Highly Cited Researcher (a listing of the world's most influential researchers). He received a Distinguished Service award from the Academy of Management in 2017 and a Distinguished Service award from the strategic management division of the Academy of Management in the same year. The Rawls College of Business, Texas Tech University, chose him as a Distinguished Alumnus in 2018. In 2017, he received the Lifetime Achievement Award for Research and Scholarship from Mays Business School.

Robert E. Hoskisson

Robert E. Hoskisson is the George R. Brown Emeritus Chair of Strategic Management at the Jesse H. Jones Graduate School of Business, Rice University. Dr. Hoskisson received his Ph.D. from the University of California-Irvine. His research topics focus on corporate governance, acquisitions and divestitures, corporate and international diversification, and cooperative strategy. He teaches courses in corporate and international strategic management, cooperative strategy, and strategy consulting. He has co-authored 26 books, including recent books on business strategy and competitive advantage. Dr. Hoskisson has served on several editorial boards for such publications as the *Strategic Management Journal* (Associate Editor), *Academy of Management Journal* (Consulting Editor), *Journal of International Business Studies* (Consulting Editor), *Journal of Management* (Associate Editor), and *Organization Science.* His research has appeared in over 130 publications, including the *Strategic Management Journal, Academy of Management Journal, Academy of Management Review, Organization Science, Journal of Management, Academy of Management Perspective, Academy of Management Executive, Journal of Management Studies, Journal of International Business Studies, Journal of Business Venturing, Entrepreneurship Theory and Practice, California Management Review,* and *Journal of World Business.* A recent article in the *Academy of Management Learning and Education* lists him among the most highly cited authors in strategic management textbooks. He is listed in the Thomson Reuters Highly Cited Researcher list that catalogues the world's most influential research scholars. Dr. Hoskisson is a fellow of the Academy of Management and a charter member of the Academy of Management Journal's Hall of Fame. He is also a fellow of the Strategic Management Society and has received awards from the American Society for Competitiveness and the William G. Dyer Alumni award from the Marriott School of Management, Brigham Young University. He completed three years of service as a Representative-at-Large on the Board of Governors of the Academy of Management. He also served as President of the Strategic Management Society, and served on the Executive Committee of its Board of Directors for six years.

Case Title	Manu-facturing	Service	Consumer Goods	Food/ Retail	High Technology	Internet	Transportation/ Communication	International Perspective	Social/ Ethical Issues	Industry Perspective
Alphabet (Google)		•			•	•	•	•		
Baidu		•			•	•		•		•
BMW	•		•		•		•		•	
CrossFit		•							•	•
Healthcare Industry (Long-Term)		•							•	•
Heise Medien		•				•	•			•
Illinois Tool Works	•				•					
Kone	•				•			•		•
MatchMove		•			•	•		•		
Movie Exhibition Industry		•	•							•
Pacific Drilling	•				•			•		•
Pfizer	•							•	•	
Publix	•		•	•		•				•
Starbucks		•		•				•		•
Sturm, Ruger and Co.	•									•
Trivago		•			•	•	•			
Volkswagen	•		•					•		
Wells Fargo		•							•	
ZF Fried-richshafen	•				•			•	•	
ZO-Rooms		•			•	•			•	•

Case Title	Chapters												
	1	2	3	4	5	6	7	8	9	10	11	12	13
Alphabet (Google)						●	●			●	●		●
Baidu				●		●		●	●				●
BMW	●	●		●	●								●
CrossFit	●	●	●	●	●							●	
Healthcare Industry (Long-Term)		●		●	●					●			
Heise Medien		●		●	●								
Illinois Tool Works						●	●				●	●	●
Kone				●				●					●
MatchMove	●		●	●	●								●
Movie Exhibition Industry		●	●	●	●								
Pacific Drilling						●			●				●
Pfizer	●	●				●	●		●	●	●	●	●
Publix	●	●		●	●					●			
Starbucks		●	●									●	●
Sturm, Ruger and Co.		●	●	●	●								
Trivago								●			●	●	●
Volkswagen	●									●		●	
Wells Fargo	●									●		●	
ZF Friedrichshafen					●		●	●			●		
ZO-Rooms		●		●	●		●		●				●

1

Strategic Management and Strategic Competitiveness

Studying this chapter should provide you with the strategic management knowledge needed to:

1-1 Define strategic competitiveness, strategy, competitive advantage, above-average returns, and the strategic management process.

1-2 Describe the competitive landscape and explain how globalization and technological changes shape it.

1-3 Use the industrial organization (I/O) model to explain how firms can earn above-average returns.

1-4 Use the resource-based model to explain how firms can earn above-average returns.

1-5 Describe vision and mission and discuss their value.

1-6 Define stakeholders and describe their ability to influence organizations.

1-7 Describe the work of strategic leaders.

1-8 Explain the strategic management process.

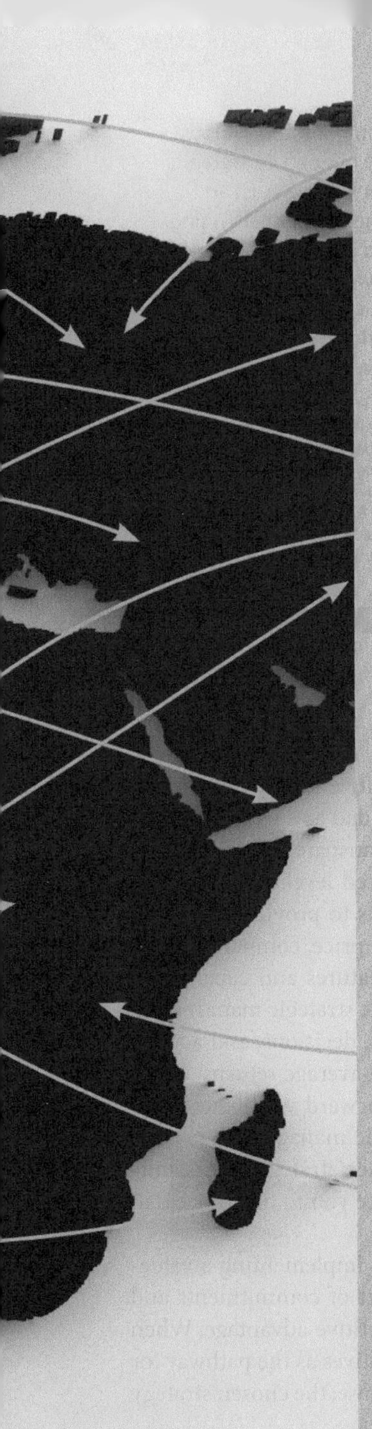

THE HONEST CO.: CAN IT BECOME AN ICONIC GLOBAL BRAND?

Launched on 2011, The Honest Co. is an eco-friendly consumer goods company co-founded by actress Jessica Alba. According to Alba, a desire as a parent to be able to purchase safe, effective products that perform as promised drove the decision to establish Honest. The firm says that it is a "wellness brand with values rooted in consciousness, community, transparency and design. We're on a mission to empower people to live happy, healthy lives."

Over the years, Honest has offered consumers products in a number of categories including diapering, vitamins, feeding, personal care, and cleaning among others. Essentially, this firm's strategy calls for it to provide unique products to customers who value that uniqueness and are willing to pay for it in the form of prices that exceed those of "mainstream" products. Implementing this strategy successfully would be the foundation for the firm achieving strategic competitiveness (we define strategy and strategic competitiveness in this chapter).

According to the firm's CEO, for the near future at least, Honest intends to concentrate on its baby and beauty products categories as a means of making progress to reach its objective of becoming an iconic global brand. Expansion into Europe in 2019 was an important strategic action taken to reach this objective. To avoid the highly competitive and low-margin diaper category, part of Honest's European expansion strategy includes its partnership with "German cosmetics and perfume chain Douglas to sell its beauty products in Germany, France, Spain, Italy, Poland, the Netherlands, and Austria."

Stefanie Keenan/WireImage/Getty Images

Co-founder of The Honest Company Jessica Alba at a special ribbon cutting ceremony in Beverly Hills, California.

The path to achieving strategic competitiveness has not been challenge- and error-free for The Honest Co. In terms of challenges, the firm has direct competitors such as Zulily (a firm offering always-fresh products for families with new babies including home décor items, clothing, gifts, etc.) and Giggle, a one-stop source for new parents seeking unique baby products. Additionally, large consumer-goods companies such as Unilever and Procter & Gamble offer products to consumers with some of the features associated with Honest's items, sometimes at a lower price. A series of lawsuits filed against The Honest Co. suggest mistakes made by the firm. In 2016, for example, a lawsuit alleged false labelling of some of the ingredients of the firm's cleaning products. Other allegations include one that the firm's sunscreen product does not work effectively. Honest also had to recall its organic baby powder for potential contamination and its baby wipes because of contamination with mold.

Recently, Honest received a $200 million dollar minority investment from L. Catterton, a private equity firm. The Honest Co. believes this investment provides the capital required to expand its supply chains and global reach. Honest thinks of L. Catterton as a perfect investment partner because of its expertise with global supply chains. The Honest Co. is the type of firm in which L. Catterton typically invests, as shown by its involvement with well-known American beauty product businesses such as Bliss, Elemis, and Tula.

Going forward, will The Honest Co. be able to use its resources to outcompete rivals as a means of reaching its objective to become an iconic global brand by offering consumers eco-friendly and effective products? While committed to regaining consumers' trust and confidence by producing products they want to buy, reaching this objective is challenging, especially in light of the competition the firm faces. On the other hand, some analysts believe Honest will succeed because the firm has three valuable capabilities (we define capabilities in this chapter): "tremendous brand equity, innovative and quality products, and a loyal customer following." Time will tell if The Honest Co. will be able to execute with these capabilities in a way that yields competitive success in the form of strategic competitiveness.

Sources: 2018, The Honest Co., About us, www.honest.com, August, 8; 2018, Jessica Alba's Honest Co. gets $200 million investment from L. Catterton, *Fortune*, www.fortune.com, June 6; A. Black, 2018, The right way for food companies to buy their way to growth, *Wall Street Journal*, www.wsj.com, June 6; W. Colville, 2018, Jessica Alba's Honest Co. gets $200 million investment, *Wall Street Journal*, www.wsj.com, June 6; A. Gasparro & J. Bunge, 2018, Food companies churn through CEOs, desperate for fresh ideas, *Wall Street Journal*, www.wsj.com, May 29; A. Stych, 2018, Jessica Alba's Honest Company gets $200M investment, *bizwomen*, www.bizwomen.com, June 7; J. Valinsky, 2018, Jessica Alba's Honest Co. just got a $200 million lifeline, *CNNMoney*, www.cnnmoney.com, June 6; A. C. Wischhover, 2018, Jessica Alba's Honest Company is relaunching products and trying to put bad PR drama behind it, *Racked*, www.racked.com, June 7.

As we see from the Opening Case, achieving strategic competitiveness by implementing a firm's chosen strategy successfully is challenging. Founded as a wellness brand with a grounding in the values of consciousness, community, transparency, and design, Honest is struggling to reach its mission and the founders' desired level of competitive success. An eco-friendly consumer goods company, Honest seeks to provide customers with unique products for which they are willing to pay a higher price, compared to the prices for consumer goods products with relatively standard features and capabilities. Honest's top management team, including Jessica Alba, is using the strategic management process (see Figure 1.1) as the foundation for the commitments, decisions, and actions the team is taking to pursue strategic competitiveness and above-average returns. Given the firm's challenges, some of its decisions and actions going forward will likely differ from some made previously. In this book, we explain the strategic management process The Honest Co. and multiple other firms use to implement a chosen strategy successfully and to achieve strategic competitiveness by doing so. We introduce you to this process in the next few paragraphs.

Firms achieve **strategic competitiveness** by formulating and implementing a value creating strategy.

A **strategy** is an integrated and coordinated set of commitments and actions designed to exploit core competencies and gain a competitive advantage.

A firm has a **competitive advantage** when by implementing a chosen strategy, it creates superior value for customers and when competitors are not able to imitate the value the firm's products create or find it too expensive to attempt imitation.

Firms achieve **strategic competitiveness** by formulating and implementing a value-creating strategy. A **strategy** is an integrated and coordinated set of commitments and actions designed to exploit core competencies and gain a competitive advantage. When choosing a strategy, firms make choices among competing alternatives as the pathway for deciding how they will pursue strategic competitiveness. In this sense, the chosen strategy indicates what the firm *will do* as well as what the firm *will not do*.

A firm has a **competitive advantage** when by implementing a chosen strategy, it creates superior value for customers and when competitors are not able to imitate the value the firm's products create or find it too expensive to attempt imitation.[1] An organization can be confident that its strategy yields a competitive advantage after competitors' efforts to duplicate it have ceased or failed. In addition, firms must understand that no competitive advantage is permanent.[2] The speed with which competitors are able to acquire the skills needed to duplicate the benefits of a firm's value-creating strategy determines how long the competitive advantage will last.[3] The Honest Co. seeks to create a competitive advantage, as do all organizations. We discuss competitive advantages and provide a few firm-specific examples of them in the Strategic Focus.

Strategic Focus

Competitive Advantage as a Source of Strategic Competitiveness

Possessing a competitive advantage, and understanding how to use it effectively in marketplace competitions, is foundational to all firms' efforts to achieve strategic competitiveness and outperform rivals in the process of doing so. Strategic leaders influence choices firms make to develop a competitive advantage. (We define strategic leaders later in this chapter and discuss strategic leadership in detail in Chapter 12.) In essence, a firm creates a competitive advantage by being as different as possible from competitors in ways that are important to customers and in ways that competitors cannot duplicate. Important differences are ones for which customers are willing to pay. Having and exploiting a competitive advantage successfully finds a firm creating superior value for its customers and superior profits for itself.

The competitive advantages firms possess differ among companies across and within industries. Drawing from Michael Porter's work, we explain in Chapter 4 that firms have a competitive advantage when they deliver the same value to customers as competitors deliver but at a lower cost, or when they deliver benefits for which customers are willing to pay that exceed the benefits competitors offer. Facilitating a firm's efforts to develop a competitive advantage is its ability to make the value its products offers customers as clear, concise, and easily recognizable as possible. In slightly different words, firms must convey effectively the value of their products, relative to competitors' offerings, to their customers. The larger is the "gap" between the value a firm's products creates for customers and the value competitors' products bring to customers, the more significant is a firm's competitive advantage.

The competitive dimensions on which firms are able to establish a competitive advantage are virtually endless. In a general sense, technological developments, which continue at a rapid pace, may be a source of competitive advantage for firms in multiple industries. Salesforce.com, the customer relationship management (CRM) firm that uses cloud computing extensively, recently "debuted a CRM solution that uses machine learning to build comprehensive data-based customer profiles, identify crucial touch points and uncover additional sales opportunities." Adaptability and flexibility are additional potential sources of competitive advantage for firms learning how to exploit newly developing technologies quickly and successfully. Netflix is building competitive advantages in terms of its original programming and its customer interface platform that creates unique experiences for individual users. Some analysts feel that trust is an important source of competitive advantage. In a recent survey, a group reported that "Unlike other online retailers, 67% of Amazon customers trust the company to protect their privacy and personal data." Home Depot officials cite the firm's culture as a competitive advantage. The culture emphasizes "excellent customer service, an entrepreneurial spirit, building strong relationships, taking care of its people, and doing the right thing." In today's globalized competitive environment, firms that learn how to develop an effective balance among economic growth, ecological balance, and social growth may have a viable competitive advantage. Finally, some argue that in the final analysis, a firm's people are the most important source of competitive advantage. The reason for this is that a firm's people think of ways to create differences between their firm and competitors; a firm's people then execute in ways that bring those differences to life.

AB Forces News Collection/Alamy Stock Photo

Volunteers with The Home Depot's Building Materials Department help to restore the memorial of Sergeant Adam Cann during the K9 upgrade project at Camp Pendleton.

We note in Chapter 4 that no competitive advantage is sustainable permanently. In some instances, a firm's advantage no longer creates value for which customers are willing to pay. In other cases, competitors will learn how to create more value for customers with respect to a valued competitive dimension for which they are willing to pay. Thus, to achieve strategic competitiveness across time, a firm must concentrate simultaneously on exploiting the competitive advantage it possesses today while contemplating decisions to make today to ensure that it will possess a competitive advantage in the future.

Sources: A. Bylund, 2018, What is Netflix, Inc's competitive advantage? *The Motley Fool*, www.fool.com, July 21; I. Hunkeler, 2018, How to turn digital disruption into a competitive advantage, *Small Business Daily*, www.smallbizdaily.com, January 26; L. Lent, 2018, Strategic sustainability focus delivers competitive advantages, *PHYS.ORG*, www.phys.org, February 8; I. Linton, 2018, Strategic moves to build a competitive advantage, *Houston Chronicle*, www.smallbusiness.chron.com, June 29; G. Pickard-Whitehead, 2018, What is competitive advantage? *Small Business Trends*, www.smallbiztrends.com, April 10; A. Rogers, 2018, Innovation case studies: How companies use technology to solidify a competitive advantage, *Forbes*, www.forbes.com, April 13; J. Silver, 2018, Culture as a competitive advantage, *Hispanic Executive*, www.hispanicexecutive.com, May 1; G. Sterling, 2018, Survey: Consumer trust may be Amazon's true competitive advantage, *Search Engine Land*, www.searchengineland.com, June 7; R. Wartzman & L. Crosby, 2018, A company's performance depends first of all on its people, *Wall Street Journal*, www.wsj.com, August 12.

Above-average returns are returns in excess of what an investor expects to earn from other investments with a similar amount of risk. **Risk** is an investor's uncertainty about the economic gains or losses that will result from a particular investment. The most successful companies learn how to manage risk effectively;[4] doing so reduces investors' uncertainty about the outcomes of their investment.[5] Firms often use accounting-based metrics, such as return on assets, return on equity, and return on sales to assess their performance. Alternatively, firms can assess their performance in terms of stock market returns, even monthly returns. (Monthly returns are the end-of-the-period stock price minus the beginning stock price divided by the beginning stock price, yielding a percentage return.) In smaller, new venture firms, returns are sometimes measured in terms of the amount and speed of growth (e.g., in annual sales) rather than more traditional profitability measures[6] because new ventures require time to earn acceptable returns (in the form of return on assets and so forth) for investors.[7]

Understanding how to exploit a competitive advantage is important for firms seeking to earn above-average returns.[8] Firms without a competitive advantage or those that do not compete in an attractive industry earn, at best, average returns. **Average returns** are returns equal to those an investor expects to earn from other investments possessing a similar amount of risk. Over time, an inability to earn at least average returns results first in decline and, eventually, failure.[9] Failure occurs because investors withdraw their investments from those firms earning less-than-average returns.

As previously noted, there are no guarantees of permanent success. Companies succeeding at a point in time must not become overconfident. Research suggests that overconfidence can lead to excessive risk taking.[10] Used as an example several times in this book, Amazon.com today continues growing and increasing its sales revenue. This firm too though must avoid assuming that success today is a guarantee of success tomorrow. Using the strategic management process effectively facilitates firms' efforts to achieve success across time.

The **strategic management process** is the full set of commitments, decisions, and actions firms take to achieve strategic competitiveness and earn above-average returns (see Figure 1.1).[11] The process involves analysis, strategy, and performance (the A-S-P model—see Figure 1.1). The firm's first step in the process is to *analyze* its external environment and internal organization to identify external opportunities and threats and to recognize its internal resources, capabilities, and core competencies. The results of these analyses influence the selection of the firm's strategy or strategies. The *strategy* portion of the model entails strategy formulation and strategy implementation.

With the information gained from external and internal analyses, the firm develops its vision and mission and formulates one or more *strategies*. To implement its strategies, the firm takes actions to enact each one with the intent of achieving strategic competitiveness and above-average returns (*performance*). Effective actions that take place in the context of integrated strategy formulation and implementation efforts result in positive performance. Firms seek to maintain the quality of what is a dynamic strategic management process as a means of dealing successfully with ever-changing markets and evolving internal conditions.[12]

In the remaining chapters of this book, we use the strategic management process to explain what firms do to achieve strategic competitiveness and earn above-average returns. We demonstrate why some firms achieve competitive success consistently while others do not. Today, global competition is a critical part of the strategic management process and influences firms' performances.[13] Indeed, learning how to compete in the globalized world is one of the most significant challenges firms face.[14]

We discuss several topics in this chapter. First, we describe the current competitive landscape. Several realities, including the emergence of a global economy, globalization

Above-average returns are returns in excess of what an investor expects to earn from other investments with a similar amount of risk.

Risk is an investor's uncertainty about the economic gains or losses that will result from a particular investment.

Average returns are returns equal to those an investor expects to earn from other investments possessing a similar amount of risk.

The **strategic management process** is the full set of commitments, decisions, and actions firms take to achieve strategic competitiveness and earn above-average returns.

Figure 1.1 The Strategic Management Process

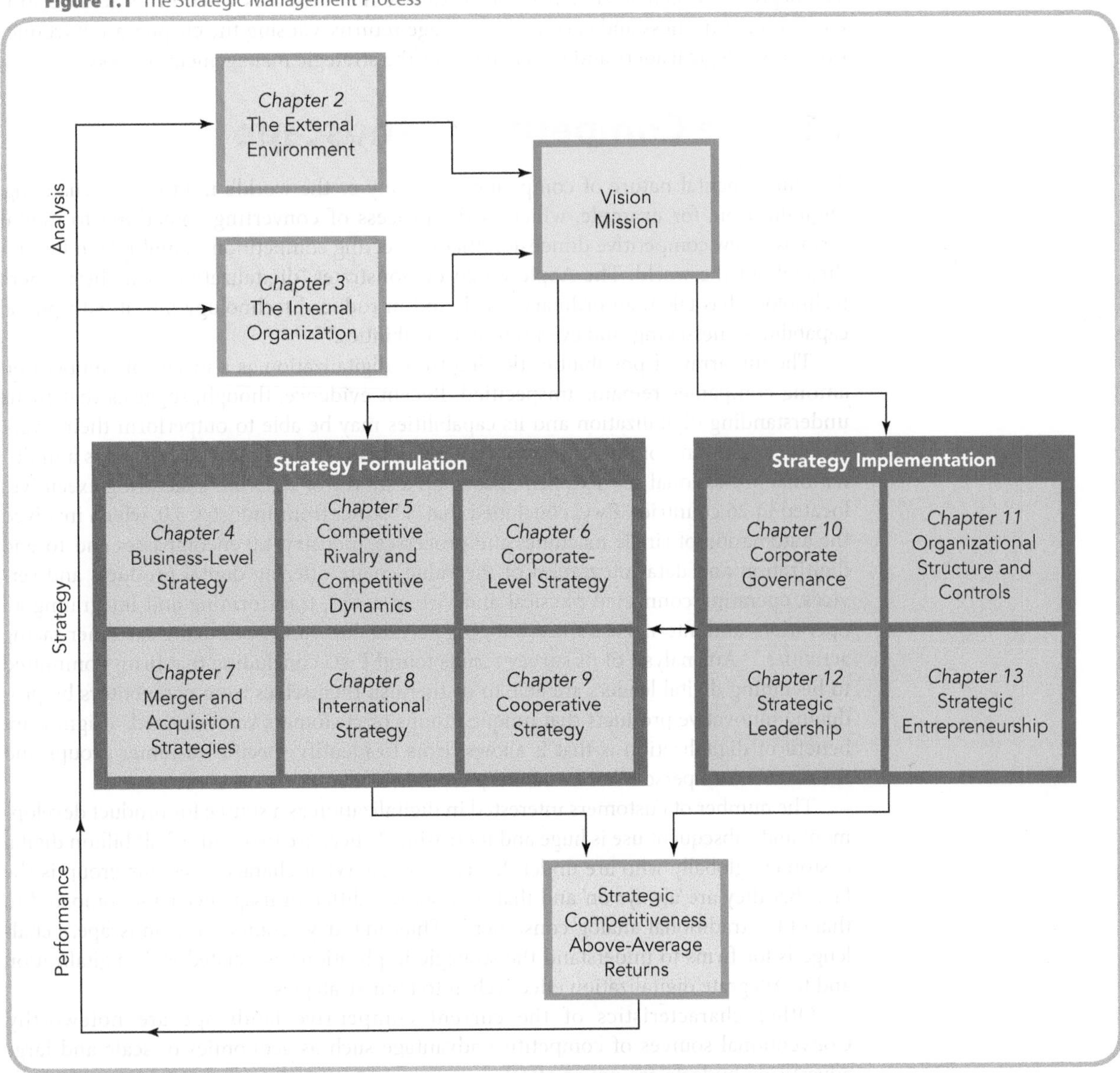

resulting from that economy, and rapid technological changes, influence this landscape. Next, we examine two models firms use to gather the information and knowledge required to choose and then effectively implement their strategies. The insights gained from these models also serve as the foundation for forming the firm's vision and mission. The first model (industrial organization or I/O) suggests that the external environment is the primary determinant of a firm's strategic actions. According to this model, identifying and then operating effectively in an attractive (i.e., profitable) industry or segment of an industry are the keys to competitive success.[15] The second model (resource-based) suggests that a firm's unique resources and capabilities are the critical link to strategic competitiveness.[16] Thus, the first model is concerned primarily with the firm's external environment while the second model is concerned primarily with the firm's internal organization. After discussing vision and mission, direction-setting statements that influence the choice and use of strategies, we describe the stakeholders that organizations serve.

The degree to which stakeholders' needs can be met increases when firms achieve strategic competitiveness and earn above-average returns. Closing the chapter are introductions to strategic leaders and the elements of the strategic management process.

1-1 The Competitive Landscape

The fundamental nature of competition in many of the world's industries is changing. Digitalization, for example, which is the process of converting something to digital form, is a new competitive dimension that is affecting competition in multiple industries throughout the world. The Apple watch demonstrates "digitalization at its best where technology has taken an ordinary watch and introduced technology into it with phone capabilities, messaging, and even Internet capabilities."[17]

The full array of possibilities flowing from digitalization as a means of competition among companies remains unspecified. Recent evidence, though, suggests that firms understanding digitalization and its capabilities may be able to outperform their rivals. Headquartered in London, PricewaterhouseCoopers (doing business as PwC) is a multinational professional services firm. Based on a survey of 1,155 manufacturing executives located in 26 countries, PwC concluded that "Distinct from Industry 3.0, which involved the automation of single machines and processes, Industry 4.0 encompasses end-to-end digitization and data integration of the value chain: offering digital products and services, operating connected physical and virtual assets, transforming and integrating all operations and internal activities, building partnerships, and optimizing customer-facing activities."[18] An analysis of its survey results found PwC concluding that firms committed to becoming digital leaders are able to distinguish themselves from competitors by producing innovative products that unique groups of customers value. Indeed, a significant benefit of digitalization is that it allows firms to identify specific customer groups and then serve their personalized and unique needs.[19]

The number of customers interested in digitalization as a source for product development and subsequent use is huge and increasing. "There are two-and-a-half billion digital customers globally who are under 25 years of age. What characterizes this group is the fact that they are 'always on' and that they show a different usage behavior compared to that of the traditional 'analog' consumer."[20] Thus, in today's competitive landscape, a challenge is for firms to understand the strategic implications associated with digitalization and to integrate digitalization effectively into their strategies.

Other characteristics of the current competitive landscape are noteworthy. Conventional sources of competitive advantage such as economies of scale and large advertising budgets are not as effective as they once were (e.g., because of social media advertising) in terms of helping firms earn above-average returns. Moreover, the traditional managerial mind-set is unlikely to lead a firm to strategic competitiveness. Managers must adopt a new mind-set that values flexibility, speed, innovation, integration, and the challenges flowing from constantly changing conditions.[21] The conditions of the competitive landscape result in a perilous business world—a world in which the investments necessary to compete on a global scale are enormous and the consequences of failure are severe.[22] Effective use of the strategic management process reduces the likelihood of failure for firms while competing against their rivals.

Hypercompetition is a condition where competitors engage in intense rivalry, markets change quickly and often, and entry barriers are low. In these environments, firms find it difficult to maintain a competitive advantage.[23] Rivalry in hypercompetitive environments tends to occur among global competitors who innovate regularly and successfully.[24] It is a condition of rapidly escalating competition based on price-quality positioning, competition to create new know-how and establish first-mover advantage, and competition to

Hypercompetition is a condition where competitors engage in intense rivalry, markets change quickly and often, and entry barriers are low.

protect or invade established product and/or geographic markets. In a hypercompetitive market, firms often challenge their competitors aggressively to strengthen their market position and ultimately, their performance.[25] Specifically how firms challenge each other in hypercompetitive markets varies across time. Recently, for example, Internet giant Tencent Holdings Ltd. of China has become one of the world's largest technology investors. Between 2013 and mid-2018, the firm took stakes in 277 startups. Analysts believe this is a calculated strategy to crowd out rivals and to increase profits.[26]

Several factors create hypercompetitive environments and influence the nature of the current competitive landscape. The emergence of a global economy and technology, specifically rapid technological change, are two primary drivers of hypercompetitive environments and the nature of today's competitive landscape.

1-1a The Global Economy

A **global economy** is one in which goods, services, people, skills, and ideas move freely across geographic borders. Relatively unfettered by artificial constraints, such as tariffs, the global economy significantly expands and complicates a firm's competitive environment.[27]

The global economy, which changes rapidly and constantly,[28] increases the scope of the competitive environment in which companies compete. Because of this, firms must study the global economy carefully as a foundation for learning how to position themselves successfully for competitive purposes.

The size of parts of the global economy is an important aspect of studying this competitive arena. In 2018 for example, the United States was the world's largest economy at a value of $20.4 trillion. At that time, China was the world's second largest economy with a value of $14 trillion while Japan was the third largest at $5.1 trillion. Following Japan were three European countries (Germany at $4.2 trillion, United Kingdom at $2.94 trillion, and France at $2.93 trillion). In observing economies' values in 2018, the World Economic Forum noted that the size of the United States economy was "larger than the combined economies of numbers four to 10 on the list. Overall, the global economy (was) worth an estimated $79.98 trillion, meaning the United States accounts for more than one-quarter of the world total."[29] Thus, companies scanning the global economy for opportunities in 2018 might conclude that markets in the United States, China, and Japan yield potentially significant opportunities for them. Of course, such an analysis also must consider entry barriers to various economies in the form of tariffs. This type of analysis must also be forward looking in that in 2018, for example, the World Economic Forum estimated that China and India's economies would exceed the size of the U.S. economy by 2050 and that the economies of Germany, United Kingdom, and France would decline in size by this time as well. Companies should study carefully predictions such as these when determining the parts of the world in which growth opportunities as well as threats to their competitive global positions may exist in future years.

U.S.-based Netflix continues studying the global economy to identify opportunities in countries and regions in which it can grow. In mid-2018, the firm continued adding subscribers, reaching 125 million globally. At that time, analysts predicted the firm would have 360 million subscribers by 2030. International markets were to be the source of much of the growth in subscribers.[30] Informing this prediction was the expectation that Netflix would achieve reasonable levels of market penetration internationally, including reaching penetration in 35 percent of all broadband households worldwide, excluding China.[31] To fuel its international plans, Netflix offers some of its original movies in languages other than English. In 2018 alone, the firm allocated $8 billion to develop original programming, with some of those programs targeted to international customers.[32]

A **global economy** is one in which goods, services, people, skills, and ideas move freely across geographic borders.

During the global recession of roughly 2007 and 2008, General Motors (GM) identified what it thought was a significant international opportunity in China. The fact that GM and its Chinese joint venture partners are now the leading manufacturers in the world's largest automobile market seems to validate GM's assessment and the actions it took in light of it. GM and its partners' decision to launch the Baojun brand is foundational to the firm's success in China. With expectations of continuing growth, "Baojun is an entry-level brand targeted at consumers who live in (China's) smaller cities and rural areas."[33] In recent times, the competitive actions GM is taking in China result in the firm outperforming its rival Ford Motor Co. in this key global market.[34]

The March of Globalization

Globalization is the increasing economic interdependence among countries and their organizations as reflected in the flow of products, financial capital, and knowledge across country borders.[35] Globalization is a product of a large number of firms competing against one another in an increasing number of global economies.

In globalized markets and industries, firms might obtain financial capital in one national market and use it to buy raw materials in another. Firms might then use manufacturing equipment purchased in a third national market to produce and deliver products that it sells in a fourth market. Thus, globalization increases the range of opportunities for companies competing in the current competitive landscape.[36]

Firms operating globally must make culturally sensitive decisions when using the strategic management process, as is the case in Starbucks' operations in European countries (we discuss additional aspects of this firm's recent decisions and actions in this Chapter's Mini-Case). Additionally, highly globalized firms must anticipate ever-increasing complexity in their operations as goods, services, people, and so forth move freely across geographic borders and throughout different economies.

Overall, globalization has led to higher performance standards with respect to multiple competitive dimensions, including quality, cost, productivity, product introduction time, and operational efficiency. In addition to firms competing in the global economy, these standards affect firms competing on a domestic-only basis. Customers will choose to buy a global competitor's product when it creates superior value for them relative to the value created by the domestic firm's product. Workers now flow rather freely among global economies. This is important in that employees are a key source of competitive advantage.[37] Firms must learn how to deal with the reality that in today's competitive landscape, only companies capable of meeting, if not exceeding, global standards typically earn above-average returns.

Although globalization offers potential benefits to firms, it is not without risks. "Liability of foreignness" is the term describing the risks of competing outside a firm's domestic markets.[38] The amount of time firms usually require to learn to compete in markets that are new to them is one risk of entering a global market. A firm's performance can suffer until it gains the knowledge needed to compete successfully in a new global market.[39] In addition, a firm's performance may suffer by entering too many global markets either simultaneously or too quickly. When this happens, the overall organization may lack the skills required to manage effectively all of its diversified global operations.[40]

The increasing opportunities available in emerging economies is a major driver of growth in the size of the global economy. Important emerging economies include the BRIC countries (Brazil, Russia, India, and China),[41] the VISTA countries (Vietnam, Indonesia, South Africa, Turkey, and Argentina),[42] as well as Mexico and Thailand.

Demonstrating the growth in size of some of these economies is the 2018 prediction that by 2050, Indonesia, Brazil, Russia, and Mexico will be the fourth, fifth, sixth, and seventh largest economies in the world by size. If this were to happen, by 2050, the size of these emerging economies would exceed those of Japan, Germany, the United Kingdom, and France.[43] Emerging economy firms now compete in global markets, some with increasing success.[44] Indeed, the emergence of emerging-market multinational corporations (MNCs) in international markets forces large MNCs based in developed markets to enrich their own capabilities to compete effectively in global markets.[45]

Thus, entry into international markets, even for firms with substantial experience in the global economy, requires effective use of the strategic management process. Moreover, while global markets are an attractive strategic option for some companies, they are not the only source of strategic competitiveness. In fact, most companies, even those capable of competing successfully in global markets, should commit to remaining competitive in their home market and in the international markets in which they choose to compete. Firms do this by remaining in tune with technological opportunities and potential disruptions innovations might create. As indicated in this chapter's Mini-Case, Starbucks is emphasizing both product innovation and international expansion as means of growing profitably.

1-1b Technology and Technological Changes

Increasingly, technology affects all aspects of how companies operate and as such, the strategies they choose to implement. Boston Consulting Group analysts describe technology's impact as follows: "No company can afford to ignore the impact of technology on everything from supply chains to customer engagement, and the advent of even more advanced technologies, such as artificial intelligence (AI) and the Internet of Things, portends more far-reaching change."[46]

There are three categories of technology-related trends and conditions affecting today's firms: technology diffusion and disruptive technologies, the information age, and increasing knowledge intensity. As noted in the paragraph above, these categories have a significant effect on the nature of competition in many industries.

Technology Diffusion and Disruptive Technologies

The rate of technology diffusion, which is the speed at which new technologies become available to firms and when firms choose to adopt them, is far greater than was the case a decade or two ago. Consider the following rates of technology diffusion:

It took the telephone 35 years to get into 25 percent of all homes in the United States. It took TV 26 years. It took radio 22 years. It took PCs 16 years. It took the Internet 7 years.[47]

The impact of technological changes on individual firms and industries is broad and significant. For example, in the not-too-distant past, people rented movies on videotapes from retail stores such as Blockbuster. (Dish Network acquired Blockbuster in 2011.) Today, customers on a global basis use electronic means almost exclusively to rent movies and games. The publishing industry (books, journals, magazines, newspapers) is moving rapidly from hard copy to electronic format. Many firms in these industries, operating with a more traditional business model, are suffering. These changes are also affecting other industries, from trucking to mail services.

Perpetual innovation is a term used to describe how rapidly and consistently new, information-intensive technologies replace older ones. The shorter product life cycles resulting from these rapid diffusions of new technologies place a competitive premium on being able to introduce quickly new, innovative products into the marketplace.[48]

In fact, when products become hard to distinguish because of the widespread and rapid diffusion of technologies, speed to market with innovative products may be the primary source of competitive advantage (see Chapter 5).[49] Indeed, some argue that continuous innovations occurring in the global economy drive much of today's rapid and substantial change. Not surprisingly, an understanding of global standards and of the expectations customers have regarding a product's functionality inform the nature of these innovations. Although some argue that large established firms may have trouble innovating, evidence suggests that today these firms are developing radically new technologies that transform old industries or create new ones.[50] In 2018, for example, Boston Consulting Group identified the 50 most innovative companies in the world. The first five firms on this list are large companies—Apple, Google, Microsoft, Amazon, and Samsung.[51] Wireless AirPods, ARKit (the firm's augmented-reality framework), and HomePod (an intelligent speaker) are some of the innovative products Apple introduced recently and for which some recognize it as the most innovative company in the world.[52]

Another indicator of rapid technology diffusion is that commonly, firms gather information quickly about their competitors' research and development (R&D) and product decisions, sometimes even within days.[53] In this sense, the rate of technological diffusion has reduced the competitive benefits of patents.[54] Today, patents may be an effective way of protecting proprietary technology in a small number of industries such as pharmaceuticals. Indeed, many firms competing in the electronics industry often do not apply for patents to prevent competitors from gaining access to the technological knowledge included in the patent application.

Disruptive technologies—technologies that destroy the value of an existing technology and create new markets[55]—surface frequently in today's competitive markets. Think of the new markets created by the technologies underlying the development of products such as Wi-Fi, iPads, and the web browser and the markets advances in artificial intelligence will create. Some believe that these types of products represent radical or breakthrough innovations (we discuss radical innovations in Chapter 13).[56] A disruptive or radical technology can create what is essentially a new industry or can harm industry incumbents. However, some industry incumbents adapt to radical innovations from competitors based on their superior resources, experience, and ability to gain access to the new technology through multiple sources (e.g., alliances, acquisitions, and ongoing internal research).[57]

The Information Age

Dramatic changes in information technology (IT) continue occurring in the global economy. Personal computers, cellular phones, artificial intelligence, virtual reality, massive databases ("big data"), data analytics, and multiple social networking sites are a few examples of how technological developments permit different uses of information. Data and information are vital to firms' efforts today to understand customers and their needs and to implement strategies in ways that satisfy those needs as well as the interests of all other stakeholders. For today's firms in virtually all industries, IT is an important capability that contributes positively to product innovation efforts[58] and may be a source of competitive advantage as well. Firms failing to harness the power of data and information are disadvantaged compared to their competitors.[59]

Both the pace of change in IT and its diffusion continue increasing on a global scale. Consider that in 2018, 36 percent of the world's population owned a smartphone. With respect to personal computers, expectations are that the number of personal computers sold annually will decline from 258.8 million in 2017 to 215.8 million in 2023. On the other hand, indications are that during the same time, technology innovations such as touch-enabled PCs, ultra-slim and convertible laptops, and hybrid machines will stimulate revenue growth among technology companies.[60] Technology-based innovations also stimulate additional markets. For example, predictions are that the global video streaming market will reach $70 billion by 2021. Contributing to this market's growth is the fact that in 2018, the percentage of Internet and mobile audiences watching live video continued to expand.[61] Trends such as these inform the work firms complete to select and implement their strategies in the global economy. The most successful firms envision information technology-derived innovations as opportunities to identify and serve new markets rather than as threats to the markets they serve currently.[62]

Increasing Knowledge Intensity

Knowledge (information, intelligence, and expertise) is the basis of technology and its application. Today, knowledge is a critical organizational resource and an increasingly valuable source of competitive advantage.[63] The shifting of the basis of competition being on tangible assets to intangible ones such as knowledge began in the early 1980s. For example, "Walmart transformed retailing through its proprietary approach to supply chain management and its information-rich relationships with customers and suppliers."[64] Relationships with customers and suppliers, such as those characterizing Walmart, are an example of an intangible resource requiring managerial attention.[65]

Individuals acquire knowledge through experience, observation, and inference. Knowledge is an intangible resource (we describe tangible and intangible resources fully in Chapter 3). The value of firms' intangible resources, including knowledge, continues increasing as a proportion of total shareholder value.[66] Some believe that "intangibles have grown from filling 20% of corporate balance sheets to 80%, due in large part to the expanding nature, and rising importance, of intangibles as represented by intellectual capital vs. bricks-and-mortar, research and development vs. capital spending, services vs. manufacturing, and the list goes on."[67] Overall, U.S. firms may hold over $8 trillion in intangible assets on their balance sheets. This amount is roughly one-half of the market capitalization of companies comprising the S&P 500 index.[68] Knowledge is a key intangible asset that when diffused quickly throughout a firm contributes to efforts to outperform rivals.[69] Therefore, firms must develop (e.g., through training programs) and acquire (e.g., by hiring educated and experienced employees) knowledge, integrate it into the organization to create capabilities, and then apply it to gain a competitive advantage.[70]

A strong knowledge base is necessary to create innovations. In fact, firms lacking appropriate internal knowledge resources are less likely to allocate sufficient financial resources to R&D.[71] Firms must continue to use learning to build their knowledge base because of the common occurrence of knowledge spillovers to competitors. Rival companies hiring personnel from a firm results in the knowledge from one firm spilling over to another company.[72] Because of the potential for spillovers, firms must move quickly to use their knowledge productively. In addition, firms must find ways for knowledge to diffuse inside the organization such that it becomes available in all places where its use creates value.[73] Strategic flexibility helps firms reach these objectives.

Strategic flexibility is a set of capabilities firms use to respond to various demands and opportunities existing in today's dynamic and uncertain competitive environment. Strategic flexibility involves coping with uncertainty and its accompanying risks.[74] Firms should try to develop strategic flexibility in all areas of their operations. However, building strategic flexibility is not an easy task, largely because of inertia that can build

Strategic flexibility is a set of capabilities firms use to respond to various demands and opportunities existing in today's dynamic and uncertain competitive environment.

over time. A firm's focus and past core competencies may actually slow change and strategic flexibility.[75]

To be strategically flexible on a continuing basis and to gain the competitive benefits of such flexibility, a firm must develop the capacity to learn. Continuous learning provides the firm with new and up-to-date skill sets, which allow it to adapt to its environment as it encounters changes.[76] Firms capable of applying quickly what they have learned exhibit the strategic flexibility and the capacity to change in ways that will increase the probability of dealing successfully with uncertain, hypercompetitive environments.

1-2 The I/O Model of Above-Average Returns

From the 1960s through the 1980s, those leading organizations believed that the external environment rather than the internal organization was the strongest influence on the choice of strategy.[77] The industrial organization (I/O) model of above-average returns explains the external environment's dominant influence on the choice of strategy and the actions associated with it. The logic of the I/O model is that a set of industry characteristics, including economies of scale, barriers to market entry, diversification, product differentiation, the degree of concentration of firms in the industry, and market frictions, determine the profitability potential of an industry or a segment of it as well as the actions firms should take to operate profitably.[78] We examine these industry characteristics and explain their influence in Chapter 2.

Grounded in economics, four underlying assumptions explain the I/O model. First, the model assumes that the external environment imposes pressures and constraints that determine the strategies that would result in above-average returns. Second, most firms competing within an industry or within a segment of that industry are assumed to control similar strategically relevant resources and to pursue similar strategies in light of those resources. Third, firms assume that their resources are highly mobile, meaning that any resource differences that might develop between firms will be short-lived. Fourth, the model assumes that organizational decision makers are rational individuals who are committed to acting in the firm's best interests, as shown by their profit-maximizing behaviors.[79]

The I/O model challenges firms to find the most attractive industry in which to compete. An assumption supporting the need to find the most attractive industry is that firms possess the same types of resources with value and that these resources are mobile across companies. This means that a firm is able to increase its performance only when it competes in the industry with the highest profit potential and learns how to use its resources to implement the strategy required by the industry's structural characteristics. The competitive realities associated with the I/O model find firms imitating each other's strategies and actions taken to implement them.[80]

The five forces model of competition is an analytical tool firms use to find the industry that is the most attractive for them. The model (explained in Chapter 2) encompasses several variables and tries to capture the complexity of competition. The five forces model suggests that an industry's profitability (i.e., its rate of return on invested capital relative to its cost of capital) is a function of interactions among five forces: suppliers, buyers, competitive rivalry among firms currently in the industry, product substitutes, and potential entrants to the industry.[81]

Firms use the five forces model to identify the attractiveness of an industry (as measured by its profitability potential) as well as the most advantageous position for the firm to take in that industry, given the industry's structural characteristics.[82] The model suggests that firms can earn above-average returns by producing either standardized products at costs below those of competitors (a cost leadership strategy) or by producing differentiated products for which customers are willing to pay a price premium (a differentiation strategy). We discuss the cost leadership and product differentiation strategies fully in Chapter 4.

As shown in Figure 1.2, the I/O model suggests that firms earn above-average returns by studying the external environment effectively as the foundation for identifying an attractive industry and implementing an appropriate strategy in it. For example, in some industries, firms can reduce competitive rivalry and erect barriers to entry by forming joint ventures. In turn, reduced rivalry increases the profitability potential of firms that are collaborating.[83] Companies that develop or acquire the internal skills needed to implement strategies required by the external environment are likely to succeed, while those that do not are likely to fail.[84] Hence, this model suggests that the characteristics

Figure 1.2 The I/O Model of Above-Average Returns

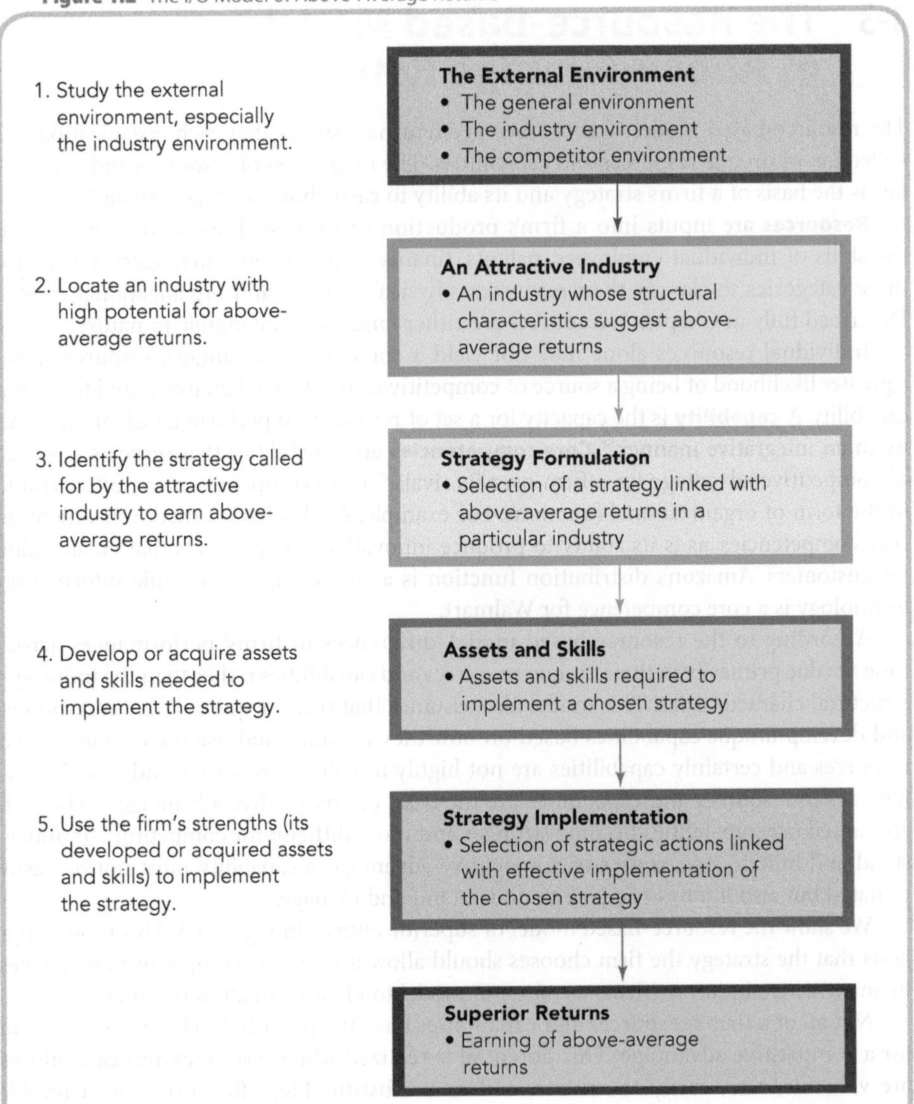

of the external environment influence returns more so than do a firm's unique internal resources and capabilities.

Research findings support the I/O model because the industry in which a firm competes explains approximately 20 percent of its profitability. However, research also shows that the firm's resources and capabilities and the actions taken by using them accounts for 36 percent of the variance in firm profitability.[85] Thus, managers' strategic actions affect the firm's performance as do the characteristics of the environment in which the firm competes.[86] These findings suggest that the external environment and a firm's resources, capabilities, core competencies, and competitive advantages (see Chapter 3) influence the company's ability to achieve strategic competitiveness and earn above-average returns.

As shown in Figure 1.2, the I/O model assumes that a firm's strategy is a set of commitments and actions flowing from the characteristics of the industry in which the firm chose to compete. The resource-based model, discussed next, takes a different view of the major influences on a firm's choice of strategy.

1-3 The Resource-Based Model of Above-Average Returns

The resource-based model of above-average returns assumes that each organization is a collection of unique resources and capabilities. The *uniqueness* of resources and capabilities is the basis of a firm's strategy and its ability to earn above-average returns.[87]

Resources are inputs into a firm's production process, such as capital equipment, the skills of individual employees, patents, finances, and talented managers. Firms use three categories to classify their resources: physical, human, and organizational capital. Described fully in Chapter 3, resources are either tangible or intangible in nature.

Individual resources alone may not yield a competitive advantage; resources have a greater likelihood of being a source of competitive advantage when integrated to form a capability. A **capability** is the capacity for a set of resources to perform a task or an activity in an integrative manner.[88] **Core competencies** are capabilities that serve as a source of competitive advantage for a firm over its rivals.[89] Core competencies are often visible in the form of organizational functions. For example, Apple's R&D function is one of its core competencies, as is its ability to produce innovative new products that create value for customers. Amazon's distribution function is a core competence while information technology is a core competence for Walmart.

According to the resource-based model, differences in firms' performances across time are due primarily to their unique resources and capabilities rather than the industry's structural characteristics. This model also assumes that firms acquire different resources and develop unique capabilities based on how they combine and use the resources; that resources and certainly capabilities are not highly mobile across firms; and that the differences in resources and capabilities are the basis of competitive advantage.[90] Through continued use, capabilities become stronger and more difficult for competitors to understand and imitate. As a source of competitive advantage, a capability must not be easily imitated but also not too complex to understand and manage.[91]

We show the resource-based model of superior returns in Figure 1.3. This model suggests that the strategy the firm chooses should allow it to use its competitive advantages in an attractive industry (firms use the I/O model to identify an attractive industry).

Not all of a firm's resources and capabilities have the potential to be the foundation for a competitive advantage. This potential is realized when resources and capabilities are valuable, rare, costly to imitate, and non-substitutable.[92] Resources are *valuable* when they allow a firm to take advantage of opportunities or neutralize threats in

Resources are inputs into a firm's production process, such as capital equipment, the skills of individual employees, patents, finances, and talented managers.

A **capability** is the capacity for a set of resources to perform a task or an activity in an integrative manner.

Core competencies are capabilities that serve as a source of competitive advantage for a firm over its rivals.

Figure 1.3 The Resource-Based Model of Above-Average Returns

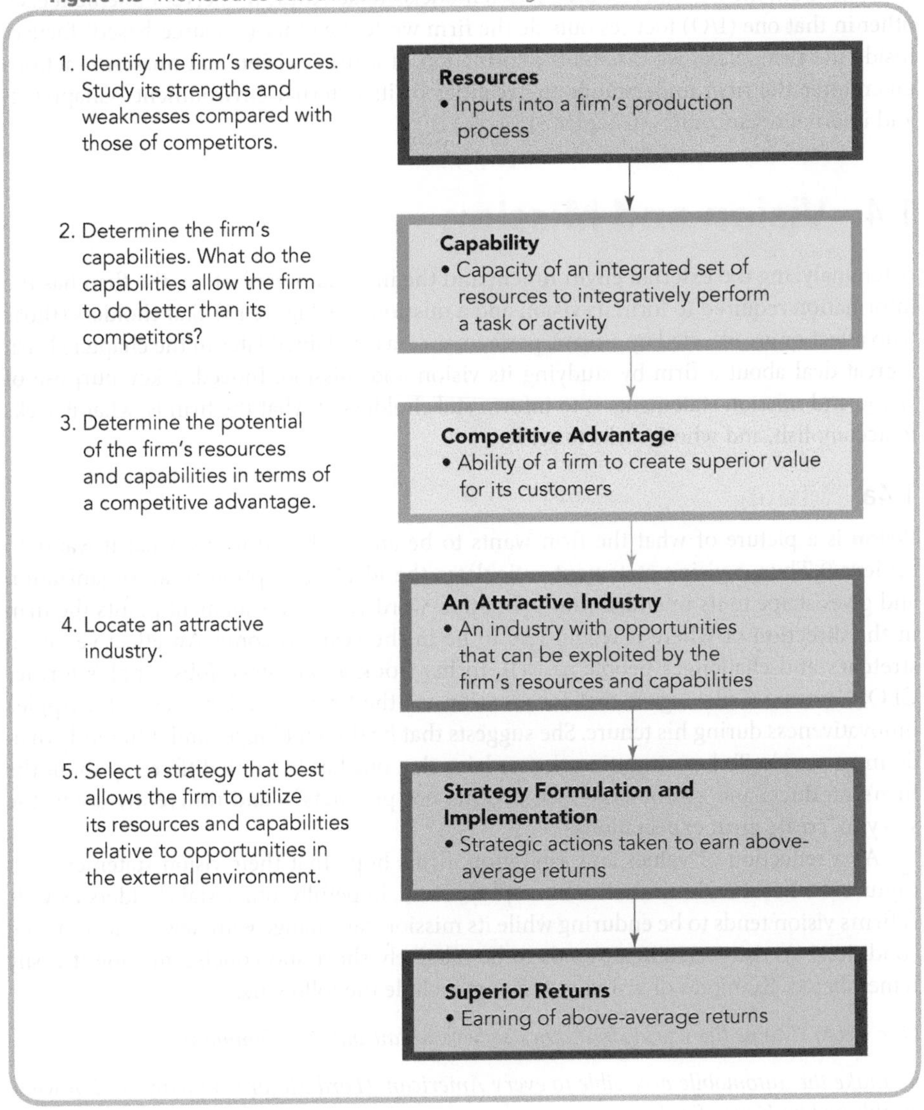

its external environment. They are *rare* when possessed by few, if any, current and potential competitors. Resources are *costly to imitate* when other firms either cannot obtain them or are at a cost disadvantage in obtaining them compared with the firm that already possesses them. They are *non-substitutable* when they have no structural equivalents. Over time, competitors find ways to imitate value-creating resources or to create new resources that yield a different type of value that creates value for customers. Therefore, it is difficult to achieve and sustain a competitive advantage based on resources alone. Firms integrate individual resources to develop configurations of resources with the potential to build capabilities. Capabilities developed in this manner have a stronger likelihood of becoming a core competence and of leading to a source of competitive advantage.[93]

Previously, we noted that research shows that both the industry environment and a firm's internal assets affect its performance over time.[94] Thus, to form a vision and mission, and subsequently to select one or more strategies and determine how to implement them, firms use both the I/O and resource-based models. In fact, these models complement each other in that one (I/O) focuses outside the firm while the other (resource-based) focuses inside the firm. Next, we discuss the formation of a firm's vision and mission—actions taken after the firm understands the realities of its external environment (Chapter 2) and internal organization (Chapter 3).

1-4 Vision and Mission

After analyzing the external environment and the internal organization, the firm has the information required to form its vision and a mission (see Figure 1.1). Stakeholders (those who affect or are affected by a firm's performance, as explained later in the chapter) learn a great deal about a firm by studying its vision and mission. Indeed, a key purpose of vision and mission statements is to inform stakeholders of what the firm is, what it seeks to accomplish, and who it seeks to serve.

1-4a Vision

Vision is a picture of what the firm wants to be and, in broad terms, what it wants to achieve.[95] Thus, a vision statement articulates the ideal description of an organization and gives shape to its intended future. In other words, a vision statement points the firm in the direction of where it would like to be in the years to come. An effective vision stretches and challenges people as well. In her book about Steve Jobs, Apple's former CEO, Carmine Gallo argues that Jobs's vision for the firm was a key reason for Apple's innovativeness during his tenure. She suggests that he thought bigger and differently than do most people. To be innovative, she explains that one has to think differently about the firm's products and customers—"sell dreams not products"—and differently about the story to "create great expectations."[96]

As a reflection of values and aspiration, firms hope that their vision statement will capture the heart and mind of each employee and, hopefully, other stakeholders as well. A firm's vision tends to be enduring while its mission can change with new environmental conditions. A vision statement tends to be relatively short and concise, making it easily remembered. Examples of vision statements include the following:

Our vision is to be the world's best quick service restaurant. (McDonald's)

To make the automobile accessible to every American. (Ford Motor Company's vision when established by Henry Ford)

Delivering happiness to customers, employees, and vendors. (Zappos.com)

As a firm's most important and prominent strategic leader, the CEO is responsible for working with others to form the firm's vision. Experience shows that the most effective vision statement results when the CEO involves a host of stakeholders (e.g., other top-level managers, employees working in different parts of the organization, suppliers, and customers) to develop it.[97] Conditions in the firm's external environment and internal organization influence the forming of a vision statement. Moreover, the decisions and actions of those involved with developing the vision, especially the CEO and the other top-level managers, must be consistent with it.

Vision is a picture of what the firm wants to be and, in broad terms, what it wants to achieve.

A **mission** specifies the businesses in which the firm intends to compete and the customers it intends to serve.

1-4b Mission

The vision is the foundation for the firm's mission. A **mission** specifies the businesses in which the firm intends to compete and the customers it intends to serve.[98] The firm's mission is more concrete than its vision. However, similar to the vision, a mission should establish a firm's individuality and should be inspiring and relevant to all stakeholders. Together, the vision and mission provide the foundation the firm needs to choose and implement one or more strategies. The probability of forming an effective mission increases when employees have a strong sense of the ethical standards that guide their behaviors as they work to help the firm reach its vision.[99] Thus, business ethics are a vital part of the firm's discussions to decide what it wants to become (its vision) as well as who it intends to serve and how it desires to serve those individuals and groups (its mission).[100]

Even though the final responsibility for forming the firm's mission rests with the CEO, the CEO and other top-level managers often involve other people to develop the mission statement. The main reason for this is that the mission deals more directly with product markets and customers. Compared to a firm's senior-level leaders, middle- and first-level managers and other employees interact frequently with customers and the markets the firm serves. Examples of mission statements include the following:

Be the best employer for our people in each community around the world and deliver operational excellence to our customers in each of our restaurants. (McDonald's)

Provide the best customer service possible. Deliver WOW through service. (Zappos.com)

McDonald's mission statement flows from its vision of being the world's best quick service restaurant. Zappos.com's mission statement indicates that the firm will reach its vision of delivering happiness to different stakeholder groups by providing service that WOWs them.

Clearly, ineffectively developed vision and mission statements fail to provide the direction a firm needs to take appropriate strategic actions. This is undesirable in that as shown in Figure 1.1, a firm's vision and mission are critical aspects of the *analysis* and the base required to engage in *strategic actions* that help the firm achieve strategic competitiveness and earn above-average returns. Therefore, firms must accept the challenge of forming effective vision and mission statements.

1-5 Stakeholders

Every organization involves a system of primary stakeholder groups with whom it establishes and manages relationships.[101] **Stakeholders** are individuals, groups, and organizations that can affect the firm's vision and mission, are affected by the strategic outcomes achieved, and have enforceable claims on the firm's performance.[102] Their ability to withhold participation that is essential to the firm's survival, competitiveness, and profitability is the source of stakeholders' ability to enforce their claims against an organization. Stakeholders continue to support an organization when its performance meets or exceeds their expectations. Research suggests that firms managing relationships with their stakeholders effectively outperform those that do not.[103] Stakeholder relationships and the firm's overall reputation among stakeholders can therefore be a source of competitive advantage.[104]

Although organizations have dependency relationships with their stakeholders, firms are not equally dependent on all stakeholders at all times. Unequal dependencies means that stakeholders possess different degrees of ability to influence an organization.[105] The more critical and valued is a stakeholder's participation, the greater is a firm's dependency on that stakeholder. Greater dependence, in turn, gives the stakeholder more potential influence over a firm's commitments, decisions, and actions. Managers must find ways to either accommodate or insulate the organization from the demands of stakeholders controlling critical resources.[106]

Stakeholders are individuals, groups, and organizations that can affect the firm's vision and mission, are affected by the strategic outcomes achieved, and have enforceable claims on the firm's performance.

1-5a Classifications of Stakeholders

Firms can separate the parties involved with their operations into at least three groups.[107] As shown in Figure 1.4, these groups are the capital market stakeholders (shareholders and the major suppliers of a firm's capital), the product market stakeholders (the firm's primary customers, suppliers, host communities, and unions representing the workforce), and the organizational stakeholders (all of a firm's employees, including both non-managerial and managerial personnel).

Each stakeholder group expects those making strategic decisions in a firm to provide the leadership that will result in the reaching of its valued objectives.[108] The objectives of stakeholder groups often differ from one another, sometimes placing those involved with a firm's strategic management process in situations where trade-offs have to be made. The most obvious stakeholders, at least in U.S. organizations, are *shareholders*—individuals and groups who have invested capital in a firm in the expectation of earning a positive return on their investments. Laws governing private property and private enterprise are the source of shareholders' rights.

In contrast to shareholders, another group of stakeholders—the firm's customers—prefers that investors receive a minimum return on their investments. Customers could have their interests maximized when the quality and reliability of a firm's products are improved, but without high prices. High returns to customers, therefore, might come at the expense of lower returns for capital market stakeholders.

Because of potential conflicts, firms seek to manage stakeholders' expectations. First, a firm must identify and then seek to understand fully each stakeholder group's interests. Second, it must prioritize those interests in case it cannot satisfy all of them. Power

Figure 1.4 The Three Stakeholder Groups

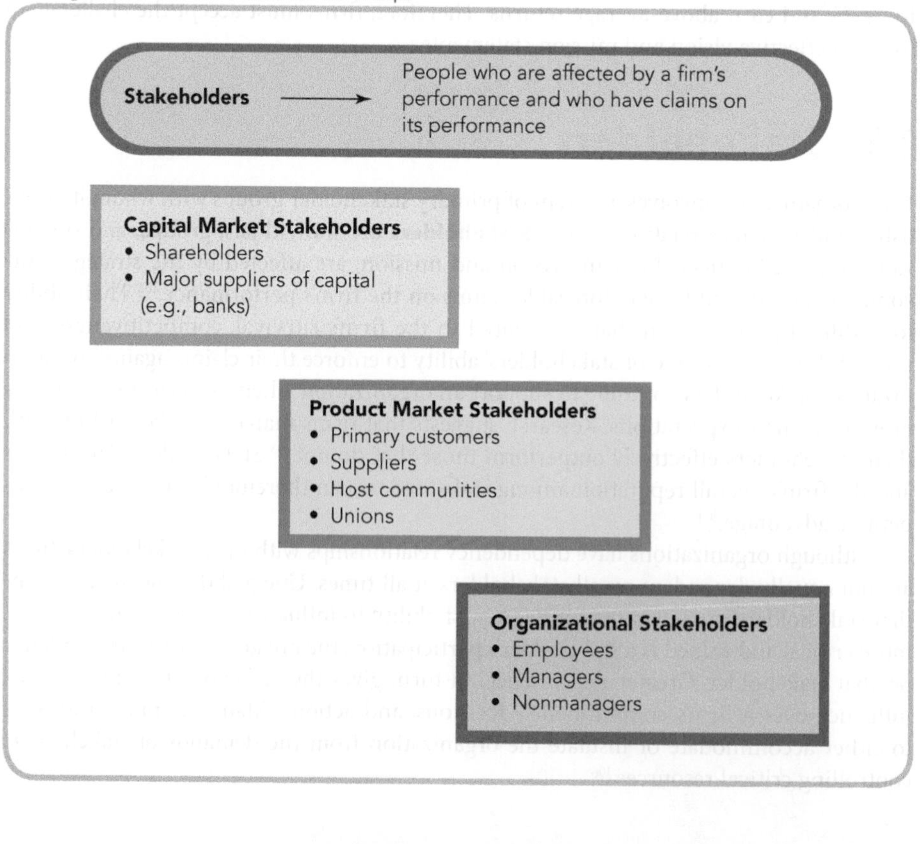

Stakeholders → People who are affected by a firm's performance and who have claims on its performance

Capital Market Stakeholders
- Shareholders
- Major suppliers of capital (e.g., banks)

Product Market Stakeholders
- Primary customers
- Suppliers
- Host communities
- Unions

Organizational Stakeholders
- Employees
- Managers
- Nonmanagers

is the most critical criterion in prioritizing stakeholders; that is to say, the stakeholder group with whom the firm has the greatest dependence for its commitment has the greatest amount of power to influence the firm's actions.[109]

When earning above-average returns, the firm is in a better position to manage stakeholder relationships effectively. With the capability and flexibility provided by above-average returns, a firm can satisfy multiple stakeholders more easily. When the firm earns only average returns, it is unable to maximize the interests of all stakeholders. The objective then becomes that of satisfying each stakeholder group's minimal expectations.

Africa Studio/Shutterstock.com

As a firm formulates its strategy, it must consider all of its primary stakeholders in the product and capital markets as well as organizational shareholders.

Stakeholders receive different levels of attention in light of how dependent the firm is on their support at a point in time. For example, environmental groups may be very important to firms in the energy industry but less important to professional service firms. A firm earning below-average returns lacks the capacity to satisfy the minimal expectations of all stakeholder groups. The managerial challenge in this case is to make trade-offs that minimize the amount of support lost from stakeholders. Societal values also influence the general weightings allocated among the three stakeholder groups shown in Figure 1.4; that is to say that cultural norms and institutional rules, regulations, and laws influence how firms interact with stakeholders in different countries and regions of the world. Next, we present additional details about each of the three major stakeholder groups.

Capital Market Stakeholders

Shareholders and lenders both expect a firm to preserve and enhance the wealth they have entrusted to it. The returns they expect are commensurate with the degree of risk they accept with those investments (i.e., lower returns are expected with low-risk investments while higher returns are expected with high-risk investments). Dissatisfied lenders may impose stricter covenants on subsequent borrowing of capital. Dissatisfied shareholders may reflect their concerns through several means, including selling their stock. Institutional investors too (e.g., pension funds, mutual funds) may choose to sell their stock if the returns fail to meet their expectations.

Alternatively, as stakeholders, these investors might take actions to improve the firm's performance. Communicating clearly their expectations regarding performance to the firm's board of directors and top-level managers is an example of such actions.[110] Some institutions owning major shares of a firm's stock may have conflicting views of the actions needed, which can be challenging for the firm's managers. This is because some may want an increase in returns in the short-term while the others desire a focus on building long-term competitiveness.[111] In these instances, managers may need to balance their desires with those of other shareholders or prioritize the importance of the institutional owners with different goals. Clearly, shareholders who hold a large share of stock (sometimes referred to as blockholders, see Chapter 10) are influential, especially in determining the firm's capital structure (i.e., the amount of equity versus the amount of debt used). Large shareholders often prefer that the firm minimize its use of debt because of its risk, its cost, and the possibility that debt holders have first call on the firm's assets relative to shareholders in case of default.[112] Because of their importance in terms of supporting needs for capital, firms typically seek to find ways to better satisfy the expectations of capital market stakeholders.

Product Market Stakeholders

Some might think that product market stakeholders (customers, suppliers, host communities, and unions) share few common interests. However, these four groups can benefit as firms engage in competitive battles. For example, depending on product and industry characteristics, marketplace competition may result in lower product prices for a firm's customers and higher prices for its suppliers (the firm might be willing to pay higher supplier prices to ensure delivery of the products linked to its competitive success).[113]

Customers, as stakeholders, seek reliable products at the lowest possible prices. Suppliers seek loyal customers who are willing to pay the highest sustainable prices for the products they receive. Although all product market stakeholders are important, without customers, the other product market stakeholders are of little value. Therefore, the firm must try to learn about and understand current and potential customers.

Host communities include the national (home and abroad), state/province, and local government entities with which the firm interacts. Governments want companies willing to be long-term employers and providers of tax revenue without placing excessive demands on public support services. These stakeholders also influence the firm through laws and regulations. In fact, firms must deal with laws and regulations developed and enforced at the national, state, and local levels (the influence is *polycentric*—multiple levels of power and influence). This means that firms encounter influence attempts from multiple regulatory sources with power.[114] The interests of unions include secure jobs and desirable working conditions for members.

In an overall sense, product market stakeholders are generally satisfied when a firm's profit margin reflects at least a balance between the returns to capital market stakeholders (i.e., the returns lenders and shareholders will accept and retain their interests in the firm) and the returns in which they share.

Organizational Stakeholders

Employees—the firm's organizational stakeholders—expect the firm to provide a dynamic, stimulating, and rewarding work environment. Employees generally prefer to work for a company that is growing and in which they can develop their skills, especially those required to be effective team members and to meet or exceed global work standards. Workers who learn how to use new knowledge productively are critical to organizational success. In a collective sense, the education and skills of a firm's workforce are competitive weapons affecting strategy implementation and firm performance.[115]

Those leading a firm bear responsibility for serving stakeholders' needs on a day-to-day basis. Using the firm's human capital successfully supports leaders' efforts to do this.[116] International assignments facilitate efforts to help a firm's employees understand competition in the global competitive landscape. "Expats" is the title given to individuals engaged in an international assignment for their company. The process of managing expatriate employees so they develop knowledge while working internationally and understand how to bring that knowledge with them upon return has the potential to enhance the firm's performance at the domestic and international levels.[117]

1-6 Strategic Leaders

Bloomberg/Getty Images

Gary Kelly, CEO of Southwest Airlines, is a recipient of the Tony Jannus Award, which recognizes outstanding contributors to the growth and improvement of the airline industry.

Strategic leaders are people located in different areas and levels of the firm using the strategic management process to select actions that help the firm achieve its vision and fulfill its mission. Regardless of their location in the firm, successful strategic leaders are decisive, committed to nurturing those around them, and committed to helping the firm create value for all stakeholder groups.[118] In this vein, research evidence suggests that employees who perceive that their CEO is a visionary leader also believe that the CEO leads the firm to operate in ways that are consistent with the values of all stakeholder groups rather than emphasizing only maximizing profits for shareholders. In turn, visionary leadership motivates employees to expend extra effort, thereby helping to increase firm performance.

When identifying strategic leaders, most of us tend to think of CEOs and other top-level managers. Clearly, these people are strategic leaders. In the final analysis, CEOs are responsible for making certain their firm uses the strategic management process successfully. The pressure on CEOs today to manage strategically is stronger than ever.[119] However, many others help choose a firm's strategy and the actions to implement it.[120] The reason for this is that the realities of twenty-first century competition mentioned earlier in this chapter (e.g., the global economy, globalization, rapid technological change, and the increasing importance of knowledge and people as sources of competitive advantage) create a need for those "closest to the action" to play a role in choosing and implementing the firm's strategy. In fact, all managers (as strategic leaders) must think globally and act locally.[121] Thus, the most effective CEOs and top-level managers understand how to delegate strategic responsibilities to people throughout the firm who influence the use of organizational resources. Delegation also helps to avoid managerial hubris at the top and the problems it causes, especially in situations allowing significant managerial discretion.[122]

Organizational culture also affects strategic leaders and their work. In turn, strategic leaders' decisions and actions shape a firm's culture. **Organizational culture** refers to the complex set of ideologies, symbols, and core values that individuals throughout the firm share and that influence how the firm conducts business. Organizational culture is the social energy that drives—or fails to drive—the organization.[123] For example, many believe that the culture at Southwest Airlines is unique and valuable. Its culture encourages employees to work hard but also to have fun while doing so. Moreover, its culture entails respect for others—employees and customers alike. The firm also places a premium on service, as suggested by its commitment to provide POS (Positively Outrageous Service) to each customer.

Strategic leaders are people located in different areas and levels of the firm using the strategic management process to select actions that help the firm achieve its vision and fulfill its mission.

Organizational culture refers to the complex set of ideologies, symbols, and core value that individuals throughout the firm share and that influence how the firm conducts business.

1-6a The Work of Effective Strategic Leaders

Perhaps not surprisingly, hard work, thorough analyses, a willingness to be brutally honest, a penchant for wanting the firm and its people to achieve success, and tenacity are prerequisites to an individual's success as a strategic leader. Individuals become top-level leaders because of their capabilities (their accumulation of human capital and

Strategic Focus

Strategic Leaders' Decisions as a Path to Firms' Efforts to Deal Successfully with Their Challenges

The rapid pace of change facing companies and those leading them in today's globalized business environment is a recurring theme in our analysis of the strategic management process. Stated simply, the pace of change organizations throughout the world encounter today is rapid, while the nature of such change induces complexity for firms as they seek strategic competitiveness. Often, change comes to firms in the form of different customer expectations. In the hotel industry for example, Hilton Worldwide Holdings, with 14 brands and more than 5,300 properties, believes that "one of its biggest challenges is keeping up with changing tastes, especially among millennials, who want high-tech amenities, bigger, hipper lobbies and a cleaner, more minimal look." For Hilton's strategic leaders, the "biggest challenge continues to be the pace of change and the rate at which, in the digital space, new capabilities get put in front of consumers."

To deal with changes such as these, top-level strategic leaders typically help their firms form strategic actions and strategic responses. For many of these strategic leaders, a global mind-set and a passion for meeting people's needs inform their decisions.

Defined and discussed in Chapter 5, strategic actions and strategic responses find firms trying to outcompete rivals in marketplace competitions. Strategic actions and responses require significant commitments of organizational resources and are decisions that are difficult for firms to reverse once executed. The strategic actions Hilton is taking to respond to changes include those of refreshing old brands and establishing new ones such as Tru, which emphasizes communal space over room size.

Consumer-goods giant Procter & Gamble (P&G) is facing fundamental challenges in its home U.S. market, including shifts in consumer preferences, retailers pushing for lower prices, and the availability of private label alternatives for consumers. In response, P&G's top-level strategic leaders decided recently to acquire the consumer health business of Germany's Merck KGaA for $4.2 billion. This unit's product portfolio includes an array of specialty dietary supplements as well as a nasal decongestant. One reason for this acquisition is declines in P&G's organic sales growth and in its all-important Gillette razors. Encountering stalling revenue growth, Pfizer's strategic leaders are considering several strategic actions including those of spinning off its consumer-health business, which sells products such as Advil pain pills, ChapStick lip balm, and Centrum vitamins, to splitting the company. Following successful stints with Volkswagen AG and Nissan Infiniti brand, Johan de Nysschen accepted the role of president of Cadillac, a General Motors unit. An indication that he intends to "mold Cadillac in the image of BMW and other luxury brands" suggests the emergence of a string of strategic actions. Global declines in beer consumption finds Dutch brewer Heineken NV engaging in a number of strategic actions. Acquiring a 20.67% stake in China's largest brewer, China Resources Beer Holdings Co., and acquiring several craft brewers are examples of decisions made to expand the firm's customer base.

helen89/iStock Editorial/Getty Images

Tru Hotel; Hilton's response to millennials who want high-tech amenities, bigger, hipper lobbies, and a cleaner, more minimal look.

Recently, the Drucker Institute, founded in 2007 to advance managerial ideals as espoused by Peter Drucker, identified the 250 most effectively managed U.S. companies. Amazon held the top spot with Apple, Google parent Alphabet, IBM, Microsoft, and Cisco rounding out the top five. These firms' positive performance relative to other companies in terms of five areas Drucker said are critical to corporate success—customer satisfaction, employee engagement and development, innovation, social responsibility, and financial strength—earned them the top spots on the list.

One might argue that these firms' strategic leaders, including the top-level leaders, rendered decisions regarding strategic actions and responses that contributed to their firms' excellence. In addition to the characteristics of strategic leaders mentioned in this chapter's text, such as hard work, a commitment to analyze situations thoroughly, and so forth, those leading the top five firms as well as the others on the list of 250 companies chosen by the Drucker Institute may have additional qualities. For example, some believe that the success of Sergio Marchionne, the leader credited with turning around Fiat and Chrysler (who recently passed away), is a function of an "unusual blend of vision, technical expertise, analytical rigor, open-mindedness, and candor." As with Steve Jobs, Apple's former CEO, Marchionne's actions earned him a recognition as being a bit of an eccentric, too. Regardless of their characteristics though, the decisions made by strategic leaders inform how their firm will use the strategic management process.

Sources: A. Back, 2018, P&G needs a workout, not vitamins, *Wall Street Journal*, www.wsj.com, April 19; M. Colias, 2018, The 10-year plan to make Cadillac cool again, *Wall Street Journal*, www.wsj.com, October 25; K. Paul, 2018, What millennials want in hotel rooms, *Wall Street Journal*, www.wsj.com, August 12; J. D. Rockoff & W. Colville, 2018, Johnson & Johnson remakes top leadership, *Wall Street Journal*, www.wsj.com, June 22; J. D. Rockoff & C. Lombardo, 2018, Pfizer revenue growth stalls as company mulls OTC unit's future, *Wall Street Journal*, www.wsj.com, May 1; J. D. Rockoff & I. Moise, 2018, Johnson & Johnson raises sales outlook, *Wall Street Journal*, www.wsj.com, April 17; S. Terlap & A. Hufford, 2018, P&G slogs through 'difficult' markets for sales growth, *Wall Street Journal*, www.wsj.com, April 19; S. Terlap & J. D. Rockoff, 2018, P&G to acquire Merck KGaA's consumer-health unit, *Wall Street Journal*, www.wsj.com, April 19; N. Trentmann, 2018, Heineken's strategy in a stagnate beer market, *Wall Street Journal*, www.wsj.com, August 9; S. Walker, 2018, Why the future belongs to 'challenge-driven leaders,' *Wall Street Journal*, www.wsj.com, August 11; S. Walker, 2018, The leader of the future: Why Sergio Marchionne fit the profile, *Wall Street Journal*, www.wsj.com, August 11; V. Fuhrmans & Y. Koh, 2017, The 250 most effectively managed U.S. companies—and how they got that way, *Wall Street Journal*, www.wsj.com, December 6.

skills over time). Effective top management teams (those with better human capital, management skills, and cognitive abilities) make better strategic decisions.[124] In addition, strategic leaders must have a strong strategic orientation while embracing change in today's dynamic competitive landscape.[125] To deal with change effectively, strategic leaders must be innovative thinkers and promote innovation in their organization.[126] A top management team representing different types of expertise and leveraging relationships with external parties promotes firm innovation.[127] Strategic leaders can best leverage partnerships with external parties and organizations when their organizations are ambidextrous; that is, when they are both innovative and skilled at execution.[128] In addition, strategic leaders need to have a global mind-set; some consider this mind-set as an ambicultural approach to management.[129]

Strategic leaders, regardless of their location in the organization, often work long hours, and ambiguous decision situations dominate the nature of their work. However, the opportunities afforded by this work are appealing and offer exciting chances to dream and to act. The following words, given as advice to the late Time Warner chair and co-CEO Steven J. Ross by his father, describe the opportunities in a strategic leader's work:

There are three categories of people—the person who goes into the office, puts his feet up on his desk, and dreams for 12 hours; the person who arrives at 5 a.m. and works for 16 hours, never once stopping to dream; and the person who puts his feet up, dreams for one hour, then does something about those dreams.[130]

As a term, vision describes a dream that challenges and energizes a company. The most effective strategic leaders provide a vision as the foundation for the firm's mission and subsequent choice and use of one or more strategies.[131]

We describe the work of some strategic leaders in the Strategic Focus. While reading this material, notice the relationship between the points mentioned in this part of the chapter about strategic leaders and the actions highlighted in the Strategic Focus. Strategic leaders work in all parts of an organization; however, in this Strategic Focus, top-level leaders are the focus of the discussion.

As you will see, the work of upper-level strategic leaders is indeed challenging, complex, and ambiguous in nature. On the other hand, these individuals play a major role in the making of a firm's competitive decisions—the types of decisions that are a part of their use of the strategic management process.

1-7 The Strategic Management Process

As suggested by Figure 1.1, the strategic management process is a rational approach firms use to achieve strategic competitiveness and earn above-average returns. Figure 1.1 also features the topics we examine in this book to present the strategic management process.

We divide this book into three parts—parts that align with the A-S-P process explained in the beginning of the chapter. In Part 1, we describe the *analyses* (A) firms use to develop strategies. Specifically, we explain how firms analyze their external environment (Chapter 2) and internal organization (Chapter 3). Firms complete these analyses to identify marketplace opportunities and threats in the external environment (Chapter 2) and to decide how to use the resources, capabilities, core competencies, and competitive advantages in their internal organization to pursue opportunities and overcome threats (Chapter 3). The analyses explained in Chapters 2 and 3 are the well-known SWOT analyses (strengths, weaknesses, opportunities, threats).[132] Firms use knowledge about their external environment and internal organization to formulate strategies in light of their vision and mission.

The firm's analyses (see Figure 1.1) provide the foundation for choosing one or more *strategies* (S) and deciding which one(s) to implement. As suggested in Figure 1.1 by the horizontal arrow linking the two types of strategic actions, firms simultaneously integrate formulation and implementation as a basis for a successful strategic management process. Integration occurs as decision makers review implementation issues when choosing strategies and when considering potential adaptations to a strategy during the implementation process itself.

In Part 2, we discuss the different strategies firms may choose to use. First, we examine business-level strategies (Chapter 4). A business-level strategy describes actions a firm takes to exploit its competitive advantage(s). A company competing in a single product market (e.g., a locally owned grocery store operating in only one location) has but one business-level strategy, while a diversified firm competing in multiple product markets (e.g., Siemens AG) forms a business-level strategy for each of its businesses. In Chapter 5, we describe the actions and reactions that occur among firms as they engage each other in competition. Competitors typically respond to and try to anticipate each other's actions. The dynamics of competition affect the strategies firms choose as well as how they intend to implement those strategies.[133] For example, one year after Amazon acquired Whole Foods, some analysts felt that this strategic action was "prompting the food industry to retool how it sells fresh food to consumers."[134] You will learn more about Amazon and Whole Foods in Chapter 5's Opening Case.

Determining the businesses in which the company intends to compete as well as how it will manage those businesses is the focus of corporate-level strategy (Chapter 6). Companies competing in more than one business experience diversification in the form of products (Chapter 7) and/or geographic markets (Chapter 8). Other topics vital to strategy formulation, particularly in the diversified company, include acquiring other businesses and, as appropriate, restructuring the firm's portfolio of businesses (Chapter 7) and selecting an international strategy (Chapter 8). With cooperative strategies (Chapter 9), firms form a partnership to share their resources and capabilities to develop a competitive advantage.

To examine actions firms take to implement strategies, we consider several topics in Part 3. First, we examine the different mechanisms companies use to govern themselves (Chapter 10). With different stakeholders (e.g., financial investors and board of directors' members) demanding improved corporate governance today, organizations seek to identify paths to follow to satisfy these demands.[135] In the last three chapters, we address the organizational structure and actions needed to control a firm's operations (Chapter 11), the patterns of strategic leadership appropriate for today's firms and competitive environments (Chapter 12), and strategic entrepreneurship (Chapter 13) as a path to continuous innovation.

Because they deal with how a firm interacts with its stakeholders, strategic management process decisions have ethical dimensions.[136] Organizational culture reveals the firm's ethics; that is to say, a firm's core values, the ones most or all employees share, influence strongly their decisions. Especially in the global economy's turbulent and often ambiguous competitive landscape, those making decisions as a part of the strategic management process must understand how their decisions affect capital market, product market, and organizational stakeholders differently and regularly evaluate the ethical implications of their decisions.[137] Decision makers failing to recognize these realities accept the risk of placing their firm at a competitive disadvantage.[138]

As you will discover, the strategic management process we present to you in this book calls for disciplined approaches to serve as the foundation for developing a competitive advantage. Therefore, the process has a major effect on the *performance* (P) of the firm.[139] The firm's ability to achieve strategic competitiveness and earn above-average returns reflects the quality of its performance. Mastery of this strategic management process contributes positively to a firm's efforts to outperform competitors and to create value for its stakeholders.

SUMMARY

- Firms use the strategic management process to achieve strategic competitiveness and earn above-average returns. Firms *analyze* the external environment and their internal organization, then formulate and implement a *strategy* to achieve a desired level of *performance* (A-S-P). The firm's level of strategic competitiveness and the extent to which it earns above-average returns reflects its performance. Firms achieve strategic competitiveness by developing and implementing a value-creating strategy. Above-average returns (in excess of what investors expect to earn from other investments with similar levels of risk) provide the foundation for satisfying all of a firm's stakeholders simultaneously.

- The fundamental nature of competition is different in the current competitive landscape. As a result, those making strategic decisions must adopt a different mind-set, one that allows them to learn how to compete in highly turbulent and chaotic environments that produce a great deal of uncertainty. The globalization of industries and their markets along with rapid and significant technological changes are the two primary factors contributing to the turbulence of the competitive landscape.

- Firms use two major models to help develop their vision and mission when choosing one or more strategies to pursue strategic competitiveness and above-average returns. The core assumption of the I/O model is that the firm's external environment has a larger influence on the choice of strategies than does its internal resources, capabilities, and core competencies. Thus, firms use the I/O model to understand the effects an industry's characteristics can have on them when selecting a strategy or strategies to use to compete against rivals. The logic supporting the I/O model suggests that firms earn above-average returns by locating an attractive industry or part of an attractive industry and then implementing the strategy dictated by that industry's characteristics successfully.

  The core assumption of the resource-based model is that the firm's unique resources, capabilities, and core competencies have more of an influence on selecting and using strategies than does the firm's external environment. When firms use their valuable, rare, costly-to-imitate, and non-substitutable resources and capabilities effectively when competing against rivals in one or more industries, they earn above-average returns. Evidence indicates that both models' insights help firms as they select and implement strategies. Thus, firms want to use their unique resources, capabilities, and core competencies as the foundation to engage in one or more strategies that allow them to compete effectively against rivals.

- The firm's vision and mission guide its selection of strategies based on the information from analyses of its external environment and internal organization. Vision is a picture of what the firm wants to be and, in broad terms, what it wants to achieve ultimately. Flowing from the vision, the mission specifies the business or businesses in which the firm intends to compete and the customers it intends to serve. Vision and mission provide direction to the firm and signal important descriptive information to stakeholders.

- Stakeholders are those who can affect, and are affected by, a firm's performance. Because a firm is dependent on the continuing support of stakeholders (shareholders, customers, suppliers, employees, host communities, etc.), they have enforceable claims on the company's performance. When earning above-average returns, a firm generally has the resources it needs to satisfy the interests of all stakeholders. However, when earning only average returns, the firm must manage its stakeholders carefully to retain their support. A firm earning below-average returns must minimize the amount of support it loses from unsatisfied stakeholders.

- Strategic leaders are people located in different areas and levels of the firm using the strategic management process to help the firm achieve its vision and fulfill its mission. In general, CEOs are responsible for making certain that their firms use the strategic management process properly. The effectiveness of the strategic management process increases when grounded in ethical intentions and behaviors. The strategic leader's work demands decision trade-offs, often among attractive alternatives. It is important for all strategic leaders, especially the CEO and other members of the top management team, to conduct thorough analyses of conditions facing the firm, be brutally and consistently honest, and work collaboratively with others to select and implement strategies.

KEY TERMS

above-average returns 6
average returns 6
capability 16
competitive advantage 4
core competencies 16
global economy 9
hypercompetition 8
mission 18
organizational culture 23
resources 16
risk 6
stakeholders 19
strategic competitiveness 4
strategic flexibility 13
strategic leaders 23
strategic management process 6
strategy 4
vision 18

REVIEW QUESTIONS

1. What are strategic competitiveness, strategy, competitive advantage, above-average returns, and the strategic management process?
2. What are the characteristics of the current competitive landscape? What two factors are the primary drivers of this landscape?
3. According to the I/O model, what should a firm do to earn above-average returns?
4. What does the resource-based model suggest a firm should do to earn above-average returns?
5. What are vision and mission? What is their value for the strategic management process?
6. What are stakeholders? How do the three primary stakeholder groups influence organizations?
7. How would you describe the work of strategic leaders?
8. What are the elements of the strategic management process? How are they interrelated?

Mini-Case

Starbucks Is "Juicing" Its Earnings per Store through Technological Innovations

The choice of a CEO signals potential actions to stakeholders about a firm's potential actions. Howard Schultz served as Starbucks CEO for many years; the firm achieved multiple successes during his service. As of April 2017, Schulz became executive chairman of Starbucks's board while Kevin Johnson, a former CEO of Juniper Networks and a 16 year veteran of Microsoft, assumed the CEO position for the coffee giant. Johnson's background may find him concentrating on the firm's digital operations, information technology practices and supply chain operations as a means of increasing Starbucks's effectiveness and efficiency.

Many brick and mortar stores have experienced decreasing sales in the United States as online traffic has increased. Interestingly, 2014 Starbucks sales store operations increased 5 percent in the fourth quarter; this 5 percent uptick in revenue came from increased traffic (2 percent from growth in sales and 3 percent in increased ticket size).

Additional and more sophisticated technology applications may be the driver of this increase in revenues. To stimulate sales, Starbucks is ramping up its digital tools such as mobile payment platforms. Customers now can place online orders and pick them up in about 150 Starbucks outlets in the Portland, OR area. Besides leadership and a focus on technology, Starbucks receives suggestions, ideas, and experimentation from its employees. Starbucks views its employees, called baristas, as partners who blend, steam, and brew the brand's specialty coffee in over 21,000 stores worldwide. Schultz credits the employees as a dominant force in helping it to build its revenue gains.

To incentivize employees further, Starbucks is among the first companies to provide comprehensive health benefits and stock option ownership opportunities to part-time employees. Currently, employees have received more than $1 billion worth of financial gain through the stock option program. An additional benefit for U.S. employees is the firm's program that pays 100 percent of workers' tuition to finish their degrees through Arizona State University. To date, one thousand workers have enrolled in this program. In mid-2018, Walmart offered subsidized college tuition to its employees as a means of attracting and retaining talent in a tight labor market. Walmart's actions may demonstrate the value of Starbucks's approach to supporting employees' efforts to earn a college degree.

When developing new storefront concepts, Starbucks innovates. For instance, it is testing smaller express stores in New York City that reduce client wait times. Today, Starbucks emphasizes online payments as a means of increasing the speed of customer transactions. It now gives Starbucks rewards for mobile payment applications to its 12 million active users. Interestingly, this puts it ahead of iTunes and American Express Serve with its Starbucks mobile payment app in terms of the number of users.

To put its innovation on display, Starbucks opened its first "Reserve Roastery and Tasting Room." This is a 15,000 square foot coffee roasting facility and a consumer retail outlet. According to Schultz, it is a retail theater where "you can watch beans being roasted, talk to master grinders, have your drink brewed in front of you in multiple ways, lounge in a coffee library, order a selection of gourmet brews and locally prepared foods." Schultz calls this store in New York the "Willie Wonka Factory of coffee." Based on this concept, Starbucks opened small "reserve" stores inspired by this flagship roastery concept across New York in 2015. To attract customers in the afternoon, the firm is "rolling out new cold coffee and tea drinks and is introducing happy hour promotions featuring cold beverages."

These technological advances and different store offerings are also taking place internationally. For example, Starbucks is expanding a new store concept in India in smaller towns and suburbs. These new outlets are about half the size of existing Starbucks cafes in India. In China, Starbucks is opening roughly one store daily and is rolling out its Roastery and Reserve brands to penetrate the country further.

Sources: D. B Klein, 2018, Here's how Starbucks plans to conquer China, *The Motley Fool*, www.fool.com, March 25; J. Jargon, 2018, Starbucks trying to woo afternoon customers, *Wall Street Journal*, www.wsj.com, May 8; S. Nassauer, 2018, Walmart to pay certain college costs for U.S. store workers, *Wall Street Journal*, www.wsj.com, May 30; I. Brat & T. Stynes, 2015, Earnings: Starbucks picks a president from technology industry, *Wall Street Journal*, www.wsj.com, January 23; A. Adamczyk, 2014, The next big caffeine craze? Starbucks testing cold-brewed coffee, *Forbes*, www.forbes.com, August 18; R. Foroohr, 2014, Go inside Starbucks' wild new "Willie Wonka Factory of coffee", *Time*, www.time.com, December 8; FRPT-Retail Snapshot, 2014, Starbucks' strategy of expansion with profitability: To debut in towns and suburbs with half the size of the new stores, *FRPT-Retail Snapshot*, September 28, 9–10; L. Lorenzetti, 2014, Fortune's world most admired companies: Starbucks where innovation is always brewing, *Fortune*, www.fortune.com, October 30; P. Wahba, 2014, Starbucks to offer delivery in 2015 in some key markets, *Fortune*, www.fortune.com, November 4; V. Wong, 2014, Your boss will love the new Starbucks delivery service, *Bloomberg Businessweek*, www.businessweek.com, November 3.

Case Discussion Questions

1. What competitive advantage or competitive advantages do you believe Starbucks seeks to establish? What are the main challenges the firm faces as it tries to maintain the advantage or advantages you identified?
2. Identify three or four capabilities you believe Starbucks possesses. Of these, are any a core competence? If so, explain your reasoning.
3. Starbucks's mission is "To inspire and nurture the human spirit—one person, one cup and one neighborhood at a time." What actions do you recommend the firm take to reach this mission?
4. As Starbucks's new chief executive officer and strategic leader, what key challenges does Kevin Johnson and his firm face?

NOTES

1. T. M. Jones, J. S. Harrison, & W. Felps, 2018, How applying instrumental stakeholder theory can provide sustainable competitive advantage, *Academy of Management Review*, 43: 371–391; N. Bhawe, V. K. Gupta, & J. M. Pollack, 2017, Founder exits and firm performance: An exploratory study, *Journal of Business Venturing Insights*, 8: 114–122.
2. H. Saranga, R. George, J. Beine, & U. Arnold, 2018, Resource configurations, product development capability, and competitive advantage: An empirical analysis of their evolution, *Journal of Business Research*, 85: 32–50; T. L. Madsen & G. Walker, 2017, Competitive heterogeneity, cohorts, and persistent advantage, *Strategic Management Journal*, 38: 184–202.
3. C. Giachetti, J. Lampel, & S. L. Pira, 2017, Red Queen competitive imitation in the U.K. mobile phone industry, *Academy of Management Journal*, 60: 1882–1914; G. Linton & J. Kask, 2017, Configurations of entrepreneurial orientation and competitive strategy for high performance, *Journal of Business Research*, 70: 168–176; G. Pacheco-de-Almeida, A. Hawk, & B. Yeung, 2015, The right speed and its value, *Strategic Management Journal*, 36: 159–176.
4. J.-M. Ross, J. H. Fisch, & E. Varga, 2018, Unlocking the value of real options: How firm-specific learning conditions affect R&D investments under uncertainty, *Strategic Entrepreneurship Journal*, in press; D. G. Ross, 2014, Taking a chance: A formal model of how firms use risk in strategic interaction with other firms, *Academy of Management Review*, 39: 202–226.
5. C. T. Gavin, G. J. Kilduff, D. Ordonez, & M. E. Schweitzer, 2018, Going for it on fourth down: Rivalry increases risk-taking, physiological arousal, and promotion focus, *Academy of Management Journal*, 61: 1281–1306; A. Nari, E. Rustambekov, M. McShane, & S. Fainshmidt, 2014, Enterprise risk management as a dynamic capability: A test of its effectiveness during a crisis, *Managerial and Decision Economics*, 35: 555–566.
6. L. DiVito & R. Bohnsack, 2017, Entrepreneurial orientation and its effects on sustainability decision tradeoffs: The case of sustainable fashion firms, *Journal of Business Venturing*, 32: 569–587; W. Qian & K. Xing, 2018, Linking environmental and financial performance for privately owned firms: Some evidence from Australia, *Journal of Small Business Management*, 56: 330–347.
7. A. M. Garcia-Cabrera, M. G. Garcia-Soto, & A. Olivares-Mesa, 2018, Entrepreneurs' resources, technology strategy, and new technology-based firms' performance, *Journal of Small Business Management*, in press; P. Gjerlov-Juel & C. Guenther, 2018, Early employment expansion and long-run survival examining employee turnover as a context factor, *Journal of Business Venturing*, in press.
8. O. Alexy, J. West, H. Klapper, & M. Reitzig, 2018, Surrending control to gain advantage: Reconciling opennesss and the resource-based view of the firm, *Strategic Management Journal*, 39: 1704–1727; R. Mudambi & T. Swift, 2014, Knowing when to leap: Transitioning between exploitative and explorative R&D, *Strategic Management Journal*, 35: 126–145.
9. A. Jenkins & A. McKelvie, 2017, Is this the end? Investigating firm and individual level outcomes post-failure, *Journal of Business Venturing Insights*, 8: 138–143; D. Ucbasaran, D. A. Shepherd, A. Lockett, & S. J. Lyon, 2013, Life after business failure: The process and consequences of business failure for entrepreneurs, *Journal of Management*, 39: 163–202.
10. C. Navis & O. V. Ozbek, 2017, Why context matters: Overconfidence, narcissism, and the role of objective uncertainty in entrepreneurship, *Academy of Management Review*, 148–153; P. M. Picone, G. B. Dagnino, & A. Mina, 2014, The origin of failure: A multidisciplinary appraisal of the hubris hypothesis and proposed research agenda, *Academy of Management Perspectives*, 28: 447–468.
11. R. Demir, K. Wennberg, & A. McKelvie, 2017, The strategic management of high-growth firms: A review and theoretical conceptualization, *Long Range Planning*, 50: 431–456; D. A. Shepherd, J. S. McMullen, & W. Ocasio, 2017, Is that an opportunity? An attention model of top managers' opportunity beliefs for strategic action, *Strategic Management Journal*, 38: 626–644.
12. M. C. Withers, R. D. Ireland, D. Miller, J. S. Harrison, & D. Boss, 2018, Competitive landscape shifts: The influence of strategic entrepreneurship on shifts in market commonality, *Academy of Management Review*, 43: 349–370; F. Monteiro & J. Birkinshaw, 2017, The external knowledge sourcing process in multinational corporations, *Strategic Management Journal*, 38: 342–362.
13. S. Junisch, M. Menz, & A. A. Cannella, Jr., 2018, The CEO as a key microfoundation of global strategy: Task demands, CEO origin and the CEO's international background, *Global Strategy Journal*, in press; S. Tallman, Y. Luo, & P. J. Buckley, 2018, Business models in global competition, *Global Strategy Journal*, in press; N. Hashai & P. J. Buckley, 2014, Is competitive advantage a necessary condition for the emergence of the multinational enterprise? *Global Strategy Journal*, 4: 35–48.
14. P. Thakur-Wernz & S. Samant, 2018, Relationship between international experience and innovation performance: The importance of organizational learning for EMNEs, *Global Strategy Journal*, in press; A. Juznetsova & O. Kuznetsova, 2014, Building professional discourse in emerging markets: Language, context and the challenge of sensemaking, *Journal of International Business Studies*, 43: 107–122.
15. S. Gerguri-Rashiti, V. Ramadani, H. Abazi-Alili, L. P. Dana, & V. Ratten, 2017, ICT, innovation and firm performance: The transition economies perspective, *Thunderbird International Review*, 59: 93–102; R. Makadok & D.G. Ross, 2013, Taking industry structuring seriously: A strategic perspective on product differentiation, *Strategic Management Journal*, 34: 509–532.
16. R. S. Nason & J. Wiklund, 2018, An assessment of resource-based theorizing on firm growth and suggestions for the future, *Journal of Management*, 44: 32–60; J. Barney, D. J. Ketchen, Jr., & M. Wright, 2011, The future of resource-based theory: Revitalization or decline? *Journal of Management*, 37: 1299–1315.
17. 2018, Digitalization, *Business Dictionary*, www.businessdictionary.com, June 6.
18. 2018, Global digital operations: 2018 survey, *PwC*, www.strategyandpwc.com, April.
19. 2018, 2018 media and entertainment industry outlook: Reaching new heights through personalization and mobility, *Deloitte Center for Technology, Media & Telecommunications*, www.deloitte.com, February.
20. J. Meffert & N. Mohr, 2017, Overwhelming OTT: Telcos' growth strategy in a digital world, *McKinsey Quarterly*, www.mckinsey.com, January.
21. P. Behrendt, S. Matz, & A. S. Goritz, 2017, An integrative model of leadership behavior, *Leadership Quarterly*, 28: 229–244; P. A. Heslin & L. A. Keating, 2017, In learning mode: The role of mindsets in derailing and enabling experiential leadership development, *Leadership Quarterly*, 28: 367–384.
22. S. F. Karabag, 2018, Factors impacting firm failure and technological development: A study of three emerging-economy firms, *Journal of Business Research*, in press; Y. Snihur, 2018, Respoding to business model innovation: Organizational unlearning and firm failure, *The Learning Organization*, in press.
23. 2018, Definition of hypercompetition, *Lexicon.ft*, www.lexicon.ft.com, April 2; R. D'Aveni, G. B. Dagnino, & K. G. Smith, 2010, The age of temporary advantage, *Strategic Management Journal*, 31: 1371–1385.

24. M. Carney, J. Zhao, & L. Zhu, 2018, Lean innovation: Family firm succession and patenting strategy in a dynamic institutional landscape, *Journal of Family Business Strategy*, in press; S. Greengard, 2015, Disruption is the new normal, *CIO Insight*, January 5.
25. K. Hoisl, M. Gruber, & A. Conti, 2017, R&D team diversity and performance in hypercompetitive environments, *Strategic Management Journal*, 38: 1455–1477; A. Kriz, R. Voola, & U. Yuksel, 2014, The dynamic capability of ambidexterity in hypercompetition: Qualitative insights, *Journal of Strategic Marketing*, 22: 287–299.
26. L. Lin & J. Steinberg, 2018, How China's Tencent uses deals to crowd out tech rivals, *Wall Street Journal*, www.wsj.com, May 15.
27. A. Cuervo-Cazurrra, R. Mudambi, & T. Pedersen, 2017, Globalization: Rising skepticism, *Global Strategy Journal*, 7: 155–158; S. J. Kobrin, 2017, Bricks and mortar in a borderless world: Globalization, the backlash, and the multinational enterprise, *Global Strategy Journal*, 7: 159–171.
28. P. J. Buckley, T. D. Craig, & R. Madumbi, 2018, Time to learn? Assignment duration in global value chain organization, *Journal of Business Research*, in press; S. Manning S. Massini, C. Peeters, & A. Y. Lewin, 2018, The changing rationale for governance choices: Early vs. late adopters of global services sourcing, *Strategic Management Journal*, in press.
29. R. Smith, 2018, The world's biggest economies in 2018, *World Economic Forum*, www.weform.org, April 18.
30. A. Shah, 2018, Netflix crushes subscriber growth estimates again and continues focus on international growth, *Forbes*, www.forbes.com, April 17.
31. D. Vena, International growth could triple Netflix's subscribers, *The Motely Fool*, www.fool.com, May 22.
32. L. M. Segarra, 2018, Netflix is adding way more original movies in 2018, *Fortune*, www.fortune.com, May 16.
33. A. Levine-Weinberg, 2018, General Motors' Baojun brand continues its massive growth in China, *The Motely Fool*, www.fool.com, March 10.
34. J. Rosevear, 2018, How General Motors is beating Ford in China, *The Motley Fool*, www.fool.com, March 15.
35. M. Miletkov, A. Poulsen, & M. B. Wintoki, 2017, Foreign independent directors and the quality of legal institutions, *Journal of International Business Studies*, 48: 267–292; M. W. Peng, D. Ahlstrom, S. M. Carraher, & W. (Stone) Shi, 2017, An institution-based view of global IPR history, *Journal of International Business Studies*, 48: 893–907.
36. S. Le & M. Kroll, 2017, CEO international experience: Effects on strategic change and firm performance, *Journal of International Business Studies*, 48: 575–595; U. Andersson, P. J. Buckley, & H. Dellestrand, 2015, In the right place at the right time! The influence of knowledge governance tools on knowledge transfer and utilization in MNEs, *Global Strategy Journal*, 5: 27–47.
37. B. S. Reiche, A. Bird, M. E. Mendenhall, & J. S. Osland, 2017, Contextualizing leadership: A typology of global leadership roles, *Journal of International Business Studies*, 48: 552–572; S. L. Wang & A. Cuervo-Cazurra, 2017, Overcoming human capital voids in underdeveloped countries, *Global Strategy Journal*, 7: 36–57.
38. E. Autio, 2017, Strategic entrepreneurial internationalization: A normative framework, *Strategic Entrepreneurship Journal*, 11: 211–227; C. H. Oh & J. Oetzel, 2017, Once bitten twice shy: Experience managing violent conflict risk and MNC subsidiary-level investment and expansion, *Strategic Management Journal*, 38: 714–731; H. Kim & M. Jensen, 2014, Audience heterogeneity and the effectiveness of market signals: How to overcome liabilities of foreignness in film exports, *Academy of Management Journal*, 57: 1360–1384.
39. H. Gorostidi-Martinez & X. Zhao, 2017, Strategies to avoid liability of foreignness when entering a new market, *Journal of Advances in Management Research*, 14: 46–68; Z. Wu & R. Salomon, 2017, Deconstructing the liability of foreignness: Regulatory enforcement actions against foreign banks, *Journal of International Business Studies*, 48: 837–861; F. Jiang, L. Liu, & B. W. Stening, 2014, Do foreign firms in China incur a liability of foreignness? The local Chines firms' perspective, *Thunderbird International Business Review*, 56: 501–518.
40. X. Luo & Q. Zheng, 2018, How firm internationalization is recognized by outsiders: The response of financial analysts, *Journal of Business Research*, 90: 87–106; S. Manning, S. Massini, C. Peeters, & A. Y. Lewin, 2018, The changing rationale for governance choices: Early vs. late adopters of global services sourcing, *Strategic Management Journal*, in press.
41. Y. Luo & R. L. Tung, 2018, A general theory of springboard MNEs, *Journal of International Business Studies*, 49: 129–152.
42. P. Williamson & F. Wan, 2018, Emerging market multinationals and the concept of ownership advantages, *International Journal of Emerging Markets*, in press.
43. Smith, 2018, The world's largest economies in 2018.
44. T. L. J. Broekhuizen, T. Bakker, & T. J. B. M. Postma, 2018, Implementing new business models: What challenges lie ahead? *Business Horizons*, 61: 555–566; S. Ray, A. Mondai, & K. Ramachandran, 2018, How does family involvement affect a firm's internationalization? An investigation of Indian family firms, *Global Strategy Journal*, in press.
45. D. E. Armanios, C. E. Eesley, J. Li, & K. M. Eisenhardt, 2017, How entrepreneurs leverage institutional intermediaries in emerging economies to acquire public resources, *Strategic Management Journal*, 38: 1373–1390; Q. Li, P. Deng, & M. Ahuja, 2017, From international new ventures to MNCs: Crossing the chasm effect on internationalization paths, *Journal of Business Research*, 70: 92–100; J. Kim, R. E. Hoskisson, & S.-H. Lee, 2015, Why strategic factor markets matter: 'New' multinationals' geographic diversification and firm profitability, *Strategic Management Journal*, 36: 518–536.
46. 2017, The 2017 M&A report: The technology makeover, *Boston Consulting Group*, www.bcg.com, September.
47. K. H. Hammonds, 2001, What is the state of the new economy? *Fast Company*, September, 101–104.
48. P. Thakur-Wernz & S. Samant, 2018, Relationship between international experience and innovation performance: The importance of organizational learning for EMNEs, *Global Strategy Journal*, in press; R. J. Jean, D. Kim, & D. C. Bello, 2017, Relationship-based product innovations: Evidence from the global supply chain, *Journal of Business Research*, 80: 127–140.
49. P. B. Le & H. Lei, 2018, The effects of innovation speed and quality on differentiation and low-cost competitive advantage: The case of Chinese firms, *Chinese Management Studies*, 12: 305–322; T. Morgan, M. Obal, & S. Anokhin, 2017, Customer participation and new product performance: Towards the understanding of the mechanisms and key contingencies, *Research Policy*, 47: 498–510; G. Pacheco-de-Almeida, A. Hawk, & B. Yeung, 2015, The right speed and its value, *Strategic Management Journal*, 36: 159–176.
50. R. (Priya) Kannan-Narasimhan & B. S. Lawrence, 2018, How innovators reframe resources in the strategy-making process to gain innovation adoption, *Strategic Management Journal*, in press.
51. M. Ringel & H. Zablit, 2018, Innovation in 2018, *Boston Consulting Group*, www.bcg.com, January 17.
52. R. Safian, 2018, The world's 50 most innovative companies, *Fast Company*, www.fastcompany.com, March 15.
53. S. Haneda & K. Ito, 2018, Organizational and human resource management and innovation: Which management practices are linked to product and/or process innovation? *Research Policy*, 47: 194–208.
54. A. De Marco, G. Scellato, E. Ughetto, & F. Caviggioli, 2017, Global markets for technology: Evidence from patent transactions, *Research Policy*, 46: 1644–1654; K. Bilir, 2014, Patent laws, product life-cycle lengths, and multinational activity, *American Economic Review*, 104: 1979–2013.
55. R. Roy, C. M. Lampert, & I. Stoyneva, 2018, When dinosaurs fly: The role of firm capabilities in the 'avianization' of incumbents during disruptive technological change, *Strategic Entrepreneurship Journal*, 12: 261–284;

C. Christensen, 2015, Disruptive innovation is a strategy, not just a technology, *Business Today* 23(26): 150–158.

56. B. Spigel & R. Harrison, 2018, Toward a process theory of entrepreneurial ecosystems, *Strategic Entrepreneurship Journal*, 12: 151–168; J. Henkel, T. Ronde, & M. Wagner, 2015, And the winner is—acquired: Entrepreneurship as a contest yielding radical innovations, *Research Policy*, 44: 295–310.
57. J. P. Eggers & A. Kaul, 2018, Motivation and ability? A behavioral perspective on the pursuit of radical invention in multi-technology incumbents, *Academy of Management Journal*, 61: 67–93; M. Moeen & R. Agarwal, 2017, Incubation of an industry: Heterogeneous knowledge bases and modes of value capture, *Strategic Management Journal*, 38: 566–587.
58. C. Hopp, D. Antons, J. Kaminski, & T. O. Salge, 2018, Disruptive innovation: Conceptual foundations, empirical evidence, and research opportunities in the digital age, *Journal of Product Innovation Management*, 35: 446–457.
59. L. Argote & M. Hora, 2017, Organizational learning and management of technology, *Production and Operations Management*, 26: 579–590.
60. 2018, Global PC market 2017—forecast to 2023, *Cision PR Newswire*, www.prnewswire.com, February 19.
61. 2018, Stats you need to know about live-streaming video in 2018, *Talk Point*, www.talkpoint.com, January 9.
62. F. Eggers, I. Hatak, S. Kraus, & T. Niemand, 2017, Technologies that support marketing and market development in SMES—Evidence from social networks, *Journal of Small Business Management*, 55: 270–302; L. Trigeorgis & J. J. Reuer, 2017, Real options theory in strategic management, *Strategic Management Joournal*, 38: 42–63.
63. P. Deshllas, M. Miozzo, H.-F. Lee, & I. Miles, 2018, Capturing value from innovation in knowledge-intensive business service firms: The role of competitive strategy, *British Journal of Management*, in press; S. R. Nair, M. Demirbag, K. Mellahi, & K. G. Pillai, 2018, Do parent units benefit from reverse knowledge transfer? *British Journal of Management*, 29: 428–444.
64. M. Gottgredson, R. Puryear, & S. Phillips, 2005, Strategic sourcing: From periphery to the core, *Harvard Business Review*, 83(2): 132–139.
65. T. Gu, N. R. Sanders, & A. Vankateswaran, 2017, CEO incentives and customer-supplier relations, *Production and Operations Management*, 26: 1705–1727; V. H. Villena & C. W. Craighead, 2017, On the same page? How asymmetric buyer-supplier relationships affect opportunism and performance, *Production and Operations Management*, 26: 491–508.
66. A.-K. Kahkonen & K. Lintukangas, 2018, Key dimensions of value creation ability of supply management, *International Journal of Operations & Production Managemnt*, 38: 979–996; C. Flammer & P. Bansal, 2017, Does a long-term orientation create value? Evidence from a regression discontinuity, *Strategic Management Journal*, 38: 1827–1847.
67. C. P. Skroupa, 2017, How intangible assets are affecting company value in the stock market, *Forbes*, www.forbes.com, November 3.
68. V. Monga, 2016, Accounting's 21st century challenge: How to value intangible assets, *Wall Street Journal*, www.wsj.com, March 21.
69. R. Eckardt, B. C. Skaggs, & D. Lepak, 2018, An examination of the firm-level performance impact of cluster hiring in knowledge-intensive firms, *Academy of Management Journal*, 61: 919–944; M. Lawrence, 2018, Taking stock of the ability to change: The effect of prior experience, *Organization Science*, 29: 489–506.
70. S. M. Riley, S. C. Michael, & J. T. Mahoney, 2017, Human capital matters: Market valuation of firm investments in training and the role of complementary assets, *Strategic Management Journal*, 38: 1895–1914; D. Laureiro-Martinez, S. Brusoni, N. Canessa, & M. Zollo, 2015, Understanding the exploration-exploitation dilemma: An fMRI study of attention control and decision-making performance, *Strategic Management Journal*, 36: 319–338.
71. X. Xie, H. Zou, & G. Qi, 2018, Knowledge absorptive capacity and innovation performance in high-tech companies: A multi-modeling analysis, *Journal of Business Research*, 88: 289–297; A. Martini, P. Neirotti, & F. P. Appio, 2017, Knowledge searching, integrating and performing: Always a tuned trio for innovation? *Long Range Planning*, 50: 200–220.
72. E. Darmon & D. Torre, 2017, Dual licensing strategy with open source competition, *Managerial and Decision Economics*, 38: 1082–1093; M. Theeke & H. Lee, 2017, Multimarket contact and rivalry over knowledge-based resources, *Strategic Management Journal*, 38: 2508–2531.
73. P. Akhtar, Z. Khan, J. G. Frynas, Y. K. Tse, & R. Rao-Nicholson, 2018, Essential micro-foundations for contemporary business operations: Top management tangible competencies, relationship-based business networks and environmental sustainability, *British Journal of Management*, 29: 43–62; S. Roper, J. H. Love, & K. Bonner, 2017, Firms' knowledge search and local knowledge externalities in innovation performance, *Research Policy*, 46: 43–56.
74. T. Vanacker, V. Collewaert, & S. A. Zahra, 2017, Slack resources, firm performance, and the institutional context: Evidence from privately held European firms, *Strategic Management Journal*, 38: 1305–1326; F. Zambuto, G. L. Nigro, & J. P. O'Brien, 2017, The importance of alliances in firm capital structure decisions: Evidence from biotechnology firms, *Managerial and Decision Economics*, 38: 3–18; D. Herhausen, R. E. Morgan, & H. W. Volberda, 2014, A meta-analysis of the antecedents and consequences of strategic flexibility, *Academy of Management Proceedings*, 1051–1057.
75. D. McIver & C. Lengnick-Hall, 2018, The causal ambiguity paradox: Deliberate actions under causal ambiguity, *Strategic Organization*, 16: 304–322; Y. Chen, Y. Wang, S. Nevo, J. Benitez, & G. Kou, 2017, Improving strategic flexibility with information technologies: Insights for firm performance in an emerging economy, *Journal of Information Technology*, 32: 10–25.
76. F. Fagerholm, A. S. Guinea, H. Maenpaa, & J. Munch, 2017, The RIGHT model for continuous experimentation, *Journal of Systems and Software*, 123: 292–305; E. G. Anderson, Jr. & K. Lewis, 2014, A dynamic model of individual and collective learning amid disruption, *Organization Science*, 25: 356–376.
77. R. E. Hoskisson, M. A. Hitt, W. P. Wan, & D. Yiu, 1999, Swings of a pendulum: Theory and research in strategic management, *Journal of Management*, 25: 417–456.
78. J. W. Medcor & T. Lee, 2017, The effects of the chief technology officer and firm and industry R&D intensity on organizational performance, *R&D Management*, 47: 767–781; S. F. Karabag & C. Berggren, 2014, Antecedents of firm performance in emerging economies: Business groups, strategy, industry structure, and state support, *Journal of Business Research*, 67: 2212–2223.
79. D. Waldman & E. Jensen, 2016, *Industrial Organization: Theory and Practice*, fourth edition, London: Routledge.
80. J.-A. Lamberg, J. Laurila, & T. Mokelainen, 2017, Institutional path dependence in competitive dynamics: The case of paper industries in Finland and the USA, *Managerial and Decision Economics*, 38: 979–991; R. Casadesus-Masanell & F. Zhu, 2013, Business model innovation and competitive imitation: The case of sponsor-based business models, *Strategic Management Journal*, 34: 464–482.
81. M. E. Porter, 1985, *Competitive Advantage*, New York: Free Press; M. E. Porter, 1980, *Competitive Strategy*, New York: Free Press.
82. W. M. Friske & M. A. Zachary, 2018, Regulation, new venture creation, and resource-advantage theory: An analysis of the U.S. brewing industry, *Entrepreneurship Theory and Practice*, in press; F. J. Mas-Ruiz, F. J. Ruiz-Moreno, & A. Ladron de Guevara Martinez, 2014, Asymmetric rivalry within and between strategic groups, *Strategic Management Journal*, 35: 419–439.
83. B. Arslan, 2018, The interplay of competitive and cooperative behavior and differential benefits in alliances, *Strategic Management Journal*, in press; S. D. Pathak, Z. Wu, & D. Johnston, 2014, Toward a structural view

of co-optition in supply networks, *Journal of Operations Management*, 32: 254–267.

84. C. Williams & A. Vrabie, 2018, Host country R&D determinants of MNE entry strategy: A study of ownership in the automobile industry, *Research Policy*, 47: 474–486; J. Y. Sun, 2017, Airline deregulation and its impacts on air travel demand and airline competition: Evidence from Korea, *Review of Industrial Organization*, 51: 343–380.
85. A. M. McGahan & M. E. Porter, 2003, The emergence and sustainability of abnormal profits, *Strategic Organization*, 1: 79–108.
86. D. Vrontis, A. Thrassou, G. Santoro, & A. Papa, 2017, Ambidexterity, external knowledge and performance in knowledge-intensive firms, *The Journal of Technology Transfer*, 42: 374–388; N. J. Foss & P. G. Klein, 2014, Why managers still matter, *MIT Sloan Management Review*, 56(1): 73–80; J. W. Upson, D. J. Ketchen, Jr., B. L. Connelly, & A. L. Ranft, 2012, Competitor analysis and foothold moves, *Academy of Management Journal*, 55: 93–110.
87. O. F. Bustinza, E. Gomes, F. Vendrell-Herrero, & T. Baines, 2018, Product-service innovation and performance: The role of collaborative partnerships and R&D intensity, *R&D Management*, in press; S. F. Wamba, A. Gunasekaran, S. Akter, S. Jifan Ren, R. Dubey, & S. J. Childe, 2017, Big data analytics and firm performance: Effects of dynamic capabilities, *Journal of Business Research*, 70: 356–365; L. A. Costa, K. Cool, & I. Dierickx, 2013, The competitive implications of the deployment of unique resources, *Strategic Management Journal*, 34: 445–463.
88. S. J. G. Girod & R. Whittington, 2017, Reconfiguration, restructuring and firm performance: Dynamic capabilities and environmental dynamism, *Strategic Management Journal*, 38: 1121–1133; M. Moeen, 2017, Entry into nascent industries: Disentangling a firm's capability portfolio at the time of investment versus market entry, *Strategic Management Journal*, 1986–2004.
89. J. P. Eggers & A. Kaul, 2018, Motivation and ability? A behavioral perspective on the pursuit of radical invention in multi-technology incumbents, *Academy of Management Journal*, 61: 67–93; D. J. Teece, 2018, Business models and dynamic capabilities, *Long Range Planning*, 51: 40–49.
90. D. J. Teece, 2017, Towards a capability theory of (innovating) firms: Implications for management and policy, *Cambridge Journal of Economics*, 41: 693–720; S. Hassan, S. M. Tang, & H. Johari, 2017, Mediating role of operational capabilities between intellectual capital and organizational performance: A proposed theoretical framework, *Academy of Strategic Management Journal*, 16: 1–12.
91. S. S. Levine, M. Bernard, & R. Nagel, 2017, Strategic intelligence: The cognitive capability to anticipate competitor behavior, *Strategic Management Journal*, 38: 2390–2423; Y. Lin & L. Wu, 2014, Exploring the role of dyamic capabilities in firm performance under the resource-based view framework, *Journal of Business Research*, 67: 407–413.
92. D. J. Teece, 2018, A capability theory of the firm: An economics and (strategic) management perspective, *New Zealand Economic Papers*, in press; C. Tsinopoulos, C. M. P. Sousa, & J. Yan, 2018, Process innovation: Open innovation and the moderating role of the motivation to achieve legitimacy, *Journal of Product and Innovation Management*, 35: 27–48.
93. B. McKnight & C. Zietsma, 2018, Finding the threshold: A configurational approach to optimal distinctiveness, *Journal of Business Venturing*, 33: 493–512; Y. Y. Kor & A. Mesko, 2013, Dynamic managerial capabilities: Configuration and orchestration of top executives' capabilities and the firm's dominant logic, *Strategic Management Journal*, 34: 233–244.
94. L. C. Leonidou, P. Christodoulides, L. Kyrgidou, & D. Palihawadana, 2017, Internal drivers and performance consequences of small firm green business strategy: The moderating role of external forces, *Journal of Business Ethics*, 140: 585–606.
95. B. Cannatelli, B. Smith, A. Giudici, J. Jones, & M. Congner 2017, An expanded model of distributed leadership in organizational knowledge creation, *Long Range Planning*, 50: 582–602; D. D. Warrick, 2017, What leaders need to know about organizational culture, *Business Horizons*, 60: 395–404.
96. C. Gallo, 2010, *The Innovation Secrets of Steve Jobs*, McGraw-Hill, New York, NY.
97. S. A. Kirkpatrick, 2017, Toward a grounded theory: A qualitative study of vision statement development, *Journal of Management Policy and Practice*, 18: 87–101; A. M. Carton, C. Murhpy, & J. R. Clark, 2014, A (blurry) vision of the future: How leader rhetoric about ultimate goals influences performance, *Academy of Management Journal*, 57: 1544–1570.
98. C. Ray & M. Bastons, 2018, Three dimensions of effective mission implementation, *Long Range Planning*, in press; S. Spear, 2017, Impression management activity in vision, mission, and values statements: A comparison of commercial and charitable organizations, *International Studies of Management & Organization*, 47: 159–175.
99. T. Ramus & A. Vaccaro, 2017, Stakeholders matter: How social enterprises address mission drift, *Journal of Business Ethics*, 143: 307–322.
100. R. Chun, 2018, How virtuous global firms say they are: A content analysis of ethical values, *Journal of Business Ethics*, in press.
101. T. M. Jones, J. S. Harrison, & W. Felps, 2018, How applying instrumental stakeholder theory can provide sustainable competitive advantage, *Academy of Management Review*, 43: 371–391; M. Cording, J. S. Harrison, R. E. Hoskisson, & K. Jonsen, 2014, "Walking the talk": A multi-stakeholder exploration of organizational authenticity, employee productivity and post-merger performance, *Academy of Management Perspectives*, 28: 38–56.
102. P. Tracey, E. Dalpiaz, & N. Phillips, 2018, Fish out of water: Translation, legitimation, and new venture creation, *Academy of Management Journal*, in press; R. Garcia-Castro & R. Aguilera, 2015, Incremental value creation and appropriation in a world with multiple stakeholders, *Strategic Management Journal*, 36: 137–147.
103. S. A. Yawar & S. Seuring, 2017, Management of social issues in supply chains: A literature review exploring social issues, actions and performance outcomes, *Journal of Business Ethics*, 141: 621–643.
104. S. Dorobantu & K. Odziemkowska, 2017, Valuing stakeholder governance: Property rights, community mobilization, and firm value, *Strategic Management Journal*, 38: 2682–2703; Y. Mishina, E. S. Block, & M. J. Mannor, 2012, The path dependence of organizational reputation: How social judgment influences assessments of capability and character, *Strategic Management Journal*, 33: 459–477.
105. J. Bundy, R. M. Vogel, & M. A. Zachary, 2108, Organization-stakeholder fit: A dynamic theory of cooperation, compromise, and conflict between an organization and its stakeholders, *Strategic Management Journal*, 39: 476–501; K. Chang, I. Kim, & Y. Li, 2014, The heterogeneous impact of corporate social responsibility activities that target different stakeholders, *Journal of Business Ethics*, 125: 211–234.
106. J. Li, J. Xia, & E. J. Zajac, 2018, On the duality of political and economic stakeholder influence on firm innovation performance: Theory and evidence from Chinese firms, *Strategic Management Journal*, 39: 193–216; A. Soleimani, W. D. Schneper, & W. Newburry, 2014, The impact of stakeholder power on corporate reputation: A cross-country corporate governance perspective, *Organization Science*, 25: 991–1008.
107. F. Zhang, L. Wei, J. Yang, & L. Zhu, 2018, Roles of relationships between large shareholders and managers in radical innovation: A stewardship theory perspective, *Journal of Product Innovation Management*, 35: 88–105; G. W. S. Dowell & S. Muthulingam, 2017, Will firms go green if it pays? The impact of disruption, cost, and external factors on the adoption of environmental initiatives, *Strategic Management Journal*, 38: 1287–1304.
108. M. R. Bowers, J. R. Hall, & M. M. Srinivasan, 2017, Organizational culture and leadership style: The missing combination for selecting the right leader for effective crisis management *Business Horizons*, 60: 551–563; J. P. Doh & N. R. Quigley, 2014,

Responsible leadership and stakeholder management: Influence pathways and organizational outcomes, *Academy of Management Perspectives*, 28: 255–274.

109. F. Testa, O. Boiral, & F. Iraldo, 2018, Internalization of environmental practices and institutional complexity: Can stakeholders pressures encourage greenwhashing? *Journal of Business Ethics*, 147: 287–307; D. F. Kuratko, J. S. McMullen, J. S. Hornsby, & C. Jackson, 2017, Is your organization conducive to the continuous creation of social value? Toward a social corporate entrepreneurship scale, *Business Horizons*, 60: 271–283; W. J. Heinsz, S. Dorobantu, & L. J. Nartey, 2014, Spinning gold: The financial returns to stakeholder engagement, *Strategic Management Journal*, 35: 1727–1748.

110. S. Dorobantu, W. J. Henisz, & L. Nartey, 2017, Not all sparks light a fire: Stakeholder and shareholder reactions to critical events in contested markets, *Administrative Science Quarterly*, 62: 561–597; M. Goranova & L. V. Ryan, 2014, Shareholder activism: A multidisciplinary review, *Journal of Management*, 40: 1230–1268.

111. W. Shi, B. L. Connelly, & K. Cirik, 2018, Short seller influence on firm growth: A threat-rigidity perspective, *Academy of Management Journal*, in press; I. Filatotchev & O. Dotsenko, 2015, Shareholder activism in the UK: Types of activists, forms of activism, and their impact on a target's performance, *Journal of Management & Governance*, 19: 5–24; B. L. Connelly, L. Tihanyi, S. T. Certo, & M. A. Hitt, 2010, Marching to the best of different drummers: The influence of institutional owners on competitive actions, *Academy of Management Journal*, 53: 723–742.

112. V. Z. Chen, B. Hobdari, & Y. Zhang, 2018, Blockholder heterogeneity and conflicts in cross-border acquisitions, 2018, *Journal of Corporate Finance*, in press; H. R. Greve & C. M. Zhang, 2017, Institutional logics and power sources: Merger and acquisition decisions, *Academy of Management Journal*, 60: 671–694.

113. M. A. Merz, L. Zarantonello, & S. Grappi, 2018, How valuable are your customers in the brand value co-creation process? The development of a customer co-creation value (CCCV) scale, *Journal of Business Research*, 82: 79–89; S. Wilkins & J. Huisman, 2014, Corporate images' impact on consumers' product choices: The case of multinational foreign subsidiaries, *Journal of Business Research*, 67: 2224–2230.

114. K. Xu, L. Tihanyi, & M. A. Hitt, 2017, Firm resources, governmental power, and privatization, *Journal of Management*, 43: 998–1024; B. Batjargal, M. A. Hitt, A. S. Tsui, J.-L. Arregle, J. Webb, & T. Miller, 2013, Institutional polycentrism, entrepreneurs' social networks and new venture growth, *Academy of Management Journal*, 56: 1024–1049.

115. S. S. Morris, S. A. Alvarez, J. B. Barney, & J. C. Molloy, 2017, Firm-specific human capital investments as a signal of general value: Revisiting assumptions about human capital and how it is managed, *Strategic Management Journal*, 38: 912–919.

116. C. Bode & J. Singh, 2018, Taking a hit to save the world? Employee participation in a corporate social initiative, *Strategic Management Journal*, 39: 1003–1030; S. E. Jackson, R. S. Schuler, & K. Jiang, 2014, An aspirational framework for strategic human resource management, *Academy of Management Annals*, 8: 1–56.

117. C. Li, F. C. Brodbeck, O. Shenkar, L. J. Ponzi, & J. H. Fisch, 2017, Embracing the foreign: Cultural attractiveness and international strategy, *Strategic Management Journal*, 38: 950–971; W. A. Schiemann, 2014, From talent management to talent optimization, *Journal of World Business*, 49: 281–288.

118. P. Gabaldon, S. B. Kanadli, & M. Bankewitz, 2018, How does job-related diversity affect boards' strategic participation? An information-processing approach, *Long Range Planning*, in press; C. S. Reina, S. J. Peterson, & Z. Zhang, 2018, Adverse effects of CEO family-to-work conflict on firm performance, *Organization Science*, 28: 211–227.

119. S. J. Miles & M. Van Clieaf, 2017, Strategic fit: Key to growing enterprise value through organizational capital, *Business Horizons*, 60: 55–65; D. J. Schepker, Y. Kim, P. C. Patel, S. M. B. Thatcher, & M. C. Campion, 2017, CEO succession, strategic change, and post-succession performance: A meta-analysis, *Leadership Quarterly*, 28: 701–720; S. Gunz & L. Thorne, 2015, Introduction to the special issue on tone at the top, *Journal of Business Ethics*, 126: 1–2.

120. C. A. de Oliveira, J. Carneiro, & F. Esteves, 2018, Conceptualizing and measuring the "strategy execution" construct, *Journal of Business Research*, in press; P. Spee & P. Jarzabkowski, 2017, Agreeing on what? Creating joint accounts of strategic change, *Organization Science*, 28: 152–176.

121. D. A. Levinthal & M. Workiewicz, 2018, When two bosses are better than one: Nearly decomposable systems and organizational adaptation, *Organization Science*, in press.

122. M. A. Hitt & K. T. Haynes, 2018, CEO overpayment and underpayment: Executives, governance and institutions, *Management Research: Journal of the Iberoamerican Academy of Management*, 16: 38–46; J.-H. Park, C. Kim, Y. K. Chang, D.-H. Lee, & Y.-D. Sung, 2018, CEO hubris and firm performance: Exploring the moderating roles of CEO power and board vigilance, *Journal of Business Ethics*, 147: 919–933.

123. S. Fainshmidt & M. L. Frazier, 2017, What facilitates dynamic capabilities? The role of organizational climate for trust, *Long Range Planning*, 50: 550–566; D. D. Warrick, 2017, What leaders need to know about organizational culture, *Business Horizons*, 60: 395–404.

124. A. Y. Ou, J. (Jamie) Seo, D. Choi, & P. W. Hom, 2017, When can humble top executives retain middle managers? The moderating role of top management team faultlines, *Academy of Management Journal*, 60: 1915–1931; D. C. Hambrick, S. E. Humphrey, & A. Gupta, 2015, Structural interdependence within top management teams: A key moderator of upper echelons predictions, *Strategic Management Journal*, 36: 449–461.

125. V. L. Glaser, 2017, Design performances: How organizations inscribe artifacts to change routines, *Academy of Management Journal*, 60: 2126–2154; M. L. M. Heyden, S. van Doorn, M. Reimer, F. J. Va Den Bosch, & H. W. Volberda, 2013, Perceived environmental dynamism, relative competitive performance, and top management team heterogeneity: Examining correlates of upper echelons' advice-seeking, *Organization Studies*, 34: 1327–1356.

126. G. Calabretta, G. Gemser, & N. W. Wijnberg, 2017, The interplay between intuition and rationality in strategic decision making: A paradox perspective, *Organization Studies*, 38: 365–401; S. J. Miles & M. Van Clieaf, 2017, Strategic fit: Key to growing enterprise value through organizational capital, *Business Horizons*, 60: 55–65.

127. G. H. Seijts & J. Gandz, 2018, Transformational change and leader character, *Business Horizons*, 61: 239–249; L. Wei & L. Wu, 2013, What a diverse top management tea means: Testing an integrated model, *Journal of Management Studies*, 50: 389–412.

128. C. Heavey & Z. Simsek, 2017, Distributed cognition in top management teams and organizational ambidexterity, *Journal of Management*, 43: 919–945.

129. O. Kyvik, 2018, The global mindset: A must for international innovation and entrepreneurship, *International Entrepreneurship and Management Journal*, 16: 309–327; N. Gaffney, D. Cooper, B. Kedia, & J. Clampit, 2014, Institutional transitions, global mindset, and EMNE internationalization, *European Management Journal*, 24: 17–37.

130. M. Loeb, 1993, Steven J. Ross, 1927–1992, *Fortune*, January 25, 4.

131. S. J. Ashford, N. Wellman, M. Sully de Luque, K. E. M. De Stobbeleir, & M. Wollan, 2018, Two roads to effectiveness: CEO feedback seeking vision articulation, and firm performance, *Journal of Organizational Behavior*, 39: 82–95; F. Jing, G. Avery, & H. Bergsteiner, 2014, Enhancing performance in small professional firms through vision communication and sharing, *Asia Pacific Journal of Management*, 31: 599–620.

132. V. Bruni-Bossio, N. T. Sheehan, & C. R. Willness, 2018, Circle mapping your firm's growth strategy, *Business Horizons*, 61: 285–296; S. W. Reid, J. C. Short, & D. J. Ketchen, Jr.,

2018, Reading the room: Leveraging popular business books to enhance organizational performance, *Business Horizons*, 61: 191–197; R. F. Everett, 2014, A crack in the foundation: Why SWOT might be less than effective in market sensing analysis, *Journal of Marketing & Management*, 1: 58–78.

133. B. L. Connelly, L. Tihanyi, D. J. Ketchen, Jr., C. M. Carnes, & W. J. Ferrier, 2017, Competitive repertoire complexity: Governance antecedents and performance outcomes, *Strategic Management Journal*, 38: 1151–1173; J. Luoma, S. Ruutu, A. W. King, & H. Tikkanen, 2017, Time delays, competitive interdependence, and firm performance, *Strategic Management Journal*, 38: 506–525.

134. H. Haddon, 2018, A year after Amazon devoured Whole Foods, rivals are pursuing countermoves, *Wall Street Journal*, www.wsj.com, June 10.

135. C. R. Greer, R. F. Lusch, & M. A. Hitt, 2017, A service perspective for human capital resources: A critical base for strategy implementation, *Academy of Management Perspectives*, 31: 137–158; W. Shi, B. L. Connelly, & R. E. Hoskisson, 2017, External corporate governance and financial fraud: Cognitive evaluation theoretical insights on agency theory prescriptions, *Strategic Management Journal*, 38: 1268–1286; L. A. Cunningham, 2015, The secret sauce of corporate leadership, *Wall Street Journal*, www.wsj.com, January 26.

136. H. Jiang, A. A. Cannella, & J. Jiao, 2018, Does desperation breed deceiver? A behavioral model of new venture opportunism, *Entrepreneurship Theory and Practice*, in press; L. C. Leonidou, P. Chirstodoulides, L. P. Kyrgidou, & D. Palihawadana, 2017, Internal drivers and performance consequences of small firm green business strategy: The moderating role of external forces, *Journal of Business Ethics*, 140: 585–606.

137. K. Hockerts, 2017, Determinants of social entrepreneurial intentions, *Entrepreneurship Theory and Practice*, 41: 105–130; B. A. Scott, A. S. Garza, D. E. Conlon, & K. Y. Jin, 2014, Why do managers act fairly in the first place? A daily investigation of "hot" and "cold" motives and discretion, *Academy of Management Journal*, 57: 1571–1591.

138. M. Lee, M. Pitesa, M. M. Pillutia, & S. Thau, 2017, Male immorality: An evolutionary account of sex differences in unethical negotiation behavior, *Academy of Management Journal*, 60: 2014–2044; M. Sharif & T. Scandura, 2014, Do perceptions of ethical conduct matter during organizational change? Ethical leadership and employee involvement, *Journal of Business Ethics*, 124: 185–196.

139. S. F. Wamba, A. Gunasekaran, S. Akter, S. J.-F. Ren, R. Dubey, & S. J. Childe, 2017, Big data analytics and firm performance: Effects of dynamic capabilities, *Journal of Business Research*, 70: 356–365; D. C. Hambrick & T. J. Quigley, 2014, Toward more accurate contextualization of the CEO effect on firm performance, *Strategic Management Journal*, 35: 473–491.

2

The External Environment: Opportunities, Threats, Industry Competition, and Competitor Analysis

Studying this chapter should provide you with the strategic management knowledge needed to:

2-1 Explain the importance of analyzing and understanding the firm's external environment.

2-2 Define and describe the general environment and the industry environment.

2-3 Discuss the four parts of the external environmental analysis process.

2-4 Name and describe the general environment's seven segments.

2-5 Identify the five competitive forces and explain how they determine an industry's profitability potential.

2-6 Define strategic groups and describe their influence on firms.

2-7 Describe what firms need to know about their competitors and different methods (including ethical standards) used to collect intelligence about them.

iStock.com/DNY59

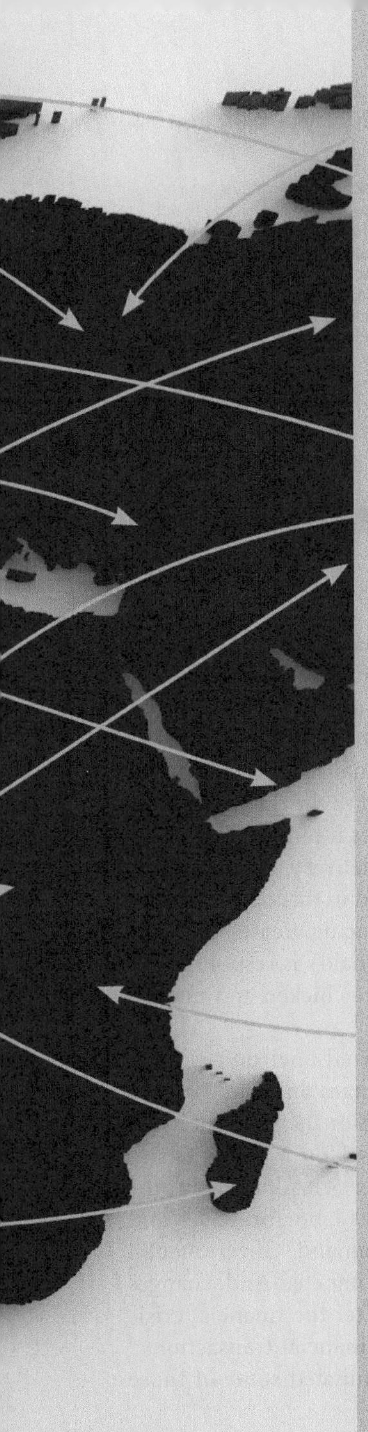

CRACKS IN THE GOLDEN ARCHES AND MCDONALD'S NEW GLUE

McDonald's is the largest restaurant chain in the world. It has 14,155 restaurants in the United States, and 36,899 restaurants worldwide—in more than 100 countries. It employs 1.5 million people and serves approximately 69 million customers daily. It sells 9 million pounds of french fries daily and sells 550 million Big Macs annually. Over the years, McDonald's was a leader, not only in market share, but also with the introduction of new menu items to the fast food market. For example, it first introduced breakfast items to this market, and its breakfast menu now accounts for about 25 percent of its sales. It successfully introduced Chicken McNuggets to this market, and also successfully introduced gourmet coffee products and began to compete against Starbucks. With all this success, what is the problem?

The problems revolve around competition and changing consumer tastes. Consumers have become more health-conscious, and competitors have been more attuned to customer desires. As a result, McDonald's suffered a decline in its total sales revenue of 18.9 percent from its high point in 2013 of $28.1 billion to $22.8 billion in 2017. It seems that McDonald's did a poor job of analyzing its environment and especially its customers and competitors. During this same time, some of McDonald's competitors flourished. For example, Sonic and Chipotle recorded significant increases in their annual sales. Other specialty burger restaurants, such as Smashburger, have stolen business from McDonald's even though their burgers are priced higher. The quality of these competitors' products is perceived to be higher, and many are "made to order" and thus customized to the customer's desires. And, partly because the volume and complexity of the McDonald's menu items have grown, the time required to provide service has also increased.

Ruaridh Stewart/ZUMA Press/Newscom

Healthier choice options now available at McDonald's to satisfy the more health-conscious consumer.

Failing to understand the changing market and competitive landscape, McDonald's was unable to be proactive and thus tried to be reactive but without much success. Because of these problems, McDonald's hired a new CEO in 2015, hoping to overcome its woes. With a thorough analysis of its customers and competition and its products and services, McDonald's developed a strategy to achieve a multi-year turnaround. It is adding new products to its menu and has enhanced the healthiness of those products along with enhancing their quality. For example, McDonald's announced that it will now use only chickens raised without antibiotics to be sensitive to human health concerns. Changing vegetables in Happy Meals (e.g., adding baby carrots) and implementing new wraps that require additional (new) vegetables (such as cucumbers) are meant to enhance the healthiness of the McDonald's menu. It has also introduced signature sandwiches, Quarter Pounders cooked with fresh meat only (not frozen), new espresso-based drinks, and other quality items.

Other parts of its multi-year strategy include renovated restaurants, digital ordering, and new delivery services. McDonald's was once a leader, and now it is fighting regain its position, trying to stem the downturn. It is now responding to its external environment, especially its customers and competitors. Sales began to pick up in the last part of 2017. Within the next few years, we will know whether these changes succeed.

Sources: C. Smith, 2018, 40 Interesting McDonald's facts and statistics, *DMR Business Statistics*, https://expanded ramblings .com/index.php/mcdonalds-statistics/, February 19; J. Wohl, 2018, McDonald's makes happy meals (slightly) healthier, *AdAge*, http://adage.com, February 15; J. Wohl, 2018, McDonald's CMO bullish on tiered value menu amid competition, *AdAge*, http://adage.com, January 5; K. Taylor, 2017, McDonald's makes 6 major changes that totally turned business around, *Business Insider*, www.businessinsider.com, October 24; S. Whitten, 2017, 4 ways McDonald's is about to change, CNBC, www.cnbc.com; A. Gasparro, 2015, McDonald's new chief plots counter attack, *Wall Street Journal*, www.wsj.com, March 1; D. Shanker, 2015, Dear McDonald's new CEO: Happy first day. Here's some (unsolicited) advice, *Fortune*, www.Fortune.com, March 2; S. Strom, 2015, McDonald's seeks its fast-food soul, *New York Times*, www.nytimes.com, March 7; S. Strom, 2015, McDonald's tests custom burgers and other new concepts as sales drop, *New York Times*, www.nytimes.com, January 23; B. Kowitt, 2014, Fallen Arches, *Fortune*, December, 106–116.

As suggested in the Opening Case and by research, the external environment (which includes the industry in which a firm competes as well as those against whom it competes) affects the competitive actions and responses firms take to outperform competitors and earn above-average returns.[1] For example, McDonald's has been experiencing a reduction in returns in recent times because of changing consumer tastes and enhanced competition. McDonald's is attempting to respond to the threats from its environment by changing its menu, revising the types of supplies it purchases, remodeling its restaurants, and implementing digital sales and home delivery of food orders. The sociocultural segment of the general environment (discussed in this chapter) is the driver of some of the changing values in society that are now placing greater emphasis on healthy food choices. As the Opening Case describes, McDonald's is responding to these changing values by, for example, using only antibiotic-free chicken and making its Happy Meals healthier.

As noted in Chapter 1, the characteristics of today's external environment differ from historical conditions. For example, technological changes and the continuing growth of information gathering and processing capabilities increase the need for firms to develop effective competitive actions and responses on a timely basis.[2] (We fully discuss competitive actions and responses in Chapter 5.) Additionally, the rapid sociological changes occurring in many countries affect labor practices and the nature of products that increasingly diverse consumers demand. Governmental policies and laws also affect where and how firms choose to compete.[3] And, changes to several nations' financial regulatory systems were enacted after the financial crisis in 2008–2009 that increased the complexity of organizations' financial transactions.[4] (However, in 2018 the Trump administration weakened or eliminated some of those regulations in the United States.)

Firms understand the external environment by acquiring information about competitors, customers, and other stakeholders to build their own base of knowledge and capabilities.[5] On the basis of the new information, firms take actions, such as building new capabilities and core competencies, in hopes of buffering themselves from any negative environmental effects and to pursue opportunities to better serve their stakeholders' needs.[6]

In summary, a firm's competitive actions and responses are influenced by the conditions in the three parts (the general, industry, and competitor) of its external environment (see Figure 2.1) and its understanding of those conditions. Next, we fully describe each part of the firm's external environment.

Figure 2.1 The External Environment

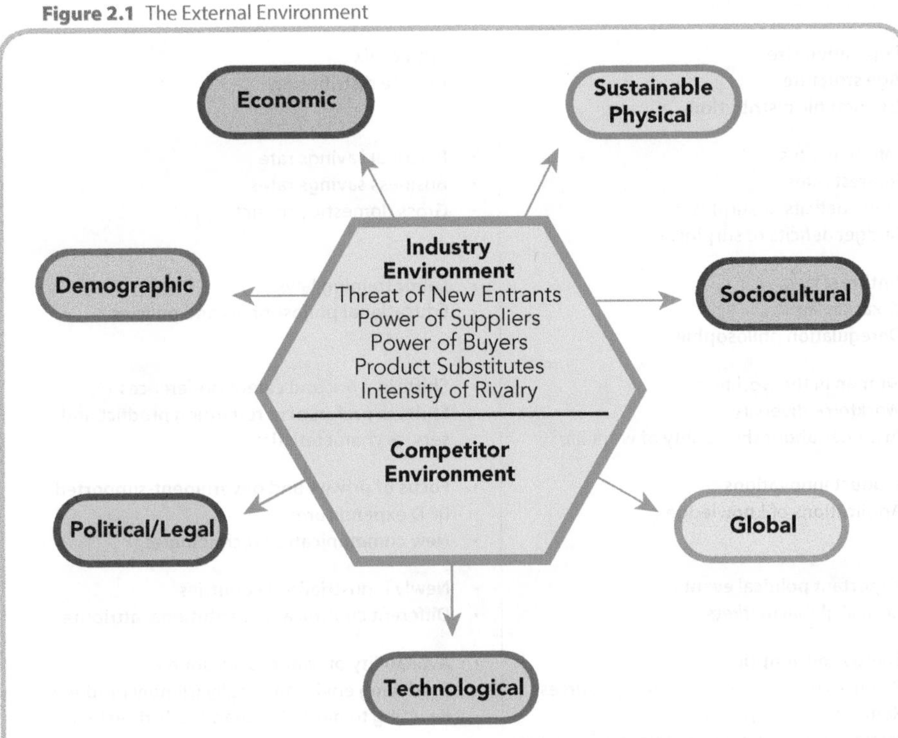

2-1 The General, Industry, and Competitor Environments

The **general environment** is composed of dimensions in the broader society that influence an industry and the firms within it.[7] We group these dimensions into seven environmental *segments*: demographic, economic, political/legal, sociocultural, technological, global, and sustainable physical. Examples of *elements* analyzed in each of these segments are shown in Table 2.1.

Firms cannot directly control the general environment's segments. Accordingly, what a company seeks to do is recognize trends in each segment of the general environment and then *predict* each trend's effect on it. For example, it has been predicted that over the next 10 to 20 years, millions of people living in emerging market countries will join the middle class. In fact, by 2030, it is predicted that two-thirds of the global middle class, about 525 million people, will live in the Asia-Pacific region of the world.[8] Of course, this is not surprising given that almost 60 percent of the world's population is located in Asia.[9] No firm, including large multinationals, is able to control where growth in potential customers may take place in the next decade or two. Nonetheless, firms must study this anticipated trend as a foundation for predicting its effects on their ability to identify strategies to use that will allow them to remain successful as market conditions change.

The **industry environment** is the set of factors that directly influences a firm and its competitive actions and responses: the threat of new entrants, the power of suppliers, the power of buyers, the threat of product substitutes, and the intensity of rivalry

The **general environment** is composed of dimensions in the broader society that influence an industry and the firms within it.

The **industry environment** is the set of factors that directly influences a firm and its competitive actions and responses: the threat of new entrants, the power of suppliers, the power of buyers, the threat of product substitutes, and the intensity of rivalry among competing firms.

Five Forces Model

Table 2.1 The General Environment: Segments and Elements

Segment	Elements	
Demographic segment	• Population size • Age structure • Geographic distribution	• Ethnic mix • Income distribution
Economic segment	• Inflation rates • Interest rates • Trade deficits or surpluses • Budget deficits or surpluses	• Personal savings rate • Business savings rates • Gross domestic product
Political/Legal segment	• Antitrust laws • Taxation laws • Deregulation philosophies	• Labor training laws • Educational philosophies and policies
Sociocultural segment	• Women in the workforce • Workforce diversity • Attitudes about the quality of work life	• Shifts in work and career preferences • Shifts in preferences regarding product and service characteristics
Technological segment	• Product innovations • Applications of knowledge	• Focus of private and government-supported R&D expenditures • New communication technologies
Global segment	• Important political events • Critical global markets	• Newly industrialized countries • Different cultural and institutional attributes
Sustainable physical environment segment	• Energy consumption • Practices used to develop energy sources • Renewable energy efforts • Minimizing a firm's environmental footprint	• Availability of water as a resource • Producing environmentally friendly products • Reacting to natural or man-made disasters

among competing firms.[10] In total, the interactions among these five factors determine an industry's profitability potential; in turn, the industry's profitability potential influences the choices each firm makes about its competitive actions and responses. The challenge for a firm is to locate a position within an industry where it can favorably influence the five factors or where it can successfully defend itself against their influence. The greater a firm's capacity to favorably influence its industry environment, the greater the likelihood it will earn above-average returns.

How companies gather and interpret information about their competitors is called **competitor analysis**. Understanding the firm's competitor environment complements the insights provided by studying the general and industry environments.[11] This means, for example, that McDonald's needs to do a better job of analyzing and understanding its general and industry environments.

How companies gather and interpret information about their competitors is called **competitor analysis**.

An analysis of the general environment focuses on environmental trends and their implications, an analysis of the industry environment focuses on the factors and conditions influencing an industry's profitability potential, and an analysis of competitors is focused on predicting competitors' actions, responses, and intentions. In combination, the results of these three analyses influence the firm's vision, mission, choice of strategies, and the competitive actions and responses it will take to implement those strategies. Although we discuss each analysis separately, the firm can develop and implement a more effective strategy when it successfully integrates the insights provided by analyses of the general environment, the industry environment, and the competitor environment.

2-2 External Environmental Analysis

Most firms face external environments that are turbulent, complex, and global—conditions that make interpreting those environments difficult.[12] To cope with often ambiguous and incomplete environmental data and to increase understanding of the general environment, firms complete an *external environmental analysis*. This analysis has four parts: scanning, monitoring, forecasting, and assessing (see Table 2.2).

Identifying opportunities and threats is an important objective of studying the general environment. An **opportunity** is a condition in the general environment that, if exploited effectively, helps a company reach strategic competitiveness. Most companies—and certainly large ones—continuously encounter multiple opportunities as well as threats.

In terms of possible opportunities, a combination of cultural, political, and economic factors is resulting in rapid retail growth in parts of Africa, Asia, and Latin America. Accordingly, Walmart, the world's largest retailer, and the next three largest global giants (France's Carrefour, UK-based Tesco, and Germany's Metro) are expanding in these regions. Walmart is expanding its number of retail units in Chile (404 units), India (20 units), and South Africa (360 units). Interestingly, Carrefour exited India after four years and in the same year that Tesco opened stores in India. While Metro closed its operations in Egypt, it has stores in China, Russia, Japan, Vietnam, and India in addition to many eastern European countries.[13]

A **threat** is a condition in the general environment that may hinder a company's efforts to achieve strategic competitiveness.[14] Intellectual property protection has become a significant issue not only within a country but also across country borders. For example, in 2018 President Trump placed tariffs on goods exported from China into the United States. The primary reason given for the tariffs was the theft of U.S. firms' intellectual property by Chinese firms. As is common in these cases, China responded by placing tariffs on a large number of U.S. products exported to China, sparking fears of a potential trade war between the two countries with the largest economies in the world. This type of threat obviously deals with the political/legal segment.

Firms use multiple sources to analyze the general environment through scanning, monitoring, forecasting, and assessing. Examples of these sources include a wide variety of printed materials (such as trade publications, newspapers, business publications, and the results of academic research and public polls), trade shows, and suppliers, customers, and employees of public-sector organizations. Of course, the information available from Internet sources is of increasing importance to a firm's efforts to study the general environment.

2-2a Scanning

Scanning entails the study of all segments in the general environment. Although challenging, scanning is critically important to the firms' efforts to understand trends in the

Table 2.2 Parts of the External Environment Analysis

Scanning	• Identifying early signals of environmental changes and trends
Monitoring	• Detecting meaning through ongoing observations of environmental changes and trends
Forecasting	• Developing projections of anticipated outcomes based on monitored changes and trends
Assessing	• Determining the timing and importance of environmental changes and trends for firms' strategies and their management

An **opportunity** is a condition in the general environment that, if exploited effectively, helps a company reach strategic competitiveness.

A **threat** is a condition in the general environment that may hinder a company's efforts to achieve strategic competitiveness.

general environment and to predict their implications. This is particularly the case for companies competing in highly volatile environments.[15]

Through scanning, firms identify early signals of potential changes in the general environment and detect changes that are already under way.[16] Scanning activities must be aligned with the organizational context; a scanning system designed for a volatile environment is inappropriate for a firm in a stable environment.[17] Scanning often reveals ambiguous, incomplete, or unconnected data and information that require careful analysis.

Many firms use special software to help them identify events that are taking place in the environment and that are announced in public sources. For example, news event detection uses information-based systems to categorize text and reduce the trade-off between an important missed event and false alarm rates. Increasingly, these systems are used to study social media outlets as sources of information.[18]

Broadly speaking, the Internet provides a wealth of opportunities for scanning. Amazon.com, for example, records information about individuals visiting its website, particularly if a purchase is made. Amazon then welcomes these customers by name when they visit the website again. The firm sends messages to customers about specials and new products similar to those they purchased in previous visits. A number of other companies, such as Netflix, also collect demographic data about their customers in an attempt to identify their unique preferences (demographics is one of the segments in the general environment). Approximately 4 billion people use the Internet in some way, including more than 738 million in China and 287 million in the United States. So, the Internet represents a healthy opportunity to gather information on users.[19]

2-2b Monitoring

When *monitoring*, analysts observe environmental changes to see if an important trend is emerging from among those spotted through scanning.[20] Critical to successful monitoring is the firm's ability to detect meaning in environmental events and trends. For example, those monitoring retirement trends in the United States learned that the median retirement savings of U.S. workers was only $5000. And for those who are aged 56-61, the median savings for retirement was only $17,000. For a reasonable retirement, Fidelity estimates that people should have saved 10 times their annual salary.[21] Firms seeking to serve retirees' financial needs will continue monitoring workers' savings and investment patterns to see if a trend is developing. If, say, they identify that saving less for retirement (or other needs) is indeed a trend, these firms will seek to understand its competitive implications.

Effective monitoring requires the firm to identify important stakeholders and understand its reputation among these stakeholders as the foundation for serving their unique needs.[22] (Stakeholders' unique needs are described in Chapter 1.) One means of monitoring major stakeholders is by using directors that serve on other boards of directors (referred to as interlocking directorates). They facilitate information and knowledge transfer from external sources.[23] Scanning and monitoring are particularly important when a firm competes in an industry with high technological uncertainty.[24] Scanning and monitoring can provide the firm with information. These activities also serve as a means of importing knowledge about markets and about how to successfully commercialize the new technologies the firm has developed.[25]

2-2c Forecasting

Scanning and monitoring are concerned with events and trends in the general environment at a point in time. When *forecasting*, analysts develop feasible projections of what might happen, and how quickly, as a result of the events and trends detected through scanning and monitoring.[26] For example, analysts might forecast the time that will be required for a new technology to reach the marketplace, the length of time before different corporate training procedures are required to deal with anticipated changes in the composition of the workforce, or how much time will elapse before changes in governmental taxation policies affect consumers' purchasing patterns.

Forecasting events and outcomes accurately is challenging. Forecasting demand for new technological products is difficult because technology trends are continually shortening product life cycles. This is particularly difficult for a firm such as Intel, whose products go into many customers' technological products, which are frequently updated. Thus, having access to tools that allow better forecasting of electronic product demand is of value to Intel as the firm studies conditions in its external environment.[27]

2-2d Assessing

When *assessing*, the objective is to determine the timing and significance of the effects of environmental changes and trends that have been identified.[28] Through scanning, monitoring, and forecasting, analysts are able to understand the general environment. Additionally, the intent of assessment is to specify the implications of that understanding. Without assessment, the firm has data that may be interesting but of unknown competitive relevance. Even if formal assessment is inadequate, the appropriate interpretation of that information is important.

Accurately assessing the trends expected to take place in the segments of a firm's general environment is important. However, accurately interpreting the meaning of those trends is even more important. In slightly different words, although gathering and organizing information is important, appropriately interpreting that information to determine if an identified trend in the general environment is an opportunity or threat is critical.[29]

2-3 Segments of the General Environment

The general environment is composed of segments that are external to the firm (see Table 2.1). Although the degree of impact varies, these environmental segments affect all industries and the firms competing in them. The challenge to each firm is to scan, monitor, forecast, and assess the elements in each segment to predict their effects on it. Effective scanning, monitoring, forecasting, and assessing are vital to the firm's efforts to recognize and evaluate opportunities and threats.

2-3a The Demographic Segment

The **demographic segment** is concerned with a population's size, age structure, geographic distribution, ethnic mix, and income distribution.[30] Demographic segments are commonly analyzed on a global basis because of their potential effects across countries' borders and because many firms compete in global markets.

Population Size

The world's population doubled (from 3 billion to 6 billion) between 1959 and 1999. Current projections suggest that population growth will continue in the twenty-first century, but at a slower pace. In 2018, the world's population was 7.6 billion, and it is projected to be 9.2 billion by 2040 and roughly 10 billion by 2055.[31] In 2018, China was the world's largest country by population with slightly more than 1.4 billion people. By

The **demographic segment** is concerned with a population's size, age structure, geographic distribution, ethnic mix, and income distribution.

2050, however, India is expected to be the most populous nation in the world followed by China, the United States, Indonesia, and Pakistan.[32] Firms seeking to find growing markets in which to sell their goods and services want to recognize the market potential that may exist for them in these five nations.

Firms also want to study changes occurring within the populations of different nations and regions of the world to assess their strategic implications. For example, 28 percent of Japan's citizens are 65 or older, while the figures for the United States and China are 15 percent and 11 percent, respectively. However, the population in both countries is aging rapidly and could match that in Japan by 2040.[33] Aging populations are a significant problem for countries because of the need for workers and the burden of supporting retirement programs. In Japan and some other countries, employees are urged to work longer to overcome these problems.

Age Structure

The most noteworthy aspect of this element of the demographic segment is that the world's population is rapidly aging, as noted above. For example, predictions are that the number of centenarians worldwide will double by 2023 and double again by 2035. Projections suggest life expectancy will surpass 100 in some industrialized countries by the second half of this century—roughly triple the lifespan of the population in earlier years.[34] In the 1950s, Japan's population was one of the youngest in the world. However, 45 is now the median age in Japan, with the projection that it will be 55 by 2040. With a fertility rate that is below replacement value, another prediction is that by 2040 there will be almost as many Japanese people 100 years old or older as there are newborns.[35] By 2050, almost 25 percent of the world's population will be aged 65 or older. These changes in the age of the population have significant implications for availability of qualified labor, health care, retirement policies, and business opportunities among others.[36]

This aging of the population threatens the ability of firms to hire and retain a workforce that meets their needs. Thus, firms are challenged to increase the productivity of their workers and/or to establish additional operations in other nations in order to access the potential working age population. A potential opportunity is represented by delayed retirements; older workers with extended life expectancies may need to work longer in order to eventually afford retirement. Delayed retirements may help companies to retain experienced and knowledgeable workers. In this sense, "organizations now have a fresh opportunity to address the talent gap created by a shortage of critical skills in the marketplace as well as the experience gap created by multiple waves of downsizing over the past decade."[37] Firms can also use their older, more experienced workers to transfer their knowledge to younger employees, helping them to quickly gain valuable skills. There is also an opportunity for firms to more effectively use the talent available in the workforce. For example, moving women into higher level professional and managerial jobs could offset the challenges created by decline in overall talent availability. And, based on research, it may even enhance overall outcomes.[38]

Geographic Distribution

How a population is distributed within countries and regions is subject to change over time. For example, over the last few decades, the U.S. population has shifted from states in the Northeast and Great Lakes region to states in the West (California), South (Florida), and Southwest (Texas). Based on data in 2018, California's population has grown by approximately 2.3 million since 2010, while Texas's population has grown by 3.2 million in the same time period.[39] These changes are characterized as moving from the "Frost

Belt" to the "Sun Belt." Outcomes from these shifts include the fact that the gross domestic product (GDP) of California in 2017 was slightly more than $2.75 trillion, an amount that makes California the sixth-largest economy in the world. In this same year, at a value of $1.6 trillion, Texas' GDP was second to that of California.[40]

The least popular states are Illinois, Vermont, and West Virginia, which experienced population declines between 2010 and 2018. During the same time period, the population of Connecticut, Maine, Michigan, Mississippi, Pennsylvania and Rhode Island grew less than one percent. In the coming years, California, Florida and Texas are forecasted to have the largest gains in population.[41]

Firms want to carefully study the patterns of population distributions in countries and regions to identify opportunities and threats. Thus, in the United States, current patterns suggest the possibility of opportunities in states on the West Coast and some in the South and Southwest. In contrast, firms competing in the Northeast and Great Lakes areas may concentrate on identifying threats to their ability to operate profitably in those areas.

Of course, geographic distribution patterns differ throughout the world. For example, in past years, the majority of the population in China lived in rural areas; however, growth patterns have been shifting to urban communities such as Shanghai and Beijing. In fact, in 2006, there were 148.7 million more people living in rural areas than in urban areas in China. However, by 2016, 203.2 million more people lived in urban than in rural areas within China, a substantial shift in a only ten-year period.[42] Recent shifts in Europe show small population gains for countries such as France, Germany, and the United Kingdom, while Greece experienced a small population decline. Overall, the geographic distribution patterns in Europe have been reasonably stable.[43]

Ethnic Mix

The ethnic mix of countries' populations continues to change, creating opportunities and threats for many companies as a result. For example, Hispanics have become the largest ethnic minority in the United States.[44] In fact, the U.S. Hispanic market is the third largest "Latin American" economy behind Brazil and Mexico. Spanish is now the dominant language in parts of the United States such as Texas, California, Florida, and New Mexico. Given these facts, some firms might want to assess how their goods or services could be adapted to serve the unique needs of Hispanic consumers. Interestingly, by 2020, more than 50 percent of children in the United States will be a member of a minority ethnic group, and the population in the United States is projected to have a majority of minority ethnic members by 2044. And, by 2060, whites are projected to compose approximately 44 percent of the U.S. population.[45] The ethnic diversity of the population is important not only because of consumer needs but also because of the labor force composition. Interestingly, research has shown that firms with greater ethnic diversity in their managerial team are likely to enjoy higher performance.[46]

Additional evidence is of interest to firms when examining this segment. For example, African countries are the most ethnically diverse in the world, with Uganda having the highest ethnic diversity rating and Liberia having the second highest. In contrast, Japan and the Koreas are the least ethnically diversified in their populations. European countries are largely ethnically homogeneous while the Americas are more diverse. "From the United States through Central America down to Brazil, the 'new world' countries, maybe in part because of their histories of relatively open immigration (and, in some cases, intermingling between natives and new arrivals) tend to be pretty diverse."[47]

Income Distribution

Understanding how income is distributed within and across populations informs firms of different groups' purchasing power and discretionary income. Of particular interest to firms are the average incomes of households and individuals. For instance, the increase in dual-career couples has had a notable effect on average incomes. Although real income has been declining in general in some nations, the household income of dual-career couples has increased, especially in the United States. These figures yield strategically relevant information for firms. For instance, research indicates that whether an employee is part of a dual-career couple can strongly influence the willingness of the employee to accept an international assignment. Worldwide it is estimated that there were almost 57 million expatriates in 2017, with Saudi Arabia, United Arab Emirates, and the United States as the top three destinations.[48]

The growth of the economy in China has drawn many firms, not only for the low-cost production, but also because of the large potential demand for products, given its large population base. However, in recent times, the amount of China's gross domestic product that makes up domestic consumption is the lowest of any major economy at less than one-third. In comparison, India's domestic consumption of consumer goods accounts for two-thirds of its economy, or twice China's level. For this reason, many western multinationals are interested in India as a consumption market as its middle class grows extensively; although India has poor infrastructure, its consumers are in a better position to spend. Because of situations such as this, paying attention to the differences between markets based on income distribution can be very important.[49] These differences across nations suggest it is important for most firms to identify the economic systems that are most likely to produce the most income growth and market opportunities.[50] Thus, the economic segment is a critically important focus of firms' environmental analysis.

2-3b The Economic Segment

The **economic environment** refers to the nature and direction of the economy in which a firm competes or may compete.[51] In general, firms seek to compete in relatively stable economies with strong growth potential. Because nations are interconnected as a result of the global economy, firms must scan, monitor, forecast, and assess the health of their host nation as well as the health of the economies outside it.

It is challenging for firms studying the economic environment to predict economic trends that may occur and their effects on them. There are at least two reasons for this. First, the global recession of 2008 and 2009 created numerous problems for companies throughout the world, including problems of reduced consumer demand, increases in firms' inventory levels, development of additional governmental regulations, and a tightening of access to financial resources. Second, the global recovery from the economic shock in 2008 and 2009 was persistently slow compared to previous recoveries. Firms must adjust to the economic shock and try to recover from it. And although the world economic prospects appear to be good in 2018, the recovery has been uneven across countries. For example, the economies in several European countries continue to struggle (e.g., Greece, Spain). And, perhaps partly due to political uncertainties (e.g., in the United States), there continue to be concerns about economic uncertainty. And again, according to some research, "it is clear that (economic) uncertainty has increased in recent times."[52] This current degree of economic uncertainty makes it challenging to develop effective strategies.

The **economic environment** refers to the nature and direction of the economy in which a firm competes or may compete.

When facing economic uncertainty, firms especially want to study closely the economic environment in multiple regions and countries throughout the world. Although economic growth remains relatively weak and economic uncertainty has been strong in Europe, economic growth has been better in the United States in recent times. For example, the projected average annual economic growth in Europe for 2018–2020 is 1.75 percent, while in the United States it is 2.25 percent. Alternatively, the projected average annual economic growth for 2018–2020 is 6.3 percent in China, 7.45 percent in India, 2.25 percent in Brazil, and 2.45 percent in Mexico. These estimates highlight the anticipation of the continuing development of emerging economies.[53] Ideally, firms will be able to pursue higher growth opportunities in regions and nations where they exist while avoiding the threats of slow growth periods in other settings.

AP Images/Brennan Linsley

A marijuana Budtender sorts strands of marijuana for sale at a retail and medical cannabis dispensary in Boulder, Colorado.

2-3c The Political/Legal Segment

The **political/legal segment** is the arena in which organizations and interest groups compete for attention, resources, and a voice in overseeing the body of laws and regulations guiding interactions among nations as well as between firms and various local governmental agencies.[54] Essentially, this segment is concerned with how organizations try to influence governments and how they try to understand the influences (current and projected) of those governments on their competitive actions and responses. Commonly, firms develop a political strategy to specify how they will analyze and the political/legal to develop approaches they can take (such as lobbying efforts) to successfully deal with opportunities and threats that surface within this segment of the environment.[55]

Regulations formed in response to new national, regional, state, and/or local laws that are legislated often influence a firm's competitive actions and responses.[56] For example, the state of California in the United States recently legalized the retail selling of cannabis (also known as marijuana). This action follows similar laws legalizing the sale of cannabis in other states such as Colorado and Washington. The immediate concern is the risk that firms take to invest capital in this business, given that it is unknown whether the U.S. Department of Justice will allow the states to proceed without enforcing federal law against the sale of this product. Thus, the relationship between national, regional, and local laws and regulations creates a highly complex environment within which businesses must navigate.[57]

For interactive, technology-based firms such as Facebook, Google, and Amazon, among others, the effort in Europe to adopt the world's strongest data protection law has significant challenges. Highly restrictive laws about consumer privacy could threaten how these firms conduct business in the European Union. Alternatively, firms must deal with quite different challenges when they operate in countries with weak formal institutions (e.g., weak legal protection of intellectual property). Laws and regulations provide structure to guide strategic and competitive actions; without such structure, it is difficult to identify the best strategic actions.[58]

The **political/legal segment** is the arena in which organizations and interest groups compete for attention, resources, and a voice in overseeing the body of laws and regulations guiding interactions among nations as well as between firms and various local governmental agencies.

2-3d The Sociocultural Segment

The **sociocultural segment** is concerned with a society's attitudes and cultural values. Because attitudes and values form the cornerstone of a society, they often drive demographic, economic, political/legal, and technological conditions and changes.

Individual societies' attitudes and cultural orientations are relatively stable, but they can and often do change over time. Thus, firms must carefully scan, monitor, forecast, and assess them to recognize and study associated opportunities and threats. Successful firms must also be aware of changes taking place in the societies and their associated cultural values in which they are competing. Indeed, firms must identify changes in cultural values, norms, and attitudes in order to "adapt to stay ahead of their competitors and stay relevant in the minds of their consumers."[59] Research has shown that sociocultural factors influence the entry into new markets and the development of new firms in a country.[60]

Attitudes about and approaches to health care are being evaluated in nations and regions throughout the world. For Europe, the European Commission has developed a health care strategy for all of Europe that is oriented to preventing diseases while tackling lifestyle factors influencing health such as nutrition, working conditions, and physical activity. This Commission argues that promoting attitudes to take care of one's health is especially important in the context of an aging Europe, as shown by the projection that the proportion of people over 65 living in Europe and in most of the developed nations throughout the world will continue to grow.[61] At issue for business firms is that attitudes and values about health care can affect them; accordingly, they must carefully examine trends regarding health care in order to anticipate the effects on their operations.

The U.S. labor force has evolved to become more diverse, with significantly more women and minorities from a variety of cultures entering the workplace. For example, women were 46.8 percent of the workforce in 2014, a number projected to grow to 47.2 percent by 2024. Hispanics are expected to be about 20 percent of the workforce by 2024. In 2005, the total U.S. workforce was slightly greater than 148 million, and it is predicted to grow to approximately 164 million by 2024.[62]

The **sociocultural segment** is concerned with a society's attitudes and cultural values.

However, the rate of growth in the U.S. labor force has declined over the past two decades largely because of slower growth of the nation's population and because of a downward trend in the labor force participation rate. More specifically, data show that the overall participation rate (the proportion of the civilian non-institutional population in the labor force) peaked at an annual average of 67.1 percent in 2000. But the rate has declined since that time and is expected to fall to 58.5 percent by 2050. Other changes in the U.S. labor force between 2010 and 2050 are expected. During this time, Asian membership in the labor force is projected to more than double in size, while the growth in Caucasian members of the labor force is predicted to be much slower compared to other racial groups. In contrast, people of Hispanic origin are expected to account for roughly 80 percent of the total growth in the labor force.[63]

Alexander Raths/Shutterstock.com

Healthcare is becoming increasingly important as the proportion of people older than 65 is growing larger in many nations throughout the world.

Greater diversity in the workforce creates challenges and opportunities, including combining the best of both men's and women's traditional leadership styles. Although diversity in the workforce has the potential to improve performance, research indicates that diversity initiatives must be successfully managed to reap these organizational benefits.

Although the lifestyle and workforce changes referenced previously reflect the attitudes and values of the U.S. population, each country is unique with respect to these sociocultural indicators. National cultural values affect behavior in organizations and thus also influence organizational outcomes such as differences in managerial styles. Likewise, the national culture influences a large portion of the internationalization strategy that firms pursue relative to one's home country.[64] Knowledge sharing is important for dispersing new knowledge in organizations and increasing the speed in implementing innovations. Personal relationships are especially important in China; the concept of *guanxi* (personal relationships or good connections) is important in doing business within the country and for individuals to advance their careers in what is becoming a more open market society. Understanding the importance of guanxi is critical for foreign firms doing business in China.[65]

2-3e The Technological Segment

Pervasive and diversified in scope, technological changes affect many parts of societies. These effects occur primarily through new products, processes, and materials. The **technological segment** includes the institutions and activities involved in creating new knowledge and translating that knowledge into new outputs, products, processes, and materials.

Given the rapid pace of technological change and risk of disruption, it is vital for firms to thoroughly study the technological segment.[66] The importance of these efforts is shown by the fact that early adopters of new technology often achieve higher market shares and earn higher returns. Thus, both large and small firms should continuously scan the general environment to identify potential substitutes for technologies that are in current use, as well as to identify newly emerging technologies from which their firm could derive competitive advantage.[67]

New technology and innovations are changing many industries.[68] These changes are exemplified by the change to digital publishing (e.g., electronic books) and retail industries moving from brick and mortar stores to Internet sales. As such, firms in all industries must become more innovative in order to survive, and must develop new or at least comparable technology—and continuously improve it.[69] In so doing, most firms must have a sophisticated information system to support their new product development efforts.[70] In fact, because the adoption and efficient use of new technology has become critical to global competitiveness in many or most industries, countries have begun to offer special forms of support, such as the development of technology business incubators, which provide several types of assistance to increase the success rate of new technology ventures.[71]

As a significant technological development, the Internet offers firms a remarkable capability in terms of their efforts to scan, monitor, forecast, and assess conditions in their general environment. Companies continue to study the Internet's capabilities to anticipate how it may allow them to create more value for customers and to anticipate future trends. Additionally, the Internet generates a significant number of opportunities and threats for firms across the world. As noted earlier, there are approximately 4 billion Internet users globally.

Despite the Internet's far-reaching effects and the opportunities and threats associated with its potential, wireless communication technology has become a significant

The **technological segment** includes the institutions and activities involved in creating new knowledge and translating that knowledge into new outputs, products, processes, and materials.

technological opportunity for companies. Handheld devices and other wireless communications equipment are used to access a variety of network-based services. The use of handheld computers (of many types) with wireless network connectivity has become the dominant form of communication and commerce, and additional functionalities and software applications are generating multiple opportunities—and potential threats—for companies of all types.

2-3f The Global Segment

The **global segment** includes relevant new global markets and their critical cultural and institutional characteristics, existing markets that are changing, and important international political events.[72] For example, firms competing in the automobile industry must study the global segment. The fact that consumers in multiple nations are willing to buy cars and trucks "from whatever area of the world"[73] supports this position.

When studying the global segment, firms should recognize that globalization of business markets may create opportunities to enter new markets, as well as threats that new competitors from other economies may also enter their market.[74] In terms of an opportunity for automobile manufacturers, the possibility for these firms to sell their products outside of their home market would seem attractive. But what markets might firms choose to enter? Currently, automobile and truck sales are expected to increase in Brazil, Russia, India, China, and Eastern Europe. In contrast, sales are expected to decline, at least in the near term, in the United States, Western Europe, and Japan. These markets, then, are the most and least attractive ones for automobile manufacturers desiring to sell outside their domestic market. At the same time, from the perspective of a threat, Japan, Germany, Korea, Spain, France, and the United States appear to have excess production capacity in the automobile manufacturing industry. In turn, overcapacity signals the possibility that companies based in markets where this is the case will simultaneously attempt to increase their exports as well as sales in their domestic market.[75] Thus, global automobile manufacturers should carefully examine the global segment to precisely identify all opportunities and threats.

In light of threats associated with participating in international markets, some firms choose to take a more cautious approach to globalization. For example, family business firms, even the larger ones, often take a conservative approach to entering international markets in a manner very similar to how they approach the development and introduction of new technology. They try to manage their risk.[76] These firms participate in what some refer to as *globalfocusing*. Globalfocusing often is used by firms with moderate levels of international operations who increase their internationalization by focusing on global niche markets.[77] This approach allows firms to build onto and use their core competencies while limiting their risks within the niche market. Another way in which firms limit their risks in international markets is to focus their operations and sales in one region of the world.[78] Success with these efforts finds a firm building relationships in and knowledge of its markets. As the firm builds these strengths, rivals find it more difficult to enter its markets and compete successfully.

Firms competing in global markets should recognize each market's sociocultural and institutional attributes.[79] For example, Korean ideology emphasizes communitarianism, a characteristic of many Asian countries. Alternatively, the ideology in China calls for an emphasis on *guanxi*—personal connections—while in Japan, the focus is on *wa*—group harmony and social cohesion.[80] The institutional context of China suggests a major emphasis on centralized planning by the government. The Chinese government

The **global segment** includes relevant new global markets and their critical cultural and institutional characteristics, existing markets that are changing, and important international political events.

provides incentives to firms to develop alliances with foreign firms having sophisticated technology, in hopes of building knowledge and introducing new technologies to the Chinese markets over time.[81] As such, it is important to analyze the strategic intent of foreign firms when pursuing alliances and joint ventures abroad, especially where the local partners are receiving technology that may in the long run reduce the foreign firms' advantages.[82]

Increasingly, the *informal economy* as it exists throughout the world is another aspect of the global segment requiring analysis. Growing in size, this economy has implications for firms' competitive actions and responses in that increasingly, firms competing in the formal economy will find that they are competing against informal economy companies as well.

2-3g The Sustainable Physical Environment Segment

The **sustainable physical environment segment** refers to potential and actual changes in the physical environment and business practices that are intended to positively respond to those changes in order to create a sustainable environment.[83] Concerned with trends oriented to sustaining the world's physical environment, firms recognize that ecological, social, and economic systems interactively influence what happens in this particular segment and that they are part of an interconnected global society.[84]

Companies across the globe are concerned about the physical environment, and many record the actions they are taking in reports with names such as "Sustainability" and "Corporate Social Responsibility." Moreover, and in a comprehensive sense, an increasing number of companies are investing in sustainable development.

There are many parts or attributes of the physical environment that firms consider as they try to identify trends in the physical environment.[85] Because of the importance to firms of becoming sustainable, certification programs have been developed to help them understand how to be sustainable organizations.[86] As the world's largest retailer, Walmart's environmental footprint is huge, meaning that trends in the physical environment can significantly affect this firm and how it chooses to operate. Because of this, Walmart's goal is to produce zero waste and to use 100 percent renewable energy to power its operations.[87] Environmental sustainability is important to all societal citizens and because of its importance, customers react more positively to firms taking actions such as those by Walmart.[88] To build and maintain sustainable operations in companies that directly service retail customers requires sustainable supply chain management practices.[89] Thus, top managers must focus on managing any of the firm's practices that have effects on the physical environment. In doing so, they not only contribute to a cleaner environment but also reap financial rewards from being an effective competitor due to positive customer responses.[90]

As our discussion of the general environment shows, identifying anticipated changes and trends among segments and their elements is a key objective of analyzing this environment. With a focus on the future, the analysis of the general environment allows firms to identify opportunities and threats. It is necessary to have a top management team with the experience, knowledge, and sensitivity required to effectively analyze the conditions in a firm's general environment—as well as other facets such as the industry environment and competitors.[91] In fact, as you noted in the Strategic Focus on Target, the lack of a commitment to analyzing the environment in depth can have serious, company-wide ramifications.

The **sustainable physical environment segment** refers to potential and actual changes in the physical environment and business practices that are intended to positively respond to those changes in order to create a sustainable environment.

Strategic Focus

Target (Tar-zhey) Is Trying to Navigate in a New and Rapidly Changing Competitive Landscape

Target became known by consumers as Tar-zhey, the retailer of cheaper but 'chic' products. The firm offered a step up in quality goods at a slightly higher price than discount retailers such as Walmart, but was targeted below major, first line retailers such Macy's and Nordstrom. Additionally, it promoted its stores to offer one-stop shopping with clothing, toys, health products, and food goods, among other products. For many years, Tar-zhey "hit the bullseye" and performed well serving this large niche in the market. But the company took its eye off the target and began losing market share (along with other poor strategic actions).

The first major crack in the ship appeared with the announcement of a massive cyberattack on Target's computer system that netted customers' personal information. Not only was this a public relations disaster, it drew a focus on Target that identified other problems. For example, careful analysis showed that Target was losing customers to established competitors and new rivals, especially Internet retailers (e.g., Amazon.com).

Target's marketing chief stated that "it's not that we became insular. We were insular." This suggests that the firm was not analyzing its environment. By allowing rivals, and especially Internet competitors, to woo the company's customers, it lost sales, market share, and profits. It obviously did not predict and prepare for the significant competition from Internet rivals that is now reshaping most all retail industries. Competitors were offering better value to customers (perhaps more variety and convenience through online sales). Thus, Target's reputation and market share were simultaneously harmed.

Because of all the problems experienced, Target hired a new CEO, Brian Cornell, in 2014. Cornell has made a number of changes, but the continued revolution in the industry, largely driven by Amazon, continued to gnaw away Target's annual sales. Target's annual sales declined by approximately 5 percent in 2017 and its stock price suffered as a result. Target was forced to develop a new strategy, which involves a major rebranding. It launched four new brands late in 2017, including A New Day, a fashionable line of women's clothes, and Goodfellow & Co, a modern line of menswear, with the intent to make an emotional connection with customers. It also plans to remodel 100 of its stores and change in-store displays to improve customer experiences. It will add 30 small stores that offer innovative designs and, to compete with Amazon, is emphasizing its digital sales and delivery of products. Up to now its digital strategy has not been highly successful, so it is narrowing its focus to increase its effectiveness.

Glen Stubbe/ZUMA Press/Minneapolis/Minnesota/USA

Goodfellow & Co menswear, a new line introduced by Target in late 2017.

Target plans to discontinue several major brands by 2019 and will continue to introduce new brands (12 in total are planned). The intent is to increase the appeal of Target and its products to millennials. These actions alone suggest the importance of gathering and analyzing data on the market and competitors' actions. The next few years will show the fruits of all of Target's changes. If they are successful, Target will still face substantial competition from Amazon and Walmart; if they are not successful, Target suffer the same fate of of many other large and formerly successful retailers that no exist.

Sources: A. Pasquarelli, 2017, Our strategy is working: Target plows into the holidays, *AdAge*, http://adage.com, October 19; S. Heller, 2017, Target's biggest brands are about to disappear from stores, *The Insider*, www.theinsider.com, July 6; 2017, Rebranding its wheel: Target's new strategy, *Seeking Alpha*, http://seeking alpha.com, July 4;K. Safdar, 2017, Target's new online strategy: Less is more, *Wall Street Journal*, www.wsj.com, May 15; 2015, What your new CEO is reading: Smell ya later; Target's new CEO, *CIO Journal/Wall Street Journal*, www.wsj.com/cio, March 6; J. Reingold, 2014, Can Target's new CEO get the struggling retailer back on target? *Fortune*, www.fortune.com, July 31; G. Smith, 2014, Target turns to PepsiCo's Brian Cornell to restore its fortunes, *Fortune*, www.fortune.com, July 31; P. Ziobro, M. Langley, & J. S. Lublin, 2014, Target's problem: Tar-zhey isn't working. *Wall Street Journal*, www.wsj.com, May 5.

As described in the Strategic Focus, Target failed to maintain a good understanding of its industry and hence, lost market share to Internet company rivals and other more established competitors. We conclude that critical to a firm's choices of strategies and their associated competitive actions and responses is an understanding of its industry environment, its competitors, and the general environment of the countries in which it operates.[92] Next, we discuss the analyses firms complete to gain such an understanding.

2-4 Industry Environment Analysis

An **industry** is a group of firms producing products that are close substitutes. In the course of competition, these firms influence one another. Typically, companies use a rich mix of different competitive strategies to pursue above-average returns when competing in a particular industry. An industry's structural characteristics influence a firm's choice of strategies.[93]

Compared with the general environment, the industry environment (measured primarily in the form of its characteristics) has a more direct effect on the competitive actions and responses a firm takes to succeed.[94] To study an industry, the firm examines five forces that affect the ability of all firms to operate profitably within a given industry. Shown in Figure 2.2, the five forces are: the threats posed by new entrants, the power of suppliers, the power of buyers, product substitutes, and the intensity of rivalry among competitors.

The five forces of competition model depicted in Figure 2.2 expands the scope of a firm's competitive analysis. Historically, when studying the competitive environment, firms concentrated on companies with which they directly competed. However, firms must search more broadly to recognize current and potential competitors by identifying potential customers as well as the firms serving them. For example, the communications industry is now broadly defined as encompassing media companies, telecoms, entertainment companies, and companies producing devices such as smartphones. In such an environment, firms must study many other industries to identify companies with capabilities (especially technology-based capabilities) that might be the foundation for producing a good or a service that can compete against what they are producing.

Figure 2.2 The Five Forces of Competition Model

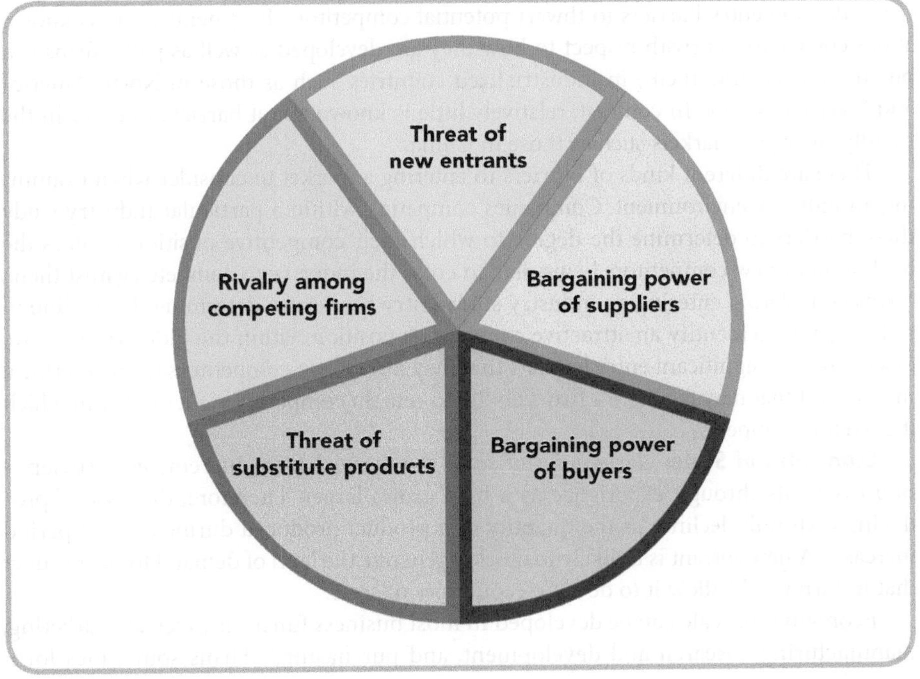

An **industry** is a group of firms producing products that are close substitutes.

When studying the industry environment, firms must also recognize that suppliers can become a firm's competitors (by integrating forward) as can buyers (by integrating backward). For example, several firms have integrated forward in the pharmaceutical industry by acquiring distributors or wholesalers. In addition, firms choosing to enter a new market and those producing products that are adequate substitutes for existing products can become a company's competitors.

Next, we examine the five forces the firm needs to analyze in order to understand the profitability potential within an industry (or a segment of an industry) in which it competes or may choose to compete.

2-4a Threat of New Entrants

Identifying new entrants is important because they can threaten the market share of existing competitors.[95] One reason new entrants pose such a threat is that they bring additional production capacity. Unless the demand for a good or service is increasing, additional capacity holds consumers' costs down, resulting in less revenue and lower returns for competing firms. Often, new entrants have a keen interest in gaining a large market share. As a result, new competitors may force existing firms to be more efficient and to learn how to compete in new dimensions (e.g., using an Internet-based distribution channel).

The likelihood that firms will enter an industry is a function of two factors: barriers to entry and the retaliation expected from current industry participants. Entry barriers make it difficult for new firms to enter an industry and often place them at a competitive disadvantage even when they can enter. As such, high entry barriers tend to increase the returns for existing firms in the industry and may allow some firms to dominate the industry.[96] Thus, firms competing successfully in an industry want to maintain high entry barriers to discourage potential competitors from deciding to enter the industry.

Barriers to Entry

Firms competing in an industry (and especially those earning above-average returns) try to develop entry barriers to thwart potential competitors. In general, more is known about entry barriers (with respect to how they are developed as well as paths firms can pursue to overcome them) in industrialized countries such as those in North America and Western Europe. In contrast, relatively little is known about barriers to entry in the rapidly emerging markets such as those in China.

There are different kinds of barriers to entering a market to consider when examining an industry environment. Companies competing within a particular industry study these barriers to determine the degree to which their competitive position reduces the likelihood of new competitors being able to enter the industry to compete against them. Firms considering entering an industry study entry barriers to determine the likelihood of being able to identify an attractive competitive position within the industry. Next, we discuss several significant entry barriers that may discourage competitors from entering a market and that may facilitate a firm's ability to remain competitive in a market in which it currently competes.

Economies of Scale *Economies of scale* are derived from incremental efficiency improvements through experience as a firm grows larger. Therefore, the cost of producing each unit declines as the quantity of a product produced during a given period increases. A new entrant is unlikely to quickly generate the level of demand for its product that in turn would allow it to develop economies of scale.

Economies of scale can be developed in most business functions, such as marketing, manufacturing, research and development, and purchasing.[97] Firms sometimes form strategic alliances or joint ventures to gain scale economies. And, other firms acquire rivals in order to build economies of scale in the operations and to increase their market share as well.

Becoming more flexible in terms of being able to meet shifts in customer demand is another benefit for an industry incumbent and a possible entry barrier for the firms considering entering the industry. For example, a firm may choose to reduce its price with the intention of capturing a larger share of the market. Alternatively, it may keep its price constant to increase profits. In so doing, it likely will increase its free cash flow, which is very helpful during financially challenging times.

Some competitive conditions reduce the ability of economies of scale to create an entry barrier such as the use of scale free resources.[98] Also, many companies now customize their products for large numbers of small customer groups. In these cases, customized products are not manufactured in the volumes necessary to achieve economies of scale. Customization is made possible by several factors, including flexible manufacturing systems. In fact, the new manufacturing technology facilitated by advanced information systems has allowed the development of mass customization in an increasing number of industries. Online ordering has enhanced customers' ability to buy customized products. Companies manufacturing customized products can respond quickly to customers' needs in lieu of developing scale economies.

Product Differentiation Over time, customers may come to believe that a firm's product is unique. This belief can result from the firm's service to the customer, effective advertising campaigns, or being the first to market a good or service.[99] Greater levels of perceived product uniqueness create customers who consistently purchase a firm's products. To combat the perception of uniqueness, new entrants frequently offer products at lower prices. This decision, however, may result in lower profits or even losses.

The Coca-Cola Company and PepsiCo have established strong brands in the markets in which they compete, and these companies compete against each other in countries throughout the world. Because each of these competitors has allocated a significant amount of resources over many decades to build its brands, customer loyalty is strong for each firm. When considering entry into the soft drink market, a potential entrant would be well advised to pause and determine actions it would take to try to overcome the brand image and consumer loyalty each of these giants possesses.

Capital Requirements Competing in a new industry requires a firm to have resources to invest. In addition to physical facilities, capital is needed for inventories, marketing activities, and other critical business functions. Even when a new industry is attractive, the capital required for successful market entry may not be available to pursue the market opportunity.[100] For example, defense industries are difficult to enter because of the substantial resource investments required to be competitive. In addition, because of the high knowledge requirements of the defense industry, a firm might acquire an existing company as a means of entering this industry, but it must have access to the capital necessary to do this.

Switching Costs *Switching costs* are the one-time costs customers incur when they buy from a different supplier. The costs of buying new ancillary equipment and of retraining employees, and even the psychological costs of ending a relationship, may be incurred in switching to a new supplier. In some cases, switching costs are low, such as when the consumer switches to a different brand of soft drink. Switching costs can vary as a function of time, as shown by the fact that in terms of credit hours toward graduation, the cost to a student to transfer from one university to another as a freshman is much lower than it is when the student is entering the senior year.

Occasionally, a decision made by manufacturers to produce a new, innovative product creates high switching costs for customers. Customer loyalty programs, such as airlines' frequent flyer miles, are intended to increase the customer's switching costs. If switching costs are high, a new entrant must offer either a substantially lower price or a much better product to attract buyers. Usually, the more established the relationships between parties, the greater the switching costs.

Access to Distribution Channels Over time, industry participants commonly learn how to effectively distribute their products. After building a relationship with its distributors, a firm will nurture it, thus creating switching costs for the distributors. Access to distribution channels can be a strong entry barrier for new entrants, particularly in consumer nondurable goods industries (e.g., in grocery stores where shelf space is limited) and in international markets.[101] New entrants have to persuade distributors to carry their products, either in addition to or in place of those currently distributed. Price breaks and cooperative advertising allowances may be used for this purpose; however, those practices reduce the new entrant's profit potential. Interestingly, access to distribution is less of a barrier for products that can be sold on the Internet.

Cost Disadvantages Independent of Scale Sometimes, established competitors have cost advantages that new entrants cannot duplicate. Proprietary product technology, favorable access to raw materials, desirable locations, and government subsidies are examples. Successful competition requires new entrants to reduce the strategic relevance of these factors. For example, delivering purchases directly to the buyer can counter the advantage of a desirable location; new food establishments in an undesirable location often follow this practice. Spanish clothing company Zara is owned by Inditex, the largest fashion clothing retailer in the world.[102] From the time of its launching, Zara relied on classy, well-tailored, and relatively inexpensive items that were produced and sold by adhering to ethical practices to successfully enter the highly competitive global clothing market and overcome that market's entry barriers. It is successful because it has used a novel business model in the industry. It also sells quality merchandise for less, offers good stores and store locations, and is well positioned in the industry.[103] Business model innovation may be the key to survival and success in current retail industries.[104]

Government Policy Through their decisions about issues such as the granting of licenses and permits, governments can also control entry into an industry. Liquor retailing, radio and TV broadcasting, banking, and trucking are examples of industries in which government decisions and actions affect entry possibilities. Also, governments often restrict entry into some industries because of the need to provide quality service or the desire to protect jobs. Alternatively, deregulating industries, such as the airline and utilities industries in the United States, generally results in additional firms choosing to enter and compete within an industry.[105] It is not uncommon for governments to attempt to regulate the entry of foreign firms, especially in industries considered critical to the country's economy or important markets within it.[106] Governmental decisions and policies regarding antitrust issues also affect entry barriers. For example, in the United States, the Antitrust Division of the Justice Department or the Federal Trade Commission will sometimes disallow a proposed merger because officials conclude that approving it would create a firm that is too dominant in an industry and would thus create unfair competition. For example, the U.S. Department of Justice filed a suit in 2017 to block the merger of AT&T and Time Warner with the trial initiated in March 2018. The actions of the Department of Justice were unsuccessful and in June 2018, the merger was approved and completed.[107] Such a negative ruling would obviously be an entry barrier for an acquiring firm.

Expected Retaliation

Companies seeking to enter an industry also anticipate the reactions of firms in the industry. An expectation of swift and vigorous competitive responses reduces the likelihood of entry. Vigorous retaliation can be expected when the existing firm has a major stake in the industry (e.g., it has fixed assets with few, if any, alternative uses), when it has substantial resources, and when industry growth is slow or constrained.[108] For example, any firm attempting to enter the airline industry can expect significant retaliation from existing competitors due to overcapacity.

Locating market niches not being served by incumbents allows the new entrant to avoid entry barriers. Small entrepreneurial firms are generally best suited for identifying and serving neglected market segments. When Honda first entered the U.S. motorcycle market, it concentrated on small-engine motorcycles, a market that firms such as Harley-Davidson ignored. By targeting this neglected niche, Honda initially avoided a significant amount of head-to-head competition with well-established competitors. After consolidating its position, Honda used its strength to attack rivals by introducing larger motorcycles and competing in the broader market.

DWImages Northern Ireland/Alamy Stock Photo

Honda's entry into the large motorcycle market is changing the competitive landscape especially for the traditional competitors in this market such as Harley-Davidson.

2-4b Bargaining Power of Suppliers

Increasing prices and reducing the quality of their products are potential means suppliers use to exert power over firms competing within an industry. If a firm is unable to recover cost increases by its suppliers through its own pricing structure, its profitability is reduced by its suppliers' actions.[109] A supplier group is powerful when:

- It is dominated by a few large companies and is more concentrated than the industry to which it sells.
- Satisfactory substitute products are not available to industry firms.
- Industry firms are not a significant customer for the supplier group.
- Suppliers' goods are critical to buyers' marketplace success.
- The effectiveness of suppliers' products has created high switching costs for industry firms.
- It poses a credible threat to integrate forward into the buyers' industry. Credibility is enhanced when suppliers have substantial resources and provide a highly differentiated product.[110]

Some buyers attempt to manage or reduce suppliers' power by developing a long-term relationship with them. Although long-term arrangements reduce buyer power, they also increase the suppliers' incentive to be helpful and cooperative in appreciation of the longer-term relationship (guaranteed sales). This is especially true when the partners develop trust in one another.[111]

The airline industry is one in which suppliers' bargaining power is changing. Though the number of suppliers is low, the demand for major aircraft is also relatively low. Boeing and Airbus aggressively compete for orders of major aircraft, creating more power for buyers in the process. When a large airline signals that it might place a "significant" order for wide-body airliners that either Airbus or Boeing might produce, both companies are likely to battle for the business and include a financing arrangement, highlighting the buyer's power in the potential transaction. And, with China's entry into the large commercial airliner industry, buyer power has increased.

2-4c Bargaining Power of Buyers

Firms seek to maximize the return on their invested capital. Alternatively, buyers (customers of an industry or a firm) want to buy products at the lowest possible price—the point at which the industry earns the lowest acceptable rate of return on its invested capital. To reduce their costs, buyers bargain for higher quality, greater levels of service, and lower prices.[112] These outcomes are achieved by encouraging competitive battles among the industry's firms. Customers (buyer groups) are powerful when:

- They purchase a large portion of an industry's total output.
- The sales of the product being purchased account for a significant portion of the seller's annual revenues.
- They could switch to another product at little, if any, cost.
- The industry's products are undifferentiated or standardized, and the buyers pose a credible threat if they were to integrate backward into the sellers' industry.

Consumers armed with greater amounts of information about the manufacturer's costs and the power of the Internet as a shopping and distribution alternative have increased bargaining power in many industries.

2-4d Threat of Substitute Products

Substitute products are goods or services from outside a given industry that perform similar or the same functions as a product that the industry produces. For example, as a sugar substitute, NutraSweet (and other sugar substitutes) places an upper limit on sugar manufacturers' prices—NutraSweet and sugar perform the same function, though with different characteristics. Other product substitutes include e-mail and fax machines instead of overnight deliveries, plastic containers rather than glass jars, and tea instead of coffee.

Newspaper firms have experienced significant circulation declines over the past 20 years. The declines are a result of the ready availability of substitute outlets for news including Internet sources and cable television news channels, along with e-mail and cell phone alerts. Likewise, satellite TV and cable and telecommunication companies provide substitute services for basic media services such as television, Internet, and phone. The many electronic devices that provide services overlapping with the personal computer (e.g., laptops) such as tablets, watches (iWatch), etc. are changing markets for PCs, with multiple niches in the market.

In general, product substitutes present a strong threat to a firm when customers face few if any switching costs and when the substitute product's price is lower or its quality and performance capabilities are equal to or greater than those of the competing product. Interestingly, some firms that produce substitutes have begun forming brand alliances, which research shows can be effective when the two products are of relatively equal quality.

If there is a differential in quality, the firm with the higher quality product will obtain lower returns from such an alliance.[113] Differentiating a product along dimensions that are valuable to customers (such as quality, service after the sale, and location) reduces a substitute's attractiveness.

2-4e Intensity of Rivalry among Competitors

Because an industry's firms are mutually dependent, actions taken by one company usually invite responses. Competitive rivalry intensifies when a firm is challenged by a competitor's actions or when a company recognizes an opportunity to improve its market position.[114]

Firms within industries are rarely homogeneous; they differ in resources and capabilities and seek to differentiate themselves from competitors. Typically, firms seek to differentiate their products from competitors' offerings in ways that customers value and in which the firms have a competitive advantage. Common dimensions on which rivalry is based include price, service after the sale, and innovation. More recently, firms have begun to act quickly (speed a new product to the market) in order to gain a competitive advantage.[115]

Next, we discuss the most prominent factors that experience shows affect the intensity of rivalries among firms.

Numerous or Equally Balanced Competitors

Intense rivalries are common in industries with many companies. With multiple competitors, it is common for a few firms to believe they can act without eliciting a response. However, evidence suggests that other firms generally are aware of competitors' actions, often choosing to respond to them. At the other extreme, industries with only a few firms of equivalent size and power also tend to have strong rivalries. The large and often similar-sized resource bases of these firms permit vigorous actions and responses. The competitive battles between Airbus and Boeing and between Coca-Cola and PepsiCo exemplify intense rivalry between relatively equal competitors.

Slow Industry Growth

When a market is growing, firms try to effectively use resources to serve an expanding customer base. Markets increasing in size reduce the pressure to take customers from competitors. However, rivalry in no-growth or slow-growth markets becomes more intense as firms battle to increase their market shares by attracting competitors' customers. Certainly, this has been the case in the fast-food industry as explained in the Opening Case about McDonald's. McDonald's, Wendy's, and Burger King use their resources, capabilities, and core competencies to try to win each other's customers. The instability in the market that results from these competitive engagements may reduce the profitability for all firms engaging in such battles. As noted in the Opening Case, McDonald's has suffered from this competitive rivalry but is taking actions to rebuild its customer base and achieve a competitive advantage or at least competitive parity.

High Fixed Costs or High Storage Costs

When fixed costs account for a large part of total costs, companies try to maximize the use of their productive capacity. Doing so allows the firm to spread costs across a larger volume of output. However, when many firms attempt to maximize their productive capacity, excess capacity is created on an industry-wide basis. To then reduce inventories, individual companies typically cut the price of their product and offer rebates and other special discounts to customers. However, doing this often intensifies competition. The pattern of excess capacity at the industry level followed by intense rivalry at the firm level is frequently observed in industries with high storage costs. Perishable products, for example, lose their value rapidly with the passage of time. As their inventories grow, producers of perishable goods often use pricing strategies to sell products quickly.

Lack of Differentiation or Low Switching Costs

When buyers find a differentiated product that satisfies their needs, they frequently purchase the product loyally over time. Industries with many companies that have successfully differentiated their products have less rivalry, resulting in lower competition for individual firms. Firms that develop and sustain a differentiated product that cannot be easily imitated by competitors often earn higher returns. However, when buyers view products as commodities (i.e., as products with few differentiated features or capabilities), rivalry intensifies. In these instances, buyers' purchasing decisions are based primarily on price and, to a lesser degree, service. Personal computers are a commodity product, and the cost to switch from a computer manufactured by one firm to another is low. Thus, the rivalry among Dell, Hewlett-Packard, Lenovo, and other computer manufacturers is strong as these companies consistently seek to find ways to differentiate their offerings.

High Strategic Stakes

Competitive rivalry is likely to be high when it is important for several of the competitors to perform well in the market. Competing in diverse businesses (such as petrochemicals, fashion, medicine, and plant construction, among others), Samsung is a formidable foe for Apple in the global smartphone market. Samsung has committed a significant amount of resources to develop innovative products as the foundation for its efforts to try to outperform Apple in selling this particular product. Only a few years ago, Samsung held a sizable lead in market share. But in 2017, in the U.S. market, it was estimated that the iPhone achieved a holiday period market share of 31.3 percent while Samsung's Galaxy held 28.9 percent. Overall, these firms are in a virtual dead heat in the smartphone market.[116] Because this market is extremely important to both firms, the smart-phone rivalry between them (and others) will likely remain quite intense.

High strategic stakes can also exist in terms of geographic locations. For example, several automobile manufacturers have established manufacturing facilities in China, which has been the world's largest car market since 2009.[117] Because of the high stakes involved in China for General Motors and other firms (including domestic Chinese automobile manufacturers) producing luxury cars (including Audi, BMW, and Mercedes-Benz), rivalry among them in this market is quite intense.

High Exit Barriers

Sometimes companies continue competing in an industry even though the returns on their invested capital are low or even negative. Firms making this choice likely face high exit barriers, which include economic, strategic, and emotional factors causing them to remain in an industry when the profitability of doing so is questionable.

Common exit barriers that firms face include the following:

- Specialized assets (assets with values linked to a business or location)
- Fixed costs of exit (such as labor agreements)
- Strategic interrelationships (relationships of mutual dependence, such as those between one business and other parts of a company's operations, including shared facilities and access to financial markets)
- Emotional barriers (aversion to economically justified business decisions because of fear for one's own career, loyalty to employees, and so forth)

- Government and social restrictions (often based on government concerns for job losses and regional economic effects; more common outside the United States)

Exit barriers are especially high in the airline industry. Fortunately, profitability has returned to the industry following the global financial crisis and is expected to reach its highest level in 2018. Industry consolidation and efficiency enhancements regarding airline alliances helped reduce airline companies' costs. This, combined with improving economic conditions in several countries, resulted in a greater demand for travel. This has helped eased the pressures on several firms that may have been contemplating leaving the airline travel industry.[118]

2-5 Interpreting Industry Analyses

Effective industry analyses are products of careful study and interpretation of data and information from multiple sources. A wealth of industry-specific data is available for firms to analyze to better understand an industry's competitive realities. Because of globalization, international markets and rivalries must be included in the firm's analyses. And, because of the development of global markets, a country's borders no longer restrict industry structures. In fact, in general, entering international markets enhances the chances of success for new ventures as well as more established firms.[119]

Analysis of the five forces within a given industry allows the firm to determine the industry's attractiveness in terms of the potential to earn average or above-average returns. In general, the stronger the competitive forces, the lower the potential for firms to generate profits by implementing their strategies. An unattractive industry has low entry barriers, suppliers and buyers with strong bargaining positions, strong competitive threats from product substitutes, and intense rivalry among competitors. These industry characteristics make it difficult for firms to achieve strategic competitiveness and earn above-average returns. Alternatively, an attractive industry has high entry barriers, suppliers and buyers with little bargaining power, few competitive threats from product substitutes, and relatively moderate rivalry.[120] Next, we explain strategic groups as an aspect of industry competition.

2-6 Strategic Groups

A set of firms emphasizing similar strategic dimensions and using a similar strategy is called a **strategic group**.[121] The competition between firms within a strategic group is greater than the competition between a member of a strategic group and companies outside that strategic group. Therefore, intra-strategic group competition is more intense than is inter-strategic group competition. In fact, more heterogeneity is evident in the performance of firms within strategic groups than across the groups. The performance leaders within groups can follow strategies similar to those of other firms in the group and yet maintain strategic distinctiveness as a foundation for earning above-average returns.[122]

The extent of technological leadership, product quality, pricing policies, distribution channels, and customer service are examples of strategic dimensions that firms in a strategic group may treat similarly. Thus, membership in a strategic group defines the essential characteristics of the firm's strategy.

The notion of strategic groups can be useful for analyzing an industry's competitive structure. Such analyses can be helpful in diagnosing competition, positioning, and the profitability of firms competing within an industry. High mobility barriers, high rivalry, and low resources among the firms within an industry limit the formation of strategic groups.[123] However, after strategic groups are formed, their membership

A set of firms emphasizing similar strategic dimensions and using a similar strategy is called a **strategic group**.

Strategic **Focus**

Toys 'R' Us Exemplifies the Apocalypse in the Retail Industries

More than 10,000 stores closed in the United States in 2017. The companies that have gone bankrupt or are in serious financial trouble read like a list of Who's Who in retailing, The ones that could default in the near term include Sears, Neiman Marcus, Payless, J. Crew, PetSmart, and Steak 'n Shake, among others. But, perhaps the bankruptcy of Toys 'R' Us in 2018 caused the most angst among consumers because they remember what it used to be and know what it could have been.

Toys 'R' Us was a dominant retailer of toys that had devoted customers and toy manufacturers. The stores had every conceivable toy and became a 'one-stop-shopping destination' for most parents. It also reached out to and fostered the development of many small and medium sized toy manufacturers who largely owed their existence to Toys 'R' Us. At one time it was perhaps the most significant toy retailer in the world. As it grew, many of its competitors went out of business. Yet, after the founder stepped down from the CEO position, a succession of CEOs became complacent. Toys 'R' Us stopped analyzing its competitors, didn't invest in and update its stores, and began to lose the devotion of its customers. This made it vulnerable to new competition. Essentially, by ignoring competition and maintaining the status quo, it let competitors take advantage by better serving its customer base.

Large retailers such as Walmart and Target began to grow their toy sales and take market share away from Toys 'R' Us. And then Internet sales began to take market share. To respond, Toys 'R' Us signed an exclusive agreement to sell its toys over the Internet with Amazon. The contract was expensive (about $50 million annually), and Amazon did not only sell the toys from Toys 'R' Us. In fact, Amazon created an Internet marketplace selling multiple brands' and companies' toys. As such, Toy 'R' Us paid Amazon to become a substantial competitor.

Andrew Harrer/Bloomberg/Getty Images

Toys 'R' Us filed for bankruptcy in 2018, closing all of its stores.

At the height of these problems, Toys 'R' Us was sold to private equity investors who completed a leveraged buyout that saddled the company with substantial debt. With large debt payments, fewer resources were available to invest in the stores and to respond to competitors. Thus, in 2018 it filed for bankruptcy, closing all of its stores.

The exit of Toys 'R' Us leaves its two biggest competitors, Walmart and Amazon, now locked in a rivalry of their own.

Sources: H. Peterson, 2018, Retailers are filing for bankruptcy at a staggering rate—and these 19 companies could be the next to default. Business Insider, www.msn.com, March 18; 2018, Toys R Us built a kingdom and the world's biggest toy store. Then, they lost it, MSN, www.msn.com, March 17; 2018, Nostalgic shoppers shed tears over Toys 'R' Us demise, CNBC, wwwcnbc.com, March 15; M. Corkery, 2018, Toys 'R' Us case is test of private equity in age of Amazon, *New York Times*, nyti.ms/2DvabV5, March 15; M. Boyle, K. Bhasin & L. Rupp, 2018, Walmart-Amazon battle takes to Manhattan with dueling showcases, Bloomberg, Bloomberg.com, February 28; K Taylor, 2017, Here are the 18 biggest bankruptcies of the 'retail apocalypse' of 2017, Business Insider, www.businessinsider.com, December 20.

remains relatively stable over time. Using strategic groups to understand an industry's competitive structure requires the firm to plot companies' competitive actions and responses along strategic dimensions, such as pricing decisions, product quality, distribution channels, and so forth. This type of analysis shows the firm how certain companies are competing similarly in terms of how they use similar strategic dimensions.

Strategic groups have several implications. First, because firms within a group offer similar products to the same customers, the competitive rivalry among them can be intense. The more intense the rivalry, the greater the threat to each firm's profitability. Second, the strengths of the five forces differ across strategic groups. Third, the closer the strategic groups are in terms of their strategies, the greater is the likelihood of rivalry between the groups.

As explained in the Strategic Focus, there is a massive 'train wreck' occurring in the retail industries. Former stalwarts such as Sears, Macy's, JCPenney, and Toys 'R' Us are all failing, largely because they ignored competition and it eventually caught up to them. Although other rivals began to erode their market share, the current problem revolves around the formidable Amazon. Amazon has been winning competitive battles against these weakened retailers, and even against other more formidable rivals Google and Walmart. Toys 'R' Us sowed the seeds of its demise a number of years ago by ignoring its competition. It was dominant in its industry, and then focused on growing its store base while paying little or no attention to what new competitors were doing. In fact, unknowingly it helped Amazon become a major competitor. The lesson in this for Amazon is that even highly successful firms must continuously analyze and understand their competitors if they are to maintain their current market leading positions. If Amazon continues to effectively analyze its competition across industries, the question becomes, can any of its rivals beat it?[124]

2-7 Competitor Analysis

The competitor environment is the final part of the external environment requiring study. Competitor analysis focuses on each company against which a firm competes directly. The Coca-Cola Company and PepsiCo, Home Depot and Lowe's, Carrefour SA and Tesco PLC, and Amazon and Google are examples of competitors that are keenly interested in understanding each other's objectives, strategies, assumptions, and capabilities. Indeed, intense rivalry creates a strong need to understand competitors.[125] In a competitor analysis, the firm seeks to understand the following:

- What drives the competitor, as shown by its *future objectives.*
- What the competitor is doing and can do, as revealed by its *current strategy.*
- What the competitor believes about the industry, as shown by its *assumptions.*
- What the competitor's capabilities are, as shown by its *strengths* and *weaknesses.*[126]

Knowledge about these four dimensions helps the firm prepare an anticipated response profile for each competitor (see Figure 2.3). The results of an effective competitor analysis help a firm understand, interpret, and predict its competitors' actions and responses. Understanding competitors' actions and responses clearly contributes to the firm's ability to compete successfully within the industry.[127] Interestingly, research suggests that executives often fail to analyze competitors' possible reactions to competitive actions their firm takes,[128] placing their firm at a potential competitive disadvantage as a result.

Critical to an effective competitor analysis is gathering data and information that can help the firm understand its competitors' intentions and the strategic implications resulting from them.[129] Useful data and information combine to form **competitor intelligence**, which is the set of data and information the firm gathers to better understand and anticipate competitors' objectives, strategies, assumptions, and capabilities. In competitor analysis, the firm gathers intelligence not only about its competitors, but also regarding public policies in countries around the world. Such intelligence facilitates an understanding of the strategic posture of foreign competitors. Through effective competitive and public policy intelligence, the firm gains the insights needed to make effective strategic decisions regarding how to compete against rivals.

Competitor intelligence is the set of data and information the firm gathers to better understand and anticipate competitors' objectives, strategies, assumptions, and capabilities.

When asked to describe competitive intelligence, phrases such as "competitive spying" and "corporate espionage" come to mind for some. These phrases underscore the fact

Figure 2.3 Competitor Analysis Components

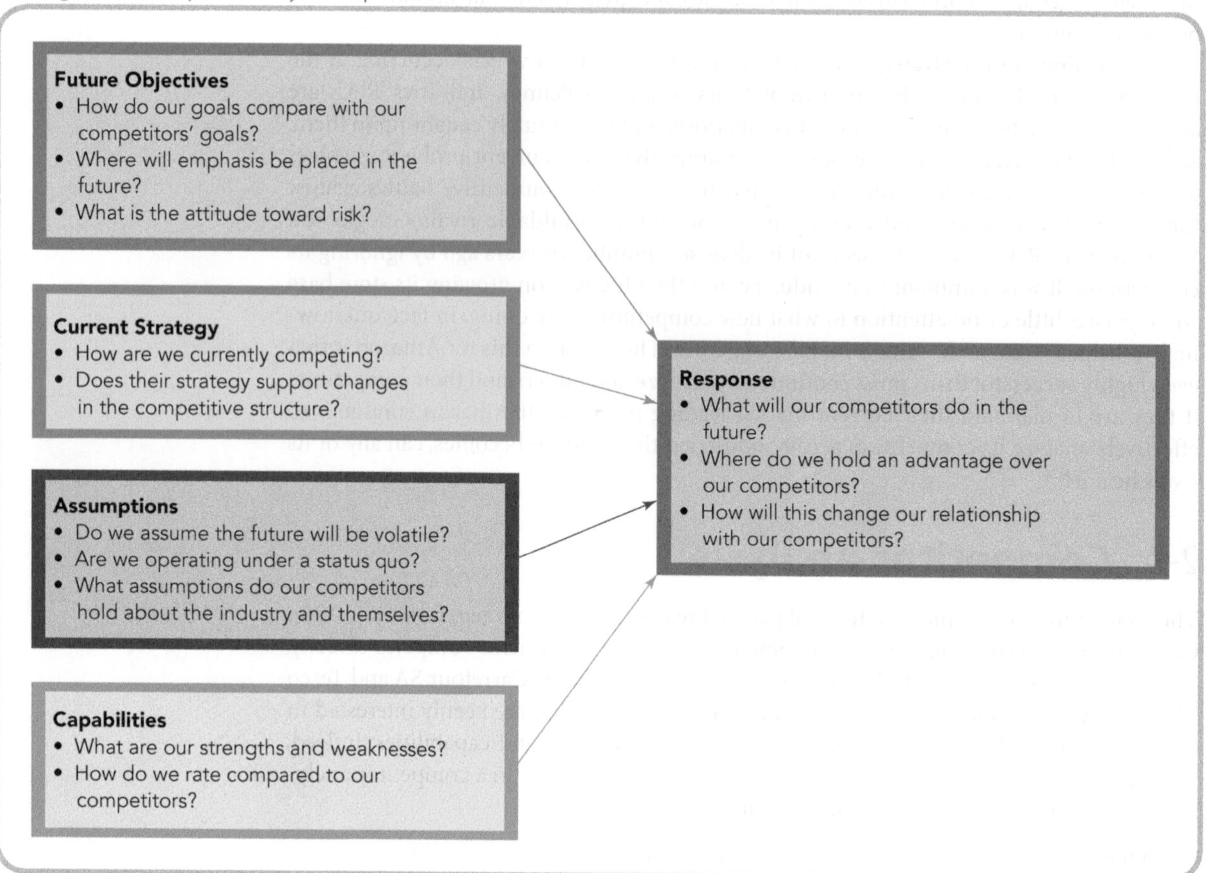

that competitive intelligence appears to involve trade-offs.[130] The reason for this is that "what is ethical in one country is different from what is ethical in other countries." This position implies that the rules of engagement to follow when gathering competitive intelligence change in different contexts.[131] To avoid the possibility of legal entanglements and ethical quandaries, firms must govern their competitive intelligence gathering methods by a strict set of legal and ethical guidelines.[132] Ethical behavior and actions, as well as the mandates of relevant laws and regulations, should be the foundation on which a firm's competitive intelligence-gathering process is formed.

When gathering competitive intelligence, a firm must also pay attention to the complementors of its products and strategy.[133] **Complementors** are companies or networks of companies that sell complementary goods or services that are compatible with the focal firm's good or service. When a complementor's good or service contributes to the functionality of a focal firm's good or service, it in turn creates additional value for that firm.

Complementors are companies or networks of companies that sell complementary goods or services that are compatible with the focal firm's good or service.

There are many examples of firms whose good or service complements other companies' offerings. For example, firms manufacturing affordable home photo printers complement other companies' efforts to sell digital cameras. Intel and Microsoft are perhaps the most widely recognized complementors. The two firms do not directly buy from or sell to each other, but their products are highly complementary.

Alliances among airline companies such as Oneworld and Star involve member companies sharing their route structures and customer loyalty programs as a means of complementing each other's operations. (Alliances and other cooperative strategies are described in Chapter 9.) In this example, each of the two alliances is a network of complementors. American Airlines, British Airways, Finnair, Japan Airlines, and Royal Jordanian are among the airlines forming the Oneworld alliance. Air Canada, Brussels Airlines, Croatia Airlines, Lufthansa, and United Airlines are five of the members forming the Star alliance. Both alliances constantly adjust their members and services offered to better meet customers' needs.

As our discussion shows, complementors expand the set of competitors that firms must evaluate when completing a competitor analysis. In this sense, American Airlines and United Airlines examine each other both as direct competitors on multiple routes but also as complementors that are members of different alliances (Oneworld for American and Star for United). In all cases though, ethical commitments and actions should be the foundation on which competitor analyses are developed.

2-8 Ethical Considerations

Firms must follow relevant laws and regulations as well as carefully articulated ethical guidelines when gathering competitor intelligence. Industry associations often develop lists of these practices that firms can adopt. Practices considered both legal and ethical include:

1. Obtaining publicly available information (e.g., court records, competitors' help-wanted advertisements, annual reports, financial reports of publicly held corporations, and Uniform Commercial Code filings)
2. Attending trade fairs and shows to obtain competitors' brochures, view their exhibits, and listen to discussions about their products

In contrast, certain practices (including blackmail, trespassing, eavesdropping, and stealing drawings, samples, or documents) are widely viewed as unethical and often are illegal as well.

Some competitive intelligence practices may be legal, but a firm must decide whether they are also ethical, given the image it desires as a corporate citizen. Especially with electronic transmissions, the line between legal and ethical practices can be difficult to determine. For example, a firm may develop website addresses that are like those of its competitors and thus occasionally receive e-mail transmissions that were intended for those competitors. The practice is an example of the challenges companies face in deciding how to gather intelligence about competitors while simultaneously determining how to prevent competitors from learning too much about them. To deal with these challenges, firms should establish principles and take actions that are consistent with them.

Professional associations are available to firms as sources of information regarding competitive intelligence practices. For example, while pursuing its mission to help firms make "better decisions through competitive intelligence," the Strategy and Competitive Intelligence Professionals association offers codes of professional practice and ethics to firms for their possible use when deciding how to gather competitive intelligence.[134]

Open discussions of intelligence-gathering techniques can help a firm ensure that employees, customers, suppliers, and even potential competitors understand its convictions to follow ethical practices when gathering intelligence about its competitors. An appropriate guideline for competitor intelligence practices is to respect the principles of common morality and the right of competitors not to reveal certain information about their products, operations, and intentions.

SUMMARY

- The firm's external environment is challenging and complex. Because of its effect on performance, firms must develop the skills required to identify opportunities and threats that are a part of their external environment.
- The external environment has three major parts:
  1. The general environment (segments and elements in the broader society that affect industries and the firms competing in them)
  2. The industry environment (factors that influence a firm, its competitive actions and responses, and the industry's profitability potential)
  3. The competitor environment (in which the firm analyzes each major competitor's future objectives, current strategies, assumptions, and capabilities)
- Scanning, monitoring, forecasting, and assessing are the four parts of the external environmental analysis process. Effectively using this process helps the firm in its efforts to identify opportunities and threats.
- The general environment has seven segments: demographic, economic, political/legal, sociocultural, technological, global, and sustainable physical. For each segment, firms have to determine the strategic relevance of environmental changes and trends.
- Compared with the general environment, the industry environment has a more direct effect on firms' competitive actions and responses. The five forces model of competition includes the threat of entry, the power of suppliers, the power of buyers, product substitutes, and the intensity of rivalry among competitors. By studying these forces, a firm can identify a position in an industry where it can influence the forces in its favor or where it can buffer itself from the power of the forces in order to achieve strategic competitiveness and earn above-average returns.
- Industries are populated with different strategic groups. A strategic group is a collection of firms following similar strategies along similar dimensions. Competitive rivalry is greater within a strategic group than between strategic groups.
- Competitor analysis informs the firm about the future objectives, current strategies, assumptions, and capabilities of the companies with which it competes directly. A thorough competitor analysis examines complementors that support forming and implementing rivals' strategies.
- Different techniques are used to create competitor intelligence: the set of data, information, and knowledge that allow the firm to better understand its competitors and thereby predict their likely competitive actions and responses. Firms absolutely should use only legal and ethical practices to gather intelligence. The Internet enhances firms' ability to gather insights about competitors and their strategic intentions.

KEY TERMS

competitor analysis 40
competitor intelligence 63
complementors 64
demographic segment 43
economic environment 46
general environment 39
global segment 50
industry 53
industry environment 39
opportunity 41
political/legal segment 47
sociocultural segment 48
strategic group 61
sustainable physical environment segment 51
threat 41
technological segment 49

REVIEW QUESTIONS

1. Why is it important for a firm to study and understand the external environment?
2. What are the differences between the general environment and the industry environment? Why are these differences important?
3. What is the external environmental analysis process (four parts)? What does the firm want to learn when using this process?
4. What are the seven segments of the general environment? Explain the differences among them.

5. How do the five forces of competition in an industry affect its profitability potential? Explain.
6. What is a strategic group? Of what value is knowledge of the firm's strategic group in formulating that firm's strategy?
7. What is the importance of collecting and interpreting data and information about competitors? What practices should a firm use to gather competitor intelligence and why?

Mini-Case

Watch Out All Retailers, Here Comes Amazon; Watch Out Amazon, Here Comes Other Competitors

Amazon's sales in 2014 were $88.99 billion, an increase of 19.4 percent over 2013. In fact, its sales in 2014 were a whopping 160 percent more than its sales in 2010, only four years prior. Amazon has been able to achieve remarkable gains in sales by providing high quality, rapid, and relatively inexpensive (relative to competitors) service. Amazon has taken on such formidable competitors as Walmart, Google, and Barnes & Noble, among others, and has come out of it as a winner, particularly in the last 4–5 years.

Walmart has been emphasizing its online sales as well. In 2014, it grew online sales by about $3 billion, for a 30 percent increase. That seems like excellent progress, until one compares it to Amazon's sales increase in 2014 of about $14.5 billion. Much opportunity remains for both to improve as total 2014 online sales were $300 billion.

Google is clearly the giant search engine with 88 percent of the information search market. However, when consumers are shopping to purchase goods, Amazon is the leader. In the third quarter of 2014, 39 percent of online shoppers in the United States began their search on Amazon, compared to 11 percent for Google. Interestingly, in 2009 the figures were 18 percent for Amazon and 24 percent for Google. So, Amazon appears to be winning this competitive battle with Google.

Barnes & Noble lost out to Google before by ignoring it as a threat. Today, B&N has re-established itself in market niches trying not to compete with Google. For example, its college division largely sells through college bookstores, which have a 'monopoly' location granted by the university. However, Amazon is now targeting the college market by developing agreements with universities to operate co-branded websites to sell textbooks, university t-shirts, etc. Most of the students already shop on Amazon, making the promotion easier to market to universities and to sell to students.

A few years ago, Amazon was referred to as the Walmart of the Internet. But, Amazon has diversified its product/service line much further than Walmart. For example, Amazon now competes against Netflix and other services providing video entertainment. In fact, Amazon won two Golden Globe Awards in 2015 for programs it produced. Amazon also markets high fashion clothing for men and women. Founder and CEO of Amazon, Jeff Bezos, stated that Amazon's goal is to become a $200 billion company, and to do that, the firm must learn how to sell clothes and food.

It appears that Amazon is beating all competitors, even formidable ones such as Google and Walmart. But, Amazon still needs to carefully watch its competition. A new company, Jet.com, is targeting Amazon. Jet.com was founded by Marc Lore, who founded the highly successful Diaper.com and a former competitor of Amazon, Quidsi. Amazon hurt Quidsi in a major price war and eventually acquired the company for $550 million. Lore worked for Amazon for two years thereafter but eventually quit to found Jet.com. Jet.com plans to market 10 million products and guarantee the lowest price. Its annual membership will be $50 compared to Amazon Prime's cost of $99. Competing with Amazon represents a major challenge. However, Jet.com has raised about $240 million in venture funding with capital from such players as Bain Capital Ventures, Google Ventures, Goldman Sachs, and Norwest Venture partners. Its current market value is estimated to be $600 million. The future competition between the two companies should be interesting.

Sources: G. Bensniger, 2015, Amazon makes a push on college campuses, *Wall Street Journal*, www.wsj.com, February 1; K. Bhasin & L. Sherman, 2015, Amazon Coutre: Jeff Bezos wants to sell fancy clothes, *Bloomberg*, www.bloomberg.com, February 18; L. Dormehl, 2015, Amazon and Netflix score big at the Golden Globe, *Fast Company*, www.fastcomany.com, January 12; S. Soper, 2015, Amazon.com rival Jet.com raises $140 million in new funding, *Bloomberg*, www.bloomberg.com, February 11; B. Stone, 2015, Amazon bought this man's company. Now he is coming for him, *Bloomberg*, www.bloomberg.com, January 7; M. Kwatinetz, 2014, In online sales, could Walmart ever top Amazon? *Fortune*, www.fortune.com, October 23; R. Winkler & A. Barr, 2014, Google shopping to counter Amazon, *Wall Street Journal*, www.wsj.com, December 15.

Mini-Case Questions

1. Can any firm beat Amazon in the marketplace? If not, why not? If so, how can they best do so?
2. How formidable a competitor is Google for Amazon? Please explain.
3. What are Amazon's major strengths? Does it have any weaknesses? Please explain.
4. Is Jet.com a potential concern for Amazon? Why or why not?

NOTES

1. R. Krause, M. Semadeni, & A. A. Cannella, 2013, External COO/presidents as expert directors: A new look at the service of role of boards, *Strategic Management Journal*, 34: 1628–1641; Y. Y. Kor & A. Mesko, 2013, Dynamic managerial capabilities: Configuration and orchestration of top executives' capabilities and the firm's dominant logic, *Strategic Management Journal*, 34: 233–234.
2. K.-Y. Hsieh, W. Tsai, & M.-J. Chen, 2015, If they can do it, why not us? Competitors as reference points for justifying escalation of commitment, *Academy of Management Journal*, 58: 38–58; R. Kapoor & J. M. Lee, 2013, Coordinating and competing in ecosystems: How organizational forms shape new technology investments, *Strategic Management Journal*, 34: 274–296.
3. J. A. Parnell, 2018 Nonmarket and market strategies, strategic uncertainty and strategic capabilities: Evidence from the USA, *Management Research Review*, doi 10.1108/MRR-05-2017-0151; C. E. Stevens, E. Xie, & M. W. Peng, 2016, Toward a legitimacy-based view of political risk: The case of Google and Yahoo in China, *Strategic Management Journal*, 37: 945–963.
4. R. J. Sawant, 2012, Asset specificity and corporate political activity in regulated industries, *Academy of Management Review*, 37: 194–210; S. Hanson, A. Kashyap, & J. Stein, 2011, A macroprudential approach to financial regulation. *Journal of Economic Perspectives*, 25: 3–28.
5. T. A. Gur & T. Greckhamer, 2018, Know thy enemy: A review and agenda for research on competitor identification, *Journal of Management*, in press; S. Garg, 2013, Venture boards: Distinctive monitoring and implications for firm performance, *Academy of Management Review*, 38: 90–108.
6. J. B. Barney & A. Mackey, 2018, Monopoly profits, Efficiency profits, and Teaching Strategic Management, *Academy of Management Learning and Education*, doi: 10.5465/amle.2017.0171; S. C. Schleimer & T. Pedersen, 2013, The driving forces of subsidiary absorptive capacity, *Journal of Management Studies*, 50: 646–672.
7. M. Taissig & A. Delios, 2015, Unbundling the effects of institutions on firm resources: The contingent value of being local in emerging economy private equity, *Strategic Management Journal*, 36: 1845–1865; C. Qian, Q. Cao, & R. Takeuchi, 2013, Top management team functional diversity and organizational innovation in China: The moderating effects of environment, *Strategic Management Journal*, 34: 110–120.
8. EY, 2015, Middle class growth in emerging markets entering the global middle class, www.ey.com, March 6; EY, 2015 Middle class growth in emerging markets hitting the sweet spot, www.ey.com, March 6.
9. 2018, Regions of the world by population (2018), Worldometers, www.worldometers.info, accessed on March 20.
10. S. Lahiri & S. Purkayastha, 2017, Impact of industry sector on corporate diversification and firm performance: Evidence from Indian business groups, *Canadian Journal of Administrative Sciences*, 34: 77–88; E. V. Karniouchina, S. J. Carson, J. C. Short, & D. J. Ketchen, 2013, Extending the firm vs. industry debate: Does industry life cycle stage matter? *Strategic Management Journal*, 34: 1010–1018.
11. R. B. MacKay & R. Chia, 2013, Choice, chance, and unintended consequences in strategic change: A process understanding of the rise and fall of NorthCo Automotive, *Academy of Management Journal*, 56: 208–230; J. P. Murmann, 2013, The coevolution of industries and important features of their environments, *Organization Science*, 24: 58–78; G. J. Kilduff, H. A. Elfenbein, & B. M. Staw, 2010, The psychology of rivalry: A relationally dependent analysis of competition, *Academy of Management Journal*, 53: 943–969.
12. R. E. Hoskisson, M. Wright, I. Filatotchev, & M. W. Peng, 2013, Emerging multinationals from mid-range economies: The influence of institutions and factor markets, *Journal of Management Studies*, 50: 127–153; A. Hecker & A. Ganter, 2013, The influence of product market competition on technological and management innovation: Firm-level evidence from a large-scale survey, *European Management Review*, 10: 17–33.
13. Walmart, 2015, Our locations. www.corporate.walmart.com, March 6; Metro Cash and Carry, 2015, International Operations, en.wikipedia.org, February 1; BBC news, 2014, Carrefour to exit India business, www.bbc.com, July 8; BBC news, 2014, Tesco signs deal to enter India's supermarket sector, www.bbc.com, March 21.
14. F. Bridoux & J. W. Stoelhorst, 2014, Microfoundations for stakeholder theory: Managing stakeholders with heterogeneous motives, *Strategic Management Journal*, 35: 107–125; B. Gilad, 2011, The power of blindspots. What companies don't know, surprises them. What they don't want to know, kills them, *Strategic Direction*, 27(4): 3–4.
15. R. Whittington, B. Yakis-Douglas, K. Ahn, & L. Cailluet, 2017, Strategic planners in

more turbulent times: The changing job characteristics of strategy professionals, 1960–2003, *Long Range Planning*, 50: 108–119.

16. J. Tang, K. M. Kacmar, & L. Busenitz, 2012, Entrepreneurial alertness in the pursuit of new opportunities, *Journal of Business Venturing*, 27: 77–94; D. Chrusciel, 2011, Environmental scan: Influence on strategic direction, *Journal of Facilities Management*, 9(1): 7–15.
17. D. E. Hughes, J. Le Bon, & A. Rapp, 2013, Gaining and leveraging customer-based competitive intelligence: The pivotal role of social capital and salesperson adaptive selling skills, *Journal of the Academy of Marketing Science*, 41: 91–110; J. R. Hough & M. A. White, 2004, Scanning actions and environmental dynamism: Gathering information for strategic decision making, *Management Decision*, 42: 781–793; V. K. Garg, B. A. Walters, & R. L. Priem, 2003, Chief executive scanning emphases, environmental dynamism, and manufacturing firm performance, *Strategic Management Journal*, 24: 725–744.
18. C.-H. Lee & T.-F. Chien, 2013, Leveraging microblogging big data with a modified density-based clustering approach for event awareness and topic ranking, *Journal of Information Science*, 39: 523–543.
19. 2018, Number of internet users worldwide from 2005 to 2017 (in millions), Statista, www.statista.com, Accessed on March 23. 2018; 2018, Countries with the highest number of internet users as of June 2017 (in millions), Statista, www.statista.com, Accessed on March 23.
20. W. Yu, R. Ramanathan & P. Nath, 2017, Environmental pressures and performance: An analysis of the roles of environmental innovation strategy and marketing capability, *Technological Forecasting and Social Change*, 117: 160–169; S. Garg, 2013, Venture boards: Distinctive monitoring and implications for firm performance, *Academy of Management Review*, 38: 90–108.
21. K. Elkins, 2017, Here's how much the average family has saved for retirement at every age, CNBC, www.cnbc.com, April 7.
22. B. L. Connelly & E. J. Van Slyke, 2012, The power and peril of board interlocks, *Business Horizons*, 55: 403–408; C. Dellarocas, 2010, Online reputation systems: How to design one that does what you need, *MIT Sloan Management Review*, 51: 33–37.
23. G. Martin, R. Gozubuyuk, & M. Becerra, 2015, Interlocks and firm performance: The role of uncertainty in the directorate interlock-performance relationship, *Strategic Management Journal*, 36: 235–253.
24. K. L. Turner & M. V. Makhija, 2012, The role of individuals in the information processing perspective, *Strategic Management Journal*, 33: 661–680; X. Zhang, S. Majid, & S. Foo, 2010, Environmental scanning: An application of information literacy skills at the workplace, *Journal of Information Science*, 36: 719–732.
25. L. Sleuwaegen, 2013, Scanning for profitable (international) growth, *Journal of Strategy and Management*, 6: 96–110; J. Calof & J. Smith, 2010, The integrative domain of foresight and competitive intelligence and its impact on R&D management, *R & D Management*, 40(1): 31–39.
26. S. Phandis, C. Caplice, Y. Sheffi, & M. Singh, 2015, Effect of scenario planning on field experts judgment of long-range investment decisions, *Strategic Management Journal*, 36: 1401–1411; A. Chwolka & M. G. Raith, 2012, The value of business planning before start-up—A decision-theoretical perspective, *Journal of Business Venturing*, 27: 385–399.
27. V. Mrass, C. Peters, & J. M. Leimeister, 2018, Managing complex work systems via crowdworking platforms: How Intel and Hyve explore future technological innovations. 2018. Hawaii International Conference on System Sciences, Waikoloa, HI, February 1; D. Wu, K. G. Kempf, M. O. Atan, B. Aytac, S. A. Shirodkar, & A. Mishra, 2010, Improving new-product forecasting at Intel Corporation, *Interfaces*, 40: 385–396.
28. K. D. Miller & S.-J. Lin, 2015, Analogical reasoning for diagnosing strategic issues in dynamic and complex environments, *Strategic Management Journal*, 36: 2000–2020; R. Klingebiel, 2012, Options in the implementation plan of entrepreneurial initiatives: Examining firms' attainment of flexibility benefit, *Strategic Entrepreneurship Journal*, 6: 307–334.
29. P. Jarzabkowski & S. Kaplan, 2015, Strategy tools-in-use: A framework for understanding "technologies of rationality" in practice, *Strategic Management Journal*, 36: 537–558; N. J. Foss, J. Lyngsie, & S. A. Zahra, 2013, The role of external knowledge sources and organizational design in the process of opportunity exploitation, *Strategic Management Journal*, 34:1453–1471.
30. D. Grewal, A. Roggeveen, & R. C. Runyan, 2013, Retailing in a connected world, *Journal of Marketing Management*, 29: 263–270; R. King, 2010, Consumer demographics: Use demographic resources to target specific audiences, *Journal of Financial Planning*, 23(12): S4–S6.
31. 2018, World population clock: World population forecast (2020–2050), www.worldometers.info/world-population, March 24.
32. World population clock, 2013, The world population and the top ten countries with the highest population, *Internet World Stats*, www.internetworldstats.com, May 21.
33. 2018, How many people have ever lived on earth, Population Reference Bureau, www.prb.org, March 24.
34. D. Bloom & D. Canning, 2012, How companies must adapt for an aging workforce, *HBR Blog Network*, www.hbr.org, December 3.
35. M. B. Dougherty, 2012, Stunning facts about Japan's demographic implosion, *Business Insider*, www.businessinsider.com, April 24.
36. M. Chand & R. L. Tung, 2014, The aging of the world's population and its effects on global business, *Academy of Management Perspectives*, 28: 409–429.
37. 2013, The aging workforce: Finding the silver lining in the talent gap, *Deloitte*, www.deloitte.com, February.
38. D. Cumming, T. Leung, & O. Rui, 2015, Gender diversity and securities fraud, *Academy of Management Journal*, 58: 1572–1593; A. Joshi, J. Son, & H. Roh, 2015, When can women close the gap? A meta-analytic test of sex differences in performance and rewards, *Academy of Management Journal*, 58: 1516–1545.
39. 2018, List of U.S. states and territories by population, *Wikipedia*, en.wikipedia.org, March 24.
40. 2018, Economy of California, *Wikipedia*, en.wikipedia.org, March 24; 2018, Texas economic forecast 2017–2018, Texas Comptroller, comptroller.texas.gov, March 24.
41. A. Nevin, 2018, 2018 Economic Outlook: California and San Diego, Our City San Diego, ourcitysd.com; 2018, List of U.S. states and territories by population.
42. 2018. Urban and rural population of China from 2006 to 2016, Statista, www.statista.com, March 24.
43. 2012, Population and population change statistics, *European Commission*, www.epp.eurostat.ec.europa.eu, October.
44. 2018, Percentage distribution of population in the United States in 2015 and 2060, by race and Hispanic origin, Statista, www.statista.com, March 24; S. Reddy, 2011, U.S. News: Latinos fuel growth in decade, *Wall Street Journal*, March 25, A2.
45. Percentage distribution of population in the United States in 2015 and 2060; 2015, New census bureau report analyzes U.S. population projects, www.census.gov, March 3.
46. G. Andrrevski, O. C. Richard, J. D. Shaw, & W. J. Ferrier, 2014, Racial diversity and firm performance: The mediating role of competitive intensity, *Journal of Management*, 40: 820–844.
47. M. Fisher, 2013, A revealing map of the world's most and least ethnically diverse countries, *The Washington Post*, www.washingtonpost.com, May 16.
48. 2018, New report shows record number of expats worldwide, Paragon Relocation, paragonrelocation.com, March 24.
49. W. Q. Judge, A. Fainschmidt, & J. L. Brown, 2014, Which model of capitalism best delivers both wealth and equality? *Journal of International Business Studies*, 45: 363–386.
50. G. A. Shinkle & B. T. McCann, 2013, New product deployment: The moderating influence of economic institutional context, *Strategic Management Journal*, 35: 1090–1101.
51. L. Fahey & V. K. Narayanan, 1986, *Macroenvironmental Analysis for Strategic Management (The West Series in Strategic*

Management), St. Paul, Minnesota: West Publishing Company, 105.

52. Chakrabarti, 2015, Organizational adaptation in an economic shock: The role of growth reconfiguration, *Strategic Management Journal*, 36: 1717–1738; N. Bloom, M. A. Kose, & M. E. Terrones, 2013, Held back by uncertainty, *Finance & Development*, 50: 38–41, March.
53. 2018. *Global Economic Prospects: Broad-Based Upturn but for How Long?* World Bank, Washington, DC: World Bank Group Flagship Report.
54. V. Marano, J.-L. Arregle, M. A. Hitt, E. Spadafora, & M. van Essen, 2016, Home country institutions and the internationalization-performance relationship: A meta-analytic review, *Journal of Management*, 42: 1075–1110.
55. S. Dorobantu, A. Kaul, & B. Zelner, 2018. Nonmarket strategy research through the lens of new institutional economics: An integrative review and future directions, *Strategic Management Journal*, in press; T. Vanacker, V. Colwaert, & S. A. Zahra, 2018, Slack resources, firm performance, and the institutional context: Evidence from privately held European firms, *Strategic Management Journal*, in press; T. A. Khoury, M. Junkunc, & S. Mingo, 2015, Navigating political hazard risks and legal system quality: Venture capital investments in Latin America, *Journal of Management*, 41: 808–840; M. R. King, 2015, Political bargaining and multinational bailouts, *Journal of International Business Studies*, 46: 206–222.
56. J.-L. Arregle, T. Miller, M. A. Hitt, & P. Beamish, 2016, How does regional institutional complexity affect MNE internationalization, *Journal of International Business Studies*, 47: 697–722; G. Lazzarini, 2015, Strategizing by the government: Can industrial policy create firm-level competitive advantage, *Strategic Management Journal*, 36: 97–112.
57. M. A. Hitt, 2016, International strategy and institutional environments, *Cross Cultural and Strategic Management*, 23: 206–215.
58. C, Geng, T. Zuzul, G. Jones, & T. Khanna, 2017, Overcoming institutional voids: A reputational view of long-run survival, *Strategic Management Journal*, 38: 2147–2167; B. C. Pinkham & M. W. Peng, 2017. Overcoming institutional voids via arbitration, *Journal of International Business Studies*, 48: 344–359.
59. L. Richards, 2013, The effects of socioculture on business, *The Houston Chronicle*, www.chron.com, May 26.
60. Hitt, International strategy and institutional environments; J. G. York & M. J. Lenox, 2014, Exploring the sociocultural determinants of *de novo* and *de alio* entry into emerging industries, *Strategic Management Journal*, 35: 1930–1951.
61. 2013, Health strategy, *European Commission Public Health*, www.europa.eu, May 23.
62. 2015, Labor force projections to 2024: the labor force is growing, but slowly, Monthly Labor Review, Bureau of Labor Statistics, www.bls.gov, December.
63. Labor force projections to 2024: the labor force is growing, but slowly; M. Toosi, 2012, Projections of the labor force to 2050: A visual essay, Monthly Labor Review, October.
64. M. A. Hitt, D. Li, & K. Xu, 2016, International Strategy: From Local to Global and Beyond, *Journal of World Business*, 51: 58–73; R. M. Holmes Jr., T. Miller, M. A. Hitt, & M. P. Salmador, 2013, The Interrelationships among Informal Institutions, Formal Institutions and Inward Foreign Direct Investment, *Journal of Management*, 39: 531–566.
65. J. Liu, C. Hui, C. Lee, & Z. X. Chen, 2013, Why do I feel valued and why do I contribute? A relational approach to employee's organization-based self-esteem and job performance, *Journal of Management Studies*, 50: 1018–1040; P. J. Buckley, J. Clegg, & H. Tan, 2006, Cultural awareness in knowledge transfer to China—The role of guanxi and mianzi, *Journal of World Business*, 41: 275–288.
66. Z. Liu, X. Chen, J. Chu, & Q. Zhu, 2018, Industrial development environment and innovation efficiency of high-tech industry: Analysis based on the framework of innovation systems, *Technology Analysis and Strategic Management*, 30: 434–446; L. Proskuryakova, D. Meissner, & P. Rudnik, 2017, The use of technology platforms as a policy tool to address research challenges and technology transfer, *Journal of Technology Transfer*, 42: 206–227; S. Grodal, 2015, The co-evolution of technologies and categories during industry emergence, *Academy of Management Review*, 40: 423–445.
67. C. Giachetti & G. Marchi, 2017, Successive changes in leadership in the worldwide mobile phone industry: The role of windows of opportunity and firm competitive action, *Research Policy*, 46: 352–364; H. Kang & J. Song, 2017, Innovation and recurring shifts in industrial leadership: Three phases of change and persistence in the camera industry, *Research Policy*, 46: 376–387; L. Fuentelsaz, E. Garrido, & J. P. Maicas, 2015, Incumbents, technological change and institutions: How the value of complementary resources varies across markets, *Strategic Management Journal*, 36: 1778–1801.
68. M. Igami, 2017, Estimating the innovator's dilemma: Structural analysis of creative destruction in the hard disk drive industry, 1981–1998, *Journal of Political Economy*, 1q25: 798–847.
69. H. Zou, H. Du, J. Ren, B. K. Sovacool, Y. Zhang, & G. Mao, 2017, Market dynamics, innovation and transition in China's solar photovoltaic (PV) industry: A critical review, *Renewable and Sustainable Energy Review*, 69: 197–206.
70. T. Mauerhoefer, S. Strese, & M. Brettel, 2018, The impact of information technology on new product development, *Journal of Product Innovation Management*, in press.
71. L. Xiao & D. North, 2017, The graduation performance of technology business incubators in China's three tier cities: The role of incubator funding, technical support and entrepreneurial mentoring, *Journal of Technology Transfer*, 42: 615–634.
72. P. Buckley & R. Strange, 2015, The governance of the global factory: Location and control of world economic activity, *Academy of Management Perspectives*, 29: 237–249; J.-E. Vahlne & I. Ivarsson, 2014, The globalization of Swedish MNEs: Empirical evidence and theoretical explanations, *Journal of International Business Studies*, 45: 227–247; E. R. Banalieva & C. Dhanaraj, 2013, Home-region orientation in international expansion strategies, *Journal of International Business Studies*, 44: 89–116.
73. K. Kyung-Tae, R. Seung-Kyu, & O. Joongsan, 2011, The strategic role evolution of foreign automotive parts subsidiaries in China, *International Journal of Operations & Production Management*, 31: 31–55.
74. S. T. Cavusgil & G. Knight, 2015, The born global firm: An entrepreneurial and capabilities perspective on early and rapid internationalization, *Journal of International Business Studies*, 46: 3–16; S. Sui & M. Baum, 2014, Internationalization strategy, firm resources and the survival of SMEs in the export market, *Journal of International Business Studies*, 45: 821–841.
75. 2018, Global automotive aftermarket set to grow in 2018, says Frost & Sullivan, Canadian Manufacturing, www.canadianmanufacturing.com, March 29; 2013, Growth and globalization: Keeping a lid on capacity, KPMG, Automotive executive survey, www.kpmb.com, January 15.
76. D. Souder, A. Zaheer, H. Sapienza, & R. Ranucci, 2018, How family influence, socioemotional wealth, and competitive conditions shape new technology adoption, *Strategic Management Journal*, in press; J.-L. Arregle, P. Duran, M. A. Hitt, & M. van Essen, 2017, Why is family firms' internationalization unique? *Entrepreneurship Theory and Practice* 41: 801–837.
77. T. J. Pukall & A. Calabro, 2014, The internationalization of family firms: A critical review and integrative model, *Family Business Review*, 27: 103–125; K. E. Meyer, 2006, Globalfocusing: From domestic conglomerates to global specialists, *Journal of Management Studies*, 43: 1110–1144.
78. How does regional institutional complexity affect MNE internationalization; R. G. Flores, R. V. Aguilera, A. Mahdian,

& P. M. Vaaler, 2013, How well do supranational regional grouping schemes fit international business research models? *Journal of International Business Studies*, 44: 451–474; Hoskisson, Wright, Filatotchev, & Peng, Emerging multinationals.

79. H. R. Greve & C. M. Zhang, 2017, Institutional logics and power sources: Merger and acquisition decisions, *Academy of Management Journal*, 60: 671–694.

80. Z. Xie, Z. Chen & R. Wu, 2017, Investing in social capital, and competing with foreign firms: Strategies of local rivals in China, *Academy of Management Proceedings*, January; F. J. Froese, 2013, Work values of the next generation of business leaders in Shanghai, Tokyo, and Seoul, *Asia Pacific Journal of Management*, 30: 297–315; M. A. Hitt, M. T. Dacin, B. B. Tyler, & D. Park, 1997, Understanding the differences in Korean and U.S. executives' strategic orientations, *Strategic Management Journal*, 18: 159–167.

81. K. Z. Zhou, G. Y. Gao, & H. Zhao, 2017, State ownership and firm innovation in China: An integrated view of institutional and efficiency logics, *Administrative Science Quarterly*, 62: 375–404; D. Ahlstrom, E. Levitas, M. A. Hitt, M. T. Dacin, & H. Zhu, 2014, The three faces of China: Strategic alliance partner selection in three Chinese economies, *Journal of World Business*, 49: 572–585.

82. M. Majidpour, 2017. International technology transfer and the dynamics of complementarity: A new approach, *Technological Forecasting and Social Change*, 122: 196–206; T. Yu, M. Subramaniam, & A. A. Cannella, Jr., 2013, Competing globally, allying locally: Alliances between global rivals and host-country factors, *Journal of International Business Studies*, 44: 117–137.

83. C. L. Franca, G. Broman, K.-H. Robert, G. Basile, & L. Trygg, 2017, An approach to business model innovation and design for strategic sustainable development, *Journal of Cleaner Production*, 140: 155–166; B. Perrott, 2014, The sustainable organization: Blueprint for an integrated model, *Journal of Business Strategy*, 35: 26–37; A. G. Scherer, G. Palazzo, & D. Seidl, 2013, Managing legitimacy in complex and heterogeneous environments: Sustainable development in a globalized world, *Journal of Management Studies*, 50: 259–284.

84. G. I. Broman & K.-H. Robert, 2017, A framework for strategic sustainable development, *Journal of Cleaner Production*, 140: 17–31; W. Lewis, J. L. Walls, & G. W. S. Dowell, 2014, Difference in degrees: CEO characteristics and firm environmental disclosure, *Strategic Management Journal*, 35: 712–722; P. Berrone, A. Fosfuri, L. Gelabert, & L. R. Gomez-Mejia, 2013, Necessity as the mother of 'green' inventions: Institutional pressures and environmental innovations, *Strategic Management Journal*, 34: 891–909.

85. P. Akhtar, Z. Khan, J. G. Frynas, Y. K. Tse, & R. Rao-Nicholson, 2018, Essential microfoundations for contemporary business operations: Top management tangible competencies, relationship-based business networks and environmental sustainability, *British Journal of Management*, 29: 43–62; J. K. Hall, G. A. Daneke, & M. J. Lenox, 2010, Sustainable development and entrepreneurship: Past contributions and future directions, *Journal of Business Venturing*, 25: 439–448.

86. M. A. Delmas & O. Gergaud, 2014, Sustainable certification for future generations: The case of family firms, *Family Business Review*, 27: 228–243.

87. 2018, Sustainability: Enhancing sustainability of operations and global value chains, Report by Walmart, corporate.walmart.com, March.

88. Y. Shin, 2017, Do corporate sustainable activities improve customer satisfaction, word-of-mouth retention and repurchase intention? Empirical evidence from the shipping industry, *International Journal of Logistics Management*, 28: 555–570.

89. A. Paulraj, I. J. Chen, & C. Blome, 2017, Motives and performance outcomes of sustainable supply chain management practices: A Multi-theoretical perspective, *Journal of Business Ethics*, 145: 239–258; A. Genovse, A. A. Acquaye, A. Figueroa, & S. C. L. Koh, 2017. Sustainable supply chain management and the transition towards a circular economy: Evidence and some applications, *Omega*, 66(B): 344–357.

90. H. Song, C. Zhao, & J. Zeng, 2017, Can environmental management improve financial performance: An empirical study of A-shares listed companies in China, *Journal of Cleaner Production*, 141: 1051–1056.

91. A. McKelvie, J. Wiklund, & A. Brattstrom, 2018, Externally acquired or internally generated? Knowledge development and perceived environmental dynamism in new venture innovation, *Entrepreneurship Theory and Practice*, in press; M. Ben-Menahern, Z. Kwee, H. W. Volberda, & F. A. J. Van Den Bosch, 2013, Strategic renewal over time: The enabling role of potential absorptive capacity in aligning internal and external rates of change, *Long Range Planning*, 46: 216–235.

92. S.-J. Chang & B. Wu, 2014, Institutional barriers and industry dynamics, *Strategic Management Journal*, 35: 1103–1121.

93. M. Schimmer & M. Brauer, 2012, Firm performance and aspiration levels as determinants of a firm's strategic repositioning within strategic group structures, *Strategic Organization*, 10: 406–435; J. Galbreath & P. Galvin, 2008, Firm factors, industry structure and performance variation: New empirical evidence to a classic debate, *Journal of Business Research*, 61: 109–117.

94. J. J. Tarzijan & C. C. Ramirez, 2011, Firm, industry and corporation effects revisited: A mixed multilevel analysis for Chilean companies, *Applied Economics Letters*, 18: 95–100; V. F. Misangyl, H. Elms, T. Greckhamer, & J. A. Lepine, 2006, A new perspective on a fundamental debate: A multilevel approach to industry, corporate, and business unit effects, *Strategic Management Journal*, 27: 571–590.

95. G. MacDonald & M. Ryall, 2018, Do new entrants sustain, destroy or create guaranteed profitability? *Strategic Management Journal*, in press; G. D. Markman & T. L. Waldron, 2014, Small entrants and large incumbents: A framework of micro entry, *Academy of Management Perspectives*, 28: 179–197.

96. J. A. Cookson, 2018, Anticipated entry and entry deterrence: Evidence from the American casino industry, *Management Science*, in press: F. Karakaya & S. Parayitam, 2013, Barriers to entry and firm performance: A proposed model and curvilinear relationships, *Journal of Strategic Marketing*, 21: 25–47; B. F. Schivardi & E. Viviano, 2011, Entry barriers in retail trade, *Economic Journal*, 121: 145–170; A. V. Mainkar, M. Lubatkin, & W. S. Schulze, 2006, Toward a product-proliferation theory of entry barriers, *Academy of Management Review*, 31: 1062–1075.

97. R. Vandaie & A. Zaheer, 2014, Surviving bear hugs: Firm capability, large partner alliances and growth, *Strategic Management Journal*, 35: 566–577; V. K. Garg, R. L. Priem, & A. A. Rasheed, 2013, A theoretical explanation of the cost advantages of multi-unit franchising, *Journal of Marketing Channels*, 20: 52–72.

98. C. G. Asmussen, 2015, Strategic factor markets, scale free resources and economic performance: The impact of product market rivalry, *Strategic Management Journal*, 36: 1826–1844.

99. G. A. Shinkle & B. T. McCann, 2014, New product deployment: The moderating influence of economic institutional context, *Strategic Management Journal*, 35: 1090–1101.

100. J. J. Ebbers & N. M. Wijnberg, 2013, Nascent ventures competing for start-up capital: Matching reputations and investors, *Journal of Business Venturing*, 27: 372–384; T. Rice & P. E. Strahan, 2010, Does credit competition affect small-firm finance? *Journal of Finance*, 65: 861–889.

101. Z. Khan, Y. K. Lew, & R. R. Sinkovics, 2015, International joint ventures as boundary spanners: Technological knowledge transfer in an emerging economy, *Global Strategy Journal*, 5: 48–68.

102. 2013, Zara-owned Inditex's profits rise by 22%, *BBC News Business*, www.bbc.co.uk, March 13. 105.

103. V. Singh, 2016, Why has the retail chain Zara been so successful? Quora, www.quora.com, October 1; M. Schlossberg, 2016, While

the rest of the industry struggles, this store has created the 'best business model in apparel'—and millennials are flocking to it, *Business Insider*, www.businessinsider.com, June 16.

104. T. Clauss, 2017, Measuring business model innovation: Conceptualization, scale development, and proof of performance, *R&D Management*, 47: 385–403.

105. Y. Pan, L. Teng, A. B. Supapol, X. Lu, D. Huang, & Z. Wang, 2014, Firms; FDI ownership: The influence of government ownership and legislative connections, *Journal of International Business*, 45: 1029–1043; 2011, Airline deregulation, revisited, *Bloomberg Businessweek*, www.businessweek.com, January 21.

106. S. H. Ang, M. H. Benischke, & J. P. Doh, 2015, The interactions of institutions on foreign market entry mode, *Strategic Management Journal*, 36: 1536–1553.

107. T. Johnson, 2018, AT&T-Time Warner merger approved, *Variety*, https://variety.com/2018/biz/news/; N. Reiff, 2018, AT&T and Time Warner merger case: What you need to know, Investopedia, www.investopedia.com, March 19.

108. J. Luoma, T. Falk, D. Totzek, H. Tikkanen, & A. Mrozek, 2018, Big splash, no waves? Cognitive mechanisms driving incumbent firms' responses to low-price market entry strategies, *Strategic Management Journal*, in press; N. Argyes, L. Bigelow, & J. A. Nickerson, 2015, Dominant designs, innovation shocks and the follower's dilemma, *Strategic Management Journal*, 36: 216–234.

109. F. Reimann & D. J. Ketchen, 2017, Power in supply chain management, *Journal of Supply Chain Management*, 53: 3–9; J. B. Heide, A. Kumar, & K. H. Wathne, 2014, Concurrent sourcing, governance mechanisms and performance outcomes in industrial value chains, *Strategic Management Journal*, 35: 1164–1185; L. Poppo & K. Z. Zhou, 2014, Managing contracts for fairness in buyer-supplier exchanges, *Strategic Management Journal*, 35: 1508–1527.

110. M. J. Mol & C. Brewster, 2014, The outsourcing strategy of local and multinational firms: A supply base perspective, *Global Strategy Journal*, 4: 20–34.

111. R. P. Brito & P. L. S. Miguel, 2017, Power, governance, and value in collaboration: Differences between buyer and supplier perspectives, *Journal of Supply Chain Management*, 53: 61–87; L. Poppo, K. Z. Zhou, & J. J. Li, 2016, When can you trust "trust?" Calculative trust, relational trust and supplier performance, *Strategic Management Journal*, 37: 724–741; J. Roloff, M. S. Aßländer, & D. Z. Nayir, 2015, The supplier perspective: Forging strong partnerships with buyers; *Journal of Business Strategy*, 36(1): 25–32.

112. S. Chae, T. Y. Choi, & D. Hur, 2017, Buyer power and supplier relationship commitment: A cognitive evaluation theory perspective, *Journal of Supply Chain Management*, 53: 39–60; M. C. Schleper, C. Blome, & D. A. Wuttke, 2017, The Dark side of buyer power: Supplier exploitation and the role of ethical climates, *Journal of Business Ethics*, 140: 97–114; F. H. Liu, 2014, OEM supplier impact on buyer competence development, *Journal of Strategy and Management*, 7: 2–18.

113. R. Yan & Z. Cao, 2017, Is brand alliance always beneficial to firms? *Journal of Retailing and Consumer Services*, 34: 193–200.

114. J. Luoma, S. Ruutu, A. W. King, & H. Tikkanen, 2017, Time delays, competitive interdependence, and firm performance, *Strategic Management Journal*, 38: 506–525; C. Giachetti & G. B. Dagnino, 2014, Detecting the relationship between competitive intensity and firm product line length: Evidence from the worldwide mobile phone industry, *Strategic Management Journal*, 35: 138–1409.

115. Y. Yi, Y. Li, M. A. Hitt, Y. Liu, & Z. Wei, 2016, The Influence of resource bundling on the speed of strategic change: Moderating effects of relational capital, *Asia Pacific Journal of Management*, 33: 435–467; G. Pacheco-de-Almeida, A. Hawk, & B. Yeung, 2015, The right speed and its value, *Strategic Management Journal*, 36: 159–176.

116. B. Lovejoy, 2017, iPhone market share grows 6.4% in USA, takes share from Android in most markets, 9to5mac, 9t05mac.com, January 11.

117. K. Bradsher, 2014, China's embrace of foreign cars, *New York Times*, www.nytimes.com, April 8; K. Bradsher, 2013, Chinese auto buyers grow hungry for larger cars, *New York Times*, www.nytimes.com, April 21.

118. 2018, Net profit of commercial airlines worldwide from 2005 to 2018 (in billion U.S. dollars), Statista, www.statista.com, March 30; H. Martin, 2014, Global airline industry expects record profits in 2014, *Los Angeles Times*, articles.latimes.com, February 9.

119. M. A. Hitt, D. Li, & K. Xu, 2016, International Strategy: From local to global and beyond, *Journal of World Business*, 51: 58–73; A. Goerzen, C. G. Asmussen, & B. B. Nielsen, 2013, Global cities and multinational enterprise location strategy, *Journal of International Business Studies*, 44: 427–450.

120. F. Bauer, M. A. Dao, K. Malzer, & S. Y. Tarba, 2017, How Industry Lifecycle sets boundary conditions for M&A integration, *Long Range Planning*, 50: 501–517; M. E. Porter, 1980, *Competitive Strategy*, New York: Free Press.

121. F. J. Mas-Ruiz, F. Ruiz-Moreno, & A. L. de Guevara Martinez, 2014, Asymmetric rivalry within and between strategic groups, *Strategic Management Journal*, 35: 419–439; M. S. Hunt, 1972, Competition in the major home appliance industry, 1960–1970 (doctoral dissertation, Harvard University); Porter, *Competitive Strategy*, 129.

122. S. Sonenshein, K. Nault, & O. Obodaru, 2017, Competition of a different flavour: How a strategic group identity shapes competition and cooperation, *Administrative Science Quarterly*, 62: 626–656; S. Cheng & H. Chang, 2009, Performance implications of cognitive complexity: An empirical study of cognitive strategic groups in semiconductor industry, *Journal of Business Research*, 62: 1311–1320.

123. B. P. S. Murthi, A. A. Rasheed, & I. Goll, 2013, An empirical analysis of strategic groups in the airline industry using latent class regressions, *Managerial and Decision Economics*, 34(2): 59–73; J. Lee, K. Lee, & S. Rho, 2002, An evolutionary perspective on strategic group emergence: A genetic algorithm-based model, *Strategic Management Journal*, 23: 727–746.

124. V. Govindarajan, 2018, Can anyone stop Amazon from winning the industrial Internet? *Harvard Business Review*, hbr.org, February 3.

125. K.-Y. Hsieh, W. Tsai, & M.-J. Chen, 2015, If they can do it, why not us? Competitors as reference points in justifying escalation of commitment, *Academy of Management Journal, 58: 38–58;* T. Keil, T. Laarmanen, & R. G. McGrath, 2013, Is a counterattack the best defense? Competitive dynamics through acquisitions, *Long Range Planning*, 46: 195–215.

126. Porter, *Competitive Strategy*, 49.

127. Know thy enemy: A review and agenda for research on competitor identification; R. L. Priem, S. Li, & J. C. Carr, 2012, Insights and new directions from demand-side approaches to technology innovation, entrepreneurship, and strategic management research, *Journal of Management*, 38: 346–374.

128. D. E. Hughes, J. Le Bon, & A. Rapp, 2013. Gaining and leveraging customer-based competitive intelligence: The pivotal role of social capital and salesperson adaptive selling skills, *Journal of the Academy of Marketing Science*, 41: 91–110; D. B. Montgomery, M. C. Moore, & J. E. Urbany, 2005, Reasoning about competitive reactions: Evidence from executives, *Marketing Science*, 24: 138–149.

129. H. Akbar & N. Tzokas, 2012, An exploration of new product development's front-end knowledge conceptualization process in discontinuous innovations, *British Journal of Management*, 24: 245–263; K. Xu, S. Liao, J. Li, & Y. Song, 2011, Mining comparative opinions from customer reviews for competitive intelligence, *Decision Support Systems*, 50: 743–754; S. Jain, 2008, Digital piracy: A competitive analysis, *Marketing Science*, 27: 610–626.

130. S. Wright, 2013, Converting input to insight: Organising for intelligence-based competitive advantage. In S. Wright (ed.),

Competitive Intelligence, Analysis and Strategy: Creating Organisational Agility. Abingdon: Routledge, 1–35; J. G. York, 2009, Pragmatic sustainability: Translating environmental ethics into competitive advantage, *Journal of Business Ethics*, 85: 97–109.

131. R. Huggins, 2010, Regional competitive intelligence: Benchmarking and policy-making. *Regional Studies*, 44: 639–658.

132. L. T. Tuan, 2013, Leading to learning and competitive intelligence, *The Learning Organization*, 20: 216–239; K. A. Sawka, 2008, The ethics of competitive intelligence, *Kiplinger Business Resource Center Online*, www.kiplinger.com, March.

133. R. B. Bouncken & S. Kraus, 2013, Innovation in knowledge-intensive industries: The double-edged sword of coopetition, *Journal of Business Research*, 66: 2060–2070; T. Mazzarol & S. Reboud, 2008, The role of complementary actors in the development of innovation in small firms, *International Journal of Innovation Management*, 12: 223–253; A. Brandenburger & B. Nalebuff, 1996, *Co-opetition*, New York: Currency Doubleday.

134. 2018, SCIP Code of ethics for CI professionals, www.scip.org, March 30.

3

The Internal Organization: Resources, Capabilities, Core Competencies, and Competitive Advantages

Studying this chapter should provide you with the strategic management knowledge needed to:

3-1 Explain why firms need to study and understand their internal organization.

3-2 Define value and discuss its importance.

3-3 Describe the differences between tangible and intangible resources.

3-4 Define capabilities and discuss their development.

3-5 Describe four criteria used to determine if resources and capabilities are core competencies.

3-6 Explain how firms analyze their value chain to determine where they are able to create value when using their resources, capabilities, and core competencies.

3-7 Define outsourcing and discuss reasons for its use.

3-8 Discuss the importance of identifying internal strengths and weaknesses.

3-9 Describe the importance of avoiding core rigidities.

iStock.com/DNY59

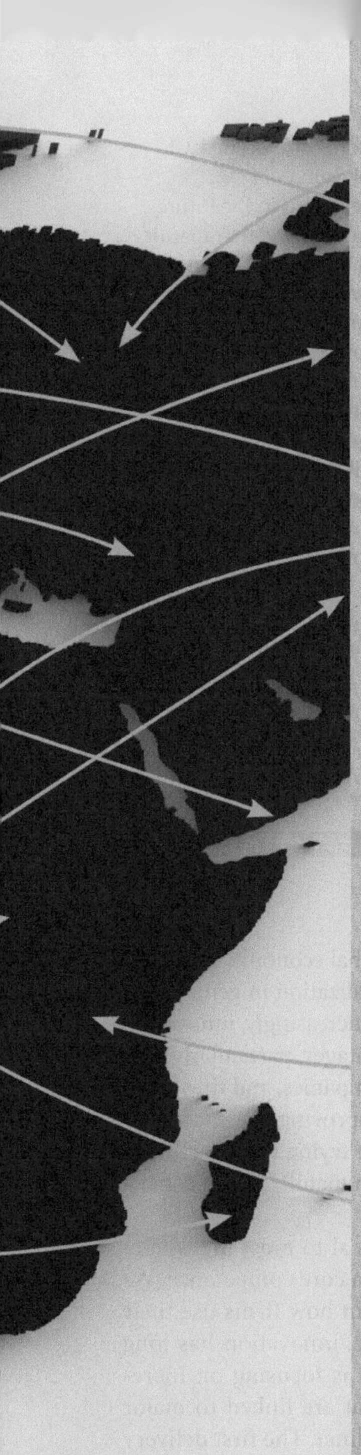

LARGE PHARMACEUTICAL COMPANIES, BIG DATA ANALYTICS, ARTIFICIAL INTELLIGENCE AND CORE COMPETENCIES: A BRAVE NEW WORLD

To date, and perhaps surprisingly, the idea of using data strategically remains somewhat novel in some organizations. However, the reality of "big data" and "big data analytics" (which is "the process of examining big data to uncover hidden patterns, unknown correlations, and other useful information that can be used to make better decisions") is becoming increasingly popular in business. Indeed, in the current competitive landscape, most businesses must use big data analytics (BDA) across all customer channels (mobile, Web, e-mail, and physical stores) throughout their supply chain to help them become more innovative.

This is the situation for large pharmaceutical companies (the firms often called "big pharma") in that many have been working to develop a core competence in BDA. (We define and discuss core competencies in this chapter.) There are several reasons they are doing this. In addition to the vast increases in the amounts of data that must be studied and interpreted for competitive purposes, "health care reform and the changing landscape of health care delivery" systems throughout the world are influencing these firms to think about developing BDA as a core competence.

AI can help analyze data on clinical trials, health records, genetic profiles, and preclinical studies. China has a goal to become the world leader in AI.

Many benefits can accrue to big pharma firms that develop BDA as a core competence. For example, having BDA as a core competence can help a firm quickly identify trial candidates and accelerate their recruitment, develop improved inclusion and exclusion criteria to use in clinical trials, and uncover unintended uses and indications for products. In terms of customer functionality, superior products can be provided at a faster pace as a foundation for helping patients live better and healthier lives.

In developing their BDA capabilities, many of the big pharma companies are investing in artificial intelligence (AI). AI provides the capability to analyze many different sets of information. For example, AI can help analyze data on clinical trials, health records, genetic profiles, and preclinical studies. AI can analyze and integrate these data to identify patterns in the data and suggest hypotheses about relationships. A new drug generally requires a decade of research and $2.6 billion of investment. And only about 5 percent of the drugs that enter experimental research make it to the market and are successful. Eventually, it is expected that the use of AI could reduce the early research development time from 4-6 years to 1 year, not only greatly reducing the time of development but also the costs.

As we discuss in this chapter, capabilities are the foundation for developing core competencies. There are several capabilities big pharma companies need for BDA to be a core competence. Supportive architecture, the proper mix of data scientists, and "technology that integrates and manages new types and sources of data flexibility and scalability while maintaining the highest standards of data governance, data quality, and data security" are examples of capabilities that big pharma need if they wish to develop BDA as a core competence. Of course, using artificial intelligence provides strong support for the application of BDA.

Having a strong BDA competence could be critical for pharmaceutical firms in the future. Most Chinese pharmaceutical firms are medium-sized and sell generic drugs and therapeutic medicines, investing in R&D at only about 25% of the amount invested by big pharma in developed countries. However, China has a plan to develop large, competitive pharmaceutical firms by 2025. In 2017, for example, China's second largest class of investments was biopharma. Interestingly, the largest Chinese investment that year was in information systems, including AI. China has a goal to become the world leader in AI.

In recent years, big pharma has been earning mediocre returns of about 3 percent ROI, down from 10 percent a decade earlier. Thus, big pharma executives feel pressure especially with the initial costs of developing BDA and AI. Hopefully, they soon will be able to reduce their costs and experience higher rates of success in the development of new drugs. Until then, however, analysts are predicting record numbers of mergers and acquisitions in the pharmaceutical industry, with big pharma acquiring successful medium-sized pharmaceuticals and biotechnology firms.

Sources: S. Mukherjee, 2018, How big pharma is using AI to make better drugs, *Fortune*, fortune.com, March 19: Z. Torrey, 2018, China prepares for big pharma, thediplomat.com, March 14; E. Corbett, 2018, European mid-sized pharma companies-biotechs and big pharma? *The Pharmaletter*, www.thepharmaletter.com, March 9; M. Jewel, 2018, Signs that 2018 will be a record year for pharma M&A, *The Pharmaletter*, www.thepharmaletter.com, March1; B. Nelson, 2018, Why big pharma and biotech are betting big on AI, *NBC News*, www.nbc.news, March 1; Big data analytics: What it is & why it matters, 2015, *SAS*, www.sas.com, April 2; Big data for the pharmaceutical industry, *Informatica*, www.informatica.com, March 17; B. Atkins, 2015, Big data and the board, *Wall Street Journal Online*, www.wsj.com, April 16; S. F. DeAngelis, 2014, Pharmaceutical big data analytics promises a healthier future, *Enterrasolutions*, www.enterrasolutions.com, June 5; T. Wolfram, 2014, Data analytics has big pharma rethinking its core competencies, *Forbes Online*, www.forbes.com, December 22.

As discussed in the first two chapters, several factors in the global economy, including the rapid development of the Internet's capabilities and globalization in general, are making it difficult for firms to develop competitive advantages.[1] Increasingly, innovation appears to be a vital path to efforts to develop competitive advantages, particularly sustainable ones.[2] Innovative actions are required by big pharma companies, and they need to develop new drugs more quickly and at lower costs while improving the success of the drugs that they develop. As the Opening Case shows, they are trying to use artificial intelligence to help develop capabilities in big data analytics that hopefully can become a core competence.

As is the case for big pharma companies, innovation is critical to most firms' success. This means that many firms seek to develop innovation as a core competence. We define and discuss core competencies in this chapter and explain how firms use their resources and capabilities to form them. As a core competence, innovation has long been critical to Boeing's success, too. Today, however, the firm is focusing on incremental innovations as well as developing new technologies that are linked to major innovations and the projects they spawn, such as the 787 Dreamliner. The first delivery of the 787-10 Dreamliner was made to Singapore Airlines on March 26, 2018. Boeing believes its incremental innovations enable the firm to deliver reliable products to customers more quickly and at a lower cost.[3] As we discuss in this chapter, firms and organizations—such as those we mention here—achieve strategic competitiveness and earn above-average returns by acquiring, bundling, and leveraging their resources for the purpose of taking advantage of opportunities in the external environment in ways that create value for customers.[4]

Even if the firm develops and manages resources in ways that create core competencies and competitive advantages, competitors will eventually learn how to duplicate the benefits of any firm's value-creating strategy; thus, all competitive advantages have a limited life.[5] Because of this, the question of duplication of a competitive advantage is not *if* it will happen, but *when*. In general, a competitive advantage's sustainability is a function of three factors:

1. The rate of core competence obsolescence because of environmental changes
2. The availability of substitutes for the core competence
3. The imitability of the core competence[6]

For all firms, the challenge is to effectively manage current core competencies while simultaneously developing new ones.[7] Only when firms are able to do this can they expect to achieve strategic competitiveness, earn above-average returns, and remain ahead of competitors in both the short and long term.

We studied the general, industry, and competitor environments in Chapter 2. Armed with knowledge about the realities and conditions of their external environment, firms have a better understanding of marketplace opportunities and the characteristics of the competitive environment in which those opportunities exist. In this chapter, we focus on the firm. By analyzing its internal organization, a firm determines what it can do. Matching what a firm *can do* (a function of its resources, capabilities, and core competencies in the internal organization) with what it *might do* (a function of opportunities and threats in the external environment) yields insights for the firm to select strategies from among those we discuss in Chapters 4 through 9.

We begin this chapter by briefly describing conditions associated with analyzing the firm's internal organization. We then discuss the roles of resources and capabilities in developing core competencies, which are the sources of the firm's competitive advantages. Included in this discussion are the techniques firms use to identify and evaluate resources and capabilities and the criteria for identifying core competencies from among them. Resources alone typically do not provide competitive advantages. Instead, resources create value when the firm uses them to form capabilities, some of which become core competencies, and hopefully competitive advantages. Because of the relationship among resources, capabilities, and core competencies, we also discuss the value chain and examine four criteria that firms use to determine if their capabilities are core competencies and, as such, sources of competitive advantage.[8] The chapter closes with comments about outsourcing as well as the need for firms to prevent their core competencies from becoming core rigidities. The existence of core rigidities indicates that the firm is too anchored to its past, a situation that prevents it from continuously developing new capabilities and core competencies.

3-1 Analyzing the Internal Organization

3-1a The Context of Internal Analysis

One of the conditions associated with analyzing a firm's internal organization is the reality that in today's global economy, some of the resources that were traditionally critical to firms' efforts to produce, sell, and distribute their goods or services—such as labor costs, access to financial resources and raw materials, and protected or regulated markets—although still important, are now less likely to be the source of competitive advantages.[9] An important reason for this is that an increasing number of firms are using their resources to form core competencies through which they successfully implement an international strategy (discussed in Chapter 8) as a means of overcoming the advantages created by more traditional resources.

Given the increasing importance of the global economy, those analyzing their firm's internal organization should use a global mind-set to do so. A **global mind-set** is the

A **global mind-set** is the ability to analyze, understand, and manage an internal organization in ways that are not dependent on the assumptions of a single country, culture, or context.

ability to analyze, understand, and manage an internal organization in ways that are not dependent on the assumptions of a single country, culture, or context.[10] Because they are able to span artificial boundaries, those with a global mind-set recognize that their firms must possess resources and capabilities that allow understanding of and appropriate responses to competitive situations that are influenced by country-specific factors and unique cultures. Using a global mind-set to analyze the internal organization has the potential to significantly help the firm in its efforts to outperform rivals.[11]

Finally, analyzing the firm's internal organization requires that evaluators examine the firm's entire portfolio of resources and capabilities. This perspective suggests that individual firms possess at least some resources and capabilities that other companies do not—at least not in the same combination. Resources are the source of capabilities, some of which lead to the development of core competencies; in turn, some core competencies may lead to a competitive advantage for the firm.[12] Understanding how to leverage the firm's unique bundle of resources and capabilities is a key outcome decision makers seek when analyzing the internal organization.[13] Figure 3.1 illustrates the relationships among resources, capabilities, core competencies, and competitive advantages and shows how their integrated use can lead to strategic competitiveness. As we discuss next, firms use the resources in their internal organization to create value for customers.

3-1b Creating Value

Firms use their resources as the foundation for producing goods or services that will create value for customers.[14] **Value** is measured by a product's performance characteristics and by its attributes for which customers are willing to pay. Firms create value by innovatively bundling and leveraging their resources to form capabilities and core competencies.[15] Firms with a competitive advantage create more value for customers than do competitors.[16] Walmart uses its "every day low price" approach to doing business (an approach that is grounded in the firm's core competencies, such as information technology and distribution

Value is measured by a product's performance characteristics and by its attributes for which customers are willing to pay.

Figure 3.1 Components of an Internal Analysis

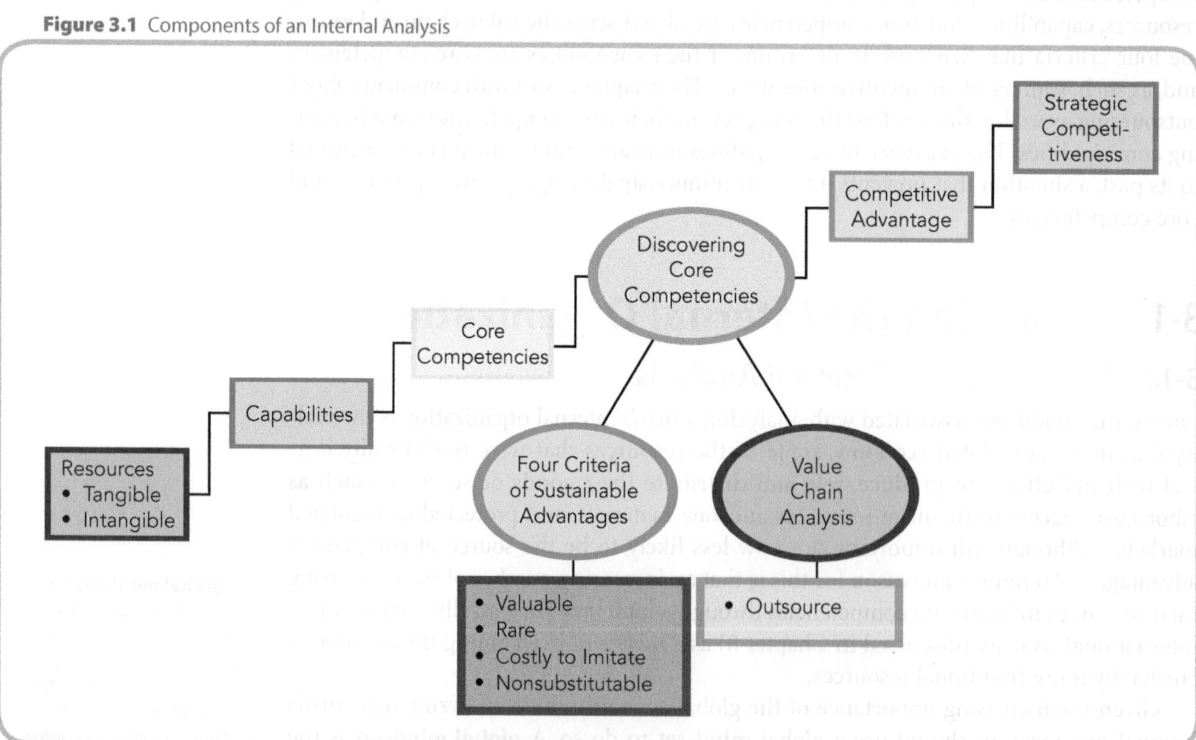

channels) to create value for those seeking to buy products at a low price compared to competitors' prices for those products. The stronger these firms' core competencies, the greater the amount of value they're able to create for their customers.[17]

Ultimately, creating value for customers is the source of above-average returns for a firm. What the firm intends regarding value creation affects its choice of business-level strategy (see Chapter 4) and its organizational structure (see Chapter 11).[18] In Chapter 4's discussion of business-level strategies, we note that value is created by a product's low cost, by its highly differentiated features, or by a combination of low cost and high differentiation compared to competitors' offerings. A business-level strategy is effective only when it is grounded in exploiting the firm's capabilities and core competencies. Thus, the successful firm continuously examines the effectiveness of current capabilities and core competencies while thinking about the capabilities and competencies it will require for future success.[19]

At one time, firms' efforts to create value were largely oriented toward understanding the characteristics of the industry in which they competed and, in light of those characteristics, determining how they should be positioned relative to competitors. This emphasis on industry characteristics and competitive strategy underestimated the role of the firm's resources and capabilities in developing core competencies as the source of competitive advantages. In fact, core competencies, in combination with product-market positions, are the firm's most important sources of competitive advantage.[20] A firm's core competencies, integrated with an understanding of the results of studying the conditions in the external environment, should drive the selection of strategies.[21] As Clayton Christensen noted, "successful strategists need to cultivate a deep understanding of the processes of competition and progress and of the factors that undergird each advantage. Only thus will they be able to see when old advantages are poised to disappear and how new advantages can be built in their stead."[22] By emphasizing core competencies when selecting and implementing strategies, companies learn to compete primarily on the basis of firm-specific differences. However, while doing so they must be simultaneously aware of changes in the firm's external environment.[23]

3-1c The Challenge of Analyzing the Internal Organization

The strategic decisions managers make about the internal organization are nonroutine,[24] have ethical implications,[25] and significantly influence the firm's ability to earn above-average returns.[26] These decisions involve choices about the resources the firm needs to collect and how to best manage and leverage them.

Making decisions involving the firm's assets—identifying, developing, deploying, and protecting resources, capabilities, and core competencies—may appear to be relatively easy. However, this task is as challenging and difficult as any other with which managers are involved; moreover, the task is increasingly internationalized.[27] Some believe that the pressure on managers to pursue only decisions that help the firm meet anticipated quarterly earnings makes it difficult to accurately examine the firm's internal organization.[28]

The challenge and difficulty of making effective decisions are implied by preliminary evidence suggesting that one-half of organizational decisions fail.[29] Sometimes, mistakes are made as the firm analyzes conditions in its internal organization.[30] Managers might, for example, think a capability is a core competence when it is not. This may have been the case at Polaroid Corporation, as decision makers continued to believe that the capabilities it used to build its instant film cameras were highly relevant at the time its competitors were preparing to introduce digital cameras. In this instance, Polaroid's decision makers may have concluded that superior manufacturing was a core competence, as was the firm's ability to innovate in terms of creating value-adding features for its instant

Gene Blevins/Polaris/Newscom

At one time, Polaroid's cameras created a significant amount of value for customers. Poor decisions may have contributed to the firm's subsequent inability to create value and its initial filing for bankruptcy in 2001.

cameras. If a mistake is made when analyzing and managing a firm's resources, decision makers must have the confidence to admit it and take corrective actions.[31]

A firm can improve by studying its mistakes; in fact, the learning generated by making and correcting mistakes can be important in the creation of new capabilities and core competencies.[32] One capability that can be learned from failure is when to quit. Polaroid should have obviously changed its strategy earlier than it did, so it could have been able to avoid demise. Another potential example concerns News Corp.'s Amplify unit (founded 2011), which was created to change the way children are taught. As of mid-2015, the firm had invested over $1 billion in the unit, which makes tablets, sells online curricula, and offers testing services. In 2014, Amplify generated a $193 million loss, facing competition from well-established textbook publishers enhancing their own ability to sell similar digital products. In September 2015, News Corp. decided to sell Amplify to a team of managers and private investors, incurring a significant loss.[33]

As we discuss next, three conditions—uncertainty, complexity, and intraorganizational conflict—affect managers as they analyze the internal organization and make decisions about resources (see Figure 3.2).

When studying the internal organization, managers face uncertainty because of a number of issues, including those of new proprietary technologies, rapidly changing economic and political trends, transformations in societal values, and shifts in customers' demands.[34] Environmental uncertainty increases the complexity and range of issues to examine when studying the internal environment.[35] Consider how uncertainty affects the ways to use resources at coal companies such as Peabody Energy Corp. and Murray Energy Corp. Coal companies have been suffering in the last decade or more with significant regulations and the competition from cleaner forms of energy such as natural gas. They have been aided some by the reduction of regulations by the Trump administration, but the competition from cleaner and cheaper forms of energy remains. Thus, they still have to deal with a complex and uncertain environment.

Figure 3.2 Conditions Affecting Managerial Decisions about Resources, Capabilities, and Core Competencies

Conditions	**Uncertainty**	**Uncertainty exists about the characteristics of the firm's general and industry environments and customers' needs.**
	Complexity	**Complexity results from the interrelationships among conditions shaping a firm.**
	Intraorganizational Conflicts	**Intraorganizational conflicts may exist among managers making decisions as well as among those affected by the decisions.**

Biases regarding how to cope with uncertainty affect decisions made about how to manage the firm's resources and capabilities to form core competencies.[36] Additionally, intraorganizational conflict may surface when decisions are made about the core competencies a firm should develop and nurture. Conflict might surface in the energy companies mentioned above about the degree to which resources and capabilities should be used to form new core competencies to support newer "clean technologies."

In making decisions affected by these three conditions, judgment is required. *Judgment* is the capability of making successful decisions when no obviously correct model or rule is available or when relevant data are unreliable or incomplete. In such situations, decision makers must be aware of possible cognitive biases, such as overconfidence. Individuals who are too confident in the decisions they make about how to use the firm's resources may fail to fully evaluate contingencies that could affect those decisions.[37]

When exercising judgment, decision makers often take intelligent risks. In the current competitive landscape, executive judgment can become a valuable capability. One reason is that, over time, effective judgment that decision makers demonstrate allows a firm to build a strong reputation and retain the loyalty of stakeholders whose support is linked to above-average returns.[38]

Finding individuals who can make the most successful decisions about using the organization's resources is challenging, and important. The quality of decisions regarding resources and their management affect a firm's ability to achieve strategic competitiveness. Individuals holding such key decision-making positions are called *strategic leaders.* Discussed fully in Chapter 12 and for our purposes in this chapter, we can think of strategic leaders as individuals with an ability to examine the firm's resources, capabilities, and core competencies and make effective choices about their use.

Next, we consider the relationships among a firm's resources, capabilities, and core competencies. While reading these sections, keep in mind that organizations have more resources than capabilities and more capabilities than core competencies.

3-2 Resources, Capabilities, and Core Competencies

Resources, capabilities, and core competencies are the foundation of competitive advantage. Resources are bundled to create organizational capabilities. In turn, capabilities are the source of a firm's core competencies, which are the basis of establishing competitive advantages.[39] We show these relationships in Figure 3.1 and discuss them next.

3-2a Resources

Broad in scope, resources cover a spectrum of individual, social, and organizational phenomena. By themselves, resources do not allow firms to create value for customers as the foundation for earning above-average returns. Indeed, resources are combined to form capabilities.[40] For example, Subway links its fresh ingredients with several other resources, including the continuous training it provides to those running the firm's fast food restaurants, as the foundation for customer service as a capability; customer service is also a core competence for Subway.

As its sole distribution channel, the Internet is a resource for Amazon.com. The firm uses the Internet to sell goods at prices that typically are lower than those offered by competitors selling the same goods through more costly brick-and-mortar storefronts. By combining other resources (such as access to a wide product inventory), Amazon has developed a reputation for excellent customer service. Amazon's capability in terms of customer service is a core competence as well in that the firm creates unique value for customers through the services it provides to them.

Some of a firm's resources (defined in Chapter 1 as inputs to the firm's production process) are tangible while others are intangible. **Tangible resources** are assets that can be observed and quantified. Production equipment, manufacturing facilities, distribution centers, and formal reporting structures are examples of tangible resources. For energy giant Kinder Morgan, its stock of oil and gas pipelines are a key tangible resource. **Intangible resources** are assets that are rooted deeply in the firm's history, accumulate over time, and are relatively difficult for competitors to analyze and imitate. Because they are embedded in unique patterns of routines, intangible resources are difficult for competitors to analyze and imitate. Knowledge, trust between managers and employees, managerial capabilities, organizational routines (the unique ways people work together), scientific capabilities, the capacity for innovation, brand name, the firm's reputation for its goods or services and how it interacts with people (such as employees, customers, and suppliers), and organizational culture are intangible resources.[41]

Intangible resources require nurturing to maintain their ability to help firms engage in competitive battles. For example, brand has long been a valuable intangible resource for Coca-Cola Company. The same is true for "logo-laden British brand Superdry," a case highlighted at the end of the chapter. As you will read, SuperGroup PLC, the owner of Superdry, encountered problems a few years ago in its efforts to maintain and enhance the value of the Superdry brand. New management and a new approach are attempting to renew the Superdry brand.[42]

As noted in the Strategic Focus, intangible resources may be even more important in the development of core competencies. Of course, three of the firms described in the Strategic Focus—Fainsbert Mase Brown & Susmann, Genpact, and Document Security Systems—were service firms, which commonly base their core competencies on their human capital. However, even Hecla Mining Company, which has significant investments in specialized mining equipment, must also have valuable human capital for its core competence in "high grade, narrow-vein underground mining."

For each analysis, tangible and intangible resources are grouped into categories. The four primary categories of tangible resources are financial, organizational, physical, and technological (see Table 3.1). The three primary categories of intangible resources are human, innovation, and reputational (see Table 3.2).

Table 3.1 Tangible Resources

Financial Resources	• The firm's capacity to borrow • The firm's ability to generate funds through internal operations
Organizational Resources	• Formal reporting structures
Physical Resources	• The sophistication of a firm's plant and equipment and the attractiveness of its location • Distribution facilities • Product inventory
Technological Resources	• Availability of technology-related resources such as copyrights, patents, trademarks, and trade secrets

Sources: Adapted from J. B. Barney, 1991, Firm resources and sustained competitive advantage, *Journal of Management*, 17: 101; R. M. Grant, 1991, *Contemporary Strategy Analysis*, Cambridge: U.K.: Blackwell Business, 100–102.

Tangible resources are assets that can be observed and quantified.

Intangible resources are assets that are rooted deeply in the firm's history, accumulate over time, and are relatively difficult for competitors to analyze and imitate.

Strategic Focus

Tangible and Intangible Resources as the Base for Core Competencies

While tangible resources are important, intangible resources are perhaps even more important in the development of firms' core competencies. Understandably, most professional service firms have few tangible resources but can have high market value primarily because of their intangible resources. For example, Fainsbert Mase Brown & Susmann, LLP is a premier law firm located in Los Angeles, California. Obviously, its goal is to provide superior legal services to its clients. Within this broad frame, however, there is a core competence. The firm provides legal advice and support on significant real estate, business, and corporate transactions for large institutions, high net-worth individuals, and privately owned businesses. For example, in 2018 the firm provided the legal services to conclude the negotiations for the Industrial Realty Group's purchase of the 3.1 million square foot IBM technology campus in Rochester, Minnesota. This complex transaction required more than one year to negotiate with a multi-level corporate legal team.

Likewise, other major service firms are heavily dependent on their intangible assets. For example, Genpact requires highly knowledgeable human capital for its core competence. Genpact provides solutions to major process problems for its clients. Genpact describes its competence as providing "digital-led innovation and digitally enabled intelligent operations" for clients. The firm solves clients' problems using data analytics, helping its clients transform their operations. Another technology-based service firm is Document Security Systems, Inc. (DSS). DSS has a core competence in the development of anti-counterfeit, authentication, and diversion software that protects organizations against Internet fraud and theft. And it tries to remain a leader in this field through continued investment in research and new technology. In 2018, it announced an agreement to partner with the Hong Kong R&D Center for Logistics and Supply Chain to develop the next generation of protection products using blockchain technology.

Firms with larger amounts of tangible resources also need valuable intangible resources. For example, Hecla Mining Company has a core competence in "high grade, narrow-vein underground mining." Obviously, the company has significant investments in specialized mining equipment in order to employ this core competence. But significant engineering and mining knowledge and expertise is required to successfully engage in this type of mining. This knowledge and expertise resides in the human capital (intangible assets) within the firm.

It is important to note that firms' reputations are often significant intangible assets. For example, professional service firms must be considered not only highly knowledgeable in the areas in which they compete, but also must be considered honest and highly trustworthy. In meeting this challenge, Genpact was selected as one of the "World's Most Ethical Companies" in 2018. Companies can also enhance intangible assets, such as their reputation, through use of their core competencies. For example, in the aftermath of Hurricane Harvey in 2017, Johnson & Johnson provided medical supplies, FedEx provided logistical support to provide bottled water, and Butterball provided 40,000 pounds of canned turkey to help citizens in the recovery. Companies that are ethical and good corporate citizens often are highly respected and are called on to use their core competencies to serve an increasing number of customers.

360b/Alamy Stock Photo

In 2018, Genpact announced an agreement to partner with the Hong Kong R&D Center for Logistics and Supply Chain to develop the next generation of protection products using blockchain technology.

Sources: Document Security Systems, Inc., 2018, DSS Partners with Hong Kong R&D Centre for logistics and supply chain management enabling technologies for blockchain research, globenewswire.com, March 19; *StreetInsider*, 2018, Hecla Mining (HL) Announces $462 million Acquisition of Klondes Mines, Ltd. (K), www.streetinsider.com, March 19; *BusinessInsider*, 2018, Genpact named one of the 2018 world's most ethical companies by the Ethisphere Institute, markets.businessinsider.com, March14; *Cision PR Newswire*, 2018, Fainsbert Mase Brown & Sussmann, LLP completes acquisition closing on 3.1 million sq. ft. IBM campus in Minnesota, www.prnewswire, February 23; P. N. Danziger, 2018, Fire, floods, hurricanes: How and why corporations must help, *Forbes*, www.forbes.com, October 20.

Table 3.2 Intangible Resources

Human Resources	• Knowledge • Trust • Skills • Abilities to collaborate with others
Innovation Resources	• Ideas • Scientific capabilities • Capacity to innovate
Reputational Resources	• Brand name • Perceptions of product quality, durability, and reliability • Positive reputation with stakeholders such as suppliers and customers

Sources: Adapted from R. Hall, 1992, The strategic analysis of intangible resources, *Strategic Management Journal*, 13: 136–139: R. M. Grant, 1991, *Contemporary Strategy Analysis*, Cambridge: U.K.: Blackwell Business, 101–104.

Tangible Resources

As tangible resources, a firm's borrowing capacity and the status of its physical facilities are visible. The value of many tangible resources can be established through financial statements, but these statements do not account for the value of all of the firm's assets because they disregard some intangible resources.[43] The value of tangible resources is also constrained because they are hard to leverage—it is difficult to derive additional business or value from a tangible resource. For example, an airplane is a tangible resource, but "you can't use the same airplane on five different routes at the same time. You can't put the same crew on five different routes at the same time. And the same goes for the financial investment you've made in the airplane."[44]

Although production assets are tangible, many of the processes necessary to use them are intangible as in the case of Hecla Mining Company described in the Strategic Focus. Thus, the learning and potential proprietary processes associated with a tangible resource, such as manufacturing facilities, can have unique intangible attributes, such as quality control processes, unique manufacturing processes, and technologies that develop over time.[45]

Intangible Resources

Compared to tangible resources, intangible resources are a superior source of capabilities and subsequently, core competencies.[46] In fact, in the global economy, a firm's intellectual capital often plays a more critical role in corporate success than do physical assets.[47] Because of this, being able to effectively manage intellectual capital is an increasingly important skill for today's leaders to develop.[48]

Because intangible resources are less visible and more difficult for competitors to understand, purchase, imitate, or substitute for, firms prefer to rely on them rather than on tangible resources as the foundation for their capabilities. In fact, the more unobservable (i.e., intangible) a resource is, the more valuable that resource is to create capabilities.[49] Another benefit of intangible resources is that, unlike most tangible resources, their use can be leveraged. For instance, sharing knowledge among employees does not diminish its value for any one person. To the contrary, two people sharing their individualized knowledge sets often can be leveraged to create additional knowledge that, although new to each individual, contributes potentially to performance improvements for the firm.

Reputational resources (see Table 3.2) are important sources of a firm's capabilities and core competencies. Indeed, some argue that a positive reputation can even be a source of competitive advantage.[50] Earned through the firm's actions as well as its words, a value-creating reputation is a product of years of superior marketplace competence as perceived by stakeholders.[51] A reputation indicates the level of awareness a firm has been able to develop among stakeholders and the degree to which they hold the firm in high esteem.[52]

iStock.com/Courtney Keating

Developing capabilities in specific functional areas can give companies a competitive edge. The effective use of social media to direct advertising to specific market segments has given some firms an advantage over their rivals.

A well-known and highly valued brand name is a specific reputational resource.[53] A continuing commitment to innovation and aggressive advertising facilitates firms' efforts to take advantage of the reputation associated with their brands.[54] Harley-Davidson has a reputation for producing and servicing high-quality motorcycles with unique designs. Because of the desirability of its reputation, the company also produces a wide range of accessory items that it sells based on its reputation for offering unique products with high quality. Sunglasses, jewelry, belts, wallets, shirts, slacks, and hats are just a few of the large variety of accessories customers can purchase from a Harley-Davidson dealer or from its online store.[55]

Taking advantage of today's technologies, some firms are using social media as a means of influencing their reputation. Recognizing that thousands of conversations occur daily throughout the world and that what is being said can affect its reputation, Coca-Cola company encourages its employees to be a part of these social media-based discussions as a means of positively influencing the company's reputation. Driving the nature of these conversations is a set of social media principles that Coca-Cola employees use as a foundation for how they will engage with various social media. Being transparent and protecting consumers' privacy are examples of the commitments the firm established.[56]

3-2b Capabilities

The firm combines individual tangible and intangible resources to create capabilities. In turn, capabilities are used to complete the organizational tasks required to produce, distribute, and service the goods or services the firm provides to customers for the purpose of creating value for them. As a foundation for building core competencies and hopefully competitive advantages, capabilities are often based on developing, carrying, and exchanging information and knowledge through the firm's human capital.[57] Hence, the value of human capital in developing and using capabilities and, ultimately, core competencies cannot be overstated.[58] In fact, it seems to be "well known that human capital makes or breaks companies."[59] At pizza-maker Domino's, human capital is critical to the firm's efforts to change how it competes. Describing this, CEO Patrick Doyle says that, in many ways, Domino's is becoming "a technology company … that has adapted the art of pizza-making to the digital age."[60]

As illustrated in Table 3.3, capabilities are often developed in specific functional areas (such as manufacturing, R&D, and marketing) or in a part of a functional area (e.g., advertising). Table 3.3 shows a grouping of organizational functions and the capabilities that some companies are thought to possess in terms of all or parts of those functions.

Table 3.3 Example of Firms' Capabilities

Functional Areas	Capabilities	Examples of Firms
Distribution	• Effective use of logistics management techniques	• Walmart
Human Resources	• Motivating, empowering, and retaining employees	• Microsoft
Management Information Systems	• Effective and efficient control of inventories through point-of-purchase data collection methods	• Walmart
Marketing	• Effective promotion of brand-name products • Effective customer service • Innovative merchandising	• Procter & Gamble • Ralph Lauren Corp. • McKinsey & Co. • Nordstrom Inc. • Crate & Barrel
Management	• Ability to envision the future of clothing	• Hugo Boss • Zara
Manufacturing	• Design and production skills yielding reliable products • Product and design quality • Miniaturization of components and products	• Komatsu • Witt Gas Technology • Sony
Research & Development	• Innovative technology • Development of sophisticated elevator control solutions • Rapid transformation of technology into new products and processes • Digital technology	• Caterpillar • Otis Elevator Co. • Chaparral Steel • Thomson Consumer Electronics

3-2c Core Competencies

Defined in Chapter 1, core competencies are capabilities that serve as a source of competitive advantage for a firm over its rivals. Core competencies distinguish a company competitively and reflect its personality. Core competencies emerge over time through an organizational process of accumulating and learning how to deploy different resources and capabilities.[61] As the capacity to take action, core competencies are the "crown jewels of a company," the activities the company performs especially well compared to competitors and through which the firm adds unique value to the goods or services it sells to customers.[62] Thus, if a big pharma company (such as Pfizer) developed big data analytics as a core competence, one could conclude that the firm had formed capabilities through which it was able to analyze and effectively use huge amounts of data in a competitively superior manner.

Innovation is thought to be a core competence at Apple. As a capability, R&D activities are the source of this core competence. More specifically, the way Apple has combined some of its tangible (e.g., financial resources and research laboratories) and intangible (e.g., scientists and engineers and organizational routines) resources to complete research and development tasks creates a capability in R&D. By emphasizing its R&D capability, Apple can innovate in ways that create unique value for customers in the form of the products it sells, suggesting that innovation is a core competence for Apple.

Excellent customer service in its retail stores is another of Apple's core competencies. In this instance, unique and contemporary store designs (a tangible resource) are combined with knowledgeable and skilled employees (an intangible resource) to provide superior service to customers. A number of carefully developed training and development procedures are capabilities on which Apple's core competence of excellent customer service is based. The procedures that are capabilities include specification of how employees are to interact with customers, carefully written training manuals to describe on-site tech support that is to be provided to customers, and deep thinking about every aspect of the store's design including music that is played. Apple has a special training program designed to build associates' knowledge of Apple products and how to sell them.[63]

3-3 Building Core Competencies

Two tools help firms identify their core competencies. The first consists of four specific criteria of sustainable competitive advantage that can be used to determine which capabilities are core competencies. Because the capabilities shown in Table 3.3 have satisfied these four criteria, they are core competencies. The second tool is the value chain analysis. Firms use this tool to select the value-creating competencies that should be maintained, upgraded, or developed and those that should be outsourced.

3-3a The Four Criteria of Sustainable Competitive Advantage

Capabilities that are valuable, rare, costly to imitate, and nonsubstitutable are core competencies (see Table 3.4). In turn, core competencies help firms to gain competitive advantages over their rivals. Capabilities failing to satisfy the four criteria are not core competencies, meaning that although every core competence is a capability, not every capability is a core competence. In slightly different words, for a capability to be a core competence, it must be valuable and unique from a customer's point of view. For a core competence to be a potential source of competitive advantage, it must be inimitable and nonsubstitutable by competitors.[64]

A sustainable competitive advantage exists only when competitors are unable to duplicate the benefits of a firm's strategy or when they lack the resources to attempt imitation. For some period of time, the firm may have a core competence by using capabilities that are valuable and rare, but imitable. For example, some firms are trying to develop a core competence and potentially, a competitive advantage by out-greening their competitors. (Interestingly, developing a "green" core competence can contribute to the firm's efforts to earn above-average returns while benefitting the broader society.) For many years, Walmart has been committed to using its resources in ways that support environmental sustainability while pursuing a competitive advantage in the process. In this regard, Walmart has three major end goals: to create zero waste, operate with 100 percent renewable energy, and sell products that sustain our resources and the environment. To facilitate these efforts, Walmart recently labeled over 10,000 products on its e-commerce site as products that are "Made by a Sustainability Leader." Initially, these items were batched into roughly 80 product categories. In addition to seeking

Table 3.4 The Four Criteria of Sustainable Competitive Advantage

Valuable Capabilities	• **Help a firm neutralize threats or exploit opportunities**
Rare Capabilities	• **Are not possessed by many others**
Costly-to-Imitate Capabilities	• **Historical: A unique and a valuable organizational culture or brand name** • **Ambiguous cause: The causes and uses of a competence are unclear** • **Social complexity: Interpersonal relationships, trust, and friendship among managers, suppliers, and customers**
Nonsubstitutable Capabilities	• **No strategic equivalent**

a competitive advantage through these actions, Walmart hoped to make it easier for customers to make "sustainable choices" when purchasing products. Walmart is also working to lead the industry in deploying clean technologies as a means of reducing fuel consumption and air pollution.[65] Of course, Walmart competitors such as Target are engaging in similar actions. Time will reveal the degree to which Walmart's green practices can be imitated.

The length of time a firm can expect to create value by using its core competencies is a function of how quickly competitors can successfully imitate a good, service, or process. Value-creating core competencies may last for a relatively long period of time only when all four of the criteria we discuss next are satisfied. Thus, Walmart would know that it has a core competence and possibly, a competitive advantage in terms of green practices if the ways the firm uses its resources to complete these practices satisfy the four criteria.

Valuable

Valuable capabilities allow the firm to exploit opportunities or neutralize threats in its external environment. By effectively using capabilities to exploit opportunities or neutralize threats, a firm creates value for customers.[66] For example, Groupon created the "daily deal" marketing space; the firm reached $1 billion in revenue faster than any other company in history. In essence, the opportunity Groupon's founders pursued was to create a marketplace through which businesses could introduce their goods or services to customers who would be able to experience them at a discounted price. Restaurants, hair and nail salons, and hotels are examples of the types of companies making frequent use of Groupon's services. Young, urban professionals desiring to affordably experience the cities in which they live are the firm's target customers. But, Groupon's financial performance has been lower than desired by investors primarily because of competition.[67] While offering value to customers, the capabilities to offer its services can be imitated and its initial success invited rivals to enter the market. Competing daily-deal websites such as LivingSocial quickly surfaced and offered similar and often less expensive deals. In fact, many competitors have entered the market, to include Yipit, Woot, RetailMeNot, Tanga, and Ebate in addition to LivingSocial.[68]

Rare

Rare capabilities are capabilities that few, if any, competitors possess. A key question to be answered when evaluating this criterion is "how many rival firms possess these valuable capabilities?" Capabilities possessed by many rivals are unlikely to become core competencies for any of the involved firms. Instead, valuable but common (i.e., not rare) capabilities are sources of competitive parity.[69] Competitive advantage results only when firms develop and exploit valuable capabilities that become core competencies and that differ from those shared with competitors. The central problem for Groupon is that its capabilities to produce the "daily deal" reached competitive parity quickly. Similarly, Walmart has developed valuable capabilities that it uses to engage in green practices; but, as mentioned previously, Target seeks to develop sustainability capabilities through which it can duplicate Walmart's green practices. Target's success in doing so, if this happens, suggests that Walmart's green practices are valuable but not rare.

Costly to Imitate

Costly-to-imitate capabilities are capabilities that other firms cannot easily develop. Capabilities that are costly to imitate are created because of one reason or a combination of three reasons (see Table 3.4). First, a firm sometimes is able to develop

Valuable capabilities allow the firm to exploit opportunities or neutralize threats in its external environment.

Rare capabilities are capabilities that few, if any, competitors possess.

Costly-to-imitate capabilities are capabilities that other firms cannot easily develop.

capabilities because of *unique historical conditions*. As firms evolve, they often acquire or develop capabilities that are unique to them.[70] A firm with a unique and valuable *organizational culture* that emerged in the early stages of the company's history "may have an imperfectly imitable advantage over firms founded in another historical period,"[71] one in which less valuable or less competitively useful values and beliefs strongly influenced the development of the firm's culture. Briefly discussed in Chapter 1, organizational culture is a set of values that are shared by members in the organization. An organizational culture is a source of advantage when employees are held together tightly by their belief in it and the leaders who helped to create it.[72] Historically, emphasizing cleanliness, consistency, and service and the training that reinforces the value of these characteristics created a culture at McDonald's that some thought was a core competence and a competitive advantage for the firm. However, as explained in Chapter 2's Opening Case, McDonald's has experienced problems with a number of strategic actions taken by competitors. McDonald's hired a new CEO in 2015 and is now making a number of menu changes to make its food offerings healthier and more attractive overall to customers.[73] McDonald's hopes these changes along with others will help it to reinvigorate its historically unique culture as a core competence.

The Washington Post/Getty Images

Southwest Airlines crew hold puppies who became homeless after Hurricane Maria damaged the island of Puerto Rico. The flight, which was donated by Southwest Airlines, carried 14,000 pounds of supplies.

A second condition of being costly to imitate occurs when the link between the firm's core competencies and its competitive advantage is *causally ambiguous*.[74] In these instances, competitors can't clearly understand how a firm uses its capabilities that are core competencies as the foundation for competitive advantage. As a result, firms are uncertain about the capabilities they should develop to duplicate the benefits of a competitor's value-creating strategy. For years, firms tried to imitate Southwest Airlines' low-cost strategy, but most have been unable to do so, primarily because they can't duplicate this firm's unique culture.

Social complexity is the third reason that capabilities can be costly to imitate. Social complexity means that at least some, and frequently many, of the firm's capabilities are the product of complex social phenomena. Interpersonal relationships, trust, friendships among managers and between managers and employees, and a firm's reputation with suppliers and customers are examples of socially complex capabilities.[75] Southwest Airlines is careful to hire people who fit with its culture. This complex interrelationship between the culture and human capital adds value in ways that other airlines cannot, such as jokes on flights by the flight attendants or the cooperation between gate personnel and pilots.

Nonsubstitutable

Nonsubstitutable capabilities are capabilities that do not have strategic equivalents. This final criterion "is that there must be no strategically equivalent valuable resources that are themselves either not rare or imitable. Two valuable firm resources (or two bundles

Nonsubstitutable capabilities are capabilities that do not have strategic equivalents.

Table 3.5 Outcomes from Combinations of the Criteria for Sustainable Competitive Advantage

Is the Capability Valuable?	Is the Capability Rare?	Is the Capability Costly to Imitate?	Is the Capability Nonsubstitutable?	Competitive Consequences	Performance Implications
No	No	No	No	• Competitive disadvantage	• Below-average returns
Yes	No	No	Yes/no	• Competitive parity	• Average returns
Yes	Yes	No	Yes/no	• Temporary competitive advantage	• Average returns to above-average returns
Yes	Yes	Yes	Yes/no	• Sustainable competitive advantage	• Above-average returns

of firm resources) are strategically equivalent when they each can be separately exploited to implement the same strategies."[76] In general, the strategic value of capabilities increases as they become more difficult to substitute. The more intangible, and hence invisible, capabilities are, the more difficult it is for firms to find substitutes and the greater the challenge is to competitors trying to imitate a firm's value-creating strategy. Firm-specific knowledge and trust-based working relationships between managers and nonmanagerial personnel, such as has existed for years at Southwest Airlines, are examples of capabilities that are difficult to identify and for which finding a substitute is challenging. However, causal ambiguity may make it difficult for the firm to learn and may stifle progress because the firm may not know how to improve processes that are not easily codified and thus are ambiguous.[77]

In summary, only using valuable, rare, costly-to-imitate, and nonsubstitutable capabilities has the potential for the firm to create sustainable competitive advantages. Table 3.5 shows the competitive consequences and performance implications resulting from combinations of the four criteria of sustainability. The analysis suggested by the table helps managers determine the strategic value of a firm's capabilities. The firm should not emphasize capabilities that fit the criteria described in the first row in the table (i.e., resources and capabilities that are neither valuable nor rare and that are imitable and for which strategic substitutes exist). Capabilities yielding competitive parity and either temporary or sustainable competitive advantage, however, should be supported. Some competitors such as Coca-Cola and PepsiCo and Boeing and Airbus may have capabilities that result in competitive parity. In such cases, the firms will nurture these capabilities while simultaneously trying to develop capabilities that can yield either a temporary or sustainable competitive advantage.[78]

3-3b Value Chain Analysis

Value chain analysis allows the firm to understand the parts of its operations that create value and those that do not.[79] Understanding these issues is important because the firm earns above-average returns only when the value it creates is greater than the costs incurred to create that value.[80]

The value chain is a template that firms use to analyze their cost position and to identify the multiple means that can be used to facilitate implementation of a chosen strategy.[81] Today's competitive landscape demands that firms examine their value chains in a global rather than a domestic-only context.[82] In particular, activities associated with supply chains should be studied within a global context.[83]

Figure 3.3 A Model of the Value Chain

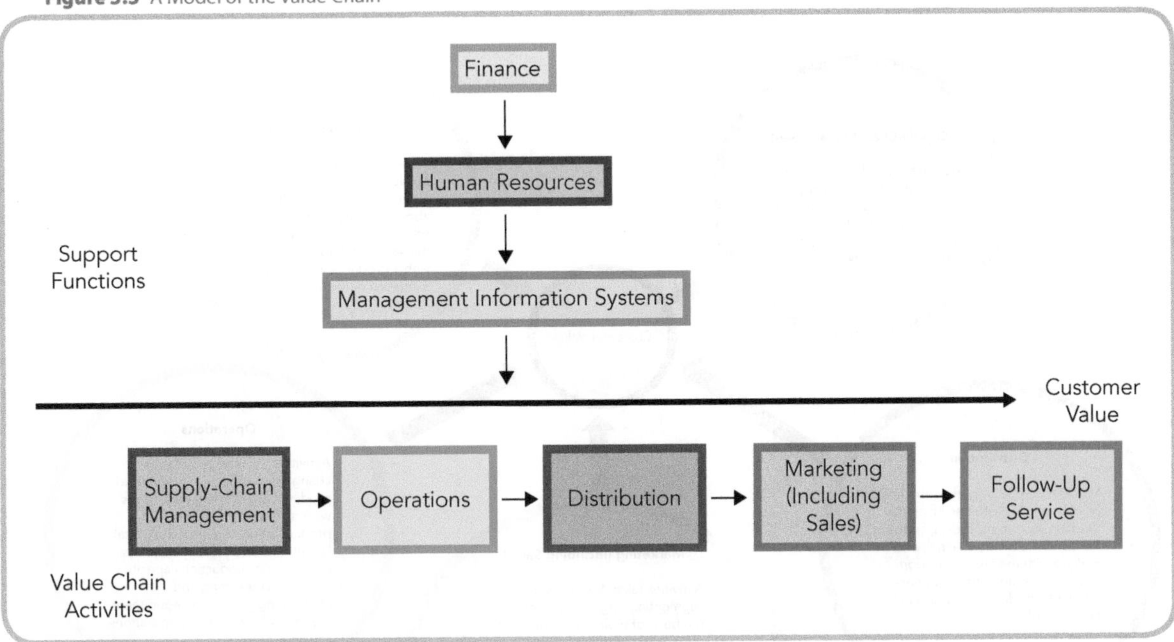

We show a model of the value chain in Figure 3.3. As depicted in the model, a firm's value chain is segmented into value chain activities and support functions. **Value chain activities** are activities or tasks the firm completes in order to produce products and then sell, distribute, and service those products in ways that create value for customers. **Support functions** include the activities or tasks the firm completes in order to support the work being done to produce, sell, distribute, and service the products the firm is producing. A firm can develop a capability and/or a core competence in any of the value chain activities and in any of the support functions. When it does so, it has established an ability to create value for customers. In fact, as shown in Figure 3.3, customers are the ones firms seek to serve when using value chain analysis to identify their capabilities and core competencies. When using their unique core competencies to create unique value for customers that competitors cannot duplicate, firms have established one or more competitive advantages.[84] Deutsche Bank believes that its application development and information security technologies are proprietary core competencies that are a source of competitive differentiation for the firm.[85] As explained in a Strategic Focus about outsourcing later in the chapter, Deutsche Bank will not outsource these two technologies given that the firm concentrates on them as a means of creating value for customers.

The activities associated with each part of the value chain are shown in Figure 3.4, while the activities that are part of the tasks firms complete when dealing with support functions appear in Figure 3.5. All items in both figures should be evaluated relative to competitors' capabilities and core competencies. To become a core competence and a source of competitive advantage, a capability must allow the firm to either:

1. Perform an activity in a manner that provides value superior to that provided by competitors, or
2. Perform a value-creating activity that competitors cannot perform.

Only under these conditions does a firm create value for customers and have opportunities to capture that value.

Value chain activities are activities or tasks the firm completes in order to produce products and then sell, distribute, and service those products in ways that create value for customers.

Support functions include the activities or tasks the firm completes in order to support the work being done to produce, sell, distribute, and service the products the firm is producing.

Figure 3.4 Creating Value through Value Chain Activities

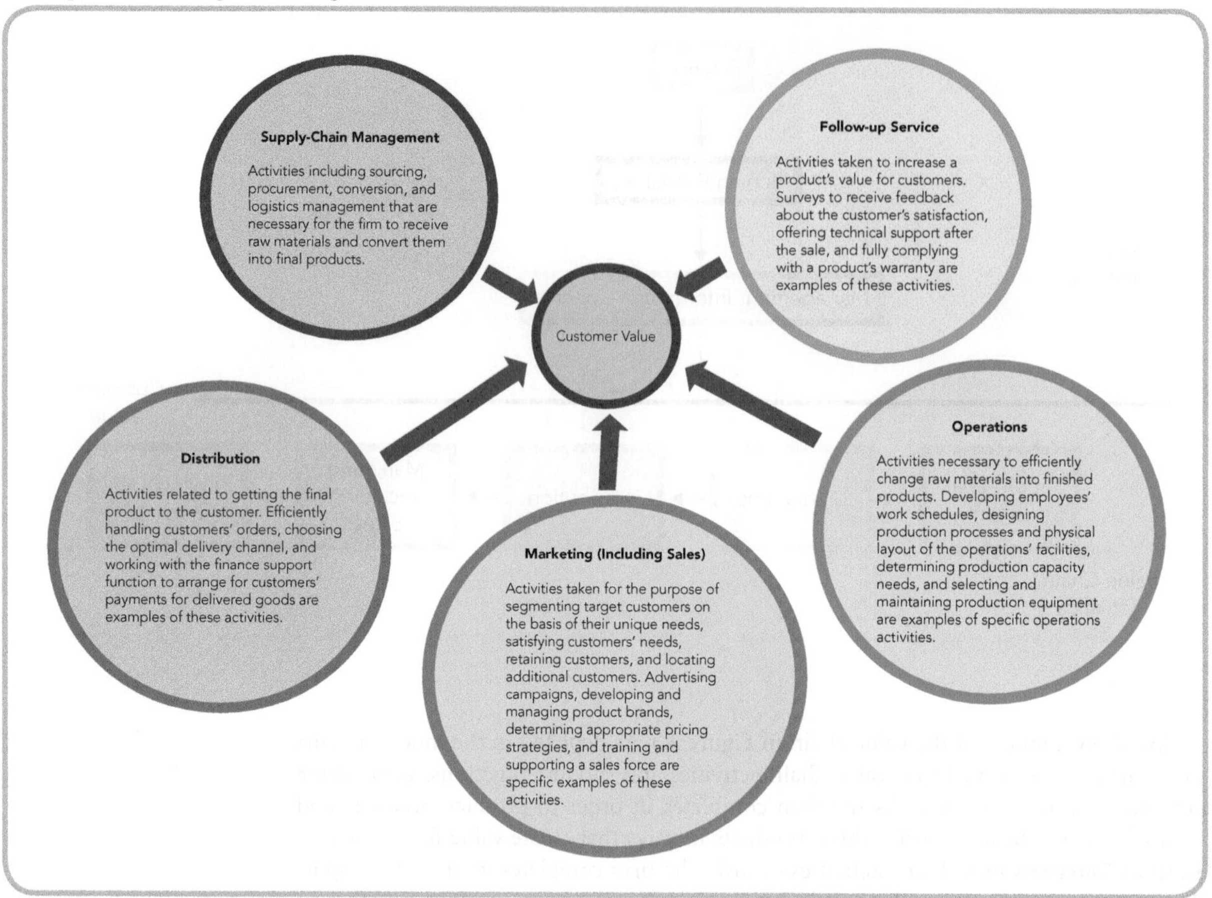

Creating value for customers by completing activities that are part of the value chain often requires building effective alliances with suppliers (and sometimes others to which the firm outsources activities, as discussed in the next section) and developing strong positive relationships with customers. When firms have strong positive relationships with suppliers and customers, they are said to have social capital.[86] The relationships themselves have value because they lead to transfers of knowledge as well as to access to resources that a firm may not hold internally.[87] To build social capital whereby resources such as knowledge are transferred across organizations requires trust between partners. Indeed, partners must trust each other to allow their resources to be used in such a way that both parties will benefit over time while neither party will take advantage of the other.[88]

Evaluating a firm's capability to execute its value chain activities and support functions is challenging. Earlier in the chapter, we noted that identifying and assessing the value of a firm's resources and capabilities requires judgment. Judgment is equally necessary when using value chain analysis, because no obviously correct model or rule is universally available to help in the process.

What should a firm do about value chain activities and support functions in which its resources and capabilities are not a source of core competence? Outsourcing is one solution to consider.

Figure 3.5 Creating Value through Support Functions

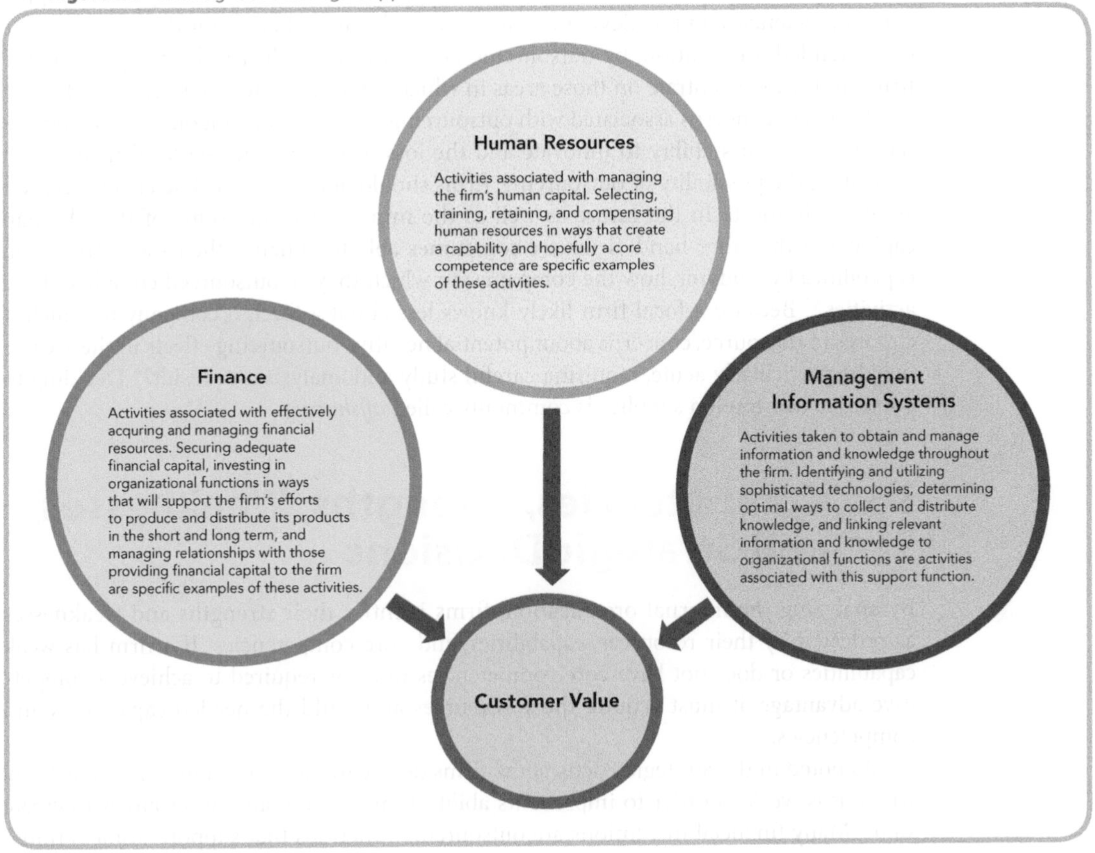

3-4 Outsourcing

Concerned with how components, finished goods, or services will be obtained, **outsourcing** is the purchase of a value-creating activity or a support function activity from an external supplier. Not-for-profit agencies as well as for-profit organizations actively engage in outsourcing.[89] Firms engaging in effective outsourcing increase their flexibility, mitigate risks, and reduce their capital investments.[90] Moreover, in some industries virtually all firms seek the value that can be captured through effective outsourcing. However, as is the case with other strategic management process decisions, careful analysis is required before the firm decides to outsource.[91] And if outsourcing is to be used, firms must recognize that only activities where they cannot create value or where they are at a substantial disadvantage compared to competitors should be outsourced.[92] Experience suggests that virtually any activity associated with the value chain functions or the support functions may fall into this category. We discuss different activities that some firms outsource in the Strategic Focus. We also consider core competencies that firms to whom others outsource activities may try to develop to satisfy customers' future outsourcing needs.

Outsourcing can be effective because few, if any, organizations possess the resources and capabilities required to achieve competitive superiority in each value chain activity and support function. For example, research suggests that few companies can afford to internally develop all the technologies that might lead to competitive advantage.[93] By

Outsourcing is the purchase of a value-creating activity or a support function activity from an external supplier.

nurturing a smaller number of capabilities, a firm increases the probability of developing core competencies and achieving a competitive advantage because it does not become overextended. In addition, by outsourcing activities in which it lacks competence, the firm can fully concentrate on those areas in which it has the potential to create value.

There are concerns associated with outsourcing.[94] Two significant ones are the potential loss in a firm's ability to innovate and the loss of jobs within the focal firm. When evaluating the possibility of outsourcing, firms should anticipate possible effects on their ability to innovate in the future as well as the impact of losing some of their human capital. On the other hand, firms are sometimes able to enhance their own innovation capabilities by studying how the companies to which they've outsourced complete those activities.[95] Because a focal firm likely knows less about a foreign company to which it chooses to outsource, concerns about potential negative outsourcing effects in these cases may be particularly acute, requiring careful study and analysis as a result.[96] Deciding to outsource to a foreign supplier is commonly called *offshoring*.

3-5 Competencies, Strengths, Weaknesses, and Strategic Decisions

By analyzing the internal organization, firms identify their strengths and weaknesses as reflected by their resources, capabilities, and core competencies. If a firm has weak capabilities or does not have core competencies in areas required to achieve a competitive advantage, it must acquire those resources and build the needed capabilities and competencies.

As noted in the Strategic Focus, some firms decide to outsource a function or activity where it is weak in order to improve its ability to use its remaining resources to create value. Many financial institutions are outsourcing functions that support cashless transaction because their IT systems cannot handle these activities efficiently. Some governments are outsourcing services to increase the quality and efficiency with which the services are delivered (e.g., U.K. outsourcing some surgeries to French healthcare providers). Outsourcing decisions must be made carefully, considering all of the options. However, when done effectively, outsourcing can provide access to needed resources.

In considering the results of examining the firm's internal organization, managers should understand that having a significant quantity of resources is not the same as having the "right" resources. The "right" resources are those with the potential to be formed into core competencies as the foundation for creating value for customers and developing competitive advantages because of doing so. Interestingly, decision makers sometimes become more focused and productive when seeking to find the right resources when the firm's total set of resources is constrained.[97]

Tools such as outsourcing help the firm focus on its core competencies as the source of its competitive advantages. However, evidence shows that the value-creating ability of core competencies should never be taken for granted. Moreover, the ability of a core competence to be a permanent competitive advantage can't be assumed. The reason for these cautions is that all core competencies have the potential to become *core rigidities*.[98] Typically, events occurring in the firm's external environment create conditions through which core competencies can become core rigidities, generate inertia, and stifle innovation.[99]

After studying its external environment to determine what it *might choose to do* (as explained in Chapter 2) and its internal organization to understand what it *can do* (as explained in this chapter), the firm has the information required to select a business-level strategy that it will use to compete against rivals. We describe different business-level strategies in the next chapter.

Strategic **Focus**

The Extreme Specialization of Outsourcing: Who Is Doing It and Who Is Not?

Outsourcing activities and functions has been growing dramatically over the last decade. With the election of Donald Trump, companies in some industries—particularly manufacturing—have reduced their outsourcing outside of the United States for fear of government actions against them. However, outsourcing remains strong in other sectors of the economy.

As we discussed in the Opening Case, big pharma companies are using some of their resources and capabilities to develop "big data analytics" as a core competence because of the value of these analytics to these firms. In contrast, these same firms are outsourcing drug safety processes and procedures to other firms, many of which are located in India or have offices located there. In fact, monitoring drug safety is "one of outsourcing's newest frontiers, and the now $2 billion business is booming as regulators require closer tracking of rare side effects and interactions between medicines." Accenture, Cognizant, and Tata Consultancy Services Ltd. are some of the firms to which big pharma companies AstraZeneca PLC, Novartis AG, and Bristol-Myers Squibb Co. are outsourcing the monitoring of drug safety. Thus, the big pharma firms have decided that data analytics processes are an activity in which they can capture value while monitoring drug safety is not.

Similar examples exist within firms competing in other industries. Deutsche Bank has outsourced some data center services to Hewlett-Packard; however, it is retaining control over certain technology application areas it believes are proprietary and, as such, are core competencies through which the firm creates value. In fact, outsourcing information technology activities has been growing in banking and the financial sector. This is due to the rapid move to cashless transaction and mobile banking. Many of the banks have "legacy" information technology systems that are difficult to change over to handle these new functions. As such, they are outsourcing many activities such as commercial credit card payments to what is referred to as fintech firms. The number of these specialized fintech firms is growing dramatically because of the increasing amount of cashless transactions and the need for help by banks and other financial institutions such as credit unions.

Interestingly, government has become a major outsourcer. Governments are trying to outsource the provision of services from government agencies to private and non-profit organizations who can perform the services more efficiently and with higher quality. In fact, even the British Health Service is outsourcing some health services (e.g., surgeries) to healthcare organizations in other European countries (e.g., France), trying to manage its own backlog of requests for healthcare services.

Wipro and Infosys have historically been successful as firms to whom others outsource activities. However, this success has been largely a product of being able to employ relatively inexpensive programmers to complete tasks lacking significant amounts of complexity. The technology service needs have become more sophisticated and challenging. And, with the reductions of outsourcing in some sectors, some of these firms are struggling. For example, Infosys and Cognizant have laid off many employees in India and Infosys is trying to establish operations in the United States.

Stuart Forster/Alamy Stock Photo

These individuals are working in a firm to which other companies have outsourced certain activities for completion.

Therefore, the nature of outsourcing is changing and firms are becoming more specialized. Additionally, some industries are outsourcing less (e.g., manufacturing) and others are outsourcing more (financial institutions). Nevertheless, outsourcing remains a critical means for firms to gain access to valuable resources that they need to seize and maintain a competitive advantage.

Sources: R. Koczkar, 2018, Governmental outsourcing a boon for service providers, *The Australian*, www.australian.com, March 22; K. Ferguson, 2018, Why outsourcing can leave a lasting mark on the US banking industry, *Payments Journal*, paymentsjournal.com, March 23; A. Frazzetto, 2018, Outsourcing in the new normal: Three trends reshaping the global industry, *Forbes*, www.forbes.com, March 21; K. de Freytas-Tamura, 2018, U.K., Land of 'brexit', quietly outsources some surgeries to France, *New York Times*, www.nytimes.com, March 17; A. Jain, 2018, This global fintech enabler has a strategy to enter India's crowded payment space, *Entrepreneur*, www.entrepreneur.com, March 9; L. Joyce, 2018, Six Strategic keys to becoming a mobile-centric bank, *The Financial Brand*, thefinancialbrand.com, March 6; 2015, Deutsche Bank, H-P divide IT responsibility in cloud deal, *Wall Street Journal Online*, www.wsj.com, February 25; D. A. Thoppil, 2015, Indian outsourcers struggle to evolve as growth slows, *Wall Street Journal Online*, www.wsj.com, February 22; S McLain, 2015, Big Pharma farms out drug safety to India, *Wall Street Journal Online*, www.wsj.com, February 2; S. McLain, 2015, New outsourcing frontier in India: Monitoring drug safety, *Wall Street Journal Online*, www.wsj.com, February 1.

SUMMARY

- In the current competitive landscape, the most effective organizations recognize that strategic competitiveness and above-average returns result only when core competencies (identified by studying the firm's internal organization) are matched with opportunities (determined by studying the firm's external environment).
- No competitive advantage lasts forever. Over time, rivals use their own unique resources, capabilities, and core competencies to form different value-creating propositions that duplicate the focal firm's ability to create value for customers. Because competitive advantages are not permanently sustainable, firms must exploit their current advantages while simultaneously using their resources and capabilities to form new advantages that can lead to future competitive success.
- Effectively managing core competencies requires careful analysis of the firm's resources (inputs to the production process) and capabilities (resources that have been purposely integrated to achieve a specific task or set of tasks). The knowledge the firm's human capital possesses is among the most significant of an organization's capabilities and ultimately provides the base for most competitive advantages. The firm must create an organizational culture that allows people to integrate their individual knowledge with that held by others so that, collectively, the firm has a significant amount of value-creating organizational knowledge.
- Capabilities are a more likely source of core competence and subsequently of competitive advantages than are individual resources. How a firm nurtures and supports its capabilities to become core competencies is less visible to rivals, making efforts to understand and imitate the focal firm's capabilities difficult.
- Only when a capability is valuable, rare, costly to imitate, and nonsubstitutable is it a core competence and a source of competitive advantage. Over time, core competencies must be supported, but they cannot be allowed to become core rigidities. Core competencies are a source of competitive advantage only when they allow the firm to create value by exploiting opportunities in its external environment. When this is no longer possible, the company shifts its attention to forming other capabilities that satisfy the four criteria of sustainable competitive advantage.
- Value chain analysis is used to identify and evaluate the competitive potential of resources and capabilities. By studying their skills relative to those associated with value chain activities and support functions, firms can understand their cost structure and identify the activities through which they are able to create value.
- When the firm cannot create value in either a value chain activity or a support function, outsourcing is considered. Used commonly in the global economy, outsourcing is the purchase of a value-creating activity from an external supplier. The firm should outsource only to companies possessing a competitive advantage in terms of the particular value chain activity or support function under consideration. In addition, the firm must continuously verify that it is not outsourcing activities through which it could create value.

KEY TERMS

REVIEW QUESTIONS

1. Why is it important for a firm to study and understand its internal organization?
2. What is value? Why is it critical for the firm to create value? How does it do so?
3. What are the differences between tangible and intangible resources? Why is it important for decision makers to understand these differences? Are tangible resources more valuable for creating capabilities than are intangible resources, or is the reverse true? Why?
4. What are capabilities? How do firms create capabilities?
5. What four criteria must capabilities satisfy for them to become core competencies? Why is it important for firms to

use these criteria to evaluate their capabilities' value-creating potential?

6. What is value chain analysis? What does the firm gain by successfully using this tool?

7. What is outsourcing? Why do firms outsource?

8. How do firms identify internal strengths and weaknesses? Why is it vital that managers have a clear understanding of their firm's strengths and weaknesses?

9. What are core rigidities? What does it mean to say that each core competence could become a core rigidity?

Mini-Case

Is Strengthening the Superdry Brand a Foundation to Strategic Success?

British-based SuperGroup, owner of Superdry and its carefully banded product lines, is taking actions to deal with recent performance problems. These problems manifested themselves in various ways, including the need for the firm to issue three profit warnings in one six-month period and a 34 percent decline in the price of its stock in 2014 compared to 2013.

Founded in 1985, the firm is recognized as a distinctive, branded fashion retailer selling quality clothing and accessories. In fact, the firm says that "the Superdry brand is at the heart of the business." The brand is targeted to discerning customers who seek to purchase "stylish clothing that is uniquely designed and well made." In this sense, the company believes that its men's and women's products have "wide appeal, capturing elements of 'urban' and 'streetwear' designs with subtle combinations of vintage Americana, Japanese imagery, and British tailoring, all with strong attention to detail." Thus, the firm's brand is critical to the image it conveys with its historical target customer—teens and those in their early twenties. Those leading SuperGroup believe that customers love the Superdry products as well as the "theatre and personality" of the stores in which they are sold. These outcomes are important given the company's intention of providing customers with "personalized shopping experiences that enhance the brand rather than just selling clothes."

As noted above, problems have affected the firm's performance. What the firm wants to do, of course, is correct the problems before the Superdry brand is damaged. Management turmoil is one of the firm's problems. In January of 2015, the CEO abruptly left. Almost simultaneously, the CFO was suspended for filing for personal bankruptcy, and the Chief Operating Officer left to explore other options. Some analysts believe that the firm's growth had been ill-conceived, signaling the possibility of ineffective strategic decisions on the part of the firm's upper-level leaders. As one analyst said: "The issue with SuperGroup is that they've expanded too quickly, without the supporting infrastructure."

Efforts are now underway to address these problems. In particular, those now leading SuperGroup intend to better control the firm as a means of protecting the value of its brand. A new CEO has been appointed who believes that "the business is very much more in control" today than has been the case recently. A well-regarded interim CFO has been appointed, and the firm's board has been strengthened by added experienced individuals. Commenting about these changes, an observer said that SuperGroup has "moved from an owner-entrepreneurial style of management to a more professional and experienced type of management. The key thing is, it is much better now than it was."

Direct actions are also being taken to enhance the Superdry brand. The appointment of Idris Elba, actor from *The Wire*, is seen as a major attempt to reignite the brand's image. In fact, SuperGroup says that Elba epitomizes what the Superdry brand is—British, grounded, and cool. The thinking here, too, is that Elba, who at the time of his selection was 42, would appeal to the customer who was "growing up" with the Superdry brand. For these customers, who are 25 and older, SuperGroup is developing Superdry products with less dramatic presentations of the brand's well-known large logos. Additional lines of clothing, for skiing and rugby for example, are being developed for the more mature Superdry customer. After correcting the recently encountered problems, SuperGroup intends to expand into additional markets, including China. In every instance though, the firm will protect the brand when entering new competitive arenas and will rely on it as the foundation for intended success.

Sources: About SuperGroup, 2015, SuperGroupPLC.com, www.supergroup.co.uk, April 5; S. Chaudhuri, 2015, Superdry brand works to iron out problems, *Wall Street Journal Online*, www.wsj.com, April 15; S. Chaudhuri, 2015, Superdry looks to U.S. to drive growth, *Wall Street Journal Online*, www.wsj.com, March 26; H. Mann, 2015, SuperGroup strategy oozes Hollywood glamour, *Interactive Investor*, www.iii.co.uk, March 26; A. Monaghan & S. Butler, 2015, Superdry signs up Idris Elba, *The Guardian Online*, www.theguardian.com, March 26; A. Petroff, 2015, Is this the worst CFO ever? *CNNMoney*, www.money.cnn.com, February 25.

Case Discussion Questions

1. What influences from the external environment over the next several years do you think might affect SuperDry's ability to compete?
2. Does Superdry have one or more capabilities that are valuable, rare, costly to imitate, and nonsubstitutable? If so, what are they? If not, on which criteria do they fall short?
3. Will the actions that Superdry is taking solve its problems? Why or why not?
4. What value does Superdry create for its customers?
5. What actions would you recommend the management of Superdry take to resolve its problems and turn around the performance of the firm?

NOTES

1. A. Gambardella, C. Panico, & G. Valentini, 2015, Strategic incentives to human capital, *Strategic Management Journal*, 36: 37–52; C. Gilbert, M. Eyring, & R. N. Foster, 2012, Two routes to resilience. *Harvard Business Review*, 90(12): 65–73; H. A. Ndofor, D. G. Sirmon, & X. He, 2011, Firm resources, competitive actions and performance: Investigating a mediated model with evidence from the in-vitro diagnostics industry, *Strategic Management Journal*, 32: 640–657.
2. M. E. Porter & M. R. Kramer, 2018, Creating shared value. In G. Lenssen & N. Smith (Eds.), *Managing Sustainable Business*, Dordrecht, Netherlands: Springer; Khanna, I. Guler, & A. Nerkar, 2016, Fail often, fail big, and fail fast: Learning from small failures and R&D performance in the pharmaceutical industry, *Academy of Management Journal*, 59: 436–459; C. Engel & M. Kleine, 2015, Who is afraid of pirates? An experiment on the deterrence of innovation by imitation, *Research Policy*, 44: 20–33; K. Wilson & Y. L. Doz, 2012, 10 rules for managing global innovation, *Harvard Business Review*, 90(10): 84–90.
3. 2018, Onboard Singapore Airlines' Boeing 787–10 'dreamliner' delivery flight, *USA Today*, www.usatoday.com, March 26; J. Ostrower, 2015, At Boeing, innovation means small steps, not giant leaps, *Wall Street Journal Online*, www.wsj.com, April 2.
4. C. Helfat & R. S. Raubitschek, 2018, Dynamic and integrative capabilities for profiting from innovation in digital platform-based ecosystems, *Research Policy*, in press; M. S. Qureshi, N. Aziz & S. A. Mian, 2017, How marketing capabilities shape entrepreneurial firm's performance? Evidence from new technology based firms in Turkey, *Journal of Global Entrepreneurship Research*, in press; D. G. Sirmon, M. A. Hitt, & R. D. Ireland, 2007, Managing firm resources in dynamic markets to create value: Looking inside the black box, *Academy of Management Review*, 32: 273–292.
5. M.-J. Chen & D. Miller, 2015, Reconceptualizing competitive dynamics: A multidimensional framework, *Strategic Management Journal*, 36: 758–775; F. Polidoro, Jr. & P. K. Toh, 2011, Letting rivals come close or warding them off? The effects of substitution threat on imitation deterrence, *Academy of Management Journal*, 54: 369–392; A. W. King, 2007, Disentangling interfirm and intrafirm causal ambiguity: A conceptual model of causal ambiguity and sustainable competitive advantage, *Academy of Management Review*, 32: 156–178.
6. I. Le Breton-Miller & D. Miller, 2015, The paradox of resource vulnerability: Considerations for organizational curatorship, *Strategic Management Journal*, 36: 397–415; M. Semadeni & B. S. Anderson, 2010, The follower's dilemma: Innovation and imitation in the professional services industry, *Academy of Management Journal*, 53: 1175–1193.
7. U. Stettner & D. Lavie, 2014, Ambidexterity under scrutiny: Exploration and exploitation via internal organization, alliances, and acquisitions, *Strategic Management Journal*, 35: 1903–1929; M. G. Jacobides, S. G. Winter, & S. M. Kassberger, 2012, The dynamics of wealth, profit, and sustainable advantage, *Strategic Management Journal*, 33: 1384–1410.
8. J. Ferreira & C. Fernandes, 2017, Resources and capabilities' effects on firm performance: What are they? *Journal of Knowledge Management*, 21: 1202–1217; M. A. Peteraf & J. B. Barney, 2003, Unraveling the resource-based tangle, *Managerial and Decision Economics*, 24: 309–323; J. B. Barney, 2001, Is the resource-based "view" a useful perspective for strategic management research? Yes, *Academy of Management Review*, 26: 41–56.
9. R. Roy & M. B. Sarkar, 2016, Knowledge, firm boundaries, and innovation: Mitigating the incumbent's curse during radical technological change, *Strategic Management Journal*, 37: 835–854; G. Zied & J. McGuire, 2011, Multimarket competition, mobility barriers, and firm performance, *Journal of Management Studies*, 48: 857–890.
10. D. Piaskowska & G. Trojanowski, 2014, Twice as smart: The importance of managers' formative-years' international experience for their international orientation and foreign acquisition decisions, *British Journal of Management*, 25: 40–57; M. Javidan, R. M. Steers, & M. A. Hitt (eds.), 2007, *The Global Mindset*: Amsterdam: Elsevier Ltd.
11. M. Andresen & F. Bergdolt, 2017, A systematic literature review on the definitions of

global mindset and cultural intelligence—merging two different research streams, *The International Journal of Human Resource management*, 28: 170–195; H. Liang, B. Ren, & S. Li Sun, 2015, An anatomy of state control in the globalization of state-owned enterprises, *Journal of International Business Studies*, 46: 223–240.

12. S. J. Miles & M. van Cleaf, 2017, Strategic fit: Key to growing enterprise value through organizational capital, Business Horizons, 60: 55–65; R. A. D'Aveni, G. B. Dagnino, & K. G. Smith, 2010, The age of temporary advantage, *Strategic Management Journal*, 31: 1371–1385; E. Danneels, 2008, Organizational antecedents of second-order competences, *Strategic Management Journal*, 29: 519–543.
13. R. Vandaie & A. Zaheer, 2015, Alliance partners and firm capability: Evidence from the motion picture industry, *Organization Science*, 26: 22–36; S. A. Zahra & S. Nambisan, 2012, Entrepreneurship and strategic thinking in business ecosystems, *Business Horizons*, 55: 219–229.
14. A. Waeraas & H. L. Sataoen, 2015, Being all things to all customers: Building reputation in an institutionalized field, *British Journal of Management*, 26: 310–326; D. G. Sirmon, M. A. Hitt, R. D. Ireland, & B. A. Gilbert, 2011, Resource orchestration to create competitive advantage: Breadth, depth, and life cycle effects, *Journal of Management*, 37: 1390–1412; R. Adner & R. Kapoor, 2010, Value creation in innovation ecosystems: How the structure of technological interdependence affects firm performance in new technology generations, *Strategic Management Journal*, 31: 306–333.
15. C. Grimpe & K. Hussinger, 2014, Resource complementarity and value capture in firm acquisitions: The role of intellectual property rights, *Strategic Management Journal*, 35: 1762–1780; M. A. Hitt, R. D. Ireland, D. G. Sirmon, & C. A. Trahms, 2011, Strategic entrepreneurship: Creating value for individuals, organizations, and society, *Academy of Management Perspectives*, 25: 57–75; D. G. Sirmon, S. Gove, & M. A. Hitt, 2008, Resource management in dyadic competitive rivalry: The effects of resource bundling and deployment, *Academy of Management Journal*, 51: 919–935.
16. B. Clarysse, M. Wright, J. Bruneel, & A. Mahajan, 2014, Creating value in ecosystems: Crossing the chasm between knowledge and business ecosystems, *Research Policy*, 43: 1164–1176; J. S. Harrison, D. A. Bosse, & R. A. Phillips, 2010, Managing for stakeholders, stakeholder utility functions, and competitive advantage, *Strategic Management Journal*, 31: 58–74; J. L. Morrow, Jr., D. G. Sirmon, M. A. Hitt, & T. R. Holcomb, 2007, Creating value in the face of declining performance: Firm strategies and organizational recovery, *Strategic Management Journal*, 28: 271–283.
17. R. L. Priem, M. Wenzel, & J. Koch, 2018, Demand-side strategy and business models: Putting value creation for consumers center stage, *Long Range Planning*, 51: 22–31; V. Rindova, W. J. Ferrier, & R. Wiltbank, 2010, Value from gestalt: How sequences of competitive actions create advantage for firms in nascent markets, *Strategic Management Journal*, 31: 1474–1497.
18. C. Tantalo & R. L. Priem, 2016, Value creation through stakeholder synergy, *Strategic Management Journal*, 37: 314–329; E. R. Brenes, D. Montoya, & L. Ciravegna, 2014, Differentiation strategies in emerging markets: The case of Latin American agribusinesses, *Journal of Business Research*, 67: 847–855; D. G. Sirmon, M. A. Hitt, J.-L. Arregle, & J. T. Campbell, 2010, The dynamic interplay of capability strengths and weaknesses: Investigating the bases of temporary competitive advantage, *Strategic Management Journal*, 31: 1386–1409.
19. S. Nadkarni & J. Chen, 2014, Bridging yesterday, today, and tomorrow: CEO temporal focus, environmental dynamism, and rate of new product introduction, *Academy of Management Journal*, 57: 1810–1833; S. Nadkarni, T. Chen, & J. Chen, 2016, The clock is ticking: Executive temporal depth, industry velocity, and competitive aggressiveness, *Strategic Management Journal*, 37: 1132–1153; F. Aime, S. Johnson, J. W. Ridge, & A. D. Hill, 2010, The routine may be stable but the advantage is not: Competitive implications of key employee mobility, *Strategic Management Journal*, 31: 75–87.
20. M. Arrfelt, R. M. Wiseman, G. McNamara, & G. T. M. Hult, 2015, Examining a key corporate role: The influence of capital allocation competency on business unit performance, *Strategic Management Journal*, 36: 1017–1034; D. Li & J. Liu, 2014, Dynamic capabilities, environmental dynamism, and competitive advantage: Evidence from China, *Journal of Business Research*, 67: 2793–2799; D. J. Teece, 2012, Dynamic capabilities: Routines versus entrepreneurial action, *Journal of Management Studies*, 49: 1395–1401.
21. A. R. Menon & D. A. Yao, 2017, Elevating Repiositioning costs: Strategy dynamics and competitive interactions, *Strategic management Journal*, 38: 1953–1963; A. M. Kleinbaum & T. E. Stuart, 2015, Network responsiveness: The social structural microfoundations of dynamic capabilities, *Academy of Management Perspectives*, 28: 353–367; M. H. Kunc & J. D. W. Morecroft, 2010, Managerial decision making and firm performance under a resource–based paradigm, *Strategic Management Journal*, 31: 1164–1182.
22. C. M. Christensen, 2001, The past and future of competitive advantage, *Sloan Management Review*, 42(2): 105–109.
23. C. Giachem & S. Torrisi, 2018, Following or running away from the market leader? The influences of environmental uncertainty and market leadership *European Management Review*, in press; J. Gomez, R. Orcos, & S. Palomas, 2016, Competitors' strategic heterogeneity and firm performance, *Long Range Planning*, 49: 145–163.
24. M. G. Butler & C. M. Callahan, 2014, Human resource outsourcing: Market and operating performance effects of administrative HR functions, *Journal of Business Research*, 67: 218–224; Y. Y. Kor & A. Mesko, 2013, Dynamic managerial capabilities: Configuration and orchestration of top executives' capabilities and the firm's dominant logic, *Strategic Management Journal*, 34: 233–244; D. P. Forbes, 2007, Reconsidering the strategic implications of decision comprehensiveness, *Academy of Management Review*, 32: 361–376.
25. T. M. Jones, J. S. Harrison, & W. Felps, 2018, How applying instrumental stakeholder theory can provide sustainable competitive advantage, *Academy of Management Review*, in press; Maitland & A. Sammartino, 2015, Decision making and uncertainty: The role of heuristics and experience in assessing a politically hazardous environment, *Strategic Management Journal*, 36: 1554–1578; T. M. Jones, W. Felps, & G. A. Bigley, 2007, Ethical theory and stakeholder-related decisions: The role of stakeholder culture, *Academy of Management Review*, 32: 137–155.
26. P. Chatzoglou, D. Chatzoudes, L. Savigiannidis, & G. Theriou, 2018, The role of firm-specific factors in the strategy-performance relationship: Revisiting the resource-based view of the firm and the VRIO framework, *Management Research Review*, 41: 46–73.
27. F. R. Cahen, M de Miranda Oliveira, & F. M. Brini, 2017, The internationalization of new technology-based firms from emerging markets, *International Journal of Technology Management*, 74: 23–44; W. Tong, J. J. Reuer, B. B. Tyler, & S. Zhang, 2015, Host country executives' assessments of international joint ventures and divestitures: An experimental approach, *Strategic Management Journal*, 36: 254–275; C. B. Bingham & K. M. Eisenhardt, 2011, Rational heuristics: The 'simple rules' that strategists learn from process experience, *Strategic Management Journal*, 32: 1437–1464.
28. M. Hughes-Morgan & W. J. Ferrier, 2017, 'Short interest pressure' and competitive behaviour, *British Journal of Management*, 28: 120–134; R. Mudambi & T. Swift, 2014, Knowing when to leap: Transitioning between exploitative and explorative R&D, *Strategic Management Journal*, 35: 126–145; Y. Zhang & J. Gimeno, 2010, Earnings pressure and competitive behavior: Evidence from the U.S. electricity industry, *Academy of Management Journal*, 53: 743–768.

29. E. Vidal & W. Mitchell, 2018, Virtuous or vicious cycles? The role of divestitures as a complementary Penrose effect within resource-based theory, *Strategic Management Journal*, 38: 131–154; P. Madsen & V. Desai, 2010, Failing to learn? The effects of failure and success on organizational learning in the global orbital launch vehicle industry, *Academy of Management Journal*, 53: 451–476; P. C. Nutt, 2002, *Why Decisions Fail*, San Francisco, Barrett-Koehler Publishers.
30. M. R. Habibi, A Davidson, & M. Laroche, 2017, What managers should know about the sharing economy, *Business Horizons*, 60: 113–121; D. Maslach, 2016, Change and persistence with failed technological innovation, *Strategic Management Journal*, 37: 714–723; A. O. Laplume & P. Dass, 2015, Outstreaming for ambidexterity: Evolving a firm's core business from components to systems by serving internal and external customers, *Long Range Planning*, 48: 135–150.
31. S. Singh, P. D. Corner, & K. Pavlovich, 2015, Failed, not finished: A narrative approach to understanding venture failure stigmatization, *Journal of Business Venturing*, 30: 150–166; S. Mousavi & G. Gigerenzer, 2014, Risk, uncertainty, and heuristics, *Journal of Business Research*, 67: 1671–1678; J. D. Ford & L. W. Ford, 2010, Stop blaming resistance to change and start using it, *Organizational Dynamics*, 39: 24–36.
32. V. Desai, 2015, Learning through the distribution of failures within an organization: Evidence from heart bypass surgery performance, *Academy of Management Journal*, 58: 1032–1050; J. P. Eggers & L. Song, 2015, Dealing with failure: Serial entrepreneurs and the costs of changing industries between ventures, *Academy of Management Journal*, 58: 1785–1803; K. Muehlfeld, P. Rao Sahib, & A. Van Witteloostuijn, 2012, A contextual theory of organizational learning from failures and successes: A study of acquisition completion in the global newspaper industry, 1981–2008, *Strategic Management Journal*, 33: 938–964.
33. News Corp, 2018, News Corp completes sale of Amplify Digital Education businesses, newscorp.com, Accessed April 14; L. Colby, 2015, News Corp.'s $1 billion plan to overhaul education is riddled with failures, *Bloomberg Online*, www.bloomberg.com, April 7.
34. R. Aguilera, W. Judge, & S. Terjesen, 2018, Corporate governance deviance, *Academy of Management Review*, 43: 87–109; V. Bamiatzi, K. Bozos, S. T. Cavusgil, & G. T. M. Hult, 2016, Revisiting the firm, industry, and country effects on profitability under recessionary and expansion periods: A multilevel analysis, *Strategic Management Journal*, 37: 1448–1471.
35. H. Chen, S. Zeng, H. Lin, & H. Ma, 2017, Munificence, dynamism and complexity: How industry context drives corporate sustainability, *Business Strategy and the Environment*, 26: 125–141; S. R. Hiatt & W. D. Sine, 2014, Clear and present danger: Planning and new venture survival amid political and civil violence, *Strategic Management Journal*, 35: 773–785; A. Arora & A. Nandkumar, 2012, Insecure advantage? Markets for technology and the value of resources for entrepreneurial ventures, *Strategic Management Journal*, 33: 231–251.
36. P. C. Patel, M. J. Guedes, N. Soares, & V. C. Goncalves, 2018, Strength of the association between R&D volatility and firm growth: The roles of corporate governance and tangible asset volatility, *Journal of Business Research*, in press; J.Winkler, C. P. Jian-Wej Kuklinski, & R. Moser, 2015, Decision making in emerging markets: The Delphi approach's contribution to coping with uncertainty and equivocality, *Journal of Business Research*, 68: 1118–1126; O. H. Azar, 2014, The default heuristic in strategic decision making: When is it optimal to choose the default without investing in information search? *Journal of Business Research*, 67: 1744–1748.
37. M. A. Hitt & K. T. Haynes, 2018, CEO overpayment and underpayment: Executives, governance and institutions, *Management Research*, in press; M. Cain, D. A. Moore, & U. Haran, 2015, Making sense of overconfidence in market entry, *Strategic Management Journal*, 36: 1–18; M. Gary, R. E. Wood, & T. Pillinger, 2012, Enhancing mental models, analogical transfer, and performance in strategic decision making, *Strategic Management Journal*, 33: 1229–1246.
38. A. D. Martinez, Z. A. Russell, L. P. Maher, S. A. Brandon-Lai, & G. R. Ferris, 2017, The socio-political implications of firm reputation: Firm financial reputation X social reputation interaction on firm financial performance, *Journal of Leadership & Organizational Studies*, 24: 55–64; D. Laureiro-Martinez, 2014, Cognitive control capabilities, routinization propensity, and decision-making performance, *Organization Science*, 25: 1111–1133; P. D. Windschitl, A. M. Scherer, A. R. Smith, & J. P. Rose, 2013, Why so confident? The influence of outcome desirability on selective exposure and likelihood judgment, *Organizational Behavior & Human Decision Processes*, 120: 73–86.
39. N. D. Tho, 2018, Firm capabilities and performance: a necessary condition analysis, *Journal of Management Development*, in press; D. Albert, M. Kreutzer, & C. Lechner, 2015, Resolving the paradox of interdependency and strategic renewal in activity systems, *Academy of Management Review*, 40: 210–234; L. Alexander & D. van Knippenberg, 2014, Teams in pursuit of radical innovation: A goal orientation perspective, *Academy of Management Review*, 39: 423–438.
40. C. A. Maritan & G. K. Lee, 2017, Bringing a resource and capability lens to resource allocation, *Journal of Management*, 43: 2609–2619; Lipparini, G. Lorenzoni, & S. Ferriani, 2014, From core to periphery and back: A study on the deliberate shaping of knowledge flows in interfirm dyads and networks, *Strategic Management Journal*, 35: 578–595.
41. L. Radulovich, R. G. Javalgi, & R. F. Scherer, 2018, Intangible resources influencing the international performance of professional service SMEs in an emerging market: Evidence from India, *International Marketing Review*, 35: 113–135; S. Raithel & M. Schwaiger, 2015, The effects of corporate reputation perceptions of the general public on shareholder value, *Strategic Management Journal*: 36: 945–956; B. S. Anderson & Y. Eshima, 2013, The influence of firm age and intangible resources on the relationship between entrepreneurial orientation and firm growth among Japanese SMEs, *Journal of Business Venturing*, 28: 413–429.
42. B.Wright, 2017, SuperGroup to rebrand as Superdry, *Just-Style*, www.juststyle.com, September 27: M. Khan, 2017, SuperGroup to launch Superdry sports stores, *FastFT*, www.ft.com, July 3.
43. D. A. Levinthal, 2017. Resource allocation and firm boundaries, *Journal of Management*, 43: 2580–2587; A. Vomberg, C. Homburg, & T. Bornemann, 2015, Talented people and strong brands: The contribution of human capital and brand equity to firm value, *Strategic Management Journal*, 36: 2122–2131.
44. A. M. Webber, 2000, New math for a new economy, *Fast Company*, January/
45. Z. Karazijiene & A. Jurgelevicuis, 2017, The impact of intangible resources on economy in the EU, *Public Policy and Administration Research Journal*, 16: 279–295; R. Sydler, S. Haefliger, & R. Pruksa, 2014, Measuring intellectual capital with financial figures: Can we predict firm profitability? *European Management Journal*, 32: 244–259; F. Neffke & M. Henning, 2013, Skill relatedness and firm diversification, *Strategic Management Journal*, 34: 297–316.
46. A. A. Haji & N. A. M. Ghazali, 2018, The role of intangible assets and liabilities in firm performance: Empirical evidence, *Journal of Applied Accounting Research*, 19: 42–59; F. Honore, F. Munari, & B. van Pottelsberghe de La Potterie, 2015, corporate governance practices and companies' R&D intensity: Evidence from European countries, *Research Policy*, 44: 533–543; J. Gómez & P. Vargas, 2012, Intangible resources and technology adoption in manufacturing firms, *Research Policy*, 41: 1607–1619.
47. B. Cuozzo, J. Dumay, M. Palmaccio, & R, Lombardi, 2017, Intellectual capital disclosure: A structured literature review, *Journal of Intellectual Capital*, 18: 9–28; J.-Y. Lee, D. G. Bachrach, & D. M. Rousseau, 2015,

Internal labor markets, firm-specif ic human capital, and heterogeneity antecedents of employee idiosyncratic deal requests, *Organization Science*, 26: 794–810.

48. B. Y. Obeidal, A. Tarhini, R. Masa'deh, & N. O. Aqqad, 2017, The impact of intellectual capital on innovation via mediating role of knowledge management: A structural equations approach, *International Journal of Knowledge Management Studies*, 8: 273–295; J. Raffiee & R. Coff, 2016, Micro-foundations of firm-specific human capital: When do employees perceive their skills to be firm-specific? *Academy of Management Journal*, 59: 766–790.
49. A. Jain & R.-A. Thietart, 2014, Capabilities as shift parameters for the outsourcing decision, *Strategic Management Journal*, 35: 1881–1890; R. E. Ployhart, C. H. Van Iddekinge, & W. I. MacKenzie, Jr., 2011, Acquiring and developing human capital in service contexts: The interconnectedness of human capital resources, *Academy of Management Journal*, 54: 353–368.
50. D. Ravasi, J. Cornelissen, V. Rindova, & M. Etter, 2018, The formation of organizational reputation, *Academy of Management Annals*, in press; N. Tracey & E. French, 2017, Influence your firm;s resilience through its reputation: Results won't happen overnight but they will happen, *Corporate Reputation Review*, 20: 57–75; S. Raithel & M. Schwaiger, 2015, The effects of corporate reputation perceptions of the general public on shareholder value, *Strategic Management Journal*, 36: 945–956.
51. E. G. Love, J. Lim, & M. K. Bednar, 2017, The face of the firm: The influence of CEOs on corporate reputation, *Academy of Management Journal*, 60: 1462–1481; G. Dowling & P. Moran, 2012, Corporate reputations: Built in or bolted on? *California Management Review*, 54(2): 25–42; M. D. Pfarrer, T. G. Pollock, & V. P. Rindova, 2010, A tale of two assets: The effects of firm reputation and celebrity on earnings surprises and investors' reactions, *Academy of Management Journal*, 53: 1131–1152; T. G. Pollock, G. Chen, & E. M. Jackson, 2010, How much prestige is enough? Assessing the value of multiple types of high-status affiliates for young firms, *Journal of Business Venturing*, 25: 6–23.
52. R. Sroufe & V. Gopalakrishna-Remani, 2018, Management, social sustainability, reputation, and financial performance relationships: An empirical examination of U.S. firms, *Organization and Environment*, in press; A. P. Petkova, A. Wadhwa, X. Yao, & S. Jain, 2014, Reputation and decision making under ambiguity: A study of U.S. venture capital firms' investments in the emerging clean energy sector, *Academy of Management Journal*, 57: 422–448; Y. Wang, G. Berens, & C. van Riel, 2012, Competing in the capital market with a good reputation, *Corporate Reputation Review*, 15: 198–221.
53. C. B. Astrachan, I. Bolero, J. H. Astrachan, & R. Prugl, 2018, Branding the family firm: A review, integrative framework proposal, and research agenda, *Journal of Family Business Strategy*, in press; P. Foroudi, T. C. Melewar, & S. Gupta, 2014, Linking corporate logo, corporate image, and reputation: An examination of consumer perceptions in the financial setting, *Journal of Business Research*, 67: 2269–2281; S. Tischer & L. Hildebrandt, 2014, Linking corporate reputation and shareholder value using the publication of reputation rankings, *Journal of Business Research*, 67: 1007–1017.
54. R. Sellers-Rubio, F. Mas-Ruiz, & F. Sancho-Esper, 2018, Firm reputation, advertising investment and price premium: The role of collective brand membership in high-quality wines, *Agribusiness*, in press; C. A. Roster, 2014, Cultural influences on global firms' decisions to cut the strategic brand ties that bind: A commentary essay, *Journal of Business Research*, 67: 486–488; N. Rosenbusch & J. Brinckmann, 2011, Is innovation always beneficial? A meta-analysis of the relationship between innovation and performance in SMEs, *Journal of Business Venturing*, 26: 441–457.
55. 2018, Harley-Davidson Online store, www.harley-davidson.com, April 17.
56. Coca-Cola online social media principles, 2018, Coca-Cola Company Home page, www.cocacolacompany.com, April 17.
57. H. Feng, N. A. Morgan, & L. L. Rego, 2017, Firm capabilities and growth: The moderating role of market conditions, *Journal of the Academy of Marketing Science*, 45: 76–92; Y. Lin & L.-Y. Wu, 2014, Exploring the role of dynamic capabilities in firm performance under the resource-based view framework, *Journal of Business Research*, 67: 407–413; R. W. Coff, 2010, The coevolution of rent appropriation and capability development, *Strategic Management Journal*, 31: 711–733.
58. J. E. Delery & D. Roumpi, 2017, Strategic human resource management, human capital and competititve advantage, Is the field going in circles? *Human Resource Management Journal*, 27: 1–21: S. Chowdhury, E. Schulz, M. Milner, & D. Van De Voort, 2014, Core employee based human capital and revenue productivity in small firms: An empirical investigation, *Journal of Business Research*, 67: 2473–2479; A. M. Subramanian, 2012, A longitudinal study of the influence of intellectual human capital on firm exploratory innovation, *IEEE Transactions on Engineering Management*, 59: 540–550.
59. K. Freeman, 2015, CEOs must prioritize human capital, *Wall Street Journal Online*, www.wsj.com, February 27.
60. S. Moore, 2015, How pizza became a growth stock, *Wall Street Journal Online*, www.wsj.com, March 13.
61. G. P. Pisano, 2017, Toward a prescript=ptive theory of dynamic capabilities: Connecting strategic choice, learning, and competition, *Industrial and Corporate Change*, 26: 747–762; D. J. Teece, 2014, The foundations of enterprise performance: Dynamic and ordinary capabilities in an (economic) theory of firms, *Academy of Management Perspectives*, 28: 328–352; K. H. Heimeriks, M. Schijven, & S. Gates, 2012, Manifestations of higher-order routines: The underlying mechanisms of deliberate learning in the context of post acquisition integration, *Academy of Management Journal*, 55: 703–726.
62. S. J. G. Girod & R. Whittington, 2017, Reconfiguration, restructuring and firm performance: Dynamic capabilities and environmental dynamism, *Strategic Management Journal*, 38: 1121–1133; Y. Zhao, E. Cavusgil, & S. T. Cavusgil, 2014, An investigation of the black-box supplier integration in new product development, *Journal of Business Research*, 67: 1058–1064; H. R. Greve, 2009, Bigger and safer: The diffusion of competitive advantage, *Strategic Management Journal*, 30: 1–23; C. K. Prahalad & G. Hamel, 1990, The core competence of the corporation, *Harvard Business Review*, 68(3): 79–93.
63. L. Moak, 2018, Associates become masters in Apple training program, *XTheExchange Post.com*, publicaffairs-sme.com, March 1; Reisinger, 2015, Apple's genius bar to get smarter with 'concierge'—report, *CNET.* com, www.cnet.com, February 24; Y. I. Kane & I. Sherr, 2011, Secrets from Apple's genius bar: Full loyalty, no negativity, *Wall Street Journal*, www.wsj. com, June 15.
64. C . M. Carnes, F. Chirico, M. A. Hitt, D. W. Huh, & V. Pisano, 2017, Resource orchestration for innovation: Structuring and bundling resources in growth and mature-stage firms, *Long Range Planning*, 50: 472–486; J. Schmidt, R. Makadok, & T. Keil, 2016, Customer-specific synergies and market convergence, *Strategic Management Journal*, 37: 870–895; S. Newbert, 2008, Value, rareness, competitive advantage, and performance: A conceptual-level empirical investigation of the resource-based view of the firm, *Strategic Management Journal*, 29: 745–768.
65. 2018, Sustainability: Enhancing sustainability of operations and global value chains, Walmart, corporatewalmart. com/global-responsibility, April 18 Walmart environmental sustainability, 2015, *Walmart Homepage*, www.walmart. com, March 30; A. Winston, 2015, Can Walmart get us to buy sustainable products? *Harvard Business Review blog*, www.hbr.org, February 24.
66. R. S. Nason & J. Wiklund, 2018, An Assessment of resource-based theorizing on firm growth and suggestions for the future, *Journal of Management*, 44: 32–60; A. Kaul & Z (Brian) Wu, 2016, A capabilities-based perspective on target selection in acquisitions, *Strategic Management Journal*: 37: 1220–1239; D. S. K. Lim, N. Celly,

E. A. Morse, & W. G. Rowe, 2013, Rethinking the effectiveness of asset and cost retrenchment: The contingency effects of a firm's rent creation mechanism, *Strategic Management Journal*, 34: 42–61.
67. 2018, Groupon stock rallies as Morgan Stanley ends beafrish call, *MarketWatch, www.marketwatch.com, March 5;* D. Roos, 2011, How does Groupon work? *Howstuffworks.com*, www.howstuffworks .com, June 12.
68. E. Moreau, 2018, Looking for more sites like Goupon? *Lifewire*, www.lifewire.com, March 4, 2018.
69. O. Alexy, J. West, H. Klapper, & M. Reitzig, 2018, Surrendering control to gain advantage: Reconciling openness and the resource-based view of the firm, *Strategic Management Journal*, in press; H. A. Ndofor, D. G. Sirmon, & X. He, 2015, Utilizing the firm's resources: How TMT heterogeneity and resulting faultlines affect TMT tasks, *Strategic Management Journal*: 36: 1636–1674.
70. A. Doha, M. Pagell, M. Swink, & D. Johnston, 2017, Measuring firms' imitation activity, *R&D Management*, 47: 522–533; S. G. Lazzarini, 2015, Strategizing by the government: Can industrial policy create firm-level competitive advantage? *Strategic Management Journal*, 36: 97–112; H. Rahmandad, 2012, Impact of growth opportunities and competition on firm-level capability development trade-offs, *Organization Science*, 23: 138–154.
71. J. B. Barney, 1991, Firm resources and sustained competitive advantage, *Journal of Management*, 17: 99–120.
72. M. E. B. Herrera, 2015, Creating competitive advantage by institutionalizing corporate social innovation, *Journal of Business Research*: 68: 1468–1474; C. M. Wilderom, P. T. van den Berg, & U. J. Wiersma, 2012, A longitudinal study of the effects of charismatic leadership and organizational culture on objective and perceived corporate performance, *Leadership Quarterly*, 23: 835–848; C. C. Maurer, P. Bansal, & M. M. Crossan, 2011, Creating economic value through social values: Introducing a culturally informed resource-based view, *Organization Science*, 22: 432–448.
73. C. Smith, 2018, 40 Interesting McDonald's facts and statistics, DMR Business Statistics, https://expanded ramblings.com/index .php/mcdonalds-statistics/, February 19; J. Wohl, 2018, McDonald's makes happy meals (slightly) healthier, AdAge, http:// adage.com, February 15;J. Wohl, 2018, McDonald's CMO bullish on tiered value menu amid competition, AdAge, http:// adage.com, January 5.
74. D. McIver & C. Lengnick-Hall, 2018, The causal ambiguity paradox: Deliberate actions under causal ambiguity, *Strategic Organization*, in press: Alnuaimi & G. George, 2016, Appropriability and the retrieval of knowledge after spillovers, *Strategic Management Journal*: 37: 1263–1279; A. W. King & C. P. Zeithaml, 2001, Competencies and firm performance: Examining the causal ambiguity paradox, *Strategic Management Journal*, 22: 75–99.
75. L. Zhang, X. Zhang, & Y. Xi, 2017, The sociality of resources: Understanding organizational competitive advantage from a social perspective, *Asia Pacific Journal of Management*, 34: 619–648.
76. Barney, Firm resources, 111.
77. A. Kaleka & N. A. Morgan, 2017, Which competitive advantage(s)? Competitive advantage—market performance relationships in international markets, *Journal of International Marketing*, 25: 25–49; Z. Erden, D. Klang, R. Sydler, & G. von Krogh, 2014, Knowledge-flows and firm performance, *Journal of Business Research*, 67: 2777–2785; E. Beleska-Spasova & K. W. Glaister, 2013, Intrafirm causal ambiguity in an international context, *International Business Review*, 22: 32–46.
78. N. T. Sheehan & N. J. Foss, 2017, Using Porterian activity analysis to understand organizational capabilities, *Journal of General Management*, 42: 41–51.
79. B. Sleuer, R. Ramusch, F. Part, & S. Salhofer, 2017, Analysis of a value chain structure of informal waste recycling in Beijing, China, *Resources, Conservation and Recycling*, 117 B: 137–150; M. G. Jacobides & C. J. Tae, 2015, Kingpins, bottlenecks, and value dynamics along a sector, *Organization Science*: 26: 889–907; J. B. Heide, A. Kumar, & K. H. Wathne, 2014, Concurrent sourcing, governance mechanisms, and performance outcomes in industrial value chains, *Strategic Management Journal*, 35: 1164–1185.
80. M. E. Porter, 1985, *Competitive Advantage*, New York: Free Press, 33–61.
81. C. F. Dunant, M. P. Drewniok, M. Sansom, S. Corbey, J. M. Cullen, & J. M. Allwood, 2018, Options to make steel reuse profitable: An analysis of cost and risk distribution across the UK construction value chain, *Journal of Cleaner Production*, 183: 102–111; R. Garcia-Castro & C. Francoeur, 2016, When more is not better: Complementarities, costs and contingencies in stakeholder management, Strategic Management Journal, 37: 406–424; P. Frow, S. Nenonen, A. Payne, & K. Storbacka, 2015, Managing co-creation design: A strategic approach to innovation, *British Journal of Management*, 26: 463–483 .
82. P. J. Buckley, T. D. Craig, & R. Mudambi, 2018, Time to learn? Assignment of duration in global value chain organization, *Journal of Business Research*, in press; Y. M. Zhou, 2015, Supervising across borders: The case of multinational hierarchies, *Organization Science*, 26: 277–292; N. Haworth, 2013, Compressed development: Global value chains, multinational enterprises and human resource development in 21st century Asia, *Journal of World Business*, 48: 251–259.
83. R. Garcia-Castro & R. V. Aguilera, 2015, Incremental value creation and appropriation in a world with multiple stakeholders, *Strategic Management Journal*, 36: 137–147; S. Manning, M. M. Larsen, & P. Bharati, 2015, Global delivery models: The role of talent, speed and time zones in the global outsourcing industry, *Journal of International Business Studies*, 46; 850–877; A. Jara & H. Escaith, 2012, Global value chains, international trade statistics and policymaking in a flattening world, *World Economics*, 13(4): 5–18.
84. J. Sheth, 2017, Revitalizing relationship marketing, *Journal of Services Marketing*, 31: 6–10.
85. C. Boulton & S. Norton, 2015, Deutsche Bank, H-P divide IT responsibility in cloud deal, *Wall Street Journal Online*, www.wsj .com, February 26.
86. J. Rietveld, 2018, Creating and capturing value from freemium business models: A demand-side perspective, *Strategic Entrepreneurship Journal*, in press; R. Lungeanu & E. Zajac, 2015, Venture capital ownership as a contingent resource: How owner/firm fit influences IPO outcomes, *Academy of Management Journal*, 59: 930–955; J.-Y. Lee, D. G. Bachrach, & K. Lewis, 2014, Social network ties, transactive memory, and performance in groups, *Organization Science*, 25: 951–967.
87. H. Wieland, N. N. Hartmann, & S. L. Vargo, 2017, Business models as service strategy, *Journal of the Academy ofMarketing Science*, 45: 925–943; S. G. Lazzarini, 2015, Strategizing by the government: Can industrial policy create firm-level competitive advantage? *Strategic Management Journal*, 36: 97–112; H. Yang, Y. Zheng, & X. Zhao, 2014, Exploration or exploitation: Small firms' alliance strategies with large firms, *Strategic Management Journal*, 35: 146–157.
88. C. Lioukas & J. Reuer, 2015, Isolating trust outcomes from exchange relationships: Social exchange and learning benefits of prior ties in alliances, *Academy of Management Journal*, 58: 1826–1847; J. Song, 2014, Subsidiary absorptive capacity and knowledge transfer within multinational corporations, *Journal of International Business Studies*, 45: 73–84.
89. R Strange & G. Magnani, 2018, Outsourcing, offshoring and the global factory, in G. Cook & F. McDonald (eds.), *The Routledge Companion on International Business and Economic Geography*, London: Routledge, in press; E. Mitchell, 2014, Collaborative propensities among transnational NGOs registered in the United States, *The American Review of Public Administration*, 44: 575–599.
90. J. J. Choi, Ming Ju, M. Kotabe, L. Trigeorgis, & X. T. Zhang, 2018, Flexibility as firm value driver: Evidence from offshore outsourcing, *Global Strategy Journal*, in press; W. Tate & L. Bals, 2017, Outsourcing/offshoring

insights: Going beyond resoring to rightshoring, *International Journal of Physical Distribution & Logistics Management*, 47: 106–113; S. M. Handley & C. M. Angst, 2015, The impact of culture on the relationship between governance and opportunism in outsourcing relationships, *Strategic Management Journal*, 36: 1412–1434.

91. M. Kotabe & J. Y. Murray, 2018, Global sourcing strategy: An evolution in global production and sourcing rationalization, in L. C. Leonidou, C. S. Katsikeas, S. Samiee, & B. Aykol (eds.) *Advances in Global Marketing: A Research Anthology*, Springer, in press; A. Gunasekaran, Z. Irani, K.-L. Choy, L. Filippi, & T. Papadopoulos, 2015, Performance measures and metrics in outsourcing decisions: A review for research and applications, *International Journal of Production Economics*, 161: 153–166; W. L. Tate, L. M. Ellram, T. Schoenherr, & K. J. Petersen, 2014, Global competitive conditions driving the manufacturing location decision, *Business Horizons*, 57: 381–390.

92. J. Pla-Barber, E. Linares, & P. N. Ghauri, 2018, The choice of offshoring operation mode: A behavioural perspective, *Journal of Business Research*, in press; Jain & R.-A. Thietart, 2014, Capabilities as shift parameters for the outsourcing decision, *Strategic Management Journal*, 35: 1881–1890; J. Li, 2012, The alignment between organizational control mechanisms and outsourcing strategies: A commentary essay, *Journal of Business Research*, 65: 1384–1386.

93. K.-J. Wu, M.-L. Tseng, A. S. F. Chiu, & M. K. Lim, 2017, Achieving competitive advantage through supply chain agility under uncertainty: A novel multi-criteria decision-making structure, *International Journal of Production Economics*, 190: 96–107; R. Kapoor & N. R. Furr, 2015, Complementarities and competition: Unpacking the drivers of entrants' technology choices in the solar photovoltaic industry, *Strategic Management Journal*, 36: 416–436; N. Raassens, S. Wuyts, & I. Geyskens, 2012, The market valuation of outsourcing new product development, *Journal of Marketing Research*, 49: 682–695.

94. S. Holloway & A. Parmigiani, 2016, Friends and profits don't mix: The performance implications of repeated partnerships, *Academy of Management Journal*, 59: 460–478; A. Arino, J. J. Reuer, K. J. Mayer, & J. Jane, 2014, Contracts, negotiation, and learning: An examination of termination provisions, *Journal of Management Studies*, 51: 379–405; A. Martinez-Noya, E. Garcia-Canal, & M. F. Guillen, 2013, R&D outsourcing and the effectiveness of intangible investments: Is proprietary core knowledge walking out of the door? *Journal of Management Studies*, 50: 67–91.

95. J. Alcacer & J. Oxley, 2014, Learning by supplying, *Strategic Management Journal*, 35: 204–223; S. Sonenshein, 2013, How organizations foster the creative use of resources, *Academy of Management Journal*, 57: 814–848; C. Grimpe & U. Kaiser, 2010, Balancing internal and external knowledge acquisition: The gains and pains from R&D outsourcing, *Journal of Management Studies*, 47: 1483–1509.

96. B. Kim, K. S. Park, S.-Y. Jung, & S. H. Park, 2018, Offshoring and outsourcing in a global supply chain: Impact of the arm's length regulation on transfer pricing, *European Journal of Operational Research*, 266: 88–98; Obloj & P. Zemsky, 2015, Value creation and value capture under moral hazard: Exploring the micro-foundations of buyer-supplier relationships, *Strategic Management Journal*, 36: 1146–1163; S. M. Handley, 2012, The perilous effects of capability loss on outsourcing management and performance, *Journal of Operations Management*, 30: 152–165.

97. L. P. K. Ade, A. Mufutau, & A. I. Tubosun, 2017, The influence of marketing intelligence on business competitive advantage (A study of Diamond Bank PLC), *Journal of Competitiveness*, 9: 51–71; M. Taussig & A. Delios, 2015, Unbundling the effects of institutions on firm resources: The contingent value of being local in emerging economy private equity, *Strategic Management Journal*, 36: 1845–1865; O. Baumann & N. Stieglitz, 2014, Rewarding value-creating ideas in organizations: The power of low-powered incentives, *Strategic Management Journal*, 35: 358–375.

98. U. Stettner & D. Lavie, 2014, Ambidexterity under scrutiny: Exploration and exploitation via internal organization, alliances, and acquisitions, *Strategic Management Journal*, 35: 1903–1929; E. Rawley, 2010, Diversification, coordination costs, and organizational rigidity: Evidence from microdata, *Strategic Management Journal*, 31: 873–891.

99. A. Schneider, C. Wickert, & E. Marti, 2017, Reducing complexity by creating complexity: A systems theory perspective on how organizations respond to their environments, *Journal of Management Studies*, 54: 182–208; D. L. Barton, 1995, *Wellsprings of Knowledge: Building and Sustaining the Sources of Innovation*, Boston: Harvard Business School Press, 30–31.

4

Business-Level Strategy

Studying this chapter should provide you with the strategic management knowledge needed to:

4-1 Discuss the relationship between customers and business-level strategies in terms of *who*, *what*, and *how*.

4-2 Explain the purpose of forming and implementing a business-level strategy.

4-3 Describe business models and explain their relationship with business-level strategies.

4-4 Explain the differences among five types of business-level strategies.

4-5 Use the five forces of competition model to explain how firms can earn above-average returns when using each business-level strategy.

4-6 Discuss the risks associated with using each of the business-level strategies.

iStock.com/DNY59

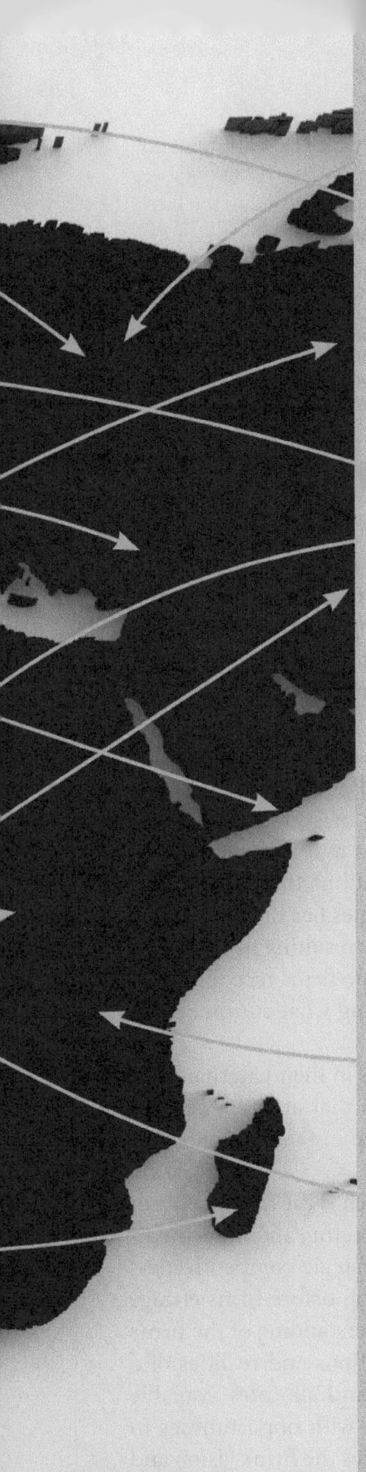

DIGITAL: AN INCREASINGLY IMPORTANT ASPECT OF STRATEGY CHOICE AND STRATEGY IMPLEMENTATION

"The pace of change is faster and more relentless, the level of uncertainty higher and the degree of complexity greater than it has even been." In the first three chapters and in other parts of the book as well, we discuss the influence of these realities on today's firms and their stakeholders. These realities challenge each type of strategy (business-level, corporate-level, merger and acquisition, international, and cooperative) a firm may choose to implement.

Each type of strategy a firm chooses to implement helps it deal with the competitive realities mentioned above. Defined in Chapter 1 as an integrated and coordinated set of commitments and actions designed to exploit core competencies and gain a competitive advantage, strategy helps companies in their efforts to change quickly and effectively and reduce the levels of uncertainty and complexity in their external environment (see Chapter 2) and internal environment (see Chapter 3). In this sense, when involved with strategy, leaders and those with whom they work seek to set a firm's direction, sequence how the firm will allocate and as necessary reallocate resources, and commit to creating a certain type of value for a certain type of customer. Business-level strategy, this chapter's topic, finds a firm choosing a strategy to use to gain a competitive advantage by exploiting its core competencies within one or more specific product markets.

Chris Batson/Alamy Stock Photo

Netflix uses data analytics to identify behavioral patterns among its customers. This data gives Netflix the ability to recommend shows and movies tailored to each individual users' preferences.

Innovation is a key part of firms' efforts to achieve success with their strategies. In turn, information and technologies play vital roles in innovation-related projects and activities. This means that firms need to have a *digital* strategy as part of what they do to implement each type of business-level strategy. Those committed to having a digital strategy believe that the world's competitive environments are increasingly information intensive and interconnected.

In essence, a digital strategy "is the application of information and technology to raise human performance." Increasing human performance is important in that, as noted in Chapters 1 and 3, human capital is one of the most significant competitive advantages a firm can develop. Thus, a digital strategy has the potential to help the firm develop a competitive advantage—human capital—as it seeks to implement its business-level strategy. People engaged with digital activities within a company help the firm become more agile and more capable of dealing with competitive challenges more quickly and effectively.

Digital principles—principles that redefine company imperatives around customers, growth, efficiency, and innovation—are the basis of an effective digital strategy. Using digitally based technologies and tools such as data analytics (which is the gathering and interpreting of data to identify behavioral patterns among customers for the purpose of serving customers' needs better during future transactions), a firm's digital strategy finds it (1) concentrating on outcomes customers repeatedly notice, value, and choose; (2) using information and technologies to derive more output from each unit of input; and (3) seeking to learn how to do new things in new ways as a means of enhancing the functionality of products it creates for customers.

Leaders committed to the importance of developing a digital strategy are foundational to a firm's efforts to develop such a strategy. Working with others, these leaders make choices about how to form an effective data analytics function, determine the degree to which cloud computing (which is the sharing of resources, software, and information via an Internet-based network) benefits the firm's digital strategy, and predict the future with the type of clarity that allows the firm to recognize what could be a viable competitive position for it in the years to come.

Sources: 2018, 5 key technology trends for 2018, *Cincinnati Business Courier*, www.bizjournals.com, March 7; 2018, Data analytics, *Techopedia*, www.techopedia.com, March 9; J. Ferguson & N. Anderson, 2018, How to build a digital strategy, *World Economic Forum*, www.weforum.org, January 10; K. Tama-Rutgliano, 2018, Mapping out your digital marketing strategy for 2018, *Forbes*, www.forbes.com, January 2; A. Bollard, E. Larrea, A. Singla, & R. Sood, 2017, The next-generation operating model for the digital world, *McKinsey & Company*, www.mckinsey.com, March; T. Oliveria, M. Alhinho, R. Rita, & G. Dhillon, 2017, Modelling and testing consumer trust dimensions in e-commerce, *Computers in Human Behavior*, 71: 153-164; M. McDonald, 2016, Becoming a truly digital organization, *Accenture*, www.accenture.com, March 31; M. McDonald, 2015, What is digital strategy? *Accenture*, www.accenture.com, March 3.

Increasingly important to firm success, strategy is concerned with making choices among two or more alternatives.[1] We noted in Chapter 1 that the choice of a strategy indicates a firm's decision to pursue one course of action instead of others. Opportunities and threats in the external environment influence the choices the firm makes[2] (see Chapter 2) as do the nature and quality of the resources, capabilities, and core competencies in the firm's internal organization[3] (see Chapter 3).

As discussed in the Opening Case, information and the technologies available to gather and analyze it are at the core of a firm's effort to form a digital strategy. Used to facilitate the selection and implementation of the firm's strategy or strategies, a digital strategy helps a firm concentrate on understanding its customers and their needs with greater clarity as a foundation for being able to develop innovations that create more value for those customers.[4] Integrating information and technologies has the potential to help employees increase their effectiveness and efficiency, possibly resulting in a competitive advantage for the firm in the form of its human capital. Astute firms recognize that information and technologies to manage it can inform determining what customers the firm will seek to serve as well as the strategy it will use to do so.

In previous chapters, we described how firms study conditions in their external environment and the resources, capabilities, and core competencies that are part of their internal environment. Studying these environments is the first step in the strategic management process.

This chapter is the first one to deal with "strategy" directly, which is the second part of the strategic management process as explained in Chapter 1. By selecting and implementing one or more strategies (see Figure 1.1), firms seek to gain strategic competitiveness and earn above-average returns.[5] Strategies are purposeful, develop before firms engage rivals in marketplace competitions, and demonstrate a shared understanding of the firm's vision and mission.[6] A strategy that is consistent with the conditions and realities of a firm's external and internal environments marshals, integrates, and allocates available resources, capabilities, and competencies to align them properly with opportunities in the external environment. When effective, a strategy also rationalizes the firm's vision and mission along with the actions taken to achieve them. In the final analysis, sound strategic choices that reduce uncertainty regarding outcomes are the foundation for building successful strategies.

A **business-level strategy** is an integrated and coordinated set of commitments and actions the firm uses to gain a competitive advantage by exploiting core competencies in a specific product market.

Business-level strategy, this chapter's focus, indicates the choices the firm has made about how it intends to compete in individual product markets. **Business-level strategy** is an integrated and coordinated set of commitments and actions the firm uses to gain a competitive advantage by exploiting core competencies in a specific product market.[7] The choices are important because the firm's strategies influence its performance, certainly its long-term performance. Given the complexity of competing successfully in the global economy, the choices about how the firm will compete are challenging. As explained later in a Strategic Focus, this is the case for Macy's as it seeks to find ways to implement its business-level strategy of differentiation with greater effectiveness.

Every firm must develop and implement a business-level strategy. However, some firms may not use all the strategies—corporate-level, merger and acquisition, international, and cooperative—we examine in Chapters 6 through 9. A firm competing in a single-product market in a single geographic location does not need a corporate-level strategy regarding product diversity or an international strategy to deal with geographic diversity. In contrast, a diversified firm will use one of the corporate-level strategies as well as a separate business-level strategy for each product market in which it competes. Every firm—ranging from the local dry cleaner to the multinational corporation—must develop and use at least one business-level strategy. Thus, business-level strategy is the *core* strategy—the strategy that the firm forms to describe how it intends to compete against rivals on a day-to-day basis in its chosen product market.[8]

We discuss several topics to examine business-level strategies. Customers are the foundation of successful business-level strategies; firms must continue creating value for their customers if they are to retain them.[9] Because of this reality, we present information about customers that is relevant to business-level strategies. In terms of customers, when selecting a business-level strategy, the firm determines

1. *who* will be served,
2. *what* needs those target customers have that it will satisfy, and
3. *how* those needs will be satisfied.

Selecting customers and deciding which of their needs the firm will try to satisfy, as well as how it will do so, are challenging tasks. Competition across the globe creates attractive options for customers. Because of this, individual firms must identify and implement a specific strategy that will best meet their target customers' needs.[10] Effective global competitors have become adept at identifying the needs of customers in different cultures and geographic regions as well as learning how to respond to changes in their needs.

Prior to describing the purpose of business-level strategies, and of the five business-level strategies, we define business models and explain their relationship with strategies, particularly business-level strategies. The five business-level strategies we then consider are *generic* in nature in that any organization competing in any industry can use any of them.[11] Our analysis describes how effective use of each strategy allows the firm to position itself favorably relative to an industry's five competitive forces (see Chapter 2). In addition, we use the value chain (see Chapter 3) to present examples of the primary and support activities that are necessary to implement specific business-level strategies. Because no strategy is risk-free,[12] we describe the different risks the firm may encounter when using these strategies. In Chapter 11, we explain the organizational structures and controls linked with the successful use of each business-level strategy.

4-1 Customers: Their Relationship with Business-Level Strategies

Strategic competitiveness results only when the firm satisfies a group of customers by using its competitive advantages as the basis for competing in individual product markets.[13] A key reason firms must satisfy customers with their business-level strategy is that returns earned from relationships with customers are the lifeblood of all organizations.[14]

The most successful companies try to find new ways to satisfy current customers and/or to meet the needs of new customers. Being able to do this can be even more difficult when firms and consumers face challenging economic conditions. During such times, firms may decide to reduce their workforce to control costs. This can lead to problems, however, because having fewer employees makes it more difficult for companies to meet individual customers' needs and expectations. In these instances, firms can follow several possible courses of action, such as paying extra attention to their best customers and developing a flexible workforce by cross-training employees so they can undertake a variety of responsibilities on their jobs.

4-1a Effectively Managing Relationships with Customers

Firms strengthen their relationships with customers by delivering superior value to them. Strong interactive relationships with customers often provide the foundation for the firm to earn profits because of how well they serve customers' unique needs.

Importantly, delivering superior value often results in increased customer satisfaction. In turn, customer satisfaction has a positive relationship with profitability because satisfied customers are more likely to be repeat customers. However, a wide variety of choices and easily accessible information about the functionality of firms' products create increasingly sophisticated and knowledgeable customers, making it difficult for companies to earn their loyalty. As such, many firms interact regularly with customers to co-create value that, in turn, results in satisfied customers.[15]

A number of companies have become skilled at the art of managing all aspects of their relationship with their customers.[16] For example, competitors and others admire Amazon for the quality of information it maintains about its customers, the services it renders, and its ability to anticipate customers' needs. Using the information it has, Amazon tries to serve what it believes are the unique needs of each customer. To date, the firm has maintained a strong reputation for being able to do this.[17]

Next, we discuss three dimensions that characterize firms' relationships with customers. Successful companies understand these dimensions and manage their relationships with customers in light of them.

4-1b Reach, Richness, and Affiliation

The *reach* dimension of relationships with customers revolves around the firm's access and connection to customers. In general, firms seek to extend their reach, adding customers in the process of doing so.

Reach is an especially critical dimension for social networking sites such as Facebook in that the value these firms create for users is to connect them with others. The number of Facebook users is increasing dramatically; access to a large number of users influences a social networking site's efforts to be successful. As of the end of January of 2018, there were close to 1.9 billion monthly active users, making Facebook the world's most popular social networking site.[18] Obviously, Facebook's reach increases opportunities for the firm to create value for those using its site.

Reach is also important to Netflix Inc. The firm acquired two million subscribers more than Wall Street analysts anticipated during the final three months of 2017. These results drove Netflix's market capitalization to more than $100 billion for the first time.[19] Overall, 2017 was a year in which the firm's international "subscriber base increased at a rapid pace once again, while domestic subscriber base growth stabilized in the low double digits."[20] Analysts and firm personnel expected subscriber growth in both domestic and international markets for Netflix in 2018 and beyond, suggesting that Netflix would gain all-important access to still additional customers.

Richness, the second dimension of firms' relationships with customers, concerns the depth and detail of the two-way flow of information between the firm and customers. The potential of the richness dimension to help the firm establish a competitive advantage in its relationship with customers leads many firms to offer online services as a means of superior management of information exchanges with them. Broader and deeper information-based exchanges allow firms to improve their understanding of customers and their needs. Such exchanges also enable customers to become more knowledgeable about how the firm can satisfy them. Internet technology and e-commerce transactions, which are part of a firm's digital strategy, have substantially reduced the costs of meaningful information exchanges with current and potential customers.

As we have noted, Amazon is a leader in using the Internet to build relationships with customers. In fact, Amazon's mission is "to be the Earth's most customer-centric company."[21] Operationally, this means that Amazon seeks "to build a place where people can come to find and discover anything they might want to buy."[22] Amazon and other firms committed to the importance of richness use information from customers to help them develop innovative new products that provide superior satisfaction of customers' needs.[23]

Affiliation, the third dimension, is concerned with facilitating useful interactions with customers. Viewing the world through the customer's eyes and constantly seeking ways to create more value for the customer have positive effects in terms of affiliation. This approach enhances customer satisfaction and has the potential to result in fewer customer complaints. This is important in that for services, for example, customers often do not complain when dissatisfied; instead, they simply go to competitors for their service needs, although a firm's strong brand can mitigate the switching.[24] To enhance their affiliation with customers, some companies now have a position called "Chief Customer Officer." Those appointed to this position previously carried the title of "Chief Marketing Officer." This is the case for Tesco, the largest retail grocer in the United Kingdom. To further interact with some of its customers, Walmart now delivers groceries to those who order items online and then come to the store to receive their items from an employee who brings them to their vehicle. The firm is also testing delivering food to customers' refrigerators. Demonstrating potentially positive outcomes from further affiliation with customers is the view of Walmart officials who believe that "the 'high touch' approach of online grocery ordering is improving people's opinion of the shopping experience at its stores, making them more likely to purchase general merchandise in addition to food."[25] Likewise, because of data available through digitization, firms have a tremendous amount of individual customer data.[26] Analyzing data about customers allows firms to find additional ways to affiliate with them through value-creating interactions.

As we discuss next, managing customer relationships effectively (along the dimensions of reach, richness, and affiliation) helps the firm answer questions related to the issues of *who, what*, and *how*.

4-1c Who: Determining the Customers to Serve

Deciding *who* the target customer is that the firm intends to serve with its business-level strategy is an important decision.[27] Companies divide customers into groups based on differences in customers' needs (needs are discussed further in the next section) to make this decision. **Market segmentation** is the process of dividing customers into groups based on their needs.[28] Market segmentation is a process used to cluster customers with similar needs into individual and identifiable groups. In the animal food products business, for example, the food-product needs of owners of companion pets (e.g., dogs and cats) differ from the needs for food and health-related products of those owning production animals (e.g., livestock). Hill's Pet Nutrition, which is a subsidiary of Colgate-Palmolive Company, sells food products for pets. The firm's vision is to "make nutrition a cornerstone of veterinary medicine" while its mission is "to help enrich and lengthen the special relationships between people and their pets."[29] Hill's categorizes its food products for cats as pets into four market segments: kitten, adult (one year-plus), mature (seven years plus), and senior (11 years plus). The food products the firm produces and sells differ based on the veterinary-determined needs of each segment of pet cats.

Firms can use almost any identifiable human or organizational characteristic to subdivide a market into segments that differ from one another on a given characteristic. In Table 4.1, we show common characteristics on which customers' needs vary.

4-1d What: Determining Which Customer Needs to Satisfy

After the firm decides *who* it will serve, it must identify the targeted customer group's needs that its products can satisfy. In a general sense, *needs (what)* are related to a product's benefits and features. Successful firms learn how to deliver to customers what they want, when they want it. For example, a number of global automobile manufacturers are attempting to build an affordable electric car for consumers in emerging economies.[30] In general, emerging markets are ones in which customers have little money to spend to buy a vehicle; in addition, the vehicle must be able to navigate roads that are part of underdeveloped infrastructures.

In the case of these automobile manufacturers—and for all firms competing in all industries—having close and frequent interactions with both current and potential customers helps them identify individuals' and groups' current and future needs. For example, knowledge gained about purchasing practices is facilitating efforts by Kroger, the largest grocery store chain in the United States, to enhance its understanding of customers' needs. Using data analytics, Kroger relies on current purchases to support

Table 4.1 Basis for Customer Segmentation

Consumer Markets
1. Demographic factors (age, income, sex, etc.)
2. Socioeconomic factors (social class, stage in the family life cycle)
3. Geographic factors (cultural, regional, and national differences)
4. Psychological factors (lifestyle, personality traits)
5. Consumption patterns (heavy, moderate, and light users)
6. Perceptual factors (benefit segmentation, perceptual mapping)
Industrial Markets
1. End-use segments (identified by Standard Industrial Classification [SIC] code)
2. Product segments (based on technological differences or production economics)
3. Geographic segments (defined by boundaries between countries or by regional differences within them)
4. Common buying factor segments (cut across product market and geographic segments)
5. Customer size segments

Source: Based on information in S. C. Jain, 2009, *Marketing Planning and Strategy*, Mason, OH: South-Western Cengage Custom Publishing.

Market segmentation is the process of dividing customers into groups based on their needs.

related sales. "If a customer is buying baby food regularly, a coupon may be generated (for the customer) for baby diapers or other baby products." In this manner, Kroger is simultaneously able to satisfy customers' needs better and increase its sales revenues. Essentially then, the firm's digital strategy finds it using information and technology to develop its promotion and marketing strategies.[31] From a strategic perspective, a basic need of all customers is to buy products that create value for them. The generalized forms of value that products provide are either low cost with acceptable features or highly differentiated features with acceptable cost. The most effective firms strive continuously to anticipate changes in customers' needs. The firm that fails to anticipate and certainly to recognize changes in its customers' needs may lose them to competitors whose products provide more value. Successful firms recognize that consumer needs change. For example, recent trends suggest that additional numbers of consumers desire to have an experience instead of simply purchasing a product. Starbucks is an example of a firm seeking to provide customers with an experience, not just a cup of coffee or a food item. Customers also prefer to buy customized products. Again, Starbucks has been doing this for some time, allowing customers to design their own drinks from a multitude of choices.

4-1e How: Determining Core Competencies Necessary to Satisfy Customer Needs

After deciding *who* the firm will serve and the specific *needs* those customers have, the firm is prepared to determine how to use its resources, capabilities, and competencies to develop products that can satisfy its target customers' needs. As explained in Chapters 1 and 3, *core competencies* are resources and capabilities that serve as a source of competitive advantage for the firm over its rivals. Firms use core competencies (*how*) to implement value-creating strategies, thereby satisfying customers' needs. Only those firms with the capacity to improve consistently, innovate, and upgrade their competencies can meet and exceed customers' expectations across time.[32] By continuously upgrading their competencies, firms are able to maintain an advantage over their rivals by providing customers with products that create value that exceeds the value created for them by competitors' offerings.[33]

Companies draw from a wide range of core competencies to produce products that satisfy customers' needs. In today's competitive environment and across industries, developing a core competence in the R&D function is critical. Apple, Amazon, Facebook, and Google recognize this reality and invest significant resources to deal with it. Recently, for example, Apple increased its spending on R&D by 30 percent, bringing that total to 5 percent of sales revenue. At the same time, Facebook was allocating 13.4 percent of revenue to R&D, Google spent 16.6 of its revenue on R&D, and Amazon increased its R&D expenditure by 28 percent. These commitments to R&D are in part to shape that function so that it is a core competence for each firm and a path through which the companies can produce and sell innovative products.[34]

SAS Institute Inc. is the world's largest privately owned software company and is the leader in business intelligence and analytics. Customers use SAS programs for data warehousing, data mining, and decision support purposes. SAS's mission is to "deliver proven solutions that drive innovation and improve performance." Thus, this firm seeks to help its customers in their efforts to innovate and improve their performance as a result. To reach its mission, SAS itself must be innovative as it develops new products. Supporting SAS's commitment to innovation is its allocation of 26 percent of its sales revenue to R&D in 2017 (up from 23 percent just a few years ago). The firm's reach is extensive in that 96 of the top 100 companies on the 2017 *Fortune Global 500* list were SAS customers. The firm's total customer base includes over 83,000 businesses, universities, and governmental agencies.[35]

Our discussion about customers shows that all organizations must use their capabilities and core competencies (the *how*) to satisfy the needs (the *what*) of the target group of customers (the *who*) the firm has chosen to serve.

4-2 The Purpose of a Business-Level Strategy

The purpose of a business-level strategy is to create differences between the firm's position and those of its competitors.[36] To position itself differently from competitors, a firm must decide if it intends to *perform activities differently* or if it will *perform different activities*. Strategy defines the path that provides the direction of actions organizational leaders take to help their firm achieve success.[37] In fact, "choosing to perform activities differently or to perform different activities than rivals" is the essence of a business-level strategy.[38] Thus, the firm's business-level strategy is a deliberate choice about how it will perform the value chain's primary and support activities to create unique value. Indeed, in the current complex competitive landscape, successful use of a business-level strategy results from the firm learning how to integrate the activities it performs in ways that create superior value for customers.

The manner in which Southwest Airlines Co. has integrated its activities is the foundation for the firm's ability to use the cost leadership strategy successfully (we discuss this strategy later in the chapter). However, as required by the cost leadership strategy, Southwest Airlines also provides customers with a set of features they find to be acceptable along with a low cost for its services. The tight integration among Southwest's activities is a key source of the firm's ability, historically, to operate more profitably than do its primary competitors. Today, Southwest flies more passengers in the United States than any other airline.[39]

Southwest Airlines has configured the activities it performs into six areas of strategic intent—limited passenger service; frequent, reliable departures; lean, highly productive ground and gate crews; high aircraft utilization with few aircraft models; very low ticket prices; and short-haul, point-to-point routes between mid-sized cities and secondary airports. Individual clusters of tightly linked activities enhance the likelihood the firm will execute its cost leadership strategy successfully. For example, no meals, no seat assignments, and no baggage transfers form a cluster of individual activities that support the objective of offering limited passenger service.

Southwest's tightly integrated activities make it difficult for competitors to imitate the firm's cost leadership strategy. The firm's unique culture and customer service are sources of competitive advantage that rivals have been unable to imitate, although some tried and failed (e.g., US Airways' MetroJet subsidiary, United Airlines' Shuttle by United, Delta's Song, and Continental Airlines' Continental Lite). Hindsight shows that these competitors offered low prices to customers, but weren't able to operate at costs close to those of Southwest or to provide customers with any notable sources of differentiation, such as a unique experience while in the air. The key to Southwest's success has been its ability to maintain low costs across time while providing customers with *acceptable* levels of differentiation such as an engaging culture. Firms using the cost leadership strategy must understand that in terms of sources of differentiation accompanying the cost leader's product, the customer defines *acceptable*. Fit among activities is a key to the sustainability of competitive advantage for all firms, including Southwest Airlines. Strategic fit among the many activities is critical for competitive advantage. It is more difficult for a competitor to match a configuration of integrated activities than to imitate a particular activity such as sales promotion, or a process technology.[40]

Next, we discuss business models, which are part of a comprehensive business-level strategy.[41] While business models inform the development and use of the other types of strategies a firm may choose to implement, their primary use is with business-level strategies. The reason for this is that as noted previously in this chapter, a business-level strategy is the firm's core strategy—the one the firm forms to describe how it intends to compete against rivals on a day-to-day basis in its chosen product market. As part of a firm's business-level strategy, the chosen business model influences the implementation of strategy, especially in terms of the interdependent processes the firm uses during implementation.[42] Developing and integrating a business model and a business-level strategy increases the likelihood of company success.[43] We use a discussion of business models and their relationship with strategy as a foundation for then describing five types of business-level strategies firms may choose to implement.

4-3 Business Models and their Relationship with Business-Level Strategies

As is the case with strategy, there are multiple definitions of a business model.[44] The consensus across these definitions is that a **business model** describes what a firm does to create, deliver, and capture value for its stakeholders.[45] As explained in Chapter 1, stakeholders value related yet different outcomes. For example, for shareholders, the firm captures and distributes value to them in the form of a return on their investment. For customers, the firm creates and delivers value in the form of a product featuring the combination of price and features for which they are willing to pay. For employees, the firm creates and delivers value in the form of a job about which they are passionate as well as through which they have opportunities to develop their skills by participating in continuous learning experiences. In a sense then, a business model is a *framework* for how the firm will create, deliver, and capture value while a business-level strategy is the set of commitments and actions that yields the *path* a firm intends to follow to gain a competitive advantage by exploiting its core competencies in a specific product market. Understanding customers in terms of *who, what,* and *how* is foundational to developing and using successfully both a business model and a business-level strategy.[46]

Regardless of the business model chosen, those leading a company should view that selection as one that will require adjustment in response to conditions that change from time to time in the firm's external environment (e.g., an opportunity to enter a new region surfaces) and its internal environment (e.g., the development of new capabilities).[47] Particularly because it is involved primarily with implementing a business-level strategy, the operational mechanics of a business model should change given the realities a firm encounters while engaging rivals in marketplace competitions.

There is an array of different business models, from which firms select one to use.[48] A franchise business model, for example, finds a firm licensing its trademark and the processes it follows to create and deliver a product to franchisees. In this instance, the firm franchising its trademark and processes captures value by receiving fees and royalty payments from its franchisees.

McDonald's and Panera Bread both use the franchise business model. McDonald's uses the model as part of its cost leadership strategy while Panera Bread uses it to implement a differentiation strategy (we discuss both strategies in detail in the next major section). McDonald's' cost leadership strategy finds it using processes detailed in its franchise business model to deliver food items to its customers that are offered at a low price but with acceptable levels of differentiation. Customers receive acceptable levels of differentiation in terms of taste quality, service quality, the cleanliness of the firm's units, and

A **business model** describes what a firm does to create, deliver, and capture value for its stakeholders.

the value the customers believe they receive when buying McDonald's food.[49] (Additional information about McDonald's and its cost leadership strategy appear later in the chapter in a Strategic Focus.)

Panera Bread also uses a franchise business model, but its model differs from the McDonald's franchise business model. One difference is that a person can purchase a single McDonald's unit. This is not the case for Panera Bread: "Panera Bread does not sell single-unit franchises, so it is not possible to open just one bakery-café. Rather, we have chosen to develop by selling market areas which require the franchise developer to open a number of units, typically 15 bakery-cafes in a period of 6 years."[50] Operating in the fast-casual part of the restaurant industry (McDonald's operates in the fast food part of the industry), Panera implements the differentiation strategy to provide customers "with good food (that) they can feel good about."[51] Through the differentiation strategy, Panera uses a carefully designed set of processes to offer differentiated food items in a differentiated setting to provide customers with value for which they are willing to pay and at a cost that is acceptable to them. Thus, while McDonald's and Panera Bread use the same business model, the franchising business model these firms use differ in actions the firms take to implement different business-level strategies.

As mentioned, there are multiple kinds of business models, such as the subscription model. In this instance, the business model finds a firm offering a product to customers on a regular basis such as once-per-month, once-per-year, or upon demand. Netflix uses a subscription business model as does Blue Apron, a firm founded on the belief that the way food is grown and distributed is complicated, making it difficult for families to make "good" choices about what they eat. Blue Apron delivers food directly to consumers, eliminating the "middleman" by doing so. The firm partners with farmers who are committed to sustainable production processes "to raise the highest-quality ingredients." Thus, Blue Apron combines the differentiation strategy with a subscription model to create, deliver, and capture value for the stakeholders (e.g., customers, suppliers, employees, and local communities) with whom the firm interacts while implementing its business-level strategy.[52] Other business models that also support the use of any of the five generic business-level strategies we discuss next include the following: (1) a freemium model (here the firm provides a basic product to customers for free and earns revenues and profits by selling a premium version of the service—examples include Dropbox and MailChimp); (2) an advertising model (where for a fee, firms provide advertisers with high-quality access to their target customers—Google and Pinterest are examples of firms using this business model); and (3) a peer-to-peer model (where a business matches those wanting a particular service with those providing that service—two examples are Task Rabbit and Airbnb).

4-4 Types of Business-Level Strategies

Firms choose between five business-level strategies to establish and defend their desired strategic position against competitors: *cost leadership, differentiation, focused cost leadership, focused differentiation*, and *integrated cost leadership/differentiation* (see Figure 4.1). Each business-level strategy can help the firm establish and exploit a *competitive advantage* (either lowest cost or distinctiveness) as the basis for how it will create value for customers within a particular *competitive scope* (broad market or narrow market). How firms integrate the activities they complete within each business level strategy demonstrates how they differ from one another.[53] For example, firms have different activity maps, and thus, a Southwest Airlines activity map differs from those of competitors JetBlue, United Airlines, American Airlines, and so forth. Superior integration of activities increases the

Figure 4.1 Five Business-Level Strategies

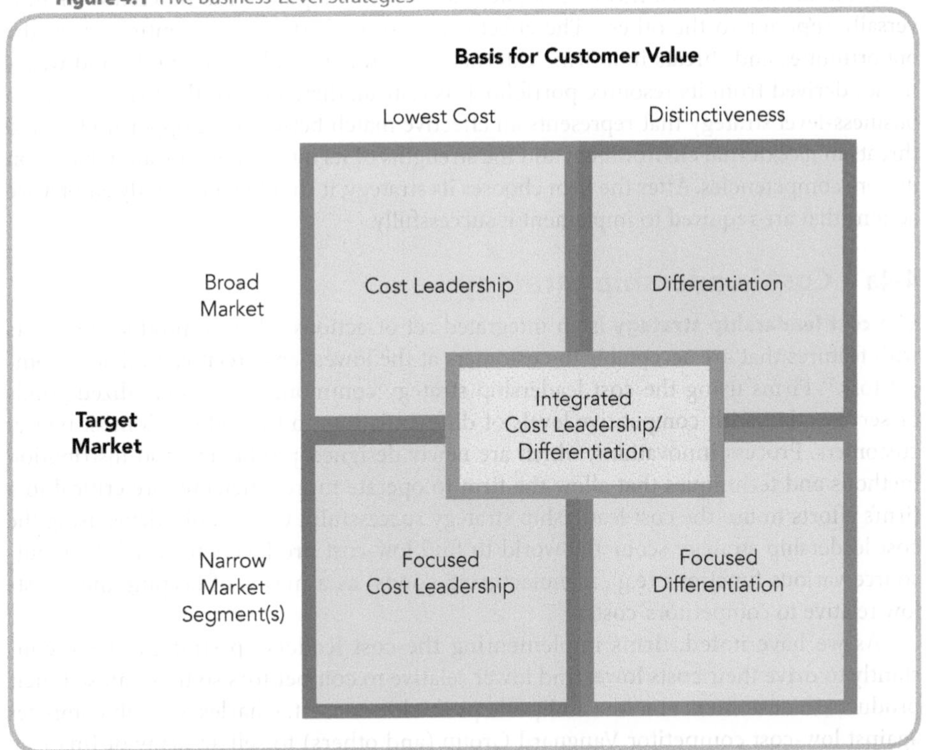

Source: Based on M. E. Porter, 1998, *Competitive Advantage: Creating and Sustaining Superior Performance*, New York: The Free Press; D. G. Sirmon, M. A. Hitt, & R. D. Ireland, 2007, Managing firm resources in dynamic environments to create value: Looking inside the black box, *Academy of Management Review*, 32: 273–292; D. G. Sirmon, M. A. Hitt, R. D. Ireland, & B. A. Gilbert, 2011, Resource orchestration to create competitive advantage: Breadth, depth and life cycles effects, *Journal of Management*, 37: 1390–1412.

likelihood a firm will develop an advantage relative to competitors as a path to earning above-average returns.

When selecting a business-level strategy, firms evaluate two types of potential competitive advantages: "lower cost than rivals or the ability to differentiate and command a premium price that exceeds the extra cost of doing so."[54] Lower costs result from the firm's ability to perform activities differently than rivals; being able to differentiate indicates the firm's capacity to perform different (and valuable) activities. Thus, based on the nature and quality of its internal resources, capabilities, and core competencies, a firm seeks to form either a cost competitive advantage or a distinctiveness competitive advantage as the basis for implementing its business-level strategy.[55]

Two types of target markets are broad market and narrow market segment(s) (see Figure 4.1). Firms serving a broad market seek to use their capabilities to create value for customers on an industry-wide basis. A narrow market segment means that the firm intends to serve the needs of a narrow customer group. With focus strategies, the firm "selects a segment or group of segments in the industry and tailors its strategy to serving them to the exclusion of others."[56] Buyers with special needs and buyers located in specific geographic regions are examples of narrow customer groups. As shown in Figure 4.1, a firm could also strive to develop a combined low cost/distinctiveness value creation approach as the foundation for serving a target customer group that is larger than a narrow market segment but not as comprehensive as a broad (or industry-wide) customer group. In this instance, the firm uses the integrated cost leadership/differentiation strategy.

None of the five business-level strategies shown in Figure 4.1 is inherently or universally superior to the others. The effectiveness of each strategy is contingent on the opportunities and threats in a firm's external environment and the strengths and weaknesses derived from its resource portfolio. It is critical, therefore, for the firm to select a business-level strategy that represents an effective match between the opportunities and threats in its external environment and the strengths of its internal organization based on its core competencies. After the firm chooses its strategy, it should consistently emphasize actions that are required to implement it successfully.

4-4a Cost Leadership Strategy

The **cost leadership strategy** is an integrated set of actions taken to produce products with features that are acceptable to customers at the lowest cost, relative to that of competitors.[57] Firms using the cost leadership strategy commonly sell standardized goods or services, but with competitive levels of differentiation, to the industry's most typical customers. Process innovations, which are newly designed production and distribution methods and techniques that allow the firm to operate more efficiently, are critical to a firm's efforts to use the cost leadership strategy successfully. Commonly, firms using the cost leadership strategy scour the world to find low-cost producers to which they outsource various functions (e.g., manufacturing goods) as a means of keeping their costs low relative to competitors' costs.[58]

As we have noted, firms implementing the cost leadership strategy strive constantly to drive their costs lower and lower relative to competitors so they can sell their products to customers at a low and perhaps the lowest cost. Charles Schwab competes against low-cost competitor Vanguard Group (and others) to sell an array of financial products. Both firms offer numerous "passively managed" rather than "actively managed" funds to customers. Recently, Schwab claimed that the costs of its market cap index mutual funds were "lower than comparable competitor funds with the lowest investment minimums."[59] To offer a source of differentiation that customers wanting to buy low-cost products with acceptable levels of differentiation would find interesting, Schwab announced in January of 2018 that the expense ratio it would charge for three new equity index funds would be zero until June 30, 2018. At that time, the expense ratios for the three new funds would increase from zero to .04 or .05 percent.[60] Along with Vanguard and other competitors such as Fidelity, Schwab also offers commission-free ETF (exchange-traded funds) trades for a number of its ETFs. As an example of a source of differentiation, waiving Schwab's standard trade commission of $4.95 per transaction for a number of ETFs allows customers to save money when buying the firm's products. Now the fifth largest U.S. ETF sponsor, analysts suggest that "one of the primary reasons Schwab has been able to ascend to the upper echelon of ETF issuers in terms of size is the provider's willingness to compete with and in many cases beat rival sponsors when it comes to low fees."[61]

As primary activities, inbound logistics (e.g., materials handling, warehousing, and inventory control) and outbound logistics (e.g., collecting, storing, and distributing products to customers) often account for significant portions of the total cost to produce some products. Research suggests that having a competitive advantage in logistics creates more value with a cost leadership strategy than with a differentiation strategy.[62]

The **cost leadership strategy** is an integrated set of actions taken to produce products with features that are acceptable to customers at the lowest cost, relative to that of competitors.

Thus, cost leaders seeking competitively valuable ways to reduce costs may want to concentrate on the primary activities of inbound logistics and outbound logistics. An example of this is the decision by a number of low-cost producers to outsource their manufacturing operations to low-cost firms with low-wage employees (e.g., China).[63] However, outsourcing also makes the firm more dependent on suppliers over which they may have little control. Because of this, firms analyze outsourcing possibilities carefully prior to committing to any of them. Outsourcing creates interdependencies between the outsourcing firm and the suppliers. If dependencies become too great, supplier power may result in higher costs for the outsourcing firm. Such actions could harm the cost leader's ability to maintain a low-cost competitive advantage.[64] Cost leaders also examine all support activities to find additional potential cost reductions. Developing new systems for finding the optimal combination of low cost and acceptable levels of differentiation in the raw materials required to produce the firm's products is an example of how the procurement support activity can help when implementing the cost leadership strategy.

As described in Chapter 3, firms use value-chain analysis to identify the parts of the company's operations that create value and those that do not. Figure 4.2 demonstrates the value-chain activities and support functions that allow a firm to create value when implementing the cost leadership strategy. Companies lacking the ability to integrate the activities and functions shown in this figure typically lack the core competencies needed to use the cost leadership strategy successfully.

Effective use of the cost leadership strategy allows a firm to earn above-average returns in spite of the presence of strong competitive forces (see Chapter 2). The next sections (one for each of the five forces) explain how firms seek to earn above-average returns by implementing the cost leadership strategy.

Figure 4.2 Examples of Value-Creating Activities Associated with the Cost Leadership Strategy

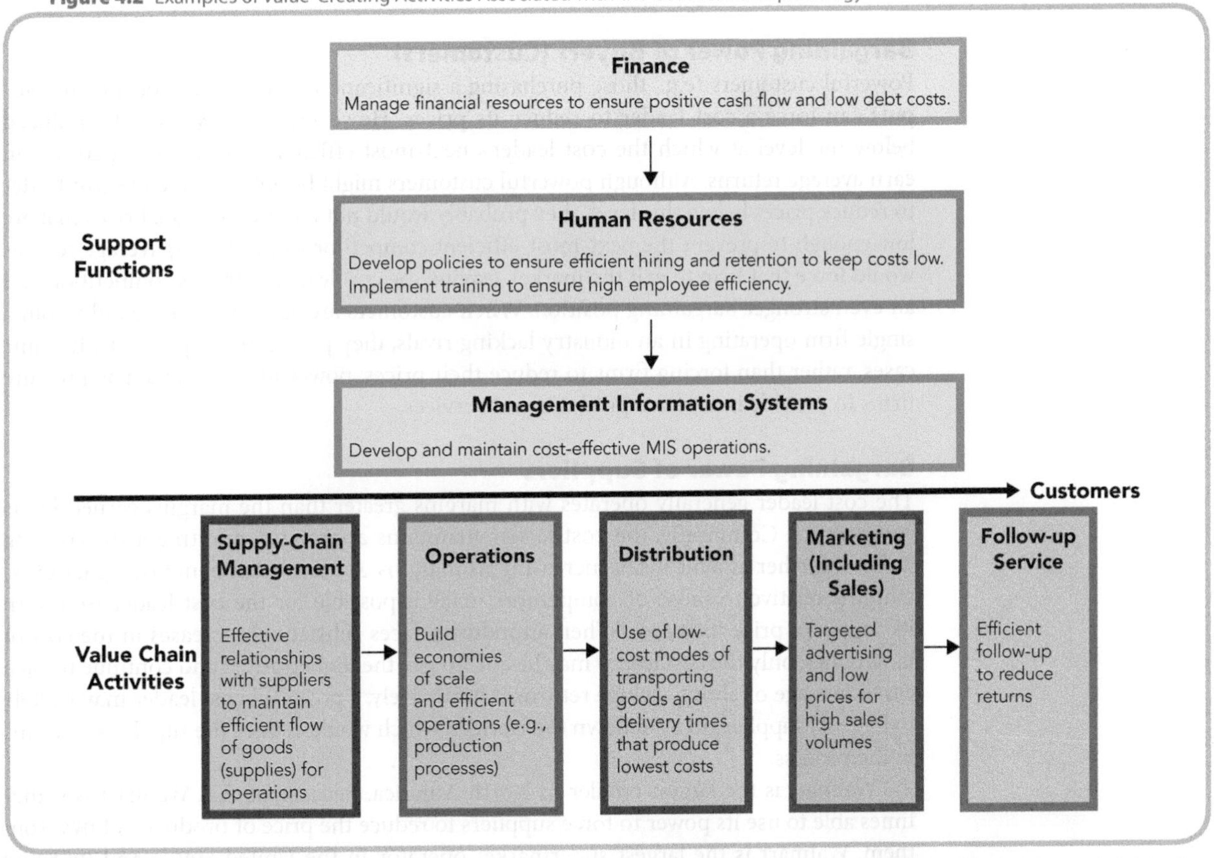

Source: Based on M. E. Porter, 1998, *Competitive Advantage: Creating and Sustaining Superior Performance*, New York: The Free Press; D. G. Sirmon, M. A. Hitt, & R. D. Ireland, 2007, Managing firm resources in dynamic environments to create value: Looking inside the black box, *Academy of Management Review*, 32: 273–292; D. G. Sirmon, M. A. Hitt, R. D. Ireland, & B. A. Gilbert, 2011, Resource orchestration to create competitive advantage: Breadth, depth and life cycles effects, *Journal of Management*, 37: 1390–1412.

Rivalry with Existing Competitors

Having the low-cost position is valuable when dealing with rivals. Because of the cost leader's advantageous position, rivals hesitate to compete on the price variable, especially before evaluating the potential outcomes of such competition.[65] Walmart and Dollar General use the cost leadership strategy. Successfully executing their strategies causes competitors to avoid focusing on the price variable as a means—and certainly as the primary means—of competing against Walmart and Dollar General.

A number of factors influence the degree of rivalry that firms encounter when implementing the cost leadership strategy. Examples of these factors include organizational size, resources possessed by rivals, a firm's dependence on a particular market, location and prior competitive interactions between firms, and a firm's reach, richness, and affiliation with its customers.[66] Walmart's size deters some competitors from competing against this firm. The richness and affiliation Amazon has with its customers create competitive challenges for competitors, even Walmart as it ramps up its effort through Walmart.com to challenge Amazon's superiority in online sales.

Those using the cost leadership strategy may also try to reduce the amount of rivalry they experience from competitors. Firms may decide to form collaborations, such as joint ventures and strategic alliances (see Chapter 9), to reduce rivalry.[67] In other instances, cost leaders try to develop strong and mutually supportive relationships with stakeholders (e.g., important government officials, suppliers, and customers) to reduce rivalry and lower their cost as a result. As noted in Chapter 2, *guanxi* is the name used to describe relationships that Chinese firms develop with others to reduce rivalry.[68]

Bargaining Power of Buyers (Customers)

Powerful customers (e.g., those purchasing a significant amount of the focal firm's output) can force a cost leader to reduce its prices. However, prices will not be reduced below the level at which the cost leader's next-most-efficient industry competitor can earn average returns. Although powerful customers might be able to force the cost leader to reduce prices below this level, they probably would not choose to do so. Prices that are low enough to prevent the next-most-efficient competitor from earning average returns would force that firm to exit the market, leaving the cost leader with less competition and an even stronger bargaining position. When customers are able to purchase only from a single firm operating in an industry lacking rivals, they pay more for products. In some cases, rather than forcing firms to reduce their prices, powerful customers may pressure firms to provide innovative products and services.

Bargaining Power of Suppliers

The cost leader generally operates with margins greater than the margins earned by its competitors. Commonly, the cost leader maintains a strong commitment to reducing its costs further as a means of increasing its margins. Among other benefits, higher gross margins relative to those of competitors make it possible for the cost leader to absorb its suppliers' price increases. When an industry faces substantial increases in the cost of its supplies, only the cost leader may be able to pay the higher prices and continue to earn either average or above average returns. Alternatively, a powerful cost leader may be able to force its suppliers to hold down their prices, which would reduce the suppliers' margins in the process.

Walmart is the largest retailer in North America. Because of this, Walmart is sometimes able to use its power to force suppliers to reduce the price of products it buys from them. Walmart is the largest supermarket operator in the United States, and its Sam's Club division is the second largest warehouse club in the United States. Its sales revenue of $495.76 billion in 2018 makes the firm an attractive outlet for suppliers to place their products. Because of its size (recently, there were 11,695 Walmart stores and 665 Sam's Club units located in 28 countries) and reach with customers (approximately 260 million customers shop at Walmart's stores weekly),[69] Walmart historically has been able to bargain for low prices from its suppliers. However, in light of increasing competition with Amazon in terms of online sales and because of the possibility of Amazon establishing storefronts, Walmart may find in the future that it has less bargaining power with suppliers than has been the case historically.[70]

To reduce costs, some firms may outsource an entire function such as manufacturing to a single or a small number of suppliers.[71] Outsourcing may take place in response to earnings pressure as expressed by shareholders, particularly institutional investors.[72] In the face of earnings pressure, a firm's decision-makers may conclude that outsourcing will be less expensive, allowing it to reduce its products' prices as a result.[73] This is not a risk-free decision though. For example, some businesspeople believe that "outsourcing can create new costs, as suppliers and partners demand a larger share of the value created."[74] This possibility highlights how important it is for the firm to select the most appropriate company to engage in outsourcing and then to manage its relationship with that company. Through effective management of the relationship between a firm and the one to which it outsources an activity, trust can develop. In turn, trust may be the foundation on which a firm might choose to integrate an outsourcing firm into its value chain to find ways to reduce its costs further.[75]

Potential Entrants

Through continuous efforts to reduce costs to levels that are lower than those against whom it competes, a cost leader becomes highly efficient. Increasing levels of efficiency (e.g., economies of scale) enhance profit margins. In turn, attractive profit margins create an entry barrier to potential competitors.[76] New entrants must be willing to accept less than average returns until they gain the experience required to approach the cost leader's efficiency. To earn even average returns, new entrants must have the competencies required to match the cost levels of competitors other than the cost leader. The low profit margins (relative to margins earned by firms implementing the differentiation strategy) make it necessary for the cost leader to sell large volumes of its product to earn above-average returns. However, firms striving to be the cost leader must avoid pricing their products so low that they cannot operate profitably, even though volume increases.

Product Substitutes

Compared with its industry rivals, the cost leader also holds an attractive position relative to product substitutes. A product substitute becomes a concern for the cost leader when its features and characteristics, in terms of cost and levels of differentiation that are acceptable to customers, are potentially attractive to the firm's customers. When faced with possible substitutes, the cost leader has more flexibility than do its competitors. To retain customers, it often can reduce its product's price. With still lower prices and competitive levels of differentiation, the cost leader increases the probability that customers will continue to prefer its product rather than a substitute.

Competitive Risks of the Cost Leadership Strategy

The cost leadership strategy is not risk-free. One risk is that the processes used by the cost leader to produce and distribute its product could become obsolete because of competitors' innovations.[77] These innovations may allow rivals to produce products at costs lower than those of the original cost leader, or to provide additional differentiated features without increasing the product's price to customers.

A second risk is that too much focus by the cost leader on cost reductions may occur at the expense of trying to understand customers' perceptions of "competitive levels of differentiation." Some believe, for example, that Walmart often has too few salespeople available to help customers and too few individuals at checkout registers. These complaints suggest that there might be a discrepancy between how Walmart's customers define "minimal acceptable levels of service" and the firm's attempts to drive its costs increasingly lower.

Imitation is a final risk of the cost leadership strategy. Using their own core competencies, competitors sometimes learn how to imitate the cost leader's strategy. When this happens, the cost leader must increase the value its product provides to customers. Commonly, the cost leader increases the value it creates by selling the current product at an even lower price or by adding differentiated features that create value for customers while maintaining price.

4-4b Differentiation Strategy

The **differentiation strategy** is an integrated set of actions taken to produce products (at an acceptable cost) that customers perceive as being different in ways that are important to them.[78] While cost leaders serve a typical customer in an industry, differentiators target customers for whom the firm creates value because of the manner in which its products differ from those produced and marketed by competitors. Product innovation, which is "the result of bringing to life a new way to solve the customer's problem—through a new product or service development—that benefits both the customer and the sponsoring company,"[79] is critical to successful use of the differentiation strategy.[80]

Firms must be able to provide customers with differentiated products at competitive costs to reduce upward pressure on the price they pay. When a firm produces differentiated features for its products at non-competitive costs, the price for the product may exceed what target customers are willing to pay. If firms have a thorough understanding of the value its target customers seek, the relative importance they attach to the satisfaction of different needs and for what they are willing to pay a premium, the differentiation strategy can be effective in helping them earn above-average returns. Of course, to achieve these returns, the firm must apply its knowledge capital (knowledge held by its employees and managers) to provide customers with a differentiated product that provides them with value for which they are willing to pay.[81]

Through the differentiation strategy, the firm produces distinctive products for customers who value differentiated features more than low cost. For example, superior product reliability, durability, and high-performance sound systems are among the differentiated features of Toyota Motor Corporation's Lexus products. (Nevertheless, Lexus does offer its vehicles to customers at a competitive purchase price relative to other luxury automobiles.)

As with Lexus products, a product's unique attributes, rather than its purchase price, provide the value for which customers are willing to pay. Now the second-largest luxury brand by revenue behind only Louis Vuitton, Gucci relies today on innovative and unique product designs from Alessandro Michele. These new designs "mix colorful streetwear, historical references and garish animal prints."[82] The firm believes that these unique designs, for which customers are willing to pay, will help it defy what is typically a boom-bust cycle with fashion-based products.

The **differentiation strategy** is an integrated set of actions taken to produce products (at an acceptable cost) that customers perceive as being different in ways that are important to them.

To maintain success by implementing the differentiation strategy, the firm must consistently upgrade differentiated features that customers value and/or create new valuable features (i.e., innovate) without significant cost increases.[83] This approach requires firms to change their product lines frequently.[84] These firms may also offer a portfolio of products that complement each other, thereby enriching the differentiation for the customer and perhaps satisfying a portfolio of consumer needs. Because a differentiated product satisfies customers' unique needs, firms following the differentiation strategy are able to charge premium prices. The ability to sell a product at a price that substantially exceeds the cost of creating its differentiated features allows the firm to outperform rivals and earn above-average returns. Rather than costs, a firm using the differentiation strategy primarily concentrates on investing in and developing features that differentiate a product in ways that create value for customers.[85] Overall, a firm using the differentiation strategy seeks to be different from its competitors in as many dimensions as possible. The less similarity between a firm's goods or services and those of its competitors, the more buffered it is from rivals' actions. Still, customers must view the prices they are paying for the differentiated products they buy from a firm as acceptable to them in order for this strategy to succeed. Commonly recognized differentiated goods include those offered by Gucci and Louis Vuitton, men's suits tailored by Brioni, Caterpillar's heavy-duty earth-moving equipment, and the differentiated consulting services McKinsey & Co. offers clients.

Yannis Vlamos/Pixelform/SIPA/SIPA France/Arles/France/Newscom

A runway model wearing creations by Alessandro Michele, Gucci's Creative Director.

Many dimensions are available to firms seeking to differentiate their products from competitors' offerings. Unusual features, responsive customer service, rapid product innovations, technological leadership, perceived prestige and status, different tastes, and engineering design and performance are examples of approaches to differentiation.[86] While the number of ways to reduce costs may be finite, virtually anything a firm can do to create real or perceived value in consumers' eyes is a basis for differentiation. Consider product design as a case in point. Because it can create a positive experience for customers, design is an important source of differentiation (even for cost leaders seeking to find ways to add functionalities to their low-cost products as a way of differentiating their products from competitors) and, hopefully for firms emphasizing it, of competitive advantage.[87] Examples of other competitive dimensions firms use to differentiate their products include Halliburton's (an oil-field services company) focus on superior execution of projects[88] and Subaru's focus on product longevity and durability.[89]

Firms use the value chain to determine if they are able to link the activities required to create value by using the differentiation strategy. In Figure 4.3, we show examples of value chain activities and support functions that firms use commonly to differentiate a product. Companies without the skills needed to link these activities cannot expect to use the differentiation strategy successfully.

Figure 4.3 Examples of Value-Creating Activities Associated with the Differentiation Strategy

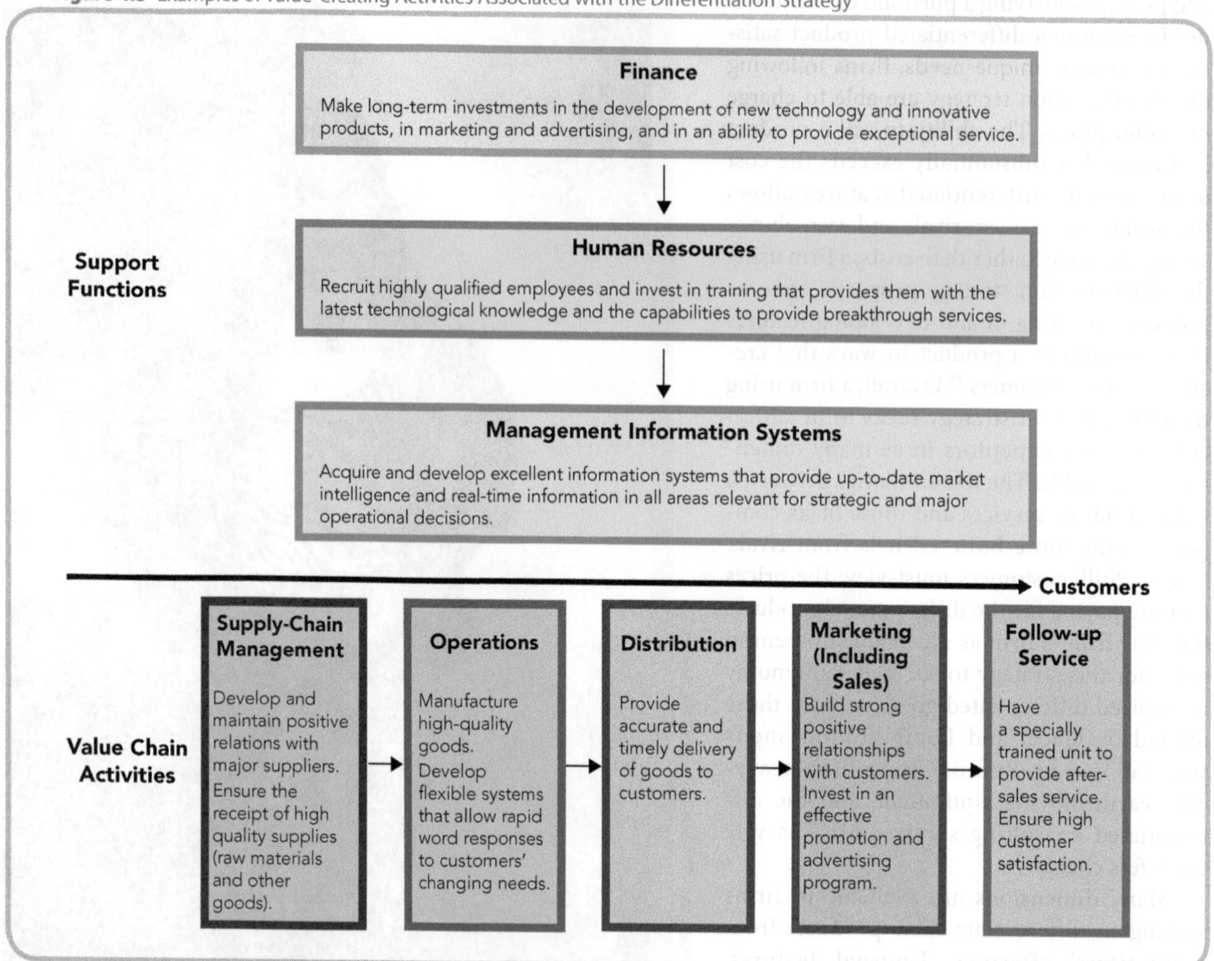

Source: Based on information from M. E. Porter, 1998, *Competitive Advantage: Creating and Sustaining Superior Performance*, New York: The Free Press; D. G. Sirmon, M. A. Hitt, & R. D. Ireland, 2007, Managing firm resources in dynamic environments to create value: Looking inside the black box, *Academy of Management Review*, 32: 273–292; D. G. Sirmon, M. A. Hitt, R. D. Ireland, & B. A. Gilbert, 2011, Resource orchestration to create competitive advantage: Breadth, depth and life cycles effects, *Journal of Management*, 37: 1390–1412.

Next, we explain how firms using the differentiation strategy can successfully position themselves in terms of the five forces of competition (see Chapter 2) to earn above-average returns.

Rivalry with Existing Competitors

Customers tend to be loyal purchasers of products differentiated in ways that are meaningful to them. As their loyalty to a brand increases, customers become less sensitive to price increases. The relationship between brand loyalty and price sensitivity insulates a firm from competitive rivalry. Thus, positive reputations with customers sustain the competitive advantage of firms using a differentiation strategy.[90] Nonetheless, firms using a differentiation strategy must be aware of imitation efforts by rivals and aware of any resulting successes. This is the case between Samsung and Apple as Samsung seeks to improve on Apple's products, potentially creating value for customers when doing so. In the context of competitive rivalry (see Chapter 5), Apple must respond to imitation efforts to improve the value its products create for customers. Simultaneously, as a firm using the differentiation strategy, Apple must develop new and novel products to maintain its reputation for producing and selling innovative and stylish products that target customers find valuable.[91]

Bargaining Power of Buyers (Customers)

The distinctiveness of differentiated products reduces customers' sensitivity to price increases. Customers are willing to accept a price increase when a product still satisfies their unique needs better than does a competitor's offering. Thus, the golfer whose needs are met by the Ping G Stretch series of clubs or Piretti Putters will likely continue buying those products even when encountering price increases. Purchasers of brand-name food items (e.g., Heinz ketchup, Sir Kensington's ketchup, and Kleenex tissues) accept price increases in those products as long as they continue to perceive that they satisfy their distinctive needs at an acceptable cost. In all of these cases, customers are relatively insensitive to price increases because they do not think an acceptable product alternative exists.

Bargaining Power of Suppliers

Because the firm using the differentiation strategy charges a premium price for its products, suppliers must provide high-quality components, driving up the differentiator's costs. However, the high margins the firm earns in these cases partially insulate it from suppliers' influence. The reason for this is that higher margins make it possible for the firm to absorb potentially higher costs from its suppliers.[92] On the other hand, because of buyers' relative insensitivity to price increases, the firm implementing a differentiation strategy might choose to pass the additional cost of supplies on to the customer by increasing the price of its unique product. However, when buyer firms outsource an entire function or large portions of it to a supplier, especially R&D for a firm following a differentiation strategy, they can become dependent on and thus vulnerable to that supplier.[93]

Potential Entrants

Customer loyalty and the need to overcome the uniqueness of a differentiated product create substantial barriers to potential entrants. Entering an industry under these conditions typically demands significant investments of resources and patience while seeking customers' loyalty. In these cases, some potential entrants decide to make smaller investments to see if they can gain a "foothold" (or a relatively secure position through which competitive progress is possible) in the market. In these cases, the firm's loss if it fails to develop a foothold is minimal while the gain from developing a foothold could be substantial.[94]

Product Substitutes

Firms selling brand-name products to loyal customers hold an attractive position relative to product substitutes. In contrast, companies without brand loyalty face a higher probability of customers switching either to products that offer differentiated features that serve the same function (particularly if the substitute has a lower price) or to products that offer more features and perform functions that create more value. In these instances, firms may be vulnerable to innovations from outside the industry that provide superior satisfaction in terms of customers' needs (e.g., Amazon's Alexa in the music industry).[95]

Competitive Risks of the Differentiation Strategy

One risk of the differentiation strategy is that customers may decide that the price differential between the differentiator's product and the cost leader's product is too large. In this instance, a firm may be offering differentiated features that exceed target customers' needs. The firm then becomes vulnerable to competitors that are able to offer customers a combination of features and price that is more consistent with their needs.

Another risk of the differentiation strategy is that a firm's means of differentiation may cease to provide value for which customers are willing to pay or that how the firm seeks to differentiate its offerings is unclear to target customers. A differentiated product becomes less valuable if imitation by rivals causes customers to perceive that competitors offer essentially the same product, but at a lower price. For example, does buying and using an iPhone create value that exceeds the costs and features of some competitors' offerings?

A third risk of the differentiation strategy is that experience can narrow customers' perceptions of the value of a product's differentiated features. For example, customers having positive experiences with generic tissues may decide that the differentiated features of the Kleenex product are not worth the extra cost. To counter this risk, firms must continue to differentiate their product (e.g., through innovation) for customers at a price they are willing to pay.[96]

Counterfeiting is the differentiation strategy's fourth risk. Counterfeits have a trademark or logo that is identical to or indistinguishable from a legal logo owned by another party, thus infringing the rights of the legal owner. When a consumer purchases such a product and discovers the deception, regret creates distrust of the branded product and reduces differentiation.[97] Because of this, firms take actions to prevent counterfeiters from imitating their products.

Failing to provide crisp and identifiable differentiation to customers in the form of a firm's products (goods and services) is a fifth risk of the differentiation strategy. When this is the case, the firm does not meet customers' expectations through its efforts to implement the differentiation strategy. Another way of viewing this is to say that firms sometimes fail to create differentiation for which the customer is willing to pay. As explained in the Strategic Focus, this may be the case for Macy's department stores. For the past few years, this firm's efforts fell short in terms of satisfying stakeholders including shareholders (who have seen the value of their ownership positions decline) and customers (who are not frequenting Macy's stores to shop). We describe actions Macy's is taking to reverse its fortunes and to become successful again by implementing the differentiation strategy.

4-4c Focus Strategies

The **focus strategy** is an integrated set of actions taken to produce products that serve the needs of a particular segment of customers. Thus, firms implementing a focus strategy utilize their core competencies to serve the needs of a particular industry segment or niche to the exclusion of others. Market segments firms may choose to serve by implementing a focus strategy include the following:

1. a particular buyer group (e.g., youth or senior citizens),
2. a different segment of a product line (e.g., products for professional painters or the do-it-yourself group), or
3. a different geographic market (e.g., northern or southern Italy).[98]

Firms can serve many types of customer needs when using a focus strategy. For example, founded in 1936 by Don Prudencio Unanue and his wife Carolina, Goya Foods, Inc. is the largest Hispanic-owned food company in the United States. Segmenting the Hispanic market into unique groups, Goya offers more than 2,500 "high-quality and affordable food products from the Caribbean, Mexico, Spain, Central and South America."[99] The firm is a leading authority on Hispanic food and seeks to be a premier source for those desiring to purchase authentic Latin cuisine. By successfully using a focus strategy, firms such as Goya gain a competitive advantage in specific market niches or segments, even though they do not possess an industry-wide competitive advantage.

The **focus strategy** is an integrated set of actions taken to produce products that serve the needs of a particular segment of customers.

Although the breadth of a target is clearly a matter of degree, the essence of the focus strategy "is the exploitation of a narrow target's differences from the balance of

Strategic **Focus**

The Differentiation Strategy—Can Macy's Again Find Ways to Achieve Success by Implementing this Strategy?

Rowland Hussey Macy established the firm known today as Macy's Inc. in 1858 at the corner of 14th Street and 6th Avenue in New York City (sales on the day the store opened totaled $11.06). R.H. Macy, the firm's original name, contributed a number of innovations to retailing. Known for its creative merchandising approaches, Macy's was the first department store to offer bath towels in an array of colors and was the first retailer in New York City to hold a liquor license. Macy's also "pioneered such revolutionary business practices as the one-price system, in which the same item was sold to every customer at one price, and quoting specific prices for goods in newspaper advertising."

At the time of its founding and on a going-forward basis, Macy's chose to implement the differentiation strategy as a means of succeeding with customers and other stakeholders. Historically, Macy's differentiated itself from competitors on several dimensions including offering private label brands, providing unique service, stocking trendier products, using specially trained experts to staff its perfume and make-up counters, and organizing the layout of its stores to promote easy access to products for customers during their shopping experience.

For many decades, Macy's was a successful department store retailer as it implemented its differentiation strategy. Times have changed for retailers such as Macy's though. Today, for example, 70 percent of merchandise found in department stores like Macy's is available from Amazon and other online vendors as well. The lack of differentiation between the inventory of a storefront retailer such as Macy's and the inventory of online retailers "is the single biggest challenge department stores face." Because of the lack of clear differentiation between what Macy's and competitors such as retail discounters (e.g., T.J. Maxx), nimble and focused firms (e.g., Ulta Beauty), and online vendors offer, it seems that Macy's is failing to meet customers' expectations regarding sharp differentiation for which they are willing to pay. Evidence for the firm's lack of success in recent times includes multiple consecutive quarters of sales declines and the decision to sell a number of stores to generate cash. Facing this type of situation, analysts believe that "the best opportunity department stores (including Macy's) have is to create products that set them apart, to give customers a reason to go." How is Macy's responding to this situation? What is the firm doing to address the challenge of finding ways to implement its differentiation strategy with greater degrees of success? As we discuss next, the firm is taking several actions, many of which return it to its commitment to innovation.

Macy's North Star Strategy is a set of commitments and actions the firm is taking to improve its execution in terms of the differentiation strategy. The North Star Strategy has five components: (1) *from familiar to favorite*—the interest here is to anticipate customers' needs and respond to them quickly and effectively by offering desirable products and enjoyable shopping experiences; (2) *must be Macy's*—the firm is again emphasizing its private brands (such as I.N.C. apparel, Hotel Collection and Impulse beauty items) as a way to offer value-creating products and services that are exclusive

Astrid Stawiarz/Getty Images Entertainment/Getty Images

NICOPANDA, known for its edgy and playful looks, launched an exclusive apparel collection with Macy's in 2018.

to Macy's; (3) *every experience matters*—the firm believes that its "competitive advantage is the ability to combine the human touch in our physical stores with cutting-edge technology" (including mobile apps and the "Buy Online Pickup in Stores" program); (4) *funding our future*—to have the financial resources needed to reinvest in innovations that will create valuable differentiation for customers, Macy's is reinvesting in innovation, reducing expenses that do not serve the customer directly, and creating value by selling units in its vast real estate portfolio; and (5) *what's new, what's next*—this commitment and actions resulting from it "explores how we innovate to turn consumer and technology trends to our advantage and drive growth." As we see, part of Macy's efforts to implement its differentiation strategy with greater degrees of success is to form a digital strategy through which it uses technology to interpret information as a means of creating more value for customers.

Overall, Macy's is trying to set itself apart from competitors in ways that create value for customers. In addition to emphasizing its private label brands, the firm established mobile checkout capabilities to speed up service to customers. It also introduced an incentive plan to its 130,000 employees, including part-time workers. Through this plan, all employees benefit when sales exceed internal benchmarks. For customers, Macy's established its Star Rewards loyalty program recently. A three-tier program, the benefits flowing to customers increase as they spend more with the firm. Collectively, those leading Macy's and its stakeholders hope that the innovations the firm is establishing and on which it is executing will be the foundation through which the differentiation strategy leads to company success.

Sources: 2018, Bluemercury, Macy's Homepage, www.macy's.com, March 9; 2018, Company history, Macy's Homepage, www.macys.com, March 9; S. Kapner & A. Prang, 2018, Holiday sales rebound at Macy's and JCPenney, *Wall Street Journal*, www.wsj.com, January 4; A. Levine-Weinberg, 2018, Macy's, Inc. real estate sales will continue in 2018, *The Motley Fool*, www.fool.com, January 16; W. Loeb, 2018, Macy's makes progress under Gennett, but much remains to be done, *Forbes*, www.forbes.com, February 28; Z. Meyer & C. Jones, 2018, Macy's buoyed by brisk sales, popular new loyalty program, *USA Today*, www.usatoday.com, February 27; E. Winkler, 2018, Macy's has a spring in its step, *Wall Street Journal*, www.wsj.com, February 27; C. Jones, 2017, Why Walmart is soaring while Macy's flounders, *USA Today*, www.usatoday.com, February 22; P. Wahba, 2017, How Macy's is turning beauty store Bluemercury into its secret weapon, *Fortune*, www.fortune.com, October 4; P. Wahba, 2017, How Macy's new CEO plans to stop the bleeding, *Fortune*, www.fortune.com, March 22; G. Petro, 2016, Macy's, JCPenney, and Sears: Where's the differentiation? *Forbes*, www.forbes.com, June 22.

the industry."[100] Firms using the focus strategy intend to serve a particular customer segment of an industry more effectively than can industry-wide competitors. Entrepreneurial firms and certainly entrepreneurial start-ups commonly serve a specific market niche or segment, partly because they do not have the knowledge or resources to serve the broader market.[101] Firms implementing a focus strategy generally prefer to operate "below the radar" of larger and more resource rich firms that serve the broader market. The focus strategy leads to success when the firm serves a segment well whose unique needs are so specialized that broad-based competitors choose not to serve that segment or when they create value for a segment that exceeds the value created by industry-wide competitors.

Firms can create value for customers in specific and unique market segments by using the focused cost leadership strategy or the focused differentiation strategy.

Focused Cost Leadership Strategy

Based in Sweden, IKEA, a global furniture retailer with 403 store locations in 49 markets and sales revenue of 38.3 billion euros in 2017,[102] uses the focused cost leadership strategy. Germany, the United States, France, Britain, and China are the firm's largest markets.[103] Using the focused cost leadership strategy, IKEA hosted 936 million store visits and 2.3 billion website visits from customers in 2017. The company's founder, Ingvar Kamprad, died recently at the age of 91.

Demonstrating the low cost part of the firm's strategy is its commitment to strive constantly "to reduce costs without compromising quality."[104] When customers see a "new lower price" announcement, IKEA says that it means that the firm has discovered a way to offer good quality, function, and better prices on its products. Highlighting the focus part of IKEA's focused cost leadership strategy is the firm's target market: young buyers desiring style at a low cost.

Design is critical to the firm's ability to provide style at a low cost to customers. Regarding design, the firm notes the following: "We feel that good design combines form, function, quality, and sustainability at a low price. We call it 'Democratic Design' because we believe good home furnishing is for everyone."[105] For these customers, the firm offers home furnishings that combine good design, function, and acceptable quality with low prices. According to the firm, it seeks "to offer a wide range of well-designed, functional home furnishing products at prices so low that as many people as possible will be able to afford them."

IKEA emphasizes several activities to keep its costs low. For example, instead of relying primarily on third-party manufacturers, the firm's engineers design low-cost, modular furniture that is ready for customers to assemble. To eliminate the need for sales associates or decorators, IKEA positions the products in its stores so that customers can view different living combinations (complete with sofas, chairs, tables, etc.) in a single room-like setting. The room-specific settings help customers imagine how furniture would look in their home. Historically, not offering delivery services was a third practice that supported efforts to keep the firm's costs low. To be more competitive though, IKEA recently offered a delivery option to customers. In the company's words: "Delivery starts at $29! Prices range from $29 to $59. The prices vary based on demand and distance from the closet IKEA retail store to your shipping address."[106]

Although the firm emphasizes low costs, IKEA offers some differentiated features that appeal to or are acceptable to its target customers. Unique furniture designs, in-store playrooms for children, wheelchairs for customer use, and extended hours are examples of the differentiated features IKEA customers like in addition to the low cost of the firm's products.

Focused Differentiation Strategy

Other firms implement the focused differentiation strategy. As noted earlier, firms can differentiate their products along many dimensions. For example, some of the new generation of food trucks populating cities such as Los Angeles use the focused differentiation strategy, serving, for example, organic food that often trained chefs and well-known restaurateurs prepare.

Headquartered in Los Angeles and in light of its mission to "heal our planet, one meal at a time," Green Truck "serves an all organic menu sourced from local organic farms."[107] To reach as many customers as possible, Green Truck uses Twitter and Facebook to inform customers of its locations as it moves from point to point in Los Angeles.[108]

With a focus strategy, firms must be able to complete various primary value-chain activities and support functions in a competitively superior manner to develop and sustain a competitive advantage and earn above-average returns. The activities required to use the focused cost leadership strategy are virtually identical to those of the industry-wide cost leadership strategy (see Figure 4.2); activities required to use the focused differentiation strategy are largely identical to those of the industry-wide differentiation strategy (see Figure 4.3). Similarly, the manner in which each of the two focus strategies allows a firm to deal successfully with the five competitive forces parallels those of the two broad strategies. The only difference is in the firm's choice of target market—that is, its competitive scope (see Figure 4.1). With a focus strategy, the firm chooses to focus on a narrow market segment. Thus, Figure 4.2 and Figure 4.3 and the text describing the five competitive forces also explain the relationship between each of the two focus strategies and competitive advantage.

In the Strategic Focus, we use a single product—hamburgers—as offered by different firms to present specific examples of the focused cost leadership and the focused differentiation strategies. For comparison purposes, we also mention firms using either the cost

Strategic **Focus**

What Type of Hamburger Would You Like to Buy and Eat Today?

Hamburgers are popular in many parts of the world. Merriam-Webster offers the following definition of a hamburger: "ground beef; a patty of ground beef; a sandwich consisting of a patty of hamburger in a split typically round bun." This informative definition seems straightforward. However, as those who consume this food product know, there are multiple varieties of hamburgers available for customers to purchase. In this Strategic Focus, we describe how firms use four of the five generic business-level strategies to make and sell hamburgers (we do not use the integrated cost leadership/differentiation strategy here).

As mentioned earlier in this chapter, the number of dimensions on which firms can differentiate products is virtually endless. Essentially, any product attribute that customers value and for which they are willing to pay is a potential source of differentiation. Companies using a focused differentiation strategy to produce and sell hamburgers seek to present a narrow or specific group of customers with a product that is distinctive in ways that are important to them.

Located in Bryan, TX, and with a geographic focus as well as a product focus, Proudest Monkey uses the focused differentiation strategy. This firm's owners say that their restaurant is "all about good times and good company." One differentiator of this firm is its location, which is a part of a downtown area that the community seeks to revitalize. Another differentiator is the fact that a historic building houses the firm. In constructing their restaurant, the owners were careful to maintain the building's integrity. Known among customers as "The Monkey," the firm differentiates its hamburgers in addition to offering customers an opportunity to dine in an establishment housed in a way that is consistent with a region's history. Quality is a key differentiator. To offer consistent quality to customers, the firm's unique menu is "simple" and "fresh." Each morning, employees make fresh patties, sauces, and toppings. An extended list of Texas craft beers is available to customers as well as are "unique to the Monkey" Ice Cream Martinis with names such as Arnold Palmer, Chocolate Covered Strawberry, and Mint Chocolate Chip. Prices for the firm's unique burgers (examples are the Willie Norris and the Yard Bird) range from $6.95 to $8.35. The restaurant also offers unique french fries that are prepared as "dirty" (salt, pepper, & sugar) or as "yuppie" (olive oil, salt, pepper, garlic powder, and parmesan cheese).

Instead of focusing on a narrow group of customers, Smashburger, founded in Colorado in 2007, uses the differentiation strategy to target a "broad market" of customers with what the firm believes are unique food items. With over 350 units located in 32 U.S. states and 5 countries, this firm differentiates its hamburgers in ways that a large set of customers finds appealing. Smashburger's mission is to "put burgers back into people's lives. We want to change the way people think about burgers and the way they feel when they have a burger." The firm's hamburgers "are always made-to-order, never frozen, smashed and seared to perfection on our grill." The fresh meat used to make a Smashburger is literally smashed on a grill using a specialized tool the firm developed. Using this process, which the firm contends increases the desirability of its meat patties, Smashburger makes hamburgers such as the Classic Smash, the BBQ, Bacon & Cheddar, the Avocado Club, and the Bacon Cheeseburger. Prices for a Smashburger range from roughly $6.59 to $7.79. Customers can order Smashfries (with rosemary and garlic integrated into the cooking of the fries) to accompany their Smashburger if so inclined.

Lee Svitak Dean/Minneapolis Star Tribune/MCT/Newscom

Smashburger's Bacon Avocado Club.

Founded in 1923 in Flint, MI, Kewpee Hamburgers is the second known hamburger chain in the United States. Now headquartered in Lima, OH where three of the firm's five remaining units are located (the other two are in Lansing, MI and Racine, WI), this firm uses geography and low prices as the basis of its focused cost leadership strategy. Interestingly, the first Kewpee storefront built in Lima, OH is a national historic site. Kewpee serves low-cost food items to a narrow segment of people located in three Midwestern states. Using locally raised beef, Kewpee makes hamburgers that are basic and that appeal to a local population wanting a basic hamburger with minimal differentiators. The firm's slogan—"Hamburger pickle on top, makes your heart go flippity-flop!" captures the standardized and non-differentiated aspect of Kewpee hamburgers. With its basic food products offered in undifferentiated buildings, the hamburgers' prices are inexpensive compared to the prices of hamburgers offered by Proudest Monkey, Smashburger, and other hamburger establishments following the focused differentiation or the differentiation strategy. The regular Kewpee hamburger is $2.20 while the special hamburger (including Miracle Whip, lettuce, and tomato) is $2.40. If not in the mood for a hamburger, Kewpee offers customers a cheese sandwich for $1.90. A double-large soft drink is $1.00. As a means of providing some differentiation when implementing its focused cost leadership strategy, Kewpee provides different slices of pie at special prices for each month of the year. February sees customers having access to Februcherry while Marchocolate is available in March.

In contrast to Kewpee, McDonald's uses the cost leadership strategy to serve a broad market of customers. As of January 2018, there were more than 36,000 McDonald's restaurants in the world. The company's 1.9 million workers serve over 69 million people daily. Ray Kroc, the founder of McDonald's, wanted to build a restaurant system that would result in customers being able to buy products of consistent quality at all of the firm's locations. Focusing on "quality, service, cleanliness and value," McDonald's offers an array of food products at lower costs that appeal to a large number of customers throughout the world. The "dollar menu" is an important part of this firm's cost leadership strategy, as is the case for other hamburger chains, such as Burger King, using the same strategy.

Sources: 2018, About us—monkey eat, monkey drink, Proudest Monkey Homepage, www.proudestmonkey.com, March 9; 2018, Our mission, About us, McDonald's Homepage, www.mcdonalds.com, March 9; 2018, Definition of hamburger, *Merriam-Webster*, www.merriam-webster.com, March 9; 2018, About us, Kewpee Homepage, www.kewpeehamburgers.com, March 9; 2018, Our story, Smashburger Homepage, www.smashburger.com, March 9; M. Rosenberg, 2018, Number of McDonald's restaurants worldwide, *ThoughtCo.*, www.thoughtco.com, February 11.

leadership or the differentiation strategy on an industry-wide basis to sell hamburgers. As this Strategic Focus demonstrates, firms can use any of these four generic business-level strategies to achieve success when making and selling hamburgers.

Competitive Risks of Focus Strategies

With either focus strategy, the firm faces the same set of general risks the company using the cost leadership or the differentiation strategy on an industry-wide basis faces. However, because of a narrow target market, focus strategies have three additional risks.

First, a competitor may be able to focus on a more narrowly defined competitive segment and thereby "out-focus" the focuser. This could be a competitive challenge for IKEA if another firm found a way to offer IKEA's customers (young buyers interested in stylish furniture at a low cost) additional sources of differentiation while charging the same price or to provide the same service with the same sources of differentiation at a lower price. Harley Davidson's recent decision to produce electric motorcycles may challenge Zero Motorcycles, a much smaller company producing only electric motorcycles.[109] Potentially enhancing the significance of this competitive challenge for Zero Motorcycles is Harley's decision to invest in Alta Motors, an electric bike start-up. Harley made this investment to "accelerate its electrification effort."[110]

A second risk is that a company competing on an industry-wide basis may decide that the market segment served by the firm using a focus strategy is attractive and worthy of competitive pursuit.[111] For example, a major restaurant in Los Angeles that serves multiple types of offerings to a range of customers might decide that serving organic foods through its own food truck is an attractive market. With capabilities to prepare a larger set of food items compared to the food offerings provided by a firm such as Green Truck (located in Los Angeles and mentioned earlier), the major restaurant might be able to prepare and sell organic foods that exceed the combination of quality and price that Green Truck is able to offer.

The third risk associated with using a focus strategy is that the needs of customers within a narrow competitive segment may become more similar to those of industry-wide customers as a whole over time. When this happens, the firm implementing a focus strategy no longer provides unique value to its target customers. This may be what happened to RadioShack in that the unique demand of do-it-yourself electronic dabblers that RadioShack traditionally focused on dissipated over time. Big-box-retailers such as Best Buy started carrying a number of the "specialty" items RadioShack stocked historically. In response, RadioShack executives struggled over many years to find the right focus and made too many strategic changes over time, which ultimately led to the firm's bankruptcy.

4-4d Integrated Cost Leadership/Differentiation Strategy

Most consumers have high expectations when purchasing products. In general, it seems that most consumers want to pay a low price for products that possess somewhat highly differentiated features. Because of these expectations, a number of firms engage in primary value-chain activities and support functions that allow them to pursue low cost and differentiation simultaneously.

The **integrated cost leadership/differentiation strategy** finds a firm engaging simultaneously in primary value-chain activities and support functions to achieve a low cost position with some product differentiation. When using this strategy, firms seek to produce products at a relatively low cost that have some differentiated features that their customers value. Efficient production is the source of maintaining low costs, while differentiation is the source of creating unique value. Firms that use the integrated cost leadership/differentiation strategy successfully usually adapt quickly to new technologies and rapid changes in their external environments. Concentrating jointly on developing two sources of competitive advantage (cost and differentiation) increases the number of primary value-chain activities and support functions in which the firm becomes competent. In these cases, firms often have strong networks with external parties that perform some of the value-chain activities and/or support functions.[112] In turn, having skills in a larger number of activities and functions increases a firm's flexibility and its adaptability.

Concentrating on the needs of its core customer group (e.g., higher-income, fashion-conscious discount shoppers), Target implements an integrated cost leadership/differentiation strategy. The firm informs customers of this strategy through its "Expect More. Pay Less." brand promise. The firm essentially describes this strategy with the following statement: "Target Corporation is an upscale discount retailer that provides high-quality, on-trend merchandise at attractive prices in clean, spacious and guest-friendly stores."[113] In addition to a relatively low price for its somewhat differentiated products, Target creates some differentiation for customers by providing them with a quick check-out experience and a dedicated team providing more personalized service.

Historically, most firms competing in emerging markets chose the cost leadership strategy to guide their actions. Influencing this strategy choice are the relatively low labor costs and other supply costs firms competing in emerging economies experience (compared to the labor and supply costs for firms competing in developed economies). The choice of strategy for emerging economy firms may soon change however, given their interest in producing capabilities through which they can develop innovations. In the short run, the newly developed innovation capabilities in emerging economy firms will likely lag innovation capabilities in developed economy firms. Combining newly developed innovation capabilities with the ability to deliver products at a lower cost may soon find a number of emerging economy firms implementing the integrated cost leadership/differentiation strategy.[114]

The **integrated cost leadership/differentiation strategy** finds a firm engaging simultaneously in primary value-chain activities and support functions to achieve a low cost position with some product differentiation.

Flexibility is required for firms to complete primary value-chain activities and support functions in ways that allow them to use the integrated cost leadership/differentiation strategy successfully. A number of Chinese firms, including some in the automobile manufacturing sector, have developed a flexible architecture system through which they produce differentiated car designs at relatively low costs.[115] For firms seeking to balance cost reductions with sources of differentiation, flexible manufacturing systems, information networks, and total quality management systems are three sources of flexibility that help them implement the integrated cost leadership/differentiation strategy successfully.

Flexible Manufacturing Systems

Using a flexible manufacturing system (FMS), firms integrate human, physical, and information resources to create somewhat differentiated products and to sell them to consumers at a relatively low price. A significant technological advance, an FMS is a computer-controlled process that firms use to produce a variety of products in moderate, flexible quantities with a minimum of manual intervention.[116] "A flexible manufacturing system gives manufacturing firms an advantage to quickly change a manufacturing environment to improve process efficiency and thus lower production cost."[117]

Automobile manufacturing processes that take place in the Ford-Changan joint venture located in Chongqing, China show the clear benefits of flexible production. This joint venture, with each firm owning 50 percent of it, manufactures Ford brand passenger cars for the Chinese market.[118] Comments from Yuan Fleng Xin, the manufacturing engineering manager for the Ford-Changan partnership, highlight the benefits of using an FMS: "We can introduce new models within hours, simply by configuring the line for production of the next model, while still being able to produce the existing models during the introduction of new models ... This allows the phasing-in of new models, and the phasing-out of old models, directly driven by market demand and not by production capacity, lead time nor a need to wait for infrastructure build-up."[119] An FMS may also affect the success of another joint venture Ford sought to form with China's Anhui Zotye Automobile Co. If approved through required regulatory processes, the two firms intend to produce electric vehicles in China in the form of a brand that would be unique to the Chinese market.[120]

The goal of an FMS is to eliminate the "low cost versus product variety" trade-off that is inherent in traditional manufacturing technologies. Firms use an FMS to change quickly and easily from making one product to making another. Used properly, an FMS allows the firm to increase its effectiveness in responding to changes in its customers' needs, while retaining low-cost advantages and consistent product quality. Because an FMS also enables the firm to reduce the lot size needed to manufacture a product efficiently, the firm has a greater capacity to serve the unique needs of a narrow competitive scope. In industries of all types, effective combinations of the firm's tangible assets (e.g., machines) and intangible assets (e.g., employees' skills) facilitate implementation of complex competitive strategies, especially the integrated cost leadership/differentiation strategy.

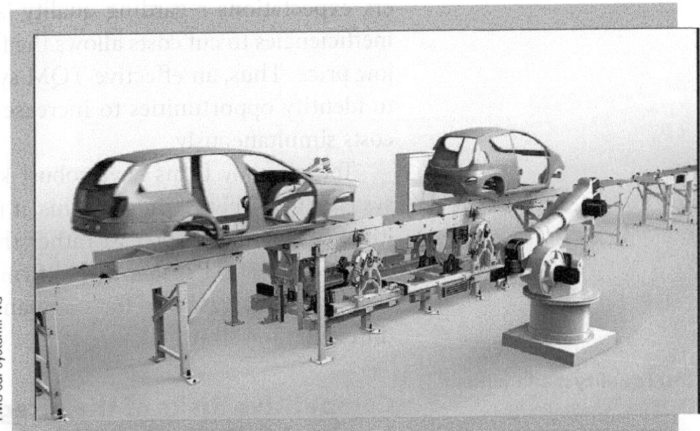
FMS car system.PNG

This photo illustrates the flexibility of computer aided manufacturing lines as two different vehicle bodies are pieced together on the same line.

Information Networks

By linking companies with their suppliers, distributors, and customers, information networks provide another source of flexibility. These networks, when used effectively, help the firm satisfy customer expectations in terms of product quality and delivery speed.[121]

Earlier, we discussed the importance of managing the firm's relationships with its customers to understand their needs. Customer relationship management (CRM) is one form of an information-based network process firms use for this purpose.[122] An effective CRM system provides a 360-degree view of the company's relationship with customers, encompassing all contact points, business processes, and communication media and sales channels.

With more than 150,000 customers, Salesforce.com is the world's largest provider of customer-relationship management services.[123] The firm is moving to the cloud,[124] allowing large database storage and access from multiple devices including smartphones. Noting that cloud computing has been around for over two decades, Salesforce.com indicated recently that over 69 percent of businesses already use cloud technology in one capacity or another. Highlighting the advantages of cloud computing when it comes to managing relationships with customers, Salesforce.com believes that there are at least 12 benefits that accrue to firms when they use this technology. Cost savings, security, flexibility, mobility, and insights are examples of these benefits.[125] Firms use information about their customers to which they gain access to determine the trade-offs they are willing to make between differentiated features and low cost—an assessment that is vital for companies using the integrated cost leadership/differentiation strategy. Firms also use information networks to manage their supply chains.[126] Through these networks, firms use their supply chain to manage the flow of somewhat differentiated inputs as they proceed through the manufacturing process in a way that lowers costs.

Total Quality Management Systems

Total quality management (TQM) "involves the implementation of appropriate tools/techniques to provide products and services to customers with best quality."[127] Firms develop and use TQM systems to

1. increase customer satisfaction,
2. cut costs, and
3. reduce the amount of time required to introduce innovative products to the marketplace.[128]

Firms able to reduce costs while enhancing their ability to develop innovative products increase their flexibility, an outcome that is particularly helpful to companies implementing the integrated cost leadership/differentiation strategy. Exceeding customers' expectations regarding quality is a differentiating feature and eliminating process inefficiencies to cut costs allows the firm to offer that quality to customers at a relatively low price. Thus, an effective TQM system helps the firm develop the flexibility needed to identify opportunities to increase its product's differentiated features and to reduce costs simultaneously.

Today, many firms have robust knowledge about how to establish and use a TQM system effectively. Because of this, it is typical for a firm's TQM system to yield competitive parity (see Chapter 3) rather than competitive advantage.[129] Nonetheless, because an effective TQM system helps firms increase product quality and reduce its costs, it is particularly valuable for companies implementing the integrated cost leadership/differentiation strategy.

Total quality management (TQM) involves the implementation of appropriate tools/techniques to provide products and services to customers with best quality.

Competitive Risks of the Integrated Cost Leadership/Differentiation Strategy

The potential to earn above-average returns by using the integrated cost leadership/differentiation strategy successfully appeals to some leaders and their firms. However, it is a risky strategy in that firms find it difficult to perform primary value-chain activities and support functions in ways that allow them to produce relatively inexpensive products with levels of differentiation that create value for the target customer. Moreover, to use this strategy effectively across time, it is necessary for firms to reduce costs incurred to produce products (as required by the cost leadership strategy) and to increase product differentiation (as required by the differentiation strategy) simultaneously.

Firms failing to perform the value-chain activities and support functions in an optimum manner when implementing the integrated cost leadership/differentiation strategy become "stuck in the middle."[130] Stuck in the middle means that the cost structure of a firm prevents it from offering its products to customers at a low enough price and that its products lack sufficient differentiation to create value for those customers.

This appears to be what happened to JCPenney in recent years. A key decision made during Ron Johnson's tenure as the firm's CEO (from November of 2011 until April of 2013) was to replace the firm's historic pricing strategy with a new one. Instead of offering sales to customers, often through coupons, Johnson decided that the firm should engage in an "everyday low prices" pricing strategy that he used with Apple Stores when he was an executive with that firm. In addition to eliminating coupon-based sales, Johnson changed the firm's floor merchandise and added boutiques/streets within the stores.[131] Because of these actions, JCPenney become "stuck in the middle" in that its prices were no longer low enough to attract the firm's historic customers and its merchandise failed to create sufficient differentiation to attract new customers. Firms that are "stuck in the middle" fail to earn above-average returns and earn average returns only when the structure of the industry in which they compete is highly favorable.[132]

Failing to implement *either* the cost leadership *or* the differentiation strategy in ways that create value for customers also finds firms stuck in the middle. In other words, industry-wide competitors too can become stuck in the middle.

In spite of the risks, the integrated strategy is becoming more common and perhaps necessary in many industries because of technological advances and global competition. This strategy often necessitates a long-term perspective to make it work effectively, and therefore requires dedicated owners that support implementation of a long-term strategy that may require several years to generate positive returns.[133]

SUMMARY

- A business-level strategy is an integrated and coordinated set of commitments and actions the firm uses to gain a competitive advantage by exploiting core competencies in specific product markets. We examine five business-level strategies (cost leadership, differentiation, focused cost leadership, focused differentiation, and integrated cost leadership/differentiation) in the chapter.
- Customers are the foundation of successful business-level strategies. When considering customers, a firm simultaneously examines three issues: *who*, *what*, and *how*. These issues, respectively, refer to the customer groups the firm intends to serve, the needs those customers have that the firm seeks to satisfy, and the core competencies the firm will use to satisfy customers' needs. Increasing segmentation of markets throughout the global economy creates opportunities for firms to identify more distinctive customer needs that they can serve by implementing their chosen business-level strategy.
- A business model, which describes what a firm does to create, deliver, and capture value for stakeholders, is part of a firm's business-level strategy. In essence, a business model is a framework for how the firm will use processes to create, deliver, and capture value, while a business-level strategy is the path the firm will follow to gain a competitive advantage by exploiting its core competencies in a specific product market. There are many types of business models including the franchise, freemium, subscription, and peer-to-peer models. Firms may pair each type of business model with any one of the five generic business-level strategies as the firm seeks to compete successfully against rivals.
- Firms seeking competitive advantage through the cost leadership strategy produce no-frills, standardized products for an industry's typical customer. Firms must offer these low-cost products to customers with competitive levels of differentiation. Firms using this strategy earn above-average returns

when they learn how to emphasize efficiency such that their costs are lower than the costs of their competitors, while providing products to customers that have levels of differentiated features that are acceptable to them.

- Competitive risks associated with the cost leadership strategy include (1) a loss of competitive advantage to newer technologies, (2) a failure to detect changes in customers' needs, and (3) the ability of competitors to imitate the cost leader's competitive advantage through their own distinct strategic actions.
- Through the differentiation strategy, firms provide customers with products that have different (and valued) features. Customers pay a price for differentiated products that they believe is competitive relative to the product's features as compared to the cost/feature combinations available from competitors' products. Because of their distinctiveness, differentiated products carry a premium price. Firms differentiate products on any dimension that some customer group values. Firms using this strategy seek to differentiate their products from competitors' products on as many dimensions as possible. The less similarity to competitors' offerings, the more buffered a firm is from competition with its rivals.
- Risks associated with the differentiation strategy include (1) a customer group's decision that the unique features provided by the differentiated product over the cost leader's product are no longer worth a premium price, (2) the inability of a differentiated product to create the type of value for which customers are willing to pay a premium price, (3) the ability of competitors to provide customers with products that have features similar to those of the differentiated product, but at a lower cost, (4) the threat of counterfeiting, whereby firms produce a cheap imitation of a differentiated product, and (5) failing to implement the differentiation strategy in ways that create value for which customers are willing to pay.
- Through the cost leadership and the differentiated focus strategies, firms serve the needs of a narrow market segment (e.g., a buyer group, product segment, or geographic area). This strategy is successful when firms have the core competencies required to provide value to a specialized market segment that exceeds the value available from firms serving customers across the total market (industry).
- The competitive risks of focus strategies include (1) a competitor's ability to use its core competencies to "out focus" the focuser by serving an even more narrowly defined market segment, (2) decisions by industry-wide competitors to focus on a customer group's specialized needs, and (3) a reduction in differences of the needs between customers in a narrow market segment and the industry-wide market.
- Firms using the integrated cost leadership/differentiation strategy strive to provide customers with relatively low-cost products that also have valued differentiated features. Flexibility is required for firms to learn how to use primary value-chain activities and support functions in ways that allow them to produce differentiated products at relatively low costs. Flexible manufacturing systems, improvements to them, and interconnectedness in information systems within and between firms (buyers and suppliers) facilitate the flexibility that supports use of the integrated strategy. Continuous improvements to a firm's work processes as brought about by a total quality management (TQM) system also facilitate use of the integrated strategy. The primary risk of this strategy is that a firm might produce products that do not offer sufficient value in terms of either low cost or differentiation. In such cases, the company becomes "stuck in the middle." Firms stuck in the middle compete at a disadvantage and are unable to earn more than average returns.

KEY TERMS

business-level strategy 106
business model 113
cost leadership strategy 116
differentiation strategy 120
focus strategy 124
integrated cost leadership/differentiation strategy 130
market segmentation 110
total quality management (TQM) 132

REVIEW QUESTIONS

1. What is a business-level strategy?
2. What is the relationship between a firm's customers and its business-level strategy in terms of *who*, *what*, and *how*? Why is this relationship important?
3. What is a business model and how do business models differ from business-level strategies?
4. What are the differences among the cost leadership, differentiation, focused cost leadership, focused differentiation, and integrated cost leadership/differentiation business-level strategies?
5. How can firms use each of the business-level strategies to position themselves favorably relative to the five forces of competition?
6. What are the specific risks associated with using each business-level strategy?

Mini-Case

Hain Celestial Group: A Firm Focused on "Organic" Differentiation

Business-level strategy, this chapter's focus, details actions a firm takes to compete successfully in a particular industry or industry segment by using its resources, capabilities, and core competencies to create a competitive advantage. Hain Celestial Group uses a differentiation strategy to compete against its rivals. As explained in this chapter, the differentiation strategy is one through which the firm seeks to differentiate itself from competitors in ways that create value for which target customers are willing to pay. By developing and using capabilities and competencies to produce and distribute unique types of natural and organic foods, Hain differentiates itself from competitors. Hain's strategy takes advantage of a newly evolving preference among some consumers in terms of the types of food products they buy. This consumer preference change, which in essence is a preference for food that is healthier and in some cases more responsive to environmental challenges, affects a number of firms including those growing food products, grocery stores that sell those products, and restaurants in which people consume the products.

Irwin Simon is Hain Celestial's founder and CEO. At the time of founding, Simon said that he "knew that the choice to eat more wholesome foods and live a healthier lifestyle wasn't a fad or a trend. It's a transformation people want to make for the long term." The company grew through a series of acquisitions of small organic and natural foods' producers. These acquisitions, as Simon puts it, are "not GE or Heinz or Campbell's . . . . Growth is coming from companies like Ell's and BluePrint—entrepreneurial start-ups." The largest acquisition to date was Celestial Seasonings, a supplier of teas and juices. The firm's successful acquisition strategy has focused on "buying brands started by someone else" and then "figuring out how to grow them from there."

Through these acquisitions and the products associated with them and because of effective marketing programs, Hain is the largest supplier to natural food retailer Whole Foods Markets (now owned by Amazon). BluePrint, the company mentioned above, focuses on natural juices marketed to consumers to 'cleanse' their bodies. Brands such as Terra vegetable chips, Dream non-dairy milk, and Celestial Seasonings tea are household names for the health-oriented shopper. Sales of Hain's portfolio of products result in Hain Celestial being the world's largest natural foods company.

The demand for natural food in general and for Hain's products in particular finds Hain selling its branded products to traditional grocery store chains; these sales account for about 60 percent of the firm's U.S. sales. In 2014, sales outside the United States accounted for the remaining 40 percent of Hain's revenue.

Meanwhile, large branded food firms without as intense of a focus on natural food products are experiencing revenue and earnings' challenges. Kraft Foods, Campbell Soup Company, and J.M. Smucker Company are examples of these firms. For these and similar firms, earnings have stalled in part because their brands do not focus on the natural and organic items that appeal to some of today customers, at least not to the degree that is the case for Hain Celestial. Partially because of this, Hain's earnings and stock price have climbed much higher on a relative basis.

To deal with the slump in revenue and earnings, large branded firm companies are implementing different strategies. Smucker's, for example, acquired Big Heart Pet Foods (maker of Milk-Bone dog treats and Meow Mix cat food) as a means of entering the pet food market quickly. Others, such as Nestlé (maker of Crunch and Butterfinger candy bars and other chocolates), are removing artificial ingredients such as colors and dyes from candy and chocolate. Hershey Company and Mars, Inc., which collectively account for approximately 65 percent of the global market share in packaged candy, are reducing the amount of high fructose corn syrup in their food items. Mondelēz is seeking to reduce saturated fats and sodium in its snacks by 10 percent. However, these changes do not allow these firms to overcome the problem of rapidly changing consumer tastes toward organic and natural foods.

Grocery stores, such as Kroger, Safeway, and Walmart, are also seeking to enter the natural or organic segment. Given its commitment to using the cost leadership strategy, Walmart's decision to introduce low-priced organic foods is not surprising. Walmart is joining Wild Oats Marketplace (an independent producer in the natural food segment) "to place about 100 organic products into its store" and the "Wild Oats line will be priced 25 percent lower than competing national organic brands." Competition from a firm with success using the cost leadership strategy (such as Walmart) will challenge Hain Celestial to emphasize the value of differentiated products to customers wanting to purchase natural or organic.

The trend toward organic foods is occurring in restaurants as well. Chipotle Mexican Grill, Inc., for example, commits to providing customers with "Food with Integrity." For Chipotle, this means serving foods made with local, sustainably produced organic products and using meats from naturally raised—not factory farm—animals.

To address what had become somewhat unimpressive sales growth beginning in 2016, Hain Celestial contemplated the possibility of selling its organic meat businesses in mid-2018. Instead of meats, executives evaluated the possibility of expanding the firm's efforts to provide protein options to customers through some of its other products such as an array of organic nuts.

Sources: 2018, Founder's message, Hain Celestial Homepage, www.hain.com, February 28; 2018, Hain Celestial reports second quarter fiscal year 2018 financial results, Hain Celestial Homepage, www.hain.com, February 7; A. Gasparro & A. Hufford, 2018, Hain looks to sell meat business as U.S. sales fall, *Wall Street Journal*, www.wsj.com, February 7; J. Bacon, 2015, Brands capitalize on health-driven resolutions, *Marketing Week*, www.marketingweek.com, January 29; A. Chen & A. Gasparro, 2015, Smucker's latest food firm hurt by changing tastes, *Wall Street Journal*, February 14–15, B4; A. Gasparro, 2015, Indigestion hits food giants, *Wall Street Journal*, February 13, B1; A. Gasparro, 2015, Nestlé bars artificial color, flavors, *Wall Street Journal*, February 18, B6; M. Esterl, 2015, PepsiCo earnings, revenue drop on foreign-exchange impact, *Wall Street Journal*, www.wsj.com, February 12; L. Light, 2015, How to revive McDonald's, *Wall Street Journal*, www.wsj.com, February 11; M. Alva, 2014, Organic growth comes naturally to Hain Celestial Group, *Investor's Business Daily*, July 24, A5; A. Kingston, 2014, Juice junkies, *Maclean's*, June 30, 64–66; *SCTWeek*, 2014, Walmart to sell low-price organic food, 2014, *SCTWeek*, April 11, 4.

Case Discussion Questions

1. We note in the Mini-Case that Hain Celestial is implementing the differentiation strategy. Provide examples of the competitive dimensions on which this firm focuses while implementing its differentiation strategy.
2. On what environmental trends did Hain Celestial base its business-level strategy? What environmental trends could have a negative effect on this firm's strategy in the future? Why?
3. In years to come, should Hain try to grow primarily organically, through collaborative strategies such as joint ventures and strategic alliances, or through mergers and acquisitions? Explain your answer. (Glance ahead to Chapter 7 to learn about mergers and acquisitions and to Chapter 9 to learn about joint ventures and strategic alliances.)
4. What are the most serious competitive challenges you anticipate Hain Celestial will face over the next ten years? How should the firm respond to these challenges?

NOTES

1. J. Irwin, B. Lahneman, & A. Parmigiani, 2018, Nested identities as cognitive drivers of strategy, *Strategic Management Journal*, 39: 269–294; L. Mirabeau, S. Maguire, & C. Hardy, 2018, Bridging practice and process research to study transient manifestations of strategy, *Strategic Management Journal*, 39: 582–605.
2. G. W. S. Dowell & S. Muthulingam, 2017, Will firms go green if it pays? The impact of disruption, cost, and external factors on the adoption of environmental initiatives, *Strategic Management Journal*, 38: 1287–1304; D. A. Shepherd, J. S. McMullen, & W. Ocasio, 2017, Is that an opportunity? An attention model of top managers' opportunity beliefs for strategic action, *Strategic Management Journal*, 38: 626–644.
3. J. P. Eggers & K. F. Park, 2018, Incumbent adaptation to technological change: The past, present, and future of research on heterogeneous incumbent response, *Academy of Management Annals*, 12: 357–389. T. Saarikko, U. H. Westergren, & T. Blomquist, 2017, The Internet of things: Are you ready for what is coming? *Business Horizons*, 60: 667–676.
4. K. Tama-Rutigliano, 2018, Mapping your digital marketing strategy for 2018, *Forbes*, www.forbes.com, January 2.
5. N. Symeonidou & N. Nicolaou, 2018, Resource orchestration in start-ups: Synchronizing human capital investment, leveraging strategy, and founder start-up experience, *Strategic Entrepreneurship Journal*, 12: 194–218; F. F. Suzrez, S. Grodal, & A. Gotsopoulos, 2015, Perfect timing? Dominant category, dominant design, and the window of opportunity for firm entry, *Strategic Management Journal*, 36: 437–448.
6. L. Achtenhagen, O. Brunninge, & L. Melin, 2017, Patterns of dynamic growth in medium-sized companies: Beyond the dichotomy of organic versus acquired growth, *Long Range Planning*, 50: 457–471; Y. Eshima & B. S. Andeerson, 2017, Firm growth, adaptive capability, and entrepreneurial orientation, *Strategic Management Journal*, 38: 770–779.

7. S. I. Carlier, R. Costamagna, P. Mendi, & J. M. Parra, 2018, Low-skilled labor markets as a constraint on business strategy choices: A theoretical approach, *Journal of Business Research*, in press; M. M. Appleyard & H. W. Chesbrough, 2017, The dynamics of open strategy: From adoption to reversion, *Long Range Planning*, 50: 310–321.
8. C. R. Greer, R. F. Lusch, & M. A. Hitt, 2017, A service perspective for human capital resources: A critical base for strategy implementation, *Academy of Management Perspectives*, 31: 137–158; R. E. Hoskisson, M. A. Hitt, R. D. Ireland, & J. S. Harrison, 2013, 3rd edition, *Competing for Advantage*, Mason, OH: Cengage Learning.
9. M. S. Rosenbaum, M. L. Otalora, & G. C. Ramirez, 2017, How to crate a realistic customer journey map, *Business Horizons*, 60: 143–150; M. Subramony & D. S. Pugh, 2015, Services management research: Review, integration, and future directions, *Journal of Management*, 41: 349–373.
10. M. Hughes, P. Hughes, J. (Karena) Yan, & C. M. P. Sousa, 2018, Marketing as an investment in shareholder value, *British Journal of Management*, in press; A. S. Cui & F. Wu, 2017, The impact of customer involvement on new product development: Contingent and substitutive effects, *Journal of Product Innovation Management*, 34: 60–80.
11. M. E. Porter, 1985, *Competitive Strategy*, New York: Free Press.
12. R. P. Lee & X. Tang, 2018, Does it pay to be innovation and imitation oriented? An examination of the antecedents and consequences of innovation and imitation orientations, *Journal of Product Innovation Management*, 35: 11–26; A. Buchner, A. Mohamed, & A. Schwienbacher, 2017, Diversification, risk, and returns in venture capital, *Journal of Business Venturing*, 32: 519–535; J. Calandro Jr., 2015, A leader's guide to strategic risk management, *Strategy & Leadership*, 43: 26–35.
13. T. L. Madsen & G. Walker, 2017, Competitive heterogeneity, cohorts, and persistent advantage, *Strategic Management Journal*, 38: 184–202; F. Zhang, Y. Wang, D. Li, & V. Cui, 2017, Configurations of innovations across domains: An organizational ambidexterity view, *Journal of Product Innovation Management*, 34: 821–841.
14. R. K. Pati, M. K. Nandakumar, A. Ghobadian, R. D. Ireland, & N. O'Regan, 2018, Business model design-performance relationship under external and internal contingencies: Evidence from SMEs in an emerging economy, *Long Range Planning*, in press; J. A. Petersen, V. Kumar, Y. Polo, & F. J. Sese, 2018, Unlocking the power of marketing: Understanding the links between customer mindset metrics, behavior, and profitability, *Journal of the Academy of Marketing Science*, in press.
15. N. Hajli, M. Shanmugam, S. Papagiannidis, D. Zahay, & M.-O. Richard, 2017, Branding co-creation with members of online brand communities, *Journal of Business Research*, 70: 136–144; F. J. Gulillart, 2014, The race to implement co-creation of value with stakeholders: Five approaches to competitive advantage, *Strategy & Leadership*, 42: 2–8.
16. A. Pansari & V. Kumar, 2017, Customer engagement: The construct, antecedents, and consequences, *Journal of the Academy of Marketing Science*, 45: 294–311; L. A. Bettencourt, C. P. Blocker, M. B. Houston, & D. J. Flint, 2015, Rethinking customer relationships, *Business Horizons*, 58: 99–108.
17. R. Wang & C. Miller, 2018, Managing relationships with a platform: An empirical study of publishers' e-book offerings on Amazon Kindle, *SSRN*, https://papers.ssrn.com/sol3/papers.cfm?abstract_id=3120686.
18. 2018, Number of Facebook users in the United States as of January 2018, *The Statistics Portal*, www.statista.com, February 15.
19. L. Richwine & A. Venugopal, 2018, Netflix crosses $100 billion market capitalization as subscribers surge, *Reuters*, www.reuters.com, January 22.
20. Treflis team, 2018, Subscriber additions propel Netflix to an all time high, *Forbes*, www.forbes.com, January 23.
21. 2018, About Amazon, Amazon Homepage, www.amazon.com, March 3.
22. B. Farfan, 2017, Amazon.com's mission statement, *The Balance*, www.thebalance.com, December 24.
23. T. J. V. Saldanha, S. Mithas, & M. S. Krishnan, 2017, Leveraging customer involvement for fueling innovation: The role of relational and analytical information processing capabilities, *MIS Quarterly*, 41: 267–286; R. Parmar, I. MacKenzie, D. Cohn, & D. Gann, 2014, The new patterns of innovation, *Harvard Business Review*, 92(1/2): 86–95.
24. R. G. S. Silva, P. L. Broilo, L. Balestrin, & K. Basso, 2017, Altruistic punishment: A consumer response to service failure, *Journal of Marketing Theory and Practice*, 25: 421–435; A.S. Balaju & B. C. Krishnan, 2015, How customers cope with service failure? A study of brand reputation and customer satisfaction, *Journal of Business Research*, 68: 665–674.
25. M. Corkery, 2017, Walmart puts its eggs in a time-saving basket: Grocery pickup, *New York Times*, www.nytimes.com, October 5.
26. K. D. Martin, A. Borah, & R. Palmatier, 2017, Data privacy: Effects on customer and firm performance, *Journal of Marketing*, 81: 36–58.
27. A. Payne, P. Frow, & A. Eggert, 2017, The customer value proposition: Evolution, development, and application in marketing, *Journal of the Academy of Marketing Science*, 45: 467–489.
28. S. Han, Y. Ye, X. Fu, & Z. Chen, 2014, Category role aided market segmentation approach to convenience store chain category management, *Decision Support Systems*, 57: 296–308; P. Adams, R. Fontana, & F. Malerba, 2017, Bridging knowledge resources: The location choices of spinouts, *Strategic Entrepreneurship Journal*, 11: 93–121.
29. 2018, Our company, Hill's Pet Nutrition Homepage, www.hillspet.com, March 3.
30. E. Bellman, 2018, Auto makers race to build a cheaper electric car for India, other growing markets, *Wall Street Journal*, www.wsj.com, February 23.
31. K. Graham, 2017, Op-E: How data analytics enhances my grocery shopping at Kroger, *Digital Journal*, www.digitaljournal.com, July 21.
32. R. G. Cooper, 2017, We've come a long way baby, *Journal of Product Innovation Management*, 34: 387–391; P. J. Holahan, Z. Z. Sullivan, & S. K. Markham, 2014, Product development as core competence: How formal product development practices differ for radical, more innovative, and incremental product innovations, *Journal of Product Innovation Management*, 31: 329–345.
33. J. Chatterjee, 2017, Strategy, human capital investments, business-domain capabilities, and performance: A study in the global software services industry, *Strategic Management Journal*, 38: 588–608; D. J. Teece, 2014, The foundations of enterprise performance: Dynamic and ordinary capabilities in an (economic) theory of firms, *Academy of Management Perspectives*, 28: 328–352.
34. R. Krause, 2016, Apple R&D spending rises but still trails Google, Facebook, Amazon, *Investor's Business Daily*, www.investors.com, May 10.
35. 2018, About us, SAS Homepage, www.sas.com, March 3.
36. M. E. Porter, *Competitive Advantage*, New York: Free Press, 26.
37. R. Rumelt, 2011, *Good Strategy/Bad Strategy*, New York: Crown Business.
38. M. E. Porter, 1996, What is strategy? *Harvard Business Review*, 74(6): 61–78.
39. 2017, How Southwest Airlines created a mass market for air travel, *Entrepreneur*, www.entrepreneur.com, February 14.
40. Porter, What is strategy?
41. 2018, What are some examples of different types of business models in major industries? *Investopedia*, www.investopedia.com, March 14.
42. R. Amit & C. Zott, 2012, Creating value through business model innovation, *MIT Sloan Management Review*, 53: 41–49.
43. N. Kokemuller, 2017, Differences between a business model & a business strategy, *bizfluent*, www.bizfluent.com, September 26.
44. N. J. Foss & T. Saebi, 2018, Business models and business model innovation: Between wicked and paradigmatic problems, *Long Range Planning*, 51: 9–21.

45. B. R. Barringer & R. D. Ireland, 2019, *Entrepreneurship: Successfully Launching New Ventures*, 6th ed., Pearson.
46. D. J. Teece & G. Linen, 2017, Business models, value capture, and the digital enterprise, *Journal of Organization Design*, 6–8.
47. C. Nielsen & M. Lund, 2018, Building scalable business models, *MIT Sloan Management Review*, Winter: 65–69.
48. Barringer & Ireland, *Entrepreneurship: Successfully Creating New Ventures*, 6h ed., 125–130.
49. 2018, Our business model, McDonald's Homepage, www.mcdonalds.com, March 14.
50. 2018, Overview, Panera Bread Homepage, www.panerabread.com, March 14.
51. 2018, We are Panera Bread, Panera Bread Homepage, www.panerabread.com, March 14.
52. 2018, We're building a better food system, Blue Apron Homepage, www.blueapron .com, March 14.
53. R. L. Priem, 2018, Demand-side strategy and business models: Putting value creation for consumers center stage, *Long Range Planning*, 51: 22–31.
54. M. E. Porter, 1994, Toward a dynamic theory of strategy. In R. P. Rumelt, D. E. Schendel, & D. J. Teece (eds.), *Fundamental Issues in Strategy*. Boston: Harvard Business School Press: 423–461.
55. Porter, What is strategy?, 62.
56. Porter, *Competitive Advantage*, 15.
57. Porter, *Competitive Strategy*, 35–40.
58. S. Tallman, Y. Luo, & P. J. Buckley, 2018, Business models in global competition, *Global Strategy Journal*, in press; G. Linton & J. Kask, 2017, Configurations of entrepreneurial orientation and competitive strategy for high performance, *Journal of Business Research*, 70: 168–176; B. Berman, 2015, How to compete effectively against low-cost competitors, *Business Horizons*, 58: 87–97.
59. 2018, The lowest cost index mutual funds in the industry with no minimums, Charles Schwab Home page, www.schwab.com, March 3.
60. B. Napach, 2017, Schwab launching 3 equity index mutual funds, waiving fees, *Think Advisor*, www.thinkadvisor.com, December 1.
61. T. Shriber, 2017, Schwab continues low-cost tradition with new ETF, *Investopedia*, www .investopedia.com, October 6.
62. M. Pietro & M. Mura, 2017, Executing strategy through comprehensive performance measurement systems, *International Journal of Operations & Production Management*, 37: 423–443; J.-K. Park & Y. K. Ro, 2013, Product architectures and sourcing decisions: Their impact on performance, *Journal of Management*, 39: 814–846.
63. P. J. Steinberg, V. D. Procher, & D. Urbig, 2017, Too much or too little of R&D offshoring: The impact of captive offshoring and contract offshoring on innovation performance, *Research Policy*, 46: 1810–1823; S. Carnahan & D. Somaya, 2013, Alumni effects and relational advantage: The impact on outsourcing when a buyer hires employees from a supplier's competitors, *Academy of Management Journal*, 56: 1578–1600.
64. I. M. B. Freitas & R. Fontana, 2018, Formalized problem-solving practices and the effects of collaboration with suppliers on a firm's product innovation performance, *Journal of Product Innovation Management*, in press.
65. H. Chung & E. Lee, 2017, Asymmetric relationships with symmetric suppliers: Strategic choice of supply chain price leadership in a competitive market, *European Journal of Operational Research*, 259: 564–575; F. Zhang, Y. Wang, D. Li, & V. Cui, 2017, Configurations of innovations across domains: An organizational ambidexterity view, *Journal of Product Innovation Management*, 34: 821–841; A. Hinterhuber & S. M. Liozu, 2014, Is innovation in pricing your next source of competitive advantage? *Business Horizons*, 57: 413–423.
66. J. Luoma, T. Falk, D. Totzek, H. Tikkanen, & A. Mrozek, 2018, Big splash, no waves? Cognitive mechanisms driving incumbent firms' responses to low-price market entry strategies, *Strategic Management Journal*, in press.
67. T.-J. A. Peng, M.-H. Yen, & M. Bourne, 2018, How rival partners compete based on cooperation? *Long Range Planning*, 51: 351–383; S. D. Patha, Z. Wu, & D. Johnston, 2014, Toward a structural view of co-opetition in supply networks, *Journal of Operations Management*, 32: 254–267.
68. S. Opper, V. Nee, & H. J. Holm, 2017, Risk aversion and Guanxi activities: A behavioral analysis of CEOs in China, *Academy of Management Journal*, 60: 1504–1530; Y. Luo, Y. Huang, & S. L. Wang, 2011, Guanxi and organizational performance: A meta-analysis, *Management and Organization Review*, 8: 139–172.
69. C. Smith, 2017, 40 amazing Walmart statistics and facts (November 2017) by the numbers, *Expanded Ramblings*, www.expandedramblings.com, November 30.
70. D. Green, 2017, Walmart and Amazon's long-simmering feud exploded in 2017—and it's redefining retail, *Business Insider*, www .businessinsider.com, December 15.
71. A. A. Tsay, J. V. Gray, I. J. Noh, & J. T. Mahoney, 2018, A review of production and operations management research on outsourcing in supply chains: Implications for the theory of the firm, *Production and Operations Management*, in press.
72. H. L. Chen, 2018, Supply chain risk's impact on corporate financial performance, *International Journal of Operations & Production Management*, 38: 713–731; Y. Zhang & J. Gimeno, 2010, Earnings pressure and competitive behavior, *Academy of Management Journal*, 53: 743–768.
73. A. Cezar, H. Cavusoglu, & S. Raghunathan, 2017, Sourcing information security operations: The role of risk interdependency and competitive externality in outsourcing decisions, *Production and Operations Management*, 26: 860–879; M. M. Larsen, S. Manning, & T. Pedersen, 2013, Uncovering the hidden costs of offshoring: The interplay of complexity, organizational design, and experience, *Strategic Management Journal*, 34: 533–552.
74. M. E. Porter & J. E. Heppelmann, 2014, How smart, connected products are transforming competition, *Harvard Business Review*, 92(11): 64–88.
75. S. M. Handley, 2017, How governance misalignment and outsourcing capability impact performance, *Production and Operations Management*, 26: 134–155; T. J. Kull, S. C. Ellis, & R. Narasimhan, 2013, Reducing behavioral constraints to supplier integration: A socio-technical systems perspective, *Journal of Supply Chain Management*, 49: 64–86.
76. B. Maury, 2018, Sustainable competitive advantage and profitability persistence: Sources versus outcomes for assessing advantage, *Journal of Business Research*, 84: 100–113; D. Wani, M. Malhotra, & S. Venkataraman, 2018, Impact of competition on process of care and resource investments, *Journal of Operations Management*, 57: 23–35.
77. T. E. Ott, K. M. Eisenhardt, & C. B. Bingham, 2017, Strategy formation in entrepreneurial settings: Past insights and future directions, *Strategic Entrepreneurship Journal*, 11: 306–325; R. J. Schonberger & K. A. Brown, 2017, Missing link in competitive manufacturing research and practice: Customer-responsive concurrent production, *Journal of Operations Management*, 49–51: 83–87.
78. Porter, *Competitive Strategy*, 35–40.
79. 2018, Product innovation, www.1000ventures.com, March 5.
80. G. Cattani, R. L. M. Dunbar, & Z. Shapira, 2017, How commitment to craftsmanship leads to unique value: Steinway & Sons' differentiation strategy, *Strategy Science*, 2: 13–38; H. Ryu, J. Lee, & B. Choi, 2015, Alignment between service innovation strategy and business strategy and its effect on firm performance: An empirical investigation, *IEEE Transactions on Engineering Management*, 62: 100–113.
81. H.-E. Lin, E. F. McDonough III, J. Yang, & C. Wang, 2017, Aligning knowledge assets for exploitation, exploration, and ambidexterity: A study of companies in high-tech parks in China, *Journal of Product Innovation Management*, 34: 122–140; M.

Terpstra & F. H. Berbeeten, 2014, Customer satisfaction: Cost driver or value driver? Empirical evidence from the financial services industry, *European Management Journal*, 32: 499–508.

82. M. Dalton, 2018, Gucci seeks to escape fashion's boom-bust, *Wall Street Journal*, www.wsj.com, February 25.

83. J.-F. Hennart, A. Majocchi, & E. Forlani, 2018, The myth of the stay-at-home family firm: How family-managed SMEs can overcome their internationalization limitations, *Journal of International Business Studies*, in press; K. Rahman & C. S. Areni, 2014, Generic, genuine, or completely new? Branding strategies to leverage new products, *Journal of Strategic Marketing*, 22: 3–15.

84. M. J. Donate & J. D. Sanchez de Pablo, 2015, The role of knowledge-oriented leadership in knowledge management practices and innovation, *Journal of Business Research*, 68: 360–370.

85. R. Bunduchi, 2017, Legitimacy-seeking mechanisms in product innovation: A qualitative study, *Journal of Product Innovation Management*, 34: 315–342.

86. D. Alfakhir, D. Haress, J. Nicholson, & T. Harness, 2018, The role of aesthetics and design in hotelscape: A phenomenological investigation of cosmopolitan consumers, *Journal of Business Research*, 85: 523–531; H. (Meg) Meng, C. Zamudio, & R. D. Jewell, 2018, Unlocking competitiveness through scent names: A data-driven approach, *Business Horizons*, 61: 385–395.

87. B. J. Allen, D. Chandrasekaran, & S. Basuroy, 2018, Design crowdsourcing: The impact on new product performance of sourcing design solutions from the "crowd," *Journal of Marketing*, 82: 106–123; R. Simons, 2014, Choosing the right customer, *Harvard Business Review*, 92(3): 48–55.

88. 2018, About us, *Halliburton Homepage*, www.halliburton.com, March 3.

89. C. Dawson, 2018, Subaru's plan to woo Americans: A roomy SUV with 19 cup holders, *Wall Street Journal*, www.wsj.com, January 4.

90. C. Giachetti, J. Lampel, & S. L. Pira, 2017, Red Queen competitive imitation in the U.K. mobile phone industry, *Academy of Management Journal*, 60: 1882–1914; Y. Mishina, E. S. Block, & M. J. Mannor, 2012, The path dependence of organizational reputation: How social judgment influences assessments of capability and character, *Strategic Management Journal*, 33: 459–477.

91. D. E. D'Souza, P. Sigdyal, & E. Struckell, 2017, Relative ambidexterity: A measure and a versatile framework, *Academy of Management Perspectives*, 31: 124–136; D. Laureiro-Martinez, S. Brusoni, N. Canessa, & M. Zollo, 2015, Understanding the exploration-exploitation dilemma: An fMRI study of attention control and decision-making performance, *Strategic Management Journal*, 36: 319–338.

92. I. Geyskens, K. O. Keller, M. G. Dekimpe, & K. de Jong, 2018, How to brand your private labels, *Business Horizons*, 61: 487–496; P. Micheli, H. Perks, & M. B. Beverland, 2018, Elevating design in the organization, *Journal of Product Management*, 35: 629–651.

93. G. Magnani, A. Zucchella, & R. Strange, 2018, The dynamics of outsourcing relationships in global value chains: Perspectives from MNEs and their suppliers, *Journal of Business Research*, in press; A. Marinez-Noya, E. Garcia-Canal, & M. F. Guillen, 2013, R&D outsourcing and the effectiveness of intangible investments: Is proprietary core knowledge walking out the door? *Journal of Management Studies*, 50: 67–91.

94. C. W. Craighead, D. J. Ketchen, Jr., M. T. Jenkins, & T. R. Holcomb, 2017, A supply chain perspective on strategic foothold moves in emerging markets, *Journal of Supply Chain Management*, 53: 3-12; J. W. Upson, D. J. Ketchen, Jr., B. L. Connelly, & A. L. Ranft, 2012, Competitor analysis and foothold moves, *Academy of Management Journal*, 55: 93–110.

95. A. Capaldo, D. Lavie, & A. M. Petruzzelli, 2017, Knowledge maturity and the scientific value of innovations, *Journal of Management*, 43: 503–533; J. Harvey, P. Cohendet, L. Simon, & S. Borzillo, 2015, Knowing communities in the front end of innovation, *Research-Technology Management*, 58: 46–54.

96. C. Castaldi, 2018, To trademark or not to trademark: The case of the creative and cultural industries, *Research Policy*, 47: 606–616; J. West & M. Bogers, 2014, Leveraging external sources of innovation: A review of research on open innovation, *Journal of Product Innovation Management*, 31: 814–831.

97. F. Marticotte & M. Arcand, 2017, Schadenfreude, attitude and the purchase intentions of a counterfeit luxury brand, *Journal of Business Research*, 77: 175–183; J. Chen, L. Teng, L. S. Liu, & H. Zhu, 2015, Anticipating regret and consumers' preferences for counterfeit luxury products, *Journal of Business Research*, 68: 507–515.

98. M. H. Meyer, O. Osiyevskyy, D. Libaers, & M. van Hugten, 2018, Does product platforming pay off? *Journal of Product Innovation Management*, 35: 66–87; S. Chen, Y. Kim, & C. Kohli, 2017, A Korean, a Chinese, and an Indian walk into an American bar: Tapping the Asian-American goldmine, *Business Horizons*, 60: 91–100.

99. 2018, Our company, *Goya Foods Homepage*, www.goya.com, March 3.

100. Porter, *Competitive Advantage*, 15.

101. Barringer & Ireland, 2019, *Entrepreneurship: Successfully Launching New Ventures*, 6th ed.

102. 2018, IKEA by the numbers, 2017, *IKEA Homepage*, www.ikea.com, March 3.

103. J. R. Hagerty, 2018, Ingvar Kamprad made IKEA a global retailer by keeping it simple, *Wall Street Journal*, www.wsj.com, February 2.

104. 2018, New lower price, *IKEA Homepage*, www.ikea.com, March 3.

105. 2018, Design for everyone, *IKEA Homepage*, www.ikea.com, March. 3.

106. 2018, IKEA services, *IKEA Homepage*, www.ikea.com, March 3.

107. 2018, About Green Truck, *Green Truck Homepage*, www.greentruck.com, March 7.

108. A. Kadet, 2015, City news-metro money: Wheelin' and dealin' from a truck, *Wall Street Journal*, www.wsj.com, February 28.

109. T. Dahl, 2018, Harley-Davidson confirms first production electric motorcycle, *Popular Mechanics*, February 2.

110. F. Lambert, 2018, Harley-Davidson invests in electric motorcycle startup Alta Motors ahead of launching its own electric bike, *Electrek*, www.electrek.com, March 1.

111. A. De Massis, D. Audretsch, L. Uhlaner, & N. Kammerlander, 2018, Innovation with limited resources: Management lessons from the German Mittelstand, *Journal of Product Innovation Management*, 35: 125–146; C. E. Armstrong, 2012, Small retailer strategies for battling the big boxes: A "Goliath" victory?, *Journal of Strategy and Management*, 4: 41–56.

112. R. P. Lee & X. Tang, 2018, Does it pay to be innovation and imitation oriented? An examination of the antecedents and consequences of innovation and imitation orientations, *Journal of Product Innovation Management*, 35: 11–26; C. Cennamo & J. Santalo, 2013, Platform competition: Strategic trade-offs in platform markets, *Strategic Management Journal*, 34: 1331–1350.

113. 2018, Corporate fact sheet, *Target Homepage*, www.target.com, March 5.

114. S. Awate, M. M. Larsen, & R. Mudambi, 2015, Accessing vs. sourcing knowledge: A comparative study of R&D internationalization between emerging and advanced economy firms, *Journal of International Business Studies*, 46: 63–86.

115. J. Zeng, C. Simpson, & B.-L. Dang, 2017, A process model of dynamic capability development: Evidence from the Chinese Manufacturing sector, *Management and Organization Review*, 13: 643–673; H. Wang & C. Kimble, 2010, Low-cost strategy through product architecture: Lessons from China, *Journal of Business Strategy*, 31(3): 12–20.

116. R. J. Schonberger & K. A. Brown, 2017, Missing link in competitive manufacturing research and practice: Customer-responsive concurrent production, *Journal of Operations Management*, 49–51: 83–87; 2016, Advantages & disadvantages of flexible manufacturing system, *CPV Manufacturing*, www.cpvmfg.com, September 23.

117. 2018, Flexible Manufacturing System—FMS, *Investopedia*, www.investipodia.com, March 8.

118. Reuters staff, 2018, Factbox: Chinese automakers' international alliances, *Reuters*, www.reuters.com, February 26.
119. 2014, Rethinking car assembly, *Automotive Manufacturing Solutions*, November, 2–3.
120. 2017, *Bloomberg News*, Ford seals big deal for Chinese electric cars in time for Trump, *Bloomberg*, www.bloomberg.com, November 8.
121. R. S. Burt & K. Burzynska, 2017, Chinese entrepreneurs, social networks, and *Guanxi*, 2017, *Management and Organization Review*, 13: 221–260; I. Filatotchev, Z. Su, & G. D. Bruton, 2017, Market orientation, growth strategy, and firm performance: The moderating effects of external connections, *Management and Organization Review*, 13: 575–601.
122. C. Prange & B. B. Schlegelmilch, 2018, Managing innovation dilemmas: The cube solution, *Business Horizons*, 61: 309–322; W. W. Moe & D. A. Schweidel, 2017, Opportunities for innovation in social media analytics, *Journal of Product Innovation Management*, 34: 697–702.
123. 2018, Thanks to our trailblazing customers, we're the world's #1 CRM, Salesforce.com Homepage, March 5.
124. P. Barlas, 2015, Salesforce.com large deals boom, fueling growth, Investors Business Daily, www.investors.com, February 26.
125. 2018, 12 benefits of cloud computing Salesforce.com Homepage, www.salesforce.com, March 5.
126. S. Ba & B. R. Nault, 2017, Emergent themes in the interface between economics of information systems and management of technology, *Production and Operations Management*, 26: 652–666; D. J. Ketchen, Jr., T. R. Crook, & C. W. Craighead, 2014, From supply chains to supply ecosystems: Implications for strategic sourcing research and practice, *Journal of Business Logistics*, 35: 165–171.
127. G. Muruganantham, S. Vinodh, C. S. Arun, & K. Ramesh, 2018, Application of interpretive structural modelling for analyzing barriers to total quality management practices: Implementation in the automotive sector, *Total Quality Management & Business Excellence*, 29: 524–545.
128. H.-H. Lee & C. Li, 2018, Supplier quality management: Investment, inspection, and incentives, *Production and Operations Management*, 27: 304–322; H. Su, K. Linderman, R. G. Schroeder, & A. H. Van de Ven, 2014, A comparative case study of sustaining quality as a competitive advantage, *Journal of Operations Management*, 32: 429–445.
129. J. Smith, S. Anderson, & G. Fox, 2017, A quality system's impact on the service experience, *International Journal of Operations & Production Management*, 37: 1817–1839; J. Singh & H. Singh, 2015, Continuous improvement philosophy—literature review and directions, *Benchmarking: An International Journal*, 22: 75–119.
130. Porter, *Competitive Advantage*, 16.
131. P. Mourdoukoutas, 2017, A strategic mistake that still haunts JCPenney, *Forbes*, www.forbes.com, February 24.
132. Porter, *Competitive Advantage*, 16.
133. Linton & Kask, Configurations of entrepreneurial orientation and competitive strategy for high performance, 2017.

iStock.com/DNY59

5

Competitive Rivalry and Competitive Dynamics

Studying this chapter should provide you with the strategic management knowledge needed to:

5-1 Define competitors, competitive rivalry, competitive behavior, and competitive dynamics.

5-2 Describe market commonality and resource similarity as the building blocks of a competitor analysis.

5-3 Explain awareness, motivation, and ability as drivers of competitive behavior.

5-4 Describe how strategic actions and tactical actions drive competitive rivalry between firms.

5-5 Discuss factors affecting the likelihood a firm will take actions to attack its competitors.

5-6 Explain factors affecting the likelihood a firm will respond to actions its competitors take.

5-7 Explain competitive dynamics in slow-cycle, fast-cycle, and standard-cycle markets.

iStock.com/DNY59

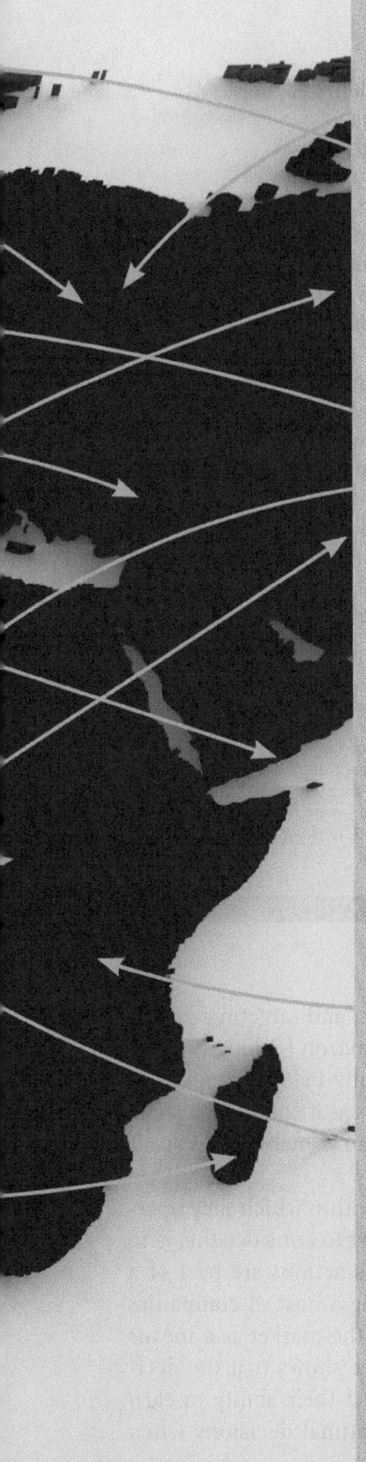

THE GROCERY INDUSTRY: WELCOME TO A NEW COMPETITIVE LANDSCAPE

Saying that his firm is "incredibly focused on the customer of the future," Kroger Co.'s CEO noted recently that investments in online ordering and the ability to stock new products in its stores were vital to the firm's desire to increase its profitability in 2020 and the years beyond. Kroger is experiencing intense competition from an array of competitors including storefront operators such as Aldi (you will learn more about Aldi in this chapter's Mini-Case), Walmart, and Safeway. Kroger now faces additional competition from online competitor Amazon through this firm's purchase of Whole Foods and from Walmart because of its efforts to enhance its online grocery-selling capability. Amazon paid approximately $13.7 billion to buy Whole Foods in 2017. (In the Opening Case for Chapter 6, we offer this acquisition as an example of Amazon's corporate-level strategy of related diversification.)

Simultaneously, Walmart was allocating additional resources to enhance its online capabilities. The additional competition from Amazon, Walmart, and others influences and stimulates Kroger's intention to enhance its online capabilities as part of a robust effort to focus with greater clarity and effectiveness on customers and their needs.

NetPhotos/Alamy Stock Photo

With rising competition from Amazon and Walmart, Kroger's online capabilities are vital to increasing its profitability in the future.

Amazon's purchase of Whole Foods is a *strategic action*. Defined and discussed later in this chapter, strategic actions find firms allocating resources to execute significant market-based actions with the potential to affect competition among rivals within an industry. Speaking about the acquisition of Whole Foods, some analysts suggested that "the impact of this in the grocery industry is going to be huge." Typically, strategic actions, such as Amazon's purchase of Whole Foods, elicit *strategic responses*. Explored in this chapter, strategic responses, which also are resource-intense, are actions competitors take to respond in the marketplace to a rival's strategic action(s). Given Amazon's strategic action, what is an appropriate strategic response for Kroger to take?

Kroger is the largest supermarket chain in the United States, with roughly 2,800 stores in 35 U.S. states in 2018. The firm has a well-known brand name, a historic ability to satisfy stakeholders through its performance, and a vision of "imagining a world with Zero hunger and Zero waste as we transform communities and improve health for millions of Americans." Because of this, Kroger appears to have the potential required to achieve its objective of serving the customer of tomorrow effectively and efficiently and to respond successfully to Amazon's strategic action in the process of doing so.

In contemplating the strategic and tactical responses (tactical actions and responses are described in this chapter) it will take regarding Amazon's purchase of Whole Foods, Kroger and other traditional grocery storefront operators such as Safeway must recognize the significance of the challenge they face. Some believe, for example, that "the shift to e-commerce is not like the other marketplace ebbs and flows Kroger has weathered over the years. It is a dramatically different business model, with a new set of competitors, logistical hurdles and profitability impediments." Recognizing this reality, Kroger's CEO observed that "investments in online ordering were critical to Kroger's future and would take two or three years to build." Examples of the strategic response Kroger is taking relative to Amazon's strategic action—and those of other competitors as well—include the following: (1) building fewer physical storefronts as a means of generating financial capital to develop e-commerce options; (2) increasing the number of its storefront locations where customers can collect groceries they ordered online; (3) working with suppliers to reduce its freight costs, with generated savings going to e-commerce investments; (4) re-engineering its supply chain to become "more omnichannel, allowing (its) customers to order via desktop or mobile, in-store, or by phone"; (5) investing in technology and infrastructure to support its emerging e-commerce operations and (6) evaluating acquisitions and partnerships as a way of expanding its reach with U.S. customers and potentially to establish international operations as well.

The reality of competitive rivalry and competitive dynamics, though, is that competitors engage continuously in a series of actions and responses. Thus, while Kroger is responding to actions launched by rivals such as Amazon and Walmart, those firms will in turn respond to Kroger's responses. For example, almost immediately after acquiring Whole Foods, Amazon assessed ways to offer Whole Foods' products to its Prime customers. This is one example of Amazon's apparent intention of using Whole Foods' physical locations to expand its grocery delivery services. Over time, we can expect to see continuing efforts (in the form of strategic and tactical actions and strategic and tactical responses) between Amazon and Kroger (and between these firms and other grocery industry competitors) for the express purpose of establishing a favorable position in the marketplace.

Sources: H. Haddon, 2018, Kroger shares drop as battle with Amazon cuts into profits, *Wall Street Journal*, www.wsj.com, March 8; H. Haddon, 2018, Kroger earnings: What to watch for, *Wall Street Journal*, www.wsj.com, March 2; E. Harper, 2018, What to expect from Amazon in 2018, *Techspot*, www.techspot.com, January 11; G. Bruno, 2017, Why Amazon really bought Whole Foods, *The Street*, www.thestreet.com, October 11; T. Kim, 2017, Amazon's booming online sales and Whole Foods acquisition make it a buy: Analysts, *CNBC*, www.cnbc.com, October 24; S. Halzack, 2017, Kroger must admit its Amazon problem, *Bloomberg*, www.blomberg.com, October 11; G. Petro, 2017, Amazon's acquisition of Whole Foods is about two things: Data and product, *Forbes*, www.forbes.com, August 2; N. Walters, 2017, 3 things Kroger must do to compete with Amazon's Whole Foods, *The Motley Fool*, www.thefool.com, November 8, 2017, What industry analysts and insiders are saying about Amazon buying Whole Foods, *Reuters*, www.reuters.com, June 16.

Firms operating in the same market, offering similar products, and targeting similar customers are **competitors**.[1] Thus, in the grocery business, Amazon (through Whole Foods) and Kroger engage in competitive behavior (defined fully below, competitive behavior is essentially the set of actions and responses a firm takes as it competes against its rivals). Of course, Whole Foods and Kroger also compete against many other rivals including Safeway, Costco, Walmart, and Aldi.

Firms interact with competitors as part of the broad context within which they operate while attempting to earn above-average returns.[2] Another way to consider this is to note that firms do not compete in a vacuum; rather, each firm's actions are part of a mosaic of competitive actions and responses taking place among a host of companies seeking the same objective—establishing a desirable position in the market as a means of having superior performance relative to competitors. Evidence shows that the decisions firms make about their interactions with competitors affect their ability to earn above-average returns.[3] Because of this, firms seek to reach optimal decisions when considering how to compete against their rivals.[4]

Competitors are firms operating in the same market, offering similar products, and targeting similar customers.

Competitive rivalry is the ongoing set of competitive actions and competitive responses that occur among firms as they maneuver for an advantageous market position.

Competitive rivalry is the ongoing set of competitive actions and competitive responses that occur among firms as they maneuver for an advantageous market position.[5] Especially in highly competitive industries, firms jockey constantly for advantage as they launch strategic actions and respond or react to rivals' moves.[6] It is important for those leading organizations to understand competitive rivalry because the reality is that some firms learn how to outperform their competitors, meaning that competitive rivalry influences an individual firm's ability to gain and sustain competitive advantages.[7] Rivalry results from firms initiating their own competitive actions and then responding to actions taken by competitors.[8]

In the Strategic Focus, we discuss competitive rivalry that is emerging among firms seeking the most advantageous market position in the energy-storage battery market. As you will see, rivalry is becoming more intense in this market as firms seek to serve customers' needs to store energy they can use later. In the Strategic Focus, we examine competitive rivalry among firms competing to establish the most attractive position in the market to provide large-scale storage capabilities to customers.

Competitive behavior is the set of competitive actions and responses a firm takes to build or defend its competitive advantages and to improve its market position.[9] As explained in the Opening Case, it appears that a desire to expand the channels through which it can deliver groceries is one reason Amazon acquired Whole Foods. In this sense, Amazon's interest in Whole Foods as a distribution channel may exceed its interest in Whole Foods' physical storefronts.[10] Also helping Amazon to improve its market position and ability to earn above-average returns by selling groceries is the expectation that in the longer term, Amazon may leverage the "Whole Foods Market brand and supply chain to source high-quality food and build demand for it, but ultimately leverage Amazon's expertise to drive efficiency in the logistics efforts, fulfilling orders outside of the Whole Foods Market store footprint."[11] In response to Amazon's competitive behavior, Kroger and other competitors are taking actions to defend their current market positions (e.g., Kroger's storefront operations) while trying to enhance their competitive ability in related market positions (e.g., Kroger's actions to improve its e-commerce operations).

Increasingly, competitors engage in competitive actions and responses in more than one market.[12] United and Delta, Google and Apple, and oil field services companies Halliburton and Schlumberger are examples of firms for whom this is the case. Firms competing against each other in several product or geographic markets engage in **multimarket competition.**[13] **Competitive dynamics** is the total set of competitive actions and responses taken by all firms competing within a market.[14] We show the relationships among all of these key concepts in Figure 5.1.

In this chapter, we focus on competitive rivalry and competitive dynamics. A firm's strategies are dynamic in nature in that actions taken by one firm elicit responses from competitors that typically result in responses from the firm that took the initial action.[15] Dynamism describes the competition occurring among four technology giants to have the leadership position in voice recognition. In the early stages of competition today, Amazon's Alexa is the market leader. However, the competition for the leadership position in voice recognition is intense as Amazon battles with Apple's Siri, Microsoft's Cortana, and Google's Assistant.[16]

Gaining the leadership position in the voice recognition market is critical in that voice recognition has the potential to be a disruptive technology. Makers of household items such as Unilever, Procter & Gamble, and Nestle SA recognize this reality and are engaging in competitive actions as a result. Unilever, for example, which owns Hellmann's mayonnaise and Domestos toilet cleaner among many products, "has developed Alexa apps that give free recipes and cleaning tips that may or may not incorporate Unilever brands." In spite of this, Unilever sees this app as a new and hopefully effective way to make consumers aware of their products as a foundation for purchasing them in the future if not today.[17] In 2018, analysts felt that "the winning virtual assistant (would) be the one that first achieves ubiquity. It's about doing everything, and being everywhere. Once people pick an assistant and start using it in their lives, they're not likely to switch. The stakes are high, and immediate."[18]

Competitive behavior is the set of competitive actions and responses a firm takes to build or defend its competitive advantages and to improve its market position.

Multimarket competition occurs when firms compete against each other in several product or geographic markets.

Competitive dynamics is the total set of competitive actions and responses taken by all firms competing within a market.

Strategic Focus

The Emergence of Competitive Rivalry among Battery Manufacturers: Who Will Establish the Most Attractive Market Position?

Although small in size today, the growth potential of the battery-storage market is substantial. "Utilities looking for less expensive alternatives to power plants that fire up during peak hours to meet power demands" are a key customer for the manufacturers of large-scale battery-storage products. Utility companies encounter the challenge of having sufficient capacity to meet peak demand for energy consumption. Commonly, mornings and evenings are the times when customers use the greatest amounts of the product utilities provide. At non-peak times though, utilities have idle capacity. Examining today's competitive scene finds IHS Markit predicting that the global market for batteries in the power sector will expand annually by 14 percent through at least 2025. Thus, energy storage on a large-scale basis is an attractive market.

Increasing levels of power generation from renewable energy sources such as wind and power and the need to store that energy influence the growth in large-scale battery-storage units. The challenge with wind and solar as energy sources is that they are intermittent energy sources. In this sense, power companies do not know exactly when the wind will blow (and for how long and at what velocity) and exactly when the sun will shine (and for how long and with what degree of intensity). Large-scale storage batteries address this issue by allowing the capture of wind- and solar-generated power when created and then storing it until needed to meet consumer demand. In the words of an industry expert: "With large grid systems, batteries can be attached directly to generation sources such as wind turbines and solar panels to store and release excess electricity that the grid can't absorb in that moment, or even be used in hybridizing conventional power generation (gas engines or turbines) in order to enhance the flexibility of and speed of response to grid intermittency." The decreasing cost of lithium-ion batteries is increasing the attractiveness of large-scale, battery-storage systems. (Small versions of lithium-ion batteries power our cell phones and a host of other products.)

Tesla, Siemens AG, and General Electric (GE) are primary competitors in the large-scale, battery-storage system market. The commercial attractiveness of this market elicits competition among these competitors as they jockey to establish the most attractive market position. In mid-2017, for example, Tesla announced that in partnership with Neoen, a French renewable energy provider, it would build, deliver, and install the world's largest lithium battery to a location north of Jamestown, South Australia in 100 days. Tesla fulfilled this promise and delivered a battery-storage product that runs constantly and provides stability services for renewable energy sources and is available for emergency backup power in case of an energy shortfall. Early operational results from using this product were positive.

Recognizing the importance of battery-storage size in what is an attractive market and to compete against Tesla, Siemens and AES combined their efforts to form an energy storage start-up called Fluence Energy. This partnership commenced operations on January 1, 2018; the firm immediately became the "supplier of AES' Alamitos power center energy storage project in Long Beach, California serving Southern California Edison and the Western Los Angeles area." Fluence's battery-storage project was to be the largest in the world, exceeding the size of Tesla's project in Southern Australia.

ZUMA Press, Inc./Alamy Stock Photo

Tesla's battery storage facility can store a megawatt of alternative energy, allowing the district to use more "green" power during peak times of the day.

Trying to catch up to rivals Tesla and Siemens, GE announced in early 2018 that it would establish a giant energy-storage platform called GE Reservoir. This platform "is expected to store electricity generated by wind turbines and solar panels for later use."

How do GE's, Tesla's, and Siemens' products differ? What position will each firm's product allow it to establish in the large-scale battery-storage market? With respect to GE, some analysts observe that "one of GE's biggest challenges will be differentiating its battery products from those offered by competitors such as Fluence." Early responses to this challenge suggest that GE's Reservoir platform lasts approximately 15 percent longer than competitors' products; faster installation of the platform is a second differentiator. Thus, product longevity and installation ease may be the foundation for GE's effort to "stake out" a viable market position. For Tesla, being a first mover (this concept is discussed later in the chapter) and being very willing to collaborate with governmental agencies to install products may be sources of differentiation (Tesla and Neoen partnered with the South Australian government to establish their battery-storage system). Siemens uses a "holistic approach" to serve battery-storage customers. In this sense, the firm notes that it offers "customers in the battery industry solutions comprising software, automation and drives spanning the entire value chain." Thus, integrated technology solutions may be a marketplace differentiator for Siemens and for Fluence, the start-up formed by Siemens and AES.

Going forward, these three major competitors will encounter competition from additional entrants to a very attractive market. Overall, "competition in the energy storage market will only improve the industry, forcing companies like Tesla and the newly-established Fluence (and GE) to continue being innovative." Thus, energy customers throughout the world will benefit from the competitive rivalry occurring among firms seeking to establish the most attractive market position.

Sources: 2018, Siemens backs efficient digitalized large-scale production of batteries, Siemens Homepage, www.siemens.co, February 22; E. Ailworth, 2018, GE Power, in need of a lift, chases Tesla and Siemens in batteries, *Wall Street Journal*, www.wsj.com, March 7; J. Cropley, 2018, GE rolls out battery-based energy storage product, *Daily Gazette*, www.dailygazette.com, March 7; T. Kellner, 2018, Making waves: GE unveils plans to build an offshore wind turbine the size of a skyscraper, the world's most powerful, *Renewables*, www.ge.com, Mary 1; F. Lambert, 2018, AES and Siemens launch new energy storage startup to compete with Tesla Energy, will supply new world's biggest battery project, *Electrek*, www.electrek.com, January 11; C. Mimms, 2018, The battery boost we've been waiting for is only a few years out, *Wall Street Journal*, www.wsj.com, March 18; S. Patterson & R. Gold, 2018, There's a global race to control batteries—and China is winning, *Wall Street Journal*, www.wsj.com, February 11; B. Spaen, 2018, New 'Fluence Energy' builds world's biggest storage system in California, *GreenMatters*, www.greenmatters.com, January 12; B. Fung, 2017, Tesla's enormous battery in Australia, just weeks old, is already responding to outages in 'record' time, *Washington Post*, www.washingtonpost.com, December 26; I. Slav, 2017, Tesla is facing stiff competition in the energy storage war, *OilPrice.com*, www.oilprice.com, July 17.

Figure 5.1 From Competition to Competitive Dynamics

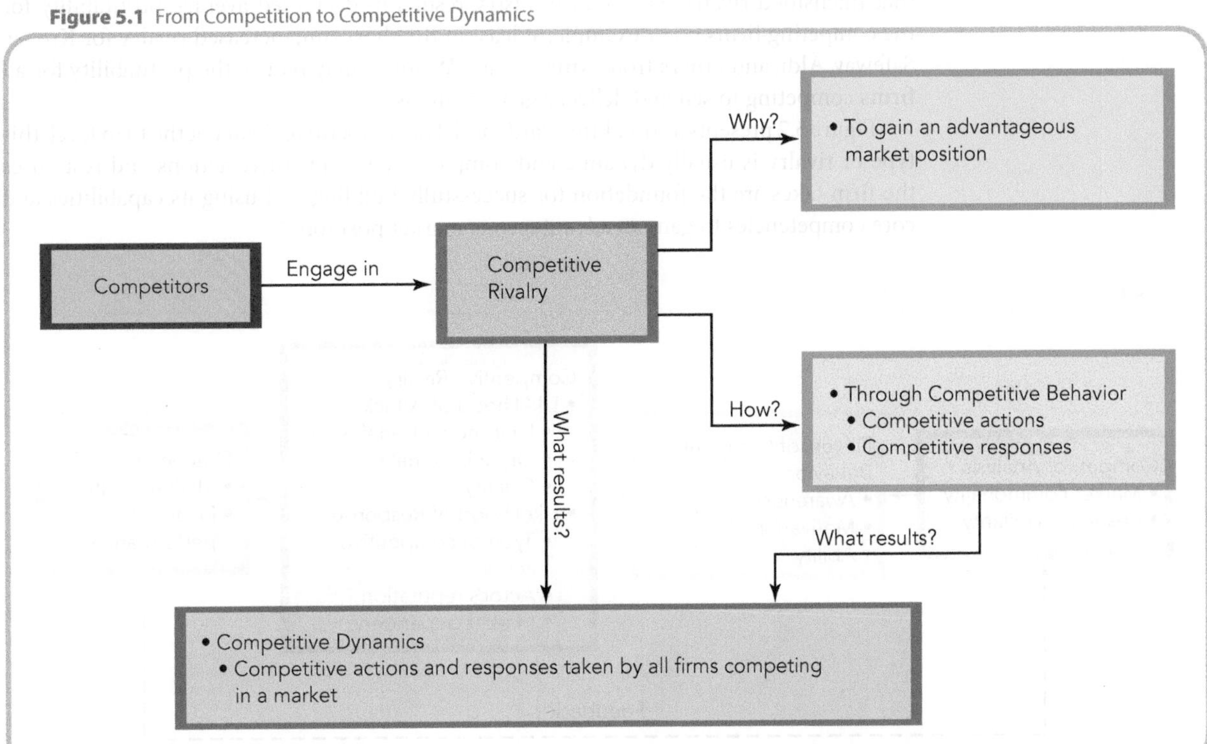

Source: Adapted from M. J. Chen, 1996, Competitor analysis and interfirm rivalry: Toward a theoretical integration, *Academy of Management Review*, 21: 100–134.

Competitive rivalries such as those among Amazon, Google, Apple, and Microsoft in the voice recognition market affect a firm's strategies. This is because a strategy's success is a function of the firm's initial competitive actions, how well it anticipates competitors' responses to them, *and* how well the firm anticipates and responds to its competitors' initial actions. ("Attacks" is another term for a firm's initial competitive actions.)[19] Competitive rivalry affects all types of strategies (e.g., corporate-level, merger and acquisition, international, and cooperative). However, its dominant influence is on business-level strategy. Indeed, firms' actions and responses to those of their rivals are part of the basic building blocks of business-level strategies.

Recall from Chapter 4 that business-level strategy is concerned with what the firm does to use its core competencies in specific product markets in ways that yield competitive success. In the global economy, competitive rivalry is intensifying, meaning that its effect on firms' strategies is increasing. However, firms that develop and use effective business-level strategies tend to outperform competitors in individual product markets, even when experiencing intense competitive rivalry.[20]

5-1 A Model of Competitive Rivalry

Competitive rivalry evolves from the pattern of actions and responses as one firm's competitive actions have noticeable effects on competitors, eliciting competitive responses from them.[21] This pattern suggests that firms are mutually interdependent, that competitors' actions and responses affect them, and that marketplace success is a function of both individual strategies and the consequences of their use.[22]

Increasingly, executives recognize that competitive rivalry can have a major effect on the firm's financial performance and market position.[23] For example, research shows that intensified rivalry within an industry results in decreased average profitability for the competing firms.[24] For example, at least in the short run, increased rivalry for Kroger, Safeway, Aldi, and others from Amazon and Walmart may reduce the profitability for all firms competing to sell and delivery grocery items.

Figure 5.2 presents a straightforward model of competitive rivalry at the firm level; this type of rivalry is usually dynamic and complex. The competitive actions and responses the firm takes are the foundation for successfully building and using its capabilities and core competencies to gain an advantageous market position.[25]

Figure 5.2 A Model of Competitive Reality

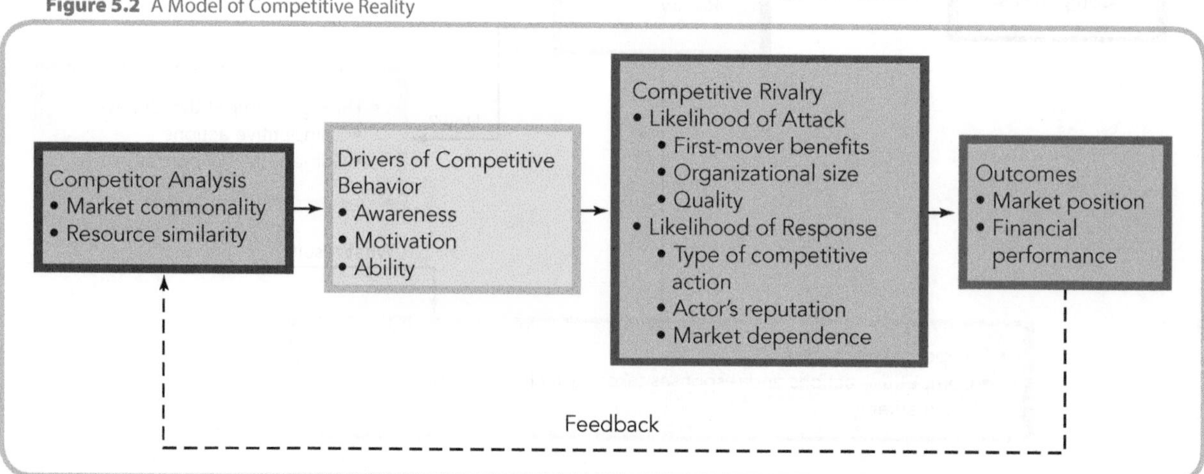

Source: Adapted from M. J. Chen, 1996, Competitor analysis and interfirm rivalry: Toward a theoretical integration, *Academy of Management Review*, 21: 100–134.

The model in Figure 5.2 presents the sequence of activities occurring as competitors compete against each other. Companies use this model to understand how to predict a competitor's behavior and reduce the uncertainty associated with it.[26] Being able to predict competitors' actions and responses has a positive effect on the firm's market position and its subsequent financial performance.[27] The total of all the individual rivalries shown in Figure 5.2 that occur in a particular market reflects the competitive dynamics in that market.

The remainder of the chapter explains components of the model shown in Figure 5.2. We first describe market commonality and resource similarity as the building blocks of a competitor analysis. Next, we discuss the effects of three organizational characteristics—awareness, motivation, and ability—on the firm's competitive behavior. We then examine competitive rivalry between firms (interfirm rivalry). To do this, we explain the factors that affect the likelihood a firm will take a competitive action and the factors that affect the likelihood a firm will respond to a competitor's action. In the chapter's final section, we turn our attention to competitive dynamics to describe how market characteristics affect competitive rivalry in slow-, fast-, and standard-cycle markets.

5-2 Competitor Analysis

As noted previously, a competitor analysis is the first step the firm takes to predict the extent and nature of its rivalry with each competitor. Competitor analyses are also important when entering a foreign market because firms doing so need to understand the local competition and foreign competitors operating in that market.[28] Without such analyses, they are less likely to be successful.

Market commonality refers to the number of markets in which firms compete against each other, while resource similarity refers to the similarity in competing firms' resource portfolios (we discuss both terms fully later in the chapter). These two dimensions of competition determine the extent to which firms are competitors. Firms with high market commonality and highly similar resources are direct and mutually acknowledged competitors. The drivers of competitive behavior—as well as factors influencing the likelihood that a competitor will initiate competitive actions and will respond to its competitors' actions—influence the intensity of rivalry.

In Chapter 2, we discussed competitor analysis as a technique firms use to understand their competitive environment. Together, the general, industry, and competitive environments comprise the firm's external environment. We also described how firms use competitor analysis to help them *understand* their competitors. This understanding results from studying competitors' future objectives, current strategies, assumptions, and capabilities (see Figure 2.3 in Chapter 2).

In this chapter, we extend the discussion of competitor analysis to describe what firms study to be able to *predict* competitors' behavior in the form of their competitive actions and responses. The discussions of competitor analysis in Chapter 2 and in this chapter are complementary in that firms must first *understand* competitors (Chapter 2) before their competitive actions and responses can be *predicted* (this chapter).

Being able to predict rivals' likely competitive actions and responses accurately helps a firm avoid situations in which it is unaware of competitors' objectives, strategies, assumptions, and capabilities. Lacking the information needed to predict these conditions for competitors creates *competitive blind spots*. Typically, competitive blind spots find a firm caught off guard by a competitor's actions, potentially resulting in negative outcomes.[29] Members of a firm's board of directors are a source of knowledge and expertise about other businesses and industry environments that can help a firm avoid competitive blind spots.

5-2a Market Commonality

Every industry is composed of various markets. The financial services industry has markets for insurance, brokerage services, banks, and so forth. To concentrate on the needs of different, unique customer groups, firms may further subdivide the markets they intend to serve. The insurance market could be broken into market segments (such as commercial and consumer), product segments (such as health insurance and life insurance), and geographic markets (such as Southeast Asia and Western Europe). In general, the capabilities that Internet technologies generate help to shape the nature of industries' markets along with patterns of competition within those industries.

Companies want to be vigilant about identifying new market segments that they may be able to serve with their product. Recently, for example, business software companies turned their attention to the blue-collar workforce to sell their product. "Knowledge workers" was the market segment these firms served historically. In the United States alone, there are over 113 million plumbers, contractors, garage-door specialists, and so forth that business software companies believe can benefit from their products and services. These workers can use the sophisticated, yet intuitive software on tablets that software companies such as UpKeep Technologies are developing to exchange data with their home office while on the job and to show customers what the cost of repairs would be as well as the appearance of the finished project. The growth potential of this market segment for business software companies is significant.[30]

Competitors such as rivals in the business software market tend to agree about the different characteristics of individual markets that form an industry. For example, in the transportation industry, the commercial air travel market differs from the ground transportation market, which is served by such firms as YRC Worldwide (one of the largest, less-than-truckload—LTL—carriers in North America with awards including selection as Walmart's LTL Carrier of the Year) and its major competitors Arkansas Best, Con-way, Inc., and FedEx Freight.[31] Although differences exist, many industries' markets share some similarities in terms of technologies used or core competencies needed to develop a competitive advantage. For example, although railroads and truck ground transport compete in different segments and can be substitutes, different types of transportation companies all need to provide reliable and timely service. Commercial air carriers such as Southwest, United, and JetBlue must therefore develop service competencies to satisfy their passengers, while ground transport companies such as YRC, railroads, and their major competitors must develop such competencies to satisfy the needs of those using their services to ship goods.

Firms sometimes compete against each other in several markets, a condition called market commonality. More formally, **market commonality** is concerned with the number of markets with which the firm and a competitor are involved jointly and the degree of importance of the individual markets to each.[32] Firms competing against one another in several markets engage in multimarket competition.[33] Coca-Cola and PepsiCo compete across a number of product markets (e.g., soft drinks, bottled water) as well as geographic markets (throughout North America and in many other countries throughout the world). Airlines, chemicals, pharmaceuticals, and consumer foods are examples of other industries with firms often competing against each other in multiple markets.

Market commonality is concerned with the number of markets with which the firm and a competitor are jointly involved and the degree of importance of the individual markets to each.

Firms competing in several of the same markets have the potential to respond to a competitor's actions within the market in which the competitor took an action as well as in other markets where they compete with the rival. This potential creates a complicated mosaic in which the firm may decide to initiate competitive actions or responses in one market with the desire to affect the outcome of its rivalry with a particular competitor in a second market.[34] This potential complicates the rivalry between competitors. In fact, research suggests that a firm with greater multimarket contact is less likely to initiate an attack, but more likely to respond aggressively when attacked. For instance, research in the computer industry found that "firms respond to competitive attacks by introducing new products but do not use price as a retaliatory weapon."[35] Thus, in general, multimarket competition reduces competitive rivalry, but some firms will still compete when the potential rewards (e.g., potential market share gain) are high.[36]

5-2b Resource Similarity

Resource similarity is the extent to which the firm's tangible and intangible resources compare favorably to a competitor's in terms of type and amount.[37] Firms with similar types and amounts of resources tend to have similar strengths and weaknesses and use similar strategies in light of their strengths to pursue what may be similar opportunities in the external environment.

"Resource similarity" describes part of the competitive relationship between FedEx and United Parcel Service (UPS). These companies compete in many of the same markets, meaning that both market commonality and resource similarity describe their relationship. For example, these firms have similar types of truck and airplane fleets, similar levels of financial capital, and rely on equally talented reservoirs of human capital along with sophisticated information technology systems (resources). In addition to competing aggressively against each other in North America, the firms share many other markets in common in various countries and regions. Thus, the rivalry between FedEx and UPS is intense.

When performing a competitor analysis, a firm analyzes each of its competitors with respect to market commonality and resource similarity. It then maps the results of its analyses for visual comparisons. In Figure 5.3, we show different hypothetical intersections between the firm and individual competitors in terms of market commonality and resource similarity. These intersections indicate the extent to which the firm and those with which it compares itself are competitors. For example, the firm and its competitor displayed in quadrant I have similar types and amounts of resources (i.e., the two firms

Figure 5.3 A Framework of Competitor Analysis

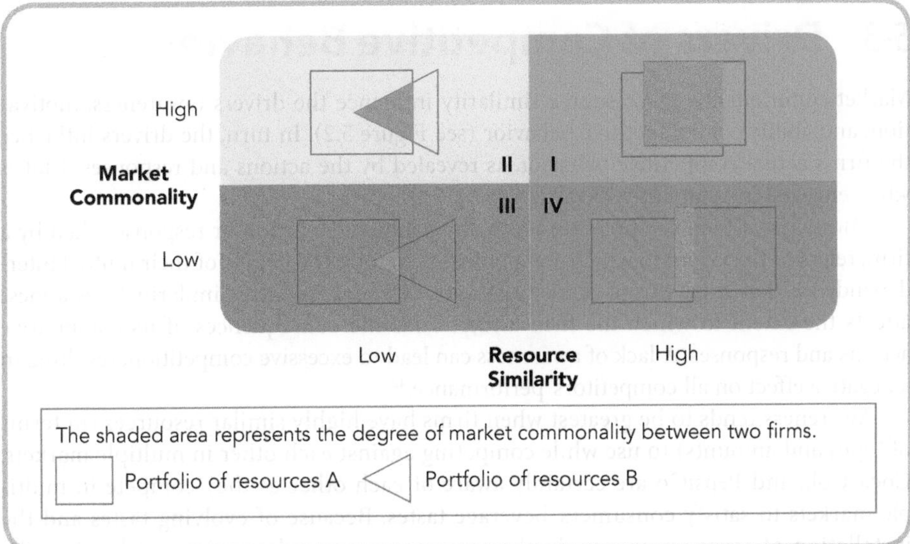

Source: Adapted from M. J. Chen, 1996, Competitor analysis and interfirm rivalry: Toward a theoretical integration, *Academy of Management Review*, 21: 100–134.

Resource similarity is the extent to which the firm's tangible and intangible resources compare favorably to a competitor's in terms of type and amount.

have a similar portfolio of resources). The firm and its competitor in quadrant I would use their similar resource portfolios to compete against each other in many markets that are important to each. These conditions lead to the conclusion that the firms modeled in quadrant I are direct and mutually acknowledged competitors.

In contrast, the firm and its competitor shown in quadrant III share few markets and have little similarity in their resources, indicating that they are not direct and mutually acknowledged competitors. Thus, a small, local, family-owned restaurant concentrating on selling "gourmet" hamburgers is not in direct competition with McDonald's. (We described this competitive situation in a Strategic Focus dealing with hamburgers in Chapter 4.) The mapping of competitive relationships is fluid as companies enter and exit markets and as rivals' resources change in type and amount, meaning that the companies with which a given firm competes change over time.

The type of relationship competitors have with each other may change over time as well. Some firms will engage each other more directly as competitors, while changes to the products they emphasize may cause some firms to become less direct competitors. Historically, General Mills and Kellogg competed against each other directly and aggressively to sell their cereal products. As a consumer, think of the competition between General Mills' cereals such as Honey Nut Cheerios, Cinnamon Toast Crunch, Lucky Charms, and Rice Chex versus those of Kellogg including Corn Flakes, Frosted Flakes, Special K, and Fruit Loops. Given the declining popularity of cereals, the competition between these firms may become less direct. General Mills, for example, recently acquired pet food company Blue Buffalo Pet Products Inc. for $8 billion. One reason for this acquisition is that the pet food business is "one of the largest center-of-the-store categories in the U.S. food and beverage market."[38] Moving into pet foods finds General Mills competing more directly with J.M. Smucker Co., in that Smucker paid $3 billion to buy Milk-Bone owner Big Heart. Similarly, Kellogg, whose CEO noted that "cereal doesn't have to be the growth engine of Kellogg,"[39] is emphasizing other products such as Pringles chips, Cheez-It crackers, Pop-Tarts, and frozen Eggo waffles to stimulate firm growth. Emphasizing snack products could find Kellogg competing more directly with PepsiCo, the owner of snack-giant Frito Lay.

5-3 Drivers of Competitive Behavior

Market commonality and resource similarity influence the drivers (awareness, motivation, and ability) of competitive behavior (see Figure 5.2). In turn, the drivers influence the firm's actual competitive behavior, as revealed by the actions and responses it takes while engaged in competitive rivalry.[40]

Awareness, which is a prerequisite to any competitive action or response taken by a firm, refers to the extent to which competitors recognize the degree of their mutual interdependence that results from market commonality and resource similarity.[41] Awareness affects the extent to which the firm understands the consequences of its competitive actions and responses. A lack of awareness can lead to excessive competition, resulting in a negative effect on all competitors' performance.[42]

Awareness tends to be greatest when firms have highly similar resources (in terms of types and amounts) to use while competing against each other in multiple markets. Coca-Cola and PepsiCo are certainly aware of each other as they compete in multiple markets to satisfy consumers' beverage tastes. Because of evolving tastes and the installation of taxes on sugary drinks some governmental agencies are levying, the companies are investing in healthier alternatives.[43] However, developing new soda products to meet consumers' interests is more critical for Coca-Cola compared to

PepsiCo. The reason for this is that PepsiCo's ownership of food products such as Frito-Lay, Quaker Oats, and so forth means that it sells a number of items to consumers in addition to sodas.

To appeal to millennials, Coca-Cola recently launched new flavors of Diet Coke including Ginger Lime and Zesty Blood Orange. These beverages are in a sleek can the firm believes millennials will value. Coca-Cola also continues to move beyond soda. The firm is one of the largest makers of bottled water in the form of its Dasani brand.[44] Aware of Coca-Cola's competitive actions, Pepsi-Co seeks to shake up competition among firms competing in the sparkling water market segment. To do this, the firm launched "bubly," a new flavored sparkling water that the firm says "has an upbeat and playful sense of humor to shake up the sparkling water category while not including artificial flavors, sweeteners or calories."[45] Initial versions of bubly included flavors like lemonbubly, orangebubly, applebubly, and mangobubly. Because of their awareness of each other and their motivation to compete against each other aggressively, rivals Coca-Cola and PepsiCo will continue to engage in direct competition to win customers when they choose a beverage.

Motivation, which concerns the firm's incentive to take action or to respond to a competitor's attack, relates to perceived gains and losses. Thus, a firm may be aware of competitors but may not be motivated to engage in rivalry with them if it perceives that its market position will neither improve nor suffer if it does not respond.[46] A benefit of lacking the motivation to engage in rivalry at a point in time with a competitor is the ability to retain resources for other purposes, including competing against a different rival.

Market commonality affects the firm's perceptions and resulting motivation. For example, a firm is generally more likely to attack the rival with whom it has low market commonality than the one with whom it competes in multiple markets. The primary reason for this is the high stakes involved in trying to gain a more advantageous position over a rival with whom the firm shares many markets. As mentioned earlier, multimarket competition can result in a competitor responding to the firm's action in a market different from the one in which the initial action occurred. Actions and responses of this type can cause both firms to lose focus on core markets and to battle each other with resources they allocated for other purposes. Because of the high competitive stakes under the condition of market commonality, the probability is high that the attacked firm will feel motivated to respond to its competitor's action in an effort to protect its position in one or more markets.[47]

In some instances, the firm may be aware of the markets it shares with a competitor and be motivated to respond to an attack by that competitor, but lack the ability to do so. *Ability* relates to each firm's resources and the flexibility they provide. Without available resources (such as financial capital and people), the firm is not able to attack a competitor or respond to its actions. For example, smaller and newer firms tend to be more innovative but generally have fewer resources to attack larger and established competitors. Local firms' social capital (relationships) with stakeholders including consumers, suppliers, and government officials create a disadvantage for foreign firms lacking the social capital of local companies.[48] However, possessing similar resources such as is the case with Coca-Cola and PepsiCo suggests similar abilities to attack and respond. When a firm faces a competitor with similar resources, careful study of a possible attack before initiating it is essential because the similarly resourced competitor is likely to respond to that action.[49]

Resource *dissimilarity* also influences the competitive actions and responses firms choose to take. The reason is that the more significant is the difference between resources owned by the acting firm and those against whom it has taken action, the longer is the delay by the firm with a resource disadvantage.[50] For example, Walmart initially used a focused cost leadership strategy to compete only in small communities (those with a population

David Grossman/Alamy Stock Photo

Small competitors, such as A&T Grocery, find it difficult to respond to the competitive threat that exists with Walmart. Yet, they must find a way to respond, perhaps by offering personalized services, in order to survive such a threat.

of 25,000 or less). Using sophisticated logistics systems and efficient purchasing practices, among other methods to gain competitive advantages, Walmart created a new type of value (primarily in the form of wide selections of products at the lowest competitive prices) for customers in small retail markets. Local competitors lacked the ability to marshal needed resources at the pace required to respond to Walmart's actions quickly and effectively. However, even when facing competitors with greater resources (greater ability) or more attractive market positions, firms should eventually respond, no matter how daunting the task seems. Choosing not to respond can ultimately result in failure, as happened with at least some local retailers who did not respond to Walmart's competitive actions. Today, with Walmart as the world's largest retailer, it is indeed difficult for smaller competitors to have the resources required to respond effectively to its competitive actions or competitive responses.[51]

5-4 Competitive Rivalry

The ongoing competitive action/response sequence between a firm and a competitor affects the performance of both companies. Because of this, it is important for companies to carefully analyze and understand the competitive rivalry present in the markets in which they compete.[52]

As we described earlier, market commonality and resource similarity are the foundation for the predictions drawn from studying competitors in terms of awareness, motivation, and ability. Studying the "Likelihood of Attack" factors (such as first-mover benefits and organizational size) and the "Likelihood of Response" factors (such as the actor's reputation) (see Figure 5.2) increases the value of the predictions the firm develops about each of its competitors' competitive actions. Evaluating and understanding these factors allow the firm to refine its predictions about competitors' actions and responses.

A **competitive action** is a strategic or tactical action the firm takes to build or defend its competitive advantages or improve its market position.

A **competitive response** is a strategic or tactical action the firm takes to counter the effects of a competitor's competitive action.

A **strategic action** or a **strategic response** is a market-based move that involves a significant commitment of organizational resources and is difficult to implement and reverse.

A **tactical action** or a **tactical response** is a market-based move that firms take to fine-tune a strategy; these actions and responses involve fewer resources and are relatively easy to implement and reverse.

5-4a Strategic and Tactical Actions

Firms use both strategic and tactical actions when forming their competitive actions and competitive responses in the course of engaging in competitive rivalry.[53] A **competitive action** is a strategic or tactical action the firm takes to build or defend its competitive advantages or improve its market position. A **competitive response** is a strategic or tactical action the firm takes to counter the effects of a competitor's competitive action. A **strategic action** or a **strategic response** is a market-based move that involves a significant commitment of organizational resources and is difficult to implement and reverse. A **tactical action** or a **tactical response** is a market-based move that firms take to fine-tune a strategy; these actions and responses involve fewer resources and are relatively easy to implement and reverse. When engaging rivals in competition, firms must recognize the differences between strategic and tactical actions and responses and develop an effective balance between them.

In mid-2018, Cigna Corp. announced that it intended to pay $54 billion to acquire Express Scripts Holding Co. This was a strategic response to a strategic action taken previously by competitors. For example, roughly at the same time, CVS planned to pay $70 billion to acquire Aetna, Inc. Both of these strategic actions are examples of "the emerging model of companies that bring together health and pharmacy benefits."[54] Today, health insurers such as Cigna believe that they must control additional parts of the value chain if they are to earn above-average returns. The vertical integration within the value chain that results by combining health insurers such as Cigna and Aetna with pharmacy benefit managers such as CVS and Express Scripts increases the opportunities for the involved companies to operate more profitably.[55]

Walmart prices aggressively as a means of increasing revenues and gaining market share at the expense of competitors. In this regard, the firm engages in a continuous stream of tactical actions to attack rivals by changing some of its products' prices and tactical responses to price changes taken by competitor Costco. Similarly, to compete against grocery retailers such as Kroger and online competitor Walmart, Amazon reduced prices for some of Whole Foods' products by as much as 43 percent almost immediately after completing the acquisition of the upper-scale grocery retailer.[56]

5-5 Likelihood of Attack

In addition to market commonality, resource similarity, and the drivers of awareness, motivation, and ability, other factors affect the likelihood a competitor will use strategic actions and tactical actions to attack its competitors. We discuss three of these factors—first-mover benefits, organizational size, and quality—next. In this discussion, we consider first movers, second movers, and late movers.

5-5a First-Mover Benefits

A **first mover** is a firm that takes an initial competitive action to build or defend its competitive advantages or to improve its market position. Work by the famous economist Joseph Schumpeter is the basis for the first-mover concept. Schumpeter argued that firms achieve competitive advantage by taking innovative actions[57] (we define and discuss innovation in Chapter 13). In general, first movers emphasize research and development (R&D) as a path to developing innovative products that customers will value.[58] Amazon was a first-mover as an online bookstore while eBay was the first major online auction site.[59]

First-mover benefits can be substantial.[60] This is especially true in fast-cycle markets (discussed later in the chapter) where changes occur rapidly, and where it is virtually impossible to sustain a competitive advantage for any length of time. A first mover in a fast-cycle market can experience many times the revenue and valuation of a second mover.[61] This evidence suggests that although first-mover benefits are never absolute, they are often critical to a firm's success in industries experiencing rapid technological developments and with relatively short product life cycles.[62] In addition to earning above-average returns until its competitors respond to its successful competitive action, the first mover can gain

- the loyalty of customers who may become committed to the products of the firm that first made them available
- market share that can be difficult for competitors to take when engaging in competitive rivalry[63]

A **first mover** is a firm that takes an initial competitive action to build or defend its competitive advantages or to improve its market position.

The general evidence that first movers have greater survival rates than later market entrants is perhaps the culmination of first-mover benefits.[64]

The firm trying to predict its rivals' competitive actions might conclude that they will take aggressive strategic actions to gain first movers' benefits. However, even though a firm's competitors might be motivated to be first movers, they may lack the ability to do so. First movers tend to be aggressive and willing to experiment with innovation and take higher yet reasonable levels of risk, and their long-term success depends on retaining the ability to do so.[65]

To be a first mover, the firm must have the readily available resources to invest significantly in R&D as well as to rapidly and successfully produce and market a stream of innovative products.[66] Organizational slack makes it possible for firms to have the ability (as measured by available resources) to be first movers. *Slack* is the buffer provided by actual or obtainable resources not in use currently and that exceed the minimum resources needed to produce a given level of organizational output.[67] As a liquid resource, slack is available to allocate quickly to support competitive actions, such as R&D investments and aggressive marketing campaigns that lead to first-mover advantages. This relationship between slack and the ability to be a first mover allows the firm to predict that a first-mover competitor likely has available slack and will probably take aggressive competitive actions as a means of introducing innovative products continuously. Furthermore, the firm can predict that as a first mover, a competitor will try to gain market share and customer loyalty rapidly to earn above-average returns until its competitors are able to respond effectively to its first move.

Firms evaluating their competitors should realize that being a first mover carries risk. For example, it is difficult to estimate accurately the returns that a firm might earn by introducing product innovations to the marketplace.[68] Additionally, the first mover's cost to develop a product innovation can be substantial, reducing the slack available to support further innovation. Thus, the firm should carefully study the results a competitor achieves as a first mover. Continuous success by the competitor suggests additional product innovations, while lack of product acceptance over the course of the competitor's innovations may indicate less willingness in the future to accept the risks of being a first mover.[69]

A **second mover** is a firm that responds to the first mover's competitive action, typically through imitation. Although its successful iPhone changed consumers' and companies' perceptions about the potential of cell phones, Apple is a well-known second mover with many of its product introductions. In fact, "Apple has been second at most stuff. They're not a true innovator in the definition of the word. They weren't the first into object-oriented computing (the mouse), they weren't the first mp3 player, they weren't the first mobile phone."[70] What Apple does extremely well though is to study products as a means of determining how to improve them by making them more user friendly for consumers.

More cautious than the first mover, the second mover such as Apple studies customers' reactions to product innovations. In the course of doing so, the second mover also tries to find any mistakes the first mover made so that it can avoid them and the problems they created. Often, successful imitation of the first mover's innovations allows the second mover to avoid the mistakes and the major investments required of the pioneering first movers.[71]

Second movers have the time needed to develop processes and technologies that are more efficient than those the first mover used or that create additional value for consumers.[72] The most successful second movers rarely act too fast (so they can study the first mover's actions carefully) nor too slow (so they do not give the first mover time to correct its mistakes and "lock in" customer loyalty). Overall, the outcomes of the first mover's competitive actions may provide a blueprint for second and even late movers as they determine the nature and timing of their competitive responses.[73]

A **second mover** is a firm that responds to the first mover's competitive action, typically through imitation.

Determining whether a competitor is effective as a second mover (based on its actions in the past) allows a first-mover firm to predict when or if the competitor will respond quickly to successful, innovation-based market entries. The first mover can expect a successful second-mover competitor to study its market entries and to respond with a new entry into the market within a short time period. As a second mover, the competitor will try to respond with a product that provides greater customer value than does the first mover's product. The most successful second movers are able to interpret market feedback with precision as a foundation for responding quickly yet successfully to the first mover's successful innovations.

Bloomua/Shutterstock.com

Apple, a well-known second mover, studies customers' reactions to product innovations, in order to avoid the mistakes of first movers.

A **late mover** is a firm that responds to a competitive action a significant amount of time after the first mover's action and the second mover's response. General Motors introduced the Hummer late into the sport utility vehicle (SUV) market; the product failed to appeal strongly to a sufficient number of customers. Although still available, the product struggles to find a target market of sufficient size to support GM's ambitions for it.

Typically, a late response is better than no response at all, although any success achieved from the late competitive response tends to be considerably less than that achieved by first and second movers. However, on occasion, late movers can be successful if they develop a unique way to enter the market and compete. For firms from emerging economies, this often means a niche strategy with lower-cost production and manufacturing. It can also mean that they need to learn from the competitors or others in the market in order to market products that allow them to compete.[74]

The firm competing against a late mover can predict that the competitor will likely enter a particular market only after both the first and second movers have achieved success in that market. Moreover, on a relative basis, the firm can predict that the late mover's competitive action will allow it to earn average returns only after the considerable time required for it to understand how to create at least as much customer value as that offered by the first and second movers' products.

5-5b Organizational Size

An organization's size affects the likelihood it will take competitive actions as well as the types and timing of those actions.[75] In general, small firms are more likely than large companies to launch competitive actions and tend to do so more quickly. Because of this tendency, smaller firms have the capacity to be nimble and flexible competitors. These firms rely on speed and surprise to defend their competitive advantages or to develop new ones while engaged in competitive rivalry, especially with large companies, to gain an advantageous market position.[76] Small firms' flexibility and nimbleness allow them to develop variety in their competitive actions; large firms tend to limit the types of competitive actions used.[77]

Large firms, however, are likely to initiate a larger total number of competitive actions and strategic actions during a given period. Thus, when studying its competitors in terms of organizational size the firm should use a measurement such as total sales revenue or total number of employees. The competitive actions the firm likely will encounter from

A **late mover** is a firm that responds to a competitive action a significant amount of time after the first mover's action and the second mover's response.

competitors larger than it is will be different from the competitive actions it will encounter from smaller competitors.

The organizational size factor adds another layer of complexity. When engaging in competitive rivalry, firms prefer to be able to have the capabilities required to take a large number of unique competitive actions. For this to be the case, a firm needs to have the amount of slack resources that a large, successful company typically holds if it is to be able to launch a greater *number* of competitive actions. Simultaneously though, the firm needs to be flexible when considering competitive actions and responses it might take if it is to be able to launch a greater *variety* of competitive actions. Collectively, a firm's effectiveness increases when its size permits it to take an appropriate number of unique or diverse competitive actions and responses.

5-5c Quality

Quality has many definitions, including well-established ones relating it to producing products with zero defects and as a cycle of continuous improvement.[78] From a strategic perspective, we consider quality to be the outcome of how a firm competes through its value chain activities and support functions (see Chapter 3). Thus, **quality** exists when the firm's products meet or exceed customers' expectations. Evidence suggests that quality is often among the most critical components in satisfying the firm's customers.[79]

In the eyes of customers, quality is about doing the right things relative to performance measures that are important to them.[80] Customers may be interested in measuring the quality of a firm's products against a broad range of dimensions. We show quality dimensions in which customers commonly express an interest in Table 5.1. Quality is

Table 5.1 Quality Dimensions of Products and Services

Product Quality Dimensions
1. *Performance*—Operating characteristics
2. *Features*—Important special characteristics
3. *Flexibility*—Meeting operating specifications over some period of time
4. *Durability*—Amount of use before performance deteriorates
5. *Conformance*—Match with pre-established standards
6. *Serviceability*—Ease and speed of repair
7. *Aesthetics*—How a product looks and feels
8. *Perceived quality*—Subjective assessment of characteristics (product image)
Service Quality Dimensions
1. *Timeliness*—Performed in the promised period of time
2. *Courtesy*—Performed cheerfully
3. *Consistency*—Giving all customers similar experiences each time
4. *Convenience*—Accessibility to customers
5. *Completeness*—Fully serviced, as required
6. *Accuracy*—Performed correctly each time

Source: Adapted from J. Evans, 2008, *Managing for Quality and Performance*, 7th Ed., Mason, OH: Thomson Publishing.

Quality exists when the firm's products meet or exceed customers' expectations.

possible only when top-level managers support it and when the organization validates its importance throughout all of its operations.[81] When all employees and managers accept its importance, they become vigilant in their efforts to improve a product's quality on a continuous basis.

Quality is a universal theme in the global economy and is a necessary but insufficient condition for competitive success.[82] Without quality, a firm's products lack credibility, meaning that customers do not think of them as viable options. Indeed, customers will not consider buying a product or using a service until they believe that it can satisfy at least their base-level expectations in terms of quality dimensions that are important to them.[83]

Quality affects competitive rivalry. The firm evaluating a competitor whose products suffer from poor quality can predict declines in the competitor's sales revenue until the quality issues are resolved. In addition, the firm can predict that the competitor likely will not be aggressive in its competitive actions until it is able to correct the quality problems as a path to gaining credibility with customers.[84] However, after correcting the problems, that competitor is likely to take aggressive competitive actions.

5-6 Likelihood of Response

The success of a firm's competitive action is a function of the likelihood that a competitor will respond to it as well as by the type of action (strategic or tactical) and the effectiveness of that response. As noted earlier, a competitive response is a strategic or tactical action the firm takes to counter the effects of a competitor's competitive action. In general, a firm is likely to respond to a competitor's action when either

- the action leads to better use of the competitor's capabilities to develop a stronger competitive advantage or an improvement in its market position,
- the action damages the firm's ability to use its core competencies to create or maintain an advantage, or
- the firm's market position becomes harder to defend.[85]

In addition to market commonality and resource similarity, and awareness, motivation, and ability, firms evaluate three other factors—type of competitive action, actor's reputation, and market dependence—to predict how a competitor is likely to respond to competitive actions (see Figure 5.2).

5-6a Type of Competitive Action

Competitive responses to strategic actions differ from responses to tactical actions. These differences allow the firm to predict a competitor's likely response to a competitive action that a firm took against it. Strategic actions commonly receive strategic responses and tactical actions receive tactical responses. In general, strategic actions elicit fewer total competitive responses because strategic responses, such as market-based moves, involve a significant commitment of resources and are difficult to implement and reverse.[86]

Another reason that strategic actions elicit fewer responses than do tactical actions is that the time needed to implement a strategic action and to assess its effectiveness can delay the competitor's response to that action. In contrast, a competitor likely will respond quickly to a tactical action, such as when an airline company almost immediately matches a competitor's tactical action of reducing prices in certain markets. Either strategic actions or tactical actions that target a large number of a rival's customers are likely to elicit strong responses.[87] In fact, if the effects of a competitor's strategic action on the focal firm are significant (e.g., loss of market share, loss of major resources such as critical employees), a response is likely to be swift and strong.[88]

The IBM brand has had a very strong positive reputation for many years.

IBM Service Software.PNG

5-6b Actor's Reputation

In the context of competitive rivalry, an *actor* is the firm taking an action or a response, while *reputation* is "the positive or negative attribute ascribed by one rival to another based on past competitive behavior."[89] A positive reputation may be a source of above-average returns, especially for consumer goods producers.[90] Thus, a positive corporate reputation is of strategic value[91] and affects competitive rivalry. To predict the likelihood of a competitor's response to a current or planned action, firms evaluate the responses that the competitor took previously when attacked. In this way, firms assume that past behavior predicts future behavior.

Competitors are more likely to respond to strategic or tactical actions when market leaders take them.[92] In particular, evidence suggests that successful actions, especially strategic actions, are ones competitors will choose to imitate quickly. For example, although a second mover, IBM committed significant resources to enter the information service market. Competitors such as Hewlett-Packard (HP), Dell Inc., and others responded with strategic actions to enter this market also.[93] IBM has invested heavily to build its capabilities in service-related software as well. As explained in the Opening Case, Kroger and others responded quickly to market leader Amazon's acquisition of Whole Foods.

In contrast to a firm with a strong reputation, competitors are less likely to respond to actions taken by a company with a reputation for risky, complex, and unpredictable competitive behavior. For example, the firm with a reputation as a price predator (an actor that frequently reduces prices to gain or maintain market share) generates few responses to its pricing tactical actions because price predators, which typically increase prices once they reach their desired market share, lack credibility with their competitors.[94]

5-6c Market Dependence

Market dependence denotes the extent to which a firm derives its revenues or profits from a particular market.[95] In general, competitors with high market dependence are likely to respond strongly to attacks threatening their market position.[96] However, the threatened firm in these instances may not always respond quickly, even though an effective response to an attack on the firm's position in a critical market is important.

Target generates approximately 19 percent of its revenue from apparel sales. Thus, the firm is somewhat dependent on the apparel market as a generator of revenue. Because of this, the firm pays attention to Amazon's efforts to increase its sales of apparel items, particularly given that these two firms are battling each other for the position as the "second-most-popular clothing and footwear retailer in the US as measured by number of shoppers."[97]

Overall, Amazon is highly dependent on the e-commerce market for its sales. While the firm is experimenting with establishing physical bookstores and purchased Whole Foods, e-commerce sales account for the vast majority of its revenue. Amazon's competitor Walmart is less dependent on e-commerce; nonetheless, Walmart is enhancing its e-commerce skills. Because of its dependence on the e-commerce market, Amazon pays close attention to Walmart's efforts to enhance its e-commerce presence and capabilities. Recent Walmart actions dealing with its e-commerce business include seeking additional traffic to its website by emphasizing paid search functions[98] and a commitment to acquiring boutique firms as a means of being able to offer differentiated products to online shoppers. Modcloth.com (a women's vintage-inspired retailer) and Moosejaw (an outdoor retailer that adds popular brands such as Patagonia and North Face to Walmart's product line) are examples of firms Walmart acquired to offer differentiated products to its e-commerce customers.[99] According to the executive in charge of Walmart's e-commerce activities, the firm "remains in buying mode as it looks to differentiate its online inventory to compete with Amazon.com."[100] Given its dependence on the e-commerce market, expecting a strong response from Amazon to Walmart's actions is reasonable.

5-7 Competitive Dynamics

Whereas competitive rivalry concerns the ongoing actions and responses between a firm and its direct competitors for an advantageous market position, *competitive dynamics* concerns the ongoing actions and responses among *all* firms competing within a market for advantageous positions. Thus, United and Delta engage in competitive rivalry while the competitive actions and responses taken by United, Delta, American, Southwest, British Airways, Lufthansa, and Emirates Airways (and many others) form the competitive dynamics of the airline passenger industry.

To explain competitive dynamics, we explore the effects of varying rates of competitive speed in different markets (called slow-cycle, fast-cycle, and standard-cycle markets) on the behavior (actions and responses) of all competitors within a given market. Competitive behaviors, as well as the reasons for taking them, are similar within each market type, but differ across types of markets. Thus, competitive dynamics differ in slow-, fast-, and standard-cycle markets.

As noted in Chapter 1, firms want to sustain their competitive advantages for as long as possible, although no advantage is sustainable permanently. However, as we discuss next, the sustainability of the firm's competitive advantages differs by market type. How quickly competitors can imitate a rival's competitive advantage and the cost to do so influences the sustainability of a focal firm's competitive advantage.

5-7a Slow-Cycle Markets

Slow-cycle markets are markets in which competitors lack the ability to imitate the focal firm's competitive advantages that commonly last for long periods, and where imitation would be costly.[101] Thus, firms may be able to sustain a competitive advantage over longer periods in slow-cycle markets. However, because no competitive advantage is sustainable permanently, firms competing in slow-cycle markets can expect eventually to see a decline in the value their competitive advantage creates for target customers.

As we explain in the Strategic Focus, this was the case for Swiss watchmakers for decades. Relying largely on the competitive advantage of exclusivity that was a function of extreme precision in the manufacture of watches, these companies lacked effective competitors for many years. However, technological innovations such as smartwatches and changes in consumers' interests (e.g., for "memorable experiences" rather than for valuable "things") are creating serious competitive challenges for Swiss watchmakers. As you will see, the strategic actions taken by Swiss manufacturers making high-end, high-quality watches to address the competitive challenges they face today may extend their historical competitive advantage.

Slow-cycle markets are markets in which competitors lack the ability to imitate the focal firm's competitive advantages that commonly last for long periods, and where imitation would be costly.

Strategic Focus

Swiss Watchmakers: The Eroding of a Long-Lasting Competitive Advantage While Competing in a Slow-Cycle Market?

Long committed to competitive dominance in the watch market, and certainly in upper-end watches, the Swiss watch industry held roughly 50 percent of the global watch market prior to the 1970s and held a virtual monopoly position in the luxury watch segment. Truly a global market, Swiss firms export almost 95 percent of their upper-end watches to countries throughout the world. Impeccable quality, aesthetic prowess, technical innovation, sophisticated manufacturing of mechanical watches as completed by craftsman, and careful branding of the watches as "Swiss Made" led to the ultimate source of differentiation and competitive advantage for high-end Swiss watches—exclusivity. Because it is seen as a status symbol, successful people wishing to convey an image of their success might choose to purchase an expensive Swiss watch. Frequently targeting individuals initially achieving notable levels of career and financial success (commonly, these individuals are in their early to mid-thirties), upper-end Swiss watches were long the foundation of strategic competitiveness for many firms such as Breguet, Richemont, TAG Heuer, Piaget SA, Patek Philippe & Co., and Parmigiani Fleurier.

Now though, Swiss watchmakers' competitive advantage of exclusivity and the cachet of the term "Swiss Made" face challenges. For a number of young, successful people today, the exclusivity of a watch does not create value. Instead, these individuals, who tend to value "experiences" over "things," might choose to book a getaway to Costa Rica and document the trip extensively on Instagram rather than buy an expensive watch with the Swiss Made label. What are Swiss watchmakers doing in response to today's competitive realities that historically took place in a slow-cycle market?

First, in collaboration with their home nation and the Federation of the Swiss Watch Industry group, Swiss watchmakers strongly support efforts to control counterfeiting of their products. A long-term challenge for Swiss watchmakers, counterfeiters sell tens of millions of their products annually on a global basis. In the Federation's words: "Essentially the theft of an intellectual property right, the problem of counterfeiting today has reached global proportions." Today, fake watches account for approximately 9 percent of customs' seizures. This makes watches the second most counterfeited product behind textiles. Working with the Swiss government that is in turn working with countries throughout the world, importing a counterfeit watch is now against the law in many nations, "even in the case of one-off pieces bought in good faith for private use." Reducing counterfeiting protects the exclusivity competitive advantage on which the makers of high-end Swiss watches rely for success.

Brandon Voight/Splash News/Sydney/AUSTRALIA/Newscom

Swiss watchmakers, such as TAG Heuer, target younger customers by using celebrities and athletes as product brand ambassadors.

Targeting younger customers, "even at the expense of traditions that have long endeared Swiss watches to older generations," is a strategic action exercised today by some Swiss watchmakers. To support their sales, TAG Heuer and Hublot (LVMH Moet Hennessy Louis Vuitton owns these brands), now use artists such as Jay-Z to design watches and signed models in their twenties (e.g., Cara Delevingne) as product brand ambassadors. Basketball stars Kobe Bryant and Dwayne Wade also are ambassadors, while street artists Alec Monopoly and Mr. Brainwash and renowned tattoo artist Maxime Buchi are others whom TAG Heuer and Hublot employ as designers. These efforts seek to present expensive Swiss watches to today's young consumers in ways that appeal to them. The "Shawn Carter by Hublot" is one of the watches designed in collaboration with Jay-Z. There are two version of this watch: "one in black for $17,900 and the other in yellow gold for $33,900." Both watches feature a transparent back displaying their complicated internal working mechanisms. Limited in quantity to only 350 to reinforce the image of exclusivity, the watches sold out quickly. In this sense, Swiss watchmakers were able to extend the "exclusivity" competitive advantage in ways that appeal to the target audience.

Audemars Piguet is taking an additional competitive action to protect the firm's advantage while competing in a historical slow-cycle market. In this instance, the firm is seeking to expand the target customer segment to whom it can sell its products. To do this, Audemars Piguet is reselling its own product so customers can buy a used version "at a fraction of the $15,000-and-up new cost." The hope is that once they become customers, individuals will later choose to purchase a "new" Audemars Piguet watch.

Overall, manufacturers of high-end, high-quality Swiss watches seek to find novel ways of executing on their historic competitive advantage of exclusivity. In this sense, the firms want to create value in the form of their watches for which individuals across the globe are willing to pay.

Sources: 2018, Stop the Fakes! Federation of the Swiss Watch Industry FH, www.fhs.swiss.com, March 28; 2018, Swiss made: The only true reference, Federation of the Swiss Watch Industry FH, www.fhs.swiss.com, March 28; M. Clerizo, 2018, The world's weirdest watches: Good luck telling the time, *Wall Street Journal*, www.wsj.com, January 17; M. Dalton, 2018, Is time running out for the Swiss watch industry? *Wall Street Journal*, www.wsj.com, March 12; T. Mulier, 2018, Swiss watchmakers' new pitch: $10,000 timepiece can be a bargain, *Bloomberg*, www.bloomberg.com, January 26.

Building a unique and proprietary capability produces a competitive advantage and success in a slow-cycle market. This type of advantage is difficult for competitors to understand. As discussed in Chapter 3, a difficult-to-understand and costly-to-imitate capability usually results from unique historical conditions, causal ambiguity, and/or social complexity. Copyrights and patents are examples of these types of capabilities. After a firm develops a proprietary advantage by using its capabilities, the competitive actions and responses it takes in a slow-cycle market are oriented to protecting, maintaining, and extending that advantage. Major strategic actions in these markets, such as acquisitions, usually carry less risk than in faster-cycle markets.[102] Clearly, firms that gain an advantage can grow more and earn higher returns than those who simply track with the industry, especially in mature and declining industries.[103]

The Walt Disney Company continues to extend its proprietary characters, such as Mickey Mouse, Minnie Mouse, and Goofy, to enhance the value its characters as a competitive advantage create for target customers. These characters have a unique historical development because of Walt and Roy Disney's creativity and vision for entertaining people. Products based on the characters seen in Disney's animated films are available to customers to buy through Disney's theme park shops as well as freestanding retail outlets called Disney Stores. Because copyrights shield it, the proprietary nature of Disney's competitive advantage in terms of animated character trademarks continues to protect the firm from imitation by competitors.

Consistent with another attribute of competition in a slow-cycle market, Disney protects its exclusive rights to its characters and their use. As with all firms competing in slow-cycle markets, Disney's competitive actions (such as building theme parks in France, Japan, and China) and responses (such as lawsuits to protect its right to fully control use of its animated characters) maintain and extend its proprietary competitive advantage while protecting it.

Patent laws and regulatory requirements in the United States requiring FDA (Food and Drug Administration) approval to launch new products shield pharmaceutical companies' positions. Competitors in this market try to extend patents on their drugs to maintain advantageous positions that patents provide. However, after a patent expires, the firm's product faces a different situation in that generic imitations become available to customers. These imitations may lead to reduced sales and profits for the firm losing a

Figure 5.4 Gradual Erosion of a Sustained Competitive Advantage

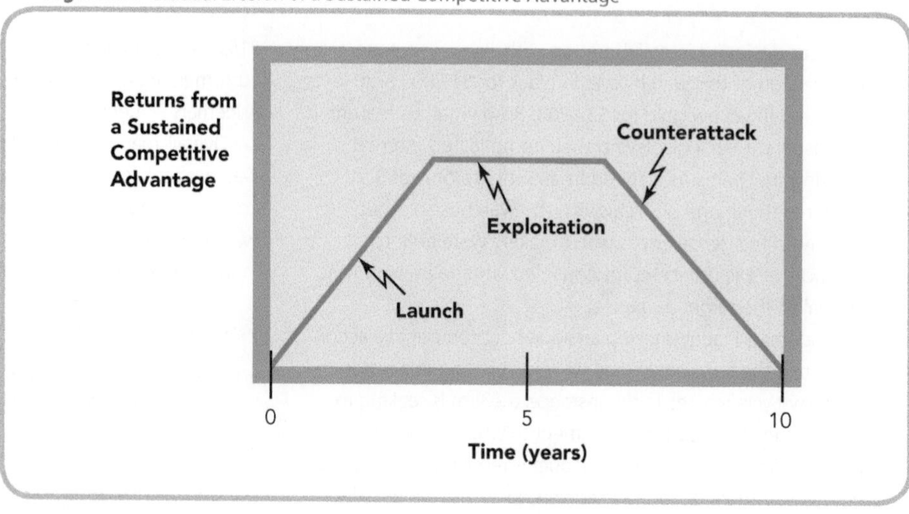

Source: Adapted from I. C. MacMillan, 1988, Controlling competitive dynamics by taking strategic initiative, *Academy of Management Executive*, II(2): 111–118.

patent on its product. This was the case for Pfizer when Lipitor (which is the best-selling drug in history) went off patent in the fall of 2011. The firm's profits declined 19 percent in the first quarter after that event. A number of prominent drugs went off patent in 2017 including Eli Lilly's Cialis and Alimta, Pfizer's Viagra, Johnson & Johnson's Prezista, and Takeda's Velcade. These drugs generated significant revenue for the firms owning them. In 2016, for example, sales revenue for Viagra was $1.2 billion.[104]

We show the competitive dynamics generated by firms competing in slow-cycle markets in Figure 5.4. In slow-cycle markets, the firm launches a product (e.g., a new drug) it developed through a proprietary advantage (e.g., R&D) and then exploits that advantage for as long as possible while the product's uniqueness shields it from competition. Eventually, competitors respond to the action with a counterattack. In markets for drugs, this counterattack commonly occurs as patents expire or are broken through legal means, creating the need for another product launch by the firm seeking a protected market position.

5-7b Fast-Cycle Markets

Fast-cycle markets are markets in which competitors can imitate the focal firm's capabilities that contribute to its competitive advantages and where that imitation is often rapid and inexpensive.[105] Thus, competitive advantages are not sustainable in fast-cycle markets. Firms competing in fast-cycle markets recognize the importance of speed; these companies appreciate that "time is as precious a business resource as money or head count—and that the costs of hesitation and delay are just as steep as going over budget or missing a financial forecast."[106] The velocity of change in fast-cycle markets places considerable pressure on top-level managers to help their firm make strategic decisions quickly that are effective. This is a challenging task for managers and the organizations they lead.[107]

Fast-cycle markets are markets in which competitors can imitate the focal firm's capabilities that contribute to its competitive advantages and where that imitation is often rapid and inexpensive.

Reverse engineering and the rate of technology diffusion facilitate the rapid imitation that takes place in fast-cycle markets. A competitor uses reverse engineering to gain quick access to the knowledge required to imitate or improve the firm's products. Technology diffuses rapidly in fast-cycle markets, making it available to competitors in a short period. The technology firms competing in fast-cycle markets use often is not proprietary, nor is it protected by patents as is the technology used by firms competing in slow-cycle markets. For example, only a few hundred parts, which are readily available on the open market, are required to build a PC. Patents protect only a few of these parts, such as microprocessor chips. However, potential entrants may hesitate to enter even a fast-cycle market when it knows that the success of one or more firms competing in the market is a function of the ability to develop valuable patents.[108]

Fast-cycle markets are more volatile than slow- and standard-cycle markets. Indeed, the pace of competition in fast-cycle markets is almost frenzied, as companies rely on innovations as growth engines. Because prices often decline quickly in these markets, companies need to profit rapidly from their product innovations.

Recognizing this reality, firms avoid "loyalty" to any of their products, preferring to cannibalize their own products before competitors learn how to do so through successful imitation. This emphasis creates competitive dynamics that differ substantially from those found in slow-cycle markets. Instead of concentrating on protecting, maintaining, and extending competitive advantages, as in slow-cycle markets, companies competing in fast-cycle markets focus on forming the capabilities and core competencies that will allow them to develop new competitive advantages continuously and rapidly. In some industries, cooperative strategies such as strategic alliances and joint ventures (see Chapter 9) are a path to firms gaining access to new technologies that lead to introducing innovative products to the market.[109] In recent years, many of these alliances have been offshore (with partners in foreign countries); gaining access to a partner's capabilities at a lower cost is a key driver in such instances. However, finding the balance between sharing knowledge and skills with a foreign partner and preventing that partner from appropriating value from the focal firm's contributions to the alliance is challenging.[110]

We show the competitive behavior of firms competing in fast-cycle markets in Figure 5.5. Competitive dynamics in this market type entail actions and responses firms take to introduce products rapidly and continuously into the market. Flowing from an ability to do this is a stream of ever-changing competitive advantages for the firm. In this sense, the firm launches a product to achieve a competitive advantage and then exploits the advantage for as long as possible. However, the firm also tries to develop another competitive advantage before competitors can respond to the first one. Thus, competitive dynamics in fast-cycle markets often result in rapid product upgrades as well as quick product innovations.[111]

Figure 5.5 Developing Temporary Advantages to Create Sustained Advantage

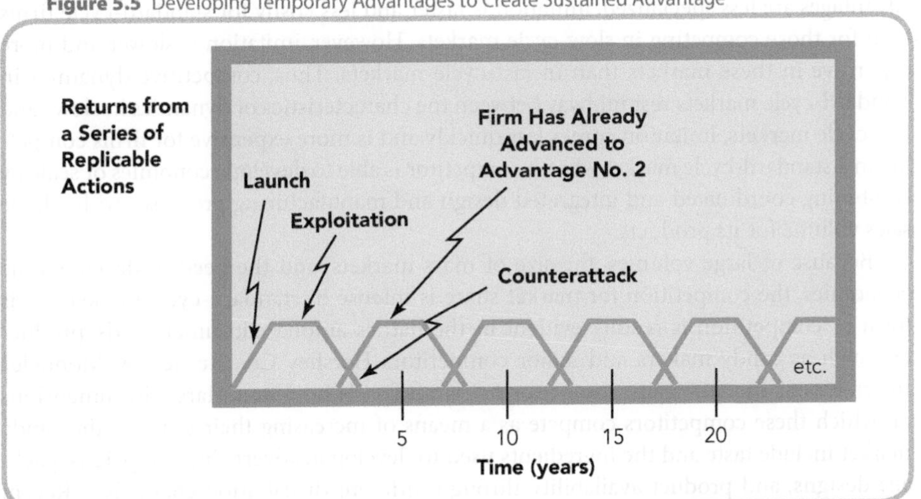

Source: Adapted from I. C. MacMillan, 1988, Controlling competitive dynamics by taking strategic initiative, *Academy of Management Executive*, II(2): 111–118.

Tech giants Alibaba Group Holding and Tencent Holdings compete against each other in a range of mobile Internet businesses. As competitors in this fast-cycle market, these direct competitors are aware of each other and have the motivation and ability to engage in aggressive competition. Some analysts believe that the competition between these giants today "is likely to reshape the landscape of China's business world and affect the lives of Chinese and the destinies of smaller companies."[112] Initially, Alibaba and Tencent dominated separate Internet spheres: messaging and games for Tencent and e-commerce for Alibaba. Largely because of a reduction in the growth in online users, the rivalry between these firms is now more direct and intense as each firm seeks control over the convergence of online and offline services. While competing aggressively with each other, Alibaba and Tencent will try to find innovative ways to serve customers.

As our discussion suggests, innovation plays a critical role in the competitive dynamics in fast-cycle markets. For individual firms, innovation is a key source of competitive advantage. Through continuous and effective innovation, firms can cannibalize their own products before competitors successfully imitate them and still maintain an advantage through next-generation products.

5-7c Standard-Cycle Markets

Standard-cycle markets are markets in which some competitors may be able to imitate the focal firm's competitive advantages and where that imitation is moderately costly. Competitive advantages are partially sustainable in standard-cycle markets. However, this is the case only when the firm can upgrade the quality of its capabilities continuously as a foundation for being able to remain ahead of competitors. Firms initiate competitive actions and responses in standard-cycle markets to seek large market shares, to gain customer loyalty through brand names, and to control a firm's operations carefully. When successful with these efforts, a firm consistently provides the same positive experience to customers.[113] This is how the retail food industry operated for many years. As explained in this chapter's Mini-Case, changes are occurring with this pattern of competition as discount competitors such as Aldi become more competitive on a global basis.

Companies competing in standard-cycle markets tend to serve many customers in what are typically highly competitive markets. Because the capabilities and core competencies on which firms competing in standard-cycle markets base their competitive advantages are less specialized, imitation is faster and less costly for standard-cycle firms than for those competing in slow-cycle markets. However, imitation is slower and more expensive in these markets than in fast-cycle markets. Thus, competitive dynamics in standard-cycle markets rest midway between the characteristics of dynamics in slow- and fast-cycle markets. Imitation comes less quickly and is more expensive for firms competing in a standard-cycle market when a competitor is able to develop economies of scale by combining coordinated and integrated design and manufacturing processes with a large sales volume for its products.

Because of large volumes, the size of mass markets, and the need to develop scale economies, the competition for market share is intense in standard-cycle markets. This form of competition is readily evident in the battles among consumer foods' producers, such as candy makers and major competitors Hershey Co., Nestlé, SA, Mondelēz International, Inc. (the name for the former Kraft Foods Inc.), and Mars. The dimensions on which these competitors compete as a means of increasing their share of the candy market include taste and the ingredients used to develop it, advertising campaigns, package designs, and product availability through different distribution channels.[114] Recent years found candy manufacturers contending with criticism from health professionals about the sugar, saturated fats, and calories their products provide. These criticisms

Standard-cycle markets are markets in which some competitors may be able to imitate the focal firm's competitive advantages and where that imitation is moderately costly.

revolve around the negative effects on individuals' health caused by the ingredients used to manufacture candy products.

Innovation can also drive competitive actions and responses in standard-cycle markets, especially when rivalry is intense. As explained in the Opening Case, we can anticipate innovation in distribution channels and in the use of data analytics to take place in the retail grocery industry as Amazon, Walmart, and others engage in competitive battles with traditional storefront operators such as Kroger and Safeway. Some innovations in standard-cycle markets are incremental rather than radical in nature. (We discuss incremental and radical innovations in Chapter 13.) Both types of innovation, though, are critical to firms' efforts to achieve strategic competitiveness when competing in standard-cycle markets.

Overall, innovation has a substantial influence on competitive dynamics as it affects the actions and responses of all companies competing within a slow-, fast-, or standard-cycle market. In previous chapters, we emphasized the importance of innovation to the firm's strategic competitiveness. In Chapter 13's discussion of strategic entrepreneurship, we emphasize this relationship and its importance again. These discussions highlight the critical role innovation plays for firms regardless of the type of competitive rivalry and competitive dynamics they encounter while competing.

SUMMARY

- Competitors are firms competing in the same market, offering similar products, and targeting similar customers. Competitive rivalry is the ongoing set of competitive actions and responses occurring between competitors as they compete against each other for an advantageous market position. The outcomes of competitive rivalry influence the firm's ability to develop and then sustain its competitive advantages as well as the level (average, below average, or above average) of its financial returns.
- Competitive behavior is the set of competitive actions and responses an individual firm takes while engaged in competitive rivalry. Competitive dynamics is the set of actions and responses taken by all firms that are competitors within a particular market.
- Firms study competitive rivalry in order to predict the competitive actions and responses each of their competitors is likely to take. Competitive actions are either strategic or tactical in nature. The firm takes competitive actions to defend or build its competitive advantages or to improve its market position. Firms take competitive responses to counter the effects of a competitor's competitive action. A strategic action or a strategic response requires a significant commitment of organizational resources, is difficult to implement successfully, and is difficult to reverse. In contrast, a tactical action or a tactical response requires fewer organizational resources and is easier to implement and reverse. For example, for an airline company, entering major new markets is an example of a strategic action or a strategic response; changing ticket prices in a particular market is an example of a tactical action or a tactical response.
- A competitor analysis is the first step the firm takes to be able to predict its competitors' actions and responses. In Chapter 2, we discussed what firms do to *understand* competitors. We extended this discussion in this chapter to describe what the firm does to *predict* competitors' market-based actions. Thus, understanding precedes prediction. Firms study market commonality (the number of markets with which competitors are involved jointly and their importance to each) and resource similarity (how comparable competitors' resources are in terms of type and amount) to complete a competitor analysis. In general, the greater the market commonality and resource similarity, the more firms acknowledge that they are direct competitors.
- Market commonality and resource similarity shape the firm's awareness (the degree to which it and its competitors understand their mutual interdependence), motivation (the firm's incentive to attack or respond), and ability (the quality of the resources available to the firm to attack and respond). Having knowledge of these characteristics of a competitor increases the quality of the firm's predictions about that competitor's actions and responses.
- In addition to market commonality, resource similarity, awareness, motivation, and ability, three more specific factors affect the likelihood a competitor will take competitive actions. The first of these is first-mover benefits. First movers, those taking an initial competitive action, often gain loyal customers and earn above-average returns until competitors can respond successfully to their action. Not all firms can be first movers because they may lack the awareness, motivation, or ability required to engage in this type of competitive behavior.

Moreover, some firms prefer to be a second mover (the firm responding to the first mover's action). By evaluating the first mover's product, customers' reactions to it, and the responses of other competitors to the first mover, the second mover may be able to avoid the early entrant's mistakes and find ways to improve upon the value created for customers by the first mover's product. Late movers (those that respond a long time after the original action was taken) commonly are lower performers and less competitive.

- Organizational size tends to reduce the variety of competitive actions that large firms launch, while it increases the variety of actions smaller competitors undertake. Ideally, a firm prefers to initiate a large number of diverse actions when engaging in competitive rivalry. Another factor, quality, is a base denominator for competing successfully in the global economy and for achieving competitive parity, at a minimum. However, quality is a necessary but insufficient condition for establishing an advantage.

- To predict a competitor's response to its actions, a firm examines the type of action (strategic or tactical) it took, the competitor's reputation for the nature of its competitive behavior, and that competitor's dependence on the market in which the focal firm took action. In general, the number of tactical responses firms take exceeds the number of strategic responses they take. Competitors respond more frequently to the actions taken by the firm with a reputation for predictable and understandable competitive behavior, especially if that firm is a market leader. In general, the firm can predict that when its competitor is highly dependent on its revenue and profitability in the market in which the firm took a competitive action, that competitor is likely to launch a strong response. However, firms with greater diversification across markets are less likely to respond to a particular action that affects only one of the markets in which they compete.

- In slow-cycle markets, firms generally can maintain competitive advantages for some amount of time. Competitive dynamics in slow-cycle markets often include actions and responses intended to protect, maintain, and extend the firm's proprietary advantages. In fast-cycle markets, competition is substantial as firms concentrate on developing a series of temporary competitive advantages. This emphasis is necessary because firms' advantages in fast-cycle markets are not proprietary; as such, they are subject to rapid and relatively inexpensive imitation. Standard-cycle markets have a level of competition between that in slow- and fast-cycle markets; firms often (but not always) have a moderate amount of protection from competition in standard-cycle markets as they use competencies that produce competitive advantages with some sustainability. Competitors in standard-cycle markets serve mass markets and try to develop economies of scale to enhance their profitability. Innovation is vital to competitive success in each of the three types of markets. Companies should recognize that the set of competitive actions and responses taken by all firms differs by type of market.

KEY TERMS

competitive action 154
competitive behavior 145
competitive dynamics 145
competitive response 154
competitive rivalry 144
competitors 144
fast-cycle markets 164
first mover 155
late mover 157
market commonality 150
multimarket competition 145
quality 158
resource similarity 151
second mover 156
slow-cycle markets 161
standard-cycle markets 166
strategic action or strategic response 154
tactical action or tactical response 154

REVIEW QUESTIONS

1. Who are competitors? How are competitive rivalry, competitive behavior, and competitive dynamics defined in the chapter?
2. What is market commonality? What is resource similarity? In what way are these concepts the building blocks for a competitor analysis?
3. How do awareness, motivation, and ability affect the firm's competitive behavior?
4. What factors affect the likelihood a firm will take a competitive action?
5. What factors affect the likelihood a firm will initiate a competitive response to a competitor's action(s)?
6. What competitive dynamics can firms expect to experience when competing in slow-cycle markets? In fast-cycle markets? In standard-cycle markets?

Mini-Case

The Ripple Effect of Supermarket Wars: Aldi Is Changing the Markets in Many Countries

Aldi started as a small, family-owned grocery store located in Essen, Germany, in 1913. Two sons, Karl and Theo, took over the store from their mother in 1946; soon after doing so, they began expanding the business. They emphasized low costs from the very beginning, allowing them to offer their products to customers at low prices relative to competitors. Over time, Aldi expanded to other European countries, and it entered the United States market in 1976. Currently, there are roughly 11,000 Aldi stores located in 20 countries; 1,750 of these units are in 35 states in the United States. In the United States alone, the firm serves 40 million customers on a monthly basis.

Aldi holds its costs down in a variety of ways. It largely sells its own brand-label products in "no frill" stores. The company limits the number of external brands it sells (usually one or two per product), and it has low packaging, transportation, and employee costs. To sell products in its stores, Aldi positions them in ways that are similar to the approach warehouse stores use, for example, placing products on pallets and in cut-away cardboard boxes. In Germany, Aldi advertises very little, but it does advertise in the United States. It produces its own ads in-house (no external agency) and advertises mostly through newspaper inserts and a few television commercials.

Aldi and another discount store, Lidl, have hurt the largest four supermarkets in the U.K. market—Tesco, Walmart's Asda, J Sainsbury, and Wm. Morrison Supermarkets. Aldi and Lidl have captured market share from these retailers, especially Tesco and Morrison, and held approximately 8.6 percent of the U.K. market in 2016. Aldi plans call for it to reach about 17 percent share of the market by 2021. Tesco has controlled about 30 percent of the discount supermarket market, but it has been declining. Morrison's recent poor performance has precipitated turnover in most of the firm's top executives. In addition, the new CEO, David Potts, has been making major changes—largely cutting costs in order to compete on prices. Because of reduced costs, Morrison cut its prices on 130 staple items such as milk and eggs. Likewise, Tesco reduced prices of 380 of its brand products by about 25 percent. Yet, because of gains in its market share, Aldi plans to invest about $900 million to open 550 new stores in Britain by 2022.

Aldi is having similar effects on the Australian market. It has gained market share from the two largest supermarkets in Australia—Coles and Woolworths. In response, Woolworths indicated that it plans to reduce its prices to avoid a perception among customers as the "expensive option." This action does not seem to concern Aldi in that the firm intends to spend $700 million to add 120–130 stores by 2020 to its current number of 300 stores in Australia.

Aldi appears to be harming some competitors in the United States as well. For example, a rival discount food retailer, Bottom Dollar owned by Delhaize from Belgium, closed all of its stores (located in New Jersey, Pennsylvania, and Ohio) and sold the locations and leases to Aldi. Aldi does have stiffer competition in the United States from Walmart, Sam's (Walmart's warehouse stores), and Costco, among other discount food retailers. Yet, Aldi is not only surviving, but also flourishing and growing in the U.S. market as well. In early 2018, Aldi announced that it would spend $1.6 billion to remodel and expand 1,300 U.S. stores by 2020. Desiring to have 2,500 stores in the United States by 2022, the firm announced in 2018 that it would spend up to $3 billion to open new stores to reach this target. If reached, a total number of 2,500 stores would result in Aldi being the third largest supermarket chain in the United States.

In addition to affecting grocery store competitive rivalry across country boundaries, Aldi's actions (and those of others as well) have an effect on wholesalers and other suppliers. For example, wholesale prices have been declining, and some of the major supermarket chains, such as Tesco and Morrison, have been reducing the number of brands on their shelves. Interestingly, manufacturers of popular products, such as Mr. Kipling cakes and Bistro gravy, stand to gain shelf space and increase sales because of stores' decisions to take some rivals' products off their shelves. Of course, the suppliers whose products lose their positions on stores' shelves will likely suffer.

The bottom line is that Aldi is having a major effect on rivals in multiple countries and on many other companies that supply products to the industry. As a result, the grocery industry's competitive dynamics are different today than they were before.

Sources: 2018, Aldi unveils $1.6 billion nationwide store remodel plan to enhance customer shopping experience, Aldi Homepage, www.aldi.com, February 8; 2017, Motley Fool staff, Setting the stage for grocery industry competition in 2018, Motley Fool Homepage, www.fool.com, December 24; 2014, Aldi targets doubling of UK stores with 600 million pound investment, *New York Times*, www.nytimes.com, November 10; T. Hua, 2015, Tesco's overhaul points to a price war, *Wall Street Journal*, www.wsj.com, January 5; L. Northrup, 2015, Bottom dollar food to close stores, sell chain to Aldi, *Consumerist*, www.consumerist.com, January 5; 2015, Mr. Kipling Maker Premier Foods sees positives in supermarket wars, *New York Times*, www.nytimes.com, January 23; 2015, Morrisons cuts prices on 130 grocery staples like milk, eggs, *New York Times*, www.nytimes.com, February 15; 2015, British shop price decline steepens in February—BRC, *New York Times*, www.nytimes.com, March 3; K. Ross, 2015, Supermarket wars: Aldi takes on market share as Woolworths drops prices, *Smart Company*, www.smartcompany.com.au, March 9; A. Felsted, 2015, Morrison chiefs take express checkout from struggling supermarket, *Financial Times*, www.ft.com, March 24; 2015, Aldi Foods, www.grocery.com, accessed March 25.

Case Discussion Questions

1. Using materials in the case and items to which you gain access through a search, describe how Aldi is creating competitive rivalry in the retail grocers' industry.
2. As explained in this chapter's Opening Case, Amazon purchased Whole Foods. How will this transaction affect Aldi as it seeks to expand its presence in the United States? What competitive actions might Aldi take in response to Amazon's purchase of Whole Foods?
3. Using concepts and actions explained in this chapter, decide if Aldi is more likely to respond to any strategic actions Amazon might initiate through Whole Foods or if Amazon through Whole Foods is more likely to respond to any strategic actions Aldi takes. Be prepared to justify your decision.
4. In a competitive rivalry sense, explain the actions (strategic and/or tactical) you believe Walmart and Costco will take to respond to Aldi's intentions to have 2,500 U.S. stores by 2020.

NOTES

1. J. P. Eggers & A. Kaul, 2018, Motivation and ability? A behavioral perspective on the pursuit of radical invention in multi-technology incumbents, *Academy of Management Journal*, 61: 67–93; P. Karhu & P. Ritala, 2018, Dilemmas and paradoxes: How managers make the toughest decisions, *Journal of Business Strategy*, 39: 24–31; M.-J. Chen & D. Miller, 2012, Competitive dynamics: Themes, trends, and a prospective research platform, *Academy of Management Annals*, 6: 135–210.
2. K.-Y. Hsieh & E. (E.J.) Hyun, 2018, Matching response to competitors' moves under asymmetric market strength, *Journal of Business Research*, 82: 202–212; M. G. Jacobides & C. J. Tae, 2015, Kingpins, bottlenecks, and value dynamics along a sector, *Organization Science*, 26: 889–907.
3. B. Power & G. C. Reid, 2018, Decision support for firm performance by real options analytics, *Managerial and Decision Economics*, 39: 56–64; J. Luoma, S. Ruutu, A. W. King, & H. Tikkanen, 2017, Time delays, competitive interdependence, and firm performance, *Strategic Management Journal*, 38: 506–525.
4. D. P. Hannah & K. M. Eisenhardt, 2018, How firms navigate cooperation and competition in nascent ecosystems, *Strategic Management Journal*, in press; R. E. Hoskisson, E. Gambeta, C. Green, & T. Li, 2018, Is my firm-specific investment protected? Overcoming the stakeholder investment dilemma in the resource based view, *Academy of Management Review*, in press.
5. M. W. Withers, R. D. Ireland, D. Miller, J. Harrison, & D. Boss, 2018, Competitive landscape shifts: The influence of strategic entrepreneurship on shifts in market commonality, *Academy of Management Review*, 43: 349–370; P. J. Derfus, P. G. Maggitti, C. M. Grimm, & K. G. Smith, 2008, The red queen effect: Competitive actions and firm performance, *Academy of Management Journal*, 51: 61–80.
6. R. Katila, S. Thatchenkery, M. Q. Christensen, & S. Zenios, 2017, Is there a doctor in the house? Expert product users, organizational roles, and innovation, *Academy of Management Journal*, 60: 2415–2437; C. Giachetti & G. B. Dagnino, 2014, Detecting the relationship between competitive intensity and firm product line length: Evidence from the worldwide mobile phone industry, *Strategic Management Journal*, 35: 1398–1409.
7. C. Giachetti, J. Lampel, & S. L. Pira, 2017, Red Queen imitation in the U.K. mobile phone industry, *Academy of Management Journal*, 60: 1992–2014; D. G. Sirmon, S. Gove, & M. A. Hitt, 2008, Resource management in dyadic competitive rivalry: The effects of resource bundling and deployment, *Academy of Management Journal*, 51: 919–935.
8. T. Chen, M. A. Tribbitt, Y. Yang, & X. Li, 2017, Does rivals' innovation matter? A competitive dynamics perspective on firms' product strategy, *Journal of Business Research*, 76: 1–7; R. Kapoor & N. R. Furr, 2015, Complementarities and competition: Unpacking the drivers of entrants' technology choices in the solar photovoltaic industry, *Strategic Management Journal*, 36: 416–436.
9. M. Hughes-Morgan, K. Kolev & G. McNamara, 2018, A meta-analytic review of competitive aggressiveness research, *Journal of Business Research*, 85: 73–82; W. Guo, T. Yu, & J. Gimeno, 2017, Language

and competition: Communication vagueness, interpretation difficulties, and market entry, *Academy of Management Journal*, 60: 2073–2098.

10. 2017, What industry analysts and insiders are saying about Amazon Buying Whole Foods, *Reuters*, www.reuters.com, June 16.
11. T. Kim, 2017, Amazon's booming online sales and Whole Foods acquisition make it a buy: Analysts, *Reuters*, www.reuters.com, October 24.
12. K.-Y. Hsieh & E. (E.J.) Hyun, 2018, Matching response to competitors' moves under asymmetric market strength, *Journal of Business Research*, 82: 2-2–212.
13. J. Han, A. V. Shipilov, & H. R. Greve, 2017, Unequal bedfellows: Gender role-based deference in multiplex ties between Korean business groups, *Academy of Management Journal*, 60: 1531–1553; T. Yu, M. Subramaniam, & A. A. Cannella, Jr., 2009, Rivalry deterrence in international markets: Contingencies governing the mutual forbearance hypothesis, *Academy of Management Journal*, 52: 127–147.
14. B. Uzunca, 2018, A competence-based view of industry evolution: The impact of submarket convergence on incumbent-entrant dynamics, *Academy of Management Journal*, 61: 738–768.
15. J. Luoma, S. Ruutu, A. W. King, & H. Tikkanen, 2017, Time delays, competitive interdependence, and firm performance, *Strategic Management Journal*, 38: 506–525; F. Bridoux, K. G. Smith, & C. M. Grimm, 2011, The management of resources: Temporal effects of different types of actions on performance, *Journal of Management*, 33: 1281–1310.
16. J. Greene & L. Stevens, 2017, Amazon plans to send Alexa to the office, *Wall Street Journal*, www.wsj.com, November 30.
17. S. Chaudhuri & S. Terlep, 2018, The next big threat to consumer brands (yes, Amazon's behind it), *Wall Street Journal*, www.wsj .com, February 27.
18. D. Pierce, The Google versus Alexa war is on at CES 2018, *Wired.com*, www .wired.com, January 8.
19. C. Hernandez-Carrion, C. Camarero-Izquierdo, & J. Gutierrez-Cillan, 2017, Entrepreneurs' social capital and the economic performance of small businesses: The moderating role of competitive intensity and entrepreneurs' experience, *Strategic Entrepreneurship Journal*, 11: 61–89; J.-A. Lamberg, J. Laurila, & T. Nokelainen, 2017, Institutional path dependence in competitive dynamics: The case of paper industries in Finland and the USA, *Managerial and Decision Economics*, 38: 971–991.
20. M. R. Gonzales-Rodriguez, J. L. Jimenez-Caballero, R. C. Martin-Samper, M. A. Koseoglu, & F. Okumns, 2018, Revisiting the link between business strategy and performance: Evidence from hotels, *International Journal of Hospitality Management*, 72: 21–31; L. Trigeorgis & J. J. Reuer, 2017, Real options theory in strategic management, *Strategic Management Journal*, 38: 42–63.
21. R. P. Lee & X. Tang, 2018, Does it pay to be innovation and imitation oriented? An examination of the antecedents and consequences of innovation and imitation orientations, *Journal of Product Innovation Management*, 35: 11–26; M. A. Abebe & A. Angriawan, 2014, Organizational and competitive influences of exploration and exploitation activities in small firms, *Journal of Business Research*, 67: 339–345.
22. A. Srinivasan & N. Venkatraman, 2018, Entrepreneurship in digital platforms: A network-centric view, *Strategic Entrepreneurship Journal*, 12: 54–71; D. P. McInture & A. Srinivasan, 2017, Networks, platforms, and strategy: Emerging views and next steps, *Strategic Management Journal*, 38: 141–160; A. E. Bass & S. Chakrabarti, 2014, Resource security: Competition for global resources, strategic intent and governments as owners, *Journal of International Business Studies*, 45: 961–979.
23. B. T. McCann & M. Bahl, 2017, The influence of competition from informal firms on new product development, *Strategic Management Journal*, 38: 1518–1535; C. Boone, F. C. Wezel, & A. van Witteloostuijn, 2013, Joining the pack or going solo? A dynamic theory of new firm positioning, *Journal of Business Venturing*, 28: 511–527; H. Ndofor, D. G. Sirmon, & X. He, 2011, Firm resources, competitive actions and performance: Investigating a mediated model with evidence from the in-vitro diagnostics industry, *Strategic Management Journal*, 32: 640–675.
24. K. Hoisl, M. Gruber, & A. Conti, 2017, R&D team diversity and performance in hypercompetitive environments, *Strategic Management Journal*, 38: 1455–1477; S.-J. Chang & B. Wu, 2014, Institutional barriers and industry dynamics, *Strategic Management Journal*, 35: 1103–1123.
25. P. J. Buckley, T. D. Craig, & R. Mudambi, 2018, Time to learn? Assignment duration in global value chain organization, *Journal of Business Research*, in press; H. Rahmandad, 2012, Impact of growth opportunities and competition on firm-level capability development trade-offs, *Organization Science*, 34: 138–154.
26. L. Cui, D. Fan, X. Liy, & Y. Li, 2017, Where to seek strategic assets for competitive catch-up? A configurational study of emerging multinational enterprises expanding into foreign strategic factor markets, *Organization Studies*, 38: 1059–1083; Y. Gao, C. Shu, X. Jiang, S. Gao, & A. L. Page, 2017, Managerial ties and product innovation: The moderating roles of macro- and micro-institutional environments, *Long Range Planning*, 50: 168–183.
27. K.-Y. Hsieh & E. (E.J.) Hyun, 2017, Matching response to competitors' moves under asymmetric market strength, *Journal of Business Research*, 82: 202–212; L. K. S. Lim, 2013, Mapping competitive prediction capability: Construct conceptualization and performance payoffs, *Journal of Business Research*, 66: 1576–1586.
28. H. Xu, H. Guo, J. Zhang, & A. Dang, 2018, Facilitating dynamic marketing capabilities development for domestic and foreign firms in an emerging economy, *Journal of Business Research*, 86: 141–152; M. A. Hitt & K. Xu, 2016, The transformation of China: Effects of the institutional environment on business actions, *Long Range Planning*, 49: 589–593.
29. C. O. Longenecker & R. D. Yonker, 2017, Leadership blind spots in rapidly changing organizations, *Industrial Management*, 59: 12–17; S. M. Thatchenkery, 2017, Executive experience and awareness of competitive blind spots, *Academy of Management Proceedings*, January; D. Ng, R. Westgren, & S. Sonka, 2009, Competitive blind spots in an institutional field, *Strategic Management Journal*, 30: 349–369.
30. D. Gage, 2018, Software for the blue-collar workforce, *Wall Street Journal*, www.wsj .com, March 9.
31. 2018, About, *YRC Freight Homepage*, www .yrc.com, March 23.
32. B. S. Aharonson & M. A. Schilling, 2016, Mapping the technological landscape: Measuring technology distance, technological footprints, and technology evolution, *Research Policy*, 45: 81–96; J. W. Upson, D. J. Ketchen, Jr., B. L. Connelly, & A. L Ranft, 2012, Competitor analysis and foothold moves, *Academy of Management Journal*, 55: 93–110; Chen, Competitor analysis, 106.
33. A. Fazli & J. D. Shulman, 2018, Implications of market spillovers, *Management Science*, in press; J. Yu & A. A. Cannella, Jr., 2013, A comprehensive review of multimarket competition research, *Journal of Management*, 39: 76–109; J. Anand, L. F. Mesquita, & R. S. Vassolo, 2009, The dynamics of multimarket competition in exploration and exploitation activities, *Academy of Management Journal*, 52: 802–821.
34. S. P. L. Fourne, J. J. P. Jansen, & T. J. M. Mom, 2014, Strategic agility in MNEs: Managing tensions to capture opportunities across emerging and established markets, *California Management Review*, 56(3): 1–26.
35. W. Kang, B. Bayus, & S. Balasubramanian, 2010, The strategic effects of multimarket contact: Mutual forbearance and competitive response in the personal computer industry, *Journal of Marketing Research*, 47: 415–427.
36. Y.-S. Peng & I.-C. Liang, 2016, A dynamic framework for competitor identification: A neglecting role of dominant design, *Journal of Business Research*, 69: 1898–1903;

V. Bilotkach, 2011, Multimarket contact and intensity of competition: Evidence from an airline merger, *Review of Industrial Organization*, 38: 95–115; H. R. Greve, 2008, Multimarket contact and sales growth: Evidence from insurance, *Strategic Management Journal*, 29: 229–249.

37. A. V. Sakhartov, 2017, Economies of scope, resource relatedness, and the dynamics of corporate diversification, *Strategic Management Journal*, 38: 2508–2531; M. Theeke & H. Lee, 2017, Multimarket contact and rivalry over knowledge-based resources, *Strategic Management Journal*, 38: 2508–2531; M. Liu, 2015, Davids against goliaths? Collective identities and the market success of peripheral organizations during resource partitioning, *Organization Science*, 26: 293–309.
38. A. Gasparro & C. Lombardo, 2018, General Mills, maker of cheerios, now wants to feed your dog, too, *Wall Street Journal*, www.wsj.com, February 23.
39. A. Gasparro, 2018, Kellogg's problem: Americans aren't eating as much cereal, *Wall Street Journal*, www.wsj.com, February 8.
40. Withers, Ireland, Miller, Harrison, & Boss, Competitive landscape shifts, 2018; S. Sonenshein, K. Nault, & O. Obodaru, 2017, Competition of a different flavor: How a strategic group identity shapes competition and cooperation, *Administrative Science Quarterly*, 62: 626-656; P. J. Patel, S. A. Fernhaber, P. P. McDougal-Covin, & R. P. Van der Have, 2014, Beating competitors to international markets: The value of geographically balanced networks for innovation, *Strategic Management Journal*, 35: 691–711.
41. L. Qian & I. K. Wang, 2017, Competition and innovation: The tango of the market and technology in the competitive landscape, *Managerial and Decision Economics*, 38: 1237–1247; K.-Y. Hsieh, W. Tsai, & M.-J. Chen, 2015, If they can do it, why not us? Competitors reference points for justifying escalation of commitment, *Academy of Management Journal*, 58: 38–58.
42. H. Gao, T. Yu, & A. A. Cannella, Jr., 2017, Understanding word responses in competitive dynamics, *Academy of Management Review*, 42: 129–144; B. Larraneta, S. A. Zahra, & J. L. Galan, 2014, Strategic repertoire variety and new venture growth: The moderating effects of origin and industry dynamism, *Strategic Management Journal*, 35: 761–772.
43. D. Wiener-Bronner, 2018, Why Coke is winning the cola wars, *CNN Money*, www.money.cnn.com, February 21.
44. P. R. La Monica, 2018, Coca-Cola's new CEO: We've got to experiment, *CNN Money*, www.money.cnn.com, February 5.
45. E. Mandel, 2018, Pepsi sees opportunity to innovate with new challenge to Coca-Cola, *Atlanta Business Chronicle*, February 9.
46. L.-D. Benyayer & M. Kupp, 2017, Responding to open business models, *Journal of Business Strategy*, 38: 33–40; A. Compagni, V. Mele, & D. Ravasi, 2015, How early implementations influence later adoptions of innovation: Social positioning and skill reproduction in the diffusion of robotic surgery, *Academy of Management Journal*, 58: 242–278.
47. K. Uhlenbruck, M. Hughes-Morgan, M. A. Hitt, W. J. Ferrier, & R. Brymer, 2016, Rivals' reactions to mergers and acquisitions, *Strategic Organization*, 15: 40–66; Chen, Competitor analysis, 113.
48. J. Rodrigo-Alarcon, P. M. Garcia-Villaverde, M. J. Ruiz-Ortega, & G. Parra-Requena, 2018, From social capital to entrepreneurial orientation: The mediating role of dynamic capabilities, *European Management Journal*, 36: 195–209; L.-H. Lin, 2014, Subsidiary performance: The contingency of the multinational corporation's strategy, *European Management Journal*, 32: 928–937.
49. T. Ritter & C. Letti, 2018, The wider implications of business-model research, *Long Range Planning*, 51: 1–8; R. Makadok, 2010, The interaction effect of rivalry restraint and competitive advantage on profit: Why the whole is less than the sum of the parts, *Management Science*, 56: 356–372.
50. G. F. A. Monteiro & N. Foss, 2018, Resources and market definition: Rethinking the "hypothetical monopolist" from a resource-based perspective, *Managerial and Decision Economics*, 39: 346–353; C. M. Grimm & K. G. Smith, 1997, *Strategy as Action: Industry Rivalry and Coordination*, Cincinnati: South-Western Publishing Co., 125.
51. S. J. Miles & M. van Clieaf, 2017, Strategic fit: Key to growing enterprise value through organizational capital, *Business Horizons*, 60: 55–65; H. Brea-Solis, R. Casadesus-Masanell, & E. Grifell-Tatje, 2015, Business model evaluation: Quantifying Walmart's sources of advantage, *Strategic Entrepreneurship Journal*, 9: 12–33.
52. P. Jarzabkowski & R. Bednarek, 2018, Toward a social practice theory of relational competing, *Strategic Management Journal*, 39: 794–819; M. S. Cusumano, S. J. Kahl, & F. F. Suarez, 2015, Services, industry evolution and the competitive strategies of product firms, *Strategic Management Journal*, 36: 559–575.
53. A. Gupta & V. F. Misangyi, 2018, Follow the leader (or not): The influence of peer CEOs' characteristics on interorganizational imitation, *Strategic Management Journal*, in press; S. Wagner & M. Goossen, 2018, Knowing me, knowing you: Inventor mobility and the formation of technology-oriented alliances, *Academy of Management Journal*, in press.
54. A. W. Mathews & J. Walker, 2018, Cigna deal shows being a health insurer isn't enough anymore, *Wall Street Journal*, www.wsj.com, March 8.
55. D. Mattioli & D. Cimilluca, 2018, Cigna agrees to buy Express Scripts for more than $50 billion, *Wall Street Journal*, www.wsj.com, March 8.
56. E. Harper, 2018, What to expect from Amazon in 2018, *Techspot*, www.techspot.com, January 11.
57. J. Schumpeter, 1934, *The Theory of Economic Development*, Cambridge, MA: Harvard University Press.
58. C. Giachetti, J. Lampel, & S. L. Pira, 2017, Red Queen competitive imitation in the U.K. mobile phone industry, *Academy of Management Journal*, 60: 1882–1914; N. Argyres, L. Bigelow, & J. A. Nickerson, 2015, Dominant designs, innovation shocks and the follower's dilemma, *Strategic Management Journal*, 36: 216–234.
59. 2018, First mover, *Investopedia*, www.investopedia.com, March 25.
60. B. H. Lee, J. Struben, & C. B. Bingham, 2018, Collective action and market formation: An integrative framework, *Strategic Management Journal*, 39: 242–266; C. B. Bingham, N. R. Furr, & K. M. Eisenhardt, 2014, The opportunity paradox, *MIT Sloan Management Review*, 56(1): 29–39.
61. M. Sabatier & B. Chollet, 2017, Is there a first move advantage in science? Pioneering behavior and scientific production in nanotechnology, *Research Policy*, 46: 522–533; G. M. McNamara, J. Haleblian, & B. J. Dykes, 2008, The performance implications of participating in an acquisition wave: Early mover advantages, bandwagon effects and the moderating influence of industry characteristics and acquirer tactics, *Academy of Management Journal*, 51: 113–130.
62. M. Bianchi, A. Di Benedetto, S. Franzo, & F. Frattini, 2017, Selecting early adopters to foster the diffusion of innovations in industrial markets: Evidence from a multiple case study, *European Journal of Innovation Management*, 20: 620–644; H. Feng, N. A. Morgan, & L. L. Rego, 2017, Firm capabilities and growth: The moderating role of market conditions, *Journal of the Academy of Marketing Science*, 45: 76–92.
63. C. Lomberg, D. Urbig, C. Stockmann, L. D. Marino, & P. H. Dickson, 2017, Entrepreneurial orientation: The dimension's shared effects in explaining firm performance, *Entrepreneurship Theory and Practice*, 41: 973–998.
64. Y.-C. Hsiao, C.-J. Chen, R.-S. Guo, & K.-K Hu, 2017, First-mover strategy, resource capacity alignment, and new product performance: A framework for mediation and moderation effects, *R&D Management*, 47: 75–87; J. C. Short & G. T. Payne, 2008, First-movers and performance: Timing is everything, *Academy of Management Review*, 33: 267–269.
65. M. H. Youssef & I. Christodoulou, 2017, Assessing Miles and Snow typology through the lens of managerial discretion, *Management and Organizational Studies*, 4: 67–73; E. de Oliveira & W. B. Werther, Jr.,

2013, Resilience: Continuous renewal of competitive advantages, *Business Horizons*, 56: 333–342.

66. S. Arunachalam, S. N. Ramaswami, P. Hermann, & D. Walker, 2018, Innovation pathway to profitability: The role of entrepreneurial orientation and marketing capabilities, *Journal of the Academy of Marketing Science*, 46: 744–766; A. Hawk, G. Pacheco-De-Almeida, & B. Yeung, 2013, Fast-mover advantages: Speed capabilities and entry into the emerging submarket of Atlantic basin LNG, *Strategic Management Journal*, 34: 1531–1550.
67. A. N. Kiss, S. Fernhaber, & P. P. McDougall-Covin, 2018, Slack, innovation, and export intensity: Implications for small- and medium-sized enterprises, *Entrepreneurship Theory and Practice*, in press; E. R. Banalieva, 2014, Embracing the second best? Synchronization of reform speeds, excess high discretion slack and performance of transition economy firms, *Global Strategy Journal*, 4: 104–126.
68. E. Montaguti & A. Zammit, 2017, Being the first entrant and getting stuck in the middle: The risks of becoming the intermediate pioneer, *European Journal of Marketing*, 51: 1178–1196; R. Mudambi & T. Swift, 2014, Knowing when to leap: Transitioning between exploitative and explorative R&D, *Strategic Management Journal*, 35: 126–145.
69. J. Gomez & B. Perez-Aradros, 2017, How does order of entry shape competitive strategy? An analysis for European mobile operators, *Academy of Management Proceedings*, January; H. R. Greve & M.-D. L. Seidel, 2015, The thin red line between success and failure: Path dependence in the diffusion of innovative production technologies, *Strategic Management Journal*, 36: 475–496.
70. M. Udland, 2015, The number one key to Apple's success? It was second, *Business Insider*, www.businessinsider.com, June 7.
71. H. Kang & J. Song, 2017, Innovation and recurring shifts in industrial leadership: Three phases of change and persistence in the camera industry, *Research Policy*, 46: 376–387; J. Y. Yang, J. Li, & A. Delios, 2015, Will a second mouse get the cheese? Learning from early entrants' failures in a foreign market, *Organization Science*, 26: 908–922.
72. R. M. Bakker & D. A. Shepherd, 2017, Pull the plug or take the plunge: Multiple opportunities and the speed of venturing decision in the Australian mining industry, *Academy of Management Journal*, 60: 130–155; O. N. Parker, R. Krause, & J. G. Covin, 2017, Ready, set, slow: How aspiration-relative product quality impacts the rate of new product introduction, *Journal of Management*, 43: 2333–2356.
73. T. Anderson, 2013, The second-mover advantage, *KelloggInsight*, www.insight .kellogg.com, November 4.
74. A. Querbes & K. Frenken, 2016, Evolving user needs and late-mover advantage, *Strategic Organization*, 15: 167–190; N. K. Park, J. M. Mezias, J. Lee, & H.-H. Han, 2014, Reverse knowledge diffusion: Competitive dynamics and the knowledge seeking behavior of Korean high-tech firms, *Asia Pacific Journal of Management*, 31: 355–377.
75. E. Golovko & G. Valentini, 2014, Selective learning-by-exporting: Firm size and product versus process innovation, *Global Strategy Journal*, 4: 161–180; G. R. Carroll, 2003, Size (and competition) among organizations: Modeling scale-based selection among automobile producers in four major countries, 1885–1981, *Strategic Management Journal*, 24: 541–558.
76. G. Linton & J. Kask, 2017, Configurations of entrepreneurial orientation and competitive strategy for high performance, *Journal of Business Research*, 70: 168–176; W. Stam, S. Arzianian, & T. Elfring, 2014, Social capital of entrepreneurs and small firm performance: A meta-analysis of contextual and methodological moderators, *Journal of Business Venturing*, 29: 152–173.
77. D. Miller & I. Le Breton-Miller, 2017, Sources of entrepreneurial courage and imagination: Three perspectives, three contexts, *Entrepreneurship Theory and Practice*, 41: 667–675; G. D. Markham & T. L. Waldron, 2014, Small entrants and large incumbents: A framework of micro entry, *Academy of Management Perspectives*, 28: 178–197.
78. H.-H. Lee & C. Li, 2018, Supplier quality management: Investment inspection, and incentives, *Production and Operations Management*, 27: 304–322.
79. J. L. Stevens, B. I. Spaid, M. Breazeale, & C. L. Esmark-Jones, 2018, Timeliness, transparency, and trust: A framework for managing online customer complaints, *Business Horizons*, 61: 375–384; F. Zhang, Y. Wang, D. Li, & V. Cui, 2017, Configurations of innovations across domains: An organizational ambidexterity view, *Journal of Product Innovation Management*, 34: 821–841.
80. O. Ceryan, I. Duenyas, & O. Sahin, 2018, Dynamic pricing and replenishment with customer upgrades, *Production and Operations Management*, 27: 663–679; C. Groenin & P. Mills, 2017, A guide to pay-what-you-wish pricing from the consumer's viewpoint, *Business Horizons*, 60: 441–445.
81. I. Sila, 2018, Linking quality with social and financial performance: A contextual, ethics-based approach, *Production and Operations Management*, 27: 1102–1123.
82. L. Argote & M. Hora, 2017, Organizational learning and management of technology, *Production and Operations Management*, April, 579–590.
83. N. N. Chau & R. Desiraju, 2017, Product introduction strategies under sequential innovation for durable goods with network effects, *Production and Operations Management*, 26: 320–340; K. R. Sarangee & R. Echambadki, 2014, Firm-specific determinants of product line technology strategies in high technology markets, *Strategic Entrepreneurship Journal*, 8: 149–166.
84. L. J. Gutierrez-Gutierrez, V. Barrales-Molina, & H. Kaynak, 2018, The role of human resource-related quality management practices in new product development: A dynamic capability perspective, *International Journal of Operations & Production Management*, 38: 43–66; D Honhon & X. A. Pan, 2017, Improving profits by bundling vertically differentiated products, *Production and Operations Management*, 26: 1481–1497.
85. C. Giachetti & G. Marchi, 2017, Successive changes in leadership in the worldwide mobile phone industry: The role of windows of opportunity and firms' competitive action, *Research Policy*, 46: 352–364; M. L. Sosa, 2013, Decoupling market incumbency from organizational prehistory: Locating the real sources of competitive advantage in R&D for radical innovation, *Strategic Management Journal*, 34: 245–255.
86. S. W. Smith, 2014, Follow me to the innovation frontier? Leaders, laggards and the differential effects of imports and exports on technological innovation, *Journal of International Business Studies*, 45: 248–274.
87. H. R. Greve & C. M. Zhang, 2017, Institutional logics and power sources: Merger and acquisition decisions, *Academy of Management Journal*, 60: 671–694; M. J. Chen & D. Miller, 1994, Competitive attack, retaliation and performance: An expectancy-valence framework, *Strategic Management Journal*, 15: 85–102.
88. F. Jell, J. Henkel, & M. W. Wallin, 2017, Offensive patent portfolio races, *Long Range Planning*, 50: 531–549.
89. D. Tzabbar & J. Margolis, 2018, Beyond the startup stage: The founding team's human capital, new venture's stage of life, founder-CEO duality, and breakthrough innovation, *Organization Science*, 28: 857–872; Smith, Ferrier, & Ndofor, Competitive dynamics research, 333.
90. J. S. Harrison, S. Boivie, N. Sharp, & R. Gentry, 2018, Saving face: How exit in response to negative press and star analyst downgrades reflects reputation maintenance by directors, *Academy of Management Journal*, in press; E. Fauchart & R. Cowan, 2014, Weak links and the management of reputational interdependencies, *Strategic Management Journal*, 35: 532–549.
91. E. G. Love & M. S. Kraatz, 2017, Failed stakeholder exchanges and corporate reputation: The case of earnings misses, *Academy of Management Journal*, 60: 880–903; Q. Gu & X. Lu, 2014, Unraveling the mechanisms of reputation and alliance

formation: A study of venture capital syndication in China, *Strategic Management Journal*, 35: 739–750; I. Stern, J. M. Dukerich, & E. Zajac, 2014, Unmixed signals: How reputation and status affect alliance formation, *Strategic Management Journal*, 35: 512–531.

92. F. J. Mas-Ruiz & F. Ruiz-Moreno, 2017, How strategic groups act competitively within and across markets, *Managerial and Decision Economics*, 38: 1017–1032; B. Larraneta, S. A. Zahra, & J. L. G. Gonzales, 2014, Strategic repertoire variety and new venture growth: The moderating effects of origin and industry dynamism, *Strategic Management Journal*, 35: 761–772; W. J. Ferrier, K. G. Smith, & C. M. Grimm, 1999, The role of competitive actions in market share erosion and industry dethronement: A study of industry leaders and challengers, *Academy of Management Journal*, 42: 372–388.

93. R. Karlgaard, 2011, Transitions: Michael reinvents Dell, *Forbes*, www.forbes.com, May 9.

94. J. Luoma, T. Falk, D. Totzek, H. Tikkanen, & A. Mrozek, 2018, Big splash, no waves? Cognitive mechanisms driving incumbent firms' responses to low-price market entry strategies, *Strategic Management Journal*, in press; M. Fassnacht & S. El Husseini, 2013, EDLP versus Hi-Lo pricing strategies in retailing—a state of the art article, *Journal of Business Economics*, 83: 259–289.

95. M. A. Josefy, J. S. Harrison, D. G. Sirmon, & C. Carnes, 2017, Living and dying: Synthesizing the literature on firm survival and failure across stages of development, *Academy of Management Annals*, 11: 770–799.

96. N. Symeonidou, J. Bruneel, & E. Autio, 2017, Commercialization strategy and internationalization outcomes in technology-based new ventures, *Journal of Business Venturing*, 32: 302–317; G. Ahrne, P. Aspers, & N. Brusson, 2014, The organization of markets, *Organization Studies*, 36: 7–27; Smith, Ferrier, & Ndofor, Competitive dynamics research, 330.

97. D. Weinswig, 2018, Why apparel's biggest battel pits Amazon against Target, not Walmart, *Forbes*, www.forbes.com, February 1.

98. T. Popomaronis, 2017, Walmart vs. Amazon: A surprising turn in the battle for e-commerce glory, *Forbes*, www.forbes.com, December 20.

99. 2017, 6 of Walmart's most recent acquisitions, *The Street*, www.thestreet.com, April 17.

100. S. Soper, 2018, Walmart remains in buying mode to fight Amazon, executive says, *Bloomberg*, www.bloomberg.com, March 20.

101. Y. Snihur & J. Tarzijan, 2018, Managing complexity in a multi-business-model organization, *Long Range Planning*, 51: 50–63; J. R. Williams, 1992, How sustainable is your competitive advantage? *California Management Review*, 34(3): 29–51.

102. M. S. Lewis & K. E. Pflum, 2017, Hospital systems and bargaining power: Evidence from out-of-market acquisitions, *The Rand Journal of Economics*, 48: 579–610; R. A. D'Aveni, G. Dagnino, & K. G. Smith, 2010, The age of temporary advantage, *Strategic Management Journal*, 31: 1371–1385.

103. W. Shi, B. L. Connelly, & K. Cirik, 2018, Short seller influence on firm growth: A threat-rigidity perspective, *Academy of Management Journal*, in press; G. N. Chandler, J. C. Broberg, & T. H. Allison, 2014, Customer value propositions in declining industries: Differences between industry representative and high-growth firms, *Strategic Entrepreneurship Journal*, 8: 234–253.

104. 2017, Leading drugs going off patent in the U.S. in 2017, by revenue (in million U.S. dollars), *The Statistics Portal*, www.statista.com, November 12.

105. P. Ozcan, 2018, Growing with the market: How changing conditions during market growth affect formation and evolution of interfirm ties, *Strategic Management Journal*, 39: 295–328; F. Giones & A. Brem, 2017, From toys to tools: The co-evolution of technological and entrepreneurial developments in the drone industry, *Business Horizons*, 60: 875–884; M. A. Schilling, 2015, Technology shocks, technological collaboration and innovation outcomes, *Organization Science*, 26: 668–686.

106. 2003, How fast is your company? *Fast Company*, June, 18.

107. M. C. Schuhmacher, S. Kuester, & E. J. Hultink, 2018, Appetizer or main course: Early market vs. majority market go-to-market strategies for radical innovations, *Journal of Product Innovation Management*, 35: 106–124; N. R. Furr & D. C. Snow, 2015, Intergenerational hybrids: Spillbacks, spillforwards and adapting to technological discontinuities, *Organization Science*, 26: 475–493.

108. A. Doha, M. Pagell, M. Swink, & D. Johnston, 2018, The imitator's dilemma: Why imitators should break out of imitation, *Journal of Product Innovation Management*, in press; C. B. Dobni, M. Klassen, & W. T. Nelson, 2015, Innovation strategy in the U.S.: Top executives offer their views, *Journal of Business Strategy*, 36(10): 3–13; G. Clarkson & P. Toh, 2010, 'Keep out' signs: The role of deterrence in the competition for resources, *Strategic Management Journal*, 31: 1202–1225.

109. W.-Y. Park, Y. K. Ro, & N. Kim, 2018, Architectural innovation and the emergence of a dominant design: The effects of strategic sourcing on performance, *Research Policy*, 47: 326–341; T. Klueter, L. F. Monteiro, & D. R. Dunlap, 2017, Standard vs. partnership licensing: Attention and the relationship between licensing and product innovations, *Research Policy*, 46: 1629–1643; A. K. Chatterji & K. R. Fabrizio, 2014, Using users: When does external knowledge enhance corporate product innovation? *Strategic Management Journal*, 35: 1427–1445.

110. P. J. Steinberg, V. D. Procher, & D. Urbig, 2017, Too much or too little of R&D offshoring: The impact of captive offshoring and contract offshoring on innovation performance, *Research Policy*, 46: 1810–1823; M. M. Larsen, S. Manning, & T. Pedersen, 2013, Uncovering the hidden costs of offshoring: The interplay of complexity, organizational design, and experience, *Strategic Management Journal*, 34: 533–552.

111. K. H. Tan & Y. Zhan, 2017, Improving new product development using big data: A case study of an electronics company, *R&D Management*, 47: 570–582; B. Wu, Z. Wan, & D. A. Leventhal, 2014, Complementary assets as pipes and prisms: Innovation incentives and trajectory choices, *Strategic Management Journal*, 35: 1257–1278.

112. L. Yuan, 2017, Tech titans wage war in China's next Internet revolution, *Wall Street Journal*, www.wsj.com, December 17.

113. S. Tallman, Y. Luo, & P. J. Buckley, 2018, Business models in global competition, *Global Strategy Journal*, in press; N. J. Foss & T. Saebi, 2018, Business models and business model innovation: Between wicked and paradigmatic problems, *Long Range Planning*, 51; 9–21.

114. E. Loutskina & G. Shapovalov, 2017, Mars, Incorporated, *Darden Business Publishing Cases*, https://doi.org/10.1108/case.darden.2016.000189.

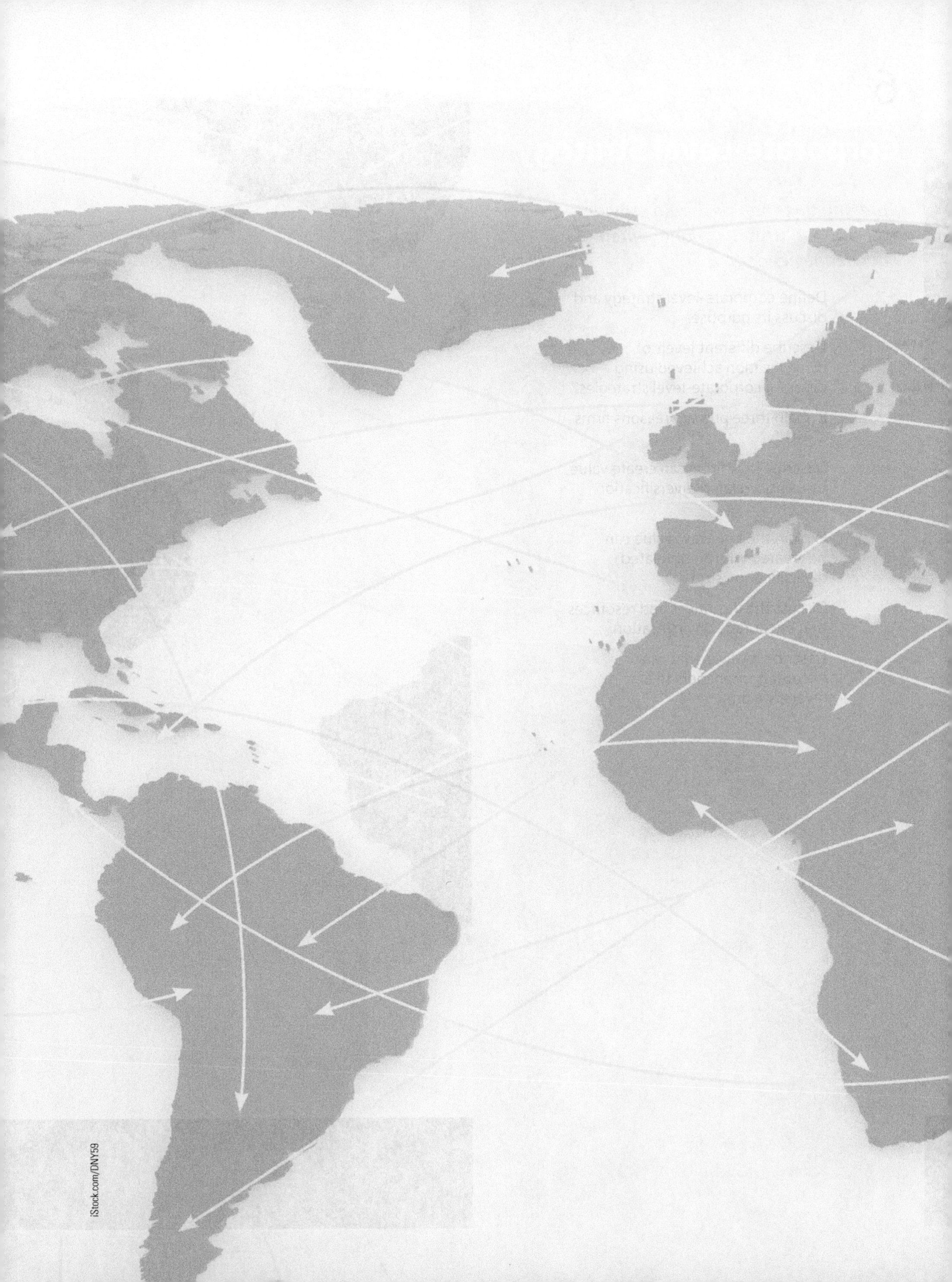

iStock.com/DNY59

6

Corporate-Level Strategy

Studying this chapter should provide you with the strategic management knowledge needed to:

6-1 Define corporate-level strategy and discuss its purpose.

6-2 Describe different levels of diversification achieved using different corporate-level strategies.

6-3 Explain three primary reasons firms diversify.

6-4 Describe how firms can create value by using a related diversification strategy.

6-5 Explain the two ways value can be created with an unrelated diversification strategy.

6-6 Discuss the incentives and resources that encourage diversification.

6-7 Describe motives that can encourage managers to over diversify a firm.

iStock.com/DNY59

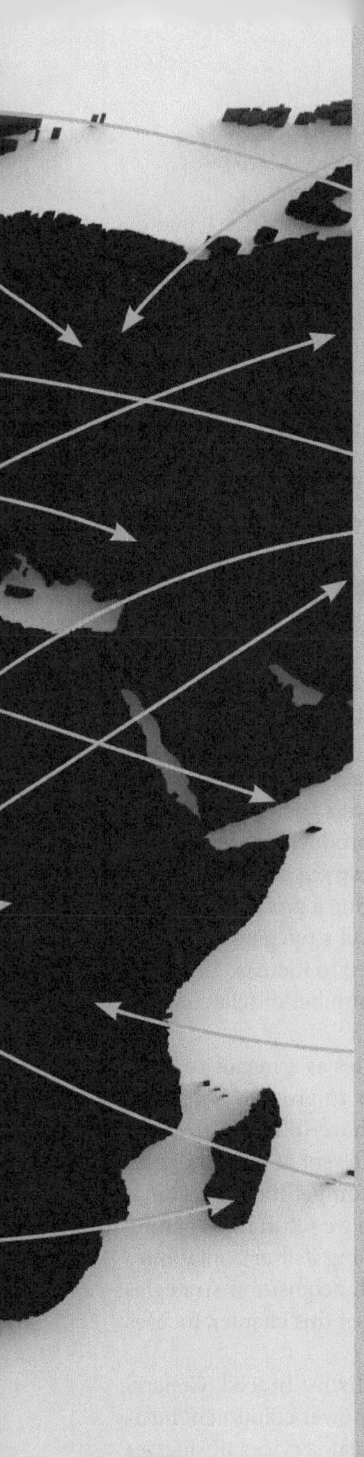

AMAZON'S SUCCESSFUL GROWTH THROUGH ITS CORPORATE DIVERSIFICATION STRATEGY

Amazon has grown from its original offering in 1997 as an online book distributor to a vast array of services and products mostly through related diversification and more recently vertical integration. Once it originally established its success exclusively as an online book seller, it was able to expand its online sales to CDs and DVDs. Relatedly, it next added toys, games, electronics, and video games to its product offerings. Following this success, it opened its site to third party sellers and labeled this business "Marketplace" similar to eBay's online product market.

Because of its requirement for data services, it had many computers and servers for backing up its product preference and customer taste information. From this, it vertically integrated into Amazon Web Services and began selling these services to other cloud computing clients. It next started to sell clothing products in a related move and expanded its ability to provide the necessary sizing information and efficient returns.

Due to the exceptional demand of its products, Amazon created a partnership with an airline leasing company to expand its ability to lower shipping costs, and to have more control over its delivery service.

In 2005, it offered Prime shipping membership at $79 per year and promised unlimited two-day shipping for no additional charge. In 2007, it produced its first Kindle reader, originally priced at $399. As competition emerged, this price decreased and new products such as Kindle Fire were later introduced. In 2009, Amazon began selling private label goods, including blank DVDs and USB cables. It also introduced its streaming video service. Amazon Studios was created in 2010, and in 2011 Prime membership included instant video streaming services.

In 2014, it offered a $99 Fire TV set-top box for streaming video as well as a smart phone, which was later discontinued due to poor sales. It also began selling its Echo speaker with voice recognition and later Alexa. Because of the exceptional demand for its products, Amazon needed to expand and vertically integrate into shipping and began its Flex delivery services. Later this included creating a partnership with an airline leasing company to expand its ability to lower shipping costs, having more control over its delivery service.

In its evolutionary process, Amazon has pursued a logical strategy of related diversification. Beginning with its original goal of selling books online, Amazon has diversified throughout to become an online retailer and provider of services, entertainment, and goods, including now even furniture and large appliances. In 2017, it acquired Whole Foods Market, an organic food retailer, giving it a large brick and mortar presence throughout the United States and elsewhere. This sent shockwaves through the retail food industry because of the disruptive effect Amazon has had on other retailers throughout its history, in particular, large department stores such as Macy's, JCPenney's, and Best Buy.

Because of the "Amazon effect," other giant retailers have beefed up their online abilities to sell products. In particular, Walmart has acquired Jet.com, and all other retailers have sought to build up their online selling presence through their websites. Amazon has signaled it is joining Berkshire Hathaway and JPMorgan Chase to create an independent health care organization that will serve their employees. This venture may disrupt drug distributors and health insurance companies as they have other companies. Because of Amazon's success, it now competes with a variety of retailers, media companies like Netflix, hardware companies like Apple, advertising companies like Google, and even a lot of its own transportation delivery suppliers such as FedEx and UPS, including the United States Postal Service. It is also looking into its own checking account-like payment system. As it has with retail shopping, in the future Amazon may do the same with payments, banking, and the way pharmaceuticals and healthcare are delivered.

Sources: D. Cameron & J. Smith, 2018, Air-Cargo space is tight as even spaghetti sauce is in an ASAP rush, *Wall Street Journal*, www.wsj.com, January 24; B. Evans, 2018, Amazon to become #1 in cloud computing revenue by beating IBM's $17 Billion, *Forbes*, www.forbes.com, January 26; E. Glazer, L. Hoffman, & L. Steven, 2018, Next Up for Amazon: Checking Accounts, *Wall Street Journal*, www.wsj.com, March 5; C. Johnston, 2018, Amazon opens a supermarket with no checkouts, *BBC News*, www.bbc.com, January 22; B. C. Koons, & R. Langreth, 2018, What stands between Bezos, Buffett, and Dimon and a health-care fix, *Bloomberg Businessweek*, www.bloomberg.com, February 14; Kowitt, 2017, The deal that made an industry shudder, *Fortune*, July 1, 7; C. Mims, 2018, The limits of Amazon, *Wall Street Journal*, www.wsj.com, January 1; P. Schoerdt, 2018, How Amazon will drastically change health care, according to futurists, *Money*, www.time.com/money, February 1; E. Winkler, 2018, Can Amazon do with clothes what it did with books?, *Wall Street Journal*, www.wsj.com, January 3.

Our discussions of business-level strategies (Chapter 4) and the competitive rivalry and competitive dynamics associated with them (Chapter 5) have concentrated on firms competing in a single industry or product market.[1] In this chapter, we introduce you to corporate-level strategies, which are strategies firms use to *diversify* their operations from a single business competing in a single market into several product markets—most commonly, into several businesses. Thus, a **corporate-level strategy** specifies actions a firm takes to gain a competitive advantage by selecting and managing a group of different businesses competing in different product markets. Corporate-level strategies help companies to select new strategic positions—positions that are expected to increase the firm's value.[2] As explained in the Opening Case, Amazon competes in a number of related retail, hardware, entertainment, and delivery industries.[3]

As is the case with Amazon, firms use corporate-level strategies as a means to grow revenues and profits, but there can be additional strategic intents to growth. Firms can pursue defensive or offensive strategies that realize growth but have different strategic intents. Firms can also pursue market development by entering different geographic markets (this approach is discussed in Chapter 8). Firms can acquire competitors (horizontal integration) or buy a supplier or customer (vertical integration). As we see in the Opening Case, Amazon has acquired Whole Foods Market, thereby increasing its horizontal integration in the retail food product and distribution business. Such acquisition strategies are discussed in Chapter 7. The basic corporate strategy, the topic of this chapter, focuses on diversification.

The decision to pursue growth is not a risk-free choice for firms. Indeed, General Electric (GE) experienced difficulty in its oil and gas service, and power equipment businesses. GE also suffered significant revenue declines in its financial services businesses and thus sold its assets in that area, choosing to seek growth in other industrial and equipment businesses and to better integrate its digitalization strategy through the Internet.[4] Effective firms carefully evaluate their growth options (including the different corporate-level strategies) before committing firm resources to any of them.

A **corporate-level strategy** specifies actions a firm takes to gain a competitive advantage by selecting and managing a group of different businesses competing in different product markets.

Because the diversified firm operates in several different and unique product markets and likely in several businesses, it forms two types of strategies: corporate-level (company-wide) and business-level (competitive).[5] Corporate-level strategy is concerned with two key issues: in what product markets and businesses the firm should compete and how corporate headquarters should manage those businesses.[6] For the diversified company, a business-level strategy (see Chapter 4) must be selected for each of the businesses in which the firm has decided to compete.

As is the case with a business-level strategy, a corporate-level strategy is expected to help the firm earn above-average returns by creating value.[7] Some suggest that few corporate-level strategies actually create value.[8] As the Opening Case indicates, realizing value through a corporate strategy can be achieved, but it is challenging to do so. Evidence suggests that a corporate-level strategy's value is ultimately determined by the degree to which "the businesses in the portfolio are worth more under the management of the company than they would be under any other ownership."[9] Thus, an effective corporate-level strategy creates, across all of a firm's businesses, aggregate returns that exceed what those returns would be without the strategy[10] and contributes to the firm's strategic competitiveness and its ability to earn above-average returns.[11]

Product diversification, a primary form of corporate-level strategies, concerns the scope of the markets and industries in which the firm competes as well as "how managers buy, create, and sell different businesses to match skills and strengths with opportunities presented to the firm."[12] Successful diversification is expected to reduce variability in the firm's profitability as earnings are generated from different businesses.[13] Diversification can also provide firms with the flexibility to shift their investments to markets where the greatest returns are possible rather than being dependent on only one or a few markets.[14] Because firms incur development and monitoring costs when diversifying, the ideal portfolio of businesses balances diversification's costs and benefits. CEOs and their top-management teams are responsible for determining the best portfolio for their company.[15]

We begin this chapter by examining different levels of diversification (from low to high). After describing the different reasons firms diversify their operations, we focus on two types of related diversification (related diversification signifies a moderate to high level of diversification for the firm). When properly used, these strategies help create value in the diversified firm, either through the sharing of resources (the related constrained strategy) or the transferring of core competencies across the firm's different businesses (the related linked strategy). We then examine unrelated diversification, which is another corporate-level strategy that can create value. Thereafter, the chapter shifts to the incentives and resources that can stimulate diversification that is value neutral. However, managerial motives to diversify, the final topic in the chapter, can actually destroy some of the firm's value.

6-1 Levels of Diversification

Diversified firms vary according to their level of diversification and the connections between and among their businesses. Figure 6.1 lists and defines five categories of businesses according to increasing levels of diversification. The single- and dominant-business categories denote no or relatively low levels of diversification; more fully diversified firms are classified into related and unrelated categories. A firm is related through its diversification when its businesses share several links. For example, businesses may share product markets (goods or services), technologies, or distribution channels. The more links among businesses, the more "constrained" is the level of diversification. "Unrelated" refers to the absence of direct links between businesses.

Figure 6.1 Levels and Types of Diversification

Low Levels of Diversification

Single business:	95% or more of revenue comes from a single business.	 A
Dominant business:	Between 70% and 95% of revenue comes from a single business.	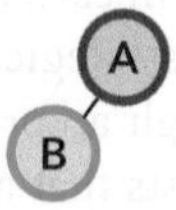 A–B

Moderate to High Levels of Diversification

Related constrained:	Less than 70% of revenue comes from the dominant business, and all businesses share product, technological, and distribution linkages.	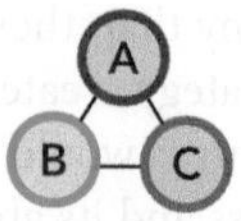 A, B, C
Related linked (mixed related and unrelated):	Less than 70% of revenue comes from the dominant business, and there are only limited links between businesses.	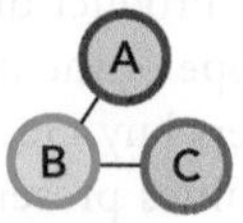 A, B, C

Very High Levels of Diversification

Unrelated:	Less than 70% of revenue comes from the dominant business, and there are no common links between businesses.	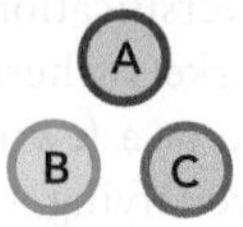 A, B, C

Source: Adapted from R. P. Rumelt, 1974, *Strategy, Structure and Economic Performance*, Boston: Harvard Business School.

6-1a Low Levels of Diversification

A firm pursuing a low level of diversification uses either a single- or a dominant-business, corporate-level diversification strategy. A *single-business diversification strategy* is a corporate-level strategy wherein the firm generates 95 percent or more of its sales revenue from its core business area.[16] For example, McIlhenny Company, headquartered on Avery Island in Louisiana and producer of Tabasco brand, has maintained its focus on its family's hot sauce products for seven generations. On its website, the following quote is provided about its products: "Back in 1868, Edmund McIlhenny experimented with pepper seeds from Mexico (or somewhere in Central America) to create his own style of Louisiana hot sauce—our Original Red Sauce. Since then we've continued this tradition of exploration and experimentation, and today McIlhenny Company crafts seven unique and distinct flavors of sauce, each with its own variety of deliciousness. From mild to wild, there's something for everyone!"[17] Historically McIlhenny has used a single-business strategy while operating in relatively few product markets. Recently, it has begun to partner with other firms so that the Tabasco taste can be found in a variety of food products such as jelly bean candies (Tabasco Jelly Belly), crackers (Hot N' Spicy Cheez-It), and ice cream (Chocolate Chipotle Rocky Road).[18]

With the *dominant-business diversification strategy*, the firm generates between 70 and 95 percent of its total revenue within a single business area. United Parcel Service (UPS) uses this strategy. Recently UPS generated 63 percent of its revenue from its U.S. package delivery business and 20 percent from its international package business, with the remaining 17 percent coming from the firm's nonpackage business.[19] Though the U.S. package delivery business currently generates the largest percentage of UPS's sales revenue, the firm anticipates that in the future its other two businesses will account for the majority of revenue growth. This expectation suggests that UPS may become more diversified, both in terms of its goods and services and in the number of countries in which those goods and services are offered.

Firms that focus on one or very few businesses and markets can earn positive returns, because they develop capabilities useful for these markets and can provide superior service to their customers. Additionally, there are fewer challenges in managing one or a very small set of businesses, allowing them to gain economies of scale and efficiently use their resources.[20] Family-owned and controlled businesses, such as McIlhenny Company's Tabasco sauce business, are commonly less diversified. They prefer the narrower focus because the family's reputation is related closely to that of the business. Thus, family members prefer to provide quality goods and services, which a focused strategy better allows.[21]

Thus, some might considered this a strategy of moderate diversification in the form of highly related constrained diversification, which is discussed next.

6-1b Moderate and High Levels of Diversification

A firm generating more than 30 percent of its revenue outside a dominant business and whose businesses are related to each other in some manner uses a related diversification corporate-level strategy. When the links between the diversified firm's businesses are rather direct—meaning they use similar sourcing, throughput, and outbound processes—it is a *related constrained diversification strategy*. Campbell Soup, Proctor & Gamble, and Merck & Co. use a related constrained strategy. With a related constrained strategy, a firm shares resources and activities across its businesses.

As noted in the Strategic Focus, Caterpillar is the largest global producer of heavy equipment. Caterpillar's construction, resource (e.g., mining), energy and transportation equipment, and machinery businesses made up about 60 percent of sales in 2016.[22] While each segment is distinct, many similar technologies and inputs are used in the production of its equipment. Furthermore, related technologies allow similarities in production processes and main equipment parts, allowing a transfer of knowledge across these businesses. In addition, customers and markets share some similarities because most relate to some form of construction, mining, and extraction industries. It also uses an R&D approach focused on product and system updates through a series of differentiated products and thus follows a product proliferation strategy. A product proliferation strategy represents a form of within-industry diversification.[23] Yet, as noted, Caterpillar also has four divisions, including a financial products segment that supports financing of its equipment and machinery sales.

The diversified company with a portfolio of businesses that have only a few links between them is called a mixed related and unrelated firm and is using the *related linked diversification strategy* (see Figure 6.1). Until recently (see Strategic Focus in Chapter 11), GE has used a related-linked corporate-level diversification strategy. Compared with related constrained firms, related linked firms share fewer resources and assets between their businesses, concentrating instead on transferring knowledge and core competencies between the businesses. GE has four strategic business units (see Chapter 11 for a definition of SBUs) it calls "divisions," each composed of related businesses. There are few relationships across the strategic business units, but many among the subsidiaries or divisions within them. As with firms using each type of diversification strategy, companies implementing the related linked strategy constantly adjust the mix in their portfolio of businesses as well as make decisions about how to manage these businesses.[24] GE's recent decline suggests that such business can be challenging to run and at times may be excessively complicated.[25]

Strategic **Focus**

Caterpillar Uses the Related Constrained Diversification Strategy

Caterpillar is the largest global producer of heavy equipment focused on the construction, resource extraction (e.g. mining), oil and gas, and energy and transportation industries. Besides its traditional earth moving equipment it also produces diesel and natural gas engines, industrial gas turbines, and diesel-electric locomotives. It classifies these businesses into the following four main business segments (with associated 2017 revenues): Construction Industries ($19,133 billion); Energy & Transportation ($15,964 billion); Resource Industries ($7,504 billion); and Financial Products ($2,786 billion). It has over 98,000 employees and almost 60 percent of its sales revenue is derived from outside of the United States. Caterpillar made a horizontal acquisition of large mining equipment producer Bucyrus International in 2011.

One of its strong competitive advantages is its global dealer network; there are 171 dealers serving 192 countries. This network provides efficient and effective parts distribution with easy-to-use eCommerce platforms throughout the world. Fast delivery of parts is important when an expensive, essential piece of equipment is down.

In 2014, 2015, and 2016, a downturn in the energy and commodity industries significantly reduced Caterpillar's revenue and profits. However, it continued to try to meet its customers' needs, while restructuring to meet the lower demand characteristics. For example, in 2016, Caterpillar's mining truck sales were down 95 percent from the peak numbers achieved in 2012. In 2017 and 2018, outlook improved and its profits and stock price likewise increased.

Caterpillar spends about 5.1 percent of its sales on R&D, focused on continually improving its products and manufacturing processes. Its product innovations, largely driven by paying attention to customer needs, has allowed the company to be competitive in developed as well as developing markets. Research suggests that such client-focused diversification comes from deep knowledge about customers. For example, Caterpillar has pursued technology that has allowed it to be a leader in autonomous trucks in the mining sector. Its technology will allow it to retrofit a competitor's truck to make it autonomous or semi-autonomous through innovations to its MineStar system. During the downturn, other competitors did not fare so well; for example, in 2017 U.S.-based competitor Joy Global was purchased by Komatsu, a global Japanese equipment producer.

Sergio Dionisio/Bloomberg/Getty Images

Caterpillar autonomous trucks transporting iron ore to and from mining sites.

Caterpillar's interrelated set of businesses are also supported by a financial products division, which facilitates sales finance and leasing and likewise helps to generate profits. In support of its business segments, it also provides servicing by remanufacturing of Caterpillar product engines and components and providing remanufacturing services for other companies with related products. Its R&D program is utilized across many of its business segments. Although its global R&D center is located near its corporate headquarters in Peoria, Illinois, it has other regional facilities in North America, Europe, and Asia-Pacific to provide technical expertise to support its manufacturing and sales opportunities around the world.

Sources: 2018 Caterpillar fact sheet, www.caterpillar.com, Accessed March 6; 2018, Caterpillar forges new value parts brand for legacy engines, machines, *Concrete Products*, 71(1): 8; J. K. Mawdsley & D. Somaya, 2018, Demand-side strategy, relational advantage and partner-driven corporate scope: The case for client-led diversification, *Strategic Management Journal*, 39: 1834–1859; M. Shunko, T. Yunes, G. Fenu, A. Scheller-Wolf, V. Tardif, & S. Tayur, 2018, Product portfolio restructuring: Methodology and application at Caterpillar, *Production & Operations Management*, 27: 100–120; 2017, Caterpillar and FTP Solutions partner to boost mine network performance, *Coal International*, 265(6): 20; A. Hiyate, 2017, CAT brings partnerships to the fore, *Canadian Mining Journal*, 138(10): 23–25; A. Tangel & J. Zumbrun, J. 2017, Caterpillar boosts outlook, signaling cautious optimism in recovery, *Wall Street Journal*, www.wsj.com, July 26.

A highly diversified firm that has no relationships between its businesses follows an *unrelated diversification strategy*. United Technologies Corporation, Textron, Samsung, and Newell Brand Corporation are examples of firms using this type of corporate-level strategy. Commonly, firms using this strategy are called *conglomerates*.[26] Newell Brand Corporation has a number of consumer businesses that are not related to each other, and the firm makes no efforts to share activities or to transfer core competencies between or among them. It has a range of businesses such as Rubbermaid household products, K2 skis, and Coleman camping equipment, which are independently run with decentralized operating divisions.[27] Successfully managing the unrelated diversification strategy can be difficult, and Newell has been recently challenged by Starboard, an activist investor, to improve its performance.[28] Another form of unrelated diversification strategy is pursued by private equity firms such Carlyle Group, Blackstone, and KKR.[29] They often have an unrelated set of portfolio firms.

6-2 Reasons for Diversification

A firm uses a corporate-level diversification strategy for a variety of reasons (see Table 6.1). Typically, a diversification strategy is used to increase the firm's value by improving its overall performance. Value is created—either through related diversification or through unrelated diversification—when the strategy allows a company's businesses to increase revenues or reduce costs while implementing their business-level strategies.[30]

Other reasons for using a diversification strategy may have nothing to do with increasing the firm's value; in fact, diversification can have neutral effects or even reduce a firm's value.

Table 6.1 Reasons for Diversification

Value-Creating Diversification

• Economies of scope (related diversification)
  • Sharing activities
  • Transferring core competencies
• Market power (related diversification)
  • Blocking competitors through multipoint competition
  • Vertical integration
• Financial economies (unrelated diversification)
  • Efficient internal capital allocation
  • Business restructuring

Value-Neutral Diversification
• Antitrust regulation • Tax laws • Low performance • Uncertain future cash flows • Risk reduction for firm • Tangible resources • Intangible resources
Value-Reducing Diversification
• Diversifying managerial employment risk • Increasing managerial compensation

Value-neutral reasons for diversification include a desire to match and thereby neutralize a competitor's market power (e.g., to neutralize another firm's advantage by acquiring a similar distribution outlet). Decisions to expand a firm's portfolio of businesses to reduce managerial risk or increase top managers' pay can have a negative effect on the firm's value. Greater amounts of diversification reduce managerial risk in that if one of the businesses in a diversified firm fails, the top executive of that business does not risk total failure by the corporation. As such, this reduces the top executives' employment risk. In addition, because diversification can increase a firm's size and thus managerial compensation, managers have motives to diversify a firm to a level that reduces its value.[31] Diversification rationales that may have a neutral or negative effect on the firm's value are discussed later in the chapter.

Operational relatedness and corporate relatedness are two diversification strategies that can create value (see Figure 6.2). Studies of these independent relatedness dimensions show the importance of resources and key competencies.[32] The figure's vertical dimension depicts opportunities to share operational activities between businesses (operational relatedness), while the horizontal dimension suggests opportunities for transferring corporate-level core competencies (corporate relatedness). The firm with a strong capability in managing operational synergy, especially in sharing assets between its businesses, falls in the upper left quadrant, which also represents vertical sharing of assets through vertical integration. The lower right quadrant represents a highly developed corporate capability for transferring one or more core competencies across businesses.

This capability is located primarily in the corporate headquarters office. Unrelated diversification is also illustrated in Figure 6.2 in the lower left quadrant. Financial economies (discussed later), rather than either operational or corporate relatedness, are the source of value creation for firms using the unrelated diversification strategy.

Figure 6.2 Value-Creating Diversification Strategies: Operational and Corporate Relatedness

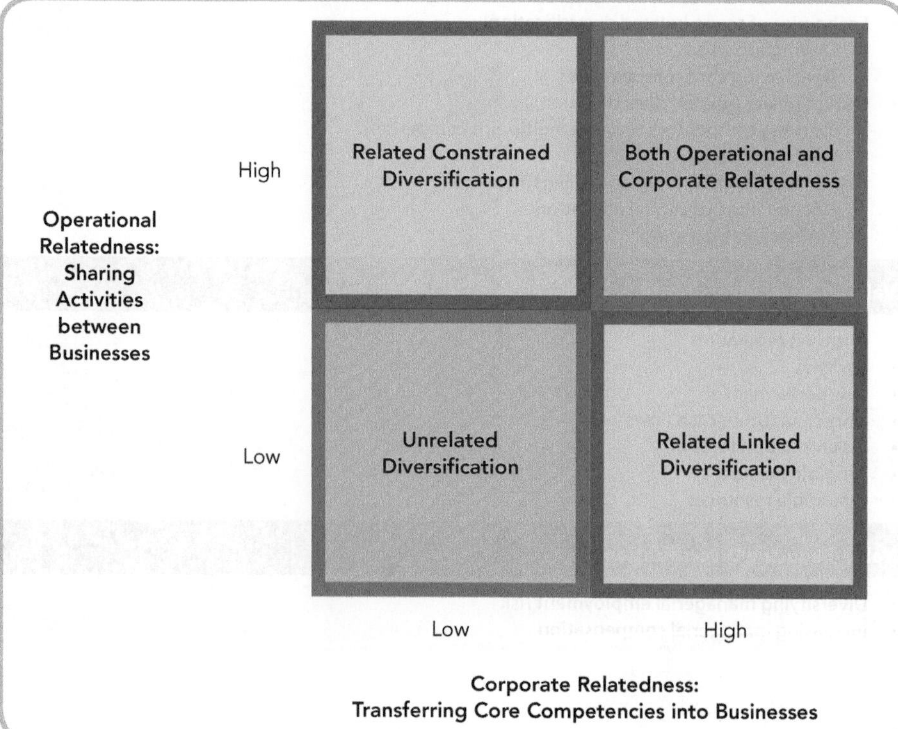

6-3 Value-Creating Diversification: Related Constrained and Related Linked Diversification

With the related diversification corporate-level strategy, the firm builds upon or extends its resources and capabilities to build a competitive advantage by creating value for customers.[33] The company using the related diversification strategy wants to develop and exploit economies of scope between its businesses.[34] In fact, even nonprofit organizations have found that carefully planned and implemented related diversification can create value.[35]

Economies of scope are cost savings a firm creates by successfully sharing resources and capabilities or transferring one or more corporate-level core competencies that were developed in one of its businesses to another of its businesses.[36]

As illustrated in Figure 6.2, firms seek to create value from economies of scope through two basic kinds of operational economies: sharing activities (operational relatedness) and transferring corporate-level core competencies (corporate relatedness). The difference between sharing activities and transferring competencies is based on how separate resources are jointly used to create economies of scope. To create economies of scope, tangible resources such as plant and equipment or other business-unit physical assets often must be shared. Less tangible resources such as manufacturing know-how and technological capabilities can also be shared. However, know-how transferred between separate activities with no physical or tangible resource involved is a transfer of a corporate-level core competence, not an operational sharing of activities.[37]

Economies of scope are cost savings a firm creates by successfully sharing resources and capabilities or transferring one or more corporate-level core competencies that were developed in one of its businesses to another of its businesses.

6-3a Operational Relatedness: Sharing Activities

Firms can create operational relatedness by sharing either a primary activity (e.g., inventory delivery systems) or a support activity (e.g., purchasing practices)—see Chapter 3's discussion of the value chain. Firms using the related constrained diversification strategy share activities in order to create value. Procter & Gamble uses this corporate-level strategy. Caterpillar, described in the Strategic Focus on page 182, also shares activities. For example, Caterpillar's various businesses share marketing activities because all of their equipment is sold to firms in the construction and mineral extraction industries.

Activity sharing is also risky because ties among a firm's businesses create links between outcomes. For instance, if demand for one business's product is reduced, it may not generate sufficient revenues to cover the fixed costs required to operate the shared facilities. These types of organizational difficulties can reduce activity-sharing success. Additionally, activity sharing requires careful coordination between the businesses involved. The coordination challenges must be managed effectively for the appropriate sharing of activities (see Chapter 11 for further discussion).[38]

Tom Uhlman/Bloomberg/Getty Images

Procter & Gamble (P&G) is a consumer products firm that shares a lot of activities among its divisions; for example, most of its products are sold through retail outlets and those sales activities can be shared among its divisions.

Although activity sharing across businesses is not risk-free, research shows that it can create value. For example, studies of acquisitions of firms in the same industry (horizontal acquisitions), such as the banking and software industries, found that sharing resources and activities and thereby creating economies of scope contributed to post-acquisition increases in performance and higher returns to shareholders. Additionally, firms that sold off related units in which resource sharing was a possible source of economies of scope have been found to produce lower returns than those that sold off businesses unrelated to the firm's core business. Still other research discovered that firms with closely related businesses have lower risk. These results suggest that gaining economies of scope by sharing activities across a firm's businesses may be important in reducing risk and in creating value. More attractive results are obtained through activity sharing when a strong corporate headquarters office facilitates it.[39]

6-3b Corporate Relatedness: Transferring of Core Competencies

Over time, the firm's intangible resources, such as its know-how, become the foundation of core competencies. **Corporate-level core competencies** are complex sets of resources and capabilities that link different businesses, primarily through managerial and technological knowledge, experience, and expertise.[40] Firms seeking to create value through corporate relatedness use the related linked diversification strategy as exemplified by Sony Corporation (see Chapter 11).

In at least two ways, the related linked diversification strategy helps firms to create value. First, because the expense of developing a core competence has already been incurred in one of the firm's businesses, transferring this competence to a second business eliminates the need for that business to allocate resources to develop it. Resource intangibility is a second source of value creation through corporate relatedness. Intangible resources are difficult for competitors to understand and imitate. Because of this difficulty, the unit receiving a transferred corporate-level competence often gains an immediate competitive advantage over its rivals.[41]

Ruby Washington/The New York Times/Redux

Virgin Group, known for its airline, has also transferred its brand through its marketing competence to other product areas such as cosmetics, music, drinks, mobile phones, health clubs, and a number of other businesses.

A number of firms have successfully transferred one or more corporate-level core competencies across their businesses. Virgin Group Ltd. transfers its marketing core competence across airlines, cosmetics, music, drinks, mobile phones, health clubs, and a number of other businesses.[42] Honda has developed and transferred its competence in engine design and manufacturing among its businesses making products such as motorcycles, lawnmowers, and cars and trucks. Company officials state that Honda is a major manufacturer of engines focused on providing products for all forms of human mobility.[43]

Corporate-level core competencies are complex sets of resources and capabilities that link different businesses, primarily through managerial and technological knowledge, experience, and expertise.

One way managers facilitate the transfer of corporate-level core competencies is by moving key people into new management positions.[44] However, the manager of an older business may be reluctant to transfer key people who have accumulated knowledge and experience critical to the business's success. Thus, managers with the ability to facilitate the transfer of a core competence may come at a premium, or the key people involved may not want to transfer. Additionally, the top-level managers from the transferring business may not want the competencies transferred to a new business to fulfill the firm's diversification objectives.[45] Research suggests that the nature of the top management team can influence the success of the knowledge and skill transfer process.[46] Research also suggests too much dependence on outsourcing can lower the usefulness of core competencies, thereby reducing their useful transferability to other business units in the diversified firm. For example, Fiat has developed a novel organizational solution in how firms can organize R&D to protect against innovation competence loss in R&D outsourcing, by maintaining certain design capabilities in cooperation with the supplier. [47]

6-3c Market Power

Firms using a related diversification strategy may gain market power when successfully using a related constrained or related linked strategy. **Market power** exists when a firm is able to sell its products above the existing competitive level or to reduce the costs of its primary and support activities below the competitive level, or both.[48] Heinz was bought by a private equity firm in Brazil called 3G Capital Partners LP, which subsequently combined Kraft Foods Group with Heinz to form Kraft-Heinz. These deals were supported by Warren Buffet's Berkshire Hathaway & Co., who teamed up with 3G to buy these food businesses. In a similar deal to build market power, 3G took private food restaurant Burger King Worldwide, Inc., and also bought Tim Hortons Inc. (a Canadian coffee and donut fast-food restaurant) through its Burger King holdings. Warren Buffet also contributed $11 million to help finance the latter deal. These deals obviously build market power for the combining firms in branded consumer foods and fast food restaurants.[49]

Ericsson for a long time had the largest share of the global market in telecommunications equipment, and for many years its leadership position afforded it considerable market power. However, that market share has eroded, due primarily to Chinese rivals. "Since 2012, Ericsson has fallen from first to third place in the $126 billion market for telecommunications equipment and software . . . In 2016, Huawei led with a 20.4 percent market share. Nokia acquired competitor Alcatel-Lucent to leap into second place, with 14 percent. Ericsson had 12.5 percent, while China's fast-rising ZTE Corp. had 9.2 percent."[50] As many customer firms move to the "cloud," all of these firms are seeking acquisitions and contracts to maintain that market power.

In addition to efforts to gain scale as a means of increasing market power, firms can foster increased market power through multipoint competition and vertical integration. **Multipoint competition** exists when two or more diversified firms simultaneously compete in the same product areas or geographical markets.[51] Through multi-point competition, rival firms often experience pressure to diversify because other firms in their dominant industry segment have made acquisitions to compete in a different market segment. The actions taken by UPS and FedEx in two markets, overnight delivery and ground shipping, illustrate multipoint competition. UPS moved into overnight delivery, FedEx's stronghold; in turn, FedEx bought trucking and ground shipping assets to move into ground shipping, UPS's stronghold. Similarly, J.M. Smucker Company, a snack food producer, in 2015 bought Big Heart Pet Brands, which specializes in snacks such as Milk-Bone dog biscuits, treats, and chews and has over $2.2 billion in annual revenue. Smucker's competitor, Mars, had acquired a significant portion of Proctor & Gamble's dog and cat food division in 2014. Apparently, Smucker's was seeking to keep up its size and cross-industry positions relative to Mars by also diversifying into snacks for pets. In 2018 following these acquisitions, General Mills announced its intent to acquire Blue Buffalo Pet Products for about $8 billion to obtain "a piece of the rapidly expanding natural pet-food market."[52]

Market power exists when a firm is able to sell its products above the existing competitive level or to reduce the costs of its primary and support activities below the competitive level, or both.

Multipoint competition exists when two or more diversified firms simultaneously compete in the same product areas or geographical markets.

When firm pursue vertical integration more information is processed at headquarters and thus more knowledge processing is needed as illustrated by these servers. External relations with suppliers are also supported by such information networks.

Some firms using a related diversification strategy engage in vertical integration to gain market power. **Vertical integration** exists when a company produces its own inputs (backward integration) or owns its own source of output distribution (forward integration). In some instances, firms partially integrate their operations, producing and selling their products by using company-owned businesses as well as outside sources.[53]

Vertical integration is commonly used in the firm's core business to gain market power over rivals. Market power is gained as the firm develops the ability to save on its operations, avoid sourcing and market costs, improve product quality, possibly protect its technology from imitation by rivals, and potentially exploit underlying capabilities in the marketplace. Vertically integrated firms are better able to improve product quality and improve or create new technologies than specialized firms because they have access to more information and knowledge that are complementary.[54] Market power also is created when firms have strong ties between their productive assets for which no market prices exist. Establishing a market price would result in high search and transaction costs, so firms seek to vertically integrate rather than remain separate businesses.[55]

Vertical integration has its limitations. For example, an outside supplier may produce the product at a lower cost. As a result, internal transactions from vertical integration may be expensive and reduce profitability relative to competitors.[56] Also, bureaucratic costs can be present with vertical integration.[57] Because vertical integration can require substantial investments in specific technologies, it may reduce the firm's flexibility, especially when technology changes quickly. Finally, changes in demand create capacity balance and coordination problems. If one business is building a part for another internal business but achieving economies of scale requires the first division to manufacture quantities that are beyond the capacity of the internal buyer to absorb, it would be necessary to sell the parts outside the firm as well as to the internal business. Thus, although vertical integration can create value, especially through market power over competitors, it is not without risks and costs.[58]

Around the turn of the twenty-first century, manufacturing firms such as Intel and Dell began to reduce vertical integration by reducing ownership of self-manufactured parts and components. This trend also occurred in some large auto companies, such as Ford and General Motors, as they developed independent supplier networks.[59] Flex (formerly known as Flextronics), a large electronics contract manufacturer, helps to support this approach to supply-chain management.[60] Such firms often manage their customers' entire product lines and offer services ranging from inventory management to delivery and after-sales service. Interestingly, however, some firms are beginning to reintegrate in order to gain better control over the quality and timing of their supplies.[61] Samsung has maintained control of its operations through a vertical integration strategy, while being a manufacturer for competitors such as Apple in consumer electronics.

Vertical integration exists when a company produces its own inputs (backward integration) or owns its own source of output distribution (forward integration).

6-3d Simultaneous Operational Relatedness and Corporate Relatedness

As Figure 6.2 suggests, some firms simultaneously seek operational and corporate relatedness to create economies of scope.[62] The ability to simultaneously create economies of scope by sharing activities (operational relatedness) and transferring core competencies (corporate relatedness) is difficult for competitors to understand and learn how to imitate. However, if the cost of realizing both types of relatedness is not offset by the benefits created, the result is diseconomies because the cost of organization and incentive structure is very expensive.[63]

As noted in the Opening Case, Amazon uses a related diversification strategy to simultaneously create economies of scope through operational and corporate relatedness. This is illustrated in how its deep customer knowledge is integrated in the various retail and media businesses along with the cloud service and shipping businesses. Amazon has pursued a related business strategy primarily through its online retail portal. For example, Amazon is deriving value through its economies of scale in cloud computing and warehouse and delivery logistics expertise. Through its purchase of Whole Foods Market, it now has other brick and mortal locations to pursue its online expertise in the grocery business.[64]

In addition, Disney, as illustrated in the mini-case at the end of the chapter, also applies this strategy. Disney has five separate but related businesses: media networks, parks and resorts, studio entertainment, consumer products, and interactive media. Within the firm's Studio Entertainment business, for example, Disney can gain economies of scope by sharing activities among its different movie distribution companies, such as Marvel, Touchstone Pictures, Hollywood Pictures, and Dimension Films. Broad and deep knowledge about its customers is a capability on which Disney relies to develop corporate-level core competencies in terms of advertising and marketing. With these competencies, Disney is able to create economies of scope through corporate relatedness as it cross-sells products that are highlighted in its movies through the distribution channels that are part of its parks and resorts and consumer products businesses. Thus, characters created in movies become figures that are marketed through Disney's retail stores (which are part of the consumer products business). In addition, themes established in movies become the source of new rides in the firm's theme parks, which are part of the parks and resorts business, and provide themes for clothing and other retail business products.[65]

Although The Walt Disney Company has been able to successfully use related diversification as a corporate-level strategy through which it creates economies of scope by sharing some activities and by transferring core competencies, it can be difficult for investors to identify the value created by a firm (e.g., The Walt Disney Company) as it shares activities and transfers core competencies. For this reason, the value of the assets of a firm using a diversification strategy to create economies of scope often is discounted by investors.[66]

Richard B.Levine/Newscom

Disney sells many products related to its movies in its own stores as well as more broadly through other retail outlets.

6-4 Unrelated Diversification

Firms do not seek either operational relatedness or corporate relatedness when using the unrelated diversification corporate-level strategy. An unrelated diversification strategy (see Figure 6.2) can create value through two types of financial economies. **Financial economies** are cost savings realized through improved allocations of financial resources based on investments inside or outside the firm.[67]

Efficient internal capital allocations can lead to financial economies. Efficient internal capital allocations reduce risk among the firm's businesses—for example, by leading to the development of a portfolio of businesses with different risk profiles. The second type of financial economy concerns the restructuring of acquired assets. Here, the diversified firm buys another company, restructures that company's assets in ways that allow it to operate more profitably, and then sells the company for a profit in the external market.[68] Next, we discuss the two types of financial economies in greater detail, efficient internal capital market allocation and asset restructuring.

6-4a Efficient Internal Capital Market Allocation

In a market economy, capital markets are believed to efficiently allocate capital. Efficiency results as investors take equity positions (ownership) with high expected future cash-flow values. Capital is also allocated through debt as shareholders and debt holders try to improve the value of their investments by taking stakes in businesses with high growth and profitability prospects.

In large diversified firms, the corporate headquarters office distributes capital to its businesses to create value for the overall corporation. As highlighted in the Strategic Focus, Berkshire Hathaway and SoftBank have used both efficient internal capital market allocation and restructuring approaches in managing its unrelated business units. The nature of these distributions can generate gains from internal capital market allocations that exceed the gains that would accrue to shareholders as a result of capital being allocated by the external capital market.[69] Because those in a firm's corporate headquarters generally have access to detailed and accurate information regarding the actual and potential future performance of the company's portfolio of businesses, they have the best information to make capital distribution decisions.[70]

Compared with corporate office personnel, external investors have relatively limited access to internal information and can only estimate the performances of individual businesses as well as their future prospects. Moreover, although businesses seeking capital must provide information to potential suppliers (e.g., banks or insurance companies), firms with internal capital markets can have at least two informational advantages. First, information provided to capital markets through annual reports and other sources emphasizes positive prospects and outcomes. External sources of capital have a limited ability to understand the operational dynamics within large organizations. Even external shareholders who have access to information are unlikely to receive full and complete disclosure.[71] Second, although a firm must disseminate information, that information also becomes simultaneously available to the firm's current and potential competitors. Competitors might attempt to duplicate a firm's value-creating strategy with insights gained by studying such information. Thus, the ability to efficiently allocate capital through an internal market helps the firm protect the competitive advantages it develops while using its corporate-level strategy as well as its various business-unit–level strategies.

Financial economies are cost savings realized through improved allocations of financial resources based on investments inside or outside the firm.

If intervention from outside the firm is required to make corrections to capital allocations, only significant changes are possible because the power to make changes by outsiders is often indirect (e.g., through members of the board of directors). External parties can try to make changes by forcing the firm into bankruptcy or changing the top management team.

Strategic Focus

Berkshire Hathaway and SoftBank Use Similar Unrelated Strategies

This Strategic Focus will examine the unrelated diversified strategies employed by Berkshire Hathaway and SoftBank. Berkshire Hathaway uses a two pronged strategy, one focused on dominant owned or wholly owned businesses as well as large—although minority—ownership positions in a number of other businesses. It has dominant or wholly owned positions in insurance, including National Fire and Marine, GEICO, and Gen Re, offering reinsurance solutions that work behind the scenes to share the risk among frontline carriers. Another dominant position is focused on regulated and capital intensive businesses, which include BNSF Railroad and Berkshire Hathaway Energy (BHE), a 90% owned utility business. Another group, Home Services, which came with the purchase of Mid America (the energy utility that led to the formation of BHE in 1999), owns 38 realty companies with 29,000 agents operating in 28 states.

Manufacturing service and retail operations is another group, with 44 businesses that report directly to the Berkshire Hathaway corporate headquarters. Included in this group is Kraft Heinz, which has been restructured, and other businesses such as Duracell, a battery business, purchased from Gillette.

Berkshire Hathaway also owns financing and financial product businesses. Included in this group are rental and leasing operations conducted by CORT Furniture (home and office furniture rental), XTRA (truck semi-trailers), and MARMON (primarily rail tank cars but also freight cars, intermodal tank controllers, and cranes); each of these is a leader in its field. Berkshire Hathaway also owns a manufactured home financing business called Clayton Homes.

Besides this unrelated set of dominant ownership position or wholly owned businesses, Berkshire Hathaway has investments in a number of other well-known businesses including: American Express Company, Apple Inc., Charter Communications, Inc., Coca-Cola Company, Delta Airlines, Goldman Sachs, Inc., International Business Machines Corp. Moody's Corporation, Phillips 66, Sanofi, Southwest Airlines Company, US Bank Corp, United Continental Holdings, Inc. (United Airlines), USG Corp, and Wells Fargo Company. It uses cash generated from the insurance business as well as other assets and finance businesses to fund its investments in these additional minority investments. It primarily invests its money in long-term holdings where the business has a strong competitive advantage relative to others in its industrial segment.

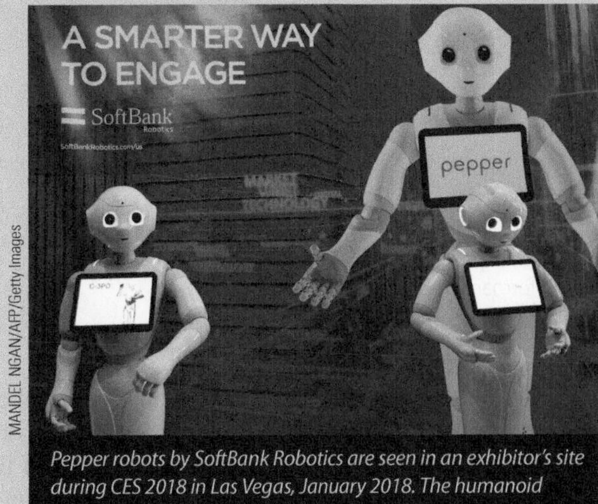

MANDEL NGAN/AFP/Getty Images

Pepper robots by SoftBank Robotics are seen in an exhibitor's site during CES 2018 in Las Vegas, January 2018. The humanoid robot is capable of recognizing human emotions.

To compare and contrast, SoftBank uses a similar strategy as noted above. However, SoftBank, a large Japanese firm, has minority investments primarily in the high-tech area rather than in large dominant and well-known businesses as found in Berkshire Hathaway. The dominant business that SoftBank has used from which to expand is the telecommunications business in Japan, which also includes Bright Start (mobile phones and other accessory device distribution). Furthermore, it has acquired Sprint, a mobile telecommunication carrier in the United States, to expand and improve on its investments in telecommunications. SoftBank also has an investment in Vodafone in Europe.

It has largely sought to turn these struggling mobile phone businesses back into money makers and use the cash flow and asset base to fund Internet and other technology-oriented businesses in its broader minority ownership portfolio. For example, DiDi is a ride-hailing giant in China (like Uber) whose platform SoftBank will likely use to help develop its ride-hailing business in Japan. Additionally, SoftBank has investments in Yahoo! Japan, Alibaba Group, among a myriad of others. To foster investments it has a number of financial companies to facilitate its investment transactions as well as engineering design companies including: Softbank Vision Fund (venture capital), Arm Holdings (semiconductors and software design), Fortress Investment Group (private equity), and Boston Dynamics (engineering and robotics). For example, the Vision

Fund "strategy is to invest in the leading company in an array of sectors, giving each company enough money to rise above competitors." Softbank has invested more than $34 billion globally across more than 20 companies. Comparatively, this is a sizable investment given that the U.S. venture-capital industry raises about $40 billion annually.

In summary, both these businesses employ an unrelated strategy whereby they use the cash flow from large insurance or utility type businesses to fund their partial investments in a range of other investments. They both use holding company structures, where most businesses are organized to report their results independently to corporate headquarters and are rewarded according to their individual business unit or subsidiary performance.

Sources: A. Abkowitz, 2018, DiDi ties up with SoftBank to give a lift to Japanese taxi companies, *Wall Street Journal*, www.wsj.com, February 8; P. Alpeyev, 2018, Masayoshi Son plans push to cut discount in Softbank's Stock, *Bloomberg*, www.bloomberg.com, February 6; E. Brown, 2018, SoftBank bets big on food delivery, *Wall Street Journal*, www.wsj.com, March 1; P. Dvorak & M. Negishi, 2018, How SoftBank, world's biggest tech investor, throws around its cash, *Wall Street Journal*, www.wsj.com, February 26; T. Lachapelle, 2018, Even Warren Buffett's magic can't help Kraft Heinz, *Bloomberg Businessweek*, www.businessweek.com, February 16; C. Leaf, 2018, Amazon-JP Morgan-Berkshire Hathaway; what their new health venture really means, *Fortune*, www.fortune.com, January 31; R. L. Ensign, 2017, It's official; Warren Buffett made about $13 billion on Bank of America deal, *Wall Street Journal*, www.wsj.com, August 30; A. Gara, 2017, Another reason to buy Berkshire Hathaway? Hedge funds can't beat Buffett on their own turf, *Forbes*, www.forbes.com, July 11; S. Grocer, 2017 Berkshire hopes its second tango with energy goes more smoothly, *Wall Street Journal*, www.wsj.com, July 7; J. Pearce, 2017, SoftBank aligned with Uber investment, *Global Telecoms Business*, August 14, 20; P. Alpeyev & T. Amano, 2015, Softbank $3 billion startup incubator, *Bloomberg*, www.bloomberg.com, November 30.

Alternatively, in an internal capital market, the corporate headquarters office can fine-tune its corrections, such as choosing to adjust business unit managerial incentives or encouraging strategic changes in one of the firm's businesses.[72] Thus, capital can be allocated according to more specific criteria than is possible with external market allocations. Because it has less accurate information, the external capital market may fail to allocate resources adequately to high-potential investments. The corporate headquarters office of a diversified company can more effectively perform such tasks as disciplining underperforming management teams through resource allocations.[73]

In spite of the challenges associated with it, a number of corporations continue to use the unrelated diversification strategy, especially in emerging markets. As an example, Siemens is a large diversified German conglomerate that engages in substantial diversification in order to balance its economic risk. In economic downturns, diversification can help some companies improve future performance.[74]

The Achilles' heel for firms using the unrelated diversification strategy in a developed economy is that competitors can imitate financial economies more easily than they can replicate the value gained from the economies of scope developed through operational relatedness and corporate relatedness. This issue is less of a problem in emerging economies, in which the absence of a "soft infrastructure" (including effective financial intermediaries, sound regulations, and contract laws) supports and encourages use of the unrelated diversification strategy.[75] In fact, in emerging economies such as those in Taiwan, India, and Chile, research has shown that diversification increases the performance of firms affiliated within large diversified business groups such as the Tata group in India.[76]

6-4b Restructuring of Assets

Financial economies can also be created when firms learn how to create value by buying, restructuring, and then selling the restructured companies' assets in the external market.[77] As in the real estate business, buying assets at low prices, restructuring them, and selling them at a price that exceeds their cost generates a positive return on the firm's invested capital. This is a strategy that has been taken up by private equity firms, who successfully buy, restructure, and then sell, often within a four-or five-year period.[78]

Unrelated diversified companies that pursue this strategy try to create financial economies by acquiring and restructuring other companies' assets, but it involves significant trade-offs. For example, both Berkshire Hathaway and Softbank as illustrated in the Strategic Focus have used this strategy. Likewise, Danaher Corp.'s success requires a focus on mature manufacturing businesses because of the uncertainty of demand for high-technology products. It has acquired hundreds of businesses since 1984 and applied the Danaher Business System to reduce costs and create a lean organization by finding firms with "secular growth drivers and opportunities for consolidation" during restructuring.[79] Danaher as noted focused on mature, low-technology businesses because resource allocation decisions are highly complex in these businesses, often creating information-processing overload on the small corporate headquarters offices that are common in unrelated diversified firms. High-technology and service businesses are often human-resource dependent; these people can leave or demand higher pay and thus appropriate or deplete the value of an acquired firm.[80]

Buying and then restructuring service-based assets so they can be profitably sold in the external market is also difficult. Thus, for both high-technology firms and service-based companies, relatively few tangible assets can be restructured to create value and sell profitably, although this is the approach used by SoftBank (see the Strategic Focus). It is difficult to restructure intangible assets such as human capital and effective relationships that have evolved over time between buyers (customers) and sellers (firm personnel). Ideally, executives will follow a strategy of buying businesses when prices are lower, such as in the midst of a recession, and selling them at late stages in an expansion. This is certainly the approach that Warren Buffett has used at Berkshire Hathaway; for example, it bought a large position in GE, Wells Fargo, and IBM during the downturn and sold its positions once the stock price improved significantly. Because of the increases in global economic activity, including more cross-border acquisitions, there is also a growing number of foreign divestitures and restructuring in internal markets (e.g., partial or full privatization of state-owned enterprises). Foreign divestitures are even more complex than domestic ones and must be managed carefully.[81]

6-5 Value-Neutral Diversification: Incentives and Resources

The objectives firms seek when using related diversification and unrelated diversification strategies all have the potential to help the firm create value through the corporate-level strategy. However, these strategies, as well as single- and dominant-business diversification strategies, are sometimes used with objectives that are value-neutral. Different incentives to diversify sometimes exist, and the quality of the firm's resources may permit only diversification that is value neutral rather than value creating.

6-5a Incentives to Diversify

Incentives to diversify come from both the external environment and a firm's internal environment. External incentives include antitrust regulations and tax laws. Internal incentives include low performance, uncertain future cash flows, the pursuit of synergy, and reduction of risk for the firm.

Antitrust Regulation and Tax Laws

Government antitrust policies and tax laws provided incentives for U.S. firms to diversify in the 1960s and 1970s.[82] Antitrust laws prohibiting mergers that created increased market power (via either vertical or horizontal integration) were stringently enforced during that period. Merger activity that produced conglomerate diversification was encouraged primarily by the Celler-Kefauver Antimerger Act (1950), which discouraged horizontal and vertical mergers. As a result, many of the mergers during the 1960s and 1970s were "conglomerate" in character, involving companies pursuing different lines of business. Between 1973 and 1977, 79.1 percent of all mergers were conglomerate in nature.[83]

During the 1980s, antitrust enforcement lessened, resulting in more and larger horizontal mergers (acquisitions of target firms in the same line of business, such as a merger between two oil companies).[84] In addition, investment bankers became more open to the kinds of mergers facilitated by regulation changes; as a consequence, takeovers increased to unprecedented numbers.[85] The conglomerates, or highly diversified firms, of the 1960s and 1970s became more "focused" in the 1980s and early 1990s as merger constraints were relaxed and restructuring was implemented.[86]

In the beginning of the twenty-first century, antitrust concerns emerged again with the large volume of mergers and acquisitions (see Chapter 7).[87] Mergers are now receiving more scrutiny than they did in the 1980s, 1990s, and the first decade of the 2000s.[88]

The tax effects of diversification stem not only from corporate tax changes, but also from individual tax rates. Some companies (especially mature ones) generate more cash from their operations than they can reinvest profitably. Some argue that *free cash flows* (liquid financial assets for which investments in current businesses are no longer economically viable) should be redistributed to shareholders as dividends.[89] However, in the 1960s and 1970s, dividends were taxed more heavily than were capital gains. As a result, before 1980, shareholders preferred that firms use free cash flows to buy and build companies in high-performance industries. If the firm's stock value appreciated over the long term, shareholders might receive a better return on those funds than if the funds had been redistributed as dividends because returns from stock sales would be taxed more lightly than would dividends.

Under the 1986 Tax Reform Act, however, the top individual ordinary income tax rate was reduced from 50 to 28 percent, and the special capital gains tax was changed to treat capital gains as ordinary income. These changes created an incentive for shareholders to stop encouraging firms to retain funds for purposes of diversification. These tax law changes also influenced an increase in divestitures of unrelated business units after 1984. Thus, while individual tax rates for capital gains and dividends created a shareholder incentive to increase diversification before 1986, they encouraged lower diversification after 1986, unless the diversification was funded by tax-deductible debt. Yet, there have been changes in the maximum individual tax rates since the 1980s. The top individual tax rate has varied from 31 percent in 1992 to 39.6 percent in 2017. There have also been some changes in the capital gains tax rates.

Corporate tax laws also affect diversification. Acquisitions typically increase a firm's depreciable asset allowances. Increased depreciation (a non-cash-flow expense) produces lower taxable income, thereby providing an additional incentive for acquisitions. At one time, acquisitions were an attractive means for securing tax benefits, but changes recommended by the Financial Accounting Standards Board (FASB) eliminated the "pooling of interests" method to account for the acquired firm's assets. It also eliminated the write-off for research and development in process, and thus reduced some of the incentives to make acquisitions, especially acquisitions in related high-technology industries (these changes are discussed further in Chapter 7).[90]

Thus, regulatory changes such as the ones we have described create incentives or disincentives for diversification. Interestingly, European antitrust laws have historically been stricter regarding horizontal mergers than those in the United States, but recently have become more similar.[91]

Low Performance

Some research shows that low returns are related to greater levels of diversification.[92] If high performance eliminates the need for greater diversification, then low performance may provide an incentive for diversification. AIG has experienced poor performance in the company's core commercial insurance businesses. While it was still recovering from the economic downturn, it recently "struck a deal to acquire Bermuda-based insurance and reinsurance group Validus Holdings for $5.56 billion." The acquisitions will "add a number of business lines that AIG currently lacks, including crop insurance, a syndicate with the Lloyd's insurance market, and the reinsurance operations."[93] AIG is hoping that this diversification move will help it recover and reduce its focus on commercial insurance. There are also risks in that the reinsurance business has had difficult to establish pricing power and AIG also paid a large premium.

Firms such as AIG, which has an incentive to diversify, there is a need to be careful because as noted there are risks to moving into areas that are new and where the company lacks operational expertise. There can be negative synergy (where potential synergy between acquiring and target firms is illusory) and problems between leaders and cultural fit difficulties with recent acquisitions.[94] Research evidence and the experience of a number of firms suggest that an overall curvilinear relationship, as illustrated in Figure 6.3, may exist between diversification and performance.[95] Although low performance can be an incentive to diversify, firms that are more broadly diversified compared to their competitors may have overall lower performance.

Uncertain Future Cash Flows

As a firm's product line matures or is threatened, diversification may be an important defensive strategy.[96] Research also suggests that during a financial downturn, diversification improves firm performance because external capital markets are costly and internal resource allocation become more important.[97] Family firms and companies in mature or maturing industries sometimes find it necessary to diversify for long-term survival of the legacy business.[98]

Diversifying into other product markets or into other businesses can reduce the uncertainty about a firm's future cash flows. Alcoa, the largest U.S. aluminum producer, has been pursuing a "multi-material" diversification strategy driven by the highly competitive nature of its basic commodity business. Alcoa has been diversifying into other metals beside aluminum while simultaneously moving into a variety of end-product industries. In 2015, for example, it announced that it would acquire RTI International

Figure 6.3 The Curvilinear Relationship between Diversification and Performance

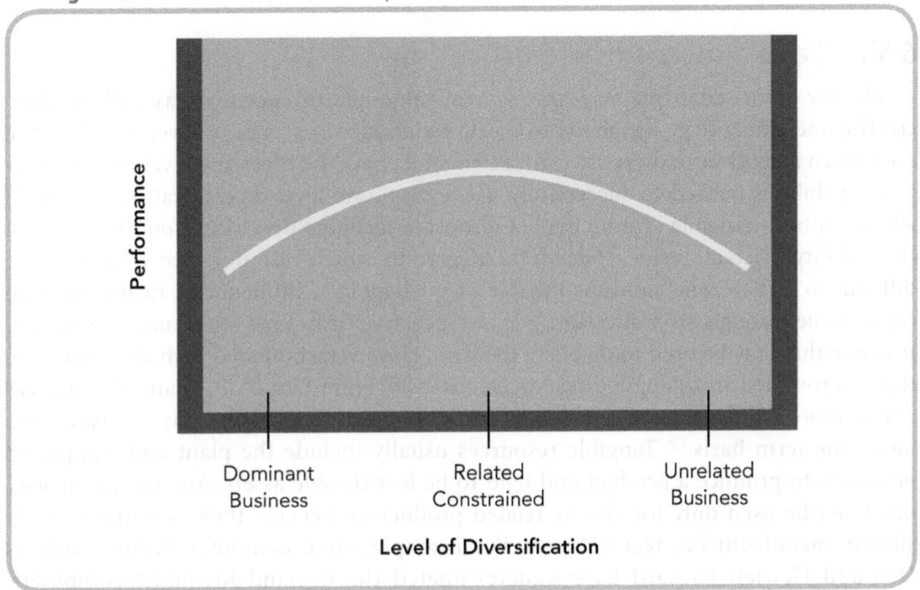

Metals, Inc., which is one of the largest titanium producers for the aerospace industry; this allowed greater ability to negotiate prices with customers.[99] However, shortly after its increased diversification, it announced it would break into two businesses, the commodity upstream business and a multi-metal downstream business, due to pressure by activist owners and stock analysts.[100]

Synergy and Firm Risk Reduction

Diversified firms pursuing economies of scope often have investments that are too inflexible as they try to realize synergy among business units. As a result, a number of problems may arise. **Synergy** exists when the value created by business units working together exceeds the value that those same units create working independently. However, as a firm increases its relatedness among business units, it also increases its risk of corporate failure because synergy produces joint interdependence among businesses that constrains the firm's flexibility to respond.[101] This threat may force two basic decisions.

First, the firm may reduce its level of technological change by operating in environments that are more certain. This behavior may make the firm risk averse and thus uninterested in pursuing new product lines that have potential but are not proven. Alternatively, the firm may constrain its level of activity sharing and forgo potential benefits of synergy. Either or both decisions may lead to further diversification.[102] Operating in environments that are more certain will likely lead to related diversification into industries that lack potential,[103] while constraining the level of activity sharing may produce additional, but unrelated, diversification, where the firm lacks expertise. Research suggests that a firm using a related diversification strategy is more careful in bidding for new businesses, whereas a firm pursuing an unrelated diversification strategy may be more likely to overbid because it is less likely to have full information about the firm it wants to acquire.[104] However, firms using either a related or an unrelated diversification strategy must understand the consequences of paying large premiums.[105] Paying excessive acquisition premiums often causes managers to become more risk averse and focus on achieving short-term returns. When this occurs, managers are less likely to be concerned about making long-term investments (e.g., developing innovation). Alternatively, diversified firms (related and unrelated) can be innovative if the firm pursues these strategies appropriately.[106]

6-5b Resources and Diversification

As already discussed, firms may have several value-neutral incentives as well as value-creating incentives (e.g., the ability to create economies of scope) to diversify. However, even when incentives to diversify exist, a firm must have the types and levels of resources and capabilities needed to successfully use a corporate-level diversification strategy.[107] Although both tangible and intangible resources facilitate diversification, they vary in their ability to create value. Indeed, the degree to which resources are valuable, rare, difficult to imitate, and nonsubstitutable (see Chapter 3) influences a firm's ability to create value through diversification. For instance, free cash flows are a tangible financial resource that may be used to diversify the firm. However, compared with diversification that is grounded in intangible resources, diversification based on financial resources only is more visible to competitors and thus more imitable and less likely to create value on a long-term basis.[108] Tangible resources usually include the plant and equipment necessary to produce a product and tend to be less-flexible assets. Any excess capacity often can be used only for closely related products, especially those requiring highly similar manufacturing technologies. For example, large computer makers such as Dell and Hewlett-Packard have underestimated the demand for tablet computers.

Synergy exists when the value created by business units working together exceeds the value that those same units create working independently.

Apple developed a tablet computer, the iPad, and many expect such tablets to eventually replace the personal computer (PC). In fact, Dell's and HP's sales of their PCs have been declining since the introduction of the iPad. Dell, HP, Lenovo, and others have responded by making cheaper tablet-like laptops and iPad-like tablets and have stayed in the game without having to diversify too much.[109]

Excess capacity of other tangible resources, such as a sales force, can be used to diversify more easily. Again, excess capacity in a sales force is more effective with related diversification because it may be utilized to sell products in similar markets (e.g., same customers). The sales force would be more knowledgeable about related product characteristics, customers, and distribution channels.[110] Tangible resources may create resource interrelationships in production, marketing, procurement, and technology, defined earlier as activity sharing. Interestingly, Dyson, which produces vacuum cleaners, has invested in battery technology. Dyson's CEO, James Dyson, has indicated that the company, besides producing a battery operated vacuum, will seek to launch products using new, more efficient battery technology, including an electric automobile.[111]

Intangible resources are more flexible than tangible physical assets in facilitating diversification. Although the sharing of tangible resources may induce diversification, intangible resources such as tacit knowledge could encourage even more diversification. Service firms also pursue diversification strategies especially through greenfield ventures (opening a new business for the firm without acquiring a previous established brand-name business). Alvarez & Marsal, a professional service firm that has focused on helping to restructure firms that experience financial distress, has diversified into several additional service businesses. It has a reputation (an intangible asset) in New York financial circles for its ability to do interim management for firms that are experiencing financial distress and often gone into bankruptcy. Alvarez & Marsal managed the largest U.S. bankruptcy in history, the wind-down of Lehman Bros. after it folded. As part of this massive wind down, it needed to manage the treasury and cash assets of the company in a way to realize the best returns possible for the remaining stakeholders and creditors who held right to debt secured assets. Through its experience over a number of bankruptcies, but in particular the Lehman Bros. bankruptcy, Alvarez & Marsal has gained a reputation and ability in investment management especially for short-term treasury deposits. These capabilities have led the firm to open a new business to manage treasury and cash assets for other companies, but also for endowments and local and state government entities. It also serves as a consultant for private equity firms that are closely associated with firms in financial distress and restructuring strategies. From its interim management business, it has moved into performance improvement consulting. Through its reputation and skills in serving private equity clients, Alvarez & Marsal also gained knowledge about investing in private equity businesses and have likewise started a private equity fund.[112] This approach to diversification is not unfamiliar to other professional service firms such as Bain Strategy Consulting, which also started Bain Capital, a private equity fund, through the support of Bain partners (owners) in their consulting business.

Sometimes, however, the benefits expected from using resources to diversify the firm for either value-creating or value-neutral reasons are not gained. Research suggests that picking the right target firm partner is critical to acquisition success.[113] For example, Paris-listed Kering has spent the past decade and a half transforming itself from a retail conglomerate into a luxury group anchored by the Florence-based Gucci brand. It purchased a majority stake in Puma, an athletic shoe and clothing brand in competition with Nike and others. It is seeking to offload its "long suffering" position in Puma and hoping to get back the $4.8 billion it paid for the brand over a decade ago.[114]

6-6 Value-Reducing Diversification: Managerial Motives to Diversify

Managerial motives to diversify can exist independent of value-neutral reasons (i.e., incentives and resources) and value-creating reasons (e.g., economies of scope). The desire for increased compensation and reduced managerial risk are two motives for top-level executives to diversify their firm beyond value-creating and value-neutral levels.[115] In slightly different words, top-level executives may diversify a firm in order to spread their own employment risk, as long as profitability does not suffer excessively.[116]

Diversification provides additional benefits to top-level managers that shareholders do not enjoy. Research evidence shows that diversification and firm size are highly correlated, and as firm size increases, so does executive compensation and social status.[117] Because large firms are complex, difficult-to-manage organizations, top-level managers commonly receive substantial levels of compensation to lead them, but the amounts vary across countries.[118] Greater levels of diversification can increase a firm's complexity, resulting in still more compensation for executives to lead an increasingly diversified organization. Governance mechanisms, such as the board of directors, monitoring by owners, executive compensation practices, and the market for corporate control, may limit managerial tendencies to over diversify.[119] These mechanisms are discussed in more detail in Chapter 10.

In some instances, though, a firm's governance mechanisms may not be strong, allowing executives to diversify the firm to the point that it fails to earn even average returns.[120] The loss of adequate internal governance may result in relatively poor performance, thereby triggering a threat of takeover. Although takeovers may improve efficiency by replacing ineffective managerial teams, managers may avoid takeovers through defensive tactics, such as "poison pills," or may reduce their own exposure with "golden parachute" agreements.[121] Therefore, an external governance threat, although restraining managers, does not flawlessly control managerial motives for diversification.[122]

Most large publicly held firms are profitable because the managers leading them are positive stewards of firm resources, and many of their strategic actions, including those related to selecting a corporate-level diversification strategy, contribute to the firm's success.[123] As mentioned, governance mechanisms should be designed to deal with exceptions to the managerial norms of making decisions and taking actions that increase the firm's ability to earn above-average returns. Thus, it is overly pessimistic to assume that managers usually act in their own self-interest as opposed to their firm's interest.[124]

Top-level executives' diversification decisions may also be held in check by concerns for their reputation. If a positive reputation facilitates development and use of managerial power, a poor reputation can reduce it. Likewise, a strong external market for managerial talent may deter managers from pursuing inappropriate diversification.[125] In addition, a diversified firm may acquire other firms that are poorly managed in order to restructure its own asset base. Knowing that their firms could be acquired if they are not managed successfully encourages executives to use value-creating diversification strategies.

As shown in Figure 6.4, the level of diversification with the greatest potential positive effect on performance is based partly on the effects of the interaction of resources, managerial motives, and incentives on the adoption of particular diversification strategies. As indicated earlier, the greater the incentives and the more flexible the resources, the higher the level of expected diversification. Financial resources (the most flexible) should have a stronger relationship to the extent of diversification than either tangible or intangible resources. Tangible resources (the most inflexible) are useful primarily for related diversification.

Figure 6.4 Summary Model of the Relationship between Diversification and Firm Performance

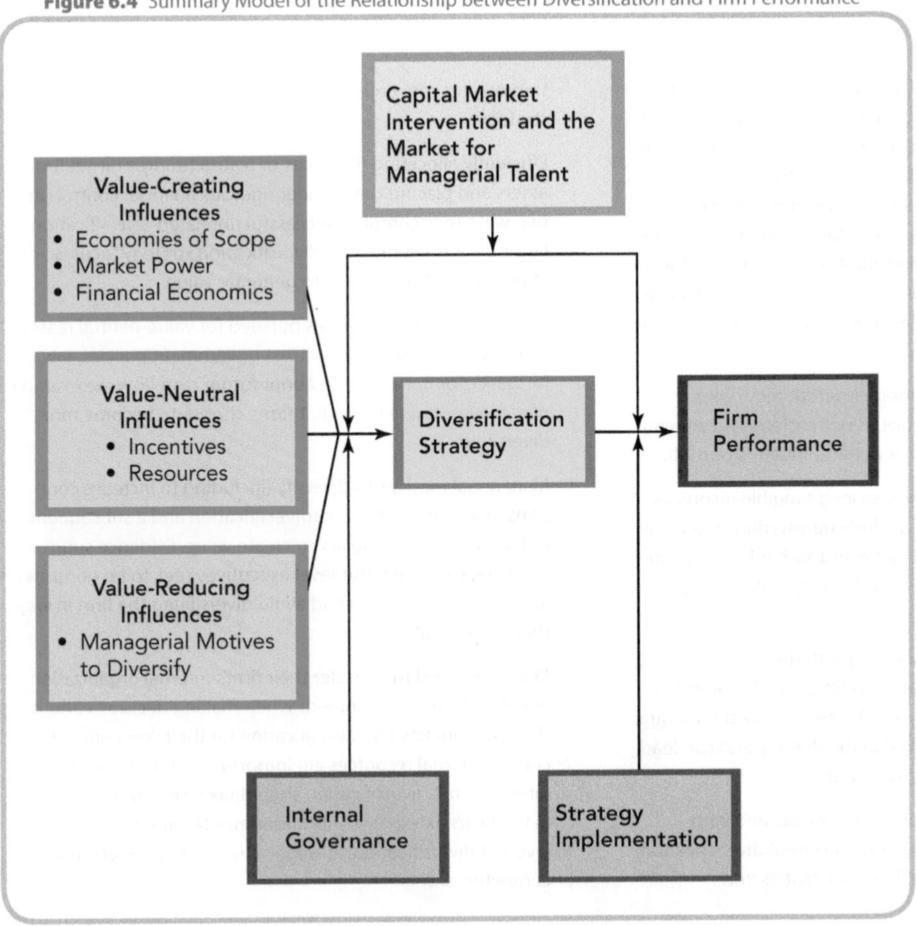

Source: Adapted from R. E. Hoskisson & M. A. Hitt, 1990, Antecedents and performace outcomes of diversification: A review and critique of theoretical perspectives, *Journal of Management*, 16: 498.

As discussed in this chapter, firms can create more value by effectively using diversification strategies. However, diversification must be kept in check by corporate governance (see Chapter 10). Appropriate strategy implementation tools, such as organizational structures, are also important for the strategies to be successful (see Chapter 11).

We have described corporate-level strategies in this chapter. In the next chapter, we discuss mergers and acquisitions as prominent means for firms to diversify and to grow profitably. These trends toward more diversification through acquisitions, which have been partially reversed due to restructuring (see Chapter 7), indicate that learning has taken place regarding corporate-level diversification strategies.[126] Accordingly, firms that diversify should do so cautiously, choosing to focus on relatively few, rather than many, businesses. In fact, research suggests that although unrelated diversification has decreased, related diversification has increased, possibly due to the restructuring that continued from the 1990s through the early twenty-first century. This sequence of diversification followed by restructuring has occurred in Europe and in countries such as Korea, following actions of firms in the United States and the United Kingdom.[127] Firms can improve their strategic competitiveness when they pursue a level of diversification that is appropriate for their resources (especially financial resources) and core competencies and the opportunities and threats in their country's institutional and competitive environments.[128]

SUMMARY

- The primary reason a firm uses a corporate-level strategy to become more diversified is to create additional value. Using a single- or dominant-business corporate-level strategy may be preferable to seeking a more diversified strategy, unless a corporation can develop economies of scope or financial economies between businesses, or unless it can obtain market power through additional levels of diversification. Economies of scope and market power are the main sources of value creation when the firm uses a corporate-level strategy to achieve moderate to high levels of diversification.
- The related diversification corporate-level strategy helps the firm create value by sharing activities or transferring competencies between different businesses in the company's portfolio.
- Sharing activities usually involves sharing tangible resources between businesses. Examples include transferring core competencies developed in one business to another business, and transferring competencies between the corporate headquarters office and a business unit.
- Sharing activities is usually associated with the related constrained diversification corporate-level strategy. Activity sharing is costly to implement and coordinate, may create unequal benefits for the divisions involved in the sharing, and can lead to fewer managerial risk-taking behaviors.
- Transferring core competencies is often associated with related linked (or mixed related and unrelated) diversification, although firms pursuing both sharing activities and transferring core competencies can also use the related linked strategy.
- Efficiently allocating resources or restructuring a target firm's assets and placing them under rigorous financial controls are two ways to accomplish successful unrelated diversification. Firms using the unrelated diversification strategy focus on creating financial economies to generate value.
- Diversification is sometimes pursued for value-neutral reasons. Incentives from tax and antitrust government policies, low performance, or uncertainties about future cash flow are examples of value-neutral reasons that firms choose to become more diversified.
- Managerial motives to diversify (including to increase compensation) can lead to overdiversification and a subsequent reduction in a firm's ability to create value. Evidence suggests, however, that many top-level executives seek to be good stewards of the firm's assets and avoid diversifying the firm in ways that destroy value.
- Managers need to consider their firm's internal organization and its external environment when making decisions about the optimum level of diversification for their company. Of course, internal resources are important determinants of the direction that diversification should take. However, conditions in the firm's external environment may facilitate additional levels of diversification, as might unexpected threats from competitors.

KEY TERMS

corporate-level core competencies 186
corporate-level strategy 178
economies of scope 185
financial economies 190
market power 187
multipoint competition 187
synergy 196
vertical integration 188

REVIEW QUESTIONS

1. What is corporate-level strategy and why is it important?
2. What are the different levels of diversification firms can pursue by using different corporate-level strategies?
3. What are three reasons firms choose to diversify their operations?
4. How do firms create value when using a related diversification strategy?
5. What are the two ways to obtain financial economies when using an unrelated diversification strategy?
6. What incentives and resources encourage diversification?
7. What motives might encourage managers to over diversify their firm?

Mini-Case

Walt Disney Company Corporate Strategy

The Walt Disney Company has a diversified set of businesses in movie-making, television show production, media distribution (e.g., ABC and ESPN), interactive and theme parks (e.g., Disneyland, Disney World, Disneyland Paris, and Shanghai Disneyland), and retail and consumer product sales. It is the second largest mass media producer after Comcast, which owns NBC and Universal Studios. While other more focused media content providers such as Discover Communications, CBS, and Viacom have seen decreasing revenues because of lower ratings and TV ad weakness, Disney was strengthened through its other businesses based on its diversification strategy. Although its ad revenues have decreased like other more focused content producers and distributors, its other businesses are growing and allow it to maintain higher earnings compared to other rival media producing firms.

Disney's strategy is successful because its corporate strategy, compared to its business-level strategy, adds value across its set of businesses above what the individual businesses could create individually. In the literature this is often known as synergy, or in the more academic literature, economies of scope (defined earlier in Chapter 6). First, Disney has a set of businesses that feed into each other: its studio entertainment, consumer products and interactive media, media network outlets, parks and resorts, studio entertainment parks, and retail enterprises have overlapping aspects. Within its studio entertainment businesses, Disney can share activities across its different production firms: Touchstone Pictures, Hollywood Pictures, Dimension Films, Pixar Films, and Marvel Entertainment. By sharing activities among these semi-independent studios, it can learn faster and gain success by the knowledge sharing and efficiencies associated with each studio's expertise. The corporation also has broad and deep knowledge about its customers, which is a corporate-level capability in terms of advertising and marketing. This capability allows Disney to cross-sell products highlighted in its movies through its media distribution outlets, parks and resorts, as well as consumer product businesses.

Recently, for example, Disney has found success in making live action movies from former comic books through its Marvel acquisition. A recent example is the success of *Black Panther*, a superhero film that deals with issues of being of African descent. Its success follows other Marvel superhero movies such as *Wonder Woman*, *Guardians of the Galaxy*, *Captain America*, and *Iron Man*. Marvel's characters have also led to TV series such as *Agency of S.H.I.E.L.D.* from *Captain America: The Winter Soldier*.

Disney has been also been moving from its historical central focus on animation in movies such as *Cinderella*, *The Jungle Book*, and *Beauty and the Beast*, into the same titles or stories using a live action approach. The recent release of *A Wrinkle in Time staring* Oprah Winfrey and Reese Witherspoon is another example. *Cinderella*, a live action version of the original 1950 animated classic, stays particularly close to the "fairy tale version of the script." This approach comes from its understanding of its customers and what they prefer. Other approaches can be found in *Alice in Wonderland* with Johnny Depp and *Maleficent* with Angelina Jolie, both of which were twists on their respective originals (*Maleficent* came from *Sleeping Beauty*). The action versions of these two movies grossed $1.3 billion and $813 million globally, respectively. Although Disney has had some relatively unsuccessful pictures—*John Carter*, *The Lone Ranger*, and *The Sorcerer's Apprentice*—its action movies based on its animated fairy tales have been relatively more successful. Disney successfully promoted *Cinderella* products in its stores and in other focused retail outlets and advertised its movie-themed products along with direct connections to *Alice*, *Maleficent*, and *Frozen*. All of these have been consumer product successes, and *A Wrinkle in Time* is likely to have the same appeal. All of these feed products not only into its Disney stores and Disney-themed sections in department stores, but also promote resort themes and thus drive interrelated revenue through cross-selling.

One of the downside problems for these fairy tale themes is that the stories are in the public domain. As such, other competitors are seeking to follow Disney's successful approach. For example, Time Warner Inc.'s Warner Bros. Studio will release *Pan*, which seems to be beating Disney to the punch on its former *Peter Pan* movie success. Likewise, Time Warner released *Jungle Book* in 2017 and has another script based on *Beauty and the Beast*. Comcast's Universal Pictures is developing *The Little Mermaid*. However, neither of these studios has the retail marketing power nor the franchising capability of Disney and its interrelated business and corporate skills. Although they are seeking to build these skills, they cannot duplicate Disney's corporate strategy and parent benefit because they are primarily focused on content and distribution.

Disney also owns ABC and its sports channel ESPN. Although ESPN subscriber numbers are down recently due to cord cutting, Disney has developed the ESPN Wide World of Sports Complex at The Walt Disney World Resort as a sports-related complex that attracts sports enthusiasts and teams to its Disney World Resort in Florida. The complex also attracts sports teams such as the Atlanta Braves during their training camp. It is planning to reduce the cord cutting by offering its own standalone streaming service, and ESPN is already an anchor tenant of emerging digital platforms, with carriage on Dish's Sling TV, DirecTV Now, PlayStation Vue, YouTube TV, and Hulu.

In summary, Disney has a current corporate parental advantage over its more focused movie and content producing and distribution competitors due to the power of its interrelated set of businesses, where the corporation facilitates customer market information sharing and skill transfer among the various business units.

Sources: E. Low, 2018, Forget ESPN, this part of Disney is 'underappreciated' by Wall Street, *Investors Business Daily*, February 7, 20; S. Mendelson, 2018, Box office: Marvel's 'Black Panther' tops $800M worldwide today, *Forbes*, www.forbes.com, March 2; A. Gara, 2017, Disney's 1995 deal for ABC made Buffett billions by marrying Mickey Mouse with SportsCenter, *Forbes*, www.forbes.com, May 23; C. Harrison, 2017, ESPN subscribers drop to 14-year low, putting pressure on Disney, *Bloomberg*, www.bloomberg.com, November 22; N. LaPorte, 2017, Marvel rules the universe, *Fast Company*, May, 60-68; B. Fritz, 2015, Disney recycles fairy tales, minus cartoons, *Wall Street Journal*, March 11, B1, B6; M. Gottfried, 2015, Walt Disney has built a better mousetrap, *Wall Street Journal*, Feb 5, C8; M. Lev-Ram, 2015, Empire of tech, *Fortune*, January 1, 48–58; C. Palmeri & A. Sakoui, 2015, Disney's princesses' give a little live action, *Bloomberg BusinessWeek*, March 9, 30–31; D. Leonard, 2014, The master of Marvel universe, *Bloomberg BusinessWeek*, April 7, 62–68; C. Palmeri & B. Faries, 2014, Big Mickey is watching, *Bloomberg BusinessWeek*, March 10, 22–23.

Case Discussion Questions

1. What corporate diversification strategy is being pursued by Disney? What evidence do you have that supports your position?
2. How does the corporate office create a parental advantage, which is difficult to duplicate by its more focused competitors?
3. What are synergies and economies of scope and how do they work at Disney to lower its overall costs?
4. Given the diversification approach that Disney uses, what are some things that they can do to deal further with the trend toward cord-cutting and competition from large streaming and content producers such at Netflix, Amazon, and other content producers?

NOTES

1. M. E. Porter, 1980, *Competitive Strategy*, New York: The Free Press, xvi.
2. T. B. Mackey, J. B. Barney, & J. P. Dotson, 2017. Corporate diversification and the value of individual firms: A Bayesian approach. *Strategic Management Journal*, 38: 322–341; J. P. O'Brien, P. David, T. Yoshikawa, & A. Delios, 2014, How capital structure influences diversification performance: A transaction cost perspective, *Strategic Management Journal*, 35: 1013–1031.
3. C. Mims, 2018, The limits of Amazon, *Wall Street Journal*, www.wsj.com, January 1.
4. G. Roumeliotis, 2017, General Electric faces long road to pruning assets. www.reuters.com, November 13.
5. M. E. Porter, 1987, From competitive advantage to corporate strategy, *Harvard Business Review*, 65(3): 43–59.
6. J. Oxley & G. Pandher, 2016, Equity-based incentives and collaboration in the modern multibusiness firm, *Strategic Management Journal*, 37: 1379–1394.
7. W. P. Wan, R. E. Hoskisson, J. C. Short, & D. W. Yiu, 2011, Resource-based theory and corporate diversification: Accomplishments and opportunities, *Journal of Management*, 37: 1335–1368.
8. S. Chang, B. Kogut, & J. Yang, 2016, Global diversification discount and its discontents: A bit of self-selection makes a world of difference. *Strategic Management Journal*, 37: 2254–2274; C. Custódio, 2014, Mergers and acquisitions accounting and the diversification discount, *Journal of Finance*, 69: 219–240.
9. Campbell, M. Goold, & M. Alexander, 1995, Corporate strategy: The question for parenting advantage, *Harvard Business Review*, 73(2): 120–132.
10. W. Su & E. W. K. Tsang, 2015, Product diversification and financial performance: The moderating role of secondary stakeholders, *Academy of Management Journal*, 58: 1128–1148.
11. S. Kunisch, 2017, Does headquarter structure follow corporate strategy? An empirical study of antecedents and consequences of changes in the size of corporate headquarters, *Journal of Business*

Economics & Management, 18: 390–411; A. M. Kleinbaum & T. E. Stuart, 2014, Inside the black box of the corporate staff: Social networks and the implementation of corporate strategy, *Strategic Management Journal*, 35: 24–47.

12. D. D. Bergh, 2001, Diversification strategy research at a crossroads: Established, emerging and anticipated paths. In M. A. Hitt, R. E. Freeman, & J. S. Harrison (eds.), *Handbook of Strategic Management*, Oxford, U.K.: Blackwell Publishers, 363–383.
13. S. F. Matusik & M. A. Fitza, 2012, Diversification in the venture capital industry: Leveraging knowledge under uncertainty, *Strategic Management Journal*, 33: 407–426.
14. Y. S. Getachew & P. W. Beamish, 2017, Foreign subsidiary exit from Africa: The effects of investment purpose diversity and orientation, *Global Strategy Journal*, 7: 58–82; J. R. Lecuona & M. Reitzig, 2014, Knowledge worth having in 'excess': The value of tacit and firm-specific human resource slack, *Strategic Management Journal*, 35: 954–973.
15. T. B. Mackey, J. B. Barney, & J. P. Dotson, Corporate diversification and the value of individual firms; D. H. Zhu & G. Chen, 2015, CEO narcissism and the impact of prior board experience on corporate strategy, *Administrative Science Quarterly*, 60: 31–65.
16. R. P. Rumelt, 1974, *Strategy, Structure, and Economic Performance*, Boston: Harvard Business School; L. Wrigley, 1970, *Divisional Autonomy and Diversification* (Ph.D. dissertation), Harvard Business School.
17. 2018, Tabasco Products, www.tabasco.com, February 3.
18. J. McLester, 2016, Fuel the Flavor, *Prepared Foods*, September, 50–51.
19. 2016, United Parcel Service 2016 Annual Report, www.ups.com, Accessed February 17.
20. R. Rumelt, 2011, *Good Strategy/Bad Strategy: The Difference and Why It Matters*, New York: Crown Business Publishing.
21. E. R. Feldman, R. Amit, & B. Villalonga, 2016, Corporate divestitures and family control. *Strategic Management Journal*, 37: 429–446; L. R. Gomez-Mejia, M. Makri, & M. L. Kintana, 2010, Diversification decisions in family controlled firms, *Journal of Management Studies*, 47: 223–252.
22. 2016, Caterpillar 2016 Annual report.
23. J. K. Mawdsley & D. Somaya, 2018, Demand-side strategy, relational advantage and partner-driven corporate scope: The case for client-led diversification, *Strategic Management Journal*, 39: 1834–1859; N. Hashai, 2015, Within-industry diversification and firm performance—an S-shaped hypothesis, *Strategic Management Journal*, 36: 1378–1400; T. Zahavi & D. Lavie, 2013. Intra-industry diversification and firm performance. *Strategic Management Journal*, 34: 978–998.
24. C. Vieregger, E. C., Larson, & P. C. Anderson, 2017, Top Management team structure and resource reallocation within the multibusiness firm, *Journal of Management*, 43: 2497–2525; J.-H. Lee & A. S. Gaur, 2013, Managing multibusiness firms: A comparison between Korean chaebols and diversified U.S. firms, *Journal of World Business*, 48: 443–454.
25. R. Messenbock, Y. Morieux, J. Backx, & D. Wunderlich, 2018, How complicated is your company? www.bcg.com, January 16.
26. R. Clough, N. Buhayar, & T. Black, 2018, Conglomerates don't work, *Bloomberg Businessweek*, February 5, 14–16.
27. D. Diakantonis, 2017, Newell sells Rubbermaid Storage Business, makes progress with portfolio restructuring. *Mergers & Acquisitions Report*, January 13, 1.
28. S. Terlep & D. Benoit, 2018, Starboard to launch proxy fight to replace entire Newell Brands board, *Wall Street Journal*, www.wsj.com, February 8.
29. P. J. Davies, 2018, Why private equity risks tripping on its own success, *Wall Street Journal*, www.wsj.com, February 13; R. E. Hoskisson, W, Shi, X. Yi, & J. Jing, 2013, The evolution and strategic positioning of private equity firms, *Academy of Management Perspectives*, 27: 22–38.
30. K. Ramaswamy, S. Purkayastha, & B. S. Petitt, 2017, How do institutional transitions impact the efficacy of related and unrelated diversification strategies used by business groups?. *Journal of Business Research*, 72: 1–13; T. M. Alessandri & A. Seth, 2014, The effects of managerial ownership on international and business diversification: Balancing incentives and risks, *Strategic Management Journal*, 35: 2064–2075.
31. S. Pathak, R. E. Hoskisson, & R. A. Johnson, 2014, Settling up in CEO compensation: The impact of divestiture intensity and contextual factors in refocusing firms, *Strategic Management Journal*, 35: 1124–1143.
32. H. Wang, S. Zhao, & G. Chen, 2017, Firm-specific knowledge assets and employment arrangements: Evidence from CEO compensation design and CEO dismissal, *Strategic Management Journal*, 38: 1875–1894.
33. J. Schmidt, R. Makadok, & T. Keil, 2016, Customer-specific synergies and market convergence, *Strategic Management Journal*, 37: 870–895.
34. F. Bauer & K. Matzler, 2014, Antecedents of M&A success: The role of strategic complementarity, cultural fit, and degree and speed of integration, *Strategic Management Journal*, 35: 269–291; M. E. Graebner, K. M. Eisenhardt, & P. T. Roundy, 2010, Success and failure of technology acquisitions: Lessons for buyers and sellers, *Academy of Management Perspectives*, 24: 73–92.
35. G. M. Kistruck, I. Qureshi, & P. W. Beamish, 2013, Geographic and product diversification in charitable organizations, *Journal of Management*, 39: 496–530.
36. A. V. Sakhartov, 2017, Economies of scope, resource relatedness, and the dynamics of corporate diversification, *Strategic Management Journal*, 38: 2168–2188; F. Neffke & M. Henning, 2013, Skill relatedness and firm diversification, *Strategic Management Journal*, 34: 297–316.
37. S. Karim & L Capron, 2016, Reconfiguration: Adding, redeploying, recombining and divesting resources and business units, *Strategic Management Journal*, 37: E54–E62.
38. F. Brahm, J. Tarzijan, & M. Singer, 2017, The Impact of frictions in routine execution on economies of scope. *Strategic Management Journal*, 38: 2121–2142.
39. M. Menz, S. Kunisch, & D. J. Collis, 2015, The corporate headquarters in the contemporary corporation: Advancing a multimarket firm perspective, *Academy of Management Annals*, 9: 633–714.
40. K. Grigoriou & F. T. Rothaermel, 2017, Organizing for knowledge generation: Internal knowledge networks and the contingent effect of external knowledge sourcing, *Strategic Management Journal*, 38: 395–414; A. Caimo & A. Lomi, 2015, Knowledge sharing in organizations: A Bayesian analysis of the role of reciprocity and formal structure. *Journal of Management*, 41: 665–691.
41. A. R. Menon & D. A. Yao, 2017, Elevating repositioning costs: Strategy dynamics and competitive interactions, *Strategic Management Journal*, 38:1953–1963.
42. C. Huston, 2013, The value of a good name, *Wall Street Journal*, July 18, B5; J. Thottam, 2008, Branson's flight plan, *Time*, April 28, 40.
43. 2018, Operations (see Mobility), Honda Motor Company, www.honda.com, Accessed February 22.
44. M. Matsuo, 2015, Human resource development programs for knowledge transfer and creation: The case of the Toyota Technical Development Corporation, *Journal of Knowledge Management*, 19: 1186–1203; N. D. Nguyen & A Aoyama, A. 2014, Achieving efficient technology transfer through a specific corporate culture facilitated by management practices, *Journal of High Technology Management Research*, 25: 108–122.
45. M. Naseer Butt, K. D. Antia, B. R. Murtha, & V. Kashyap, 2018, Clustering, knowledge sharing, and intrabrand competition: A multiyear analysis of an evolving franchise system, *Journal of Marketing*, 82: 74–92; U. Andersson, P. J. Buckley, & H. Dellestrand, 2015, In the right place at the right time!: The influence of knowledge governance tools on knowledge transfer and utilization in MNEs, *Global Strategy Journal*, 5: 27–47.
46. C. Vieregger, E. C. Larson, & P. C. Anderson, 2017, Top management team structure and resource reallocation within the multibusiness firm, *Journal of Management*, 43: 2497–2525; T. Hutzschenreuter & J.

Horstkotte, 2013, Performance effects of top management team demographic faultlines in the process of product diversification, *Strategic Management Journal*, 34: 704–726.

47. M. C. Becker & F. Zirpoli, 2017, How to avoid innovation competence loss in R&D outsourcing, *California Management Review*, 59(2): 24–44.
48. Y. Alhenawi & S. Krishnaswami, 2015, Long-term impact of merger synergies on performance and value, *Quarterly Review of Economics & Finance*, 58: 93–118.
49. S. Daneshkhu, L. Whipp, & J. Fontanella-Khan, 2017, The lean and mean approach of 3G Capital, *Financial Times*, www.ft.com, May 7.
50. S. Woo, 2018, Ericsson, humbled by Huawei, takes another $1.8 billion in charges, *Wall Street Journal*, www.wsj.com, January 17; A. Ewing, 2014, Ericsson looks for a home in the cloud, *Bloomberg Businessweek*, November 17, 36–37.
51. H. Kai-Yu & F. Vermeulen, 2014, The structure of competition: How competition between one's rivals influences imitative market entry, *Organization Science*, 25: 299–319; J. Gimeno & C. Y. Woo, 1999, Multimarket contact, economies of scope, and firm performance, *Academy of Management Journal*, 42: 239–259.
52. A. Gasparro & C. Lombardo, 2018, General Mills, maker of Cheerios, now wants to feed your dog, too, *Wall Street Journal*, www.wsj .com, February 23.
53. K. Grigoriou & F. T. Rothaermel, 2017, Organizing for knowledge generation: Internal knowledge networks and the contingent effect of external knowledge sourcing, *Strategic Management Journal*, 38: 395–414.
54. N. Argyres & R. Mostafa, 2016,. Knowledge inheritance, vertical integration, and entrant survival in the early U.S. auto industry, *Academy of Management Journal*, 59: 1474–1492.
55. B. Gulbrandsen, C. J. Lambe, & K. Sandvik, 2017, Firm boundaries and transaction costs: The complementary role of capabilities, *Journal of Business Research*, 78: 193–203.
56. R. Kapoor, 2013, Persistence of integration in the face of specialization: How firms navigated the winds of disintegration and shaped the architecture of the semiconductor industry, *Organization Science*, 24: 1195–1213; S. Novak & S. Stern, 2008, How does outsourcing affect performance dynamics? Evidence from the automobile industry, *Management Science*, 54: 1963–1979.
57. T. Wang & Y. Chen, 2018, Capability stretching in product innovation, *Journal of Management*, 44: 784–810; C. Weigelt & D. J. Miller, 2013, Implications of internal organization structure for firm boundaries *Strategic Management Journal*, 34: 1411–1434; E. Rawley, 2010, Diversification, coordination costs and organizational rigidity: Evidence from microdata, *Strategic Management Journal*, 31: 873–891.
58. F. Brahm & J. Tarziján, 2016, Toward an integrated theory of the firm: The interplay between internal organization and vertical integration, *Strategic Management Journal*, 37: 2481–2502.
59. W. L. Tate, L. M. Ellram, T. Schoenherr, & K. L. Petersen, 2014, Global competitive conditions driving the manufacturing location decision, *Business Horizons*, 57: 381–390.
60. 2018, Flex, www.flex.com, Accessed February 23.
61. Y. M. Zhou & X. Wan, 2017, Product variety and vertical integration, *Strategic Management Journal*, 38: 1134–1150.
62. T. Wang & Y. Chen, 2018, Capability stretching in product innovation, *Journal of Management*, 44: 784–810.
63. O. Schilke, H. Songcui, & C. E. Helfat, 2018, Quo vadis, dynamic capabilities? A content-analytic review of the current state of knowledge and recommendations for future research, *Academy of Management Annals*, 390–439; O. Schilke, 2014, On the contingent value of dynamic capabilities for competitive advantage: The nonlinear moderating effect of environmental dynamism, *Strategic Management Journal*, 35: 179–203.
64. H. Haddon, 2018, Amazon's grocery sales increased after it devoured Whole Foods, *Wall Street Journal*, www.wsj.com, January 14.
65. N. LaPorte, 2017, Marvel rules the universe, *Fast Company*, May, 60–68; M. Gottfried, 2015, Walt Disney has built a better mousetrap, *Wall Street Journal*, Feb 5, C8.
66. M. J. Benner & T. Zenger 2016, The lemons problem in markets for strategy, *Strategy Science*, 1: 71–89.
67. M. Flickinger & M. Zschoche, 2018, Corporate divestiture and performance: An institutional view. *Journal of Management & Governance*, 22: 111–131; C. Rudolph & B. Schwetzler, 2013, Conglomerates on the rise again? A cross-regional study on the impact of the 2008–2009 financial crisis on the diversification discount, *Journal of Corporate Finance*, 22: 153–165.
68. E. Vidal & W. Mitchell, 2018, Virtuous or vicious cycles? The role of divestitures as a complementary Penrose effect within resource-based theory, *Strategic Management Journal*, 39: 131–154; Porter, *Competitive Advantage*.
69. B.S. Vanneste, 2017, How much do industry, corporation, and business matter, really? A meta-analysis, *Strategy Science*, 2: 121–139.
70. T. C. Ambos & G. Muller-Stewens, 2017, Rethinking the role of the centre in the multidivisional firm: A retrospective, *Long Range Planning*, 50: 8–16; M. B. Lieberman G. Matvos & A. Seru, 2014, Resource allocation within firms and financial market dislocation: Evidence from diversified conglomerates, *Review of Financial Studies*, 27: 1143–1189.
71. M. B. Lieberman, G. K. Lee, & T. B. Folta, 2017, Entry, exit, and the potential for resource redeployment, *Strategic Management Journal*, 38: 526–544; B. N. Cline, J. L. Garner, & S. A. Yore, 2014, Exploitation of the internal capital market and the avoidance of outside monitoring, *Journal of Corporate Finance*, 25: 234–250.
72. D. A. Levinthal, 2017, Resource allocation and firm Boundaries, *Journal of Management*, 43: 2580–2587.
73. Wang, Zhao, Chen, Firm-specific knowledge assets and employment arrangements: Evidence from CEO compensation design and CEO dismissal; M. Sengul & J. Gimeno, 2013, Constrained delegation: Limiting subsidiaries' decision rights and resources in firms that compete across multiple industries, *Administrative Science Quarterly*, 58: 420–471; M. E. Raynor & J. L. Bower, 2001, Lead from the center: How to manage divisions dynamically, *Harvard Business Review*, 79(5): 92–100.
74. Z. Turner & W. Boston, 2017, Germany's Siemens to Slash 6,900 jobs amid shift to renewable energy, *Wall Street Journal*, www.wsj.com, November 17; G. Smith, 2015, Siemens' long-feared slimdown isn't as drastic as feared, *Fortune*, www.fortune.com.
75. B. Larrain & I. F. Urzúa 2016, Do business groups change with market development?, *Journal of Economics & Management Strategy*, 25: 750–784.
76. R. M. Holmes Jr., T. R. Holcomb, R. E. Hoskisson, H. Kim, & W. Wan, 2018, International strategy and business groups: A review and future research agenda, *Journal of World Business*, 53: 134–150; S. F. Karabag & C. Berggren, 2014, Antecedents of firm performance in emerging economies: Business groups, strategy, industry structure, and state support, *Journal of Business Research*, 67: 2212–2223.
77. S. Chiu, R. A. Johnson, R. E. Hoskisson, & S. Pathak, 2016, The impact of CEO successor origin on corporate divestiture scale and scope change, *Leadership Quarterly*, 27: 617–633.
78. P. J. Davies, 2018, Does private equity really beat the stock market? *Wall Street Journal*, www.wsj.com, February 13.
79. 2018, Our approach, Danaher, www.danaher.com, Accessed February 22; S. Ward, 2014, Danaher's best recent deal: Its shares, *Barron's*, June 9, 21.
80. J. Kim, C. Lee, & Y. Cho, 2016, Technological diversification, core-technology competence, and firm growth, *Research Policy*, 45: 113–124; R. Coff, 2003, Bidding wars over R&D-intensive firms: Knowledge, opportunism, and the market for corporate control, *Academy of Management Journal*, 46: 74–85.
81. M. Kaprielyan, 2016, Valuation consequences of the decision to divest in the globalized world, *Journal of Multinational Financial Management*, 36:

16–29; J. Xia, & S. Li, 2013, The divestiture of acquired subunits: A resource-dependence approach, *Strategic Management Journal*, 34: 131–148.

82. P. Pautler, 2015, A brief history of the FTC's Bureau of Economics: Reports, mergers, and information regulation. *Review of Industrial Organization*, 46: 59–94; M. Lubatkin, H. Merchant, & M. Srinivasan, 1997, Merger strategies and shareholder value during times of relaxed antitrust enforcement: The case of large mergers during the 1980s, *Journal of Management*, 23: 61–81.
83. R. M. Scherer & D. Ross, 1990, *Industrial Market Structure and Economic Performance*, Boston: Houghton Mifflin.
84. A. Shleifer & R. W. Vishny, 1994, Takeovers in the 1960s and 1980s: Evidence and implications. In R. P. Rumelt, D. E. Schendel, & D. J. Teece (eds.), *Fundamental Issues in Strategy*, Boston: Harvard Business School Press, 403–422.
85. S. Chatterjee, J. S. Harrison, & D. D. Bergh, 2003, Failed takeover attempts, corporate governance and refocusing, *Strategic Management Journal*, 24: 87–96; Lubatkin, Merchant, & Srinivasan, Merger strategies and shareholder value; D. J. Ravenscraft, & R. M. Scherer, 1987, *Mergers, Sell-Offs and Economic Efficiency*, Washington, DC: Brookings Institution, 22.
86. R. T. Miller, 2013, Inefficient results in the market for corporate control: Highest bidders, highest-value users, and socially optimal owners, *Journal of Corporation Law*, 39: 71–128; D. A. Zalewski, 2001, Corporate takeovers, fairness, and public policy, *Journal of Economic Issues*, 35: 431–437.
87. E. J. Lopez, 2001, New anti-merger theories: A critique, *Cato Journal*, 20: 359–378; 1998, The trustbusters' new tools, *The Economist*, May 2, 62–64.
88. L Silvia, 2018, Economics and antitrust enforcement: The last 25 years. *International Journal of the Economics of Business*, 25: 119–129; D. Bush & B. D. Gelb, 2012 Anti-trust enforcement: An inflection point? *Journal of Business Strategy*, 33: 15–21.
89. M. C. Jensen, 1986, Agency costs of free cash flow, corporate finance, and takeovers, *American Economic Review*, 76: 323–329.
90. S. Zheng, 2017, Can corporate diversification induce more tax avoidance? *Journal of Multinational Financial Management*, 41: 47–60; M. A. Hitt, J. S. Harrison, & R. D. Ireland, 2001, *Mergers and Acquisitions: A Guide to Creating Value for Stakeholders*, NY: Oxford University Press.
91. M. T. Brouwer, 2008, Horizontal mergers and efficiencies; theory and antitrust practice, *European Journal of Law and Economics*, 26: 11–26.
92. G. Matvos, A. Seru, & R. C. Silva, 2018, Financial market frictions and diversification, *Journal of Financial Economics*, 127: 21–50; J. M. Shaver, 2006, A paradox of synergy: Contagion and capacity effects in mergers and acquisitions, *Academy of Management Journal*, 31: 962–976.
93. A Back, 2018, Is Growth Worth the Risk at AIG? *Wall Street Journal*, www.wsj.com, January 22.
94. M. R. Rabier, 2017, Acquisition Motives and the Distribution of Acquisition Performance. *Strategic Management Journal*, 38: 2666–2681; C. Sundaramurthy, K. Pukthuanthong, & Y. Kor, 2014, Positive and negative synergies between the CEO's and the corporate board's human and social capital: A study of biotechnology firms, *Strategic Management Journal*, 35: 845–868.
95. S. Ali, S. H. Hashmi, & T. Mehmood, 2016, Corporate diversification and firm performance: An inverted U-shaped hypothesis, *International Journal of Organizational Leadership*, 5: 381–398; L. E. Palich, L. B. Cardinal, & C. C. Miller, 2000, Curvilinearity in the diversification-performance linkage: An examination of over three decades of research, *Strategic Management Journal*, 21: 155–174.
96. I. Galavotti, D. Depperu, & D. Cerrato, 2017, Acquirer-to-target relatedness and target country unfamiliarity in acquisitions. *Management Decision*, 55: 892–914; J. P. O'Brien, P. David, T. Yoshikawa, & A. Delios, 2014, How capital structure influences diversification performance: A transaction cost perspective, *Strategic Management Journal*, 35: 1013–1031; A. E. Bernardo & B. Chowdhry, 2002, Resources, real options, and corporate strategy, *Journal of Financial Economics*, 63: 211–234.
97. V. Kuppuswamy & B. Villalonga, 2016, Does diversification create value in the presence of external financing constraints? Evidence from the 2007–2009 financial crisis, *Management Science*, 62: 905–923.
98. K. Craninckx & N. Huyghebaert, 2015, Large shareholders and value creation through corporate acquisitions in Europe. The identity of the controlling shareholder matters, *European Management Journal*, 33: 116–131; T. B. Mackey & J. B. Barney, 2013, Incorporating opportunity costs in strategic management research: The value of diversification and payout as opportunities forgone when reinvesting in the firm, *Strategic Organization*, 11: 347–363.
99. James, D. 2016, Alcoa flexes RTI acquisition muscle with Airbus 3D parts deal, *Investors Business Daily*, www.investor.com, April 8.
100. L. Whiteman, 2016, Alcoa trades diversification for specialization, www.thestreet.com, June 29.
101. W. Sun & R. Govind, 2017, Product market diversification and market emphasis, *European Journal of Marketing*, 51: 1308–1331.
102. Sakhartov, Economies of scope, resource relatedness, and the dynamics of corporate diversification; I. Galavotti, D. Depperu, & D. Cerrato, 2017, Acquirer-to-target relatedness and target country unfamiliarity in acquisitions, *Management Decision*, 55: 892–914.
103. N. M. Kay & A. Diamantopoulos, 1987, Uncertainty and synergy: Towards a formal model of corporate strategy, *Managerial and Decision Economics*, 8: 121–130.
104. G. Ahuja & E. Novelli, 2017, Activity overinvestment: The case of R&D, *Journal of Management*, 43: 2456–2468; R. W. Coff, 1999, How buyers cope with uncertainty when acquiring firms in knowledge-intensive industries: Caveat emptor, *Organization Science*, 10: 144–161.
105. J. H. Kim, 2018, Asset specificity and firm value: Evidence from mergers, *Journal of Corporate Finance*, 48: 375–412; P. B. Carroll & C. Muim 2008, 7 ways to fail big, *Harvard Business Review*, 86(9): 82–91.
106. B. Orlando, A. Renzi, G. Sancetta, & N. Cucari, N. 2018, How does firm diversification impact innovation?, *Technology Analysis & Strategic Management*, 30: 391–404; S. K. Kim, J. D. Arthurs, A. Sahaym, & J. B. Cullen, 2013, Search behavior of the diversified firm: The impact of fit on innovation, *Strategic Management Journal*, 34: 999–1009; J. Kang, 2013, The relationship between corporate diversification and corporate social performance, *Strategic Management Journal*, 34: 94–109.
107. S. Pratap & B. Saha, 2018, Evolving efficacy of managerial capital, contesting managerial practices, and the process of strategic renewal, *Strategic Management Journal*, 39: 759–793; Lieberman, Lee, & Folta, Entry, exit, and the potential for resource redeployment, D. G. Sirmon, S. Gove, & M. A. Hitt, 2008, Resource management in dyadic competitive rivalry: The effects of resource bundling and deployment, *Academy of Management Journal*, 51: 919–935.
108. Vidal & Mitchell, Virtuous or vicious cycles? The role of divestitures as a complementary Penrose effect within resource-based theory; T. Nguyen, C. Cai, & P. McColgan, 2017, How firms manage their cash flows: An examination of diversification's effect, *Review of Quantitative Finance & Accounting*, 48: 701–724; G. Ertug & F. Castellucci, 2015, Who shall get more? How intangible assets and aspiration levels affect the valuation of resource providers, *Strategic Organization*, 13: 6–31.
109. S. K. White, 2017, Microsoft vs. Apple: Strategies change but the battle continues, *CIO*, www.cio.com, April 17; C. Zillman, 2014, Michael Dell: Long live the PC, *Fortune*, www.fortune.com, May 23.
110. L. Capron & J. Hull 1999, Redeployment of brands, sales forces, and general marketing management expertise following horizontal acquisitions: A resource-based view, *Journal of Marketing*, 63: 41–54.

111. R. Adams, 2017, Dyson's electric car dreams hinge on battery development. His not-so-secret weapon: Ann Marie Sastry, *Forbes*, www.forbes.com, September 26; C. Mims, 2015, In battery revolution, a clean leap forward, *Wall Street Journal*, March 16, B4.
112. 2018, Expertise, www.alvarezandmarsal.com, Accessed March 1; J. Chekler, 2015, Alvarez & Marsal to launch investment arm, *Wall Street Journal*, www.wsj.com, March 25.
113. Z. Chen, P. Kale, & R. E. Hoskisson, 2018, Geographic overlap and acquisition pairing, *Strategic Management Journal*, 39: 329–355; M. Rogan & O. Sorenson, 2014, Picking a (poor) partner: A relational perspective on acquisitions, *Administrative Science Quarterly*, 59: 301–329; C. Moschieri, 2011, The implementation and structuring of divestitures: The unit's perspective, *Strategic Management Journal*, 32: 368–401.
114. S. Wilmot, 2018, Why Gucci owner wants to kick off its Pumas, *Wall Street Journal*, www.wsj.com, January 12.
115. A. L. Steinbach, T. R. Holcomb, R. M. Holmes Jr., C. E. Devers, & A. A. Cannella, 2017, Top management team incentive heterogeneity, strategic investment behavior, and performance: A contingency theory of incentive alignment, *Strategic Management Journal*, 38: 1701–1720.
116. R. Martin, 2016, M&A: The one thing you need to get right, *Harvard Business Review*, 94(6): 42–48.
117. W. Shi, Y. Zhang, & R. E. Hoskisson, 2017, Ripple effects of CEO awards: Investigating the acquisition activities of superstar CEOs' competitors, *Strategic Management Journal*, 38: 2080–2102.
118. T. Greckhamer, 2016, CEO compensation in relation to worker compensation across countries: The configurational impact of country-level institutions, *Strategic Management Journal*, 37: 793–815; D. E. Black, S. S. Dikolli, & S. D. Dyreng, 2014, CEO pay-for-complexity and the risk of managerial diversion from multinational diversification, *Contemporary Accounting Research*, 31: 103–135.
119. E. Teti, A. Dell'Acqua, L. Etro, & M. Volpe, 2017, The impact of board independency, CEO duality and CEO fixed compensation on M&A performance, *Corporate Governance: The International Journal of Effective Board Performance*, 17: 947–971; R. Krause, K. A. Whitler, & M. Semadeni, 2014, Power to the principals! An experimental look at shareholder say-on-pay voting, *Academy of Management Journal*, 57: 94–115.
120. E. Xie, K. Reddy, & J. Liang, J. 2017, Country-specific determinants of cross-border mergers and acquisitions: A comprehensive review and future research directions, *Journal of World Business*, 52: 127–183; D. H. Zhu & G. Chen, 2015, CEO narcissism and the impact of prior board experience on corporate strategy, *Administrative Science Quarterly*, 60: 31–65.
121. M. D. Cain, S. B. McKeon, & S. D. Solomon, 2017, Do takeover laws matter? Evidence from five decades of hostile takeovers, *Journal of Financial Economics*, 124: 464–485; E. Y. Rhee & P. C. Fiss, 2014, Framing controversial actions: Regulatory focus, source credibility, and stock market reaction to poison pill adoption, *Academy of Management Journal*, 57: 1734–1758.
122. B. W. Benson, W. N. Davidson, T. R. Davidson, & H. Wang, 2015, Do busy directors and CEOs shirk their responsibilities? Evidence from mergers and acquisitions, *Quarterly Review of Economics & Finance*, 55: 1–19.
123. F. Rubino, P. Tenuta, & D. Cambrea, 2017, Board characteristics effects on performance in family and non-family business: A multi-theoretical approach, *Journal of Management & Governance*, 21, 623–658; C. E. Devers, G. Mcnamara, J. Haleblian, & M. E. Yoder, 2013, Do they walk the talk? Gauging acquiring CEO and director confidence in the value creation potential of announced acquisitions, *Academy of Management Journal*, 56: 1679–1702.
124. M. Cording, J. S. Harrison, R. E. Hoskisson, & K. Jonsen, 2014, Walking the talk: A multistakeholder exploration of organizational authenticity, employee productivity, and post-merger performance. *Academy of Management Perspectives*, 28: 38–56.
125. E. F. Fama, 1980, Agency problems and the theory of the firm, *Journal of Political Economy*, 88: 288–307.
126. M. Brauer, J. Mammen, & J. Luger, 2017, Sell-offs and firm performance: A matter of experience? *Journal of Management*, 43: 1359–1387.
127. R. E. Hoskisson, R. A. Johnson, L. Tihanyi, & R. E. White, 2005, Diversified business groups and corporate refocusing in emerging economies, *Journal of Management*, 31: 941–965.
128. S. L. Sun, M. W. Peng, & W. Tan 2017, Institutional relatedness behind product diversification and international diversification, *Asia Pacific Journal of Management*, 34: 339–366; R. Chittoor, P. Kale, & P. Puranam, 2015. Business groups in developing capital markets: Towards a complementarity perspective, *Strategic Management Journal*, 36: 1277–1296.

iStock.com/DNY59

7

Merger and Acquisition Strategies

Studying this chapter should provide you with the strategic management knowledge needed to:

7-1 Explain the popularity of merger and acquisition strategies in firms competing in the global economy.

7-2 Discuss reasons why firms use an acquisition strategy to achieve strategic competitiveness.

7-3 Describe seven problems that work against achieving success when using an acquisition strategy.

7-4 Name and describe the attributes of effective acquisitions.

7-5 Define the restructuring strategy and distinguish among its common forms.

7-6 Explain the short- and long-term outcomes of the different types of restructuring strategies.

iStock.com/DNY59

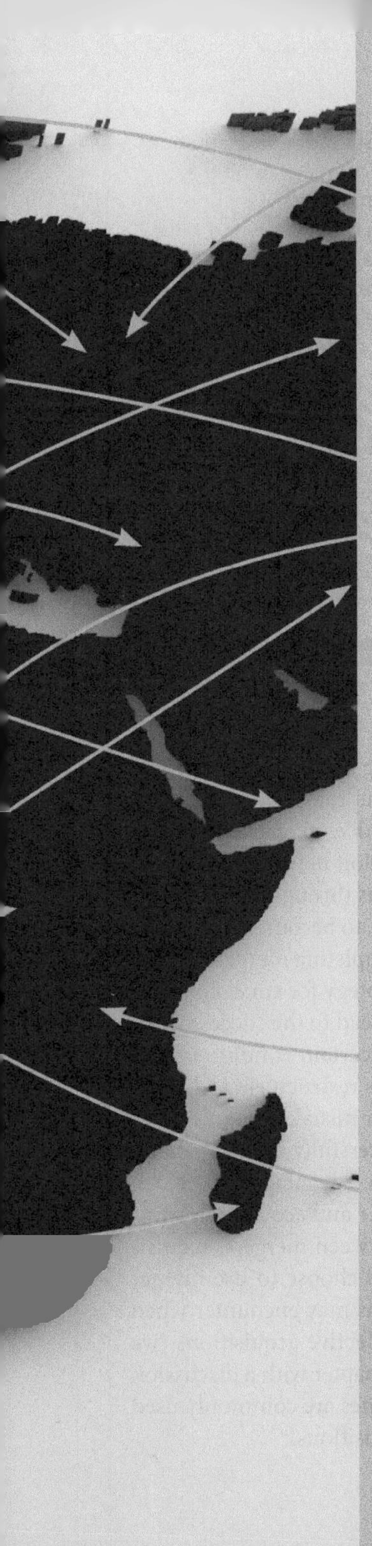

CISCO SYSTEMS: STRATEGIC ACQUISITIONS TO ADAPT TO A CHANGING MARKET

Cisco Systems has traditionally been in the business of building the infrastructure that allows the Internet to work. As the Internet evolved, however, Cisco's business was required to change with this evolution. As part of its advancement, Cisco Systems has used an acquisition strategy to build network products and extend its reach into new areas, both related and unrelated. In the beginning, digital connectivity was important through e-mail and Web browsing and searches. This evolved into a network economy facilitating e-commerce, digital supply chains, and digital collaboration. Subsequently, the digital interaction phase moved Cisco into developing infrastructure for social media, mobile and cloud computing, and digital video. The next stage seemed to be "the Internet of everything" connecting people, processes, and data. This will require the basic core in routing, switching, and services, as well as large data centers to facilitate visualization through cloud computing. Video and collaboration as well as basic architecture of the business will be transforming to become the base strategic business blocks. Furthermore, the need to have strong digital security will be paramount.

John Chambers, seen here at a January 2014 Consumer Electronics show in Las Vegas, led Cisco away from its basic business of network gear and routers, and into businesses that were farther from its core competencies.

This vision by John Chambers led to Cisco moving away from its basic business of network sales and routers and into businesses that were farther from its core competencies. Although in the IT sector about 90 percent of acquisitions fail, Chambers noted optimistically, "we know that a third of our acquisitions won't work." In fact, "Cisco bought cable set-top box market Scientific-Atlanta for nearly $7 billion in 2005 and sold it for just $600 million ten years later to French telco equipment firm Technicolor." It also bought Linksys, a producer of routers for home networks a consumer business, in 2003 for $500 million and sold it in 2013 to Belkin for less than it paid. Additionally, Cisco bought video maker Pure Digital for about $600 million in 2009, but the timing was poor because consumers were starting to buy iPhones and Android devices that also made it seamless to record and post videos. Cisco closed this business in 2011. While Chambers was optimistic, its acquisition failures increased when it moved away from its core business.

In 2015, Chuck Robbins became the CEO, and more recently has made acquisitions that are supportive of its core business and but also has sought to strengthen new strategic emphases. Cisco bought cloud software firm BroadSoft and AI monitoring manager AppDynamics in 2017. These as well as many other acquisitions support Cisco's move toward a cloud-centric company, which is not only focused on physical network upgrades such as routers but on software solutions that make the network more efficient (such as its Springpath and ContainerX acquisitions). Likewise, it has pursued software acquisitions that protect the movement to cloud computing from attacks. For example, it purchased CloudLock and Lancope, and more recently Skyport, "a physical server platform that provides an end-to-end set of security guarantees." The software strategy seeks to provide Cisco more recurring revenue relative to selling network hardware.

In the process of its rapid changes over time, Cisco has developed a distinct ability to integrate acquisitions. When Cisco contemplates an acquisition, along with financial due diligence to make sure that it is paying the right price, it develops a detailed plan for possible post-merger integration. It begins communicating early with stakeholders about integration plans and conducts rigorous post-mortems to identify ways "to make subsequent integrations more efficient and effective." Once a deal is completed, this allows the company to hit the ground running when the deal becomes public. During the integration process, it is important to know how far the integration should go. Sometimes integration is too deep, and value that was being sought in the acquisition is destroyed. Sometimes it may even pay to keep the business separate from Cisco's other operations to allow the business to function without integration until the necessary learning is complete. "Cisco learned the hard way that complex deals require you to know at a high level of detail how you're going to drive value."

Sources: S. M. Kerner, 2018, Cisco acquires Skyport as cyber-security investments continue, *Eweek*, www.eweek.com January 25; P. R. La Monica, 2018, Cisco is the market's comeback kid, *CNNMoney*, www.money.cnn.com, March 15; M. Cooney, 2017, Cisco closes AppDynamics deal, increases software weight, CIO, www.cio.com, March 23; Credit Suisse, 2017, Investors' soapbox: Cisco's 2017 acquisitions hit $4.3 billion, *Barrons*, www.barrons.com, May 3; R. King, 2017, Cisco steers further into cloud with $1.73 billion deal for BroadSoft, *Wall Street Journal*, www.wsj.com, October 24; F. Caviggioli, A. De Marco, G. Scellato, & E. Ughetto, 2017, Corporate strategies for technology acquisition: Evidence from patent transactions, *Management Decision*, 55(6): 1163–1181; A. Konrad, 2017, What Cisco's $3.7B splurge for AppDynamics means for tech's other unicorns, *Forbes*, www.forbes.com, January 26; C. Preimesberger, 2017, Cisco boards HCI train with Springpath acquisition, *Eweek*, www.eweek.com, August 21; S. Karim & L Capron, 2016, Reconfiguration: Adding, redeploying, recombining and divesting resources and business units, *Strategic Management Journal*, 37: E54–E62; L. Capron, 2013, Cisco's corporate development portfolio: A blend of building, borrowing, and buying, *Strategy & Leadership*, 41(2): 27–30.

We examined corporate-level strategy in Chapter 6, focusing on types and levels of product diversification strategies firms use to create value for stakeholders and competitive advantages for the firms. As noted in that chapter, diversification allows a firm to create value by productively using excess resources to exploit new opportunities.[1] In this chapter, we explore merger and acquisition strategies. Firms throughout the world use these strategies, often in concert with diversification strategies, to become more diversified. In other words, firms often become more diversified by completing mergers and/or acquisitions. As we discuss in this chapter, although a popular strategy for small corporations[2] as well as large ones, using these strategies does not always lead to the success firms seek.[3] And as described in the Opening Case focused on Cisco, certain conditions may necessitate that a firm engage in merger and acquisition as well as restructuring (divestiture) activity in order to move into new markets or correct poor or mistaken acquisitions.

A key objective of this chapter is to explain how firms can successfully use merger and acquisition strategies to create stakeholder value and competitive advantages.[4] To reach this objective, we first explain the continuing popularity of merger and acquisition strategies. As part of this explanation, we describe the differences between mergers, acquisitions, and takeovers. We next discuss specific reasons why firms choose to use merger and acquisition strategies and some of the problems organizations may encounter when doing so. We then describe the characteristics associated with effective acquisitions (we focus on acquisition strategies in the chapter) before closing the chapter with a discussion of different types of restructuring strategies. Restructuring strategies are commonly used to correct or deal with the results of ineffective mergers and acquisitions.

7-1 The Popularity of Merger and Acquisition Strategies

Merger and acquisition (M&A) strategies have been popular among U.S. firms for many years. Some believe that these strategies played a central role in the restructuring of U.S. businesses during the 1980s and 1990s and that they continue generating these types of benefits in the twenty-first century. In fact, 2018 is on track for a record with deals worth $4.8 trillion expected (possibly more than the record set in 2007).[5] As discussed in other parts of this chapter, mergers and acquisitions are also occurring with greater frequency in many regions of the world.[6] In the final analysis, firms use these strategies for the purpose of trying to create more value for all firm stakeholders.[7]

Although popular as a way of creating value and earning above-average returns, it is challenging to effectively implement merger and acquisition strategies. This is particularly true for the acquiring firms in that some research results indicate that shareholders of the acquired firms often earn above-average returns from acquisitions, while shareholders of the acquiring firms typically earn returns that are close to zero.[8] Moreover, in approximately two-thirds of all acquisitions, the acquiring firm's stock price falls immediately after the intended transaction is announced. This negative response reflects investors' skepticism about the likelihood that the acquirer will be able to achieve the synergies required to justify the premium to purchase the target firm.[9]

Discussed more fully later in the chapter, paying excessive premiums to acquire firms can negatively influence the results a firm achieves through an acquisition strategy. Determining the worth of a target firm is difficult; this difficulty increases the likelihood a firm will pay a premium to acquire a target. Premiums are paid when those leading an acquiring firm conclude that the target firm would be worth more under its ownership than it would be as part of any other ownership arrangement or if it were to remain as an independent company. Recently, for example, Cigna Corp., an insurance company, has sought to acquire Express Scripts, a pharmacy-benefit manager, or PBM. Such companies serve as middlemen that help negotiate discounts with drugmakers. The deal is worth $54 billion and Cigna is offering a 31 percent premium to Express Scripts' shareholders. On the day of the announcement, Express Scripts share price increased 9.3 percent, while Cigna share price decreased 12 percent. It remains to be seen whether this deal will be allowed, given that another deal between Cigna and Anthem (two insurance companies) was disapproved by regulators.[10] Overall though, paying a premium that exceeds the value of a target once integrated with the acquiring firm can result in negative outcomes.[11]

Jansos/Alamy Stock Photo

The Dell acquisition of EMC was completed in September of 2017.

7-1a Mergers, Acquisitions, and Takeovers: What Are the Differences?

A **merger** is a strategy through which two firms agree to integrate their operations on a relatively coequal basis. A proposed merger of equals between Dell Technologies, focused on PC and smaller companies, and EMC, focused on servers and storage serving large companies, was announced in 2016. Because of cloud computing both firms were in consolidation mode due to market shrinkage. Because they were able to cross-sell their products and both were under pressure, it allowed them to improve sales opportunities while consolidating.[12]

A **merger** is a strategy through which two firms agree to integrate their operations on a relatively coequal basis.

Even though the transaction between Dell and EMC was to be a merger of equals, evidence suggests that finalizing a proposal for firms to merge on an equal or a relatively equal basis is difficult. One thing that helped the integration process of this transaction was that the two firms had a preexisting technology sharing partnership. On a practical basis, deciding who will lead the merged firm, how to fuse what are often disparate corporate cultures, and how to reach an agreement about the value of each company prior to the merger are issues that commonly affect firms' efforts to merge on a coequal basis.

An **acquisition** is a strategy through which one firm buys a controlling, or 100 percent, interest in another firm with the intent of making the acquired firm a subsidiary business within its portfolio. After the acquisition is completed, the management of the acquired firm reports to the management of the acquiring firm.

Although most mergers that are completed are friendly in nature, acquisitions can be friendly or unfriendly. A **takeover** is a special type of acquisition where the target firm does not solicit the acquiring firm's bid; thus, takeovers are unfriendly acquisitions. As explained in Chapter 10, firms have developed defenses (mostly corporate governance devices) that can be used to prevent an unrequested and undesired takeover bid from being successful.[13]

Commonly, firms think of unsolicited bids as "hostile" takeovers. When such a bid is received, the takeover target may try to determine the highest amount the acquiring firm is willing to pay, even while simultaneously using defense mechanisms to prevent a takeover attempt from succeeding. Multiple exchanges may take place between a potential acquirer and its target before a resolution to the unsolicited bid is reached, and these exchanges can become quite complicated. The exchanges outlined in the Strategic Focus between Broadcom and Qualcomm, two semiconductor producers, initiated in the late 2017 demonstrate this complexity. Broadcom made an offer for Qualcomm while Qualcomm's price was depressed due to regulator challenges over Qualcomm's dominance as a critical cell phone component supplier. At the same time, Qualcomm was seeking to close a deal for NPX, a semiconductor producer focused on automobiles and self-driving cars, which led to Broadcom lowering is offer price.[14] Ultimately, Broadcom withdrew its offer because it was disallowed by regulators due to government intellectual property and security concerns.[15]

On a comparative basis, acquisitions are more common than mergers and takeovers. Accordingly, we focus the remainder of this chapter's discussion on acquisitions.

7-2 Reasons for Acquisitions

In this section, we discuss reasons why firms decide to acquire another company. As this discussion shows, there are many unique reasons that firms choose to use an acquisition strategy.[16]

An **acquisition** is a strategy through which one firm buys a controlling, or 100 percent, interest in another firm with the intent of making the acquired firm a subsidiary business within its portfolio.

A **takeover** is a special type of acquisition where the target firm does not solicit the acquiring firm's bid; thus, takeovers are unfriendly acquisitions.

7-2a Increased Market Power

Achieving greater market power is a primary reason for acquisitions.[17] Defined in Chapter 6, *market power* exists when a firm is able to sell its goods or services above competitive levels or when the costs of its primary or support activities are lower than those of its competitors. Market power usually is derived from the size of the firm, the quality of the resources it uses to compete, and its share of the market(s) in which it competes.[18] Therefore, most acquisitions that are designed to achieve greater market power entail buying a competitor, a supplier, a distributor, or a business in a highly related industry so that a core competence can be used to gain competitive advantage in the acquiring firm's primary market.

Strategic Focus

Broadcom's Failed Hostile Takeover Attempt of Qualcomm

In late 2017 Broadcom made a hostile takeover offer for Qualcomm, which has focused on cellphone chips and is investing in the next generation network, 5G technology. Through a series of five large acquisitions since 2013 including Freescale and Brocade Communications Systems, Broadcom, headquartered in Singapore, has become the fifth largest semiconductor firm in the world. With the Qualcomm acquisition, it would become third largest, after Intel and Samsung Electronics. The CEO, Hock Tan, has used a private equity approach (discussed later in the chapter) focused on acquisition integration and restructuring; this external approach reduced Broadcom's focus on internal R&D and, instead, focused on making more acquisitions to build the business. Qualcomm itself has purchased additional chipmakers including a potential acquisition of NXP, a Netherlands-based producer, for $47 billion. The NXP deal is focused on producing semiconductors for the automotive industry, particularly self-driving cars, which is a promising area for chipmakers. Qualcomm later withdrew its offer for NXP because it was unlikely to be approved by Chinese regulators in a timely fashion.

One reason that Broadcom took an opportunity to make a hostile offer for Qualcomm was that Qualcomm's stock price was discounted due to regulatory challenges. Qualcomm has traditionally sought to make significant revenues through patent licensing. This approach has been problematic for the firm in that many countries have sought substantial fines for alleged anti-competitive behavior. These include regulatory bodies in China, South Korea, and Taiwan. Additionally, Apple has sued Qualcomm over its licensing terms and has started to withhold royalty payments, depriving Qualcomm of billions in sales. Accordingly, with Qualcomm's lower stock market prices due to regulatory and patent infringement uncertainties, Broadcom was able to offer a relatively significant premium to Qualcomm shareholders.

Although Qualcomm rejected the initial $130 billion offer, it looked as if a Qualcomm shareholder vote would favor Broadcom's position and elect Broadcom's slate as Qualcomm board members. Broadcom, however, withdrew its offer when the Committee for Foreign Investment in the United States (CFIUS) chose not to support the deal. CFIUS is an interagency committee working under the jurisdiction of the U.S. Treasury Department and operates under strict confidentially requirements. Qualcomm does some classified research work for the U.S. government. Additionally, an apparent concern of this committee was that Qualcomm will help to set the standard for next generation cellular network, 5G Internet. The 5G network update will make possible what is labelled "The Internet of Things," which would support advances such as autonomous cars and home appliances that run over networks. The two leaders in 5G are Qualcomm and Chinese firm Huawei, a giant network and telecom company. Because Broadcom does significant business with Huawei, CFIUS members were worried that once in control of Qualcomm, Broadcom would strike a deal with Huawei, which would make U.S. 5G network leadership and other technological intellectual property available to the Chinese.

It is interesting to note that Broadcom had promised to move its headquarters to the United States; had it completed this move prior to the offer for Qualcomm, it would no longer be under CFIUS review. It's also interesting to note that even though Broadcom CEO Tan is a U.S. citizen, Broadcom has not invested as much on lobbying as Qualcomm. In fact, Qualcomm's expenditures were over 100 times those of Broadcom. Though some have the opinion that Qualcomm has more sway in Washington, D.C. than does Broadcom, Broadcom has significant U.S. assets.

Thierry Monasse/Polaris Images/Brussels/Belgium/Newscom

In January of 2018, the European Union fined Qualcomm $1.2 billion for allegedly abusing its dominant market position to squeeze out competitors.

In summary, hostile takeovers can be very complex and involve government bodies for approval and may even involve security concerns between governments. For instance, Qualcomm's NXP deal also needs to be approved by Chinese authorities and may have been rejected in retaliation for the CFIUS rejection of the Qualcomm hostile takeover by Broadcom. Although the deal with NXP was ultimately nixed by both Qualcomm and NXP, company officials justified dropping the deal based on regulatory approval delays by the Chinese.

Sources: J. Burt, 2018, Qualcomm offered to buy NXP complicates Broadcom's hostile takeover bid, *eWeek*, www.eweek.com, February 22; T. Greenwald, 2018, Qualcomm warms to Broadcom bid, but price is sticking point, *Wall Street Journal*, www.wsj.com, February 26; T. Greenwald & A. Hufford, 2018, Broadcom cuts offer for Qualcomm over new NXP deal price, *Wall Street Journal*, www.wsj.com, February 22; I. King, B. Brody, & S. Mohsin, 2018, Qualcomm outspent Broadcom about 100 to 1 in lobbying, *Bloomberg*, www.bloomberg.com, March 14; A. Lashinsky, 2018, The merits of blocking Broadcom's acquisition of Qualcomm, *Fortune*, www.fortune.com, March 15; L. Qi, 2018, China to Qualcomm: Don't blame us for failed NXP deal, *Wall Street Journal*, www.wsj.com, July 27; Economist, 2017, Welcome to the wild; Broadcom's $130bn Qualcomm bid highlights a ruthless chips industry, *Economist*, www.economist.com, November 9; P. Seitz, 2017, Qualcomm rejects Broadcom's buyout offer, says it's undervalued, *Investors Business Daily*, www.investor.com, November 13.

Next, we discuss how firms use horizontal, vertical, and related types of acquisitions to increase their market power. Active acquirers simultaneously pursue two or all three types of acquisitions in order to do this. Evidence suggests, for example, that Amazon has been expanding the scale and scope of its operation (see the Opening Case for Chapter 6), both horizontally (new products to sell online) and vertically (its moving into shipping).[19] These three types of acquisitions are subject to regulatory review by various governmental entities. Sometimes these reviews bring about the dissolution of proposed transactions as illustrated in the Strategic Focus on the Broadcom takeover attempt of Qualcomm. For example, AT&T is attempting to acquire Time Warner (a media cable and movie content producer) and have gone to court after the U.S. Department of Justice rejected its proposal.[20]

Horizontal Acquisitions

The acquisition of a company competing in the same industry as the acquiring firm is a *horizontal acquisition*. Horizontal acquisitions increase a firm's market power by exploiting cost-based and revenue-based synergies.[21] Horizontal acquisitions occur frequently in the semiconductor industry as illustrated in the Strategic Focus. Both Broadcom and Qualcomm have increased their scale and market power through a series of acquisitions. Likewise, industry leader Intel has improved its scale and product differentiation with horizontal acquisitions. It acquired Mobileye in 2107 for $15.3 billion and Altera for $16.7 billion in 2015. The Mobileye acquisition puts Intel in a stronger position "in the booming market for autonomous-vehicle technology."[22] Research suggests that horizontal acquisitions result in higher performance when the firms have similar characteristics,[23] such as strategy, managerial styles, and resource allocation patterns. Similarities in these characteristics, as well as previous alliance management experience as in the merger between Dell and EMC noted earlier, support efforts to integrate the acquiring and the acquired firm. Horizontal acquisitions are often most effective when the acquiring firm effectively integrates the acquired firm's assets with its own, but only after evaluating and divesting excess capacity and assets that do not complement the newly combined firm's core competencies.[24]

Vertical Acquisitions

A *vertical acquisition* refers to a firm acquiring a supplier or distributor of one or more of its products. Through a vertical acquisition, the newly formed firm controls additional parts of the value chain (see Chapter 3),[25] which is how vertical acquisitions lead to increased market power.

Through vertical integration, a firm has an opportunity to appropriate value being generated in a part of the value chain in which it does not currently compete and to better control its own destiny in terms of costs and access. These factors influenced the attempted acquisition of Aetna, a large health insurance company, by CVS, the largest

U.S. drug store chain. "Already, CVS has 1,100 MinuteClinics in its pharmacies, where nurse practitioners and physician assistants provide routine care such as flu shots or wrapping sprained ankles. It's also trying out hearing and vision centers in a handful of locations. If the merger goes through, CVS plans to build mini-health centers in many more of its 9,700 stores, turning them into places where Aetna members—and customers of rival insurers—get convenient low-level care for ailments and chronic diseases."[26] This acquisition has "the potential to help bend the cost curve, while making health care more convenient and effective,"[27] but also give CVS and Aetna more market power, so it will be interesting to see if the Justice Department approves the transaction.[28]

Related Acquisitions

Acquiring a firm in a highly related industry is called a *related acquisition*. Through a related acquisition, firms seek to create value through the synergy that can be generated by integrating some of their resources and capabilities.

As illustrated in the Opening Case, Cisco Systems designs, manufacturers, and sells networking equipment. Over time though, the firm has engaged in related acquisitions, primarily as a foundation for being able to compete aggressively in other product markets. For example, as software becomes a more integral aspect of all networking products, the firm is acquiring software companies that support and protect cloud computing, its newest emphasis under CEO Chuck Robbins. As noted, Cisco bought cloud software firm BroadSoft and AI monitoring manager AppDynamics in 2017. Cisco also sought to make networks more efficient through its acquisitions of Springpath and ContainerX, both software companies.[29]

7-2b Overcoming Entry Barriers

Barriers to entry (introduced in Chapter 2) are factors associated with a market, or the firms currently operating in it, that increase the expense and difficulty new firms encounter when trying to enter that particular market. For example, well-established competitors may have economies of scale in manufacturing or servicing their products. In addition, enduring relationships with customers often create loyalties and customer information that are difficult for new entrants to overcome.[30] When facing differentiated products, new entrants typically must spend considerable resources to advertise their products and may find it necessary to sell below competitors' prices to entice new customers.

Facing the entry barriers that economies of scale and differentiated products create, a new entrant may find that acquiring an established company is more effective than entering the market as a competitor offering a product that is unfamiliar to current buyers. In fact, the higher the barriers to market entry, the greater the probability that a firm will acquire an existing firm to overcome them. For example, China's agriculture technology is antiquated and yet its government has to feed 19 percent of the world's population with 7 percent of the arable land. Because patents and intellectual property rights protect much of agriculture technology, there are strong barriers to entry. Additionally, recent mergers between Dow and DuPont (now DowDuPont) and a potential merger between Bayer and Monsanto, a large genetically modified seed producer, have spurred China to act. In 2017, as depicted in the Strategic Focus, Chinese state-owned enterprise (SOE) ChemChina succeeded in merging with Syngenta, the third largest agriculture technology firm by sales, headquartered in Switzerland. This deal is by far the largest acquisition by a Chinese company outside of China.[31]

As this discussion suggests, a key advantage of using an acquisition strategy to overcome entry barriers is that the acquiring firm gains immediate access to a market that is attractive to it. This can be especially important for firms seeking to enter global markets, as was the case for ChemChina. We further discuss cross-border acquisitions next.

Cross-Border Acquisitions

Acquisitions made between companies with headquarters in different countries are called *cross-border acquisitions*.[32] Historically, North American and European companies were the most active acquirers of companies outside their domestic markets. However, today's global competitive landscape is one in which firms from economies throughout the world are engaging in cross-border acquisitions, and for a host of reasons. In the Strategic Focus, we discuss different cross-border acquisitions that are being pursued or have been completed recently and are products of different strategic rationales even though they are in closely related sectors.

Firms should recognize that cross-border acquisitions such as the ones discussed in the Strategic Focus are not risk-free, even when a strong strategic rationale undergirds the completed transactions. China, for example, is a country with political and legal obstacles that increase acquisition risk.[33] Being able to conduct an effective due-diligence process when acquiring a company in China can be difficult, because the target firm's financial data and corporate governance practices may lack complete transparency. However, research shows that foreign acquisitions by Chinese multinational firms into more developed countries lead to better governance, especially for Chinese SOEs.[34] However, because Chinese acquisitions of foreign firms have not had a stellar record, Chinese regulators hesitate to approve deals, especially if the acquiring firm did not have expertise in managing the potential target business. For instance, Anbang Insurance attempted to take over Starwood Hotels & Resorts of the United States for $14 billion but the deal was blocked by Chinese authorities.[35] Thus, firms must carefully study the risks as well as the potential benefits when contemplating cross-border acquisitions.

7-2c Cost of New Product Development and Increased Speed to Market

Developing new products internally and successfully introducing them into the marketplace often requires significant investment of a firm's resources, including time, making it difficult to quickly earn a profitable return.[36] Because an estimated 88 percent of innovations fail to achieve adequate returns, concerns exist in firms about their ability to achieve adequate returns from the capital they invest to develop and commercialize new products. These types of outcomes may lead managers to perceive internal product development as a high-risk activity.[37]

An acquisition strategy is another course of action a firm can take to gain access to new products and to current products that are new to it. Compared with internal product development processes, acquisitions provide more predictable returns as well as faster market entry. Returns are more predictable because the performance of the acquired firm's products can be assessed prior to completing the acquisition.[38]

Celanese, a chemical-based materials firm, seeks to improve its engineered materials business in the United States through both acquisitions and internal innovation as it develops a portfolio of materials and resins to more fully meet emerging needs of its customers. It has found that in some changing areas it can more quickly gain access to products that are related to its own and that target the changing needs of historic customers. For example, the company was interested in entering into the emerging autonomous vehicle market. It purchased Nilit Plastics, a deal that increased the company's nylon compounding capability, so Celanese can now design and provide the plastics used to make the housings for the large number of sensors and cameras that autonomous vehicles use.[39]

Strategic Focus

Cross-Border Mega Mergers in the Agricultural Chemical and Technology Sectors

The agricultural chemical and technology sectors are in flux because of three mega-acquisitions, which have potential to affect, for example, approximately 50 percent of the commercial seed market. The first merger between Dow Chemical and DuPont Corporation was proposed in early 2015, but was not consummated until 2017. In 2016, Monsanto tried to buy the third largest agricultural technology company, Syngenta; however, the Monsanto acquisition of Syngenta was blocked based on anti-trust concerns. Subsequently, ChemChina offered to pay the price that Syngenta was asking and the deal ultimately was consummated because the regulators found that ChemChina did not have the agricultural technology market power that both Monsanto and Syngenta would have had together. ChemChina, a Chinese SOE, was allowed to consummate the merger and pay the premium necessary, due to government concern for food security in China with its large population base (19 percent of the world) versus its small percentage of arable land (7 percent of the world). Over the years, China has experienced significant famines, including one in the 1950s and 1960s in which an estimated 34 million people starved to death. The Chinese concern for food security drove Chinese leaders to pursue policies that led to storing of agricultural foodstuffs as well as to increasing its ability to be more globally competitive in agricultural chemistry, technology, and data-driven farming for efficiency purposes.

There are some complications to the deal, in that ChemChina will have to focus on developing genetically modified organism (GMO) seeds. At present, China does not allow GMO agricultural products to enter the country, thanks in part to the many food production and contamination scandals in China over the years. But this likely will have to change with this large-scale acquisition. The new Chinese strategy for food security includes controlling its global supply chain from beginning to end, and since the chain obviously begins with seeds, the focus now on efficiency requires GMO varieties. So, this will create a dilemma that may require compromise on many sides.

Interestingly, the acquisition of Syngenta would leave Europe with significantly less power among global food technology producers. As such Bayer, a large German chemical firm with significant food technology assets, put forth an offer to buy U.S.-based Monsanto. This transaction has largely been approved by most regulatory bodies around the world because it was not anti-competitive though it was a very large transaction. Although Bayer had a small agricultural seed business, it has a global agricultural chemicals division. On the other hand, Monsanto is the world's leader in agricultural seeds and genetics, but was quite small in agricultural chemicals. Thus the combination will make Bayer strong in both types of technology. Additionally, Monsanto has a huge big-data advantage; Monsanto has become the leading provider of analytics for growers and is at the forefront of digital farming. This business provides analysis as to the appropriate combination of seed types, fertilizers, and chemicals for improving farm efficiency around the world.

Jonathan Weiss/Alamy Stock Photo

Mycogen Seeds is a subsidiary of Dow AgroSciences.

The Dow-DuPont merger was completed in 2017 after a complex process of obtaining regulatory approval in most of the large countries in the world. In part, the merger won approval by suggesting that after integration it would spin off into three separate firms: material science, specialty chemical products, and seeds and agricultural chemicals (more detail on this restructuring strategy will be addressed later in the chapter).

In summary, these three deals leave one large company in China, Europe, and the United States, ChemChina(Syngenta), Bayer(Monsanto), and DowDuPont (future spin-off), respectively. These large cross-border acquisitions will largely determine the future of the agricultural chemical and seed businesses, as well as technological efficiency through big-data analytics in farming.

Sources: B. Gomes-Casseres, 2018, What the big mergers in 2017 tell us about 2018, *Harvard Business Review*, www.hbr.org, January 2; F. Y. Chee, 2018, Bayer wins EU approval for $62.5 billion Monsanto buy, *Reuters*, www.reuters.com, March 21; C. Jing, 2018, DowDuPont names three planned spin offs, *Chemical Week*, February 26, 10; Z. Turner & N. Drozdiak, 2018, Bayer to sell more assets to win approval for Monsanto deal, *Wall Street Journal*, www.wsj.com, February 28; S. Chatterjee & C. Alzhu, 2017, As Syngenta deal closes, ChemChina and Sinochem press $120 billion deal, *Reuters*, www.reuters.com, May 23; G. Colvin, 2017, Inside China's $43 billion bid for food security, *Fortune*, www.fortune.com, April 21; B. Tita & J. S. Lublin, 2016, Breen's Tyco experience will guide him in dismantling DowDuPont, *Wall Street Journal*, www.wsj.com, January 6.

7-2d Lower Risk Compared to Developing New Products

The outcomes of an acquisition can be estimated more easily and accurately than the outcomes of an internal product development process; as such, managers may view acquisitions as less risky.[40] However, firms should be cautious: even though research suggests acquisition strategies are a common means of avoiding risky internal ventures (and therefore risky R&D investments), acquisitions may also become a substitute for internal innovation.

Over time, being dependent on others for innovation leaves a firm vulnerable and less capable of mastering its own destiny when it comes to using innovation as a driver of wealth creation. Thus, a clear strategic rationale, such as the ones influencing the cross-border acquisitions described in the Strategic Focus above, should drive each acquisition a firm chooses to complete. If a firm is being acquired to gain access to a specific innovation or to a target's innovation-related capabilities, the acquiring firm should be able to specify how the innovation is or the innovation-based skills are to be integrated with its operations for strategic purposes.[41]

7-2e Increased Diversification

Acquisitions are also used to diversify firms. Based on experience and the insights resulting from it, firms typically find it easier to develop and introduce new products in markets they are currently serving. In contrast, it is difficult for companies to develop products that differ from their current lines for markets in which they lack experience. Thus, it is relatively uncommon for a firm to develop new products internally to diversify its product lines.[42]

Acquisition strategies can be used to support the use of both related and unrelated diversification strategies. As we mentioned in the Opening Case, Cisco became excessively diversified and sought to refocus by divestitures and further acquisitions focused on software, which was more complementary to its basic network equipment business.[43]

Samsung Group, a huge conglomerate, uses an unrelated diversification strategy to further diversify its operations. Headquartered in Suwon, South Korea, Samsung's portfolio recently included almost 70 companies competing in unrelated areas such as electronics, construction, life insurance, and fashion. It is South Korea's largest chaebol, or business conglomerate. Samsung Electronics, one of the firm's three core units, features three businesses that are well known to consumers throughout the world—mobile devices such as smartphones, consumer electronics (televisions and home appliances), and electronics components such as semiconductors and display panels. In 2017, Samsung bought Harman, focused on automotive and audio electronics, which gave it "more confidence" to pursue other deals in the future. In particular, it signaled that it was interested in expansion "in automotive markets, digital health and industrial automation."[44]

David Paul Morris/Bloomberg/Getty Images

Dinesh Paliwal, President and CEO of Harman, announces the autonomous driving platforms he's developing at the Consumer Electronics Show in Las Vegas, January 8, 2018.

Firms using acquisition strategies should be aware that, in general, the more related the acquired firm is to the acquiring firm, the greater is the probability that the acquisition will be successful. Thus, horizontal acquisitions and related acquisitions tend to contribute more to the firm's strategic competitiveness than do acquisitions of companies operating in product markets that differ from those in which the acquiring firm competes. Nonetheless, the unrelated diversification strategy, such as the one Samsung is implementing, can also lead to success when used in ways that enhance firm value.

7-2f Reshaping the Firm's Competitive Scope

As discussed in Chapter 2, the intensity of competitive rivalry is an industry characteristic that affects a firm's profitability. To reduce the negative effect of an intense rivalry on financial performance, firms may use acquisitions to lessen their product and/or market dependencies.[45] Reducing a company's dependence on specific products or markets shapes the firm's competitive scope. For example, Dean Foods was built through the acquisition of many smaller dairies, and that effort has left its supply chain fragmented and decentralized. As firms like Walmart move into private brand label fluid milk, Dean Foods has faced significant pressure to deal with the necessary economies of scale. As such, it is seeking to pursue diversification and acquisitions "into such categories as ice cream, cottage cheese, sour cream and juices [that] show promise, but are still in the early days of development and execution."[46]

7-2g Learning and Developing New Capabilities

Firms sometimes complete acquisitions to gain access to capabilities they lack. Research shows that firms can broaden their knowledge base and reduce inertia through acquisitions[47] and that they increase the potential of their capabilities when they acquire diverse talent through cross-border acquisitions.[48] Of course, firms are better able to learn these acquired capabilities if they share some similar properties with the firm's current capabilities. Thus, firms should seek to acquire companies with different but related and complementary capabilities as a path to building their own knowledge base.

As illustrated in the Opening Case, Cisco has used acquisitions to build new capabilities as its market has changed, most recently it has made software acquisitions in its pursuit of becoming more cloud computing-centric.[49] Likewise, ChemChina is seeking to increase its capabilities in agriculture genetics and technology through its acquisition of Syngenta as described in the Strategic Focus.[50]

7-3 Problems in Achieving Acquisition Success

Effective and appropriate use of the acquisition strategies discussed in this chapter can facilitate firms' efforts to earn above-average returns. However, even when pursued for value-creating reasons, acquisition strategies are not problem-free.[51] Reasons for the use of acquisition strategies and potential problems with such strategies are shown in Figure 7.1.

Research suggests that perhaps 20 percent of mergers and acquisitions are successful, approximately 60 percent produce disappointing results, and the remaining 20 percent are clear failures; evidence suggests that technology acquisitions have even higher failure rates.[52] In general, though, companies appear to be increasing their ability to achieve success with acquisition strategies. Later, we discuss a number of attributes

Figure 7.1 Reasons for Acquisitions and Problems in Achieving Success

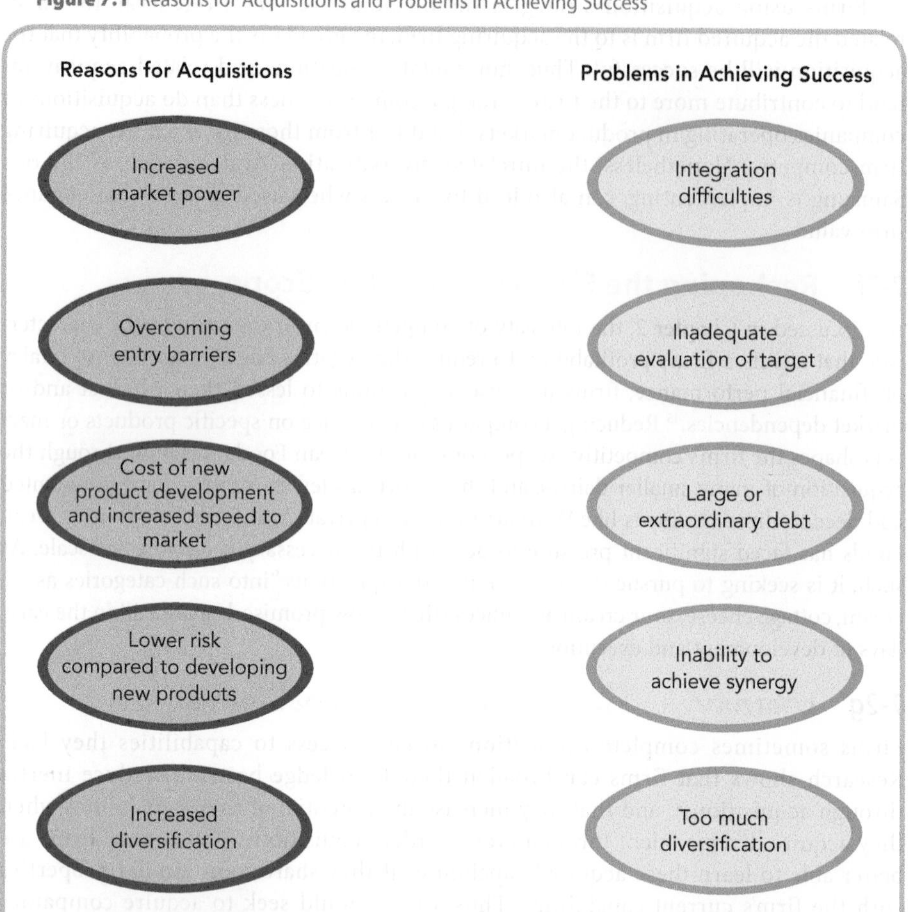

that are associated with successful acquisitions (the attributes appear in Table 7.1 on page 225). In spite of this increasing success, firms using acquisition strategies should be aware of problems that tend to affect acquisition success when problems do surface. We show these problems in Figure 7.1 and discuss them next.

7-3a Integration Difficulties

The importance of a successful integration should not be underestimated.[53] Indeed, some believe that the integration process is the strongest determinant of whether either a merger or an acquisition will be successful. This belief highlights the fact that post-acquisition integration is often a complex set of organizational processes that is difficult and challenging. The processes tend to generate uncertainty and often resistance because of cultural clashes and organizational politics.[54] How people are treated during the integration process relative to perceptions of fairness is an important issue to consider when trying to integrate the acquiring and acquired firms. Among the challenges associated with integration processes are the need to:

- meld two or more unique corporate cultures
- link different financial and information control systems
- build effective working relationships (particularly when management styles differ)
- determine the leadership structure and those who will fill it for the integrated firm.[55]

7-3b Inadequate Evaluation of Target

Due diligence is a process through which a potential acquirer evaluates a target firm for acquisition. In an effective due-diligence process, hundreds of items are examined in areas as diverse as the financing for the intended transaction, differences in cultures between the acquiring and target firm, tax consequences of the transaction, and actions that would be necessary to successfully meld the two workforces. Research finds that when there is geographic overlap in the operational activities of the acquiring and target firms, informal due diligence between the deal firms is facilitated.[56] Due diligence is commonly performed by investment bankers such as Deutsche Bank, Goldman Sachs, and Morgan Stanley, as well as accountants, lawyers, and management consultants specializing in that activity, although firms actively pursuing acquisitions may form their own internal due-diligence team. Even in instances when a company does its own due diligence, companies almost always work with intermediaries such as large investment banks to facilitate their due-diligence efforts. Interestingly, research suggests that acquisition performance increases with the number of due-diligence–related transactions facilitated by an investment bank, but decreases when the relationship with a particular investment bank becomes exclusive.[57] Thus, using investment banks as part of the due-diligence process a firm completes to examine a proposed merger or acquisition is a complex matter requiring careful managerial attention.

Although due diligence often focuses on evaluating the accuracy of the financial position and accounting standards used (a financial audit), due diligence also needs to examine the quality of the strategic fit and the ability of the acquiring firm to effectively integrate the target to realize the potential gains from the deal.[58] A comprehensive due-diligence process reduces the likelihood that an acquiring firm will have the experience Teva did as a result of acquiring Actavis Generics from Allergan for $40.5 billion. The deal saddled Teva with significant debt at the same time generic drugs were under a price squeeze due to increased competition from faster regulator generic drug approval.[59] Additionally, Teva acquired a smaller Mexican generic producer, Rimsa, which lost significant value after finding previously undiscovered "fraud" once the deal closed.[60]

Commonly, firms are willing to pay a premium to acquire a company they believe will increase their ability to earn above-average returns. Determining the precise premium that is appropriate to pay is challenging. While the acquirer can estimate the value of anticipated synergies, it is just that—an estimate. Only after working to integrate the firms and then engaging in competitive actions in the marketplace will the real value of synergies be known.

When firms overestimate the value of synergies or the value of future growth potential associated with an acquisition, the premium they pay may prove to be too large. Excessive premiums can have dilutive effects on the newly formed firm's short- and long-term earning potential. In November 2011, for example, Gilead Sciences paid an 89 percent premium to acquire Pharmasset.[61] At first glance, this premium seems excessive. However, since the acquisition was completed, Gilead's stock price has soared. Moreover, the firm's hepatitis C drug franchise, to which Gilead obtained access by acquiring Pharmasset, met with huge success and created a large pile of cash. In this instance then, it seems that the premium Gilead paid to acquire Pharmasset was not excessive. Gilead recently made another acquisition with its available capital, Kite Pharma. Although it paid a 29 percent premium this time, Kites stock price had risen 200 percent over the eight months before making the deal. The acquisition provided Gilead with assets that offer highly specialized cell therapies for late-stage cancer victims, diversifying it away from its mature hepatitis C business. It remains to be seen whether this acquisitions will be a similar blockbuster.[62] The managerial challenge is to effectively examine each acquisition target in order to determine the amount of premium that is appropriate for the acquiring firm to pay.

7-3c Large or Extraordinary Debt

To finance a number of acquisitions completed during the 1980s and 1990s, some companies significantly increased their debt levels. Although firms today are more prudent about the amount of debt they'll accept to complete an acquisition, those evaluating the possibility of an acquisition for their company need to be aware of the problem that taking on too much debt can create. In this sense, firms using an acquisition strategy want to verify that their purchases do not create a debt load that overpowers their ability to remain solvent and vibrant as a competitor.

A financial innovation called junk bonds supported firms' earlier efforts to take on large amounts of debt when completing acquisitions. *Junk bonds*, which are used less frequently today and are now more commonly called high-yield bonds, are a financing option through which risky acquisitions are financed with money (debt) that provides a large potential return to lenders (bondholders). Because junk bonds are unsecured obligations that are not tied to specific assets for collateral, interest rates for these high-risk debt instruments sometimes reached between 18 and 20 percent during the 1980s.[63] Additionally, interest rates for these types of bonds tend to be quite volatile, a condition that potentially exposes companies to greater financial risk.[64] Some prominent financial economists viewed debt as a means to discipline managers, causing the managers to act in the shareholders' best interests.[65] Managers adopting this perspective are less concerned about the amount of debt their firm assumes when acquiring other companies. However, the perspective that debt disciplines managers is not as widely supported today as was the case in the past.[66]

Bidding wars, through which an acquiring firm overcommits to the decision to acquire a target, can result in large or extraordinary debt. While finance theory suggests that managers will make rational decisions when seeking to complete an acquisition, other research suggests that rationality may not always drive the acquisition decision. Hubris, escalation of commitment to complete a particular transaction, and self-interest sometimes influence executives to pay a large premium, which, in turn, may result in taking on too much debt to acquire a target.[67] Given Teva's excessive acquisition debt load, it appears that Teva's leaders may have been subject to some of these problems.[68] Executives need to be aware of these possibilities and challenge themselves to engage in rational decision making when making an acquisition.

7-3d Inability to Achieve Synergy

Derived from *synergos*, a Greek word that means "working together," *synergy* exists when the value created by units working together exceeds the value that those units could create working independently (see Chapter 6). That is, synergy exists when assets are worth more when used in conjunction with each other than when they are used separately. For shareholders, synergy generates gains in their wealth that they could not duplicate or exceed through their own portfolio diversification decisions.[69] Synergy is created by the efficiencies derived from economies of scale and economies of scope and by sharing resources (e.g., human capital and knowledge) across the businesses in the newly created firm's portfolio.[70]

A firm develops a competitive advantage through an acquisition strategy only when a transaction generates private synergy. *Private synergy* is created when combining and integrating the acquiring and acquired firms' assets yield capabilities and core competencies that could not be developed by combining and integrating either firm's assets with another company. Private synergy is possible when firms' assets are complementary in unique ways; that is, the unique type of asset complementarity is not always possible simply by combining two companies' sets of assets with each other.[71] Although difficult to create, the attractiveness of private synergy is that because of its uniqueness, it is difficult for competitors to understand and imitate, meaning that a competitive advantage results for the firms able to create it.

A firm's ability to account for costs that are necessary to create anticipated revenue and cost-based synergies affects its efforts to create private synergy. Firms experience several expenses when seeking to create synergy through acquisitions. Called transaction costs, these expenses are incurred when firms use acquisition strategies to create synergy.[72] Transaction costs may be direct or indirect. Direct costs include legal fees and charges from investment bankers who complete due diligence for the acquiring firm. Indirect costs include managerial time to evaluate target firms and then to complete negotiations, as well as the loss of key managers and employees following an acquisition.[73] French financial giant AXA SA has signaled it would buy XL Group Ltd. to form the largest global property insurance company. Thomas Buberl, AXA CEO, said that there are "significant synergies on the cost side and on the capital side" with the deal. However, the market is not too favorable on its potential. One analysis said, "From my calls with investors so far, they all point to three things: wrong asset, wrong timing and wrong price." At the time of the announcement AXA was potentially paying a 33 percent premium for the transaction.[74] Although it remains to be seen if the deal will be successful, often firms tend to underestimate the sum of indirect costs when specifying the value of the synergy that may be created by integrating the acquired firm's assets with the acquiring firm's assets.

7-3e Too Much Diversification

As explained in Chapter 6, diversification strategies, when used effectively, can help a firm earn above-average returns. In general, firms using related diversification strategies outperform those employing unrelated diversification strategies. However, conglomerates formed by using an unrelated diversification strategy also can be successful.

At some point, however, firms can become overdiversified. The level at which this happens varies across companies because each firm has different capabilities to manage diversification. Recall from Chapter 6 that related diversification requires more information processing than does unrelated diversification. Because of this need to process additional amounts of information, related diversified firms become overdiversified with a smaller number of business units than do firms using an unrelated diversification strategy.[75] Regardless of the type of diversification strategy implemented, however, the firm that becomes overdiversified will experience a decline in its performance and likely a decision to divest some of its units.[76] Commonly, such divestments, which tend to reshape a firm's competitive scope, are part of a firm's restructuring strategy. (Restructuring is discussed in greater detail later in the chapter.)

Even when a firm is not overdiversified, a high level of diversification can have a negative effect on its long-term performance. For example, the scope created by additional amounts of diversification often causes managers to rely on financial rather than strategic controls to evaluate business units' performance (financial and strategic controls are discussed in Chapters 11 and 12). Top-level executives often rely on financial controls to assess the performance of business units when they do not have a rich understanding of business units' objectives and strategies. Using financial controls, such as return on investment (ROI), causes individual business-unit managers to focus on short-term outcomes at the expense of long-term investments. Reducing long-term investments to generate short-term profits can negatively affect a firm's overall performance ability.[77]

Another problem resulting from overdiversification is the tendency for acquisitions to become substitutes for innovation. Typically, managers have no interest in acquisitions substituting for internal R&D efforts; however, a reinforcing cycle evolves. Costs associated with acquisitions may result in fewer allocations to activities, such as R&D, that are linked to innovation. Without adequate support, a firm's innovation skills begin to atrophy. Without internal innovation skills, a key option available to a firm to gain access to innovation is to complete additional acquisitions. Evidence suggests that a firm using acquisitions as a substitute for internal innovations eventually encounters performance problems.[78]

7-3f Managers Overly Focused on Acquisitions

Typically, a considerable amount of managerial time and energy is required for acquisition strategies to be used successfully. Activities with which managers become involved include:

- searching for viable acquisition candidates
- completing effective due-diligence processes
- preparing for negotiations
- managing the integration process after completing the acquisition

Top-level managers do not personally gather all of the information and data required to make acquisitions. However, these executives do make critical decisions regarding the targeted firms, the nature of the negotiations, and so forth.[79] Company experiences show that participating in and overseeing the activities required for making acquisitions can divert managerial attention from other matters that are necessary for long-term competitive success, such as identifying and taking advantage of other opportunities and interacting with important external stakeholders.[80]

Both theory and research suggest that managers can become overly involved in the process of making acquisitions.[81] One observer suggested, "some executives can become preoccupied with making deals—and the thrill of selecting, chasing, and seizing a target."[82] The over-involvement can be surmounted by learning from mistakes and by not having too much agreement in the boardroom. Dissent is helpful to make sure that all sides of a question are considered. For example, research suggests that CEOs who are not challenged substantially in their decision making, either by the CFO or the board, realize more value destructive acquisitions.[83] When failure does occur, leaders may be tempted to blame the failure on others and on unforeseen circumstances rather than on their excessive involvement in the acquisition process. Finding the appropriate degree of involvement with the firm's acquisition strategy is a challenging, yet important, task for top-level managers.

7-3g Too Large

Most acquisitions result in a larger firm, which should create or enhance economies of scale. In turn, scale economies can lead to more efficient operations—for example, two sales organizations can be integrated using fewer sales representatives because the combined sales force can sell the products of both firms (particularly if the products of the acquiring and target firms are highly related).[84] However, size can also increase the complexity of the managerial challenge and create diseconomies of scope—that is, not enough economic benefit to outweigh the costs of managing the more complex organization created through acquisitions.

Thus, while many firms seek increases in size because of the potential economies of scale and enhanced market power size creates, at some level, the additional costs required to manage the larger firm will exceed the benefits of the economies of scale and additional market power. The complexities generated by the larger size often lead managers to implement more bureaucratic controls to manage the combined firm's operations. *Bureaucratic controls* are formalized supervisory and behavioral rules and policies designed to ensure consistency of decisions and actions across a firm's units. However, across time, formalized controls often lead to relatively rigid and standardized managerial behavior.[85] Certainly, in the long run, the diminished flexibility that accompanies rigid and standardized managerial behavior may produce less innovation. Because of innovation's importance to competitive success, the bureaucratic controls resulting from a large organization that might be built at least in part by using an acquisition strategy can negatively affect a firm's performance. Thus, managers may decide their firm should complete acquisitions in the pursuit of increased size as a path to profitable growth. At the same time, managers should avoid allowing their firm to get to a point where acquisitions are creating a degree of size that increases its inefficiency and ineffectiveness.

7-4 Effective Acquisitions

As noted, acquisition strategies do not always lead to above-average returns for the acquiring firm's shareholders.[86] Nonetheless, some companies are able to create value when using an acquisition strategy.[87] Research evidence suggests that the probability of being able to create value through acquisitions increases when the nature of the acquisition and the processes used to complete it are consistent with the "attributes of successful acquisitions" shown in Table 7.1.[88] For example, when the target firm's assets

Table 7.1 Attributes of Successful Acquisitions

Attributes	Results
1. Acquired firm has assets or resources that are complementary to the acquiring firm's core business	1. High probability of synergy and competitive advantage by maintaining strengths
2. Faster and more effective integration and possibly lower premiums	2. Acquisition is friendly
3. Acquiring firm conducts effective due diligence to select target firms and evaluate the target firm's health (financial, cultural, and human resources)	3. Firms with strongest complementarities are acquired and overpayment is avoided
4. Financing (debt or equity) is easier and less costly to obtain	4. Acquiring firm has financial slack (cash or a favorable debt position)
5. Merged firm maintains low to moderate debt position	5. Lower financing cost, lower risk (e.g., of bankruptcy), and avoidance of trade-offs that are associated with high debt
6. Acquiring firm maintains long-term competitive advantage in markets	6. Acquiring firm has a sustained and consistent emphasis on R&D and innovation
7. Acquiring firm manages change well and is flexible and adaptable	7. Faster and more effective integration facilitates achievement of synergy

are complementary to the acquired firm's assets, an acquisition is more successful. With complementary assets, the integration of two firms' operations has a higher probability of creating synergy. In fact, integrating two firms with complementary assets frequently produces unique capabilities and core competencies. With complementary assets, the acquiring firm can maintain its focus on core businesses and leverage the complementary assets and capabilities from the acquired firm. In effective acquisitions, targets are often selected and "groomed" by establishing a working relationship prior to the acquisition.[89] As discussed in Chapter 9, firms sometimes form strategic alliances to test the feasibility of a future merger or acquisition between them, an experience that can also contribute to acquisition success.

Research evidence also shows that friendly acquisitions facilitate integration of the acquiring and acquired firms. Of course, a target firm's positive reaction to a bid from the acquiring firm increases the likelihood that a friendly transaction will take place. For example, AdvancedCath responded positively to being acquired by TE Connectivity, a world leader in designing and managing highly engineered connectors, sensors, and electronic components that are sold to manufacturers who integrate them into their products. Total, a large French energy firm, completed a friendly acquisition of Saft Group to expand its renewable energies business and complement the acquisition in 2011 of a majority stake in U.S. solar power systems maker SunPower.[90] After completing a friendly acquisition, firms collaborate to create synergy while integrating their operations with more speed than hostile acquisitions.[91] Friendly deals also allow for easier leadership and operational combinations and thus facilitate the ability to create synergy in the integration process.

Additionally, effective due-diligence processes involving the deliberate and careful selection of target firms and an evaluation of the relative health of those firms (financial health, cultural fit, and the value of human resources) contribute to successful acquisitions.[92] Financial slack in the form of debt equity or cash, in both the acquiring and acquired firms, also frequently contributes to acquisition success. Even though financial slack provides access to financing for the acquisition, it is still important to maintain a low or moderate level of debt after the acquisition to keep debt costs low. When substantial debt is used to finance acquisitions, companies with successful acquisitions reduce the debt quickly, partly by selling off assets from the acquired firm, especially noncomplementary or poorly performing assets. For these firms, debt costs do not preclude long-term investments in areas such as R&D, and managerial discretion in the use of cash flow is relatively flexible.

Another attribute of successful acquisition strategies is an emphasis on innovation, as demonstrated by continuing investments in R&D activities.[93] As noted in the Strategic Focus, one of the government concerns about the Broadcom acquisition of Qualcomm was that Broadcom has not had a strong tradition of R&D investment after its past acquisitions and Qualcomm, as a leader in 5G network implementation, would need strong innovation investment to maintain that leadership.[94]

Flexibility and adaptability are the final two attributes of successful acquisitions. When executives of both the acquiring and the target firms have experience in managing change and learning from acquisitions, they are more skilled at adapting their capabilities to new environments.[95] As a result, they are more adept at integrating the two organizations, which is particularly important when firms have different organizational cultures.

As we have explained, firms using an acquisition strategy seek to create wealth and earn above-average returns. Sometimes, though, the results of an acquisition strategy fall short of expectations. When this happens, firms consider using restructuring strategies.

7-5 Restructuring

Restructuring is a strategy through which a firm changes its set of businesses or its financial structure.[96] Restructuring is a global phenomenon.[97] Historically, divesting businesses from company portfolios and downsizing have accounted for a large percentage of firms' restructuring strategies. Commonly, firms focus on fewer products and markets following restructuring.

Although restructuring strategies are generally used to deal with acquisitions that are not reaching expectations, firms sometimes use restructuring strategies because of changes they have detected in their external environment. For example, opportunities sometimes surface in a firm's external environment that a diversified firm can pursue because of the capabilities it has formed by integrating firms' operations. In such cases, restructuring may be appropriate to position the firm to create more value for stakeholders, given environmental changes and the opportunities associated with them.[98]

As discussed next, firms use three types of restructuring strategies: downsizing, downscoping, and leveraged buyouts.

7-5a Downsizing

Downsizing is a reduction in the number of a firm's employees and, sometimes, in the number of its operating units; but, the composition of businesses in the company's portfolio may not change through downsizing. Thus, downsizing is an intentional managerial strategy that is used for the purpose of improving firm performance. In contrast, organizational decline, which too often results in a reduction of a firm's resources including the number of its employees and potentially in the number of its units, is an unintentional outcome of what turned out to be a firm's ineffective competitive actions.[99] When downsizing, firms make intentional decisions about resources to retain and resources to eliminate. Organizational decline, on the other hand, finds firms losing access to an array of resources, many of which are critical to current and future performance. Thus, downsizing is a legitimate strategy to appropriately adjust firm size and is not necessarily a sign of organizational decline.[100]

Downsizing can be an appropriate strategy to use after completing an acquisition, particularly when there are significant operational and/or strategic relationships between the acquiring and the acquired firm. In these instances, the newly formed firm may have excess capacity in functional areas such as sales, manufacturing, distribution, human resource management, and so forth. In turn, excess capacity may prevent the combined firm from realizing anticipated synergies and the reduced costs associated with them.[101] Managers should remember that, as a strategy, downsizing will be far more effective when they consistently use human resource practices that ensure procedural justice and fairness in downsizing decisions.[102]

7-5b Downscoping

Downscoping refers to divestiture, spin-off, or some other means of eliminating businesses that are unrelated to a firm's core businesses. Downscoping has a more positive effect on firm performance than does downsizing[103] because firms commonly find that downscoping causes them to refocus on their core business.[104] As noted above, the DowDuPont merger plans to downscope by splitting into three separate firms. The largest of those three will focus on plastic resins and other materials; the other two spinoff firms will concentrate on agriculture and specialty products, respectively.[105] Managerial effectiveness increases because the firm has become less diversified, allowing the top management team to better understand and manage the remaining businesses.[106]

Restructuring is a strategy through which a firm changes its set of businesses or its financial structure.

Firms often use the downscoping and downsizing strategies simultaneously. As noted above, Teva Pharmaceuticals is restructuring; the company has suggested that it needs to lay off 14,000 employees and is likewise considering divesting former acquisitions.[107] When downsizing, firms need to avoid layoffs of key employees, as such layoffs might lead to a loss of one or more core competencies. Instead, a firm that chooses simultaneously to engage in downscoping and downsizing should intentionally become smaller as a result of decisions made to reduce the diversity of businesses in its portfolio, allowing it to focus on its core areas as a result.[108]

In general, U.S. firms use downscoping as a restructuring strategy more frequently than do European companies—in fact, the trend not too long ago in Europe, Latin America, and Asia was to build conglomerates. In Latin America, these conglomerates are called *grupos*. More recently though, many Asian and Latin American conglomerates have chosen to downscope their operations as a path to refocusing on their core businesses. This recent downscoping trend has occurred simultaneously with increasing globalization and with more open markets that have greatly enhanced competition.[109]

7-5c Leveraged Buyouts

A *leveraged buyout* (LBO) is a restructuring strategy whereby a party (typically a private equity firm) buys all of a firm's assets in order to take the firm private.[110] Once a private equity firm completes this type of transaction, the target firm's company stock is no longer traded publicly.

Traditionally, leveraged buyouts were used as a restructuring strategy to correct for managerial mistakes or because the firm's managers were making decisions that primarily served their own interests rather than those of shareholders.[111] However, some firms complete leveraged buyouts for the purpose of building firm resources and expanding their operations rather than simply to restructure a distressed firm's assets.

Significant amounts of debt are commonly incurred to finance a buyout; hence, the term *leveraged* buyout.[112] To support debt payments and to downscope the company to concentrate on the firm's core businesses, the new owners may quickly sell a number of assets. Indeed, it is not uncommon for those buying a firm through an LBO to restructure the firm to the point that it can be sold at a profit within a five- to eight-year period.

Management buyouts (MBOs), employee buyouts (EBOs), and whole-firm buyouts, in which one company or partnership purchases an entire company instead of a part of it, are the three types of LBOs. In part because of managerial incentives, MBOs, more so than EBOs and whole-firm buyouts, have been found to lead to downscoping, increased strategic focus, and improved performance.[113] Research shows that management buyouts can lead to greater entrepreneurial activity and growth.[114] As such, buyouts can represent a form of firm rebirth to facilitate entrepreneurial efforts and stimulate strategic growth and productivity.[115]

7-5d Restructuring Outcomes

The short- and long-term outcomes that result from use of the three restructuring strategies are shown in Figure 7.2. As indicated, downsizing typically does not lead to higher firm performance.[116] In fact, some research results show that downsizing contributes to lower returns for both U.S. and Japanese firms. The stock markets in the firms' respective nations evaluate downsizing negatively, believing that it has long-term negative effects on the firms' efforts to achieve strategic competitiveness. Investors also seem to conclude that downsizing occurs as a consequence of other problems in a company.[117] This assumption may be caused by a firm's diminished corporate reputation when a major downsizing is announced.[118]

Figure 7.2 Restructuring and Outcomes

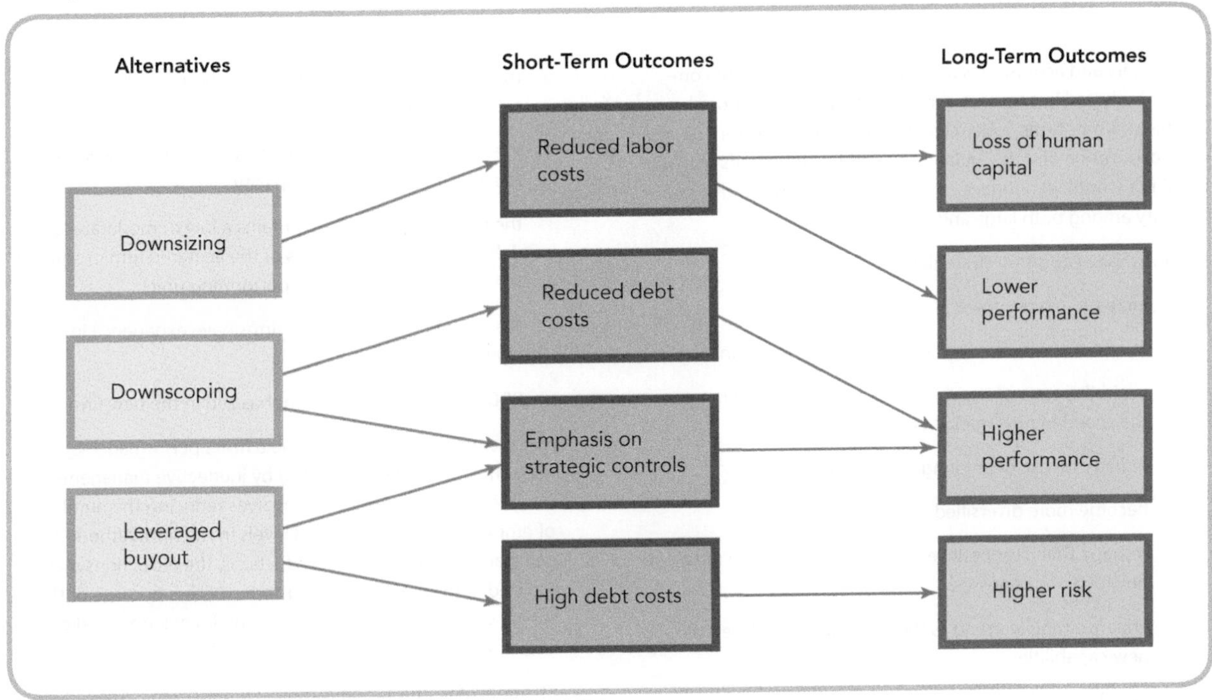

The loss of human capital is another potential problem of downsizing (see Figure 7.2). Losing employees with many years of experience with the firm represents a major loss of knowledge. As noted in Chapter 3, knowledge is vital to competitive success in the global economy. Research also suggests that a loss of valuable human capital can spill over into dissatisfaction of customers.[119] Thus, in general, downsizing may be of more tactical (or short-term) value than strategic (or long-term) value, meaning that firms should exercise caution when restructuring through downsizing.

Compared to downsizing and leveraged buyouts, downscoping generally leads to more positive outcomes in both the short term and long term. Downscoping's desirable long-term outcome of higher performance is a product of reduced debt costs and the emphasis on strategic controls derived from concentrating on the firm's core businesses. In so doing, the refocused firm should be able to increase its ability to compete.[120]

Whole-firm LBOs have been hailed as a significant innovation in the financial restructuring of firms. However, this type of restructuring can be complicated, especially when cross-border transactions are involved;[121] moreover, they can involve negative trade-offs.[122] First, the resulting large debt increases the firm's financial risk, as is evidenced by the number of companies that filed for bankruptcy in the 1990s after executing a whole-firm LBO. Sometimes, the intent of the owners to increase the efficiency of the acquired firm and then sell it within five to eight years creates a short-term and risk-averse managerial focus.[123] As a result, these firms may fail to invest adequately in R&D or take other major actions designed to maintain or improve the company's ability to compete successfully against rivals.[124] Because buyouts more often result in significant debt, most LBOs have been completed in mature industries where stable cash flows are the norm. Stable cash flows support the purchaser's efforts to service the debt obligations assumed as a result of taking a firm private.

SUMMARY

- Mergers and acquisitions as a strategy are popular for companies based in countries throughout the world. Through this strategy, firms seek to create value and outperform rivals. Globalization and deregulation of multiple industries in many of the world's economies are two of the reasons for this popularity among both large and small firms.
- Firms use acquisition strategies to
    - increase market power
    - overcome entry barriers to new markets or regions
    - avoid the costs of developing new products and increase the speed of new market entries
    - reduce the risk of entering a new business
    - become more diversified
    - reshape their competitive scope by developing a different portfolio of businesses
    - enhance their learning as the foundation for developing new capabilities
- Among the problems associated with using an acquisition strategy are
    - the difficulty of effectively integrating the firms involved
    - incorrectly evaluating the target firm's value
    - creating debt loads that preclude adequate long-term investments (e.g., R&D)
    - overestimating the potential for synergy
    - creating a firm that is too diversified
    - creating an internal environment in which managers devote increasing amounts of their time and energy to analyzing and completing the acquisition
    - developing a combined firm that is too large, necessitating extensive use of bureaucratic, rather than strategic, controls
- Effective acquisitions have the following characteristics:
    - the acquiring and target firms have complementary resources that are the foundation for developing new capabilities
    - the acquisition is friendly, thereby facilitating integration of the firm's resources
    - the target firm is selected and purchased on the basis of completing a thorough due-diligence process
    - the acquiring and target firms have considerable slack in the form of cash or debt capacity
    - the newly formed firm maintains a low or moderate level of debt by selling off portions of the acquired firm or some of the acquiring firm's poorly performing units
    - the acquiring and acquired firms have experience in terms of adapting to change
    - R&D and innovation are emphasized in the new firm
- Restructuring is used to improve a firm's performance by correcting for problems created by ineffective management. Restructuring by downsizing involves reducing the number of employees and hierarchical levels in the firm. Although it can lead to short-term cost reductions, the reductions may be realized at the expense of long-term success because of the loss of valuable human resources (and knowledge) and overall corporate reputation.
- The goal of restructuring through downscoping is to reduce the firm's level of diversification. Often, the firm divests unrelated businesses to achieve this goal. Eliminating unrelated businesses makes it easier for the firm and its top-level managers to refocus on the core businesses.
- Through a leveraged buyout (an LBO), a firm is purchased so that it can become a private entity. LBOs usually are financed largely through debt, although limited partners (institutional investors) are becoming more prominent. General partners have a variety of strategies, and some emphasize equity versus debt when minority partners have a longer time horizon. Management buyouts (MBOs), employee buyouts (EBOs), and whole-firm LBOs are the three types of LBOs. Because they provide clear managerial incentives, MBOs have been the most successful of the three. Often, the intent of a buyout is to improve efficiency and performance to the point where the firm can be sold successfully within five to eight years.
- Commonly, restructuring's primary goal is gaining or reestablishing effective strategic control of the firm. Of the three restructuring strategies, downscoping is aligned most closely with establishing and using strategic controls and usually improves performance more on a comparative basis.

KEY TERMS

acquisition 212
merger 211
restructuring 227
takeover 212

REVIEW QUESTIONS

1. Why are merger and acquisition strategies popular in many firms competing in the global economy?
2. What reasons account for firms' decisions to use acquisition strategies as a means to achieving strategic competitiveness?
3. What are the seven primary problems that affect a firm's efforts to successfully use an acquisition strategy?
4. What are the attributes associated with a successful acquisition strategy?
5. What is the restructuring strategy, and what are its common forms?
6. What are the short- and long-term outcomes associated with the different restructuring strategies?

Mini-Case

Cementing a Merger of Equals between Lafarge and Holcim Has Been Difficult

Founded in France in 1833, Lafarge became a successful global industrial company specializing in three product areas—cement, construction aggregates, and concrete. The other party in a "merger of equals," which required well over a year to design and bring to the conclusion the firms intended, is Holcim, a materials and aggregates company that was founded in Switzerland in 1912. Holcim's global ambitions were obvious early when the firm expanded into France and throughout Europe and the Middle East during the 1920s. This expansion resulted in long-term and active competitions between Lafarge and Holcim.

In April of 2014, Lafarge and Holcim announced that they had settled on terms that would result in a merger of equals and that, accordingly, they were prepared to seek regulatory approval of the proposed transaction. Obtaining such approvals was anticipated to be challenging given that the diversity of the independent firms' global operations meant that 15 or so different jurisdictions could potentially object to a merger between the firms.

What influenced Lafarge and Holcim to want to merge as coequals given the difficulties of doing so? The prevailing thought is that mergers of equals are always more fragile to bring about in light of the need to effectively meld what are commonly two different cultures and specify the leadership structure that will be used to operate the newly created firm. These issues are in addition to a core one of identifying the financial aspects of the transactions that will appeal to each firm's shareholders.

In spite of challenges such as these, Lafarge and Holcim thought that merging as equals would create a firm with enhanced and significant competitive abilities. Leaders of the two firms concluded that together LafargeHolcim, the agreed-upon name for the combined firm, would have the most balanced and diversified portfolio in the building materials industry. The firms anticipated that integrating their operations would generate approximately $1.5 billion in annual cost savings. In an overall sense, company leaders thought that the anticipated positive benefits of merging would come about primarily as a result of being able to meld Holcim's marketing strengths with Lafarge's innovation capabilities.

Perhaps not unexpectedly, the transaction proposed between Lafarge and Holcim almost fell apart. This happened in March of 2015 when Holcim's board, "after first agreeing to a $44 billion merger with Lafarge, rejected the deal's terms as undervaluing Holcim. Corporate leadership also was a concern." This objection surfaced after the firms had received regulatory approvals from key jurisdictions, including the European Union, India, and the United States, regarding the number of divestitures of units they would make to prevent them from having highly concentrated positions in different global markets. At the core of the dispute was the conviction among Holcim's board members that the financial terms should be more attractive for their shareholders and that Lafarge's CEO should not be appointed as CEO of the newly created firm. One reason for these convictions was that in the nearly one year since terms of the initial merger were agreed upon, Holcim's "operating performance and share price had outperformed those of Lafarge." After restructuring the financing of the transaction and agreeing that a different CEO would be appointed for the new firm, 94 percent of Holcim's shareholders approved the transaction's terms.

After dealing with challenges, LafargeHolcim became a firm that was a merger of equals in July 2015. Speaking to the future, one board member said that "this isn't just another merger. It is an opportunity to create a new Number One in our industry." Assuming that this merger of equals achieves the potential some anticipate, all of the work required to bring it about will be validated. Going forward though, implementation challenges may come into play, at least in the short term, given the potential incompatibility of Holcim's decentralized management approach with the more centralized approach that characterized Lafarge when it competed as an independent firm.

In fact, in 2016 one year after the merger, the merged firm was not performing well relative to smaller competitors. At its one year anniversary, "LafargeHolcim has fallen 39 percent since its forerunner, Switzerland's Holcim, revealed plans to combine with France's Lafarge in April 2014. Irish building materials group CRH is up 29 percent in the period; HeidelbergCement is up by 13 percent. The Bloomberg European 500 index has shed just 1.5 percent." Given the progress that the firm said that they were making in regard to the integration, their market valuation should have been higher. There are questions about the ability of LafargeHolcim to create economies of scale from its large size. One observer noted that "cement is inherently a local business and so scale economies aren't so easy," given that transporting it long distances is expensive.

In September 2017, a new CEO, Jan Jenisch, was hired. When he launched the strategy to revive the company's fortunes, he announced that LafargeHolcim would be "cutting costs, selling assets and focusing on fewer markets as the world's biggest cement maker." The firm also announced that it would write off $4 billion in assets and the "stock fell more than 7 percent after the strategy was revealed."

Sources: J. Revill, 2018, LafargeHolcim's new CEO writes off over $4 billion and sets out strategy, *Reuters*, www.reuters.com; C. Hughes, 2016, Many unhappy returns for a $50 billion merger, *Bloomberg*, www.bloomberg.com, July 13; 2015, Holcim and Lafarge obtain merger clearances in the United States and Canada paving the way to closing their merger, *Holcim Home Page*, www.holcim. com, May 4; 2015, Lafarge to cut 380 jobs ahead of merger with Holcim, *Global Cement*, www.globalcement.com, May 19; M. Curtin, 2015, Holcim-Lafarge shows 'merger of equals' doesn't equal smooth sailing, *Wall Street Journal*, www.wsj. com, March 16; M. Curtin, 2015, A 'merger of equals' is more fragile, *Wall Street Journal*, www.wsj.com, March 16; J. Franklin, 2015, Holcim and Lafarge name post-merger board candidates, *Reuters*, www.reuters.com, April 14; J. Revill, 2015, Holcim moves step closer to Lafarge merger, *Wall Street Journal*, www.wsj.com, May 8.

Case Discussion Questions

1. Of the "Reasons for Acquisitions" discussed in the chapter, which reasons are the primary drivers of Lafarge-Holcim merger strategy?
2. Given that there have been performance difficulties of this "merger of equals," which of the "Problems in Achieving Acquisition Success" do you believe have most likely affected this deal?
3. The new CEO, Jan Jenisch, has undertaken a restructuring strategy. Why do you think the market reacted negatively to this plan?
4. What would you suggest the firm do to improve it restructuring plan and ultimately its poor performance?

NOTES

1. F. Castellaneta & R. Conti, 2017, How does acquisition experience create value? Evidence from a regulatory change affecting the information environment. *European Management Journal*, 35: 60–68; M. Menz, S. Kunisch, & D. J. Collis, 2015, The corporate headquarters in the contemporary corporation: Advancing a multimarket firm perspective, *Academy of Management Annals*, 9: 633–714.
2. M. Worek, 2017, Mergers and acquisitions in family businesses: Current literature and future insights, *Journal of Family Business Management*, 7: 177–206; R. Ragozzino & D. P. Blevins, 2015, Venture-backed firms: How does venture capital involvement affect their likelihood of going public or being acquired? *Entrepreneurship Theory and Practice*, 40: 991–1016.
3. J. Benitez, G. Ray, & J. Henseler, J. 2018, Impact of information technology infrastructure flexibility on mergers and acquisitions, *MIS Quarterly*, 42: 25–43; P.-X. Meschi & E. Metais, 2015, Too big to learn: The effects of major acquisition failures on subsequent acquisition divestment, *British Journal of Management*, 26: 408–423.
4. E. M. Bettinazzi & M. Zollo, 2017, Stakeholder orientation and acquisition performance, *Strategic Management Journal*, 38: 2465–2485; D. A. Basuil & D. K. Datta, 2015, Effects of industry- and region-specific acquisition experience on value creation in cross-border acquisitions: The moderating role of cultural similarity, *Journal of Management Studies*, 52: 766–795.

5. D. Mattioli & D. Cimilluca, 2018, M&A market headed for a record, powered by tech disruption, AT&T ruling, *Wall Street Journal*, www.wsj.com, July 1; B. Gomes-Casseres 2018, What the big mergers in 2017 tell us about 2018, *Harvard Business Review Digital Articles*, www.hbr.org, January 2; C. Moschieri & J. M. Campa, 2014, New trends in mergers and acquisitions: Idiosyncrasies of the European market, *Journal of Business Research*, 67: 1478–1485.
6. J. Li, J. Xia, & Z. Lin, 2017, Cross-border acquisitions by state-owned firms: How do legitimacy concerns affect the completion and duration of their acquisitions?, *Strategic Management Journal*, 38: 1915–1934.
7. L. Berchicci, G. Dowell, & A. A. King, 2017, Environmental performance and the market for corporate assets, *Strategic Management Journal*, *38*: 2444–2464.
8. S. Y. Cho, J. D. Arthurs, D. M. Townsend, D. R. Miller, & J. Q. Barden, 2016, Performance deviations and acquisition premiums: The impact of CEO celebrity on managerial risk-taking, *Strategic Management Journal*, 37: 2677–2694; J. S. Ang & A. K. Ismail, 2015, What premiums do target shareholders expect? Explaining negative returns upon offer announcement, *Journal of Corporate Finance*, 30: 245–256.
9. L. Li & W. H. Tong, 2018, Information uncertainty and target valuation in mergers and acquisitions, *Journal of Empirical Finance*, 45: 84–107.
10. D. Mattioli & D. Cimilluca, 2018, Cigna agrees to buy Express Scripts for more than $50 billion, *Wall Street Journal*, www.wsj.com, March 8.
11. J. H. Kim, 2018, Asset specificity and firm value: Evidence from mergers, *Journal of Corporate Finance*, 48: 375–412; J.-Y. (Jay) Kim, S. Finkelstein, & J. Haleblian, 2015, All aspirations are not created equal: The differential effects of historical and social aspirations on acquisition behavior, *Academy of Management Journal*, 58: 1361–1388.
12. Deloitte, 2017, The Dell-EMC deal: Anatomy of a "merger of equals," *CFO Journal*, www.wsj.com, November 6; R. King, 2016, Dell Closes $60 Billion Merger with EMC, Walls Street Journal, www.wsj.com, September 7.
13. M. D. Cain, S. B. McKeon, & S. D. Solomon, 2017, Do takeover laws matter? Evidence from five decades of hostile takeovers, *Journal of Financial Economics*, 124: 464–485; N. Aktas, E. Croci, & S. A. Simsir, 2016, Corporate governance and takeover outcomes, *Corporate Governance: An International Review*, 24: 242–252.
14. T. Greenwald & A. Hufford, 2018, Broadcom cuts offer for Qualcomm over new NXP deal price, *Wall Street Journal*, www.wsj.com, February 22.
15. M. Freeman, 2018, Broadcom-Qualcomm: What's the fallout of epic takeover battle? *San Diego Union Tribune*, www.sandiegouniontribune.com, March 18.
16. M. R. Rabier, 2017, Acquisition motives and the distribution of acquisition performance, *Strategic Management Journal*, 38: 2666–2681.
17. J. Clougherty, J. U. Kim, B. R. Skousen, & F. Szücs, 2017, The foundations of international business: Cross-border investment activity and the balance between market-power and efficiency effects, *Journal of Management Studies*, 54: 340–365; K. Huschelrath & K. Muller, 2015, Market power, efficiencies, and entry evidence from an airline merger, *Managerial and Decision Economics*, 36: 239–255.
18. B. A. Blonigen & J. R. Pierce, 2016, Evidence for the effects of mergers on market power and efficiency, Finance and Economics Discussion Series 2016–082. Washington: Board of Governors of the Federal Reserve.
19. C. Mims, 2018, The limits of Amazon, *Wall Street Journal*, www.wsj.com, January 1.
20. E. Winkler, 2018, Judge will decide two media merger cases in one, *Wall Street Journal*, www.wsj.com, February 23.
21. M. B. Lieberman, G. K. Lee, & T. B. Folta, 2017, Entry, exit, and the potential for resource redeployment, *Strategic Management Journal*, 38: 526–544.
22. T. Greenwald, 2017, Deal for Mobileye puts Intel's spotty record of acquisitions on the line, *Wall Street Journal*, www.wsj.com, March 15.
23. W. Moatti, C. R. Ren, J. Anand, & P. Dussauge, 2015, Disentangling the performance effects of efficiency and bargaining power in horizontal growth strategies: An empirical investigation in the global retail industry, *Strategic Management Journal*, 36: 745–757.
24. T. H. Reus, B. T. Lamont, & K. M. Ellis, 2016, A darker side of knowledge transfer following international acquisitions, *Strategic Management Journal*, 37: 932–944; L. Capron, 1999, The long-term performance of horizontal acquisitions. *Strategic Management Journal*, 20: 987–1018.
25. D. McGowan, 2017, Digging deep to compete: Vertical integration, product market competition and prices, *Journal of Industrial Economics*, 65: 683–718; C.-H. Chou, 2014, Strategic delegation and vertical integration, *Managerial and Decision Economics*, 35: 580–586; J. Shenoy, 2012, An examination of the efficiency, foreclosure, and collusion rationales for vertical takeovers, *Management Science*, 58: 1482–1501.
26. Z. Tracer, R. Lnagreth, & P. Coy, 2017, CVS brings one-stop shopping to health care, *Bloomberg Businessweek*, December 11: 21–22.
27. J. Woldt, 2017, CVS, Aetna take on health care challenge. *MMR*, December 18: 10.
28. A. W. Mathews, 2017, Will CVS health deal to buy Aetna hold up to antitrust scrutiny?, *Wall Street Journal*, www.wsj.com, December 4.
29. P. R. La Monica, 2018, Cisco is the market's comeback kid, *CNNMoney*, www.money.cnn.com, March 15.
30. S. K. Bhaumik, O. Oluwarotimi, & S. Pal, 2018, Private information, institutional distance, and the failure of cross-border acquisitions: Evidence from the banking sector in Central and Eastern Europe, *Journal of World Business*, 53: 504–513.
31. G. Colvin, 2017, Inside China's $43 Billion Bid for Food Security, *Fortune*, www.fortune.com, April 21.
32. T. A. Luong, 2018, Picking cherries or lemons: A unified theory of cross-border mergers and acquisitions, *World Economy*, 41: 653–666; D. A. Basuil & D. K. Datta, 2017, Value creation in cross-border acquisitions: The role of outside directors' human and social capital, *Journal of Business Research*, 80: 35–44; B. B. Fancis, I. Hasan, X. Sun, & M. Waisman, 2014, Can firms learn by observing? Evidence from cross-border M&As, *Journal of Corporate Finance*, 25: 202–215.
33. H. R. Greve & C. M. Zhang, 2017, Institutional logics and power sources: Merger and acquisition decisions, *Academy of Management Journal*, 60: 671–694; Y. Chen, W. Li, & K. J. Lin, 2015, Cumulative voting: Investor protection or antitakeover? Evidence from family firms in China, *Corporate Governance: An International Review*, 23: 234–238.
34. X. (Sara) Ding, J. Mo, & L. Zhong, 2017, The effect of cross-border mergers and acquisitions on earnings quality: Evidence from China, *Thunderbird International Business Review*, 59: 519–531.
35. J. Espinoza, T. Hancock, & C. Jones, 2017, Foreign deals with China worth $75bn canned amid crackdown on outflows, Financial Times, www.ft.com, February 6.
36. Lieberman, Lee, & Folta, Entry, exit, and the potential for resource redeployment; G. K. Lee & M. B. Lieberman, 2010, Acquisition vs. internal development as modes of market entry, *Strategic Management Journal*, 31: 140–158.
37. A. McKelvie, J. Wiklund, & A. Brattström, 2018, Externally acquired or internally generated? Knowledge development and perceived environmental dynamism in new venture innovation, *Entrepreneurship: Theory & Practice*, 42: 24–46; H. Berends, M. Jelinek, I. Reymen, & R. Stultiens, 2014, Product innovation processes in small firms: Combining entrepreneurial effectuation and managerial causation, *Journal of Product Innovation Management*, 31: 616–635.
38. J. B. Sears, 2017, When are acquired technological capabilities complements rather than substitutes? A study on value creation, *Journal of Business Research*, 78: 33–42; U. Stettner & D. Lavie, 2014, Ambidexterity under scrutiny: Exploration and exploitation via internal organization, alliances, and acquisitions, *Strategic Management Journal*, 35: 1903–1929.
39. A. Greenwood, 2017, Celanese expected to grow via M&A and products, *ICIS Chemical Business*, April 14, 1.

40. K. Grigoriou & F. T. Rothaermel, 2017, Organizing for knowledge generation: Internal knowledge networks and the contingent effect of external knowledge sourcing, *Strategic Management Journal*, 38: 395–414; C. Grimpe & K. Hussinger, 2014, Resource complementarity and value capture in firm acquisitions: The role of intellectual property rights, *Strategic Management Journal*, 35: 1762–1780.
41. Q. Ai & H.Tan, 2017, Acquirers' prior related knowledge and post-acquisition integration, *Journal of Organizational Change Management*, 30: 647–662.
42. J. J. Haleblian, M. D. Pfarrer, & J. T. Kiley, 2017, High-reputation firms and their differential acquisition behaviors, *Strategic Management Journal*, 38: 2237–2254; O. Koryak, K. F. Mole, A. Lockett, J. C. Hayton, D. Ucbasaran, & G. P. Hodgkinson, 2015, Entrepreneurial leadership, capabilities and firm growth, *International Small Business Journal*, 33: 89–105.
43. P. R. La Monica, 2018, Cisco is the market's comeback kid, *CNNMoney*, www.money.cnn.com, March 15.
44. Reuters, 2017, Samsung Is Eyeing Big Acquisitions, *Fortune*, www.fortune.com, December 1.
45. K. Uhlenbruck, M. Hughes-Morgan, M. A. Hitt, W. J. Ferrier, & R. Brymer, 2017, Rivals' reactions to mergers and acquisitions, *Strategic Organization*, 15: 40–66.
46. K. Nunes, 2018, Cost reduction remains central to Dean Foods' strategy, *Food Business News*, www.foodbusinessnew.net, March 1.
47. A. Kaul & X. (Brian) Wu, 2016, A capabilities-based perspective on target selection in acquisitions, *Strategic Management Journal*, 37: 1220–1239.
48. S. Banerjee, J. C. Prabhu, & R. K. Chandy, 2015, Indirect learning: How emerging-market firms grow in developed markets, *Journal of Marketing*, 79: 10–28.
49. S. M. Kerner, 2018, Cisco acquires Skyport as cyber-security investments continue, *Eweek*, www.eweek.com January 25.
50. Colvin, Inside China's $43 Billion Bid for Food Security.
51. R. L. Martin, 2016, M&A: The one thing you need to get right, *Harvard Business Review*, 94(6): 42–48.
52. O. Zaks, 2016, Success and failure in M&As: Is there a place for a paradigm change? Evidence from the Israeli hi-tech industry, *Economics & Business Review*, 2: 85–106; M. G. Colombo & L. Rabbiosi, 2014, Technological similarity, post-acquisition R&D reorganization, and innovation performance in horizontal acquisitions, *Research Policy*, 43: 1039–1054.
53. J. Bodner & L. Capron, 2018, Post-merger integration, *Journal of Organization Design*, 7: 1–20; A. Trichterborn, D. Z. Knyphausen-Aufseb, & L. Schweizer, 2016, How to improve acquisition performance: The role of a dedicated M&A function, M&A learning process, and M&A capability, *Strategic Management Journal*, 37: 763–773.
54. N. Vuori, T. O. Vuori, & Q. N. Huy, 2018, Emotional practices: How masking negative emotions impacts the post-acquisition integration process, *Strategic Management Journal*, 39: 859–893.
55. M. Graebner, K. Heimeriks, Q. N. Huy, & E. Vaara, 2017. The process of post-merger integration: A review and agenda for future research, *Academy of Management Annals*, 11: 1–32; H. Zhu, J. Xia, & S. Makino, 2015, How do high-technology firms create value in international M&A? Integration, autonomy and cross-border contingencies, *Journal of World Business*, 50: 718–728.
56. Z. Chen, P. Kale, & R. E. Hoskisson, 2018 Geographic overlap and acquisition pairing, *Strategic Management Journal*, 39: 329–355.
57. H. Johnson, 2017, Cross-border deals drive M&A, *Global Finance*, 31(4): 43–44; A. Sleptsov, J. Anand, & G. Vasudeva, 2013, Relationship configurations with information intermediaries: The effect of firm-investment bank ties on expected acquisition performance, *Strategic Management Journal*, 34: 957–977.
58. Bhaumik, Owolabi, & Pal, Private information, institutional distance, and the failure of cross-border acquisitions: Evidence from the banking sector in Central and Eastern Europe.
59. N. Bach, 2017, Struggling Israeli generics maker Teva finally names new CEO. *Fortune*. www.fortune.com, November 11.
60. C. Helfand, 2017, Mexican regulator undermines Teva's Rimsa fraud claims with 'all clear' memorandum, *FiercePharma*, www.fiercepharma.com, April 11.
61. J. Wieczner, 2015, Fat pharma: Pfizer-Hospira and the top 10 overpriced drug deals ever, *Fortune*, www.fortune.com, February 6.
62. N. K. Taylor, 2017, Kite's CAR-T medication, cancer candidates draw choosy Gilead for $12B pipeline-building buyout, *FierceBiotech*, www.fiercebiotech.com, August 28.
63. M. W. Simpson & A. Grossmann, 2017, The value of restrictive covenants in the changing bond market dynamics before and after the financial crisis, *Journal of Corporate Finance*, 46: 307–319; B. Becker & V. Ivashiina, 2015, Reaching for yield in the bond market, *Journal of Finance*, 70: 1863–1901; G. Yago, 1991, *Junk Bonds: How High Yield Securities Restructured Corporate America*, NY: Oxford University Press, 146–148.
64. Simpson & Grossmann, The value of restrictive covenants in the changing bond market dynamics before and after the financial crisis; D. H. Kim & D. Stock, 2014, The effect of interest rate volatility and equity volatility on corporate bond yield spreads: A comparison of noncallables and callables, *Journal of Corporate Finance*, 26: 20–35.
65. J. O'Brien & A. Sasson, 2017, A contingency theory of entrepreneurial debt governance, *Journal of Business Research*, 81: 118–129; M. C. Jensen, 1986, Agency costs of free cash flow, corporate finance, and takeovers, *American Economic Review*, 76: 323–329.
66. Ni, X. & S. Yin, 2018, Shareholder litigation rights and the cost of debt: Evidence from derivative lawsuits, *Journal of Corporate Finance*, 48:169–186; S. Guo, E. S. Hotchkiss, & W. Song, 2011, Do buyouts (still) create value? *Journal of Finance*, 66: 479–517.
67. W. Shi, Y. Zhang, & R. E. Hoskisson, 2017, Ripple effects of CEO awards: Investigating the acquisition activities of superstar CEOs' competitors, *Strategic Management Journal*, 38: 2080–2102.
68. Fortune, 2018, Teva is drowning in debt and firing thousands of employees. Now warren Buffett is interested, *Fortune, www.fortune.com*, February 15.
69. M. R. Rabier, Acquisition motives and the distribution of acquisition performance; K. Craninckx & N. Huyghebaert, 2015, Large shareholders and value creation through corporate acquisitions in Europe: The identity of the controlling shareholder matters, *European Management Journal*, 33: 116–131.
70. C. Tantalo & R. L. Priem, 2016, Value creation through stakeholder synergy, *Strategic Management Journal*, 37: 314–329; J. Jaffe, J. Jindra, D. Pedersen, & T. Voetmann, 2015, Returns to acquirers of public and subsidiary targets, *Journal of Corporate Finance*, 31: 246–270.
71. G. Chondrakis, 2016, Unique synergies in technology acquisitions, *Research Policy*, 45: 1873–1889; J. B. Barney, 1988, Returns to bidding firms in mergers and acquisitions: Reconsidering the relatedness hypothesis, Strategic Management Journal, 9(Summer Special Issue), 71–78.
72. M. F. Ahammad, V. Leone, S. Y. Tarba, K. W. Glaister, & A. Arslan, 2017, Equity ownership in cross-border mergers and acquisitions by British firms: An analysis of real options and transaction cost factors, *British Journal of Management*, 28: 180–196; O. E. Williamson, 1999, Strategy research: Governance and competence perspectives, *Strategic Management Journal*, 20: 1087–1108.
73. L. Frantz, 2017, Dissecting post-merger integration risk: The PMI risk framework, In C. L. Cooper & S. Finkelstein (eds.) *Advances in Mergers and Acquisitions (Volume 16)*, Bingley, UK: Emerald Publishing Limited, 33–164; S. Chatterjee, 2007, Why is synergy so difficult in mergers of related businesses? *Strategy & Leadership*, 35(2): 46–52.
74. M. Dalton & B. Dummett, 2018, AXA to buy insurer XL Group for $15.3 billion, *Wall Street Journal*, www.wsj.com, March 5.
75. P.-X. Meschi & E. Metais, 2015, Too big to learn: The effects of major acquisition failures on subsequent acquisition divestment, *British Journal of Management*,

26: 408–423; W. P. Wan, R. E. Hoskisson, J. C. Short, & D. W. Yiu, 2011, Resource-based theory and corporate diversification: Accomplishments and opportunities, *Journal of Management*, 37: 1335–1368.

76. S. J. G. Girod & R. Whittington, 2017, Reconfiguration, restructuring and firm performance: Dynamic capabilities and environmental dynamism, *Strategic Management Journal*, 38: 1121–1133; S. Pathak, R. E. Hoskisson, & R. A. Johnson, 2014, Settling up in CEO compensation: The impact of divestiture intensity and contextual factors in refocusing firms, *Strategic Management Journal*, 35: 1124–1143.

77. M. Miozzo, L. DiVito, & P. Desyllas, 2016, When do acquirers invest in the R&D assets of acquired science-based firms in cross-border acquisitions? The role of technology and capabilities similarity and complementarity, *Long Range Planning*, 49: 221–240; R. E. Hoskisson & R. A. Johnson, 1992, Corporate restructuring and strategic change: The effect on diversification strategy and R&D intensity, *Strategic Management Journal*, 13: 625–634.

78. J. Stiebale, 2016, Cross-border M&As and innovative activity of acquiring and target firms, *Journal of International Economics*, 99: 1–15; F. Szucs, 2014, M&A and R&D: Asymmetric effects on acquirers and targets? *Research Policy*, 43: 1264–1273; R. D. Banker, S. Wattal, & J. M. Plehn-Dujowich, 2011, R&D versus acquisitions: Role of diversification in the choice of innovation strategy by information technology firms, *Journal of Management Information Systems*, 28: 109–144.

79. I. R. P. Cuypers, Y. Cuypers, & Z. Martin, 2017, When the target may know better: Effects of experience and information asymmetries on value from mergers and acquisitions, *Strategic Management Journal*, 38: 609–625.

80. H. T. J. Smit & J. M. Kil, 2017, Toehold Acquisitions as Behavioral Real Options, *California Management Review*, 59(3): 42–73; B. E. Perrott, 2015, Building the sustainable organization: An integrated approach, *Journal of Business Strategy*, 36: 41–51; A. Kacperczyk, 2009, With greater power comes greater responsibility? Takeover protection and corporate attention to stakeholders, *Strategic Management Journal*, 30: 261–285.

81. N. Aktas, E. de Bodt, H. Bollaert, & R. Roll, 2016, CEO narcissism and the takeover process: From private initiation to deal completion, *Journal of Financial & Quantitative Analysis*, 51: 113–137; M. V. S. Kumar, J. Dixit, & B. Francis, 2015, The impact of prior stock market reactions on risk taking in acquisitions, *Strategic Management Journal*, 36: 2111–2121.

82. F. Vermeulen, 2007, Business insight (a special report): Bad deals: Eight warning signs that an acquisition may not pay off, *Wall Street Journal*, www.wsj.com, April 28, R10.

83. W. Shi, Y. Zhang, & R. E. Hoskisson, 2018. Examination of CEO-CFO social interaction through language style matching: Outcomes for the CFO and the organization Investigating. *Academy of Management Journal*, in press; D. H. Zhu, 2013, Group polarization on corporate boards: Theory and evidence on board decisions about acquisition premiums, *Strategic Management Journal*, 34: 800–822.

84. N. Fannon, 2017, What makes a business valuation firm an attractive acquisition target?, *Business Valuation Update*, 23(7): 1–4; G. Kling, A. Ghobadian, M. A. Hitt, U. Weitzel, & N. O'Regan, 2014, The effects of cross-border and cross-industry mergers and acquisitions on home-region and global multinational enterprises, *British Journal of Management*, 25: S116–S132.

85. A. Marrewijk, 2016, Conflicting subcultures in mergers and acquisitions: A longitudinal study of integrating a radical internet firm into a bureaucratic telecoms firm, *British Journal of Management*, 27: 338–354.

86. P. Kale & H. Singh, 2017, Management of overseas acquisitions by developing country multinationals and its performance implications: The Indian example, *Thunderbird International Business Review*, 59: 153–172; D. N. Angwin, S. Paroutis, & R. Connell, 2015, Why good things don't happen: The micro-foundations of routines in the M&A process, *Journal of Business Research*, 68: 1367–1381.

87. Z. Huang, H. Zhu, & D. J. Brass, 2017, Cross-border acquisitions and the asymmetric effect of power distance value difference on long-term post-acquisition performance, *Strategic Management Journal*, 38, 972–991; D. Gamache, G. McNamara, M. Mannor, & R. Johnson, 2015, Motivated to acquire? The impact of CEO regulatory focus on firm acquisitions, *Academy of Management Journal*, 58: 1261–1282.

88. V. Cherepanova, 2017, M&A proposal geared to success: Matters, aspects and theories to be considered by acquirer, *Journal of Accounting, Finance & Management Strategy*, 12: 41–64; M. A. Hitt, R. D. Ireland, J. S. Harrison, & A. Best, 1998, Attributes of successful and unsuccessful acquisitions of U.S. firms, *British Journal of Management*, 9: 91–114.

89. R. Zakaria, 2017, Alliances to acquisitions: A road map to advance the field of strategic management, In C. L. Cooper & S. Finkelstein (eds.), *Advances in Mergers and Acquisitions (Volume 16)*, Bingley, UK: Emerald Publishing Limited, 1–20.

90. G. De Clercq & B. Felix, 2016, Total to acquire battery maker Saft for $1.1 billion, *Reuters*, www.reuters.com, May 9.

91. O. Meglio, D. R. King, & A. Risberg, 2017, Speed in acquisitions: A managerial framework, *Business Horizons*, 60: 415–425.

92. A. Herzfeldt, V. Tritschler, M. Dieterle, & C. M. Seubert, 2017, Effectively realizing synergies: Lessons learned from 10 years of M&A activities, *Management Accounting Quarterly*, 18: 8–18; S. Graffin, J. Haleblian, & J. T. Kiley, 2016, Ready, AIM, acquire: Impression offsetting and acquisitions, *Academy of Management Journal*, 59: 232–252.

93. A. R. Saboo, A. Sharma, A. Chakravarty, & V. Kumar, 2017, Influencing acquisition performance in high-technology industries: The role of innovation and relational overlap, *Journal of Marketing Research*, 54(2): 219–238; F. Szucs, 2014, M&A and R&D: Asymmetric effects on acquirers and targets? *Research Policy*, 43: 1264–1273; Y. Suh, J. You, & P. Kim, 2013, The effect of innovation capabilities and experience on cross-border acquisition performance, *Global Journal of Business Research*, 7: 59–74.

94. D. Gallagher, 2018, Qualcomm's spending buys the right friends, *Wall Street Journal*, www.wsj.com, March 6.

95. A. Bansal, 2017, A revelation of employee feelings of alienation during post-mergers and acquisition, *Journal of Organizational Change Management*, 30: 417–439; D. N. Angwin & M. Meadows, 2015, New integration strategies for post-acquisition management, *Long Range Planning*, 48: 235–251.

96. M. Brauer, J. Mammen, & J. Luger, 2017, Sell-Offs and firm performance: A matter of experience? *Journal of Management*, 43: 1359–1387; C. Moschieri & J. Mair, 2017, Corporate entrepreneurship: Partial divestitures as a real option, *European Management Review*, 14: 67–82.

97. S. B. Baziki , P.-J. Norbäck , L. Persson, & J. Tåg, 2017, Cross-border acquisitions and restructuring: Multinational enterprises and private equity-firms, *European Economic Review*, 94: 166–184; N. Kavadis & X. Castaner, 2015, Who drives corporate restructuring? Co-existing owners in French firms, *Corporate Governance: An International Review*, 23: 417–433.

98. P. Kuusela, T. Keil, & M. Maula, 2017, Driven by aspirations, but in what direction? Performance shortfalls, slack resources, and resource-consuming vs. resource-freeing organizational change, *Strategic Management Journal*, 38: 1101–1120; E. R. Feldman, 2016, Corporate spinoffs and analysts' coverage decisions: The implications for diversified firms, *Strategic Management Journal*, 37: 1196–1219.

99. M. A. Abebe & C. Tangpong, 2018, Founder-CEOs and corporate turnaround among declining firms, *Corporate Governance: An International Review*, 26: 45–57; W. McKinley, S. Latham, & M. Braun, 2014, Organizational decline and innovation: Turnarounds and downward spirals, *Academy of Management Review*, 39: 88–110.

100. O. Bergström & R. Arman, 2017, Increasing commitment after downsizing: The role of involvement and voluntary redundancies, *Journal of Change Management*, 17: 297–320; C. Tangpong, M. Agebe, & Z. Li, 2015, A temporal approach to retrenchment and

successful turnaround in declining firms, *Journal of Management Studies*, 52: 647–677.

101. A. Schenkel & R. Teigland, 2017, Why doesn't downsizing deliver? A multi-level model integrating downsizing, social capital, dynamic capabilities, and firm performance, *International Journal of Human Resource Management*, 28: 1065–1107; I. Paeleman & T. Vanacker, 2015, Less is more, or not? On the interplay between bundles of slack resources, firm performance and firm survival, *Journal of Management Studies*, 52: 819–848.
102. R. E. Hoskisson & M. A. Hitt, 1990, Antecedents and performance outcomes of diversification: A review and critique of theoretical perspectives, *Journal of Management*, 16: 461–509.
103. M. Flickinger & M. Zschoche, 2018, Corporate divestiture and performance: An institutional view. *Journal of Management & Governance*, 22: 111–131.
104. E. Vidal & W. Mitchell, 2018, Virtuous or vicious cycles? The role of divestitures as a complementary Penrose effect within resource-based theory, *Strategic Management Journal*, 39: 131–154; E. R. Feldman, R. (Raffi) Amit, & B. Villalonga, 2016, Corporate divestitures and family control, *Strategic Management Journal*, 37: 429–446.
105. C. Jing, 2018, DowDuPont names three planned spin offs, *Chemical week*, February 26.
106. S. Chiu, R. A. Johnson, R. E. Hoskisson, & S. Pathak, 2016, The impact of CEO successor origin on corporate divestiture scale and scope change, *Leadership Quarterly*, 27: 617–633; R. E. Hoskisson & M. A. Hitt, 1994, *Downscoping: How to Tame the Diversified Firm*, NY: Oxford University Press.
107. R. Jones & A. Hufford, 2017, Teva Pharmaceutical to cut 14,000 jobs, *Wall Street Journal*, www.wsj.com, December 14.
108. J. K. Mawdsley & D. Somaya, 2018, Demand-side strategy, relational advantage and partner-driven corporate scope: The case for client-led diversification, *Strategic Management Journal*, 39: 1834–1859; E. Vidal & W. Mitchell, 2015, Adding by subtracting: The relationship between performance feedback and resource reconfiguration through divestitures, *Organization Science*, 26: 1101–1118.
109. R. M. Holmes Jr., T. R. Holcomb, R. E. Hoskisson, H. Kim, & W. Wan, 2018, International strategy and business groups: A review and future research agenda, *Journal of World Business*, 53: 134–150; W. G. Xavier, R. Bandeira-de-Mello, & R. Marcon, 2014, Institutional environment and business groups' resilience in Brazil, *Journal of Business Research*, 67: 900–907; H. Berry, 2013, When do firms divest foreign operations? *Organization Science*, 24: 246–261.
110. P. J. Davies, 2018, Does private equity really beat the stock market? *Wall Street Journal*, www.wsj.com, February 13; H. D. Park & P. C. Patel, 2015, How does ambiguity influence IPO underpricing? The role of the signaling environment, *Journal of Management Studies*, 52: 796–818.
111. E. Battistin, P. Bortoluzzi, F. Buttignon, & M. Vedovato, M. 2017, Minority and majority private equity investments: Firm performance and governance, *Journal of Management & Governance*, 21: 659–684; S. N. Kaplan & P. Stromberg, 2009, Leveraged buyouts and private equity, *Journal of Economic Perspectives*, 23: 121–146.
112. P. J. Davies, 2018, Why private equity risks tripping on its own success, *Wall Street Journal*, www.wsj.com, February 13; S. N. Kaplan & P. Stromberg, 2009, Leveraged buyouts and private equity, *Journal of Economic Perspectives*, 23: 121–146.
113. E. R. Feldman, 2016, Managerial compensation and corporate spinoffs, *Strategic Management Journal*, 37: 2011–2030; Pathak, Hoskisson, & Johnson, Settling up in CEO compensation: The impact of divestiture intensity and contextual factors in refocusing.
114. P. Toma & S. Montanari, 2017, Corporate governance effectiveness along the entrepreneurial process of a family firm: The role of private equity, *Journal of Management & Governance*, 21: 1023–1052; E. Autio, M. Kenney, P. Mustar, D. Siegel, & M. Wright, 2014, Entrepreneurial innovation: The importance of context, *Research Policy*, 43: 1097–1108; H. Bruining, E. Verwaal, & M. Wright, 2013, Private equity and entrepreneurial management in management buy-outs, *Small Business Economics*, 40: 591–605.
115. F. Castellaneta & O. Gottschalg, 2016, Does ownership matter in private equity? The sources of variance in buyouts' performance, *Strategic Management Journal*, 37: 330–348; M. Wright, R. E. Hoskisson, & L. W. Busenitz, 2001, Firm rebirth: Buyouts as facilitators of strategic growth and entrepreneurship, *Academy of Management Executive*, 15: 111–125.
116. Schenkel & Teigland, Why doesn't downsizing deliver?; Y.-Y. Ji, J. P. Guthrie, & J. G. Messersmith, 2014, The tortoise and the hare: The impact of employment instability on firm performance, *Human Resource Management Journal*, 24: 355–373.
117. M. Brauer & T. Laamanen, 2014, Workforce downsizing and firm performance: An organizational routine perspective, *Journal of Management Studies*, 51: 1311–1333.
118. S. López Bohle, P. M. Bal, P. W. Jansen, P. I. Leiva, & A. M. Alonso, 2017, How mass layoffs are related to lower job performance and OCB among surviving employees in Chile: An investigation of the essential role of psychological contract, *International Journal of Human Resource Management*, 28(20): 2837–2860; H. A. Krishnan & D. Park, 2002, The impact of work force reduction on subsequent performance in major mergers and acquisitions: An exploratory study, *Journal of Business Research*, 55: 285–292.
119. C. Tsao, A. Newman, S. Chen, & M. Wang, 2016, HRM retrenchment practices and firm performance in times of economic downturn: Exploring the moderating effects of family involvement in management, *International Journal of Human Resource Management*, 27: 954–973; S. Mariconda & F. Lurati, 2015, Ambivalence and reputation stability: An experimental investigation on the effects of new information, *Corporate Reputation Review*, 18: 87–98; D. J. Flanagan & K. C. O'Shaughnessy, 2005, The effect of layoffs on firm reputation, *Journal of Management*, 31: 445–463.
120. D. Kim & T. K. Tan, 2016, Ex-post stock return behaviour of corporate restructurings and corporate control, *Review of Accounting & Finance*, 15: 484–498; F. Bertoni & A. P. Groh, 2014, Cross-border investments and venture capital exits in Europe, *Corporate Governance: An International Review*, 22: 84–99.
121. J. X. Cao, D. Cumming, M. Qian, & X. Wang, 2015, Cross-border LBOs, *Journal of Banking and Finance*, 50: 69–80.
122. F. Suffge & R. Braun, 2017, Corporate raiders at the gates of Germany? Value drivers in buyout transactions, *Journal of Private Equity*, 20(2): 28–45; P. G. Klein, J. L. Chapman, & M. P. Mondelli, 2013, Private equity and entrepreneurial governance: Time for a balanced view, *Academy of Management Perspectives*, 27: 39–51; D. T. Brown, C. E. Fee, & S. E. Thomas, 2009, Financial leverage and bargaining power with suppliers: Evidence from leveraged buyouts, *Journal of Corporate Finance*, 15: 196–211.
123. Y. Hung & M. Tsai, 2017, Value creation and value transfer of leveraged buyouts: A review of recent developments and challenges for emerging markets, *Emerging Markets Finance & Trade*, 53: 877–917; H.-C. Huang, Y.-C. Su, & Y.-H. Chang, 2014, Dynamic return-order imbalance relationship response to leveraged buyout announcements, *Global Journal of Business Research*, 8: 55–63; S. B. Rodrigues & J. Child, 2010, Private equity, the minimalist organization and the quality of employment relations, *Human Relations*, 63: 1321–1342.
124. J. Lerner, M. Sorensen, & P. Strömberg, 2011, Private Equity and long-run investment: The case of innovation. *Journal of Finance*, 66: 445–477; M. Goergen, N. O'Sullivan, & G. Wood, 2011, Private equity takeovers and employment in the UK: Some empirical evidence, *Corporate Governance: An International Review*, 19: 259–275; W. F. Long & D. J. Ravenscraft, 1993, LBOs, debt, and R&D intensity, *Strategic Management Journal*, 14 (Special Issue): 119–135.

iStock.com/DNY59

8

International Strategy

Studying this chapter should provide you with the strategic management knowledge needed to:

8-1 Explain incentives that can influence firms to use an international strategy.

8-2 Identify three basic benefits firms gain by successfully implementing an international strategy.

8-3 Explore the determinants of national advantage as the basis for international business-level strategies.

8-4 Describe the three international corporate-level strategies.

8-5 Discuss environmental trends affecting the choice of international strategies, particularly international corporate-level strategies.

8-6 Identify and explain the five modes firms use to enter international markets.

8-7 Discuss the two major risks of using international strategies.

8-8 Discuss the strategic competitiveness outcomes associated with international strategies, particularly with an international diversification strategy.

8-9 Explain two important issues firms should have knowledge about when using international strategies.

iStock.com/DNY59

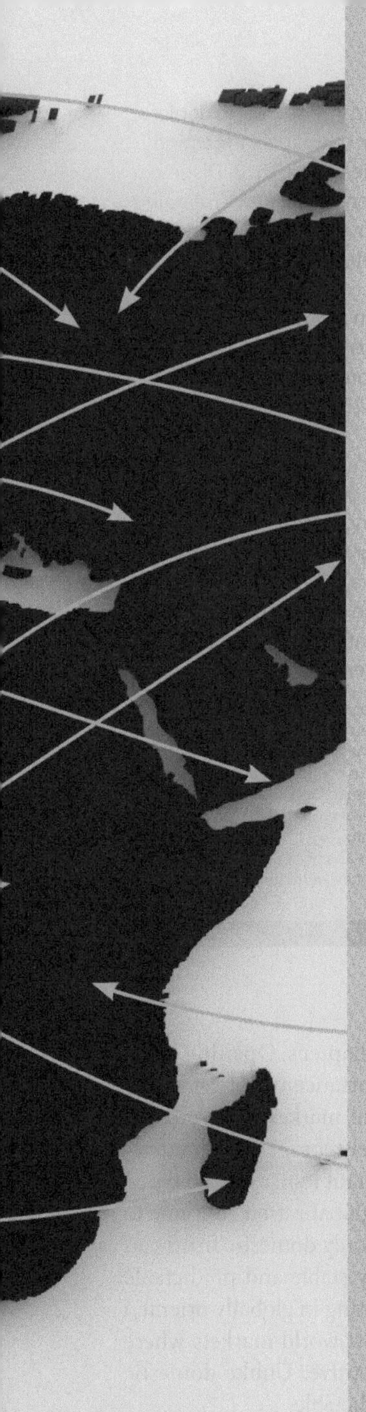

NETFLIX ACHIEVES SUBSTANTIAL GROWTH THROUGH INTERNATIONAL EXPANSION, BUT SUCH GROWTH ALSO IS ATTRACTING SIGNIFICANT COMPETITION

Netflix has ramped up its international expansion in recent years. The base of its international strategy includes strong capabilities in technological innovation, which it uses to expand abroad. Its technology is focused on understanding customer viewing patterns and providing content that matches those patterns. It has a broad selection of content produced by network television and movie studios in addition to its own original content, which has become a strong force in the market that, with its advancing investments, will likely become even stronger.

Given that Netflix has reached a near saturation point in the domestic U.S. market, it is extending its services abroad. It began to do so in countries that are close culturally and geographically to its U.S. customer base, such as Canada, Nordic, and Latin American countries. Netflix's primary growth is coming from its international expansion efforts, which allow it to share its cost across a broader range of countries and a larger subscriber base. In the fourth quarter of 2017, Netflix added 8.3 million streaming subscribers, primarily driven by growth in foreign markets. In 2017, CEO Reed Hastings announced that Netflix added 130 new countries in which it provides its services. Basically, Netflix now serves all countries but Crimea, North Korea, Syria and China. In 2016 the company invested $6 billion and plans to spend another $8 billion to acquire new content to serves its various geographic markets. For example, its plans call for adding approximately 700 new shows/programs to its original content in 2018 with 80 of those targeted for international markets.

Felipe Caicedo/Getty Images

Netflix CEO Reed Hastings talks to the international press during the launch of Netflix in Colombia.

Netflix's international growth strategy has had to overcome challenges. First, Netflix had to seek global licenses with its contract video and movie content providers. The content providers want to distribute their content in international markets as well, so Netflix generally must pay more for the content in order to obtain a global license. In addition, the expenses of initial start-up and licensing in new foreign countries drive up the costs of pursuing its global strategy, at least in the short term.

Second, Netflix must make its substantial English language content accessible in local languages for many international subscribers. Currently, Netflix provides content accessible in 20 different languages but it must rapidly increase this number to grow its subscriber base. To facilitate this transition, it has developed a new translation tool, HERMES, and hired many people to help with the translations.

Third, as it pursues its global streaming strategy, there are both increased domestic competition for subscriber growth and new entrants into foreign markets. Market success attracts rivals as they see the opportunities available. Netflix has many other current domestic streaming competitors, including Amazon and Hulu. And, it is now facing the entry of new formidable rivals in Disney and Apple. Disney has announced that it is opening its new video streaming service in 2019 and withdrawing all Disney content from Netflix at the end of 2018. Disney also planned to invest $1 billion to acquire and develop original content for its new streaming service. And, its planned acquisition of Twenty-First Century Fox will provide access to significant content as well. Apple has been investing heavily to develop new content to compete in these markets as well.

In 2018, Netflix had 117 million subscribers, with 62 million of them from outside the United States. Netflix is currently focusing heavily on expanding its business in India. India is projected to have 650 million Internet users by 2021 compared to approximately 300 million in the United States. Netflix hopes to double its subscriber base by 2023, with 100 million of those coming from India.

Netflix has profited handsomely from its international expansion. For example, in recent years its average annual revenue growth has been 26.5 percent and its annual average growth in net income has been 100 percent. It has increased the size of its board, adding international expertise. However, although the international expansion strategy has facilitated growth and profits for Netflix through sharing costs and expenses across a large subscriber base, it has also increased the complexity of its management structure. Additionally, the difficulty in global contracting for top-level domestic U.S. content continues to grow with increased international and domestic competition. While Netflix has challenges, it has become the global leader in its industry.

Sources: N. Walters, 2018, Apple and Disney gear up to pounce on Netflix, *The Motley Fool*, http://host.madison.com, March 23; R. Krause, 2018, Netflix takes on media giants as video streaming war goes global, *Investor's Business Daily*, https://www.investors.com, March 8; 2018, Netflix, Inc's (NFLX) international expansion puts pressure on media competitors, *Stocknews.com*, https://stocknews.com, March 1; E. Gruenwedel, 2018, Netflix putting global growth focus on India, *MediaPlayNews*, https://www.mediaplaynews.com, February 26; W. Healy, 2018, Netflix, Inc. faces widening competition amid a narrowing moat, *InvestorPlace*, http://investorplace.com, February 26; F. DiPietro, 2017, How Netflix Inc. is overcoming this key obstacle to its international expansion, *The Motley Fool*, https://.www.fool.com, May 9; S. Ramachandran, 2015, Netflix steps up foreign expansion, subscriber additions top streaming service's forecast, helped by growth in markets abroad, *Wall Street Journal*, www.wsj.com, January 21; F. Video, 2015, Netflix eyes China for continued global expansion, *Fortune*, www.fortune.com, June 11.

Our description of Netflix's competitive actions in this chapter's Opening Case (e.g., international expansion strategy) highlights the importance of international markets for this firm. Netflix is using its growth in international markets to overcome slowing subscriber growth in its U.S. market. Being able to effectively compete in countries and regions outside a firm's domestic market is increasingly important to firms of all types, as exemplified by Netflix. One reason for this is that the effects of globalization continue to reduce the number of industrial and consumer markets in which only domestic firms can compete successfully. In place of what historically were relatively stable and predictable domestic markets, firms across the globe find they are now competing in globally oriented industries—industries in which firms must compete in all or most world markets where a consumer or commercial good or service is sold to be competitive.[1] Unlike domestic markets, global markets are relatively unstable and much less predictable.

The purpose of this chapter is to discuss how international strategies can be a source of strategic competitiveness for firms competing in global markets. To do this, we examine several topics (see Figure 8.1). After describing incentives that influence firms to identify international opportunities, we discuss three basic benefits that can accrue to firms that successfully use international strategies. We then turn our attention to the international strategies available to firms. Specifically, we examine both international business-level strategies and international corporate-level strategies. The five modes of entry firms can use to enter international markets for implementing their international strategies are then examined. Firms encounter economic and political risks when using international strategies. Some refer to these as economic and political institutions.[2] These

Figure 8.1 Opportunities and Outcomes of International Strategy

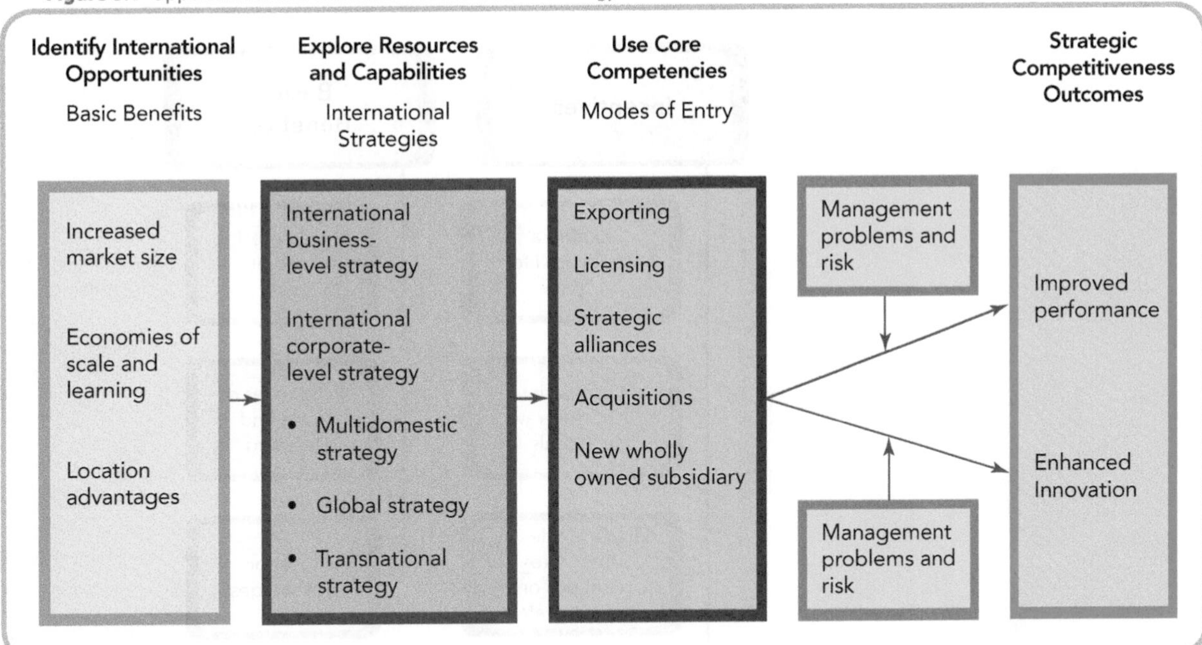

risks must be effectively managed if the firm is to achieve the desired outcomes of higher performance and enhanced innovation. After discussing the outcomes firms seek when using international strategies, the chapter closes with mention of two cautions about international strategy that should be kept in mind.

8-1 Identifying International Opportunities

An **international strategy** is a strategy through which the firm sells its goods or services outside its domestic market.[3] In some instances, firms using an international strategy become quite diversified geographically as they compete in numerous countries or regions outside their domestic market. This is the case for Netflix in that it competes now in all but a few countries. In other cases, firms engage in less international diversification because they focus on a smaller number of markets outside their "home" market.

There are incentives for firms to use an international strategy and to diversify their operations geographically, and they can gain three basic benefits when they successfully do so.[4] We show international strategy's incentives and benefits in Figure 8.2.

8-1a Incentives to Use International Strategy

Raymond Vernon expressed the classic rationale for an international strategy.[5] He suggested that typically a firm discovers an innovation in its home-country market, especially in advanced economies such as those in Germany, France, Japan, Sweden, Canada, and the United States. Often demand for the product then develops in other countries, causing a firm to export products from its domestic operations to fulfil demand. Continuing increases in demand can subsequently justify a firm's decision to establish operations outside of its domestic base, as illustrated in the Opening Case on Netflix. As Vernon noted, engaging in an international strategy has the potential to help a firm extend the life cycle of its product(s).

An **international strategy** is a strategy through which the firm sells its goods or services outside its domestic market.

Figure 8.2 Incentives and Basic Benefits of International Strategy

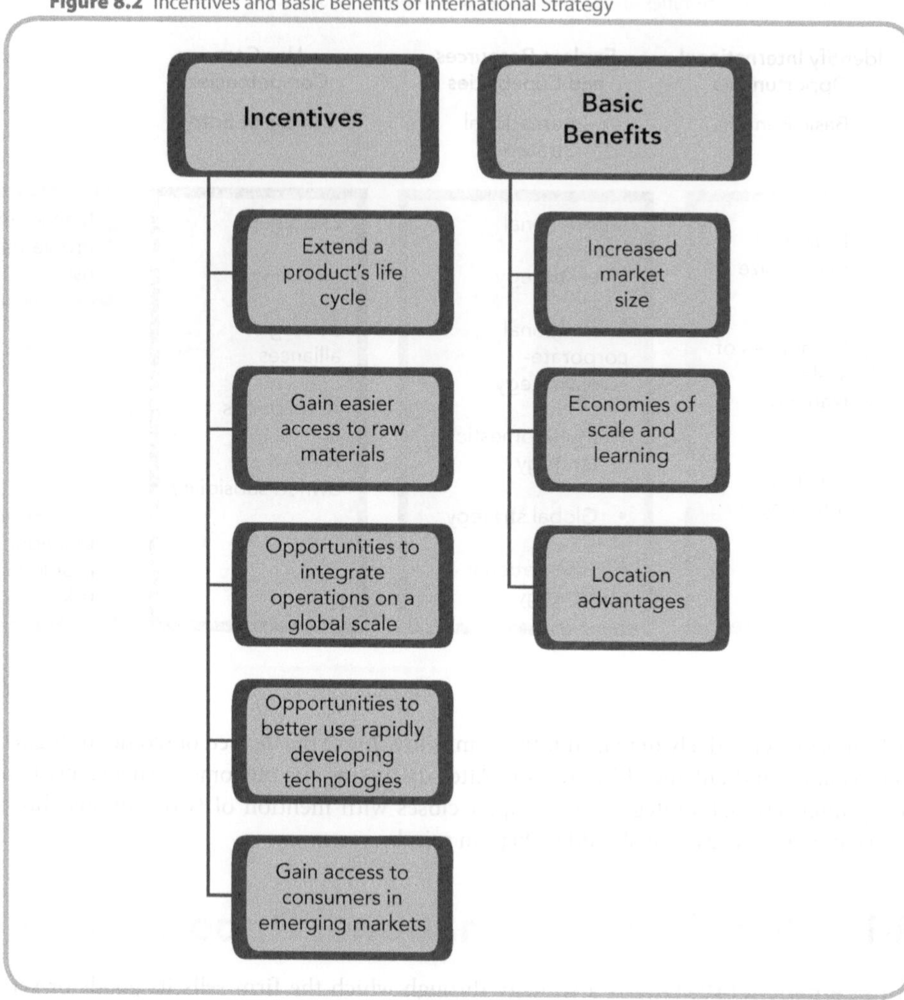

Gaining access to needed and potentially scarce resources is another reason that firms use an international strategy. Key supplies of raw material—especially minerals and energy—are critical to firms' efforts in some industries to manufacture their products. Energy and mining companies have access to the raw materials, through their worldwide operations, which they in turn sell to manufacturers requiring those resources. Rio Tinto Group is a leading international mining corporation. Operating as a global organization, the firm has 55,000 employees across six continents and operating in more than 40 countries. Rio Tinto uses its capabilities of technology and innovation (see first incentive noted above), exploration, marketing, and operational processes to identify, extract, and market mineral resources throughout the world.[6] In other industries where labor costs account for a significant portion of a company's expenses, firms may choose to establish facilities in other countries to gain access to less expensive labor. Clothing and electronics manufacturers are examples of firms pursuing an international strategy for this reason.

Increased pressure to integrate operations on a global scale is another factor influencing firms to pursue an international strategy. As nations industrialize, the demand for some products and commodities appears to become more similar. This borderless demand for globally branded products may be due to growing similarities in lifestyle in developed nations. Increases in global communications also facilitate the ability of people in different countries to visualize and model lifestyles in other cultures. In an increasing number of industries, technology drives globalization because the economies of scale necessary to reduce costs to the lowest level often require an investment greater than that needed to meet domestic market demand. Moreover, in emerging markets, the increasingly rapid adoption of technologies such as the Internet and mobile applications permits greater integration of trade, capital, culture, and labor. For instance, Vietnam is experiencing a "mobile revolution." In 2017, 28.8 million people had smartphones and access to the Internet, compared to 20.7 million in 2015. That number is projected to increase to 42.7 million people by 2022.[7] In this sense, technologies are the foundation for efforts to bind together disparate markets and operations across the world. International strategy also makes it possible for firms to use technologies to organize their operations into a seamless whole.[8]

The potential of large demand for goods and services from people in emerging markets such as China and India is another strong incentive for firms to use an international strategy.[9] This is the case for French-based Carrefour S.A. This firm is the world's second-largest retailer (behind only Walmart) and the largest retailer in Europe. Carrefour operates five main grocery store formats—hypermarkets, supermarkets, cash & carry, hypercash stores, and convenience stores. The firm also sells products online. Carrefour operates 12,300 stores in 30 countries.[10] In 2018, it announced a major strategic alliance with Tesco, a British multinational firm that operates in similar domains as Carrefour. In the alliance they plan to cooperate in several areas, especially in their supply chains. By sharing their expertise, they believe that they will be able to obtain higher quality supplies at lower costs.[11]

Even though India differs from Western countries in many respects, such as culture, politics, and the precepts of its economic system, it offers a huge potential market, and the government has become more supportive of foreign direct investment.[12] Differences among Chinese, Indian, and Western-style economies and cultures make the successful use of an international strategy challenging. As such, firms seeking to meet customer demands in emerging markets must learn how to manage an array of political and economic risks, which we discuss later in the chapter.[13]

We've now discussed incentives that influence firms to use international strategies. Firms derive three basic benefits by successfully using international strategies:

1. increased market size
2. increased economies of scale and learning
3. development of a competitive advantage through location (e.g., access to low-cost labor, critical resources, or customers)

These benefits will be examined here in terms of both their costs (e.g., higher coordination expenses and limited access to knowledge about host country political influences)[14] and their challenges.

8-1b Three Basic Benefits of International Strategy

As noted, effectively using one or more international strategies can result in three basic benefits for the firm. These benefits facilitate the firm's effort to achieve strategic competitiveness (see Figure 8.1) when using an international strategy.

Increased Market Size

Firms can expand the size of their potential market—sometimes dramatically—by using an international strategy to establish stronger positions in markets outside their domestic market.[15] As noted, access to additional consumers is a key reason Carrefour sees international markets such as China as a major source of growth.

Firms such as Netflix, Carrefour, and WH Group understand that effectively managing different consumer tastes and practices linked to cultural values or traditions in different markets is challenging. Nonetheless, they accept this challenge because of the potential to enhance the firms' size and performance. Other firms accept the challenge of successfully implementing an international strategy largely because of limited growth opportunities in their domestic market. This appears to be at least partly the case for major competitors Coca-Cola and PepsiCo, firms that have not been able to generate significant growth in their U.S. domestic and North American markets for some time. Indeed, most of these firms' growth is occurring in international markets. An international market's overall size also has the potential to affect the degree of benefit a firm can accrue because of using an international strategy. In general, larger international markets offer higher potential returns and pose less risk for the firm choosing to invest in those markets. Also related is the strength of the science base of the international markets in which a firm may compete. This is important because scientific knowledge and human capital are needed to facilitate efforts to more effectively sell and/or deliver products that create value for customers.[16]

Economies of Scale and Learning

By expanding the number of markets in which they compete, firms may be able to enjoy economies of scale, particularly in manufacturing operations. More broadly, firms able to make continual process improvements enhance their ability to reduce costs while, hopefully, increasing the value their products create for customers.[17] For example, rivals Airbus SAS and Boeing have multiple manufacturing facilities and outsource some activities to firms located throughout the world, partly for developing economies of scale as a source of being able to create value for customers.

Economies of scale are critical in a number of settings in addition to the airline manufacturing industry. For example, economies of scale are a critical component of Costco's business model. Costco is a subscription business that sells a service to its customers. The service it provides is buying goods in large quantities at low costs (because of its economies of scale), thus allowing the firm to sell the goods to consumers at lower prices, passing on the savings provided by Costco's purchases.[18] In fact, Costco is so popular that it is experiencing some of the diseconomies of scale in that some people prefer not to shop in crowded stores. This causes Costco to continue to expand the number of its stores. Firms may also be able to exploit core competencies in international markets through resource and knowledge sharing between units and network partners across country borders.[19] By sharing resources and knowledge in this manner, firms can learn how to create synergy, which in turn can help each firm learn how to deliver higher quality products at a lower cost.

Operating in multiple international markets also provides firms with new learning opportunities,[20] perhaps even in terms of research and development (R&D) activities. Increasing the firm's R&D ability can contribute to its efforts to enhance innovation, which is critical to both short- and long-term success. However, research results suggest that to take advantage of international R&D investments, firms need to have a strong R&D system already in place to absorb knowledge resulting from effective R&D activities.[21]

Location Advantages

Locating facilities outside their domestic market can sometimes help firms reduce costs. This benefit of an international strategy accrues to the firm when its facilities in international locations provide easier access to lower cost labor, energy, and other natural resources. Other location advantages include access to critical supplies and to customers. Once positioned in an attractive location, firms must manage their facilities effectively to gain the full benefit of a location advantage.[22]

A firm's costs, particularly those dealing with manufacturing and distribution, as well as the nature of international customers' needs affect the degree of benefit it can capture through a location advantage.[23] The influences of cultural and formal country institutions (e.g., laws and regulations) may also affect location advantages and disadvantages. International business transactions are easier for a firm to complete when there is a strong cultural match and similar country institutions with which the firm is involved while implementing its international strategy.[24] Finally, physical distances influence a firm's location choices as well as how it manages facilities in the chosen locations.[25]

In recent times, there has been pressure in some countries for firms to reduce the scale and scope of their internationalization and focus on producing goods in the domestic market. For example, the Trump administration in the United States has pressured firms to move their internationally based manufacturing operations to the United States in order to provide more jobs for U.S. citizens. As a result, some firms have begun searching for ways that they can reverse some of their internationalization efforts while doing so efficiently and serving all domestic and international markets.[26]

8-2 International Strategies

Firms choose to use one or both basic types of international strategy: business-level international strategy and corporate-level international strategy. At the business level, firms select from among the generic strategies of cost leadership, differentiation, focused cost leadership, focused differentiation, and integrated cost leadership/differentiation. At the corporate level, multidomestic, global, and transnational international strategies (the transnational is a combination of the multidomestic and global strategies) are considered. To contribute to the firm's efforts to achieve strategic competitiveness in the form of improved performance and enhanced innovation (see Figure 8.1), each international strategy the firm uses must be based on one or more core competencies.[27]

8-2a International Business-Level Strategy

Firms considering the use of any international strategy first develop domestic-market strategies (at the business level and at the corporate level if the firm has diversified at the product level). This is important because the firm may be able to use some of the capabilities and core competencies it has developed in its domestic market as the foundation for competitive success in international markets, as illustrated in the Opening Case on Netflix. However, research results indicate that the value created by relying on capabilities and core competencies developed in domestic markets as a source of success in international markets diminishes as a firm's geographic diversity increases.[28]

As we know from our discussion of competitive dynamics in Chapter 5, firms do not select and then use strategies in isolation of market realities. In the case of international strategies, conditions in a firm's domestic market affect the degree to which the firm can build on capabilities and core competencies it established to create capabilities and core competencies in international markets. The reason is grounded in Michael Porter's analysis of why some nations are more competitive than other nations and why and how some industries within nations are more competitive relative to those industries in other nations. Porter's core argument is that conditions or factors in a firm's home base—that is, in its domestic market—either hinder or support the firm's efforts to use an international business-level strategy for the purpose of establishing a competitive advantage in international markets. Porter identifies four factors as determinants of a national advantage that some countries possess (see Figure 8.3).[29] Interactions among these four factors influence a firm's choice of international business-level strategy.

Figure 8.3 Determinants of National Advantage

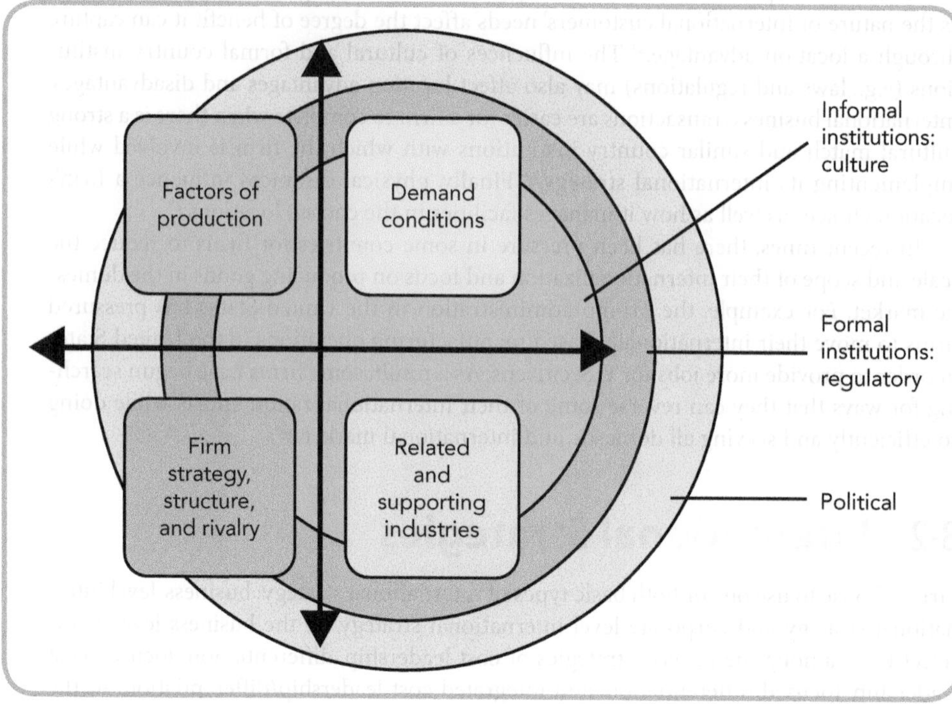

The first determinant of national advantage is factors of production. This determinant refers to the inputs necessary for a firm to compete in any industry. Labor, land, natural resources, capital, and infrastructure (transportation, delivery, and communication systems) represent such inputs. There are basic factors (natural and labor resources) and advanced factors (digital communication systems and a highly educated workforce). Other factors of production are generalized (highway systems and the supply of debt capital) and specialized (skilled personnel in a specific industry, such as the workers in a port that specialize in handling bulk chemicals). If a country possesses advanced and specialized production factors, it is likely to serve an industry well by spawning strong home-country competitors that also can be successful global competitors.

Ironically, countries often develop advanced and specialized factors because they lack critical basic resources. For example, South Korea lacks abundant natural resources but has a workforce with a strong work ethic, a large number of engineers, and systems of large firms to create an expertise in manufacturing. Similarly, Germany developed a strong chemical industry, partly because Hoechst and BASF spent years creating a synthetic indigo dye to reduce their dependence on imports, unlike the United Kingdom, whose colonies provided large supplies of natural indigo.[30]

The second factor or determinant of national advantage, demand conditions, is characterized by the nature and size of customers' needs in the home market for the products firms competing in an industry produce. Meeting the demand generated by many customers creates conditions through which a firm can develop scale-efficient facilities and enhance the capabilities, and perhaps core competencies, required to use those facilities. Once enhancements are in place, the probability that the capabilities and core competencies will benefit the firm as it diversifies geographically increases.[31]

This is the case for Chiquita Brands International, which spent years building its businesses and developing economies of scale and scale efficient facilities. It diversified into too many different product lines and its profits suffered. In recent years it has refocused the firm on its bananas and packaged salad product lines. Now, Chiquita produces almost one-third of the bananas it sells on its own farms in Latin America. It is the market leader in bananas in Europe and is number two in the market in North America. Chiquita is using its capabilities and core competencies in growing and distributing its brand of bananas in its international markets. In 2015 it was purchased by Brazil's Cutrale Group, which added Chiquita brand bananas and fresh packaged salads to its fruit business in oranges, apples, and peaches.[32]

The third factor in Porter's model of the determinants of national advantage is related and supporting industries. Italy has become the leader in the shoe industry because of related and supporting industries. For example, a well-established leather-processing industry provides the leather needed to construct shoes and related products. Also, many people travel to Italy to purchase leather goods, providing support in distribution. Supporting industries in leather-working machinery and design services also contribute to the success of the shoe industry. In fact, the design services industry supports its own related industries, such as ski boots, fashion apparel, and furniture. In Japan, cameras and copiers are related industries. Similarly, Germany is known for the quality of its machine tools and Belgium is known for skilled manufacturing (supporting and related industries are important in these two settings also).

Firm strategy, structure, and rivalry make up the final determinant of national advantage and foster the growth of certain industries. The types of strategy, structure, and rivalry among firms vary greatly from nation to nation. The excellent technical training system in Germany fosters a strong emphasis on continuous product and process improvements. In Italy, the national pride of the country's designers spawns strong industries not only in shoes but also sports cars, fashion apparel, and furniture. In the United States, competition among computer manufacturers and software producers contributes to further development of these industries.

The four determinants of national advantage (see Figure 8.3) emphasize the structural characteristics of a specific economy that contribute to some degree to national advantage and influence the firm's selection of an international business-level strategy. Policies of individual governments also affect the nature of the determinants as well as how firms compete within the boundaries governing bodies establish and enforce within a particular economy.[33] While studying their external environment (see Chapter 2), firms considering the possibility of using an international strategy need to gather information and data that will allow them to understand the effects of governmental policies and their enforcement on the nation's ability to establish advantages relative to other nations. Likewise, firms need to understand the relative degree of increased competitiveness the entering firm might receive by examining the country resources necessary to help the firm compete on a global basis in a focal industry.

Leading companies should recognize that a firm based in a country with a national competitive advantage is not guaranteed success as it implements its chosen international business-level strategy. The actual strategic choices managers make may be the most compelling reasons for success or failure as firms diversify geographically. Accordingly, the factors illustrated in Figure 8.3 are likely to produce the foundation for a firm's competitive advantages only when it develops and implements an appropriate international business-level strategy that takes advantage of distinct country factors. Thus, these distinct country factors should be thoroughly considered when deciding about which international business-level strategy to use. The firm will then make continuous adjustments to its international business-level strategy considering the nature of competition it encounters in different international markets and in light of customers' needs. Lexus, for example, does not have the share of the luxury car market in China that it desires. Accordingly, Toyota (which manufactures Lexus) is adjusting how it implements its international differentiation business-level strategy in China to better serve customers. However, it lagged far behind other luxury brands such as BMW, Audi, and Cadillac. Toyota decided not to put a production facility in China, thus having to pay a 25 percent tariff for each vehicle sold. However, its differentiation strategy has been paying off with a 27% increase in sales in 2017. It sold approximately 140,000 autos in China during that year. It is the second largest market for Lexus cars behind the United States.[34]

8-2b International Corporate-Level Strategy

A firm's international business-level strategy is also based, at least partially, on its international corporate-level strategy. Some international corporate-level strategies give individual country units the authority to develop their own business-level strategies, while others dictate the business-level strategies to standardize the firm's products and sharing of resources across countries.[35]

International corporate-level strategy focuses on the scope of a firm's operations through geographic diversification.[36] International corporate-level strategy is required when the firm operates in multiple industries that are located in multiple countries or regions (e.g., Southeast Asia or the European Union) and in which it sells multiple products. The headquarters unit guides the strategy, although as noted, business-or country-level managers can have substantial strategic input depending on the type of international corporate-level strategy the firm uses. The three international corporate-level strategies are shown in Figure 8.4; they vary in terms of two dimensions—the need for global integration and the need for local responsiveness.[37]

Multidomestic Strategy

A **multidomestic strategy** is an international strategy in which strategic and operating decisions are decentralized to the strategic business units in individual countries or

Figure 8.4 International Corporate-Level Strategies

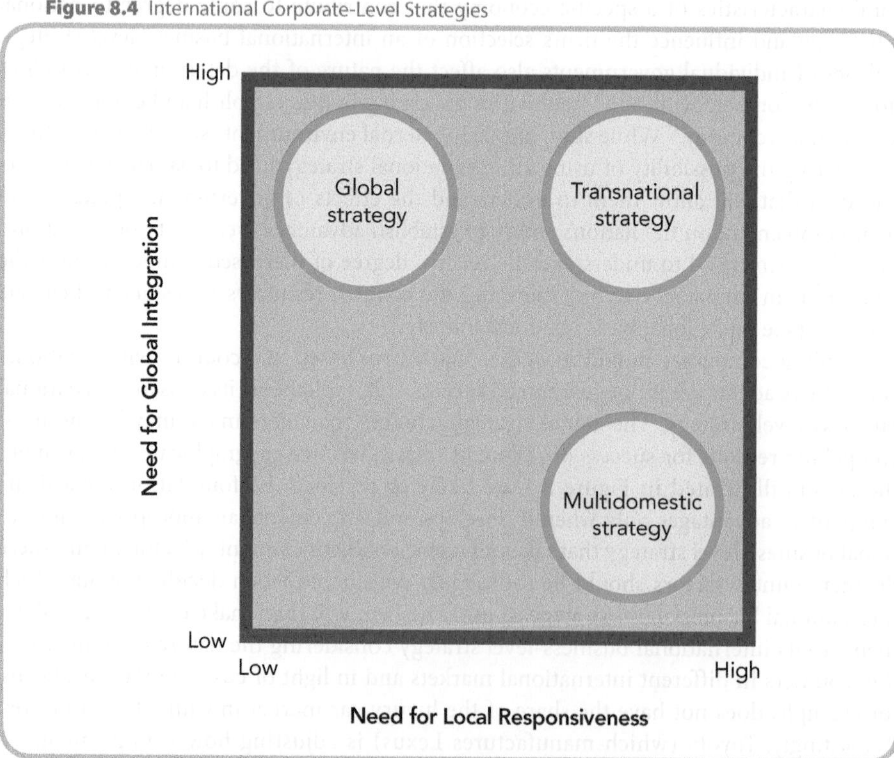

A **multidomestic strategy** is an international strategy in which strategic and operating decisions are decentralized to the strategic business units in individual countries or regions for allowing each unit the opportunity to tailor products to the local market

regions, allowing each unit the opportunity to tailor products to the local market.[38] With this strategy, the firm's need for local responsiveness is high while its need for global integration is low. Influencing these needs is the firm's belief that consumer needs and desires, industry conditions (e.g., the number and type of competitors), political and legal structures, and social norms vary by country. Thus, a multidomestic strategy focuses on competition within each country because market needs are thought to be segmented by country boundaries. To meet the specific needs and preferences of local customers, country or regional managers have the autonomy to customize the firm's products. Therefore, these strategies should maximize a firm's competitive response to the idiosyncratic requirements of each market.[39] The multidomestic strategy is most appropriate for use when the differences between the markets a firm serves and the customers in them are significant.

The use of multidomestic strategies usually expands the firm's local market share because the firm focuses its attention on the local clientele's needs. However, using a multidomestic strategy results in less knowledge sharing for the corporation as a whole because of the differences across markets, decentralization, and the different international business-level strategies employed by local units.[40] Moreover, multidomestic strategies do not allow the development of economies of scale and thus can be more costly.

Unilever is a large European consumer products company selling products in over 100 countries. The firm has more than 240 global brands that are grouped into three business units—foods, home care, and personal care. Historically, Unilever has used a highly decentralized approach for the purpose of managing its global brands. This approach allows regional managers considerable autonomy to adapt the characteristics of specific products to satisfy the unique needs of customers in different markets. More recently, however, Unilever has sought to increase the coordination between its independent subsidiaries in order to establish an even stronger global brand presence. One way that coordination is achieved is by having the presidents of each of the five global regions serve as members of the top management team.[41] As such, Unilever may be transitioning from a multidomestic strategy to a transnational strategy.

Global Strategy

A **global strategy** is an international strategy in which a firm's home office determines the strategies that business units are to use in each country or region.[42] This strategy indicates that the firm has a high need for global integration and a low need for local responsiveness. These needs indicate that, compared to a multidomestic strategy, a global strategy seeks greater levels of standardization of products across country markets. The firm using a global strategy seeks to develop economies of scale as it produces the same, or largely the same, products for distribution to customers throughout the world who are assumed to have similar needs. The global strategy offers greater opportunities to take innovations developed at the corporate level, or in one market, and apply them in other markets.[43] Improvements in global accounting and financial reporting standards have facilitated the use of this strategy.[44] A global strategy is most effective when the differences between markets and the customers the firm is serving are insignificant.

Efficient operations are required to successfully implement a global strategy. Increasing the efficiency of a firm's international operations mandates resource sharing and greater coordination and cooperation across market boundaries. Centralized decision making as designed by headquarters details how resources are to be shared and coordinated across markets. Research results suggest that the outcomes a firm achieves by using a global strategy become more desirable when the strategy is used in areas in which regional integration among countries is occurring.[45]

As illustrated in the following Strategic Focus, IKEA has implemented the global strategy. IKEA uses a standardized set of products worldwide and has centralized several

A **global strategy** is an international strategy in which a firm's home office determines the strategies that business units are to use in each country or region.

Strategic Focus

Ikea's Global Strategy in the Age of Digitalization and Urbanization

Founded in Sweden, IKEA has pursued a global strategy in developing its well-designed, inexpensive retail furniture strategy. As with most companies pursuing a global strategy, it emphasizes global efficiencies.

One particular approach that IKEA has used is to reduce shipping weight by efficient packaging. Standardization of the product offerings, efficient packaging, and the associated benefit of lower transportation costs are "at the heart of IKEA's ability to stay affordable." "Instead of changing products once they have hit shelves, IKEA is increasingly designing things with packaging and manufacturing in mind from the start." A tradeoff IKEA has experienced is that packaging can become too efficient at the expense of consumer frustration at the complexity of assembly once the product is in the home. So, simple assembly is also an important criterion.

IKEA continues to grow with annual sales of $45.7 billion, and more than 400 stores across 49 countries. It has also continued to enter new countries, with special focus recently on Latin America—such as Chile, Colombia, and Peru—and India. Furthermore, the firm is ramping up its focus on online shopping, because of the increasing emphasis on digital sales in the marketplace. The number of visitors to IKEA stores has plateaued, with expected heightened sales coming from online shopping in future years. IKEA is expanding this strategy by increasing its "click-and-collect merchandising approach where people order online and pick up the merchandise at a physical location."

Also, because of increased urbanization, IKEA is developing smaller city-center stores with a lower range of products compared to its majority of suburban store locations. One of these stores, which recently opened in the central part of Madrid, offers only bedroom furnishings while another one in Stockholm specializes in kitchen furniture and fixtures. Even with suburban locations, IKEA seeks to be within walking distance of transportation hubs such as subway stations.

Although IKEA is focused on efficiency, it also invests a significant amount of time studying each new country market entry. It focuses on where a growing middle-class is developing. It has entered China and India and is considering other South American countries such as Brazil. All of these economies have a growing middle class. Even in these countries, IKEA is focusing on flat packing, transporting, and reassembling its Swedish-styling furniture offered globally.

One of IKEA's latest strategies to improve its image is to develop a sounder approach to sustainability. Accordingly, its store roofs are outfitted with solar panels, and it will operate 314 wind turbines in 9 countries, putting the company on track to be energy independent by 2020. With its multiple actions to enhance sustainability, IKEA expects to be perceived as a socially and environmentally responsible company. These costs have reduced its operating income in the short term, yet they should lower overall costs in the longer term.

Face to Face/UPPA/Photoshot

The founding CEO of IKEA, Ingvar Kamprad, in front of one of IKEA's store fronts.

IKEA has many challenges and hopes to continue to grow, especially in its largest markets such as the United States. Although the recent tariffs placed on some European goods by the U.S. government cause IKEA operations in the United States concern, the company is well positioned. It has 13,000 employees in the United States and produces many of its products there. Although the founder's family continues to play a role in the company, they do not have ownership control. Thus, IKEA is a family influenced—not a family-controlled—firm. It has the advantages of a family firm without many of the disadvantages.

Sources: J. R, Hagerty, 2018, Ingvar Kamprad made IKEA a global retailer by keeping it simple, *Wall Street Journal*, https://www.wsj.com, February 2; R. Milne, 2018, What will Ikea build next? *Financial Times*, https://www.ft.com, January 31; C. Matlack, 2018, The tiny Ikea of the future, without meatballs of showroom mazes, *Bloomberg News*, https://www/Bloomberg.com, January 10; R. Milne, 2017, Ikea moves focus to centre city stores, *Financial Times*, https://www.ft.com, November 28; T. Gillies, 2017, Ikea's strategy: Stick to the basics, and expand in the US, *CNBC*, https://www.cnbc.com, January 16; S. Chaudhuri, 2015, IKEA's favorite design idea: Shrink the box, Wall Street Journal, June 18, B10; B. Kowitt, 2015, How IKEA took over the world, Fortune, www.fortune.com, March 13; A. Molin, 2015, C. Zillman, 2015, Here's how IKEA is fighting climate change, Fortune, www.fortune.com, June 11.

of its activities, including design and packaging. Accordingly, it integrates and centralizes some support functions from the firm's value chain (see Chapter 3). This integration and centralization foster economies of scale benefiting IKEA. Alternatively, IKEA is having to implement changes because of increasing digitalization and urbanization. As future growth may come largely from these types of sales, it has increased its online sales and continues to invest in the technology needed. It also has developed smaller and more specialized stores in the urban parts of cities, catering to new customers. Unlike many retailers, IKEA's annual sales continue to grow, albeit at a slower pace in recent years.

Because of increasing global competition and the need to simultaneously be cost efficient and produce differentiated products, the number of firms using a transnational international corporate-level strategy is increasing.

Transnational Strategy

A **transnational strategy** is an international strategy through which the firm seeks to achieve both global efficiency and local responsiveness. Realizing the twin goals of global integration and local responsiveness is difficult because global integration requires close global coordination while local responsiveness requires local flexibility. "Flexible coordination"—building a shared vision and individual commitment through an integrated network—is required to implement the transnational strategy. Such integrated networks allow a firm to manage its connections with customers, suppliers, partners, and other parties more efficiently rather than using arm's-length transactions.[46] The transnational strategy is difficult to use because of its conflicting goals (see Chapter 11 for more on the implementation of this and other corporate-level international strategies). On the positive side, effectively implementing a transnational strategy can produce higher performance than implementing either the multidomestic or global strategies if the circumstances are right.[47]

Transnational strategies are becoming increasingly necessary to successfully compete in international markets. Reasons for this include the continuing increases in the number of viable global competitors that challenge firms to reduce their costs. Simultaneously, the increasing sophistication of markets with greater information flows, made possible largely by the diffusion of the Internet and the desire for specialized products to meet consumers' unique needs, pressures firms to differentiate their products in local markets. Differences in culture and institutional environments also require firms to adapt their products and approaches to local environments. However, some argue that transnational strategies are not required to successfully compete in international markets. Those holding this view suggest that most multinational firms try to compete at the regional level (e.g., the European Union) rather than at the country level. To the degree this is the case, the need for the firm to simultaneously offer relatively unique products that are adapted to local markets and to produce those products at lower costs permitted by developing scale economies is reduced.[48]

Pictured above are many of the international brands that Mondelez manages globally while implementing the transnational strategy.

The complexities of competing in global markets increase the need for the use of a transnational strategy. Mondelēz International was created as a spinoff company from Kraft, which separated its domestic grocery products to focus on its high-growth snack foods business, in which 74 percent of sales come from outside North America. Mondelēz had \$26 billion in revenue in 2017 and about 80,000 employees; it has power brands (brands that are globally known and respected) and local brands.[49] So, because it globally integrates its operations to

A **transnational strategy** is an international strategy through which the firm seeks to achieve both global efficiency and local responsiveness.

standardize and maintain its power brands while simultaneously developing and marketing local brands that are specialized to meet the needs of local customers, Mondelēz pursues the transnational strategy. It is the global market leader in biscuits, chocolate, candy, and powdered beverages, and it holds the number two position in the global markets for chewing gum and coffee. About 45 percent of its sales come from fast-growing, emerging markets and with the variety of brands offered, it must adjust its strategy accordingly.

Next, we discuss trends in the global environment that are affecting the choices firms make when deciding which international corporate-level strategies to use and in which international markets to compete.

8-3 Environmental Trends

Although the transnational strategy is difficult to implement, an emphasis on global efficiency is increasing as more industries, and the companies competing within them, encounter intensified global competition. Magnifying the scope of this issue is the fact that, simultaneously, firms are experiencing demands for local adaptations of their products. These demands can be from customers (for products to satisfy their tastes and preferences) and from governing bodies (for products to satisfy a country's regulations). In addition, most multinational firms desire coordination and sharing of resources across country markets to hold down costs, as demonstrated in the Opening Case on Netflix.[50]

Because of these conditions, some large multinational firms with diverse products use a multidomestic strategy with certain product lines and a global strategy with others when diversifying geographically. Many multinational firms may require this type of flexibility if they are to be strategically competitive, in part due to trends that change over time.

Liability of foreignness and regionalization are two important trends influencing a firm's choice and use of international strategies, particularly international corporate-level strategies. We discuss these trends next.

8-3a Liability of Foreignness

The dramatic success of Japanese firms such as Toyota and Sony in the United States and other international markets in the 1980s was a powerful jolt to U.S. managers. This success awakened U.S. managers to the importance of international competition and the fact that many markets were rapidly becoming globalized. In the twenty-first century, Brazil, Russia, India, and China (BRIC) represent major international market opportunities for firms from many countries, including the United States, Japan, Korea, and members of the European Union. In addition, emerging economies such as Indonesia, Malaysia, Mexico, Colombia, Kenya, and Poland have shown rapid growth, Internet penetration, and improving rule of law.[51] However, even if foreign markets seem attractive, as appears to be the case with the BRIC countries and other growing economies, there are legitimate concerns for firms considering entering these markets. This is the *liability of foreignness*,[52] a set of costs associated with various issues firms face when entering foreign markets, including unfamiliar operating environments; economic, administrative, and cultural differences from their home institutional environments; and the challenges of coordination over distances.[53] Four types of distances commonly associated with liability of foreignness are cultural, administrative, geographic, and economic.[54]

Walt Disney Company's experience while opening theme parks in foreign countries demonstrates the liability of foreignness. For example, Disney suffered "lawsuits in France, at Disneyland Paris, because of the lack of fit between its transferred personnel policies and the French employees charged to enact them."[55] Disney executives learned from this experience and from building the firm's theme park in Hong Kong, and the company "went out of its way to tailor the park to local tastes."[56] Thus, as with Walt Disney Company, firms thinking about using an international strategy to enter foreign markets must be aware of the four types of distances they'll encounter when doing so and determine actions to take to reduce the potentially negative effects associated with those distances.

8-3b Regionalization

Regionalization is a second global environmental trend influencing a firm's choice and use of international strategies. This trend is becoming prominent largely because *where* a firm chooses to compete can affect its strategic competitiveness.[57] As a result, the firm considering using international strategies must decide if it should enter individual country markets or if it would be better served by competing in one or more regional markets.

Currently, the global strategy is used less frequently. It remains difficult to successfully implement even when the firm uses Internet-based strategies, although country borders matter less when e-commerce matters more.[58] In addition, the amount of competition vying for a limited amount of resources and customers can limit a firm's focus to a specific region rather than on country-specific markets that are in multiple parts of the world. A regional focus allows a firm to marshal its resources to compete effectively rather than spreading their limited resources across multiple country-specific international markets.[59]

However, a firm that competes in industries where the international markets differ greatly (in which it must employ a multidomestic strategy) may wish to narrow its focus to a particular region of the world. In so doing, it can better understand the cultures, legal and social norms, and other factors that are important for effective competition in those markets. For example, a firm may focus on Asian markets only, rather than competing simultaneously in the Middle East, Europe, and Asia or the firm may choose a region of the world where the markets are more similar and coordination and sharing of resources would be possible. In this way, the firm may be better able to understand the markets in which it competes, as well as achieve some economies, even though it may have to employ a multidomestic strategy. Firms commonly focus much of their international market entries on countries adjacent to their home country, which might be referred to as their home region.[60]

Countries that develop trade agreements to increase the economic power of their regions may promote regional strategies. The European Union and South America's Organization of American States (OAS) are country associations that developed trade agreements to promote the flow of trade across country boundaries within their respective regions.[61] Many European firms acquire and integrate their businesses in Europe to better coordinate pan-European brands as the European Union tries to create unity across the European markets. This process is likely to continue as new countries are added to the agreement.

The North American Free Trade Agreement (NAFTA), signed by the United States, Canada, and Mexico in 1993, facilitates free trade across country borders in North America. NAFTA loosens restrictions on international strategies within this region and provides greater opportunity for regional international strategies.[62] However, the Trump administrations has expressed doubts about the agreement and is in the process of trying to renegotiate it. It is unclear if the agreement will survive but if it fails, all three countries will suffer lost jobs. For example, it is estimated that the United States will lose 300,000 jobs if NAFTA is lost.[63]

Most firms enter regional markets sequentially, beginning in markets with which they are more familiar. They also introduce their largest and strongest lines of business into these markets first, followed by other product lines once the initial efforts are deemed successful. The additional product lines typically are introduced in the original investment location.[64] However, research also suggests that the size of the market and industry characteristics can influence this decision.[65]

Regionalization is important to most multinational firms, even those competing in many regions across the globe. For example, most large multinational firms have organizational structures that group operations within the same region (across countries) for managing and coordination purposes. Managing businesses by regions helps multinational enterprises (MNEs) deal with the complexities and challenges of operating in multiple international markets. As the Opening Case on Netflix suggests, managing across regions creates more costs, notwithstanding the benefits.

After selecting its business- and corporate-level international strategies, the firm determines how it will enter the international markets in which it has chosen to compete. We turn to this topic next.

8-4 Choice of International Entry Mode

Five modes of entry into international markets are available to firms. We show these entry modes and their characteristics in Figure 8.5. Each means of market entry has its advantages and disadvantages, suggesting that the choice of entry mode can affect the degree of

Figure 8.5 Modes of Entry and Their Characteristics

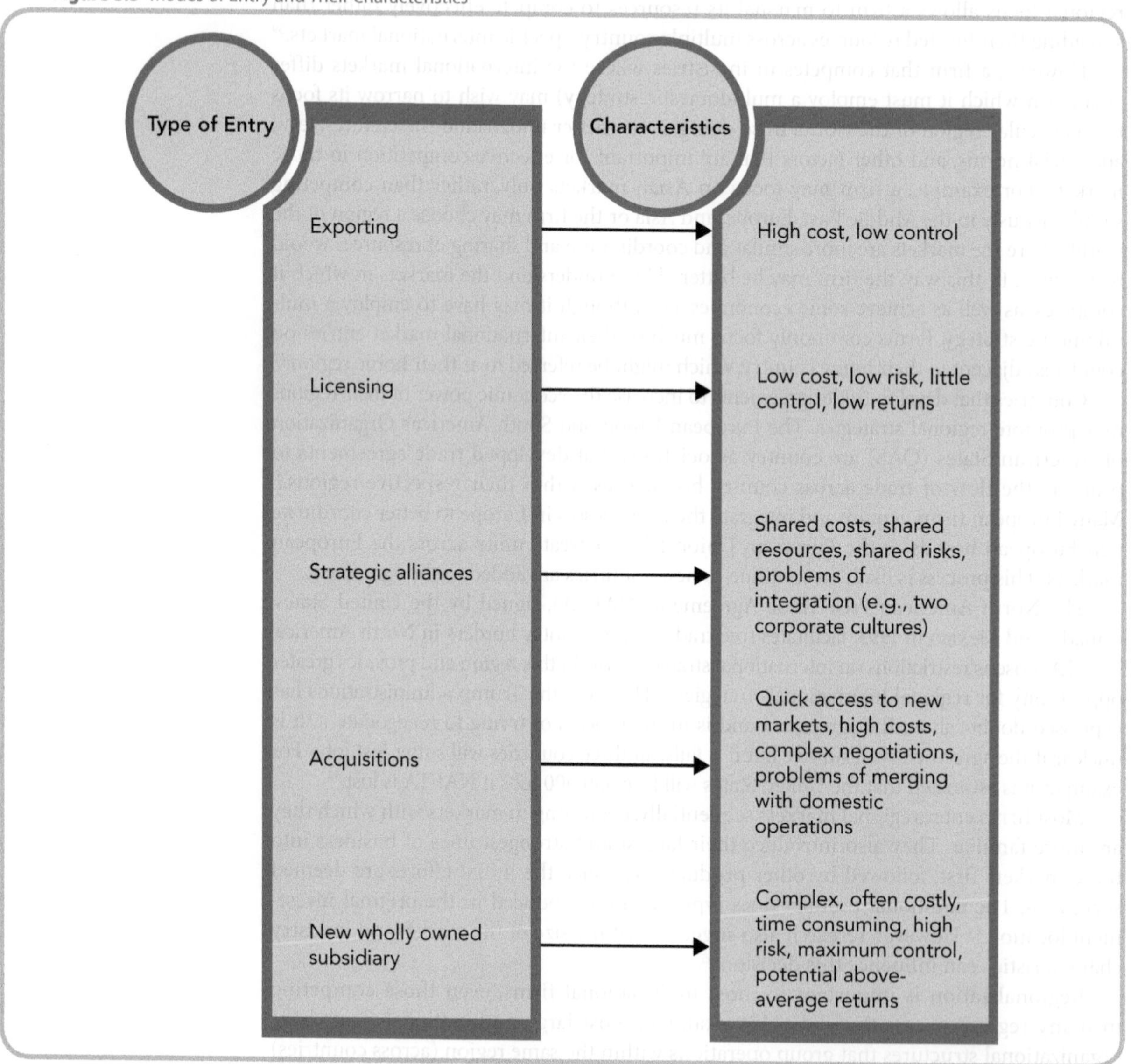

success the firm achieves by implementing an international strategy.[66] Many firms competing in multiple markets may use one or more or all five entry modes.[67]

8-4a Exporting

For many firms, exporting is the initial mode of entry used.[68] *Exporting* is an entry mode through which the firm sends products it produces in its domestic market to international markets. Exporting is a popular entry mode choice for small businesses to initiate an international strategy.[69]

The number of small U.S. firms using an international strategy is increasing; for example, 97 percent of U.S. firms exporting goods in 2018 are small businesses.[70] By exporting, firms avoid the expense of establishing operations in host countries (e.g., in countries outside their home country) in which they have chosen to compete. However, firms must establish some means of marketing and distributing their products when exporting. Usually, contracts are formed with host-country firms to handle these activities. Potentially high transportation costs to export products to international markets and the expense of tariffs placed on the firm's products because of host countries' policies are examples of exporting costs. The loss of some control when the firm contracts with local companies in host countries for marketing and distribution purposes can be expensive, making it harder for the exporting firm to earn profits.[71] Evidence suggests that, in general, using an international cost leadership strategy when exporting to developed countries has the most positive effect on firm performance, while using an international differentiation strategy with larger scale when exporting to emerging economies leads to the greatest amount of success. In either case, younger firms with a strong management team and market orientation capabilities are more successful.[72]

Firms export mostly to countries that are closest to their facilities because usually transportation costs are lower and there is greater similarity between geographic neighbors. For example, the United States' NAFTA partners, Mexico and Canada, account for more than half of the goods exported from the state of Texas. The Internet has also made exporting easier. Firms of any size can use the Internet to access critical information about foreign markets, examine a target market, research the competition, and find lists of potential customers.[73] Governments also use the Internet to support the efforts of those applying for export and import licenses, facilitating international trade among countries while doing so.

8-4b Licensing

Licensing is an entry mode in which an agreement is formed that allows a foreign company to purchase the right to manufacture and sell a firm's products within a host country's market or a set of host countries' markets.[74] The licensor is normally paid a royalty on each unit produced and sold. The licensee takes the risks and makes the monetary investments in facilities for manufacturing, marketing, and distributing products. As a result, licensing is possibly the least costly form of international diversification. As with exporting, licensing is an attractive entry mode option for smaller firms, and potentially for newer firms as well.[75]

Philip Morris International (PMI) and the China National Tobacco Corporation (CNTC) completed a licensing agreement at the end of 2005. This agreement provides CNTC access to the most famous brand in the world, Marlboro.[76] This agreement was quite important for the continued growth of PMI because its domestic sales were declining. Licensing agreements continue to be quite common in the marketplace. For example, an Australian company, Stan, signed a licensing agreement in 2018 for the rights to stream Starz originals and additional programming from Lionsgate and Starz premium.[77]

Another potential benefit of licensing as an entry mode is the possibility of earning greater returns from product innovations by selling the firm's innovations in international markets as well as in the domestic market.[78] Firms can obtain a larger market for their innovative new products, which helps them to pay off the R&D costs to develop them and to earn a faster return on the innovations than if they only sell them in domestic markets. This is done with little risk and without additional investment costs.

Licensing also has disadvantages. For example, after a firm licenses its product or brand to another party, it has little control over selling and distribution. Developing licensing agreements that protect the interests of both parties, while supporting the relationship embedded within an agreement, helps prevent this potential disadvantage.[79] In addition, licensing provides the least potential returns because returns must be shared between the licensor and the licensee. Another disadvantage is that the international firm may learn the technology of the party with whom it formed an agreement and then produce and sell a similar competitive product after the licensing agreement expires. In a classic example, Komatsu first licensed much of its technology from International Harvester, Bucyrus-Erie, and Cummins Engine to compete against Caterpillar in the earthmoving equipment business. Komatsu then dropped these licenses and developed its own products using the technology it gained from the U.S. companies.[80] Because of potential disadvantages, the parties to a licensing arrangement should finalize an agreement only after they are convinced that both parties' best interests are protected.

8-4c Strategic Alliances

Increasingly popular as an entry mode among firms using international strategies,[81] a *strategic alliance* involves a firm collaborating with another company in a different setting in order to enter one or more international markets.[82] Firms share the risks and the resources required to enter international markets when using strategic alliances.[83] Moreover, because partners bring their unique resources together for the purpose of working collaboratively, strategic alliances can facilitate developing new capabilities and possibly core competencies that may contribute to the firm's strategic competitiveness.[84] Indeed, developing and learning how to use new capabilities and/or competencies (particularly those related to technology) is often a key purpose for which firms use strategic alliances as an entry mode.[85] Firms should be aware that establishing trust between partners is critical for developing and managing technology-based capabilities while using strategic alliances.[86]

French-based Limagrain is the fourth largest seed company in the world through its subsidiary Vilmorin & Cie. An international agricultural cooperative group specializing in field seeds, vegetable seeds, and cereal products, part of Limagrain's strategy calls for it to continue to enter and compete in additional international markets. Limagrain is using strategic alliances as an entry mode. In 2011, the firm formed a strategic alliance with the Brazilian seed company Sementes Guerra in Brazil. The joint venture is named Limagrain Guerra do Brasil. Corn is the focus of the joint venture between these companies. Guerra is a family-owned company engaged in seed research; the production of corn, wheat, and soybeans; and the distribution of those products to farmers in Brazil and neighboring countries. Limagrain also had an earlier, successful joint venture with KWS in the United States. This venture, called AgReliant Genetics, focused primarily on corn and soybeans, is the third largest seed company in the United States.[87]

Not all alliances formed to enter international markets are successful.[88] Incompatible partners and conflict between the partners are primary reasons for failure when firms use strategic alliances as an entry mode. Another issue is that international strategic alliances are especially difficult to manage. Trust is an important aspect of alliances and must be carefully managed. The degree of trust between partners strongly influences alliance success. The probability of alliance success increases as the amount of trust between partners expands. Efforts to build trust are affected by at least four fundamental issues: the initial condition of the relationship, the negotiation process to arrive at an agreement, partner interactions, and external events.[89] Trust is also influenced by the country cultures involved and the relationships between the countries' governments (e.g., degree of political differences) where the firms in the alliance are home based.[90] Firms should be aware of these issues when trying to appropriately manage trust.

Research has shown that equity-based alliances, over which a firm has more control, are more likely to produce positive returns.[91] (We discuss equity-based and other types of strategic alliances in Chapter 9.) However, if trust is required to develop new capabilities through an alliance, equity positions can serve as a barrier to the necessary relationship building. Trust can be an especially important issue when firms have multiple partners supplying raw materials and/or services in their value chain (often referred to as outsourcing).[92] If conflict in a strategic alliance formed as an entry mode is not manageable, using acquisitions to enter international markets may be a better option.[93]

8-4d Acquisitions

When a firm acquires another company to enter an international market, it has completed a cross-border acquisition. Specifically, a *cross-border acquisition* is an entry mode through which a firm from one country acquires a stake in or purchases all of a firm located in another country.[94]

As free trade expands in global markets, firms throughout the world are completing a larger number of cross-border acquisitions. The ability of cross-border acquisitions to provide rapid access to new markets is a key reason for their growth. In fact, of the five entry modes, acquisitions often are the quickest means for firms to enter international markets.[95]

For example, two European supermarket chains merged in 2016 with important implications for the U.S. market. The $29 billion merger between Ahold, the Dutch owner of the Stop and Shop and Giant chains in the United States, with Delhaize, the Belgian operator of American chains Food Lion and Hannaford, gave the merged Ahold Delhaize company a 4.6 percent share of the U.S. grocery market, making it the fourth-largest competitor by revenue. This gave the combined European-based firm a major footprint on the East Coast and over 2,000 stores in the United States. Ahold also owns Peapod, a large online grocer in the United States, thus strengthening its stake in United States markets. Ahold Delhaize employs 369,000 associates across 6,637 stores operating in 11 different countries and serves 50 million customers per week.[96]

LAURIE DIEFFEMBACQ/AFP/Getty Images

The CEOs of Ahold, Dick Boer (left), and Belgian rival Delhaize, Frans Mullerand Delhaize, shake hands prior to announcing the merger of these giant food distribution chains in a significant cross-border merger.

Interestingly, firms use cross-border acquisitions less frequently to enter markets where corruption affects business transactions and, hence, the use of international strategies. A firm's preference is to use joint ventures to enter markets in which corruption is an issue, rather than using acquisitions. (Discussed fully in Chapter 9, a joint venture is a type of strategic alliance in which two or more firms create a legally independent company and share their resources and capabilities to operate it.) However, these ventures often fail, although this is less frequently the case for firms experienced with entering "corrupt" markets. When acquisitions are made in such countries, acquirers commonly pay smaller premiums to purchase firms.[97]

Although increasingly popular, acquisitions as an entry mode are not without costs, nor are they easy to successfully complete and operate. Cross-border acquisitions have some of the disadvantages of domestic acquisitions (see Chapter 7). In addition, they often require debt financing to complete, which carries an extra cost. Another issue for firms to consider is that negotiations for cross-border acquisitions can be exceedingly complex and are generally more complicated than are the negotiations associated with domestic acquisitions.[98] Dealing with the legal and regulatory requirements in the target firm's country and obtaining appropriate information to negotiate an agreement are also frequent problems. Finally, the merging of the new firm into the acquiring firm is often more complex than is the case with domestic acquisitions. The firm completing the cross-border acquisition must deal not only with different corporate cultures, but also with potentially different social cultures and practices.[99] These differences make integrating the two firms after the acquisition more challenging because it is difficult to capture the potential synergy when integration is slowed or stymied because of cultural differences.[100] Therefore, while cross-border acquisitions are popular as an entry mode primarily because they provide rapid access to new markets, firms considering this option should be fully aware of the costs and risks associated with using it.

8-4e New Wholly Owned Subsidiary

A **greenfield venture** is an entry mode through which a firm invests directly in another country or market by establishing a new wholly owned subsidiary. The process of creating a greenfield venture is often complex and potentially costly, but this entry mode affords maximum control to the firm and has the greatest amount of potential to contribute to the firm's strategic competitiveness as it implements international strategies. This potential is especially true for firms with strong intangible capabilities that might be leveraged through a greenfield venture.[101] Moreover, having additional control over its operations in a foreign market is especially advantageous when the firm has proprietary technology.

Research also suggests that "wholly owned subsidiaries and expatriate staff are preferred" in service industries where "close contacts with end customers" and "high levels of professional skills, specialized know-how, and customization" are required.[102] Other research suggests that, as investments, greenfield ventures are used more prominently when the firm's business relies significantly on the quality of its capital-intensive manufacturing facilities. In contrast, cross-border acquisitions are more likely to be used as an entry mode when a firm's operations are human-capital intensive—for example, if a strong local union and high cultural distance (between the countries involved) would cause difficulty in transferring knowledge to a host nation through a greenfield venture.[103]

The risks associated with greenfield ventures are significant in that the costs of establishing a new business operation in a new country or market can be substantial. To support the operations of a newly established operation in a foreign country, the firm may have to acquire knowledge and expertise about the new market by hiring either host-country nationals, possibly from competitors, or through consultants, which can be costly. This new knowledge and expertise often is necessary to facilitate the building of new facilities, establishing distribution networks, and learning how to implement marketing strategies that can lead to competitive success in the new market.[104] Importantly, while taking these actions, the firm seeks to maintain control over the technology, marketing,

A **greenfield venture** is an entry mode through which a firm invests directly in another country or market by establishing a new wholly owned subsidiary.

and distribution of its products. Research also suggests that when the country risk is high, firms prefer to enter with joint ventures instead of greenfield investments. However, if firms have previous experience in a country, they prefer to use a wholly owned greenfield venture rather than a joint venture.[105]

China has been an attractive market for foreign retailers (e.g., Walmart) because of its large population, the growing economic capabilities of Chinese citizens, and the opening of the Chinese market to foreign firms. Many foreign retailers have entered China, many of them using greenfield ventures. Of course, China is a unique environment, partly because of its culture, but more so because of the government control and intervention. Good relationships with local and national government officials are quite important to foreign firms' success in China. Because of these complexities and the challenges they present, foreign retailers' success in this market has been mixed despite the substantial opportunities that exist there. Expansion, however, is going to be more difficult, given how popular the online retailer Alibaba and its affiliates and competitors have become. Thus, great care should be exercised when selecting the best mode for entering particular markets, as we discuss next.[106]

8-4f Dynamics of Mode of Entry

Several factors affect the firm's choice about how to enter international markets. Market entry is often achieved initially through exporting, which requires no foreign manufacturing expertise and investment only in distribution. Licensing can facilitate the product improvements necessary to enter foreign markets, as in the Komatsu example. Strategic alliances are a popular entry mode because they allow a firm to connect with an experienced partner already in the market. Partly because of this, geographically diversifying firms often use alliances in uncertain situations, such as an emerging economy where there is significant risk (e.g., Venezuela). However, if intellectual property rights in the emerging economy are not well protected, the number of firms in the industry is growing fast, and the need for global integration is high, other entry modes such as a joint venture (see Chapter 9) or a wholly owned subsidiary are preferred.[107] In the final analysis though, all three modes—export, licensing, and strategic alliance—can be effective means of initially entering new markets and for developing a presence in those markets.

Acquisitions, greenfield ventures, and sometimes joint ventures are used when firms want to establish a strong presence in an international market. Aerospace firms Airbus and Boeing have used joint ventures, especially in large markets, to facilitate entry, while military equipment firms such as Thales SA have used acquisitions to build a global presence. Japanese auto manufacturer Toyota largely established a presence in the United States through both greenfield ventures and joint ventures. Because of Toyota's highly efficient manufacturing processes, the firm wants to maintain control over manufacturing when possible. As such, it opened a new regional center that combines supplier coordination and regional North American research in Michigan and a new North American headquarters facility in Texas. Toyota has ten manufacturing plants in the United States with 136,000 employees (direct and indirect). Overall, Toyota has invested almost $22 billion in its U.S. operations.[108] Both acquisitions and greenfield ventures are likely to come at later stages in the development of a firm's international strategies.

Thus, to enter a global market, a firm selects the entry mode that is best suited to its situation. In some instances, the various options will be followed sequentially, beginning with exporting and eventually leading to greenfield ventures. In other cases, the firm may use several, but not all, of the different entry modes, each in different markets. The decision regarding which entry mode to use is primarily a result of the industry's competitive conditions; the country's situation and government policies; and the firm's unique set of resources, capabilities, and core competencies.

8-5 Risks in an International Environment

International strategies are risky, particularly those that would cause a firm to become substantially more diversified in terms of geographic markets served. Firms entering markets in new countries often encounter several complex institutional risks.[109] Political and economic risks cannot be ignored by firms using international strategies (see specific examples of political and economic risks in Figure 8.6).

8-5a Political Risks

Political risks "denote the probability of disruption of the operations of multinational enterprises by political forces or events whether they occur in host countries, home country, or result from changes in the international environment."[110] Possible disruptions to a firm's operations when seeking to implement its international strategy create numerous problems, including uncertainty created by government regulation; the existence of many, possibly conflicting, legal authorities or corruption; and the potential nationalization of private assets.[111] Firms investing in other countries, when implementing their international strategy, may have concerns about the stability of the national government and the effects of unrest and government instability on their investments or assets.[112] A recent study also suggests that political risk in one country often spreads to others, as in the Arab Spring revolutions among many Middle Eastern countries.[113] To deal with these concerns, firms should conduct a political risk analysis of the countries or regions they may enter using one of the five entry modes. Through political risk analysis, the firm examines potential sources and factors of non-commercial disruptions of their foreign investments and the operations flowing from them.[114] However, occasionally firms might use political (institutional) weaknesses as an opportunity to transfer

Figure 8.6 Risks in the International Environment

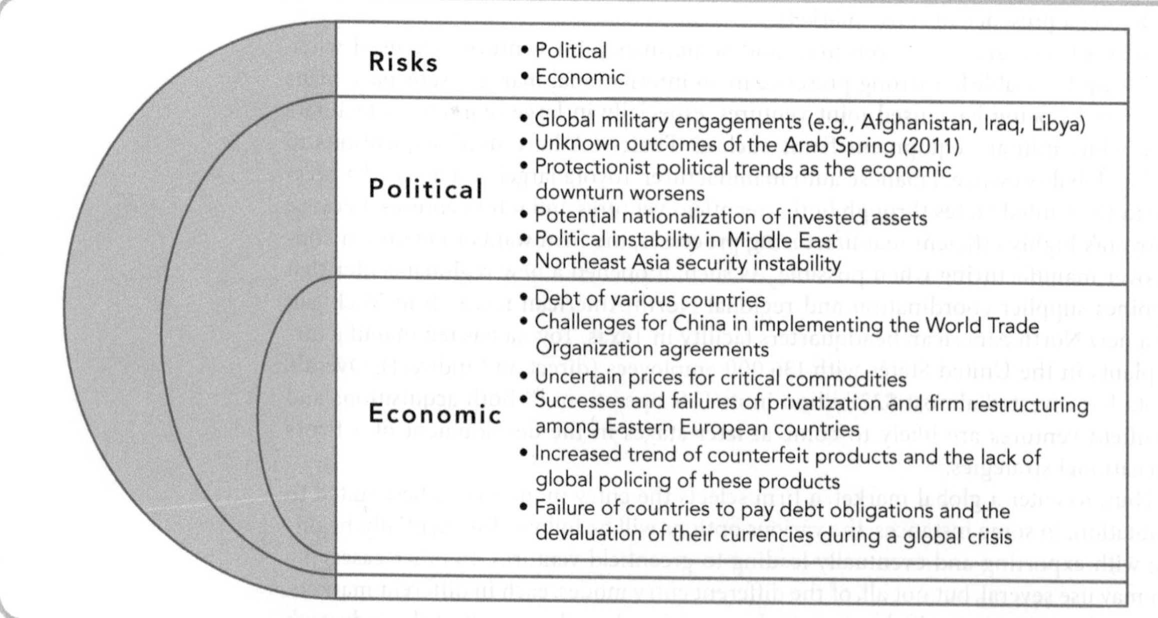

activities or practices that stakeholders see as undesirable for their operations in the home country to a new market so they can continue earning returns on these questionable practices.[115]

FIFA, the international soccer federation that sponsors World Cup soccer matches along with its regional and country affiliates, has come under heavy scrutiny for possible corrupt practices, as illustrated in the Mini Case at the end of the chapter. Much of the alleged corruption that has taken place has been indirectly supported by the nature of the governments and institutions in which soccer is popular, especially in less developed countries. Bribes were alleged to have been paid for Africa to receive the World Cup, and the recent decisions by FIFA to host the games in Russia and Qatar in 2018 and 2022 have come under question.[116] Many of the countries, for example Brazil and Paraguay, are seeking to overhaul their country soccer regulating bodies because of the scandal.[117]

Russia has experienced a relatively high level of institutional instability in the years following its revolutionary transition to a more democratic government. To regain more central control and reduce the decentralized chaos, Russian leaders took actions such as prosecuting powerful private firm executives, seeking to gain state control of firm assets, and not approving some foreign acquisitions of Russian businesses. The initial institutional instability, followed by the actions of the central government, caused some firms to delay or avoid significant foreign direct investment in Russia. The riskiness of the situation worsened when Russia took Crimea from the Ukraine and used proxy rebels to fight in Eastern Ukraine. Russia's economy has suffered under sanctions placed on them by the United States and other Western countries. The situation has been exacerbated by concerns about Russia's meddling in the 2016 U.S. Presidential election. In fact, the probe of this activity has resulted in the indictment of a number of Russians by Special Prosecutor Robert Mueller. The outcome of these actions is currently unclear.[118]

As suggested by the information in the Strategic Focus, DHL, FedEx, and UPS have a difficult task ahead. They face unusual economic risks in mostly developed economies from which they have a substantial amount of business. They must predict which economies, industries, and companies are the most vulnerable to declines from tariffs and in turn how tariffs will affect the demand for their company's services. And, they need to forecast the likelihood of a full-scale trade war and determine how they can best prepare to deal with this challenge.

8-5b Economic Risks

Economic risks include fundamental weaknesses in a country or region's economy with the potential to cause adverse effects on firms' efforts to successfully implement their international strategies. As illustrated in the example of Russian institutional instability and property rights, political risks and economic risks are interdependent. If firms cannot protect their intellectual property, they are highly unlikely to use a means of entering a foreign market that involves significant and direct investments. Therefore, countries need to create, sustain, and enforce strong intellectual property rights to attract foreign direct investment.[119]

In emerging economies, one of the significant economic risks is the availability of important infrastructure to allow large industry players, such as miners, to have sufficient electrical power in national grids to meet their power usage requirements. Often, inefficient, state-owned electric power producers are forced to run intermittent blackouts, which is devastating for continuous process manufacturing and refining such as found in the mining industry. South Africa used to have a reliable electrical power grid. However, the state-owned electrical utility, Eskom Holdings Ltd., neglected to build new

Strategic **Focus**

The Global Delivery Services Industry: Economic Disruption of Tariffs and Trade Wars

The global delivery service industry has been booming in the last few years, primarily because of the significant increase in online sales. The three largest global market shares in this industry are held by DHL at 38 percent, FedEx at 24 percent, and UPS at 22 percent. DHL is a German-based company and both FedEx and UPS are home based in the United States. The four largest markets for delivery services are in the United States, Europe, China, and Japan. These three companies are major participants in each one, but they play a much smaller role in the local delivery services in China than the other three. And, although DHL has the largest global market share, it has a much smaller share of the U.S. market. There UPS is number one and FedEx is a close second. The U.S. Postal Service (USPS) is the third largest in the U.S. market. DHL currently handles about 500 million packages annually in the United States. That sounds very large until it is compared to the 750 million packages that UPS delivered during the 2017 Christmas season alone. However, DHL has made major investments in 2017 and 2018 to increase its business in the U.S. market.

In many ways, the future for this industry looks to be bright with the increasing amount of online sales that then require the goods to be delivered. Of course, a major portion of online sales are made by Amazon, which has its own delivery service. And it supplements its delivery service with local deliveries by the USPS. Still, many other retail and other firms are selling their goods online. New technology is being developed and used to facilitate deliveries such as drones and robotics. With the significant growth in the market that is expected, the future should look bright especially for the three companies with the largest global market shares. However, they also face some unusual economic risks and uncertainties. As noted earlier in the chapter, the future of NAFTA is uncertain. If, by chance, the trade agreement is extinguished, economists predict negative economic consequences for all three countries involved, Canada, Mexico and the United States. And, a number of specific industries are likely to suffer lower sales revenue, which will translate into fewer packages shipped within and across these countries' boundaries.

An additional and potentially even larger and more disruptive economic risk is on the horizon. In 2018, the U.S. government implemented tariffs on specific goods imported from European countries, Canada, Mexico, and China. In response, the European Union, Canada, China, and Mexico all instituted tariffs on specific goods imported into their countries from the United States. In return, the U.S. government has threatened to implement even larger tariffs on a greater number of goods. There are fears of a major trade war among these countries. If that happens, economists predict that the gross domestic product (GDP) of each country is likely to decline. In other words, no country is likely to come out of a trade war as a winner (based on the outcomes of past trade wars). If economies decline, the demand for delivery services will also decline. However, the negative effects are likely to be uneven in a trade war, partly because tariffs are commonly placed on specific products and so some sectors suffer more than others. The delivery services have little or no control over the changes in demand that are likely to occur from a trade war, and it may be difficult to predict the industries/sectors and companies that will be harmed the most. This is partly because some of the goods on which tariffs are placed may be used in the manufacture of multiple products. And the demand for these products will vary because of the price increases due to the tariffs. Additionally, some companies in the same industry may import more of these goods than others. Some companies may rely more on local suppliers and thus avoid the price increases due to tariffs on imported goods.

dpa picture alliance/Alamy Stock Photo

DHL, FedEx, and UPS hold the 3 largest market shares in the global delivery service industry.

Sources: P. R. La Monica, 2018, Wall street's $6.3 trillion man is worried about a trade war, *CNNMoney*, https://www.cnnmoney.com, July 16; D. Shine, 2018, China's economy slows just as the trade fight begins, *CNNMoney*, https://www.cnnmoney.com, July 16; 2018, Couriers and local delivery service providers' global market share in 2017, *Statistica*, https://www.statistica.com, July 15; 2018, China express delivery market size trends and forecasts 2018–2022, EMailWire.com, https://www.reportsweb.com, July 2; 2018, Deutsche Post's DHL expands U.S. delivery service in swipe at FedEx, UPS, *New York Times*, https://www.nytimes.com, March 15; E. E. Phillips, 2018, DHL steps back into U.S. package delivery in challenge to UPS, FedEx, *Wall Street Journal*, https://www.wsj.com, March 15; E. E. Phillips, E-commerce spurs push for speedier shipping payments, *Wall Street Journal*, https://www.wsj.com, March 13; J. Berman, 2018, 2018 parcel express roundtable: Business boom, *Logistics Management*, https://www.logisticsmgmt.com; March 2; 2017, Japan-Express delivery, International Trade Administration, https://www.export.gov, September 25; 2017, Express delivery market 2017 key players (UPS, FedEx, DHL. TNT. USPS, Deppon) competitive analysis, product demand, applications, Future growth by 2022, *Reuters*, https://www.reuters.com, August 8; A. Marder, 2017, UPS vs FedEx: Who ships more? *Capterra Logistics*, https://blog.captura.com, June 7; 2017, Express delivery market in Europe 2017–2021, *PRNewswire*, https://www.prnewswire.com, Jan 24.

power plants and sufficiently maintain current operating generating plants. As such, intermittent power outages have occurred lasting up to 12 hours, resulting in significant productivity decreases in the mining industry, which produces 60 percent of South Africa's exports. This problem has been significant because Eskom produces 95 percent of the country's electricity and 45 percent of the electricity in Africa. As this example suggests, infrastructure can be a significant economic risk in emerging or partially developed economies such as South Africa.[120]

Dean Hutton/Bloomberg/Getty Images

Darkness surrounding residential homes due to blackout by Eskom Holdings SOC Ltd. in the Troyeville suburb of Johannesburg, South Africa, in 2014.

Another economic risk is the perceived security risk of a foreign firm acquiring companies that have key natural resources or firms that may be considered strategic with regard to intellectual property. For instance, many Chinese firms have been buying natural resource firms in Australia and Latin America. as well as manufacturing assets in the United States. This has made the governments of the key resource firms concerned about such strategic assets falling under the control of state-owned Chinese firms.[121] Terrorism has also been of concern. Indonesia has difficulty competing for investment against China and India, countries that are viewed as having fewer security risks.

As noted earlier, the differences and fluctuations in the value of currencies is among the foremost economic risks of using an international strategy.[122] This is especially true as the level of the firm's geographic diversification increases to the point where the firm is trading in many currencies. The value of the dollar relative to other currencies can affect the value of the international assets and earnings of U.S. firms. For example, an increase in the value of the U.S. dollar can reduce the value of U.S. multinational firms' international assets and earnings in other countries. Furthermore, the value of different currencies can, at times, dramatically affect a firm's competitiveness in global markets because of its effect on the prices of goods manufactured in different countries. An increase in the value of the dollar can harm U.S. firms' exports to international markets because of the price differential of the products. Currency value can be affected by the institution of tariffs and trade wars as experienced recently in the United States and China. And, the concerns about the tariffs implemented can affect the amount of foreign firm's investment even in developed economies (e.g., Western European countries).[123] This could be the case of the major express delivery service companies, DHL, FedEx, and UPS, as discussed in the Strategic Focus. Thus, government oversight and control of economic and financial capital, as well as corporate governance rules in a country, affect not only local economic activity, but also foreign investments in the country.[124]

8-6 Strategic Competitiveness Outcomes

As previously discussed, international strategies can result in three basic benefits (increased market size; economies of scale and learning; and location advantages) for firms. These basic benefits are gained when the firm successfully manages political, economic, and other institutional risks while implementing its international strategies. In turn, these benefits are critical to the firm's efforts to achieve strategic competitiveness (as measured by improved performance and enhanced innovation—see Figure 8.1).[125]

Overall, the degree to which firms achieve strategic competitiveness through international strategies is expanded or increased when they successfully implement an international diversification strategy. As an extension or elaboration of international strategy, an **international diversification strategy** is a strategy through which a firm expands the sales of its goods or services across the borders of global regions and countries into a potentially large number of geographic locations or markets. Instead of entering one or just a few markets, the international diversification strategy finds firms using international business-level and international corporate-level strategies for the purpose of entering multiple regions and markets in order to sell their products.

8-6a International Diversification and Returns

Evidence suggests numerous reasons for firms to use an international diversification strategy,[126] meaning that international diversification should be related positively to a firm's performance as measured by the returns it earns on its investments. Research has shown that as international diversification increases, a firm's returns decrease initially but then increase quickly as it learns how to manage the increased geographic diversification it has created.[127] In fact, the stock market is particularly sensitive to investments in international markets. Firms that are broadly diversified into multiple international markets usually achieve the most positive stock returns, especially when they diversify geographically into core business areas.[128]

Many factors contribute to the positive effects of international diversification, such as private versus government ownership, potential economies of scale and experience, location advantages, increased market size, and the opportunity to stabilize returns. The stabilization of returns through international diversification helps reduce a firm's overall risk.[129] Large, well-established firms and entrepreneurial ventures can both achieve these positive outcomes by successfully implementing an international diversification strategy.

8-6b Enhanced Innovation

In Chapter 1, we indicated that developing new technology is at the heart of strategic competitiveness. As noted in our discussion of the determinants of national advantage (see Figure 8.3), a nation's competitiveness depends, in part, on the capacity of its industries to innovate. Eventually and inevitably, competitors outperform firms that fail to innovate. Therefore, the only way for individual nations and individual firms to sustain a competitive advantage is to upgrade it continually through innovation.[130]

An international diversification strategy creates the potential for firms to achieve greater returns on their innovations (through larger or more numerous markets) while reducing the often-substantial risks of R&D investments. Additionally, international diversification may be necessary to generate the resources required to sustain a large-scale R&D operation. An environment of rapid technological obsolescence makes it difficult to invest in new technology and the capital-intensive operations necessary to compete in such an environment. Firms operating solely in domestic markets may find such investments difficult because of the length of time required to recoup the original investment. However, diversifying into several international markets improves a firm's ability to appropriate additional returns from innovation before domestic competitors can overcome the initial competitive advantage created by the innovation.[131] In addition, firms moving into international markets are exposed to new products and processes. If

As an extension or elaboration of international strategy, an **international diversification strategy** is a strategy through which a firm expands the sales of its goods or services across the borders of global regions and countries into a potentially large number of geographic locations or markets.

they learn about those products and processes and integrate this knowledge into their operations, further innovation can be developed. To incorporate the learning into their own R&D processes, firms must manage those processes effectively to absorb and use the new knowledge to create further innovations.[132] For a number of reasons then, international strategies and certainly an international diversification strategy provide incentives for firms to innovate.

The relationship among international geographic diversification, innovation, and returns is complex. Some level of performance is necessary to provide the resources the firm needs to diversify geographically; in turn, geographic diversification provides incentives and resources to invest in R&D. Effective R&D should enhance the firm's returns, which then provide more resources for continued geographic diversification and investment in R&D.[133] Of course, the returns generated from these relationships increase through effective managerial practices. Evidence suggests that more culturally diverse top management teams often have a greater knowledge of international markets and their idiosyncrasies, but their orientation to expand internationally can be affected by the nature of their incentives.[134] Moreover, managing the business units of a geographically diverse multinational firm requires skill, not only in managing a decentralized set of businesses, but also coordinating diverse points of view emerging from businesses located in different countries and regions. Firms able to do this increase the likelihood of outperforming their rivals.[135]

8-7 The Challenge of International Strategies

Effectively using international strategies creates basic benefits and contributes to the firm's strategic competitiveness. However, for several reasons, attaining these positive outcomes is difficult.[136]

8-7a Complexity of Managing International Strategies

Pursuing international strategies, particularly an international diversification strategy, typically leads to growth in a firm's size and the complexity of its operations. In turn, larger size and greater operational complexity make a firm more difficult to manage. At some point, size and complexity either cause the firm to become virtually unmanageable or increase the cost of its management beyond the value created using international strategies. Different cultures and institutional practices (e.g., those associated with governmental agencies) that are part of the countries in which a firm competes when using an international strategy also can create difficulties.[137]

Firms must build on their capabilities and other advantages to overcome the challenges encountered in international markets. For example, some firms from emerging economies that hold monopolies in their home markets can invest the resources gained there to enhance their competitiveness in international markets (because they don't have to be concerned about competitors in home markets).[138] The key is for firms to overcome the various liabilities of foreignness regardless of their source.

8-7b Limits to International Expansion

Learning how to effectively manage an international strategy improves the likelihood of achieving positive outcomes such as enhanced performance. However, at some point, the degree of geographic and possibly product diversification the firm's international strategies bring about causes the returns from using the strategies to level off and eventually become negative.[139]

There are several reasons for the limits to the positive effects of the diversification associated with international strategies. First, greater geographic dispersion across country borders increases the costs of coordination between units and the distribution of products. This is especially true when firms have multiple locations in countries that have diverse subnational institutions. Second, trade barriers, logistical costs, cultural diversity, and other differences by country (e.g., access to raw materials and different employee skill levels) greatly complicate the implementation of an international strategy.[140]

Institutional and cultural factors can be strong barriers to the transfer of a firm's core competencies from one market to another.[141] Marketing programs often must be redesigned and new distribution networks established when firms expand into new markets. In addition, firms may encounter different labor costs and capital expenses. In general, it becomes increasingly difficult to effectively implement, manage, and control a firm's international operations with increases in geographic diversity.[142]

The amount of diversification in a firm's international operations that can be managed varies from company to company and is affected by managers' abilities to deal with ambiguity and complexity. The problems of central coordination and integration are mitigated if the firm's international operations compete in friendly countries that are geographically close and have cultures like its own country's culture. In that case, the firm is likely to encounter fewer trade barriers, the laws and customs are better understood, and the product is easier to adapt to local markets.[143] For example, U.S. firms may find it less difficult to expand their operations into Mexico, Canada, and Western European countries than into Asian countries.

The relationships between the firm using an international strategy and the governments in the countries in which the firm is competing can also be constraining.[144] The reason for this is that the differences in host countries' governmental policies and practices can be substantial, creating a need for the focal firm to learn how to manage what can be a large set of different enforcement policies and practices. At some point, the differences create too many problems for the firm to be successful. Using strategic alliances is another way that firms can deal with this limiting factor. Partnering with companies in different countries allows the foreign-entering firm to rely on its partner to help deal with local laws, rules, regulations, and customs. But these partnerships are not risk free and managing them tends to be difficult.[145]

SUMMARY

- The use of international strategies is increasing. Multiple factors and conditions are influencing the increasing use of these strategies, including opportunities to:
  - extend a product's life cycle
  - gain access to critical raw materials, sometimes including relatively inexpensive labor
  - integrate a firm's operations on a global scale to better serve customers in different countries
  - better serve customers whose needs appear to be more alike today as a result of global communications media and the Internet's capabilities to inform
  - meet increasing demand for goods and services that is surfacing in emerging markets
- When used effectively, international strategies yield three basic benefits: increased market size, economies of scale and learning, and location advantages. Firms use international business-level and international corporate-level strategies to geographically diversify their operations.
- International business-level strategies are usually grounded in one or more home-country advantages. Research suggests that there are four determinants of national advantage: factors of production; demand conditions; related and supporting industries; and patterns of firm strategy, structure, and rivalry.
- There are three types of international corporate-level strategies. A multidomestic strategy focuses on competition within each country in which the firm competes. Firms using a multidomestic strategy decentralize strategic and operating decisions

to the business units operating in each country, so that each unit can tailor its products to local conditions. A global strategy assumes more standardization of products across country boundaries; therefore, a competitive strategy is centralized and controlled by the home office. Commonly, large multinational firms, particularly those with multiple diverse products being sold in many different markets, use a multidomestic strategy with some product lines and a global strategy with others.

- A transnational strategy seeks to integrate characteristics of both multidomestic and global strategies for the purpose of being able to simultaneously emphasize local responsiveness and global integration.
- Two global environmental trends—liability of foreignness and regionalization—are influencing firms' choices of international strategies as well as their implementation. Liability of foreignness requires firms to analyze how distance between their domestic market and international markets affects their ability to compete. Some firms choose to concentrate their international strategies on regions (e.g., the EU, Asia, Latin America) rather than on individual country markets.
- Firms can use one or more of five entry modes to enter international markets. Exporting, licensing, strategic alliances, acquisitions, and new wholly owned subsidiaries, often referred to as greenfield ventures, are the five entry modes. Most firms begin with exporting or licensing because of their lower costs and risks. Later they tend to use strategic alliances and acquisitions as well. The most expensive and risky means of entering a new international market is establishing a new wholly owned subsidiary (greenfield venture). On the other hand, such subsidiaries provide the advantages of maximum control by the firm and, if successful, the greatest returns. Large, geographically diversified firms often use most or all five entry modes across different markets when implementing international strategies.
- Firms also encounter risks when implementing international strategies. The two major categories of risks firms need to understand and address when diversifying geographically through international strategies are political risks (risks concerned with the probability that a firm's operations will be disrupted by political forces or events, whether they occur in the firm's domestic market or in the markets the firm has entered) and economic risks (risks resulting from fundamental weaknesses in a country's or a region's economy with the potential to adversely affect a firm's ability to implement its international strategies).
- Successful use of international strategies (especially an international diversification strategy) contributes to a firm's strategic competitiveness in the form of improved performance and enhanced innovation. International diversification facilitates innovation in a firm because it provides a larger market to gain greater and faster returns from investments in innovation. In addition, international diversification can generate the resources necessary to sustain a large-scale R&D program.
- In general, international diversification helps to achieve above-average returns, but this assumes that the diversification is effectively implemented and that the firm's international operations are well managed. International diversification provides greater economies of scope and learning which, along with greater innovation, help produce above-average returns.
- A firm using international strategies to pursue strategic competitiveness often experiences complex challenges that must be overcome. Some limits also constrain the ability to manage international expansion effectively. International diversification increases coordination and distribution costs, and management problems are exacerbated by trade barriers, logistical costs, and cultural diversity, among other factors.

KEY TERMS

global strategy 249
greenfield venture 258
international diversification strategy 264
international strategy 241
multidomestic strategy 248
transnational strategy 251

REVIEW QUESTIONS

1. What incentives influence firms to use international strategies?
2. What are the three basic benefits firms can gain by successfully implementing an international strategy?
3. What four factors are determinants of national advantage and serve as a basis for international business-level strategies?
4. What are the three international corporate-level strategies? What are the advantages and disadvantages associated with these strategies?
5. What are some global environmental trends affecting the choice of international strategies, particularly international corporate-level strategies?

6. What five entry modes do firms use to enter international markets? What is the typical sequence in which firms use these entry modes?
7. What are political risks and what are economic risks? How should firms deal with these risks?
8. What are the strategic competitiveness outcomes firms can achieve through international strategies, and particularly through an international diversification strategy?
9. What are two important issues that can potentially affect a firm's ability to successfully use international strategies?

Mini-Case

The Global Soccer Industry and the Effect of the FIFA Scandal

The Fédération Internationale de Football Association (FIFA) was founded in Paris in 1904 and was initially comprised of only European nations. By World War II, FIFA had added a few South American members. Newly independent states in Africa, Asia, and the Caribbean joined later. However, it continued to be governed "as though it was an exclusive European club"—until 1974 when João Havelange, a Brazilian, won the election as FIFA's president. Havelange was able to transform the organization and expand the World Cup competition to teams from nations outside Europe and South America and made the tournament a major money-making enterprise. With the amount of exposure and money involved, companies desired sponsorship rights because of the advertising potential. Adidas AG and Coca-Cola were original sponsors. Havelange also oversaw significant increases in revenue from television rights. In the process, Havelange was alleged to have participated in much corruption and eventually was suspected of amassing $50 million in bribes.

Havelange facilitated the election of Sepp Blatter who became FIFA president in 1998 and continued to follow Havelange's approach to politics. After FIFA became a worldwide organization, especially in developing countries in Latin America, Africa, and the Caribbean, more allegations of corruption surfaced. One analyst suggested that "FIFA could not have developed soccer in poorer countries without corrupt practices." Of course, there has also been corruption in more developed countries, such as the United Kingdom and the United States, although normally not through blatant bribery. On May 27, 2015, the United States Department of Justice and the FBI announced a long list of indictments, and simultaneous arrests of FIFA officials were made at the Zurich FIFA meetings in Switzerland. Several days after the indictment, though he was not officially indicted, Blatter stepped down from his long presidency.

In order to understand the amount of exposure and money involved, an estimated one billion people watched at least some of the 2010 World Cup Final. In the same year the National Football League's Super Bowl accumulated only 114.4 million worldwide viewers. Given the massive exposure, it is no wonder that sponsors along with television and media outlets want to be involved. However, sponsors do not want to be associated with a large scandal. Coca-Cola, Adidas, Nike, McDonald's, and Hyundai Motor were all said to be "deeply concerned" about the FBI allegations—and by indictments brought recently by the United States Department of Justice against many regional and country-level FIFA-affiliated executives who were identified as having participated in the alleged corruption.

Many of the sponsors are cautious about supporting an organization that has been tainted politically such as FIFA. Apparently, the way the corruption has been pursued is through intermediaries who are paid exorbitant amounts for contracts that they helped to establish; these intermediaries funnel the bribes to the leaders of the regional and country FIFA-related associations. For example, in order for Nike to get a contract in the soccer-crazed country of Brazil, it paid a sports marketing agency, Traffic Brazil, $30 million between 1996 and 1999, which Traffic Brazil used, in part, for bribes and kick-backs. This allowed Nike to sign a 10-year, $160 million agreement to become a co-sponsor of the CBF, the Brazilian soccer confederation. Nike's strategic intent for the deal was to better compete with its chief overseas rival, Adidas. In 2014, the World Cup was held in Brazil, and Nike had $2.3 billion in sales of soccer products, an annual increase of 21 percent, compared with $2.29 billion in sales for Adidas, which was up 20 percent over its previous year. These figures illustrate how strong the incentives are for sponsors as well as for media outlets to participate; the advertising potential and selling opportunities are enormous for those involved.

However, because of the weak institutional infrastructure in many countries around the world where the game of soccer is played, there is opportunity for corruption. Apparently, many involved in the FIFA infrastructure globally, regionally, and within specific countries have taken advantage of this opportunity. For example, Paraguay has been the headquarters for the Latin American regional confederation known as CONMEBOL since 1998 when Nicolás Leoz, a Paraguayan businessman and president of the Latin American Confederation, negotiated to have the confederation headquartered there. As part of the agreement, he obtained prosecutorial immunity for the organization through the Paraguay parliament. In essence, this gave the federation license to act in ways that would protect it against local law enforcement officials, similar to local embassies that have exemption from prosecution in a particular foreign country. As such, this allowed the local confederation to pursue deals under the table. Leoz was charged in the FIFA indictments by the U.S. Department of Justice, along with 13 other FIFA officials, of bribery and money laundering schemes related to funds he received from sports marketing firms during his tenure at CONMEBOL. Interestingly, following the indictment, Paraguay's congress moved quickly to repeal the prosecutorial immunity for the CONMEBOL federation.

Likewise, many other legal and investigative organizations in Switzerland, Latin America, and around the world, including INTERPOL, an international investigation organization, have begun to initiate their own enquiries. Many fans in the soccer world have been excited about these indictments because they felt that the corruption was hurting the game. People were profiting in illegal ways that tainted many organizations associated with the game of soccer. This outlines a main danger of working in countries where many participate in corrupt practices indirectly sponsored by the government. This is not to say officials in more developed governments are not also corrupt, but the rule of law is not as strong in many developing countries.

Sources: 2015, A timeline of the FIFA scandal, *Los Angeles Times*, www.latimes.com, June 2; P. Blake, 2015, FIFA scandal: Why the US is policing a global game, *BBC News*, www.bbc.com, May 28; M. Futterman, A. Viswanatha, & C. M. Matthews, 2015, Soccer's geyser of cash, *Wall Street Journal*, May 28, A1, A10; S. Germano, 2015, Nike is cooperating with investigators, *Wall Street Journal*, May 28, A11; P. Keirnan, R. Jelmayer, & L. Magalhaes, 2015, Soccer boss learned ropes from his Brazilian mentor, *Wall Street Journal*, May 30–31, A4; K. Malic, 2015, The corruption rhetoric of the FIFA scandal, *New York Times*, www.nytimes.com, June 16; S. S. Munoz, 2015, FIFA pro shows soccer state within a state, *Wall Street Journal*, June 20–21, A7; S. Vranica, T. Micklel, & J. Robinson, 2015, Scandal pressures soccer's sponsors, *Wall Street Journal*, May 29, A1, A8; A. Viswanatha, S. Germano, & P. Kowsmann, 2015, U.S. probes Nike Brazil money, *Wall Street Journal*, June 13–14, B1, B4; M. Yglesias & J. Stromberg, 2015, FIFA's huge corruption and bribery scandal, explained, *VOX*, www.vox.com, June 3; C. Zillman, 2015, Here's how major FIFA sponsors are reacting to the scandal, *Fortune*, www.fortune.com, May 28.

Case Discussion Questions

1. How does the FIFA scandal represent a form of political risk for companies operating in foreign countries?
2. What are the benefits to companies such as Nike and Coca-Cola acting as sponsors of soccer organizations in foreign countries?
3. What international strategy is being used by the major companies holding these sponsorships? Please explain.
4. Given the process described for gaining sponsorships (e.g., through sports marketing agencies), should Nike and other major companies realize that bribes and other corrupt practices were taking place?
5. How can companies handle corrupt practices in foreign practices? Can they find ways to compete there without engaging in these practices? Please explain.

NOTES

1. J.-E. Vahlne & J. Johanson, 2017, From internationalization to evolution: The Uppsala model at 40 years, *Journal of international Business Studies*, 48: 1087–1102; C. G. Asmussen & N. J. Foss, 2014, Competitive advantage and the existence of the multinational corporation: Earlier research and the role of frictions, *Global Strategy Journal*, 4: 49–54.
2. E. Newman, 2018, The EU global strategy in a transitional International order, *Global Society*, 32: 198–209; S. K. Majumdar & A. Bhattacharjee, 2014, Firms, markets, and the state: Institutional change and manufacturing sector profitability variances in India, *Organization Science*, 25: 509–528; R. M. Holmes Jr., T. Miller, M. A. Hitt, & M. P. Salmador, 2013, The interrelationship among informal institutions, formal institutions and inward foreign direct investment, *Journal of Management*, 39: 531–566.
3. L. Hakanson & P. Kappen, 2017, The 'casino model' of internationalization: An alternative Uppsala paradigm, *Journal of International Business Studies*, 48: 1103–1113; A. Gaur & A. Delios, 2015, International diversification of emerging market firms: The role of ownership structure and group affiliation, *Management International Review*, 55: 235–253; M. A. Hitt, L. Tihanyi, T. Miller, & B. Connelly, 2006, International diversification: Antecedents, outcomes and moderators, *Journal of Management*, 32: 831–867.
4. C. Elosge, M.-J. Oesterle, C. M. Stein, & S. Hattula, 2018, CEO succession and firms' internationalization processes: Insights from German companies, *International Business Review*, 27: 367–379; M. Hilmersson, M. Johanson, H. Lundberg & S. Papaioannou, 2017, Time, temporality and internationalization: The relationship among a point in time of, time to and speed of international expansion, *Journal of International Marketing*, 25: 22–45; H. Kim, R. E. Hoskisson, & S. Lee, 2015, Why strategic factor markets matter: 'New' multinationals' geographic diversification and firm profitability, *Strategic Management Journal*, 36: 518–536.
5. R. Vernon, 1996, International investment and international trade in the product cycle, *Quarterly Journal of Economics*, 80: 190–207.
6. 2018, Performance with purpose, Rio Tinto homepage, www.riotinto.com, accessed on July 12.
7. *Statistica*, 2018, number of smartphone users in Vietnam from 2015–2022 (in millions), https://www.statistic.com, accessed, July 12.
8. S. He, Z. Khan, Y. K. Lew, & G. Fallon, 2018, Technological innovation as a source of Chinese multinationals' firm-specific advantages and internationalization, *International Journal of Emerging Markets*, in press; M. J. Mol & C. Brewster, 2014, The outsourcing strategy of local and multinational firms: A supply base perspective, *Global Strategy Journal*, 4: 20–34.
9. J. P. Murmann, S. Z. Ozdemir, & D. Sardana, 2015, The role of home country demand in the internationalization of new ventures, *Research Policy*, 44: 1207–1225; K. E. Meyer, R. Mudambi, & R. Nanula, 2011, Multinational enterprises and local contexts: The opportunities and challenges of multiple embeddedness, *Journal of Management Studies*, 48: 235–252.
10. 2018, Carrefour stores worldwide, Carrefour Group homepage, www.carrefour.com, July 12.
11. 2018, Current news, Carrefour Group homepage, www.carrefour.com, July 12.
12. R. Dubbudu, 2017, These are the sectors in which FDI is allowed in India, *Factly*, https://factly.in, August 29; V. Mallet, 2014, Narendra Modi prepares to raise India's FDI limits, *Financial Times*, www.ft.com, May 30.
13. S. L. Fourné, J. J. P. Jansen, & T. M. Mom, 2014, Strategic agility in MNEs: Managing tensions to capture opportunities across emerging and established markets, *California Management Review*, 56(3): 13–38; R. Ramamurti, 2012, What is really different about emerging market multinationals? *Global Strategy Journal*, 2: 41–47.
14. P. Regnér & J. Edman, 2014, MNE institutional advantage: How subunits shape, transpose and evade host country institutions, *Journal of International Business Studies*, 45: 275–302; M. Carney, E. R. Gedajlovic, P. P. M. A. R. Heugens, M. van Essen, & J. van Oosterhout, 2011, Business group affiliation, performance, context, and strategy: A meta-analysis, *Academy of Management Journal*, 54: 437–460; B. Elango, 2009, Minimizing effects of "liability of foreignness": Response strategies of foreign firm in the United States, *Journal of World Business*, 44: 51–62.
15. A. Mohr & G. Batsakas, 2017, Internationalization speed and firm performance: A study of the market-seeking expansion of retail MNEs, *Management International Review*, 57: 153–177.
16. R. Garcia-Garcia, E. Garcia-Canal, & M. F. Guillen, 2017, Rapid internationalization and long-term performance The knowledge link, *Journal of World Business*, 52: 87–110; K. Kalasin, P. Dussauge, & M. Rivera-Santos, 2014, The expansion of emerging economy firms into advanced markets: The influence of intentional path-breaking change, *Global Strategy Journal*, 4: 75–103; A. Verbeke & W. Yuan, 2013, The drivers of multinational enterprise subsidiary entrepreneurship in China: A resource-based view perspective, *Journal of Management Studies*, 50: 236–258.
17. J. Carneiro, V. Bamiatzi & S. T. Cavusgil, 2018, Organizational slack as an enabler of internationalization: The case of large Brazilian firms, *International Business Review*, in press.
18. V. Page, 2018. Costco's business model is smarter than you think, *Investopedia*, https://www.investopedia.com, accessed July 12.
19. R. Erkelens, B. Hooff, M. Huysman, & P. Vlaar, 2015, Learning from locally embedded knowledge: Facilitating organizational learning in geographically dispersed settings, *Global Strategy Journal*, 5: 177–197; A. H. Kirka, G. T. M. Hult, S. Deligonul, M. Z. Perry, & S. T. Cavusgil, 2012, A multilevel examination of the drivers of firm multinationality: A meta-analysis, *Journal of Management*, 38: 502–530.
20. M. Kim, 2016, Geographic scope, isolating mechanisms, and value appropriation, *Strategic Management Journal*, 37: 695–713; G. Qian, T. A. Khoury, M. W. Peng, & Z. Qian, 2010, The performance implications of intra- and inter-regional geographic diversification, *Strategic Management Journal*, 31: 1018–1030; H. Zou & P. N. Ghauri, 2009, Learning through international acquisitions: The process of knowledge acquisition in China, *Management International Review*, 48: 207–226.
21. R. M. Holmes, H. Li, M. A. Hitt, K. DeGhetto & T. Sutton, 2016, The effects of location and MNC attributes on MNCs' Establishment of foreign R&D centers: Evidence from China, *Long Range Planning*, 49: 594–613: R. Sambharya & J. Lee, 2014, Renewing dynamic capabilities globally: An empirical study of the world's largest MNCs, *Management International Review*, 54: 137–169; Y. Zhang, H. Li, Y. Li, & L.-A. Zhou, 2010, FDI spillovers in an emerging market: The role of foreign firms' country origin diversity and domestic firms' absorptive capacity, *Strategic Management Journal*, 31: 969–989.
22. A. Cuervo-Cazurra & R. Ramamurti, 2017, Home country underdevelopment and internationalization: Innovation-based and escape-based internationalization, *Competitiveness Review*, 27: 217–230: N. Hashai & P. J. Buckley, 2014, Is competitive advantage a necessary condition for the emergence of the multinational enterprise? *Global Strategy Journal*, 4: 35–48.
23. F. Lo & F. Lin, 2015, Advantage transfer on location choice and subsidiary performance, *Journal of Business Research*, 68: 1527–1531; A. Gambardella

& M. S. Giarratana, 2010, Localized knowledge spillovers and skill-based performance, *Strategic Entrepreneurship Journal*, 4: 323–339.

24. J.-L. Arregle, T. Miller, M. A. Hitt & P. Beamish, 2016, How does regional institutional complexity affect MNE internationalization? *Journal of International Business Studies*, 47: 697–722; C. Peeters, C. Dehon, & P. Garcia-Prieto, 2015, The attention stimulus of cultural differences in global services sourcing, *Journal of International Business Studies*, 46: 241–251; O. Shenkar, 2012, Cultural distance revisited: Towards a more rigorous conceptualization and measurement of cultural differences, *Journal of International Business Studies*, 43: 1–11.
25. L. Kano & A. Verbeke, 2017, Family firm internationalization: Heritage assets and the impact of bifurcation bias, *Global Strategy Journal*, 8: 158–183; S. L. Sun, M. W. Peng, R. P. Lee, & W. Tan, 2015, Institutional open access at home and outward internationalization, *Journal of World Business*, 50: 234–246.
26. I. Gnizy & A. Shonham, 2018, Reverse internationalization: A review and suggestions for future research, in L.C. Leonidou, C. S. Katsikeas, S. Samiee, & B. Aykol (Eds.), *Advances in Global Marketing*, Cham Switzerland, 59–75.
27. Sambharya & Lee, Renewing dynamic capabilities globally: An empirical study of the world's largest MNCs; Y. Y. Chang, Y. Gong, & M. Peng, 2012, Expatriate knowledge transfer, subsidiary absorptive capacity and subsidiary performance, *Academy of Management Journal*, 55: 927–948; P. Kappen, 2011, Competence-creating overlaps and subsidiary technological evolution in the multinational corporation, *Research Policy*, 40: 673–686.
28. H. Liang, B. Ren, & S. L. Sun, 2015, An anatomy of state control in the globalization of state-owned enterprises, *Journal of International Business Studies*, 46: 223–240; Y. Fang, M. Wade, A. Delios, & P. W. Beamish, 2013, An exploration of multinational enterprise knowledge resources and foreign subsidiary performance, *Journal of World Business*, 48: 30–38; A. Arino, 2011, Building the global enterprise: Strategic assembly, *Global Strategy Journal*, 1: 47–49.
29. M. Hanafi, D. Wibisono, K. Mangkusubroto, M. Siallagan, & M. J. K. Badriyah, 2017, Modelling competitive advantage of nation: A literature review, *Competitiveness Review*, 27: 335–365; M. E. Porter, 1990, *The Competitive Advantage of Nations*, NY: The Free Press.
30. Ibid., 84.
31. S. Yan & G. Liu, 2017, Competitive strategy, market entry mode and international performance: The case of construction firms in China, *Business and Management Studies*, 3: 1–9.
32. D. Dulaney, 2014, Chiquita agrees to $742 million buyout, *Wall Street Journal*, www.wsj.com, October 28; D. Englander, 2013, Chiquita Brands—Stocks with appeal, *Wall Street Journal*, www.wsj.com, April 28.
33. A. Cuervo-Cazurra, Y Luo, R. Ramamurti & S. H. ang, 2018, Impact of the home country on internationalization, *Journal of World Business*, 28: in press; M. Bucheli & M. Kim, 2015, Attacked from both sides: A dynamic model of multinational corporations' strategies for protection of their property rights, *Global Strategy Journal*, 5: 1–26; C. Wang, J. Hong, M. Kafouros, & M. Wright, 2012, Exploring the role of government involvement in outward FDI from emerging economies, *Journal of International Business Studies*, 43: 655–676.
34. 2017. Lexus sales booming in China, *Lexus Enthusiast*, https://lexusenthusiast.com, August 22; C. Trundell & Y Hagiwara, 2015, Lexus flag China ambitions with new ES's Shanghai debut, *Bloomberg Business*, www.bloombergbusiness.com, April 9.
35. S. Lakshman & C. Lakshman, 2017, The dynamic change in expatriate roles: strategy type and stage of internationalization, *Management Decision*, 55: 1770–1784; S. Song, M. Makhija, & S. Lee, 2014, Within-country growth options versus across-country switching options in foreign direct investment, *Global Strategy Journal*, 4: 127–142.
36. Kim, Hoskisson, & Lee, Why strategic factor markets matter: 'New multinationals' geographic diversification and firm profitability; M. Musteen, D. K. Datta, & J. Francis, 2014, Early internationalization by firms in transition economies into developed markets: The role of international networks, *Global Strategy Journal*, 4: 221–237.
37. T.-C. Chou & J.-L. Liao, 2015, IT governance balancing global integration and local responsiveness for multinational companies, *Total Quality Management & Business Excellence*, 28: 32–46.
38. R. Qu & Z. Zhang, 2015, Market orientation and business performance in MNC foreign subsidiaries—moderating effects of integration and responsiveness, *Journal of Business Research*, 68: 919–924.
39. J. Siegel, L. Pyun, & B. Y. Cheon, 2018, Multinational firms, labor market discrimination, and the capture of outsider's advantage by exploiting the social divide, *Administrative Science Quarterly*, in press; W. Aghina, A. De Smet, & S. Heywood, 2014, The past and future of global organizations, *McKinsey Quarterly*, March, 97–106; S. Zaheer & L. Nachum, 2011, Sense of place: From location resources to MNE locational capital, *Global Strategy Journal*, 1: 96–108.
40. S. C. Schleimer & T. Pedersen, 2014, The effects of MNC parent effort and social structure on subsidiary absorptive capacity, *Journal of International Business Studies*, 45: 303–320; J.-S. Chen & A. S. Lovvorn, 2011, The speed of knowledge transfer within multinational enterprises: The role of social capital, *International Journal of Commerce and Management*, 21: 46–62; H. Kasper, M. Lehrer, J. Muhlbacher, & B. Muller, 2009, Integration-responsiveness and knowledge-management perspectives on the MNC: A typology and field study of cross-site knowledge-sharing practices, *Journal of Leadership & Organizational Studies*, 15: 287–303.
41. 2018, About-Who we are-Our strategy, Unilever homepage, www.unilever. com, accessed on July13; J. Neff, 2008, Unilever's CMO finally gets down to business, *Advertising Age*, July 11.
42. A. Cuervo-Cazurra, R. Mudambi, & T. Pedersen, 2018, The boundaries of the firm in global strategy, *Global Strategy Journal*, 8: 211–219; K. E. Meyer & S. Estrin, 2014, Local context and global strategy: Extending the integration responsiveness framework to subsidiary strategy, *Global Strategy Journal*, 4: 1–19
43. S. Lakshman, C. Lakshman, & C. Estay, 2017, The relationship between MNCs' strategies and executive staffing, *International Journal of Organizational Analysis*, 25: 233–250; H. Berry, 2014, Global integration and innovation: Multicountry knowledge generation within MNCs, *Strategic Management Journal*, 35: 869–890.
44. C. Wang, 2014, Accounting standards harmonization and financial statement comparability: Evidence from transnational information transfer, *Journal of Accounting Research*, 52: 955–992; L. Hail, C. Leuz, & P. Wysocki, 2010, Global accounting convergence and the potential adoption of IFRS by the U.S. (part II): Political factors and future scenarios for U.S. accounting standards, *Accounting Horizons*, 24: 567–581; R. G. Barker, 2003, Trend: Global accounting is coming, *Harvard Business Review*, 81(4): 24–25.
45. J.-L. Arregle, T. Miller, M. A. Hitt, & P. Beamish, 2018, The role of MNEs' internationalization patterns in their regional integration of FDI locations, *Journal of World Business*, in press; J. U. Kim & R. V. Aguilera, 2015, The world is spiky: An internationalization framework for a semi-globalized world, *Global Strategy Journal*, 5: 113–132; J.-L. Arregle, T. Miller, M. A. Hitt, & P. W. Beamish, 2013, Do regions matter? An integrated institutional and semiglobalization perspective on the internationalization of MNEs, *Strategic Management Journal*, 34: 910–934.
46. S. Morris, R. Hammond, & S. Snell, 2014, A microfoundations approach to transnational capabilities: The role of knowledge search in an ever-changing world, *Journal of International Business Studies*, 45: 405–427; R. Greenwood, S. Fairclough, T. Morris, & M. Boussebaa,

2010, The organizational design of transnational professional service firms, *Organizational Dynamics*, 39: 173–183.

47. C. A. Bartlett & P. W. Beamish, 2018, *Transnational management: Text and cases in cross-border management,* Cambridge: Cambridge University Press; K. J. Breunig, R. Kvålshaugen, & K. M. Hydle, 2014, Knowing your boundaries: Integration opportunities in international professional service firms, *Journal of World Business*, 49: 502–511.
48. X. Zhang, W. Zhong, & S. Makino, 2015, Customer involvement and service firm internationalization performance: An integrative framework, *Journal of International Business Studies,* 46: 355–380; 2010, Regional resilience: Theoretical and empirical perspectives, *Cambridge Journal of Regions, Economy and Society*, 3–10; Rugman & Verbeke, A regional solution to the strategy and structure of multinationals.
49. 2018, 2018 fact sheet, Mondelez International, Https://www.mondelezinternational.com, accessed July 13: 2015, Unleashing a global snacking powerhouse, Mondelez International, www.mondelezinternational.com, accessed on June 22.
50. J. Doh, S. Rodrigues, A. Saka-Helmhout, & M. Makhija, 2017, International business responses to institutional voids, *Journal of International Business Studies,* 48: 293–307; M. W. Peng & Y. Y. Jiang, 2010, Institutions behind family ownership and control in large firms, *Journal of Management Studies*, 47: 253–273; A. M. Rugman & A. Verbeke, 2003, Extending the theory of the multinational enterprise: Internationalization and strategic management perspectives, *Journal of International Business Studies*, 34: 125–137.
51. I. Bremmer, E. Fry, & D. Shanker, 2015 The new world of business, *Fortune*, February 1, 86–92; D. Klonowski, 2011, Private equity in emerging markets: Stacking up the BRICs, *Journal of Private Equity*, 14: 24–37.
52. M. Buchelli & E. Salvaj, 2018, Political connections, the liability of foregnness, and legitimacy: A business historical analysis of multinationals' strategy in Chile, *Global Strategy Journal,* in press; F. Jiang, L. Liu, & B. W. Stening, 2014, Do Foreign Firms in China Incur a Liability of Foreignness? The Local Chinese Firms' Perspective, *Thunderbird International Business Review*, 56: 501–518; J. Mata & E. Freitas, 2012, Foreignness and exit over the life cycle of firms, *Journal of International Business Studies*, 43: 615–630. R. G. Bell, I. Filatotchev, & A. A. Rasheed, 2012, The liability of foreignness, in capital markets: Sources and remedies, *Journal of International Business Studies*, 43: 107–122.
53. Y. Gu, R. G. Bell, I. Filatotchev, & A. A. Rasheed, 2018, The liability of foreignness, in capital markets: Institutional distance and capital markets, *Journal of Corporate Finance,* in press; V. Marano, J.-L. Arregle, M. A. Hitt, E. Spadafora & M. van Essen, 2016, Home country Institutions and the internationalization-performance relationship: A meta-analytic review, *Journal of Management*, 42: 1075–1110; J. Aguilera-Caracuel, E. M. Fedriani, & B. L. Delgado-Márquez, 2014, Institutional distance among country influences and environmental performance standardization in multinational enterprises, *Journal of Business Research*, 67: 2385–2392; R. Salomon & Z. Wu, 2012, Institutional distance and local isomorphism strategy, *Journal of International Business Studies,* 43: 347–367.
54. C. H. Tupper, O. Guldiken, & M. Benischke, 2018, Capital market liability of foreignness of IPO firms, *Journal of World Business,* 53: 555–567; J.-L. Arregle, P. Duran, M. A. Hitt, & M. van Essen, 2017, Why is family firms' internationalization unique? *Entrepreneurship Theory and Practice*, 41: 801–837; Z. Wu & R. Salomon, 2017, Deconstructing the liability of foreignness: Regulatory enforcement actions against foreign banks, *Journal of International Business Studies,* 48: 837–861; T. Hutzschenreuter, I. Kleindienst, & S. Lange, 2014, Added psychic distance stimuli and MNE performance: Performance effects of added cultural, governance, geographic, and economic distance in MNEs' international expansion, *Journal of International Management*, 20: 38–54.
55. N. Y. Brannen, 2004, When Mickey loses face: Recontextualization, semantic fit and semiotics of foreignness, *Academy of Management Review*, 29: 593–616.
56. M. Schuman, 2006, Disney's Hong Kong headache, *Time*, www.time.com, May 8.
57. G. Suder, P. W. Liesch, S. Inomata, I. Mihailova, & B. Meng, 2015, The evolving geography of production hubs and regional value chains across East Asia: Trade in value-added, *Journal of World Business*, 50: 404–416; Arregle, Miller, Hitt, & Beamish, Do regions matter?; J. Cantwell & Y. Zhang, 2011, Innovation and location in the multinational firm, *International Journal of Technology Management*, 54: 116–132.
58. Y. Kim & S. J. Gray, 2017, Internationalization strategy and the home-regionalization hypothesis: The case of Australian multinational enterprises, *Austalian Journal of Management,* 42: 673–691; L. Stevens, 2015, Borders matter less and less in e-commerce, *Wall Street Journal*, June 24, B8; K. Ito & E. L. Rose, 2010, The implicit return on domestic and international sales: An empirical analysis of U.S. and Japanese firms, *Journal of International Business Studies*, 41: 1074–1089.
59. A. Ghobadian, A. M. Rugman, & R. L. Tung, 2014, Strategies for firm globalization and regionalization, *British Journal of Management*, 25: S1–S5; Arregle, Miller, Hitt, & Beamish, Do regions matter?; E. R. Banalieva, M. D. Santoro, & J. R. Jiang, 2012, Home region focus and technical efficiency of multinational enterprises: The moderating role of regional integration, *Management International Review*, 52: 493–518.
60. Y. Liu & Y. Yu, 2018, Institutions, firm resources and foreign establishment mode choices of Chinese firms: The moderating role of home regional institutional development, *Journal of Business Research*, in press; D. E. Westney, 2006, Review of the regional multinationals: MNEs and global strategic management (book review), *Journal of International Business Studies*, 37: 445–449.
61. S. Arita & K. Tanaka, 2014, Heterogeneous multinational firms and productivity gains from falling FDI barriers, *Review of World Economics*, 150: 83–113; R. D. Ludema, 2002, Increasing returns, multinationals and geography of preferential trade agreements, *Journal of International Economics*, 56: 329–358.
62. L Caliendo & F. Parro, 2015, Estimates of the trade and welfare effects of NAFTA, *Review of Economic Studies*, 82: 1–44; M. Aspinwall, 2009, NAFTA-ization: Regionalization and domestic political adjustment in the North American economic area, *Journal of Common Market Studies*, 47: 1–24.
63. N. P. Flannery, 2018, Will NAFTA survive? *Forbes,* https://www.forbes.com, February 1.
64. N. Åkerman, 2015, Knowledge-acquisition strategies and the effects on market knowledge—profiling the internationalizing firm, *European Management Journal*, 33: 79–88; D. Zu & O. Shenar, 2002, Institutional distance and the multinational enterprise, *Academy of Management Review, 27*: 608–618.
65. P. J. Buckley & N. Hashai, 2014, The role of technological catch up and domestic market growth in the genesis of emerging country-based multinationals, *Research Policy*, 43: 423–437; A. Ojala, 2008, Entry in a psychically distant market: Finnish small and medium-sized software firms in Japan, *European Management Journal*, 26: 135–144.
66. D. Cai & Y. Karasawa-Ohtashiro, 2018, Greenfield, merger and acquisition, or export? Regulating the entry of multinational enterprises to a host-country market, *International Review of Economics & Finance,* 56: 397–407; V. Hernández & M. J. Nieto, 2015, The effect of the magnitude and direction of institutional distance on the choice of international entry modes, *Journal of World Business*, 50: 122–132; K. D. Brouthers, 2013, Institutional, cultural and transaction cost influences on entry mode choice and performance, *Journal of International Business Studies*, 44: 1–13.
67. J.-F. Hennart & A. H. L. Slangen, 2015, Yes, we really do need more entry mode studies! A commentary on Shaver, *Journal of International Business Studies*, 46: 114–122; B. Maekelburger, C. Schwens, & R. Kabst,

2012, Asset specificity and foreign market entry mode choice of small and medium-sized enterprises: The moderating influence of knowledge safeguards and institutional safeguards, *Journal of International Business Studies*, 43: 458–476.

68. B. Jin, J.-E. Chung, H. Yang, & S. W. Jeong, 2018, Entry market choices and post-entry growth patterns among born globals in consumer goods sectors, *International Marketing Review*, in press; S. Gerschewski, E. L. Rose, & V. J. Lindsay, 2015, Understanding the drivers of international performance for born global firms: An integrated perspective, *Journal of World Business*, 50: 558–575.

69. M.-C. Stoian, J. Rialp, & P. Dimitratos, SME networks and international performance: Unveiling the significance of foreign market entry mode, *Journal of Small Business Management*, 55: 128–148; S. T. Cavusgil & G. Knight, 2015, The born global firm: An entrepreneurial and capabilities perspective on early and rapid internationalization, *Journal of International Business Studies*, 46: 3–16; P. Ganotakis & J. H. Love, 2012, Export propensity, export intensity and firm performance: The role of the entrepreneurial founding team, *Journal of International Business Studies*, 43: 693–718.

70. S. Bose, 2018, Nearly all U.S. exporters are small businesses, *Small Business Trends*, https://www.smallbiztrends.com, March 28; I. Zander, P. McDougall-Covin, & E. L. Rose, 2015, Born globals and international business: Evolution of a field of research, *Journal of International Business Studies*, 46: 27–35; M. Bandyk, 2008, Now even small firms can go global, *U.S. News & World Report*, March 10, 52.

71. S. Sui & M. Baum, 2014, Internationalization strategy, firm resources and the survival of SMEs in the export market, *Journal of International Business Studies*, 45: 821–841; B. Cassiman & E. Golovko, 2010, Innovation and internationalization through exports, *Journal of International Business Studies*, 42: 56–75.

72. E. Golovko & G. Valentini, 2014, Selective learning-by-exporting: Firm size and product versus process innovation, *Global Strategy Journal*, 4: 161–180; X. He, K. D. Brouthers, & I. Filatotchev, 2013, Resource-based and institutional perspectives on export channel selection and export performance, *Journal of Management*, 39: 27–47; M. Hughes, S. L. Martin, R. E. Morgan, & M. J. Robson, 2010, Realizing product-market advantage in high-technology international new ventures: The mediating role of ambidextrous innovation, *Journal of International Marketing*, 18: 1–21.

73. A. Troianovski, 2014, German seeds web shopping in the developing world, *Wall Street Journal*, January 14, A1, A12; P. Ganotakis & J. H. Love, 2011, R&D, product innovation, and exporting: Evidence from UK new technology-based firms, *Oxford Economic Papers*, 63: 279–306; M. Gabrielsson & P. Gabrielsson, 2011, Internet-based sales channel strategies of born global firms, *International Business Review*, 20: 88–99.

74. B. Bozeman, H. Rimes, & J. Youtie, J. 2015, The evolving state-of-the-art in technology transfer research: Revisiting the contingent effectiveness model, *Research Policy*, 44: 34–49; P. S. Aulakh, M. Jiang, & Y. Pan, 2010, International technology licensing: Monopoly rents transaction costs and exclusive rights, *Journal of International Business Studies*, 41: 587–605; R. Bird & D. R. Cahoy, 2008, The impact of compulsory licensing on foreign direct investment: A collective bargaining approach, *American Business Law Journal*, 45: 283–330.

75. M. Bianchi, M. Frattini, J. Lejarraga, & A. Di Minin, 2014, Technology exploitation paths: combining technological and complementary resources in new product development and licensing, *Journal of Product Innovation Management*, 31: 146–169; M. S. Giarratana & S. Torrisi, 2010, Foreign entry and survival in a knowledge-intensive market: Emerging economy countries' international linkages, technology competences, and firm experience, *Strategic Entrepreneurship Journal*, 4: 85–104; U. Lichtenthaler, 2008, Externally commercializing technology assets: An examination of different process stages, *Journal of Business Venturing*, 23: 445–464.

76. N. Byrnes & F. Balfour, 2009, Philip Morris unbound, *BusinessWeek*, May 4, 38–42.

77. 2018, Stan and Lionsgate announce new multi-year licensing agreement in Australia, *Consumer Electronics Net*, www.consumerelectronicsnet.com, June 5.

78. A. Filippetti, M. Frenz, & G. Letto-Gillies, 2017, The impact of internationalization on innovation at countries' level: The role of absorptive capacity, *Cambridge Journal of Economics*, 41: 413–439; J. Li-Ying & Y. Wang, 2015, Find them home or abroad? The relative contribution of international technology in-licensing to "indigenous innovation" in China, *Long Range Planning*, 48: 123–134; S. Hagaoka, 2009, Does strong patent protection facilitate international technology transfer? Some evidence from licensing contrasts of Japanese firms, *Journal of Technology Transfer*, 34: 128–144.

79. A. Agarwal, I. Cockburn, & I. Zhang, L. Deals not done: Sources of failure in the market for ideas, *Strategic Management Journal*, 36: 976–986; U. Lichtenthaler, 2011, The evolution of technology licensing management: Identifying five strategic approaches, *R&D Management*, 41: 173–189; M. Fiedler & I. M. Welpe, 2010, Antecedents of cooperative commercialisation strategies of nanotechnology firms, *Research Policy*, 39: 400–410.

80. C. A. Barlett & S. Rangan, 1992, Komatsu Limited. In C. A. Bartlett & S. Ghoshal (eds.), *Transnational Management: Text, Cases and Readings in Cross-Border Management*, Homewood, IL: Irwin, 311–326.

81. F. J. Contractor & J. J. Reuer, 2018, *Frontiers of strategic alliance research: Negotiating, structuring and governing partnerships*, Cambridge, UK: Cambridge University Press; F. J. Contractor & J. J. Reuer, 2014, Structuring and governing alliances: New directions for research, *Global Strategy Journal*, 4: 241–256; S. Veilleux, N. Haskell, & F. Pons, 2012, Going global: How smaller enterprises benefit from strategic alliances, *Journal of Business Strategy*, 33(5): 22–31.

82. A. Goerzen, 2018, Small-firm boundary-spanning via bridging ties: Achieving international connectivity via cross-border inter-cluster alliances, *Journal of international Management*, 24: 153–164; J. J. Reuer & R. Ragozzino, 2014, Signals and international alliance formation: The roles of affiliations and international activities, *Journal of International Business Studies*, 45: 321–337; T. Barnes, S. Raynor, & J. Bacchus, 2012, A new typology of forms of international collaboration, *Journal of Business and Strategy*, 5: 81–102.

83. F. J. Contractor & J. A. Woodley, 2015, How the alliance pie is split: Value appropriation by each partner in cross-border technology transfer alliances, *Journal of World Business*, 50: 535–547; Z. Bhanji & J. E. Oxley, 2013, Overcoming the dual liability of foreignness and privateness in international corporate citizenship partnerships, *Journal of International Business Studies*, 44: 290–311; J. S. Harrison, M. A. Hitt, R. E. Hoskisson, & R. D. Ireland, 2001, Resource complementarity in business combinations: Extending the logic to organization alliances, *Journal of Management*, 27: 679–690.

84. L. Hollender, F. B. Zapkau & C. Schwens, 2017, SME foreign market entry mode choice and foreign venture performance: The moderating effect of international experience and product adaptation, *International Business Review*, 26: 250–263; W. Shi, S. L. Sun, B. C. Pinkham, & M. W. Peng, 2014, Domestic alliance network to attract foreign partners: Evidence from international joint ventures in China, *Journal of International Business Studies*, 45: 338–362; M. A. Hitt, D. Ahlstrom, M. T. Dacin, E. Levitas, & L. Svobodina, 2004, The institutional effects on strategic alliance partner selection in transition economies: China versus Russia, *Organization Science*, 15: 173–185.

85. F. Vendrell-Herrero, E. Gomes, O. F. Bustinza, & K. Melllahi, 2018, Uncovering the role of cross-border strategic alliances and expertise decision centralization in enhancing product-service innovation in MNEs, *International Business Review*, 27: 814–825; Z. Khan, R. R. Sinkovics, & Y. K. Lew, 2015, International joint ventures as boundary spanners: Technological knowledge transfer in an emerging economy, *Global Strategy*

Journal, 5: 48–68; G. Vasudeva, J. W. Spencer, & H. J. Teegen, 2013, Bringing the institutional context back in: A cross-national comparison of alliance partner selection and knowledge acquisition, *Organization Science*, 24: 319–338.

86. M. Hsiao-Wen Ho, P. N. Ghauri, & J. A. Larimo, 2018, Institutional distance and knowledge acquisition in international buyer-supplier relationships: The moderating role of trust, *Asia Pacific Journal of Management*, 35: 427–447; X. Jiang, F. Jiang, X. Cai, & H. Liu, 2015, How does trust affect alliance performance? The mediating role of resource sharing, *Industrial Marketing Management*, 45: 128–138; J.-P. Roy, 2012, IJV partner trustworthy behavior: The role of host country governance and partner selection criteria, *Journal of Management Studies*, 49: 332–355.

87. 2018, History and ownership, AgReliant Genetics, https://agreliantgenetics.com, accessed July 14; 2015, A culture of partnership in favor of collective intelligence, Limagrain, www.limagrain.com, accessed on June 23; 2011, Limagrain signs strategic alliance to enter Brazilian corn market, *Great Lakes Hybrids*, www.greatlakeshybrids.com, February 14.

88. M. del Mar Benavides-Espinosa & D. Ribeiro-Soriano, 2014, Cooperative learning in creating and managing joint ventures, *Journal of Business Research*, 67: 648–655; S. Kotha & K. Srikanth, 2013, Managing a global partnership model: Lessons from the Boeing 787 'dreamliner' program, *Global Strategy Journal*, 3: 41–66; C. Schwens, J. Eiche, & R. Kabst, 2011, The moderating impact of informal institutional distance and formal institutional risk on SME entry mode choice, *Journal of Management Studies*, 48: 330–351.

89. R. Kumar, 2014, Managing ambiguity in strategic alliances, *California Management Review*, 56(4): 82–102; Y. Luo, O. Shenkar, & H. Gurnani, 2008, Control-cooperation interfaces in global strategic alliances: A situational typology and strategic responses, *Journal of International Business Studies*, 39: 428–453.

90. I. Arikan & O. Shenkar, 2013, National animosity and cross-border alliances, *Academy of Management Journal*, 56:516–1544; T. K. Das, 2010, Interpartner sensemaking in strategic alliances: Managing cultural differences and internal tensions, *Management Decision*, 48: 17–36.

91. G. Lojacono, N. Misani, & S. Tallman, 2017, Offshoring, local market entry, and the strategic context of cross-border alliances: The impact of governance mode, *International Business Review*, 26: 435–447; A. Iriyama & R. Madhavan, 2014, Post-formation inter-partner equity transfers in international joint ventures: the role of experience, *Global Strategy Journal*, 4: 331–348; D. Li, L. Eden, M. A. Hitt, & R. D. Ireland, 2008, Friends, acquaintances and stranger? Partner selection in R&D alliances, *Academy of Management Journal*, 51: 315–334.

92. A. M. Joshi & N. Lahiri, 2015, Language friction and partner selection in cross-border R&D alliance formation, *Journal of International Business Studies*, 46: 123–152; P. D. O. Jensen & B. Petersen, 2013, Global sourcing of services: Risk, process and collaborative architecture, *Global Strategy Journal*, 3: 67–87.

93. T. W. Tong, J. J. Reuer, B. B. Tyler, & S. Zhang, 2015, Host country executives' assessments of international joint ventures and divestitures: An experimental approach, *Strategic Management Journal*, 36: 254–275; S.-F. Chen, 2010, A general TCE model of international business institutions; market failure and reciprocity, *Journal of International Business Studies*, 41: 935–959; J. Wiklund & D. A. Shepherd, 2009, The effectiveness of alliances and acquisitions: The role of resource combination activities, *Entrepreneurship Theory and Practice*, 33: 193–212.

94. G. Kling, A. Ghobadian, M. A. Hitt, U. Weitzel, & N. O'Regan, 2014, The effects of cross-border and cross-industry mergers and acquisitions on home-region and global multinational enterprises, *British Journal of Management*, 25: S116–S132.

95. I. Surdu, K. Mellahi, & K. Glaister, 2018, Emerging market multinationals' international equity-based entry mode strategies: Review of theoretical foundations and future directions, *International Marketing Review*, 35: 342–359; A. Guar, S. Malhotra, & P. Zhu, 2013, Acquisition announcements and stock market valuations of acquiring firms' rivals: A test of the growth probability hypothesis in China, *Strategic Management Journal*, 34: 215–232; M. A. Hitt & V. Pisano, 2003, The cross-border merger and acquisition strategy, *Management Research*, 1: 133–144.

96. 2018, Company overview, Ahold Delhaize, https://www.aholddelhaize.com, accessed July 14; I. Walker & A. Gasparro, 2015, Merger unites major supermarket players, *Wall Street Journal*, June 25, B1.

97. M. A. Sartor & P. W. Beamish, 2018, Host market government corruption and the equity-based foreign entry strategies of multinational enterprises, *Journal of International Business Studies*, 48: 346–370; P. C. Narayan & M. Thenmozhi, 2014, Do cross-border acquisitions involving emerging market firms create value: Impact of deal characteristics, *Management Decision*, 52: 1–23; S. Malhotra, P.-C. Zhu, & W. Locander, 2010, Impact of host-country corruption on U.S. and Chinese cross-border acquisitions, *Thunderbird International Business Review*, 52: 491–507.

98. M. F. Ahammad, V. Leone, S. Y Tarba, K. W. Glaister, & A. Arslan, 2017, Equity ownership in cross-border mergers and acquisitions by British firms: An analysis of real options and transaction cost factors, *British Journal of Management*, 28: 180–196.

99. A. Chikhouni, G. Edwards, & M. Farashahi, 2017, Psychic distance and ownership in acquisitions: Direction matters, *Journal of International Management*, 23: 32–42; F. J. Contractor, S. Lahiri, B. Elango, & S. K. Kundu, Institutional, cultural and industry related determinants of ownership choices in emerging market FDI acquisitions, *International Business Review*, 23: 931–941; J. Li & C. Qian, 2013, Principal-principal conflicts under weak institutions: A study of corporate takeovers in China, *Strategic Management Journal*, 34: 498–508.

100. S. Lee, J. Kim, & B. I. Park, 2015, Culture clashes in cross-border mergers and acquisitions: A case study of Sweden's Volvo and South Korea's Samsung, *International Business Review*, 24: 580–593; E. Vaara, R. Sarala, G. K. Stahl, & I. Bjorkman, 2012, *Journal of Management Studies*, 49: 1–27; D. R. Denison, B. Adkins, & A. Guidroz, 2011, Managing cultural integration in cross-border mergers and acquisitions. In W. H. Mobley, M. Li, & Y. Wang (eds.), *Advances in Global Leadership*, vol. 6, Bingley, U.K.: Emerald Publishing Group, 95–115.

101. U. Stettner & D. Lavie, 2014, Ambidexterity under scrutiny: Exploration and exploitation via internal organization, alliances, and acquisitions, *Strategic Management Journal*, 35: 1903–1929; S.-J. Chang, J. Chung, & J. J. Moon, 2013, When do wholly owned subsidiaries perform better than joint ventures? *Strategic Management Journal*, 34: 317–337; Y. Fang, G.-L. F. Jiang, S. Makino, & P. W. Beamish, 2010, Multinational firm knowledge, use of expatriates, and foreign subsidiary performance, *Journal of Management Studies*, 47: 27–54.

102. S. Lahiri, B. Elango, & S. K. Kundu, 2014, Cross-border acquisition in services: Comparing ownership choice of developed and emerging economy MNEs in India, *Journal of World Business*, 49: 409–420; C. Bouquet, L. Hebert, & A. Delios, 2004, Foreign expansion in service industries: Separability and human capital intensity, *Journal of Business Research*, 57: 35–46.

103. A. Arslan & J. Larimo, 2017, Greenfield entry strategy of multinational enterprises in the emerging markets: Influences of institutional distance and international trade freedom, *Journal of East-West Business*, 23: 140–170; O. Bertrand & L. Capron, L. 2015, Productivity enhancement at home via cross-border acquisitions: The roles of learning and contemporaneous domestic investments, *Strategic Management Journal*, 36: 640–658; C. Schwens, J. Eiche, & R. Kabst, 2011, The moderating impact of informal institutional distance and formal institutional risk on SME entry mode choice, *Journal of Management Studies*, 48: 330–351.

104. G. O. White, T. A. Hemphill, J. R. Joplin, & L. A. Marsh, 2014, Wholly owned foreign subsidiary relation-based strategies in volatile environments, *International Business Review*, 23: 303–312; Chang,

Chung & Moon, When do wholly owned subsidiaries perform better than joint ventures?; K. D. Brouthers & D. Dikova, 2010, Acquisitions and real options: The greenfield alternative, *Journal of Management Studies*, 47: 1048–1071.

105. V. Shirodkar & P. Konara, 2017, Institutional distance and foreign subsidiary performance in emerging markets: Moderating effects of ownership strategy and host-country experience, *Management International Review*, 57: 179–207; Y. Parke & B. Sternquist, 2008, The global retailer's strategic proposition and choice of entry mode, *International Journal of Retail & Distribution Management*, 36: 281–299.

106. X. He, J. Zhang, & J. Wang, 2015, Market seeking orientation and performance in China: The impact of institutional environment, subsidiary ownership structure and experience. *Management International Review*, 55: 389–419; L. Q. Siebers, 2012, Foreign retailers in China: The first ten years, *Journal of Business Strategy*, 33(1): 27–38.

107. G. F. Jiang, G. L. F. Holburn & P. W. Beamish, 2018, Repeat market entries in the internationalization process: The impact of investment motives and corporate capabilities, *Global Strategy Journal*, in press; A. M. Rugman, 2010, Reconciling internalization theory and the eclectic paradigm, *Multinational Business Review*, 18: 1–12; J. Che & G. Facchini, 2009, Cultural differences, insecure property rights and the mode of entry decision, *Economic Theory*, 38: 465–484.

108. 2018, Toyota in the U.S., Toyota newsroom, corporatenews.pressroom.toyota.com, accessed July 14; J. Muller, 2015, Toyota is laying down deeper roots in Michigan. *Forbes*, June 11, 24.

109. J. E. Clarke & P. W. Liesch, 2017, Wait-and-see strategy: Risk management in the internationalization process, *Journal of International Business Studies*, 48: 923–940; A. Cuervo-Cazurra, A. Inkpen, A. Musacchio, & K. Ramaswamy, 2014, Governments as owners: State-owned multinational companies, *Journal of International Business Studies*, 45: 919–942; B. Batjargal, M. Hitt, A. S. Tsui, J.-L. Arregle, J. Webb, & T. Miller, 2013, Institutional polycentrism, entrepreneurs' social networks and new venture growth, *Academy of Management Journal*, 56: 1024–1049.

110. C. Giersch, 2011, Political risk and political due diligence, *Global Risk Affairs*, www.globalriskaffairs.com, March 4.

111. K. J. Mayer, 2017, Political hazards and firms' geographic concentration, *Strategic Management Journal*, 38: 203–231; G. G. Goswami & S. Haider, 2014, Does political risk deter FDI inflow? An analytical approach using panel data and factor analysis, *Journal of Economic Studies*, 41: 233–252; P. Rodriguez, K. Uhlenbruck, & L. Eden, 2003, Government corruption and the entry strategies of multinationals, *Academy of Management Review*, 30: 383–396.

112. M A. De Villa, T. Rajwani, T. C. Lawton & K. Mellahi, 2018, To engage or not to engage with host governments: Corporate political activity and host country political risk, *Global Strategy Journal*, in press; A. Jiménez, I. Luis-Rico, & D. Benito-Osorio, 2014, The influence of political risk on the scope of internationalization of regulated companies: Insights from a Spanish sample, *Journal of World Business*, 49: 301–311; D. Quer, E. Claver, & L. Rienda, 2012, Political risk, cultural distance, and outward foreign direct investment: Empirical evidence from large Chinese firms, *Asia Pacific Journal of Management*, 29: 1089–1104; O. Branzei & S. Abdelnour, 2010, Another day, another dollar: Enterprise resilience under terrorism in developing countries, *Journal of International Business Studies*, 41: 804–825.

113. G. Bekaert, C. R. Harvey, C. T. Lundblad, & S. Siegel, 2014, Political risk spreads, *Journal of International Business Studies*, 45: 471–493.

114. C. L. Brown, S. T. Cavusgil, & A. W. Lord, 2015, Country-risk measurement and analysis: A new conceptualization and managerial tool, *International Business Review*, 24: 246–265; Giersch, Political risk and political due diligence.

115. D. L. Keig, L. E. Brouthers, & V. B. Marshall, 2015, Formal and informal corruption environments and multinational enterprise social irresponsibility, *Journal of Management Studies*, 52: 89–116; J. Surroca, J. A. Tribo, & S. A. Zahra, 2013, Stakeholder pressure on MNEs and the transfer of socially irresponsible practices to subsidiaries, *Academy of Management Journal*, 56: 549–572.

116. A. Flynn, 2015, Questions re-emerge on World Cup venues, *Wall Street Journal*, May 28, A10.

117. R. Johnson, R. Jelmaye, & L. Magalhaes, Scandal spurs overhaul of Brazil's soccer body, *Wall Street Journal*, June 12, A9.

118. M. Mazzeti & K. Benner, 2018, 12 Russian agents indicted in Mueller investigation, *New York Times*, https://www.nytimes.com, July 13.

119. C. Grimpe & K. Hussinger, 2014, Resource complementarity and value capture in firm acquisitions: The role of intellectual property rights, *Strategic Management Journal*, 35: 1762–1780.

120. 2018, Company information overview, Eskom Holdings Ltd., https://www.eskom.co.za, accessed, July 16; A. Wexler, 2015, Power outages mar South Africa's economic expansion, *Wall Street Journal*, www.wsj.com, May 8.

121. P. Kiernan & P. Trevisani, 2015, China seeks to keep its ties tight with South America, *Wall Street Journal*, May 20, A14; G. Fornes & A. Butt-Philip, 2011, Chinese MNEs and Latin America: A review, *International Journal of Emerging Markets*, 6: 98–117; S. Globerman & D. Shapiro, 2009, Economic and strategic considerations surrounding Chinese FDI in the United States, Asia Pacific *Journal of Management*, 26: 163–183.

122. E. Beckmann & H. Stix, 2015, Foreign currency borrowing and knowledge about exchange rate risk, *Journal of Economic Behavior & Organization*, 11: 21–16; C. R. Goddard, 2011, Risky business: Financial-sector liberalization and China, *Thunderbird International Business Review*, 53: 469–482; I. G. Kawaller, 2009, Hedging currency exposures by multinationals: Things to consider, *Journal of Applied Finance*, 18: 92–98.

123. P. R. La Monica, 2018, Wall street's $6.3 trillion man is worried about a trade war, CNNMoney, https://www.cnnmoney.com, July 16; L.G. Barbopoulos & J. Danbolt, 2018, The role of earnout financing on the valuation effects of global diversification, *Journal of International Business Studies*, 49: 523–551.

124. R. G. Bell, I. Filatotchev, & R. Aguilera, 2014, Corporate governance and investors' perceptions of foreign IPO value: An institutional perspective, *Academy of Management Journal*, 57: 301–320.

125. S. J. Castro-Gonzales, M. I. Espina, & R. M. Tinoco-Egas, 2018, Strategies and competitiveness for emerging countries: A comparative study among three Sougth American countries, *International Journal of Emerging Markets*, in press; M. Carney, P. Duran, M. van Essen & D. Shapiro, 2017, Family firms, internationalization, and national competitiveness: Does family firm prevalence matter? *Journal of Family Business Strategy*, 8: 123–136.

126. S. McDowell, 2017, The benefits of international diversification: Re-examining the effect of market allocation constraints, *The North American Journal of Economics and Finance*, 41: 190–203; M. Alessandri & A. Seth, 2014, The effects of managerial ownership on international and business diversification: Balancing incentives and risks, *Strategic Management Journal*, 35: 2064–2075; F. J. Contractor, 2012, Why do multinational firms exist? A theory note about the effect of multinational expansion on performance and recent methodological critiques, *Global Strategy Journal*, 2: 318–331.

127. J. Hojnik, M. Ruzzier, & T. S. Manolova, 2018, Internationalization and economic performance: The mediating role of eco-innovation, *Journal of Cleaner Production*, 171: 1312–1323; Marano, Arregle, Hitt, Spadafora, & van Essen, Home country Institutions and the internationalization-performance relationship; L. Zhou & A. Wu, 2014, Earliness of internationalization and performance outcomes: Exploring the moderating effects of venture age and international commitment, *Journal of World Business*, 49: 132–142; L. Li, 2007, Multinationality and performance:

A synthetic review and research agenda, *International Journal of Management Reviews*, 9: 117–139.

128. H. Tan & J. A. Mathews, 2015, Accelerated internationalization and resource leverage strategizing: The case of Chinese wind turbine manufacturers, *Journal of World Business*, 50: 417–427; J. H. Fisch, 2012, Information costs and internationalization performance, *Global Strategy Journal*, 2: 296–312; S. E. Christophe & H. Lee, 2005, What matters about internationalization: A market-based assessment, *Journal of Business Research*, 58: 636–643.

129. C. H. Oh & J. Oetzel, 2016, Once bitten twice shy? Experience managing violent conflict risk and MNC subsidiary-level investment expansion, *Strategic Management Journal*, 38: 714–731; S. Kraus, T. C. Ambos, F. Eggers, & B. Cesinger, 2015, Distance and perceptions of risk in internationalization decisions, *Journal of Business Research*, 68: 1501–1505; H. Berry, 2013, When do firms divest foreign operations? *Organization Science*, 24: 246–261.

130. L. Gagliardi & S. Lammarino, 2018, Innovation in risky markets: Ownership and location advantages in the UK regions, *Journal of Economic Geography*, in press; N. Nuruzzaman, A. S. Guar, & R. B. Sambharya, 2018, A microfoundations approach to studying innovation in multinational subsidiaries, *Global Strategy Journal*, in press.

131. J. Freixaneta & J. Churakova, 2018, Exploring the relationship between internationalization stage, innovation and performance: The case of Spanish companies, *International Journal of Business*, 23: 131–150; V. Ratten & K. Tajeddini, 2017, Innovativeness in family firms: An internationalization approach, *Review o f International Business and Strategy*, 27: 217–230; P. C. Patel, S. A. Fernhaber, P. P. McDougal-Covin, & R. P. van der Have, 2014, Beating competitors to international markets: The value of geographically balanced networks for innovation, *Strategic Management Journal*, 35: 691–711.

132. V. Braga, A. Correia, A. Braga, & S. Lemos, 2017, The innovation and internationalization processes of family businesses, *Review of International Business and Strategy*, 27: 231–247; S. Awate, M. M. Larsen, & R. Mudambi, 2015, Accessing vs sourcing knowledge: A comparative study of R&D internationalization between emerging and advanced economy firms, *Journal of International Business Studies*, 46: 63–86; O. Bertrand & M. J. Mol, 2013, The antecedents and innovation effects of domestic and offshore R&D outsourcing: The contingent impact of cognitive distance and absorptive capacity, *Strategic Management Journal*, 34: 751–760.

133. R. Belderbos, B. Lokshin, & B. Sadowski, 2015, The returns to foreign R&D, *Journal of International Business Studies*, 46, 491–504; I. Guler & A. Nerkar, 2012, The impact of global and local cohesion on innovation in the pharmaceutical industry, *Strategic Management Journal*, 33: 535–549.

134. M. Alessandri & A. Seth, 2014, The effects of managerial ownership on international and business diversification: Balancing incentives and risks, *Strategic Management Journal*, 35: 2064–2075; B. B. Nielsen & S. Nielsen, 2013, Top management team nationality diversity and firm performance: A multilevel study. *Strategic Management Journal*, 34, 373–382; M. Halme, S. Lindeman, & P. Linna, 2012, Innovation for inclusive business: Intrapreneurial bricolage in multinational corporations, *Journal of Management Studies*, 49: 743–784; I. Filatotchev & M. Wright, 2010, Agency perspectives on corporate governance of multinational enterprises, *Journal of Management Studies*, 47: 471–486.

135. T. Meelen, A. M. Hermann & J. Faber, 2017, Disentangling patterns of economic, technological and innovative specialization of Western economies: An assessment of the varieties-of-capitalism theory on comparative institutional advantages, *Research Policy*, 40: 667–677.

136. P. J. Buckley, J. P. Doh & M. H. Benischke, 2017, Towards a renaissance in international business research? Big questions, grand challenges, and the future of IB scholarship, *Journal ofInternational Business Studies*, 48: 1045–1064.

137. K. J. Alter & K. Raustiala, 2018, The rise of international regime complexity, *Annual Review of Law and Social Science*, 14: in press; J. Wu & S. H. Park, 2018, The role of international institutional complexity on emerging market companies' innovation, *Global Strategy Journal*, in press; J. I. Siegel & S. H. Schwartz, 2013, Egalitarianism, cultural distance and foreign direct investment: A new approach, *Organization Science*, 24: 1174–1194.

138. R. Chittoor, P. S. Aulakh, & S. Ray, 2015, Accumulative and assimilative learning, institutional infrastructure, and innovation orientation of developing economy firms, *Global Strategy Journal*, 5: 133–153; P. C. Nell & B. Ambos, 2013, Parenting advantage in the MNC: An embeddedness perspective on the value added by headquarters, *Strategic Management Journal*, 34: 1086–1103; J.-F. Hennart, 2012, Emerging market multinationals and the theory of the multinational enterprise, *Global Strategy Journal*, 2: 168–187.

139. J.-E. Vahlne, I. Ivarsson, & C. G. Alvstam, 2018, Are multinational enterprises in retreat? *Multinational Business Review*, 55: 128–148; S. Schmid & T. Dauth, 2014, Does internationalization make a difference? Stock market reaction to announcements of international top executive appointments, *Journal of World Business*, 49: 63–77.

140. N. Irwin, 2018, Globalization's backlash is here, at just the wrong time, *New York Times*, http://www.nytimes.com, March 23; J. U. Kim & R. V. Aguilera, 2015, The world is spiky: An internationalization framework for a semi-globalized world, *Global Strategy Journal*, 5: 113–132; R. Belderbos, T. W. Tong, & S. Wu, 2014, Multinationality and downside risk: The roles of option portfolio and organization, *Strategic Management Journal*, 35: 88–106.

141. P. Regnér & J. Edman, 2014, MNE institutional advantage: How subunits shape, transpose and evade host country institutions, *Journal of International Business Studies*, 45: 275–302; B. Baik, J.-K. Kang, J.-M. Kim, & J. Lee, 2013, The liability of foreignness in international equity investments: Evidence from the U.S. stock market, *Journal of International Business Studies*, 44: 391–411.

142. S. Zhao & C.-V. Priporas, 2017, Information technology and marketing performance within international market-entry alliances: A review and an integrated conceptual framework, *International Marketing Review*, 34: 5–28; S. Song, 2014, Entry mode irreversibility, host market uncertainty, and foreign subsidiary exits, *Asia Pacific Journal of Management*, 31: 455–471; S.-H. Lee & S. Song, 2012, Host country uncertainty, intra-MNC production shifts, and subsidiary performance, *Strategic Management Journal*, 33: 1331–1340.

143. D. W. Williams & D. A. Grégoire, 2015, Seeking commonalities or avoiding differences? Re-conceptualizing distance and its effects on internationalization decisions, *Journal of International Business Studies*, 46: 253–284; L. Berchicci, A. King, & C. L. Tucci, 2011, Does the apple always fall close to the tree? The geographical proximity choice of spin-outs, *Strategic Entrepreneurship Journal*, 5: 120–136; A. Ojala, 2008, Entry in a psychically distant market: Finnish small and medium-sized software firms in Japan, *European Management Journal*, 26: 135–144.

144. W. Shi, R. E. Hoskisson, & Y. Zhang, 2016. A geopolitical perspective into the opposition to globalizing state-owned enterprises in target states. *Global Strategy Journal*, 6: 13–30; M. L. L. Lam, 2009, Beyond credibility of doing business in China: Strategies for improving corporate citizenship of foreign multinational enterprises in China, *Journal of Business Ethics*, 87: 137–146.

145. M. H. Ho & F. Wang, 2015, Unpacking knowledge transfer and learning paradoxes in international strategic alliances: Contextual differences matter, *International Business Review*, 24: 287–297; E. Fang & S. Zou, 2010, The effects of absorptive capacity and joint learning on the instability of international joint ventures in emerging economies, *Journal of International Business Studies*, 41: 906–924; D. Lavie & S. Miller, 2009, Alliance portfolio internationalization and firm performance, *Organization Science*, 19: 623–646.

iStock.com/DNY59

9

Cooperative Strategy

Studying this chapter should provide you with the strategic management knowledge needed to:

9-1 Define cooperative strategies and explain why firms use them.

9-2 Define and discuss the three major types of strategic alliances.

9-3 Name the business-level cooperative strategies and describe their use.

9-4 Discuss the use of corporate-level cooperative strategies.

9-5 Understand why firms use cross-border strategic alliances as an international cooperative strategy.

9-6 Explain cooperative strategies' risks.

9-7 Describe two approaches used to manage cooperative strategies.

iStock.com/DNY59

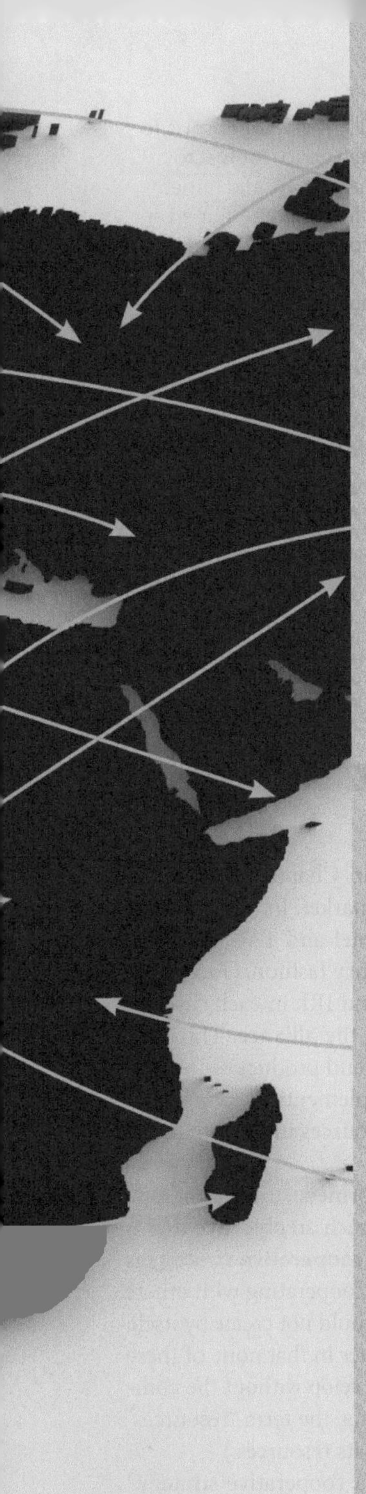

GOOGLE'S DIVERSIFIED ALLIANCE PORTFOLIO: A RESPONSE TO COMPETITORS AND AN ATTEMPT TO BE A DOMINANT FORCE

When using different types of cooperative strategies, firms commit to sharing some of their unique resources in order to reach an objective that is important to all participants. A key reason that cooperative strategies are used is that individual firms sometimes identify opportunities they can't pursue because they lack the type and/or quantity of resources (e.g., technological capabilities or special expertise) needed to do so or the access to markets.

Some partnerships are formed between similar firms who desire to develop scale economies to enhance their competitiveness. For years, automobile manufacturers have formed large numbers of partnerships for this reason. In other instances, firms competing in different industries uniquely combine their unique resources to pursue what they believe is a value-creating shared objective. It was for this reason that Google, Intel, and TAG Heuer formed a partnership several years ago to design and produce a smartwatch.

In part, the decision Google, Intel, and TAG Heuer made to collaborate was a strategic action taken in response to Apple's introduction of the iWatch. They have now produced a high-end smartwatch, with the most expensive version priced at about $17,000. They have also more recently produced a lower-priced smartwatch named the Connected Modular 45 beginning at a price of $1,650. Still this watch serves a special luxury market niche, in keeping with the TAG Heuer market focus.

Fabrice Coffrini/AFP/Getty Images

Guy Semon (Tag Heuer), Jean-Claude Biver (Tag Heuer), Michael Bell (Intel) and David Singleton (Google) pose with a block of swiss cheese, at the announcement of the new partnership between the watch brand and the two giants of Silicon Valley.

Google has parlayed the knowledge it has gained in the alliance with Intel and TAG Heuer into another alliance with Fitbit. For example, Fitbit has agreed to use Google's new 'health data standards for apps.' Fitbit will begin using Google's cloud data storage platform, which is in compliance with the U.S. Health Standards and Accountability Act. This legislation regulates the use of medical records. The partnership allows Fitbit to avoid building its own system to comply with this law. Fitbit CEO James Park says that "working with Google gives us the opportunity to transform how we scale our business, allowing us to reach more people around the world faster, while also enhancing the experience we offer to our users and the healthcare system."

Fitbit was established in the fitness tracker market, but has lost customers to smartphones by Apple and Samsung that now are able to track physical exercise and travel. Thus, Fitbit has been expanding to the broader healthcare market, and its alliance with Google exemplifies this change. Google is also working with Fitbit because its Android Wear software was unsuccessful in the market. After the Google alliance was announced, the price of Fitbit shares on the market increased by 8%. This alliance is even more important as a counter to Apple as it is now using its smartwatch for digital health services.

Google has developed an increasingly diversified portfolio of strategic alliances. For example, it recently signed agreements to form alliances with Carrefour, a large French retailer, and Repsol, a major energy firm in Spain. The alliance with Carrefour is intended to help the firm increase its e-commerce presence. Alternatively, the goal of the alliance with Repsol is to use Google's machine learning tool to deploy big data and artificial intelligence tools across Repsol's refineries. Google shut down its search engine activity in China in 2010, and rather than taking actions to re-enter the market, it started a research center in China and signed an agreement to form an alliance with Tencent, a large Chinese Internet conglomerate. Additionally, it recently formed an alliance partnership with IRI to conduct marketing mix analyses. This work will be a part of Google's new Google Measurement Partners program. The intent of this program (and its alliance with IRI) is to provide high quality and choice to its advertisers across multiple areas of specialization. IRI will help bolster Google's marketing efforts.

In addition to its multiple and diversified alliances, Google continues to invest heavily in R&D to develop new technologies and services (e.g., in artificial intelligence and many other areas). Thus, we can expect Google to be a dominant force in high technology for years to come.

Sources: S. Hughes, 2018, Google selects IRI to join new measurement partners program, *Odessa American*, https://www.oaoa.com, July 18: R. Zhong, 2018, Google, rebuilding its presence in China, invests in retailer, JD.com, *New York Times*, https://www.nytimes.com, June 18; H Agnew, 2018, French retailer Carrefour boosts e-commerce aspirations with Google partnership, *Financial Times*, https://www.ft.com, June 11: A. Raval, 2018, Google and Repsol team up to boost oil refinery efficiency, *Financial Times*, https://www.ft.com, June 3; T. Bradshaw, 2018, Fitbit shares jump on Google alliance, *Financial Times*, https://www.ft.com, April 30; A. Pressman, 2018, Fitbit strikes deal with Google that could lead to wearables collaboration, *Fortune*, http://fortune.com, April 30; 2017, Tag Heuer teams up with Google, Intel for new $1650 android smartwatch, *PYMNTS.com*, https://www.pymnts.com, March 15; D Pierce 2017, Tag Heuer's new $1600 smartwatch (almost) worth it, *Wired*, https://www.wired.com, March 14; Chen, 2015, Google, Intel, TAG Heuer to collaborate on Swiss smartwatch, *Wall Street Journal* Online, //www.wsj.com, March 19; M. Clerizo, 2015, There's something in the way they move, *Wall Street Journal Online*, www.wsj.com, March 18; L. Dignan, 2015, Can TAG Heuer, Intel, Google collaborate and create a smart enough watch? ZDNET Online, www.zdnet.com, March 19.

In describing the multiple arenas in which Google competes in Chapter 5's Opening Case, we mentioned the firm's plans to enter the smartwatch market. In this chapter's Opening Case, we describe the actions Google is taking with Intel and TAG Heuer to develop technological innovations to compete in the world of luxury fashion. Google has also developed alliances with Fitbit, Carrefour, Repsol, Tencent, and IRI; in each case the firms and Google have complementary resources to be used in the alliance. Thus, the specific combination of each firm's unique resources through the end product of the alliance will be developed. Thus, as is the case for all companies implementing cooperative strategies, Google and its alliance partners intend to use their resources in ways that will create the greatest amount of value for stakeholders.[1]

Forming a cooperative strategy like those that Google has formed, such as the one with Intel and TAG Heuer, have the potential to help companies reach an objective that is important to all of the partners, such as firm growth. Specifically, a **cooperative strategy** is a means by which firms collaborate to achieve a shared objective.[2] Cooperating with others is a strategy a firm uses to create value for a customer that it likely could not create by itself. As noted above, this is the situation for Google, Intel, and TAG Heuer in that none of these firms could create the specific smartwatch the firms intended to develop without the combination of the three companies' resources. (Throughout this chapter, the term "resources" is used comprehensively and refers to a firm's capabilities as well as its resources.)

Firms also try to create competitive advantages when using a cooperative strategy.[3] A competitive advantage developed through a cooperative strategy often is called a *collaborative* or *relational* advantage,[4] indicating that the relationship that develops among collaborating partners is commonly the basis on which to build a competitive advantage. Importantly, successfully using cooperative strategies often helps a firm to outperform its rivals in terms of strategic competitiveness and earn above-average returns,[5] often because they've been able to form a competitive advantage.

A **cooperative strategy** is a means by which firms collaborate to achieve a shared objective.

We examine several topics in this chapter. First, we define and offer examples of different strategic alliances as primary types of cooperative strategies. We focus on strategic alliances because firms use them more frequently than other types of cooperative relationships. In succession, we describe business-level, corporate-level, international, and network cooperative strategies. The chapter closes with a discussion of the risks of using cooperative strategies as well as how effectively managing the strategies can reduce these risks.

9-1 Strategic Alliances as a Primary Type of Cooperative Strategy

A **strategic alliance** is a cooperative strategy in which firms combine some of their resources to create a competitive advantage. Strategic alliances involve firms with some degree of exchange and sharing of resources to jointly develop, sell, and service goods or services.[6] In addition, firms use strategic alliances to leverage their existing resources while working with partners to develop additional resources as the foundation for new competitive advantages.[7] To be certain, the reality today is that strategic alliances are a vital strategy that firms use as a means to try to outperform rivals.[8]

Several successful alliances provide examples of partnerships that were formed to combine the individual firm's unique resources with the intent to create competitive advantages as a path to outperforming rivals. Among those alliances were partnerships formed by Barnes & Noble and Starbucks and by Hewlett Packard and Disney. Having Starbucks coffee shops in Barnes & Noble bookstores allowed customers to peruse new books while enjoying a fresh cup of coffee. Both firms profited from this partnership. Additionally, Disney realized early the value of technology for use in its theme parks and other Disney innovations. Thus, the partnership with Hewlett Packard has been a major success for both companies for many years.[9]

Before describing three types of major strategic alliances and reasons for their use, we need to note that, for all cooperative strategies, success is more likely when partners behave cooperatively. Actively solving problems, being trustworthy, and consistently pursuing ways to combine partners' resources to create value are examples of cooperative behavior known to contribute to alliance success.[10]

9-1a Types of Major Strategic Alliances

Joint ventures, equity strategic alliances, and nonequity strategic alliances are the three major types of strategic alliances that firms use. The ownership arrangement is a key difference among these alliances.

A **joint venture** is a strategic alliance in which two or more firms create a legally independent company to share some of their resources to create a competitive advantage. Typically, partners in a joint venture own equal percentages and contribute equally to the venture's operations. Often formed to improve a firm's ability to compete in uncertain competitive environments, joint ventures can be effective in establishing long-term relationships and in transferring tacit knowledge between partners.[11]

GM and China-based SAIC Motor Corp., China's largest automobile manufacturer by sales volume, recently formed a joint venture to develop new cars that cater specifically to Chinese tastes. Called Shanghai GM Co., each partner controls 50 percent of this cooperative strategy. The partners intend to invest a total of 100 billion yuan, or approximately $16.4 billion, between 2016 and 2020 for the purpose of developing at least "10 all-new or face-lift" models during each of the five years included within the investment time horizon. These companies have partnered in other ways. For example, SAIC and GM recently agreed for SAIC to take over GM's Opel manufacturing plant in India, which allows SAIC to enter India's automobile market.[12] Demonstrating the complexities associated with being a successful competitor in today's business environment is the fact

A **strategic alliance** is a cooperative strategy in which firms combine some of their resources to create a competitive advantage.

A **joint venture** is a strategic alliance in which two or more firms create a legally independent company to share some of their resources to create a competitive advantage.

Shanghai GM facility where the work of the firms' joint venture takes place.

that SAIC also has a joint venture with Volkswagen AG. Among other products, the SAIC–VW joint venture manufactures the Tiguan sport-utility model, which is the number one foreign-brand SUV being sold in China. The joint venture began producing Audi vehicles for China in 2018. VW is introducing a new platform to use for the vehicles it produces in cooperation with SAIC for the Chinese market.[13]

Because it can't be codified, tacit knowledge, which is increasingly critical to firms' efforts to develop competitive advantages, is learned through experiences such as those taking place when people from partner firms work together in a joint venture.[14] Overall, a joint venture may be the optimal type of cooperative arrangement when firms need to combine their resources to create a competitive advantage that is substantially different from any they possess individually and when the partners intend to compete in highly uncertain environments.

An **equity strategic alliance** is an alliance in which two or more firms own different percentages of a company that they have formed by combining some of their resources to create a competitive advantage. As with most alliances, the partners are seeking complementary resources and/or capabilities, hopefully allowing them to learn from each other.[15] Companies commonly form equity alliances because they want to ensure that they have control over assets that they commit to the alliance. This is particularly the case with firms from developed countries entering less developed countries. Yet, firms from emerging market countries such as China also use equity alliances when entering foreign markets.[16] Control of firms' resources, especially intellectual capital, can be quite important when R&D alliances are formed. In fact, equity-based alliances are common when the resources and relationships among partners is complex, which is the case with R&D alliances. Thus, most R&D alliances are equity strategic alliances.[17]

A **nonequity strategic alliance** is an alliance in which two or more firms develop a contractual relationship to share some of their resources to create a competitive advantage.[18] In this type of alliance, firms do not establish a separate independent company and therefore do not take equity positions. For this reason, nonequity strategic alliances are less formal, demand fewer partner commitments than do joint ventures and equity strategic alliances, and generally do not foster an intimate relationship between partners; nonetheless, research evidence indicates that they can create value for the involved firms.[19] The relative informality and lower commitment levels characterizing nonequity strategic alliances make them unsuitable for complex projects where success requires partners to be able to effectively transfer tacit knowledge to each other.[20] Licensing agreements, distribution agreements, and supply contracts are examples of nonequity strategic alliances.

An **equity strategic alliance** is an alliance in which two or more firms own different percentages of a company that they have formed by combining some of their resources to create a competitive advantage.

A **nonequity strategic alliance** is an alliance in which two or more firms develop a contractual relationship to share some of their resources to create a competitive advantage.

Commonly, outsourcing arrangements are organized in the form of a nonequity strategic alliance. (Discussed in Chapter 3, *outsourcing* is the purchase of a value-chain activity or a support-function activity from another firm.) Apple Inc. and most other companies involved with selling computers, tablets, and smartphones use nonequity strategic alliances to outsource most or all of the activities required to manufacture their products. Apple, for example, has traditionally outsourced most of its manufacturing to Foxconn Technology Group.[21] Firms often choose to use nonequity strategic alliances to outsource manufacturing activities to emerging market companies because of the cost efficiencies those firms generate through scale economies. Normally, the collaborative pattern between a product designer such as Apple and a manufacturer such as Foxconn should be expected to continue. For example, Foxconn built more Apple MacBooks in 2018 than in any previous year. However, the trade war between the United States and China is causing problems for this alliance. For this and other reasons, Foxconn is trying to reduce its dependence on Apple by acquiring other companies and customers.[22]

ZDnet

Foxconn manufacturer working to produce iPhones for Apple.

9-1b Reasons Firms Develop Strategic Alliances

Cooperative strategies are an integral part of the competitive landscape and are quite important to many companies. The fact that alliances can account for up to 25 percent or more of a typical firm's sales revenue demonstrates their importance. In addition to partnerships among for-profit organizations, alliances are also formed between educational institutions and individual companies for the purpose of commercializing ideas flowing from basic research projects that are completed at universities.[23] Moreover, in addition to dyadic partnerships where two firms form a collaborative relationship for competitive purposes, competition now occurs between large alliances in some industries. This pattern of competition exists in the global airline industry where individual airlines compete against each other but simultaneously join alliances (such as Star, Oneworld, and SkyTeam), which in turn compete against each other.[24] The array of alliances with which firms are involved highlights the various options available to companies seeking to increase their competitiveness by cooperating with others.

Overall, there are many reasons firms choose to participate in strategic alliances. We mention two key reasons here and discuss additional ones below by explaining how strategic alliances may help firms improve their competitiveness while competing in either slow-, fast-, or standard-cycle markets.

The first important reason firms form strategic alliances is to create value they couldn't generate by acting independently and entering markets more rapidly.[25] The partnership formed among online news publishers such as *The Guardian*, *CNN International*, *Financial Times*, and *The Economist* to allow advertisers to reach online audiences with scale demonstrates this. Those forming this alliance, called Pangaea, concluded that the collaboration would help the firms efficiently expand on a global basis. The Pangaea alliance has become a significant force in the industry with 220 million users across 140 countries.[26]

A second major reason firms form strategic alliances is that most (if not all) companies lack the full set of resources needed to pursue all identified opportunities and reach their objectives in the process of doing so on their own.[27] Given constrained resources, firms can collaborate for a number of purposes, including those of reaching new customers and broadening both the product offerings and the distribution of their products without adding significantly to their cost structures. Alternatively, firms with greater cash and other resources might form alliances to enter multiple markets, allowing them to compete more effectively with rivals across markets and/or to forestall rivals' entrance or certain competitive actions in certain markets.[28]

Through the partnership between Expedia and Latin American online travel leader Decolar.com, which operates the Portuguese Decolar.com and Spanish Despegar.com websites, both firms are deriving important benefits that neither could access acting independently. Expedia has acquired a number of rivals such as Travelocity, Trivago, and Orbitz to become a global market player in the travel platform industry.[29]

As we discussed in Chapter 5, when considering competitive rivalry and competitive dynamics, unique competitive conditions characterize slow-, fast-, and standard-cycle markets.[30] As shown in Figure 9.1, these unique market types create different reasons for firms to use strategic alliances.

In short, *slow-cycle markets* are markets where the firm's competitive advantages are shielded from imitation for relatively long periods of time and where imitation is costly. Railroads and, historically, telecommunications, utilities, and financial services are industries characterized as slow-cycle markets. In *fast-cycle markets*, the firm's competitive advantages are not shielded from imitation, preventing their long-term sustainability. Competitive advantages are moderately shielded from imitation in *standard-cycle markets*, typically allowing them to be sustained for a longer period of time than in fast-cycle market situations, but for a shorter period of time than in slow-cycle markets.

Figure 9.1 Reasons for Strategic Alliances by Market Type

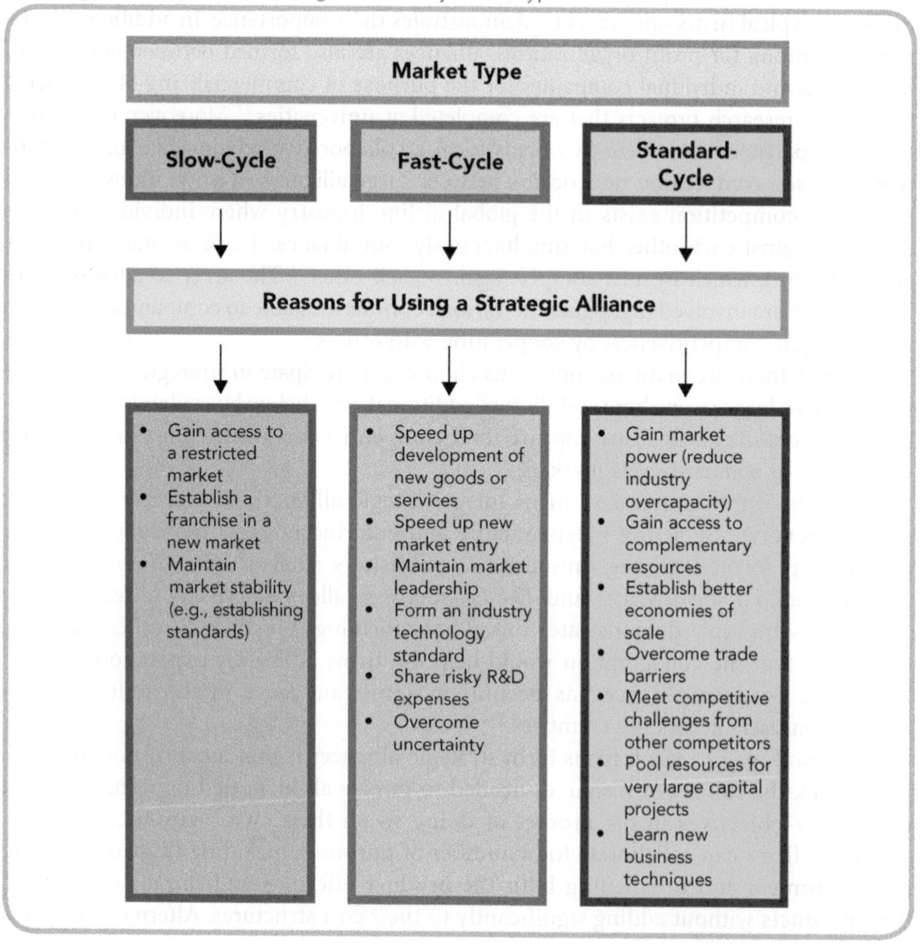

Slow-Cycle Markets

Firms in slow-cycle markets often use strategic alliances to enter restricted markets or to establish a franchise in a new market. For example, Carnival Corporation, owner and operator of Carnival Cruise Line, formed two joint ventures with state-owned China Merchants Group, which is a conglomerate with businesses in financial investments and property development as well as transportation. One venture between the two firms focuses on shipbuilding while the second concentrates on developing new ports and travel destinations in and around China. The launching of China's first domestic cruise brand that will target Chinese customers is one outcome associated with the collaborations between the two companies. Carnival's interest with these joint ventures is to compete in China where the cruise industry is beginning to grow rapidly. Interestingly, Carnival has delayed a major entry into the cruise market in China, citing high demand for its cruise ships in Australia. However, Carnival's commitment to the Chinese market continues as it signed a contract for the manufacture of two large cruise ships in China to be delivered in 2023.[31]

Slow-cycle markets are becoming rare in the twenty-first century competitive landscape for several reasons, including the privatization of industries and economies, the rapid expansion of the Internet's capabilities for quick dissemination of information, and the speed with which advancing technologies make quickly imitating even complex products possible.[32] Firms competing in slow-cycle markets should recognize the likelihood that in the future, they will encounter situations in which their competitive advantages become partially sustainable (in the instance of a standard-cycle market) or unsustainable (in the case of a fast-cycle market). Cooperative strategies can help firms transition from relatively sheltered markets, such as the travel cruise market in which Carnival Corporation competes, to more competitive ones.[33]

Fast-Cycle Markets

Fast-cycle markets are unstable, unpredictable, and complex; in a word, hypercompetitive.[34] Combined, these conditions virtually preclude establishing sustainable competitive advantages, forcing firms to constantly seek sources of new competitive advantages while creating value by using current ones. Alliances between firms with current excess resources and those with promising resources help companies competing in fast-cycle markets effectively transition from the present to the future and gain rapid entry into new markets. Alliances can also help firms to gain legitimacy more quickly in new markets.[35]

Micron Technology, Inc. and Seagate Technology LLC are competitors in manufacturing storage solutions, a competitive arena in which establishing sustainable competitive advantages is all but impossible. Because of this, innovation is critical to their success as well as for others operating in this industry given the fast-cycle nature of the storage-solution market. Micron and Seagate formed a strategic alliance to combine the firms' innovation and expertise. Resulting from this collaboration, the

Think4photop/Shutterstock.com

A Carnival Cruise Line ship that may soon transport Chinese customers through the firm's joint venture with China Merchants Group.

partners believe, will be an ability to provide customers with "industry-leading" storage solutions. In turn, Micron and Seagate believe that customers buying the products that will flow from the collaboration will be able to innovate faster while producing their goods and services. Micro also has other alliances designed to provide technological solutions for specialized markets which is the goal of a joint development program it has with Intel.[36]

Standard-Cycle Markets

In standard-cycle markets, alliances are more likely to be made by partners that have complementary resources.[37] The alliances formed by airline companies are an example of standard-cycle market alliances.

When initially established, airline alliances were intended to allow firms to share their complementary resources to make it easier for passengers to fly between secondary cities in the United States and Europe. Today, airline alliances are mostly global in nature and are formed primarily so members can gain marketing clout, have opportunities to reduce costs, and have access to additional international routes.[38] Of these reasons, international expansion by having access to more international routes is the most important because these routes are the path to increased revenues and potential profits. To support efforts to control costs, alliance members jointly purchase some items and share facilities such as passenger gates, customer service centers, and airport passenger lounges when possible. For passengers, airline alliances create benefits such as less complicated ticket buying processes, easier connections for international flights, and the earning of frequent flyer miles.

There are three major airline alliances operating today. Star Alliance is the largest with 28 members, followed by SkyTeam Alliance with 20 and Oneworld Alliance with 13. All three alliances continue to expand their geographic coverage and to respond to market trends, such as the increasing amount of travel from regions throughout the world to Asia. In general, most airline alliances, such as the three we mention here, are formed to help firms gain economies of scale and meet competitive challenges (see Figure 9.1). Code sharing agreements and the ability to reduce costs associated with operations, maintenance, and purchases are examples of how airline alliances help members gain economies of scale as a path to increasing their competitiveness.[39]

9-2 Business-Level Cooperative Strategy

A **business-level cooperative strategy** is a strategy through which firms combine some of their resources to create a competitive advantage by competing in one or more product markets. As discussed in Chapter 4, business-level strategy details what the firm intends to do to gain a competitive advantage in specific product markets. Thus, the firm forms a business-level cooperative strategy when it believes that combining some of its resources with those of one or more partners will create competitive advantages that it can't create alone and will lead to success in a specific product market. We present the four business-level cooperative strategies in Figure 9.2.

A **business-level cooperative strategy** is a strategy through which firms combine some of their resources to create a competitive advantage by competing in one or more product markets.

9-2a Complementary Strategic Alliances

Complementary strategic alliances are business-level alliances in which firms share some of their resources in complementary ways to create a competitive advantage.[40] Vertical and horizontal are the two dominant types of complementary strategic alliances (see Figure 9.2).

Complementary strategic alliances are business-level alliances in which firms share some of their resources in complementary ways to create a competitive advantage.

Figure 9.2 Business-Level Cooperative Strategies

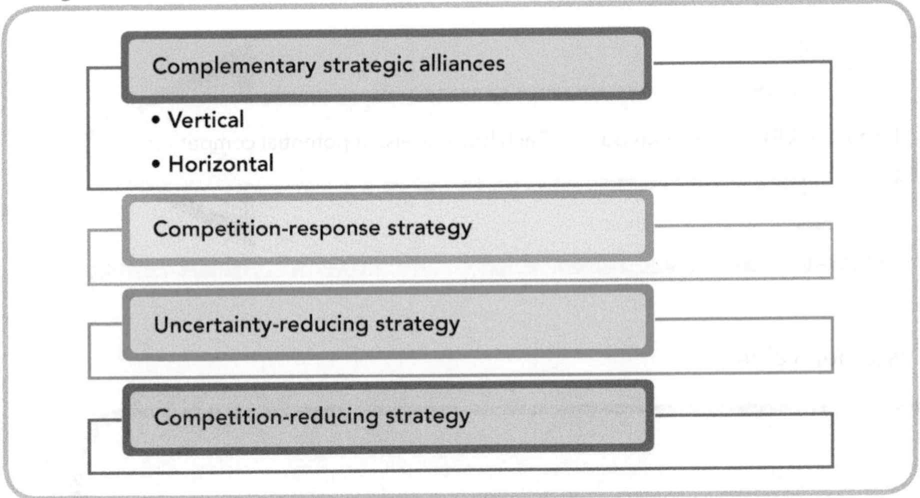

Vertical Complementary Strategic Alliance

In a *vertical complementary strategic alliance*, firms share some of their resources from different stages of the value chain to create a competitive advantage (see Figure 9.3).[41] Oftentimes, vertical complementary alliances are formed to adapt to environmental changes;[42] sometimes the changes represent an opportunity for partnering firms to innovate while adapting.[43]

Companies recognize that today's consumers are more connected than ever as they use various devices such as smartphone applications, GPS systems, and the wireless Internet. AT&T has built alliances with multiple companies, such as Rockwell automation, Emerson, and LoJack, an anti-car-theft company, to develop technology-based products that satisfy the needs of current and future customers. It is integrating the technology-based products with AT&T's network such as sprinkler heads made by HydroPoint to develop smart irrigation systems. Ralph de la Vega, CEO of AT&T's mobile and business solutions, explained that "This is much, much different from trying to procure a piece of technology and trying to optimize the price. This is about trying to optimize a business process and reinvesting in the business."[44]

Horizontal Complementary Strategic Alliance

A *horizontal complementary strategic alliance* is an alliance in which firms share some of their resources from the same stage (or stages) of the value chain for creating a competitive advantage. Pharmaceutical companies make frequent use of this type of alliance. Such alliances often help them to weather economic recessions and rivals' actions.[45] More comprehensively, some of the world's largest pharmaceutical firms, including Pfizer, Bristol-Myers Squibb, GlaxoSmithKline, and Eli Lilly, are sharing some of their proprietary assets through a collaboration organized by the U.S.-based National Institutes of Health. The primary purpose of this five-year partnership is to more quickly discover and produce drugs that cure challenging and historically intractable diseases. This example of horizontal alliances involves competitors cooperating, which some refer to as coopetition.[46]

Commonly, firms use complementary strategic alliances to focus on joint long-term product development and distribution opportunities.[47] Sometimes the desired outcomes of horizontal alliances are difficult to achieve; the parties may not agree

Figure 9.3 Vertical and Horizontal Complementary Strategic Alliances

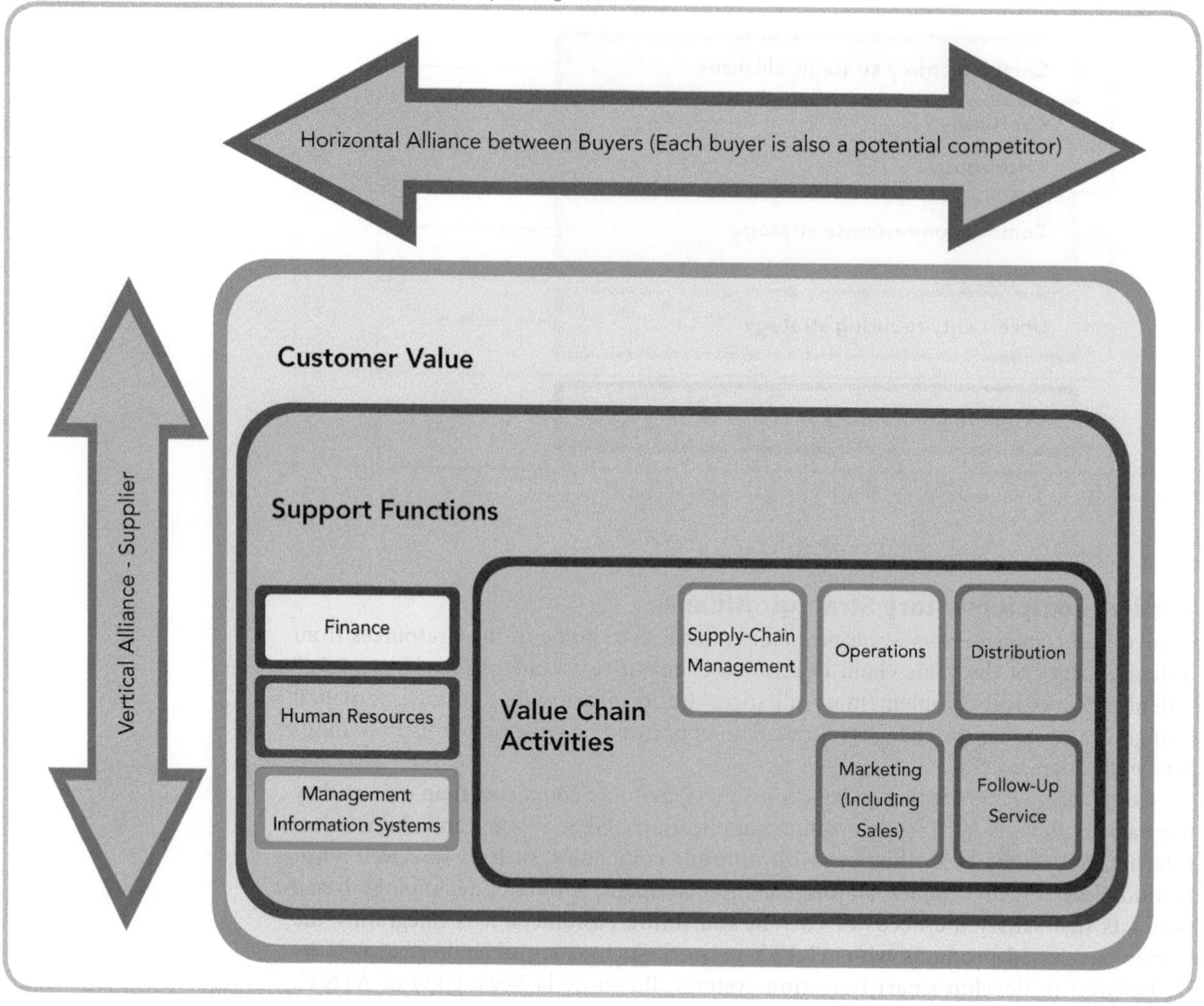

on how to combine their complementary resources, and the other alliances each partner has in its alliance portfolio can also affect the performance of the alliance over time.[48]

9-2b Competition Response Strategy

As discussed in Chapter 5, competitors initiate competitive actions (strategic and tactical) to attack rivals and launch competitive responses (strategic and tactical) to their competitors' actions. Strategic alliances can be used at the business level to respond to competitors' attacks. The alliance among Google, Intel, and TAG Heuer that is discussed in the Opening Case is a strategic response to Apple's strategic action of introducing the iWatch. Because they can be difficult to reverse and expensive to operate, strategic alliances are primarily formed to take strategic rather than tactical actions and to respond to competitors' actions in a like manner.

In October of 2007, SABMiller and Molson Coors Brewing Company formed a partnership. At the time, these firms held the second and third largest shares of the U.S. brew market. When formed, MillerCoors LLC, the name of the partnership, commanded roughly 29 percent of the U.S. brew market. However, Anheuser-Busch held 49 percent of the market. Indeed, the MillerCoors collaboration was a response to the size and scale of Anheuser-Busch's operations. (Anheuser-Busch itself was acquired by InBev in 2008, an acquisition that created the world's largest brewer.) Indicating that the collaboration would result in significant cost reductions and an ability to generate economies of scale through the firms' combined operations, a company official said that "Miller and Coors will be a stronger, more competitive U.S. brewer than either company can be on its own." Analysts agreed with this assessment, with one person noting that the partnership would give the two companies "substantially more scale, which helps them with their retailers and their distributors and helps erode Anheuser-Busch's No. 1 competitive advantage, which is their (market) share." However, the reduction in competition within the industry resulting from the MillerCoors joint venture led to price increases unexpected by outsiders. In fact, a study conducted by economists found that prices of beer products were 17–18 percent higher after the joint venture was consummated and as much as 8 percent higher than can be explained by other factors. Thus, some alliances formed as competitive responses, particularly those that reduce overall competition, may have some unintended consequences.[49] A successful collaboration in response to competitors for many years, MillerCoors today is struggling as it tries to compete against consumers' emerging preference for craft brews and cocktails instead of domestic lagers.[50] Perhaps customer responses to the price effects is one reason why. Thus, finding ways to effectively manage this alliance going forward is critical to its future.

9-2c Uncertainty-Reducing Strategy

Firms sometimes use business-level strategic alliances to hedge against risk and uncertainty, especially in fast-cycle markets.[51] These strategies are also used where uncertainty exists, such as in entering new product markets, especially those within emerging economies. The development of new products to enter new markets and the entry into emerging markets often carry with them significant risks. Thus, to reduce or mollify these risks, firms often develop R&D alliances and alliances with emerging market firms, respectively.[52]

The relationship between hybrid vehicles and batteries that are needed to power them created a situation for which alliances were formed to reduce uncertainty. More specifically, industry capacity among battery manufacturers was originally inadequate to meet the demand for the type of batteries used in hybrids. This lack of a sufficient supply created uncertainty for automobile manufacturers. To reduce this uncertainty, auto manufacturers formed alliances. For example, Daimler AG formed a partnership with Tesla through which it bought Tesla batteries to use in its "smart" minicar as well as its Freightliner trucks. Daimler originally bought a 9 percent stake in Tesla and gradually sold off shares until it sold its final 4 percent ownership stake in 2014. Daimler and other auto manufacturers are now bringing a number of new electric vehicles to the market, creating significant competition for Tesla.[53]

We further discuss Tesla in the Strategic Focus. As noted in this discussion, alliances were critical to Tesla's early operations and several have not been successful over time.

Strategic Focus

Tesla Losing Critical Strategic Alliances and Experiencing Challenges Creating Efficient Operations

Founded in 2003, Tesla Motors, manufacturer of electric vehicles, has formed many alliances as a means of competing during the early years of its life. For example, the company created an R&D partnership with Dana Holding Corporation initially for the purpose of jointly designing and producing a system capable of controlling the build-up of heat in its car batteries. Overall, Tesla originally partnered with many companies working in the value chain that is used to produce its products. Alliances were formed with multiple suppliers, R&D experts, and other original equipment manufacturers such as Daimler. One of the projects on which Daimler and Tesla originally collaborated was the B-Class Electric Drive, an all-electric vehicle from Mercedes-Benz. Essentially, Daimler needed Tesla's capability to produce the batteries for the car. Other partnerships were formed over the years such as Tesla's nonequity strategic alliance with Sotira, a French company, and an equity alliance with Panasonic, a Japanese-based firm. The purpose of the partnership with Sotira was to manufacture the carbon fiber bodies for its cars, while battery cells for the Tesla battery pack are produced through the collaboration with Panasonic.

Interestingly, with its expertise in batteries Tesla may, at is core, become a battery company rather than an automobile manufacturer. Supporting this contention is Tesla's intent to make and sell mega-batteries for homes and electric utility companies. The firm's decision to build and operate a 10-million-square-foot facility (dubbed the Gigafactory) to build batteries afforded Tesla the capacity to manufacture an array of batteries with different functionalities. Interestingly, the Gigafactory's size and scale allow Tesla to produce a quantity of batteries exceeding the firm's needs for its cars.

In early 2015, Apple announced an internal project that was aimed at developing an Apple-branded electric vehicle. Code-named "Titan," the initial work was oriented to designing a vehicle that resembles a minivan. Early assessments were that Apple intended to compete directly against Tesla if it decided to enter the electric vehicle market space. The complexity of designing and producing an electric vehicle is such that several years would be required for Apple to introduce its product to the market, even if it chose to do so. Some analysts predicted that Apple might eventually partner with Tesla in this venture. But, Apple recently announced it was partnering with Volkswagen to develop an autonomous electric vehicle.

Apple is not Tesla's biggest problem; however, it is losing its partnerships. Recently, both Daimler and Toyota extinguished their partnerships with Tesla and sold their original stakes in the company. Both companies along with BMW and Volvo have major plans to compete heavily in the electric car market. Thus, they are likely to be major competitors for Tesla, and some analysts have predicted that these four companies will have a larger share of the electric car market by 2021.

Tesla's problems go much deeper than these four rivals. Importantly, Tesla has had major production problems and fallen far short of its goals in the number of autos produced (its goal is 500,000 produced annually but it has produced only about 40,000 to date). These problems are exemplified by the fact that Tesla requires more than 90 hours of labor to produce one auto, whereas Toyota requires about 30 hours of labor to produce one. Tesla also has had problems with its alliances, especially with suppliers, placing heavy pressures on them to provide more of the parts needed and to do so faster. Interestingly, Tesla is also trying to insource many of the parts to avoid using many suppliers, whereas most other automakers use thousands of external suppliers. Tesla has not maintained good relationships with many of its suppliers and in 2018 even requested refunds from them in an attempt to reduce its costs and become profitable. Even with all of Tesla's problems, in 2018 it signed agreements to begin building a new manufacturing plant in Shanghai, China with 100 percent ownership (no joint venture such as was required by the Chinese government for all of the other major foreign automakers entering the Chinese market).

Doug Cheeseman/Photolibrary/Getty Images

A Tesla Roadster and the electric battery pack that powers the car.

Only time will tell if Tesla will succeed. It has an uphill battle, thanks to losing many of its major alliance partners and trying to deal with all of the challenges of creating efficient manufacturing operations.

Sources: L. Kehnscherper, 2018, German electric cars could catch up with Tesla in just a few years, *Bloomberg*, https://www.bloomberg.com, July 12; N. E. Boudette, 2018, Tesla's latest aim: Build 500,000 cars a year in China, *New York Times*, https://www.nytimes.com, July 10; T. Randall, J. Eidelson, D. Hull & J. Lippert, 2018, Harder than rocket science, *Bloomberg BusinessWeek*, pp. 36–41; A. Wahlman, 2018, Apple ignores Tesla, instead partners with Volkswagen, Seeking Alpha, https://seekingalpha.com, May 24; R. Harding, 2017, Toyota sells stake in Tesla as partnership dies, *Financial Times*, https://www.ft.com, June 4; C. Bryant, 2017, Mercedes vs. Tesla is an epic tale, *Bloomberg*, https://www.bloomberg.com, April 12; K. Finley, 2015, Tesla isn't an automaker. It's a battery company, *Wired*, www.wired.com, April 22; D. Wakabayashi & M. Ramsey, 2015, Apple gears up to challenge Tesla in electric cars, *Wall Street Journal Online*, www.wsj.com, February 13.

9-2d Competition-Reducing Strategy

Used to reduce competition, collusive strategies differ from strategic alliances in that collusive strategies are often an illegal cooperative strategy. Explicit collusion and tacit collusion are the two types of collusive strategies.

Explicit collusion exists when two or more firms negotiate directly to jointly agree about the amount to produce as well as the prices for what is produced.[54] Explicit collusion strategies are illegal in the United States and most developed economies (except in regulated industries). Accordingly, companies choosing to explicitly collude with other firms should recognize that competitors and regulatory bodies likely will challenge the acceptability of their competitive actions.

Tacit collusion exists when several firms in an industry indirectly coordinate their production and pricing decisions by observing each other's competitive actions and responses.[55] Tacit collusion tends to take place in industries dominated by a few large firms. Tacit collusion results in production output that is below fully competitive levels and above fully competitive prices. In addition to the effects on competition within a particular market, research suggests that tacit collusion between two firms can lead to less competition in other markets in which both firms operate.[56]

As suggested above, tacit collusion tends to be used as a competition-reducing, business-level strategy in industries with a high degree of concentration, such as the airline and breakfast cereal industries. Research in the airline industry suggests that tacit collusion reduces service quality and on-time performance.[57] Firms in these industries recognize their interdependence, which means that their competitive actions and responses significantly affect competitors' behavior toward them. Understanding this interdependence and carefully observing competitors can lead to tacit collusion. It can occur in other industries as well. For example, we noted earlier that the MillerCoors joint venture led to a large price increase on the MillerCoors and Anheuser-Busch beers. When prices are above the competitive level in an industry, it is logical to assume that the dominant firms use a tacit collusion cooperative strategy.

Mutual forbearance is a form of tacit collusion in which firms do not take competitive actions against rivals they meet in multiple markets. Rivals learn a great deal about each other when engaging in multimarket competition, including how to deter the effects of their rivals' competitive attacks and responses. Given what they know about each other as competitors, firms choose not to engage in what could be destructive competition in multiple product markets.[58]

In general, governments in free-market economies seek to determine how rivals can form cooperative strategies to increase their competitiveness without violating established regulations about competition.[59] However, this task is challenging when evaluating collusive strategies, particularly tacit ones. For example, the regulation of securities analysts through Regulation Fair Disclosure (Reg-FD) as established in the United States promoted more potential competition through competitive parity by eliminating privileged access to proprietary firm information as a critical source of competitive advantage. In doing so, research suggests that it led to more mutual forbearance among competing firms because they had greater awareness of information possessed by their competitors, thus leading to more tacit collusion.[60]

Other actions can be taken to reduce competition other than collusion. For example, firms may engage in alliances to build their knowledge. In doing so, they can create capabilities that allow them to out-maneuver their competitors, perhaps even forestalling their entry into market niches or disallowing their access to market share.[61] Also, some firms may forestall competition through rapid actions that capture and hold customers. For example, some firms rapidly introduced greener technology strategies throughout their supply chains (including alliance partners), satisfying customers' desires for a cleaner environment.[62] In the final analysis, individual companies must analyze the effect of a competition-reducing strategy on their performance and competitiveness and decide if pursuing such a strategy facilitates or inhibits their competitive success.

9-2e Assessing Business-Level Cooperative Strategies

Firms use business-level cooperative strategies to develop competitive advantages that can contribute to successful positions in individual product markets. Evidence suggests that complementary business-level strategic alliances, especially vertical ones, have the greatest probability of creating a competitive advantage and possibly even a sustainable one.[63] Horizontal complementary alliances are sometimes difficult to maintain because often they are formed between firms that compete against each other at the same time they are cooperating.[64] Airline companies, for example, want to compete aggressively against others serving their markets and customers. However, the need to develop scale economies and to share resources (such as scheduling systems) dictates that alliances be formed so the companies can compete by using cooperative actions and responses, while they simultaneously compete against one another through competitive actions and responses. The challenge in these instances is for each firm to find ways to create the greatest amount of value from their simultaneous competitive and cooperative actions.

Although strategic alliances designed to respond to competition and to reduce uncertainty can also create competitive advantages, these advantages often are more temporary than those developed through complementary (both vertical and horizontal) alliances. The primary reason for this is that complementary alliances have a stronger focus on creating value than do competition-reducing and uncertainty-reducing alliances, which are formed to respond to competitors' actions or reduce uncertainty rather than to attack competitors.[65]

9-3 Corporate-Level Cooperative Strategy

A **corporate-level cooperative strategy** is a strategy through which a firm collaborates with one or more companies to expand its operations. Diversifying alliances, synergistic alliances, and franchising are the most commonly used corporate-level cooperative strategies (see Figure 9.4).

Figure 9.4 Corporate-Level Cooperative Strategies

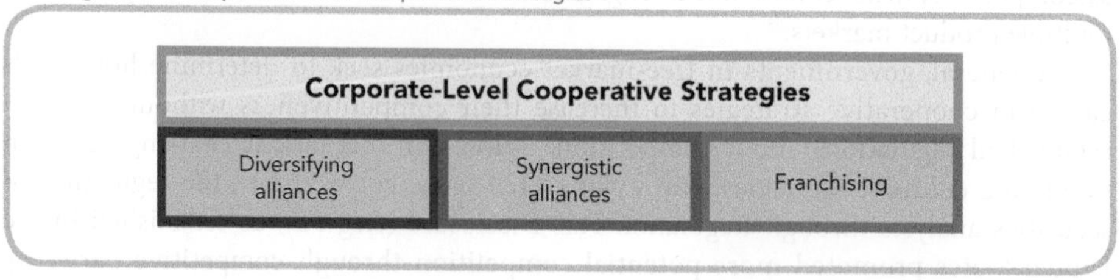

Corporate-Level Cooperative Strategies

Diversifying alliances | Synergistic alliances | Franchising

A **corporate-level cooperative strategy** is a strategy through which a firm collaborates with one or more companies to expand its operations.

Firms use diversifying and synergistic alliances to improve their performance by diversifying their operations through a means other than or in addition to internal organic growth or a merger or acquisition.[66] When a firm seeks to diversify into markets in which the host nation's government prevents mergers and acquisitions, alliances become an especially appropriate option. Corporate-level strategic alliances are also attractive compared with mergers, and particularly acquisitions, because they require fewer resource commitments and permit greater flexibility in terms of efforts to diversify partners' operations.[67] An alliance can be used to determine whether the partners might benefit from a future merger or acquisition between them. This "testing" process often characterizes alliances formed to combine firms' unique technological resources and capabilities.[68]

9-3a Diversifying Strategic Alliance

A **diversifying strategic alliance** is a strategy in which firms share some of their resources to engage in product and/or geographic diversification. Companies using this strategy typically seek to enter new markets (either domestic or outside of their home setting) with existing products or with newly developed products. Managing diversity gained through alliances has fewer financial costs but often requires more managerial expertise. The need for expertise in managing diversity is heightened by the fact that the focal firm has less control over the partner. Managers must coordinate and build trust in order to coordinate alliance activities. Additionally, they have to work at understanding their diverse partners and their capabilities in order to successfully coordinate within the alliance.[69]

9-3b Synergistic Strategic Alliance

A **synergistic strategic alliance** is a strategy in which firms share some of their resources to create economies of scope. Similar to the business-level horizontal complementary strategic alliance, synergistic strategic alliances create synergy across multiple functions or multiple businesses between partner firms.[70] A common example of a synergistic alliance is when firms partner across the value chain. When supply chain partners co-align, they often can create synergistic benefits enjoyed by both partners.[71] Synergy in sharing resources is more common in alliances that provide resources to help firms become ambidextrous and thereby satisfy multiple needs (e.g., help them create multiple capabilities). In fact, some firms that have developed strong ambidexterity (perhaps through alliances) in turn are able to form alliances and search for their partner's special skills or resources (prospective resourcing).[72]

The partnership between French-based Renault SA and Japan-based Nissan Motor Company that was formed in 1999 is a synergistic strategic alliance because, among other outcomes, the firms seek to create economies of scope by sharing their resources to develop manufacturing platforms that can be used to produce cars that will carry either the Renault or the Nissan brand. Later the firms added Mitsubishi to this alliance to become the largest automotive alliance in the world. In 2017, the partners sold more than 10.6 million vehicles.[73] BMW relies on its collaboration with Chinese auto maker Brilliance (BBA is the name of this partnership) to produce engines in China as well as models including "BMW's 3-series and 5-series vehicles as well as the small X1 SUV." In fact, BMW recently signed a new agreement with Brilliance to expand the production of BMW brand vehicles in China to 520,000 in 2019.[74] This relationship is critical to BMW's efforts to maintain strong sales in China, a market in which about 20 percent of its total global output is sold.

9-3c Franchising

Franchising is a strategy in which a firm (the franchisor) uses a franchise as a contractual relationship to describe and control the sharing of its resources with its partners (the franchisees).[75] A *franchise* is a "form of business organization in which a firm that already

A **diversifying strategic alliance** is a strategy in which firms share some of their resources to engage in product and/or geographic diversification.

A **synergistic strategic alliance** is a strategy in which firms share some of their resources to create economies of scope.

Franchising is a strategy in which a firm (the franchisor) uses a franchise as a contractual relationship to describe and control the sharing of its resources with its partners (the franchisees).

has a successful product or service (the franchisor) licenses its trademark and method of doing business to other businesses (the franchisees) in exchange for an initial franchise fee and an ongoing royalty rate."[76] Often, the effectiveness of these strategic alliances is a product of how well the franchisor can replicate its success across multiple partners in a cost-effective way.[77] As with diversifying and synergistic strategic alliances, franchising is an alternative to pursuing growth through mergers and acquisitions. McDonald's, Choice Hotels International, Hilton International, Marriott International, Mrs. Fields Cookies, Subway, and Ace Hardware are well-known firms using the franchising corporate-level cooperative strategy.

Franchising is a particularly attractive strategy to use in fragmented industries, such as retailing, hotels and motels, and commercial printing. In fragmented industries, many small and medium-sized firms compete as rivals; however, no firm or small set of firms has a dominant share, making it possible for a company to gain a large market share by consolidating independent companies through the contractual relationships that are a part of a franchise agreement.

In the most successful franchising strategy, the partners (the franchisor and the franchisees) work closely together.[78] A primary responsibility of the franchisor is to develop programs to transfer to the franchisees the knowledge and skills that are needed to successfully compete at the local level.[79] In return, franchisees should provide feedback to the franchisor regarding how their units could become more effective and efficient.[80]

Working cooperatively, the franchisor and its franchisees find ways to strengthen the core company's brand name, which is often the most important competitive advantage for franchisees operating in their local markets.[81]

9-3d Assessing Corporate-Level Cooperative Strategies

Costs are incurred to implement each type of cooperative strategy.[82] Compared with their business-level counterparts, corporate-level cooperative strategies commonly are broader in scope and more complex, making them relatively more challenging and costly to use.

Despite these costs, firms can create competitive advantages and value for customers by effectively using corporate-level cooperative strategies.[83] Internalizing successful alliance experiences makes it more likely that the strategy will attain the desired advantages. In other words, those involved with forming and using corporate-level cooperative strategies can also use them to develop useful knowledge about how to succeed in the future. To gain maximum value from this knowledge, firms should organize it and verify that it is always properly distributed to those involved with forming and using alliances.

We explained in Chapter 6 that firms answer two questions when dealing with corporate-level strategy: in which businesses and product markets will the firm choose to compete and how will those businesses be managed? These questions are also answered as firms form corporate-level cooperative strategies. Thus, firms able to develop corporate-level cooperative strategies and manage them in ways that are valuable, rare, imperfectly imitable, and nonsubstitutable (see Chapter 3) develop a competitive advantage that is in addition to advantages gained through the implementation of business-level cooperative strategies. (Later in the chapter, we further describe alliance management as another potential competitive advantage.)

9-4 International Cooperative Strategy

In the new competitive landscape, firms use cross-border transactions for several purposes. In Chapter 7, we discussed cross-border acquisitions—actions through which a company located in one country acquires a firm located in a different country. In

Chapter 8, we described how firms use cross-border acquisitions as a way of entering international markets. Here in Chapter 9, we examine cross-border strategic alliances as a type of international cooperative strategy. Thus, as the discussions in Chapters 7, 8 and 9 show, firms engage in cross-border activities to achieve several related and often complementary objectives.

A **cross-border strategic alliance** is a strategy in which firms with headquarters in different countries decide to combine some of their resources to create a competitive advantage. Taking place in virtually all industries, the number of cross-border alliances firms are completing continues to increase.[84] These alliances are sometimes formed instead of mergers and acquisitions, which can be riskier. Even though cross-border alliances can themselves be complex and difficult to manage,[85] they have the potential to help firms use some of their resources to create value in locations outside their home market. Through this collaboration, the partners often cooperate in one or more areas such as development, procurement, and production processes, partly with the intent to create value in markets throughout the world that neither firm could create operating independently. Ford and Mahindra formed a strategic alliance that will allow both of them to combine their complementary capabilities in the development of new vehicles for the Indian market. Ford will gain Mahindra's knowledge of designing and manufacturing cars for emerging markets and Mahindra will gain access to Ford's technological capabilities. While both companies are poised to benefit from this alliance, perhaps greatly so, they will also face multiple challenges to achieve the desired success.

Limited domestic growth opportunities and foreign government economic policies are key reasons firms use cross-border alliances. As discussed in Chapter 8, local ownership is an important national policy objective in some nations. In India and China, for example, governmental policies reflect a strong preference to license local companies. Thus, in some countries, the full range of entry mode choices we described in Chapter 8 may not be available to firms seeking to geographically diversify. Indeed, investment by foreign firms in these instances may be allowed only through a partnership with a local firm, such as in a cross-border alliance. Important too is the fact that strategic alliances with local partners can help firms overcome certain liabilities of moving into a foreign country, including those related to a lack of knowledge of the local culture or institutional norms. Yet, to overcome the liabilities requires that the two partners develop trust, which is even more difficult to achieve than in domestic alliances. Establishing trust may require highly effective boundary spanners who can build trusting relationships with partners.[86] A cross-border strategic alliance can also help foreign partners from an operational perspective, because the local partner has significantly more information about factors contributing to competitive success such as local markets, sources of capital, legal procedures, and politics.[87] Interestingly, research results suggest that firms with foreign operations have longer survival rates than domestic-only firms, although this is reduced if there are competition problems between foreign subsidiaries.[88]

In general, cross-border strategic alliances are more complex and riskier than domestic strategic alliances. Complexity and, perhaps, risk may be factors associated with the alliance formed in 2015 between Airbus Group NV and Korea Aerospace Industries Ltd. The goal of this partnership is to build at least 300 military and civilian helicopters in South Korea.[89] Complexity is suggested by the fact that the partners are committed to designing and producing "next-generation light civilian and military helicopters" that will satisfy South Korean customers. Risks include those of relying on unique, firm-specific cultures and practices as the foundation for designing next-generation products in an acceptable time and producing those products at acceptable costs. Despite the risks, firms such as Airbus and Korea Aerospace have developed cross-border strategic alliances partly because companies competing internationally tend to outperform domestic-only competitors.

A **cross-border strategic alliance** is a strategy in which firms with headquarters in different countries decide to combine some of their resources to create a competitive advantage.

Strategic **Focus**

The Cross-Border Alliance between Ford and Mahindra: Developing the Automobile of the Future

Ford has been producing and selling automobiles in India for a number of years. In fact, in 2018 Ford sold its one millionth car in India. All told, Ford has invested almost $2 billion to build in India. In 2010 it began building two new manufacturing plants in India to accommodate the growth in that market over time. However, Ford's sales in India were disappointing, so it began to export cars made in its new plants. Ford is not alone in failing to navigate the Indian automobile market effectively; Fiat Chrysler, General Motors, and Volkswagen have all experienced problems in the Indian market. Suzuki and Hyundai have out-maneuvered all of them to gain dominant market shares.

Ford remains committed to the Indian market and decided to take a different approach. It has developed an alliance with Mahindra and Mahindra Ltd. to cooperate in the development of specific vehicles for India and other emerging markets. They agreed to cooperate on the following:

- Jointly develop a new SUV using an existing Mahindra platform.
- Co-develop a new compact SUV and a new electric vehicle.
- Share powertrains including engines and transmissions.

This new alliance is intended to provide Ford the knowledge and expertise to better serve emerging markets, including India, as Mahindra is the leading manufacturer of pickups and SUVs in India. Alternatively, the alliance will provide Mahindra access to Ford's technology, which may be especially helpful in the development of the electric vehicle. Mahindra would like to penetrate the U.S. vehicle markets. It is already third in the tractor market in the United States, and is trying to break into the U.S. off-the-road vehicle and pickup markets as well.

Ford is extremely positive about the potential success of this alliance. It expects the Indian auto market to grow 8–10 percent annually for the foreseeable future, and it expects its own growth in Indian auto sales to exceed the market growth rate. Yet, industry analysts are skeptical partly because of the challenges involved in cross-border alliances. The two companies must overcome different corporate cultures and different processes and find ways to coordinate and collaborate. To do this will require building trust between the leaders of the alliance in each company. Obviously, Ford has much experience working with alliance partners. Ford has alliances with other industry leaders such as General Motors and is considering another with Volkswagen. Although Ford and GM are major rivals, they have cooperated in the development of a 10-speed automatic transmission that each will use in its own vehicles. The alliance being considered with VW may entail the development of several products, but one primary focus is expected to be a van. Alliances with industry rivals serve as a means of responding to a dynamic and increasingly demanding global market.

Time will tell if Ford and Mahindra enjoy a successful alliance and achieve the benefits from the alliance that they expected.

Kyodo News/Getty Images

Mahindra's new version of their electric hatchback, the e20, was revealed at the Auto Expo 2018.

Sources: P. Luthra, 2018, Ford India expects to grow faster than sector, working with Mahindra on electric vehicle, *CNBC*, https://wwwcnbctv18.com, July 17; A. Tsang, 2018, As auto industry transforms, Ford and Volkswagen consider an alliance, *New York Times*, https://www.nytimes.com, June 20; S. S. Mohile, 2018, Mahindra, Ford Motor enter second phase for a potential alliance, *Business Standard*, https://www.business-standard.com, March 23; D. Kiley, 2018, Ford and Mahindra to build SUVs and EV together, *Forbes*, https://www.forbes.com, March 22; J. Rosevear, 2018, Why Ford and Mahindra are teaming up on SUVs and EVs for India, *The Motley Fool*, https://www.fool.com, March 22; 2017, Ford explores strategic alliance with India's Mahindra, *Automotive News*, http://www.autonews.com, September 18; J. Rosevear, 2016, Why Ford and General Motors teamed up on transmissions, *The Motley Fool*, https://www.fool.com, May 22.

9-5 Network Cooperative Strategy

In addition to forming their own alliances with individual companies, an increasing number of firms are collaborating in multiple alliances called networks.[90] A **network cooperative strategy** is a strategy by which several firms agree to form multiple partnerships to achieve shared objectives.

Through its Global Partner Network, Cisco has formed alliances with a host of companies including IBM, Emerson, Hitachi, CA Technologies, Fujitsu, Intel, Nokia, and Wipro. Cisco uses alliances to drive its growth, differentiate itself from competitors, enter new businesses areas, and create competitive advantages. Recently, Cisco's annual revenues earned from its alliances exceeded $5 billion. Sometimes, several of the firms with which Cisco has formed individual alliances partner together to form a network to achieve shared objectives.[91]

Demonstrating the complexity of network cooperative strategies is the fact that Cisco also competes against several firms with whom it has formed cooperative agreements, including network strategies. For example, Cisco and IBM compete against each other. However, Cisco and IBM also collaborate such that IBM security works with Cisco's security to deliver a more secure environment for their customers, better enabling operators and partner communities to reduce security threats.[92] Overall, the example of the simultaneous "cooperative and competitive" relationships between Cisco and IBM demonstrates how firms use network cooperative strategies more extensively as a way of creating value for customers by offering many goods and services in many geographic (domestic and international) markets.

A network cooperative strategy is particularly effective when it is formed by geographically clustered firms,[93] as in California's Silicon Valley and Rome, Italy's aerospace cluster. Fostering effective social relationships and interactions among partners while sharing their resources makes it more likely that a network cooperative strategy will be successful,[94] as does having a productive *strategic center firm* (we discuss strategic center firms in detail in Chapter 11). Firms involved in networks gain information and knowledge from multiple sources. They can use these heterogeneous knowledge sets to produce more and better innovation. As a result, firms involved in networks of alliances tend to be more innovative.[95] However, there are disadvantages to participating in networks as a firm can be locked into its partnerships, precluding the development of alliances with others. In certain network configurations, such as Japanese *keiretsus*, firms in a network are expected to help other firms in that network whenever support is required. Such expectations can become a burden and negatively affect the focal firm's performance over time.[96]

9-5a Alliance Network Types

An important advantage of a network cooperative strategy is that firms gain access to their partners' other partners. Having access to multiple collaborations increases the likelihood that additional competitive advantages will be formed as the set of shared resources expands.[97] In turn, being able to develop new resources further stimulates product innovations that are critical to strategic competitiveness in the global economy.

The set of strategic alliance partnerships that firms develop when using a network cooperative strategy is called an *alliance network*. Companies' alliance networks vary by industry characteristics. A *stable alliance network* is formed in mature industries where demand is relatively constant and predictable. Through a stable alliance network, firms try to extend their competitive advantages to other settings while continuing to profit from operations in their core, relatively mature industry. Thus, stable networks are built primarily to *exploit*

A **network cooperative strategy** is a strategy by which several firms agree to form multiple partnerships to achieve shared objectives.

Mathias Rosenthal/Shutterstock.com

Shown in the middle here is representation of a strategic center firm with links to other firms in an alliance network.

the economies (scale and/or scope) that exist between the partners, such as in the airline and automobile industries.[98]

Dynamic alliance networks are used in industries characterized by frequent product innovations and short product life cycles.[99] The industries in which Apple and IBM compete are examples of this situation. Apple and IBM each partner with a host of other firms to develop component parts that are critical to providing the products that are central to their success. Thus, a network of relationships among multiple companies is foundational to achieving the objectives Apple and IBM each seek.

In dynamic alliance networks, partners typically *explore* new ideas with the potential to lead to product innovations, entries to new markets, and the development of new markets. Research suggests that firms that help to broker relationships between companies remain important network participants as these networks change.[100] Often, large firms in industries such as software and pharmaceuticals create networks of relationships with smaller entrepreneurial start-up firms in their search for innovation-based outcomes. Also, small general practice law firms are partnering with larger firms to provide their clients with legal advice on intellectual property protection. In this way, the small firm better serves its client without having to add an expensive group of patent lawyers to its staff.[101] An important outcome for small firms successfully partnering with larger firms in an alliance network is the credibility they build by being associated with their larger collaborators.[102]

9-6 Competitive Risks with Cooperative Strategies

Stated simply, many cooperative strategies fail. In fact, evidence shows that two-thirds of cooperative strategies have serious problems in their first two years and that as many as 50 percent of them fail. This failure rate suggests that even when the partnership has potential complementarities and synergies, alliance success is elusive.[103] Although failure is undesirable, it can be a valuable learning experience, meaning that firms should carefully study a cooperative strategy's failure to gain insights with respect to how to form and manage future cooperative arrangements.[104] We show prominent cooperative strategy risks in Figure 9.5. We discuss a few cooperative strategies that have failed and possible reasons for those failures in the Strategic Focus.

One cooperative strategy risk is that a firm may act in a way that its partner thinks is opportunistic. BP plc and OAO Rosneft developed a joint venture to explore Russia's Arctic Ocean in search of oil. However, the investment by minority partners of this joint venture was driven down in value at one point by 50 percent over concern that the Russian government, Rosneft's dominant owner, would expropriate value from the deal.[105] In general, opportunistic behaviors surface either when formal contracts fail to prevent them or when an alliance is based on a false perception of partner trustworthiness. Typically, an opportunistic firm wants to acquire as much of its partner's tacit

Figure 9.5 Managing Competitive Risks in Cooperative Strategies

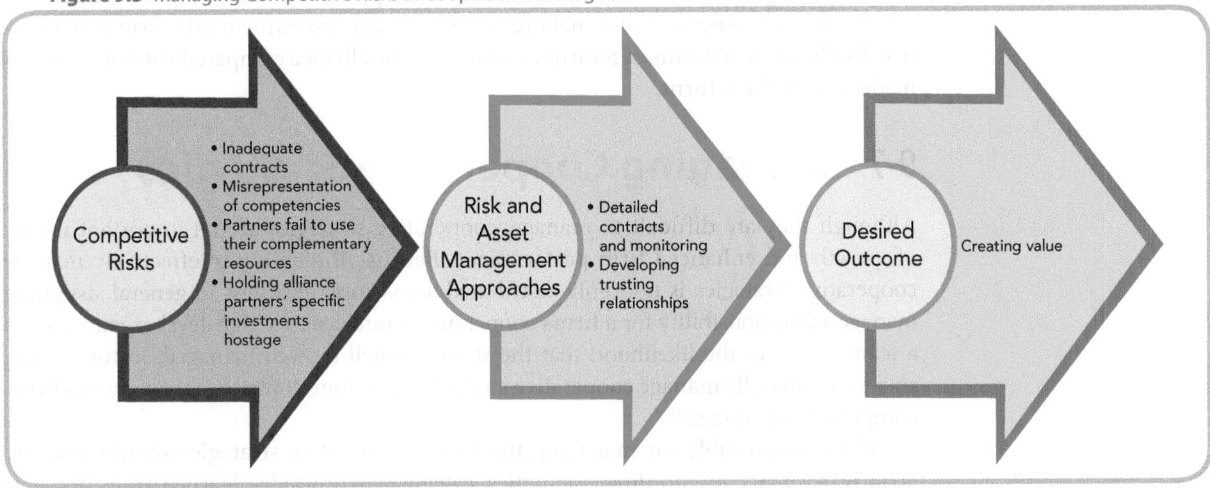

knowledge as it can.[106] Full awareness of what a partner wants in a cooperative strategy reduces the likelihood that a firm will suffer from another's opportunistic actions.[107] Interestingly, BP and Rosneft agreed to dissolve their joint venture focused on refining and petrochemicals in Germany as of 2017. Yet, BP and Rosneft still had three other active joint ventures in 2018, despite the past problems and the challenges created by the economic sanctions placed on Russia by the U.S. and Western European countries. Obviously, BP perceives major opportunities in these alliances and is trying to manage the potentially extensive risks of working with this Russian firm.[108]

Some cooperative strategies fail when it is discovered that a firm has misrepresented the resources it can bring to the partnership. This risk is more common when the partner's contribution is based on some of its intangible assets. Superior knowledge of local conditions is an example of an intangible asset that partners often fail to deliver. This type of risk suggests the importance of carefully selecting alliance partners. Some firms may guard against this risk by identifying other potential partners in case the original alliance is unsuccessful. Having "backup" suppliers available is a common approach used in supply chain alliances.[109]

The cooperative relationships in the form of nonequity strategic alliances that are being created between some large pharmaceutical companies and outsourcing firms is potentially an example of the "misrepresentation of available resources" risk. Pharmaceutical companies are outsourcing the monitoring of drug safety to firms claiming to have the requisite human capital skills needed to successfully complete various monitoring tasks. But there are critics of this approach who argue that drug monitoring is difficult, requiring deep experience as well as knowledge of biochemistry and pharmacology. Also, they may not identify side effects, some of which might be very serious. Nonetheless, one study found that approximately 66 percent of the companies outsourced at least some portion of their drug safety activities.[110] Thus, pharmaceutical companies may need to carefully monitor the quality of the human capital resource their partners provide for the purpose of completing what appears to be complicated monitoring work.

A firm's failure to make available to its partners the resources (such as the most sophisticated technologies) that it committed to the cooperative strategy is a third risk. This particular risk surfaces most commonly when firms form an international cooperative strategy, especially in emerging economies.[111] In these instances, different cultures and languages can cause misinterpretations of contractual terms or trust-based expectations.

A final risk is that one firm may make investments that are specific to the alliance while its partner does not. For example, the firm might commit resources to develop manufacturing equipment that can be used only to provide products associated with the alliance. If the partner isn't also making alliance-specific investments, the firm is at a relative disadvantage in terms of returns earned from the alliance compared with investments made to earn the returns.

9-7 Managing Cooperative Strategies

Although they are difficult to manage, cooperative strategies are an important means of growth and enhanced firm performance. Because the ability to effectively manage cooperative strategies is unevenly distributed across organizations in general, assigning managerial responsibility for a firm's cooperative strategies to a high-level executive or to a team improves the likelihood that the strategies will be well managed. In turn, being able to successfully manage cooperative strategies can alone contribute strongly to a firm's competitive advantage.[112]

Those responsible for managing the firm's cooperative strategies should take the actions necessary to coordinate activities, categorize knowledge learned from previous experiences, and make certain that what the firm knows about how to effectively form and use cooperative strategies is in the hands of the right people at the right time. Firms must also learn how to manage both the tangible and intangible assets (such as knowledge) that are involved with a cooperative arrangement. Too often, partners concentrate on managing tangible assets at the expense of taking action also to manage a cooperative relationship's intangible assets.[113]

Cost minimization and opportunity maximization are the two primary approaches firms use to manage cooperative strategies (see Figure 9.5).[114] In the *cost-minimization* approach, the firm develops formal contracts with its partners. These contracts specify how the cooperative strategy is to be monitored and how partner behavior is to be controlled. The joint venture between GM China and SAIC Motor Corp. is being managed largely through formal contractual relationships. The goal of the cost-minimization approach is to minimize the cooperative strategy's cost and to prevent opportunistic behavior by a partner.

Maximizing a partnership's value-creating opportunities is the focus of the *opportunity-maximization* approach. In this case, partners are prepared to take advantage of unexpected opportunities to learn from each other and to explore additional marketplace possibilities. Less formal contracts, with fewer constraints on partners' behaviors, make it possible for partners to explore how their resources can be shared in multiple value-creating ways. This appears to be the approach being used by the BMW and Brilliance alliance discussed earlier as they expand their footprint of luxury vehicles in China. Finding additional ways to collaborate was one of the objectives associated with the decision to organize this team.

Firms can successfully use both approaches to manage cooperative strategies. However, the costs to monitor the cooperative strategy are greater with cost minimization because writing detailed contracts and using extensive monitoring mechanisms is expensive, even though the approach is intended to reduce alliance costs. Although monitoring systems may prevent partners from acting in their own self-interests, they also often preclude positive responses to new opportunities that surface to productively use each alliance partner's unique resources. Thus, formal contracts and extensive monitoring systems tend to stifle partners' efforts to gain maximum value from their participation in a cooperative strategy and require significant resources to be put into place and used.[115]

The relative lack of detail and formality that is a part of the contract developed when using the opportunity-maximization approach means that firms need to trust that each party will act in the partnership's best interests. The psychological state of *trust* in the context of cooperative arrangements is the belief that a firm will not do anything to exploit its partner's vulnerabilities, even if it has an opportunity to do so. When partners trust each other, there is less need to write detailed formal contracts to specify each firm's alliance behaviors,[116] and the cooperative relationship tends to be more stable.[117] On a relative basis, trust tends to be more difficult to establish in international cooperative strategies than in domestic ones. Differences in trade policies, cultures, laws, and politics that are part of cross-border alliances account for the increased difficulty.

Research showing that trust between partners increases the likelihood of success when using alliances highlights the benefits of the opportunity-maximization approach to managing cooperative strategies. Trust may also be the most efficient way to influence and control alliance partners' behaviors. Thus, firms known to be trustworthy can have a competitive advantage in terms of how they develop and use cooperative strategies. Increasing the importance of trust in alliances is the fact that it is not possible to specify all operational details of a cooperative strategy in a formal contract. As such, being confident that its partner can be trusted reduces the firm's concern about its inability to contractually control all alliance details.[118]

SUMMARY

- A cooperative strategy is one in which firms work together to achieve a shared objective. Strategic alliances, whereby firms combine some of their resources for the purpose of creating a competitive advantage, are the primary form of cooperative strategies. Joint ventures (whereby firms create and own equal shares of a new venture), equity strategic alliances (in which firms own different shares of a newly created venture), and nonequity strategic alliances (whereby firms cooperate through a contractual relationship) are the three major types of strategic alliances. Outsourcing, discussed in Chapter 3, commonly occurs through nonequity strategic alliances.
- Collusive strategies are the second type of cooperative strategies (with strategic alliances being the other). In many economies, explicit collusive strategies are illegal unless sanctioned by government policies. Increasing globalization has led to fewer government-sanctioned situations involving explicit collusion. Tacit collusion, also called mutual forbearance, is a cooperative strategy through which firms tacitly cooperate to reduce industry output below the potential competitive output level, thereby increasing prices above the competitive level.
- The reasons firms use strategic alliances vary by slow-cycle, fast-cycle, and standard-cycle market conditions. To enter restricted markets (slow cycle), to move quickly from one competitive advantage to another (fast cycle), and to gain market power (standard cycle) are among the reasons firms decide to use strategic alliances.
- Four business-level cooperative strategies are used to help the firm improve its performance in individual product markets:
    - Through vertical and horizontal complementary alliances, companies combine some of their resources to create value in different parts (vertical) or the same parts (horizontal) of the value chain.
    - Competition response strategies are formed to respond to competitors' actions, especially strategic actions.
    - Uncertainty-reducing strategies are used to hedge against the risks created by the conditions of uncertain competitive environments (such as new product markets).
    - Competition-reducing strategies are used to avoid excessive competition while the firm marshals its resources to improve its strategic competitiveness.

  Complementary alliances have the highest probability of helping a firm to create a competitive advantage; competition-reducing alliances have the lowest probability.
- Firms use corporate-level cooperative strategies to engage in product and/or geographic diversification. Through diversifying strategic alliances, firms agree to share some of their resources to enter new markets or provide new products. Synergistic alliances are ones in which firms share some of their resources to develop economies of scope. Synergistic alliances are similar to business-level horizontal complementary alliances whereby firms try to develop operational synergy, except that synergistic alliances are used to develop synergy at the corporate level. Franchising is a corporate-level cooperative strategy in which the franchisor uses a franchise as a contractual relationship to specify how resources will be shared with franchisees.
- As an international cooperative strategy, a cross-border strategic alliance is used for several reasons, including the performance superiority of firms competing in markets outside their domestic market and governmental restrictions on a firm's efforts to grow through mergers and acquisitions. Commonly, cross-border strategic alliances are riskier than their domestic counterparts, because of the differences in companies and their cultures and the frequent difficulty of building trust in order to share resources among the partners.

- In a network cooperative strategy, several firms agree to form multiple partnerships to achieve shared objectives. A firm's opportunity to gain access "to its partner's other partnerships" is a primary benefit of a network cooperative strategy. Network cooperative strategies are used to form either a stable alliance network or a dynamic alliance network. In mature industries, stable networks are used to extend competitive advantages into new areas. In rapidly changing environments where frequent product innovations occur, dynamic networks are used primarily as a tool of innovation.
- Cooperative strategies often carry risk. If a contract is not developed appropriately, or if a partner misrepresents its resources or fails to make them available, failure is likely. Furthermore, a firm may be held hostage through asset-specific investments made in conjunction with a partner, which may then be exploited.
- Trust is an increasingly important aspect of successful cooperative strategies. Firms place high value on opportunities to partner with companies known for their trustworthiness. When trust exists, a cooperative strategy is managed to maximize the pursuit of opportunities between partners. Without trust, formal contracts and extensive monitoring systems are used to manage cooperative strategies. In this case, the interest is "cost minimization" rather than "opportunity maximization."

KEY TERMS

business-level cooperative strategy 286
complementary strategic alliances 286
cooperative strategy 280
corporate-level cooperative strategy 292
cross-border strategic alliance 295
diversifying strategic alliance 293
equity strategic alliance 282
franchising 293
joint venture 281
network cooperative strategy 297
nonequity strategic alliance 282
strategic alliance 281
synergistic strategic alliance 293

REVIEW QUESTIONS

1. What is the definition of cooperative strategy, and why is this strategy important to firms competing in the current competitive landscape?
2. What is a strategic alliance? What are the three major types of strategic alliances that firms form for the purpose of developing a competitive advantage?
3. What are the four business-level cooperative strategies? What are the key differences among them?
4. What are the three corporate-level cooperative strategies? How do firms use each of these strategies for the purpose of creating a competitive advantage?
5. Why do firms use cross-border strategic alliances?
6. What risks are firms likely to experience as they use cooperative strategies?
7. What are the differences between the cost-minimization approach and the opportunity-maximization approach to managing cooperative strategies?

Mini-Case

Failing to Obtain Desired Levels of Success with Cooperative Strategies

The complexity associated with most cooperative strategies increases the difficulty of successfully using them. One cause of this complexity is the fact that often, firms collaborating on certain projects are simultaneously competing with each other as well. As explained earlier, this reality describes the relationship between Cisco and IBM as well as those existing with airline companies that have joined alliance networks (such as

Star, Oneworld, and SkyTeam). Another complication is that firms sometimes form a partnership with a company that is itself a collaboration between other companies. For example, Ford Motor Company formed a joint venture with carbon manufacturer DowAksa, a firm that is a joint venture organized by Dow Chemical Company and Istanbul-based Aksa Akrilik Kimya Sanayii A.S. The purpose of the Ford/DowAksa collaboration is to find ways to develop cheaper grades of carbon fiber components that can be integrated into Ford's automobiles and trucks. Because it is much lighter than steel, carbon fiber helps auto manufacturers reduce the weight of their products, which in turn facilitates their efforts to increase products' gas mileage. We see then that, for multiple reasons, the complexities of cooperative strategies increase the challenge of effectively implementing them and may contribute to alliance failure.

Redbox and Verizon terminated their relationship that was originally developed to become the streaming subscription components of Redbox's rental business after only two years. (Outerwall founded Redbox in partnership with McDonald's Ventures, LLC. McDonald's hoped to distribute DVDs through rental kiosks at its restaurants as a means of attracting customers and providing them with a unique service.) Competing against the likes of Netflix and Hulu Plus, Redbox's streaming service failed to attract a sufficient number of customers, perhaps in part because it was able to stream to customers only items that its competitors were also streaming. Unlike Netflix and Hulu Plus, Redbox was not developing its own original content as a means of creating unique value for customers. Because the service made available through the Redbox and Verizon collaboration was losing money and was not gaining a sufficient number of subscribers, the partners chose to terminate their relationship.

Carefully executing the operational details of a planned cooperative strategy is foundational to its performance and influences if it will succeed or fail. In mid-2015 for example, First Solar, Inc. and SunPower Corporation, the two largest U.S. solar-panel manufacturers, were in the planning stages to form a joint venture that would own and operate some of the firms' projects. The proposed partners believed that the collaboration would create value by combining "SunPower's polysilicon technology with First Solar's thin-film panels." However, SunPower recorded a loss in the first quarter of 2015, partly because of costs it was incurring to structure the proposed relationship with First Solar. This demonstrates the importance of identifying efficient as well as effective ways to structure a proposed collaboration between companies as a means of increasing the likelihood of operational success.

Earlier, we noted that MillerCoors, the joint venture formed between Molson Coors and SABMiller, is encountering difficulties. Some analysts believe that a reason for this is that, while the partnership had been very successful during its first six years in terms of substantially reducing costs by creating economies of scale, it had failed to increase the market shares held by two of its important products, Miller Lite and Coors Light. The situation with the MillerCoors partnership suggests that long-term cooperative strategy success results when partners find unique ways to create value for customers in addition to finding ways to reduce operating costs.

Sources: M. Armental, 2015, SunPower swings to loss on costs related to planned joint venture, *Wall Street Journal Online*, www.wsj.com, April 30; D. Harris, 2015, China joint ventures: How not to get burned, Above the Law, www.abovethelaw.com, February 9; Molson Coors, U.S. joint venture MillerCoors facing stiff challenges, *Wall Street Journal Online*, www.wsj.com, May 7; J. D. Stoll, 2015, Ford to develop carbon-fiber material for cars, *Wall Street Journal Online*, www.wsj.com, April 17; P. E. Farrell, 2014, The 7 deadly sins of joint ventures, *Entrepreneur*, www.entrepreneur.com, September 2; Q. Plummer, 2014, Redbox instant will be killed Oct. 7: A failed joint venture, *Tech Times*, www.techtimes. com, October 6.

Case Discussion Questions

1. What are some of the major complexities encountered in developing cooperative strategies such as strategic alliances and joint ventures?
2. What role does competition from rivals play in the eventual success of cooperative strategies? Please explain.
3. What costs are incurred in developing strategic alliances? How can these costs be managed?
4. Should cost minimization or opportunity maximization be the primary goal of a cooperative strategy? Can both be achieved simultaneously? Why or why not?

NOTES

1. L. Cabral & G. Pacheco-de-Almeida, 2018, Alliance formation and firm value, *Management Science*, in press; B. B. Tyler & T. Caner, 2016, New product introductions below aspirations, slack and R&D alliances: A behavioral perspective, *Strategic Management Journal*, 37: 896–910.
2. A. L. Brito, E. P. Z. Brito, & L. H. Hashiba, 2014, What type of cooperation with suppliers and customers leads to superior performance? *Journal of Business Research*, 67: 952–959; R. A. Heidl, H. K. Steensma, & C. Phelps, 2014, Divisive faultlines and the unplanned dissolutions of multipartner alliances, *Organization Science*, 25: 1351– 1371.
3. A. Ferreira & M. Franco, 2017, Strategic alliances, intellectual capital and organisational performance in technology-based SMEs: Is there really a connection? *International Journal of Business and Globalisation*, 18: 130–151; Z. Khan, O. Shenkar, & Y. K. Lew, 2015, Knowledge transfer from international joint ventures to local suppliers in a developing economy, *Journal of International Business Studies*, 46: 656–675.
4. S. J. D. Schillebeeckx, S. Chaturvedi, G. George, & Z. King, 2016, What do I want? The effects of individual aspiration and relational capability on collaboration preferences, *Strategic Management Journal*, 37: 1493–1506; R. J. Arend, P. C. Patel, & H. D. Park, 2014, Explaining post-IPO venture performance through a knowledge-based view typology, *Strategic Management Journal*, 35: 376–397; J. H. Dyer & H. Singh, 1998, The relational view: Cooperative strategy and sources of interorganizational competitive advantage, *Academy of Management Review*, 23: 660–679.
5. A. Ferreira & M. Franco, 2017, The mediating effect of intellectual capital in the relationship between strategic alliances and organizational performance in Portuguese technology-based SMEs, *European Management Review*, 14: 303–318; R. Vandaie & A. Zaheer, 2014, Surviving bear hugs: Firm capability, large partner alliances, and growth, *Strategic Management Journal*, 35: 566–577; J. Walter, F. W. Kellermanns, & C. Lechner, 2012, Decision making within and between organizations: Rationality, politics, and alliance performance, *Journal of Management*, 38: 1582–1610.
6. C. Lioukas & J. Reuer, 2015, Isolating trust outcomes from exchange relationships: Social exchange and learning benefits of prior ties in alliances, *Academy of Management Journal*, 58:1826–1847; J. Charterina & J. Landeta, 2013, Effects of knowledge-sharing routines and dyad-based investments on company innovation and performance: An empirical study of Spanish manufacturing companies, *International Journal of Management*, 30: 197–216.
7. J. Wu & P. Olk, 2014, Technological advantage, alliances with customers, local knowledge and competitor identification, *Journal of Business Research*, 67: 2106–2114; J. L. Cummings & S. R. Holmberg, 2012, Best-fit alliance partners: The use of critical success factors in a comprehensive partner selection process, *Long Range Planning*, 45: 136–159.
8. N. Rahman & H. J. Korn, 2014, Alliance longevity: Examining relational and operational antecedents, *Long Range Planning*, 47: 245–261; S. Xu, A. P. Fenik, & M. B. Sarkar, 2014, Multilateral alliances and innovation output: The importance of equity and technological scope, *Journal of Business Research*, 67: 2403–2410.
9. K. Leonard, 2018, Examples of successful strategic alliances, *Houston Chronicle*, https://smallbusiness.chron.com, June 29.
10. R. Shakeri & R. Radfar, 2017, Antecedents of strategic alliances Performance in biopharmaceutical industry: A comprehensive model, *Technological Forecasting and Social Change*, 122: 289–302; Y. Liu & T. Ravichandran, 2015, Alliance experience, IT-enabled knowledge integration, and ex-ante value gains, *Organization Science*, 26: 511–530.
11. F. Kwok, P. Sharma, S. S. Gaur & A. Ueno, 2018, Interactive effects of information exchange, relationship capital and environmental uncertainty on international joint venture (IJV) performance: An emerging markets perspective, *International Business Review*, in press: C. J. Chen, B. W. Lin, J-Y. Lin & Y.-C. Hsiao, 2018, Learning-from-parents: Exploitive knowledge acquisition and the innovation performance of joint venture, *Journal of Technology Transfer*, in press.
12. G. Wankar, 2017, SAIC signs deal with General Motors to take over Halol plant, *Hindustantimes*, https://www.hindustantimes.com, April 5; C. Murphy, 2015, GM China venture to spend $16 billion to develop new products, *Wall Street Journal Online*, www.wsj.com, April 19.
13. C. Randall, 2018, VW to introduce the MEB platform in China with FAW & SAIC, *electrive.com*, https://www.electrive.com, March 9; 2017, Volkswagen won't make Audi cars with SAIC in China before 2018, *Yahoo Finance*, https://finance.yahoo.com, January 17; R. Yu, 2015, SAIC Motor's tie-ups with Volkswagen, GM rev up 2014 profit, *Wall Street Journal Online*, www.wsj.com, April 2.
14. J.-Y. Lin, 2017, Knowledge creation through joint venture investments: The contingent role of organizational slack, *Journal of Engineering and Technology Management*, 46: 1–25; J. H. Love, S. Roper, & P. Vahter, 2014, Learning from openness: The dynamics of breadth in external innovation linkages, *Strategic Management Journal*, 35: 1703–1716; E. Chrysostome, R. Nigam, & C. Jarilowski, 2013, Revisiting strategic learning in international joint ventures: A knowledge creation perspective, *International Journal of Management*, 30(1): 88–98.
15. H. Belgraver & E, Verwaal, 2018, Organizational capital, production factor resources, and relative firm size in strategic equity alliances, *Small Business Economics*, 50: 825–849; A. M. Subramanian, W. Bo & C. Kah-Hin, 2018, The role of knowledge base homogeneity in learning from strategic alliances, *Research Policy*, 47: 158–168.
16. I. Surdu, K. Mellahi & K. Glaister, 2018, Emerging market multinationals' international equity based entry modes: Review of theoretical foundations and future directions, *International Marketing Review*, 35: 342–359; W. (Stone) Shi, S. L. Sun, B. C. Pinkham, & M. W. Peng, 2014, Domestic alliance network to attract foreign partners: Evidence from international joint ventures in China, *Journal of International Business Studies*, 45: 338–362; L. Cui & F. Jiang, 2012, State ownership effect on firms' FDI ownership decisions under institutional pressure: A study of Chinese outward-investing firms, *Journal of International Business Studies*, 43: 264–284.
17. W. Ryu, B. T. McCann & J. J. Reuer, 2018, Geographic co-location of partners and rivals: Implications for the design of R&D alliances, *Academy of Management Journal*, 61: 945–965; D. Li, L. Eden & M. Josefy, 2017, Agent and task complexity in multilateral alliances: The safeguarding role of equity governance, *Journal of International Management*, 23: 227–241.
18. J. Reuer & S. V. Devarakonda, 2016, Mechanisms of hybrid governance: Administrative committees in non-equity alliances, *Academy of Management Journal*, 59: 510–533; A. Majocchi, U. Mayrhofer, & J. Camps, 2013, Joint ventures or non-equity alliances? Evidence from Italian firms, *Management Decision*, 51: 380–395.
19. B. T. McCann, J. J. Reuer, & N. Lahiri, 2016, Agglomeration and the choice between acquisitions and alliances: An information economics perspective, *Strategic Management Journal*, 37: 1085–1106; S. P. Gudergan, T. Devinney, N. Richter, & R. Ellis, 2012, Strategic implications for (non-equity) alliance performance, *Long Range Planning*, 45: 451–476.
20. M. G. Colombo & E. Piva, 2018, Knowledge misappropriation risks and contractual complexity in entrepreneurial ventures' non-equity alliances, *Small Business Economics*, in press; J. Choi & F. Contractor,

2018, Improving the progress of research & development (R&D) projects by selecting an optimal alliance structure and partner type, *British Journal of Management*, in press; F. J. Contractor & J. J. Reuer, 2014, Structuring and governing alliances: New directions for research, *Global Strategy Journal*, 4: 241–256.

21. 2015, Will Tim Cook stop outsourcing the manufacture of Apple products to homophobic China? *Ricochet*, www.ricochet.com, March 31.
22. D. Wu, 2018, Foxconn Chairman sees biggest challenge in U.S.-China trade war, *Bloomberg*, https://www.bloomberg.com, June 22; T. Culpan, 2018, Belcan, Nokia, Nostalgia and Foxcoon, *Bloomberg*, https://www.bloomberg.com, March 26; C. Victorino, 2018, Apple MacBook 2018: Foxcoon building more units this year, *International Business Times*, https://www.ibtimes.com.
23. D. Aristie, M. Vecchi, & F. Venturini, 2016, University and inter-firm R&D collaborations: Propensity and intensity of cooperation in Europe, *Journal of Technology Transfer*, 41: 841–871; D. Mindruta, 2013, Value creation in university-firm research collaborations: A matching approach, *Strategic Management Journal*, 34: 644–665.
24. 2018, Airline alliances 2018, *Boomer Traveler*, boomertraveler.com, accessed on August 2; K. Lange, M. Geppert, A. Saka-Helmhout, & F. Becker-Ritterspach, 2015, Changing business models and employee representation in the airline industry: A comparison of British Airways and Deutsche Lufthansa, *British Journal of Management*, 26: 388–407; X. Hu, R. Caldentey, & G. Vulcano, 2013, Revenue sharing in airline alliances, *Management Science*, 59: 1177–1195.
25. W. Yang & K. E. Meyer, 2015, Competitive dynamics in an emerging economy: Competitive pressures, resources, and the speed of action, *Journal of Business Research*, 68: 1176–1185; T. de Leeuw, B. Lokshin, & G. Duysters, 2014, Returns to alliance portfolio diversity: The relative effects of partner diversity on firm's innovative performance and productivity, *Journal of Business Research*, 67: 1839–1849.
26. 2018, Pagaea Alliance website, www.pagaeaaliance,com, accessed on August 2; J. Marshall, 2015, News publishers for programmatic advertising alliance, *CMO Today*, www.blogs.wsj.com/cmo, March 18.
27. H. M. Khamseh, D. Jolly, & L. Moril, 2017, The effect of learning approaches on the utilization of external knowledge in strategic alliances, *Industrial Marketing Management*, 63: 92–104.
28. Y.-T. Chuang, K. B. Dahlin, K. Thomson, Y.-C. Lai, & C.C. Yang, 2018, Multimarket contact, strategic alliances, and firm performance, *Journal of Management*, 44: 1551–1572; L. Bizzi, 2017, The strategic role of financial slack on alliance formation, *Management Decision*, 55: 383–399.
29. 2018, Expedia Group website, https://www.expediagroup.com, accessed on August 2; Treflis team, 2015, Expedia seeks Latin American dominance: Strengthens partnership with Decolar.com, *Forbes Online*, www.forbes.com, March 12.
30. D. J. Teece, 2014, A dynamic capabilities-based entrepreneurial theory of the multinational enterprise, *Journal of International Business Studies*, 45: 8–37; J. R. Williams, 1998, *Renewable Advantage: Crafting Strategy Through Economic Time*, New York: Free Press.
31. 2017, Carnival Corporation Cruise joint venture in China to order first-ever cruise ships built in China, *Cision PR Newswire*, https://www.prnewswire.com, February 22; L. Burkitt, 2015, Carnival in talks with China Merchants on cruise ports, ships, *Wall Street Journal Online*, www.wsj.com, January 26.
32. J. Min, 2017, Sensitivity of alliance termination to prealliance conditions: Expectation of alliance partners, *Organization Studies*, 38: 917–936; S. Artinger & T. C. Powell, 2016, Entrepreneurial failure: Statistical and psychological explanations, *Strategic Management Journal*, 37: 1047–1064; H. Rahmandad & N. Repenning, 2016, Capability erosion dynamics, *Strategic Management Journal*, 37: 649–672.
33. J. J. Reuer & R. Ragozzino, 2014, Signals and international alliance formation: The roles of affiliations and international activities, *Journal of International Business Studies*, 45: 321–337; H. K. Steensma, J. Q. Barden, C. Dhanaraj, M. Lyles, & L. Tihanyi, 2008, The evolution and internalization of international joint ventures in a transitioning economy, *Journal of International Business Studies*, 39: 491–507.
34. A. Cozzolino & F. T. Rothaermel, 2018, Discontinuities, competition and cooperation: Coopetitive dynamics between incumbents and entrants, *Strategic Management Journal*, in press; G. B. Dagnino, D. R. King & J. Tienari, 2017, Strategic management of dynamic growth, *Long Range Planning*, 50: 427–430; C. B. Bingham, K. H. Heimeriks, M. Schijven, & S. Gates, 2015, Concurrent learning: How firms develop multiple dynamic capabilities in parallel, *Strategic Management Journal*, 36: 1802–1825.
35. A. T. H. Kuah & P. Wang, 2017, Fast-expanding "online" markets in South Korea and China: Are they worth pursuing? *Thunderbird International Business Review*, 59: 63–77; M. Kishna, E. Niesten, S. Negro, & M. P. Hekkert, 2017, The role of alliances in creating legitimacy of sustainable technologies: A study of the field of bio-plastics, *Journal of Cleaner Production*, 155: 7–16; H. Milanov & S. A. Fernhaber, 2014, When do domestic alliances help ventures abroad? Direct and moderating effects from a learning perspective, *Journal of Business Venturing*, 29: 377–391.
36. 2018, Micron website, Micron Technology, Inc. https://www.micron.com, accessed on August 2; 2015, Micron, Seagate announce strategic alliance, *Micron Home Page*, www.micron. com, February 12.
37. D. Lee, K. Kirkpatrick-Husk & R. Madhaven, 2017, Diversity in Alliance portfolios and performance outcomes: A meta-analysis, *Journal of Management*, 43: 1472–1497.
38. V. Iurkov & G. R. G. Benito, 2018, Domestic alliance networks and regional strategies of MNEs: A structural embeddedness perspective, *Journal of International Business Studies*, in press; H. M. Khameseh & M. Nasiriyar, 2014, Avoiding alliance myopia: Forging learning outcomes for long-term success, *Journal of Business Strategy*, 35: 37–44; A.-P. de Man, N. Roijakkers, & H. de Graauw, 2010, Managing dynamics through robust alliance governance structures: The case of KLM and Northwest Airlines, *European Management Journal*, 28: 171–181.
39. 2018, Airline alliances 2018. *Boomer Traveller*, https://boomertraveller.com, accessed August 4.
40. S. Carnovale, S. Yeniyurt, & D. S. Rogers, 2017, Network connectedness in vertical and horizontal manufacturing joint venture formations: A power perspective, *Journal of Purchasing and Supply Management*, 23: 67–81.
41. U. Stettner & D. Lavie, 2014, Ambidexterity under scrutiny: Exploration and exploitation via internal organization, alliances, and acquisitions, *Strategic Management Journal*, 35: 1903–1929; N. Lahiri & S. Narayanan, 2013, Vertical integration, innovation and alliance portfolio size: Implications for firm performance, *Strategic Management Journal*, 34: 1042–1064; S. M. Mudambi & S. Tallman, 2010, Make, buy or ally? Theoretical perspectives on knowledge process outsourcing through alliances, *Journal of Management Studies*, 47: 1434–1456.
42. R. Kapoor & P. J. McGrath, 2014, Unmasking the interplay between technology evolution and R&D collaboration: Evidence from the global semiconductor manufacturing industry, 1990–2010, *Research Policy*, 43: 555–569; J. Hagedoorn & N. Wang, 2012, Is there complementarity or substitutability between internal and external R&D strategies? *Research Policy*, 41: 1072–1083; M. Meuleman, A. Lockett, S. Manigart, & M. Wright, 2010, Partner selection decisions in interfirm collaborations: The paradox of relational embeddedness, *Journal of Management Studies*, 47: 995–1019.
43. S. Ozdemir, D. Kandemir, & T.-Y. Eng, 2017, The role of horizontal and vertical new product alliances in responsive and proactive market orientations and performance if industrial manufacturing firms, *Industrial Marketing Management*, 64: 25–35; J. Zhang & C. Baden-Fuller, 2010, The influence of technological knowledge

base and organizational structure on technology collaboration, *Journal of Management Studies*, 47: 679–704.

44. S. Higginbotham, 2015, AT&T's plan for the Internet of things goes way beyond the network, *Fortune*, http://fortune.com, September 15.
45. T. Xia & D. Dimov, 2018, Alliances and survival of new biopharmaceutical ventures in the wake of the global financial crisis, *Journal of Small Business Management*, in press.
46. M. Robert, P. Chiambaretto, B. Mira, & F. Le Roy, 2018, Better, faster, stronger: The impact of market-oriented coopetition on product commercial performance, *M@n@gement*, 21: 574–60; J. Wieczner, 2014, Can drugmakers find profit in collaboration? *Fortune Online*, www.fortune.com, February 11.
47. H. Parker & Z. Brey, 2015, Collaboration costs and new product development performance, *Journal of Business Research*, 68: 1653–1656; C. Häeussler, H. Patzelt, & S. A. Zahra, 2012, Strategic alliances and product development in high technology new firms: The moderating effect of technological capabilities, *Journal of Business Venturing*, 27: 217–233; M. Makri, M. A. Hitt, & P. J. Lane, 2010, Complementary technologies, knowledge relatedness, and invention outcomes in high technology mergers and acquisitions, *Strategic Management Journal*, 31: 602–628.
48. N. K. Park, X. Martin, & J. Lee, 2018, Effects of functional focus on bounded momentum: Examining firm- and industry-level alliances, *Strategic Organization*, in press; B. Bos, D. Faems, & F. Noseleit, 2017, Alliance concentration in multinational companies: Examining Alliance portfolios, firm structure, and firm performance, *Strategic Management Journal*, 38: 2258–2309.
49. N. H. Miller & M. C. Weinberg, 2017, Understanding the price effects of the MillerCoors joint venture, *Econometrica*, 85: 1763–1791; A. Martin, 2007, Merger for SABMiller and Molson Coors, *New York Times Online*, www.nytimes.com, October 10.
50. T. Mickle, 2015, Molson Coors, U.S. joint venture MillerCoors facing stiff challenges, *Wall Street Journal Online*, www.wsj.com, May 7.
51. D. K. Dutta & M. Hora, 2017, From invention success to commercialization success: Technology ventures and the benefits of upstream and downstream supply-chain alliances, *Journal of Small Business Management*, 55: 216–235; J. Xia, Y. Wang, & Y. Lin, 2017, Alliance formation in the midst of market and network: Insights from resource dependence and network perspectives, *Journal of Management*, 38: 917–936; H. Yang & H. K. Steensma, 2014, When do firms rely on their knowledge spillover recipients for guidance in exploring unfamiliar knowledge? *Research Policy*, 43: 1496–1507.
52. S. Juasrikul, A. Sahaym, H. Yim, & R. L. Liu, 2018, Do cross border alliances with MNEs from developed economies create firm value for MNEs from emerging economies? *Journal of Business Research*, in press; A. Martinez-Noya & R. Narula, 2018, What more can we learn from R&D alliances? A review and research agenda, *BRQ Business Research Quarterly*, in press.
53. C. Bryant, 2017, Mercedes vs. Tesla is an epic tale, *Bloomberg*, https://www.bloomberg.com, April 12; 2014, Tesla Motors in talks with BMW, possible alliance in batteries, carbon fiber body parts, Tesla Home Page, www.myteslamotors.com, November 23.
54. L. Garrod & M. Olczak, 2018, Explicit vs tacit collusion: The effects of firm numbers and asymmetries, *International Journal of Industrial Organization*, 56: 1–25; H.-T. Normann, J. Rosch, & L. M. Schultz, 2015, Do buyer groups facilitate collusion? *Journal of Economic Behavior & Organization*, 109: 72–84; M. A. Fonseca & H. Normann, 2012, Explicit vs. tacit collusion—The impact of communication in oligopoly experiments, *European Economic Review*, 56: 1759–1772.
55. J. Boone & K. Zigic, 2015, Trade policy in markets with collusion: The case of North-South R&D spillovers, *Research in Economics*, 69: 224–237; M. Van Essen & W. B. Hankins, 2013, Tacit collusion in price-setting oligopoly: A puzzle redux, *Southern Economic Journal*, 79: 703–726; Y. Lu & J. Wright, 2010, Tacit collusion with price-matching punishments, *International Journal of Industrial Organization*, 28: 298–306.
56. A. Capobianco & A. Nyeso, 2017, Challenges for competition law enforcement and policy in the digital economy, *Journal of European Competition, Law & Practice*, 9: 19–27; F. J. Mas-Ruiz, F. Ruiz-Moreno, & A. L. de Guevara Martinez, 2014, Asymmetric rivalry within and between strategic groups, *Strategic Management Journal*, 35: 419–439.
57. M. T. Gustafson, I. T. Ivanov, & J. Ritter, 2015, Financial condition and product market cooperation, *Journal of Corporate Finance*, 31: 1–16; L. Zou, C. Yu, & M. Dresner, 2012, Multimarket contact, alliance membership, and prices in international airline markets, Transportation Research Part E: *Logistics and Transportation Review*, 48: 555–565; J. T. Prince & D. H. Simon, 2009, Multimarket contact and service quality: Evidence from on-time performance in the U.S. airline industry, *Academy of Management Journal*, 52: 336–354.
58. B. C. Konduk, 2018, The elephant in the room of mutual forbearance: How a multimarket firm develops the motivation for forbearance, *Journal of Business and Strategy*, 11: 257–279; K. Uhlenbruck, M. Hughes-Morgan, M. A. Hitt, W. J. Ferrier & R. Brymer, 2017, Rivals reaction to mergers and acquisitions, *Strategic organization*, 15: 40–66; Z. Guedri & J. McGuire, 2011, Multimarket competition, mobility barriers, and firm performance, *Journal of Management Studies*, 48: 857–890.
59. I. K. Wang, H.-S. Yang, & D. J. Miller, 2015, Collaboration in the shadow of the technology frontier: Evidence from the flat panel display industry, *Managerial and Decision Economics*, 36: 456–469; P. Massey & M. McDowell, 2010, Joint dominance and tacit collusion: Some implications for competition and regulatory policy, *European Competition Journal*, 6: 427–444.
60. A. H. Bowers, H. R. Greve, H. Mitsuhashi, & J. A. C. Baum, 2014, Competitive parity, status disparity, and mutual forbearance: Securities analysts' competition for investor attention, *Academy of Management Journal*, 57: 38–62.
61. E. Bolisani & C. Bratianu, 2017, Knowledge strategy planning: An integrated approach to manage uncertainty, turbulence and dynamics, *Journal of Knowledge Management*, 21: 233–253.
62. H.-L. Chan, B. Shen, & Y. Cai, 2018, Quick response strategy with cleaner technology in a supply chain: Coordination and win-win situation analysis, *International Journal of Production Research*, 56: 3397–3408.
63. A. Martynov, 2017, Alliance portfolios and firm performance: The moderating role of firms' strategic positioning, *Journal of Strategy and Management*, 10: 206–226; Y. Liu & T. Ravichandran, 2015, Alliance experience, IT-enabled knowledge integration, and ex-ante value gains, *Organization Science*, 26: 511–530; P. Dussauge, B. Garrette, & W. Mitchell, 2004, Asymmetric performances: The market share impact of scale and link alliances in the global auto industry, *Strategic Management Journal*, 25: 701–711.
64. H. Gao, J. Yang, H. Yin, & Z. Ma, 2017, The impact of partner similarity on alliance management capability stability and performance Empirical evidence of horizontal logistics alliance in China, *International Journal of Physical Distribution & Logistics Management*, 47: 906–926.
65. M. O'Dwyer & A. Gilmore, 2018, Value and alliance capability and the formation of strategic alliances in SMEs: The impact of customer orientation and resource optimization, *Journal of Business Research*, 87: 58–68; C.-H. Liu, J.-S. Horng, S.F. Chou Y.-C. Huang, & A. Y. Chang, 2018, How to create competitive advantage: The moderating role of organizational learning as a link between shared value, dynamic capability, differential strategy and social capital, *Asia Pacific Journal of Tourism Research*, 23: 747–764.
66. M. Rogan & H. R. Greve, 2014, Resource dependence dynamics: Partner reactions to mergers, *Organization Science*, 26: 239–255; L. Capron & W. Mitchell, 2012, Build, Borrow or Buy: Solving the Growth Dilemma, Cambridge: *Harvard Business Review Press*;

C. Häussler, 2011, The determinants of commercialization strategy: Idiosyncrasies in British and German biotechnology, *Entrepreneurship Theory and Practice*, 35: 653–681.

67. B. T. McCann, J. J. Reuer, & N. Lahiri, 2016, Agglomeration and the choice between acquisitions and alliances: An information economics perspective, *Strategic Management Journal*, 37: 1085–1106; S. Chang & M. Tsai, 2013, The effect of prior alliance experience on acquisition performance, *Applied Economics*, 45: 765–773; J. Anand, R. Oriani, & R. S. Vassolo, 2010, Alliance activity as a dynamic capability in the face of a discontinuous technological change, *Organization Science*, 21: 1213–1232.

68. K. Marhold & J. Kang, 2017, The effects of internal technological diversity and external uncertainty on technological alliance portfolio diversity, *Industry and Innovation*, 24: 122–142; B. T. McCann, J. J. Reuer, & N. Lahiri, 2016, Agglomeration and the choice between acquisitions and alliances: An information economics perspective, *Strategic Management Journal*, 37: 1085–1106; S. Chang & M. Tsai, 2013, The effect of prior alliance experience on acquisition performance, *Applied Economics*, 45: 765–773.

69. J. Hagedoorn, B. Lokshin, & A.-K. Zobel, 2018, Partner type diversity in alliance portfolios: Multiple dimensions, boundary conditions and firm innovation performance, *Journal of Management Studies*, 55: 806–836; C. Penney, 2018, Alliance portfolio diversity and dominant logic theory, *Journal of Business Strategy*, 35: 31–47; C.-H. Tseng & S.-F. Chen, 2017, Do firms with more alliance experience outperform others with less? A three-level sigmoid model and the moderating effects of diversification, *Canadian Journal of Administrative Sciences*, 34: 229–243.

70. C. Panico, 2017, Strategic interaction in alliances, *Strategic Management Journal*, 38: 1646–1667.

71. P. Srivastava, K. N. S. Iyer, & M. Y. A. Rawwas, 2017, Performance impact of supply chain partnership strategy-environment co-alignment, *International Journal of Operations & Production Management*, 37: 927–949.

72. F. D. Berends, G. Gemser, & K. Lauche, 2018, Strategizing and the initiation of interorganizational collaboration through prospective resourcing, *Academy of Management Journal*, in press; U. Wassmer, S. Li, & A. Madhok, 2017, Resource ambidexterity through alliance portfolios and firm performance, *Strategic Management Journal*, 38: 384–394.

73. 2018, The Alliance Renault Nissan Mitsubishi, The Alliance, https://www.alliance-2022.com, accessed on August 4.

74. 2018, BMW & Brilliance expanding China venture BBA, *Electrive.com*, https://www.electrive.com, July 10; 2014, BMW expands joint venture with Chinese carmaker Brilliance, *DW*, www.dw.de, December 14.

75. N. Gorovaia & J. Windsperger, 2018, The choice of contract duration in franchising networks: A transaction cost and resource-based view, *Industrial Marketing Management*, in press; F. Sadeh & M. Kacker, 2018, Quality signalling through ex-ante voluntary information disclosure in entrepreneurial networks: Evidence from franchising, *Small Business Economics*, 50: 729–748; J. G. Combs, D. J. Ketchen, Jr., C. L. Shook, & J. C. Short, 2011, Antecedents and consequences of franchising: Past accomplishments and future challenges, *Journal of Management*, 37: 99–126.

76. B. R. Barringer & R. D. Ireland, 2019, *Entrepreneurship: Successfully Launching New Ventures*, 6th ed., Prentice-Hall, 510.

77. Y. Fan, K.-U. Kuhn, & F. LaFontaine, 2017, Financial constraints and moral hazard: The case of franchising, *Journal of Political Economy*, 125: 208202125; C.-W. Wu, 2015, Antecedents of franchise strategy and performance, *Journal of Business Research*, 68: 1581–1588; W. E. Gillis, J. G. Combs, & D. J. Ketchen, Jr., 2014, Using resource-based theory to help explain plural form franchising, *Entrepreneurship Theory and Practice*, 38: 449–472.

78. M. J. McDermott & T. Boyd, 2017, The influence of human capital factors on franchising, *Small Business Institute Journal*, 13: 31–50; J.-S. Chiou & C. Droge, 2015, The effects of standardization and trust on franchisee's performance and satisfaction: A study on franchise systems in the growth stage, *Journal of Small Business Management*, 53: 129–144; N. Mumdziev & J. Windsperger, 2013, An extended transaction cost model of decision rights allocation in franchising: The moderating role of trust, *Managerial and Decision Economics*, 34: 170–182.

79. A. Rosado-Serrano, J. Paul, & D. Dikova, 2018, Internatiional franchising: A literature review and research agenda, *Journal of Business Research*, 85: 238–257; A. El Akremi, R. Perrigot, & I. Piot-Lepetit, 2015, Examining the drivers for franchised chains performance through the lens of the dynamic capabilities approach, *Journal of Small Business Management*, 53: 145–165; B. Merrilees & L. Frazer, 2013, Internal branding: Franchisor leadership as a critical determinant, *Journal of Business Research*, 66: 158–164.

80. M. Madanoglu, I. Alon, & A. Shorham, 2017, Push and pull factors in international franchising, *International Marketing Review*, 34: 29–45; I. Alon, M. Boulanger, E. Misati, & M. Madanoglu, 2015, Are the parents to blame? Predicting franchisee failure, *Competitiveness Review*, 25: 205–217; D. Grace, S. Weaven, L. Frazer, & J. Giddings, 2013, Examining the role of franchisee normative expectations in relationship evaluation, *Journal of Retailing*, 89: 219–230.

81. M. W. Nyadzayo, M. J. Matanda, & M. T. Ewing, 2015, The impact of franchisor support, brand commitment, brand citizenship behavior, and franchisee experience on franchisee-perceived brand image, *Journal of Business Research*, 68: 1886–1894; N. Gorovaia & J. Windsperger, 2013, Real options, intangible resources and performance of franchise networks, *Managerial and Decision Economics*, 34: 183–194; T. W. K. Leslie & L. S. McNeill, 2010, Towards a conceptual model for franchise perceptual equity, *Journal of Brand Management*, 18: 21–33.

82. N. Pangarkar, L. Yuan, & S. Hussain, 2017, Too much of a good thing? Alliance portfolio size and alliance expansion, *European Management Journal*, 35: 477–485; H. Parker & Z. Brey, 2015, Collaboration costs and new product development performance, *Journal of Business Research*, 68: 1653–1656; S. Demirkan & I. Demirkan, 2014, Implications of strategic alliances for earnings quality and capital market investors, *Journal of Business Research*, 67: 1806–1816; M. Onal Vural, L. Dahlander, & G. George, 2013, Collaborative benefits and coordination costs: Learning and capability development in science, *Strategic Entrepreneurship Journal*, 7: 122–137.

83. O. F. Bustinza, E. Gomes, F. Vendrell-Herrero, & T. Baines, 2018, Product-service innovation and performance: The role of collaborative partnerships and R&D intensity, *R&D Management*, in press; A. W. Clopton, 2017, Strategic alliance: Maximizing the path to effectiveness in sport organizations, *Journal of Contemporary Athletics*, 11: 17–30; C. Choi & P. Beamish, 2013, Resource complementarity and international joint venture performance in Korea, *Asia Pacific Journal of Management*, 30: 561–576.

84. Z. Khan, O. Shenkar, & Y. K. Lew, 2015, Knowledge transfer from international joint ventures to local suppliers in a developing economy, *Journal of International Business Studies*, 46: 656–675; R. Belderbos, T. W. Tong, & S. Wu, 2014, Multinationality and downside risk: The roles of option portfolio and organization, *Strategic Management Journal*, 35: 88–106; S. Veilleux, N. Haskell, & F. Pons, 2012, Going global: How smaller enterprises benefit from strategic alliances, *Journal of Business Strategy*, 33(5): 22–31.

85. W. Han, Y. Huang, & D. Macbeth, 2018, Performance measurement of cross-culture supply chain partnership: A case study in the Chinese automotive industry, *International Journal of Production Research*, 56: 2437–2451; A. Dechezlepretre, E. Neumayer, & R. Perekins, 2015, Environmental regulation and the cross-border diffusion of new technology: Evidence from automobile patents, *Research Policy*, 44: 244–257; I. Arikan & O. Shenkar, 2013, National animosity and cross-border alliances, *Academy of Management Journal*, 56: 1516–1544.

86. D. Minbaeva & G. D. Santangelo, 2018, Boundary spanners and intr-MNC knowledge sharing: The roles of controlled motivation and immediate organizational context, *Global Strategy Journal*, 8: 220–241; W. Zhong, C. Su, & J. Peng, 2017, Trust in interporganizatinal relationships: A meta-analytic integration, *Journal of Management*, 43: 1050–1075; L. Li, G. Qian, & Z. Qian, 2013, Do partners in international strategic alliances share resources, costs, and risks? *Journal of Business Research*, 66: 489–498; A. Zaheer & E. Hernandez, 2011, The geographic scope of the MNC and its alliance portfolio: Resolving the paradox of distance, *Global Strategy Journal*, 1: 109–126.
87. M.-C. Stoian, J. Rialp, & P. Dimitratos, 2017, SME Networks and international performance: Unveiling the significance of foreign market entry mode, *Journal of Small Business Management*, 55: 128–148; Z. Khan, Y. K. Lew, & R. R. Sinkovics, 2015, International joint ventures as boundary spanners: Technological knowledge transfer in an emerging economy, *Global Strategy Journal*, 5: 48–68; M. Meuleman & M. Wright, 2011, Cross-border private equity syndication: Institutional context and learning, *Journal of Business Venturing*, 26: 35–48.
88. M. Abdi & P. S. Aulakh, 2017, Locus of uncertainty and the relationship between contractual and relational governance in cross-border interfirm relationships, *Journal of Management*, 43: 771–803; J. J. Hotho, M. A. Lyles, & M. Easterby-Smith, 2015, The mutual impact of global strategy and organizational learning: Current themes and future directions, *Global Strategy Journal*, 5: 85–112; B. B. Nielsen & S. Gudergan, 2012, Exploration and exploitation fit and performance in international strategic alliances, *International Business Review*, 21: 558–574.
89. I.-S. Nam & R. Wall, 2015, Airbus, Korea Aerospace sign helicopter deal, *Wall Street Journal Online*, www.wsj.com, March 16.
90. D. R. Quatrin & B. A. D. Perrira, 2018, Who should they relate to? A study for the identification and analysis of Criteria to the partners' selection in inter-organizational networks, *Brazilian Business Review*, 14: in press.
91. 2018, Cisco Partner Summit, Cisco homepage, www.cisco.com, accessed August 5.
92. 2018, Cisco and IBM Security: Partnering to provide integrated threat defense, *SecurityIntelligence Podcast*, https://securityintelligence.com, May 31.
93. D. P. McIntyre & A. Srinivsan, 2017, Networks, platforms, and strategy: Emerging views and next steps, *Strategic Management Journal*, 38: 141–160; C. Geldes, C. Felzensztein, E. Turkina, & A. Durand, 2015, How does proximity affect interfirm marketing cooperation? A study of an agribusiness cluster, *Journal of Business Research*, 68: 263–272; W. Fu, J. Revilla Diez, & D. Schiller, 2013, Interactive learning, informal networks and innovation: Evidence from electronics firm survey in the Pearl River Delta, China, *Research Policy*, 42: 635–646.
94. S. Paruchurl & S. Awate, 2017, Organizational knowledge networks and local search: The role of intra-organizational inventor networks, *Strategic Management Journal*, 38: 657–675; A. Phene & S. Tallman, 2014, Knowledge spillovers and alliance formation, *Journal of Management Studies*, 51: 1058–1090; C. Casanueva, I. Castro, & J. L. Galán, 2013, Informational networks and innovation in mature industrial clusters, *Journal of Business Research*, 66: 603–613.
95. M. I. Roldan Bravo, F. J. Llorens Montes, & A. Ruiz Moreno, 2017, Open innovation in supply networks: An expectation disconfirmation theory perspective, *Journal of Business & industrial Marketing*, 32: 432–444; Y. Zheng & H. Yang, 2015, Does familiarity foster innovation? The impact of alliance partner repeatedness on breakthrough innovations, *Journal of Management Studies*, 52: 213–230; L. Dobusch & E. Schübler, 2013, Theorizing path dependence: A review of positive feedback mechanisms in technology markets, regional clusters, and organizations, *Industrial & Corporate Change*, 22: 617–647.
96. J. R. Lincoln, D. Guillot, & M. Sargent, 2017, Business groups, networks, and embeddedness: Innovation and implementation alliances in Japanese electronics, 1985–1998, *Industrial and Corporate Change*, 26: 357–378; S. Perkins, R. Morck, & B. Yeung, 2014, Innocents abroad: The hazards of international joint ventures with pyramidal group firms, *Global Strategy Journal*, 4: 310–330; H. Kim, R. E. Hoskisson, & W. P. Wan, 2004, Power, dependence, diversification strategy and performance in keiretsu member firms, *Strategic Management Journal*, 25: 613–636.
97. J. A. Belso-Martinez, A. Mas-Tur, & N. Roig-Tierno, 2017, Synergistic effects and the co-existence of networks in clusters, *Entrepreneurship and Regional Development*, 29: 137–154; B. Kang & K. Motohashi, 2015, Essential intellectual property rights and inventors' involvement in standardization, *Research Policy*, 44: 483–492; A. V. Shipilov, 2009, Firm scope experience, historic multimarket contact with partners, centrality, and the relationship between structural holes and performance, *Organization Science*, 20: 85–106.
98. K.-H. Huarng & A. Mas-Tur, 2015, Sprit of strategy (S.O.S.): The new S.O.S. for competitive business, *Journal of Business Research*, 68: 1383–1387; S. Gupta & M. Polonsky, 2014, Inter-firm learning and knowledge-sharing in multinational networks: An outsourced organization's perspective, *Journal of Business Research*, 67: 615–622; A. S. Cui & G. O'Connor, 2012, Alliance portfolio resource diversity and firm innovation, *Journal of Marketing*, 76: 24–43.
99. F. Collet & D. Philippe, 2014, From hot cakes to cold feet: A contingent perspective on the relationship between market uncertainty and status homophily in the formation of alliances, *Journal of Management Studies*, 51: 406–432; G. Cuevas-Rodriguez, C. Cabello-Medina, & A. Carmona-Lavado, 2014, Internal and external social capital for radical product innovation: Do they always work well together? *British Journal of Management*, 25: 266–284; G. Soda, 2011, The management of firms' alliance network positioning: Implications for innovation, *European Management Journal*, 29: 377–388.
100. I. Castro & J. L. Roldan, 2015, Alliance portfolio management: Dimensions and performance, *European Management Review*, 12: 63–81; C. Martin-Rios, 2014, Why do firms seek to share human resource management knowledge? The importance of inter-firm networks, *Journal of Business Research*, 67: 190–199.
101. A. Fernandez, 2018, Strategic alliances bring big ip power to gp firms, *Daily Business Review*, https://www.law.com/dailybusinessreview, April 26; A. G. Karamanos, 2012, Leveraging micro-and macro-structures of embeddedness in alliance networks for exploratory innovation in biotechnology, *R&D Management*, 42: 71–89; D. Somaya, Y. Kim, & N. S. Vonortas, 2011, Exclusivity in licensing alliances: Using hostages to support technology commercialization, *Strategic Management Journal*, 32: 159–186.
102. U. Ozmel & I. Guler, 2015, Small fish, big fish: The performance effects of the relative standing in partners' affiliate portfolios, *Strategic Management Journal*, 36: 2039–2057; M. J. Nieto & L. Santamaría, 2010, Technological collaboration: Bridging the innovation gap between small and large firms, *Journal of Small Business Management*, 48: 44–69.
103. M. Russo & M. Cesarani, 2017, Strategic alliance success factors: A literature review on alliance lifecycle, *International Journal of Business Administration*, 8 (3): 1–9; H. R. Greve, H. Mitsuhashi, & J. A. C. Baum, 2013, Greener pastures: Outside options and strategic alliance withdrawal, *Organization Science*, 24: 79–98; H. R. Greve, J. A. C. Baum, H. Mitsuhashi, & T. J. Rowley, 2010, Built to last but falling apart: Cohesion, friction, and withdrawal from interfirm alliances, *Academy of Management Journal*, 53: 302–322.
104. P. C. van Fenema & B. M. Keers, 2018, Interorganizational performance management: A co-evolutionary model, *International Journal of Management Reviews*, 20: 772–799; G. Vasudeva & J. Anand, 2011, Unpacking absorptive capacity: A study of knowledge utilization

from alliance portfolios, *Academy of Management Journal*, 54: 611–623; J.-Y. Kim & A. S. Miner, 2007, Vicarious learning from the failures and near-failures of others: Evidence from the U.S. commercial banking industry, *Academy of Management Journal*, 50: 687–714.

105. J. Marson, 2013, TNK-BP investors appeal to Rosneft's chief over shares, *Wall Street Journal Online*, www.wsj.com, April 17.
106. B. Kang & R. P. Jindal, 2015, Opportunism in buyer-seller relationships: Some unexplored antecedents, *Journal of Business Research*, 68: 735–742; L.-Y. Wu, P.-Y. Chen, & K.-Y. Chen, 2015, Why does loyalty-cooperation behavior vary over buyer-seller relationship? *Journal of Business Research*, 68: 2322–2329; K. Zhou & D. Xu, 2012, How foreign firms curtail local supplier opportunism in China: Detailed contracts, centralized control, and relational governance, *Journal of International Business Studies*, 43: 677–692.
107. A. Spithoven & P. Teirlinck, 2015, Internal capabilities, network resources and appropriate mechanisms as determinants of R&D outsourcing, *Research Policy*, 44: 711–725; A. V. Werder, 2011, Corporate governance and stakeholder opportunism, *Organization Science*, 22: 1345–1358; T. K. Das & R. Kumar, 2011, Regulatory focus and opportunism in the alliance development process, *Journal of Management*, 37: 682–708.
108. C. Turcan, 2018, 3 JVs between BP and Rosneft, *Seeking Alpha*, https://seekingalpha.com, May 23.
109. Z. Yin & C. Wang, 2018, Strategic cooperation with a backup supplier for the mitigation of supply disruptions, *International Journal of Production Research*, in press; I. Stern, J. M. Dukerich, & E. Zajac, 2014, Unmixed signals: How reputation and status affect alliance formation, *Strategic Management Journal*, 35: 512–531; A. S. Cui, 2013, Portfolio dynamics and alliance termination: The contingent role of resource dissimilarity, *Journal of Marketing*, 77: 15–32.
110. S. McLain, 2015, New outsourcing frontier in India: Monitoring drug safety, *Wall Street Journal Online*, www.wsj.com, February 1; 2010, Pharmacovigilance benchmarking report highlights pharma's drug safety efforts, *Pharmaceutical Commerce*, http://pharmaceuticalcommerce.com, June 1.
111. L. Li & G. Qian, 2018, Strategic alliances in technology industries: A different rationale, *Journal of Business Strategy*, 39: 3–11; M. Kafouros, C. Wang, P. Piiperopoulos, & M. Zhang, 2015, Academic collaborations and firm innovation performance in China: The role of region-specific institutions, *Research Policy*, 44: 803–817; S. Kraus, T. C. Ambos, F. Eggers, & B. Cesinger, 2015, Distance and perceptions of risk in internationalization decisions, *Journal of Business Research*, 68: 1501–1505.
112. M. Kohtamaki, R. Rabetino, & K. Moller, 2018, Alliance capabilities: A systematic review and future research directions, *Industrial Marketing Management*, 68: 188–201; I. Neyens & D. Faems, 2013, Exploring the impact of alliance portfolio management design on alliance portfolio performance, *Managerial & Decision Economics*, 34: 347–361; M. H. Hansen, R. E. Hoskisson, & J. B. Barney, 2008, Competitive advantage in alliance governance: Resolving the opportunism minimization-gain maximization paradox, *Managerial and Decision Economics*, 29: 191–208.
113. K. Stouthuysen, H. Slabbinck, & F. Roodhooft, 2017, Formal controls and alliance performance: The effects of alliance motivation and informal controls, *Management Accounting Research*, 37: 49–63; G. Speckbacher, K. Neumann, & W. H. Hoffmann, 2015, Resource relatedness and the mode of entry into new businesses: Internal resource accumulation vs. access by collaborative arrangement, *Strategic Management Journal*, 36: 1675–1687.
114. J. Windsberger, G. W. J. Hendrikse, G. Cliquet, & T. Ehrmann, 2018, Governance and strategy of entrepreneurial networks, *Small Business Networks*, 50: 671–676; D. J. Harmon, P. H. Kim, & K. J. Mayer, 2015, Breaking the letter vs. spirit of the law: How the interpretation of contract violations affects trust and the management of relationships, *Strategic Management Journal*, 36: 497–517; M. H. Hansen, R. E. Hoskisson, & J. B. Barney, 2008, Competitive advantage in alliance governance: Resolving the opportunism minimization-gain maximization paradox, *Managerial and Decision Economics*, 29: 191–208.
115. C. Panico, 2017, Strategic interactions in alliances, *Strategic Management Journal*, 38: 1646–1667; T. Felin & T. R. Zenger, 2014, Closed or open innovation? Problem solving and the governance choice, *Research Policy*, 43: 914–925; N. N. Arranz & J. C. F. de Arroyabe, 2012, Effect of formal contracts, relational norms and trust on performance of joint research and development projects, *British Journal of Management*, 23: 575–588.
116. A. Wu, Z. Wang, & S. Chen, 2017, Impact of specific investments, governance mechanisms and behaviors on the performance of cooperative innovation projects, *International Journal of Project Management*, 35: 504–515; B. S. Vanneste, P. Puranam, & T. Kretschmer, 2014, Trust over time in exchange relationships: Meta-analysis and theory, *Strategic Management Journal*, 35: 1891–1902; G. Ertug, I. Cuypers, N. Noorderhaven, & B. Bensaou, 2013, Trust between internation al joint venture partners: Effects of home countries, *Journal of International Business Studies*, 44: 263–282.
117. M. Mandell, R. Keast, & D. Chamberlain, 2017, Collaborative networks and the need for a new management language, *Public Management Review*, 19: 326–341; S. E. Fawcett, S. L. Jones, & A. M. Fawcett, 2012, Supply chain trust: The catalyst for collaborative innovation, *Business Horizons*, 55: 163–178; H. C. Dekker & A. Van den Abbeele, 2010, Organizational learning and interfirm control: The effects of partner search and prior exchange experience, *Organization Science*, 21: 1233–1250.
118. Y. Zhao, Y. Feng, & C. Li, 2018, Effect of organizational cultural differences and mutual trust on contract management of nonequity construction project alliances, *Advances in Civil Engineering*, in press.

10

Corporate Governance

Studying this chapter should provide you with the strategic management knowledge needed to:

10-1 Define corporate governance and explain why it is used to monitor and control top-level managers' decisions.

10-2 Explain why ownership is largely separated from managerial control in organizations.

10-3 Define an agency relationship and managerial opportunism and describe their strategic implications.

10-4 Explain the use of three internal governance mechanisms to monitor and control managers' decisions.

10-5 Discuss the types of compensation top-level managers receive and their effects on managerial decisions.

10-6 Describe how the external corporate governance mechanism—the market for corporate control—restrains top-level managers' decisions.

10-7 Discuss the nature and use of corporate governance in international settings, especially in Germany, Japan, and China.

10-8 Describe how corporate governance fosters ethical decisions by a firm's top-level managers.

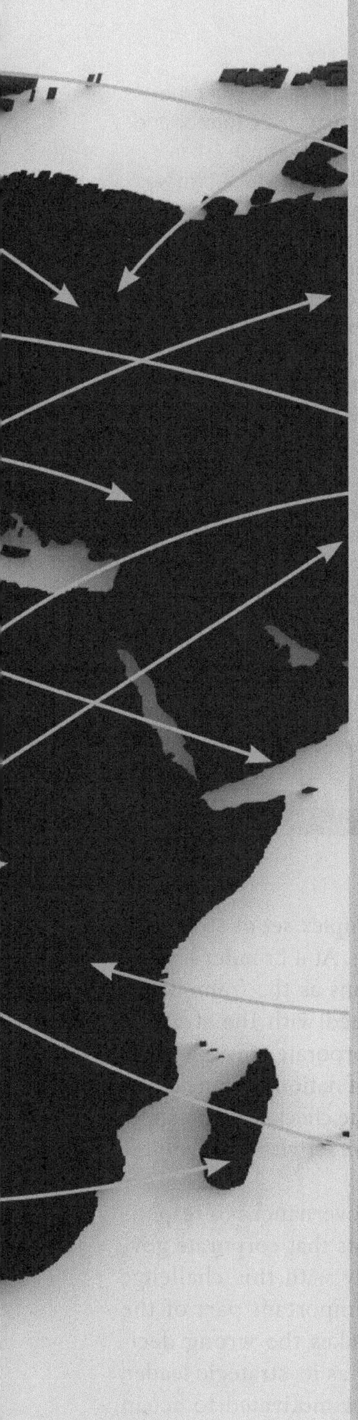

SHAREHOLDER ACTIVISTS AND CORPORATE GOVERNANCE

In the 1980s, large activist shareholders, labelled "corporate raiders," would buy significant stakes in companies and often seek to increase the debt load, sell off business units reducing diversification, and downsize by laying off many workers. If the firms did not respond as the activist shareholders required, they would make the company pay a premium on the shares they bought, often called "greenmail." Today activist investors are doing many of the same things, but they are often supported by institutional investors who follow the activist investors' lead or support them in their activities, especially shareholder votes. The number of activist firms is growing as is the amount of money being deployed. In 2017, activist fund groups deployed $62 billion in their campaigns, more than twice the amount of money spent in 2016. Approximately 20 percent of U.S. activists' funds was spent on buying shares of global companies, as opportunities in the United States decrease.

One of the strategies these activist investors pursue is to pressure firms to allow activist nominated representatives to stand for election for the targeted company's board. Another strategy gaining momentum is access to the proxy process to include shareholder resolutions for shareholder votes. This access has been allowed by the courts, and encouraged by U.S. Securities and Exchange Commission (SEC) efforts to require more proxy voting action opportunities to shareholders. Thus, regulators' decisions have allowed more open proxy voting access by shareholders. As such, firm shareholders are able to vote on strategic issues presented by activist shareholders as well as directly nominating board members who represent their interests.

Heidi Gutman/CNBC/NBCU Photo Bank/Getty Images

Nelson Peltz, CEO of Trian Fund Management L.P., now sits on the board at P&G.

Activist firms are challenging large and visible firms such as DuPont, Proctor & Gamble (P&G), Nestlé, General Electric, and Lowe's among others. For example, P&G fought a proxy battle with Trian Fund Management L.P. representatives, headed by CEO Nelson Peltz, for board seats. Even though P&G won the proxy vote, P&G still offered Peltz a board seat. In taking the board seat, Peltz personally also dropped a board seat (possibly because he was sitting on too many boards to be effective) on Mondolez, a food company, which board position Trian had gained on a previous investment.

Often activist investors seek stock buybacks and increases in dividends as well as selling off "non-performing businesses." For example, Carl Icahn, a famous activist investor, held 6.7 percent in Newell Brands and in a settlement was allowed four board seats in addition to appointing a new board chair. However, Starboard and its allied funds hold a stake of just under 5 percent in Newell brands and are trying to oust the remaining board members and replace the CEO. Starboard has been among the most aggressive activist investors in seeking to remove all board members when it buys shares. It described Newell as "a conglomerate that makes everything from Elmer's glue to Mr. Coffee machines" and declared that Newell's sprawling set of businesses needs to be narrowed and the top executives replaced. Over time, in part due to such activism, objections to corporate governance arrangements have become more strident and monitoring of top executives more intense.

However, there are risks to activist approaches, as William Ackman's Pershing Square Capital Management L.P. has found. Although typically activist investors push companies to improve short-term value through leadership changes, stock buybacks, and break-ups, others want the opposite to happen; they first "short" the stock and then make arguments that create turmoil and a perception of weakness within the company, resulting in the lowering of the company share price and increasing the value of a short position. Pershing Square Capital Management firm was shorting Herbalife, but instead of going down the stock increased. Ackman's fund has been losing shareholders because it has made some large but poor investments such as the one in Herbalife.

Although activism has caused some chaos among firms' board of directors, it has made for overall better, albeit more intense, governance and has given more voice to shareholders on strategy issues, points that are pertinent to the topic of our book. For example, activists have pursued more intense long-term compensation packages, which have provided better long-term performance such as more investment in R&D activities. On the other hand, the greatly added pressure to perform has led some firm leaders to "cook the books" and thus has led to more fraud. As you read through this chapter, these issues will become clearer as the various governance devices are defined and their purpose explained.

Sources: C. English, 2018, Activist Peltz leaving Mondelez board to join P&G's, *New York Post*, www.nypost,com, February 13; L. Fortado, 2018, Investing: activism enters the mainstream, *Financial Times*, www.ft.com, February 13; C. Lombardo, 2018, Starboard pursuing proxy fight at Newell Brands despite deal with Icahn, *Wall Street Journal*, www.wsj.com, April 4; E. Price, 2018, Investors are pulling out of Bill Ackman's hedge fund at a 'rapid pace', *Fortune*, www.fortune.com, April 5; S. Terlep & D. Benoit, 2018, Starboard to launch proxy fight to replace entire Newell brands board, *Wall Street Journal*, www.wsj.com, February 8; S. Dean, 2017, What is an activist investor? *Telegraph*, www.telegraph.co.uk, May 10; M. R. Denes, J. M. Karpoff, & V. B. McWilliams, 2017, Thirty years of shareholder activism: A survey of empirical research, *Journal of Corporate Finance*, 44: 405–424; C. Flammer & P. Bansal, 2017, Does a long-term orientation create value? Evidence from a regression discontinuity, *Strategic Management Journal*, 38(9): 1827–1847; C. P. Skroupa, 2017, 2017 and beyond—major trends shaping shareholder activism, *Forbes*, www.forbes.com, October 27; W. Shi, B. L. Connelly, & R. E. Hoskisson, 2017, External corporate governance and financial fraud: Cognitive evaluation theory insights on agency theory prescriptions, *Strategic Management Journal*, 38(6): 1268–1286; S. Terlep, 2017, Activist Nelson Peltz gets key boost in P&G proxy fight, *Wall Street Journal*, www.wsj.com, September 29.

As the Opening Case suggests, corporate governance is a complex set of structures designed to provide firm oversight of major strategic issues. At a broader level, it reflects the type of infrastructure provided by individual nations as the frameworks within which companies compete. Given that we are concerned with the strategic management process firms use, our focus in this chapter is on corporate governance in companies (although we do also address governance at the level of nations). Some of the potential pitfalls of corporate governance, such as establishing true checks and balances in the system of governance, are highlighted by the discussion of activist shareholders in the Opening Case.

Comprehensive in scope and complex in nature, corporate governance is a responsibility that challenges firms and their leaders. Evidence suggests that corporate governance is critical to firms' success, and dealing appropriately with this challenge is important. Because of this, governance is an increasingly important part of the strategic management process.[1] For example, if the board makes the wrong decisions in selecting, governing, and compensating the firm's CEO as its strategic leader, the shareholders and firm stakeholders suffer. When CEOs are motivated to act in the best interests of firm—in particular, the shareholders—the company's value is more likely to increase. Additionally, effective leadership succession plans and appropriate monitoring and direction-setting efforts by the board of directors contribute positively to a firm's performance.

Corporate governance is the set of mechanisms used to manage the relationships among stakeholders and to determine and control the strategic direction and performance of organizations.

Corporate governance is the set of mechanisms used to manage the relationships among stakeholders and to determine and control the strategic direction and performance of organizations.[2] At its core, corporate governance is concerned with identifying ways to ensure that decisions (especially strategic decisions) are made effectively and that they facilitate a firm's efforts to achieve strategic competitiveness.[3] Governance can also be thought of as a means to establish and maintain harmony between parties (the firm's owners and its top-level managers) whose interests may conflict.

In modern corporations—especially those in nations with "westernized" infrastructures and business practices such as in the United States and the United Kingdom—ensuring that top-level managers' interests are aligned with other stakeholders' interests, particularly those of shareholders, is a primary objective of corporate governance. Thus, corporate governance involves oversight in areas where owners, managers, and members of boards of directors may have conflicts of interest. Processes used to elect members of the firm's board of directors, the general management of CEO pay and more focused supervision of director pay, and the corporation's overall strategic direction are examples of areas in which oversight is sought.[4] Because corporate governance is an ongoing process concerned with how a firm is to be managed, its nature evolves in light of the types of never-ending changes in a firm's external environment that we discussed in Chapter 2.

The recent global emphasis on corporate governance stems mainly from the apparent failure of corporate governance mechanisms to adequately monitor and control top-level managers' decisions (as exemplified by the growing focus on governance issues among activist investors in the Opening Case). In turn, undesired or unacceptable consequences resulting from using corporate governance mechanisms cause changes such as electing new members to the board of directors with the hope of providing more effective governance. A second and more positive reason for this interest comes from evidence that a well-functioning corporate governance system can create a competitive advantage for an individual firm.[5]

As noted earlier, corporate governance is of concern to nations as well as to individual firms.[6] Although corporate governance reflects company standards, it also collectively reflects the societal standards of nations.[7] For example, the independence of board members and practices a board should follow to exercise effective oversight of a firm's internal control efforts are changes to governance standards that have been fostered even in emerging economies.[8] Efforts such as these are important because research shows that firms seek to invest in nations with national governance standards that are acceptable to them.[9] This is particularly the case when firms consider the possibility of expanding geographically into emerging markets.

In the chapter's first section, we describe the relationship on which the modern corporation is built—namely, the relationship between owners and managers. We use the majority of the chapter to explain various mechanisms owners use to govern managers and to ensure that they comply with their responsibility to satisfy stakeholders' needs, especially those of shareholders.

Three internal governance mechanisms and a single external one are emphasized in the modern corporation. The three internal governance mechanisms described in this chapter are

1. ownership concentration, represented by types of shareholders and their different incentives to monitor managers;
2. the board of directors; and
3. executive compensation.

We then consider the market for corporate control, an external corporate governance mechanism. Essentially, this market is a set of potential owners seeking to acquire undervalued firms and earn above-average returns on their investments by replacing ineffective top-level management teams.[10] The chapter's focus then shifts to the issue of international corporate governance. We briefly describe governance approaches used in several countries outside of the United States and United Kingdom. In part, this discussion suggests that the structures used to govern global companies competing in both developed and emerging economies are becoming more, rather than less, similar. Closing our analysis of corporate governance is a consideration of the need for these control mechanisms to encourage and support ethical and socially responsible behavior in organizations.

10-1 Separation of Ownership and Managerial Control

Historically, U.S. firms were managed by founder-owners and their descendants. In these cases, corporate ownership and control resided with the same group of people. As firms grew larger, "the managerial revolution led to a separation of ownership and control in most large corporations, where control of the firm shifted from entrepreneurs to professional managers while ownership became dispersed among thousands of unorganized stockholders who were removed from the day-to-day management of the firm."[11] These changes created the modern public corporation, which is based on the efficient separation of ownership and managerial control. Supporting the separation is a basic legal premise suggesting that the primary objective of a firm's activities is to increase the corporation's profit and, thereby, the owners' (shareholders') financial gains.[12]

The separation of ownership and managerial control allows shareholders to purchase stock, which entitles them to income (residual returns) from the firm's operations after paying expenses. This right, however, requires that shareholders take a risk that the firm's expenses may exceed its revenues. To manage this investment risk, shareholders maintain a diversified portfolio by investing in several companies to reduce their overall risk.[13] The poor performance or failure of any one firm in which they invest has less overall effect on the value of the entire portfolio of investments. Thus, shareholders specialize in managing their investment risk.

Commonly, those managing small firms also own a significant percentage of the firm. In such instances, there is less separation between ownership and managerial control. Moreover, in a large number of family-owned firms, ownership and managerial control are not separated to any significant extent. Research shows that family-owned firms perform better when a member of the family is the CEO rather than when the CEO is an outsider.[14]

In many regions outside the United States, such as in Latin America, Asia, and some European countries, family-owned firms dominate the competitive landscape.[15] The primary purpose of most of these firms is to increase the family's wealth, which explains why a family CEO often is better than an outside CEO. Still, family ownership remains significant in U.S. companies; at least one-third of the S&P 500 firms have substantial family ownership, holding on average about 18 percent of a firm's equity.[16]

Family-controlled firms face at least two critical issues related to corporate governance. First, as they grow, they may not have access to all of the skills needed to effectively manage the firm and maximize returns for the family. Thus, outsiders may be required to facilitate growth. Second, as they grow, they may need to seek outside capital and thus give up some of the ownership. In these cases, protecting the minority owners' rights becomes important.[17] To avoid these potential problems, when family firms grow and become more complex, their owner-managers may contract with managerial specialists. These managers make major decisions in the owners' firm and are compensated on the basis of their decision-making skills. Research suggests that firms in which families own enough equity to have influence without major control tend to make the best strategic decisions.[18]

Without owner (shareholder) specialization in risk bearing and management specialization in decision making, a firm may be limited by its owners' abilities to simultaneously manage it and make effective strategic decisions relative to risk. Thus, the separation and specialization of ownership (risk bearing) and managerial control (decision making) should produce the highest returns for the firm's owners.

10-1a Agency Relationships

The separation between owners and managers creates an agency relationship. An agency relationship exists when one or more persons (the principal or principals) hire another person or persons (the agent or agents) as decision-making specialists to perform a service.[19] Thus, an **agency relationship** exists when one party delegates decision-making responsibility to a second party for compensation (see Figure 10.1).

In addition to shareholders and top-level managers, other examples of agency relationships are top managers who hire subsidiary managers, client firms engaging consultants, and the insured contracting with an insurer. Moreover, within organizations, an agency relationship exists between managers and their employees, as well as between top-level managers and the firm's owners.[20] However, in this chapter we focus on the agency relationship between the firm's owners (the principals) and top-level managers (the principals' agents) because these managers are responsible for formulating and implementing the firm's strategies, which have major effects on firm performance.[21]

The separation between ownership and managerial control can be problematic. Research evidence documents a variety of agency problems in the modern corporation.[22] Problems can surface because the principal and the agent have different interests and goals or because shareholders lack direct control of large publicly traded corporations. Problems also surface when an agent makes decisions that result in pursuing goals that conflict with those of the principals. Thus, the separation of ownership and control potentially allows divergent interests (between principals and agents) to occur, which can lead to managerial opportunism.

Managerial opportunism is the seeking of self-interest with guile (i.e., cunning or deceit).[23] Opportunism is both an attitude (i.e., an inclination) and a set of behaviors

An **agency relationship** exists when one party delegates decision-making responsibility to a second party for compensation.

Managerial opportunism is the seeking of self-interest with guile (i.e., cunning or deceit).

Figure 10.1 An Agency Relationship

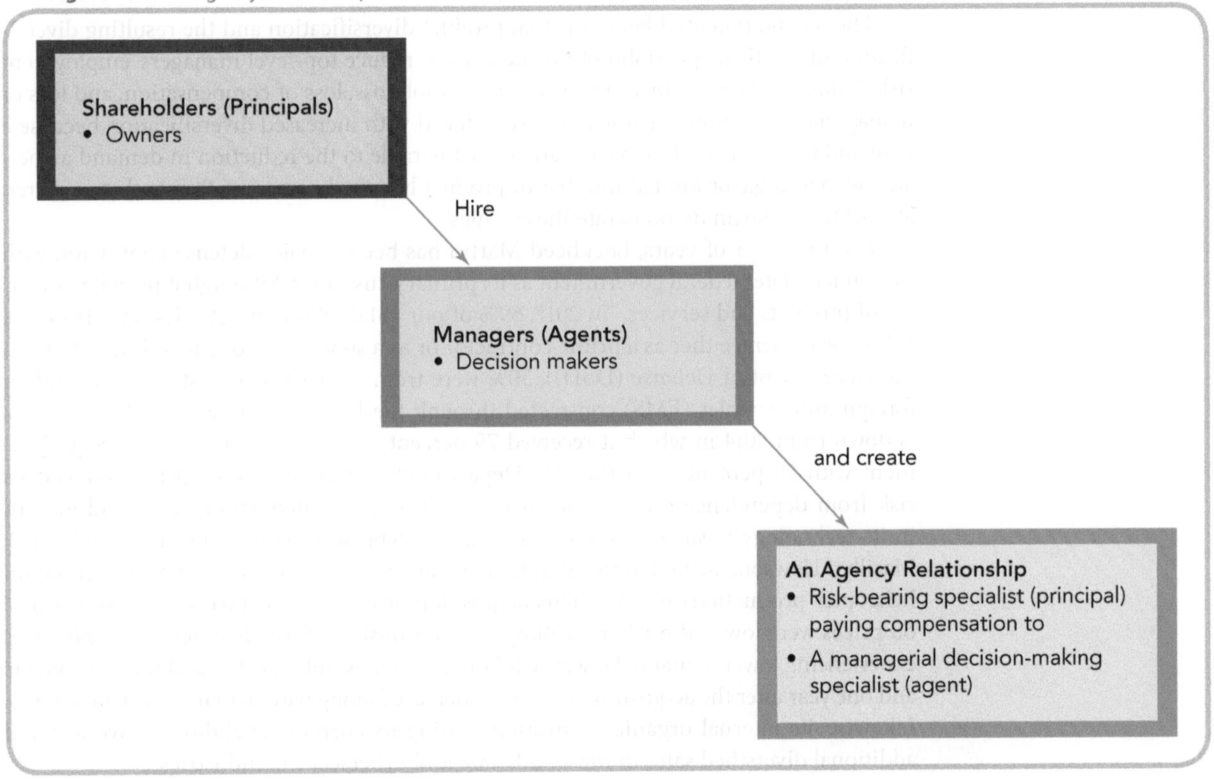

(i.e., specific acts of self-interest).[24] Principals do not know beforehand which agents will or will not act opportunistically. A top-level manager's reputation is an imperfect predictor; moreover, opportunistic behavior cannot be observed until it has occurred. Thus, principals establish governance and control mechanisms to prevent agents from acting opportunistically, even though only a few are likely to do so. Interestingly, research suggests that when CEOs feel constrained by governance mechanisms, they are more likely to seek external advice that, in turn, helps them make better strategic decisions.[25]

The agency relationship suggests that any time principals delegate decision-making responsibilities to agents, the opportunity for conflicts of interest exists. Top-level managers, for example, may make strategic decisions that maximize their personal welfare and minimize their personal risk.[26] Decisions such as these prevent maximizing shareholder wealth. Decisions regarding product diversification demonstrate this situation.

10-1b Product Diversification as an Example of an Agency Problem

As explained in Chapter 6, a corporate-level strategy to diversify the firm's product lines can enhance a firm's strategic competitiveness and increase its returns, both of which serve the interests of all stakeholders and certainly shareholders and top-level managers. However, product diversification can create two benefits for top-level managers that shareholders do not enjoy, meaning that they may prefer product diversification more than shareholders do.[27]

One reason managers prefer more diversification compared to shareholders is the fact that it usually increases the size of a firm and size is positively related to executive compensation. Diversification also increases the complexity of managing a firm and its network of businesses, possibly requiring additional managerial pay because of this complexity.[28] Thus, increased product diversification provides an opportunity for top-level managers to increase their compensation.[29]

The second potential benefit is that product diversification and the resulting diversification of the firm's portfolio of businesses can reduce top-level managers' employment risk. *Managerial employment risk* is the risk of job loss, loss of compensation, and loss of managerial reputation.[30] These risks are reduced with increased diversification because a firm and its upper-level managers are less vulnerable to the reduction in demand associated with a single or limited number of product lines or businesses. Events that occurred at Lockheed Martin demonstrate these issues.

For a number of years, Lockheed Martin has been a major defense contractor, with the United States federal government as its primary customer. Although it provides a variety of products and services, "in 2017, 69% of our $51.0 billion in net sales were from the U.S. Government, either as a prime contractor or as a subcontractor (including 58% from the Department of Defense (DoD)), 30% were from international customers (including foreign military sales (FMS) contracted through the U.S. Government)."[31] However, this is down from 2014 in which it received 79 percent of its revenue from the U.S. government with 59 percent from the U.S. Department of Defense alone. It has reduced its risk from dependence on a single customer, through related acquisitions and growth in its technology businesses such as a focus on cybersecurity. Lockheed Martin's CEO, Marillyn Hewson, facilitated the $9 billion acquisition of Sikorsky (primarily focused on helicopter production) in 2016. This acquisition at the time seemed expensive because oil prices were low and offshore drilling, a major business for helicopter companies, was experiencing lower demand. However, Sikorsky also has military demand for its products and one year after the acquisition oil prices increased along with demand for helicopters.[32] Likewise, its internal organic innovations (using its current capabilities) have fostered additional diversified sales in the health care and cybersecurity industries.

Free cash flow is the source of another potential agency problem. Calculated as operating cash flow minus capital expenditures, free cash flow represents the cash remaining after the firm has invested in all projects that have positive net present value within its current businesses.[33] Top-level managers may decide to invest free cash flow in product lines that are not associated with the firm's current lines of business to increase the firm's degree of diversification (as is currently being done at Lockheed Martin). However, when managers use free cash flow to diversify the firm in ways that do not have a strong possibility of creating additional value for shareholders, the firm can become overdiversified. Overdiversification is an example of self-serving and opportunistic managerial behavior. In contrast to managers, shareholders may prefer that free cash flow be distributed to them as dividends or stock buybacks, so they can control how the cash is invested.[34]

In Figure 10.2, Curve *S* shows shareholders' optimal level of diversification. As the firm's owners, shareholders seek the level of diversification that reduces the risk of the firm's total failure while simultaneously increasing its value by developing economies of scale and scope (see Chapter 6). Of the four corporate-level diversification strategies shown in Figure 10.2, shareholders likely prefer the diversified position noted by point *A* on Curve *S*—a position that is located between the dominant business and related-constrained diversification strategies. Of course, the optimum level of diversification owners seek varies from firm to firm.[35] Factors that affect shareholders' preferences include the firm's primary industry, the intensity of rivalry among competitors in that industry, the top management team's experience with implementing diversification strategies, and the firm's perceived expertise in the new business and its effects on other firm strategies, such as its entry into international markets.[36]

As is the case for principals, top-level managers—as agents—also seek an optimal level of diversification. Declining performance resulting from too much diversification increases the probability that external investors (representing the market for corporate control) will purchase a substantial percentage of or the entire firm for the purpose of controlling it. In fact, this situation is illustrated in the Strategic Focus on General

Figure 10.2 Manager and Shareholder Risk and Diversification

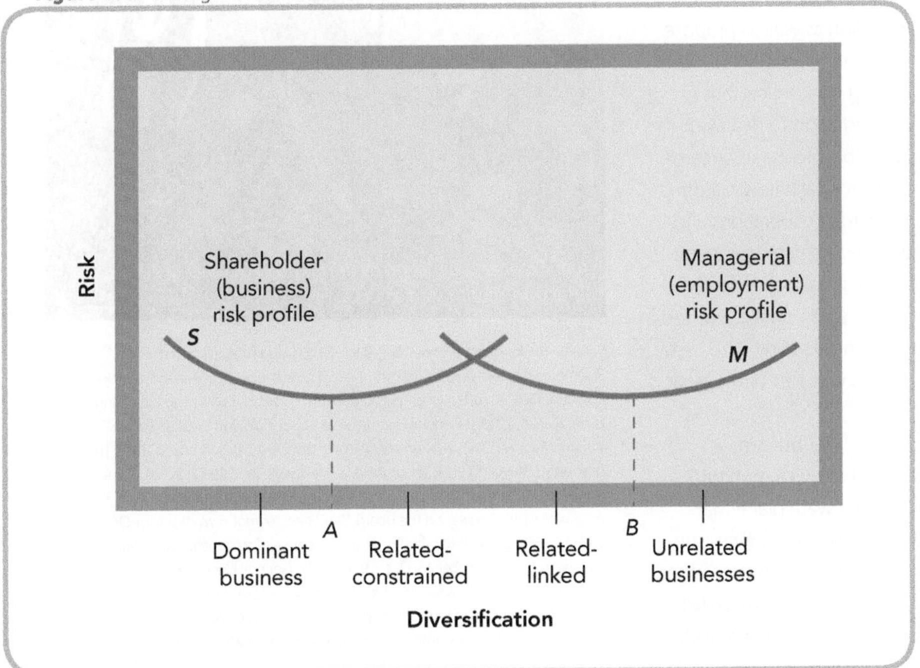

Strategic **Focus**

General Electric's Complex Diversification Strategy Makes Evaluation Difficult for Board Directors

As noted in Chapter 6, diversified firms can be complex, given the number of businesses a firm is trying to manage simultaneously. This is not only a difficult task for managers, but is more difficult for board directors, especially when they come from outside the firm. Outside directors largely have to depend on the analyses managers present, given the overall complexity of large diversified firms. Concerning General Electric, former CEO Jack Welch formed a large set of businesses in the 1980s and 1990s. Although his successor, Jeffery Immelt, largely dealt with the financial crisis and the divestiture of GE Capital, there were still significant problems from the excess diversification. In December 2016, the earnings reports started raising alarms. Nelson Peltz, from Trian Partners, had invested heavily in the firm in 2015. When this investment began to decrease in value in 2016, Trian and other activist shareholders forced CEO Jeffrey Immelt's dismissal, and John Flannery took over as CEO. Edward Garden of Trian Partners subsequently became a board member to watch over Trian's investment, which had shrunk to $1.7 billion from its original $2.5 billion in value.

In early 2018, as Flannery sought to overcome GEs performance difficulties, nine new board members were proposed on GEs proxy statement, which meant half of the board was targeted for replacement. Although there had already been significant restructuring under Immelt—including selling the majority of GE Capital, NBCUniversal, and GE's appliance business—Flannery announced that he would seek to sell more assets worth an additional $80 billion as well as propose layoffs and other cost improvements. In addition, GE had been paying a significant dividend and buying back shares, but much of this capital came from increased debt. To deal with this, Flannery has reduced the dividend payment and become more transparent with how GE uses its free cash flow. Garden's board seat gives Trian access to the board's deliberations and detailed financial results just as the 300,000-person company is conducting a strategic review of its business portfolio and deciding how to cut costs and spend its cash flow. GE also took a large $6 billion charge against its earnings in early 2018 associated with its insurance business, which was part of the legacy GE Capital business.

Apparently, along with the increased debt burden and this $6 billion charge, the board had failed to monitor other things carefully, including an extra private plane that Mr. Immelt used. Additionally, there were problems with earning calculations that the board failed to catch, so much so that GE had to restate its earnings from 2016 and 2017. These failings led to significant governance restructuring—particularly the replacement of the nine outside board members including an activist board member, Mr. Garden.

In late 2017, Flannery announced that GE would focus on three core segments, aviation, power and power distribution, and healthcare, going forward. One of the difficulties in restructuring the firm is that GE is saddled with $97.5 billion in debt. Furthermore, it has $31 billion in unfunded pension liabilities. To fund the debt and pension liabilities, GE needs substantial cash flow from its remaining businesses, making it difficult to sell all the assets Flannery is seeking to restructure. To deal with this dilemma GE has set up a new board committee focused on restructuring its portfolio and working through the legal ramifications. When you build a business such as General Electric, you build it for specific strategic reasons; breaking it up cannot be readily undone, despite shareholder wishes or demands.

In summary, General Electric is in a bind, largely because the board members seemed not to understand the complexity that the company's strategic leaders were pursuing. Because they missed these warning signs, they could not thereby shelter the firm from bad strategic acquisitions. More painful decisions are probably ahead.

Prashanth Vishwanathan/Bloomberg/Getty Images

John Flannery was let go by the board in October of 2018, after a 14-month stint as CEO.

Sources: R. Clough, N. Buhayar, & T. Black, 2018, Conglomerates don't work, *Bloomberg Businessweek*, February 5, 14-16; R. Messenbock, Y. Morieux, J. Backx, & D. Wunderlich, 2018, How complicated is your company? www.bcg.com, January 16; A. Narayanan, 2018, If General Electric breaks up should you breakup with GE stocks?, *Investors Business Daily*, www.investors.com, January 19; B. Sutherland, 2018, The slow ugly unraveling of GE, *Bloomberg Businessweek*, January 22, 30; 2017, The right mechanic? *Economist*, November 18, 54-55; T. Gryta, D. Benoit, J.S. Lublin, 2017, GE gives activist Trian a seat on the board, *Wall Street Journal*, www.wsj.com, October 9; T. Gryta, 2017, GE probed who knew about spare jet for Immelt, *Wall Street Journal*, www.wsj.com, December 13; D. Z. Morris, 2017, General Electric to lose 9 board members, *Fortune*, www.fortune.com, November 19; G. Roumeliotis, 2017, General Electric faces long road to pruning assets. www.reuters.com, November 13; L. Shen, 2017, Biggest breakup: General Electric, *Fortune*, www.fortune.com, December 20.

Electric, where Trian Partners bought a substantial portion of stock and ultimately won a board seat seeking to foster a more coherent strategy with narrower diversified scope.[37] If a firm is acquired, the employment risk for its top-level managers increases significantly. Furthermore, these managers' employment opportunities in the external managerial labor market (discussed in Chapter 12) are affected negatively by a firm's poor performance. Therefore, top-level managers prefer that the firms they lead be diversified. However, their preference is that the firm's diversification falls short of the point at which it increases their employment risk and reduces their employment opportunities.[38] Curve *M* in Figure 10.2 shows that top-level managers prefer higher levels of product diversification than do shareholders. Point *B* on Curve *M* represents where top-level managers might locate their perceived optimal level of diversification.

In general, shareholders prefer riskier strategies and more focused diversification. Shareholders reduce their risk by holding a diversified portfolio of investments. Alternatively, managers cannot balance their employment risk by working for a diverse portfolio of firms; therefore, managers may prefer a level of diversification that maximizes firm size and their compensation while also reducing their employment risk. Finding the appropriate level of diversification is difficult for managers. Research has shown that too much diversification can have negative effects on the firm's ability to create innovation (managers' unwillingness to take on higher risks). Alternatively, diversification that strategically fits the firm's capabilities can enhance its innovation output.[39] However, too much or inappropriate diversification can also divert managerial attention from other important firm activities such as corporate social responsibility.[40] Product diversification, therefore, is a potential agency problem that could result in principals incurring costs to control their agents' behaviors.

10-1c Agency Costs and Governance Mechanisms

The potential conflict between shareholders and top-level managers shown in Figure 10.2, coupled with the fact that principals cannot easily predict which managers might act opportunistically, demonstrates why principals establish governance mechanisms. However, the firm incurs costs when it uses one or more governance mechanisms. **Agency costs** are the sum of incentive costs, monitoring costs, enforcement costs, and individual financial losses incurred by principals because governance mechanisms cannot guarantee total compliance by the agent. Because monitoring activities within a firm is difficult, the principals' agency costs are larger in diversified firms given the additional complexity of diversification.[41]

In general, managerial interests may prevail when governance mechanisms are weak and therefore ineffective, such as in situations where managers have a significant amount of autonomy to make strategic decisions. If, however, the board of directors controls managerial autonomy, or if other strong governance mechanisms are used, the firm's strategies should better reflect stakeholders and certainly shareholders' interests.[42] For example, effective corporate governance may encourage managers to develop strategies that demonstrate a concern for the environment (i.e., "green strategies").[43]

In the recent past, observers of firms' governance practices have been concerned about more egregious behavior beyond mere ineffective corporate strategies, such as that discovered at Enron, WorldCom, and Volkswagen and the more recent actions by major financial institutions. Partly in response to these behaviors, the U.S. Congress enacted the Sarbanes-Oxley Act (SOX) in 2002 and passed the Dodd-Frank Wall Street Reform and Consumer Protection Act (Dodd-Frank) in mid-2010.

Because of these two acts, corporate governance mechanisms have received greater scrutiny.[44] While the implementation of SOX has been controversial to some, most believe that its use has led to generally positive outcomes in terms of protecting stakeholders

Agency costs are the sum of incentive costs, monitoring costs, enforcement costs, and individual financial losses incurred by principals because governance mechanisms cannot guarantee total compliance by the agent.

and certainly shareholders' interests. For example, Section 404 of SOX, which prescribes significant transparency improvement on internal controls associated with accounting and auditing, has arguably improved the internal auditing scrutiny (and thereby trust) in firms' financial reporting. Moreover, research suggests that internal controls associated with Section 404 increase shareholder value.[45] Nonetheless, some argue that the Act, especially Section 404, creates excessive costs for firms. In addition, a decrease in foreign firms listing on U.S. stock exchanges occurred at the same time as listing on foreign exchanges increased. In part, this shift may be because of the costs SOX generates for firms seeking to list on U.S. exchanges.

Dodd-Frank is recognized as the most sweeping set of financial regulatory reforms in the United States since the Great Depression. The Act is intended to align financial institutions' actions with society's interests. Dodd-Frank includes provisions related to the categories of consumer protection, systemic risk oversight, executive compensation, and capital requirements for banks. The Act creates a Financial Stability Oversight Council headed by the Treasury Secretary, establishes a new system for liquidation of certain financial companies, provides for a new framework to regulate derivatives, establishes new corporate governance requirements, and regulates credit rating agencies and securitizations. However, Congress has been seeking to pass relief for regional banks by lowering the capital requirements and requiring less obligations for big stress tests.[46]

More intensive application of governance mechanisms as mandated by legislation such as SOX and Dodd-Frank affects firms' choice of strategies. For example, more intense governance might find firms choosing to pursue fewer risky projects, possibly decreasing shareholder wealth as a result, although some research suggests that tighter governance associated with SOX regulation increases innovation, especially for firms with previously weaker governance.[47] Determining governance practices that strike an appropriate balance between protecting stakeholders' interests and allowing firms to implement strategies with some degree of risk is difficult.

Next, we explain the effects of the three internal governance mechanisms on managerial decisions regarding the firm's strategies.

10-2 Ownership Concentration

Ownership concentration is defined by the number of large-block shareholders and the total percentage of the firm's shares they own. **Large-block shareholders** typically own at least 5 percent of a company's issued shares. Ownership concentration as a governance mechanism has received considerable interest, because large-block shareholders are increasingly active in their demands that firms adopt effective governance mechanisms to control managerial decisions so that they will best represent owners' interests.[48] In recent years, the number of individuals who are large-block shareholders has declined. Institutional owners have replaced individuals as large-block shareholders.

In general, diffuse ownership (a large number of shareholders with small holdings and few, if any, large-block shareholders) produces weak monitoring of managers' decisions. One reason for this is that diffuse ownership makes it difficult for owners to effectively coordinate their actions. As noted earlier, diversification beyond the shareholders' optimum level can result from ineffective monitoring of managers' decisions. Higher levels of monitoring could encourage managers to avoid strategic decisions that harm shareholder value, such as too much diversification. Research evidence suggests that ownership concentration is associated with lower levels of firm product diversification.[49] Thus, with high degrees of ownership concentration, the probability is greater that managers' decisions will be designed to maximize shareholder value.[50] However,

Ownership concentration is defined by the number of large-block shareholders and the total percentage of the firm's shares they own.

Large-block shareholders typically own at least 5 percent of a company's issued shares.

the influence of large-block shareholders is mitigated to a degree in Europe by strong labor representation on boards of directors.[51]

As noted, ownership concentration influences decisions made about the strategies a firm will use and the value created by their use. In general, ownership concentration's influence on strategies and firm performance is positive. For example, when large-block shareholders have a high degree of wealth, they have power relative to minority shareholders to appropriate the firm's wealth; this is particularly the case when they are in managerial positions. Excessive appropriation at the expense of minority shareholders is somewhat common in emerging economy countries, where minority shareholder rights often are not as protected as they are in the United States. In fact, in some of these countries, state ownership of an equity stake (even minority ownership) can be used to control these potential problems.[52] The importance of boards of directors to mitigate excessive appropriation of minority shareholder value has been found in firms with strong family ownership, where family members have incentives to appropriate shareholder wealth, especially in the second generation after the founder has departed.[53] In general, family-controlled businesses will outperform nonfamily-controlled businesses, especially smaller and private firms, because of the importance of enhancing the family's wealth and maintaining the family legacy.[54] However, families often try to balance the pursuit of economic and noneconomic objectives such that they sometimes may be moderately risk averse (thereby influencing their innovative output).[55]

10-2a The Increasing Influence of Institutional Owners

A classic work published in the 1930s argued that a separation of ownership and control had come to characterize the "modern" corporation.[56] This change occurred primarily because growth prevented founder-owners from maintaining their dual positions in what were increasingly complex companies. More recently, another shift has occurred: ownership of many modern corporations is now concentrated in the hands of institutional investors rather than individual shareholders.[57]

Institutional owners are financial institutions, such as mutual funds and pension funds, that control large-block shareholder positions. Because of their prominent ownership positions, institutional owners, as large-block shareholders, have the potential to be a powerful governance mechanism. Estimates of the amount of equity in U.S. firms held by institutional owners range from 60 to 75 percent. In particular pension funds are critical drivers of growth and economic activity in the United States because they are one of the most significant sources of long-term, patient capital.[58]

These percentages suggest that as investors, institutional owners have both the size and the incentive to discipline ineffective top-level managers and that they can significantly influence a firm's choice of strategies and strategic decisions.[59] As the Opening Case indicates, institutional and other large-block shareholders are becoming more active in their efforts to influence a corporation's strategic decisions, unless they have a business relationship with the firm. Initially, these shareholder activists and institutional investors concentrated on the performance and accountability of CEOs and contributed to the dismissal of a number of them. More recently, activists have targeted the actions of boards more directly via proxy vote proposals that are intended to give shareholders more decision rights because they believe board processes have been ineffective.[60] A rule approved by the SEC allowing large shareholders (owning 1 to 5 percent of a company's stock) to nominate up to 25 percent of a company's board of directors enhances shareholders' decision rights.[61]

Institutional owners are financial institutions, such as mutual funds and pension funds, that control large-block shareholder positions.

The institutional investor BlackRock, Inc. is the largest manager of financial assets in the world, with just under $6 trillion invested and holdings in most of the largest global corporations. Interestingly, it was once described as a "silent giant" because it did not engage in activism. However, recently the silent giant has been awakened, as it has begun asking more questions of the firms in which it holds significant investments. Most of its actions are "behind the scenes," only voting against a director or a company proposal when its unobtrusive actions have failed to change the firm's behavior. BlackRock has become more "confrontational" in order to ensure the value of its investments, and some wish that it would become even more active because of the power of its large equity holdings.[62] To date, research suggests that institutional activism may not have a strong direct effect on firm performance, but it may indirectly influence a targeted firm's strategic decisions, including those concerned with social issues. Thus, to some degree at least, institutional activism has the potential to discipline managers and to enhance the likelihood of a firm taking future actions that are not only in shareholders' best interests but also those of all stakeholders including society at large.[63]

10-3 Board of Directors

Shareholders elect the members of a firm's board of directors. The **board of directors** is a group of elected individuals whose primary responsibility is to act in the owners' best interests by formally monitoring and controlling the firm's top-level managers.[64]

Those elected to a firm's board of directors are expected to oversee managers and to ensure that the corporation operates in ways that will best serve stakeholders' interests, and particularly the owners' interests. Helping board members reach their expected objectives are their powers to direct the affairs of the organization and reward and discipline top-level managers.

Board of directors is a group of elected individuals whose primary responsibility is to act in the owners' best interests by formally monitoring and controlling the firm's top level managers.

Though important to all shareholders, a firm's individual shareholders with small ownership percentages are very dependent on the board of directors to represent their interests. Unfortunately, evidence suggests that boards have not been highly effective in monitoring and controlling top-level managers' decisions and subsequent actions.[65]

Because of their relatively ineffective performance and in light of the recent financial crisis, boards are experiencing increasing pressure from shareholders, lawmakers, and regulators to become more forceful in their oversight role to prevent top-level managers from acting in their own best interests. Moreover, in addition to their monitoring role, board members increasingly are expected to provide resources to the firms they serve. These resources include their personal knowledge and expertise and their relationships with a wide variety of organizations.[66]

Peter Foley/Bloomberg/Getty Images

Larry Fink, CEO of BlackRock, the largest mutual fund provider, has suggested that managers need to focus on long-term strategy rather than responding to short-term trader proposals.

Generally, board members (often called directors) are classified into one of three groups (see Table 10.1). *Insiders* are active top-level managers in the company who are elected to the board because they are a source of information about the firm's day-to-day operations.[67] *Related outsiders* have some relationship with the firm, contractual or otherwise, that may create questions about their independence, but these individuals are not involved with the corporation's day-to-day activities. *Outsiders*

Table 10.1 Classification of Board of Directors' Members

Insiders
• **The firm's CEO and other top-level managers**
Related outsiders
• **Individuals not involved with the firm's day-to-day operations, but who have a relationship with the company**
Outsiders
• **Individuals who are independent of the firm in terms of day-to-day operations and other relationships**

provide independent counsel to the firm and may hold top-level managerial positions in other companies or may have been elected to the board prior to the beginning of the current CEO's tenure.[68]

Historically, inside managers dominated a firm's board of directors. A widely accepted view is that a board with a significant percentage of its membership from the firm's top-level managers provides relatively weak monitoring and control of managerial decisions.[69] With weak board monitoring, managers sometimes use their power to select and compensate directors and exploit their personal ties with them. In response to the SEC's proposal, in 1984 the New York Stock Exchange (NYSE) implemented a rule requiring outside directors to head the audit committee. Subsequently, after SOX was passed, other new rules required that independent outsider directors lead important committees such as the audit, compensation, and nomination committees.[70] Policies of the NYSE now require companies to maintain boards of directors that are composed of a majority of outside independent directors and to maintain full independent audit committees. Thus, additional scrutiny of corporate governance practices is resulting in a significant amount of attention being devoted to finding ways to recruit quality independent directors and to encourage boards to take actions that fully represent shareholders' best interests.[71]

Critics advocate reforms to ensure that independent outside directors are a significant majority of a board's total membership; research suggests this has been accomplished.[72] However, others argue that having outside directors is not enough to resolve the problems in that CEO power can strongly influence a board's decision. One proposal to reduce the power of the CEO is to separate the chair's role and the CEO's role on the board so that the same person does not hold both positions.[73] A situation in which an individual holds both the CEO and chair of the board title is called *CEO duality*. As is shown in the CEO duality at JPMorgan Chase with Jamie Dimon, it is often very difficult to separate the CEO and chair positions after they have been given to one person.[74] Unfortunately, having a board that actively monitors top-level managers' decisions and actions does not ensure high performance. The value that the directors bring to the company also influences the outcomes. For example, boards with members having significant relevant experience and knowledge are the most likely to help the firm formulate and implement effective strategies.[75]

Alternatively, having a large number of outside board members can also create some problems. For example, because outsiders typically do not have contact with the firm's day-to-day operations and do not have ready access to detailed information about managers and their skills, they may lack the insights required to fully and effectively evaluate their decisions and initiatives, especially when they are busy serving on multiple boards.[76] Outsiders can, however, obtain valuable information through frequent interactions with inside board members and during board meetings to enhance their understanding of managers and their decisions.

Because they work with and lead the firm daily, insiders have access to information that facilitates forming and implementing appropriate strategies. Accordingly, some evidence suggests that boards with a critical mass of insiders typically are better informed about intended strategic initiatives, the reasons for the initiatives, and the outcomes expected from pursuing them.[77] Without this type of information, outsider-dominated boards may emphasize financial, as opposed to strategic, controls to gather performance information to evaluate managers' and business units' performances. A virtually exclusive reliance on financial evaluations shifts risk to top-level managers who, in turn, may make decisions to maximize their interests and reduce their employment risk. Reducing investments in R&D, further diversifying the firm, and pursuing higher levels of compensation are some of the results of managers' actions to reach the financial goals set by outsider-dominated boards.[78] Additionally, boards can make mistakes in strategic decisions because of poor decision processes, and in CEO succession decisions because of the lack of important information about candidates as well as the firm's specific needs. Overall, knowledgeable and balanced boards are likely to be the most effective over time.[79]

10-3a Enhancing the Effectiveness of the Board of Directors

Because of the importance of boards of directors in corporate governance and as a result of increased scrutiny from shareholders—in particular, large institutional investors—the performances of individual board members and of entire boards are being evaluated more formally and with greater intensity.[80] The demand for greater accountability and improved performance is stimulating many boards to voluntarily make changes. Among these changes are:

1. increases in the diversity of the backgrounds of board members (e.g., a greater number of directors from public service, academic, and scientific settings; a greater percentage of ethnic minorities and women; and members from different countries on boards of U.S. firms);
2. the strengthening of internal management and accounting control systems;
3. establishing and consistently using formal processes to evaluate board members' performance;
4. modifying the compensation of directors, especially reducing or eliminating stock options as a part of their package; and
5. creating the "lead director" role[81] that has strong powers with regard to the board agenda and oversight of non-management board member activities.

An increase in the board's involvement with a firm's strategic decision-making processes creates the need for effective collaboration between board members and top-level managers. Some argue that improving the processes used by boards to make decisions and monitor managers and firm outcomes is important for board effectiveness.[82] Moreover, because of the increased pressure from owners and the potential conflict among board members, procedures are necessary to help boards function effectively while seeking to discharge their responsibilities.

Increasingly, outside directors are being required to own significant equity stakes as a prerequisite to holding a board seat. In fact, some research suggests that firms perform better if outside directors have such a stake; the trend is toward higher pay for directors with more stock ownership, but with fewer stock options. One study found that director stock ownership leads to better firm acquisition outcomes.[83] However, other research suggests that too much ownership can lead to lower independence for board members.[84] In addition, other research suggests that diverse boards help firms make more effective strategic decisions and perform better over time.[85] Although questions remain about whether more independent and diverse boards enhance board effectiveness, the trends for greater independence and increasing diversity among board members are likely to continue.

10-3b Executive Compensation

The compensation of top-level managers, and especially of CEOs, generates a great deal of interest and strongly held opinions. Some believe that top-management team members, and certainly CEOs, have a great deal of responsibility for a firm's performance and that they should be rewarded accordingly.[86] Others conclude that these individuals (and again, especially CEOs) are greatly overpaid and that their compensation is not as strongly related to firm performance as should be the case.[87] One of the three internal governance mechanisms attempts to deal with these issues. Specifically, **executive compensation** is a governance mechanism that seeks to align the interests of managers and owners through salaries, bonuses, and long-term incentives such as stock awards and options.

Long-term incentive plans (typically involving stock options and stock awards) are an increasingly important part of compensation packages for top-level managers, especially those leading U.S. firms. Theoretically, using long-term incentives facilitates the firm's efforts (through the board of directors' pay-related decisions) to avoid potential agency problems by linking managerial compensation to the wealth of common shareholders.[88] Effectively designed long-term incentive plans have the potential to prevent large-block stockholders (e.g., institutional investors) from pressing for changes in the composition of the board of directors and the top-management team because they assume that, when exercised, the plans will ensure that top-level managers will act in shareholders' best interests. Additionally, shareholders typically assume that top-level managers' pay and the firm's performance are more properly aligned when outsiders are the dominant block of a board's membership. Research results suggesting that fraudulent behavior can be associated with stock option incentives, such as earnings manipulation,[89] demonstrate the importance of the firm's board of directors (as a governance mechanism) actively monitoring the use of executive compensation as a governance mechanism.

Effectively using executive compensation as a governance mechanism is particularly challenging for firms implementing international strategies. For example, the interests of the owners of multinational corporations may be best served by less uniformity in the firm's foreign subsidiaries' compensation plans.[90] Developing an array of unique compensation plans requires additional monitoring, potentially increasing the firm's agency costs. Importantly, pay levels vary by regions of the world. For example, managerial pay is highest in the U.S. and much lower in Asia. Historically, compensation for top-level managers has been lower in India partly because many of the largest firms have strong family ownership and control.[91] Also, acquiring firms and participating in joint ventures in other countries increases the complexity associated with a board of directors' efforts to use executive compensation as an effective internal corporate governance mechanism.[92]

10-3c The Effectiveness of Executive Compensation

As an internal governance mechanism, executive compensation—especially long-term incentive compensation—is complicated, for several reasons. First, the strategic decisions top-level managers make are complex and nonroutine, meaning that direct supervision (even by the firm's board of directors) is likely to be ineffective as a means of judging the quality of their decisions. The result is a tendency to link top-level managers' compensation to outcomes the board can easily evaluate, such as the firm's financial performance. This leads to a second issue in that, typically, the effects of top-level managers' decisions are stronger on the firm's long-term performance than its short-term performance. This reality makes it difficult to assess the effects of their decisions on a regular basis (e.g., annually). Third, a number of other factors affect a

Executive compensation is a governance mechanism that seeks to align the interests of managers and owners through salaries, bonuses, and long-term incentives such as stock awards and options.

firm's performance besides top-level managerial decisions and behavior. Unpredictable changes in segments (economic, demographic, political/legal, etc.) in the firm's general environment (see Chapter 2) make it difficult to separate the effects of top-level managers' decisions and the effects (both positive and negative) of changes in the firm's external environment on the firm's performance.

Properly designed and used incentive compensation plans for top-level managers may increase the value of a firm in line with shareholder expectations, but such plans are subject to managerial manipulation.[93] Additionally, annual bonuses may provide incentives to pursue short-run objectives at the expense of the firm's long-term interests. Although long-term, performance-based incentives may reduce the temptation to underinvest in the short run, they increase executive exposure to risks associated with uncontrollable events, such as market fluctuations and industry decline. The longer term the focus of incentive compensation, the greater are the long-term risks top-level managers bear. Also, because long-term incentives tie a manager's overall wealth to the firm in a way that is inflexible, such incentives and ownership may not be valued as highly by a manager as by outside investors who have the opportunity to diversify their wealth in a number of other financial investments.[94] Thus, firms may have to overcompensate for managers using long-term incentives.[95] The media often focuses on the size of the CEO compensation package, especially if it is exceptionally large, and compares it to the pay of the average worker.

Much of the size of CEO pay has been driven by stock options and long-term incentives. Even though some stock option-based compensation plans are well designed with option strike prices substantially higher than current stock prices (strike prices are the prices at which the option holder can sell the underlying security), some have been developed for the primary purpose of giving executives more compensation. Research of stock option repricing, where the strike price value of the option has been lowered from its original position, suggests that action is taken more frequently in high-risk situations. However, repricing also happens when firm performance is poor, to restore the incentive effect for the option. Evidence also suggests that politics are often involved, which has resulted in "option backdating."[96] While this evidence shows that no internal governance mechanism is perfect, some compensation plans accomplish their purpose. For example, recent research suggests that long-term pay designed to encourage managers to be environmentally friendly has been linked to higher success in preventing pollution.[97]

As the Strategic Focus suggests, this internal governance mechanism is likely to continue receiving a great deal of scrutiny in the years to come. When designed properly and used effectively, each of the three internal governance mechanisms can contribute positively to the firm operating in ways that best serve stakeholders and especially shareholders' interests. By the same token, because none of the three mechanisms are perfect in design or execution, the market for corporate control, an external governance mechanism, is sometimes needed.

10-4 Market for Corporate Control

The **market for corporate control** is an external governance mechanism that is active when a firm's internal governance mechanisms fail.[98] The market for corporate control is composed of individuals and firms that buy ownership positions in or purchase all of potentially undervalued corporations typically for the purpose of forming new divisions in established companies or merging two previously separate firms. Because the top-level managers are assumed to be responsible for the undervalued firm's poor performance, they are usually replaced. An effective market for corporate control ensures that ineffective and/or opportunistic top-level managers are disciplined.[99]

Strategic Focus

Has More Governance Scrutiny Made Large CEO Compensation Packages More Reasonable?

This question often circulates in the media regarding the large compensation packages that CEOs receive as leaders of large publicly traded firms. Reporters in the media are often focused on the growing inequality between the top executives' pay and the average wages of U.S. workers. In 1983, average pay for leaders of the six largest banks was 40 times the average of all U.S. workers, while the average pay for leaders of the largest Fortune 500 companies was about 38 times. However, CEO compensation has grown significantly compared to the average worker, and now the median CEO-to-median-worker pay ratio stands at 140 to 1. It is easy to see why the media would focus on this issue.

Moreover, because of the oversized compensation packages, the 2010 Dodd-Frank Act requires that public companies disclose their CEO-to-median-employee pay ratio in their annual proxy statement. But there are huge differences in this ratio even among companies in the same industry. For example, Marathon Corporation, the second-largest oil refiner in the United States, paid its CEO, Gary Heminger, $19.7 million in 2017. His salary is 900 times that of the average employee at about $21,000 per year. However, Marathon runs Speedway retail gas stations with many part-time and low-wage employees; if the Speedway workers are excluded employee median pay at Marathon shoots up to nearly $126,000 per year, which translates into a CEO-to-worker pay ratio of 156 to 1, much closer to the overall median. As noted, there are large differences within sectors. "Processed-food giant Kraft Heinz Co. last year paid its CEO $4.2 million, about 91 times its median worker's $46,000 compensation. Kellogg Co., a smaller food maker, paid its CEO an annualized $7.3 million, or 183 times its median employee, who was paid about $40,000."

Along with Dodd Frank, the Security and Exchange Commission has given shareholders the opportunity to vote on the compensation the CEO receives; the so-called "Say on Pay" regulation. This has given more ownership scrutiny to top executive compensation. As such, board members can be disciplined and even lose board seats if the compensation plan receives a negative vote. Of course, as explained in this chapter, CEO compensation is more complex than might be deduced from media headlines. However, because of the increased transparency, firms and boards of directors making compensation decisions for CEOs are more sensitive to issues associated with executive compensation. Notwithstanding the complexities, CEO compensation continues to rise, although not as much as in the pre-financial crisis period, primarily due to the emphasis on long-term incentive compensation versus cash compensation (salary and annual bonus).

Research from the finance discipline finds that the make-up of the pay package that most top executives receive has been changing. Instead of an over-emphasis on stock options, top executives have been receiving compensation that is based on restricted stock ownership, which cannot be realized unless they meet significant performance targets over time. As such, research finds that managers are taking much more measured risks now than before, with far less of the oversized risk-taking that can result in disastrous consequences for a large firm.

Christopher Goodney/Bloomberg/Getty Images

Gary Heminger, CEO of Marathon, earns a salary which is 156 times that of the average employee, partly because the firm has a lot of low wage part-time employees.

In summary, executive compensation is a complex issue that cannot be simply determined by the overall size of the package. Although executive compensation has grown dramatically, there are both legitimate and illegitimate reasons for such huge pay packages. Each case needs to be examined closely. However, the perception will certainly linger that top management executive compensation relative to the average worker has added to the inequality in our society. As such, care should be taken to manage this issue from a policy point of view. Managerial human capital should be rewarded for its capability and the value it creates, but lower-level workers and their human capital should also have opportunities to make progress.

Sources: K. Bouslah, J. Liñares-Zegarra, B. M'Zali, & B. Scholtens, 2018, CEO risk-taking incentives and socially irresponsible activities, *British Accounting Review*, 50: 76–92; T. Francis & V. Fuhrmans, 2018, Are you underpaid? In a first, U.S. firms reveal how much they pay workers, *Wall Street Journal*, www.wsj.com, March 11; T. Francis & V. Fuhrmans, 2018, Median CEO pay hit record of nearly $12 million in 2017, juiced by markets, *Wall Street Journal*, www.wsj.com, March 21; B. Tuttle, 2018, This CEO makes 900 times more than his typical employee, *Money*, www.time.com/money, March 12; A. Gande & S. Kalpathy, 2017, CEO compensation and risk-taking at financial firms: Evidence from U.S. federal loan assistance, *Journal of Corporate Finance*, 47: 131–150; M. Grosse, S. Kean, & T. Scott, 2017, Shareholder say on pay and CEO compensation: Three strikes and the board is out. *Accounting & Finance*, 57(3): 701–725; K. Shue & R. R. Townsend, 2017, Growth through rigidity: An explanation for the rise in CEO pay, *Journal of Financial Economics*, 123: 1–21; H. Wang, S. Zhao, & G. Chen, 2017, Firm-specific knowledge assets and employment arrangements: Evidence from CEO compensation design and CEO dismissal, *Strategic Management Journal*, 38(9): 1875–1894; T. Greckhamer, 2016, CEO compensation in relation to worker compensation across countries: The configurational impact of country-level institutions, *Strategic Management Journal*, 37(4): 793–815.

Commonly, target firm managers and board members are sensitive about takeover bids emanating from the market for corporate control, since being a target suggests that they have been ineffective in fulfilling their responsibilities. For top-level managers, a board's decision to accept an acquiring firm's offer typically finds them losing their jobs because the acquirer usually wants different people to lead the firm. At the same time, rejection of an offer also increases the risk of job loss for top-level managers because the pressure from the board and shareholders for them to improve the firm's performance becomes substantial. For example, as noted in Chapter 7, Qualcomm was able to escape the hostile takeover attempt of Broadcom. But Qualcomm shareholders now have higher expectations for improved Qualcomm performance because the stock price offered was higher under the takeover bid than after the deal was disapproved by regulators.[100]

As illustrated in the Opening Case, activist investors with significant funding from institutional investors are often the head of the spear when it comes to the market for corporate control. Activist firms have enough funding to challenging large firms such as DuPont, Proctor & Gamble (P&G), Nestlé, General Electric, and Lowe's among others.[101]

In general, activist pension funds (as institutional investors and as an internal governance mechanism) are reactive in nature, taking actions when they conclude that a firm is underperforming. In contrast, activist hedge funds (as part of the market for corporate control) are proactive; they identify firms whose performance could be improved and then invest in them.[102] For example in the Opening Case, Carl Icahn, a famous activist investor, held 6.7 percent in Newell Brands and in a settlement was allowed four board seats in addition to appointing a new board chair. Starboard, a hedge fund allied with Icahn, is going further and trying to oust the remaining board members and replace the CEO.[103]

Another possibility is suggested by research results—namely, that as a governance mechanism, investors sometimes use the market for corporate control to take an ownership position in firms that are performing well.[104] A study of active corporate raiders in the 1980s showed that takeover attempts often were focused on above-average-performance firms in an industry.[105] This work and other recent research suggest that the market for corporate control is an imperfect governance mechanism.[106] Actually, mergers and acquisitions are highly complex strategic actions with many purposes and potential outcomes. As discussed in Chapter 7, some are successful and many are not—even when they have potential to do well—because implementation challenges when integrating two diverse firms can limit their ability to realize their potential.[107]

The **market for corporate control** is an external governance mechanism that is active when a firm's internal governance mechanisms fail.

In summary, the market for corporate control is a blunt instrument for corporate governance; nonetheless, this governance mechanism does have the potential to represent shareholders' best interests. Accordingly, top-level managers want to lead their firms in ways that make disciplining by activists outside the company unnecessary and/or inappropriate.

There are a number of defense tactics top-level managers can use to fend off a takeover attempt. Managers leading a target firm that is performing well are almost certain to try to thwart the takeover attempt. Even in instances when the target firm is underperforming its peers, managers might use defense tactics to protect their own interests. In general, managers' use of defense tactics is considered to be self-serving in nature.

10-4a Managerial Defense Tactics

In the majority of cases, hostile takeovers are the principal means by which the market for corporate control is activated. A *hostile takeover* is an acquisition of a target company by an acquiring firm that is accomplished "not by coming to an agreement with the target company's management but by going directly to the company's shareholders or fighting to replace management in order to get the acquisition approved."[108]

Firms targeted for a hostile takeover may use multiple defense tactics to fend off the takeover attempt. Increased use of the market for corporate control has enhanced the sophistication and variety of managerial defense tactics that are used in takeovers.

Because the market for corporate control tends to increase risk for managers, managerial pay may be augmented indirectly through golden parachutes (where a CEO can receive up to three years' salary if his or her firm is taken over). Golden parachutes, similar to most other defense tactics, are controversial. Another takeover defense strategy is traditionally known as a "poison pill." This strategy usually allows shareholders (other than the acquirer) to convert "shareholders' rights" into a large number of common shares if an individual or company acquires more than a set amount of the target firm's stock (typically 10 to 20 percent). Increasing the total number of outstanding shares dilutes the potential acquirer's existing stake. This means that, to maintain or expand its ownership position, the potential acquirer must buy additional shares at premium prices, increasing the potential acquirer's costs. Some firms amend the corporate charter so board member elections are staggered, resulting in only one third of members being up for reelection each year. Research shows that this results in reduced vulnerability to hostile takeovers but also provides for better long-term investments.[109] Additional takeover defense strategies are presented in Table 10.2.

Most institutional investors oppose the use of defense tactics because such defenses are generally seen as a way to entrench top managers in their positions.[110] Many institutional investors also oppose severance packages (golden parachutes), and the opposition is increasing significantly in Europe as well.[111] However, an advantage to severance packages is that they may encourage top-level managers to accept takeover bids with the potential to best serve shareholders' interest.[112] Alternatively, research results show that using takeover defenses reduces the amount of pressure managers feel to seek short-term performance gains, resulting in them concentrating on developing strategies with a longer time horizon and a high probability of serving stakeholders' interests. Such firms are more likely to invest in and develop innovation; when they do so, the firm's market value increases, thereby rewarding shareholders.[113]

An awareness on the part of top-level managers about the existence of external investors in the form of individuals (e.g., Carl Icahn) and groups (e.g., hedge funds) often positively influences them to align their interests with those of the firm's stakeholders, especially the shareholders. Moreover, when active as an external governance mechanism, the market for corporate control has brought about significant changes in many firms' strategies and, when used appropriately, has served shareholders' interests. Of course, the goal is to have the managers develop the psychological ownership of principals.[114] However, such sense of ownership can be taken too far such that narcissistic (i.e., egotistical) top executives can feel that they are personally central to the identity of the firm.[115]

Table 10.2 Hostile Takeover Defense Strategies

Defense strategy	Success as a strategy	Effects on shareholder wealth
Capital structure change: Dilution of the target firm's stock, making it more costly for an acquiring firm to continue purchasing the target's shares. Employee stock option plans (ESOPs), recapitalization, issuance of additional debt, and share buybacks are actions associated with this strategy.	Medium	Inconclusive
Corporate charter amendment: An amendment to the target firm's charter for the purpose of staggering the elections of members to its board of directors so that all are not elected during the same year. This change to the firm's charter prevents a potential acquirer from installing a completely new board in a single year.	Very low	Negative to Negligible
Golden parachute: A lump-sum payment of cash that is given to one or more top-level managers when the firm is acquired in a takeover bid.	Low	Negligible
Greenmail: The repurchase of the target firm's shares of stock that were obtained by the acquiring firm at a premium in exchange for an agreement that the acquirer will no longer target the company for takeover.	Medium	Negative
Litigation: Lawsuits that help the target firm stall hostile takeover attempts. Antitrust charges and inadequate disclosure are examples of the grounds on which the target firm could file.	Low	Positive
Poison pill: An action the target firm takes to make its stock less attractive to a potential acquirer.	High	Positive
Standstill agreement: A contract between the target firm and the potential acquirer specifying that the acquirer will not purchase additional shares of the target firm for a specified period of time in exchange for a fee paid by the target firm.	Low	Negative

Sources: Y. Amihud & S. Stoyanov, 2017, Do staggered boards harm shareholders? *Journal of Financial Economics*, 123: 432–439; S. Bhojraj, P. Sengupta, & S. Zhang, 2017, Takeover defenses: Entrenchment and efficiency, *Journal of Accounting & Economics*, 63: 142–160; A. Cohen & C. C. Wang, 2017, Reexamining staggered boards and shareholder value, *Journal of Financial Economics*, 125(3): 637–647; J. M. Karpoff, R. J. Schonlau, & E. W. Wehrly, 2017, Do takeover defense indices measure takeover deterrence? *Review of Financial Studies*, 30(7): 2359–2412; H. Wang, S. Zhao, & J. He, 2016, Increase in takeover protection and firm knowledge accumulation strategy, *Strategic Management Journal*, 37(12): 2393-2412; L. Guo, P. Lach, & S. Mobbs, 2015, Tradeoffs between internal and external governance: Evidence from exogenous regulatory shocks. *Financial Management*, 44: 81–114; H. Sapra, A. Subramanian, & K. V. Subramanian, 2014, Corporate governance and innovation: Theory and evidence, *Journal of Financial & Quantitative Analysis*, 49: 957–1003; M. Straska & G. Waller, 2014, Antitakeover provisions and shareholder wealth: A survey of the literature, *Journal of Financial & Quantitative Analysis*, 49: 1–32; R. Campbell, C. Ghosh, M. Petrova, & C. F. Sirmans, 2011, Corporate governance and performance in the market for corporate control: The case of REITS, *Journal of Real Estate Finance & Economics*, 42: 451–480; M. Ryngaert & R. Scholten, 2010, Have changing takeover defense rules and strategies entrenched management and damaged shareholders? The case of defeated takeover bids, *Journal of Corporate Finance*, 16: 16–37; N. Ruiz-Mallorqui & D. J. Santana-Martin, 2009, Ultimate institutional owner and takeover defenses in the controlling versus minority shareholders context, *Corporate Governance: An International Review*, 17: 238–254; J. A. Pearce II & R. B. Robinson, Jr., 2004, Hostile takeover defenses that maximize shareholder wealth, *Business Horizons*, 47(5): 15–24.

10-5 International Corporate Governance

Corporate governance is an increasingly important issue in economies around the world, including emerging economies. Globalization in trade, investments, and equity markets increases the potential value of firms throughout the world using similar mechanisms to govern corporate activities. Moreover, because of globalization, major companies want to attract foreign investment. For this to happen, foreign investors must be confident that adequate corporate governance mechanisms are in place to protect their investments.

Although globalization is stimulating an increase in the intensity of efforts to improve corporate governance and potentially to reduce the variation in regions' and nations' governance systems,[116] the reality remains that different nations do have different governance systems in place. Recognizing and understanding differences in various countries' governance systems, as well as changes taking place within those systems, improves the likelihood a firm will be able to compete successfully in the international markets it chooses to enter. Next, to highlight the general issues of differences and changes taking place in governance systems, we discuss corporate governance practices in two developed economies (Germany and Japan) and in the emerging economy of China.

10-5a Corporate Governance in Germany and Japan

In many private German firms, the owner and manager may be the same individual. In these instances, agency problems are not as prevalent.[117] Even in publicly traded German corporations, a single shareholder is often dominant, although this is changing. Thus, the concentration of ownership is an important means of corporate governance in Germany, as it is in the United States.[118]

Historically, banks occupied the center of the German corporate governance system. This is the case in other European countries as well, such as Italy and France. As lenders, banks become major shareholders when companies they financed seek funding on the stock market or default on loans. This is not the case in the United States because of the Glass Stiegel Act banning bank ownership of common stocks. Although the stakes are usually less than 10 percent, banks can hold a single ownership position up to, but not exceeding 15 percent of the bank's capital. Although shareholders can tell banks how to vote their ownership position, they generally do not do so. The banks monitor and control managers, both as lenders and as shareholders, by electing representatives to supervisory boards.

German firms with more than 2,000 employees are required to have a two-tiered board structure that places the responsibility for monitoring and controlling managerial (or supervisory) decisions and actions in the hands of a separate group.[119] All the functions of strategy and management are the responsibility of the management board (the Vorstand); however, appointment to the Vorstand is the responsibility of the supervisory tier (the Aufsichtsrat). Employees, union members, and shareholders appoint members to the Aufsichtsrat. Proponents of the German structure suggest that it helps prevent corporate wrongdoing and rash decisions by "dictatorial CEOs." However, critics maintain that it slows decision making and often ties a CEO's hands. The corporate governance practices in Germany make it difficult to restructure companies as quickly as can be done in the United States. Because of the role of local government (through the board structure) and the power of banks in Germany's corporate governance structure, private shareholders rarely have major ownership positions in German firms. Additionally, there is a significant amount of cross-shareholdings among firms, which makes takeovers more difficult.[120] However, large institutional investors, such as pension funds (outside of banks and insurance companies), are also relatively insignificant owners of corporate stock. Thus, at least historically, German executives generally have not been dedicated to maximizing shareholder wealth to the degree that is the case for top-level managers in the United States and United Kingdom.[121]

However, corporate governance practices used in Germany have been changing in recent years. A manifestation of these changes is that a number of German firms are gravitating toward U.S. governance mechanisms. Recent research suggests that the traditional system in Germany produced some agency costs because of a lack of external ownership power. Interestingly, German firms with listings on U.S. stock exchanges have increasingly adopted executive stock option compensation as a long-term incentive pay policy.[122]

The concepts of obligation, family, and consensus affect attitudes toward corporate governance in Japan. As part of a company family, individuals are members of a unit that envelops their lives; families command the attention and allegiance of parties throughout corporations. In addition, Japanese firms are concerned with a broader set of stakeholders than are firms in the United States, including employees, suppliers, and customers.[123] Moreover, a *keiretsu* (a group of firms tied together by cross-shareholdings) is more than an economic concept—it, too, is a family. Some believe, though, that extensive cross-shareholdings impede the type of structural change that is needed to improve the nation's corporate governance practices. However, recent changes in the governance code in Japan have been fostering better opportunities from improved corporate governance.[124] Consensus, another important influence in Japanese corporate governance, calls for the expenditure of significant amounts of energy to win the hearts and minds of people whenever possible, as opposed to top-level managers issuing edicts. Consensus is highly valued, even when it results in a slow and cumbersome decision-making process.

As in Germany, banks in Japan have an important role in financing and monitoring large public firms. Because the main bank in the keiretsu owns a large share position and holds a large amount of corporate debt, it has the closest relationship with a firm's top-level managers. The main bank provides financial advice to the firm and also closely monitors managers, although they have become less salient in fostering corporate restructuring.[125] Thus, although it is changing, Japan has traditionally had a bank-based financial and corporate governance structure, whereas the United States has a market-based financial and governance structure. Commercial banks in the United States by regulation are not allowed to own shares of publicly traded firms.

Japan's corporate governance practices have been changing in recent years. For example, because of Japanese banks' continuing development as economic organizations, their role in the monitoring and control of managerial behavior and firm outcomes is less significant than in the past.[126] Also, deregulation in the financial sector has reduced the cost of mounting hostile takeovers, although the activity has not been too salient.[127] As such, deregulation facilitated additional activity in Japan's market for corporate control, which was nonexistent in past years. And there are pressures for more changes because of weak performance by many Japanese companies. In fact, the Tokyo Electric Power Company faced significant criticism about its corporate governance practices after the meltdown at the Fukushima Daiichi nuclear power plant following the earthquake and tsunami in 2011. Most Japanese firms have boards that are largely composed of internal management, so they reflect the upper echelon of management. However, independent, nonexecutive board members are increasingly important in Japanese firms because they have adopted a new corporate governance code.[128] Also, long-term executive compensation (e.g., stock options) is increasingly important to foster improved performance.[129]

10-5b Corporate Governance in China

China has a unique and large economy, mixed with both socialist and market-oriented traits. Over time, the government has done much to improve the corporate governance of listed companies, particularly in light of the increasing privatization of businesses and the development of equity markets. However, the stock markets in China remain young and are continuing to develop. In their early years, these markets were weak because of significant insider trading, but with stronger governance these markets have improved.[130]

There has been a gradual decline in China in the equity held in state-owned enterprises while the number and percentage of private firms has grown, but the state still relies on direct and/or indirect controls to influence the strategies firms use. Even private firms try to develop political ties with the government because of their role in providing access to resources and to the economy.[131] In terms of long-term success, these conditions may affect firms' performance. Research shows that firms with higher state ownership tend to have lower market value and more volatility across time, because of agency conflicts within the firms and because executives must, at times, emphasize satisfying government-mandated social goals above maximizing shareholder returns.[132] Such a model sets up potential conflict between the principals, particularly the state owner and the private equity owners of such enterprises.[133]

Some evidence suggests that corporate governance in China may be tilting toward the western model. Changing a nation's governance systems is a complicated task that will inevitably encounter setbacks. Still, corporate governance in Chinese companies continues to evolve and likely will do so for some time to come as parties (e.g., the Chinese government and those seeking further movement toward free-market economies) interact to form governance mechanisms that are best for their nation, business firms, and citizens. However, along with changes in the governance systems of specific countries, multinational companies' boards and managers are also evolving. For example, firms that have entered more international markets are likely to have more top executives with greater international experience and to have a larger proportion of foreign owners and foreign directors on their boards.[134]

10-6 Governance Mechanisms and Ethical Behavior

The three internal and one external governance mechanisms are designed to ensure that the agents of the firm's owners—the corporation's top-level managers—make strategic decisions that best serve the interests of all stakeholders. In the United States, shareholders are commonly recognized as the company's most significant stakeholders. Increasingly though, top-level managers are expected to lead their firms in ways that will also serve the needs of product market stakeholders (e.g., customers, suppliers, and host communities) and organizational stakeholders (e.g., managerial and non-managerial employees).[135] Therefore, the firm's actions and the outcomes flowing from them should result in, at least, minimal satisfaction of the interests of all stakeholders; otherwise a firm risks seeing its dissatisfied stakeholders withdraw their support from the firm and provide it to another (e.g., customers will purchase products from a supplier offering an acceptable substitute).

Some believe that the internal corporate governance mechanisms designed and used by ethically responsible leaders and companies increase the likelihood the firm will be able to, at least, minimally satisfy all stakeholders' interests.[136] Scandals at companies such as Enron, WorldCom, HealthSouth, Volkswagen, and Satyam (a large information technology company based in India), among others, illustrate the negative effects of poor ethical behavior on a firm's efforts to satisfy stakeholders. Stakeholder governance of ethical behavior by top-level managers is being taken seriously in countries throughout the world.[137]

The decisions and actions of the board of directors can be an effective deterrent to unethical behaviors by top-level managers. Indeed, evidence suggests that the most effective boards set boundaries for their firms' business ethics and values.[138] After the boundaries for ethical behavior are determined, and likely formalized in a code of ethics, the board's ethics-based expectations must be clearly communicated to the firm's top-level managers and to other stakeholders (e.g., customers and suppliers) with whom interactions are necessary for the firm to produce and sell its products. Moreover, as agents of the firm's owners, top-level managers must understand that the board, acting as an internal governance mechanism, will hold them fully accountable for developing and supporting an organizational culture in which only ethical behaviors are permitted. As explained in Chapter 12, CEOs can be positive role models for improved ethical behavior.[139]

A major issue confronted by multinational companies operating in international markets is that of bribery.[140] As a whole, countries with weak institutions that have greater bribery activity tend to have fewer exports as a result. In addition, small- and medium-sized firms are the most harmed by bribery. Thus, bribery tends to limit entrepreneurial activity that can help a country's economy grow. While larger multinational firms tend to experience fewer negative outcomes, their power to exercise more ethical leadership allows them greater flexibility in selecting which markets they will enter and how they will do so.[141]

Through effective governance that results from well-designed governance mechanisms and the appropriate country institutions, top-level managers, working with others, are able to select and use strategies that result in strategic competitiveness and earning above-average returns. Such governance also provides long-term shareholder wealth and improved stakeholder cooperation.

SUMMARY

- Corporate governance is a relationship among stakeholders that is used to determine a firm's direction and control its performance. How firms monitor and control top-level managers' decisions and actions affects the implementation of strategies. Effective governance that aligns managers' decisions with shareholders' interests can help produce a competitive advantage for the firm.

- Three internal governance mechanisms are used in the modern corporation:
  - ownership concentration
  - the board of directors
  - executive compensation

  The market for corporate control is an external governance mechanism influencing managers' decisions and the outcomes resulting from them.

- Ownership is separated from control in the modern corporation. Owners (principals) hire managers (agents) to make decisions that maximize the firm's value. As risk-bearing specialists, owners diversify their risk by investing in multiple corporations with different risk profiles. Owners expect their agents (the firm's top-level managers, who are decision-making specialists) to make decisions that will help to maximize the value of their firm. Thus, modern corporations are characterized by an agency relationship that is created when one party (the firm's owners) hires and pays another party (top-level managers) to use its decision-making skills.

- Separation of ownership and control creates an agency problem when an agent pursues goals that conflict with the principals' goals. Principals establish and use governance mechanisms to control this problem.

- Ownership concentration is based on the number of large-block shareholders and the percentage of shares they own. With significant ownership percentages, such as those held by large mutual funds and pension funds, institutional investors often are able to influence top-level managers' strategic decisions and actions. Thus, unlike diffuse ownership, which tends to result in relatively weak monitoring and control of managerial decisions, concentrated ownership produces more active and effective monitoring. Institutional investors are a powerful force in corporate America and actively use their positions of concentrated ownership to force managers and boards of directors to make decisions that best serve shareholders' interests.

- In the United States and the United Kingdom, a firm's board of directors, composed of insiders, related outsiders, and outsiders, is a governance mechanism expected to represent shareholders' interests. The percentage of outside directors on many boards now exceeds the percentage of inside directors. Through implementation of the SOX Act, outsiders are expected to be more independent of a firm's top-level managers compared with directors selected from inside the firm. Relatively recent rules formulated and implemented by the SEC to allow owners with large stakes to propose new directors are beginning to change the balance even more in favor of outside and independent directors. Additional governance-related regulations have resulted from the Dodd-Frank Act.

- Executive compensation is a highly visible and often criticized governance mechanism. Salary, bonuses, and long-term incentives are used for the purpose of aligning managers' and shareholders' interests. A firm's board of directors is responsible for determining the effectiveness of the firm's executive compensation system. An effective system results in managerial decisions that are in shareholders' best interests.

- In general, evidence suggests that shareholders and boards of directors have become more vigilant in controlling managerial decisions. Nonetheless, these mechanisms are imperfect and sometimes insufficient. When the internal mechanisms fail, the market for corporate control—as an external governance mechanism—becomes relevant. Although it, too, is imperfect, the market for corporate control has been effective in improving corporations' diversification portfolios and implementing more effective strategic decisions.

- Corporate governance structures used in Germany, Japan, and China differ from each other and from the structure used in the United States. Historically, the U.S. governance structure focused on maximizing shareholder value. In Germany, employees, as a stakeholder group, take a more prominent role in governance. By contrast, until recently, Japanese shareholders played virtually no role in monitoring and controlling top-level managers. However, Japanese firms are now being challenged by "activist" shareholders. In China, the central government still plays a major role in corporate governance practices. Internationally, all these systems are becoming increasingly similar, as are many governance systems both in developed countries, such as France and Spain, and in transitional economies, such as China.

- Effective governance mechanisms ensure that the interests of all stakeholders are served. Thus, strategic competitiveness results when firms are governed in ways that permit at least minimal satisfaction of capital market stakeholders (e.g., shareholders), product market stakeholders (e.g., customers and suppliers), and organizational stakeholders (e.g., managerial and non-managerial employees; see Chapter 2). Moreover, effective governance produces ethical behavior in the formulation and implementation of strategies.

KEY TERMS

agency costs 319
agency relationship 315
board of directors 322
corporate governance 312
executive compensation 325
institutional owners 321
large-block shareholders 320
managerial opportunism 315
market for corporate control 328
ownership concentration 320

REVIEW QUESTIONS

1. What is corporate governance? What factors account for the considerable amount of attention corporate governance receives from several parties, including shareholder activists, business press writers, and academic scholars? Why is governance necessary to control managers' decisions?
2. What is meant by the statement that ownership is separated from managerial control in the corporation? Why does this separation exist?
3. What is an agency relationship? What is managerial opportunism? What assumptions do owners of corporations make about managers as agents?
4. How is each of the three internal governance mechanisms—ownership concentration, boards of directors, and executive compensation—used to align the interests of managerial agents with those of the firm's owners?
5. What trends exist regarding executive compensation? What is the effect of the increased use of long-term incentives on top-level managers' strategic decisions?
6. What is the market for corporate control? What conditions generally cause this external governance mechanism to become active? How does this mechanism constrain top-level managers' decisions and actions?
7. What is the nature of corporate governance in Germany, Japan, and China?
8. How can corporate governance foster ethical decisions and behaviors on the part of managers as agents?

Mini-Case

Governance and Activist Investors Outside of the United States

Governance in Japan, Germany, and China has been changing as "western" governance systems have increasingly been adopted. Traditionally, boards of directors in these nations have largely been composed of insider manager directors. In 2015, Japan adopted a new governance code that strongly emphasized the importance of firms to elect many more independent outside directors. Activist shareholders and a strong market for corporate control have traditionally been absent in Japan. More recently, shareholders have been more active and the most successful ones have been labelled "engagement" funds. The change is signaled, for example, by the Japanese Government Pension Investment Fund choosing an activist investor, the Taiyo Pacific Partners LP—a U.S. based engagement fund—to manage some of its $1 trillion in assets. Furthermore, the Japanese Financial Services Agency has introduced a "stewardship code" that calls on investors to "press for greater returns." As such, the Japanese environment is becoming more oriented toward "shareholder rights," although the approach comparatively is not as "activist" as found elsewhere in the world.

Besides a new brand of activism in Japan, activism is spreading around the globe including Germany. Again, a revised governance code pushed for more shareholder-friendly governance arrangements, including an emphasis on outside directors and stronger emphasis on executive long-term incentive compensation. With stronger emphasis on shareholders' rights, activist funds pursued more activity. Cevian Capital, an activist fund, is involved in ownership with ThyssenKrupp and Bilfinder. Likewise, Elliott Management, another activist fund, is involved with Celesio and Kabel Deutschland. Although management teams are quite suspicious of activists in Germany and other continental European countries, "Germany is an area where activists may look because of its protections for minority investors in takeover deals." However, research shows that activist investors have less influence on top management teams because of restrictive governance regulation. For example, one study found that activist investors' involvement did not lead to increased CEO turnover.

Although some activism has taken place in mainland China, firms in Hong Kong have been targeted more by activist funds. Hong Kong-listed companies have been loosening rules for foreign ownership and, therefore, companies have been paying more attention to what investors think in regard to governance and transparency. In mainland China, however, often shares are mostly owned by parent business group firms as well as the government or, because they are often younger, they are still owned by the firm's founders. As such, there is less potential influence for foreign investors on company decisions. However, the Shanghai-Hong Kong Stock Connect program has accelerated opportunities for activists on the mainland. Through the Connect program, foreign financial institutions can have direct access to mainland China's capital markets. This means that foreign ownership will have more activist influence because of shareholder voting rights in local mainland China-listed firms. Also, many home-grown Chinese activist funds thrived due to their recent investments in the technology sector with the success of Alibaba, Tencent, and many other high technology firms.

But how do owners from emerging market countries and countries with significant government ownership influence the firms they invest in overseas? Interestingly, sovereign wealth funds, many from emerging economies, are playing a dominant role by investing in developed economies as well as other emerging economies. In their own way, they are playing an activist role. For example, since the global financial crisis, many German firms have sought investment from sovereign wealth firms from Gulf States in the Mideast. In particular, many German major automobile firms have recruited Gulf Cooperation Council (GCC) sovereign wealth fund investments during the stresses of financial restructuring spurred by the financial crisis. These sovereign wealth funds are long-term investors and reduce the possibility of a hostile takeover, which has become a more prominent feature in the German corporate governance landscape.

Sovereign wealth funds are also taking active roles in climate change. For instance, the Norwegian sovereign wealth fund is divesting its assets in coal and other fossil fuels. Its strategy is to focus its wealth to have an influence on salient sustainability issues, such as climate change.

Another example is the acquisition activity of Brazilian multinationals, which have been supported by its sovereign wealth fund, the Brazilian Development Bank (BNDES). BNDES has been "involved in several large-scale operations and helped orchestrate mergers and acquisitions to build large 'national champions' in several industries." For example, "BNDES helped rescue Brazilian meatpacker JBS-Friboi, which aggressively expanded internationally by acquiring large U.S. producers Swift and Pilgrim's Pride, among others. In summary, western governance devices and shareholder activism have been spreading globally, and owners in emerging economies are participating in the market for corporate control and in restructuring investments, especially sovereign wealth funds that also exercise influence in developed as well as developing countries. These funds often focus to support government strategies, such as in China's energy sector, where the Chinese government is seeking to acquire more energy assets and natural resources to support its economy. Sometimes these sovereign funds also support government positions, such as Norway, which is using assets to emphasize sustainability, an important social and political movement.

Sources: M. Almadi & P. Lazic, 2016, CEO incentive compensation and earnings management, *Management Decision*, 54(10): 2447–2461; J. Braunstein, 2017, The domestic drivers of state finance institutions: Evidence from sovereign wealth funds, *Review of International Political Economy*, 24(6): 980–1003; L. Fletcher & E. Johanningsmeier, 2017, Hedge funds prosper on China tech but bubble fears emerge, *Wall Street Journal*, www.wsj.com, September 12; N. Hasegawa, H. Kim, & Y. Yasuda, 2017, The adoption of stock option plans and their effects on firm performance during Japan's period of corporate governance reform, *Journal of the Japanese and International Economies*, 44: 13–25; T. Kaspereit, K. Lopatta, & D. Onnen, 2017, Shareholder Value Implications of Compliance with the German Corporate Governance Code, *Managerial and Decision Economics*, 38: 166–177; K. Nagata & P. Nguyen, 2017, Ownership structure and disclosure quality: Evidence from management forecasts revisions in Japan, *Journal of Accounting and Public Policy*, 36(6): 451–467; O. Noreng, 2017, Norway's diversification, *World Oil*, 238(12): 23; M. Stancati & M. Farrell, 2017, Saudi Sovereign Wealth Fund sets growth targets, *Wall Street Journal*, www.wsj.com, October 26; X. Geng, T. Yoshikawa, & A. M. Colpan, 2016, Leveraging foreign institutional logic in the adoption of stock option pay among Japanese firms, *Strategic Management Journal*, 37(7): 1472–1492; B. Alhashel, 2015, Sovereign wealth funds: A literature review, *Journal of Economics and Business*, 78: 1–13; K. Narioka, 2015, Activist investors in Japan find some doors cracking open, *Wall Street Journal*, www.wsj.com, January 29; S. G. Lazzarini, A. Musacchio, R. Bandeira-de-Mello, & R. Marcon, R. 2015, What do state-owned development banks do? Evidence from BNDES, 2002–09 *World Development*, 66: 237–253; A. Musacchio & S. G. Lazzarini, 2014, *Reinventing State Capitalism: Leviathan in Business, Brazil and Beyond*, Cambridge: Harvard University Press; X. Sun, J. Li, Y. Wang, & W. Clark, 2014, China's sovereign wealth fund investments in overseas energy: The energy security perspective, *Energy Policy*, 65: 654–661.

Case Discussion Questions

1. Why are many countries adopting "western" governance systems similar to those found in the United States and the United Kingdom that are more shareholder friendly?
2. What particular governance devices are helping or hindering good governance in these countries that are changing their governance systems?
3. How do sovereign wealth funds affect governance of firms in home and foreign countries?
4. What would you recommend to improve the governance systems in Japan, Germany, and China, respectively, given the governance devices described in Chapter 10?

NOTES

1. S. Singh, N. Tabassum, T. K. Darwish, & G. Batsakis, 2018, Corporate governance and Tobin's Q as a measure of organizational performance, *British Journal of Management*, 29: 171–190.
2. P. Klein, J. Mahoney, A. McGahan, & C. Pitelis, 2018, Organizational governance adaptation: Who is in, who is out, and who gets what, *Academy of Management Review*, in press; I. Filatotchev & C. Nakajima, 2014, Corporate governance, responsible managerial behavior, and corporate social responsibility: Organizational efficiency versus organizational legitimacy? *Academy of Management Perspectives*, 28: 289–306.
3. F. Rubino, P. Tenuta, & D. Cambrea, 2017, Board characteristics effects on performance in family and non-family business: A multi-theoretical approach, *Journal of Management & Governance*, 21, 623–658; J. Joseph, W. Ocasio & M. McDonnell, 2014, The structural elaboration of board independence: Executive power, institutional logics, and the adoption of CEO-only board structures in U.S. corporate governance, *Academy of Management Journal*, 57: 1834–1858.
4. J. Paniagua, R. Rivelles, & J. Sapena, 2018, Corporate governance and financial performance: The role of ownership and board structure, *Journal of Business Research*, 89: 229–234; J. Obermann & P. Velte, 2018, Determinants and consequences of executive compensation-related shareholder activism and say-on-pay votes: A literature review and research agenda, *Journal of Accounting Literature*, 40: 116–151.
5. F. Zona, L. R. Gomez-Mejia, & M. C. Withers, 2018, Board interlocks and firm performance: Toward a combined agency–resource dependence perspective, *Journal of Management*, 44: 589–618.
6. S. Foley, 2017, The battle of the US corporate governance codes, *Financial Times*, www.ft.com, February 5; B. Soltani & C. Maupetit, 2015, Importance of core values of ethics, integrity and accountability in the European corporate governance codes, *Journal of Management & Governance*, 19: 259–284.
7. R. V. Aguilera, W. Q. Judge, & S. A. Terjesen, 2018, Corporate governance deviance, *Academy of Management Review*, 43: 87–109.
8. J. Oehmichen, 2018, East meets west—Corporate governance in Asian emerging markets: A literature review and research agenda, *International Business Review*, 27: 465–480; L. S. Tsui-Auch & T. Yoshikawa, 2015, Institutional change versus resilience: A study of incorporation of independent directors in Singapore banks, *Asian Business & Management*, 14: 91–115.
9. R. V. Aguilera, K. Desender, M. Lamy, & J. Lee, 2017, The governance impact of a changing investor landscape, *Journal of International Business Studies*, 48: 195–221; G. Bell, I. Filatotchev, & R. Aguilera, 2014, Corporate governance and investors' perceptions of foreign IPO value: An institutional perspective, *Academy of Management Journal*, 57: 301–320.
10. W. Shi, B. L. Connelly, & R. E. Hoskisson, 2017, External corporate governance and financial fraud: Cognitive evaluation theory insights on agency theory prescriptions, *Strategic Management Journal*, 38: 1268–1286; M. R. Denes, J. M. Karpoff, & V. B. McWilliams, 2017, Thirty years of shareholder activism: A survey of empirical research, *Journal of Corporate Finance*, 44: 405–424.
11. G. E. Davis & T. A. Thompson, 1994, A social movement perspective on corporate control, *Administrative Science Quarterly*, 39: 141–173.
12. M. Goranova, R. Abouk, P. C. Nystrom, & E. S. Soofi, 2017, Corporate governance antecedents to shareholder activism: A zero-inflated process, *Strategic Management Journal*, 38: 415–435; V. V. Acharya, S. C. Myers, & R. G. Rajan, 2011, The internal governance of firms, *Journal of Finance*, 66: 689–720; R. Bricker & N. Chandar, 2000, Where Berle and Means went wrong: A reassessment of capital market agency and financial reporting, *Accounting, Organizations, and Society*, 25: 529–554.
13. R. E. Hoskisson, F. Chirico, J. Zyung, & E. Gambeta, 2017, Managerial risk taking: A multi-theoretical review and future research agenda, *Journal of Management*, 43: 137–169; T. M. Alessandri & A. Seth, 2014, The effects of managerial ownership on international and business diversification: Balancing incentives and risks, *Strategic Management Journal*, 35: 2064–2075.
14. F. Visintin, D. Pittino, & A. Minichilli, 2017, Financial performance and non-family CEO turnover in private family firms under different conditions of ownership and governance, *Corporate Governance: An International Review*, 25: 312–337; M. Essen, M. Carney, E. R. Gedajlovic, & P. P. M. A. R. Heugens, 2015, How does family control influence firm strategy and performance? A meta-analysis of US publicly listed firms, *Corporate Governance: An International Review*, 23: 3–24.
15. S. Belenzon, A. Patacconi, & R. Zarutskie, R. 2016, Married to the firm? A large-scale investigation of the social context of ownership, *Strategic Management Journal*, 37: 2611–2638; D. Miller, I. Le Breton-Miller, & R. Lester, 2013, Family firm governance, strategic conformity and performance: Institutional vs. strategic perspectives, *Organization Science*, 24: 189–209.
16. D. Souder, A. Zaheer, H. Sapienza, & R. Ranucci, 2017, How family influence, socioemotional wealth, and competitive conditions shape new technology adoption, *Strategic Management Journal*, 38: 1774–1790; E. Gedajlovic, M. Carney, J. J. Chrisman, & F. W. Kellermans, 2012, The adolescence of family firm research: Taking stock and planning for the future, *Journal of Management*, 38: 1010–1037.
17. G. Martin, L. R. Gómez-Mejía, P. Berrone, & M. Makri, 2017, Conflict between controlling family owners and minority shareholders: Much ado about nothing?, *Entrepreneurship: Theory & Practice*, 41: 999–1027; Y. Cheung, I. Haw, W. Tan, & W. Wang, 2014, Board Structure and intragroup propping: Evidence from family

business groups in Hong Kong. *Financial Management*, 43: 569–601.

18. G. Cacciotti & D. Ucbasaran, 2018, Commentary: Blockholder structures and power mechanisms in family firms, *Entrepreneurship: Theory & Practice*, 42: 252–258; J. L. Arregle, L. Naldi, M. Nordquvist, & M. A. Hitt, 2012, Internationalization of family controlled firm: A study of the effects of external involvement in governance, *Entrepreneurship Theory and Practice*, 36: 1115–1143.
19. A. Zardkoohi, J. Harrison, & M. Josefy, 2017, Conflict and confluence: The multidimensionality of opportunism in principal-agent relationships, *Journal of Business Ethics*, 146: 405–417; R. M. Wiseman, G. Cuevas-Rodriguez, & L. R. Gomez-Mejia, 2012, Towards a social theory of agency, *Journal of Management Studies*, 49: 202–222.
20. R. E. Hoskisson, E. Gambeta, C. D. Green, & T. X. Li, 2018, Is my firm-specific investment protected? Overcoming the stakeholder investment dilemma in the resource-based view, *Academy of Management Review*, 43: 284–306; A. K. Hoenen & T. Kostova, 2014, Utilizing the broader agency perspective for studying headquarters-subsidiary relations in multinational companies, *Journal of International Business Studies*, 46: 104–113.
21. B. L. Connelly, W. Shi, & J. Zyung, 2017, Managerial response to constitutional constraints on shareholder power, *Strategic Management Journal*, 38: 1499–1517; Z. Goshen & R. Squire, 2017, Principal costs: A new theory for corporate law and governance, *Columbia Law Review*, 117: 767–829.
22. L. L. Lan & L. Heracleous, 2010, Rethinking agency theory: The view from law, *Academy of Management Review*, 35: 294–314; D. R. Dalton, M. A. Hitt, S. T. Certo, & C. M. Dalton, 2008, The fundamental agency problem and its mitigation: Independence, equity and the market for corporate control, in J. P. Walsh and A. P. Brief (eds.), *The Academy of Management Annals*, NY: Lawrence Erlbaum Associates, 1–64.
23. Zardkoohi, Harrison, & Josefy, Conflict and confluence: The multidimensionality of opportunism in principal-agent relationships; K. Vafai, 2010, Opportunism in organizations, *Journal of Law, Economics, and Organization*, 26: 158–181; O. E. Williamson, 1996, *The Mechanisms of Governance*, NY: Oxford University Press, 6.
24. J. R. Pierce, 2018, Reexamining the cost of corporate criminal prosecutions, *Journal of Management*, 44: 892–918; F. Lumineau & D. Malhotra, 2011, Shadow of the contract: How contract structure shapes interfirm dispute resolution, *Strategic Management Journal*, 32: 532–555.
25. Connelly, Shi, & Zyung, Managerial response to constitutional constraints on shareholder power; B. Balsmeier, A. Buchwald, & J. Stiebale, 2014, Outside directors on the board and innovative firm performance, *Research Policy*, 43: 1800–1815; M. L. McDonald, P. Khanna, & J. D. Westphal, 2008, Getting them to think outside the circle: Corporate governance CEOs' external advice networks, and firm performance, *Academy of Management Journal*, 51: 453–475.
26. M. L. Zorn, C. Shropshire, J. A. Martin, J. G. Combs, & D. Ketchen, 2017, Home alone: The effects of lone-insider boards on CEO pay, financial misconduct, and firm performance, *Strategic Management Journal*, 38: 2623–2646.
27. S. Chang, B. Kogut, & J. Yang, 2016, Global diversification discount and its discontents: A bit of self-selection makes a world of difference. *Strategic Management Journal*, 37: 2254–2274; T. J. Boulton, M. V. Braga-Alves, & F. P. Schlingemann, 2014, Does equity-based compensation make CEOs more acquisitive?, *Journal of Financial Research*, 37: 267–294.
28. W. Hou, R. L. Priem, & M. Goranova, 2017, Does one size fit all? Investigating pay-future performance relationships over the "seasons" of CEO tenure, *Journal of Management*, 43: 864–891; D. E. Black, S. S. Dikolli, & S. D. Dyreng, 2014, CEO pay-for-complexity and the risk of managerial diversion from multinational diversification, *Contemporary Accounting Research*, 31: 103–135 P. David, J. P. O'Brien, T. Yoshikawa, &. A. Delios, 2010, Do shareholders or stakeholders appropriate the rents from corporate diversification? The influence of ownership structure, *Academy of Management Journal*, 53: 636–654; S. W. Geiger & L. H. Cashen, 2007, Organizational size and CEO compensation: The moderating effect of diversification in downscoping organizations, *Journal of Managerial Issues*, 9: 233–252.
29. Z. Chen, W. Hung, D. Li, & L. Xing, 2017, The impact of bank merger growth on CEO compensation, *Journal of Business Finance & Accounting*, 44(9/10): 1398–1442; J. Seo, D. L. Gamache, C. E. Devers, & M. A. Carpenter, 2015, The role of CEO relative standing in acquisition behavior and CEO pay, *Strategic Management Journal*, 37: 1877–1894; A. S. Hornstein & Z. Nguyen, 2014, Is more less? Propensity to diversify via M&A and market reaction, *International Review of Financial Analysis*, 34: 76–88.
30. Hoskisson, Chirico, Zyung, & Gambeta, Managerial risk taking: A multi-theoretical review and future research agenda; B. W. Benson, J. C. Park, & W. N. Davidson, 2014, Equity-based incentives, risk aversion, and merger-related risk-taking behavior, *Financial Review*, 49: 117–148.
31. 2017, Lockheed Martin Annual Report, www.lockheedmartin.com, 10-K, page 3.
32. Trefis, 2017, Lockheed Martin: The Sikorsky acquisition one year on, *Forbes*, www.forbes.com, February 1.
33. T. Nguyen, C. Cai, & P. McColgan, 2017, How firms manage their cash flows: An examination of diversification's effect, *Review of Quantitative Finance & Accounting*, 48: 701–724; M. S. Jensen, 1986, Agency costs of free cash flow, corporate finance, and takeovers, *American Economic Review*, 76: 323–329.
34. T.-E. Bakke & T. Gu, 2017. Diversification and cash dynamics, *Journal of Financial Economics*, 123: 580–601; J. P. O'Brien, P. David, T. Yoshikawa, & A. Delios, 2014, How capital structure influences diversification performance: A transaction cost perspective, *Strategic Management Journal*, 35: 1013–1031.
35. T. B. Mackey, J. B. Barney, & J. P. Dotson, 2017. Corporate diversification and the value of individual firms: A Bayesian approach. *Strategic Management Journal*, 38: 322–341; T. B. Mackey & J. B. Barney, 2013, Incorporating opportunity costs in strategic management research: The value of diversification and payout as opportunities forgone when reinvesting in the firm. *Strategic Organization*, 11: 347–363.
36. C. Stadler, M. J. Mayer, J. Hautz, & K. Matzler, 2018, International and product diversification: Which strategy suits family managers?, *Global Strategy Journal*, 8: 184–207; T. M. Alessandri & A. Seth, 2014, The effects of managerial ownership on international and business diversification: Balancing incentives and risks, *Strategic Management Journal*, 35: 2064–2075.
37. T. Gryta, D. Benoit, & J. S. Lublin, 2017, GE gives activist Trian a seat on the board, *Wall Street Journal*, www.wsj.com, October 10.
38. B. Liu, 2016, The disciplinary role of failed takeover attempts, *Journal of Financial Research*, 39: 63–85; S. Pathak, R. E. Hoskisson, & R. A. Johnson, 2014, Settling up in CEO compensation: The impact of divestiture intensity and contextual factors in refocusing firms, *Strategic Management Journal*, 35: 1124–1143.
39. B. Orlando, A. Renzi, G. Sancetta, & N. Cucari, 2018, How does firm diversification impact innovation?, *Technology Analysis & Strategic Management*, 30: 391–404; S. K. Kim, J. D. Arthurs, A. Sahaym, & J. B. Cullen, 2013, Search behavior of the diversified firm: The impact of fit on innovation, *Strategic Management Journal*, 34: 999–1009.
40. Serbera, J.-P., 2017, A new strategy against hostile takeovers: A model of defense in participations, *Managerial & Decision Economics*, 38: 832–844; J. Kang, 2013, The relationship between corporate diversification and corporate social performance, *Strategic Management Journal*, 34: 94–109.
41. E. R. Feldman, 2016, Corporate spinoffs and analysts' coverage decisions: The implications for diversified firms, *Strategic Management Journal*, 37: 1196–1219; M. J. Benner & T. Zenger 2016, The lemons problem in markets for strategy, *Strategy Science*, 1: 71–89.
42. S. Dorobantu & K. Odziemkowska, 2017, Valuing stakeholder governance: Property rights, community mobilization, and firm

value, *Strategic Management Journal*, 38: 2682–2703; W. Rees & T. Rodionova, 2015, The Influence of family ownership on corporate social responsibility: An international analysis of publicly listed companies, *Corporate Governance: An International Review*, 23: 184–202; J. L. Walls, P. Berrone, & P. H. Phan, 2012, Corporate governance and environmental performance: Is there really a link? *Strategic Management Journal*, 33: 885–913.

43. C. Francoeur, A. Melis, S. Gaia, & S. Aresu, 2017, Green or greed? An alternative look at CEO compensation and corporate environmental commitment, *Journal of Business Ethics*, 140: 439–453; C. Flammer & J. Luo, J. 2017, Corporate social responsibility as an employee governance tool: Evidence from a quasi-experiment, *Strategic Management Journal*, 38: 163–183; J. L. Walls, P. Berrone, & P. H. Phan, 2012, Corporate governance and environmental performance: Is there really a link? *Strategic Management Journal*, 33: 885–913.

44. V. Chhaochharia, Y. Grinstein, G. Grullon, & R. Michaely, 2017, Product market competition and internal governance: Evidence from the Sarbanes-Oxley Act, *Management Science*, 63: 1405–1424; J. C. Coates & S. Srinivasan, 2014, SOX after ten years: A multidisciplinary review, *Accounting Horizons*, 28: 627–671; M. Hossain, S. Mitra, Z. Rezaee, & B. Sarath, 2011, Corporate governance and earnings management in the pre- and post-Sarbanes-Oxley act regimes: Evidence from implicated option backdating firms, *Journal of Accounting Auditing & Finance*, 28: 279–315.

45. A. Paletta & G. Alimehmeti, 2018, SOX disclosure and the effect of internal controls on executive compensation, *Journal of Accounting, Auditing & Finance*, 33: 277–295; S. C. Rice, D. P. Weber, & W. Biyu, 2015, Does SOX 404 have teeth? Consequences of the failure to report existing internal control weaknesses, *Accounting Review*, 90: 1169–1200.

46. K. Freking & M. Gordon, 2018, The Senate has passed a bill dialing back Dodd-Frank banking regulations, *Time*, www.time.com, March 15; 2010, The Dodd-Frank Act: Financial reform update index, Faegre & Benson, www.faegre.com, September 7.

47. G. Yuqi & Z. Ling, 2017, The impact of the Sarbanes-Oxley Act on corporate innovation, *Journal of Economics & Business*, 90: 17–30.

48. A. K. Prevost, U. Wongchoti, & B. R. Marshall, 2016, Does institutional shareholder activism stimulate corporate information flow? *Journal of Banking & Finance*, 70: 105–117; B. J. Bushee, M. E. Carter, & J. Gerakos, 2014, Institutional investor preferences for corporate governance mechanisms, *Journal of Management Accounting Research*, 26: 123–149; M. Goranova, R. Dhanwadkar, & P. Brandes, 2010, Owners on both sides of the deal: Mergers and acquisitions and overlapping institutional ownership, *Strategic Management Journal*, 31: 1114–1135.

49. T. J. Chemmanur & S. He, 2016, Institutional trading, information production, and corporate spin-offs, *Journal of Corporate Finance*, 38: 54–76; J. C. Hartzell, L. Sun, & S. Titman, S. 2014, Institutional investors as monitors of corporate diversification decisions: Evidence from real estate investment trusts, *Journal of Corporate Finance*, 25: 61–72; B. L. Connelly, R. E. Hoskisson, L. Tihanyi, & S. T. Certo, 2010, Ownership as a form of corporate governance, *Journal of Management Studies*, 47: 1561–1589.

50. P. Borochin & J. Yang, 2017, The effects of institutional investor objectives on firm valuation and governance, *Journal of Financial Economics*, 126: 171–199.

51. S. Baker, 2017, Institutional investors fill activism gap in Europe, *Pensions & Investments*, 45(10): 6; I. Busta, E. Sinani, & S. Thomsen, 2014, Ownership concentration and market value of European banks, *Journal of Management & Governance*, 18: 159–183.

52. T. Wang, H. Jiao, Z. Xu, & X. Yang, 2018, Entrepreneurial finance meets government investment at initial public offering: The role of minority state ownership, *Corporate Governance: An International Review*, 26: 97–117; C. Inoue, S. Lazzarni, & A. Musacchio, 2013, Leviathan as a minority shareholder: Firm-level implications of equity purchases by the state, *Academy of Management Journal*, 56: 1775–1801.

53. L. Che & P. Zhang, 2017, The impact of family CEO's ownership and the moderating effect of the second largest owner in private family firms, *Journal of Management & Governance*, 21: 757–784; C. Singla, R. Veliyath, & R. George, 2014, Family firms and internationalization governance relationships: Evidence of secondary agency issues, *Strategic Management Journal*, 35: 606–616.

54. M. Quinn, M. R. W. Hiebl, K. Moores, & J. B. Craig, 2018, Future research on management accounting and control in family firms: Governance, entrepreneurship and stewardship, *Journal of Management Control*, 28: 529–546; A. Zattoni, L. Gnan, & M. Huse, 2015, Does family involvement influence firm performance? Exploring the mediating effects of board processes and tasks, *Journal of Management*, 41: 1214–1243.

55. L. R. Kabbach de Castro, R. V. Aguilera, & R. Crespí-Cladera, 2017, family firms and compliance: Reconciling the conflicting predictions within the socioemotional wealth perspective, *Family Business Review*, 30: 137–159; L. R. Gomez-Mejia, J. T. Campbell, G. Martin, R. E. Hoskisson, M. Makri, & D. G. Sirmon, 2014, Socioemotional wealth as a mixed gamble: Revisiting family firm R&D investments with the behavioral agency model, *Entrepreneurship: Theory & Practice*, 38: 1351–1374.

56. A. Berle & G. Means, 1932, *The Modern Corporation and Private Property*, NY: Macmillan.

57. L. A. Bebchuk, A. Cohen, & S. Hirst, 2017, The agency problems of institutional investors, *Journal of Economic Perspectives*, 31: 89–112; R. A. Johnson, K. Schnatterly, S. G. Johnson, & S.-C. Chiu, 2010, Institutional investors and institutional environment: A comparative analysis and review, *Journal of Management Studies*, 47: 1590–1613.

58. W. Shi, B. L. Connelly, R. E. Hoskisson, & B. Koka, 2018. Shareholder influence on joint venture exploration, *Journal of Management*, in press; M. Alda, 2018, Pension fund manager skills over the economic cycle: The (non-)specialization cost, *European Journal of Finance*, 24: 36–58.

59. C. Brooks, Z. Chen, & Y. Zeng, 2018, Institutional cross-ownership and corporate strategy: The case of mergers and acquisitions, *Journal of Corporate Finance*, 48: 187–216.

60. K. Stathopoulos & G. Voulgaris, 2016, The importance of shareholder activism: The case of say-on-pay, *Corporate Governance: An International Review*, 24: 359–370; R. Krause, K. A. Whitler, & M. Semadeni, 2014, Power to the principals! An experimental look at shareholder say-on-pay voting, *Academy of Management Journal*, 57: 94–115.

61. N. Malenko & S. Yao, 2016, The role of proxy advisory firms: Evidence from a regression-discontinuity design, *Review of Financial Studies*, 29: 3394–3427; C. Mallin, 2012, Institutional investors: the vote as a tool of governance, *Journal of Management & Governance*, 16: 177–196.

62. A. R. Sorkin, 2018, Blackrock's message: Contribute to society, or risk losing our support, *New York Times*, www.nytimes.com, January 15.

63. D. Weil, 2018, Passive investors, don't vote, *Wall Street Journal*, www.wsj.com, March 8.

64. F. Vallascas, S. Mollah, & K. Keasey, 2017, Does the impact of board independence on large bank risks change after the global financial crisis?, *Journal of Corporate Finance*, 44: 149–166; M. L. Heyden, J. Oehmichen, S. Nichting, & H. W. Volberda, 2015, Board background heterogeneity and exploration-exploitation: The role of the institutionally adopted board model, *Global Strategy Journal*, 5: 154–176.

65. E. H. Kim & L. Yao, 2018, Executive suite independence: Is it related to board independence?, *Management Science*, 64: 1015–1033; D. Barton & M. Wiseman, 2015, Where boards fall short, *Harvard Business Review*, 93(1/2): 98–104.

66. D. Singh & A. Delios, 2017, Corporate governance, board networks and growth in domestic and international markets: Evidence from India, *Journal of World Business*, 52: 615–627; A. Tushke, W. G. Sanders, & E. Hernandez, 2014, Whose experience matters in the boardroom? The effects of experiential and vicarious learning on emerging market entry, *Strategic Management Journal*, 35: 398–418.

67. I. A. Shaikh, J. P. O'brien, & L. Peters, 2018, Inside directors and the underinvestment

of financial slack towards R&D-intensity in high-technology firms, *Journal of Business Research*, 82: 192–201; P. Khanna, C. D. Jones, & S. Boivie, 2014, Director human capital, information processing demands, and board effectiveness, *Journal of Management*, 40: 557–585.

68. W. Shi, R. E. Hoskisson, & Y. A. Zhang, 2017, Independent director death and CEO acquisitiveness: Build an empire or pursue a quiet life?, *Strategic Management Journal*, 38: 780–792; C. Sundaramurthy, K. Pukthuanthong & Y. Kor, 2014, Positive and negative synergies between the CEO's and the corporate board's human and social capital: A study of biotechnology firms, *Strategic Management Journal*, 35: 845–868.

69. J. Vithayathil & V. Choudhary, 2018, Governance of corporate takeovers: Time for say-on-takeovers?, *MIS Quarterly*, 42: 45–62; E. Peni, 2014, CEO and Chairperson characteristics and firm performance, *Journal of Management & Governance*, 18: 185–205.

70. M. C. Withers & M. A. Fitza, 2017, Do board chairs matter? The influence of board chairs on firm performance, *Strategic Management Journal*, 38: 1343–1355.

71. S. Shekshnia, 2018, How to be a good board chair, *Harvard Business Review*, 96(2): 96–105; D. H. Zhu, W. Shen, & A. J. Hillman, 2014, Recategorization into the in-group: The appointment of demographically different new directors and their subsequent positions on corporate boards, *Administrative Science Quarterly*, 59: 240–270; A. Holehonnur & T. Pollock, 2013, Shoot for the stars? Predicting the recruitment of prestigious directors at newly public firms, *Academy of Management Journal*, 56: 1396–1419.

72. R. Krause, 2017, Being the CEO's boss: An examination of board chair orientations, *Strategic Management Journal*, 38: 697–713; J. Joseph, W. Ocasio, & M. McDonnell, 2014, The structural elaboration of board independence: Executive power, institutional logics, and the adoption of CEO-only board structures in U.S. corporate governance, *Academy of Management Journal*, 57: 1834–1858.

73. P. Nguyen, N. Rahman, & Z. Ruoyun, 2018, CEO characteristics and firm valuation: A quantile regression analysis, *Journal of Management & Governance*, *22*: 133–151; J. Tang, 2017, CEO duality and firm performance: The moderating roles of other executives and blockholding outside directors, *European Management Journal*, 35: 362–372; E. Teti, A. Dell'Acqua, L. Etro, & M. Volpe, 2017, The impact of board independency, CEO duality and CEO fixed compensation on M&A performance, *Corporate Governance: The International Journal of Effective Board Performance*, 17: 947–971.

74. L. Moyer, 2018, JP Morgan says Jamie Dimon will continue to serve as CEO for five more years, CNBC, www.cnbc.com, January 29; E. Glazer, 2014, J.P. Morgan's decade of Dimon, *Wall Street Journal*, June 30, C1.

75. S. Garg & K. M. Eisenhardt, 2017, Unpacking the CEO-board relationship: How strategy making happens in entrepreneurial firms, *Academy of Management Journal*, 60: 1828–1858; Barton & Wiseman, Where boards fall short; M. Huse, R. E. Hoskisson, A. Zattoni, & R. Vigano, 2011, New perspectives on board research: Changing the research agenda, *Journal of Management and Governance*, 15: 5–28.

76. R. Hauser, 2018, Busy directors and firm performance: Evidence from mergers, *Journal of Financial Economics*, 128: 16–37.

77. Garg & Eisenhardt, Unpacking the CEO-board relationship: How strategy making happens in entrepreneurial firms; S. Muthusamy, P. A. Bobinski, & D. Jawahar, 2011, Toward a strategic role for employees in corporate governance, *Strategic Change*, 20: 127–138.

78. F. Bravo & N. Reguera-Alvarado, 2017. The effect of board of directors on R&D intensity: Board tenure and multiple directorships, *R&D Management*, 47: 701–714; R. Krause & G. Bruton, 2014, Agency and monitoring clarity on venture boards of directors, *Academy of Management Review*, 39: 111–114; B. Baysinger & R. E. Hoskisson, 1990, The composition of boards of directors and strategic control: Effects on corporate strategy, *Academy of Management Review*, 15: 72–87.

79. J. Lu & W. Wang, 2018, Managerial conservatism, board independence and corporate innovation, *Journal of Corporate Finance*, 48: 1–16; B. Balsmeier, A. Buchwald, & J. Stiebale, 2014, Outside directors on the board and innovative firm performance, *Research Policy*, 43: 1800–1815.

80. M. L. Goranova, R. L. Priem, H. A. Ndofor, & C. A. Trahms, 2017, Is there a 'Dark Side' to monitoring? Board and shareholder monitoring effects on M&A performance extremeness, *Strategic Management Journal*, 38: 2285–2297; C. Shropshire, 2010, The role of the interlocking director and board receptivity in the diffusion of practices, *Academy of Management Review*, 35: 246–264.

81. 2018, Lead director charter, www.franklinresources.com, accessed on April 10.

82. M. Van Peteghem, L. Bruynseels, & A. Gaeremynck, 2018, Beyond diversity: A tale of faultlines and frictions in the board of directors, *Accounting Review*, 93: 339–367; A. J. Hillman, 2015, Board diversity: Beginning to unpeel the onion, *Corporate Governance: An International Review*, 23: 104–107.

83. I. Lahlou & P. Navatte, 2017, Director compensation incentives and acquisition performance, *International Review of Financial Analysis*, 53: 1–11; E. K. Lim & B. T. Mccann, 2013, The influence of relative values of outside director stock options on firm strategic risk from a multiagent perspective, *Strategic Management Journal*, 34: 1568–1590.

84. E. Redor, 2016, Board attributes and shareholder wealth in mergers and acquisitions: A survey of the literature, *Journal of Management & Governance*, 20: 789–821; Y. Deutsch & M. Valente, 2013, The trouble with stock compensation, *MIT Sloan Management Review*, 54(4): 19–20; Y. Deutsch, T. Keil, & T. Laamanen, 2007, Decision making in acquisitions: The effect of outside directors' compensation on acquisition patterns, *Journal of Management*, 33: 30–56.

85. G. Bernile, V. Bhagwat, & S. Yonker, 2018, Board diversity, firm risk, and corporate policies, *Journal of Financial Economics*, 127: 588–612; J. S. Lublin, 2018, Why breaking into the boardroom is harder for women, *Wall Street Journal*, www.wsj.com, February 7; C. Post & K Byron, 2015, Women on boards and firm financial performance: A meta-analysis, *Academy of Management Journal*, 58: 1546–1571.

86. L. Wang & W. Jiang, 2017, How CEO underpayment influences strategic change: The equity perspective, *Management Decision*, 55: 2277–2292; E. A. Fong, X. Xing, W. H. Orman, & W. I. MacKenzie, 2015, Consequences of deviating from predicted CEO labor market compensation on long-term firm value, *Journal of Business Research*, 68: 299–305.

87. K. Shue & R. R. Townsend, 2017, Growth through rigidity: An explanation for the rise in CEO pay, *Journal of Financial Economics*, 123: 1–21; M. van Essen, J. Otten, & E. J. Carberry, 2015, Assessing managerial power theory: A meta-analytic approach to understanding the determinants of CEO compensation, *Journal of Management*, 41: 164–202.

88. V. K. Gupta, S. C. Mortal, & X. Guo, 2018, Revisiting the gender gap in CEO compensation: Replication and extension of Hill, Upadhyay, and Beekun's (2015) work on CEO gender pay gap, *Strategic Management Journal*, 39: 2036–2050; B. Glover & O. Levine, 2017, Idiosyncratic risk and the manager, *Journal of Financial Economics*, 126: 320–341; E. Croci & D. Petmezas, 2015, Do risk-taking incentives induce CEOs to invest? Evidence from acquisitions, *Journal of Corporate Finance*, 32: 1–23.

89. W. Shi, B. L. Connelly, & W. G. Sanders, 2016, Buying bad behavior: Tournament incentives and securities class action lawsuits, *Strategic Management Journal*, 37: 1354–1378; M. Almadi & P. Lazic, 2016, CEO incentive compensation and earnings management, *Management Decision*, 54: 2447–2461; S. Jayaraman & T. Milbourn, 2015, CEO equity incentives and financial misreporting: The role of auditor expertise, *Accounting Review*, 90: 321–350.

90. J. J. Gerakos, J. D. Piotroski, & S. Srinivasan, 2013, Which U.S. market interactions affect CEO pay? Evidence from UK companies, *Management Science*, 59: 2413–2434; Y. Du, M. Deloof, & A Jorissen, 2011, Active boards of directors in foreign subsidiaries, *Corporate Governance: An International Review*, 19: 153–168; J. J. Reuer, E. Klijn, F. A. J. van den Bosch, & H. W. Volberda,

2001, Bringing corporate governance to international joint ventures, *Global Strategy Journal*, 1: 54–66.

91. S. Banerjee & S. Homroy, 2018, Managerial incentives and strategic choices of firms with different ownership structures, *Journal of Corporate Finance*, 48: 314–330; A. Ghosh, 2006, Determination of executive compensation in an emerging economy: Evidence from India, *Emerging Markets, Finance & Trade*, 42: 66–90.
92. H. S. Bhabra & A. T. Hossain, 2018, Does location influence executive compensation? Evidence from Canadian SMEs, *Journal of Management & Governance*, 22: 89–109; J. J. Reuer, E. Klijn, & C. S. Lioukas, 2014, Board involvement in international joint ventures, *Strategic Management Journal*, 35: 1626–1644; M. Ederhof, 2011, Incentive compensation and promotion-based incentives of mid-level managers: Evidence from a multinational corporation, *The Accounting Review*, 86: 131–154.
93. J. H. Joo & S. L. Chamberlain, 2017, The effects of governance on classification shifting and compensation shielding, *Contemporary Accounting Research*, 34: 1779–1811; G. Pandher & R. Currie, 2013, CEO compensation: A resource advantage and stakeholder-bargaining perspective, *Strategic Management Journal*, 34: 22–41.
94. J. Obermann & P. Velte, 2018, Determinants and consequences of executive compensation-related shareholder activism and say-on-pay votes: A literature review and research agenda, *Journal of Accounting Literature*, 40: 116–151; I. Dittmann, Y. Ko-Chia, & Z. Dan, 2017, how important are risk-taking incentives in executive compensation?, *Review of Finance*, 21: 1805–1846.
95. K. Button, 2017, Balance due: Boards seek the optimal compensation formula to satisfy all sides in the conflict over executive pay packages, *CFO*, July/August, 24–29; 2013, The experts: Do companies spend too much on 'superstar' CEOs? *Wall Street Journal*, www.wsj.com, March 14.
96. A. Gupta, L. Misra, & Y. Shi, 2018, Do scandals trigger governance changes? Evidence from option backdating, *Journal of Financial Research*, 41: 91–111; C. Veld & B. H. Wu, 2014, What drives executive stock option backdating?, *Journal of Business Finance & Accounting*, 41: 1042–1070; T. G. Pollock, H. M. Fischer, & J. B. Wade, 2002, The role of politics in reprising executive options, *Academy of Management Journal*, 45: 1172–1182.
97. C. Flammer & P. Bansal, 2017, Does a long-term orientation create value? Evidence from a regression discontinuity, *Strategic Management Journal*, 38: 1827–1847; P. Berrone & L. R. Gomez-Mejia, 2009, Environmental performance and executive compensation: An integrated agency-institutional perspective, *Academy of Management Journal*, 52: 103–126.
98. M. Darrough, R. Huang, & E. Zur, 2018, Acquirer internal control weaknesses in the market for corporate control, *Contemporary Accounting Research*, 35: 211–244; R. V. Aguilera, K. Desender, M. K. Bednar, & J. H. Lee, 2015, Connecting the dots: Bringing external corporate governance into the corporate governance puzzle, *Academy of Management Annals*, 9:483–573.
99. M. M. Heyden, N. Nikolaos Kavadis, & Q. Neuman, 2017, External corporate governance and strategic investment behaviors of target CEOs, *Journal of Management*, 43: 2065–2089; T. Laamanen, M. Brauer, & O. Junna, 2014, Performance of divested assets: Evidence from the U.S. software industry, *Strategic Management Journal*, 35: 914–925.
100. T. Greenwald, 2018, Qualcomm evaded Broadcom's bid; now, CEO has a lot to prove, *Wall Street Journal*, www.wsj.com, March 20.
101. L. Fortado, 2018, Investing: Activism enters the mainstream, *Financial Times*, www.ft.com, February 13.
102. V. Agarwal, T. C. Green, & H. Ren, 2018, Alpha or beta in the eye of the beholder: What drives hedge fund flows? *Journal of Financial Economics*, 127: 417–434.
103. C. Lombardo, 2018, Starboard pursuing proxy fight at Newell Brands despite deal with Icahn, *Wall street journal*, www.wsj.com, April 4.
104. J. M. Karpoff & V. B. McWilliams, 2017, Thirty years of shareholder activism: A survey of empirical research, *Journal of Corporate Finance*, 44: 405–424; M. Cremers & A. Ferrell, 2014, Thirty years of shareholder rights and firm value, *Journal of Finance*, 69: 1167–1196.
105. J. P. Walsh & R. Kosnik, 1993, Corporate raiders and their disciplinary role in the market for corporate control, *Academy of Management Journal*, 36: 671–700.
106. Y. Wang & H. Lahr, 2017, Takeover law to protect shareholders: Increasing efficiency or merely redistributing gains?, *Journal of Corporate Finance*, 43: 288–315; K. Amess, S. Girma, & M. Wright, 2014, The wage and employment consequences of ownership change, *Managerial & Decision Economics*, 35: 161–171; M. Schijven & M. A. Hitt, 2012, The vicarious wisdom of crowds: Toward a behavioral perspective on investor reactions to acquisition announcements, *Strategic Management Journal*, 33: 1247–1268.
107. M. Graebner, K. Heimeriks, Q. Huy, & E. Vaara, 2017, The process of post-merger integration: A review and agenda for future research, *Academy of Management Annals*, 11: 1–32; F. Bauer & K. Matzler, 2014, Antecedents of M&A success: The role of strategic complementarity, cultural fit and degree and speed of integration, *Strategic Management Journal*, 35: 269–291.
108. 2018, Hostile takeover, *Investopedia*, www.investopedia.com, accessed on April 12.
109. K. M. Cremers, L. P. Litov, & S. M. Sepe, 2017, Staggered boards and long-term firm value, revisited, *Journal of Financial Economics*, 126: 422–444; M. Straska & G. Waller, 2014, Antitakeover provisions and shareholder wealth: A survey of the literature, *Journal of Financial & Quantitative Analysis*, 49: 1–32.
110. I. R. Appel, T. A. Gormley, & D. B. Keim, 2016, Passive investors, not passive owners, *Journal of Financial Economics*, 121: 111–141.
111. K. R. Cremers, S. Masconale, & S. M. Sepe, 2016, Commitment and entrenchment in corporate governance, *Northwestern University Law Review*, 110: 727–810; M. Holmén, E. Nivorozhkin, & R. Rana, 2014, Do anti-takeover devices affect the takeover likelihood or the takeover premium? *European Journal of Finance*, 20: 319–340.
112. B. Cumberland & A. Hoeinghaus, 2016, Despite strong winds, golden parachutes still holding steady, *Journal of Compensation & Benefits*, 32: 5–10; P. C. Fiss, M. T. Kennedy, & G. F. Davis, 2012, How golden parachutes unfolded: Diffusion and variation of a controversial practice, *Organization Science*, 23: 1077–1099; J. A. Pearce II & R. B. Robinson, Jr., 2004, Hostile takeover defenses that maximize shareholder wealth, *Business Horizons*, 47(5): 15–24.
113. Cremers, Litov, & Sepe, Staggered boards and long-term firm value, revisited; M. Humphery-Jenner, 2014, Takeover defenses, innovation and value creation: Evidence from acquisition decisions, *Strategic Management Journal*, 35: 668–690.
114. D. Pittino, A. Barroso Martínez, F. Chirico, & R. Sanguino Galván, 2018, Psychological ownership, knowledge sharing and entrepreneurial orientation in family firms: The moderating role of governance heterogeneity, *Journal of Business Research*, 84: 312–326; P. Sieger, T. Zellweger, & K. Aquino, 2013, Turning agents into psychological principals: Aligning interests of non-owners through psychological ownership, *Journal of Management Studies*, 50: 361–388.
115. Y. Tang, D. Z. Mack, & G. Chen, 2018, The differential effects of CEO narcissism and hubris on corporate social responsibility, *Strategic Management Journal*, 39: 1370–1387; A. Chatterjee & Pollock, T. G. 2017, Master of puppets: How narcissistic CEOs construct their professional worlds, *Academy of Management Review*, 42: 703–725.
116. D. Cumming, I. Filatotchev, A. Knill, D. Reeb, & I. Senbet, 2017, Law, finance, and the international mobility of corporate governance, *Journal of International Business Studies*, 48: 123–147; E. Schiehll, C. Ahmadjian, & I. Filatotchev, 2014, National governance bundles perspective: Understanding the diversity of corporate governance practices at the firm and country levels, *Corporate Governance: An International Review*, 22: 179–184.
117. K. Madison, F. W. Kellermanns, & T. P. Munyon, 2017, Coexisting agency and stewardship governance in family firms: An empirical investigation of individual-level and firm-level effects, *Family Business*

Review, 30: 347–368; M. P. Leitterstorf & S. B. Rau, 2014, Socioemotional wealth and IPO underpricing of family firms, *Strategic Management Journal*, 35: 751–760.

118. J. Seldeslachts, M. Newham, & A. Banal-Estanol, 2017, Changes in common ownership of German companies, *DIW Economic Bulletin*, 7(30): 303–311; A. Haller, 2013, German corporate governance in international and European context, *International Journal of Accounting*, 48: 420–423.

119. B. Albersmann & D. Hohenfels, 2017, Audit committees and earnings management - evidence from the German two-tier board system, *Schmalenbach Business Review (SBR)*, 18: 147–178; A. Tushke, W. G. Sanders, & E. Hernandez, 2014, Whose experience matters in the boardroom? The effects of experiential and vicarious learning on emerging market entry, *Strategic Management Journal*, 35: 398–418.

120. S. Chen, C. Hsu, & C. Huang, 2016, The white squire defense: Evidence from private investments in public equity, *Journal of Banking & Finance*, 64: 16–35.

121. S. Petry, 2018, Mandatory worker representation on the board and its effect on shareholder wealth, *Financial Management (Wiley-Blackwell)*, 47: 25–54; T. Duc Hung, 2014, Multiple corporate governance attributes and the cost of capital—Evidence from Germany, *British Accounting Review*, 46: 179–197; P. C. Fiss & E. J. Zajac, 2004, The diffusion of ideas over contested terrain: The (non)adoption of a shareholder value orientation among German firms, *Administrative Science Quarterly*, 49: 501–534.

122. M. Almadi & P. Lazic, 2016, CEO incentive compensation and earnings management, *Management Decision*, 54: 2447–2461; C. Engelen, 2015, The effects of managerial discretion on moral hazard related behaviour: German evidence on agency costs, *Journal of Management & Governance*, 19: 927–960; A. Chizema, 2010, Early and late adoption of American-style executive pay in Germany: Governance and institutions, *Journal of World Business*, 45: 9–18; W. G. Sanders & A. C. Tuschke, 2007, The adoption of the institutionally contested organizational practices: The emergence of stock option pay in Germany, *Academy of Management Journal*, 50: 33–56.

123. J. R. Lincoln, D. Guillot, & M. Sargent, M. 2017, Business groups, networks, and embeddedness: Innovation and implementation alliances in Japanese electronics, 1985–1998, *Industrial & Corporate Change*, 26: 357–378; J. P. O'Brien & P. David, 2014, Reciprocity and R&D search: Applying the behavioral theory of the firm to a communitarian context, *Strategic Management Journal*, 35: 550–565.

124. A. Chie & G. Giovanni, 2017, Unstash the cash! Corporate governance reform in Japan, *Journal of Banking & Financial Economics*, 37: 51–69; N. Kosaku, 2014, Japan seeks to lure investors with improved corporate governance, *Wall Street Journal*, www.wsj.com, June 28.

125. H. Miyajima, R. Ogawa, & T. Saito, T. 2018, Changes in corporate governance and top executive turnover: The evidence from Japan, *Journal of the Japanese & International Economies*, 47: 17–31.

126. T. Hoshi, S. Koibuchi, & U. Schaede, 2018, The decline in bank-led corporate restructuring in Japan: 1981–2010, *Journal of The Japanese & International Economies*, 47: 81–90.

127. M. Becht, J. Franks, J. Grant, & H. F. Wagner, 2017, Returns to hedge fund activism: An international study, *Review of Financial Studies*, 30: 2933–2971; K. Harrigan, 2014, Comparing corporate governance practices and exit decisions between US and Japanese firms, *Journal of Management & Governance*, 18: 975–988.

128. J. L. Badaracco & L G. Goldberg, 2017, Elements of Japanese corporate governance, *Harvard Business School Cases*, January 1.

129. X. Geng, T. Yoshikawa, & A. M. Colpan, 2016, Leveraging foreign institutional logic in the adoption of stock option pay among Japanese firms, *Strategic Management Journal*, 37: 1472–1492.

130. L. Lai & H. Tam, 2017, Corporate governance, ownership structure and managing earnings to meet critical thresholds among Chinese listed firms, *Review of Quantitative Finance & Accounting*, 48: 789–818; R. Morck & B. Yeung, 2014, Corporate governance in China, *Journal of Applied Corporate Finance*, 26: 20–41.

131. D. A. Schuler, W. Shi, R. E. Hoskisson, & T. Chen, 2017, Windfalls of emperors' sojourns: Stock market reactions to Chinese firms hosting high-ranking government officials, *Strategic Management Journal*, 38: 1668–1687; W. Lee & L. Wang, 2017, Do political connections affect stock price crash risk? Firm-level evidence from China, *Review of Quantitative Finance & Accounting*, 48: 643–676; X. Yu, P. Zhang, & Y. Zheng, 2015, Corporate governance, political connections, and intra-industry effects: Evidence from corporate scandals in China, *Financial Management*, 44: 49–80.

132. T. Wang, H. Jiao, Z. Xu, & X. Yang, 2018, Entrepreneurial finance meets government investment at initial public offering: The role of minority state ownership, *Corporate Governance: An International Review*, 26: 97–117; M. Rooker, 2015, Corporate governance or governance by corporates? Testing governmentality in the context of China's national oil and petrochemical business groups, *Asia Pacific Business Review*, 21: 60–76.

133. H. Farag & C. Mallin, 2016, The Impact of the dual board structure and board diversity: Evidence from Chinese initial public offerings (IPOs), *Journal of Business Ethics*, 139: 333–349; J. Li & C. Qian, 2013, Principal-principal conflicts under weak institutions: A study of corporate takeovers in China, *Strategic Management Journal*, 34: 498–508; G. Jiang, P. Rao, & H. Yue, 2015, Tunneling through non-operational fund occupancy: An investigation based on officially identified activities, *Journal of Corporate Finance*, 32: 295–311.

134. X. Du, W. Jian, & S. Lai, 2017, Do Foreign directors mitigate earnings management? Evidence from China, *International Journal of Accounting*, 52: 142–177; H. Berkman, R. A. Cole, & L. J. Fu, 2014, Improving corporate governance where the state is the controlling block holder: Evidence from China, *European Journal of Finance*, 20: 752–777.

135. S. Dorobantu & K. Odziemkowska, 2017, Valuing stakeholder governance: property rights, community mobilization, and firm value, *Strategic Management Journal*, 38: 2682–2703.

136. E. M. Bettinazzi & M. Zollo, 2017, Stakeholder orientation and acquisition performance, *Strategic Management Journal*, 38: 2465–2485; G. K. Stahl & M. S. De Luque, 2014, Antecedents of responsible leader behavior: A research synthesis, conceptual framework, and agenda for future research, *Academy of Management Perspectives*, 28: 235–254.

137. A. M. Adnan & H. Tandigalla, 2017, The dramatic shift in emphasis from a shareholder-dominated approach to a stakeholder-oriented corporate governance model, *European Journal of Business & Economics*, 12: 1–8; A. Soleimani, W. D. Schneper, & W. Newburry, 2014, The impact of stakeholder power on corporate reputation: A cross-country corporate governance perspective, *Organization Science*, 25: 991–1008.

138. J. Cohen, L. Holder-Webb, & S. Khalil, 2017, A further examination of the impact of corporate social responsibility and governance on investment decisions, *Journal of Business Ethics*, 146: 203–218.

139. L. Jiao, G. Harrison, M. Dyball, & J. Chen, 2017, CEO values, stakeholder culture, and stakeholder-based performance, *Asia Pacific Journal of Management*, 34: 875–899.

140. K. V. Tuliao & C. Chen, 2017, CEO duality and bribery: the roles of gender and national culture, *Management Decision*, 55: 218–231; Y. Li, F. Yao, & D. Ahlstrom, 2015, The social dilemma of bribery in emerging economies: A dynamic model of emotion, social value, and institutional uncertainty, *Asia Pacific Journal of Management*, 32: 311–334.

141. K. Lopatta, R. Jaeschke, M. Tchikov, & S. Lodhia, 2017, Corruption, corporate social responsibility and financial constraints: international firm-level evidence, *European Management Review*, 14: 47–65; S.-H. Lee & D. H. Weng, 2013, Does bribery in the home country promote or dampen firm exports? *Strategic Management Journal*, 34: 1472–1487.

iStock.com/DNY59

11

Organizational Structure and Controls

Studying this chapter should provide you with the strategic management knowledge needed to:

11-1 Define organizational structure and controls and discuss the difference between strategic and financial controls.

11-2 Describe the relationship between strategy and structure.

11-3 Discuss the different functional structures used to implement business-level strategies.

11-4 Explain the use of three versions of the multidivisional (M-form) structure to implement different diversification strategies.

11-5 Discuss the organizational structures used to implement three international strategies.

11-6 Define strategic networks and discuss how strategic center firms implement such networks at the business, corporate, and international levels.

iStock.com/DNY59

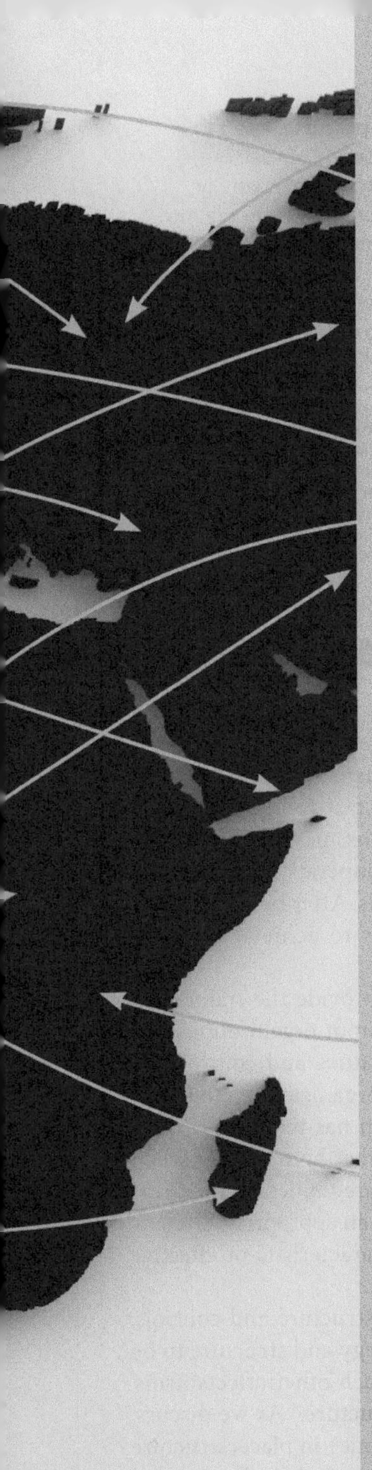

CHANGING MCDONALD'S ORGANIZATIONAL STRUCTURE AND CONTROLS: A PATH TO IMPROVED PERFORMANCE

McDonald's is a huge fast food restaurant chain—several times larger than Burger King and Wendy's, its closest competitors. In addition to the United States and Canada, McDonald's is present in over 100 countries worldwide. However, Steve Easterbrook, current CEO, appointed in 2015, has been working to adjust the firm's strategy and structure. As outlined in the Opening Case in Chapter 2, the external and competitive environments of McDonald's are turbulent. Its established competitors are fierce and others are entering the market; for example, International House of Pancakes (IHOP) placed an advertisement suggesting it may change its name to IHOb, International House of Burgers, signalling that it is now competing with McDonald's and others. This is probably due to McDonald's and others offering its breakfast menu items anytime during the day.

Chapter 4 also indicates that McDonald's is pursuing the low-cost strategy to deal with its competitive environment. To improve its performance, McDonald's needs structures and controls that match the strategy it is seeking to implement. At the same time, McDonald's is largely financed by franchisees who purchase a franchise contract to manage one or many locations worldwide. Franchising is an alliance strategy outlined in Chapter 9. The effectiveness of this alliance strategy is dependent on how well the franchisor can replicate its success across multiple partners in a cost-effective way. This is especially important to the low-cost strategy McDonald's employs, where it is desirable for customers to have a similar experience at any of its locations.

Hannelore Foerster/Getty Images/Getty Images Entertainment/Getty Images

Steve Easterbrook, CEO of McDonald's, poses with Ronald McDonald.

The firm is reducing the number of layers between the CEO and the franchisee from eight to six, especially in the regional structure. There will be a number of unspecified layoffs to reduce costly bureaucracy. The remaining regional and corporate staff will "spend more time helping operators figure out ways to boost restaurant profitability rather than just grading restaurants on such things as cleanliness, customer service and order accuracy." As noted above, the focus of the controls has largely been on enforcing replicability across franchisees. The company is now fine-tuning its corporate controls to focus on supply chain and process innovation at the franchisee level, giving more support to franchisees rather than penalizing them for not meeting exact specifications.

For example, "McDonald's assembled a panel of sensory experts consisting of suppliers, chefs and employees to compare rivals' burgers against theirs. They discovered that McDonald's burgers just weren't hot and fresh enough." So, they adjusted "the supply chain and distribution system to handle fresh—rather than frozen—hamburger patties." "McDonald's also altered its grilling methods, began toasting its buns longer and changed its preparation procedures so that burgers would be cooked upon request rather than held in warming cabinets."

For a number of years, McDonald's was structured around geographic segments including the United States, Europe, Asia/Pacific, Middle East, and Africa (APMEA). Easterbrook wants to strip away the bureaucracy at McDonald's so the firm can anticipate trends as a foundation for moving nimbly, and fully understand and appropriately respond to customers' interests. Additionally, Easterbrook specified that the new structure should be built on "commercial logic" rather than simply geography.

McDonald's has implemented this new organizational structure as part of its effort to increase revenues and profitability and improving its stock value. Corporate officials are confident the new structure will enable individual segments to identify and successfully address what are common needs of their markets and customers, and that those operating units within each segment will have the flexibility they need to innovate in ways that will create value for customers and, in turn, for the entire corporation.

As the new structure and controls reduce costs and increase effectiveness, McDonald's is using some of these cost savings to implement a digital transition to online ordering and in-store kiosks. Thus, not only are the structure and control more simplified and effective, but technology is speeding and improving the customer experience.

Sources: H. Detrick, 2018, McDonald's new Chicago headquarters is officially open. Why it moved back to the city after 47 years, *Fortune*, www.fortune.com, June 5; L. Grossman, 2018, Wendy's got all savage on McDonald's with the perfect meme, *Time*, www.time.com, May 9; J. Jargon, J. 2018, McDonald's shares details of restructuring plan in new memo, *Wall Street Journal*, www.wsj.com, June 12; L. Patton, 2018. McDonald's high-tech makeover is stressing workers out, *Bloomberg*, www.bloomberg.com, March 13; B. Peters, 2018, McDonald's plans more corporate job cuts amid tech push: Report, *Investors Business Daily*. www.investor.com, June 7; J. Sperling, 2018, McDonald's plans to eliminate a number of corporate jobs as part of reorganization plan, *Fortune*, www.fortune.com, June 7; C. Choi, 2015, McDonald's to simplify structure, focus on customers, *Spokesman*, www.spokesman.com, May 5; R. Neate, 2015, McDonald's plans huge shakeup as CEO admits: 'Our performance has been poor,' *The Guardian*, www.theguardian.com, May 4.

As we explained in Chapter 4, all firms use one or more business-level strategies. McDonald's uses the low-cost leadership strategy for its fast food business. In Chapters 6 through 9, we discussed other strategies that firms may choose to use (corporate-level, merger and acquisition, international, and cooperative), depending on the decisions made by those leading individual organizations. After being selected, strategies must be implemented effectively for organizations to achieve intended outcomes.

Organizational structure and controls, this chapter's topic, provide the framework within which strategies are implemented and used in both for-profit organizations and not-for-profit agencies.[1] However, as we explain, separate structures and controls are required to successfully implement different strategies. In all organizations, top-level managers have the final responsibility for ensuring that the firm has matched each of its strategies with the appropriate organizational structure and that both change when necessary. The match or degree of fit between strategy and structure influences the firm's attempts to earn above-average returns.[2] Thus, the ability to select an appropriate strategy and match it with the appropriate structure is an important characteristic of effective strategic leadership.[3]

This chapter opens with an introduction to organizational structure and controls. We then provide more details about the need for the firm's strategy and structure to be properly matched. The influence of strategy and structure on each other affects firms' efforts to match individual strategies with their appropriate structure.[4] As we discuss, strategy has a more important influence on structure, although once in place, structure influences strategy.[5] Next, we describe the relationship between growth and structural change successful firms experience. We then discuss the different organizational structures firms use to implement separate business-level, corporate-level, international, and cooperative strategies. We present a series of figures to highlight the different structures firms match with different strategies. Across time and based on their experiences, organizations, especially large and complex ones, customize these general structures to meet their unique needs.[6] Typically, firms try to form a structure that is complex enough to facilitate implementation of their strategies but simple enough for all parties to understand and use.[7]

11-1 Organizational Structure and Controls

Research shows that organizational structure and the controls that are a part of the structure affect firm performance.[8] In particular, evidence suggests that performance declines when the firm's strategy is not matched with the most appropriate structure and controls.[9] Even though mismatches between strategy and structure do occur, research indicates that managers try to act rationally when forming or changing their firm's structure.[10]

In Chapter 2's Opening Case, we talked about problems McDonald's is encountering when trying to cope effectively with changes that are taking place in the external environment. As we noted then, the firm is changing to better meet the competition. Additionally though and more broadly, as explained in the Opening Case, changes are being made to the organizational structure at McDonald's with the expectation that doing so will lead to enhanced firm performance. Defined comprehensively below, organizational structure essentially specifies the functions that must be completed so the firm can implement its strategy.

The leadership at McDonald's, including CEO Steve Easterbrook, believe that changes being made to the firm's structure will increase its efficiency (that is, its daily operations will improve) and its effectiveness (that is, it will better serve customers' needs). In the Opening Case, we discuss changes that have been made to the company's organizational structure, controls, and processes.

11-1a Organizational Structure

Organizational structure specifies the firm's formal reporting relationships, procedures, controls, and authority and decision-making processes.[11] A firm's structure determines and specifies the decisions that are to be made and the work that is to be completed by everyone within an organization as a result of those decisions.[12] Organizational routines serve as processes that are used to complete the work required by individual strategies.[13]

Developing an organizational structure that effectively supports the firm's strategy is difficult, especially because of the uncertainty (or unpredictable variation) about cause–effect relationships in the global economy's rapidly changing competitive environments.[14] When a structure's elements (e.g., reporting relationships, procedures, etc.) are properly aligned with one another, the structure increases the likelihood that the firm will operate in ways that allow it to better understand the challenging cause/effect relationships it encounters when competing against its rivals. Thus, helping the firm effectively cope with environmental uncertainty is an important contribution organizational structure makes to a firm as it seeks to successfully implement its strategy or strategies as a means of outperforming competitors.[15]

Appropriately designed organizational structures provide the stability a firm needs to successfully implement its strategies and maintain its current competitive advantages while simultaneously providing the flexibility to develop advantages it will need in the future.[16] More specifically, *structural stability* provides the capacity the firm requires to consistently and predictably manage its daily work routines,[17] while *structural flexibility* makes it possible for the firm to identify opportunities and then allocate resources to pursue them as a way of being prepared to succeed in the future.[18] Thus, an effectively flexible organizational structure allows the firm to *exploit* current competitive advantages while *developing* new advantages that can be used in the future. Alternatively, an ineffective structure that is inflexible may drive productive employees away because of frustration and an inability to create value while completing their work.[19] Losing productive employees can result in a loss of knowledge within a firm. This is an especially damaging outcome when a departing employee, who may accept employment with a competitor, possesses a significant amount of tacit knowledge.

Organizational structure specifies the firm's formal reporting relationships, procedures, controls, and authority and decision-making processes.

Pictured here is Alfred Chandler, a scholar whose work enhanced our understanding of organizational structure and strategy.

Modifications to the firm's current strategy or selection of a new strategy call for changes to its organizational structure. However, research shows that once in place, organizational inertia often inhibits efforts to change structure, even when the firm's performance suggests that it is time to do so.[20] In his pioneering work, Alfred Chandler found that organizations change their structures when inefficiencies force them to do so.[21] Chandler's contributions to our understanding of organizational structure and its relationship to strategies and performance are significant. Indeed, some believe that Chandler's emphasis on "organizational structure so transformed the field of business history that some call the period before Chandler's work was published 'B.C.,' meaning 'before Chandler.' "[22]

Firms seem to prefer the structural status quo and its familiar working relationships until their performance declines to the point where change is absolutely necessary.[23] Moreover, top-level managers often hesitate to conclude that the firm's structure or its strategy is the problem because doing so suggests that their previous choices were not the best ones.[24] Because of these inertial tendencies, structural change is often induced instead by actions from stakeholders (e.g., those from the capital market and customers) who are no longer willing to tolerate the firm's performance. For example, department store operators JCPenney and Sears have been unable to make a strong transition to online sales while other outlets such as Kohl's and Macy's have done better.[25] Evidence shows that appropriate timing of structural change happens when top-level managers recognize that a current organizational structure no longer provides the coordination and direction needed for the firm to successfully implement its strategies.[26] Interestingly, many organizational changes take place in economic downturns because poor performance reveals organizational weaknesses. As we discuss next, effective organizational controls help managers recognize when it is time to adjust the firm's structure.

11-1b Organizational Controls

Organizational controls are an important aspect of structure.[27] **Organizational controls** guide the use of strategy, indicate how to compare actual results with expected results, and suggest corrective actions to take when the difference is unacceptable. It is difficult for a firm to successfully exploit its competitive advantages without effective organizational controls. Properly designed organizational controls provide clear insights regarding behaviors that enhance firm performance.[28] Firms use both strategic controls and financial controls to support implementation of their strategies.

Strategic controls are largely subjective criteria intended to verify that the firm is using appropriate strategies for the conditions in the external environment and the company's competitive advantages. Thus, strategic controls are concerned with examining the fit between what the firm *might do* (as suggested by opportunities in its external environment) and what it *can do* (as indicated by its internal organization in the form of its resources, capabilities, and core competencies). Effective strategic controls help the firm understand what it takes to be successful, especially where significant strategic change is needed.[29] Strategic controls demand rich communications between managers responsible for using them to judge the firm's performance and those with primary responsibility for

Organizational controls guide the use of strategy, indicate how to compare actual results with expected results, and suggest corrective actions to take when the difference is unacceptable.

Strategic controls are largely subjective criteria intended to verify that the firm is using appropriate strategies for the conditions in the external environment and the company's competitive advantages.

implementing the firm's strategies (such as middle- and first-level managers). These frequent exchanges between managers are both formal and informal in nature.[30]

Strategic controls are also used to evaluate the degree to which the firm focuses on the requirements to implement its strategies. For a business-level strategy, for example, strategic controls are used to study value chain activities and support functions (see Figures 3.3, 3.4, and 3.5, in Chapter 3) to verify that the critical activities and functions are being emphasized and properly executed. When implementing related diversification strategies at the corporate level, strategic controls are used to verify the sharing of activities (in the case of the related-constrained strategy) or the transferring of core competencies (in the case of the related-linked strategy) across businesses. To effectively use strategic controls when evaluating either of these related diversification strategies, headquarter executives must have a deep understanding of the business-level strategies being implemented within individual strategic business units.[31]

Financial controls are largely objective criteria used to measure the firm's performance against previously established quantitative standards. When using financial controls, firms evaluate their current performance against previous outcomes as well as against competitors' performance and industry averages. Accounting-based measures, such as return on investment (ROI) and return on assets (ROA), as well as market-based measures, such as economic value added, are examples of financial controls. Partly because strategic controls are difficult to use with extensive diversification,[32] financial controls are emphasized to evaluate the performance of the firm using the unrelated diversification strategy. The unrelated diversification strategy's focus on financial outcomes (see Chapter 6) requires using standardized financial controls to compare performances between business units and those responsible for leading them.[33]

Both strategic and financial controls are important aspects of a firm's structure; as noted previously, any structure's effectiveness is determined using a "balanced" combination of strategic and financial controls. But, determining the most appropriate balance to have in place between strategic and financial controls at specific points in time is challenging, partly because the relative use of controls varies by type of strategy. For example, companies and business units of large diversified firms using the cost leadership strategy emphasize financial controls (such as quantitative cost goals), while companies and business units using the differentiation strategy emphasize strategic controls (such as subjective measures of the effectiveness of product development teams).[34] As previously explained, a corporation-wide emphasis on sharing among business units (as called for by related diversification strategies) results in an emphasis on strategic controls, while financial controls are emphasized for strategies in which activities or capabilities are not shared (e.g., in an unrelated diversification strategy). Those determining how strategies are to be implemented must keep these relative degrees of balance between controls by type of strategy in mind when making implementation-related decisions.

11-2 Relationships between Strategy and Structure

Strategy and structure have a reciprocal relationship, and if aligned properly, performance improves.[35] This relationship highlights the interconnectedness between strategy formulation (Chapters 4, 6–9) and strategy implementation (Chapters 10–13). In general, this reciprocal relationship finds structure flowing from or following selection of the firm's strategy. Once in place though, structure can influence current strategic actions as well as choices about future strategies. The new structure being put in place at McDonald's that we mentioned earlier has the potential to influence implementation of strategies that are,

Financial controls are largely objective criteria used to measure the firm's performance against previously established quantitative standards.

in part, aimed to better identify and satisfy customers' changing needs.[36] Overall, those involved with a firm's strategic management process should understand that the general nature of the strategy/structure relationship means that changes to the firm's strategy create the need to change how the organization completes its work.

Moreover, because structure can influence strategy by constraining the potential alternatives considered, firms must be vigilant in their efforts to verify how their structure not only affects implementation of chosen strategies, but also the limits the structure places on possible future strategies. Overall though, the effect of strategy on structure is stronger than is the effect of structure on strategy.

Regardless of the strength of the reciprocal relationships between strategy and structure, those choosing the firm's strategy and structure should be committed to matching each strategy with a structure that provides the stability needed to use current competitive advantages as well as the flexibility required to develop future advantages. Therefore, when changing strategies, the firm should simultaneously consider the structure that will be needed to support use of the new strategy; properly matching strategy and structure can create a competitive advantage. This process can be influenced by outside forces, such as significant media attention, which may either hinder the change or foster it.[37]

11-3 Evolutionary Patterns of Strategy and Organizational Structure

Research suggests that most firms experience a certain pattern of relationships between strategy and structure. Chandler[38] found that firms tend to grow in somewhat predictable patterns: "first by volume, then by geography, then integration (vertical, horizontal), and finally through product/business diversification"[39] (see Figure 11.1). Chandler interpreted his findings as an indication that firms' growth patterns determine their structural form.

As shown in Figure 11.1, sales growth creates coordination and control problems the existing organizational structure cannot efficiently handle. Organizational growth creates the opportunity for the firm to change its strategy to try to become even more successful. However, the existing structure's formal reporting relationships, procedures, controls, and authority and decision-making processes lack the sophistication required to support using the new strategy,[40] meaning that a new organizational structure is needed.[41]

Firms choose from among three major types of organizational structures—simple, functional, and multidivisional—to implement strategies. Across time, successful firms move from the simple, to the functional, to the multidivisional structure to support changes in their growth strategies.

11-3a Simple Structure

The **simple structure** is a structure in which the owner-manager makes all major decisions and monitors all activities, while the staff serves as an extension of the manager's supervisory authority.[42] Typically, the owner-manager actively works in the business on a daily basis. Informal relationships, few rules, limited task specialization, and unsophisticated information systems characterize this structure. Frequent and informal communications between the owner-manager and employees make coordinating the work to be completed relatively easy. The simple structure is matched with focus strategies and business-level strategies, as firms implementing these strategies commonly compete by offering a single product line in a single geographic market. Local restaurants, repair businesses, and other specialized enterprises are examples of firms using the simple structure.

The **simple structure** is a structure in which the owner-manager makes all major decisions and monitors all activities, while the staff serves as an extension of the manager's supervisory authority.

Figure 11.1 Strategy and Structure Growth Pattern

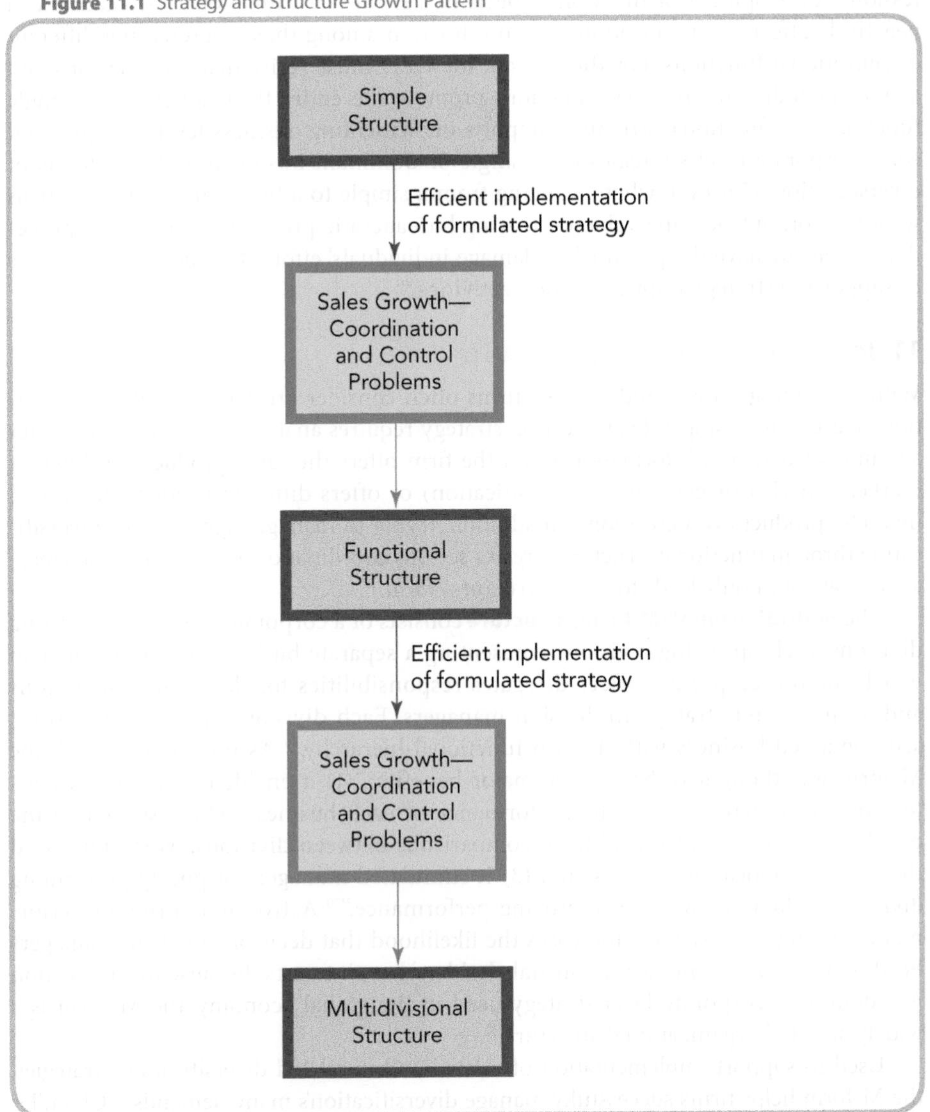

As the small firm grows larger and becomes more complex, managerial and structural challenges emerge. For example, the amount of competitively relevant information requiring analysis substantially increases, placing significant pressure on the owner-manager. Additional growth and success may cause the firm to change its strategy. Even if the strategy remains the same, the firm's larger size dictates the need for more sophisticated workflows and integrating mechanisms. At this evolutionary point, firms tend to move from the simple structure to a functional organizational structure.[43]

The **functional structure** consists of a chief executive officer and a limited corporate staff, with functional line managers in dominant organizational areas such as production, accounting, marketing, R&D, engineering, and human resources.

11-3b Functional Structure

The **functional structure** consists of a chief executive officer and a limited corporate staff, with functional line managers in dominant organizational areas such as production, accounting, marketing, R&D, engineering, and human resources.[44] This structure allows for functional specialization,[45] thereby facilitating active sharing of knowledge within each functional area. Knowledge sharing facilitates career paths as well as professional development of functional specialists. However, a functional orientation can negatively affect communication and coordination among those representing different organizational functions. For this reason, the CEO must verify that the decisions and actions of individual business functions promote the entire firm rather than a single function. The functional structure supports implementing business-level strategies and some corporate-level strategies (e.g., single or dominant business) with low levels of diversification. However, when changing from a simple to a functional structure, firms want to avoid introducing value-destroying bureaucratic procedures since such procedures typically have the potential to damage individuals' efforts to innovate as a means of supporting strategy implementation activities.[46]

11-3c Multidivisional Structure

With continuing growth and success, firms often consider greater levels of diversification. Successfully using a diversification strategy requires analyzing substantially greater amounts of data and information when the firm offers the same products in different markets (market or geographic diversification) or offers different products in several markets (product diversification). In addition, trying to manage high levels of diversification through functional structures creates serious coordination and control problems,[47] a fact that commonly leads to a new structural form.[48]

The **multidivisional (M-form) structure** consists of a corporate office and operating divisions, each operating division representing a separate business or profit center in which the top corporate officer delegates responsibilities for day-to-day operations and business-unit strategy to division managers. Each division represents a distinct, self-contained business with its own functional hierarchy.[49] As initially designed, the M-form was thought to have three major benefits: "(1) it enabled corporate officers to more accurately monitor the performance of each business, which simplified the problem of control; (2) it facilitated comparisons between divisions, which improved the resource allocation process; and (3) it stimulated managers of poorly performing divisions to look for ways of improving performance."[50] Active monitoring of performance through the M-form increases the likelihood that decisions made by managers heading individual units will be in stakeholders' best interests. Because diversification is a dominant corporate-level strategy used in the global economy, the M-form is a widely adopted organizational structure.[51]

Used to support implementation of related and unrelated diversification strategies, the M-form helps firms successfully manage diversification's many demands.[52] Chandler viewed the M-form as an innovative response to coordination and control problems that surfaced during the 1920s in the functional structures then used by large firms such as DuPont and General Motors.[53] Research shows that the M-form is appropriate when the firm grows through diversification.[54] Partly because of its value to diversified corporations, some consider the multidivisional structure to be one of the twentieth century's most significant organizational innovations.[55]

No single organizational structure (simple, functional, or multidivisional) is inherently superior to the others. Peter Drucker says the following about this matter:

"There is no one right organization.... Rather the task ... is to select the organization for the particular task and mission at hand."[56]

This statement suggests that the firm must select a structure that is "right" for successfully using the chosen strategy. Because no single structure is optimal in all instances, managers concentrate on developing proper matches between strategies and organizational structures rather than searching for an "optimal" structure. We now describe the strategy/structure matches that contribute positively to firm performance.

The **multidivisional (M-form) structure** consists of a corporate office and operating divisions, each operating division representing a separate business or profit center in which the top corporate officer delegates responsibilities for day-to-day operations and business-unit strategy to division managers.

11-3d Matches between Business-Level Strategies and the Functional Structure

Firms use different forms of the functional organizational structure to support implementing the cost leadership, differentiation, and integrated cost leadership/differentiation strategies. The differences in these forms are accounted for primarily by different uses of three important structural characteristics: *specialization* (concerned with the type and number of jobs required to complete work[57]), *centralization* (the degree to which decision-making authority is retained at higher managerial levels[58]), and *formalization* (the degree to which formal rules and procedures govern work[59]).

Using the Functional Structure to Implement the Cost Leadership Strategy

Firms using the cost leadership strategy sell large quantities of standardized products to an industry's typical customer. Firms using this strategy need a structure that allows them to achieve efficiencies and deliver their products at costs lower than those of competitors.[60] Simple reporting relationships, a few layers in the decision-making and authority structure, a centralized corporate staff, and a strong focus on process improvements through the manufacturing function rather than the development of new products by emphasizing product R&D help to achieve the needed efficiencies and thus characterize the cost leadership form of the functional structure (see Figure 11.2).[61] This structure contributes to the emergence of a low-cost culture—a culture in which employees constantly try to find ways to reduce the costs incurred to complete their work.[62] They can do this through the development of a product design that is simple and easy to manufacture, as well as through the development of efficient processes to produce the goods.[63]

Figure 11.2 Functional Structure for Implementing a Cost Leadership Strategy

Office of the President

Centralized Staff

Engineering | Marketing | Operations | Personnel | Accounting

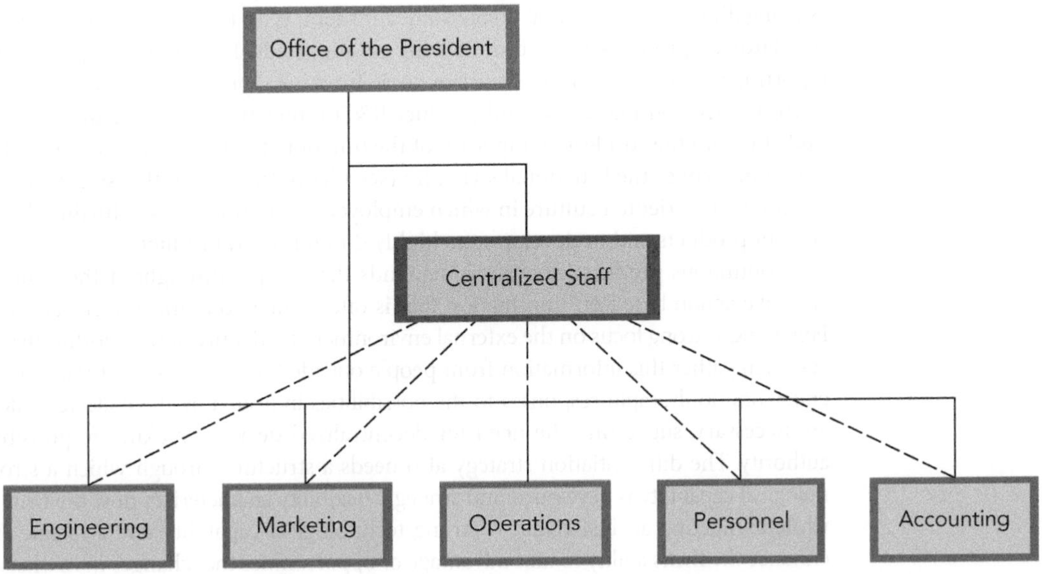

Notes:
- Operations is the main function.
- Process engineering is emphasized rather than new product R&D.
- Relatively large centralized staff coordinates functions.
- Formalized procedures allow for emergence of a low-cost culture.
- Overall structure is mechanistic; job roles are highly structured.

In terms of centralization, decision-making authority is centralized in a staff function to maintain a cost-reducing emphasis within each organizational function (engineering, marketing, etc.). While encouraging continuous cost reductions, the centralized staff also verifies that further cuts in costs in one function won't adversely affect the productivity levels in other functions.[64]

Jobs are highly specialized in the cost leadership functional structure; work is divided into homogeneous subgroups. Organizational functions are the most common subgroup, although work is sometimes batched on the basis of products delivered or clients served. Specializing in their work allows employees to increase their efficiency, resulting in reduced costs. Guiding individuals' work in this structure are highly formalized rules and procedures, which often emanate from the centralized staff.

Walmart Stores, Inc. uses the functional structure to implement cost leadership strategies in each of its three operating segments (Walmart U.S., Sam's Clubs, and Walmart International). In the Walmart U.S. segment (which generates the largest share of the firm's total sales), the cost leadership strategy is used in the firm's Supercenter, Discount, Neighborhood Market, and digital retail formats.[65] For the entire corporation, the firm says that it is committed to "bringing value to customers and communities around the world."[66] Over the years, competitors' efforts to duplicate the success Walmart has achieved by implementing its cost leadership strategies have generally failed, partly because of the effective strategy/structure matches the firm has formed between the cost leadership strategy and the functional structure that is specific to the mandates of that strategy. Although Walmart has recently been playing catch-up in online sales to Amazon, it still maintains a strong match between its structure and strategy.[67]

Using the Functional Structure to Implement the Differentiation Strategy

Firms using the differentiation strategy seek to deliver products that customers perceive as being different in ways that create value for them. With this strategy, the firm sells nonstandardized products to customers with unique needs. Relatively complex and flexible reporting relationships, frequent use of cross-functional product development teams, and a strong focus on marketing and product R&D rather than manufacturing and process R&D (as with the cost leadership form of the functional structure) characterize the differentiation form of the functional structure (see Figure 11.3). From this structure emerges a development-oriented culture in which employees try to find ways to further differentiate current products and to develop new, highly differentiated products.[68]

Continuous product innovation demands that people throughout the firm interpret and take action based on information that is often ambiguous, incomplete, and uncertain. Following a strong focus on the external environment to identify new opportunities, employees often gather this information from people outside the firm (e.g., customers and suppliers). Commonly, rapid responses to the possibilities indicated by the collected information are necessary, suggesting the need for decentralized decision-making responsibility and authority. The differentiation strategy also needs a structure through which a strong technological capability is developed and strategic flexibility characterizes how the firm operates while competing against rivals. A strong technological capability and strategic flexibility enhance the firm's ability to take advantage of opportunities that changes in markets create.[69]

To support the creativity needed and the continuous pursuit of new sources of differentiation and new products, jobs in this structure are not highly specialized. This lack of specialization means that workers have a relatively large number of tasks in their job descriptions. Few formal rules and procedures also characterize this structure. Low formalization, decentralization of decision-making authority and responsibility, and low specialization of work tasks combine to create a structure in which people interact

Figure 11.3 Functional Structure for Implementing a Differentiation Strategy

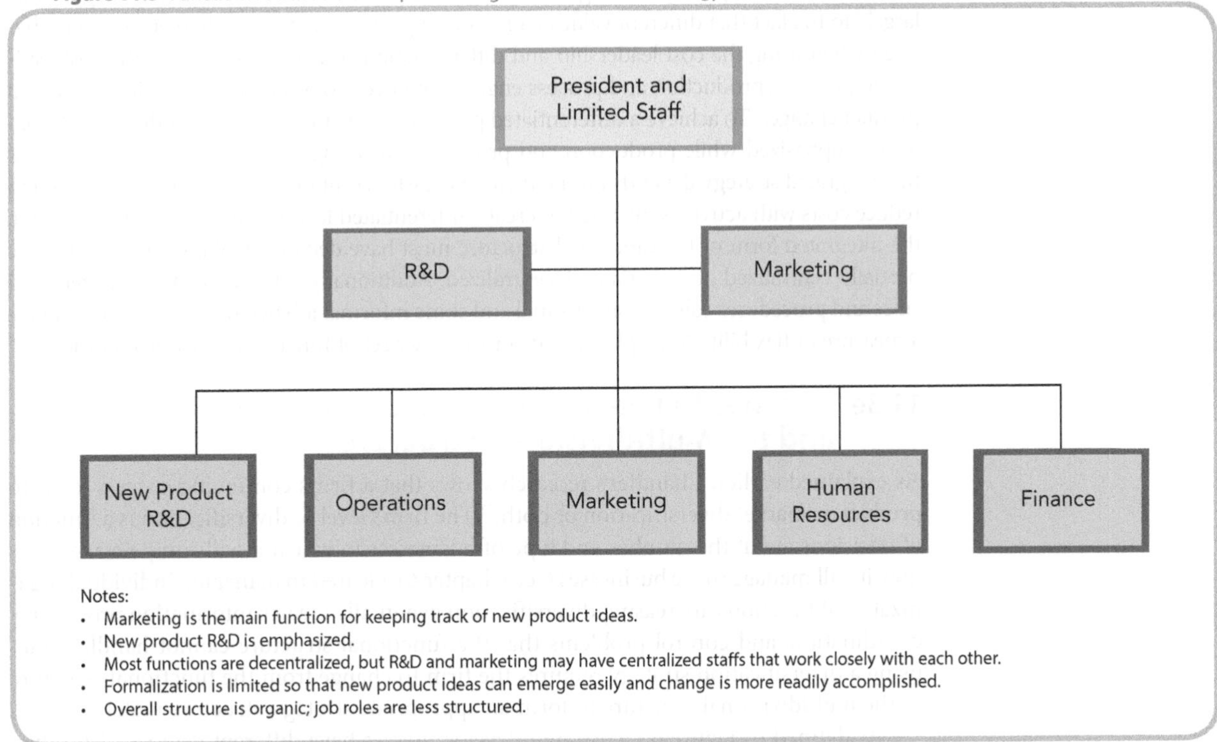

frequently to exchange ideas about how to further differentiate current products while developing ideas for new products that can be crisply differentiated at a point in the future. These structural aspects usually lead to a flatter structure than that implemented in a comparably sized firm using the low cost strategy.

Steinway & Sons pianos uses a differentiation strategy and matching structure to achieve success in piano manufacturing and distribution. Although many piano makers evolved toward mass production methods and lower costs to find a new way of meeting customer needs, Steinway "continued to use craft-based production methods to make and sell higher-priced pianos to virtuoso concert pianists and a wealthier clientele."[70]

TIMOTHY A. CLARY/AFP/Getty Images

A Steinway & Sons worker manually strings the soundboard of a Concert Grand Model D Piano.

Using the Functional Structure to Implement the Integrated Cost Leadership/Differentiation Strategy

Firms using the integrated cost leadership/differentiation strategy sell products that create value because of their relatively low cost and reasonable sources of differentiation. The cost of these products is low "relative" to the cost leader's prices, while their differentiation is "reasonable" when compared to the clearly unique features of the differentiator's products.

Although challenging to implement, the integrated cost leadership/differentiation strategy is used frequently in the global economy. The challenge of using this strategy is due largely to the fact that different value chain and support activities (see Chapter 3) are emphasized when using the cost leadership and differentiation strategies. To achieve the cost leadership position, production and process engineering need to be emphasized, with infrequent product changes. To achieve a differentiated position, marketing and new product R&D need to be emphasized while production and process engineering are not. Thus, effective use of the integrated strategy depends on the firm's successful combination of activities intended to reduce costs with activities intended to create differentiated features for a product. As a result, the integrated form of the functional structure must have decision-making patterns that are partially centralized and partially decentralized. Additionally, jobs are semispecialized, and rules and procedures call for some formal and some informal job behavior. All of this requires a measure of flexibility to emphasize one or the other set of functions at any given time.[71]

11-3e Matches between Corporate-Level Strategies and the Multidivisional Structure

As explained earlier, Chandler's research shows that a firm's continuing success leads to product or market diversification or both.[72] The firm's level of diversification is a function of decisions about the number and type of businesses in which it will compete as well as how it will manage those businesses (see Chapter 6). Geared to managing individual organizational functions, increasing diversification eventually creates information processing, coordination, and control problems that the functional structure cannot handle. Thus, using a diversification strategy requires the firm to change from the functional structure to the multidivisional structure to form an appropriate strategy/structure match.

As defined in Figure 6.1, corporate-level strategies have different degrees of product and market diversification. The demands created by different levels of diversification highlight the need for a unique organizational structure to effectively implement each strategy (see Figure 11.4). We discuss the relationships between three diversification strategies and the unique organizational structure that should be matched with each one in the next three sections.

Using the Cooperative Form of the Multidivisional Structure to Implement the Related Constrained Strategy

The **cooperative form** is an M-form structure in which horizontal integration is used to bring about interdivisional cooperation. Divisions in a firm using the related constrained

Figure 11.4 Three Variations of the Multidivisional Structure

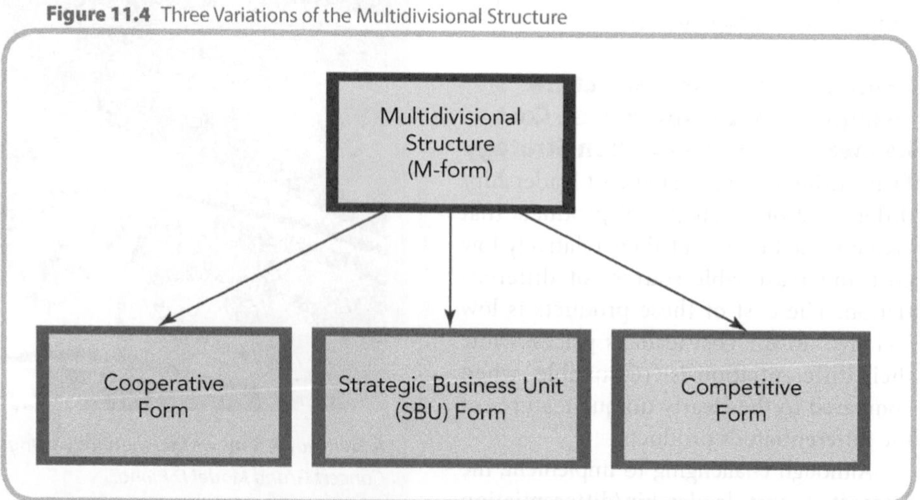

The **cooperative form** is an M-form structure in which horizontal integration is used to bring about interdivisional cooperation.

diversification strategy commonly are formed around products, markets, or both. In Figure 11.5, we use product divisions as part of the representation of the cooperative form of the multidivisional structure, although market divisions could be used instead of or in addition to product divisions to develop the figure.

We mentioned in Chapter 6 that Procter & Gamble (P&G) uses a related constrained strategy. We note here that the firm matches the cooperative form of the multidivisional structure to this strategy in order to effectively implement it.

As explained in Chapter 6, the related constrained strategy finds a firm sharing resources and activities across its businesses. Consumer understanding, scale, innovation, go-to-market capabilities, and brand-building are what P&G has identified as its six "core strengths" (or core resources). These strengths are shared across ten global product business units including "Baby Care, Fabric Care, Family Care, Feminine Care, Grooming, Hair Care, Home Care, Oral Care, Personal Health Care, and Skin and Personal Care" that form the core of P&G's cooperative multidivisional organizational structure. The reason P&G shares its six core strengths across the four industry-based sectors is that, according to the firm, the scale of these sectors allows the firm "to share knowledge, transfer technologies, optimize our spending and flow resources to better serve consumers and continually improve our efficiency and productivity."[73] Thus, through its organizational structure, P&G integrates its operations horizontally for the purpose of developing cooperation across the ten product sectors in which it competes.

Figure 11.5 Cooperative Form of the Multidivisional Structure for Implementing a Related Constrained Strategy

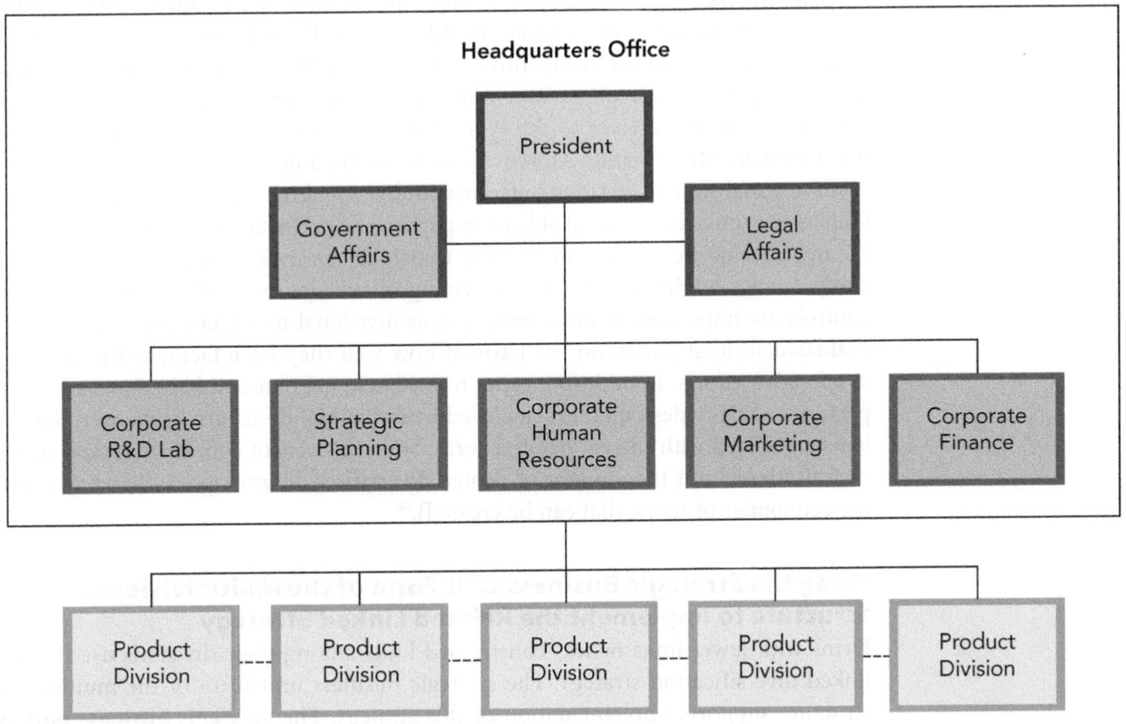

Notes:

- Structural integration devices create tight links among all divisions.
- Corporate office emphasizes centralized strategic planning, human resources, and marketing to foster cooperation between divisions.
- R&D is likely to be centralized.
- Rewards are subjective and tend to emphasize overall corporate performance in addition to divisional performance.
- Culture emphasizes cooperative sharing.

Sharing divisional competencies facilitates a firm's efforts to develop economies of scope. As explained in Chapter 6, economies of scope (cost savings resulting from the sharing of competencies developed in one division with another division) are linked with successful use of the related constrained strategy. Interdivisional sharing of competencies, such as takes place within P&G, depends on cooperation, suggesting the use of the cooperative form of the multidivisional structure.[74]

The cooperative structure uses different characteristics of structure (centralization, standardization, and formalization) as integrating mechanisms to facilitate interdivisional cooperation. Frequent, direct contact between division managers, another integrating mechanism, encourages and supports cooperation and the sharing of knowledge, capabilities, or other resources that could be used to create new advantages.[75] Sometimes, liaison roles are established in each division to reduce the time division managers spend integrating and coordinating their unit's work with the work occurring in other divisions. Temporary teams or task forces may be formed around projects whose success depends on sharing resources that are embedded within several divisions. Formal integration departments might be established in firms frequently using temporary inter-business unit teams or task forces.

Ultimately, a matrix organization may evolve in firms implementing the related constrained strategy. A *matrix organization* is an organizational structure in which there is a dual structure combining both functional specialization and business product or project specialization.[76] Although complicated, an effective matrix structure can lead to improved coordination among a firm's divisions.[77]

The success of the cooperative multidivisional structure is significantly affected by how well divisions process information. Additionally, this form creates more information processing costs than the competitive form described later. However, because cooperation among divisions implies a loss of managerial autonomy, division managers may not readily commit themselves to the type of integrative information-processing activities that this structure demands. Moreover, coordination among divisions sometimes results in an unequal flow of positive outcomes to divisional managers. In other words, when managerial rewards are based at least in part on the performance of individual divisions, the manager of the division that is able to benefit the most by the sharing of corporate competencies might be viewed as receiving relative gains at others' expense. Strategic controls are important in these instances, as divisional managers' performances can be evaluated, at least partly, on the basis of how well they have facilitated interdivisional cooperative efforts. In addition, using reward systems that emphasize overall company performance, besides outcomes achieved by individual divisions, helps overcome problems associated with the cooperative form. Still, the costs of coordination and inertia in organizations limit the amount of related diversification attempted (i.e., they constrain the economies of scope that can be created).[78]

Using the Strategic Business Unit Form of the Multidivisional Structure to Implement the Related Linked Strategy

Firms with fewer links or less constrained links among their divisions use the related linked diversification strategy. The strategic business unit form of the multidivisional structure supports implementation of this strategy. The **strategic business unit (SBU) form** is an M-form consisting of three levels: corporate headquarters, strategic business units (SBUs), and SBU divisions (see Figure 11.6). The SBU structure is used by large firms and can be complex, given associated organization size and product and market diversity.

The **strategic business unit (SBU) form** is an M-form consisting of three levels: corporate headquarters, strategic business units (SBUs), and SBU divisions.

The divisions within each SBU are related in terms of shared products or markets or both, but the divisions of one SBU have little in common with the divisions of the other SBUs. Divisions within each SBU share product or market competencies to develop

Figure 11.6 SBU Form of the Multidivisional Structure for Implementing a Related Linked Strategy

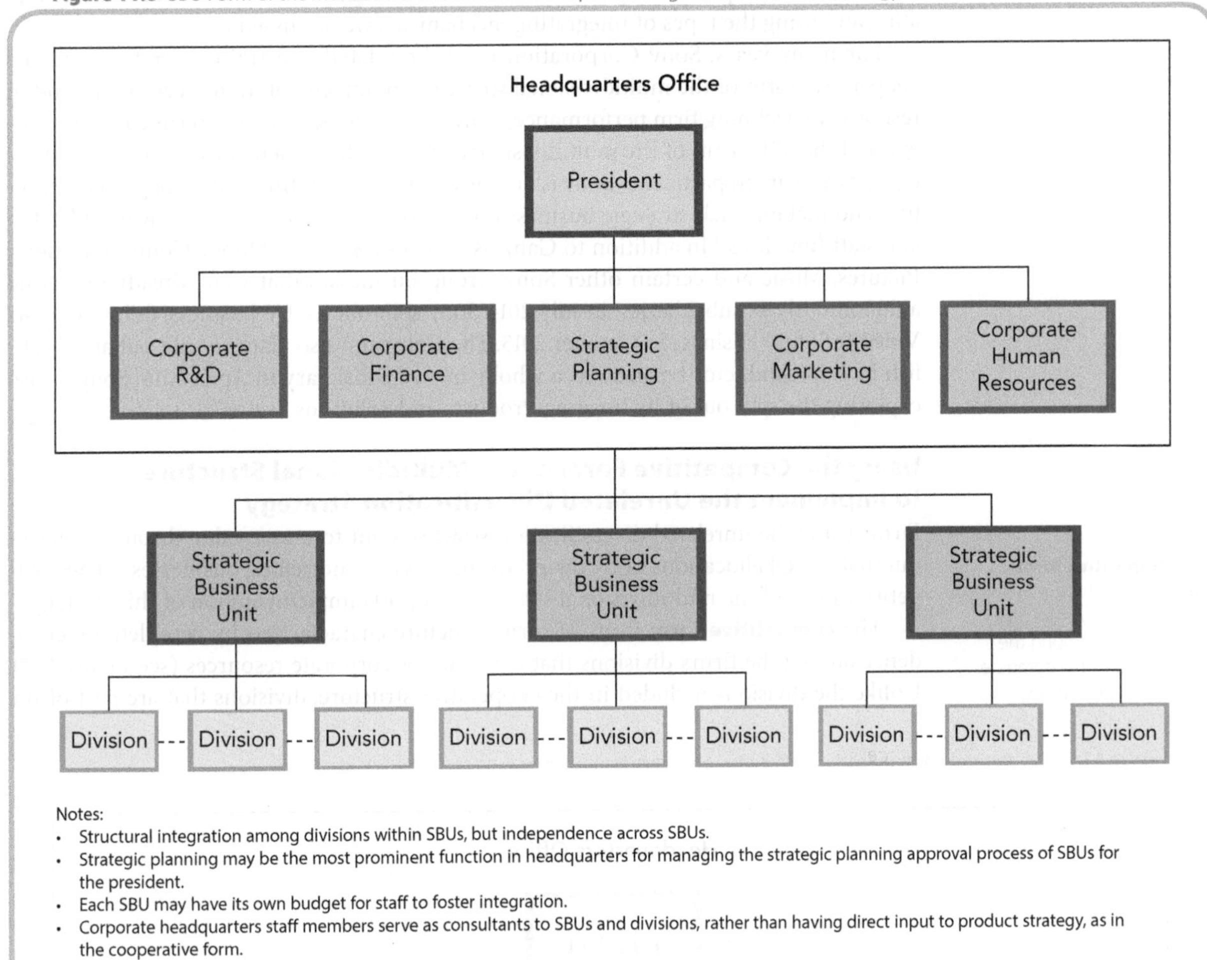

Notes:

- Structural integration among divisions within SBUs, but independence across SBUs.
- Strategic planning may be the most prominent function in headquarters for managing the strategic planning approval process of SBUs for the president.
- Each SBU may have its own budget for staff to foster integration.
- Corporate headquarters staff members serve as consultants to SBUs and divisions, rather than having direct input to product strategy, as in the cooperative form.

economies of scope and possibly economies of scale. The integrating mechanisms discussed earlier can be used by the divisions within the individual strategic business units that are part of the SBU form of the multidivisional structure. In this structure, each SBU is a profit center that is controlled and evaluated by the headquarters office. Although both financial and strategic controls are important, on a relative basis, financial controls are vital to headquarters' evaluation of each SBU; strategic controls are critical when the heads of SBUs evaluate their divisions' performances. Strategic controls are also critical to the headquarters' efforts to evaluate the quality of the portfolio of businesses that has been formed and to determine if those businesses are being successfully managed. Sharing competencies among units within individual SBUs is an important characteristic of the SBU form of the multidivisional structure (see the notes to Figure 11.6).

A disadvantage associated with the related linked diversification strategy is that, even when efforts to implement it are being properly supported by use of the SBU form of the multidivisional structure, firms using this strategy and structure combination find it challenging to effectively communicate the value of their operations to shareholders and to other investors due to its complexity.[79] Furthermore, if coordination between SBUs is required, problems can surface because the SBU structure, similar to the competitive form discussed next, does not readily foster cooperation across SBUs. Accordingly, those responsible for implementing the related linked strategy must focus on successfully creating and using the types of integrating mechanisms we discussed earlier.

For many years, Sony Corporation used the related constrained strategy and the cooperative form of the multidivisional structure to implement it. In recent years, and in response to declining firm performance, Sony appears to be using the related linked strategy and the SBU form of the multidivisional structure to implement what is a new strategy for the firm. In particular, Sony is decentralizing its operating and management structure and making each strategic business unit more independent, with its own leadership and staff functions. "In addition to Game & Network Services, Mobile Communications, Pictures, Music and certain other Sony Group businesses that were already operating autonomously as subsidiaries, in July 2014 Sony split out its TV business, followed by its Video & Sound business in October 2015. The Company also plans to split out and establish its semiconductor business as a wholly owned subsidiary in April 2016. Sony is also exploring the split out of its Imaging Products and Solutions Sector."[80]

Using the Competitive Form of the Multidivisional Structure to Implement the Unrelated Diversification Strategy

The **competitive form** is an M-form structure characterized by complete independence among the firm's divisions that compete for corporate resources.

Firms using the unrelated diversification strategy want to create value through efficient internal capital allocations or by restructuring, buying, and selling businesses.[81] The competitive form of the multidivisional structure supports implementation of this strategy.

The **competitive form** is an M-form structure characterized by complete independence among the firm's divisions that compete for corporate resources (see Figure 11.7). Unlike the divisions included in the cooperative structure, divisions that are part of the

Figure 11.7 Competitive Form of the Multidivisional Structure for Implementing an Unrelated Strategy

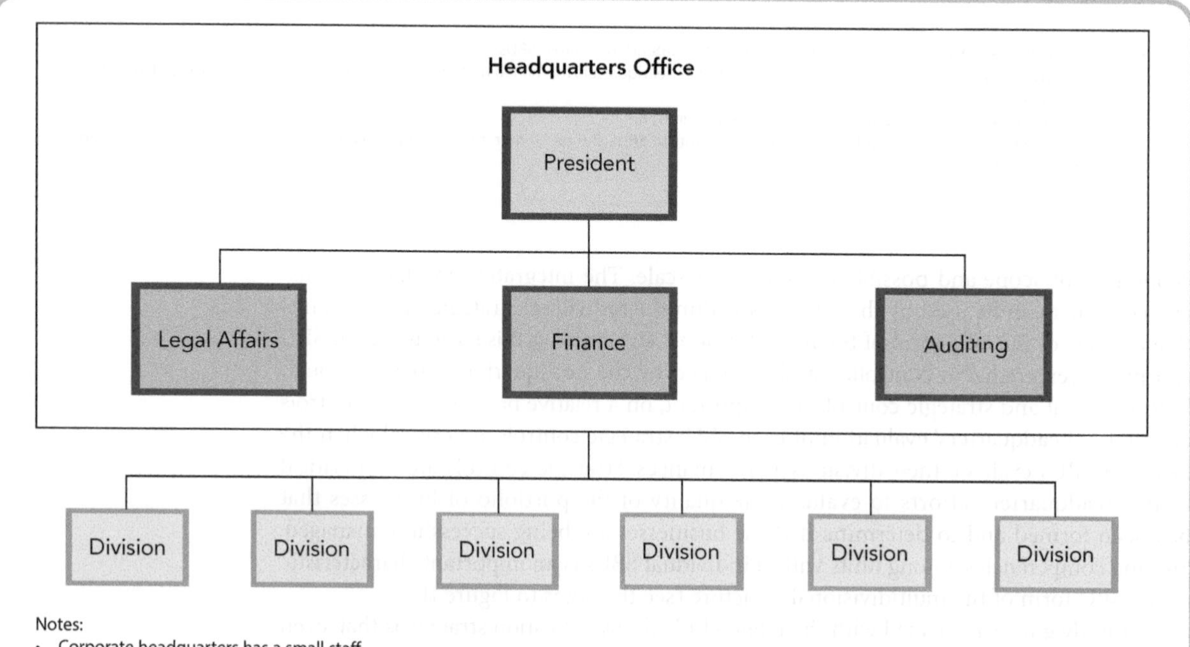

Notes:

- Corporate headquarters has a small staff.
- Finance and auditing are the most prominent functions in the headquarters office to manage cash flow and assure the accuracy of performance data coming from divisions.
- The legal affairs function becomes important when the firm acquires or divests assets.
- Divisions are independent and separate for financial evaluation purposes.
- Divisions retain strategic control, but cash is managed by the corporate office.
- Divisions compete for corporate resources.

competitive structure do not share common corporate strengths. Accordingly, integrating mechanisms are not part of the competitive form of the multidivisional structure.

The efficient internal capital market that is the foundation for using the unrelated diversification strategy requires organizational arrangements emphasizing divisional competition rather than cooperation.[82] Three benefits are expected from the internal competition. First, internal competition creates flexibility (e.g., corporate headquarters can have divisions working on different technologies and projects to identify those with the greatest potential). Resources can then be allocated to the division appearing to have the most potential to drive the entire firm's success. Second, internal competition challenges the status quo and inertia because division heads know that future resource allocations are a product of excellent current performance as well as superior positioning in terms of future performance. Third, internal competition motivates effort in that the challenge of competing against internal peers can be as great as the challenge of competing against external rivals.[83] In this structure, organizational controls (primarily financial controls) are used to emphasize and support internal competition among separate divisions and as the basis for allocating corporate capital based on divisions' performances. However, this structure can be limited by too much emphasis on divisional rewards and can create disharmony due to social comparison about rewards based on personal effort.[84]

As noted in the Strategic Focus on General Electric, GE's new structure will be more like the competitive M-form structure. Similarly, Textron Inc., a large "multi-industry" company, seeks to identify, research, select, acquire, and integrate companies and has developed a set of rigorous criteria to guide decision making. Textron continuously looks to enhance and reshape its portfolio by divesting noncore assets and acquiring branded businesses in attractive industries with substantial long-term growth potential. Textron operates a number of independent businesses including Textron Aviation, Bell (helicopters), Textron Systems and Industrial, which represent manufacturing businesses, and Finance, which represents Textron's product financing worldwide. Leaders of these businesses are responsible for effectively guiding the day-to-day competitive actions of their units. Consistent with the mandates of the competitive form of the multidivisional structure, "Textron's Corporate Office provides oversight, direction, and assistance to its businesses."[85] The profit earned by individual business units within Textron is an important measure the firm uses to decide future capital allocations.

To emphasize competitiveness among divisions, the headquarters office maintains an arm's-length relationship with them, intervening in divisional affairs only to audit operations and discipline managers whose divisions perform poorly. In emphasizing competition between divisions, the headquarters office relies on strategic controls to set rate-of-return targets and financial controls to monitor divisional performance relative to those targets. The headquarters office then allocates cash flow on a competitive basis, rather than automatically returning cash to the division that produced it. Thus, the focus of the headquarters' work is on performance appraisal, resource allocation, and long-range planning to verify that the firm's portfolio of businesses will lead to financial success.

mobil11/Shutterstock.com

Pictured here is a Bell Helicopter, a product manufactured by one of Textron's business units.

Strategic **Focus**

General Electric's Decline, New Strategy, and Reorganization

As noted in Chapter 6, General Electric (GE) has been declining and has had to restructure its portfolio of businesses. In doing so, GE CEO John Flannery announced a new orientation in its implemented structure. How did it get to this point of significant peril, requiring such restructuring?

GE has been historically run from the top; its many acquisitions over the years had to be approved by top managers, and often were businesses outside areas that GE had run before and whose acquisitions were ill timed. "GE became the great counterexample to a growing skepticism among investors and economists about giant diversified companies. During the 1980s, as conglomerates were increasingly written off as lumbering and opaque, GE was lauded as what researchers at the Boston Consulting Group called a 'premium conglomerate'—focused despite its diversity, nimble despite its scale, and armored against cyclical downturns in individual industries." However, in the wake of the dot-com bubble and right before the attacks of Sept. 11, 2001, a new CEO, Jeffrey Immelt, took over the company. Under pressure from Wall Street to do something impressive, he undertook a series of splashy acquisitions, for example paying $5.5 billion for the entertainment assets of Vivendi Universal and $9.5 billion for the British medical imaging company, Amersham. Although there were bargains such as Enron Corp.'s wind-turbine business (picked up in a bankruptcy auction), for the most part the deals proved more expensive and less synergistic than promised. One analyst calculated that GE's total return on Immelt's acquisitions turned out to be half what the company would have earned by simply investing in stock index mutual funds.

During the financial crisis, many problems appeared in GE Capital's financial businesses and Immelt sought to divest them, while at the same time trying to return the company to its industrial roots. While GE Capital was severely downsized, Immelt acquired a $10 billion power turbine business from French company Alstom. GE made a massive investment in natural gas power plants just as the market for them was contracting. Similarly, in oil and gas, GE bought Vetco Gray, Dresser, and Lufkin Industries, and then tried to merge them with Baker-Hughes at a time when oil and gas extraction revenues were depressed.

This legacy has continued to weigh GE down under its new CEO, Flannery. In order to change the strategy and structure of the firm, Flannery announced in June of 2018 that GE "will spin off its core health business within 12–18 months, fully separate Baker Hughes (BHGE), and narrow its focus to aviation, power and renewable energy, among the most salient portfolio changes." Thus, GE's strategic approach will be much less diversified. Although heath care is still a good business, it has "the least amount of synergies with the rest of GE." Meanwhile, the aviation and power businesses "share engine technology synergies," with the former boasting growth while the latter has a path to recovery.

At the same time, Flannery noted that "his plan calls for GE to change how it is run, shifting from a centralized, top-down approach to a culture where the business units are the center of gravity." He is quoted as saying GE's business has been run "from the center for decades," but that is being inverted. With fewer businesses to run, the headquarters should be much smaller, and resources and investment responsibility would be pushed out to the business units to make sure that acquisitions are more in line with business segment strategies. As such, the new structure appears to be more in line with the competitive M-form rather than the former SBU M-form structure that has been the historic structural form at GE.

Jonathan Weiss/Alamy Stock Photo

In October of 2018, GE Aviation reported eight consecutive quarters of double-digit growth.

Sources: 2018, John Flannery gets down to business restructuring General Electric, *Economist*, www.economist.com, June 27; D. Bennett & R Clough, 2018, What the hell is wrong with General Electric? *Bloomberg Businessweek*, www.bloombergbusinessweek.com, February 5; J. Collins, 2018, GE Capital's painful legacy curbs my enthusiasm for the company's restructuring, *Forbes*, www.forbes.com, June 26; G. Colvin, 2018, What the hell happened at GE?, *Fortune*, www.fortune.com, May 24; E. Crook, 2018, Flannery resists pressure for quick fixes at GE, *Financial Times*, www.ft.com, June 25; T. Gryta, 2018, T. Gryta, 2018, Q&A: GE CEO explains strategy, smaller HQ, *Wall Street Journal*, www.wsj.com, June 27; T. Gryta, J. S. Lublin, & D. Benoit, 2018, How Jeffrey Immelt's 'success theater' masked the rot at GE. *Wall Street Journal*, www.wsj.com, February 22; A. Narayanan, 2018, GE finishes restructuring, but another sharp dividend cut is expected, *Investors Business Daily*, www.investors.com, June 26.

As is the case with the related linked diversification strategy, investors and shareholders find it challenging to understand the underlying value of the set of business units associated with a firm implementing the unrelated diversification strategy.[86] Because of this, upper-level managers must find effective ways of communicating their firm's underlying value to those investing capital in the firm.[87]

The three major forms of the multidivisional structure should each be paired with a particular corporate-level strategy. Table 11.1 shows these structures' characteristics. Differences exist in the degree of centralization, the focus of the performance evaluation, the horizontal structures (integrating mechanisms), and the incentive compensation schemes. The most centralized and most costly structural form is the cooperative structure. The least centralized, with the lowest bureaucratic costs, is the competitive structure. The SBU structure requires partial centralization and involves some of the mechanisms necessary to implement the relatedness between divisions. Also, the divisional incentive compensation awards are allocated according to both SBUs and corporate performance.

11-3f Matches between International Strategies and Worldwide Structure

In Chapter 8 we explained that international strategies are increasingly important for companies' long-term competitive success in what is today virtually a borderless global economy.[88] Among other benefits, firms are able to search for new markets and then form the competencies necessary to serve them when implementing an international strategy.[89]

As with business-level and corporate-level strategies, unique organizational structures are necessary to successfully implement individual international strategies, given the different cultural, institutional, and legal environments around the world.[90] Forming proper matches between international strategies and organizational structures facilitates the firm's efforts to effectively coordinate and control its global operations. More importantly, research findings confirm the validity of the international strategy/structure matches we discuss here.[91]

Using the Worldwide Geographic Area Structure to Implement the Multidomestic Strategy

The *multidomestic strategy* decentralizes the firm's strategic and operating decisions to business units in each country so that product characteristics can be tailored to local preferences.[92] Firms using this strategy try to isolate themselves from global

Table 11.1 Characteristics of the Structures Necessary to Implement the Related Constrained, Related Linked, and Unrelated Diversification Strategies

	Overall Structural Form		
Structural Characteristics	**Cooperative M-Form (Related Constrained Strategy)**	**SBU M-Form (Related Linked Strategy)**	**Competitive M-Form (Unrelated Diversification Strategy)**
Centralization of operations	Centralized at corporate office	Partially centralized (in SBUs)	Decentralized to divisions
Use of integration mechanisms	Extensive	Moderate	Nonexistent
Divisional performance evaluation	Emphasizes subjective (strategic) criteria	Uses a mixture of subjective (strategic) and objective (financial) criteria	Emphasizes objective (financial) criteria
Divisional incentive compensation	Linked to overall corporate performance	Mixed linkage to corporate, SBU, and divisional performance	Linked to divisional performance

competitive forces by establishing protected market positions or by competing in industry segments that are most affected by differences among local countries. The worldwide geographic area structure is used to implement this strategy. The **worldwide geographic area structure** emphasizes national interests and facilitates the firm's efforts to satisfy local differences (see Figure 11.8).

Using the multidomestic strategy requires little coordination between different country markets, meaning that formal integrating mechanisms among divisions around the world are not needed. Indeed, the coordination among units in a firm's worldwide geographic area structure that does take place is informal in nature.

From a historical perspective, we note that the multidomestic strategy/worldwide geographic area structure match evolved as a natural outgrowth of the multicultural European marketplace. Friends and family members of the main business who were sent as expatriates to foreign countries to develop the independent country subsidiary often adopted the worldwide geographic area structure. The relationship to corporate headquarters by divisions took place through informal communication.

Founded in San Francisco, CA, in 2009, Uber Technologies, Inc. has pursued a multidomestic structure and in 2018 operates in 600 U.S. cities and in 78 countries; however, it has been countered by rival Lyft, especially in the United States, although it remains the market leader.[93] Uber pursued an aggressive strategy to grow rapidly outside its U.S. home market. However, it often flouted local country regulations in the process, leading to local rivals gaining strength. Although it targeted key markets in Asia, it ultimately had to cede its strategy to local rivals, ceding ownership in its Russian, Chinese, and Southeast Asian businesses as it sought to focus on its core markets. It is also under scrutiny for gender

Figure 11.8 Worldwide Geographic Area Structure for Implementing a Multidomestic Strategy

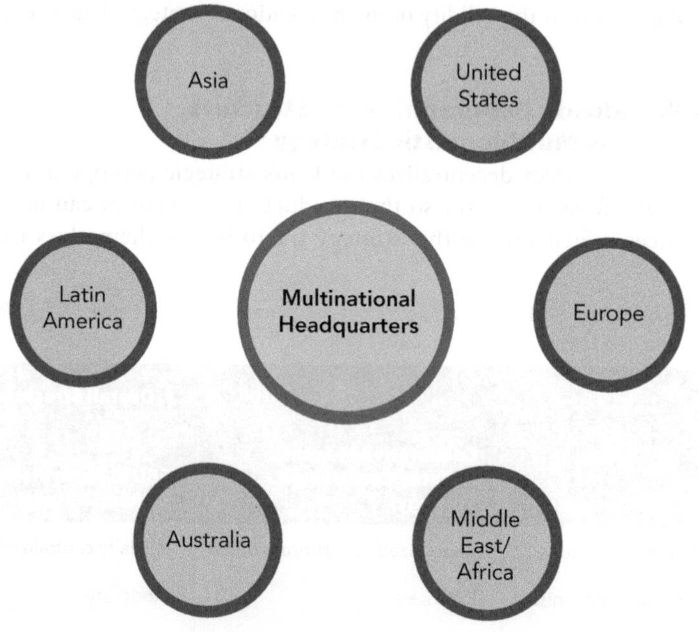

Notes:
- The perimeter circles indicate decentralization of operations.
- Emphasis is on differentiation by local demand to fit an area or country culture.
- Corporate headquarters coordinates financial resources among independent subsidiaries.
- The organization is like a decentralized federation.

The **worldwide geographic area structure** emphasizes national interests and facilitates the firm's efforts to satisfy local differences.

discrimination in the United States. Its aggressive tactics have led to the replacement of its founding CEO, Travis Kalanick, with Dara Khosrowshahi.[94]

There is a key challenge associated with effectively using the multidomestic strategy/worldwide geographic area structure match—namely, the inability to create global efficiencies. This inability is a product of companies' focus on serving unique customer needs particularly well. The inability to create global efficiencies in this match challenges firms to find ways to control costs while trying to serve local customers' unique needs.

It seems that creating global efficiencies has been a problem for Uber, as it has been unable to deal with big differences in regulations around the globe as well as with local firms that were imitating Uber's strategy successfully. By the same token, as long as the firm can continue to identify and serve the unique needs of customers in different markets in ways that create value for them, being unable to develop scale economics will not be a fatal blow to Uber's efforts to succeed in international markets. For example, it has included on its app, the opportunity to take motor scooter taxis in emerging economies where that is a usual means of transportation.[95]

In other instances, the nature of products companies seek to sell in international markets and market conditions themselves demand that a firm be able to develop economies of scale on a worldwide basis. This need calls for firms to use the global strategy and its structural match, the worldwide product divisional structure.

Using the Worldwide Product Divisional Structure to Implement the Global Strategy

With the corporation's home office dictating competitive strategy, the *global strategy* is one through which the firm offers standardized products across country markets.[96] The firm's success depends principally on its ability to develop economies of scale while competing on a global basis and while serving customers without specific and unique needs relative to the firm's standardized product.

The worldwide product divisional structure supports use of the global strategy. In the **worldwide product divisional structure**, decision-making authority is centralized in the worldwide division headquarters to coordinate and integrate decisions and actions among divisional business units (see Figure 11.9).

Integrating mechanisms are important to the effective use of the worldwide product divisional structure. Direct contact between managers, liaison roles between departments, and both temporary task forces and permanent teams are examples of these mechanisms. The disadvantages of the global strategy/worldwide structure combination are the difficulties involved with coordinating decisions and actions across country borders and the inability to quickly respond to local needs and preferences. To deal with these types of disadvantages, firms sometimes choose to try to simultaneously focus on geography and products. This simultaneous focus is similar to the combination structure that we discuss next.

In the **worldwide product divisional structure**, decision-making authority is centralized in the worldwide division headquarters to coordinate and integrate decisions and actions among divisional business units.

Using the Combination Structure to Implement the Transnational Strategy

The *transnational strategy* calls for the firm to combine the multidomestic strategy's local responsiveness with the global strategy's efficiency. Firms using this strategy are trying to gain the advantages of both local responsiveness and global efficiency.[97] The combination structure is used to implement the transnational strategy. The **combination structure** is a structure drawing characteristics and mechanisms from both the worldwide geographic area structure and the worldwide product divisional structure. The transnational strategy is often implemented through two possible combination structures: a global matrix structure and a hybrid global design.[98]

The **combination structure** is a structure drawing characteristics and mechanisms from both the worldwide geographic area structure and the worldwide product divisional structure.

Figure 11.9 Worldwide Product Divisional Structure for Implementing a Global Strategy

Notes:
- The "headquarters" circle indicates centralization to coordinate information flow among worldwide products.
- Corporate headquarters uses many intercoordination devices to facilitate global economies of scale and scope.
- Corporate headquarters also allocates financial resources in a cooperative way.
- The organization is like a centralized federation.

The global matrix design brings together both local market and product expertise into teams that develop and respond to the global marketplace. The global matrix design promotes flexibility in designing products in response to customer needs. However, it has severe limitations in that it places employees in a position of being accountable to more than one manager. At any given time, an employee may be a member of several functional or product group teams. Relationships that evolve from multiple memberships can make it difficult for employees to be simultaneously loyal to all of them. Although the matrix places authority in the hands of the managers who are most able to use it, it creates problems in regard to corporate reporting relationships that are so complex and vague that it is difficult and time-consuming to receive approval for major decisions.

We illustrate the hybrid structure in Figure 11.10. In this design, some divisions are oriented toward products while others are oriented toward market areas. Thus, in cases when the geographic area is more important, the division managers are area-oriented. In other divisions where worldwide product coordination and efficiencies are more important, the division manager is more product-oriented.

The fit between the multidomestic strategy and the worldwide geographic area structure and between the global strategy and the worldwide product divisional structure is apparent. However, when a firm wants to implement the multidomestic and global strategies simultaneously through a combination structure, the appropriate integrating mechanisms are less obvious. The structure used to implement the transnational strategy must be simultaneously centralized and decentralized, integrated and nonintegrated, formalized and nonformalized. Sometimes the structure becomes extremely complex,

Figure 11.10 Hybrid Form of the Combination Structure for Implementing a Transnational Strategy

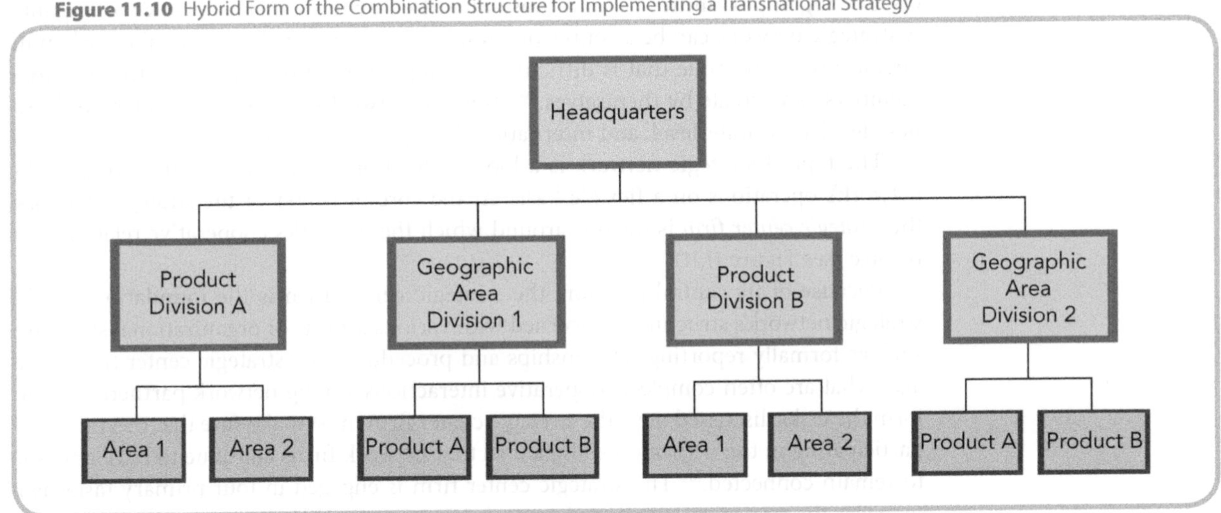

a reality that challenges managers to remain vigilant in efforts to verify that the hybrid structure is effectively supporting use of their firm's transnational strategy.

FMC Subsea—a supplier to oil companies around the world that develop marine oil fields—was a division of FMC Technologies, a U.S. technology firm, which merged with the French engineering firm Technip in 2017. FMC Subsea was the largest division of FMC Technologies before the merger, representing about 66% of total revenues and operated as an independent subsidiary. The primary purpose of a subsea "tree" is to control the flow of oil or gas out of a well on the seabed. FMC Subsea is the market leader and has the largest installed base of subsea trees (around 2000) of all companies operating in this market. The initial challenge was to establish an organization that could serve international markets and adapt to local and regional customer requirements. As such, a multidomestic structure was chosen. However, the company experienced challenges in improving cost effectiveness—as noted above, often a problem with the multidomestic strategy. To overcome the problems a combination strategy with a matrix structure was chosen with dual reporting for both geographic market and product units. However, "people found it difficult having to ask one manager about what they should do, and another about when they should do it." Accordingly, they simplified the structure to reduce the dual reporting requirements and instead introduced "internal customer-supplier linkages between internal units, with the benefits of the matrix—but without the costs."[99]

11-3g Matches between Cooperative Strategies and Network Structures

As discussed in Chapter 9, a network strategy exists when partners form several alliances in order to improve the performance of the alliance network itself through cooperative endeavors.[100] The greater levels of environmental complexity and uncertainty facing companies in today's competitive environment are causing more firms to use cooperative strategies such as strategic alliances.[101] Firms can form cooperative relationships with many of their stakeholders, including customers, suppliers, and competitors. When a firm becomes involved with combinations of cooperative relationships, it is part of a strategic network, or what others call an alliance constellation or portfolio.[102]

A *strategic network* is a group of firms that has been formed to create value by participating in multiple cooperative arrangements. An effective strategic network facilitates discovering opportunities beyond those identified by individual network participants. A strategic network can be a source of competitive advantage for its members when its operations create value that is difficult for competitors to duplicate and that network members can't create by themselves.[103] Strategic networks are used to implement business-level, corporate-level, and international cooperative strategies.

The typical strategic network is a loose federation of partners participating in the network's operations on a flexible basis. At the core or center of the strategic network, the *strategic center firm* is the one around which the network's cooperative relationships revolve (see Figure 11.11).

Because of its central position, the strategic center firm is the foundation for the strategic network's structure. Concerned with various aspects of organizational structure, such as formally reporting relationships and procedures, the strategic center firm manages what are often complex, cooperative interactions among network partners. To perform the tasks discussed next, the strategic center firm must make sure that incentives for participating in the network are aligned so that network firms continue to have a reason to remain connected.[104] The strategic center firm is engaged in four primary tasks as it manages the strategic network and controls its operations.[105]

Strategic Outsourcing The strategic center firm outsources and partners with more firms than other network members. At the same time, the strategic center firm requires network partners to be more than contractors. Members are expected to find opportunities for the network to create value through its cooperative work.[106]

Competencies To increase network effectiveness, the strategic center firm seeks ways to support each member's efforts to develop core competencies with the potential of benefiting the network.

Technology The strategic center firm is responsible for managing the development and sharing of technology-based ideas among network members. The structural

Figure 11.11 A Strategic Network

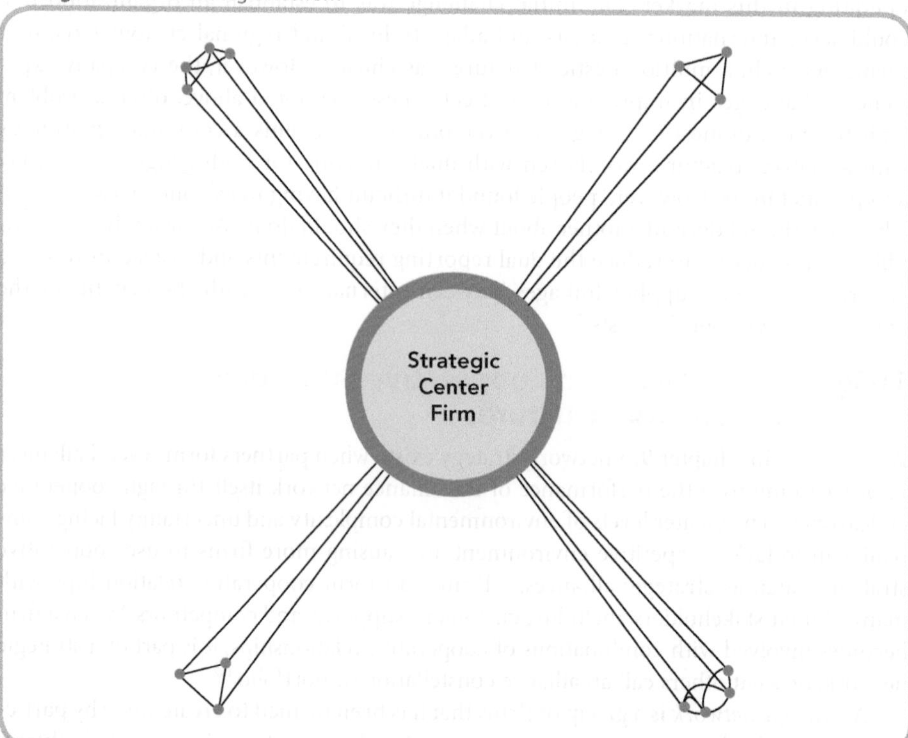

requirement that members submit formal reports detailing the technology-oriented outcomes of their efforts to the strategic center firm facilitates this activity.

Race to Learn The strategic center firm emphasizes that the principal dimensions of competition are between value chains and between networks of value chains. Because of these interconnections, an individual strategic network is only as strong as its weakest value-chain link. With its centralized decision-making authority and responsibility, the strategic center firm guides participants in efforts to form network-specific competitive advantages. The need for each participant to have capabilities that can be the foundation for the network's competitive advantages encourages friendly rivalry among participants seeking to develop the skills needed to quickly form new capabilities that create value for the network.[107]

Interestingly, strategic networks are being used more frequently, partly because of the ability of a strategic center firm to execute a strategy that effectively and efficiently links partner firms. Improved information systems and communication capabilities (e.g., the Internet) facilitate effective organization and use of strategic networks. One of the best illustrations of a network is illustrated in the global airline alliances exampled in the Strategic Focus.

11-4 Implementing Business-Level Cooperative Strategies

As explained in Chapter 9, there are two types of business-level complementary alliances—vertical and horizontal. Firms with competencies in different stages of the value chain form a vertical alliance to cooperatively integrate their different, but complementary, skills. Firms combining their competencies to create value in the same stage of the value chain are using a horizontal alliance. Vertical complementary strategic alliances such as those developed by Toyota Motor Corporation are formed more frequently than horizontal alliances.[108]

A strategic network of vertical relationships, such as the network in Japan between Toyota and its suppliers, often involves a number of implementation issues.[109] First, the strategic center firm encourages subcontractors to modernize their facilities and provides them with technical and financial assistance to do so, if necessary. Second, the strategic center firm reduces its transaction costs by promoting longer-term contracts with subcontractors, so that supplier-partners increase their long-term productivity. This approach differs from that of continually negotiating short-term contracts based on unit pricing. Third, the strategic center firm enables engineers in upstream companies (suppliers) to have better communications with those companies with whom it has contracts for services. As a result, suppliers and the strategic center firm become more interdependent and less independent.

The lean production system (a vertical complementary strategic alliance) pioneered by Toyota and others has been diffused throughout many industries.[110] In vertical complementary strategic alliances, such as the one between Toyota and its suppliers, the strategic center firm is obvious, as is the structure that firm establishes. However, the same is not always true with horizontal complementary strategic alliances where firms try to create value in the same part of the value chain. For example, airline alliances are commonly formed to create value in the marketing and sales primary activity segment of the value chain. Because air carriers commonly participate in multiple horizontal complementary alliances, such as the Oneworld alliance among American Airlines, British Airways, Iberia, Japan Airlines, TAM Airlines, and others, it is difficult to determine the strategic center firm. Moreover, participating in several alliances can cause firms to question partners' true loyalties and intentions.

Strategic **Focus**

Global Airline Alliances, Airline Joint Ventures, and Network Difficulties

Star Alliance (initiated by United Airlines) became the first multi-airline global network where member carriers could book seamless schedules and share frequent flyer benefits among their passengers. It was a convenient way for airlines to expand and maintain market share internationally without having to invest billions of dollars in market growth initiatives. It gave alliance partners airport access in regions where it might be difficult to obtain. Many of the partners also have aircraft maintenance agreements, which can create savings as well as avoiding expensive duplicative maintenance facilities around the globe. The Star Alliance was followed by Oneworld (headed by American Airlines and British Airways) and SkyTeam (headed by Delta Airlines and Air France-KLM).

In 2016, Star Alliance topped the list of alliances with 23 percent of total traffic, followed by SkyTeam with 20.4 percent and Oneworld with 18.8 percent, leaving a 38.8 percent market share divided among smaller alliances and unaligned carriers. This shows the importance of these global networks to the travel system and to the airlines involved. These alliance networks exist largely due to regulatory ownership restrictions; for example, foreign airlines cannot own over 25 percent of U.S.-flagged airlines and foreign carriers cannot own over 49 percent in EU countries. These restrictions are often justified in terms of country security and military needs; for instance, if a war breaks out, the national military system may need airline capacity to move troops in an emergency.

These alliances are, however, quite mature and they are trying to stay relevant as many of the flagship airlines have merged and have large systems in their own right, such as the Air France-KLM merger, Delta's acquisition of Northwest in 2008, and United's acquisition of Continental in 2010. Delta Airlines, for example, is continuing to enter into separate joint venture (JV) ownership arrangements to improve its scale and control. Delta has recently launched JVs with Aeromexico and Korean Air. It also formed a very large JV with Virgin Atlantic of Britain and Air France-KLM. It is also seeking to make deals with low-cost carriers such as Canada's WestJet, China Eastern, and GOL of Brazil. One analyst noted that these JVs "produce 90 percent of the cost savings of a full merger," where the global alliances can only participate up to 25 percent due to the ownership restrictions noted above. These JVs work for the regulators because the parent firms are still independent airlines. As such, although the global alliances are still important, many airlines are pursuing additional joint ventures as the Delta Airlines example suggests.

Kai Pfaffenbach/Reuters

Jets from Thai Airways, United Airlines, Lufthansa, Air Canada, and Scandinavian Airlines Systems, form a star to mark the launch of Star Alliance.

Because of the maturity of these dominant global alliances, they are expanding with more flexibility to gain share. For example, the Star Alliance added Chinese carrier Juneyao Airlines recently, as an experiment with a "connecting partner" model, which allows regional, low-cost, or hybrid airlines to link to the Star Alliance network without becoming a full member, which can be expensive for a small carrier. SkyTeam and Oneworld are also working on affiliate member schemes. These "affiliate" members would not be required to take on expensive technology improvements, which the large alliances are developing, such as a common digital services platform allowing passengers to always be connected to the Internet. Full membership in these alliances also usually requires "fast-track security, priority boarding and check-in, as well as lounge access" which low-cost airlines often do not pursue.

Frequent flyer programs among some airlines are also changing from a focus on distance to a focus on revenue produced by the customer. For example, Air France-KLM customers were told in April 2018 that the airline would no longer offer distance-based mileage credits for their flights. Air France-KLM will join the roughly 20% of airlines already operating schemes on a revenue basis. Most of these are low-cost airlines, but Air France-KLM is a leader in the SkyTeam alliance. Of course, this makes integration with other partners in the SkyTeam network more difficult and complex given the difficulty of obtaining revenue information from partner airlines that accrue loyalty on a mileage basis. This is also creating problems with regard to which frequent fliers gain lounge access; some top frequent flyers are finding that they do not have access to the most prestigious first-class lounges around the world. So, coordination has grown more difficult as changes at individual airlines create network integration challenges.

Sources: 2018, Come fly with me; airline joint ventures, *Economist*, March 17, 62; M. B. Baker, 2018, Korean Air's new terminal & JV, *Business Travel News*, February 12, 17; R. Silk, 2018, Star Alliance and SkyTeam focusing on technology, *Travel Weekly*, June 11, 10; M. Campbell & D. Kamel, 2017, The world is not enough, *Bloomberg Businessweek*, January 9, 34–41; S. Clemence, 2017, Norwegian Air takes flight, *Fast Company*, July/August, 40–42; I. Douglas & D. Tan, 2017, Global airline alliances and profitability: A difference-in-difference analysis, *Transportation Research Part A: Policy & Practice*, 103: 432–443; J. Min, 2017, Sensitivity of alliance termination to prealliance conditions: Expectation effects of alliance partners. *Organization Studies*, 38: 917–936; R. W. Moorman & K. Walker, K. 2017, The alliance question: Global alliances are an established part of the airline business, but is it time for change?, *Air Transport World*, 54(5): 28–32; I. Taylor, 2017, Delta chief says US consolidation 'great for market', *Travel Weekly*, October 26, 71.

These issues are discussed more fully in the Strategic Focus on global airline networks alliances and joint ventures. Also, if rivals band together in too many collaborative activities, one or more governments may suspect the possibility of explicit collusion among partnering firms (see Chapter 9). For these reasons, horizontal complementary alliances are used less often and less successfully than their vertical counterpart, although there are examples of success, such as some of the collaborations among automobile and aircraft manufacturers.

11-5 Implementing Corporate-Level Cooperative Strategies

Some corporate-level strategies are used to reduce costs. This was the objective with the collaboration that was formed initially between Walgreens and Swiss-based Alliance Boots, a pharmacy-led health and beauty group. This partnership helped the firms negotiate lower prices with drug suppliers, reducing their overall costs as a result of doing so.[111]

Unilever is partnering with some firms to reach a different objective. Committed to decoupling its growth from negative environmental and social effects from its operations, Unilever formed an alliance with Jacobs Engineering Group Inc. in 2010 to reduce the company's carbon, water, and waste footprint across its manufacturing locations throughout the world. Still other corporate-level cooperative strategies (such as franchising) are used to facilitate product and market diversification. As a cooperative strategy, franchising allows the firm to use its competencies to extend or diversify its product or market reach without completing a merger or acquisition.[112]

The potential to create synergy is a key reason corporate-level cooperative strategies, such as those involving Walgreens, Unilever, and active franchisers including McDonald's, are formed.[113] Historically, McDonald's approach to franchising as a corporate-level cooperative strategy found the firm emphasizing a limited value-priced menu. However, as mentioned in Opening Case, the firm's structure is being changed. One objective of these structural changes is to strip out significant firm costs. Overall, McDonald's headquarters serves as the strategic center firm for the network's franchisees. The headquarters office uses strategic and financial controls to verify that the franchisees' operations create the greatest value for the entire network.

11-6 Implementing International Cooperative Strategies

Strategic networks formed to implement international cooperative strategies result in firms competing in several countries.[114] Differences among countries' regulatory environments increase the challenge of managing international networks and verifying that, at a minimum, a network's operations comply with all legal requirements.[115]

Figure 11.12 A Distributed Strategic Network

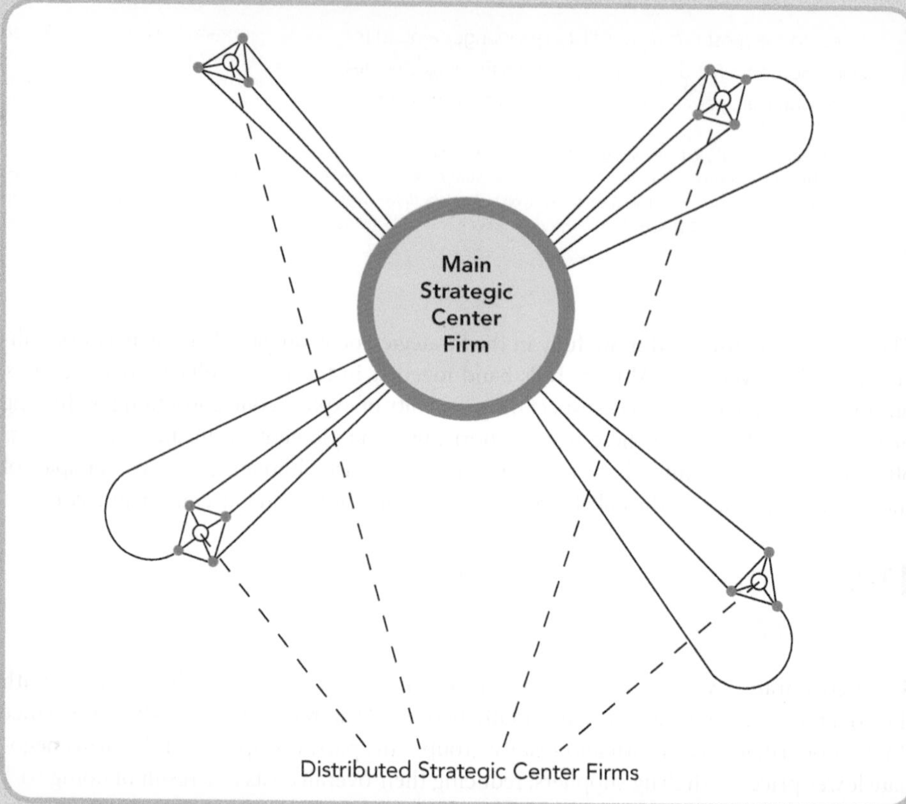

Distributed strategic networks are the organizational structure used to manage international cooperative strategies. As shown in Figure 11.12, several regional strategic center firms are included in the distributed network to manage partner firms' multiple cooperative arrangements.[116] The structure used to implement the international cooperative strategy is complex and demands careful attention to be used successfully. An example is the regional structure of Visa credit cards, which coordinates bank affiliated credit cards and transactions in Asia Pacific, Canada, Europe, Latin America and United States regions.

SUMMARY

- Organizational structure specifies the firm's formal reporting relationships, procedures, controls, and authority and decision-making processes. Essentially, organizational structure details the work to be done in a firm and how that work is to be accomplished. Organizational controls guide the use of strategy, indicate how to compare actual and expected results, and suggest actions to take to improve performance when it falls below expectations. A proper match between strategy and structure can lead to a competitive advantage.
- Strategic controls (largely subjective criteria) and financial controls (largely objective criteria) are the two types of organizational controls used to support the implementation of a strategy. Both controls are critical, although their degree of emphasis varies based on individual matches between strategy and structure.
- Strategy and structure influence each other; overall though, strategy has a stronger influence on structure. Research indicates that firms tend to change structure when declining performance forces them to do so. Effective managers anticipate the need for structural change and quickly modify structure to better accommodate the firm's strategy when evidence calls for that action.
- The functional structure is used to implement business-level strategies. The cost leadership strategy requires a centralized functional structure—one in which manufacturing efficiency

and process engineering are emphasized. The differentiation strategy's functional structure decentralizes implementation-related decisions, especially those concerned with marketing, to those involved with individual organizational functions. Focus strategies, often used in small firms, require a simple structure until such time that the firm diversifies in terms of products and/or markets.

- Unique combinations of different forms of the multidivisional structure are matched with different corporate-level diversification strategies to properly implement these strategies. The cooperative M-form, used to implement the related constrained corporate-level strategy, has a centralized corporate office and extensive integrating mechanisms. Divisional incentives are linked to overall corporate performance to foster cooperation among divisions. The related linked SBU M-form structure establishes separate profit centers within the diversified firm. Each profit center or SBU may have divisions offering similar products, but the SBUs are often unrelated to each other. The competitive M-form structure, used to implement the unrelated diversification strategy, is highly decentralized, lacks integrating mechanisms, and utilizes objective financial criteria to evaluate each unit's performance.
- The multidomestic strategy, implemented through the worldwide geographic area structure, emphasizes decentralization and locates all functional activities in the host country or geographic area. The worldwide product divisional structure is used to implement the global strategy. This structure is centralized in order to coordinate and integrate different functions' activities to gain global economies of scope and economies of scale. Decision-making authority is centralized in the firm's worldwide division headquarters.
- The transnational strategy—a strategy through which the firm seeks the local responsiveness of the multidomestic strategy and the global efficiency of the global strategy—is implemented through the combination structure. Because it must be simultaneously centralized and decentralized, integrated and nonintegrated, and formalized and nonformalized, the combination structure is difficult to organize and successfully manage. Two structures can be used to implement the transnational strategy: the matrix and the hybrid structure with both geographic and product-oriented divisions.
- Increasingly important to competitive success, cooperative strategies are implemented through organizational structures framed around strategic networks. Strategic center firms play a critical role in managing strategic networks. Business-level strategies are often employed in vertical and horizontal alliance networks. Corporate-level cooperative strategies are used to pursue product and market diversification. Franchising is one type of corporate strategy that uses a strategic network to implement this strategy. This is also true for international cooperative strategies, where distributed networks are often used.

KEY TERMS

combination structure 365
competitive form 360
cooperative form 356
financial controls 349
functional structure 351
multidivisional (M-form) structure 352
organizational controls 348
organizational structure 347
simple structure 350
strategic business unit (SBU) form 358
strategic controls 348
worldwide geographic area structure 364
worldwide product divisional structure 365

REVIEW QUESTIONS

1. What is organizational structure and what are organizational controls? What are the differences between strategic controls and financial controls? What is the importance of these differences?
2. What does it mean to say that strategy and structure have a reciprocal relationship?
3. What are the characteristics of the different functional structures used to implement the cost leadership, differentiation, integrated cost leadership/differentiation, and focused business-level strategies?
4. What are the differences among the three versions of the multidivisional (M-form) organizational structures that are used to implement the related constrained, the related linked, and the unrelated corporate-level diversification strategies?
5. What organizational structures are used to implement the multidomestic, global, and transnational international strategies?
6. What is a strategic network? What is a strategic center firm? How is a strategic center firm used in business-level, corporate-level, and international cooperative strategies?

Mini-Case

Sony's Dilemma, Matching Strategy and Structure

Launched in 1946 in Japan, Sony gained a reputation for producing innovative products that were sold throughout the world. In fact, the firm's success was instrumental to Japan's development as a powerful exporter during the 1960s, 1970s, and 1980s. Sony was sometimes "first to market" with an innovative product, while sometimes being able to rapidly enhance a product's capabilities by innovating. Introduced in 1979, the Sony Walkman, which was a personal stereo tape deck, is an example of a "first to market" product from Sony. On the other hand, Sony innovated the transistor radio—initially developed by Regency Electronics and Texas Instruments—in a way that made the product commercially viable. Regardless of the type, innovation has been critical to how Sony competes in multiple product areas.

Realizing the value that could be gained by sharing resources, capabilities, and core competencies across types of businesses, Sony's success for many decades was a product of its commitment to "convergence," which the firm operationalized by linking its activities across businesses such as film, music, and digital electronics. In essence, Sony was successful for many years as a result of being able to effectively implement the related constrained strategy. But as we noted in the chapter when discussing the related constrained strategy and the structure needed to implement it, an inability to efficiently process information and coordinate an array of integrated activities between units are problems that may surface when using the cooperative form of the multidivisional structure. This appears to be the case for Sony. In response to performance problems that have plagued the firm for over a decade, Sony put into place significant structural changes in October 2015, intended to be the foundation for improvements to Sony's ability to create value for customers and enhance wealth for shareholders. At the core of the structural changes are efforts to group the firm's businesses in ways that allow Sony's upper-level leaders to more effectively allocate financial capital. A key objective is to allocate capital to the businesses with the strongest potential not just to grow, but to grow profitably. In essence, the new structure is an example of the SBU form of the multidivisional structure.

However, in 2018, with new CEO Kenichiro Yoshida (formerly the CFO), Sony is again making a strategic shift. Yoshida laid out a strategy shift away from hardware and toward content in outlining a three-year business plan. This is not a shock; Sony sold 81 million electronic devices in 2011, but only half that volume in 2017. This plan also dispels rumors that Yoshida would sell Sony Pictures, which had successes in a remake of Jumanji, and continued production of the Spiderman movie series. In fostering this shift, Sony recently bolstered its entertainment assets by buying the majority of shares it did not own in EMI Music from Mubadala Investment Co.

The problem is that cooperation among the business units is going to be more salient. One of its central competitors, Disney has been very successful in integrating its content businesses such that its movies and TV show characters feed well into its theme parks and retail sales of cartoon and action figures (see the Mini-case at the end of Chapter 6). However, Sony has not been very successful at such integration attempts. For example, Sony's attempt to build a global content-delivery platform via the PlayStation gaming console has not been very fruitful. As Media Partners Asia executive director Vivek Couto suggested, "the company has missed an opportunity to leverage IP from PlayStation games for movies and TV." Sony "also comes off poorly in utilizing properties across divisions: that integration needs to happen."

Sony's new strategy is playing out in video game controllers, currently in its PlayStation 4 console. "Sony has been shifting its PlayStation focus from hardware to online subscription services, including a $60 annual package that includes games and multiplayer features. That service, PlayStation Plus, had 34 million users as of March 2018, fitting the new CEO's goal of adding revenue sources that are more stable than volatile hardware and software sales." The leader of this business unit, Tsuyoshi Kodera, has noted that Sony will take its time in coming out with the fifth generation PlayStation console; "We're no longer in a time when you can think just about the console or just about the network like they're two different things." Thus, there

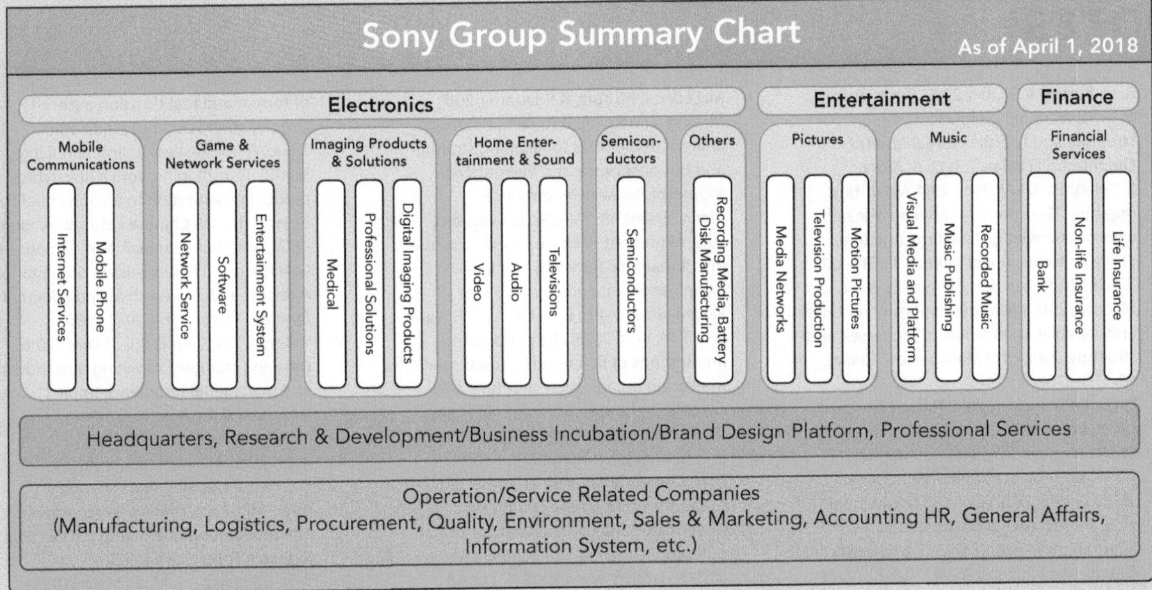

Source: https://www.sony.net/SonyInfo/CorporateInfo/Data/organization.html

needs to be better connections between the hardware and the myriad of content associated with video games, movies, and online games as well as mobility; the PlayStation has been traditionally a living-room console and demand for many games suggests the need to be available on mobile devices.

This new strategic emphasis obviously will require more integration than has been utilized in the recent past with Sony's SBU multidivisional structure. It is important to remember that Sony has other businesses besides the hardware and content businesses that need increased integration to stay competitive. It is now structured into three core sectors or business units—electronics, entertainment, and finance (see the Sony organization chart). The problem is that better integration is going to be required between two SBUs, electronics and entertainment. That will be difficult as all three units are judged on a performance criterion within the separate SBUs, which does not inspire cooperation.

Sources: 2018, Corporate Information, Organization Data, www.sony.com, Accessed July 26; J. Beckerman, 2018, Sony to buy Mubadala's stake in EMI Music Publishing, *Wall Street Journal*, www.wsj.com, May 22; G. J. Blair, 2018, Sony's strategy shift shuts down sale rumors, *Hollywood Reporter*, May 30, 22; G. J. Blair, 2018, What does Sony's new CEO have planned?, *Hollywood Reporter*, February 7, 22; T. Mochizuki, 2018, Sony says the next PlayStation is three years off, *Wall Street Journal*, www.wsj.com, May 24; T. Mochizuki, 2018, Sony chief hands over reins after resurgence, *Wall Street Journal*, www.wsj.com, February 3; Y. Wang, 2018, Tech giants are creating their own labels to conquer China's digital music market, *Forbes*, www.forbes.com, February 8; 2015, Here's Sony's new business strategy, *Business Insider*, www.businessinsider.com, February 21; T. Mochizuki & E. Pfanner, How Sony makes money off Apple's iPhone, *Wall Street Journal*, www.wsj.com, April 28; E. Pfanner & T. Mochizuki, 2015, Sony's mobile unit seeks profit, innovation, *Wall Street Journal*, www.wsj.com, March 2; M. Schilling, 2015, Sony strategy centers on splitting businesses, not selling—for now, *Variety*, www.variety.com, February 26.

Case Discussion Questions

1. To implement a corporate strategy, a firm needs to have a strong set of capabilities to "parent" the set of business units that the firm has established or acquired. Given Sony's history and organization structure, what would you argue are Sony's strongest parenting or corporate capabilities? How will the new strategy utilize these capabilities?
2. Do you think that Sony has the right organization structure to foster the necessary integration among its electronic and entertainment content businesses that its revamped strategy seems to entail?
3. What additional organizational structure and/or process adjustments will Sony need to make to realize its revised strategic objectives?

NOTES

1. R. M. Burton & B. Obel, 2018, The science of organizational design: Fit between structure and coordination, *Journal of Organization Design*, 7: 1–13; A. Arora, S. Belenzon, & L. A. Rios, 2014, Make, buy, organize: The interplay between research, external knowledge, and firm structure, *Strategic Management Journal*, 35: 317–337; T. Felin, N. J. Foss, K. H. Heimeriks, & T. L. Madsen, 2012, Microfoundations of routines and capabilities: Individuals, processes, and structure, *Journal of Management Studies*, 49: 1351–1374.
2. E. Lee & P. Puranam, 2016, The implementation imperative: Why one should implement even imperfect strategies perfectly, *Strategic Management Journal*, 37: 1529–1546; D. A. Levinthal & A. Marino, 2015, Three facets of organizational adaptation: Selection, variety, and plasticity, *Organization Science*, 26: 743–755; R. E. Miles & C. C. Snow, 1978, *Organizational Strategy, Structure and Process*, NY: McGraw-Hill.
3. S. Le & M. Kroll, 2017, CEO international experience: Effects on strategic change and firm performance, *Journal of International Business Studies*, 48: 573–595; C. Heavey & Z. Simsek, 2015, Transactive memory systems and firm performance: An upper echelons perspective, *Organization Science*, 26: 941–959.
4. N. Eva, S. Sendjaya, D. Prajogo, A. Cavanagh, & M. Robin, 2018, Creating strategic fit, *Personnel Review*, 47: 166–186; M. Josefy, S. Kuban, R. D. Ireland, & M. A. Hitt, 2015, All things great and small: Organizational size, boundaries of the firm, and a changing environment, *Academy of Management Annals*, 9: 715–802.
5. Y. M. Zhou & X. Wan, 2017, Product variety, sourcing complexity, and the bottleneck of coordination, *Strategic Management Journal*, 38: 1569–1587; M. Menz, S. Kunisch, & D. J. Collis, 2015, The corporate headquarters in the contemporary corporation: Advancing a multimarket firm perspective, *Academy of Management Annals*, 9: 633–714; B. Keats & H. O'Neill, 2001, Organizational structure: Looking through a strategy lens, in M. A. Hitt, R. E. Freeman, & J. S. Harrison (eds.), *Handbook of Strategic Management*, Oxford, U.K.: Blackwell Publishers, 520–542.
6. J. Oxley & G. Pandher, 2016, Equity-based incentives and collaboration in the modern multibusiness firm, *Strategic Management Journal*, 37: 1379–1394; A. Shipilov, R. Gulati, M. Kilduff, S. Li, & W. Tsai, 2014, Relational pluralism within and between organizations, *Academy of Management Journal*, 57: 449–459; R. E. Hoskisson, C. W. L. Hill, & H. Kim, 1993, The multidivisional structure: Organizational fossil or source of value? *Journal of Management*, 19: 269–298.
7. M. Lederer, M. Kurz, & P. Lazarov, 2017, Making strategy work: a comprehensive analysis of methods for aligning strategy and business processes, *International Journal of Business Performance Management*, 18: 274–292; B. Grøgaard, 2012, Alignment of strategy and structure in international firms: An empirical examination, *International Business Review*, 21: 397–407; E. M. Olson, S. F. Slater, & G. T. M. Hult, 2005, The performance implications of fit among business strategy, marketing organization structure, and strategic behavior, *Journal of Marketing*, 69: 49–65.
8. B. L. Connelly, L. Tihanyi, D. J. Ketchen, C. M. Carnes, & W. J. Ferrier, 2017, Competitive repertoire complexity: Governance antecedents and performance outcomes, *Strategic Management Journal*, 38: 1151–1173; M. Ahearne, S. K. Lam, & F. Kraus, 2014, Performance impact of middle managers' adaptive strategy implementation: The role of social capital, *Strategic Management Journal*, 35: 68–87; F. A. Csaszar, 2012, Organizational structure as a determinant of performance: Evidence from mutual funds, *Strategic Management Journal*, 33: 611–632.
9. J. Bundy, R. M. Vogel, & M. A. Zachary, 2018, Organization–stakeholder fit: A dynamic theory of cooperation, compromise, and conflict between an organization and its stakeholders, *Strategic Management Journal*, 39: 476–501; A. K. Hoenen & T. Kostova, 2014, Utilizing the broader agency perspective for studying headquarters-subsidiary relations in multinational companies, *Journal of International Business Studies*, 46: 104–113; A. M. Rugman & A. Verbeke, 2008, A regional solution to the strategy and structure of multinationals, *European Management Journal*, 26: 305–313.
10. Ø. D. Fjeldstad & C. C. Snow, 2018, Business models and organization design, *Long Range Planning*, 51: 32–39; B. McEvily, G. Soda, & M. Tortoriello, 2014, More formally: Rediscovering the missing link between formal organization and informal social structure, *Academy of Management Annals*, 8: 299–345.
11. T. Felin, N. J. Foss, & R. E. Ployhart, 2015, The microfoundations movement in strategy and organization theory, *Academy of Management Annals*, 9: 575–632.
12. E. Jaakkola & A. Hallin, 2018, Organizational Structures for new service development, *Journal of Product Innovation Management*, 35: 280–297; M. Dobrajska, S. Billinger, & S. Karim, 2015, Delegation within hierarchies: How information processing and knowledge characteristics influence the allocation of formal and real decision authority, *Organization Science*, 26: 687–704.
13. J. Luo, A. Van de Ven, R. Jing, & Y. Jiang, Y. 2018, Transitioning from a hierarchical product organization to an open platform organization: A Chinese case study, *Journal of Organization Design*, 7: 1–14; M. Loock & G. Hinnen, 2015, Heuristics in organizations: A review and a research agenda, *Journal of Business Research*, 68: 2027–2036.
14. S. Karim, T N. Carroll, & C. P. Long, 2016, Delaying change: Examining how industry and managerial turbulence impact structural realignment, *Academy of Management Journal*, 59: 791–817.
15. A. Engelen, H. Kube, S. Schmidt, & T. C. Flatten, 2014, Entrepreneurial orientation in turbulent environments: The moderating role of absorptive capacity, *Research Policy*, 43: 1353–1369.
16. R. D. Gonzalez & T. M. de Melo, 2018, The effects of organization context on knowledge exploration and exploitation, *Journal of Business Research*, 90: 215–225; J. B. Craig, C. Dibrell, & R. Garrett, 2014, Examining relationships among family influence, family culture, flexible planning systems, innovativeness and firm performance, *Journal of Family Business Strategy*, 5: 229–238; R. Kapoor & J. Lee, 2013, Coordinating and competing in ecosystems: How organizational forms shape new technology investments, *Strategic Management Journal*, 34: 274–296.
17. F. Vermeulen, 2018, A basic theory of inheritance: How bad practice prevails, *Strategic Management Journal*, 39: 1603–1629; H. Merchant, 2014, Configurations of governance structure, generic strategy, and firm size: Opening the black box of value creation in international joint ventures, *Global Strategy Journal*, 4: 292–309.
18. S. B. Ivory & S. B. Brooks, 2018, managing corporate sustainability with a paradoxical lens: Lessons from strategic agility, *Journal of Business Ethics*, 148: 347–361; A. N. Kiss & P. S. Barr, 2015, New venture strategic adaptation: The interplay of belief structures and industry context, *Strategic Management Journal*, 36: 1245–1263.
19. C. Loderer, R. Stulz, & U. Waelchli, 2017, Firm rigidities and the decline in growth opportunities, *Management Science*, 63: 3000–3020; S. A. Fernhaber & P. C. Patel, 2012, How do young firms manage product portfolio complexity? The role of absorptive capacity and ambidexterity, *Strategic Management Journal*, 33: 1516–1539; S. Raisch & J. Birkinshaw, 2008, Organizational ambidexterity: Antecedents, outcomes, and moderators, *Journal of Management*, 34: 375–409.
20. C.-A. Chen, 2014, Revisiting organizational age, inertia, and adaptability: Developing

and testing a multi-stage model in the nonprofit sector, *Journal of Organizational Change Management*, 27: 251–272; M. Zhao, S. H. Park, & N. Zhour, 2014, MNC strategy and social adaptation in emerging markets, *Journal of International Business Studies*, 45: 842–861; B. W. Keats & M. A. Hitt, 1988, A causal model of linkages among environmental dimensions, macro organizational characteristics, and performance, *Academy of Management Journal*, 31: 570–598.

21. A. D. Chandler, 1962, *Strategy and Structure*, Cambridge, MA: MIT Press.
22. D. Martin, 2007, Alfred D. Chandler, Jr., A Business historian, dies at 88, *New York Times*, www.nytimes.com, May 12.
23. N. Stieglitz, T. Knudsen, & M. C. Becker, M. 2016, Adaptation and inertia in dynamic environments, *Strategic Management Journal*, 37: 1854–1864; D. Albert, M. Kreutzer, & C. Lechner, 2015, Resolving the paradox of interdependency and strategic renewal in activity systems, *Academy of Management Review*, 40: 210–234; B. T. Pentland, M. S. Feldman, M. C. Becker, & P. Liu, 2012, Dynamics of organizational routines: A generative model, *Journal of Management Studies*, 49: 1484–1508.
24. D. Laureiro-Martínez & S. Brusoni, 2018, Cognitive flexibility and adaptive decision-making: Evidence from a laboratory study of expert decision makers, *Strategic Management Journal*, 39: 1031–1058.
25. E. Winkler, 2018, Winners in traditional retailing are also winning online, *Wall Street Journal*, www.wsj.com, June 8.
26. C. Ten Brink, B. D. Gelb, & R. Keller, 2018, Successful rebounds: How firms overcome their middle age crisis, *Journal of Business Strategy*, 39(3): 3–8; S. Sonenshein, 2014, How organizations foster the creative use of resources, *Academy of Management Journal*, 57: 814–848.
27. B. Dattée, O. Alexy, & E. Autio, 2018, Maneuvering in poor visibility: How firms play the ecosystem game when uncertainty is high, *Academy of Management Journal*, 61: 466–498; M. R. Allen, G. K. Adomdza, & M. H. Meyer, 2015, Managing for innovation: Managerial control and employee level outcomes, *Journal of Business Research*, 68: 371–379.
28. K. Baird & S. Su, 2018, The association between controls, performance measures and performance, *International Journal of Productivity and Performance Management*, 67: 967–984; Allen, Adomdza, & Meyer, Managing for innovation: Managerial control and employee level outcomes.
29. L. Thomas & V. Ambrosini, 2015, Materializing strategy: The role of comprehensiveness and management controls in strategy formation in volatile environments, *British Journal of Management*, 26: S105–S124; R. MacKay & R. Chia, 2013, Choice, chance, and unintended consequences in strategic change: A process understanding of the rise and fall of Northco Automotive, *Academy of Management Journal*, 56: 208–230.
30. J. Puck, M. Hödl, I. Filatotchev, H. Wolff, & B. Bader, 2016, Ownership mode, cultural distance, and the extent of parent firms' strategic control over subsidiaries in the PRC, *Asia Pacific Journal of Management*, 33: 1075–1105; S. Groda., A. J. Nelson, & R. M. Slino, 2015, Help-seeking and help-giving as an organizational routine: Continual engagement in innovative work, *Academy of Management Journal*, 58: 136–168; Hoskisson, R. E. & Hitt, M. A. 1988. Strategic control systems and relative R&D investment in large multiproduct firms. *Strategic Management Journal*, 9: 605–621.
31. Y. Lin, C. Chen, & B. Lin, 2017, The influence of strategic control and operational control on new venture performance, *Management Decision*, 55: 1042–1064; M. Menz & C. Scheef, 2014, Chief strategy officers: Contingency analysis of their presence in top management teams, *Strategic Management Journal*, 35: 461–471; M. A. Hitt, R. E. Hoskisson, R. A. Johnson, & D. D. Moesel, 1996, The market for corporate control and firm innovation, *Academy of Management Journal*, 39: 1084–1119.
32. S. Karim & A. Kaul, 2015, Structural recombination and innovation: Unlocking intraorganizational knowledge synergy through structural change, *Organization Science*, 26: 439–455; W. P. Wan, R. E. Hoskisson, J. C. Short, & D. W. Yiu, 2011, Resource-based theory and corporate diversification: Accomplishments and opportunities, *Journal of Management*, 37: 1335–1368.
33. K. A. Bentley-Goode, N. J. Newton, & A. M. Thompson, 2017, Business strategy, internal control over financial reporting, and audit reporting quality, *Auditing: A Journal of Practice & Theory*, 36: 49–69; W. Su & E. Tsang, 2015, Product diversification and financial performance: The moderating role of secondary stakeholders, *Academy of Management Journal*, 58: 1128–1148.
34. G. Linton & J. Kask, J. 2017, Configurations of entrepreneurial orientation and competitive strategy for high performance, *Journal of Business Research*, 70: 168–176; R. Amit & C. Zott, 2015, Crafting business architecture: The antecedents of business model design, *Strategic Entrepreneurship Journal*, 9: 331–350; X. S. Y. Spencer, T. A. Joiner, & S. Salmon, 2009, Differentiation strategy, performance measurement systems and organizational performance: Evidence from Australia, *International Journal of Business*, 14: 83–103.
35. L. Ambroise, I. Prim-Allaz, C. Teyssier, & S. Peillon, 2018, The environment-strategy-structure fit and performance of industrial servitized SMEs, *Journal of Service Management*, 29: 301–328; P. Almodovar & A. M. Rugman, 2014, The M curve and the performance of Spanish international new ventures, *British Journal of Management*, 25: S6–S23; M. Dass & S. Kumar, 2014, Bringing product and consumer ecosystems to the strategic forefront, *Business Horizons*, 57: 225–234; X. Yin & E. J. Zajac, 2004, The strategy/governance structure fit relationship: Theory and evidence in franchising arrangements, *Strategic Management Journal*, 25: 365–383.
36. J. Jargon, 2018, McDonald's shares details of restructuring plan in new memo, *Wall Street Journal*, www.wsj.com, June 12.
37. G. Shani & J. Westphal, 2016, Persona non grata? Determinants and consequences of social distancing from journalists who engage in negative coverage of firm leadership, *Academy of Management Journal*, 59: 302–329; E. Kulchina, 2014, Media coverage and location choice, *Strategic Management Journal*, 35: 596–605; M. K. Bednar, S. Boivie, & N. R. Prince, 2013, Burr under the saddle: How media coverage influences strategic change, *Organization Science*, 24: 910–925.
38. D. C. Mowery, 2010, Alfred Chandler and knowledge management within the firm, *Industrial & Corporate Change*, 19: 483–507; Chandler, *Strategy and Structure*.
39. Keats & O'Neill, Organizational structure, 524.
40. G. C. Kane, D. Palmer, A. Nguyen Phillips, D. Kiron, & N. Buckley, 2016, Aligning the organization for its digital future, *MIT Sloan Management Review*, 58(1): 1–28; K. Srikanth & P. Puranam, 2014, The firm as a coordination system: Evidence from software services offshoring, *Organization Science*, 25: 1253–1271; E. Rawley, 2010, Diversification, coordination costs and organizational rigidity: Evidence from microdata, *Strategic Management Journal*, 31: 873–891.
41. M. Cianni & S. Steckler, 2017, Organization alignment: The prerequisite for successful transformation, *People & Strategy*, 40: 6; S. M. Wagner, K. K. R. Ullrich, & S. Transchel, 2014, The game plan for aligning the organization, *Business Horizons*, 57: 189–201; A. Campbell & H. Strikwerda, 2013, The power of one: Towards the new integrated organization, *Journal of Business Strategy*, 34(2): 4–12.
42. C. Prange & J. C. Pinho, 2017, How personal and organizational drivers impact on SME international performance: The mediating role of organizational innovation, *International Business Review*, 26: 1114–1123; S. Amdouni & S. Boubaker, 2015, Multiple large shareholders and owner-manager compensation: Evidence from French listed firms, *Journal of Applied Business Research*, 31: 1111–1129; C. Levicki, 1999, *The Interactive Strategy Workout*, 2nd ed., London: Prentice Hall.

43. R. Wiesner, D. Chadee, & P. Best, 2018, Managing change toward environmental sustainability: A conceptual model in small and medium enterprises, *Organization & Environment*, 31: 152–177; M. Perkmann & A. Spicer, 2014, How emerging organizations take form: The role of imprinting and values in organizational bricolage, *Organization Science*, 25: 1785–1806; P. L. Drnevich & D. C. Croson, 2013, Information technology and business-level strategy: Toward an integrated theoretical perspective, *MIS Quarterly*, 37: 483–509.
44. A. Maciejczyk, 2016, Challenges of control in functional organization structures: Example of outsourcing sector, *Journal of Economics & Management*, 25: 48–62; J. Davoren, 2015, Functional structure organization strength & weaknesses, *Small Business*, http://smallbusiness.chron.com, May 10.
45. L. Picci & L. Savorelli, 2018, The 'inventor balance' and the functional specialization in global inventive activities, *Economics of Innovation & New Technology*, 27: 39–61; D. Antons & F. Piller, 2015, Opening the black box of 'not-invented-here': *Academy of Management Perspectives*, 29: 193–217.
46. A. Loderer, R. Stulz, & U. Waelchli, 2017, Firm rigidities and the decline in growth opportunities, *Management Science*, 63: 3000–3020.
47. O. E. Williamson, 1975, *Markets and Hierarchies: Analysis and Anti-Trust Implications*, NY: The Free Press.
48. J. R. Busenbark, R. M. Wiseman, M. Arrfelt, & W. Hyun-Soo, 2017, Review of the internal capital allocation literature: Piecing together the capital allocation puzzle, *Journal of Management*, 43: 2430–2455; M. J. Sanchez-Bueno & B. Usero, 2014, How may the nature of family firms explain the decisions concerning international diversification? *Journal of Business Research*, 67: 1311–1320; T. Hutzschenreuter & J. Horstkotte, 2013, Performance effects of top management team demographic faultlines in the process of product diversification, *Strategic Management Journal*, 34: 704–726; Chandler, *Strategy and Structure.*
49. T. C. Ambos & G. Muller-Stewens, 2017, Rethinking the role of the centre in the multidivisional firm: A retrospective, *Long Range Planning*, 50: 8–16; Y. M. Zhou, 2015, Supervising across borders: The case of multinational hierarchies, *Organization Science*, 26: 277–292; J. Joseph & W. Ocasio, 2012, Architecture, attention, and adaptation in the multibusiness firm: General Electric from 1951 to 2001, *Strategic Management Journal*, 33: 633–660.
50. R. E. Hoskisson, C. E. Hill, & H. Kim, 1993, The multidivisional structure: Organizational fossil or source of value?, *Journal of Management*, 19: 269–298.
51. S. Hu, Z. He, D. P. Blettner, & R. A. Bettis, 2017, Conflict inside and outside: Social comparisons and attention shifts in multidivisional firms, *Strategic Management Journal*, 38: 1435–1454; A. Zimmermann, S. Raisch, & J. Birkinshaw, 2015, How is ambidexterity initiated? The emergent charter definition process, *Organization Science*, 26: 1119–1139; V. Binda, 2012, Strategy and structure in large Italian and Spanish firms, 1950–2002, *Business History Review*, 86: 503–525.
52. J. Hautz, M. Mayer, & C. Stadler, 2014, Macro-competitive context and diversification: The impact of macroeconomic growth and foreign competition, *Long Range Planning*, 47: 337–352; C. E. Helfat & K. M. Eisenhardt, 2004, Inter-temporal economies of scope, organizational modularity, and the dynamics of diversification, *Strategic Management Journal*, 25: 1217–1232; A. D. Chandler, 1994, The functions of the HQ unit in the multibusiness firm, in R. P. Rumelt, D. E. Schendel, & D. J. Teece (eds.), *Fundamental Issues in Strategy*, Cambridge, MA: Harvard Business School Press, 327.
53. O. E. Williamson, 1994, Strategizing, economizing, and economic organization, in R. P. Rumelt, D. E. Schendel, & D. J. Teece (eds.), *Fundamental Issues in Strategy*, Cambridge, MA: Harvard Business School Press, 361–401.
54. V. A. Aggarwal & B. Wu, 2014, Organizational constraints to adaptation: Intrafirm asymmetry in the locus of coordination, *Organization Science*, 26: 218–238; Hoskisson, Hill, & Kim, The multidivisional structure: Organizational fossil or source of value?
55. D. J. Teece, 2014, A dynamic capabilities-based entrepreneurial theory of the multinational enterprise, *Journal of International Business Studies*, 45: 8–37; R. Duchin & D. Sosyura, 2013, Divisional managers and internal capital markets, *Journal of Finance*, 68: 387–429; O. E. Williamson, 1985, *The Economic Institutions of Capitalism: Firms, Markets, and Relational Contracting*, New York: Macmillan.
56. M. F. Wolff, 1999, In the organization of the future, competitive advantage will lie with inspired employees, *Research Technology Management*, 42(4): 2–4.
57. S. Albers, F. Wohlgezogen, & E. J. Zajac, 2016, Strategic alliance structures, *Journal of Management*, 42: 582–614; S. Y. Lee, M. Pitesa, S. Thau, & M. Pillutla, 2015, Discrimination in selection decisions: Integrating stereotype fit and interdependence theories, *Academy of Management Journal*, 58: 789–812; E. Schulz, S. Chowdhury, & D. Van de Voort, 2013, Firm productivity moderated link between human capital and compensation: The significance of task-specific human capital, *Human Resource Management*, 52: 423–439.
58. J. Joseph, R. Klingebiel, & A. J. Wilson, 2016, Organizational structure and performance feedback: Centralization, aspirations, and termination decisions, *Organization Science*, 27: 1065–1083; N. Malhotra, C. R. (Bob) Hinings, 2015, Unpacking continuity and change as a process of organizational transformation, *Long Range Planning*, 48: 1–22; L. G. Love, R. L. Priem, & G. T. Lumpkin, 2002, Explicitly articulated strategy and firm performance under alternative levels of centralization, *Journal of Management*, 28: 611–627.
59. Y. Gabriel, 2018, For formal organization: The past in the present and future of organization theory, *Organization Studies*, 39: 147–150; S. Biancani, D. A. McFarland, & L. Dahlander, 2014, The semiformal organizational, *Organization Science*, 25: 1306–1324; T. F. Gonzalez-Cruz, A. Huguet-Roig, & S. Cruz-Ros, 2012, Organizational technology as a mediating variable in centralization-formalization fit, *Management Decision*, 50: 1527–1548.
60. Eva, Sendjaya, Prajogo, Cavanagh, & Robin, Creating strategic fit, D. G. Sirmon, M. A. Hitt, R. D. Ireland, & B. A. Gilbert, 2011, Resource orchestration to create competitive advantage: Breadth, depth and life cycle effects, *Journal of Management*, 37: 1390–1412.
61. J. M. Walter & J. M. Peterson, 2017, Strategic R&D and the innovation of products: Understanding the role of time preferences and product differentiation, *Economics of Innovation & New Technology*, 26: 575–595; N. J. Foss, J. Lyngsie, & S. A. Zahra, 2015, Organizational design correlates of entrepreneurship: The roles of decentralization and formalization for opportunity discovery and realization, *Strategic Organization*, 123: 32–60.
62. B. Berman, 2015, How to compete effectively against low-cost competitors, *Business Horizons*, 58: 87–97; H. Brea-Solis, R. Casadesus-Masanell, & E. Grifell-Tatje, 2015, Business model evaluation: Unifying Walmart's sources of advantage, *Strategic Entrepreneurship Journal*, 9: 12–33.
63. D. Martinez-Simarro, C. Devece, & C. Liopis-Albert, 2015, How information systems strategy moderates the relationship between business strategy and performance, *Journal of Business Research*, 68: 1592–1594.
64. M. Dobrajska, S. Billinger, & S. Karim, 2015, Delegation within hierarchies: How information processing and knowledge characteristics influence the allocation of formal and real decision authority, *Organization Science*, 26: 687–704.
65. A. Spicer & D. Hyatt, 2017, Walmart's emergent low-cost sustainable product strategy, *California Management Review*, 59(2): 116–141.
66. 2018, Our story, Walmart Corporate, www.walmartstores.com, June 29.
67. A. Ignatius, 2017, We need people to lean into the future, *Harvard Business Review*, 95(2): 94–100.
68. J. Schmidt, R. Makadok, & T. Keil, 2016, Customer-specific synergies and market

convergence, *Strategic Management Journal*, 37: 2003–2007; A. Ma, Z. Yang, & M. Mourali, 2014, Consumer adoption of new products: Independent versus interdependent self-perspectives, *Journal of Marketing*, 78: 101–117.

69. V. Biloshapka & O. Osiyevskyy, 2018, Three value-focused strategic questions for continuously updating your business model, *Strategy & Leadership*, 46(3): 45–51; P. C. Patel, S. Thorgren, & J. Wincent, 2015, Leadership, passion, and performance: A study of job creation projects during the recession, *British Journal of Management*, 26: 211–224; K. Z. Zhou & F. Wu, 2010, Technological capability, strategic flexibility and product innovation, *Strategic Management Journal*, 31: 547–561.
70. G. Cattani, R. L. M. Dunbar, & Z. Shapira, 2017, How commitment to craftsmanship leads to unique value: Steinway & Sons' differentiation strategy, *Strategy Science*, 2: 13–38.
71. J. H. Burgers & J. G. Covin, 2016, The contingent effects of differentiation and integration on corporate entrepreneurship, *Strategic Management Journal*, 37: 521–540; L. Mirabeau & S. Maguire, 2014, From autonomous strategic behavior to emergent strategy, *Strategic Management Journal*, 35: 1202–1229.
72. C. Vieregger, E. C. Larson, & P. C. Anderson, 2017, Top management team structure and resource reallocation within the multibusiness firm, *Journal of Management*, 43: 2497–2525; Chandler, *Strategy and Structure*.
73. 2018, Core strengths, Procter & Gamble Home Page, www.pg.com, July 13.
74. D. Maslach, 2016, Change and persistence with failed technological innovation, *Strategic Management Journal*, 37: 714–723; S. Wagner, K. Hoisl, & G. Thoma, 2014, Overcoming localization of knowledge—the role of professional service firms, *Strategic Management Journal*, 35: 1671–1688.
75. S. Pratap & B. Saha, 2018, Evolving efficacy of managerial capital, contesting managerial practices, and the process of strategic renewal, *Strategic Management Journal*, 39: 759–793; M. Tortoriello, 2015, The social underpinnings of absorptive capacity: The moderating effects of structural holes on innovation generation based on external knowledge, *Strategic Management Journal*, 36: 586–597; M. Makri, M. A. Hitt, & P. J. Lane, 2010, Complementary technologies, knowledge relatedness and invention outcomes in high technology mergers and acquisitions, *Strategic Management Journal*, 31: 602–628.
76. D. A. Levinthal & M. Workiewicz, 2018, When two bosses are better than one: nearly decomposable systems and organizational adaptation, *Organization Science*, 29: 207–224; M. Palmie, M. M. Keupp, & O. Gassmann, 2014, Pull the right levers: Creating internationally "useful" subsidiary competence by organizational architecture, *Long Range Planning*, 47: 32–48.
77. T. J. Winkler & P. Kettunen, 2018, Five principles of industrialized transformation for successfully building an operational backbone, *MIS Quarterly Executive*, 17: 123–140; T. W. Tong, J. J. Reuer, B. B. Tyler, & S. Zhang, 2015, Host country executives' assessments of international joint ventures and divestitures: An experimental approach, *Strategic Management Journal*, 36: 254–275; S. H. Appelbaum, D. Nadeau, & M. Cyr, 2009, Performance evaluation in a matrix organization: A case study (part three), *Industrial and Commercial Training*, 41: 9–14.
78. A. V. Sakhartov, 2017, Economies of scope, resource relatedness, and the dynamics of corporate diversification, *Strategic Management Journal*, 38: 2168–2188; A. V. Sakhartov & T. B. Folta, 2014, Resource relatedness, redeployability, and firm value, *Strategic Management Journal*, 35: 1781–1797; O. Alexy, G. George, & A. J. Salter, 2013, Cui bono? The selective revealing of knowledge and its implications for innovative activity, *Academy of Management Review*, 38: 270–291.
79. E. Knight & S. Paroutis, 2017, Becoming salient: The TMT leader's role in shaping the interpretive context of paradoxical tensions, *Organization Studies*, 38(3–4): 403–432; E. R. Feldman, S. C. Gilson, & B. Villalonga, 2014, Do analysts add value when they most can? Evidence from corporate spin-offs, *Strategic Management Journal*, 35: 1446–1463; M. Kruehler, U. Pidun, & H. Rubner, 2012, How to assess the corporate parenting strategy? A conceptual answer, *Journal of Business Strategy*, 33(4): 4–17.
80. Press release, 2016, Sony Corporation announces changes to organizational and management structure, www.sony.net, March 25.
81. M. Schommer, A. Richter, & A. Karna, 2018, Does the diversification-firm performance relationship change over time? A meta-analytical review, *Journal of Management Studies*, in press; T. M. Alessandri & A. Seth, 2014, The effects of managerial ownership on international and business diversification: Balancing incentives and risks, *Strategic Management Journal*, 35: 2064–2075.
82. T. B. Mackey, J. B. Barney, & J. P. Dotson, 2017. Corporate diversification and the value of individual firms: A Bayesian approach, *Strategic Management Journal*, 38: 322–341; Hoskisson, Hill, & Kim, The multidivisional structure: Organizational fossil or source of value.
83. Busenbark, Wiseman, Arrfelt, & Hyun-Soo, Review of the internal capital allocation literature: Piecing together the capital allocation puzzle; M. Arrfelt, R. M. Wiseman, G. McNamara, & G. T. M. Hult, 2015, Examining a key corporate role: The influence of capital allocation competency on business unit performance, *Strategic Management Journal*, 36: 1017–1034.
84. C. Gartenberg & J. Wulf, 2017, Pay Harmony? Social comparison and performance compensation in multibusiness firms, *Organization Science*, 28: 39–55.
85. 2018, How is Textron organized and operated? Textron Home Page, www.textron.com, July 14.
86. Ambos & Mueller-Stewens, Rethinking the role of the centre in the multidivisional firm: A retrospective; C. Custodio, 2014, Mergers and acquisitions accounting and the diversification discount, *Journal of Finance*, 69: 219–240.
87. M. J. Benner & T. Zenger 2016, The lemons problem in markets for strategy, *Strategy Science*, 1:71–89.
88. A. R. Reuber, G. A. Knight, P. W. Liesch, & L. Zhou, 2018, International entrepreneurship: The pursuit of entrepreneurial opportunities across national borders, *Journal of International Business Studies*, 49: 395–406; R. Belderbos, T. W. Tong, & S. Wu, 2014, Multinationality and downside risk: The roles of option portfolio and organization, *Strategic Management Journal*, 35: 88–106.
89. T. Schubert, E. Baier, & C. Rammer, 2018, Firm capabilities, technological dynamism and the internationalisation of innovation: A behavioural approach, *Journal of International Business Studies*, 49: 70–95; R. Ramamurti, 2016, Internationalization and innovation in emerging markets, *Strategic Management Journal*, 37: E74–E83.
90. P. Buckley, J. Doh, & M. Benischke, 2017, Towards a renaissance in international business research? Big questions, grand challenges, and the future of IB scholarship, *Journal of International Business Studies*, 48: 1045–1064; L. Zhang, X. Zhang, & Y. Xi, 2017, The sociality of resources: Understanding organizational competitive advantage from a social perspective, *Asia Pacific Journal of Management*, 34: 619–648; G. Vasudeva, E. A. Alexander, & S. L. Jones, 2015, Institutional logics and interorganizational learning in technological arenas: Evidence from standard-setting organizations in the mobile handset industry, *Organization Science*, 26: 830–846; J.-L. Arregle, T. Miller, M. A. Hitt, & P. W. Beamish, 2013, Do regions matter? An integrated institutional and semiglobalization perspective on the internationalization of MNEs, *Strategic Management Journal*, 34: 910–934.
91. P. C. Nell, P. Kappen, & T. Laamanen, 2017, Reconceptualising hierarchies: The disaggregation and dispersion of headquarters in multinational corporations, *Journal of Management Studies*. 54: 1121–1143; A. H. Kirca, G. T. M. Hult, S. Deligonul,

M. Z. Perryy, & S. T. Cavusgil, 2012, A multilevel examination of the drivers of firm multinationality: A meta-analysis, *Journal of Management*, 38: 502–530.

92. S. Morris, S. Snell, & I. Björkman, 2016, An architectural framework for global talent management, *Journal of International Business Studies*, 47: 723–747.

93. B. Carson, 2018, Lyft doubled rides in 2017 as its rival Uber stumbled, *Forbes*, www.forbes.com, January 16.

94. P. Marinova, 2018, Uber CEO on gender discrimination investigation: 'I take sole responsibility', *Fortune*, www.fortune.com. July 16; G. Bensinger & M. Farrell, 2017, How Uber backers orchestrated Kalanick's ouster as CEO, *Wall Street Journal*, www.wsj.com, June 22.

95. R. Heilweil, 2018, For the American sharing economy, the future of motorcycles might be imitating Airbnb, not Uber. *Forbes*, www.forbes.com, July 9.

96. A. Cuervo-Cazurra, R. Mudambi, & T. Pedersen, 2018, The boundaries of the firm in global strategy, *Global Strategy Journal*, 8: 211–219; J. Y. Yang, J. Lu, & R. Jiang, 2017, Too slow or too fast? Speed of FDI expansions, industry globalization, and firm performance, *Long Range Planning*, 50(1): 74–92.

97. C. A. Bartlett & P. W. Beamish, 2018, *Transnational management: Text and cases in cross-border management*, Cambridge: Cambridge University Press; H. Merchant, 2014, Configurations of governance structure, generic strategy, and firms size: Opening the black box of value creation in international joint ventures, *Global Strategy Journal*, 4: 292–309; B. Brenner & B. Ambos, 2013, A question of legitimacy? A dynamic perspective on multinational firm control, *Organization Science*, 24: 773–795.

98. Levinthal & Workiewicz, When two bosses are better than one: Nearly decomposable systems and organizational adaptation; K. Bondy & K. Starkey, 2014, The dilemmas of internationalization: Corporate social responsibility in the multinational corporation, *British Journal of Management*, 25: 4–22; J. Qiu & L. Donaldson, 2012, Stopford and Wells were right! MNC matrix structures do fit a "high-high" strategy, *Management International Review*, 52: 671–689.

99. N. Worren, 2017, The matrix as a transitory form: the evolution of FMC Technologies 2001–2016, *Journal of Organization Design*, 6: 1–14.

100. A. Srinivasan & N. Venkatraman, 2018, Entrepreneurship in digital platforms: A network-centric view, *Strategic Entrepreneurship Journal*, 12: 54–71; Y. Lku & T. Ravichandran, 2015, Alliance experience, IT-enable knowledge integration, and ex-ante value gains, *Organization Science*, 26: 511–530.

101. G. B. Dagnino, G. Levanti, & A. M. Li Destri, 2016, Structural dynamics and intentional governance in strategic interorganizational network evolution: A multilevel approach, *Organization Studies*, 37: 349–373; D. Filiou & S. Golesorkhi, 2016, Influence of institutional differences on firm innovation from international alliances, *Long Range Planning*, 49(1): 129–144.

102. J. Bundy, R. M. Vogel, & M. A. Zachary, 2018, Organization-stakeholder fit: A dynamic theory of cooperation, compromise, and conflict between an organization and its stakeholders, *Strategic Management Journal*, 39: 476–501; W. (Stone) Shi, S. L. Sun, B. C. Pinkham, & M. W. Peng, 2014, Domestic alliance network to attract foreign partners: Evidence from international joint ventures in China, *Journal of International Business Studies*, 45: 338–362.

103. K. Ji Youn, M. Howard, E. C. Pahnke, & W. Boeker, W. 2016, Understanding network formation in strategy research: Exponential random graph models, *Strategic Management Journal*, 37: 22–44; F. J. Contractor & J. J. Reuer, 2014, Structuring and governing alliances: New directions for research, *Global Strategy Journal*, 4: 241–256; L. Dooley, D. Kirk, & K. Philpott, 2013, Nurturing life-science knowledge discovery: Managing multiorganisation networks, *Production Planning & Control*, 24: 195–207.

104. F. J. Contractor & J. J. Reuer, 2014, Structuring and governing alliances: New directions for research, *Global Strategy Journal*, 4: 241–256; Dooley, Kirk, & Philpott, Nurturing life-science knowledge discovery: Managing multiorganisation networks.

105. C. Bellavitis, I. Filatotchev, & D. S. Kamuriwo, 2014, The effects of intra-industry and extra-industry networks on performance: A case of venture capital portfolio firms, *Managerial and Decision Economics*, 35: 129–144.

106. C. V. Bustamente, 2018, Strategic choices: Accelerated startups' outsourcing decisions, *Journal of Business Research*, in press.

107. S. Balachandran & E. Hernandez, 2018, Networks and innovation: Accounting for structural and institutional sources of recombination in brokerage triads, *Organization Science*, 29: 80–99; Z. Kahn, Y. K. Lew, & R. R. Sinkovics, 2015, International joint ventures as boundary spanners: Technological knowledge transfer in an emerging economy, *Global Strategy Journal*, 5: 48–68; R. Gulati, F. Wohlgezogen, & P. Zhelyazkov, 2012, The two facets of collaboration: Cooperation and coordination in strategic alliances, *Academy of Management Annals*, 6: 531–583; M. H. Hansen, R. E. Hoskisson, & J. B. Barney, 2008, Competitive advantage in alliance governance: Resolving the opportunism minimization-gain maximization paradox, *Managerial and Decision Economics*, 29: 191–208; G. Lorenzoni & C. Baden-Fuller, 1995, Creating a strategic center to manage a web of partners, *California Management Review*, 37: 146–163.

108. S. Ozdemir, D. Kandemir, & T.-Y. Eng, 2017, The role of horizontal and vertical new product alliances in responsive and proactive market orientations and performance of industrial manufacturing firms, *Industrial Marketing Management*, 64: 25–35; F. Zambuto, G. L. Nigro, & J. P. O'Brien, 2017, The importance of alliances in firm capital structure decisions: Evidence from biotechnology firms, *Managerial and Decision Economics*, 38: 3–18; A. C. Inkpen, 2008, Knowledge transfer and international joint ventures: The case of NUMMI and General Motors, *Strategic Management Journal*, 29: 447–453; J. H. Dyer & K. Nobeoka, 2000, Creating and managing a high-performance knowledge-sharing network: The Toyota case, *Strategic Management Journal*, 21: 345–367.

109. M. Hsiao-Wen Ho, P. N. Ghauri, & J. A. Larimo, 2018, Institutional distance and knowledge acquisition in international buyer-supplier relationships: The moderating role of trust, *Asia Pacific Journal of Management*, 35: 427–447; J. Xia, Y. Wang, Y. Lin, H. Yang, & S. Li, 2018, Alliance formation in the midst of market and network: Insights from resource dependence and network perspectives, *Journal of Management*, 44: 1899–1925; Y. Liu, Y. Li, L. H. Shi, & T. Liu, 2017, Knowledge transfer in buyer-supplier relationships: The role of transactional and relational governance mechanisms, *Journal of Business Research*, 78: 285–293.

110. K. Shin, S. Kim, & G. Park, 2016, How does the partner type in R&D alliances impact technological innovation performance? A study on the Korean biotechnology industry, *Asia Pacific Journal of Management*, 33: 141–164; Y. Luo, Y. Liu, Q. Yang, V. Maksimov, & J. Hou, 2015, Improving performance and reducing cost in buyer-supplier relationships: The role of justice in curtailing opportunism, *Journal of Business Research*, 68: 607–615; S. G. Lazzarini, D. P. Claro, & L. F. Mesquita, 2008, Buyer-supplier and supplier-supplier alliances: Do they reinforce or undermine one another? *Journal of Management Studies*, 45: 561–584.

111. 2018, Work starts to 'build an even better Walgreens', *MMR*, May 21, 66.

112. M. J. Brand, E. M. Croonen, & R. J. Leenders, 2018, Entrepreneurial networking: a blessing or a curse? Differential effects for low, medium and high performing franchisees, *Small Business Economics*, 50: 783–805; F. Sadeh, & M. Kacker, 2018, Quality signaling through ex-ante voluntary information disclosure in entrepreneurial networks: Evidence from franchising, *Small Business Economics*, 50: 729–748; W. E. Gillis, J. G. Combs, & D. J. Ketchen, Jr., 2014, Using resource-based theory to help explain plural form franchising, *Entrepreneurship Theory and Practice*, 38: 449–472.

113. S. V. Devarakonda & J. J. Reuer, 2018, Knowledge sharing and safeguarding in R&D collaborations: The role of steering committees in biotechnology alliances, *Strategic Management Journal*, 39: 1912–1934; R. Hahn & S. Gold, 2014, Resources and governance in "base of the pyramid"-partnerships: Assessing collaborations between businesses and non-business actors, *Journal of Business Research*, 67: 1321–1333; W. Vanhaverbeke, V. Gilsing, & G. Duysters, 2012, Competence and governance in strategic collaboration: The differential effect of network structure on the creation of core and noncore technology, *Journal of Product Innovation Management*, 29: 784–802.

114. M.-C. Stoian, J. Rialp, & P. Dimitratos, 2017, SME networks and international performance: Unveiling the significance of foreign market entry mode, *Journal of Small Business Management*, 55: 128–148.

115. J. Li, K. E. Meyer, H. Zhang, & Y. Ding, 2018, Diplomatic and corporate networks: Bridges to foreign locations, *Journal of International Business Studies*, 49: 659–683; A. Peterman, A. Kourula, & R. Levitt, 2014, Balancing act: Government roles in an energy conservation network, *Research Policy*, 43: 1067–1082; H. Liu, X. Jiang, J. Zhang, & X. Zhao, 2013, Strategic flexibility and international venturing by emerging market firms: The moderating effects of institutional and relational factors, *Journal of International Marketing*, 21: 79–98; M. W. Hansen, T. Pedersen, & B. Petersen, 2009, MNC strategies and linkage effects in developing countries, *Journal of World Business*, 44: 121–130.

116. J.-L. Arregle, T. Miller, M. A. Hitt, & P. Beamish, 2018, The role of MNEs' internationalization patterns in their regional integration of FDI locations, *Journal of World Business*, in press; M. de Vaan, 2014, Interfirm networks in periods of technological turbulence and stability, *Research Policy*, 43: 1666–1680; C. C. Phelps, 2010, A longitudinal study of the influence of alliance network structure and composition on firm exploratory innovation, *Academy of Management Journal*, 53: 890–913.

12

Strategic Leadership

Studying this chapter should provide you with the strategic management knowledge needed to:

12-1 Define strategic leadership and describe top-level managers' importance.

12-2 Explain what top management teams are and how they affect firm performance.

12-3 Describe the managerial succession process using internal and external managerial labor markets.

12-4 Discuss the value of strategic leadership in determining the firm's strategic direction.

12-5 Describe the importance of strategic leaders in managing the firm's resources.

12-6 Explain what a firm does to sustain an effective culture.

12-7 Describe what strategic leaders can do to establish and emphasize the need for everyone to demonstrate ethical practices in their firms.

12-8 Discuss the importance and use of organizational controls.

iStock.com/DNY59

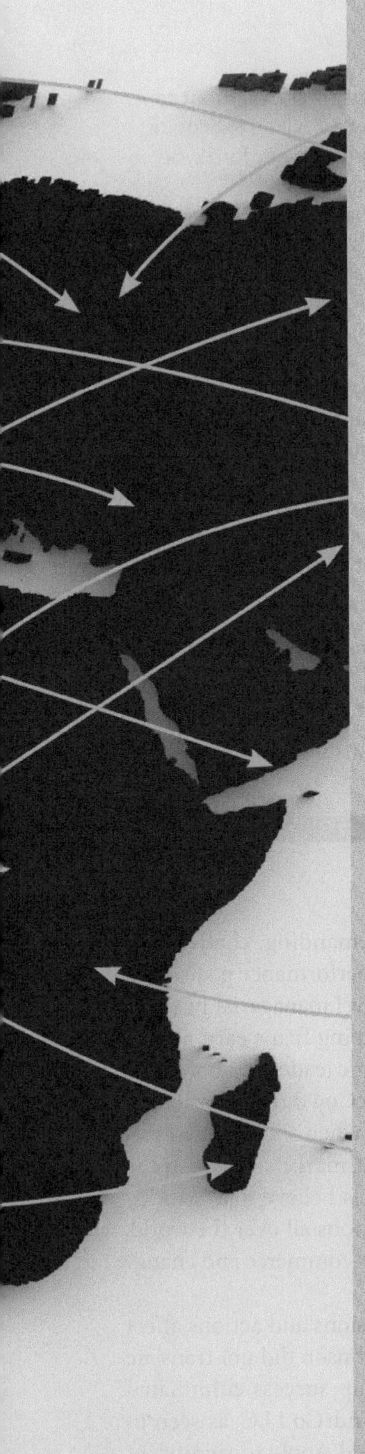

MEG WHITMAN: A PIONEERING STRATEGIC LEADER

Meg Whitman, the only female to serve as the CEO for two major U.S. corporations, announced in November of 2017 that she would step down from her CEO position at Hewlett Packard Enterprise Co. on February 1, 2018. Saying that she was returning to what she considers her "start-up roots," she had decided to join with Hollywood executive and long-time friend Jeffrey Katzenberg to run a mobile-video company called WndrCo NewTV. This firm is part of Katzenberg's WndrCo LLC, a media and tech venture that plans to develop a portfolio of companies. In her position, Whitman is to build "an online service, securing production partnerships and building a team at NewTV, which will target the 18- to 34-year-olds who have driven the rise in mobile-video viewing over the past several years." In essence, the firm intends to develop a platform through which high-budget short videos will be available to users to watch while standing in a line, riding a bus, and so forth. Some videos will be one-off stories while others will be part of richer and longer stories.

The path Whitman travelled to become one of the most prominent women in American business and an experienced CEO in Silicon Valley is enlightening. Her path as a leader demonstrates increasing levels of responsibility and decision-making authority while moving from one opportunity to another.

VCG/Getty Images

Meg Whitman, former CEO of Hewlett-Packard, led the turnaround plan to split HP into two companies; Hewlett Packard Enterprises (HPE) and Hewlett Packard Inc. (HPQ).

A graduate of Princeton University and Harvard Business School, Whitman started her career in 1979 as a brand manager at Procter & Gamble. She later worked as a consultant in Bain & Company's San Francisco office, rising to a position as senior vice president in this firm. In 1989, she accepted a position as vice president for strategic planning at Walt Disney Corporation. She met Jeffrey Katzenberg while working for Disney. After two years, she joined Stride Rite Corporation prior to becoming president and CEO of Florists' Transworld Delivery in 1995. After another two years, she accepted the role of General Manager for Hasbro's Playskool division, where she had responsibility for global management and marketing for two brands targeted to children—Playskool and Mr. Potato Head. From Hasbro, Whitman became CEO of eBay (the pioneering company that made it possible for strangers to exchange goods online) in March 1998. At the time, the firm had only 30 employees and annual revenue of approximately $4 million. Prior to resigning as eBay's CEO in November 2007, the firm's revenues had increased to $8 billion annually and the workforce numbered around 15,000.

Whitman become CEO of Hewlett-Packard in September 2011. She remained in this role for a bit over six years. During those years, "she led a turnaround plan that involved the largest split in corporate history, tens of thousands of layoffs, $18 billion in write-offs and a leadership shake-up." Deciding in 2015 to split Hewlett-Packard into Hewlett Packard Enterprises (HPE) and Hewlett Packard Inc. (HPQ) was the most prominent strategic action she took as HP's CEO. HPQ took the printer and PC businesses while business-focused HPE works in a variety of markets such as servers, storage, networking, consulting and support, and financial services. Whitman, her team, and HP's board chose to split into two companies because of declining sales in what was a complicated conglomerate. The leaders believed that breaking the firm into two units would allow each to focus more as a means of unlocking the full value embedded in the portfolios that formed the two new firms. Results achieved across time will show if the decision to break HP into two firms was one of Whitman's best strategic actions or one that failed to deliver increased value to shareholders.

As is the case for virtually all leaders serving as a CEO, Whitman's career is not without controversy. During her tenure at eBay, for example, the firm paid roughly $4.1 billion to acquire Skype in 2005. Later admitting that the premium she and her team agreed to pay for Skype was too large, eBay sold Skype to a group of investors for $2.75 billion.

In Whitman's view, failing to recognize the market potential for eBay in Japan was a major error. Instead of investing in Japan, Whitman chose to invest in eBay's existing website. At the time, Japan was the world's second largest Internet consumer market. In commenting about this, Whitman said that "I had a sense that the technology underpinning eBay was not going to help us scale where we needed to. That miss of eBay Japan is one of the big failures of my time at eBay."

Some also question a few decisions Whitman made during her tenure as HP's CEO: "Meg Whitman's tenure at Hewlett-Packard was marked by a series of splits and sales that reshaped the storied Silicon Valley company. Now, her successor Antonio Neri must take the remnants and reignite innovation." Others observed the continuing weakness in server sales at Hewlett Packard Enterprise as Whitman departed, suggesting that she was at least partly responsible for this situation. On the other hand, many view Whitman's career as a strategic leader as one through which she played a major role in commercializing the Internet industry.

Sources: D. Gallagher, 2018, New HPs give fresh life to old businesses, *Wall Street Journal*, www.wsj.com, February 23; E. Shwartzel, 2018, Meg Whitman to lead mobile-video startup NewTv, *Wall Street Journal*, www.wsj.com, January 24; D. Gallagher, 2017, Meg Whitman's latest turn signal, *Wall Street Journal*, www.wsj.com, November 22; R. King, 2017, Can Antonio Neri revive HP Enterprise after Meg Whitman? *Wall Street Journal*, www.wsj.com, November 30; R. King, 2017, Meg Whitman to step down as Hewlett Packard Enterprise CEO, *Wall Street Journal*, www.wsj.com, November 21; G. Hall, 2014, Hewlett Packard CEO talks biggest fails, *bizwomen*, www.bizjournals.com, May 2; M. Ames & Y. Levine, 2010, How Meg Whitman failed her way to the top at eBay, collecting billions while nearly destroying the company, *Alternet*, www.alternet.org, October 25; M. Mangalindan, 2008, EBay chief Whitman, web pioneer, plans to retire, *Wall Street Journal*, www.wsj.com, January 22.

As the Opening Case suggests, strategic leaders' work is demanding, challenging, and requires the balancing of desired short- and long-term performance goals. Meg Whitman is a CEO who has taken strategic actions in each top-level managerial position she held to deal with challenging situations in the pursuit of helping firms earn above-average returns. Sometimes though, for a variety of reasons, strategic leaders do not attain the level of success they desire. This is likely the case for Sheri McCoy during her tenure as Avon Products' CEO. A 30-year veteran of Johnson & Johnson when she assumed this role, McCoy had early successes at Avon, such as deciding to exit markets in which the firm was not meeting expectations. Overall, though, some analysts believe that "McCoy was trying to fix an unimaginable mess at a company with operations all over the world, and proved slow to react to market changes such as the impact of e-commerce and changing demographics."[1]

Regardless of the length of their tenure, strategic leaders' decisions and actions affect a firm's performance. Sheri McCoy's effectiveness at Johnson & Johnson did not translate into success at Avon. Meg Whitman's upward trend of leadership success culminated in her appointment as the initial CEO for Jeffrey Katzenberg's WndrCo LLC, as seen in the Opening Case.[2] Many—though not all—thought Steve Jobs led Apple to significant levels of success as the firm's CEO. There were questions about whether anyone could follow Jobs as CEO and come close to achieving his levels of success. Those questions dogged Tim Cook, who became Apple's CEO after Jobs passed away. Concerns about Cook may have been unnecessary in that after three and one-half years into his tenure as CEO, Apple's performance was noteworthy. An indicator of this performance is the fact that during this time, Apple became the first company with a $1 trillion market value (additional information about Tim Cook as Apple's CEO appears in this chapter's Mini-Case). A major message in this chapter is that effective strategic leadership is critical to leaders' efforts to use the strategic management process successfully. As implied in Figure 1.1 in Chapter 1 and through the Analysis-Strategy-Performance model, strategic leaders guide the firm in ways that result in forming a vision and mission. Often, this guidance involves leaders creating goals that stretch everyone in the organization as a foundation for enhancing firm performance. A positive outcome of stretch goals is their ability to provoke breakthrough thinking—thinking that often leads to innovation.[3] In addition, strategic leaders work with others to verify that the firm uses the analysis and strategy parts of the A-S-P model effectively to increase the likelihood it will achieve strategic competitiveness and earn above-average returns. We show how effective strategic leadership makes this possible in Figure 12.1.[4]

In this chapter, we first define strategic leadership and discuss its importance and the possibility of strategic leaders as a source of competitive advantage. These introductory comments include a brief consideration of different styles strategic leaders may use. We

Figure 12.1 Strategic Leadership and the Strategic Management Process

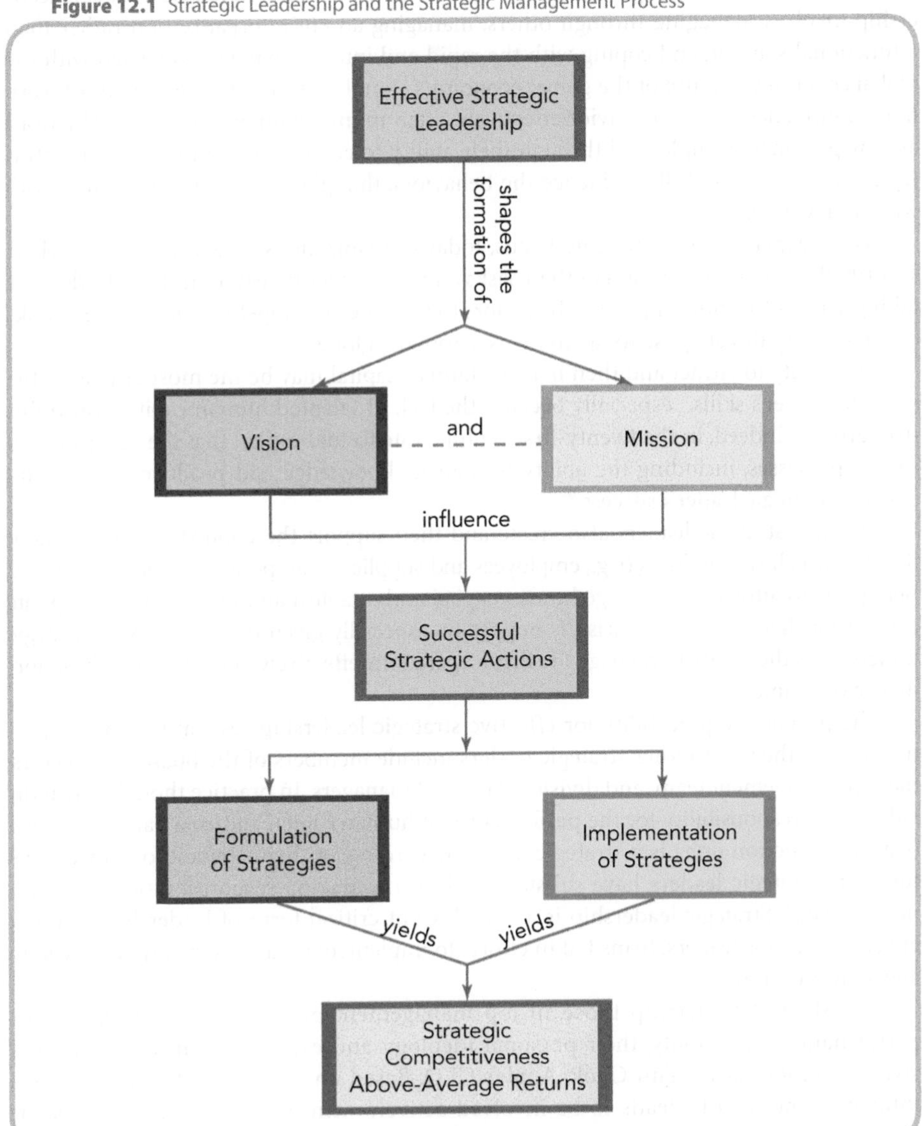

then examine the role of top-level managers and top management teams and their effects on innovation, strategic change, and firm performance. Following this discussion is an analysis of managerial succession, particularly in the context of the internal and external managerial labor markets from which firms select strategic leaders. Closing the chapter are descriptions of five key leadership actions that contribute to effective strategic leadership: determining strategic direction, effectively managing the firm's resource portfolio, sustaining an effective organizational culture, emphasizing ethical practices, and establishing balanced organizational controls.

12-1 Strategic Leadership and Style

Strategic leadership is the ability to anticipate, envision, maintain flexibility, and empower others to create strategic change as necessary. **Strategic change** is change resulting from selecting and implementing a firm's strategies.[5] Multifunctional in nature, strategic leadership involves managing through others, managing an entire organization rather than a functional subunit, and coping with the rapid and intense changes associated with the global economy. Because of the global economy's complexity, strategic leaders must learn how to influence human behavior effectively, often in uncertain environments.[6] By word and by personal example, and through their ability to envision the future, effective strategic leaders meaningfully influence the behaviors, thoughts, and feelings of those with whom they work.[7]

As we explain in the Strategic Focus, today's organizations face a new risk—cyber-security threats. In recognition of these risks and their severity, astute strategic leaders are taking actions to guide employees' behaviors to mitigate and hopefully eliminate the risks cyber-security threats pose today to firms across the globe.

The ability to attract and then manage human capital may be the most critical of the strategic leader's skills,[8] especially because the lack of talented human capital constrains firm growth. Indeed, in the twenty-first century, intellectual capital that the firm's human capital possesses, including the ability to manage knowledge and produce innovations, affects a strategic leader's success.[9]

Effective strategic leaders also create and then support the context or environment through which stakeholders (e.g., employees and suppliers) can perform at peak efficiency. Being able to attract and manage human capital and establish and nurture an appropriate context for that capital to flourish is important, especially given that the crux of strategic leadership is the ability to manage the firm's operations effectively and sustain high performance over time.[10]

The primary responsibility for effective strategic leadership rests at the top, in particular with the CEO. Other strategic leaders include members of the board of directors, the top management team, and divisional general managers. In practice though, any individual with responsibility for the performance of human capital and/or a part of the firm (e.g., a production unit) is a strategic leader. Regardless of their title and organizational function, strategic leaders have substantial decision-making responsibilities they cannot delegate.[11] Strategic leadership is a complex but critical form of leadership. Without effective strategic leaders, firms fail in efforts to implement strategies in ways that lead to above-average returns.

Strategic leadership is the ability to anticipate, envision, maintain flexibility, and empower others to create strategic change as necessary.

Strategic change is change resulting from selecting and implementing a firm's strategies.

The style of leadership those in top management positions use affects a firm's performance. Commonly, their personal ideology and experience influence leaders' style.[12] Consider again Tim Cook, Apple's CEO. Based on his personal ideology, Cook influences the firm he leads to be involved actively with philanthropic activities. He also expresses his opinion regarding what he views as important social issues, such as

Strategic Focus

Cybersecurity Risk: A Significant and Expanding Challenge for Strategic Leaders and Their Firms

For organizations engaged with rivals to achieve competitive success, new challenges appear regularly. Today, cybersecurity risks threaten firms' ability to conduct business without external interference with their operations. Cybersecurity risk "means any risk of financial loss, disruption or damage to the reputation of an organization from some sort of failure of its information technology systems."

Cyber risks are systemic in that they affect all types of firms—large and small, public and private, startups, and those with long histories. Commonly, cyber risk, which is concerned with the unique risk a firm faces because of using technological systems with interconnections, is defined as "threat X vulnerability X consequence." Cyber *threats* emerge from various actors including nation states, hackers, criminal syndicates and enterprises, lone wolf actors, and even insiders. Processes, procedures, and technologies are the sources of *vulnerabilities* that attackers seek out to find ways to threaten a firm. *Consequence* is concerned with the harm an organization experiences if it loses sensitive data to cyber-attacks and/or if disruptions affect its ability to operate its networks.

Perhaps not surprisingly, top-level executives as well as members of a firm's board of directors are prime targets for hackers seeking access to valuable information about individuals leading a company. In these instances, hackers seek to find ways to influence and perhaps to extort monies from these leaders.

Overall, the volume of cyber threats and attacks is increasing. Recently, AT&T Cybersecurity Insights reported that over a 12-month period, nearly 80 percent of surveyed organizations experienced negative effects from a cybersecurity attack. Ransomware; malware, worms, and viruses; and unauthorized access to corporate data were the types of cyber-attacks these organizations expected to experience with the greatest frequency.

Some analysts believe that organizations must change their culture as a foundation for developing processes and procedures through which they will be able to deal consistently and effectively with cybersecurity risks and the threats associated with them. Firms can take several actions to embed cybersecurity practices into their culture. First, everyone within the firm should understand cybersecurity risk as a reality and should be aware of specific risks to which their firm is exposed. Additionally, leaders must commit to the position that cybersecurity is an integral part of their firms' Information Technology capability. Providing cybersecurity training to employees is a part of developing such a capability. This is challenging in that cybersecurity specialists require unique skill sets. Currently, many organizations lack the ability to provide this type of training with an acceptable degree of effectiveness. In this sense, organizations need their own training so they can then train employees to be cybersecurity specialists.

Andrew Harrer/Bloomberg/Getty Images

In 2017, Equifax experienced a data breach that exposed the sensitive personal information of 143 million Americans.

In some instances, firms are developing strategic alliances as a path to forming a cyber-security capability. In February of 2018, for example, "AT&T and five other communications and security vendors joined forces to form the IoT (the Internet of Things) Cybersecurity Alliance, which will educate on IoT best practices and raise awareness of how to better secure the IoT ecosystem." Regardless of how a firm develops an IT capability in terms of cybersecurity, it will strive to maintain confidentiality regarding its practices. Of course, some firms, perhaps especially those competing in markets where sophisticated technologies influence organizational performance, could seek to focus on their cybersecurity practices in ways that are superior to competitors' practices, allowing those practices to become a source of competitive advantage.

Sources: 2018, Cyber risk and risk management, Institute of Risk Management, www.theirm.org, February 20; G. Baker, 2018, View from the top: How CEOs see their fields and the world, *Wall Street Journal*, www.wsj.com, January 17; A. Loten, 2018, Cyber's 'flaming sword of justice' won't save companies, says Akamai security expert, *Wall Street Journal*, www.wsj.com, January 25; G. Rometty, 2018, Ginni Rometty on how AI is going to transform jobs—all of them, *Wall Street Journal*, www.wsj.com, January 17; S. Rosenbush, 2018, The morning download: AI may not decimate job market, but it will change nature of work, *Wall Street Journal*, www.wsj.com, January 24; 2017, The corporate board's role when it comes to cybersecurity, *Wall Street Journal*, www.wsj.com, December 18; 2017, The C-suite as prime target for cyberattacks, *Wall Street Journal*, www.wsj.com, December 18; 2017, Where the jobs are: Cybersecurity, *Wall Street Journal*, www.wsj.com, December 18; D. Davis, 2017, What's next for cybersecurity in 2018? *Cybersecurity Insights*, www.csoonline.com, December 1.

David Paul Morris/Bloomberg/Getty Images

Tim Cook, CEO of Apple, is an advocate for people's privacy, and a firm believer in equal education with limits to the use of technology in the classroom.

treating all people equally regardless of ethnicity, gender, or sexual orientation. Cook says that Apple "advocates for human rights," "believes that education is a great equalizer," and "advocates for people's privacy" in a world where technology's capabilities are far-reaching in nature.[13] Cook also opines that there should be limits to the use of technology in schools and that his nephew should not use social network sites given his relatively young age.[14] He also delegated responsibility and authority to other members of Apple's leadership team and empowered them to act in ways that demonstrate the firm's commitments to socially oriented issues and projects. In this way, Cook displayed forms of what some call responsible leadership (that is, demonstrating concern for the firm's stakeholders and the broader society).[15] Others think this type of leadership orientation demonstrates concern for the triple bottom line, where firms seek returns for "people, profits, and planet," which is also thought of as generating economic, social, and environmental returns through a firm's performance.[16]

Given that he is affecting Apple's culture and employees' perspectives and actions, Tim Cook may be a transformational leader. This is potentially important for the firm he leads in that transformational leadership is one of the most effective strategic leadership styles. This style entails motivating followers to exceed the expectations others have of them, to strengthen their capabilities through continuous training, and to place the interests of the organization above their own.[17] Transformational leaders develop and communicate an organizational vision and work with others to formulate and execute a strategy to achieve it.

Transformational leaders have a high degree of integrity and recognize its importance. James Hackett, newly appointed CEO of Ford Motor Company who believes that innovation is the key to his firm's success, [18] says that "if you want to lead others, you've got to have their trust, and you can't have their trust without integrity." [19] Transformational leaders also respect their employees. Jeffrey Katzenberg, a Hollywood executive, highlights the importance of this leadership trait, saying that "by definition if there's leadership, it means there are followers. I believe the quality of the followers is in direct correlation to the respect you hold them in. It's not how much they respect you that is most important. It's actually how much you respect them. It's everything."[20]

Transformational leaders also have emotional intelligence. Emotionally intelligent leaders understand themselves well, have strong motivation, empathize with others, and have effective interpersonal skills.[21] These characteristics contribute to transformational leaders' efforts to promote and nurture innovation in firms.[22]

12-2 The Role of Top-Level Managers

In their role, top-level managers make many decisions, such as the strategic actions and responses associated with their firm's competitive rivalries (see Chapter 5). In a comprehensive sense, top-level managers make multiple decisions regarding the strategies their firms will choose and then the implementation of those strategies.

When making decisions related to using the strategic management process, managers (certainly top-level ones) often use their discretion (or latitude for action).[23] Managerial discretion differs among managers leading firms in different industries. The primary factors that determine the amount of decision-making discretion a manager has (especially a top-level manager) are

1. external environmental sources such as industry structure, the rate of market growth in the firm's primary industry, and the degree to which product differentiation is possible
2. organizational characteristics, including size, age, resources, and culture
3. managerial characteristics, including commitment to the firm, tolerance for ambiguity, skills in working with different people, and aspiration levels (see Figure 12.2)

Because strategic leaders make decisions to help the firm outperform competitors, how they exercise discretion when making decisions is critical to the firm's success[24] and affects or shapes its culture as well.

Appointed in 2017 to succeed Jeff Immelt as GE's CEO, John Flannery's early actions demonstrate use of decision-making discretion. Some analysts concluded that Flannery is deciding to back away from the ambitions of Immelt and Jack Welch before him and to

Figure 12.2 Factors Affecting Managerial Discretion

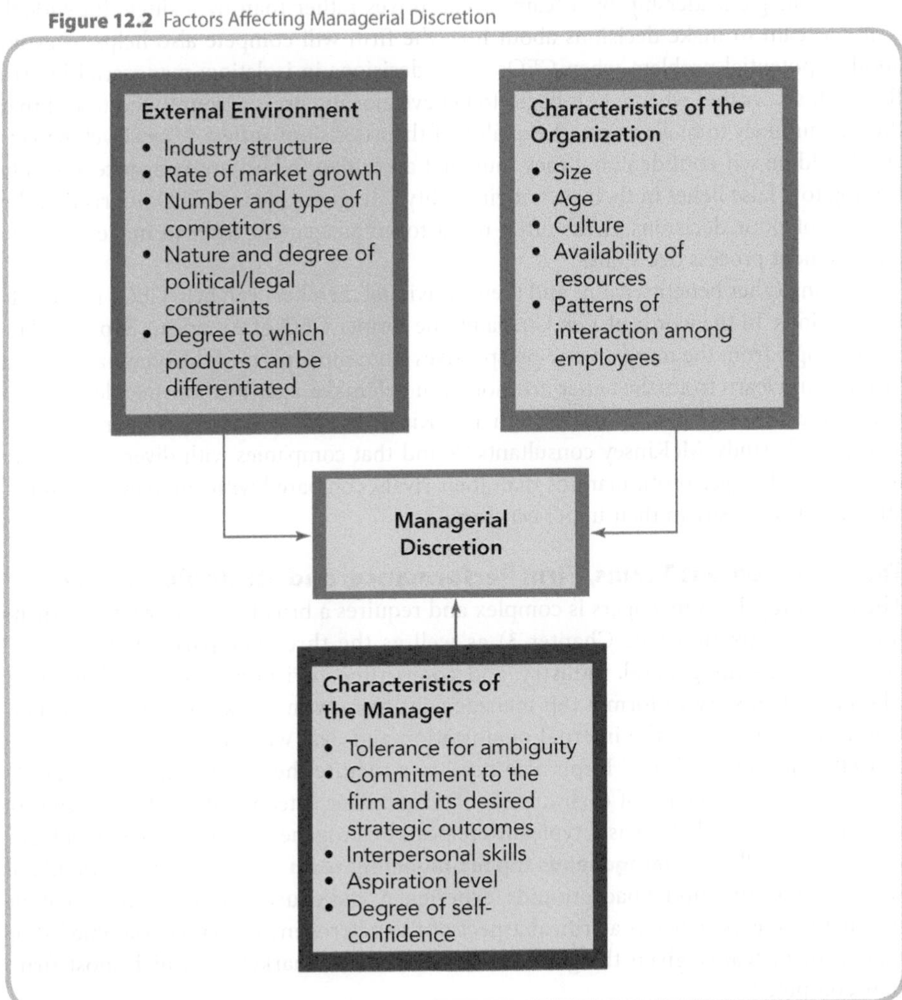

Source: Adapted from S. Finkelstein & D C. Hambrick, 1996, *Strategic Leadership: Top Executives and Their Effects on Organizations*, St. Paul, MN: West Publishing Company.

reduce GE's size. In the process, Flannery intends for GE to become a more focused company with fewer business units. He seeks to make GE "simpler and easier to operate"; in his view, complexity has hurt the firm. He is working with the firm's board of directors and people throughout GE to bring about the changes he seeks, including greater financial discipline.[25]

Top-level managers' roles in verifying that their firm uses the strategic management process effectively are complex and challenging. Because of this, top management teams, rather than a single top-level manager, typically make these types of decisions.[26]

12-2a Top Management Teams

The **top management team** is composed of the individuals responsible for making certain the firm uses the strategic management process, especially to select and implement strategies. Typically, the top management team includes the officers of the corporation, defined by the title of vice president and above or by service as a member of the board of directors.[27] Among other outcomes, the quality of a top management team's decisions affects the firm's ability to innovate and change in ways that help its efforts to earn above-average returns.[28]

As noted earlier, the complex challenges facing most organizations require the exercise of strategic leadership by a team of executives rather than by a single individual. Using a team to make decisions about how the firm will compete also helps to avoid another potential problem when CEOs make decisions in isolation: managerial hubris. Research shows that when CEOs begin to believe glowing press accounts and to feel that they are unlikely to make errors, the quality of their decisions suffers.[29] Top-level managers should be self-confident; but they must not allow that to become arrogance, possibly leading to a false belief in their own invincibility.[30] To guard against CEO hubris and the making of poor decisions, firms often use a top management *team* to make strategic management process decisions.

Among other benefits, teams and their individual members can help CEOs make better decisions. In the words of Ken Chenault, the former CEO of American Express, "The more people from the more diverse perspectives from more parts of the organization you listen to and learn from, the better decisions you will make, and the more people will help you with executing them."[31] Results from a McKinsey & Co. analysis are similar. Based on a large-scale study, McKinsey consultants "found that companies with diverse executive teams posted bigger profit margins than their rivals, compared with companies with relatively little diversity in their upper echelons."[32]

Top Management Teams, Firm Performance, and Strategic Change

The job of top-level managers is complex and requires a broad knowledge of the firm's internal organization (see Chapter 3) as well as the three key parts of its external environment—the general, industry, and competitor environments (see Chapter 2). Therefore, firms try to form a top management team with the knowledge and expertise needed to operate the internal organization and deal with the firm's stakeholders as well as its competitors.[33] Firms also need to structure the top management team to best utilize the expertise of each member.[34] Organizing a team with different types of expertise and knowledge bases typically creates a heterogeneous top management team. More specifically, a **heterogeneous top management team** is composed of individuals with different functional backgrounds, experience, and education. Increasingly, having international experience is a critical aspect of the heterogeneity that is desirable in top management teams, given the globalized nature of the markets in which most firms now compete.[35]

Members of a heterogeneous top management team benefit from discussing their different perspectives. In many cases, these discussions, and the debates they engender,

A **top management team** is composed of the individuals responsible for making certain the firm uses the strategic management process, especially to select and implement strategies.

A **heterogeneous top management team** is composed of individuals with different functional backgrounds, experience, and education.

increase the quality of the team's decisions, especially when a synthesis emerges within the team after evaluating different perspectives.[36] In effect, top management team members learn from each other and thereby develop better decisions.[37] In turn, higher-quality decisions lead to stronger firm performance.[38]

Interestingly though, the more heterogeneous and larger the top management team, the more difficult it is for the team to cohesively implement strategies.[39] Communication difficulties within larger top management teams account for some of this difficulty. Overall then, a group of top executives with diverse backgrounds may inhibit effective decision-making processes if the team lacks the ability to manage itself effectively. Without effective management, top management teams may fail to study threats and opportunities with a sufficient amount of intensity, leading to suboptimal decisions. Seeking to integrate team members' unique backgrounds is a managerial approach CEOs take to deal with these potential problems.

Having members with substantive expertise in the firm's core businesses is also important to a top management team's effectiveness.[40] In a high-technology industry, for example, it may be critical for top management team members to have R&D expertise, particularly when a firm seeks to grow. In the final analysis though, the top management team's effect on decisions it makes depends on its expertise and how it manages the team as well as the context in which the team makes decisions (the governance structure, incentive compensation, etc.).[41]

The characteristics of top management team members, and even the personalities of the CEO and other team members, have a relationship with innovation and strategic change.[42] For example, decisions reached by more heterogeneous top management teams have a positive relationship with innovation and strategic change, perhaps in part because heterogeneity may influence the team, or at least some of its members, to think more creatively when making decisions and taking actions.[43] Supporting these expectations are results from a recent Boston Consulting Group study, where the researchers found that "increasing the diversity of leadership teams leads to more and better innovation and improved financial performance" in firms competing in both developed and emerging economies.[44]

Therefore, firms that could benefit by changing their strategies are more likely to make those changes if they have top management teams with diverse backgrounds and expertise. Evidence suggests that, compared to selecting a CEO from within the firm or from within the firm's industry, hiring a CEO from outside the firm and its industry increases the probability strategic change will take place.[45] On the other hand, although hiring a new CEO from outside the industry adds diversity to the top management team such a change can affect the firm's relationships with important stakeholders, especially customers and employees.[46] Astute managers recognize any changes of this nature and deal with them in ways that demonstrate how, say, additional heterogeneity among the team in terms of functional backgrounds benefits stakeholders. Consistent with earlier comments, we highlight here the value of transformational leadership to strategic change as the CEO helps the firm match environmental opportunities with its capabilities and core competencies as a foundation for selecting and/or implementing new strategies.[47]

The CEO and Top Management Team Power

We noted in Chapter 10 that the board of directors is an important governance mechanism for monitoring a firm's strategic direction and for representing stakeholders' interests, especially shareholders. In fact, firm performance tends to improve when the board of directors is involved more directly in helping to shape the firm's strategic direction.[48]

Boards of directors, however, may find it difficult to direct the decisions and resulting actions of powerful CEOs and top management teams. Often, a powerful CEO appoints a number of sympathetic outside members to the board or may have inside board members who are also on the top management team and report to her or him.[49] In either case, the CEO may significantly influence actions such as appointments to the board. Overall, the board of directors and the decision latitude it provides to the CEO and other top management team members influence the amount of discretion a CEO and the top management team possess when making decisions.[50]

CEOs and top management team members can also achieve power in other ways. For example, a CEO who also serves as chair of the firm's board of directors usually has more power than the individual who is CEO only.[51] Some analysts and corporate "watchdogs" criticize the practice of *CEO duality* (when the same person holds the positions of CEO and board chair). The reason for this criticism is the conclusion that CEO duality can lead to poor performance and slow responses to change, partly because the board often reduces its efforts to monitor the CEO and other top management team members in instances of CEO duality.[52]

Although it varies across industries, CEO duality occurs most commonly in larger firms. CEO duality is under scrutiny and attack in both U.S. and European firms due to increased shareholder activism. In this regard, we noted in Chapter 10 that a number of analysts, regulators, and corporate directors believe that an independent board leadership structure without CEO duality has a net positive effect on the board's efforts to monitor top-level managers' decisions and actions, particularly with respect to financial performance. However, CEO duality's actual effect on firm performance (and particularly financial performance) remains inconclusive.[53] Moreover, some evidence suggests that, at least in a sample of firms in European countries, CEO duality can positively affect performance when a firm encounters a crisis.[54] Yet, recent evidence suggests that some firms have begun to separate the CEO and board chair positions. Some, but not all, of the separations occur because of poor performance. In other cases, this type of separation occurs to allow an experienced board chair to mentor a new CEO, who for some time serves as an apprentice.[55] Thus, decision makers should consider nuances or situational conditions when studying the outcomes of CEO duality on firm performance. For example, power differentials can occur among top management team members when a family holds an important ownership position; this is the case even in large public firms. Typically, top managers who are also members of the family may have a special form of power that can cause conflict unless managers try to balance family and firm interests across the top management team.[56]

Individuals with long tenure as the CEO and as a member of the top management team have greater influence on board decisions. Interestingly though, long tenure may constrain the breadth of an executive's knowledge base. Some evidence suggests that with the limited perspectives associated with a restricted knowledge base, long-tenured top executives typically develop fewer alternatives to evaluate when making strategic decisions.[57] However, long-tenured CEOs and top management team members may be able to exercise strategic control with greater effectiveness. When this is the case, there is less need for board members' involvement with decisions made by upper-level managers because effective strategic control generally leads to higher performance.[58] It may be then that "the liabilities of short tenure … appear to exceed the advantages, while the advantages of long tenure—firm-specific human and social capital, knowledge, and power—seem to outweigh the disadvantages of rigidity and maintaining the status quo."[59] Overall then, the relationship between CEO tenure and firm performance is complex and nuanced.[60] This reality indicates the need for a board of directors to develop an effective working relationship with the top management team as a means of enhancing firm performance.

Another nuance or situational condition to consider is the case in which a CEO acts as a *steward* of the firm's assets. In this instance, holding the dual roles of CEO and board chair facilitates efforts to make decisions and take actions that are in stakeholders' interests. The logic here is that the CEO, desiring to be the best possible steward of the firm's assets, gains efficiency through CEO duality.[61] In addition, because of this person's positive orientation and actions, extra governance and the coordination costs resulting from an independent board leadership structure become unnecessary.[62]

In summary, an individual firm's situation should influence choices about the relative degrees of power held by the board and top management team members. For example, the abundance of resources in a firm's external environment and the volatility of that environment may affect the ideal balance of power between the board and the top management team. Moreover, a volatile and uncertain environment has the potential to create a situation calling for a powerful CEO to move quickly. In such an instance, a diverse top management team may result in less cohesion among team members, perhaps stalling or even preventing the making of decisions in a timely manner. In the final analysis, an effective working relationship between the board and the CEO and other top management team members increases the likelihood of the firm making decisions that are in stakeholders' interests.[63]

12-3 Managerial Succession

The choice of top-level managers—particularly CEOs—is a critical decision with important implications for the firm's performance. As discussed in Chapter 10, selecting the CEO has been and remains one of the most important responsibilities for a board of directors as it seeks to represent the firm's stakeholders. As a recent article indicates: "Succession planning has always been defined as the number one responsibility of board members followed closely by strategic plan development."[64] Succession management is equally important in governmental agencies and family-owned firms. Speaking to the issue of succession planning in governmental agencies, Deloitte consultants note that based on their research, governmental agencies "with well-defined succession management practices realize significant employee engagement and retention gains, due to transparency in career paths and development opportunities, as well as more preparation time for leadership roles."[65]

In family firms, CEO succession requires discussion early in a family member's career, according to J. W. Marriott, chair of the Marriott International board of directors. Working with others, Marriott chose a strategic leader from the external managerial labor market (rather than selecting a family member from the internal managerial labor market) to succeed him as CEO of Marriott International. Marriott indicated that the choice of the firm's new CEO was in the company's best interests—the criterion that must, he believes, drive the successor decision.[66]

Corepics VOF/Shutterstock.com

Managers participating in a leadership training program.

Many companies use leadership-screening systems to identify individuals with strategic leadership potential as well as to determine the criteria individuals should satisfy to be a candidate for the CEO position. The most effective of these screening systems assesses people within the firm and produces valuable information about the capabilities of other companies' strategic leaders.[67] Based on the results of these assessments, firms place certain individuals into training and development programs as a means of shaping their potential as strategic leaders.

A number of firms have high-quality leadership programs in place, including Procter & Gamble (P&G), GE, IBM, and Dow Chemical. For example, some believe that P&G has talented individuals throughout the organization, with skills gained from training that will allow them to accept the next level of leadership responsibility when the time comes. Managing talent on a global basis, P&G is an example of a company providing leaders at all levels in the firm with meaningful work and significant responsibilities as a means of simultaneously challenging and developing them.

In spite of the value high-quality leadership training programs can create, many companies do not have training and succession plans in place for their top-level managers or for others holding key leadership positions (e.g., department heads, sections heads). With respect to family-owned firms operating in the United States, Deloitte found that only 41 percent of those surveyed have established leadership contingency plans while 49 percent indicated that they "review succession plans (only) when a change in management requires it."[68] The results are similar for family firms on a global basis, as a broader survey of family firms in Asia, Europe, and Latin America found that only the most successful companies have a clear understanding of the party responsible for managing the CEO succession process. In 44 percent of the firms surveyed, the board of directors had that responsibility.[69] This information about percentages of firms without succession plans in place is interesting in that without effective succession planning, continuity in using the firm's strategic management process, even a successful one, is unlikely.

Organizations select managers and strategic leaders from two types of managerial labor markets—internal and external.[70] An **internal managerial labor market** consists of a firm's opportunities for managerial positions and the qualified employees within it. An **external managerial labor market** is the collection of managerial career opportunities and the qualified people who are external to the organization in which the opportunities exist.

Employees commonly prefer that firms use the internal managerial labor market for selection purposes, particularly when choosing a CEO and top management team members. Evidence suggests that firms commonly follow these preferences. For example, about 86 percent of new CEOs selected in 2016 were from the internal managerial labor market.[71] As explained in this chapter's Mini-Case, Tim Cook came from Apple's internal managerial labor market as Steve Jobs' replacement as CEO.

With respect to the CEO position, some believe that several benefits accrue to those using the internal labor market to select a new CEO, one of which is the continuing commitment to the firm's existing vision, mission, and strategies. In addition, because of their experience with the firm and the industry in which it competes, inside CEOs are familiar with company products, markets, technologies, and operating procedures. Another benefit is that choosing a new CEO from within usually results in lower turnover among existing personnel, many of whom possess valuable firm-specific knowledge and skills. In summary, CEOs selected from inside the firm tend to benefit from their

An **internal managerial labor market** consists of a firm's opportunities for managerial positions and the qualified employees within it.

An **external managerial labor market** is the collection of managerial career opportunities and the qualified people who are external to the organization in which the opportunities exist.

1. clear understanding of the firm's personnel and their capabilities
2. appreciation of the company's culture and its associated core values
3. deep knowledge of the firm's core competencies as well as abilities to develop new ones as appropriate
4. "feel" for what will and will not "work" in the firm[72]

In spite of the understandable and legitimate reasons to select CEOs from inside the firm, boards of directors sometimes prefer to choose a new CEO from the external managerial labor market. This was the case recently with luxury retailer Neiman Marcus.[73] In another example, Sam Adams Beer preferred to hire from the external market to find an individual with a strong sales-and-marketing orientation to balance the firm's historical focus on operations to produce its products. The company was willing to take over a year to make its choice.[74] Broadly, conditions suggesting a potentially appropriate preference to hire from outside include

1. the firm's need to enhance its ability to innovate
2. the firm's need to reverse its recent poor performance
3. the fact that the industry in which the firm competes is experiencing rapid growth
4. the need for strategic change[75]

Overall, the decision to use either the internal or the external managerial labor market to select a firm's new CEO is one that should be based on expectations; in other words, what does the board of directors want the new CEO and top management team to accomplish? We address this issue in Figure 12.3 by showing how the composition of the top management team and the CEO succession source (managerial labor market) interact to affect strategy. For example, when the top management team is homogeneous (its members have similar functional experiences and educational backgrounds) and the new CEO comes from the internal managerial labor market, the firm's current strategy is unlikely to change. If the firm is performing well, absolutely and relative to peers, continuing to implement the current strategy may be precisely what the board of directors wants. Alternatively, when a new CEO comes from outside the firm and the top management team is heterogeneous, the probability is high that strategy will change. This, of course, would be a board's preference when the firm's performance is declining, both in absolute terms and relative to rivals. When the new CEO is from inside the firm and a heterogeneous top management team is in place, the strategy may not change, but innovation is likely to continue. An external CEO succession with a homogeneous team creates a more ambiguous situation. Furthermore, outside CEOs who lead moderate change often achieve increases in performance, but high strategic change by outsiders frequently leads to performance declines.[76] In summary, a firm's board of directors should use the insights reflected in Figure 12.3 to inform its decision about which of the two managerial labor markets to use to select a new CEO.

Figure 12.3 Effects of CEO Succession and Top Management Team Composition on Strategy

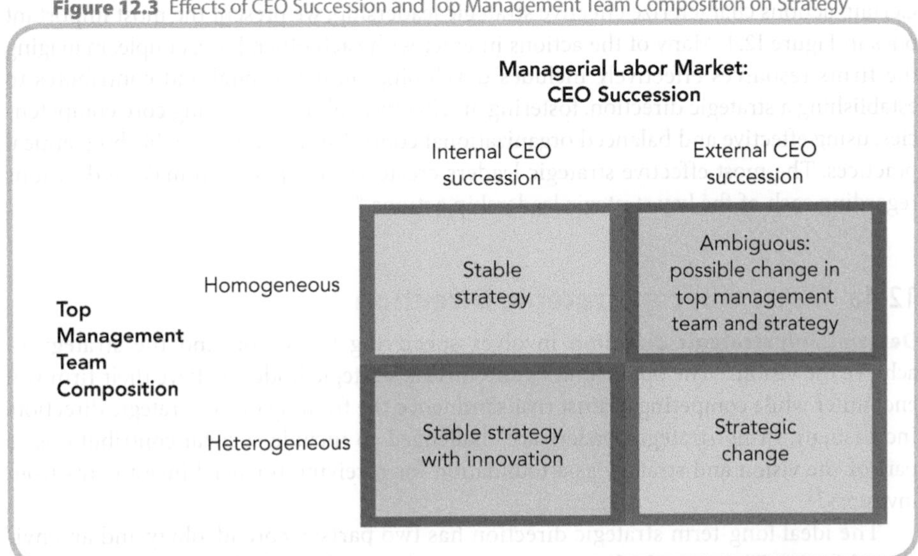

Helga Esteb/Shutterstock.com

Sir Howard Stringer, the first foreign CEO of Sony in Japan.

In companies throughout the world, an interim CEO is commonly appointed when a firm lacks a succession plan or when an emergency occurs requiring an immediate appointment of a new CEO.[77] In most cases, interim CEOs come from inside the firm. Their familiarity with the company's operations supports their efforts to "maintain order" as the firm searches for a permanent CEO. Indeed, a primary advantage of appointing an interim CEO is that doing so can generate the amount of time the board of directors requires to conduct a thorough search to find the best candidate from the external and internal markets.

Not all changes in CEOs are successful. For example, some Japanese firms have experimented with foreign CEOs largely to encourage strategic change. Managers' and employees' acceptance of a CEO from outside the firm's host country increases the likelihood that her/his proposed changes to the firm's strategies will receive enthusiastic support. Thus, most Japanese firms that hire foreign CEOs search for one who has work experience in Japan so that he or she understands the culture and the typical styles used in Japanese firms.[78] In addition, firms have learned that in general, retaining executives in a target firm following its acquisition is important. Without them, integration of the newly acquired firm into the acquiring firm is commonly more difficult. Moreover, the executives often have valuable knowledge and capabilities that are lost to the acquirer if they depart. Thus, turnover among these executives makes the acquisition less valuable to the acquiring firm.[79]

Next, we discuss key actions that effective strategic leaders demonstrate while helping their firm use the strategic management process.

12-4 Key Strategic Leadership Actions

Certain actions characterize effective strategic leadership; we present the most important ones in Figure 12.4. Many of the actions interact with each other. For example, managing the firm's resources effectively includes developing human capital and contributes to establishing a strategic direction, fostering an effective culture, exploiting core competencies, using effective and balanced organizational control systems, and establishing ethical practices. The most effective strategic leaders create viable options in making decisions regarding each of the key strategic leadership actions.[80]

12-4a Determining Strategic Direction

Determining strategic direction involves specifying the vision and the strategy to achieve the vision.[81] The opportunities and threats strategic leaders believe their firm will encounter while competing against rivals influence the framing of the strategic direction. Increasingly, firms' strategic leaders are challenged to include societal contributions as part of the vision and strategy as a foundation for receiving financial investments from investors.[82]

Determining strategic direction involves specifying the vision and the strategy to achieve the vision.

The ideal long-term strategic direction has two parts: a core ideology and an envisioned future. The core ideology motivates employees through the company's heritage

Figure 12.4 Exercise of Effective Strategic Leadership

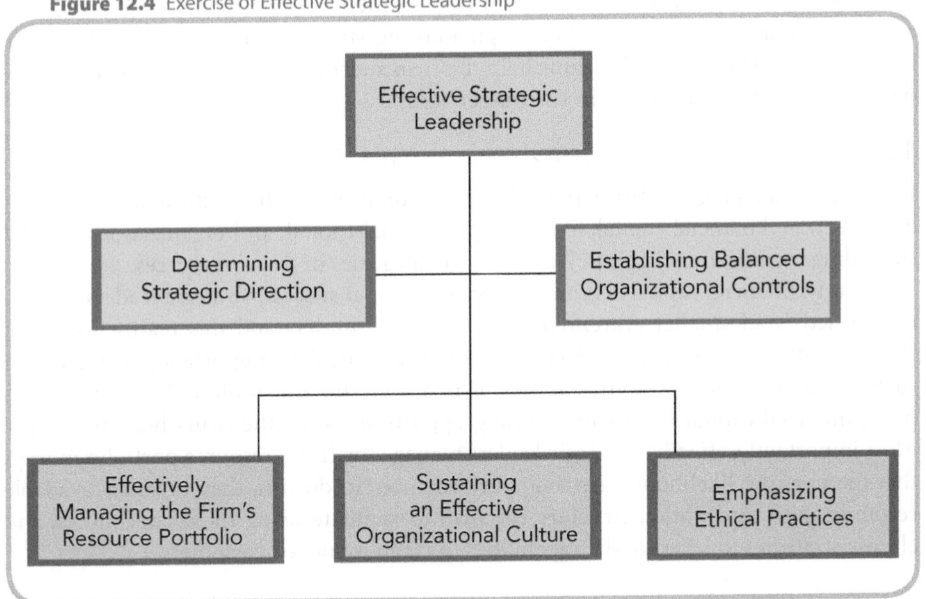

while the envisioned future encourages them to stretch beyond their expectations of accomplishment.[83] The envisioned future serves as a guide to many aspects of a firm's strategy implementation process, including motivation, leadership, employee empowerment, and organizational design. The strategic direction could include a host of actions such as entering new international markets and developing a set of new suppliers to add to the firm's value chain.[84]

Sometimes though, strategic leaders fail to select a strategy that helps a firm achieve its strategic direction. This can happen when top management team members and, certainly, the CEO are too committed to the status quo. A firm's strategic direction remains relatively stable across time. However, actions taken to use strategies to pursue the direction are somewhat fluid, largely so the firm can deal with unexpected opportunities and threats from the external environment. An aversion to what decision makers conclude are risky actions creates an inability to adjust strategies as appropriate to deal with environmental changes. An aversion to risky actions tends to be common in firms that have performed well across time and firms with long-serving CEOs.[85] Research also suggests that some CEOs are erratic or even ambivalent when choosing their firm's strategic direction. This is particularly the case when a firm faces a turbulent competitive environment, making it difficult to identify the best strategy.[86] Of course, these erratic or ambivalent behaviors are unlikely to produce high performance and may lead to CEO turnover. Interestingly, research has found that incentive compensation in the form of stock options encourages talented executives to select strategies that contribute to strong firm performance. However, the same incentives used with less talented executives produce lower performance.[87]

In contrast to risk-averse CEOs, charismatic ones may foster stakeholders' commitment to a new vision and strategic direction. Nonetheless, even when being guided by a charismatic CEO, it is important for the firm not to lose sight of its strengths and weaknesses when making changes required by a new strategic direction. The most effective charismatic CEO leads a firm in ways that are consistent with its culture and with the actions permitted by its capabilities and core competencies.[88]

Finally, being ambicultural can facilitate efforts to determine the firm's strategic direction and to choose and implement strategies to reach it. Being ambicultural means that strategic leaders are committed to identifying the best organizational activities to take particularly when implementing strategies, regardless of their cultural origin.[89] Ambicultural actions help the firm succeed in the short term as a foundation for reaching its vision in the longer term.[90]

12-4b Effectively Managing the Firm's Resource Portfolio

Effectively managing the firm's portfolio of resources is another critical strategic leadership action. Financial capital, human capital, social capital, and organizational capital (including organizational culture) are the four categories of firms' resources.

Clearly, financial capital is critical to organizational success; strategic leaders in both established[91] and smaller entrepreneurial ventures[92] understand this reality. However, the most effective strategic leaders recognize the equivalent importance of managing each remaining type of resource as well as managing the integration of resources (e.g., using financial capital to provide training opportunities for the firm's human capital). Most importantly, effective strategic leaders manage the firm's resource portfolio in ways that increase the likelihood of strong performance. To do this, they organize available resources into capabilities, structure the firm to facilitate using those capabilities, and choose strategies to leverage the capabilities to create value for customers.

Exploiting and Maintaining Core Competencies

Examined in Chapters 1 and 3, *core competencies* are capabilities that serve as a source of competitive advantage for a firm over its rivals. The reason a core competency is a source of competitive advantage for a firm is that it is a "deep proficiency that enables a company to deliver unique value to customers."[93] Typically, core competencies relate to skills within organizational functions, such as manufacturing, finance, marketing, and research and development. Strategic leaders must verify that employees understand the firm's core competencies when selecting strategies and that the competencies are central to strategy implementation efforts. This suggests, for example, that with respect to their strategies, Apple emphasizes its design competence, while Netflix recognizes and concentrates on its competence of being able to deliver physical, digital, and original content.[94]

Firms develop core competencies over time as they learn from the results of the competitive actions and responses taken while competing against their rivals. Using what they have learned, firms continuously reshape their capabilities to verify that they are, indeed, the path through which core competencies are being developed and used to establish one or more competitive advantages.

Developing Human Capital and Social Capital

Human capital refers to the knowledge and skills of a firm's entire workforce. From the perspective of human capital, firms should view employees as a capital resource requiring continuous investment.[95]

Bringing talented human capital into the firm and then developing that capital has the potential to yield positive outcomes. A key reason for this is that individuals' knowledge and skills are critical to the success of firms competing in many global industries (e.g., automobile manufacturing) as well as industries within countries (e.g., leather and shoe manufacturing in Italy). This reality suggests that people may be a highly significant source of competitive advantage for firms, especially those competing in turbulent and fast-changing environments.[96] In all types of organizations—large and small, new and established—human capital's increasing importance suggests a significant role for the firm's human resource management function.[97] As a support function on which firms rely to create value (see Chapter 3), human resource management practices have the capacity to facilitate selecting and especially implementing the firm's strategies.[98]

Human capital refers to the knowledge and skills of a firm's entire workforce. From the perspective of human capital, firms view employees as a capital resource requiring continuous investment.

Effective training and development programs increase the probability that some of the firm's human capital will become effective strategic leaders. Increasingly, the link between effective programs and firm success is becoming stronger because the knowledge gained by participating in these programs is integral to forming and then sustaining a firm's competitive advantage.[99] In addition to building human capital's knowledge and skills, these programs inculcate a common set of core values and present a systematic view of the organization, thus promoting its vision and helping form an effective organizational culture.

Effective training and development programs also contribute positively to the firm's efforts to form core competencies.[100] Furthermore, the programs help strategic leaders improve their skills that are critical to completing other tasks associated with effective strategic leadership, such as determining the firm's strategic direction, exploiting and maintaining the firm's core competencies, and developing an organizational culture that supports ethical practices. Thus, building human capital is vital to effective strategic leadership practices.

When investments in human capital (such as providing high-quality training and development programs) are successful, the outcome is a workforce capable of learning continuously. This is important in that continuous learning and leveraging the firm's expanding knowledge base have a positive influence on firm success.[101]

Learning also can preclude errors. Interestingly though, strategic leaders may learn more from failure than success. A key reason for this is that leaders sometimes make the wrong attributions for successes.[102] For example, the effectiveness of certain approaches and knowledge can be context specific. Thus, some "best practices" may not work well in all situations. We know that using teams to make decisions can be effective, but sometimes it is better for leaders to make decisions alone, especially when rapid implementation of the decisions benefits the firm (e.g., in a crisis). As such, effective strategic leaders recognize the importance of learning from success *and* from failure as a means of helping their firm use the strategic management process. Being committed to learning from failure is as important for smaller entrepreneurial ventures as it is for large, well-established organizations.[103]

When facing challenging conditions, firms may decide to lay off some of their human capital, a decision that can result in a significant loss of knowledge. Research shows that moderate-sized layoffs may improve firm performance primarily in the short run, but large layoffs result in stronger performance downturns in firm performance because of the loss of human capital.[104] Although it is common for restructuring firms to reduce their investments in training and development programs when encountering a downturn, the restructuring resulting from layoffs may actually yield an important opportunity to increase investments in these programs. The reason for this is that restructuring firms have less slack and cannot absorb as many errors; moreover, the employees who remain after layoffs may find themselves in positions without all the skills or knowledge they need to create value through their work. Viewing employees as a resource to maximize rather than as a cost to minimize facilitates successful implementation of a firm's strategies, as does the strategic leader's ability to approach layoffs in a manner that employees believe is fair and equitable, especially compared to the treatment of their peers.[105]

Social capital involves relationships inside and outside the firm that help in efforts to complete tasks that create value for stakeholders.[106] Social capital is a critical asset given that employees must cooperate with one another and others outside the firm, such as suppliers and customers, in order to complete their work. In multinational organizations, employees often must cooperate across country boundaries on activities such as R&D to achieve performance objectives (e.g., developing new products).[107]

Social capital involves relationships inside and outside the firm that help in efforts to accomplish tasks that create value for stakeholders.

External social capital is increasingly critical to firm success in that few if any companies possess all the resources needed to compete successfully against their rivals. When using cooperative strategies, such as strategic alliances (see Chapter 9), firms may develop social capital by sharing complementary resources. Transparency between firms regarding the specifics of how they will share resources creates trust and further encourages additional sharing of resources.[108] Social capital created this way yields many benefits. For example, firms with strong social capital are able to be more ambidextrous; that is, they can develop or have access to multiple capabilities, providing them with the flexibility to take advantage of opportunities and to respond to threats.[109]

Organizations' experiences and research evidence suggest that the success of many types of firms may partially depend on social capital. Large multinational firms, for example, often must establish alliances in order to enter new foreign markets while entrepreneurial firms often must establish alliances to gain access to resources, venture capital, or other types of resources (e.g., special expertise that the entrepreneurial firm cannot afford to maintain in-house).[110] However, a firm's culture affects its ability to retain quality human capital and maintain strong internal social capital.

12-4c Sustaining an Effective Organizational Culture

In Chapter 1, we defined *organizational culture* as the complex set of ideologies, symbols, and core values that individuals and groups share throughout the firm and that influence how the firm conducts business. Because organizational culture influences how the firm conducts its business and helps to regulate and control employees' behavior, it can be a source of competitive advantage.[111] Every organization has a unique culture; because of this, it is possible that a vibrant organizational culture is an increasingly important source of differentiation for firms to emphasize when pursuing strategic competitiveness and above-average returns. Thus, shaping the context within which the firm formulates and implements its strategies—that is, shaping the organizational culture—is another key strategic leadership action.[112] We describe actions leaders take to help their firms develop and sustain an effective organizational culture in the Strategic Focus.

Entrepreneurial Mind-Set

Especially in large organizations, an organizational culture often encourages (or discourages) strategic leaders and those with whom they work to pursue (or not pursue) entrepreneurial opportunities. (We define and discuss entrepreneurial opportunities in Chapter 13.) This is the case in both for-profit and not-for-profit organizations.[113] This issue is important because entrepreneurial opportunities are a vital source of growth and innovation.[114] Therefore, a key action for strategic leaders to take is to encourage and promote innovation by pursuing entrepreneurial opportunities.

Investing in opportunities as real options is one way of encouraging innovation. Investing in real options finds a firm investing in an opportunity now to provide the potential option of taking advantage of the opportunity at a point in the future.[115] For example, a firm might buy a piece of land to have the option to build on it at some time in the future should the company need more space and should that location increase in value to the company. Firms might enter strategic alliances for similar reasons. In this instance, a firm might form an alliance to have the option of acquiring the partner later or of building a stronger relationship with it (e.g., developing a new joint venture).[116]

Strategic Focus

Organizational Culture: Is It Really That Important?

The answer to the title of this Strategic Focus is yes! The reason for this is that organizational culture has a significant influence on employees and, in turn, on a firm's performance as it interacts with strategy and structure. In this regard, "organizational culture sets the context for everything an enterprise does." Strategic leaders recognize the important relationship among organizational culture, employees' actions, and firm performance. For example, based on its recent survey of CEOs, the U.S. Conference Board reported that these leaders view culture and quality talent to be the critical enablers of organizational success. The CEOs also believe that an open and inclusive culture is one in which organizational talent can thrive. As discussed in the chapter's earlier Strategic Focus, recognizing the effect of cybersecurity threats and deciding how to deal with them are vital aspects of organizational culture today.

Effective strategic leaders also know, though, that the type of culture that leads to positive outcomes requires time and effort to build. Indeed, leaders must work diligently and consistently to build an effective organizational culture. Building this type of culture "takes patience, sacrifice and vision. It requires that leaders have the passion to improve their organization and to motivate, engage, and inspire their people with more than simply words or perks." Once developed, culture changes in response to efforts needed to implement the firm's strategy within the context provided by the structures that are in place to support strategy execution efforts.

Research results support leaders' belief about culture's importance and its relationship with strategy and structure. Some researchers have found, for example, that "the key to running a successful organization is to have a culture based on a strongly held and widely shared set of beliefs that are appropriately supported by strategy and structure." Among other benefits, a strong culture informs employees how leaders want them to respond to situations that may develop; gives employees confidence that the responses they initiate will be the correct ones; and assures employees that they will be recognized and rewarded for acting in manners that demonstrate the firm's values as embedded in its culture. Thus, there is a strong link between leaders and the actions they take and the nature of a firm's culture.

Building and supporting an effective culture yields multiple specific benefits for an organization. As examples, culture (1) increases employee loyalty in that individuals working in a firm with a strong culture like the challenges associated with their job and enjoy the atmosphere in which they work; (2) attracts and retains talent in that strong cultures are environments in which people want to work and are passionate about their role in helping a firm reach its vision and mission; (3) reflects a firm's identity in that it demonstrates "how the company views itself and how the company wishes to be viewed by the outside world"; and (4) creates intrinsic motivation for employee behavior.

AP Images/dycj

Google is known for their extraordinary workspace designs, which are designed to promote social interaction and collaboration.

The most effective strategic leaders understand that their firm's culture can be a source of competitive advantage; as such, they proactively work to form an effective culture. At its best, "culture expresses goals through values and beliefs and guides activity through shared assumptions and group norms." Going a step further, Bain & Company consultants suggest that "company culture is at the heart of competitive advantage, because it determines how things are done and how people behave." Importantly, the consultants also say, culture "is the hardest thing for competitors to copy." Culture's imperfect imitability (see Chapter 3) explains why it can be a source of competitive advantage and perhaps a sustainable one. To develop such a culture, leaders work with others to create an environment in which people have a passion to perform at high levels and to develop a culture with a unique personality and soul in the process of doing so. With an effective culture, firms are able to attract and retain high-quality talent and serve loyal customers. Overall, developing and sustaining an effective organizational culture is indeed a key strategic leadership action.

Sources: 2018, Performance culture, *Bain & Company*, www.bain.com, February 20; 2018, Understanding and developing organizational culture, *Society for Human Resource Management*, www.shrm.org, February 12; B. Groysberg, J. Lee, J. Price, & Y.-J. Cheng, 2018, The leader's guide to corporate culture, *Harvard Business Review*, 96(1): 44-57; 2017, Survey finds CEOs leaning on talent and organizational culture to survive and thrive amid global volatility, Conference Board, www.conference-board-org, January 31; W. A. Levenson, 2017, Culture: A decisive competitive advantage, *QualityDigest*, www.qualitydigest.com, October 3; S. Patel, 2017, The importance of building culture in your organization, *Inc.com*, wwwlinc.com, October 24; D. Smith, 2017, How to define and build a great organizational culture in 2018, *Medium.com*, www.medium.com, December 18.

In Chapter 13, we describe how firms of all sizes use strategic entrepreneurship to pursue entrepreneurial opportunities as a means of earning above-average returns. Companies are more likely to achieve the success they desire by using strategic entrepreneurship when their employees have an entrepreneurial mind-set.[117]

Five dimensions characterize a firm's entrepreneurial mind-set: autonomy, innovativeness, risk taking, proactiveness, and competitive aggressiveness.[118] In combination, these dimensions influence the actions a firm takes to be innovative when using the strategic management process.

Autonomy, the first of an entrepreneurial orientation's five dimensions, allows employees to take actions that are free of organizational constraints and encourages them to do so. The second dimension, *innovativeness*, "reflects a firm's tendency to engage in and support new ideas, novelty, experimentation, and creative processes that may result in new products, services, or technological processes."[119] Cultures with a tendency toward innovativeness encourage employees to think beyond existing knowledge, technologies, and parameters to find creative ways to add value. *Risk taking* reflects a willingness by employees and their firm to accept measured levels of risks when pursuing entrepreneurial opportunities. The fourth dimension of an entrepreneurial orientation, *proactiveness*, describes a firm's ability to be a market leader rather than a follower. Proactive organizational cultures constantly use processes to anticipate future market needs and to satisfy them before competitors learn how to do so. Finally, *competitive aggressiveness* is a firm's propensity to take actions through which it is able to outperform rivals consistently and substantially.[120]

Changing the Organizational Culture and Restructuring

Changing a firm's organizational culture is more difficult than maintaining it; however, effective strategic leaders recognize the need for cultural change. Commonly, firms make incremental changes to their culture when implementing strategies. More significant and sometimes even radical changes to organizational culture support selecting strategies that differ from those the firm has implemented historically. Regardless of the reasons for change, shaping and reinforcing a new culture requires effective problem solving and communication practices. In addition, selecting the right people (those who have the values the organization desires), engaging in effective performance appraisals (establishing goals that support the new core values and measuring individuals' progress toward reaching them), and using appropriate reward systems (rewarding the desired behaviors that reflect the new core values) also facilitate the forming and shaping of organizational culture.[121]

Evidence suggests that cultural changes succeed only when the firm's CEO, other key top management team members, and middle-level managers actively support them.[122] Some believe that middle-level managers "are essential in a change process" and that employees become more committed to supporting change when middle-level managers are involved actively with those changes.[123] For cultural change to occur, middle-level managers in particular need to be highly disciplined to energize the culture and foster alignment with the firm's vision and mission.[124] In addition, managers working at all organizational levels must be sensitive to the effects of other changes to the firm's culture. For example, downsizings can have a negative effect on organizational culture, especially if firms fail to implement them in accordance with the dominant organizational values.[125]

The realities associated with the need to change an organization's culture partly through restructuring—and the downsizing that often accompanies it—confronted Mary Barra when she became General Motors' CEO in 2014. Since assuming this role, Barra has been trying to reorient GM's culture and structure toward superior performance in order to ward off serious competitive challenges. Some believe that "Barra's global restructuring isn't only a clean break from GM's history, it's a downsizing almost as big as the painful transformation the company underwent during its 2009 bankruptcy."[126] With a continuing focus on profitability, GM announced early in 2018 that it intended to close its factory in South Korea. This decision represents "the latest step in a broad global downsizing implemented by Chief Executive Mary Barra, who has closed, shrunk or sold unprofitable business units in India, Russia, Western Europe and Southeast Asia."[127] In all instances, Barra and her top management team will want to implement various restructuring and downsizing decisions in ways that employees view as just and reasonable as well as necessary for GM to succeed.

12-4d Emphasizing Ethical Practices

When based on ethical practices, the effectiveness of processes used to implement the firm's strategies increases. Ethical companies encourage and enable people at all levels to act ethically when taking actions to implement strategies. In turn, ethical practices and the judgment informing their development and use create "social capital" in organizations. Social capital increases the amount of goodwill that is available to individuals as well as groups in the organization.[128] Alternatively, over time as unethical practices evolve in an organization, some managers may begin to perceive them as neutral or even ethical in nature.[129] Once unethical practices become acceptable, individuals are more likely to engage in them to meet their goals when other efforts to meet them are insufficient.

To influence employees' judgment and behavior properly, ethical practices must shape the firm's decision-making process and be an integral part of organizational culture. In fact, a values-based culture is the most effective means of ensuring that employees comply with the firm's ethical standards. However, developing such a culture requires constant nurturing and support.[130]

As explained in Chapter 10, some in leadership positions may occasionally act opportunistically, making decisions that are in their own best interests. This tends to happen when firms have lax expectations in place for individuals to follow regarding ethical behavior. In other words, individuals acting opportunistically take advantage of their positions, making decisions that benefit themselves to the detriment of the firm's stakeholders.[131] Sometimes executives take such actions due to their own greed and hubris.[132] However, when there is evidence of executive wrongdoing, such as having to restate the financial earnings, stockholders and other investors often react very negatively. The hiring of a new CEO commonly follows these negative reactions by investors.[133]

Strategic leaders as well as others in the organization are most likely to integrate ethical values into their decisions when the company has explicit ethics codes, when extensive ethics training results in integration of the codes into how the firm conducts business, and when shareholders expect ethical behavior.[134] Thus, establishing and enforcing a meaningful code of ethics is an important action to take to encourage ethical decision-making and actions when using the strategic management process.

Strategic leaders can take several actions to develop and support an ethical organizational culture. Examples of these actions include

1. establishing and communicating specific goals to describe the firm's ethical standards (e.g., developing and disseminating a code of conduct)
2. continuously revising and updating the ethics code, based on inputs from people throughout the firm and from other stakeholders
3. disseminating the ethics code to all stakeholders to inform them of the firm's ethical standards and practices
4. developing and implementing methods and procedures to use in achieving the firm's ethical standards (e.g., using internal auditing practices that are consistent with the standards)
5. creating and using explicit reward systems that recognize acts of courage (e.g., rewarding those who use proper channels and procedures to report observed wrongdoings)
6. creating a work environment in which all people are treated with dignity[135]

When firms pursue these actions simultaneously, causing them to be mutually supportive, their effectiveness tends to increase. When strategic leaders and others throughout the firm fail to take actions such as these—perhaps because of a lack of an ethical culture—problems are likely to occur.

12-4e Establishing Balanced Organizational Controls

Organizational controls (discussed in Chapter 11) are an important part of the strategic management process, particularly the parts related to implementation (see Figure 1.1). Controls are necessary to help ensure that firms achieve their desired outcomes. Defined as the "formal, information-based … procedures used by managers to maintain or alter patterns in organizational activities," controls help strategic leaders build credibility, demonstrate the value of strategies to the firm's stakeholders, and promote and support strategic change.[136] Most critically, controls provide the parameters for implementing strategies as well as the corrective actions to take when implementation-related adjustments are required. For example, allegations surfaced in 2017 that a small number of KPMG employees received leaks of confidential information that allowed them to better prepare for audits conducted by the Public Company Accounting Oversight Board.[137] In response to the allegations, KPMG immediately committed to full participation with authorities to identify any problems and to correct them. The firm's chairperson and CEO said that, "Quality and integrity are the cornerstones of all we do and that includes operating with the utmost respect and regard for the regulatory process." With respect to new controls, the CEO also noted that the firm was "taking additional steps to ensure that such a situation should not happen again."[138]

In this chapter, we focus on two organizational controls—strategic and financial—that we introduced in Chapter 11. Strategic leaders are responsible for helping the firm develop and properly use these two types of controls.

As we explained in Chapter 11, financial control focuses on short-term financial outcomes while strategic control focuses on the *content* of strategic actions rather than their *outcomes*. Some strategic actions can be correct but still result in poor financial outcomes because of external conditions, such as an economic recession, unexpected domestic or foreign government actions, or natural disasters that a firm's leaders do not control directly. Because of this, emphasizing financial controls often produces more short-term and risk-averse decisions. Alternatively, strategic control encourages lower-level managers to make decisions that incorporate moderate and acceptable levels of risk because leaders and managers throughout the firm share the responsibility for the outcomes of those decisions and actions resulting from them.

The challenge for strategic leaders is to balance the use of strategic and financial controls to support efforts to improve the firm's performance. The balanced scorecard is a tool to use to achieve the sought-after balance.

The Balanced Scorecard

As noted, the **balanced scorecard** is a tool firms, including family-owned firms,[139] use to determine if they are achieving an appropriate balance when using strategic and financial controls as a means of positively influencing performance.[140] This tool is most appropriate when evaluating business-level strategies; however, it is also useful when assessing other strategies that firms implement (e.g., corporate, international, and cooperative).

The underlying premise of the balanced scorecard is that firms jeopardize their future performance when they emphasize financial controls at the expense of strategic controls.[141] This occurs because financial controls provide feedback about outcomes achieved from past actions but fail to communicate the drivers of future performance. Thus, an overemphasis on financial controls may promote behavior that sacrifices the firm's long-term, value-creating potential for short-term performance gains. In effect, managers can make self-serving decisions when they focus on the short term. Research shows that decisions balancing short-term goals with long-term goals—so, balancing strategic and financial controls—generally lead to higher performance.[142]

The balanced scorecard is a product of integrating four perspectives:

- *financial* (concerned with growth, profitability, and risk from the shareholders' perspective)
- *customer* (concerned with the amount of value customers perceive the firm's products create for them)
- *internal business processes* (concerned with the priorities for various business processes that create customer and shareholder satisfaction)
- *learning and growth* (concerned with the firm's efforts to create a climate that supports change, innovation, and growth)

Thus, using the balanced scorecard finds the firm seeking to understand how it responds to shareholders (financial perspective), how customers view it (customer perspective), what processes to emphasize to successfully use its competitive advantage (internal perspective), and what it can do to improve its performance by innovating and growing (learning and growth perspective).[143] In general, firms tend to emphasize strategic controls when assessing their performance relative to the learning and growth perspective and financial controls when assessing performance in terms of the financial perspective.

Firms use different criteria to measure their standing relative to the balanced scorecard's four perspectives. We show sample criteria in Figure 12.5. The firm should select

The **balanced scorecard** is a tool firms, including family-owned firms, use to determine if they are achieving an appropriate balance when using strategic and financial controls as a means of positively influencing performance.

Figure 12.5 Strategic Controls and Financial Controls in a Balanced Scorecard Framework

Perspectives	Criteria
Financial	• Cash flow • Return on equity • Return on assets
Customer	• Assessment of ability to anticipate customers' needs • Effectiveness of customer service practices • Percentage of repeat business • Quality of communications with customers
Internal Business Processes	• Asset utilization improvements • Improvements in employee morale • Changes in turnover rates
Learning and Growth	• Improvements in innovation ability • Number of new products compared to competitors • Increases in employees' skills

the number of criteria that allow it to have both a strategic and financial understanding of its performance without immersing itself in too many details.[144]

Strategic leaders play an important role in determining a proper balance between strategic and financial controls, whether they are in single-business firms or large diversified firms. A proper balance between controls is important, in that "wealth creation for organizations where strategic leadership is exercised is possible because these leaders make appropriate investments for future viability (through strategic control), while maintaining an appropriate level of financial stability in the present (through financial control)."[145] In fact, most firms use restructuring to refocus on their core businesses, thereby allowing top executives to re-establish strategic control in individual business units.[146]

Firms often find success using strategic control when they provide each business unit with the level of autonomy needed to develop a competitive advantage.[147] Firms use strategic control to promote the sharing of both tangible and intangible resources among interdependent business units. In addition, the autonomy provided allows the flexibility necessary to take advantage of specific marketplace opportunities. As a result, strategic leadership promotes simultaneous use of strategic control and autonomy, which in turn, provides employees with experience-based learning opportunities.[148]

As we have explained in this chapter, strategic leaders are critical to a firm's ability to use all parts of the strategic management process, including strategic entrepreneurship, successfully. Strategic entrepreneurship is the final topic included in the "strategy" part of this text's Analysis-Strategy-Performance model. We turn our attention to this topic in Chapter 13.

SUMMARY

- Effective strategic leadership is a prerequisite to using the strategic management process successfully. Strategic leadership entails the ability to anticipate events, envision possibilities, maintain flexibility, and empower others to create strategic change.
- Top-level managers are an important resource for firms to develop. In addition, when they and their work are valuable, rare, imperfectly imitable, and nonsubstitutable, strategic leaders are also a source of competitive advantage.
- Key managers, who play a critical role in selecting and implementing the firm's strategies, form the top management team. Generally, these managers are officers of the corporation and/or members of the board of directors.
- The top management team's characteristics, a firm's strategies, and the firm's performance are interrelated. For example, a top management team with significant marketing and research and development (R&D) knowledge positively contributes to the firm's ability to use a growth strategy. Overall, having diverse skills increases the effectiveness of most top management teams.
- Typically, performance improves when the board of directors and the CEO are involved in shaping a firm's strategic direction. However, when the CEO has a great deal of power, the board may be less involved in decisions about strategy formulation and implementation. By appointing people to the board and simultaneously serving as CEO and chair of the board, CEOs increase their power.
- In managerial succession, the internal managerial labor market and the external managerial labor market are the sources for new CEOs. Because of their effect on firm performance, the selection of strategic leaders has implications for a firm's effectiveness. In most instances, firms use the internal market to select their CEO. Today, however, the number of instances in which new CEOs come from the external managerial labor market is increasing. Commonly, firms select outsiders as their new CEO because of the belief that they will initiate major changes in strategy.
- Effective strategic leadership has five key leadership actions: determining the firm's strategic direction, effectively managing the firm's resource portfolio (including exploiting and maintaining core competencies and managing human capital and social capital), sustaining an effective organizational culture, emphasizing ethical practices, and establishing balanced organizational controls.
- Strategic leaders must develop the firm's strategic direction, typically working with the board of directors to do so. The strategic direction specifies the image and character the firm wants to develop over time. To form the strategic direction, strategic leaders evaluate the conditions (e.g., opportunities and threats in the external environment) they expect their firm to face over the next three to five years.
- Effective strategic leaders ensure that their firm exploits its core competencies, which employees use to produce and deliver products that create value for customers, when implementing its strategies. In related diversified and large firms in particular, effective use of core competencies occurs by sharing them across units and products.
- The ability to manage the firm's resource portfolio and the processes used to implement its strategy are critical elements of strategic leadership. Managing the resource portfolio includes integrating resources to create capabilities and leveraging those capabilities through strategies to build competitive advantages. Human capital and social capital are perhaps the most important resources.
- As a part of managing resources, strategic leaders must develop a firm's human capital. Effective strategic leaders view human capital as a resource to maximize—not as a cost to minimize. Such leaders develop and use programs designed to train current and future strategic leaders to build the skills needed to nurture the rest of the firm's human capital.
- Effective strategic leaders build and maintain internal and external social capital. Internal social capital promotes cooperation and coordination within and across the firm's units. External social capital provides access to resources from external parties that the firm needs to compete effectively.
- Shaping the firm's culture is a central task of effective strategic leadership. An appropriate organizational culture encourages the development of an entrepreneurial mind-set among employees and an ability to change the culture as necessary.
- In ethical organizations, employees are encouraged to exercise ethical judgment as a foundation for their ethical actions. Improved ethical practices foster social capital. Setting specific goals to meet the firm's ethical standards, using a code of conduct, rewarding ethical behaviors, and creating a work environment where the firm treats all people with dignity are actions that facilitate and support ethical behavior.
- Developing and using balanced organizational controls is the final key leadership action associated with effective strategic leadership. The balanced scorecard is a tool that measures the effectiveness of the firm's strategic and financial controls. An effective balance between these two controls allows for flexible use of core competencies, but within the parameters of the firm's financial position.

KEY TERMS

balanced scorecard 405
determining strategic direction 396
external managerial labor market 394
heterogeneous top management team 390
human capital 398
internal managerial labor market 394
social capital 399
strategic change 386
strategic leadership 386
top management team 390

REVIEW QUESTIONS

1. What is strategic leadership? Why are top-level managers important resources for an organization?
2. What is a top management team, and how does it affect a firm's performance and its abilities to innovate and design and bring about effective strategic change?
3. What is the managerial succession process? How important are the internal and external managerial labor markets to this process?
4. What is the effect of strategic leadership on determining the firm's strategic direction?
5. How do strategic leaders manage their firm's resource portfolio effectively to exploit its core competencies and leverage its human capital and social capital to achieve a competitive advantage?
6. What must strategic leaders do to develop and sustain an effective organizational culture?
7. As a strategic leader, what actions could you take to establish and emphasize ethical practices in your firm?
8. Why are strategic controls and financial controls important aspects of strategic leadership and the firm's strategic management process?

Mini-Case

Can You Follow an Icon and Succeed? Apple and Tim Cook After Steve Jobs

Steve Jobs was Apple's co-founder and iconic CEO. A number of observers feel that much of Apple's phenomenal success, especially after 2000, is a product of his "genius" and leadership. Because of this and a leadership style that varies significantly from his predecessor's, some have questioned Tim Cook's ability to succeed Jobs as Apple's CEO. Yet, in 2014, several years after assuming the CEO position, Apple had what Tim Cook referred to as an "unbelievable year" given that the firm sold 200 million iPhones and generated $200 billion in revenue. Apple's stock price increased by 65 percent, and the company's market value reached more than $700 billion, the largest ever of any U.S. firm. At the time, Apple's market value more than doubled that of Microsoft. Prior to assuming the CEO position, Cook's primary experience had been as manager of operations; his success in this domain led to his appointment as COO prior to assuming the CEO role. Interestingly, a significant percentage of Apple's sales flow from products developed and introduced to the market under Jobs' leadership. As such, the jury is still out on Cook, especially with regard to developing marketplace successes in the form of new products, tasks at which Jobs excelled.

Jobs and Cook have different leadership styles. Some thought Jobs was ruthless, impulsive, and almost maniacal in developing new products and finding paths through which they became marketplace successes. Cook's knowledge and skills do not make him an expert in product development, design, or marketing. Because of this, he delegates those responsibilities. As the firm's key strategic leader, Cook tries to buffer and maintain Apple's corporate culture that developed largely during Jobs' tenure. Thus, the emphasis remains on innovation that is valued in the marketplace. To support this emphasis and to nurture the firm's all-important culture, Cook hires talented individuals to join the top management team who blend well with the culture. He has made some very good hires, such as Angela Ahrendts who now heads Apple's very important retail stores. As a leader, Cook is less emotional in his style and actions compared to Jobs. Some refer to this aspect of Cook's style as a "measured emotional approach to leadership." He empowers his top management team members in ways that allow each of them to manage the functional area for which they have responsibility. He also encourages each team member to adopt a long-run perspective while leading.

Observers have been able to highlight other differences between Cook's and Jobs' strategic leadership approaches. Compared to Jobs, Cook more regularly shares the limelight with his leadership team, spotlighting their contributions while doing so. One analyst suggested that Cook is a good leader who builds an effective team around him. With respect to strategic choices, Cook's decisions have resulted in major acquisitions (e.g., an audio company for $3 billion) and developing enterprise solutions for corporate IT units; Jobs opposed actions of these types. Under Cook, Apple formed an alliance with IBM to develop enterprise applications with a focus on the iPad, especially the new and larger versions.

During Cook's early tenure as CEO, Apple introduced several innovations including the Apple watch, which entered the market in April 2015. This product's marketplace success is yet to be determined; initial reports suggested that demand exceeded supply, causing Apple to increase production. In addition, hints provided by Cook suggest that Apple may be planning to enter the television market. Most importantly, Cook claims that Apple's goal is to change the way people work. The firm intends to focus research and development efforts to develop products to achieve this objective.

In mid-2018, some analysts were questioning the delays Apple was encountering when introducing products to the marketplace. Of three major product launches under Cook since becoming the firm's CEO in 2011, AirPods earbuds and the HomePod speaker missed publicly announced shipping dates. The Apple Watch, mentioned above, entered the market later than the firm desired, initially causing customers to experience long wait times to buy the product. The Apple Pencil and Smart Keyboard, two critical accessories for the iPad Pro, also entered the market later than announced initially. On the other hand, Apple's first quarter 2018 results yielded all-time highs in both revenue and earnings. In an overall sense, only the march of time will yield insights needed to determine if as CEO, Tim Cook was a success as Steve Jobs' successor. With a market value of over $900 billion in early 2018, it seems that as Apple's key strategic leader, Cook's effect on the firm he was leading was positive.

Sources: 2018, Transcript: Apple CEO Tim Cook on the company's 2018 Q1 earnings, *iMore*, www.imore.com, February 1; T. Mickle, 2018, Tim Cook stumbles at his specialty, shipping Apple products on time, *Wall Street Journal*, www.wsj.com, January 6; R. Safian, 2018, Why Apple is the world's most innovative company, *Fast Company*, www.fastcompany.com, February 21; T. Loftus, 2015, The morning download: Apple will 'change the way people work,' CEO Tim Cook says, *CIO Journal*, blogs.wsj.com, January 28: 2015, Apple's Tim Cook cites record sales and 'unbelievable' year, *New York Times*, www.nytimes.com, March 10; A. Chang, 2015, Apple CEO Tim Cook is forging an unusual path as a social activist, *Los Angeles Times*, www.latimes.com, March 31; A. Lashinsky, 2015, Becoming Tim Cook, *Fortune*, April 1, 60–72; T. Higgins, 2015, Apple iPhones sales in China outsell the U.S. for first time, *BloombergBusiness*, www.bloomberg.com, April 27; J. Lewis, 2015, Tim Cook: A courageous innovator, *Time*, April 27, 26; J. D'Onfro, 2015, Tim Cook dropped a major clue about Apple's next big product, *Yahoo Finance*, finance.yahoo.com, April 28.

Case Discussion Questions

1. What makes a CEO's job so complex? Use the challenge Tim Cook faces as Steve Jobs' successor to provide examples that support your answer.

2. Tim Cook came from Apple's internal managerial labor market to succeed Steve Jobs. In your view, was using the internal managerial labor market the best approach to follow when replacing Jobs? Use materials in the chapter regarding the internal and external managerial labor markets to explain your answer.

3. Given their different leadership styles, describe the differences you see in Apple's culture under Tim Cook's leadership compared to the culture in Apple when Steve Jobs was CEO.

4. Using information in this Mini-Case as well as additional materials available to you via searches, how do you evaluate Tim Cook as a CEO? Is he an effective strategic leader or not? Use examples from the chapter's discussion of "Key Strategic Leadership Actions" to justify your answer to this question.

NOTES

1. P. Wahba, 2017, How Avon's CEO failed to fix the company, *Yahoo! Finance*, https://yahoofinance.com, August 3.
2. E. Schwartzel, 2018, Meg Whitman to lead mobile-video startup NewTV, *Wall Street Journal*, www.wsj.com, January 24.
3. C. J. McMillan & J. S. Overall, 2017, Crossing the chasm and over the abyss: Perspectives on organizational failure, *Academy of Management Perspectives*, 31: 271–287; V. Govindarajan, 2012, The timeless strategic value of unrealistic goals, *HBR Blog*, https://hbr.org/2012/10/the-timeless-strategic-value-of-unrealistic-goals.html, October 22.
4. G. Parmentier & R. Gandia, 2017, Redesigning the business model: From one-sided to multi-sided, *Journal of Business Strategy*, 38(2): 52–61; D. Martin, 2014, Thinking about thinking, *Journal of Business Strategy*, 35(5): 49–54.
5. W. Ocasio, T. Laamanen, & E. Vaara, 2018, Communication and attention dynamics: An attention-based view of strategic change, *Strategic Management Journal*, 39: 155–167.
6. M. D. Packard, B. B. Clark, & P. G. Klein, 2017, Uncertainty types and transitions in the entrepreneurial process, *Organization Science*, 28: 840–856; D. Cooper, P. C. Patel, & S. M. B. Thatcher, 2014, It depends: Environmental context and the effects of faultlines on top management team performance, *Organization Science*, 25: 633–652.
7. M. A. Hitt, C. Miller, A. Colella, & M. Triana, 2018, *Organizational Behavior*, 5th ed., Hoboken, NJ: John Wiley & Sons; M. Subramony, J. Segers, C. Chadwick, & A. Shyamsunder, 2018, Leadership development practice bundles and organizational performance: The mediating role of human capital and social capital, *Journal of Business Research*, 83: 120–129.
8. R. R. Kehoe & C. J. Collins, 2017, Human resource management and unit performance in knowledge-intensive work, *Journal of Applied Psychology*, 102: 1222–1236; D. Frank & T. Obloj, 2014, Firm-specific human capital, organizational incentives, and agency costs: Evidence from retail banking, *Strategic Management Journal*, 35: 1279–1301.
9. A. Kianto, J. Saenzy, & N. Aramburu, 2017, Knowledge-based human resource management practices, intellectual capital and innovation, *Journal of Business Research*, 81: 11–20; M. A. Axtle-Ortiz, 2013, Perceiving the value of intangible assets in context, *Journal of Business Research*, 56: 417–424.
10. A. L. Steinbach, T.R. Holcomb, R. M. Holmes, Jr., C. E. Devers, & A. A. Cannella, Jr., 2017, Top management team incentive heterogeneity, strategic investment behavior, and performance: A contingency theory of incentive alignment, *Strategic Management Journal*, 38: 1701–1720; C. Chadwick, J. F. Super, & K. Kwon, 2015, Resource orchestration in practice: CEO emphasis on SHRM, commitment-based HR systems and firm performance, *Strategic Management Journal*, 36: 360–376.
11. J. Detjen & S. Webber, 2017, Strategic shifts that build executive leadership, *Business Horizons*, 60: 335–343; R. M. Stock, N. A. Zacharias, & A. Schnellbaecher, 2017, How do strategy and leadership styles jointly affect co-development and its innovation outcomes? *Journal of Product Innovation and Management*, 34: 201–222.
12. A. Gupta, F. Briscoe, & D. C. Hambrick, 2017, Red, blue, and purple firms: Organizational political ideology and corporate social responsibility, *Strategic Management Journal*, 38: 1018–1040; C. Crossland, J. Zyung, N. J. Hiller, & D. C. Hambrick, 2014, CEO career variety: Effects on firm-level strategic and social novelty, *Academy of Management Journal*, 57: 652–674.
13. A. Lashinsky, 2017, Tim Cook on how Apple champions the environment, education, and health care, *Fortune*, www.fortune.com, September 11.
14. S. Gibbs, 2018, Apple's Tim Cook: I don't want my nephew on a social network, *theguardian*, www.theguardian.com, January 19.
15. S. Grewatsch & I. Kleindienst 2018, How organizational cognitive frames affect organizational capabilities: The context of corporate sustainability, *Long Range Planning*, in press; J. P. Doh & N. R. Quigley, 2014, Responsible leadership and stakeholder management: Influence pathways and organizational outcomes, *Academy of Management Perspectives*, 28: 255–274.
16. K. Hejjas, G. Miller, & C. Scarles, 2018, "It's like hating puppies!" Employee disengagement and corporate social responsibility, *Journal of Business Ethics*, in press.
17. M. J. Sousa & A. Rocha, 2018, Leadership styles and skills developed through game-based learning, *Journal of Business Research*, in press; X. Zhang, N. Li, J. Ulrich, & R. von Dick, 2015, Getting everyone on board: The effect of differentiated transformational leadership by CEOs on top management team effectiveness and leader-rated firm performance, *Journal of Management*, 41: 1898–1933.
18. 2017, James Hackett, CEO of Ford, is dedicated to innovation, *Chief Executive*, www.chiefexecutive.com, September 11.
19. A. Bryant, 2017, How to be a C.E.O., from a decade's worth of them, *New York Times*, www.nytimes.com, October 27.
20. Ibid., 2017, How to be a C.E.O.
21. R. M. M. I. Chowdhury, 2017, Emotional intelligence and consumer ethics: The mediating role of personal moral philosophies *Journal of Business Ethics*, 142: 527–548; Y. Dong, M.-G. Seo, & K. Bartol, 2014, No pain, no gain: An affect-based model of developmental job experience and the buffering effects of emotional intelligence, *Academy of Management Journal*, 57: 1056–1077.
22. E. Riivari & A.-M. Lamsa, 2018, Organizational ethical virtues of innovativeness, *Journal of Business Ethics*, in press.
23. J. M. Knippen, J. Palar, & R. J. Gentry, 2018, Breaking the mold: An examination of board discretion in female CEO appointments, *Journal of Business Research*, 84: 11–23; A. J. Wowak, L. R. Gomez-Mejia, & A. L. Steinbach, 2017, Inducements and motives at the top: A holistic perspective on the drivers of executive behaviour, *Academy of Management Annals*, 11(2): 669–702.
24. V. Gupta, S. C. Mortal, & T. Yang, 2018, Entrepreneurial orientation and firm value: Does managerial discretion play a role? *Review of Managerial Science*, 12: 1–26; M. Abraham, 2017, Pay formalization revisited: Considering the effects of manager gender and discretion on closing the gender wage gap, *Academy of Management Journal*, 60: 29–54.
25. S. Lohr, 2017, G.E. rolls back the breadth of its ambitions, *New York Times*, www.nytimes.com, November 13.
26. D. Laureiro-Martinez & S. Brusoni, 2018, Cognitive flexibility and adaptive decision-making: Evidence from a laboratory study of expert decision-makers, *Strategic Management Journal*, 39: 1031–1058; O. R. Mihalache, J. J. P. Jansen, F. A. J. van den Bosch, & H. W. Volberda, 2014, Top management team shared leadership and organizational ambidexterity: A moderated mediation framework, *Strategic Entrepreneurship Journal*, 8: 128–148.
27. X. Hollandts, 2018, Friend or foe? Employee ownership and CEO dismissal, *Managerial and Decision Economics*, 39: 377–388; J. W. Ridge, S. Johnson, A. D. Hill, & J. Bolton, 2017, The role of top management team attention in new product introductions, *Journal of Business Research*, 70: 17–24.
28. A. Protogerou, Y. Caloghirou, & N. S. Vonortas, 2017, Determinants of young firms' innovative performance: Empirical evidence from Europe, *Research Policy*, 46: 1312–1326; J. Oehmichen, S. Schrapp, & M. Wolff, 2017, Who needs experts most? Board industry expertise and strategic change—a contingency perspective, *Strategic Management Journal*, 38: 645–656.

29. Y. Tang, D. Z. Mack, & G. Chen, 2018, The differential effects of CEO narcissism and hubris on corporate social responsibility, *Strategic Management Journal*, 39: 1370–1387; K. T. Haynes, M. A. Hitt, & J. T. Campbell, 2015, The dark side of leadership: Toward a mid-range theory of hubris and greed in entrepreneurial contexts, *Journal of Managerial Studies*, 52: 479–505.
30. M. Sousa & D. van Dierendonck, 2017, Servant leadership and the effect of the interaction between humility, action, and hierarchical power on follower engagement, *Journal of Business Ethics*, 141: 13–25; A. Y. Ou, A. S. Tsui, A. J. Kinicki, D. A. Waldman, Z. Xiao, & L. J. Song, 2014, Humble chief executive officers' connections to top management team integration and middle manager response, *Administrative Science Quarterly*, 59: 34–72.
31. 2017, From the macro to the personal: Lessons from five top leaders, *Knowledge@ Wharton*, www.knowledge.wharton.upenn.edu, December 12.
32. V. Fuhrmans, 2018, Companies with diverse executive teams posted bigger profit margins, study shows, *Wall Street Journal*, www.wsj.com, January 18.
33. F. Bridoux, R. Coeurderoy, & R. Durand, 2017, Heterogeneous social motives and interactions: The three predictable paths of capability development, *Strategic Management Journal*, 38: 1755–1773; X. Wang & M. Dass, 2017, Building innovation capability: The role of top management innovativeness and relative-exploration orientation, *Journal of Business Research*, 76: 127–135.
34. A. Y. Ou, J. (Jamie) Seo, D. Choi, & P. W. Hom, 2017, When can humble top executives retain middle managers? The moderating role of top management team faultlines, *Academy of Management Journal*, 60: 1915–1931; D. C. Hambrick, S. E. Humphrey, & A. Gupta, 2015, Structural interdependence within top management teams: A key moderator of upper echelon predictions: *Strategic Management Journal*, 36: 449–461.
35. T. Hutzschenreuter & T. Matt, 2017, MNE internationalization patterns, the roles of knowledge stocks and the portfolio of MNE subsidiaries, *Journal of International Business Studies*, 48: 1131–1150; S. Le & M. Kroll, 2017, CEO international experience: Effects on strategic change and firm performance, *Journal of International Business Studies*, 48: 573–595.
36. J.-P. Ferguson & G. Camabuci, 2017, Risky recombinations: Institutional gatekeeping in the innovation process, *Organization Science*, 28: 133–151.
37. A. Nadolska & H. G. Barkema, 2014, Good learners: How top management teams affect the success and frequency of acquisitions, *Strategic Management Journal*, 35: 1483–1507.
38. C. Samba, D. Van Knippenberg, & C. C. Miller, 2018, The impact of strategic dissent on organizational outcomes: A meta-analytic integration, *Strategic Management Journal*, 39: 379–402.
39. S. Finkelstein, D. C. Hambrick, & A. A. Cannella, Jr., 2008, *Strategic Leadership: Top Executives and Their Effects on Organizations*, NY: Oxford University Press.
40. M. Reimer, S. Van Doorn, & M. L. M. Heyden, 2018, Unpacking functional experience complementarities in senior leaders' influences on CSR strategy: A CEO-top management team approach, *Journal of Business Ethics*, in press; S. Garg & K. M. Eisenhardt, 2017, Unpacking the CEO-board relationship: How strategy making happens in entrepreneurial firms, *Academy of Management Journal*, 60: 1828–1858.
41. P. Klein, J. Mahoney, A. McGahan, & C. Pitelis, 2018, Organizational governance adaptation: Who is in, who is out, and who gets what, *Academy of Management Review*, in press; J. W. Ridge, F. Aime, & M. A. White, 2015, When much more of a difference makes a difference: Social comparison and tournaments in the CEO's top team, *Strategic Management Journal*, 36: 618–636.
42. J. Lygsie & N. J. Foss, 2017, The more, the merrier: Women in top-management teams and entrepreneurship in established firms, *Strategic Management Journal*, 38: 487–505; P. Herrmann & S. Nadkarni, 2014, Managing strategic change: The duality of CEO personality, *Strategic Management Journal*, 35: 1318–1342; A. E. Colbert, M. R. Barrick, & B. H. Bradley, 2014, Personality and leadership composition in top management teams: Implications for organizational effectiveness, *Personnel Psychology*, 67: 351–387.
43. C. Williams, P.-L. Chen, & R. Agarwal, 2017, Rookies and seasoned recruits: How experience in different levels, firms, and industries shapes strategic renewal in top management, *Strategic Management Journal*, 38: 1391–1415; C. Shalley, M. A. Hitt, & J. Zhou, 2015, Integrating creativity, innovation and entrepreneurship to successfully navigate in the new competitive landscape, in C. Shalley, M. A. Hitt, & J. Zhou (eds.) *Handbook of Creativity, Innovation and Entrepreneurship*, NY: Oxford University Press, 1–14.
44. R. Lorenzo, N. Voigt, M. Tsusaka, M. Krentz, & K. Abouzahr, 2018, How diverse leadership teams boost innovation, *Boston Consulting Group*, www.bc.com, January 23.
45. X. Hollandts, 2018, Friend or foe? Employee ownership and CEO dismissal, *Managerial and Decision Economics*, 39: 377–388; J. Oehmichen, S. Schrapp, & M. Wolff, 2017, Who needs experts? Board industry expertise and strategic change—a contingency perspective, *Strategic Management Journal*, 38: 645–656.
46. B. Gruhn, S. Strese, T. C. Flatten, N. A. Jaeger, & M. Brettel, 2017, Temporal change patterns of entrepreneurial orientation: A longitudinal investigation of CEO successions, *Entrepreneurship Theory and Practice*, 41: 591–619; X. Luo, V. K. Kanuri, & M. Andrews, 2014, How does CEO tenure matter? The mediating role of firm-employee and firm-customer relationships, *Strategic Management Journal*, 35: 492–511.
47. S. J. Ashford, N. Wellman, M. S. de Luque, K. E. M. De Stobbeieir, & M. Wollan, 2018, Two roads to effectiveness: CEO feedback seeking, vision articulation, and firm performance, *Journal of Organizational Behavior*, 39: 82–95; M. Subramony, J. Segers, C. Chadwick, & A. Shyamsunder, 2018, Leadership development practice bundles and organizational performance: The mediating role of human capital and social capital, *Journal of Business Research*, 83: 120–129.
48. C. P. Green & S. Homroy, 2018, Female directors, board committees and firm performance, *European Economic Review*, 102: 19–38; A. Chatterjee & T. G. Pollock, 2017, Master of puppets: How narcissistic CEOs construct their professional worlds, *Academy of Management Review*, 42: 703–725; D. H. Zhu & G. Chen, 2015, CEO narcissism and the impact of prior board experience on firm strategy, *Administrative Science Quarterly*, 60: 31–65.
49. J. Joseph, W. Ocasio, & M.-H. McDonnell, 2014, The structural elaboration of board independence: Executive power, institutional logics, and the adoption of CEO-only board structures in U.S. corporate governance, *Academy of Management Journal*, 57: 1834–1858.
50. R. V. Aguilera, W. Q. Judge, & S. A. Terjesen, 2018, Corporate governance deviance, *Academy of Management Review*, 43: 87–109; J. M. Knippen, J. Palar, & R. J. Gentry, 2018, Breaking the mold: An examination of board discretion in female CEO appointments, *Journal of Business Research*, 84: 11–23.
51. J.-K. Kang, W.-L. Liu, A. Low, & L. Zhang, 2018, Friendly boards and innovation, *Journal of Empirical Finance*, 45: 1–25; R. Krause, 2017, Being the CEO's boss: An examination of board chair orientations, *Strategic Management Journal*, 38: 697–713; M. C. Withers & M. A. Fitza, 2017, Do board chairs matter? The influence of board chairs on firm performance, *Strategic Management Journal*, 38: 1343–1355; C. S. Tuggle, D. G. Sirmon, C. R. Reutzel, & L. Bierman, 2010, Commanding board of director attention: Investigating how organizational performance and CEO duality affect board members' attention to monitoring, *Strategic Management Journal*, 32: 640–657.
52. J. Paniagua, R. Rivelles, & J. Sapena, 2018, Corporate governance and financial performance: The role of ownership and board structure, *Journal of Business Research*, 89: 229–234.

53. S. Singh, N. Tabassum, T. K. Darwish, & G. Batsakis, 2018, Corporate governance and Tobin's Q as a measure of organizational performance, *British Journal of Management*, 29: 171–190; R. Krause & M. Semadeni, 2014, Last dance or second chance? Firm performance, CEO career horizon, and the separation of board leadership roles, *Strategic Management Journal*, 35: 808–825.
54. M. van Essen, P.-J. Engelen, & M. Carey, 2013, Does "good" corporate governance help in a crisis? The impact of country- and firm-level governance mechanisms in the European financial crisis, *Corporate Governance: An International Review*, 21: 201–224.
55. R. Krause & M. Semadeni, 2013, Apprentice, departure, and demotion: An examination of the three types of CEO-board chair separation, *Academy of Management Journal*, 56: 805–826.
56. S. Firfiray, C. Cruz, I. Neacsu, & L. R. Gomez-Mejia, 2018, Is nepotism so bad for family firms? A socioemotional wealth approach, *Human Resource Management Review*, 28: 83–97; K. Madison, J. J. Daspit, D. Turner, & F. W. Kellermanns, 2018, Family firm human resource practices: Investigating the effects of professionalization and bifurcation bias on performance, *Journal of Business Research*, 84: 327–336; P. C. Patel & D. Cooper, 2014, Structural power equality between family and non-family TMT members and the performance of family firms, *Academy of Management Journal*, 57: 1624–1649.
57. M. Leong, Z. Chen, & Z. Yao, 2018, CEO tenure and stock returns performance, *SSRN Papers*, https://papers.ssrn.com/sol3/papers.cfm?abstract_id=3100746; A. J. Wowak, L. R. Gomez-Mejia, & A. L. Steinback, 2017, Inducements and motives at the top: A holistic perspective on the drivers of executive behavior, *Academy of Management Annals*, 11(2): 669–702.
58. L. B. Cardinal, M. Kreutzer, & C. C. Miller, 2017, An aspirational view of organizational control research: Re-invigorating empirical work to better meet the challenges of 21st century organizations, *Academy of Management Annals*, 11(2): 559–592; W. Lewis, J. L. Walls, & G. W. S. Dowell, 2014, Difference in degrees: CEO characteristics and firm environmental disclosure, *Strategic Management Journal* 35: 712–722.
59. Z. Simsek, 2007, CEO tenure and organizational performance: An intervening model, *Strategic Management Journal*, 28: 653–662.
60. W. Hou, R. L. Priem, & M. Goranova, 2017, Does one size fit all? Investigating pay-future performance relationships over the "seasons" of CEO tenure, *Journal of Management*, 43: 864–891; M. A. Fitza, 2014, The use of variance decomposition in the investigation of CEO effects: How large must the CEO effect be to rule out chance? *Strategic Management Journal*, 35: 1839–1852.
61. F. Zhang, L. Wei, J. Yang, & L. Zhu, 2018, Roles of relationships between large shareholders and managers in radical innovation: A stewardship theory perspective, *Journal of Product Innovation Management*, 35: 88–105; M. Hernandez, 2012, Toward an understanding of the psychology of stewardship, *Academy of Management Review*, 37: 172–193.
62. C. Francoeur, A. Melis, S. Gaia, & S. Aresu, 2017, Green or greed? An alternative look at CEO compensation and corporate environmental commitment, *Journal of Business Ethics*, 140: 439–453; W. Ridge & A. Ingram, 2015, Modesty in the top management team: Investor reaction and performance implications, *Journal of Management*, 43: 1283–1306.
63. R. Krause, 2017, Being the CEO's boss: An examination of board chair orientations, *Strategic Management Journal*, 38: 697–713; M. Menz & C. Scheef, 2014, Chief strategy officers: Contingency analysis of their presence in top management teams, *Strategic Management Journal*, 35: 461–471.
64. S. R. Levine, 2017, Succession planning needs to be your no. 1 priority, *Forbes*, www.forbes.com, May 24.
65. L. Hilliter, E. Anderson, A. Laster, & D. Jellerette, 2018, Succession management: Developing the next generation of federal leaders, *Deloitte*, www.deloitte.com, October 27.
66. 2017, Succession planning in a family business, *Wall Street Journal*, www.wsj.com, May 9.
67. K. V. D. Berns & P. Klarner, 2017, A review of the CEO succession literature and a future research program, *Academy of Management Perspectives*, 31: 83–108; D. J. Schepker, Y. Kim, P. C. Patel, S. M. B. Thatcher, & M. C. Campion, 2017, CEO succession, strategic change, and post-succession performance: A meta-analysis, *The Leadership Quarterly*, 28: 701–720; S. D. Graffin, S. Boivie, & M. A. Carpenter, 2013, Examining CEO succession and the role of heuristics in early-stage CEO evaluation, *Strategic Management Journal*, 34: 383–403.
68. 2013, Deloitte, Perspectives on family-owned businesses: Governance and succession planning, www.deloitte.com, January.
69. C. Peterson-Withorn, 2015, New survey pinpoints what keeps family businesses going for generations, *Forbes*, www.forbes.com, April 23.
70. C. E. Fee, C. J. Hadlock, & U. J. R. Pierce, 2018, New evidence on managerial labor markets: An analysis of CEO retreads, *Journal of Corporate Finance*, 48: 428–441; X. Cao, X. Pan, M. Qian, & G. G. Tian, 2017, Political capital and CEO entrenchment: Evidence from CEO turnover in Chinese non-SOEs, *Journal of Corporate Finance*, 42: 1–14.
71. J. McGregor, 2017, It's a dangerous time to be a bad CEO, *Washington Post*, www.washingtonpost.com, July 11.
72. M. Nakauchi & M. F. Wiersema, 2015, Executive succession and strategic change, *Strategic Management Journal*, 36: 298–306.
73. S. Kapner & J. S. Lublin, 2018, Neiman Marcus CEO to step aside, *Wall Street Journal*, www.wsj.com, January 4.
74. C. Lombardo & J. S. Lublin, 2018, Sam Adams Beer isn't rushing the search for its next CEO, *Wall Street Journal*, www.wsj.com, January 28;
75. D. Schepker, A. Nyberg, M. Ulrich, & P. Wright, 2018, Planning for future leadership: Procedural rationality, formalized succession processes, and CEO influence in Chief Executive Officer succession planning, *Academy of Management Journal*, 61: 523–552; D. Georgakakis & W. Ruigrok, CEO succession origin and firm performance: A multi-level study, *Journal of Management Studies*, 54: 58–87.
76. D. Georgakakis & W. Ruigrok, 2017, CEO succession origin and firm performance: A multilevel study, *Journal of Management Studies*, 54: 58–87; J. J. Marcel, A. P. Cowen, & G. A. Ballinger, 2017, Are disruptive CEO successions viewed as a governance lapse? Evidence from board turnover, *Journal of Management*, 43: 1313–1334.
77. C. H. Mooney, M. Semadeni, & I. F. Kesner, 2017, The selection of an interim CEO: Boundary conditions and the pursuit of temporary leadership, *Journal of Management*, 43: 455–475.
78. S. Pandey & S. Rhee, 2015, An inductive study of foreign CEOs of Japanese firms, *Journal of Leadership and Organizational Studies*, 22: 202–216.
79. I. R. P. Cuypers, Y. Cuypers, & Z. Martin, 2017, When the target may know better: Effects of experience and information asymmetries on value from mergers and acquisitions, *Strategic Management Journal*, 38: 609–625; P. Kale & H. Singh, 2017, Management of overseas acquisitions by developing country multinationals and its performance implications: The Indian example, *Thunderbird International Business Review*, 59: 153–172.
80. K. A. Arnold, C. E. Connelly, I. R. Gellatly, M. M. Walsh, & M. J. Withey, 2017, Using a pattern-oriented approach to study leaders: Implications for burnout and perceived role demand, *Journal of Organizational Behavior*, 38: 1038–1056; D. H. Weng & Z. Lin, 2014, Beyond CEO tenure: The effect of CEO newness on strategic changes, *Journal of Management*, 40: 2009–2032.
81. C. Wolf & S. W. Floyd, 2017, Strategic planning research: Toward a theory-driven agenda, *Journal of Management*, 43: 1754–1788; F. F. Jing, G. C. Avery, & H. Bergsteiner, 2014, Enhancing performance in small professional firms through vision communication and sharing,

Asia Pacific Journal of Management, 31: 599–620.

82. A. R. Sorkin, 2018, Blackrock's message: Contribute to society, or risk losing our support, *New York Times*, www.nytimes.com, January 15.

83. R. Rohrbeck & M. E. Kum, 2018, Corporate foresight and its impact on firm performance: A longitudinal analysis, *Technological Forecasting and Social Change*, 129: 105–116; S. J. C. Siren, H. Makala, J. Wincent, & D. Grichnik, 2017, Breaking the routines: Entrepreneurial orientation, strategic learning, firm size, and age, *Long Range Planning*, 50: 145–167.

84. P.-Y. Li, 2018, Top management team characteristics and firm internationalization: The moderating role of the size of middle managers, *International Business Review*, 27: 125–138.

85. I. A. Shaikh, J. P. O'Brien, & L. Peters, 2018, Inside directors and the underinvestment of financial slack towards R&D-intensity in high-technology firms, *Journal of Business Research*, 82: 192–201; P. Chaigneau, 2013, Explaining the structure of CEO incentive pay with decreasing relative risk aversion, *Journal of Economics and Business*, 67: 4–23.

86. S. J. G. Girod & R. Whittington, 2017, Reconfiguration, restructuring and firm performance: Dynamic capabilities and environmental dynamism, *Strategic Management Journal*, 38: 1121–1133; S. Nankarni & J. Chen, 2014, Bridging yesterday, today and tomorrow: CEO temporal focus, environmental dynamism and rate of new product introduction, *Academy of Management Journal*, 57: 1810–1833.

87. E. G. Love, J. Lim, & M. K. Bednar, 2017, The face of the firm: The influence of CEOs on corporate reputation, *Academy of Management Journal*, 60: 1462–1481; R. Mudambi & T. Swift, 2014, Knowing when to leap: Transitioning between exploitative and explorative R&D, *Strategic Management Journal*, 31: 803–821.

88. E. G. Love, J. Lim, & M. K. Bednar, 2017, The face of the firm: The influence of CEOs on corporate reputation, *Academy of Management Journal*, 60: 1462–1481; G. A. Shinkle & B. T. McCann, 2014, New product deployment: The moderating influence of economic institutional context, *Strategic Management Journal*, 31: 803–821.

89. A. Nicholson, C. Spiller, & E. Pio, 2018, Ambicultural governance: Harmonizing indigenous and Western approaches, *Journal of Management Inquiry*, in press; M.-J. Chen & D. Miller, 2012, West meets east: Toward an ambicultural approach to management, *Academy of Management Perspectives*, 24: 17–24.

90. M.-J. Chen & G. Yemen, 2017, Ambiculture: Seeking the multicultural middle, *SSRN Papers*, https://papers.ssrn.com/sol3/papers.cfm?abstract_id=2975250; U. Stettner & D. Lavie, 2014, Ambidexterity under scrutiny: Exploration and exploitation via internal organization, alliances and acquisitions, *Strategic Management Journal*, 35: 1903–1925.

91. M. M. Hasan & A. (Wai-Kong) Cheung, 2018, Organizational capital and firm life cycle, *Journal of Corporate Finance*, 48: 556–578.

92. A. C. O. Siqueira, N. Guenste, T. Vanacker, & S. Crucke, 2018, A longitudinal comparison of capital structure between young for-profit social and commercial enterprises, *Journal of Business Venturing*, 33: 225–240.

93. 2017, Core competencies, *Bain & Company*, www.bain.com, November, 7.

94. A. Carr, 2013, Death to core competency: Lessons from Nike, Apple, Netflix, *Fast Company*, www.fastcompany.com, February 14.

95. S. S. Morris, S. A. Alvarez, J. B. Barney, & J. C. Molloy, 2017, Firm-specific human capital investments as a signal of general value: Revisiting assumptions about human capital and how it is managed, *Strategic Management Journal*, 38: 912–919; P. M. Wright, R. Coff, & T. P. Moliterno, 2014, Strategic human capital: Crossing the great divide, *Journal of Management*, 40: 353–370.

96. C. Chadwick, 2017, Toward a more comprehensive model of firms' human capital rents, *Academy of Management Review*, 42: 499–519; M. A. Hitt, L. Bierman, K. Uhlenbruck, & K. Shimizu, 2006, The importance of resources in the internationalization of professional service firms: The good, the bad and the ugly, *Academy of Management Journal*, 49: 1137–1157.

97. R. S. Nason, 2018, An assessment of resource-based theorizing on firm growth and suggestions for the future, *Journal of Management*, 44: 32–60; J. E. Delery & D. Roumpi, 2017, Strategic human resource management, human capital and competitive advantage: Is the field going in circles? *Human Resource Management*, 27: 1–21; A. Mackey, J. C. Molloy, & S. S. Morris, 2014, Scarce human capital in managerial labor markets, *Journal of Management*, 40: 399–421.

98. A. Chatterji & A. Patro, 2014, Dynamic capabilities and managing human capital, *Academy of Management Perspectives*, 28: 395–408; R. R. Kehoe & P. M. Wright, 2013, The impact of high-performance human resource practices on employees' attitudes and behaviors, *Journal of Management*, 39: 366–391.

99. J. C. Canedo, G. Graen, & M. Grace, 2018, Let's make performance management work for new hires: They are the future, *Organizational Dynamics*, in press; M. Moeen & R. Agarwal, 2017, Incubation of an industry: Heterogeneous knowledge bases and modes of value capture, *Strategic Management Journal*, 38: 566–587.

100. J. Chatterjee, 2017, Strategy, human capital investments, business-domain capabilities, and performance: A study in the global software services industry, *Strategic Management Journal*, 38: 588–608; R. Demir, K. Wennberg, & A. McKelvie, 2017, The strategic management of high-growth firms: A review and theoretical conceptualization, *Long Range Planning*, 50: 431–456.

101. L. Weber, 2017, A sociocognitive view of repeated interfirm exchanges: How the coevolution of trust and learning impacts subsequent contracts, *Organization Science*, 28: 744–759; J. R. Lecuona & M. Reitzig, 2014, Knowledge worth having in 'excess': The value of tacit and firm-specific human resource slack, *Strategic Management Journal*, 35: 954–973.

102. S. T. Hunter, L. D. Cushenbery, & B. Jayne, 2017, Why dual leaders will drive innovation: Resolving the exploration and exploitation dilemma with a conservation of resources solution, *Journal of Organizational Behavior*, 38: 1183–1195; Y. Zheng, A. S. Miner, & G. George, 2013, Does the learning value of individual failure experience depend on group-level success? Insights from a university technology transfer office, *Industrial and Corporate Change*, 22: 1557–1586.

103. J.-M. Ross, J. H. Fisch, & E. Varga, 2018, Unlocking the value of real options: How firm-specific learning conditions affect R&D investments under uncertainty, *Strategic Entrepreneurship Journal*, in press.

104. C. Gao, T. Zuzul, G. Jones, & T. Khanna, 2017, Overcoming institutional voids: A reputation-based view of long-run survival, *Strategic Management Journal*, 38: 2147–2167; R. E. Hoskisson, W. Shi, H. Yi, & J. Jin, 2013, The evolution and strategic positioning of private equity firms, *Academy of Management Perspectives*, 27: 22–38; P. M. Norman, F. C. Butler, & A. L. Ranft, 2013, Resources matter: Examining the effects of resources on the state of firms following downsizing, *Journal of Management*, 39: 2009–2038.

105. L. J. Barclay, M. R. Bashshur, & M. Fortin, 2017, Motivated cognition and fairness: Insights, integration, and creating a path forward, *Journal of Applied Psychology*, 102: 867–889; M. Richter & C. J. Konig, 2017, Explaining individuals' justification of layoffs, *Journal of Applied Social Psychology*, 47: 331–346; R. J. Bies, 2013, The delivery of bad news in organizations: A framework for analysis, *Journal of Management*, 39: 136–162.

106. S. Tasheva & A. Hillman, 2018, Integrating diversity at different levels: Multi-level human capital, social capital, and demographic diversity and their implications for team effectiveness, *Academy of Management Review*, in press; D. A. Basuil & D. K. Datta, 2017, Value creation in cross-border acquisitions: The role of outside directors' human and social

capital, *Journal of Business Research*, 80: 35–44.

107. V. Lurkov & G. R. G. Benito, 2018, Domestic alliance networks and regional strategies of MNEs: A structural embeddedness perspective, *Journal of International Business Studies*, in press; D. W. Elfenbein & T. Zenger, 2017, Creating and capturing value in repeated exchange relationships: The second paradox of embeddedness, *Organization Science*, 28: 894–914.
108. O. Alexy, J. West, H. Klapper, & M. Reitzig, 2018, Surrendering control to gain advantage: Reconciling openness and the resource-based view of the firm, *Strategic Management Journal*, in press; V. M. Desai, 2018, Collaborative stakeholder engagement: An integration between theories of organizational legitimacy and learning, *Academy of Management Journal*, 61: 220–244.
109. A. M. Kleinbaum & T. E. Stuart, 2014, Inside the black box of the corporate staff: Social networks and the implementation of corporate strategy, *Strategic Management Journal*, 35: 24–47.
110. J. Fortwengel, 2017, Practice transfer in organizations: The role of governance mode for internal and external fit, *Organization Science*, 28: 690–710; D. K. Panda, 2014, Managerial networks and strategic orientation in SMEs: Experience from a transition economy, *Journal of Strategy and Management*, 7: 376–397; B. J. Hallen & K. M. Eisenhardt, 2012, Catalyzing strategies and efficient tie formation: How entrepreneurial firms obtain investment ties, *Academy of Management Journal*, 55: 35–70.
111. R. H. Hamilton & H. K. Davison, 2018, The search for skills: Knowledge stars and innovation in the hiring process, *Business Horizons*, 61: 409–419; S. Fainshmidt & M. L. Frazier, 2017, What facilitates dynamic capabilities? The role of organizational climate for trust, *Long Range Planning*, 50: 550–566; J. B. Barney, 1986, Organizational culture: Can it be a source of sustained competitive advantage? *Academy of Management Review*, 11: 656–665.
112. S. Chattopadhyay & P. Choudhury, 2017, Sink or swim: The role of workplace context in shaping career advancement and human-capital development, *Organization Science*, 28: 211–227; B. Schneider, M. G. Ehrhard, & W. H. Macey, 2013, Organizational climate and culture, *Annual Review of Psychology*, 64: 361–388.
113. B. Spigel & R. Harrison, 2018, Toward a process theory of entrepreneurial ecosystems, *Strategic Entrepreneurship Journal*, 12: 151–168; M. S. Wood & W. McKinley, 2017, After the venture: The reproduction and destruction of entrepreneurial opportunity, *Strategic Entrepreneurship Journal*, 11: 18–35; C. B. Dobni, M. Klassen, & W. T. Nelson, 2015, Innovation strategy in the US: Top executives offer their views, *Journal of Business Strategy* 36(1): 3–13.
114. D. A. Lerner, R. A. Hunt, & D. Dimov, 2018, Action: Moving beyond the intendedly-rational logics of entrepreneurship, *Journal of Business Venturing*, 33: 52–69; P. Vogel, 2017, From venture idea to venture opportunity, *Entrepreneurship Theory and Practice*, 41: 943–971; M. S. Wood, A. McKelvie, & J. M. Haynie, 2014, Making it personal: Opportunity individuation and the shaping of opportunity beliefs, *Journal of Business Venturing*, 29: 252–272.
115. L. Trigeorgis & J. J. Reuer, 2017, Real options theory in strategic management, *Strategic Management Journal*, 38: 42–63; Y. Tang, J. Li, & H. Yang, 2015, What I see, what I do: How executive hubris affects firm innovation, *Journal of Management*, 41: 1698–1723.
116. P. Ozcan, 2018, Growing with the market: How changing conditions during market growth affect formation and evolution of interfirm ties, *Strategic Management Journal*, 39: 295–328; H. T. J. Smit & L. Trigeorgis, 2017, Strategic NPV: Real options and strategic games under different information structures, *Strategic Management Journal*, 38: 2555–2578; T. W. Tong & S. Li, 2013, The assignment of call option rights between partners in international joint ventures, *Strategic Management Journal*, 34: 1232–1243.
117. M. Gruber & I. C. MacMillan, 2017, Entrepreneurial behavior: A reconceptualization and extension based on identity theory, *Strategic Entrepreneurship Journal*, 11: 271–286; C. Bjornskov & N. Foss, 2013, How strategic entrepreneurship and the institutional context drive economic growth, *Strategic Entrepreneurship Journal*, 7: 50–69; M. A. Hitt, R. D. Ireland, D. G. Sirmon, & C.A. Trahms, 2011, Strategic entrepreneurship: Creating value for individuals, organizations, and society, *Academy of Management Perspectives*, 25: 57–75.
118. T. Wang, S. Thornhill, & J. O. de Castro, 2017, Entrepreneurial orientation, legitimation, and new venture performance, *Strategic Entrepreneurship Journal*, 11: 373–392; G. T. Lumpkin & G. G. Dess, 1996, Clarifying the entrepreneurial orientation construct and linking it to performance, *Academy of Management Review*, 21: 135–172.
119. Lumpkin & Dess, Clarifying the entrepreneurial orientation construct, 142.
120. M. Hughes-Morgan, K. Kolev, & G. McNamara, 2018, A meta-analytic review of competitive aggressiveness research, *Journal of Business Research*, 85: 73–82.
121. R. Wiedner, M. Barrett, & E. Oborn, 2017, The emergence of change in unexpected places: Resourcing across organizational practices in strategic change, *Academy of Management Journal*, 60: 823–854; C. O'Kane & J. Cunningham, 2014, Turnaround leadership core tensions during the company turnaround process, *European Management Review*, 32: 968–980.
122. D. Fan, C. K. Y. Lo, A. C. L. Yeung, & T. C. E. Cheng, 2018, The impact of corporate label change on long-term labor productivity, *Journal of Business Research*, 86: 96–108; C. R. Greer, R. F. Lusch, & M. A. Hitt, 2017, A service perspective for human capital resources: A critical base for strategy implementation, *Academy of Management Perspectives*, 31: 137–158.
123. B. Koene, 2017, Why middle managers, rather than senior leaders, should initiate organizational change, *Forbes*, www.forbes.com, November 17.
124. E. M. Anicich & J. B. Hirsh, 2017, The psychology of middle power: Vertical code-switching, role conflict, and behavioral inhibition, *Academy of Management Review*, 42: 659–682; R. Wiedner, M. Barrett, & E. Oborn, 2017, The emergence of change in unexpected places: Resourcing across organizational practices in strategic change, *Academy of Management Journal*, 60: 823–854.
125. A. Kornelakis, 2018, Why are your reward strategies not working? The role of shareholder value, country context, and employee voice, *Business Horizons*, 61: 107–113; S. Oreg, J. M. Bartunek, G. Lee, & B. Do, 2018, An affect-based model of recipients' responses to organizational change events, *Academy of Management Review*, 43: 65–86.
126. D. Welch, 2017, At Mary Barra's GM, it's profit before all else, *BloombergBusinessweek*, www.bloomberg.com, May 18.
127. M. Colias, 2018, General Motors to shutter South Korea plant, *MarketWatch*, www.marketwatch.com, February 13.
128. Z. Liu, Q. Huang, J. Dou, & X. Zhao, 2017, The impact of informal social interaction on innovation capability in the context of buyer-supplier dyads, *Journal of Business Research*, 78: 314–322..
129. S. Arjoon, A. Turriago-Hoyos, & U. Thoene, 2017, Virtuousness and the common good as a conceptual framework for harmonizing the goals of the individual, organizations, and the economy, *Journal of Business Ethics*, 147: 143–163; P. Schneider & G. Bose, 2017, Organizational cultures of corruption, *Journal of Public Economic Theory*, 19: 59–80; J. L. Campbell & A. S. Goritz, 2014, Culture corrupts! A qualitative study of organizational culture in corrupt organizations, *Journal of Business Ethics*, 120: 291–311.
130. D. Lee, Y. Choi, S. Youn, & J. U. Chun, 2017, Ethical leadership and employee moral voice: The mediating role of moral efficacy and the moderating role of leader-follower value congruence, *Journal of Business Ethics*, 141: 47–57; M. Zhao, 2013, Beyond cops and robbers: The contextual challenge driving the multinational corporation public crisis in China and Russia, *Business Horizons*, 56: 491–501.

131. P. Deb, P. David, & J. O'Brien, 2017, When is cash good or bad for firm performance? *Strategic Management Journal*, 38: 436–454; H. A. Ndofor, C. Wesley, & R. L. Priem, 2015, Providing CEOs with opportunities to cheat: The effects of complexity based information asymmetries on financial reporting fraud, *Journal of Management*, 41: 1774–1797.

132. H. Park & Y. Yoo, 2017, A literature review on chief executive officer hubris and related constructs: Is the theory of chief executive officer hubris an antecedent or consequence? *Journal of Applied Business Research*, 33: 705–720; K. T. Haynes, J. T. Campbell, & M. A. Hitt, 2015, When more is not enough: Executive greed and its influence on shareholder wealth, *Journal of Management*, 43: 555–584, G. B. Dagnino & A. Mina, 2014, The origin of failure: A multidisciplinary appraisal of the hubris hypothesis and proposed research agenda, *Academy of Management Perspectives*, 28: 447–468.

133. W. Shi, B. L. Connelly, & R. E. Hoskisson, 2017, External corporate governance and financial fraud: Cognitive evaluation theory insights on agency theory prescriptions, *Strategic Management Journal*, 38: 1268–1286; K. A. Gangloff, B. L. Connelly, & C. L. Shook, 2016, Of scapegoats and signals: Investor reactions to CEO succession in the aftermath of wrongdoing, *Journal of Management*, 42: 1614–1634; D. Gomulya & W. Boeker, 2014, How firms respond to financial restatement: CEO successors and external reactions, *Academy of Management Journal*, 57: 1759–1785.

134. B. Cuardrado-Ballesteros, L. R. Ariza, I.-M. Garcia-Sanchez, & J. Martinez-Ferrero, 2017, The mediating effect of ethical codes on the link between family firms and their social performance, *Long Range Planning*, 50: 756–765; M. S. Schwartz, 2013, Developing and sustaining an ethical corporate culture: The core elements, *Business Horizons*, 118: 635–637.

135. S. Mo & J. Shi, 2017, Linking ethical leadership to employees' organizational citizenship behavior: Testing the multilevel mediation role of organizational concern, *Journal of Business Ethics*, 141: 151–162; D. D. Warrick, 2017, What leaders need to know about organizational culture, *Business Horizons*, 60: 395–404; W. H. Bishop, 2013, The role of ethics in 21st century organizations, *Journal of Business Ethics*, 33: 670–684.

136. 2018, Control (management), https://en.wikipedia.org/wiki/Management_control_system *Wikipedia*, February 16.

137. R. D. O'Brien, D. Michaels, & M. Rapoport, 2018, Former KPMG executives charged with conspiracy, *Wall Street Journal*, www.wsj.com, January 22.

138. C. Bray, KPMG fires 6 over ethics breach on audit warnings, 2017, *New York Times*, www.wsj.com, April 12.

139. M. Quinn, M. R. W. Hiebl, K. Moores, & J. B. Craig, 2018, Future research on management accounting and control in family firms: Governance, entrepreneurship and stewardship, *Journal of Management Control*, 28: 529–546.

140. 2018, Balanced scorecard, *Wikipedia*, https://en.wikipedia.org/wiki/Balanced_scorecard, February 16; J. Sun, S. Wu, & K. Yang, 2018, An ecosystem framework for business sustainability, *Business Horizons*, 61: 59–72.

141. J. Pryshlakivsky & C. Searcy, 2017, A heuristic model for establishing trade-offs in corporate sustainability performance measurement systems, *Journal of Business Ethics*, 144: 323–342; B. E. Becker, M.A. Huselid, & D. Ulrich, 2001, *The HR Scorecard: Linking People, Strategy, and Performance*, Boston, MA: Harvard Business Press, 21.

142. D. Wang, T. Feng, & A. Lawton, 2017, Linking ethical leadership with firm performance: A multi-dimensional perspective, *Journal of Business Ethics*, 145: 95–109; K. T. Haynes, M. A. Josefy, & M. A. Hitt, 2015, Tipping point: Managers' self-interest, greed, and altruism, *Journal of Leadership & Organizational Studies*, 22: 265–279.

143. R. G. Bento, L. Mertins, & L. F. White, 2017, Ideology and the balanced scorecard: An empirical exploration of the tension between shareholder value maximization and corporate social responsibility, *Journal of Business Ethics*, 142: 769–789; R. S. Kaplan, 2012, The balanced scorecard: Comments on balanced scorecard commentaries, *Journal of Accounting and Organizational Change*, 8: 539–545.

144. D. J. Cooper, M. Ezzamel, & S. Q. Qu, 2017, Popularizing a management accounting idea: The case of the balanced scorecard, *Contemporary Accounting Research*, 34: 991–1025; A. Danaei & A. Hosseini, 2013, Performance measurement using balanced scorecard: A case study of the pipe industry, *Management Science Letters*, 3: 1433–1438.

145. G. Rowe, 2001, Creating wealth in organizations: The role of strategic leadership, *Academy of Management Executive*, 15: 81–94.

146. S. J. G. Girod & R. Whittington, 2017, Reconfiguration, restructuring and firm performance: Dynamic capabilities and environmental dynamism, *Strategic Management Journal*, 38: 1121–1133; J. Xia & S. Li, 2013, The divestiture of acquired subunits: A resource dependence approach, *Strategic Management Journal*, 34: 131–148.

147. O. Alexy, J. West, H. Klapper, & M. Reitzig, 2018, Surrendering control to gain advantage: Reconciling openness and the resource-based view of the firm, *Strategic Management Journal*, June, 1704–1727; J. Wincent, S. Thorgren, & S. Anokhin, 2013, Managing maturing government-supported networks: The shift from monitoring to embeddedness controls, *British Journal of Management*, 24: 480–497.

148. J. Leitch, D. Lancefield, & M. Dawson, 2016, 10 principles of strategic leadership, *Strategy+business*, www.strategy-business.com, May 18.

13

Strategic Entrepreneurship

Studying this chapter should provide you with the strategic management knowledge needed to:

13-1 Define strategic entrepreneurship and corporate entrepreneurship.

13-2 Define entrepreneurship and entrepreneurial opportunities and explain their importance.

13-3 Define invention, innovation, and imitation, and describe the relationship among them.

13-4 Describe entrepreneurs and the entrepreneurial mind-set.

13-5 Explain international entrepreneurship and its importance.

13-6 Describe how firms internally develop innovations.

13-7 Explain how firms use cooperative strategies to innovate.

13-8 Describe how firms use acquisitions as a means of innovation.

13-9 Explain how strategic entrepreneurship helps firms create value.

iStock.com/DNY59

TODAY IT IS GAS AND DIESEL: TOMORROW IT IS LIKELY TO BE ELECTRIC VEHICLES, PLUG-IN HYBRIDS, AND DRIVERLESS CARS AND TRUCKS

As explained in this chapter, firms engaging in strategic entrepreneurship concentrate on advantage-seeking and opportunity-seeking behaviors simultaneously. In essence, this concentration finds firms seeking entrepreneurial opportunities in their external environment that they can exploit through innovations and by successfully executing their chosen strategies. When engaging in strategic entrepreneurship, firms develop innovations through internal investments, by using cooperative strategies and acquisitions strategies. Focusing on advantage- and opportunity-seeking behaviors simultaneously is challenging in that by doing so, a firm concentrates on selling its current products while seeking to identify needs in the marketplace that it can serve by innovating. As an example, consider the fact that currently, Ford Motor Co. earns the bulk of its profits by selling large pick-up trucks and sport-utility vehicles. However, for a number of reasons including environmental sustainability, consumer demand, and governmental regulations, the firm sees electric and plug-in hybrids along with driverless cars and trucks as an opportunity that it should pursue through product innovations. To do this, Ford intends to allocate $11 billion to R&D between 2018 and 2022 to develop new and innovative transportation products. Volkswagen AG too identified producing electric, plug-in hybrid, and driverless products as an opportunity to pursue through innovation and chose to commit $40 billion to R&D between 2018 and 2023 to develop these products.

Chris Ratcliffe/Bloomberg/Getty Images

Sedric, the first autonomous automobile from Volkswagen, on display in Geneva, Switzerland.

The situation for global automobile manufacturers, such as Ford and Volkswagen, who are today earning the majority of their profits by selling gasoline and diesel powered cars and trucks, is likely to be far different in the future. Resulting from environmental concerns, some changes in consumer preferences, and anticipated regulations are opportunities for these companies to innovate in ways that will result in competitive success. Demonstrating this opportunity are predictions of increases in the sales volume of electric and hybrid vehicles along with the continuing advances with driverless cars and trucks. At the end of 2017, for example, worldwide sales of electric and plug-in hybrid models exceeded three million units. Predictions at that time were that the total number of these units would exceed 5 million by the end of 2018 and that the rate of annual growth in sales of these types of vehicles beginning in 2019 and continuing would be significant. These predictions yield significant opportunities to innovate as a way to satisfy consumer and societal demands in terms of transportation vehicles.

Driverless vehicles are another opportunity for companies to pursue. In about 2007, General Motors was the first major automaker to envision driverless vehicles as a viable and important opportunity to pursue through innovation. Today, a multitude of companies, including Internet firms (e.g., Amazon), chipmakers (e.g., Microsoft), and software vendors (e.g., Cisco) , see driverless vehicles as a viable opportunity to pursue by innovating.

Firms are using different approaches to pursue the driverless vehicle opportunity. Aptiv, the automotive-technology company previously named Delphi Automotive, initially partnered with Lyft, Inc., the ride-sharing firm. Ford also established a partnership with Lyft as a means of testing its driverless products.

Given the complexity of the opportunity, driverless vehicles require additional testing and development before becoming a viable option for a significant number of customers. In 2018, some predicted that Ford and General Motors had the highest probability of first introducing a meaningful number of viable driverless products into global markets. Ford, in fact, intends to roll out a fleet of driverless vehicles in 2021 that provides ride-sharing and ride-hailing services.

Automotive companies are not the only ones visualizing electric vehicles, plug-in hybrids, and self-driving products as an opportunity to pursue. 3M, for example, is focusing on how to tailor many of its products for what it sees as "auto electrification," such as developing cooling fluids for batteries. 3M also sees driverless vehicles as an opportunity. In early 2018, the firm tested stickers that are "transparent to the naked eye but actually contain bar codes that autonomous cars will be able to read" as a means of keeping track of their position. PPG Industries, the Pittsburgh-based paints and coatings manufacturer, is committed to developing car paints "to become more visible to electronic sensors that guide autonomous vehicles."

Sources: M. Colias, 2018, Ford increasing electric vehicle investment to $11 billion by 2022, *Wall Street Journal*, www.wsj.com, January 14; T. Higgins, 2018, Driverless-car companies try to rev their engines on commercial prospects, *Wall Street Journal*, www.wsj.com, January 8; T. Higgins, VW, Hyundai turn to driverless-car startup in Silicon Valley, *Wall Street Journal*, www.wsj.com, January 4; A. Levy & L. Kolodny, 2018, Self-driving cars take over CES: Here's how big tech is playing the market, *CNBC News*, www.cnbc.com, January 12; J. C. Reindl, 2018, Next step in driverless cars: Boot the driver, *USA Today*, www.usatoday.com, January 10; D. Muoio, 2017, Ranked: The 18 companies most likely to get self-driving cars on the road first, *Business Insider*, www.businessinsider.com, September 27; J. Stern & C. Mims, 2017, Tech that will change your life in 2018, *Wall Street Journal*, www.wsj.com, December 27; A. Tangel, 2017, Latest entrants into electric car race: Makers of Post-It notes, paint, *Wall Street Journal*, www.wsj.com, December 26.

The focus of this chapter is on strategic entrepreneurship, which is a framework firms use to integrate effectively their entrepreneurial and strategic actions.[1] More formally, **strategic entrepreneurship** involves taking entrepreneurial actions using a strategic perspective. In this process, the firm tries to find opportunities in its external environment that it can exploit through innovations. Identifying opportunities to exploit through innovations is the *entrepreneurship* dimension of strategic entrepreneurship; determining the best way to manage the firm's innovation efforts competitively is the *strategic* dimension.[2]

As explained in the Opening Case, 3M identified electrified and driverless vehicles as an opportunity for it to pursue through innovations. Demonstrating the size of this opportunity for 3M and others is the prediction in 2018 that the market "for cockpit electronics; crash-avoidance and automation systems; and components for electric, hybrid and fuel-cell powered vehicles will nearly triple to $183 billion by 2022."[3] While continuing to develop product innovations to address this opportunity, such as new types of road markings and signs that will allow better communication with cars' navigation systems as well as coatings for exterior sensors, 3M is simultaneously considering strategies to use to sell these products to automotive manufacturers. Ford has a new CEO in place whose charge includes developing and managing the strategies the firm will use to introduce its electrified and driverless products to the marketplace.[4] Interestingly, the new CEO comes from an office furniture background. His choice as the person to lead development of Ford's strategy for taking advantage of its innovations in terms of electrified and driverless vehicles is partly a function of his ability to transform how people work and how they think about using new products.[5] As these examples show, firms using strategic entrepreneurship integrate their actions to find opportunities, innovate, and then implement strategies for the purpose of appropriating value from the innovations they have developed to pursue identified opportunities.[6]

Strategic entrepreneurship involves taking entrepreneurial actions using a strategic perspective.

We consider several topics to explain strategic entrepreneurship. First, we examine entrepreneurship and innovation in a strategic context. We present definitions of entrepreneurship, entrepreneurial opportunities, and entrepreneurs (those who engage in entrepreneurship to pursue entrepreneurial opportunities). We then describe international entrepreneurship, a process through which firms take entrepreneurial actions outside their home market. After this, the chapter shifts to descriptions of the three ways firms innovate—internally, through cooperative strategies, and by acquiring other companies.[7] We discuss these methods separately. Not surprisingly though, most large firms use all three methods to innovate. The chapter closes with summary comments about how firms use strategic entrepreneurship to create value.

Before turning to the chapter's topics, we note that a major portion of the material in this chapter deals with entrepreneurship and innovation that takes place in established organizations. Corporate entrepreneurship is the term describing entrepreneurship and innovation taking place in ongoing firms. More formally, **corporate entrepreneurship** is the use or application of entrepreneurship within an established firm.[8] Corporate entrepreneurship is critical to the survival and success of for-profit organizations[9] as well as public agencies.[10] Of course, innovation and entrepreneurship play a critical role in the degree of success achieved by start-up entrepreneurial ventures as well. Because of this, what we discuss in this chapter is equally important in both entrepreneurial ventures and established organizations.

13-1 Entrepreneurship and Entrepreneurial Opportunities

Entrepreneurship is the process by which individuals, teams, or organizations identify and pursue entrepreneurial opportunities without being immediately constrained by the resources they currently control.[11] **Entrepreneurial opportunities** are conditions in which new goods or services can satisfy a need in the market. These opportunities exist because of competitive imperfections in markets and among the factors of production used to produce them, or because they were independently developed by entrepreneurs.[12] Entrepreneurial opportunities come in many forms, such as the chance to develop and sell a new product and the chance to sell an existing product in a new market.[13] Firms should be receptive to pursuing entrepreneurial opportunities whenever and wherever they may surface. In 2005, for example, Amazon launched Amazon Prime. Initially $79 annually, this fee gave customers free two-day delivery on a large number of items. The entrepreneurial opportunity Amazon identified was to satisfy customers' needs for faster delivery of a host of products. A significant benefit the firm has gained through Amazon Prime is that these customers tend to spend more with the firm compared to non-Prime members.[14]

As the definitions of entrepreneurship and entrepreneurial opportunities suggest, the essence of entrepreneurship is to identify and exploit entrepreneurial opportunities—that is, opportunities others do not see or for which they do not recognize the commercial potential—and manage risks appropriately as they arise.[15] As a process, entrepreneurship results in the "creative destruction" of existing products (goods or services) or methods of producing them and replaces them with new products and production methods.[16] Crypto currencies such as Bitcoin and Ripple may have the potential to replace long established methods of financial transactions. Start-up firm Ripple claims that it provides a "frictionless experience to send money globally using the power of blockchain. By joining Ripple's growing global network," the firm suggests, "financial institutions can process their customers' payments anywhere in the world instantly, reliably and cost-effectively."[17]

Corporate entrepreneurship is the use or application of entrepreneurship within an established firm.

Entrepreneurship is the process by which individuals, teams, or organizations identify and pursue entrepreneurial opportunities without being immediately constrained by the resources they currently control.

Entrepreneurial opportunities are conditions in which new goods or services can satisfy a need in the market.

Time will tell if crypto currencies bring about the "creative destruction" of existing means of global finance. Overall, firms committed to entrepreneurship place high value on individual innovations as well as the ability to innovate across time.[18]

We study entrepreneurship at the level of the individual firm. However, evidence suggests that entrepreneurship is the economic engine driving many nations' economies in the global competitive landscape.[19] Thus, entrepreneurship and the innovation it spawns are important for companies competing in the global economy and for countries seeking to stimulate economic climates with the potential to enhance the living standard of their citizens.

13-2 Innovation

In his classic work, *The Theory of Economic Development*, Joseph Schumpeter argued that firms engage in three types of innovative activities.[20] **Invention** is the act of creating or developing a new product or process. **Innovation** is a process used to create a commercial product from an invention. Thus, innovation follows invention[21] in that invention brings something new into being while innovation brings something new into use. Accordingly, firms use technical criteria to determine the success of an invention whereas they use commercial criteria to determine the success of an innovation.[22] Finally, **imitation** is the adoption of a similar innovation by different firms. Imitation usually leads to product standardization; commonly, imitative products have fewer features and a lower price for customers. Entrepreneurship is critical to innovative activity because it acts as the linchpin between invention and innovation.[23]

For most companies, innovation is the most critical of the three types of innovative activities. The reason for this is that while many companies are able to create ideas that lead to inventions, commercializing those inventions sometimes proves to be difficult.[24] Patents are a strategic asset, and the ability to produce them regularly can be an important source of competitive advantage, especially when a firm intends to commercialize an invention and when a firm competes in a knowledge-intensive industry (e.g., pharmaceuticals).[25] In a competitive sense, patents create entry barriers for a firm's potential competitors.[26] However, in general, entry barriers provide less protection from competition for firms competing in the global economy. In the view of the chief information officer for Unilever, the giant consumer foods manufacturer, "basically there are no entry barriers" to prevent start-ups from entering the markets in which his firm competes.[27] Reasons for fewer entry barriers in Unilever's case include consumers' demands for natural ingredients in healthier products and the fact that costs associated with manufacturing consumer goods have declined. Thus, the challenge for today's firms is to understand the degree to which their innovations create entry barriers for potential and existing competitors.

Peter Drucker argued that "innovation is the specific function of entrepreneurship, whether in an existing business, a public service institution, or a new venture started by a lone individual."[28] Moreover, Drucker suggested that innovation is "the means by which the entrepreneur either creates new wealth-producing resources or endows existing resources with enhanced potential for creating wealth."[29] Thus, entrepreneurship and the innovation resulting from it are critically important for all firms as they engage rivals in competitive battles.

The realities of global competition suggest that, to be market leaders, companies must innovate regularly. This means that innovation should be an intrinsic part of virtually all of a firm's activities. Moreover, firms should recognize the importance of their human capital's efforts to innovate.[30] Evidence suggests that particularly for radical innovation, workforce diversity increases human capital's ability to develop value-creating innovations.[31]

Invention is the act of creating or developing a new product or process.

Innovation is a process used to create a commercial product from an invention. Thus, innovation follows invention in that invention brings something new into being while innovation brings something new into use.

Imitation is the adoption of a similar innovation by different firms.

Thus, as this discussion suggests, innovation is a key outcome firms seek through entrepreneurship, and it is often the source of competitive success, especially for companies competing in highly competitive and turbulent environments.[32]

13-3 Entrepreneurs

Entrepreneurs are individuals, acting independently or as part of an organization, who perceive an entrepreneurial opportunity and then take risks to develop an innovation and exploit it. Entrepreneurs exist throughout different parts of organizations—from top-level managers to those working to produce a firm's products.[33]

Entrepreneurs tend to demonstrate several characteristics: they are highly motivated, willing to take responsibility for their projects, self-confident, and often optimistic.[34] In addition, entrepreneurs tend to be passionate and emotional about the value and importance of their innovation-based ideas.[35] They are able to deal with uncertainty and are more alert to opportunities than are others.[36] To be successful, entrepreneurs often need to have good social skills and to plan exceptionally well (e.g., to obtain venture capital).[37]

Being committed to and engaging in entrepreneurship within organizations demands significant effort from entrepreneurs. On the other hand, pursuing entrepreneurial opportunities by working as an entrepreneur can be highly satisfying—particularly when entrepreneurs recognize and follow their passions. According to Jeff Bezos, Amazon.com's founder:

Smith Collection/Gado/Getty Images

Jeff Bezos's strategy of continuous evolution earned Amazon the title of Most Innovative Company in 2017.

"One of the huge mistakes people make is that they try to force an interest on themselves. You don't choose your passions; your passions choose you."[38]

Evidence suggests that successful entrepreneurs have an entrepreneurial mind-set. An individual with an **entrepreneurial mind-set** values uncertainty in markets and continuously seeks to identify opportunities in those markets to pursue through innovation.[39] In contrast, those without an entrepreneurial mind-set tend to view opportunities to innovate as threats. Importantly, an entrepreneurial mind-set also includes recognition of the importance of competing internationally as well as domestically.[40]

Because it has the potential to lead to continuous innovations, an individual's entrepreneurial mind-set can be a source of competitive advantage for a firm. Knowledge to which individuals throughout a firm have easy access facilitates development and use of an entrepreneurial mind-set. Indeed, research shows that units within firms are more innovative when people have access to new knowledge.[41] Transferring knowledge, however, can be difficult, often because the receiving party must have adequate absorptive capacity (or the ability) to understand the knowledge and to use it productively.[42] Learning requires a link between the new knowledge and the existing knowledge. Thus,

Entrepreneurs are individuals, acting independently or as part of an organization, who perceive an entrepreneurial opportunity and then take risks to develop an innovation and exploit it.

Entrepreneurial mind-set values uncertainty in markets and continuously seeks to identify opportunities in those markets to pursue through innovation.

managers need to develop the capabilities of their human capital to build on their current knowledge base while incrementally expanding it.

Some companies demonstrate a strong commitment to entrepreneurship, suggesting that many working within them have an entrepreneurial mind-set. In 2017, *Fast Company* identified Amazon as the most innovative company, with Google, Uber, Apple, Snap, Facebook, Netflix, Twilio, Chobani, and Spotify rounding out the top ten most innovative firms.[43] Amazon's selection as the most innovative company in 2017 is largely a function of the firm's ability to "offer even more, even faster, and smarter." A strong commitment to continuous improvement and innovation results in Amazon being nimble enough to act creatively as it moves into sector after sector as a means of serving ever-increasing types of customers' needs.

13-4 International Entrepreneurship

International entrepreneurship is a process in which firms creatively discover and exploit opportunities that are outside their domestic markets.[44] Entrepreneurship is a process that many firms exercise at both the domestic and international levels. This is true for entrepreneurial ventures as suggested by the fact that an increasing number of them (perhaps as much as 50 percent) move into international markets early in their life cycle. Large, established companies commonly have significant foreign operations and often start new ventures in international markets as well.[45]

A key reason that firms choose to engage in international entrepreneurship is that, in general, doing so enhances their performance.[46] Nonetheless, those leading firms generally understand that taking entrepreneurial actions in markets outside the firm's home setting is challenging and not without risks, including risks of unstable foreign currencies, market inefficiencies, insufficient infrastructures to support businesses, and limitations on market size.[47] Thus, the decision to engage in international entrepreneurship needs to be a product of careful analysis.

Even though entrepreneurship is a global phenomenon, its rate of use differs within individual countries. For example, one source ranked the world's 10 most entrepreneurial countries in 2017 in the following order (beginning with the most entrepreneurial): Switzerland, Sweden, Netherlands, United States, United Kingdom, Denmark, Singapore, Finland, Germany, and Ireland.[48] Switzerland's selection as the most innovative country is because of its knowledge-based economy and ability to convert innovative thinking into projects that yield value-creating products for customers. Those compiling the rankings suggest that in general, the most innovative countries engage students through creative teaching techniques, enforce progressive laws, conduct business through intellectually designed practices, and are willing to take risks. Revealing the difficulty of knowing the criteria to use to identify the world's most innovative countries is the fact that in another survey, the ten most innovative countries in 2017 from the most to the least creative were South Korea, Sweden, Germany, Switzerland, Finland, Singapore, Japan, Denmark, United States, and Israel.[49] Examining the two surveys' results highlights the innovativeness of Nordic countries and reveals a reasonable degree of consistency in that Sweden, Switzerland, Germany, United States, Singapore, and Denmark appear on both lists. Growth rates in the wealth of citizens and national wealth too, in the most entrepreneurial countries, suggest the possibility of a positive relationship between entrepreneurship and economic productivity.

International entrepreneurship is a process in which firms creatively discover and exploit opportunities that are outside their domestic markets.

Culture is one reason for differential rates of entrepreneurship among countries across the globe. More specifically, cultures balancing individual initiative and a spirit of cooperation and group ownership of innovation encourage entrepreneurial behaviors within organizations. This means that for firms to be entrepreneurial, they must provide appropriate autonomy and incentives for individual initiative to surface while simultaneously promoting cooperation and group ownership of an innovation as a foundation for successfully exploiting it. Thus, international entrepreneurship often requires teams of people with unique skills and resources, especially in cultures that place high value on either individualism or collectivism. In addition to a balance of values for individual initiative and cooperative behaviors, firms engaging in international entrepreneurship must concentrate more than companies engaging only in domestic entrepreneurship on building the capabilities needed to innovate and on acquiring the resources needed to make strategic decisions through which innovations can be exploited successfully.[50]

The level of investment outside of the home country made by young ventures is also an important dimension of international entrepreneurship. In fact, with increasing globalization, a larger number of new ventures have been "born global."[51] One reason for this is that new ventures that enter international markets increase their learning of new technological knowledge and thereby enhance their performance.[52] They increase their knowledge through the external networks (e.g., suppliers, customers) that they establish in the new foreign markets, including strategic alliances in which they participate.[53]

The probability of entering and successfully competing in international markets increases when the firm's strategic leaders, and especially its top-level managers, have international experience. Because of the learning and economies of scale and scope afforded by operating in international markets, both young and established internationally diversified firms often are stronger competitors in their domestic market as well. Additionally, as research has shown, internationally diversified firms are generally more innovative.[54]

A firm's ability to develop and sustain a competitive advantage may be based partly or largely on its ability to innovate. This is true for firms engaging in international entrepreneurship as well as those that have yet to do so. As we discuss next, firms can follow different paths to innovate internally. Internal innovation is the first of three approaches firms use to innovate, with cooperative strategies and acquisitions strategies being the other two.

13-5 Internal Innovation

Efforts in firms' research and development (R&D) function are one primary source of internal innovations. Through effective R&D, firms are able to generate patentable processes and products that are innovative in nature. Increasingly, successful R&D results from integrating the skills available in the global workforce. Thus, the ability to have a competitive advantage based on innovation is more likely to accrue to firms capable of integrating the talent of human capital from countries around the world.[55]

R&D and the new products and processes it can spawn affect a firm's efforts to earn above-average returns while competing in today's global environment. Because of this, firms try to use their R&D labs to create disruptive technologies and products. Although critical to long-term competitive success, the outcomes of R&D investments are uncertain and often not achieved in the short term, meaning that patience is required as firms evaluate the outcomes of their R&D efforts.[56]

As noted earlier, successful R&D programs must have high-quality human capital—star scientists. Yet, not all ideas begin in the laboratory. For example, firms have learned that customers are often good sources for new products that will satisfy their needs. Firms also use external networks such as other scientists, published research, and even alliance partners (discussed later in this chapter).[57] They may even be able to use public knowledge, such as that on a current technology, that can be combined to create an improved technology or perhaps even a new technology.

Companies use several methods to obtain employees' ideas for new products and other types of innovation. At Google, employees have "20 Percent Time," which allows them to dedicate up to 20 percent of their working hours to projects they believe have the greatest potential to benefit the firm through innovation.[58] GE Appliances built an innovation lab to be able to rapidly prototype new products. Called FirstBuild, this innovation lab and micro factory is a freestanding entrepreneurial start-up embedded within GE's appliance unit. FirstBuild team members collaborate with other GE industrial designers, scientists, engineers, and others to "design, build, and sell innovative home appliances."[59] At Ericsson, employees are encouraged to participate in "ideaboxes." After employees submit an idea, they form a partnership with "idea-to-innovation" managers to develop it further and determine if it is feasible and valuable. Ericsson then has an internal venture-funding group that provides startup capital to the best ideas.[60]

13-5a Incremental and Novel Innovation

Firms invest in R&D to produce two primary types of innovations—incremental and novel. Most innovations are *incremental*—that is, they build on existing knowledge bases and provide small improvements in current products. Incremental innovations are evolutionary and linear in nature.[61] In general, firms introduce incremental innovations into established markets where customers understand and accept a product's characteristics. In essence, incremental innovations exploit an existing technology to provide an improvement over a current product. From the firm's perspective, incremental innovations tend to yield lower profit margins compared to those associated with the outcomes of novel or breakthrough innovations, largely because competition among firms offering products to customers that have incremental innovations is primarily on the price variable.[62] Adding a different kind of whitening agent to a soap detergent is an example of an incremental innovation, as are minor improvements in the functionality in televisions (e.g., slightly better picture quality). Companies introduce to markets a larger number of incremental than radical innovations, largely because they are cheaper, easier to produce quickly, and involve less risk. Yet, firms normally cannot rely solely on incremental innovations. If they do so, they move from being market leaders to market laggards.[63] However, incremental innovation can be risky for firms if its frequency of introduction creates more change than can be appropriately absorbed.[64]

In contrast to incremental innovations, *radical innovations* usually provide significant technological changes and create new knowledge.[65] Revolutionary and nonlinear in nature, radical innovations typically use new technologies to serve newly created markets. The development of the original personal computer is an example of such an innovation as are the driverless cars discussed in the Opening Case. Additional examples of radical innovations include: (1) Salesforce's Customer Relationship Management system (highly innovative were the firm's launching of a new cloud computing technology platform and its business model of selling its software as a service), (2) Metromile's way of selling its product (a U.S. automobile insurance company, Metromile developed a new technology—a plug-in telematics device for a customer's car—as a foundation for using it so people can buy insurance on a per-mile-basis), and (3) Amazon's Dash button (this product, which is a small Wi-Fi connected device, allows customers to reorder household essentials such as razors, toilet paper, and washing powder at the click of a button).[66]

Developing new processes is a critical part of producing radical innovations. Both types of innovations can create value, meaning that firms should determine when it is appropriate to emphasize either incremental or radical innovation. However, radical innovations have the potential to contribute more significantly to a firm's efforts to earn above-average returns, although they also are more risky.

Radical innovations are rare because of the difficulty and risk involved in their development. The value of the technology and the market opportunities are highly uncertain.[67] Because radical innovation creates new knowledge and uses only some or little of a firm's current product or technological knowledge, creativity is required; creativity is as important to efforts to innovate in not-for-profit organizations as it is in for-profit firms.[68] Creativity is an outcome of using one's imagination. In the words of Jay Walker, founder of Priceline.com, "Imagination is the fuel. You're not going to get innovation if you don't have imagination." Imagination finds firms thinking about what customers will want in a changing world. For example, Walker says, those seeking to innovate within a firm could try to imagine "what the customer is going to want in a world where, for instance, their cellphone is in their glasses."[69] Imagination is more critical to radical than incremental innovations.

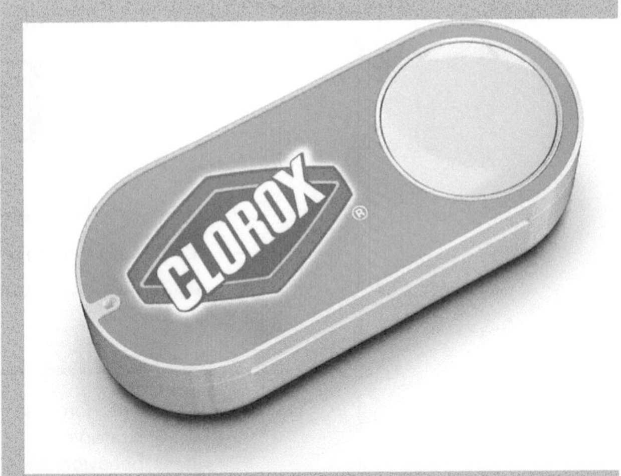

Amazon/Splash News/Newscom

An Amazon Dash Button allows customers to quickly reorder household items. Pictured here is a Dash Button for Clorox.

Surveys suggest that "creativity and innovation are the number 1 strategic priorities for organizations the world over."[70] However, creativity alone does not directly lead to innovation. Rather, creativity as generated through imagination discovers, combines, or synthesizes current knowledge, often from diverse areas.[71] Increasingly, when trying to innovate, firms seek knowledge from current users to understand their perspective about what could be beneficial innovations to the firm's products.[72] Collectively, employees use gathered knowledge to develop new, innovative products to introduce to new markets and to capture new customers—and gain access to new resources while doing so. Often, separate business units that start internal ventures produce the types of innovations that lead to these positive outcomes.

Strong, supportive leadership is required for the type of creativity and imagination needed to develop radical innovations. The fact that creativity is "messy, chaotic, sometimes even disgusting, and reeks of failure, experimentation, and disorganization"[73] is one set of reasons why leadership is so critical to its success.

This discussion highlights the fact that internally developed incremental and radical innovations result from using a set of deliberate activities. *Internal corporate venturing* is the name used to capture this set of deliberate activities—activities that firms use to develop internal inventions and particularly internal innovations.[74]

As shown in Figure 13.1, autonomous and induced strategic behaviors are the two types of internal corporate venturing. Each venturing type facilitates development of both incremental and radical innovations. However, a larger number of radical innovations spring from autonomous strategic behavior, while a larger number of incremental innovations come from induced strategic behavior.

In essence, autonomous strategic behavior results in influences to change aspects of the firm's strategy and the structure in place to support its implementation. In contrast, induced strategic behavior results from the influences of the strategy and structure the firm currently has in place to support efforts to innovate (see Figure 13.1). We emphasize these points in the discussions below.

Figure 13.1 Model of Internal Corporate Venturing

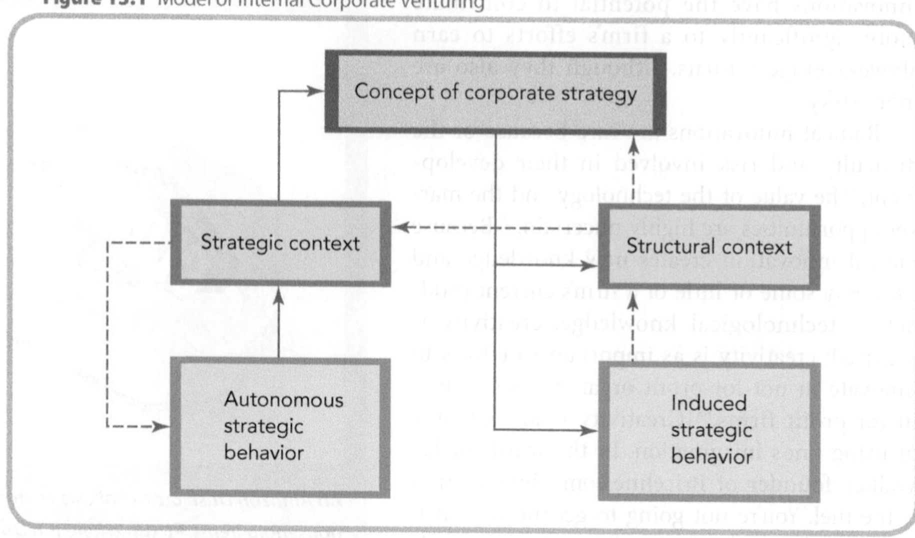

Source: Adapted from R. A. Burgelman, 1983, A model of the interactions of strategic behavior, corporate context, and the concept of strategy, *Academy of Management Review*, 8: 65.

13-5b Autonomous Strategic Behavior

Autonomous strategic behavior is a bottom-up process in which a *product champion* pursues a new idea, often through a political process, by means of which she/he develops and coordinates the actions required to convert an invention into an innovative product and to introduce that product into the market.[75] Product champions rely on their entrepreneurial mind-set to complete these actions. Product champions play critical roles in moving innovations forward. Consider Post-it Notes as an example of an innovation that reached the market because of the tireless efforts of a product champion. 3M's Post-it Notes evolved from the work of Dr. Spencer Silver, a 3M scientist. In trying to develop a bigger, stronger, tougher adhesive, Dr. Silver actually discovered something called microspheres, which retain their stickiness while having a "removable" characteristic. This characteristic allows attached surfaces to peel apart easily (think of your Post-it Notes). It took years, and the forming of a partnership with Art Fry, another 3M scientist, for the company to see the innovation-related potential of Dr. Silver's invention. In describing how this result came about, Dr. Silver said that he become known as Mr. Persistent because he would not stop trying to sell his product inside 3M.[76] His persistence indicates that Dr. Silver indeed was a product champion. As this example shows, internal innovations springing from autonomous strategic behavior differ from the firm's current strategy and structure, taking it into new markets and perhaps new ways of creating value (see Figure 13.1). As a means of innovating, the effectiveness of autonomous strategic behavior increases when new knowledge, especially tacit knowledge, diffuses continuously throughout the firm.[77]

As discussed in the Strategic Focus, agencies or bodies other than individual organizations sometimes seek innovation through autonomous strategic behavior. This is the case with the Public Investment Fund (PIF), which provides financial support to projects of strategic importance to the Kingdom of Saudi Arabia (KSA).[78] While reading about the Public Investment Fund's actions, notice that developing innovation throughout the Kingdom of Saudi Arabia is the force driving the fund's investment choices. In this regard, the PIF hopes that product champions will surface in Noon, an e-commerce platform in which it invested $500 million, as a means of developing and exploiting innovations. Mohamed Alabbar, a major investor in Noon, may be the product champion through which new ideas surface as a source of marketplace innovations.

Strategic **Focus**

Seeking Innovation through Autonomous Strategic Behavior at the Country Level

The Public Investment Fund (PIF) is a sovereign wealth fund (SWF) established by the Kingdom of Saudi Arabia (KSA). Created to invest funds derived from a country's reserves in ways that benefit that country's economy and citizens, SWFs are somewhat common. For example, because of an aging population and a declining workforce, Japan's Government Pension Investment Fund seeks returns from its investments that are capable of financially supporting its elderly citizens. Likewise, with over $800 billion in investable assets, the China Investment Corporation seeks returns that will benefit the state and its citizenry in multiple ways.

KSA's vision is "to be a global investment powerhouse and the world's most impactful investor, enabling the creation of new sectors and opportunities that will shape the future global economy, while driving the economic transformation of Saudi Arabia." This economic transformation is important as the KSA seeks to reduce its dependence on oil income as the foundation for its economy. The structure of the PIF allows it to invest in companies with the potential to innovate because of their talent. The fund notes that to date, it has "invested in some of the world's most innovative companies, forming partnerships that will ensure Saudi Arabia is at the forefront of emerging trends." The degree to which autonomous strategic behavior may emerge in a company as a means of developing innovations influences the PIF's decisions as it evaluates firms in which it may invest.

E-commerce venture Noon is a billion dollar project, with 50 percent of the investment coming from the PIF. In partnership with Dubai businessman Mohamed Alabbar and other investors, Noon's permanent operational base is in Riyadh. One of the most expensive tech ventures in the Middle East, Noon is a competitive response to Amazon's strategic action of acquiring Dubai-based Souq.com as a means of boldly entering the Middle East markets. Described by Mr. Alabbar as an Arabic-first e-commerce platform, Noon offers a range of clothing, home goods, grocery staples, and multiple other items. In 2018, online sales in the Middle East accounted for only an estimated two percent of overall retail sales, but the e-commerce sector is growing faster in the Middle East than in all other parts of the world. Thus, Amazon felt a strong incentive to enter the market quickly through an acquisition. Likewise, the PIF's managers believe that Noon will innovate in ways that will lead to commercial success in this emerging sector. In turn, Noon's commercial success would provide one avenue to reducing the KSA's dependence on oil revenue.

To achieve its goal, Noon offers over 20 million products "ranging from fashion and baby goods to books and electronics." It uses a 3.5 million square foot fulfillment order center in Dubai to distribute its products. Mr. Alabbar is committed to "creating a different kind of infrastructure: a viable competitor to Amazon.com Inc. and other global e-commerce giants, which are moving into the Middle East to capitalize on an online shopping boom." To make Noon the only Arabic-first e-commerce platform competing in the Middle East, Mr. Alabbar and his colleagues seek to identify innovations to use as the foundation for outcompeting their rivals. With Amazon's Souq.com as a competitor, the battle to innovate as a means of capturing market share will be intense.

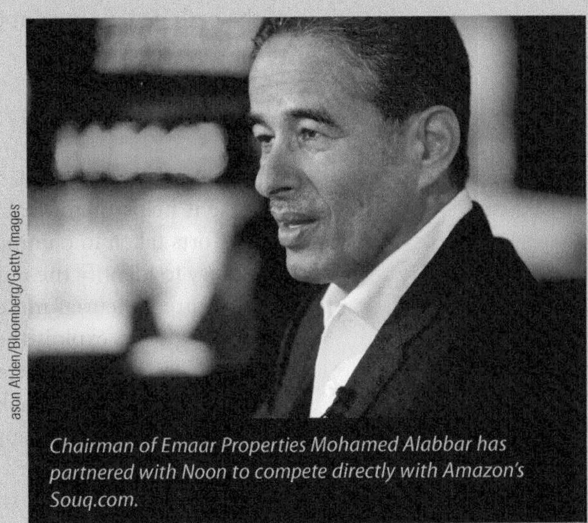

ason Alden/Bloomberg/Getty Images

Chairman of Emaar Properties Mohamed Alabbar has partnered with Noon to compete directly with Amazon's Souq.com.

Sources: 2018, Public Investment Fund, http://pif.gov.sa; 2018, Bests and bloopers from the year in deals, *Wall Street Journal*, www.wsj.com, December 28; 2018, Sovereign Wealth Fund – SWF, *Investopedia*, www.investopedia.com, January 28; N. Al Ali, 2017, Alabbar Noon venture with Saudi fund said to let Dubai staff go, *Bloomberg*, www.bloomberg.com, May 18; O. Hasan, 2017, Gulf retailer Noon.com to ignite e-commerce race, *Phys.org*, www.phys.org, October 2; M. Kassem & N. Nanji, 2017, Noon launches in the UAE, tapping into regional e-commerce boom, *The National*, www.thenational.ae, October 1; N. Parasie, 2017, Dubai billionaire's tech startup takes on Amazon, *Wall Street Journal*, www.wsj.com, December 28; M. Read, 2017, CEO, some staff leave MidEast e-commerce venture Noon – sources, *Reuters*, www.reuters.com, May 18; Z. Alkhalisi, 2016, Saudi Arabia and Burj Khalifa developer launch Gulf answer to Amazon, *CNN Tech*, www.money.cnn.com, November 13.

13-5c Induced Strategic Behavior

Induced strategic behavior, the second form of corporate venturing through which firms develop innovations internally, is a top-down process whereby the firm's current strategy and structure foster innovations that are associated closely with that strategy and structure.[79] In this form of venturing, the strategy in place filters through a matching structural hierarchy. In essence, induced strategic behavior results in internal innovations that are consistent with the firm's current strategy. Thus, the firm's CEO and its top management team play an active and key role in induced strategic behavior.[80] This is the case at IBM, where CEO Virginia (Ginni) Rometty challenged the firm's employees "to move faster and respond more quickly to customers" as a foundation for developing innovations that will facilitate the firm's efforts to "shift to new computing models."[81]

Induced innovation allows the firm and its managers to determine the type and amount of innovation desired.[82] For example, the firm could develop an intense innovation process in order to be the industry leader by introducing new products regularly even if they cannibalize currently successful products. Intel is an example of a firm following this practice. A firm uses an induced approach to innovation to determine if it wishes to create open innovation, where innovation becomes the source of industry standards, or closed innovation, which the firm uses to generate returns disallowing others to use it.[83] The majority of innovation is closed innovation, but open innovation is becoming more common, especially in some industries. Often, firms engage in evolutionary, path dependent R&D, which over time becomes more incremental (because of the path dependence in the knowledge base used).[84]

13-6 Implementing Internal Innovations

An entrepreneurial mind-set is critical to firms' efforts to innovate internally, partly because it helps them deal with the environmental and market uncertainty associated with efforts taken to commercialize inventions.[85] When facing uncertainty, firms continuously try to identify the most attractive opportunities to pursue strategically. Thus, firms use an entrepreneurial mind-set to identify opportunities and then develop innovations and strategies to exploit them in the marketplace.[86] Often, firms provide incentives to individuals to be more entrepreneurial as a foundation for successfully developing internal innovations. Additionally, firms sometimes encourage work teams to specify what they believe are the most appropriate incentives for the firm to use as a means of encouraging innovative behavior.[87]

Having processes and structures in place through which a firm can exploit its innovations is critical. In the context of internal corporate ventures, managers must allocate resources, coordinate activities, communicate with many different parties in the organization, and make a series of decisions to convert the innovations resulting from either autonomous or induced strategic behaviors into successful market entries.[88] As we describe in Chapter 11, an organizational structure depicts the sets of formal relationships that support processes managers use to exploit the firm's innovations.

To implement the incremental and radical innovations resulting from internal corporate ventures, firms integrate the functions involved in internal innovation efforts—from engineering to manufacturing and distribution. Increasingly, firms use product development teams to achieve the desired integration across organizational functions. Such integration involves coordinating and applying the knowledge and skills of different functional areas to maximize innovation and to create a culture of continuous improvement.[89] Teams must help make decisions about which projects to continue supporting and those to terminate. Emotional commitments sometimes increase the difficulty of deciding to terminate an innovation-based project.

13-6a Cross-Functional Product Development Teams

Cross-functional product development teams facilitate efforts to integrate activities associated with different organizational functions, such as design, manufacturing, and marketing. A number of individuals, representing a wide swath of the organization, are members of cross-functional new product development teams. The reason for this is that, "in today's globally interconnected, fast-paced business environment, nearly every important initiative—whether it's revenue growth, cost reduction, or new product innovation—requires insights and actions from people working across an organization."[90] As team members, research scientists, for example, bring technological content knowledge to decisions made by product development teams.[91] Those from marketing bring insights about products that appeal to millennials compared to members of the baby boomer generation. In addition to members from the organization, cross-functional product development teams may also include people from major suppliers because they have knowledge that can meaningfully inform a firm's innovation processes.[92] In addition, it is possible to complete new product development processes more quickly and to commercialize the products resulting from the processes more easily when cross-functional teams work collaboratively.[93] Using cross-functional teams, the firm batches product development stages into parallel processes so that it can tailor its product development efforts to its unique core competencies and to the market's needs.

Horizontal organizational structures support cross-functional teams in their efforts to integrate innovation-based activities across organizational functions.[94] Therefore, instead of using vertical hierarchical functions or departments as the design framework, core horizontal processes, which are relied on to produce and manage innovations, are the foundation for building the organization. Some of the horizontal processes that are critical to innovation efforts are formal and documented as procedures and practices. More commonly, however, these important processes are informal and supported properly through horizontal organizational structures—structures that typically find individuals communicating frequently on a face-to-face basis.

Team members' independent frames of reference and organizational politics are two barriers with the potential to prevent effective use of cross-functional teams.[95] Team members working within a distinct specialization (e.g., a particular organizational function) may have an independent frame of reference—one that common backgrounds and experiences influence. Such team members are likely to use the same decision criteria to evaluate issues, such as product development efforts, when making decisions within their functional units.

Additionally, individuals working in various organizational functions differ from one another in areas such as their goals, formality of the structure guiding their work, and the amount of time needed to complete their work. In turn, these differences influence how individuals working in an organization's functional departments view innovation-related activities. For example, a design engineer may consider the characteristics that make a product functional and workable to be the most important ones. Alternatively, a person from the marketing function may judge characteristics that satisfy customer needs to be most important. These different orientations can create barriers to effective communication across functions and may even generate intra-team conflict as different parts of the firm try to work together to innovate.[96]

Some organizations experience a considerable amount of political activity (i.e., organizational politics) when using cross-functional product development teams. Determining how to allocate resources to different functions is a key source of such activity. This means that inter-unit conflict may result from aggressive competition for resources among those representing different organizational functions. This type of conflict between functions creates a barrier to cross-functional integration efforts. Those trying to form effective cross-functional product development teams seek ways to mitigate the damaging effects of organizational politics. Emphasizing the critical role each function plays in the firm's overall efforts to innovate is a method firms use to help individuals appreciate the value of inter-unit collaborations.

13-6b Facilitating Integration and Innovation

Shared values and effective leadership are important for achieving cross-functional integration and implementing internal innovations.[97] As part of culture, shared values are consistent with the firm's vision and mission and become the glue that promotes integration between functional units.

Strategic leadership is also important to efforts to achieve cross-functional integration and promote internal innovation. Working with others, leaders must set goals and allocate resources needed to achieve them. The goals include integrated development and commercialization of new products. Effective strategic leaders also ensure a high-quality communication system to facilitate cross-functional integration. A critical benefit of effective communication is the sharing of knowledge among team members, who in turn are then able to communicate an innovation's existence and importance to others in the organization. Shared values and leadership practices shape the communication routines that make it possible to share innovation-related knowledge throughout the firm.[98]

13-6c Creating Value from Internal Innovation

The model in Figure 13.2 shows how firms try to create value through internal innovation processes (autonomous strategic behavior and induced strategic behavior). As shown, an entrepreneurial mind-set is foundational to efforts to identify entrepreneurial opportunities the firm can pursue to create value through innovations.[99] As we have discussed, cross-functional teams are important for promoting integrated new product design

Figure 13.2 Creating Value through Internal Innovation Processes

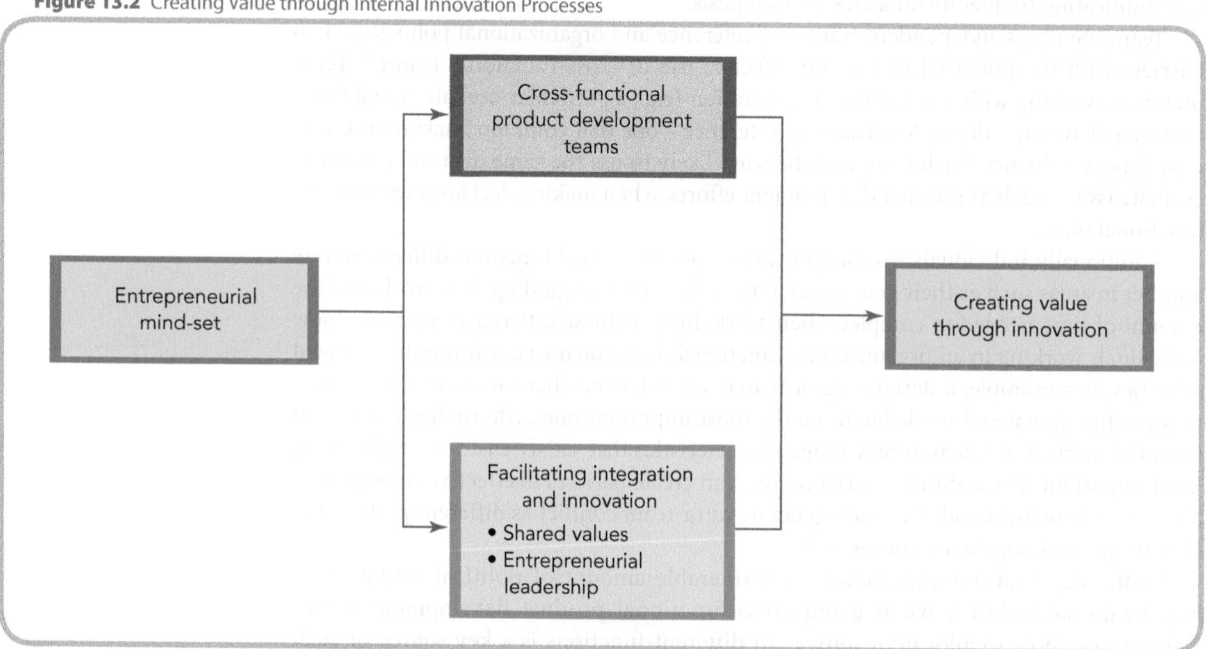

ideas and gaining commitment to their subsequent implementation. Effective leadership and shared values promote integration and vision for innovation and commitment to it. However, competitive rivalry (see Chapter 5) affects the degree of success a firm achieves through innovation. Thus, firms must carefully study competitors' responses to their innovations to have the knowledge required to know how to adjust their innovation-based efforts, and even when to abandon those efforts if market conditions indicate the need to do so.[100]

In the next two sections, we discuss the other approaches firms use to innovate—cooperative strategies and acquisitions.

13-7 Innovation through Cooperative Strategies

Alliances with other firms can contribute to innovations in several ways. First, they provide information on new business opportunities and the innovations the firm might develop to exploit them.[101] In other instances, firms use cooperative strategies to align what they believe are complementary assets that have potential to lead to future innovations. Compared to other approaches to innovation, combining complementary assets through alliances has the potential to result more frequently in radical innovations.[102]

Rapidly changing technologies, globalization, and the need to innovate in ways that satisfy global standards influence firms' decisions to innovate by cooperating with other companies. Indeed, some believe that, because of these conditions, firms are becoming increasingly dependent on cooperative strategies as a path to innovation and, ultimately, to competitive success in the global economy.[103] Both entrepreneurial ventures and established firms use cooperative strategies to innovate. An entrepreneurial venture, for example, may seek investment capital as well as established firms' distribution capabilities to introduce successfully one of its innovative products to the market. Alternatively, more-established companies may need new technological knowledge and can gain access to it by forming a cooperative strategy with entrepreneurial ventures. Large pharmaceutical firms and biotechnology companies form alliances to integrate their knowledge and resources to develop new products and bring them to market.

In some instances, large established firms form an alliance to innovate. For example, EY and Microsoft extended their alliance to combine digital and cloud technologies to serve the agricultural industry with innovative products. The focus of this alliance is on helping agricultural firms turn their digital strategies into action. In a press release, EY and Microsoft stated that this "initiative will combine EY's technology consulting experience and its agribusiness knowledge with Microsoft's digital suite of tools and the Microsoft Azure cloud platform to help companies innovate and transform their business."[104]

Marriott International, Inc.

The first Moxy Hotel that is innovative in both its design and the value it creates for customers.

An alliance formed between Inter IKEA Group, the parent company of the IKEA furniture brand, and Marriott International, Inc. is another example of large firms using a cooperative strategy to innovate. These firms formed an alliance to develop Moxy, a new hotel brand that the companies believe is innovative in its design and the value it creates for customers.[105] In this alliance, IKEA provides novel and innovative construction techniques (such as its famed flat-pack technology through which it can quickly deliver and assemble furniture) to keep manufacturing costs down while Marriott provides value in the form of unique design. Thus, IKEA and Marriott collaborated to form the Moxy brand. The innovative foundation of the brand is combining value (IKEA's contribution) with style (Marriott's contribution). The hotel serves millennials with moderate prices and an open lobby/restaurant/bar with music at one end and space where guests can work on their devices at the other. Established initially in European countries, there are to be 150 Moxy Hotels by 2026 with locations in London, Oslo, Berlin, Frankfurt, Chicago, and Nashville among others.[106] Customers seem to value Moxy's "small-but-smartly built rooms; airport-style, tablet-based check-ins; and no-frills service" among other characteristics.[107]

However, alliances formed to foster innovation carry risk. In addition to conflict that is natural when firms try to collaborate to reach a mutual goal, alliance members also take a risk that a partner might appropriate their technology or knowledge and use it for its own benefit.[108] Carefully selecting partner firms mitigates this risk. The ideal partnership is one in which the firms have complementary skills as well as compatible strategic goals.[109] When this is the case, firms encounter fewer challenges and risks as they try to manage successfully the partnership they formed to develop innovations. Companies also want to constrain the number of cooperative arrangements they form to innovate, in that becoming involved in too many alliances puts them at risk of losing the ability to manage each one successfully.[110]

Acquisitions are the final approach firms use to innovate. Evidence suggests that this approach is gaining in popularity as firms seek to enhance their technological capabilities on a continuous basis. The Boston Consulting Group offers the following commentary about this issue: "For an increasing number of organizations the answer is to buy rather than to build. Acquisitions of high-tech targets have become an instrument of choice for buyers in all sectors looking to boost innovation, streamline operations and processes, shape customer journeys, and personalize products, services, and experiences. (Indeed), high-tech deals represented almost 30% of the total $2.5 trillion of completed M&A transactions in 2016."[111]

We discuss acquisitions firms completed to gain access to others' innovations and/or innovative capability in the Strategic Focus. You will see that companies sometimes pay large premiums to acquire firms and their innovations and/or innovative capabilities. Reasons firms acquire companies to innovate and risks associated with doing so appear in the "Innovation through Acquisitions" section.

13-8 Innovation through Acquisitions

As noted in the Strategic Focus, one reason companies choose to acquire others as a means of innovating[112] is that capital markets value growth; acquisitions provide a means to rapidly extend one or more product lines and increase the firm's revenues.[113] Nonetheless, a strategic rationale should drive the decision to acquire a company. Typically, the rationale is to gain ownership of an acquired company's innovations and access to its innovative capabilities. A number of large technology-based companies have acquired firms largely for these purposes. Netflix acquired Millarworld to gain access to the firm's current stable of innovative products and to its ability to construct and tell innovative stories across time.

Similar to internal corporate venturing and strategic alliances, acquisitions are not a risk-free approach to innovation. A key risk of acquisitions is that a firm may substitute an ability to acquire innovations for an ability to develop them internally. Some analysts

Strategic **Focus**

Will These Acquisitions Lead to Innovation Success or to Strategic Failure?

As stakeholders, investors value corporate growth. Innovations have the capacity to contribute to firm growth. Compared to internal innovation and innovation resulting from cooperative strategies, firms grow quicker and have immediate access to another company's innovations when using an acquisition strategy. Because of this, acquisitions remain a popular approach to innovation, particularly for large established organizations.

In 2018, merger and acquisition activity was strong. Growing by gaining access to others' innovations and their innovating capabilities was as a key reason for this. At this time, the pharmaceuticals industry was engaged in what analysts called a "deal frenzy," including such acquisitions as Celgene's intended purchase of cancer specialist Juno Therapeutics and Sanofi SA's decision to acquire Bioverativ Inc. Celgene agreed to pay an approximate 90 percent premium to acquire Juno, while Sanofi paid a 63 percent premium to purchase Bioverativ. Driving these acquisitions was Celgene's desire to gain access to Juno's innovative capabilities in the area of developing cancer treatments and, specifically, to acquire ownership of the firm's new lymphoma treatment. Expected to gain regulatory approval in 2019, the treatment, called JCAR017, had the potential to reach $3 billion in global sales quickly. To stimulate future innovations, Celgene planned to integrate some of the firms' research and development capabilities into Juno's laboratories located in Seattle, WA. Speaking about the firms' combined interest and skills, Celgene's CEO said that by acquiring Juno, he was "bringing together two organizations with a shared vision to make cancer a chronic illness while we work toward a cure." For Sanofi, its interest in part was to gain access to Bioverativ's hemophilia drugs. In commenting about this, an analyst said the following: "Bioverativ's hemophilia drugs will fit in Sanofi's rare-disease business and complement the company's collaboration with biotech Alnylam Pharmaceuticals Inc. in developing a new kind of hemophilia therapy using an emerging technology called RNA interference." Here then, an acquiring and acquired company's innovation capabilities will be integrated partly to continue collaborating with a third company to develop innovative medical products.

The premiums these firms paid to acquire innovations and innovative capabilities are significant. Nonetheless, they were consistent with the average premium of 89 percent paid in the pharmaceutical industry at this time—a premium almost double the median paid in this industry in 2010. The premiums paid reflect the need for pharmaceutical companies to acquire others to plug holes in their product lines and to gain access to promising products and innovations. Also stimulating acquisitions here is the failure to develop new products through internal efforts. In 2018, for example, Pfizer Inc. announced that it would "stop trying to discover new drugs for Alzheimer's disease and Parkinson's disease, abandoning costly but futile efforts to find effective treatments for the disorders." The future might find Pfizer trying to acquire firms with promising products and/or with capabilities to develop successful treatments for these diseases.

Susanne Doepke/ZUMA Press/San Diego/California/USA/Newscom

Mark Millar, comic book creator of iconic characters such as Thor, Peter Parker, and Kick-Ass, speaks at Comic Con. In February of 2018, Netflix and Millarworld announced that The Magic Order comic book would be the companies' first collaboration, which appeared in stores June of that year.

Of course, firms in industries other than pharmaceuticals acquire innovation. Netflix recently completed its first acquisition by buying Millarworld, a streaming media company. "Millarworld is the independent comic publishing company founded by Mark Millar, a storied comic book creator who is behind a host of iconic characters and series, including Kick-Ass and Kingsman, as well as the creative force behind some of Marvel's best story arcs, including The Ultimates and Old Man Logan." In essence, Netflix wanted access to Millarworld's innovative story-telling ability on a going-forward basis. In the short term, the firm intended to bring Millarworld's portfolio to the screen through films, TV series, and kids' shows.

In what many call "the innovation obsessed technology industry," Broadcom Ltd. CEO Hock Tan "unapologetically favors surefire profits over visionary projects." Through what analysts saw as an increasingly bold acquisition strategy, Mr. Tan made Broadcom the industry's most visible deal-maker. In building his firm, Mr. Tan clearly prefers to acquire innovation rather than to develop it internally or via cooperative strategies.

Sources: C. Grant, 2018, High prices won't deter biotech deals, *Wall Street Journal*, www.wsj.com, January 22; T. Greenwald, 2018, Is Broadcom's CEO, a champion deal maker, innovative enough? *Wall Street Journal*, www.wsj.com, January 25; C. Lombardo, 2018, Celgene to buy Juno Therapeutics for $9 billion, *Wall Street Journal*, www.wsj.com, January 22; J. D. Rockoff, 2018, Big drugmakers pay big prices for promising biotechs, *Wall Street Journal*, www.wsj.com, January 22; J. D. Rockoff, 2018, Pfizer ends hunt for drugs to treat Alzheimer's and Parkinson's, *Wall Street Journal*, www.wsj.com, January 6; J. D. Rockoff, D. Cimilluca, & B. Dummett, 2018, Celgene nears deal to buy Impact Biomedicines for as much as $7 billion, *Wall Street Journal*, www.wsj.com, January 7; A. Bylund, 2017, Netflix, Inc. just made its first-ever acquisition, *Motley Fool*, www.fool.com, August 7.

fear this is the case for Broadcom Ltd.—a firm described in the Strategic Focus—because the firm focuses almost exclusively on acquiring other firms to gain access to their innovations. Individuals with positions in the acquired companies sometimes indicate that, as part of the Broadcom integration process, fewer allocations flow to the research and development function.[114] Reducing allocations to R&D may result when a firm concentrates on financial controls to identify, evaluate, and then manage acquisitions. Of course, strategic controls are the ones through which a firm identifies a strategic rationale to acquire another company as a means of developing innovations. Thus, the likelihood a firm will achieve success through its efforts to innovate increases by developing an appropriate balance between financial and strategic controls.

In spite of the risks though, choosing to acquire companies with complementary capabilities and knowledge sets can support a firm's efforts to innovate successfully. This is especially the case when strategic purposes drive the acquisitions and when the process to integrate the acquired firm into the focal firm proceeds without difficulty.[115] If sufficient financial capital is available, firms lacking success with internal innovation efforts are more likely to acquire companies possessing strong technological capabilities or that have new, potentially valuable innovations.[116]

The ability to learn new capabilities that can facilitate innovation-related activities from acquired companies is an important benefit for an acquiring firm. Additionally, firms that emphasize innovation, and carefully select companies to acquire that also emphasize innovation and the technological capabilities that are often the source of innovations, are likely to remain innovative.[117] Thus, some firms produce innovations internally, or use cooperative strategies to innovate, while others use external knowledge and external sources for innovations. Not surprisingly, large organizations use all three approaches to innovate. However, the quality of actions used to implement each approach influences their success.[118]

13-9 Creating Value through Strategic Entrepreneurship

Entrepreneurial ventures and younger firms often are more effective at recognizing opportunities than are larger established companies.[119] This means that entrepreneurial ventures often produce more radical innovations than do larger, more established organizations. Entrepreneurial ventures' strategic flexibility and willingness to take risks account partially for their ability to do this. Yet, because they tend to be novel, radical innovations are also risky. Thus, these innovations sometimes fail, which frequently means that the new venture fails because such firms have little slack.[120] Alternatively, larger, well-established firms often have more resources and capabilities to manage recognized opportunities strategically in the marketplace, but these efforts generally result in a larger number of incremental than radical innovations.

Thus, younger, entrepreneurial ventures generally excel in the opportunity-seeking part of strategic entrepreneurship while larger, more established firms generally excel in the advantage-seeking part. However, as we have discussed in this chapter, competitive success and superior performance relative to competitors accrues to firms capable of recognizing and exploiting opportunities. When able to do this, firms establish a competitive advantage relative to their rivals.[121] On a relative basis then, entrepreneurial ventures should seek to enhance their strategic skills, while older, more established firms should try to become more entrepreneurial.

Firms trying to learn how to be more entrepreneurial and strategic simultaneously (that is, firms trying to use strategic entrepreneurship) understand that, after recognizing opportunities, entrepreneurs within entrepreneurial ventures and established organizations must help their firms develop capabilities that are valuable, rare, difficult to imitate, and nonsubstitutable (see Chapter 3). When capabilities satisfy these four criteria, the firm has the foundation in place through which strategic actions become the pathway to exploiting innovations in the marketplace and developing a competitive advantage.

As we explained in Chapter 1, without a competitive advantage, firm success is only temporary.[122] If grounded in a recognized and viable market opportunity, an innovation may be valuable and rare early in its life; but, by itself, an innovation does not result in a competitive advantage. Indeed, strategic actions taken to introduce the new product to the market and protect its position against competitors are the source of competitive advantage. In combination, these actions (recognizing viable opportunities and using strategic actions to exploit them in the marketplace) constitute strategic entrepreneurship.

Today, a number of companies are trying to become more capable of using strategic entrepreneurship effectively. For example, an increasing number of large, well-known firms, including Wendy's International, Gucci Group, Starbucks, and Perry Ellis International among others, have established a top-level managerial position commonly called president or executive vice president of emerging brands. Other companies such as Coca-Cola, GE, Whirlpool, and Humana have established a position within their top management teams to focus on innovation.[123] Commonly, these individuals carry a title of chief innovation officer.

The essential responsibility of top-level managers focusing on emerging brands or innovation is to verify that their firm identifies entrepreneurial opportunities consistently. Additionally, they manage the firm's portfolio of innovation projects, selecting those for which further investment is appropriate while terminating unattractive projects.[124] These managers understand that some innovation projects fail; they try to learn from those failures to enhance the success of future projects.[125] For projects that are to continue receiving support, chief innovation officers collaborate with others to integrate the innovation into the firm's strategy. In this sense, those responsible for identifying opportunities the firm might want to pursue and those responsible for selecting and implementing the strategies the company would use to pursue those opportunities share responsibility for verifying that the firm is taking entrepreneurial actions using a strategic perspective. Chief innovation officers and those working in their unit also help the firm select the innovations to use to pursue opportunities, and whether those innovations should be developed internally, through a cooperative strategy, or by completing an acquisition. In the final analysis, the objective of

Ford's new 2019 Edge ST showcased at the Geneva International Motor show in March of 2018.

these top-level managers is to help firms recognize entrepreneurial opportunities and then develop successful incremental and radical innovations and strategies to exploit them.

When engaging in strategic entrepreneurship, firms develop an innovation portfolio. In part, this portfolio facilitates efforts to determine the number of incremental innovations required to continue supporting existing products that are successful in marketplace competitions. Simultaneously, the innovation portfolio includes efforts oriented to developing radical innovations—the kind that result in development of unique products in the future. This is the situation for global automobile manufacturers such as those described in the Opening Case. In that case we noted, for example, that Ford Motor Co. earns a significant percentage of its profits by selling large trucks and sport-utility vehicles (SUVs). Because of this, the company "plans to expand its lineup of SUVs and crossover vehicles in the U.S. to 13 models from seven by 2020 in response to rapid growth in SUV sales."[126] Incremental innovations will be critical to the success of these efforts to continue earning profits based on a potential competitive advantage in terms of selling SUVs to U.S. customers. Simultaneously, Ford recognizes an opportunity to develop radical innovations for future products including hybrids, electric vehicles, and hydrogen fuel cell-powered vehicles among other possibilities.[127] While identifying entrepreneurial opportunities, companies practicing strategic entrepreneurship, which appears to be the case for Ford, form strategies allowing them to achieve success with products they sell today and through which they can be successful in the future.

In this chapter, we focused on innovation's link to organizational success. Throughout the book, we examined decisions and actions firms exercise when practicing strategic management. Both skills (the ability to innovate and the ability to be strategic in marketplace competitions) are vital for organizational success. For example, firms able to innovate but lacking the skills required to achieve marketplace success with their innovations by exercising appropriate strategic actions do not perform as desired. At the same time, firms with superior strategic skills cannot achieve desired levels of success without the benefit of continuous innovations. Thus, today's organizations must learn how to engage simultaneously in opportunity-seeking and advantage-seeking behaviors. By seeking opportunities continuously, organizations recognize product attributes that can serve future customer needs. By developing their advantage-seeking behaviors, firms introduce streams of new products to customers in ways that yield a competitive advantage for the company. Strategic entrepreneurship is the combination of opportunity- and advantage-seeking behavior. Thus, the most "entrepreneurial" and the most "strategic" companies are poised to achieve marketplace success at the expense of competitors lacking the ability to engage simultaneously in opportunity- and advantage-seeking behaviors.

SUMMARY

- Strategic entrepreneurship involves taking entrepreneurial actions using a strategic perspective. Firms using strategic entrepreneurship simultaneously engage in opportunity-seeking and advantage-seeking behaviors. The purpose is to continuously find new opportunities and quickly develop and exploit innovations while simultaneously exploiting competitive advantages that are creating value through the products the firm sells currently.

- Entrepreneurship is a process used by individuals, teams, and organizations to identify entrepreneurial opportunities without being immediately constrained by the resources they control. Corporate entrepreneurship is the application of entrepreneurship (including the identification of entrepreneurial opportunities) within ongoing, established organizations. Entrepreneurial opportunities are conditions in which new goods or services can satisfy a need in the market. Entrepreneurship positively contributes to individual firms' performance and stimulates growth in countries' economies.

- Firms engage in three types of innovative activities:
  - invention, which is the act of creating a new good, process, or service
  - innovation, or the process of creating a commercial product from an invention
  - imitation, which is the adoption of similar innovations by different firms

  Invention brings something new into being while innovation brings something new into use.

- Entrepreneurs see or envision entrepreneurial opportunities and then take actions to develop innovations and exploit them. The most successful entrepreneurs (whether they are establishing their own venture or are working in an established organization) have an entrepreneurial mind-set, which is an orientation that values the potential associated with opportunities that are available because of marketplace uncertainties.

- International entrepreneurship, or the process of identifying and exploiting entrepreneurial opportunities outside the firm's domestic markets, is important to firms around the globe. Evidence suggests that firms capable of engaging effectively in international entrepreneurship generally outperform those competing only in their domestic markets.

- Firms use three basic approaches to produce innovation:
  - internal innovation, which involves R&D and forming internal corporate ventures
  - cooperative strategies such as strategic alliances
  - acquisitions

- Autonomous strategic behavior and induced strategic behavior are the two forms of internal corporate venturing. Autonomous strategic behavior is a bottom-up process through which a product champion facilitates the commercialization of an innovation. Induced strategic behavior is a top-down process in which a firm's current strategy and structure facilitate the development and implementation of innovations. Thus, the firm's current strategy and structure drives induced strategic behavior while autonomous strategic behavior can result in a change to the firm's current strategy and structure.

- Firms create two types of innovations—incremental and radical—through internal innovation that takes place in the form of autonomous strategic behavior or induced strategic behavior. Overall, firms produce more incremental innovations, but radical innovations have a higher probability of significantly increasing sales revenue and profits. Cross-functional integration is often vital to a firm's efforts to develop and implement internal corporate venturing activities and to commercialize the resulting innovation. Cross-functional teams now commonly include representatives from external organizations, such as suppliers. Additionally, developing shared values and engaging in successful strategic leadership practices facilitate integration and innovation efforts.

- To gain access to the specialized knowledge required to innovate in the global economy, firms may form a cooperative relationship, such as a strategic alliance with other companies, some of which may be competitors.

- Acquisitions are another method firms use to obtain innovation. Acquisitions can lead to direct access to an acquired firm's innovations, and/or firms can learn new capabilities from an acquisition, thereby enriching their internal innovation abilities.

- The practice of strategic entrepreneurship by all types of firms, large and small, new and more established, creates value for all stakeholders, especially for shareholders and customers. Strategic entrepreneurship also contributes to the economic development of countries.

KEY TERMS

corporate entrepreneurship 419
entrepreneurial mind-set 421
entrepreneurial opportunities 419
entrepreneurs 421
entrepreneurship 419
imitation 420
innovation 420
international entrepreneurship 422
invention 420
strategic entrepreneurship 418

REVIEW QUESTIONS

1. What is strategic entrepreneurship? What is corporate entrepreneurship?
2. What is entrepreneurship, and what are entrepreneurial opportunities? Why are they important aspects of the strategic management process?
3. What are invention, innovation, and imitation? How are these concepts interrelated?
4. What is an entrepreneur, and what is an entrepreneurial mind-set?
5. What is international entrepreneurship? Why is it important?
6. How do firms develop innovations internally?
7. How do firms use cooperative strategies to innovate and to have access to innovative capabilities?
8. How does a firm acquire other companies to increase the number of innovations it produces and improve its capability to innovate?
9. How does strategic entrepreneurship help firms create value?

Mini-Case

What Explains the Lack of Innovation at American Express? Is It Hubris, Inertia, or Lack of Capability?

The lack of innovation and entrepreneurial focus at American Express (AmEx) may be because of hubris, inertia, *and* a lack of capability. The firm's performance in 2014 was not, by any means, what stakeholders expect. Partly in response to its poor financial performance, the firm announced plans to reduce its workforce by up to 4,000 employees.

The loss of two of its major partnerships, with Costco and JetBlue, contributed to AmEx's poor performance in 2014. Its partnership with Costco, which had involved an exclusive co-branded credit card, was particularly damaging. At its peak, this collaborative relationship had accounted for approximately eight percent of AmEx's total revenues. Interestingly, cardholders used this co-branded card for many other purchases outside of Costco, as about 70 percent of the revenue generated by the card came from its use in other venues besides Costco.

Losing a major court case also affected AmEx's 2014 performance. In part, the case in question surfaced because AmEx charges each merchant higher fees when a customer uses its card to make a purchase than do other major credit card companies such as Visa and MasterCard. AmEx has a contract with each merchant using its card that does not allow the merchant to recommend to the customer to use a different card or to offer discounts that increase the attractiveness of other cards. A federal judge ruled that this requirement by AmEx was in "restraint of trade" and, therefore, violated antitrust laws. This is important because AmEx may have to reduce its fees charged to merchants, and if so, it may have to decrease the rewards paid back to customers. In turn, it could lose some customers if the rewards become equal to or less than competitors' cards.

AmEx has not enhanced its purchasing technology in some time. For instance, some have expressed concern that AmEx has lagged competitors relative to technological advances that facilitate customers' processing of car rentals and making restaurant reservations. Historically, customers and potential customers viewed AmEx as the most prestigious company from which to hold a card. This belief resulted in a strong brand image for AmEx cards. In part because of the brand, customers with higher income levels preferred to use an AmEx card. Recently though, some of its higher-income clients have chosen to leave AmEx and to use other firms' cards instead. Demonstrating this problem is a long-time client's decision to conduct business with another card company because the rewards benefits associated with that card are superior to those offered by the AmEx card. After studying card offerings available to him, this customer concluded that by switching to a different card, he would gain thousands of dollars in additional rewards. The fact that he uses the card for almost all of his purchases increased the importance of having access to a card with higher rewards in response to frequent card use.

In response to its poor 2014 performance, AmEx announced a renewed focus on affluent customers and more benefits for those holding (and using) the firm's 'Gold Card.' It will offer double points for restaurant purchases and a personalized travel service.

Additional innovations in 2015 and beyond appear to be a foundation for reversing the firm's fortunes. Committing to creative use of data analytics is an example of an innovation enhancing the firm's performance. In commenting about this, a business writer said the following: "American Express is harnessing the power of its data to migrate many traditional processes from legacy mainframes to Big Data processing environments, resulting in dramatic improvements in speed and performance." The firm is also expanding its efforts to deliver exclusive access and benefits to its cardholders. The following examples demonstrate these efforts: "Consumers can be forgiven if they forget American Express is a financial services firm and not an event producer. From staging concerts at the Apollo Theater to designing an interactive video experience featuring NBA plays to providing U.S. Open tennis fans a professional swing analysis, the company's activations touch several areas of its cardholder' lives." Thus, while failing to innovate continuously contributed to AmEx's poor performance in 2014, the firm now appears to be emphasizing innovation as a means to provide the outcomes stakeholders expect.

Sources: 2017, American Express serves up new, innovative experiences and benefits to help card members and fans ace the 2017 US Open Tennis Championships, American Express Homepage, www.americanexpress.com, August 16; C. Manglani, 2017, American Express: Using data analytics to redefine traditional banking, *Digital Innovation and Transformation*, www.digit.hbs.org, April 2; E. Dexheimer, 2015, AmEx is losing its millionaires, *BloombergBusiness*, www.bloomberg.com, February 12; J. Davidson, 2015, Why American Express users should be worried about their rewards, *Money*, www.money.com, February 20; H. Stout, 2015, With revamped gold cards, bruised American Express returns focus to affluent, *New York Times*, www.nytimes.com, February 26; J. Kell, 2015, Visa replaces American Express as Costco's credit card, *Fortune*, www.fortune.com, March 2; H. Tabuchi, 2015, Amex to ask for stay of ruling prohibiting merchants from promoting other cards, *New York Times*, www.nytimes.com, March 25; J. Carney, 2015, American Express struggles to keep up, *Wall Street Journal*, www.wsj.com, April 6; 2015, Stronger dollar drives revenue down at American Express, *New York Times*, www.nytimes.com, April 16.

Case Discussion Questions

1. This Mini-Case suggests that a lack of continuous innovation contributed to American Express's (AmEx) poor performance in 2014. Assuming this is true, what factors might prevent a firm the size and scope of AmEx from being able to innovate continuously?
2. Use material from Chapter 4 to identify the business-level strategy AmEx uses. What dimensions do you believe AmEx should emphasize to use the strategy you identified successfully across time?
3. What actions do you believe AmEx should take to establish an entrepreneurial mind-set among employees throughout the company?
4. This Mini-Case includes descriptions of recent AmEx innovations. Do you anticipate that most of these innovations resulted from autonomous strategic behavior or from induced strategic behavior? Why?

NOTES

1. M. Withers, R. D. Ireland, D. Miller, J. S. Harrison, & D. Boss, 2018, Competitive landscape shifts: The influence of strategic entrepreneurship on shifts in market commonality, *Academy of Management Review*, 43: 349–370; M. A. Hitt, R. D. Ireland, S. M. Camp, & D. L. Sexton, 2001, Strategic entrepreneurship: Entrepreneurial strategies for wealth creation. *Strategic Management Journal*, 22: 479–491.
2. M. Wright & M. A. Hitt, 2017, Strategic entrepreneurship and the *SEJ*: Development and current progress, *Strategic Entrepreneurship Journal*, 11: 200–210.
3. A. Tangel, 2017, Latest entrants into electric car race: Makers of Post-It Notes, paint, *Wall Street Journal*, www.wsj.com, December 26.
4. M. Colias, 2018, Ford increasing electric vehicle investment to $11 billion by 2022, *Wall Street Journal*, www.wsj.com, January 14.
5. 2017, Retail upheaval, data breaches and tech innovations, *Wall Street Journal*, www .wsj.com, December 19.
6. R. Agarwal, G. Dushnitsky, G. T. Lumpkin, M. Wright, & C. Zott, 2017, *Strategic Entrepreneurship Journal* at 10: Retrospect and prospect, *Strategic Entrepreneurship Journal*, 11: 197–199; M. A. Hitt, R. D. Ireland, D. G. Sirmon, & C. A. Trahms, 2011, Strategic entrepreneurship: Creating value for individuals, organizations, and societies, *Academy of Management Perspectives*, 25: 57–75.
7. A. De Massis, D. Audretsch, L. Uhlaner, & N. Kammerlander, 2018, Innovation with limited resources: Management lessons from the German Mittelstand, *Journal of Product Innovation Management*, 35: 125–146; C. Tsinopoulos, C. M. P. Sousa, & J. Yan, 2018, Process innovation: Open innovation and the moderating role of the motivation to achieve legitimacy, *Journal of Product Innovation Management*, 35: 27–48; H. Jiang, J. Xia, A. A. Cannella, & T. Xiao, 2018, Do ongoing networks block out new friends? Reconciling the embeddedness constraint dilemma on new alliance partner selection, *Strategic Management Journal*, 39: 217–241.
8. W. An, X. Zhao, Z. Cao, J. Zhang, & H. Liu, 2018, How Bricolage drives corporate entrepreneurship: The roles of opportunity identification and learning orientation, *Journal of Product Innovation Management*, 35: 49–65; D. F. Kuratko, J. S. McMullen, J. S. Hornsby, & C. Jackson, 2017, Is your organization conducive to the continuous creation of social value? Toward a social corporate entrepreneurship scale, *Business Horizons*, 60: 271–283.
9. D. F. Kuratko & M. H. Morris, 2018, Examining the future trajectory of entrepreneurship, *Journal of Small Business Management*, 56: 11–23.
10. M. A. Demircioglu, 2017, Reinventing the wheel: Public sector innovation in the age of governance, *Public Administration Review*, 77: 800–805.
11. B. R. Barringer & R. D. Ireland, 2019, *Entrepreneurship: Successfully Launching New Ventures*, 6th edition, Pearson, Englewood Cliffs, N. J.; J. S. Hornsby, J. Messersmith, M. Rutherford, & S. Simmons, 2018, Entrepreneurship everywhere: Across campus, across communities, and across borders, *Journal of Small Business Management*, 56: 4–10.
12. P. Munoz & B. Cohen, 2018, Entrepreneurial narratives in sustainable venturing: Beyond people, profit, and plant, *Journal of Small Business Management*, 56: 154–176; P. Davidsson, 2017, Entrepreneurial opportunities as propensities: Do Ramoglou & Tsang move the field forward? *Journal of Business Venturing Insights*, 7: June, 82–85.
13. U. Uygur, 2018, An analogy explanation for the evaluation of entrepreneurial opportunities, *Journal of Small Business Management*, in press; M. S. Wood & W. McKinley, 2017, After the venture: The reproduction and destruction of entrepreneurial opportunity, *Strategic Entrepreneurship Journal*, 11: 18–35.
14. About Amazon Prime, 2018, Amazon Homepage, www.amazon.com, January 16.
15. D. Goss & E. Sadler-Smith, 2018, Opportunity creation: Entrepreneurial agency, interaction, and affect, *Strategic Entrepreneurship Journal*, in press; K. M. Kacmar & L. Busenitz, 2012, Entrepreneurial alertness in the pursuit of new opportunities, *Journal of Business Venturing*, 27: 77–94.
16. M. D. Packard & P. L. Bylund, 2018, On the relationship between inequality and entrepreneurship, *Strategic Entrepreneurship Journal*, 12: 3–22; J. Schumpeter, 1964, *The Theory of Economic Development*, Cambridge, MA: Harvard University Press.
17. Ripple, 2018, Our Company, Ripple Homepage, www.ripple.com; P. Vigna, 2018, Ripple steals Bitcoin's thunder, surges 1,184% in a month, *Wall Street Journal*, www.wsj.com, January 5.
18. F. Zhang, L. Wei, J. Yang, & L. Zhu, 2018, Roles of relationships between large shareholders and managers in radical innovation: A stewardship theory perspective, *Journal of Product Innovation Management*, 35: 88–105; J. E. Perry-Smith, 2017, From creativity to innovation: The social network drivers of the four phases of the idea journey, *Academy of Management Review*, 42: 53–79.
19. D. S. Lucas & C. S. Fuller, 2017, Entrepreneurship: Productive, unproductive, and destructive—Relative to what? *Journal of Business Venturing Insights*, 7: 45–49; C. Bjornskov & N. Foss, 2013, How strategic entrepreneurship and the institutional context drive economic growth, *Strategic Entrepreneurship Journal*, 7: 50–69; W. J. Baumol, R. E. Litan, & C. J. Schramm, 2007, *Good Capitalism, Bad Capitalism, and the Economics of Growth and Prosperity*, New Haven, CT: Yale University Press.
20. Schumpeter, *The Theory of Economic Development*.
21. J. Grafstrom & A. Lindman, 2017, Invention, innovation and diffusion in the European wind power sector, *Technological Forecasting and Social Change*, 114: 176–191; L. Aarikka-Stenroos & B. Sandberg, 2012, From new-product development to commercialization through networks, *Journal of Business Research*, 65: 198–206.
22. S. Hoornaert, M. Ballings, E. C. Malthouse, & D. Van den Poel, 2017, Identifying new product ideas: Waiting for the wisdom of the crown or screening ideas in real time, *Journal of Product Innovation Management*, 34: 580–597; Y. Chen 2017, Dynamic ambidexterity: How innovators manage exploration and exploitation, *Business Horizons*, 60: 385–394.
23. L. Huang & A. P. Knight, 2017, Resources and relationships in entrepreneurship: An exchange theory of the development and effects of the entrepreneur-investor relationship, *Academy of Management Review*, 42: 80–102; S. Nambisan, 2017 Digital entrepreneurship: Toward a digital technology perspective of entrepreneurship, *Entrepreneurship Theory and Practice*, 41: 1020–1055.
24. D. K. Dutta & M. Hora, 2017, From invention success to commercialization success: Technology ventures and the benefits of upstream and downstream supply-chain alliances, *Journal of Small Business Management*, 55: 216–235; C. Grimpe, W. Sofka, M. Shargava, & R. Chatterjee 2017, R&D, marketing innovation, and new product performance: A mixed methods study, *Journal of Product Innovation Management*, 34: 360–383.
25. A. Arora, S. Belenzon, & A. Patacconi, 2018, The decline of science in corporate R&D, *Strategic Management Journal*, 39: 3–32; B. Lev, 2017, Evaluating sustainable competitive advantage *Journal of Applied Corporate Finance*, 29: 70–75.
26. D. Heger & A. K. Zaby, 2018, Patent breadth as effective barrier to market entry, *Economics of Innovation and New Technology*, 27: 174–188; B. Maury, 2018, Sustainable competitive advantage and profitability persistence: Sources versus outcomes for assessing advantage, *Journal of Business Research*, 84: 100–113.

27. S. Chaudhuri, 2018, Outfoxed by small-batch upstarts, Unilever decides to imitate them, *Wall Street Journal*, www.wsj.com, January 2.
28. P. F. Drucker, 1998, The discipline of innovation, *Harvard Business Review*, 76(6): 149–157.
29. Ibid.
30. S. Fitz-Koch & M. Nordqvist, 2017, The reciprocal relationship of innovation capabilities and socioemotional wealth in a family firm, *Journal of Small Business Management*, 55: 547–570; R. R. Kehoe & C. J. Collins, 2017, Human resource management and unit performance in knowledge-intensive work, *Journal of Applied Psychology*, 102: 1222–1236.
31. A. Mohammadi, A. Brostrom, & C. Franzoni, 2017, Workforce composition and innovation: How diversity in employees' ethnic and educational backgrounds facilitates firm-level innovativeness, *Journal of Product Innovation Management*, 34: 406–426.
32. T. Chen, M. A. Tribbitt, Y. Yang, & Z. Li, 2017, Does rivals' innovation matter? A competitive dynamics perspective on firms' product strategy, *Journal of Business Research*, 76: 1–7; C. P. Skroupa, 2017, Competitive advantage—how innovation is shaping the 21st century company, *Forbes*, www.forbes.com, October 4.
33. A. Giudici, P. Reinmoeller, & D. Ravasi, 2018, Open-system orchestration as a relational source of sensing capabilities: Evidence from a venture association, *Academy of Management Journal*, in press.
34. A. DeSantola & R. Gulati, 2017, Scaling: Organizing and growth in entrepreneurial ventures, *Academy of Management Annals*, 11: 640–668; E. E. Powell & T. Baker, 2017, In the beginning: Identity processes and organizing in multi-founder nascent ventures, *Academy of Management Journal*, 60: 2381–2414.
35. M. Ashan, 2017, The right people at the right time—the place does not matter, *Academy of Management Review*, 42: 145–148; Y. Yamakawa, M. W. Peng, & D. L. Deeds, 2015, Rising from the ashes: Cognitive determinants of venture growth after entrepreneurial failure, *Entrepreneurship Theory and Practice*, 39: 209–236.
36. G. Linton & J. Kask, 2017, Configurations of entrepreneurial orientation and competitive strategy for high performance, *Journal of Business Research*, 70: 168–176; C. Schlaegel & M. Koenig, 2014, Determinants of entrepreneurial intent: A meta-analytic test and integration of competing models, *Entrepreneurship Theory and Practice*, 38: 291–332.
37. C. Hernandez-Carrion, C. Camarero-Izquierdo, & J. Gutierrez-Cillan, 2017, Entrepreneurs' social capital and the economic performance of small businesses: The moderating role of competitive intensity and entrepreneurs' experience, *Strategic Entrepreneurship Journal*, 11: 61–89; Y. Bammens & V. Collewaert, 2014, Trust between entrepreneurs and angel investors: Exploring the positive and negative implications for venture performance assessments, *Journal of Management*, 40: 1980–2008.
38. T. Prive, 2013, Top 32 quotes every entrepreneur should live by, *Forbes*, www.forbes.com, May 2.
39. M. Gruber & I. C. MacMillan, 2017, Entrepreneurial behavior: A reconceptualization and extension based on identity theory, *Strategic Entrepreneurship Journal*, 11: 271–286; Kuratko & Morris, Examining the future trajectory of entrepreneurship.
40. S. Tallman, Y. Luo, & P. J. Buckley, 2018, Business models in global competition, *Global Strategy Journal*, in press; J. G. Covin & D. Miller, 2014, International entrepreneurial orientation: Conceptual considerations research themes, measurement issues, and future research directions, *Entrepreneurship Theory and Practice*, 38: 11–44.
41. P. Thakur-Wernz & S. Samant, 2018, Relationship between international experience and innovation performance: The importance of organizational learning in EMNEs, *Global Strategy Journal*, in press; P. Choudhury, 2017, Innovation outcomes in a distributed organization: Intrafirm mobility and access to resources, *Organization Science*, 28: 339–354; W. Tsai, 2001, Knowledge transfer in intraorganizational networks: Effects of network positon and absorptive capacity on business unit innovation performance, *Academy of Management Journal*, 44: 996–1004.
42. C. Myers, 2018, Coactive vicarious learning: Towards a relational theory of vicarious learning in organizations, *Academy of Management Review*, in press; Y. Li, V. Cui, & H. Liu, 2017, Dyadic specific investments, absorptive capacity, and manufacturers' market knowledge acquisition: Evidence from manufacturer-distributor dyads, *Journal of Business Research*, 78: 323–331.
43. The world's 50 most innovative companies in 2017, *Fast Company*, www.fastcompany.com, February 13.
44. H. (David) Yoon, N. Kim, B. Buisson, & F. Phillips, 2018, A cross-national study of knowledge, government intervention, and innovative nascent entrepreneurship, *Journal of Business Research*, 84: 243–252; H. M. Morgan, S. Sui, & M. Baum, 2018, Are SMEs with immigrant owners exceptional exporters? *Journal of Business Venturing*, 33: 241–260.
45. M. A. Rodriguez-Serrano & E. Martin-Armario, 2018, Born-global SMEs, performance, and dynamic absorptive capacity: Evidence from Spanish firms, *Journal of Small Business Management*, in press; H. Berry, 2014, Global integration and innovation: Multicountry knowledge generation within MNCs, *Strategic Management Journal*, 35: 869–890.
46. D. O'Brien, P. S. Scott, U. Andersson, T. Ambos, & N. Fu, 2018, The micro-foundations of subsidiary initiatives: How subsidiary-manager activities unlock entrepreneurship, *Global Strategy Journal*, in press; N. Symeonidou, J. Bruneel, & E. Autio, 2017, Commercialization strategy and internationalization outcomes in technology-based new ventures, *Journal of Business Venturing*, 32: 302–317.
47. R. E. Evert, J. B. Sears, J. A. Martin, & G. T. Payne, 2018, Family ownership and family involvement as antecedents of strategic action: A longitudinal study of initial international entry, *Journal of Business Research*, 84: 301–311; H. Li, X. Yi, & G. Cui, 2017, Emerging market firms' internationalization: How do firms' inward activities affect their outward activities? *Strategic Management Journal*, 38: 2704–2725.
48. A. Wiegmann, 2017, The 16 most innovative countries in the world, *Business Insider*, www.businessinsider.com, June 15.
49. M. Jamrisko & W. Lu, 2017, These are the world's most innovative economies, *Bloomberg*, www.bloomberg.com, January 16.
50. C. Cheng & M. Yang, 2018, Enhancing performance of cross-border mergers and acquisitions in developed markets: The role of business ties and technological innovation capability, *Journal of Business Research*, 81: 107–117; H. M. T. S. Herath & H. D. Karunaratne, 2017, The effect of learning orientation on born global performance: A developing country context, *The Business & Management Review*, 8: 157–166; W. Q. Judge, Y. Liu-Thompkins, J. L. Brown, & C. Pongpatipat, 2015, The impact of home country institutions on corporate technological entrepreneurship via R&D investments and virtual world presence, *Entrepreneurship Theory and Practice*, 39: 237–266.
51. C. Schwens, F. B. Zapkau, M. Bierwerth, R. Isidor, G. Knight, & R. Kabst, 2018, International entrepreneurship: A meta-analysis on the internationalization and performance relationship, *Entrepreneurship Theory and Practice*, in press; J.-F. Hennart, 2014, The accidental internationalists: A theory of born globals, *Entrepreneurship Theory and Practice*, 38: 117–135.
52. T. Schubert, E. Baier, & C. Rammer, 2018, Firm capabilities, technological dynamism and the internationalisation of innovation: A behavioral approach, *Journal of International Business Studies*, 49: 70–95; S. T. Cavusgil & G. Knight, 2015, The born global firm: An entrepreneurial and capabilities perspective on early and rapid internationalization, *Journal of International Business Studies*, 46: 3–16.
53. P. Li & H. Bathelt, 2018, Location strategy in cluster networks, *Journal of International*

Business Studies, in press; A. M. Bojica, M. del Mar Fuentes-Fuentes, & V. F. Perez, 2017, Corporate entrepreneurship and codification of the knowledge acquired from strategic partners in SMEs, *Journal of Small Business Management*, 55: 205–230.

54. W.-L. Hsieh, P. Ganotakis, M. Kafouros, & C. Wang, 2018, Foreign and domestic collaboration product innovation novelty, and firm growth, *Journal of Product Innovation Management*, 35: 652–672; R. Belderbos, B. Lokshin, & B. Sadowski, 2015, The returns to foreign R&D, *Journal of International Business Studies*, 46: 491–504.
55. A. Aagaard, 2017, Facilitating radical front-end innovation through targeted HRM practices: A case study of pharmaceutical and biotech companies, *Journal of Product Innovation Management*, 34: 427–449; S. J. Miles & M. van Clieaf, 2017, Strategic fit: Key to growing value through organizational capital, *Business Horizons*, 60: 55–65.
56. T. Kang, C. Baek, & J.-D. Lee, 2018, The persistency and volatility of the firm R&D investment: Revisited from the perspective of technological capability, *Research Policy*, 47: 307–324; J.-M. Ross, J. H. Fisch, & E. Varga, 2018, Unlocking the value of real options: How firm-specific learning conditions affect R&D investments under uncertainty, *Strategic Entrepreneurship Journal*, in press.
57. T. E. Brown, 2017, Sensor-based entrepreneurship: A framework for developing new products and services, *Business Horizons*, 60: 819–830; C. S. R. Chan & A. Parhankangas, 2017, Crowdfunding innovative ideas: How incremental and radical innovativeness influence funding outcomes, *Entrepreneurship Theory and Practice*, 41: 237–263.
58. S. Thomas, 2017, How Google encourages innovation among its employees, *Engageme*, www.engageme.com, September 13.
59. B. Kapoor, K. Nolan, & N. (Venkat) Venkatakrishnan, 2017, How GE Appliances built an innovation lab to rapidly prototype products, *Harvard Business Review blog*, www.hbr.org, July 21.
60. J. Morgan, 2015, Five examples of companies with internal innovation programs, *Huffington Post*, www.huffingtonpost.com, April 9.
61. R. M. U. S. Udagedara & K. Allman, 2018, Organizational dynamics and adoption of innovations: A study within the context of software firms in Sri Lanka, *Journal of Small Business Management*, in press; S. Fitz-Koch & M. Nordqvist, 2017, The reciprocal relationship of innovation capabilities and socioemotional wealth in a family firm, *Journal of Small Business Management*, 55: 547–570.
62. C. Prange & B. B. Schlegelmilch, 2018, Managing innovation dilemmas: The cube solution, *Business Horizons*, 61: 309–322.
63. S. W. Smith, 2014, Follow me to the innovation frontier? Leaders, laggards and the differential effects of imports and exports on technological innovation, *Journal of International Business Studies*, 45: 248–274.
64. T. Lafay & C. Maximin, 2017, How R&D competition affects investment choices, *Managerial and Decision Economics*, 38: 109–124.
65. J. P. Eggers & A. Kaul, 2018, Motivation and ability? A behavioral perspective on the pursuit of radical invention in multi-technology incumbents, *Academy of Management Journal*, 61: 67–93; G. Radaelli, G. Currie, F. Frattini, & E. Lettieri, 2017, The role of managers in enacting two-step institutional work for radical innovation in professional organizations, *Journal of Product Innovation Management*, 34: 450–470.
66. E. Muckersie, 2016, 3 examples of radical innovation, *Business 2 Community*, www.business2community.com, August 20.
67. M. Mohan, K. E. Voss, & F. R. Jimenez, 2017, Managerial disposition and front-end innovation success, *Journal of Business Research*, 70: 193–201; R. Roy & M. B. Sarkar, 2016, Knowledge, firm boundaries, and innovation: Mitigating the incumbent's curse during radical technological change, *Strategic Management Journal*, 37: 835–854.
68. S. Nicholson-Crotty, J. Nicholson-Crotty, & S. Fernandez, 2017, Performance and management in the public sector: Testing a model of relative risk aversion, *Public Administration Review*, 77: 603–614.
69. 2013, The power of imagination, *Wall Street Journal*, www.wsj.com, February 25.
70. M. Batey, 2012, Creativity is the key skill for the 21st century, *The Creativity Post*, www.creativitypost.com, March 28.
71. 2017, Creativity and imagination are as crucial for science as they are in the arts, *Firstpost*, www.firstpost.com, December 18.
72. A. Martini, P. Neirotti, & F. P. Appio, 2017, Knowledge searching, integrating and performing: Always a tuned trio for innovation? *Long Range Planning*, 50: 200–220; A. K. Chatterji & K. Fabrizio, 2012, How do product users influence corporate invention? *Organization Science*, 23: 971–987.
73. J. Brady, 2013, Some companies foster creativity, others fake it, *Wall Street Journal*, www.wsj.com, May 21.
74. I. Uzuegbunam, B. Ofem, & S. Nambisan, 2018, Do corporate investors affect entrepreneurs' IP portfolio? Entrepreneurial finance and intellectual property in new firms, *Entrepreneurship Theory and Practice*, in press; R. M. Bakker & D. A. Shepherd, 2017, Pull the plug or take the plunge: Multiple opportunities and the speed of venturing decisions in the Australian mining industry, *Academy of Management Journal*, 60: 130–155.
75. L. A. Bettencourt, E. U. Bond, III, M. S. Cole, & M. B. Houston, 2017, Domain-relevant coomitment and individual technical innovation performance, *Journal of Product Innovation Management*, 34: 159–180.
76. 2018, History timeline: Post-it Notes, 3M Homepage, www.3m.com, January 16.
77. M. D. Howard, M. C. Withers, & L. Tihanyi, 2017, Knowledge dependence and the formation of director interlocks, *Academy of Management Journal*, 60: 1986–2013.
78. 2018, Public Investment Fund, http://pif.gov.sa, January 26.
79. S. Paruchuri & S. Awate, 2017, Organizational knowledge networks and local search: The role of intra-organizational inventor networks, *Strategic Management Journal*, 38: 657–675; L. Mirabeau & S. Maguire, 2014, From autonomous strategic behavior to emergent strategy, *Strategic Management Journal*, 35: 1202–1229.
80. X. Wang & M. Dass, 2017, Building innovation capability: The role of top management innovativeness and relative-exploration orientation, *Journal of Business Research*, 76: 127–135; N. Anderson, K. Potocnik, & J. Zhou, 2014, Innovation and creativity in organizations: A state-of-the-art review, prospective commentary and guiding framework, *Journal of Management*, 40: 1297–1333.
81. S. E. Ante, 2013, IBM's chief to employees: Think fast, move faster, *Wall Street Journal*, www.wsj.com, April 24.
82. A. L. Merono-Cerdan & C. Lopez-Nicolas, 2017, Innovation objectives as determinants of organizational innovations, *Innovation: Organization & Management*, 19: 124–139; A. Caldart, R. W. Vassolo, & L. Silvestri, 2014, Induced variation in administrative systems: Experimenting with contexts for innovation, *Management Research*, 12: 123–151.
83. M. Bogers, N. J. Foss, & J. Lyngsie, 2018, The "human side" of open innovation: The role of employee diversity in firm-level openness, *Research Policy*, 47: 218–237; P. T. Gianidodis, J. E. Ettlie, & J. J. Urbana, 2014, Open service innovation in the global banking industry: Inside-out versus outside-in strategies, *Academy of Management Perspectives*, 28: 76–91.
84. H. Kang & J. Song, 2017, Innovation and recurring shifts in industrial leadership: Three phases of change and persistence in the camera industry, *Research Policy*, 46: 376–387; A. Compagni, V. Mele, & D. Ravasi, 2015, How early implementations influence later adoptions of innovation: Social positioning and skill reproduction in the diffusion of robotic surgery, *Academy of Management Journal*, 58: 242–278.
85. S. P. Clayton, M. Feldman, & N. Lowe, 2018, Behind the scenes: Intermediary organizations that facilitate science commercialization through entrepreneurship, *Academy of Management Perspectives*, 32: 104–124; S. Morricone, F. Munari, R. Oriani, & G. de Rassenfosse, 2018, Commercialization strategy and IPO underpricing, *Research Policy*, 46: 1133–1141.

86. J. E. Perry-Smith & P. V. Mannucci, 2017, From creativity to innovation: The social network drivers of the four phases of the idea journey, *Academy of Management Review*, 42: 53–79.
87. M. S. Cardon, C. Post, & W. R. Forster, 2017, Team entrepreneurial passion: Its emergence and influence in new venture teams, *Academy of Management Review*, 42: 283–205.
88. R. Veugelers & C. Schneider, 2018, Which IP strategies do young highly innovation firms choose? *Small Business Economics*, 50: 113–129; A. Martini, P. Neirotti, & F. P. Appio, 2017, Knowledge searching integrating and performing: Always a tuned trio for innovation? *Long Range Planning*, 50: 200–220.
89. J. P. Eggers & K. Park, 2018, Incumbent adaptation to technological change: The past, present, and future of research on heterogeneous incumbent response, *Academy of Management Annals*, 12: 357–389; T. G. Schweisfurth, 2017, Comparing internal and external lead users as sources of innovation, *Research Policy*, 46: 238–248.
90. S. Blount & P. Leinwand 2017, Reimagining effective cross-functional teams, *strategy & business*, www.strategy-business.com, November 20.
91. A. Agrawal, J. McHale, & A. Oetti, 2017, How stars matter: Recruiting and peer effects in evolutionary biology, *Research Policy*, 46: 853–867; P. R. Kehoe & D. Tzabbar, 2015, Lighting the way or stealing the shrine? An examination of the duality in star scientists' effects on firm innovation performance, *Strategic Management Journal*, 36: 709–727.
92. W.-Y. Park, Y. K. Ro, & N. Kim, 2018, Architectural innovation and the emergence of a dominant design: The effects of strategic sourcing on performance, *Research Policy*, 47: 326–341, K. Aoki & M. Wilheim, 2017, The role of ambidexterity in managing buyer-supplier relationships: The Toyota case, *Organization Science*, 28: 1080–1097.
93. A.-S. Fernandez, F. Le Roy, & P. Chiambaretto, 2018, Implementing the right project structure to achieve cooperative innovation projects, *Long Range Planning*, 51: 384–405; P. V. Mannucci, 2017, Drawing Snow White and animating Buzz Lightyear: Technological toolkit characteristics and creativity in cross-disciplinary teams, *Organization Science*, 28: 711–728.
94. T. Young-Hyman, 2017, How formal organizational power moderates cross-functional interaction in project teams, *Administrative Science Quarterly*, 62: 179–214; F. Aime, S. Humphrey, D. DeRue, & J. Paul, 2014, The riddle of heterarchy: Power transitions in cross-functional teams, *Academy of Mangement Journal*, 57: 327–352.
95. L. van Bundersen, L. Greer, & D. van Knippenberg, 2018, When inter-team conflict spirals into intra-team power struggles: The pivotal role of team power structures, *Academy of Management Journal*, 61: 1100–1130; G. L. Stewart, S. L. Astrove, C. J. Reeves, E. R. Crawford, & S. L. Solimeo, 2017, Those with the most find it hardest to share: Exploring leader resistance to the implementation of team-based empowerment, *Academy of Management Journal*, 60: 2266–2293.
96. D. Liu, Y. Gong, J. Zhou, & J.-C. Huang, 2017, Human resource systems, employee creativity, and firm innovations: The moderating role of firm ownership, *Academy of Management Journal*, 60: 1164–1188; J. Wombacher & J. Felfe, 2017, The interplay of team and organizational commitment in motivating employees' interteam conflict handling, *Academy of Management Journal*, 60: 1554–1581.
97. B. V. Todeschini, M. N. Cortimiglia, D. Callegaro-de-Menezes, & A. Ghezzi, 2017, Innovation and sustainable business models in the fashion industry: Entrepreneurial drivers, opportunities, and challenges, *Business Horizons*, 60: 759–770; V. Gupta & S. Singh, 2015, Leadership and creative performance behaviors in R&D laboratories: Examining the mediating role of justice perceptions, *Journal of Leadership and Organizational Studies*, 22: 21–36.
98. W. Barley, J. Treem, & T. Kuhn, 2018, Valuing multiple trajectories of knowledge: A critical review and agenda for knowledge management research, *Academy of Management Annals*, 12: 278–317; W. Sun, A. Su, & Y. Shang, 2014, Transformational leadership, team climate, and team performance within the NPD team: Evidence from China, *Asia Pacific Journal of Management*, 31: 127–147.
99. H. G. Gemunden, P. Lehner & A. Kock, 2018, The project-oriented organization and its contribution to innovation, *International Journal of Project Management*, 36: 147–160; F. Hacklin, U. Bjorkdahl, & M. W. Wallin, 2018, Strategies for business model innovation: How firms reel in migrating value, *Long Range Planning*, 51: 82–110.
100. C. Giahetti, J. Lampel, & S. L. Pira, 2017, Red Queen competitive imitation in the U.K. mobile phone industry, *Academy of Management Journal*, 60: 1882–1914; T. Lafay & C. Maximin, 2017, How R&D competition affects investment choices, *Managerial and Decision Economics*, 38: 109–124.
101. F. Meulman, I. M. M. J. Reyman, K. S. Podoynitsyna, & A. G. L. Romme, 2018, Searching for partners in open innovation settings: How to overcome the constraints of local search, *California Management Review*, 60: 71–97; U. Stettner & D. Lavie, 2014, Ambidexterity under scrutiny: Exploration and exploitation via internal organization alliances and acquisitions, *Strategic Management Journal*, 35: 1902–1929.
102. R. Roy, C. M. Lampert, & I. Stoyneva, 2018, When Dinosaurs fly: The role of firm capabilities in the 'Avianization' of incumbents during disruptive technological change, *Strategic Entrepreneurship Journal*, 12: 261–284; S. M. Riley, S. C. Michael, & J. T. Mahoney, 2017, Human capital matters: Market valuation of firm investments in training and the role of complementary assets, *Strategic Management Journal*, 38: 1895–1914.
103. T. L. Galloway, D. R. Miller, A. Sahaym, & J. D. Arthurs, 2017, Exploring the innovation strategies of young firms: Corporate venture capital and venture capital impact on alliance innovation strategy, *Journal of Business Research*, 71: 55–65; M. N. Hoehn-Weiss, S. Karim, & C.-H. Lee, 2017, Examining alliance portfolios beyond the dyads: The relevance of redundancy and nonuniformity across and between partners, *Organization Science*, 28: 56–73.
104. 2017, EY is extending alliance with Microsoft to bring innovative digital solutions to the agribusiness industry, EY Homepage, www.ey.com, October 19.
105. 2016, With IKEA's savvy, Marriott expands 'bare maximum' Moxy hotels, *Brandchannel*, www.brandchannel.com, July 8.
106. N. Trejos, 2016, First look at Marriott's new Moxy hotel brand in New Orleans, *USA Today*, www.usatoday.com, July 21.
107. P. Brady, 2017, Moxy Hotels, Marriott's millennial-friendly answer to Airbnb, opens in Times Square, *Conde Nast Traveler*, www.cntraveler.com, September 20.
108. W. Ryu, B. McCann, & J. Reuer, 2018, Geographic co-location of partners and rivals: Implications for the design of R&D alliances, *Academy of Management Journal*, 61: 945–965.
109. A. M. Subramanian, W. Bo, & C. Kah-Hin, 2018, The role of knowledge base homogeneity in learning from strategic alliances, *Research Policy*, 47: 158–168.
110. C. Salvato, J. Reuer, & P. Battigalli, 2017, Cooperation across disciplines: A multilevel perspective on cooperative behavior in governing interfirm relations, *Academy of Management Annals*, 11: 960–1004; B. B. Tyler & T. Caner, 2016, New product introductions below aspirations, slack and R&D alliances: A behavioral perspective, *Strategic Management Journal*, 37: 896–910.
111. J. Kengelback, G. Keienburg, T. Schid, S. Sievers, K. Gjerstad, J. Nielsen, & D. Walker, 2017, The 2017 M&A report: The technology takeover, *Boston Consulting Group*, www.bcg.com, September 15.
112. J.-S. Lee, J.-H. Park, & Z.-T. Bae, 2017, The effects of licensing-in on innovative performance in different technological regimes, *Research Policy*, 46: 485-496; J. Sears & G. Hoetker, 2014, Technological overlap, technological capabilities and resource recombinations by technological acquisitions, *Strategic Management Journal*, 35: 48–67.
113. L. Huang & A. P. Knight, 2017, Resources and relationships in entrepreneurship: An exchange theory of the development

and effects of the entrepreneur-investor relationship, *Academy of Management Review*, 42: 80–102; J. Li, J. Xia, & Z. Lin, 2017, Cross-border acquisitions by state-owned firms: How do legitimacy concerns affect the completion and duration of their acquisitions? *Strategic Management Journal*, 38: 1915–1934.

114. T. Greenwald, 2018, Is Broadcom's CEO, a champion deal maker, innovative enough? *Wall Street Journal*, www.wsj.com, January 25.

115. S. Choi & G. McNamara, 2018, Repeating a familiar pattern in a new way: The effect of exploitation and exploration on knowledge leverage behaviors in technology acquisitions, *Strategic Management Journal*, 39: 356–378; Y. Chen, 2017, Dynamic ambidexterity: How innovators manage exploration and exploitation, *Business Horizons*, 60: 385–394.

116. R. Lungeanu, I. Sgtern, & E. J. Zajac, 2016, When do firms change technology-sourcing vehicles? The role of poor innovative performance and financial slack, *Strategic Management Journal*, 37: 855–869.

117. B. Spigel & R. Harrison, 2018, Toward a process theory of entrepreneurial ecosystems, *Strategic Entrepreneurship Journal*, 12: 151–168; R. Lee, J.-H. Lee, & T. C. Garrett, 2018, Synergy effects of innovation on firm performance, *Journal of Business Research*, in press.

118. A. McKelvie, J. Wiklund, & A. Brattstrom, 2018, Externally acquired or internally generated? Knowledge development and perceived environmental dynamism in new venture innovation, *Entrepreneurship Theory and Practice*, 42: 24–46; A. Arora, S. Belenzon, & L. A. Rios, 2014, Make, buy, organize: The interplay between research, external knowledge, and firm structure, *Strategic Management Journal*, 35: 317–337.

119. S. Khalid & T. Sekiguchi, 2018, The role of empathy in entrepreneurial opportunity recognition: An experimental study in Japan and Pakistan, 2018, *Journal of Business Venturing Insights*, June: 1–9; R. Shu, S. Ren, & Y. Zheng, 2018, Building networks into discovery: The link between entrepreneur network capability and entrepreneurial opportunity discovery, *Journal of Business Research*, 85: 197–208.

120. C. S. R. Chan & A. Parhankangas, 2017, Crowdfunding innovative ideas: How incremental and radical innovativeness influence funding outcomes, *Entrepreneurship Theory and Practice*, 41: 237–263; A. Hyytinen, M. Pajarinen, & P. Rouvinen, 2014, Does innovativeness reduce startup survival rates? *Journal of Business Venturing*, 29: 564–581.

121. M. Wright & M. A. Hitt, 2017, Strategic entrepreneurship and *SEJ*: Development and current progress, *Strategic Entrepreneurship Journal*, 11: 200–210.

122. R. E. Hoskisson, E. Gambeta, C. Green, & T. Li, 2018, Is my firm-specific investment protected? Overcoming the stakeholder investment dilemma in the resource based view, *Academy of Management Review*, 43: 284–306.

123. T. Montgomery, 2017, "How much is this worth?" Humana's Chief Innovation Officer explains why this is the wrong question, *Muma Business Review*, 1: 31–38; R. B. Tucker, 2013, Are chief innovation officers delivering results? *Innovation Excellence*, www.innovationexcllence.com, March. 22.

124. G. Pellegrino & M. Savona, 2017, No money, no honey? Financial versus knowledge and demand constraints on innovation, *Research Policy*, 46: 510–521; J. Behrens & H. Patzelt, 2016, Corporate entrepreneurship managers' project terminations: Integrating portfolio-level, individual-level and firm-level effects, *Entrepreneurship Theory and Practice*, 40: 815–842.

125. D. A. Shepherd & T. A. Williams, 2018, Hitting rock bottom after job loss: Bouncing back to create a new positive work identity, *Academy of Management Review*, 43: 28–49; C. Aranda & J. Arellano, Organizational learning in target setting, *Academy of Management Journal*, 60: 1189–1211; J. P. Eggers, 2014, Competing technologies and industry evolution: The benefits of making mistakes in the flat panel display industry, *Strategic Management Journal*, 35: 159–178.

126. P. Lienert, 2017, Ford plans to nearly double SUV models in U.S. by 2020, *Automotive News*, www.autonews.com, February 7.

127. G. Brooks, 2017, Analysis: Ford's future global cars and minivans, *Just Auto*, www.just-auto.com, August 22.

CASE STUDIES

Case Title	Manu-facturing	Service	Consumer Goods	Food/ Retail	High Technology	Internet	Transportation/ Communication	International Perspective	Social/ Ethical Issues	Industry Perspective
Alphabet (Google)		•			•	•	•	•		
Baidu		•			•	•		•		•
BMW	•		•		•		•		•	
CrossFit		•							•	•
Healthcare Industry (Long-Term)		•							•	•
Heise Medien		•				•	•			•
Illinois Tool Works	•				•					
Kone	•				•			•		•
MatchMove		•			•	•		•		
Movie Exhibition Industry		•	•							•
Pacific Drilling	•				•			•		•
Pfizer	•				•			•	•	
Publix	•		•	•		•				•
Starbucks		•		•				•		•
Sturm, Ruger and Co.	•								•	•
Trivago		•			•	•	•			
Volkswagen	•		•					•	•	
Wells Fargo		•							•	
ZF Friedrichshafen	•				•			•	•	
ZO-Rooms		•			•	•			•	•

Case Title	Chapters 1	2	3	4	5	6	7	8	9	10	11	12	13
Alphabet (Google)						●	●			●	●		●
Baidu				●		●		●	●				●
BMW	●	●		●	●								●
CrossFit	●	●	●	●	●							●	
Healthcare Industry (Long-Term)		●		●	●								
Heise Medien		●			●								
Illinois Tool Works						●	●				●	●	●
Kone								●					●
MatchMove	●		●	●	●								●
Movie Exhibition Industry		●	●	●	●								
Pacific Drilling						●			●				●
Pfizer	●	●				●	●		●	●	●	●	●
Publix	●	●								●			
Starbucks		●	●									●	●
Sturm, Ruger and Co.		●	●	●	●								
Trivago								●					●
Volkswagen	●									●		●	
Wells Fargo	●											●	
ZF Friedrichshafen					●			●			●		
ZO-Rooms		●		●	●		●		●				●

Preparing an Effective Case Analysis

What to Expect from In-Class Case Discussions

As you will learn, classroom discussions of cases differ significantly from lectures. The case method calls for your instructor to guide the discussion and to solicit alternative views as a way of encouraging your active participation when analyzing a case. When alternative views are not forthcoming, your instructor might take a position just to challenge you and your peers to respond thoughtfully as a way of generating still additional alternatives. Often, instructors will evaluate your work in terms of both the quantity and the quality of your contributions to in-class case discussions. The in-class discussions are important in that you can derive significant benefit by having your ideas and recommendations examined against those of your peers and by responding to thoughtful challenges by other class members and/or the instructor.

During case discussions, your instructor will likely listen, question, and probe to extend the analysis of case issues. In the course of these actions, your peers and/or your instructor may challenge an individual's views and the validity of alternative perspectives that have been expressed. These challenges are offered in a constructive manner; their intent is to help all parties involved with analyzing a case develop their analytical and communication skills. Developing these skills is important in that they will serve you well when working for all types of organizations. Commonly, instructors will encourage you and your peers to be innovative and original when developing and presenting ideas. Over the course of an individual discussion, you are likely to form a more complex view of the case as a result of listening to and thinking about the diverse inputs offered by your peers and instructor. Among other benefits, experience with multiple case discussions will increase your knowledge of the advantages and disadvantages of group decision-making processes.

Both your peers and instructor will value comments that contribute to identifying problems as well as solutions to them. To offer relevant contributions, you are encouraged to think independently and, through discussions with your peers outside of class, to refine your thinking. We also encourage you to avoid using "I think," "I believe," and "I feel" to discuss your inputs to a case analysis process. Instead, consider using a less emotion laden phrase, such as "My analysis shows.... This highlights the logical nature of the approach you have taken to analyze a case. When preparing for an in-class case discussion, you should plan to use the case data to explain your assessment of the situation. Assume that your peers and instructor are familiar with the basic facts included in the case. In addition, it is good practice to prepare notes regarding your analysis of case facts before class discussions and use them when explaining your perspectives. Effective notes signal to classmates and the instructor that you are prepared to engage in a thorough discussion of a case. Moreover, comprehensive and detailed notes eliminate the need for you to memorize the facts and figures required to successfully discuss a case.

The case analysis process described above will help prepare you effectively to discuss a case during class meetings. Using this process results in consideration of the issues required to identify a focal firm's problems and to propose strategic actions through which the firm can increase the probability it will outperform its rivals. In some instances, your instructor may ask you to prepare either an oral or a written analysis of a particular case. Typically, such an assignment demands even more thorough study and analysis of the case contents. At your instructor's discretion, oral and written analyses may be completed by individuals or by groups of three or more people. The information and insights gained by completing the six steps shown in Table 1 often are of value when developing an oral or a written analysis. However, when preparing an oral or written presentation, you must consider the overall framework in which your information and inputs will be presented. Such a framework is the focus of the next section.

Preparing an Oral/Written Case Presentation

Experience shows that two types of thinking (analysis and synthesis) are necessary to develop an effective oral or written presentation (see Exhibit 1). In the analysis stage, you should first analyze the general external environmental issues affecting the firm. Next, your environmental analysis should focus on the particular industry (or industries, in the case of a diversified company) in which a firm operates. Finally, you should examine companies against which the focal firm competes. By studying the three levels of the external environment (general, industry, and competitor), you will be able to identify a firm's opportunities and threats. Following the external environmental analysis is the analysis of the firm's internal organization. This analysis provides the insights needed to identify the firm's strengths and weaknesses.

Table 1 An Effective Case Analysis Process

Step 1: Gaining Familiarity	a. In general—determine who, what, how, where, and when (the critical facts of the case). b. In detail—identify the places, persons, activities, and contexts of the situation. c. Recognize the degree of certainty/uncertainty of acquired information.
Step 2: Recognizing Symptoms	a. List all indicators (including stated "problems") that something is not as expected or as desired. b. Ensure that symptoms are not assumed to be the problem (symptoms should lead to identification of the problem).
Step 3: Identifying Goals	a. Identify critical statements by major parties (for example, people, groups, the work unit, and so on). b. List all goals of the major parties that exist or can be reasonably inferred.
Step 4: Conducting the Analysis	a. Decide which ideas, models, and theories seem useful. b. Apply these conceptual tools to the situation. c. As new information is revealed, cycle back to substeps a and b.
Step 5: Making the Diagnosis	a. Identify predicaments (goal inconsistencies). b. Identify problems (discrepancies between goals and performance). c. Prioritize predicaments/problems regarding timing, importance, and so on.
Step 6: Doing the Action Planning	a. Specify and prioritize the criteria used to choose action alternatives. b. Discover or invent feasible action alternatives. c. Examine the probable consequences of action alternatives. d. Select a course of action. e. Design an implementation plan/schedule. f. Create a plan for assessing the action to be implemented.

Source: C. C. Lundberg and C. Enz, 1993, A framework for student case preparation, *Case Research Journal,* 13 (Summer): 144, NACRA, North American Case Research Association.

As noted in Exhibit 1, you must then change the focus from analysis to synthesis. Specifically, you must synthesize information gained from your analysis of the firm's external environment and internal organization. Synthesizing information allows you to generate alternatives that can resolve the significant problems or challenges facing the focal firm. Once you identify a best alternative, from an evaluation based on predetermined criteria and goals, you must explore implementation actions.

In Table 2, we outline the sections that should be included in either an oral or a written presentation: strategic profile and case analysis purpose, situation analysis, statements of strengths/weaknesses and opportunities/threats, strategy formulation, and strategy implementation. These sections are described in the following discussion. Familiarity with the contents of your book's 13 chapters is helpful because the general outline for an oral or a written presentation shown in Table 2 is based on an understanding of the strategic management process detailed in those chapters. We follow the discussions of the parts of Table 2 with a few comments about the "process" to use to present the results of your case analysis in either a written or oral format.

Strategic Profile and Case Analysis Purpose

You will use the strategic profile to briefly present the critical facts from the case that have affected the focal firm's historical strategic direction and performance. The case facts should not be restated in the profile; rather, these comments should show how the critical facts lead to a particular focus for your analysis. This primary focus should be emphasized in this section's conclusion. In addition, this section should state important assumptions about case facts on which your analyses are based.

Situation Analysis

As shown in Table 2, a general starting place for completing a situation analysis is the general environment.

General Environmental Analysis. Your analysis of the general environment should focus on trends in the seven segments of the general environment (see Table 3). Many of the segment issues shown in Table 3 for the seven segments are explained more fully in Chapter 2 of your book. The objective you should have in evaluating these trends is to be able to *predict* the segments that you expect

Exhibit 1 Types of Thinking in Case Preparation: Analysis and Synthesis

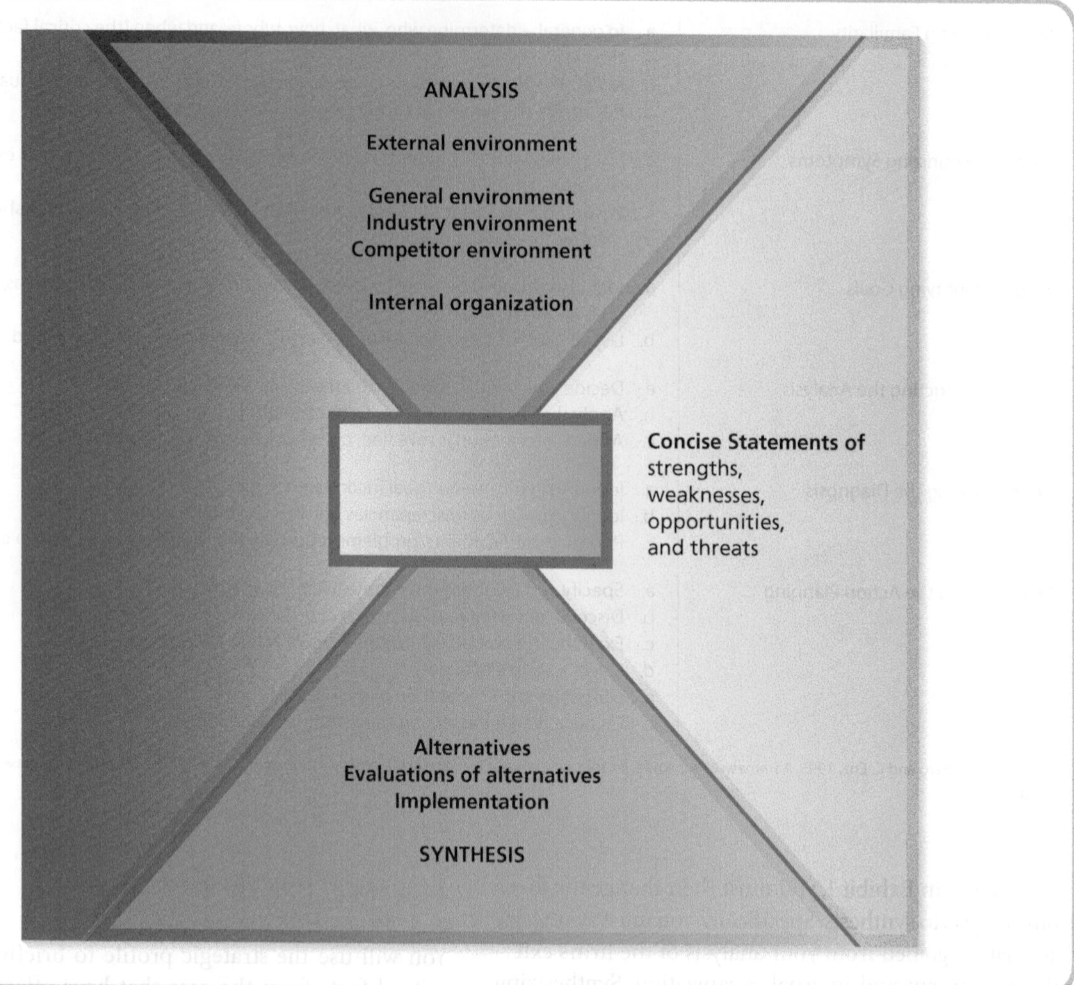

to have the most significant influence on your focal firm over the next several years (say three to five years) and to explain your reasoning for your predictions.

Industry Analysis. Porter's five forces model is a useful tool for analyzing the industry (or industries) in which your firm competes. We explain how to use this tool in Chapter 2. In this part of your analysis, you want to determine the attractiveness of an industry (or a segment of an industry) in which your firm is competing. As attractiveness increases, so does the possibility your firm will be able to earn profits by using its chosen strategies. After evaluating the power of the five forces relative to your firm, you should make a judgment as to *how* attractive the industry is in which your firm is competing.

Table 2 General Outline for an Oral or Written Presentation

I. Strategic Profile and Case Analysis Purpose
II. Situation Analysis
   A. General environmental analysis
   B. Industry analysis
   C. Competitor analysis
   D. Internal analysis
III. Identification of Environmental Opportunities and Threats and Firm Strengths and Weaknesses (SWOT Analysis)
IV. Strategy Formulation
   A. Strategic alternatives
   B. Alternative evaluation
   C. Alternative choice
v. Strategic Alternative Implementation
   A. Action items
   B. Action plan

Table 3 Sample General Environmental Categories

Technological Trends

- Information technology continues to become cheaper with more practical applications
- Database technology enables organization of complex data and distribution of information
- Telecommunications technology and networks increasingly provide fast transmission of all sources of data, including voice, written communications, and video information
- Computerized design and manufacturing technologies continue to facilitate quality and flexibility

Demographic Trends

- Regional changes in population due to migration
- Changing ethnic composition of the population
- Aging of the population
- Aging of the "baby boom" generation

Economic Trends

- Interest rates
- Inflation rates
- Savings rates
- Exchange rates
- Trade deficits
- Budget deficits

Political/Legal Trends

- Antitrust enforcement
- Tax policy changes
- Environmental protection laws
- Extent of regulation/deregulation
- Privatizing state monopolies
- State-owned industries

Sociocultural Trends

- Women in the workforce
- Awareness of health and fitness issues
- Concern for overcoming poverty
- Concern for customers

Global Trends

- Currency exchange rates
- Free-trade agreements
- Trade deficits

Physical Environment Trends

- Environmental sustainability
- Corporate social responsibility
- Renewable energy
- Goals of zero waste
- Ecosystem impact of food and energy production

Competitor Analysis. Firms also need to *analyze* each of their primary competitors. This analysis should identify competitors' current strategies, strategic intent, strategic mission, capabilities, core competencies, and a competitive response profile (see Chapter 2). This information is useful to the focal firm in formulating an appropriate strategy and in predicting competitors' probable responses. Sources that can be used to gather information about an industry and companies with whom the focal firm competes are listed in Appendix I. Included in this list is a wide range of publications, such as periodicals, newspapers, bibliographies, directories of companies, industry ratios, forecasts, rankings/ratings, and other valuable statistics.

Internal Analysis. Assessing a firm's strengths and weaknesses through a value chain analysis facilitates moving from the external environment to the internal organization. Analysis of the value chain activities and the support functions of the value chain provides opportunities to understand how external environmental trends affect the specific activities of a firm. Such analysis helps highlight strengths and weaknesses (see Chapter 3 for an explanation and use of the value chain).

For purposes of preparing an oral or a written presentation, it is important to note that strengths are internal resources and capabilities that have the potential to be core competencies. Weaknesses, on the other hand, are internal resources and capabilities that have the potential to place a firm at a competitive disadvantage relative to its rivals. Thus, some of a firm's resources and capabilities are strengths; others are weaknesses.

When evaluating the internal characteristics of the firm, your analysis of the functional activities emphasized is critical. For instance, if the strategy of the firm is primarily technology driven, it is important to evaluate the firm's R&D activities. If the strategy is market driven, marketing functional activities are of paramount importance. If a firm has financial difficulties, critical financial ratios would require careful evaluation. In fact, because of the importance of financial health, most cases require financial analyses. Appendix II lists and operationally defines several common financial ratios. Included are tables describing profitability, liquidity, leverage, activity, and shareholders' return ratios. Leadership, organizational culture, structure, and control systems (see Chapters 11 and 12) are other characteristics of firms you should examine to fully understand the "internal" part of your firm.

Identification of Environmental Opportunities and Threats and Firm Strengths and Weaknesses (SWOT Analysis)

The outcome of the situation analysis is the identification of a firm's strengths and weaknesses and its environmental threats and opportunities. The next step requires that you *analyze* the strengths and weaknesses and the opportunities and threats for configurations that benefit or do not benefit your firm's efforts to perform well. Case analysts and organizational strategists as well seek to match a firm's strengths with its opportunities. In addition, strengths are chosen to prevent any serious environmental threat from negatively affecting the firm's performance. The key objective of conducting a SWOT analysis is to determine how to position the firm so it can take advantage of opportunities, while simultaneously avoiding or minimizing environmental threats. Results from a SWOT analysis yield valuable insights into the selection of a firm's strategies. The analysis of a case should not be overemphasized relative to the synthesis of results gained from your analytical efforts. There may be a temptation to spend most of your oral or written case analysis on results from the analysis. It is important, however, that you make an equal effort to develop and evaluate alternatives and to design implementation of the chosen strategy.

Strategy Formulation—Strategic Alternatives, Alternative Evaluation, and Alternative Choice

Developing alternatives is often one of the most difficult steps in preparing an oral or a written presentation. Developing three to four alternative strategies is common (see Chapter 4 for business-level strategy alternatives and Chapter 6 for corporate-level strategy alternatives). Each alternative should be feasible (i.e., it should match the firm's strengths, capabilities, and especially core competencies), and feasibility should be demonstrated. In addition, you should show how each alternative takes advantage of the environmental opportunity or avoids/buffers against environmental threats. Developing carefully thought out alternatives requires synthesis of your analyses' results and creates greater credibility in oral and written case presentations.

Once you develop strong alternatives, you must evaluate the set to choose the best one. Your choice should be defensible and provide benefits over the other alternatives. Thus, it is important that both alternative development and the evaluation of alternatives be thorough. The choice of the best alternative should be explained and defended.

Strategic Alternative Implementation-Action Items and Action Plan

After selecting the most appropriate strategy (that is, the strategy with the highest probability of helping your firm in its efforts to earn profits), implementation issues require attention. Effective synthesis is important to ensure that you have considered and evaluated all critical implementation issues. Issues you might consider include the structural changes necessary to implement the new strategy. In addition, leadership changes and new controls or incentives may be necessary to implement strategic actions. The implementation actions you recommend should be explicit and thoroughly explained. Occasionally, careful evaluation of implementation actions may show the strategy to be less favorable than you thought originally. A strategy is only as good as the firm's ability to implement it.

Process Issues

You should ensure that your presentation (either oral or written) has logical consistency throughout. For example, if your presentation identifies one purpose, but your analysis focuses on issues that differ from the stated purpose, the logical inconsistency will be apparent. Likewise, your alternatives should flow from the configuration of strengths, weaknesses, opportunities, and threats you identified by analyzing your firm's external environment and internal organization.

Thoroughness and clarity also are critical to an effective presentation. Thoroughness is represented by the comprehensiveness of the analysis and alternative generation. Furthermore, clarity in the results of the analyses, selection of the best alternative strategy, and design of implementation actions are important. For example, your statement of the strengths and weaknesses should flow clearly and logically from your analysis of your firm's internal organization.

Presentations (oral or written) that show logical consistency, thoroughness, and clarity of purpose, effective analyses, and feasible recommendations (strategy and implementation) are more effective and are likely to be more positively received by your instructor and peers. Furthermore, developing the skills necessary to make such presentations will enhance your future job performance and career success.

Appendix I Sources for Industry and Competitor Analyses

Abstracts and Indexes	
Periodicals	ABI/*Inform* *Business Periodicals Index* *InfoTrac* Custom Journals *InfoTrac* Custom Newspapers *InfoTrac* OneFile EBSCO Business Source Premiere Lexis/Nexis Academic *Public Affairs Information Service Bulletin* (PAIS) *Reader's Guide to Periodical Literature*
Newspapers	*NewsBank—Foreign Broadcast Information* *NewsBank-Global NewsBank* *New York Times Index* *Wall Street Journal Index* *Wall Street Journal/Barron's Index* *Washington Post Index*
Bibliographies	*Encyclopedia of Business Information Sources*
Directories	
Companies—General	*America's Corporate Families and International Affiliates* *Hoover's Online: The Business Network* www.hoovers.com/free D&B Million Dollar Directory (databases: http://www.dnbmdd.com) *Standard & Poor's Corporation Records* *Standard & Poor's Register of Corporations, Directors, and Executives* (http://www.netadvantage.standardandpoors.com for all of *Standard & Poor's*) *Ward's Business Directory of Largest U.S. Companies*
Companies—International	*America's Corporate Families and International Affiliates* *Business Asia* *Business China* *Business Eastern Europe* *Business Europe* *Business International* *Business International Money Report* *Business Latin America*

(Continued)

Appendix I (Continued) Sources for Industry and Competitor Analyses

Abstracts and Indexes	
	Directory of American Firms Operating in Foreign Countries *Directory of Foreign Firms Operating in the United States* *Hoover's Handbook of World Business* *International Directory of Company Histories* *Mergent's International Manual* Mergent Online (http://www.fisonline.com—for "Business and Financial Information Connection to the World") *Who Owns Whom*
Companies—Manufacturers	*Thomas Register of American Manufacturers* U.S. Office of Management and Budget, Executive Office of the President, *Standard Industrial Classification Manual* *U.S. Manufacturer's Directory, Manufacturing & Distribution, USA*
Companies—Private	*D&B Million Dollar Directory* *Ward's Business Directory of Largest U.S. Companies*
Companies—Public	Annual Reports and 10-K Reports *Disclosure* (corporate reports) *Q-File* Securities and Exchange Commission Filings & Forms (EDGAR) http://www.sec.gov/edgar.shtml *Mergent's Manuals:* ■ *Mergent's Bank and Finance Manual* ■ *Mergent's Industrial Manual* ■ *Mergent's International Manual* ■ *Mergent's Municipal and Government Manual* ■ *Mergent's OTC Industrial Manual* ■ *Mergent's OTC Unlisted Manual* ■ *Mergent's Public Utility Manual* ■ *Mergent's Transportation Manual* Standard & Poor's Corporation, *Standard Corporation Descriptions:* http://www.netadvantage.standardandpoors.com ■ *Standard & Poor's Analyst Handbook* ■ *Standard & Poor's Industry Surveys* ■ *Standard & Poor's Statistical Service*
Companies—Subsidiaries and Affiliates	*America's Corporate Families and International Affiliates* *Ward's Directory* *Who Owns Whom* *Mergent's Industry Review* *Standard & Poor's Analyst's Handbook* *Standard & Poor's Industry Surveys* (2 volumes) U.S. Department of Commerce, *U.S. Industrial Outlook*
Industry Ratios	Dun & Bradstreet, *Industry Norms and Key Business* *Ratios RMA's Annual Statement Studies* *Troy Almanac of Business and Industrial Financial Ratios*
Industry Forecasts	International Trade Administration, *U.S. Industry & Trade Outlook*
Rankings & Ratings	Annual Report on American Industry in *Forbes Business Rankings Annual* *Mergent's Industry Review* http://www.worldcatlibraries.org *Standard & Poor's Industry Report Service* http://www.netadvantage.standardandpoors.com *Value Line Investment Survey* *Ward's Business Directory of Largest U.S. Companies*
Statistics	*American Statistics Index (ASI)* Bureau of the Census, U.S. Department of Commerce, *Economic Census Publications* Bureau of the Census, U.S. Department of Commerce, *Statistical Abstract of the United States* Bureau of Economic Analysis, U.S. Department of Commerce, *Survey of Current Business* Internal Revenue Service, U.S. Treasury Department, *Statistics of Income: Corporation Income Tax* *Returns* *Statistical Reference Index (SRI)*

Appendix II Financial Analysis in Case Studies

Table A-1 Profitability Ratios

Ratio	Formula	What It Shows
1. Return on total assets	$\frac{\text{Profits after taxes}}{\text{Total assets}}$ or $\frac{\text{Profits after taxes + Interest}}{\text{Total assets}}$	The net return on total investments of the firm or The return on both creditors' and shareholders' investments
2. Return on stockholders' equity (or return on net worth)	$\frac{\text{Profits after taxes}}{\text{Total stockholders' equity}}$	How profitably the company is utilizing shareholders' funds
3. Return on common equity	$\frac{\text{Profits after taxes} - \text{Preferred stock dividends}}{\text{Total stockholders' equity} - \text{Par value of preferred stock}}$	The net return to common stockholders
4. Operating profit margin (or return on sales)	$\frac{\text{Profits before taxes and before interest}}{\text{Sales}}$	The firm's profitability from regular operations
5. Net profit margin (or net return on sales)	$\frac{\text{Profits after taxes}}{\text{Sales}}$	The firm's net profit as a percentage of total sales

Table A-2 Liquidity Ratios

Ratio	Formula	What It Shows
1. Current ratio	$\frac{\text{Current assets}}{\text{Current liabilities}}$	The firm's ability to meet its current financial liabilities
2. Quick ratio (or acid-test ratio)	$\frac{\text{Current assets} - \text{Inventory}}{\text{Current liabilities}}$	The firm's ability to pay off short-term obligations without relying on sales of inventory
3. Inventory to net working capital	$\frac{\text{Inventory}}{\text{Current assets} - \text{Current liabilities}}$	The extent to which the firm's working capital is tied up in inventory

Table A-3 Leverage Ratios

Ratio	Formula	What It Shows
1. Debt-to-assets	$\frac{\text{Total debt}}{\text{Total assets}}$	Total borrowed funds as a percentage of total assets
2. Debt-to-equity	$\frac{\text{Total debt}}{\text{Total shareholders' equity}}$	Borrowed funds versus the funds provided by shareholders
3. Long-term debt-to-equity	$\frac{\text{Long-term debt}}{\text{Total shareholders' equity}}$	Leverage used by the firm
4. Times-interest-earned (or coverage ratio)	$\frac{\text{Profits before interest and taxes}}{\text{Total interest charges}}$	The firm's ability to meet all interest payments
5. Fixed charge coverage	$\frac{\text{Profits before taxes and interest + Lease obligations}}{\text{Total interest charges + Lease obligations}}$	The firm's ability to meet all fixed-charge obligations including lease payments

Table A-4 Activity Ratios

Ratio	Formula	What It Shows
1. Inventory turnover	$\frac{\text{Sales}}{\text{Inventory of finished goods}}$	The effectiveness of the firm in employing inventory
2. Fixed assets turnover	$\frac{\text{Sales}}{\text{Fixed assets}}$	The effectiveness of the firm in utilizing plant and equipment
3. Total assets turnover	$\frac{\text{Sales}}{\text{Total assets}}$	The effectiveness of the firm in utilizing total assets
4. Accounts receivable turnover	$\frac{\text{Annual credit sales}}{\text{Accounts receivable}}$	How many times the total receivables have been collected during the accounting period
5. Average collecting period	$\frac{\text{Accounts receivable}}{\text{Average daily sales}}$	The average length of time the firm waits to collect payment after sales

Table A-5 Shareholders' Return Ratios

Ratio	Formula	What It Shows
1. Dividend yield on common stock	$\frac{\text{Annual dividend per share}}{\text{Current market price per share}}$	A measure of return to common stockholders in the form of dividends
2. Price-earnings ratio	$\frac{\text{Current market price per share}}{\text{After-tax earnings per share}}$	An indication of market perception of the firm; usually, the faster-growing or less risky firms tend to have higher PE ratios than the slower-growing or more risky firms
3. Dividend payout ratio	$\frac{\text{Annual dividends per share}}{\text{After-tax earnings per share}}$	An indication of dividends paid out as a percentage of profits
4. Cash flow per share	$\frac{\text{After-tax profits + Depreciation}}{\text{Number of common shares outstanding}}$	A measure of total cash per share available for use by the firm

CASE 1

ICMR
IBS Center for Management Research
www.icmrindia.org

Alphabet Inc.: Reorganizing Google

In October 2015, in an unexpected move, global technology giant Google Inc (Google) restructured itself as Alphabet Inc (Alphabet), a new holding company under which Google's non-core businesses, including self-driving cars, life sciences research, high-speed Internet access, and investment divisions, were spun off as distinct entities and separated from the company's Internet operations such as Android, YouTube, and the Google search engine. The businesses were reorganized into two reporting segments: 'Google' and 'Other Bets'. This marked a massive shift from the earlier setup in which Google was in charge of a number of diverse companies, some of which carried it far afield from its core search business. Under the new structure, a number of businesses including Google operated as subsidiaries of Alphabet and were run independently, each with its own CEO. According to a statement posted by Larry Page co-founder of Google, on the company's official blog, *"Fundamentally, we believe this allows us more management scale, as we can run things independently that aren't very related. Alphabet is about businesses prospering through strong leaders and independence [. . .]. This new structure will allow us to keep tremendous focus on the extraordinary opportunities we have inside of Google."*[1]

Co-founded by Page and Sergey Brin in 1998, Google provided Internet-related services and products including web-based search, cloud computing, software applications, online advertising technologies, mobile operating systems, consumer content, enterprise solutions, and hardware products. Since its inception it had focused on innovation and come out with disruptive technologies from time to time. The company had branched out into hosting services like video and mapping, enterprise services, e-mail and chat, social networking space, payment gateway services, mobile operating software, and wireless device sales. Google's technological innovations made it one of the most recognized and valuable brands in the world.

However, over a period of time investors had begun to voice strong concern over Google expanding into areas unrelated to its core search business and into unknown territory in terms of profitability. They felt that Google had got distracted from its core web search and was hemorrhaging money in pursuing projects fancied by its founders such as developing robots and self-driving cars and studying life sciences. Investors began to question the heavy investments the company had been making in non-core businesses and the lack of clarity concerning risky investments. Analysts too found it difficult to evaluate the company's broad set of businesses and figure out their individual performances. Eventually, the senior management realized that the company had become too complex to manage and that a change was required to allow for cleaner operations and more accountability. Subsequently, they announced a radical shake-up of Google's corporate structure and management, and created a new holding company called Alphabet that would manage a collection of companies, the largest of these being Google.

Industry observers saw this move as being a response to Google's stagnant share price and an attempt to pacify investors. Some analysts lauded the move saying Google's decision to restructure itself under a new holding company would protect its core brand Google, increase the operational independence of the individual businesses, and usher in greater financial transparency across divisions. On the other hand, some analysts criticized the change and questioned how the restructuring would make the company's businesses competitively stronger and increase profitability and company valuation.

Post restructuring, Alphabet pushed for more financial discipline and accountability from its riskiest ventures. The non-core companies were struggling as they faced unprecedented pressure to bring their costs in line with their revenue. In fiscal 2016, 'Other Bets' posted a loss of about $3.6 billion. Moreover, some key executives who were chosen to turn the riskier 'Other Bets' into reality departed from Alphabet, allegedly over pressure to perform. Going forward, investors would likely pile up the pressure if the company faltered and nothing profitable emerged from 'Other Bets', said analysts.[2] The questions being asked were: Will the creation of Alphabet spell a new successful era for Google? Can Alphabet maintain Google's lead as an innovator and challenge competitors in a wide array of industries?

This case was written by **Syeda Maseeha Qumer and Debapratim Purkayastha**, IBS Hyderabad. It was compiled from published sources, and is intended to be used as a basis for class discussion rather than to illustrate either effective or ineffective handling of a management situation.

Background Note

Google's roots lay in a research project on search engines taken up by two PhD students at Stanford University, Larry Page and Sergey Brin, in 1996. Google pioneered a new technology called 'PageRank', which determined the importance of the website by the number of other pages linked to it and their importance that linked back to the original site. This new technology marked a shift from the earlier method followed by other search engines which ranked the results by the number of times the search terms appeared on the page. The search engine was initially called 'BackRub' as it determined a website's relevance by checking its back links. The name was finally changed to Google, based on the word 'Googol'—the number one followed by a hundred zeroes.

Google's primary domain 'www.google.com' was registered in September 1997 and the company was incorporated in September 1998 in a friend's garage in California, USA. In 1999, Google moved its headquarters to Palo Alto, California, home to several other technology companies. Google's mission was "to organize the world's information and make it universally accessible and useful."[3] In August 2001, Eric E. Schmidt succeeded Page as the CEO of Google, just five months after joining the company as chairman of the board.

Google started to sell advertisements associated with search keywords. This advertising model was successful and the company started getting a major part of its revenues from search-related advertising. From 2001, Google based its growth strategies on acquiring many small companies with innovative products. It added many other products to its product portfolio like Google Earth[a] and YouTube[b] in this way. Apart from acquiring other companies, Google also launched its own products like the free webmail, called 'Gmail', in April 2004. Gmail was also well received by the web community due to the massive increase in storage space provided by Google (initially one GB). The success of Gmail and YouTube made Google the undisputed leader on the Internet, with the company overtaking many other established Internet companies like Yahoo! Inc.[c]

Google's promoters were hesitant to go in for an Initial Public Offering (IPO) as they were apprehensive that public scrutiny and financial regulations would make the company less agile.[4] But, due to the demands of venture capitalists who wanted to cash out, Google filed for an IPO in April 2004. In the IPO prospectus, Google's founders attached a letter subtly warning potential subscribers that Google was not a conventional company and did not aim to be one.[5] The dual class equity structure proposed by Google's founders proved controversial. Google's IPO comprised only the issue of Class A shares, each of which was entitled to a single vote. Google's founders, venture capitalists, and other insiders held Class B shares which were entitled to 10 votes per share.[6] Class C shares had no voting rights, except as required by applicable law. Critics lambasted this share structure as they felt that it gave the founders significant management control and could lead to potential management abuse. But Page and Brin defended the structure on the grounds that it would help them fulfill their long-term vision for the company without getting bogged down by short-term financial demands.[7]

By the mid-2000s, Google faced a new challenge in the form of the ever-expanding high-end mobile phones dubbed as smartphones. Developing applications for the variety of platforms on which these smartphones were available proved to be cumbersome for Google. The company therefore decided to launch its own open-source platform for mobile phones, which would give application developers the freedom to develop applications for various mobile phones without depending on any handset manufacturer or service provider. Hence, Google acquired an open-source mobile platform called Android from Android, Inc. and released its first version in the market in 2009. Android proved to be an instant hit in the market and soon emerged as the dominant mobile operating system in the world.

In April 2009, Google launched a venture capital arm called Google Ventures to invest in a diverse array of industries, including the consumer Internet, software, clean tech, and healthcare. In January 2011, Schmidt stepped down as CEO of Google and Page took over. Schmidt continued as Executive Chairman of the company. In August 2011, Google acquired Motorola Mobility LLC[d] for \$12.5 billion in order to make its own hardware for smartphones, tablets, and other devices.[8]

Other than acquiring other smaller companies for launching new products, Google also focused on innovation and spent huge sums of money on developing

[a]Google Earth is a virtual globe, map, and geographic information application owned by Google.

[b]YouTube is a video sharing website owned by Google. Users can upload, share, and view videos on the website.

[c]Yahoo! Inc., headquartered in Sunnyvale, California, USA, is an Internet company which provides services like search engine, webmail, online mapping, etc.

[d]Motorola Mobility LLC, headquartered in Libertyville, Illinois, USA is a leading telecommunications company in the world.

new services. However, rather than a simple iterative approach to innovation, Page wanted Google to develop a 'moonshot mentality' where it would be inspired to create products and services that were 10 times better than the competition. Google X, a separate division which was established in early 2010 to come out with 'moonshot' projects, was Page's brainchild. In 2010, Google started to invest heavily in developing technologies which were both related and unrelated to its core business. Most of these products were innovative and were totally new to the world. One of the most hyped up technologies developed by Google was 'Google Glass', a wearable computer which came with its own optical head-mounted display (OHMD).[e] This wearable computer performed many of the tasks traditionally performed by other portable gadgets like smartphones and tablets.[9] Another important technology that Google had been working on was the Google Driverless Car project. This project was aimed at developing autonomous cars which would drive on their own without the need for any physical drivers. Google was testing cars which ran using this technology across the world and was expected to release it for the mass market once it obtained the legal clearances.

In September 2013, Google entered into healthcare research by creating a new company called **Calico** to make advancements in human health and well-being, in particular understanding the aging process and increasing the longevity of people. There were two other innovative technology projects of Google aimed at improving accessibility to people around the world. The more ambitious of the two was **Project Loon** which aimed to bring Internet access within the reach of people living in remote parts of the world. Another new service that Google was experimenting with was **Google Fiber** which promised to bring very high-speed Internet access (100 times greater than the prevalent broadband speeds) within the reach of everyone.

In order to make its mark in smart-home systems, in January 2014, Google acquired Nest Labs, Inc., a smart-home appliances maker of thermostats and smoke alarms, for $3.2 billion. Less than three years after acquiring Motorola, Google sold the smartphone maker to Chinese PC manufacturer Lenovo for $2.9 billion in January 2014.

In June 2015, Google started an urban innovation company called **Sidewalk Labs** that used technology and innovation to improve urban life. Google's revenues for the year 2015 were $74.5 billion with over 90% of the earnings coming from online advertising. The company had more than 59,976 employees worldwide as of October 2015.

Why Google Became Alphabet

Since its inception, Page and Brin had massively diversified Google from its origins as an Internet search engine to invest in several projects that were unrelated to its core business such as self-driving cars, renewable energy, wearable technology, artificial intelligence, mapping services, and the Android operating system. According to them, Google being just a search company, no matter how successful, would not be able to consolidate its position in the highly competitive tech market without diversifying. The duo began to pour money into far-off fields by increasing their spending on research and development. In the 2004 Founders' IPO Letter, they wrote, "*Google is not a conventional company. We do not intend to become one. Do not be surprised if we place smaller bets in areas that seem very speculative or even strange when compared to our current businesses. Although we cannot quantify the specific level of risk we will undertake, as the ratio of reward to risk increases, we will accept projects further outside our current businesses, especially when the initial investment is small relative to the level of investment in our current businesses.*"[10]

Though Google's diversification strategy drove the company forward and benefited customers, it created several issues. Google was tight-lipped about its riskier and non-core investments, including the moonshot projects, which left investors feeling uneasy. "*Historically, Google has notoriously been a black box. Larry Page and company consistently marched to the beat of their own drum,*"[11] said James Cakmak, an analyst at equity research and trading company Monness Crespi Hardt & Co. Moreover, the financial returns of the search engine and advertising business were not observed separately from the investments in all of the new businesses. This appeared to limit transparency, accountability, and discipline across the company. The moonshot projects lost $1.9 billion in 2014.[12]

Google came under some pressure from Wall Street as investors began to question the heavy investments it was making in non-core businesses and complained about the lack of clarity regarding risky investments. The shareholders were upset as there were no paybacks to them in the form of dividends or buybacks. Profits

[e]OHMD displays use an optical mixer made of silvered mirrors. These displays have the capability to reflect projected images besides allowing the user to look through them.

from the search and ad business were plowed into vague innovation projects leaving investors worried and this led to stagnation in Google's stock price despite the company's long-term value creation. Observers felt that Google had become a vast and diverse company and its mission statement—"to organize the world's information and make it universally accessible and useful"—no longer made sense. According to Michael Quirke, senior consultant at brand agency Brand Union, "*Their ambitions in health, hardware and drones are too far from their search core to keep under the Google name, and that name was beginning to get tarnished for its world-eating ambitions.*"[13]

As Google continued to grow at a rapid pace, problems began to emerge in its organizational structure. Prior to restructuring, Google had adopted a cross-functional organizational structure which was more of a team approach to management and was structured horizontally wherein Google, the parent company, was in charge of a number of diverse companies ***(See Exhibit 1).*** Google implemented a centralized decision-making system wherein Brin and Page along with Schmidt made all the major decisions together. Though the system made sense in the beginning, it turned problematic as Google grew in size. On many occasions, the trio used to discuss and debate for long hours, making the product teams wait and stalling all the dependent processes. Sometimes these meetings would end with no tangible decision being arrived at because one of the three was missing, making one more discussion inevitable. This slowed down the decision-making process at the company. Some analysts also criticized Google for maintaining an opaque and monolithic structure, where no outsider would know the developments behind the scenes. Analysts themselves found it difficult to evaluate the broad set of businesses and to figure out the performance of the core business. As managing such a diverse set of business operations under a single organization was creating bottlenecks, experts felt that the company was in need of a strong and accountable management structure and strategy.

Eventually the senior management at Google realized that the company had become too complex to manage as it was pursuing potentially big new businesses in industries far from its search-engine roots. They wanted to improve the transparency and provide an oversight of what the company was doing. Page admitted that Google's original mission statement had become somewhat obsolete. "*We're in a bit of uncharted territory. We're trying to figure it out. How do we use all these resources . . . and have a much more positive impact on the world,*"[14] he said.

In August 2015, Page announced a plan to draw a dividing line between Google and its other ventures by creating a new public holding company under which Google's non-core businesses would be spun off as

Exhibit 1 Google's Structure 2014–2015 (Before Reorganization)

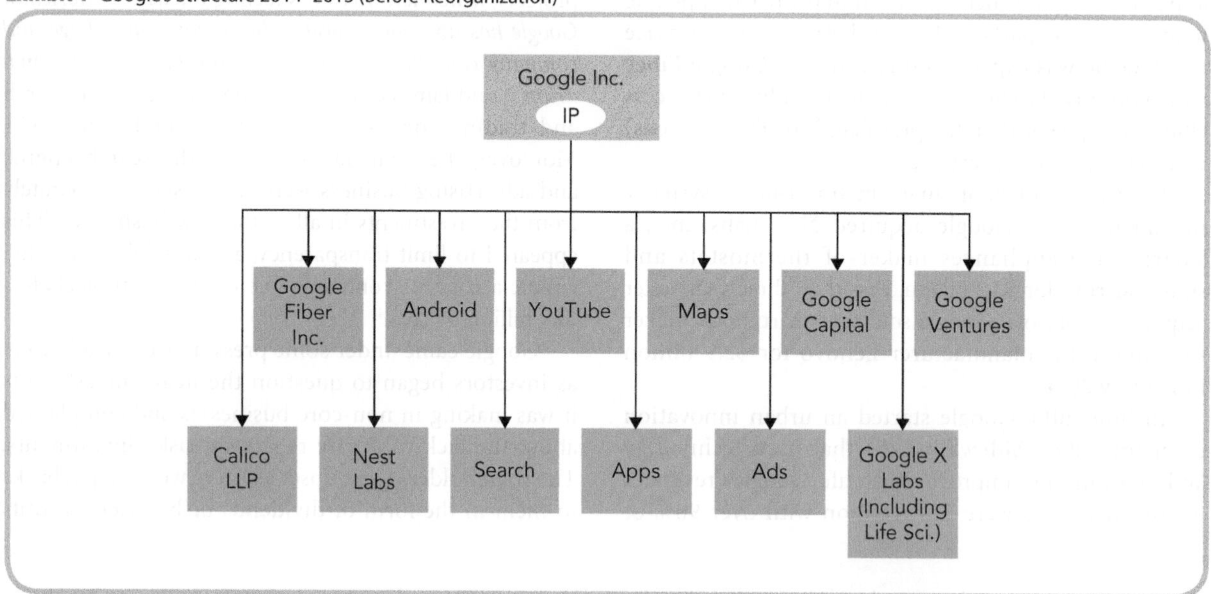

Source: hbtlj.org/articlearchive/v16i1/16HousBusTaxLJ1.pdf

distinct entities and separated from the company's main Internet-related businesses. He said, "*We've long believed that over time companies tend to get comfortable doing the same thing, just making incremental changes. But in the technology industry, where revolutionary ideas drive the next big growth areas, you need to be a bit uncomfortable to stay relevant. Our company is operating well today, but we think we can make it cleaner and more accountable. So we are creating a new company, called Alphabet.*"[15]

The A To Z of Alphabet

On October 2, 2015, Alphabet became the parent holding company of Google and its diverse set of businesses with no business operations of its own. The restructuring was carried out under a Delaware General Corporation Law called Section 251(g), according to which a company incorporated in the state could create and merge with a holding company without the consent of shareholders. Under Section 251(g) DGCL, Google incorporated Alphabet Holding as its wholly-owned subsidiary and, in turn, caused Alphabet to merge with Maple Technologies[f] (a Merger Sub), to form a Google Merger Sub. Following the Alphabet Merger, Google Merger Sub, an indirect, wholly-owned subsidiary of Google, merged with and into Google. Upon consummation of the reorganization, Google became a direct, wholly owned subsidiary of Alphabet and the transitory existence of Google Merger Sub was disregarded ***(See Exhibit 2).*** Thereafter, Google shareholders transferred their stocks to Alphabet in exchange for New Alphabet stock.

Experts said that Google's molding into Alphabet was uniquely possible because of the company's rare stock-holding structure, where its founders controlled the direction of the business without majority economic ownership of the company's stock. Since Google shareholders had few voting rights, they were unable to block the transaction by filing a lawsuit in the Delaware Court of Chancery.

Under the new structure, a number of companies, including Google, operated as subsidiaries of Alphabet. Alphabet's only significant assets were the outstanding equity interests in Google and other future subsidiaries of Alphabet ***(See Exhibit 3).*** The businesses were reorganized into two reporting segments: 'Google' and 'Other Bets'. Google's mature businesses and main Internet products such as Search, Ads, Commerce, Maps, YouTube, Apps, Cloud, Android, Chrome, Google Play, as well as hardware products such as Chromecast, Chromebooks, and Nexus and technical infrastructure and efforts like Virtual Reality remained under Google. What got separated were companies that were far afield of the core search products. These formed 'Other Bets' and included Access/Google Fiber, Calico, Nest, Verily (formerly Google Life Sciences), Google Ventures, Google Capital, X (formerly Google [X]), and other initiatives.

Addressing a group of shareholders, Page said that Google's new structure was inspired by and modeled

Exhibit 2 Google's Reorganization under DGCL Section 251 (g)

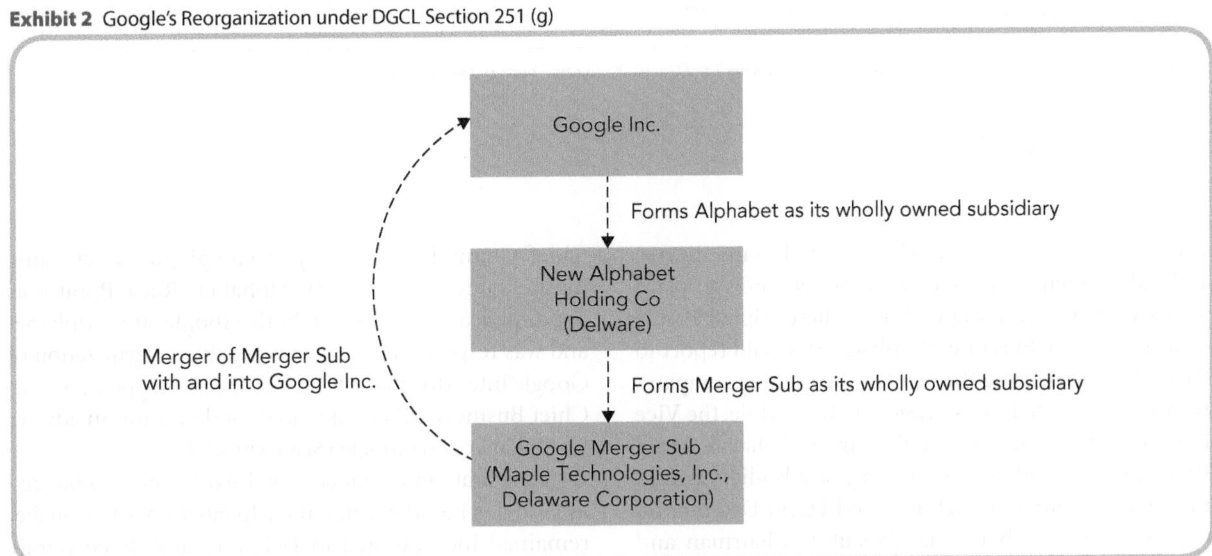

Source: hbtlj.org/articlearchive/v16i1/16HousBusTaxLJ1.pdf

[f]Maple Technologies, a Delaware corporation (Merger Sub), was created as a wholly-owned subsidiary of Alphabet.

Exhibit 3 Structure of Alphabet Inc.

Note: The list of Google departments is non-exhaustive, as is the list of Google X projects – because they're so secretive.

Source: http://www.businessinsider.in

after Berkshire Hathaway,[g] which owned many diverse and independent businesses with strong CEOs in place for each of its operating entities. Where Alphabet was concerned, the CEOs of each subsidiary would report to Page who had become the CEO of the holding company. Brin was appointed as its president. Meanwhile, the Vice President of products at Google, Sundar Pichai, replaced Page as the CEO of Google, the largest subsidiary within the Alphabet umbrella. Schmidt and David Drummond transitioned from being the Executive Chairman and Chief Counsel respectively at Google, to functioning in the same capacities at Alphabet. Ruth Porat was appointed as the CFO of both Google and Alphabet and was responsible for overseeing the reorganization of Google into Alphabet. Omid Kordistani stepped down as Chief Business Officer of Google and become an adviser to Alphabet and Google ***(See Exhibit 4).***

Corporate governance remained largely unchanged as Google's board became the Alphabet board. Alphabet remained incorporated in Delaware and its corporate

[g]Berkshire Hathaway Inc. is a US-based holding company owning subsidiaries that engage in a number of diverse business activities including insurance and reinsurance, freight rail transportation, utilities and energy, finance, manufacturing, services and retailing. Berkshire's revenue in 2016 was $223,604 million.

Exhibit 4 Alphabet's Top Management

Name	Position
Larry Page	Chief Executive Officer, Alphabet, Co-Founder and Director
Sergey Brin	President, Alphabet, Co-Founder and Director
Eric E. Schmidt	Executive Chairman of the Board of Directors
L. John Doerr	Director
Diane B. Greene	Senior Vice President, Google, and Director
John L. Hennessy	Lead Independent Director
Ann Mather	Director
Alan R. Mulally	Director
Paul S. Otellini	Director
K. Ram Shriram	Director
Shirley M. Tilghman	Director
David C. Drummond	Senior Vice President, Corporate Development, Chief Legal Officer, and Secretary, Alphabet
Sundar Pichai	Chief Executive Officer, Google
Ruth M. Porat	Senior Vice President and Chief Financial Officer, Alphabet and Google

Source: https://www.sec.gov/Archives/edgar/data/1652044/000130817916000384/lgoog_def14a.htm

website was named www.abc.xyz. As part of the identity shift, Alphabet posted a new code of conduct for its employees and replaced Google's famous "Don't Be Evil" motto with "Do the right thing" ***(See Exhibit 5)***. Talking about the new organization, Page said, "*For Sergey and me this is a very exciting new chapter in the life of Google—the birth of Alphabet. We liked the name Alphabet because it means a collection of letters that represent language, one of humanity's most important innovations, and is the core of how we index with Google search! We also like that it means alpha-bet (Alpha is investment return above benchmark), which we strive for! I should add that we are not intending*

Exhibit 5 Alphabet Inc-Code of Conduct for Employees

I. Avoid Conflicts of Interest

A conflict of interest may arise any time competing loyalties could cause you to pursue a personal benefit for you, your friends, or your family at the expense of Alphabet or our customers. Avoid conflicts of interest and circumstances that reasonably appear to be a conflict. Sometimes a situation that previously didn't present a conflict of interest may develop into one.

When faced with a potential conflict, ask yourself:

Would this activity create an actual or apparent incentive for me to benefit myself, my friends, or my family?

Would this activity harm my reputation or hurt my ability to do my job?

Would this activity embarrass Alphabet or me if it showed up in the press?

If the answer to any of these questions is "yes," the relationship or situation is likely to constitute a conflict of interest, and you should avoid it.

II. Ensure Financial Integrity and Responsibility

Ensure that money is appropriately spent, our financial records are complete and accurate, and our internal controls are honored.

If your job involves the financial recording of our transactions, make sure that you're familiar with all relevant policies, including those relating to revenue recognition.

Never interfere with the auditing of financial records. Similarly, never falsify any company record or account.

If you suspect or observe any irregularities relating to financial integrity or fiscal responsibility, no matter how small, immediately report them.

III. Obey the Law

Comply with all applicable legal requirements and understand the major laws and regulations that apply to your work.

Source: https://abc.xyz/investor/other/code-of-conduct.html

for this to be a big consumer brand with related products—the whole point is that Alphabet companies should have independence and develop their own brands."[16]

Alphabet retained Google's multi-class share structure. As part of the reorganization, Alphabet replaced Google as the publicly traded entity and all shares of Google automatically got converted into the same number of shares of Alphabet with the same designations, rights, powers, and limitations as the corresponding share of Google stock. The company's two classes of shares continued to trade on Nasdaq as GOOGL and GOOG. After the restructuring was announced, shares of the class A common stock of the company climbed 6%, thereby adding more than $28 billion to the company's market valuation. According to Erich Joachimsthaler, founder and CEO of Vivaldi Partners Group,[h] "*This corporate structure will work. It is a rather painless exercise relative to the alternative—mergers and integration. Integrating large, existing businesses into Google is time-consuming, unattractive and costly. The Alphabet structure simplifies. Simplicity wins!*"[17]

A Good Move?

According to some analysts, the new structure was a smart way for Google to pursue long-term growth while simultaneously increasing transparency and management focus on the core business. According to Eric Bradlow, co-director of the Wharton Customer Analytics Initiative, "*On net, [the restructuring] is probably a good move for branding, positioning, P&L [profit and loss reporting] and also for Sundar Pichai. It allows Google to have many uncertain, but high potential, ventures without damaging the parent brand. It also allows them the opportunity to keep the P&L separate for different areas of the company.*"[18]

More Focus

The move would ensure clearer oversight of the company's ambitious and risky research projects and allow greater focus and control of unrelated companies like Calico, X, Google Capital, Nest Labs etc., said analysts. Jeff Kagan, an independent industry analyst, said, "*This is what they should have done years ago. They've gotten out of control . . . As Google gets bigger with all of these different businesses, they get sluggish. They've gotten too big with too many arms and they're going in too many directions. This should deal with that.*"[19]

While Alphabet would give the company's moonshot bets new opportunities to grow, it would also segment them as distinct subsidiaries, each with its own liability, management, and profit stream. The subsidiaries would be freed from the matrix management of a large company such as Google. Each entity within Alphabet could be assessed on its own merits and flourish without the distraction of the potential impact on the core business. For instance, Google would not have the burden of the potential liability for X Labs and could focus on its core services like advertising and YouTube which had been money spinners for the company.

Innovation at Alphabet would also get a boost as founders Page and Brin stepped back from the day-to-day operations of Google and focused on the immense opportunities inside of Alphabet. They could dedicate their time to developing smaller emerging business lines, launching path-breaking products that might result in windfall gains for Alphabet shareholders and keep them happy. Eventually, these founders felt that becoming Alphabet could help them stay in control of the larger vision for the company and experiment and grow into areas that might be seen as unlikely for Google.

Under the new structure, Google could give operating divisions more leeway to make their own decisions and keep the businesses more nimble. Subsidiaries would get their own legal departments and be able to set their own benefit structures and culture to some extent. With each division headed by its own CEO, leaders would be able make independent decisions and drive the company forward. Stepan Khzrtian, co-founder and Managing Partner of international business law firm LegalLab Law Boutique, said, "*Putting its many projects into separate companies and donning each with a strong CEO, Alphabet can be seen as sparking robust competition and entrepreneurial spirit among its many arms. Although not necessarily direct competitors, these different projects (or different companies, I should say) will be fighting hard to bring their red financials into the black, become profitable, and remain favorable in the eyes of the senior management at Alphabet . . . or risk being scrapped as a failed enterprise.*"[20]

The moonshot projects would no longer have to justify themselves as adding value to Google's core search business as they would be standalone operations, to rise or fall on their own, opined analysts. They had to support themselves in the market rather than be falsely buoyed by the Google brand name. Rik Moore, head of creative strategy at Havas Media, said, "*It allows the*

[h]Vivaldi Partners Group is a brand strategy consulting firm.

best of both worlds—to both protect Google from association with any future false starts, while giving new projects breathing space to find their own identity away from the Google mega-brand."[21]

Limiting Liability

The restructuring would limit liability. Alphabet as a holding company would not be liable for the debts of its subsidiaries, while the subsidiaries would not be liable for each other's debts. Moreover, the creation of subsidiaries implied that potential legal fallouts or the failure of any risky bet would not impact the rest of the holding. Prior to restructuring, if one of the new projects failed, Google had to bear the loss but with its new structure, Alphabet would shield itself from the liability of its risky moonshots, said analysts. "*With its new structure, Alphabet is insulating its vague and risky businesses (Calico, Sidewalk, Fiber, Google X) from the tried and true ones (Search, Ads, Apps, Android, YouTube, Maps). So, if one or more of these 'bets' fails (big?), it would be sinking its own boat rather than bringing down the entire ship,*"[22] remarked Stepan. Moreover, having several subsidiaries might yield more tax advantages than having one large company with combined profit and losses, felt some analysts.

Corporate Transparency. According to analysts, greater transparency of both cash flows and investments would prompt greater discipline and accountability across the company, allow better analysis and valuation of the individual businesses, and increase shareholder value. Investors would be better able to value Alphabet's individual companies based solely on their financial performance. There would also be more disclosure around operations of the company's main search business, including YouTube, mobile search, and online advertising, which Google had not disclosed earlier. Analysts said the new structure would improve corporate transparency, providing investors with a clear oversight of the company's businesses, thereby fueling better decisions and increasing the stock price of the company.

Averting Anti-trust Regulation. Over the years, Google as a single entity, had been the target of anti-trust legislation in the US and Europe. European regulators were hostile toward Google and viewed its growing footprint and Internet monopoly as a threat to their local business interests. The company had faced inquiries from a number of different governments regarding its business practices, data collection methods, and privacy policies. In fact, the European Commission had accused Google of engaging in anti-competitive practices by privileging its own products and services over those of competitors in its search engine. Analysts felt that by spinning off its arms, Google might be able to pre-empt anti-trust regulation and placate regulators who were worried about Google becoming too powerful as a single entity.

Moreover, for some years, Google had been criticized for its approach to tax, data protection, and international secrecy. Experts said the shift from a single 'Branded House' approach toward a pure 'House of Brands' architecture would make Alphabet less vulnerable to scandals. "*By creating a house of brands and the Alphabet holding company they distance corporate risk from brand equity and reduce any potential impact of corporate misdeeds on its consumer brands,*"[23] observed columnist Mark Ritson.

Talent Retention and Employee Acquisition. According to some analysts, the reorganization would allow entrepreneurship within the company to flourish, promote good talent, and prevent talent loss. More talented senior executives, who otherwise might get poached by other powerful competitors, would be promoted within the company. Reportedly social networking service Twitter Inc. had been pursuing Pichai as its future CEO around the time the reorganization was announced. "*You have a number of long-time people who've been at Google, and eventually they want to run their own things, run their own shows. It's hard when top management is locked in and you can't really change it,*"[24] said Danny Sullivan, an industry expert on search engines.

By creating a portfolio of separate businesses, Alphabet would also open up many more high ranking executive openings. There would be more opportunities to hire responsible managers with in-depth knowledge in certain areas for the individual companies in the holding. The move would also allow Alphabet to employ different leadership styles and develop different cultural variations for each of its businesses. Google had created a highly distinctive culture such as its popular HR policy called 'Innovation Time Off'[i] and its campus-based community approach. The new Alphabet would allow each subsidiary to alter the company's unique culture according to the needs of each business. For instance, visionaries, risk-takers, and engineering whiz kids might better fit in with moonshot companies while disciplined go-getters would do better in its more mature businesses.

[i]Introduced in 2010, 'Innovation Time Off' allowed Google's employees to work on any company related work of their choice other than their regular job tasks for 20% percent of their total working time.

Paving Way for More Acquisitions. Industry observers felt that Google's acquisitions over a period of time had been overshadowed by doubts on how these new aspects of the business would fit in with the pre-existing facets of the business. Although some acquisitions such as YouTube were successful, many acquisitions had been either wholly swallowed up like Keyhole Inc.[j] or simply shut down as in the case of Dodgeball.[k]

Analysts said the new holding company structure would make it easier to bring in new acquisitions, since the new businesses could be added without having to be bundled together with Google's core business. The opportunity to gain access to Google's talent pool, corporate relationships, and high level of independence that could not easily be offered by Google's former management structure would create an unparalleled value proposition for future acquisitions targets, they added. *"What Silicon Valley values is innovation and scale, which is what acquisitions can help heighten. This concept is something that Google perhaps could not offer other companies. In order for Google to increase its chances of purchasing a multi-billion-dollar company, it must promote—at the forefront of their agenda—that a company along with its employees could exist under Google without losing sight of its uniqueness. The Alphabet structure could make this easier to implement, with its guarantee of generally neutral fiefdoms,"*[25] wrote author Katie Wong.

Criticism

Some analysts were, however, skeptical about the level of clarity the reorganization would actually bring as it was not clear how much of its quarterly financial information Alphabet was willing to share. They felt that the financial details disclosed by the new company were more or less similar to the ones discussed in Google's earlier earnings reports with only the labels being changed and other minor details added. Alice Truong, deputy growth editor at Quartz, Asia, commented, *"On balance the news is positive as this provides for incremental transparency into Google's business and suggests the company is looking for ways to balance founder and employee interests with those of investors. It may be overly optimistic at this point to hope for discrete business unit breakouts for the display network business GDN, YouTube, other Doubleclick-related activities, Google Play, Android, etc. Further, it remains to be seen whether or not key cash flow items such as capital expenditures—which are not commonly broken out by companies with multiple reporting segments, but which are particularly critical for Google—will be disclosed at the segment level."*[26]

According to some critics, the name 'Alphabet' was neither innovative nor catchy and it made it look as if the company was starting from scratch. They wondered why the new holding company had defected from the extremely valuable core name, Google. The spinoff businesses could have benefited from the powerful brand name, they added. Jim Prior, CEO of international brand consulting agencies The Partners and Lambie-Nairn, said, *"As a Brand Consultant I do understand how that familiarisation process works—I just think it could have, should have, been something better and cooler than the overly simplistic Alphabet. What this name fails to convey to me is any sense of the specialness of the corporation, nor its ambition, long-term view, empowerment, scale, transparency, focus or humanity—which are the things Larry writes in his memo that they are excited about."*[27]

Some analysts felt it was not yet clear how the reorganization would increase the profitability and valuation of Google. They said other than the name change, there was not much happening differently. Experts opined that the restructuring had not led to a compelling tangible corporate strategy for the overall enterprise. Moreover, according to them, the reorganization failed to address how Alphabet's businesses would become economically stronger and its projects more likely to succeed as they operated under a holding company. *"Yes, the company's new structure is now clearer to the outside world, but its strategy remains as opaque as ever. As long as that's the case, Alphabet is just a new dog trying an old trick to appease the outside world and cope with internal complexity,"*[28] remarked Ken Favaro, a Forbes contributor.

Moreover some experts felt that disclosing the financial details for risky bets might lead to investors calling for the closure of some underperforming units. Allowing investors to know the particulars of cash flows might not be the wisest thing to do for a company like Google that spent heavily on an uncertain variable like innovation, they said. Some analysts felt that post restructuring, Alphabet might lose its purpose and unifying vision because some of its high profile moonshot projects supported the company's core activity of creating audiences for ads. For instance, the self-driving car project could allow users to free up commute time that they could use to access the Internet. Project Loon, which aimed to bring the Internet to remote areas, would add more

[j]Google acquired Keyhole, a digital mapping firm, in 2004 and integrated it into Google Maps in 2005.
[k]Dodgeball, a location-based social networking software provider for mobile devices, was acquired by Google in 2005 and later shut down in 2009.

customers to Google's search business. Calling the move a risky bet, Julian Birkinshaw, Professor of Strategy and Entrepreneurship, London Business School, said, *"I suspect that by creating Alphabet, Page and Brin are opening up a Pandora's box of commentary and criticism that they could well do without. The only sustainable model for all Google's really creative business ideas is a Private Equity model, or perhaps a foundation, where they can work on their 'moonshot' ventures away from the glare of the public capital markets."*[29]

Initial Results

Beginning the fourth quarter 2015, Alphabet reported separate financial results for the core Google business and the remaining Alphabet businesses as 'Other Bets'. In the fourth quarter, Google's revenues were $21.3 billion, topping analyst expectations of $20.77 billion, up by 18% year-over-year.[30] A majority of Alphabet's earnings were derived from Google's core search business. In fiscal 2015, Google's revenues were $74.5 billion and it generated profits of $23.4 billion. In contrast, "Other Bets" posted revenues of $448 million and reported an operating loss of $3.56 billion.

Shortly after it announced its first quarterly results in February 2016, Alphabet briefly became the world's most valuable company by stock-market capitalization ***(See Exhibit 6).*** Topping analysts' expectations, the fourth quarter results drove up the company's shares by as much as 8%. On February 2, 2016, Alphabet surpassed Apple Inc.[1] to become the world's most valuable company, after reporting higher profit and sales fueled by a flourishing advertising business that supported ambitious new projects. Alphabet's shares rose 1.7% pushing its market capitalization to $531 billion, while Apple's market value was $523.9 billion. Reportedly, in the six months since Google restructured to become Alphabet, the company's market capitalization had increased by $200 billion, almost doubling its total value despite its products line-up remaining much the same. *"Alphabet's core business looks very healthy. That's going to build investors' confidence about the other bets they've been making,"*[31] said Josh Olson, an analyst at investing company Edward Jones & Co.

In fiscal 2016, Alphabet brought in $90.3 billion in revenue, a 20% growth from $75 billion in 2015 ***(See Exhibit 7).*** Revenues from the Google segment were $89.5 billion while that of 'Other Bets' were

Exhibit 6 Alphabet vs Apple

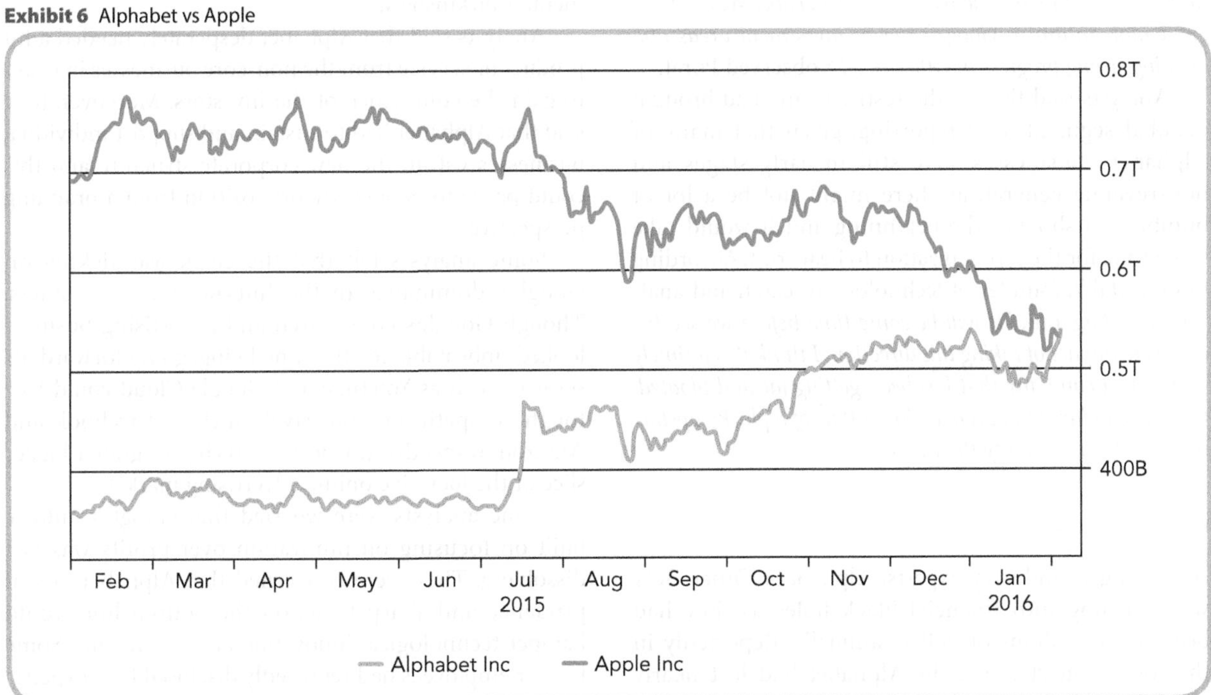

Source: https://www.bloomberg.com/news/articles/2016-02-02/google-parent-to-overtake-apple-as-world-s-most-valuable-company

[1]Apple Inc., headquartered in Cupertino, California, USA, is one of the biggest technology companies in the world. It mainly focuses on designing and selling consumer electronics products.

Exhibit 7 Alphabet Inc-Segment Wise Consolidated Revenues

Amount in millions of US Dollars

	Year Ended December 31,		
	2014	**2015**	**2016**
Google Segment			
Google properties	45,085	52,357	63,785
Google Network Members' properties	14,539	15,033	15,598
Google advertising revenues	59,624	67,390	79,383
Google Other revenues	6,050	7,154	10,080
Google segment revenues	**65,674**	**74,544**	**89,463**
Other Bets			
Other Bets revenues	327	445	809
Consolidated revenues	66,001	74,989	90,272

Source : https://abc.xyz/investor/

$809 million. According to industry observers, Porat had instilled a sense of financial discipline across the company and cut costs, thereby increasing the company's financial strength and stability. *"Our growth in the fourth quarter was exceptional—with revenues up 22% year on year and 24% on a constant currency basis. This performance was led by mobile search and YouTube. We're seeing great momentum in Google's newer investment areas and ongoing strong progress in Other Bets,"*[32] observed Porat.

Analysts said though the restructuring had brought detailed segment level reporting, given that many of Alphabet's businesses were still in early stages and non-revenue generating, there might not be a lot of numbers to show at the beginning and it would take some time for the reorganization to bear fruit. According to Om Malik, founder of technology research and analysis firm Gigaom, *"It will be some time before we see the complete impact of taking this direction, I think it is a timely move for a company that has been getting fat and bloated. Google of today is not even a faint outline of a plucky upstart that wanted to simplify the web search."*[33]

Challenges

According to industry experts, Alphabet's 'Other Bets' were turning into financial black holes as they had been losing billions of dollars annually. Reportedly in the fourth quarter of 2016, Alphabet had lost nearly $1.1 billion from its 'Other Bets' division. In 2016, the total loss posted by this division was about $3.6 billion. *"Even if the amounts of money involved in some of Google's crazier ventures are relatively small, investors will be saying "why is Google doing this stuff with my money?" This is one of the dark sides of transparency. We don't want to see sausages being made, but we are quite happy to consume the end product. Investors will struggle to understand Page and Brin's big ideas, especially while they are still being developed. And they will have no patience for failure,*[34] commented Birkinshaw.

Analysts said that Alphabet desperately needed a hit product or service from the non-core businesses in order to gain the confidence of the investors. Moreover, they said that Alphabet had to sustain and support individual businesses within the new corporate structure and this could prove to be a costly proposition from a branding perspective.

Some analysts felt that the clock was ticking on Google's dominance in the Internet search business. Though Google's core search and advertising business looked unbeatable for the time being, going forward, its services such as YouTube and Google Cloud could face tough competition from rivals such as Facebook and Amazon, respectively, who were trying to grab a bigger slice of the lucrative online advertising market.

Some analysts were worried that Google's culture built on focusing on innovation over profits was fast dissolving. They were concerned that Alphabet's fiscal prudence and sharp focus on the bottom line would hamper technological innovation at the company. Some former employees had reportedly disclosed how expense and revenue expectations, once rare at the moonshot divisions, had become common since the Alphabet reorganization. Moreover, some analysts felt that the new structure might create new obstacles to innovation and create unhealthy competition within Alphabet as creation of new cost centers might raise incentives for each business unit to compete among themselves, removing the possibility of employees allocated in a given division participating in new ventures elsewhere. According to Nelson Alves, Financial Controller at EDP, *"Firstly, will the usual freedom for employees to invest time in new projects be maintained? Employees are considered a cost in the companies where they belong, therefore, to have them working for other units for free is helping others at the cost of our own budget. You can extrapolate the previous example to other types of resources. This myopic view is very common when the management allow silos within the organization."*[35]

Though the new holding structure would allow subsidiaries to co-exist with Google under the Alphabet holding, the culture, compensation, and expansion strategy of these businesses would be fundamentally different from that of Google. These issues might become significant management challenges going forward. Moreover, some Alphabet businesses might compete against each other or overlap in ways that might lead to conflicts of interest.

Some observers felt that the demand for financial discipline and accountability across the company had taken a toll on the moonshot businesses as these ventures were facing unprecedented pressure to bring their costs in line with their revenue ***(See Exhibit 8)***. Reportedly, Porat had been scaling back or shutting down projects that had been losing money or were seeking heavy investments. For instance, Alphabet had decided to put its Boston Dynamics robotics business unit up for sale as the company felt it was not likely to produce a marketable product and make money in the future. Alphabet also scaled back its efforts with drones and scrapped its modular smartphone project Project Ara[m] as part of a larger effort to consolidate its hardware operations, which included products like its Nexus smartphones and Chromebook computers. Amid a shift in strategy, Google Fiber also decided to trim its high-speed Internet service plans in 11 US cities and planned to lay off 9% of its workforce. According to Dieter Bohn, founding editor of *The Verge*, *"It occurs to me that it's just the latest in a string of missteps and corrections for both Alphabet and Google. You can look at all this as a company flailing, or you can look at it as a sign of a company that's cleaning house and locking things down without being willing to publicly say so. Alphabet has been a confusing company from the jump, a mix of random product ideas from crazy moonshots to utilitarian smartphone appliances. Perhaps it's simply time for said company to start demanding the kind of focus and fiscal responsibility that we historically haven't seen a ton of with Google's weirder projects."*[36]

Alphabet's changing priorities pushed some key executives to quit the company. Nearly a third of the Alphabet subsidiaries (as of February 2016, there were ten Alphabet subsidiaries apart from Google) were facing major leadership challenges. In June 2016, Nest founder Tony Fadell left the company saying that the "the fiscal-discipline era has now descended upon everything" and that each business within Alphabet had to depend on Google for the capital in order to grow. According to some reports, the increased pressure on Nest to perform and deliver profitable results as a standalone unit inside the new Alphabet operating structure limited its ability to innovate and led to the departure of Fadell. Marwan Fawaz, a cable and telecom industry veteran, was appointed as the new CEO of Nest while Fadell continued as an adviser to Alphabet.

This was followed by the exit of some key executives from Alphabet's prestigious self-driving car project. In August 2016, CTO Chris Urmson, who had been the face of the self-driving car project since its launch in 2009, left the company. His departure raised a host of questions about the future of Alphabet's driverless vehicles. In December 2016, Alphabet spun off the

Exhibit 8 Alphabet Inc: 2015–2016 Quarterly Revenues

Amount in millions of US Dollars

	Q1 2015	Q1 2016	Q2 2015	Q2 2016	Q3 2015	Q3 2016	Q4 2015	Q4 2016
Google segment revenues	17,178	20,091	17,653	21,315	18,534	22,254	21,179	25,802
Google operating income	5,188	6,272	5,608	6,994	5,807	6,778	6,744	7,883
Other Bets revenues	80	166	74	185	141	197	150	262
Other Bets operating loss	(633)	(802)	(660)	(859)	(980)	(865)	(1,213)	(1,088)

Source: https://abc.xyz/investor/

[m]Project Ara, one of the flagship efforts of Google's Advanced Technology and Projects group, aimed to build fully modular smartphones with interchangeable components.

self-driving car division, earlier a unit of X, into an independent company called Waymo. During the same period, Bill Maris, founder and head of Google's investing arm GV, stepped aside after running the company for close to eight years. He was replaced by David Krane, managing partner of the venture arm. This was followed by the departure of CEO of Google Fiber Craig Barratt in October 2016. Reportedly, Barratt left Google Fiber because he was worried about procuring resources for his company post restructuring. In October 2016, Dave Vos, head of Project Wing, a drone delivery program of Alphabet managed by X, also stepped down.

The company's research lab X too had been struggling to get products out the door amidst internal politics. Several executives who left X said that instead of accelerating the moonshot divisions, the reshuffle had clogged up many of X's projects including Project Loon, drones, and robotics which since then had become rudderless. Alphabet's life sciences company Verily was also facing turbulence with many employees quitting the startup reportedly over CEO Andy Conrad whose allegedly divisive practices were said to be driving off top talent.[37] However, Porat played down analysts' concerns of instability at 'Other Bets' stressing that these ventures were on a "longer time horizon" and that Alphabet was resetting some of them as they were trying to build sustainable business models. *"As we reach for moonshots that will have a big impact in the longer term, it's inevitable that there will be course corrections along the way, and that some efforts will be more successful than others,"*[38] Porat said.

The Road Ahead

As of November 2016, Alphabet was the second most valuable company in the world, worth around $528 billion, not far behind Apple, valued at $589 billion, and ahead of Microsoft Corporation,[n] valued at $468 billion. Analysts said Alphabet's other companies were wildly ambitious and they would hardly make a dent in Google's finances owing to the huge profitability of Google's search business. According to them, Alphabet was a catalyst that could bring together human talent, technology scale, long-horizon venture and investment approaches to build new business models that could challenge rivals in a wide array of industries in the future. For instance, Alphabet could be attractive to technologists working at GE and Microsoft Research and if the company could scale up ventures like Google Fiber and Project Loon, telecommunication giants such as AT&T, Verizon, and Comcast would be at risk. *"But just because the projects do not bring in much money, it does not mean they have no effect on the company's performance. If anything, it is the opposite: Alphabet is now the largest company in the world not because of the money it makes today, which pales in comparison to the former reigning champion Apple, but because of the money it could make tomorrow, the day after, or in 50 years,"*[o] remarked Alex Hern, a technology reporter for *the Guardian*.

Going forward, the company planned to focus on cloud-based computing and artificial-intelligence initiatives and cull investment in non-profitable bets. Pichai said cloud would be one of the largest areas of investment and growth for Google in 2017. A strong digital ad market and the company's expertise in artificial intelligence to sell cloud-based computing and analytics to big businesses could push Alphabet shares to over $1,000 in a period of one year ***(See Exhibit 9).*** Some industry observers predicted that Alphabet would likely be one of the dominant conglomerates in the world in the future. Given the resources remaining at its disposal, the company should have no worries about its financial future, they said. According to Stepan, "*Today, tech companies like Alibaba and Alphabet are redefining this conventional wisdom, (re)creating conglomerates which sprawl industries, customers, and geographies. Call it innovation: not in technology, but instead in the tech business. These structures make sense from a business, finance, and legal perspective, and could well become guiding case studies for similar giants. Like Facebook. Or Apple.*"[39]

However, some analysts pointed out that the transformation of Alphabet was still a work in progress and its long-term goals still remained unclear. With the search going on for sustainable business models for its moonshot divisions ventures, Alphabet had held back from making any disclosures about if or when some of these projects would pay off. Moreover, it was unclear how the group's divisions would be ultimately managed as they become more freestanding. Analysts said the lack of a precedent for each entity under the Alphabet umbrella and the vagueness of their aims would further add to the risks of failure of the company. As Michael A.

[n]Microsoft Corporation, headquartered in Redmond, Washington, USA, is a leading multinational software corporation.
[o]Alex Hern, "X Projects: Alphabet's 'Moonshot' Ventures that Could Change the World," February 5, 2016.

Exhibit 9 Stock Price Chart of Alphabet Inc. (April 2014–February 2017)

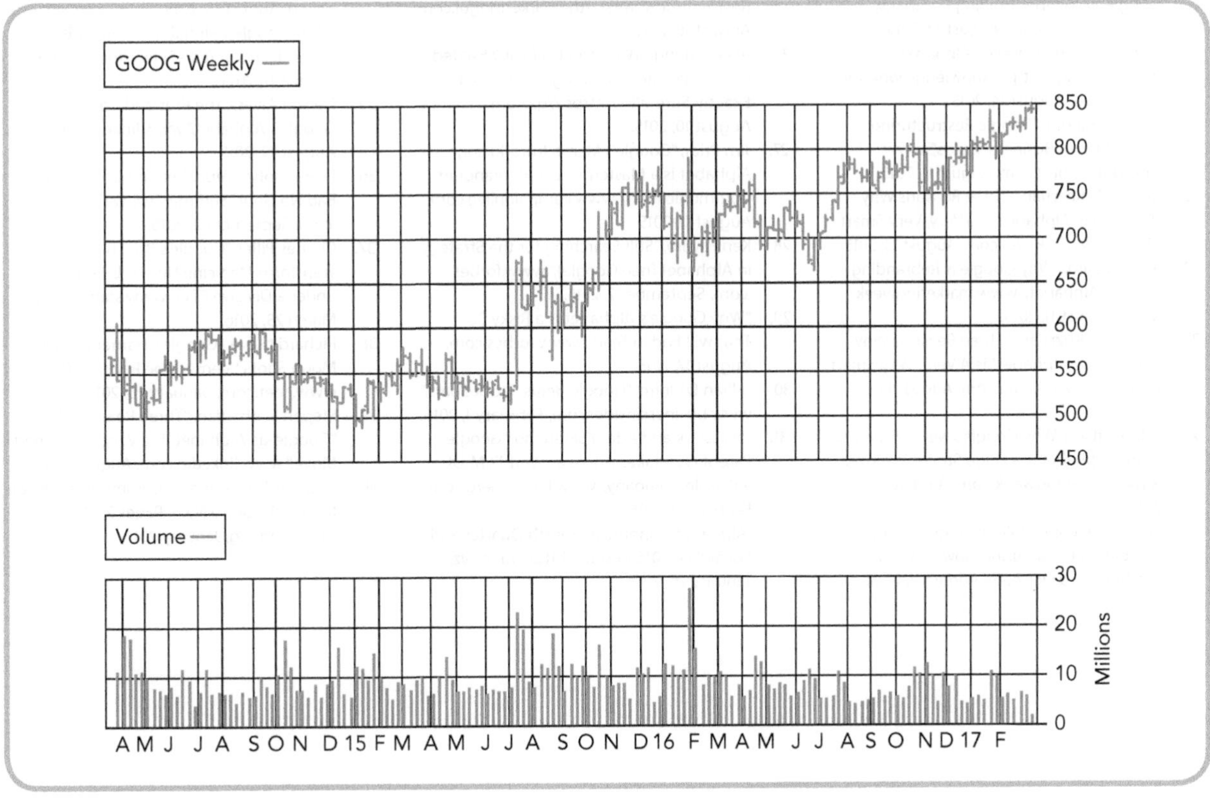

Source: http://bigcharts.marketwatch.com

Cusumano, Communications of the ACM, noted, *"But is Google's transformation into Alphabet Inc. a good bet—for Google investors and users, and society more broadly? That simple question raises big issues, such as how much should we expect large corporations to invest in research that might benefit society but not their bottom lines, and how might large corporations better use the money they do invest in research and new ventures?"*[40]

NOTES

1. https://googleblog.blogspot.in/2015/08/google-alphabet.html.
2. "What's Behind Google's Alphabet Restructuring?" http://knowledge.wharton.upenn.edu, August 14, 2015.
3. http://www.google.co.in/about/company/
4. Michael S. Malone, "Surviving IPO Fever," www.wired.com, March 12, 2003.
5. Eric Schmidt, "How I Did It: Google's CEO on the Enduring Lessons of a Quirky IPO," http://hbr.org, May 2010.
6. Caroline Thomas, "Google: The IR Behind its IPO," www.insideinvestorrelations.com, September 1, 2004.
7. Simon London, "U.S. Fund Criticizes Google's IPO Structure," www.msnbc.msn.com, May 4, 2004.
8. Robin Wauters, "Google Buys Motorola Mobility for $12.5B, Says 'Android will Stay Open," http://techcrunch.com, August 15, 2011.
9. James Rivington, "Google Glass: What You Need to Know," http://www.techradar.com, August 8, 2013.
10. https://abc.xyz/investor/founders-letters/2004/ipo-letter.html.
11. Brian Womack, "The Top Questions Facing Alphabet, the New Google Conglomerate," www.bloomberg.com, August 12, 2015.
12. Alexei Oreskovic, "Google-Parent Alphabet's Moonshots Lost $3.6 billion in 2015," www.businessinsider.com, February 1, 2016.
13. Sarah Vizard, "Why Google is Rebranding Itself as Alphabet," www.marketingweek.com, August 11, 2015.
14. https://abc.xyz/investor/founders-letters/2015/
15. https://abc.xyz/investor/founders-letters/2015/
16. https://abc.xyz/investor/founders-letters/2015/index.html#2015-larry-alphabet-letter

17. Louis Bedigian, "The Pros and Cons of Google's Alphabet Holding Company," www.benzinga.com, August 12, 2015.
18. "What's Behind Google's Alphabet Restructuring?" http://knowledge.wharton.upenn.edu, August 14, 2015.
19. Sharon Gaudin, "Google Restructuring Could Rein in Business 'Chaos,'" www.computerworld.com, August 11, 2015.
20. Stepan S. Khzrtian, "Three Reasons Why "Google-as-Alphabet" is a Very, Very Smart Move," www.linkedin.com, August 13, 2015.
21. Sarah Vizard, "Why Google is Rebranding Itself as Alphabet," www.marketingweek.com, August 11, 2015.
22. Stepan S. Khzrtian, "Three Reasons Why "Google-as-Alphabet" is A Very, Very Smart Move," www.linkedin.com, August 13, 2015.
23. "Mark Ritson: Why Google's New Corporate Brand Alphabet is a Huge Strategic Move," www.marketingweek.com, August 11, 2015.
24. Sarah Jeong and Kaleigh Rogers, "Why Google is Restructuring Now," https://motherboard.vice.com, August 11, 2015.
25. Katie Wong, "The Benefits of Google's Restructuring," http://themarketmogul.com, August 16, 2015.
26. Alice Truong, "Wall Street is Really Excited by Google's Restructuring—But it isn't Exactly Sure Why," https://qz.com, August 10, 2015.
27. Jim Prior, "Google's Memo Introducing Alphabet is a Masterpiece in Rebranding Communication," www.campaignlive.com, August 11, 2015.
28. Ken Favaro, "Still Searching for the Strategy in Alphabet (nee Google)," www.forbes.com, September 7, 2015.
29. "Why Google's Alphabet is a Risky Bet That will End in Tears," www.forbes.com, August 17, 2015.
30. "Jillian D'Onfro, "Google Beats, Stock Soars," www.businessinsider.com, February 1, 2016.
31. Jack Clark and Adam Satariano, "Google Parent Overtakes Apple as World's Most Valuable Company," www.bloomberg.com, February 2, 2016.
32. "Alphabet Announces Fourth Quarter and Fiscal Year 2016 Results," https://abc.xyz, January 26, 2017.
33. Om Malik, "The Big AlphaBet," https://om.co, August 10, 2015.
34. "Why Google's Alphabet is a Risky Bet that will End in Tears," www.forbes.com, August 17, 2015.
35. Nelson Alves, "The Pros and Cons about Google's Alphabet," www.linkedin.com, August 19, 2015.
36. Dieter Bohn, "Alphabet and Google's Very Bad No Good Summer," www.theverge.com, September 2, 2016.
37. Charles Piller, "Google's Bold Bid to Transform Medicine Hits Turbulence under a Divisive CEO," www.statnews.com, March 28, 2016.
38. Richard Nieva, "Google's Harder Look at Moon Shots Seems to be Paying Off," www.cnet.com,, January 26, 2017.
39. Stepan S. Khzrtian, "Three Reasons Why "Google-as-Alphabet" is a Very, Very Smart Move," www.linkedin.com, August 13, 2015.
40. Michael A. Cusumano, Communications of the ACM, Vol. 60 No. 1, Pages 22-25, http://cacm.acm.org, January 2017.

CASE 2

Baidu's Business Model and Its Evolution

In the second quarter of 2016 ended July, Baidu, Inc., the leading Chinese language Internet search engine, reported a 34% fall in its quarterly net income—its biggest quarterly decline since going public in August 2005. The company's net income fell to RMB 2.41 billion (US$362 million) in the quarter from RMB 3.66 billion a year earlier. The poor performance of the company was attributed to curbs on online advertising in China following the death of a 21-year-old Chinese student in April 2016 who had tried an experimental cancer therapy advertised on Baidu's website. *"The challenges Baidu faced in the second quarter served as a healthy reminder to stay focused on the key drivers of growth, sustainability and leadership: delivering the best user experience and staying at the forefront of technology. The implementation of new regulations and the stricter standards that we proactively imposed to make our platform more robust will likely suppress revenue for the next two to three quarters. This period of uncertainty will pass,"*[1] said Robin Li Yanhong, Chairman and CEO of Baidu.

Co-founded by Li and his friend Eric Xu in 2000, Baidu was China's first home-grown search engine and was created with the mission of providing the best way for people to find information. The company offered a broad range of products and services including search services, Online-to-Offline[a] (O2O) services, and an online video platform. Baidu's investments in technology along with its focus on local content helped it maintain a dominant position in the rapidly growing search engine market in China. In order to establish a global footprint, Baidu forayed into emerging markets such as Brazil, Indonesia, Japan, Egypt, India, and Thailand where Internet usage continued to climb. As of July 2016, Baidu commanded over 80% of the Chinese search market, and was among the world's top five search engines in terms of market share ***(see Exhibit I).***

Exhibit I Market Share of Top Search Engines in the World and in China

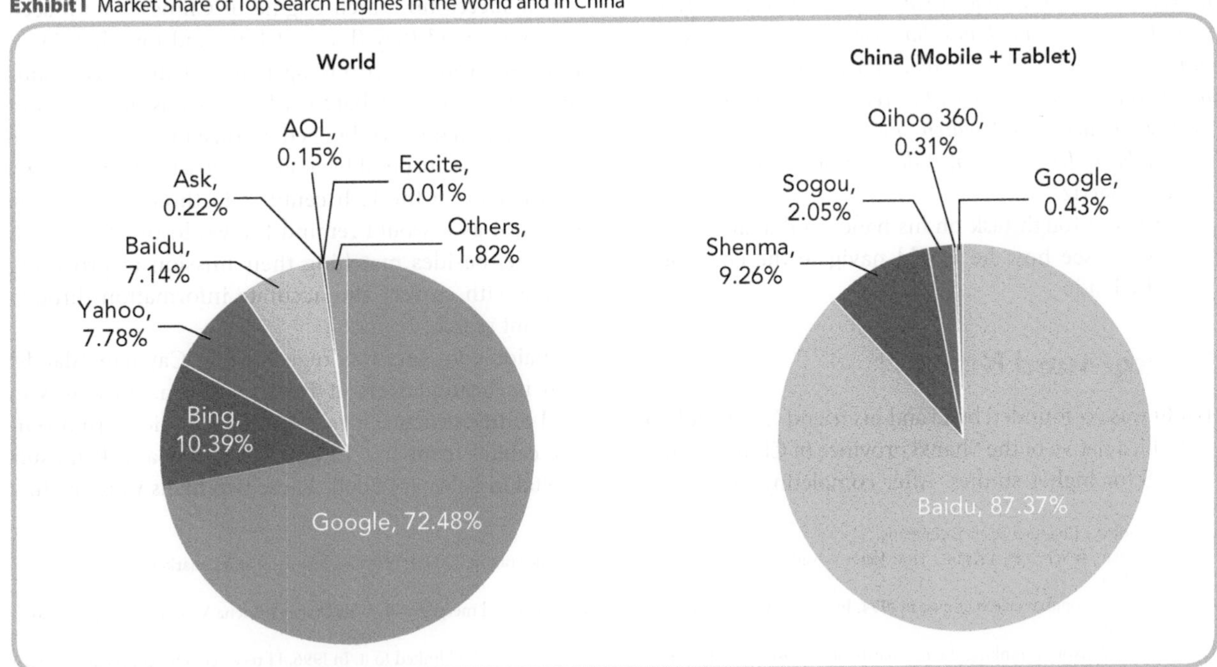

**Data as of August 2016.*
Adapted from https://searchenginewatch.com

[a]O2O is an online platform that drives online shoppers to buy products and services offline.

This case was written by **Syeda Maseeha Qumer** and **Debapratim Purkayastha,** IBS Hyderabad. It was compiled from published sources, and is intended to be used as a basis for class discussion rather than to illustrate either effective or ineffective handling of a management situation.

In May 2016, Baidu planned to overhaul its business model from a search-oriented model to one based on Artificial Intelligence (AI) due to a slowing revenue growth in its core search business. The company planned to focus on developing products in areas such as automatic translation, voice search, and driverless vehicles. Li also planned to emphasize user experience over income and set up a department to root out any behavior that might hurt user experience. Analysts said that the move would affect Baidu's short-term profitability, which in turn would make it more challenging for the company's new business model to gain momentum. Moreover, they felt that Baidu's standing as the top Internet giant in China was on shaky ground as the company battled slowing sales growth due to lack of profitability in non-core divisions like O2O services, regulatory uncertainty, an ongoing cash burn from diversification, intense competition, loss of user trust, and rapid shift toward mobile Internet usage in China. However, some analysts were confident that Baidu would bounce back. "*There's naturally going to be a fair deal of skepticism about Baidu, but it's not going to change its role as the undisputed top dog in the world's most populous nation. Everyone will have to play by the same rules, and this may actually make it even harder for smaller rivals to grow and diversify the way that Baidu can. Baidu has overcome similar hiccups in the past, and it's a more diversified company these days in terms of businesses as well as regions [....] It's no longer merely China's largest search engine provider. Baidu will bounce back. It's just what it does,*"[2] noted Motley Fool's[b] Rick Munarriz.

Li had a tough task on his hands and analysts were waiting to see how he would navigate the challenges faced by Baidu.

Background Note

Baidu was co-founded by Li and his friend Xu in 2000. In 1991, Li, a native of the Shanxi province of China, went to the US for higher studies. After completing his studies, he worked with IDD Information Services[c] between 1994 and 1997, and as a staff engineer at Infoseek[d] between 1997 and 1999. Right from the beginning, Li had a passion for Internet-based search and while working at Infoseek he developed a search mechanism called 'Link Analysis'.[e] After this, he was given an assignment to supervise search engine development. But in 1999, Walt Disney Co. acquired a stake in Infoseek after which the company's focus shifted from search to content. In order to further his interests in search engines, Li decided to start his own search engine along with Xu, a Chinese national working in the US, who had a PhD in biochemistry and good contacts in Silicon Valley.[f]

Li analyzed the Internet search industry and sensed that there was a big business opportunity in a search engine in Chinese as the number of people who used the Internet for search in China was growing. He noticed that all the major portals including the indigenous Sina Corp[g] and Sohu.com[h] were not able to get a foothold in China despite huge investments mainly because of their failure to understand the local culture and preferences. As both Li and Xu were natives of China, they felt that they had better understanding of Chinese culture and the language and it would help them start a successful search engine in Chinese. With seed money in hand they flew to China and founded Baidu in a hotel room overlooking Beijing University's campus. They named it Baidu, which means 'hundreds of times'. The name symbolized a constant search for the ideal and was inspired by a Song Dynasty[i] poem written by Xin Qiji[j] in the 12th century. Li thought the name was ideal as it would remind the world of China's rich heritage, besides matching their mission of providing people with correct and accurate information through constant search.

Baidu.com Inc. was registered in Cayman Islands[k] with its headquarters at Beijing, China. As it was in need of investments, it raised US$1.2 million[3] from venture capital firms like Integrity Partners and Peninsula Capital in February 2000. These two firms were the first

[b]Motley Fool is a financial service company.

[c]IDD Information Services, a former Dow Jones subsidiary, relaunched itself as Tradeline.com in 2000. It provides historical stock market quotes and company data.

[d]Infoseek was a popular search engine in 1994. In 1999, it was acquired by Walt Disney Co. and merged with Walt Disney's Buena Vista Internet group to form Go.com.

[e]'Link analysis' involved ranking the popularity of a website based on how many other websites had linked to it. In 1996, Li received a patent related to what he called link analysis, a way to rank search listings by the number of incoming links to sites.

[f]Silicon Valley is the southern part of the San Francisco Bay Area in Northern California, USA. The term is now used to refer to all the high-tech businesses in the area.

[g]Sina Corporation operates as an online media company and is an information services provider in China. It is an infotainment web portal.

[h]Sohu is a search engine in China which offers advertising and online gaming services.

[i]The Song dynasty flourished between 960 and 1279 AD.

[j]Xin Qiji was a Chinese soldier and a poet.

[k]The Cayman Islands are located in the western Caribbean Sea, comprising the islands of Grand Cayman, Cayman Brac, and Little Cayman.

outside investors in Baidu. In September 2000,[4] two other venture capital firms, Draper Fisher Jurvetson and IDG Technology Venture, invested US$10 million in Baidu.[5] In June 2004,[6] Google, Inc.[l] obtained a 2.6% stake in Baidu for US$5 million. However, in 2006, Google sold its stake for more than US$60 million in order to focus on developing its own operations in the country.

When Baidu was launched in January 2000, there were already many Internet portals in China like Sina, Sohu, and Yahoo! China,[m] offering multiple services like online advertising and online messaging besides search. Initially, Baidu started out by offering search services to these Chinese portals and charged them each time a user conducted a search. Later, it developed its own standalone search engine. As per Chinese censorship laws, the Chinese government blocked content deemed to be controversial and unethical. Baidu understood local issues like censorship laws and abided by them. It even had teams employed to block such content. On its web page, Baidu allowed advertisers to bid for ad space and then pay it every time a customer clicked on an ad. By the mid-2000s, Baidu had grown significantly. Its total net revenues increased from RMB 10.5 million in 2002 to RMB 110.9 million in 2004.[7] By March 31, 2005, it generated net revenues of RMB 42.6 million. Baidu, which had come to be called "China's Google", quickly strengthened its hold on China's search market and used the profits to expand into a range of other online services.

Baidu went public in August 2005. On the very first day of trading on Nasdaq[n] its stock price shot up by 354% from US$27 to US$122.4,[8] valuing the company at more than US$4 billion. By the end of 2007, Baidu had 210 million Internet users. In October 2008, Baidu launched a beta version of its online Consumer-to-Consumer (C2C) platform, called Baidu Youa.[o] In December 2008, Baidu.com was renamed Baidu, Inc.

In July 2011, Baidu acquired a majority stake in China's leading online travel company Qunar Cayman Islands Ltd.[p] for US$306 million. In September 2011, to gain a foothold in the rapidly expanding mobile-Internet market, Baidu launched its own Android-based mobile OS called Baidu Yi which allowed users quick and easy use of search-related functions on mobile devices. With Chinese users increasingly shifting from desktop search to mobile search owing to the popularity of the smartphone, Baidu began investing heavily in the mobile search business. In May 2012, the company launched a low-cost smartphone that ran on a forked version of Android powered by the Baidu Cloud Smart Terminal platform. In October 2013, the company acquired a 100% equity interest in app store 91 Wireless for US$1.9 billion from NetDragon Websoft Inc.[q] in order to gain a bigger share of the mobile user market.

In 2012, Baidu acquired a controlling interest in iQiyi,[r] an online video platform company, through a joint venture with Providence Equity Partners.[s] Later in May 2013, Baidu acquired the online video business of PPStream Inc.[t] for US$370 million and merged it with iQiyi to form the largest online video streaming platform in China. In September 2015, Baidu entered into a deal with US technology giant Microsoft Inc. under which Baidu became the default homepage and search for the Microsoft Edge browser in Windows 10 in China. As of December 2015, Baidu.com was the largest website in China and the fourth largest website globally, as measured by average daily visitors and page views by Alexa.com, an Internet analytics firm. As of March 31, 2016, the company had a dedicated workforce of about 43,500 employees.

Business Model

Baidu generated revenues mainly from online marketing services which included pay-for-placement (P4P) services, performance-based online marketing, and time-based online advertising services. The company's P4P Program was one of the core tenets of its business model. The auction-based P4P platform was an online marketplace that enabled customers to bid for priority placement of their links in the search results and reach

[l]Google, Inc. is a US-based technology giant that offers Internet-related services and products including web-based search, cloud computing, software applications, online advertising technologies, mobile operating systems, consumer content, enterprise solutions, and hardware products. Google is the world's most popular English language search engine.

[m]Yahoo!China is the Chinese version of Yahoo!Founded in 1994, Yahoo, Inc. is a US-based technology company globally known for its search engine Yahoo.com.

[n]National Association of Securities Dealers Automated Quotation (NASDAQ) is the American stock exchange.

[o]BaiduYoua is an online shopping system through which merchants can sell their products and services at Baidu-registered stores.

[p]Founded in 2005, Qunar is an online travel company that offers real-time searches for air and train tickets, hotels, and tour packages.

[q]NetDragon Websoft Inc. is one of the largest third-party mobile applications distribution platforms in China.

[r]Launched in April 2010, iQiyi is an online video platform in China that focuses exclusively on fully licensed, high-definition and professionally produced content.

[s]Providence Equity Partners LLC is a US-based global private equity investment company.

[t]Based in Shanghai, China, PPStream, Inc. offers online video, games, information, downloads, and community and other diversified products and services.

users who searched for information related to their products or services. Baidu was the first auction-based P4P service provider in China. The P4P model helped Baidu monitor each click, understand the tastes and preferences of Chinese Internet users better, and improve user experiences in order to drive traffic to its sites.

In October 2009, Baidu switched from its old advertising system based on price bid ranking to a new online advertising keyword bidding system called Phoenix Nest system. The new advertising system contributed to a strong revenue growth along with an increase in the number of Internet users. Between 2010 and 2014, Baidu's average revenue per customer grew at 33% annually, increasing from RMB 19,200 per customer per year to RMB 59,600. According to Li, *"If an advertiser wants to pay a lot of money that probably says something. The best measure for this is our growth pattern. If users keep coming back to our service, we're doing the right thing."*[s]

In addition, Baidu also offered performance-based online marketing services and time-based online advertising services, whereby the customers paid Baidu based on performance criteria such as the number of telephone calls brought to the customers, the number of bookings of air tickets or hotel rooms, the number of users registered with the customers, or the number of minimum click-throughs. Baidu's online marketing services generally included text links, images, multimedia files, and interactive forms. The advertisements were displayed through both organic Baidu websites and its affiliated website partners such as Baidu Union.[u] Between 2006 and 2014, Baidu's online marketing customer base was growing by 29% annually, and had reached 1,049,000 by December 2015. In 2015, search revenues were RMB 55.7 billion (US$11 billion), about 84% of Baidu's total sales. Total revenues and operating profit was RMB66.4 billion and RMB11.7 billion respectively ***(see Exhibit II.)*** In the

Exhibit II Baidu-Consolidated Statements of Comprehensive Income Data

(In thousands of RMB except per share and per ADS data)	For the year ended December 31				
	2011	**2012**	**2013**	**2014**	**2015**
Revenues:					
Search Services	14,500,786	22,306,026	29,590,276	43,727,459	55,667,478
Transaction Services			1,319,187	3,822,456	7,005,941
iQiyi			1,345,042	2,873,552	5,295,760
Inter Segment			(310,581)	(1,371,149)	(1,587,450)
Total revenues	14,500,786	22,306,026	31,943,924	49,052,318	66,381,729
Operating Costs and Expenses:					
Search Services			15,411,424	23,179,666	27,549,641
Transaction Services			2,841,466	9,796,434	20,151,386
iQiyi			2,088,055	3,983,851	7,679,198
Total Operating Costs and Expenses	(6,924,127)	(11,254,706)	(20,752,204)	(36,248,554)	(54,710,175)
Operating profit	7,576,659	11,051,320	11,191,720	12,803,764	11,671,554
Interest income	418,201	866,465	1,308,542	1,992,818	2,362,632
Interest expense	(82,551)	(107,857)	(447,084)	(628,571)	(1,041,394)
Income (loss) from equity method investments	(179,408)	(294,229)	22,578	(19,943)	3,867
	2011	**2012**	**2013**	**2014**	**2015**
Other income, net, including exchange gains or losses	76,278	449,738	140,951	336,338	24,909,964
Income before income taxes	7,809,179	11,965,437	12,216,707	14,484,406	37,906,623
Income taxes	(1,188,861)	(1,574,159)	(1,828,930)	(2,231,172)	(5,474,377)
Net income	6,620,318	10,391,278	10,387,777	12,253,234	32,432,246
Less: Net loss attributable to non-controlling interests	(18,319)	(64,750)	(162,880)	(943,698)	(1,231,927)
Net Income Attributable to Baidu, Inc.	**6,638,637**	**10,456,028**	**10,550,657**	**13,196,932**	**33,664,173**

Adapted from http://ir.baidu.com/phoenix.zhtml?c=188488&p=irol-sec Baidu 20F

[u]Baidu Union comprises a large number of third-party websites and software applications. It directs traffic to the Baidu website by integrating a Baidu search box into third party websites or by displaying relevant contextual promotional links for customers.

first quarter of 2016, Baidu's online marketing revenues were RMB14.931 billion (US$2.316 billion), a 19.3% increase compared to the corresponding quarter of the previous year.

Secret of Success

Since its inception, Baidu had positioned itself as a Chinese language search engine which allowed users to find information, products, and services using Chinese. According to industry observers, it was a challenging task for Baidu because of the complexity of the Chinese language. To make search easier for users, it introduced the 'pinyin' search in 2001 that allowed users to type in Chinese keywords using English alphabets when the user was not sure of a written form of a keyword. This gave relevant results and made Baidu's search reliable.

Baidu designed strategies to appeal to the Chinese web user by leveraging on the concept of 'nationalism' and 'Chinese heritage' in its business model. Its awareness of the Chinese language and culture gave it an advantage over foreign search engines operating in China. Baidu created a dominant position for itself by providing features that appealed to Chinese users. Li said, *"We think search is not just about technology. It's also about language. It's also about culture."*[10] According to some analysts, Baidu's success could be attributed to unique products like Baidu Post Bar, the world's first and largest Chinese-language query-based searchable online community platform; Baidu Knows, the world's largest Chinese-language interactive knowledge-sharing platform; and Baidu Encyclopedia, the world's largest user-generated Chinese-language encyclopedia and MP3[v] search ***(see Exhibit III).***

According to some industry watchers, one of the reasons for Baidu's rapid growth was, ironically enough, its competitor Google which began operating in China in September 2000 and offered millions of pages in the Chinese language. By 2002, Google had become the leading search engine in China and Baidu was relatively unknown to many Chinese Internet users. But slowly, Google began to face problems in China. The Chinese government began to intermittently block several websites through IP filters. However, users of Google still managed to circumvent government censorship and browse the content through cached pages.[w]

By late August 2002, ahead of the 16th Communist Party Congress,[x] users trying to use www.google.com for

Exhibit III Baidu Products and Services

Search Products	Web Search, Image Search, Video Search, News, Web Directory, Hao123.com, Dictionary, Top Searches and Search Index, Open Platform
Social Products	Post Bar, Space, Album
UGC-based Knowledge Products	Knows, Encyclopaedia, Wenku, Experience
Location-based Products and Services	Maps, Group Buy Directory, Travel
Music Products	Baidu Music, Baidu FM, TT Player
PC Client Software	Browser, Input Method Editor, Toolbar and Baidu Companion, Baidu Hi, Media Player, Reader
Mobile-Related Products and Services	Mobile Search, Cloud Smart Terminal Platform, Mobile Browser, Palm, Mobile Phone Input Method Editor, Contacts, Netdisk, Photo Wonder, Wallpaper, Desktop, One Click Root, Voice Assistant
Products and Services for Developers	Developer Center, Personal Cloud Storage, Baidu App Engine, TS browsing engine, Mobile Test Center, LBS Open Platform, Baidu Webmaster Platform, Statistics, Share
Other Products and Services	Qunar, iQiyi, Baijob, Baidu Pay, Games, Search and Store, Application Store, Ads Manager, Data Research Center, Sky, Senior Citizen Search, Search for Visually Impaired, Patent Search, Translation, Missing Person Search Site
Major Products and Services by Associated or Cooperative Websites	Leho, Leju

Adapted from http://ir.baidu.com/phoenix.zhtml?c=188488&p=irol-products

[v]MP3 or MPEG-1 Audio Layer 3 is a digital audio encoding format.

[w]Google stored pages in its own servers that could be accessed through its site. In China, even when the websites were blocked, users were able to access the content through cached pages. By providing cached pages, Google was making content that was restricted by the Chinese authorities accessible to users in the country.

[x]The Communist Party Congress held every five years by the Communist Party of China (CPC) is a significant event in Chinese politics since it decides the leadership of CPC and announces the vision and policies of the party for the next five years.

search were redirected to Baidu, which recorded a sudden rise in popularity. Later on, the access to Google's site was restored, but a search for some particular terms still led to users being directed to websites approved by the government. By early 2004, users in China began considering Google as unreliable and started using Baidu, which was similar to Google in appearance, with a largely uncluttered white page and few colors. By 2005, Google's market share had fallen to below 30%, while Baidu's share in the market had increased to 46%. Google left the country in 2010, after refusing to cooperate with censors. However, Li cited different reasons for Baidu's growth: "*The market has exploded in a very short time. User information needs to change very quickly. Because we were local and focused, we were able to catch the changes quickly. We understand the Chinese language and culture better.*"[11]

Moreover, Baidu worked closely with the Chinese government in blocking content considered inappropriate by them. Reportedly in 2009, Baidu won an award from the Internet Society of China for practicing *Zilu* (self-regulation). According to some industry observers, Li's focused and driven attitude with his emphasis on technology and investment in new ideas had led to Baidu becoming the leading search engine in China. "*However much Baidu has benefited from offering pirated music, questionable government interference, or even any conscious home-team bias the Chinese market can be accused of, no company becomes so successful without at least some competency. Market inertia or even market ignorance but no matter what you say, it will never change the basic fact that Baidu has thus far read and played its market more successfully than its competitors,*"[12] commented Kai Pan, a moderator on the Chinese online forum ChinaSmack.

Foray into O2O Services

O2O was one of the fastest growing segments in the Chinese e-commerce market and was projected to grow at an annual rate of 25% from US$390 billion in 2014 to US$718 billion in 2017[13] ***(see Exhibit IV)***. A growing population, an increasing number of Internet users, and the rapid shift toward smartphones from personal computers were driving the O2O trend in China. With the PC search business maturing and the Chinese economy slowing down, Li was looking to diversify as he wanted to reduce Baidu's dependence on the desktop search business. His goal was to transform Baidu from connecting people with information to connecting people with services. He decided to invest in O2O services (online to offline, digital marketing to describe systems enticing consumers within a digital environment to make purchases of goods or services from physical businesses) as he wanted Baidu to capture a substantial market share in

Exhibit IV Online-to-Offline Ecommerce Sales in China (2011–2018)

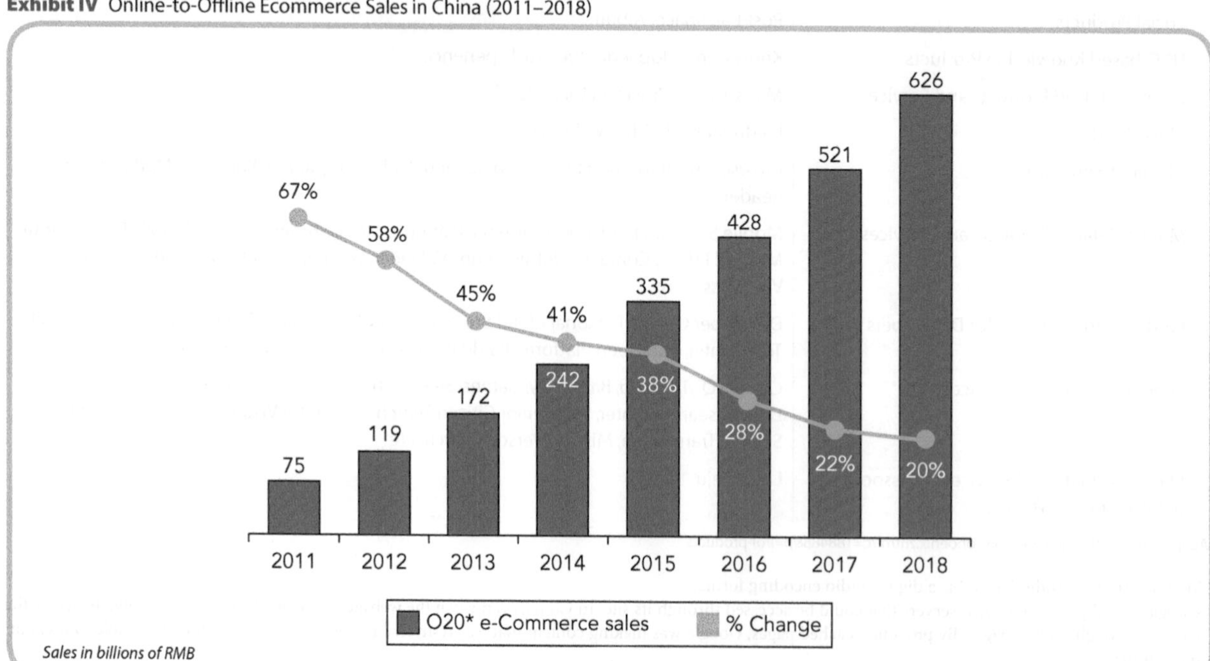

Adapted from iResearch Consulting Group2015 China O2O Services Model Research Report January 19, 2016.

the surging but highly competitive e-commerce space in China. According to Li, the Chinese O2O represented a US$1.6 trillion market opportunity.[14]

As part of the diversification, in May 2013, Baidu rolled out an online food delivery service called Baidu Waimai (Baidu Takeout), wherein customers could place food delivery orders with restaurants. As of 2016, Baidu Waimai had 30 million customers across 140 cities in China. In August 2013, Baidu acquired a 59% equity interest in a group buying site Nuomi from Renren, Inc.[y] for US$160 million. Subsequently, it acquired the remaining shares in January 2014. Baidu Nuomi offered multiple services including ticket booking, dining, hotel reservation, and health and beauty services. In 2015, Li announced that Baidu planned to invest over RMB 20 billion (US$3.2 billion) over a period of three years in Nuomi. In addition, Baidu rolled out other O2O services such as Baidu Wallet (online and mobile payment services), Baidu Maps[z] (desktop and mobile web mapping service), Baidu Connect (third-party login open API), and Baidu Cloud (personal cloud computing service). Baidu consolidated its major O2O reporting segments into a single line item called 'Transaction Services' in its financial reports.

In December 2014, Baidu made an undisclosed investment in US-based car-hailing service Uber Technologies Inc. in order to leverage its strengths in mobile search, mobile mapping, and app distribution. The integration of the Uber app with Baidu Maps, Baidu Wallet, and Baidu mobile search was expected to bring more customers to Uber and more traffic-related income to Baidu. In August 2015, Baidu invested US$100 million in the Chinese online laundry company Edaixi,[aa] as part of its efforts to position itself in the rapidly growing O2O space in China. Continuing its O2O quest, in October 2016, Baidu-backed Chinese online travel firm Qunar entered into a share swap deal with Ctrip.com International Ltd.[bb] under which Baidu would hold a 25% controlling stake in Ctrip, which in turn would gain a 45% share in Qunar. According to industry observers, the deal would make Baidu a dominant player in the O2O travelling market in China with an estimated 80% market share.

However, some analysts said that Baidu's deepening investment in the O2O sector would drive up its costs and affect margins in the short term. According to them, breaking into China's competitive O2O market would not be easy for Baidu as the market was already dominated by two Chinese Internet giants—Tencent, Inc.[cc] and Alibaba Group Holding Limited.[dd] *"Basically, there's a land grab going on. It is expensive. But you can't (gain dominance) if you don't spend the money to build and promote,"*[15] remarked Kevin Carter, founder of The Emerging Markets Internet & Ecommerce.[ee] Despite such concerns, Li said the company planned to increase its spending in O2O businesses as such initiatives could drive revenues in future. He said that the company was ready to forgo short-term profitability to invest in opportunities that might result in huge long-term gains.

Global Expansion

Though Baidu was the biggest search engine in China, its presence outside the country was limited. In 2007, it entered Japan but eventually succumbed to market pressures and shut down its Japanese search engine in March 2015. In Japan, Baidu could not compete against Yahoo and Google and eventually reported losses that amounted to RMB 260 million in 2010. Despite the setback, Li said that he wanted Baidu to become a global brand with a presence in over half the world's countries. Baidu's president, Zhang Yaqin, said the company was targeting emerging markets like Brazil, Indonesia, and India with their huge populations and rapidly growing mobile usage so that the company could attract a new wave of users who were coming online for the first time on their smartphones. He said that in such markets Baidu planned to roll out specific products for each country rather than coming out with a generic, across-the-board service offering. *"Baidu has more than 700 million users abroad, with over 250 million*

[y]Renren, Inc. is an online social networking service in China.

[z]As of March 2016, Baidu Map had about 500 million users in China and enjoys a 70% market share. It was available in more than 18 countries and regions, mostly in the Asia Pacific, such as Japan, South Korea, Thailand, and Singapore.

[aa]Launched in 2013, Edaixi is a Chinese O2O laundry services company which picks up laundry after customers send orders on smartphones and returns it in 72 hours.

[bb]Headquartered in Shanghai, Ctrip.com International Ltd. (CTRP) is a leading provider of travel services.

[cc]Founded in 1998, Tencent is a leading provider of Internet value-added services in China. Tencent's leading Internet platforms in China include QQ (QQ Instant Messenger), Weixin/WeChat, QQ.com, QQ Games, Qzone, and Tenpay. In fiscal 2015, the company's revenues were RMB102,863 million (USD15,841 million).

[dd]Established in 1999, Alibaba Group Holding Limited is a leading e-commerce company in China. Its business includes core commerce, cloud computing, and mobile media and entertainment. For the fiscal year ending in March 2015, Alibaba reported a US$5.5 billion profit.

[ee]The Emerging Markets Internet & Ecommerce is an exchange traded fund that records index of leading Internet and e-commerce companies operating in emerging markets.

active users in a month. Over the past three decades, we have virtualized the physical world, but in the next three decades, we will go the reverse process, applying the Internet technology and business model to the physical world,"[16] said Yaqin.

According to industry observers, Baidu had been expanding into foreign markets with a focus on mobile phones. Li said that he was looking for underserved markets where globally dominant search engines like Google or Yahoo had not made much of a mark. Baidu's global strategy was to venture into those markets where English was not the dominant language, build capabilities in that market, and then expand. Commenting on the choice of countries that Baidu was looking out for as part of its global expansion plans, Jennifer Li, Chief Financial Officer of Baidu, said, *"Before we make a decision, obviously we do market research to understand the country's general demographic situation, the Internet situation, the line connections and the user growth profile, whether there are some main players in there and what are the opportunities. [...]. At the end of the day it is an Internet service and the Internet is borderless. If we feel the market has a need that is not filled and the market has great potential that can become a very meaningful place, the population is there, it's those kind of factors that make us think we can try these markets."*[17]

As part of its expansion plan in the Southeast Asian market, Baidu launched local services in Thailand, Vietnam, and Indonesia such as a search engine (in Thailand) or security and PC services (Vietnam and Indonesia). In 2013, Baidu opened a local development center in Jakarta, Indonesia, as part of a long-term move to settle down in the region and create long-term relationships with the local merchants, Internet users, and governments. It also launched an Indonesian version of its web links portal Hao12. Earlier in July 2012, Baidu opened its research center Baidu-I2R Research Centre (BIRC), in Singapore in order to develop web products for Southeast Asia. Baidu's international products such as DU Speed Booster, DU Battery Saver, ES File Explorer, Photo Wonder, MoboMarket, Simeji, Baidu Antivirus, Baidu PC Faster were popular in mobile-first nations such as Thailand and Indonesia.

In 2013, Baidu entered Egypt by launching a local Arabic site and opening a local office. However, Baidu's expansion into the Middle East was put on hold due to the political unrest in the region. In January 2013, Baidu entered in to an agreement with France Telecom to pre-install Baidu's browser on low-end smartphones to be sold in Africa and the Middle East, by France Telecom's operators there. France Telecom had about 80 million customers across Africa. In July 2014, Baidu entered the South American market by launching a local Portuguese language search engine named Baidu Busca in Brazil. It also opened its local development office in Sao Paulo, Brazil. Li felt that Brazil was a promising market as it was the fifth largest Internet market in the world with 107 million Internet users and 53% Internet penetration that was expected to grow to 59.5% by 2017. In October, Baidu acquired the Brazilian daily deals site PeixeUrbano in order to penetrate the e-commerce market in Brazil.

Li was also eyeing the Indian market as he felt that the country had a strong mobile Internet market. In fact, some of Baidu's mobile apps such as the DU Speed Booster and Battery Saver were already available in India. Li said that Baidu was planning to expand in India through mergers and acquisitions and other investments. Reportedly, the company was in talks to invest in Indian e-commerce start-ups including Zomato, BookMyShow, and BigBasket. In the future, Li planned to expand Baidu to the US and Europe as well. As its rival Google was the dominant search engine in both the US and Europe, Baidu planned to focus on other channels, such as finance and its Baidu Maps service, when targeting these markets. *"I think eventually we will go into Europe, U.S. and then many other places. We are in a number of countries, but we need to find a new battleground. Search is maturing, and mobile is very different from desktop. We need to find ways to access this kind of new market,"*[18] he said. However, some analysts felt that getting a foothold in these markets would be tough, particularly on mobile where Google's Android operating system was the dominant operating system in both the US and Europe. According to them, it would be difficult for Chinese companies that dealt with content and aimed to become global brands to get anyone to trust them outside of China. *"(It is) still early stages for the global efforts, and (there are) a lot of challenges for Chinese companies to go beyond their borders—cultural, managerial, familiarity with the local market—but it's worth experimenting,"*[19] said Jennifer Li.

As part of Baidu's global strategy, CEO Li announced that the company would launch its mapping services, Baidu Map, in more than 150 countries and regions by the end of 2016 in order to serve more than 100 million Chinese outbound travellers. The internationalization plan would put Baidu Map in direct competition with the top global mapping service provider, Google Maps. As of July 2016, Baidu Map was available in more than 18 countries, mostly in the Asia Pacific, such as Japan, South Korea, Thailand, and Singapore.

As of December 2015, Baidu had over 700 million users across 200 countries and regions globally. Some analysts wondered whether it would be able to withstand competition from technology giants like Google and Amazon.com, Inc.[ff] which possessed superior technology and global work forces as it looked to attract new customers in global markets. They felt that Baidu could face more regulatory and market risks than globally diversified competitors. A bigger challenge for Baidu in its global expansion plan was the perceived image of Chinese brands as low-cost copycat brands by some global consumers.

Growing Pains

Regulatory Challenges

Though Baidu dominated the online search engine market in China, its reputation was at stake as the company became involved in some serious medical and healthcare-related scandals in China. In April 2016, a 21-year-old college student, Wei Zexi, died of cancer after reportedly receiving experimental treatment from a hospital in Beijing that advertised on the Baidu search engine. Reportedly, the hospital offering the treatment paid Baidu for the high placement in its search results. Wei contended that the hospital's claims to cure cancer were dishonest and before his death, accused Baidu of promoting false medical information online, in a post that was widely circulated among Internet users in China. To the question "What do you think is the greatest evil of human nature?" on Chinese Q&A site Zhihu, Wei replied "Baidu," saying the company was evil and he never should have trusted medical ads on the search engine. The incident sparked a huge outcry on social media in China where netizens criticized Baidu for promoting false information in an area as critical as healthcare and putting profits before morals. However, Baidu said the hospital in question was a first-tier public hospital licensed by the Beijing municipal government.

Following the public outcry, Chinese authorities including China's Cyberspace Administration Office, along with China's Industry and Commerce Administration and National Health and Family Planning Commission, launched an investigation to probe the matter. Thereafter, the Chinese government authorities ordered Baidu to block ads from unlicensed or unqualified healthcare providers and add risk warnings to health-related paid advertising. The government also announced a new stricter guidance over Internet advertising effective from September 1, 2016. The new rules required Internet search companies to explicitly identify paid search results as advertisements. All online ads also had to be clearly designated as such to help users differentiate between sponsored and organic search results. The government also imposed a 30% cap on the amount of space on each web page that could be used for advertising. The new rules also prohibited search engines operating in China from displaying banned information in various formats including links, summaries, cached pages, associative words, related searches, and relevant recommendations. After the incident, Baidu removed 126 million paid results from 2,518 medical institutions from its searches. Li also set up a RMB 1 billion fund for any future damage claims that might arise.

Analysts said this was not the first time the company had fallen foul of regulators and public opinion for its handling of healthcare ads and blogs. In January 2010, Baidu was accused of selling control of some of its hemophilia-related Tieba forums[gg] to private hospitals, which allegedly used the platform for self-promotion and provided misleading information to the forum users. As early as 2008, the company was criticized on state television CCTV for allowing medical paid search results for treatments that were not in the best interests of users.

Medical advertising was estimated to have contributed to 20–30% of Baidu's revenues. Heightened regulation in the Chinese healthcare sector took a toll on Baidu's second-quarter results in 2016. In the April–June 2016 period, Baidu's net profit slumped 34.1% on the year to RMB 2.41 billion (US$362 million), the biggest fall in the company's 11-year history as a publicly traded entity ***(see Exhibit V and Exhibit VI).*** Revenue from its core business of online marketing, which included search engine ads, dropped 6.7% to RMB 16.4 billion. The number of clients decreased by 15.9% to 524,000 companies as Baidu enhanced scrutiny of ad content in line with the government regulation. Baidu's stock price valued at US$217.97 in November 2015 fell to a 52-week low of US$100 in August 2016. *"I feel for Baidu here. It is, and always has been, in a difficult position. It needs to generate advertising revenue, and medical ads are a big enough part of that that it cannot simply ban them outright. If Baidu tries to regulate the ads, it faces angry pushback from its private hospital advertisers, and it also faces the difficult*

[ff]Based in Seattle, Amazon.com, Inc. is a leading e-commerce company in the world.

[gg]Launched in 2003, Baidu Post Bar, or Tieba, is a massive online community with about 19 million discussion groups. Tieba's illness-related post bars serve as online support groups, where patients share experiences about their diseases and treatment.

Exhibit V Baidu, Inc. Consolidated Statement of Income

(In RMB thousands except for share, per share (or ADS) information)				Three Months Ended	
	June 30, 2015	**September 30, 2015**	**March 30, 2016**	**June 30, 2016**	**September 30, 2016**
Revenues:					
Online marketing services	16,227,496	17,680,374	14,930,530	16,938,794	16,490,040
Other services	347,742	702,707	890,042	1,324,854	1,762,719
Total revenues	**16,575,238**	**18,383,081**	**15,820,572**	**18,263,648**	**18,252,759**
Operating costs and expenses:					
Cost of revenues	(6,503,020)	(7,479,580)	(7,563,184)	(8,737,821)	(9,256,370)
Selling, general and administrative	(3,889,844)	(5,701,859)	(3,945,944)	(4,194,489)	(3,595,985)
Research and development	(2,712,681)	(2,689,970)	(2,100,707)	(2,464,952)	(2,613,573)
Total operating costs and expenses	**(13,105,545)**	**(15,871,409)**	**(13,609,835)**	**(15,397,262)**	**(15,465,928)**
Operating profit	**3,469,693**	**2,511,672**	**2,210,737**	**2,866,386**	**2,786,831**
Other income:					
Interest income	612,523	616,171	596,120	486,857	627,308
Interest expense	(213,522)	(329,372)	(268,389)	(275,081)	(319,899)
Foreign exchange income, net	5,396	61,407	(66,166)	243,911	20,361
Loss from equity method investments	(2,417)	(8,856)	(117,092)	(554,533)	(248,460)
Other income, net	142,382	200,625	298,119	427,738	1,271,932
Total other income	**544,362**	**539,975**	**442,592**	**328,892**	**1,351,242**
Income before income taxes	**4,014,055**	**3,051,647**	**2,653,329**	**3,195,278**	**4,138,073**
Income taxes	(762,951)	(590,517)	(674,750)	(792,723)	(1,045,184)
Net income	**3,251,104**	**2,461,130**	**1,978,579**	**2,402,555**	**3,092,889**
Less: net loss attributable to noncontrolling interests	**(410,909)**	**(379,939)**	**(8,252)**	**(11,268)**	**(9,441)**
Net income attributable to Baidu	**3,662,013**	**2,841,069**	**1,986,831**	**2,413,823**	**3,102,330**

Adapted from http://ir.baidu.com/phoenix.zhtml

question of how, exactly, an Internet search company is supposed to effectively assess the medical legitimacy of a particular hospital or treatment. There is no easy option here, no way that Baidu could have left its users and its advertisers completely satisfied,"[20] said C. Custer, editor of *Tech in Asia.*

Li in an internal letter to employees promised to emphasize user experience over income and asked employees to put values before profit, even though the decision might have a negative impact on the company's income. "*The management and employees' obsession with KPI (key performance index) has twisted our values . . . and distanced ourselves from users. If we lose the support of users, we lose hold of our values, and Baidu will truly go bankrupt in just 30 days,"*[21] he wrote. CEO Li said that Baidu's troubles with online medical advertising were a temporary problem, and business would improve once regulations were figured out and clients returned. In order to regain the trust of users, CEO Li planned to set up a department to edge out any behavior that might damage user experience.

Rising Competition

Baidu's market share on desktop search dropped significantly from 80.4% in August 2012 to 54.0% in August 2014[22] ***(see Exhibit VII).*** Though Baidu has been able to retain its market leadership on mobile search, this business could come under increased threat from rivals such as Qihoo 360 and Sohu. The company had been losing market share to search engines such as So.com[hh] and

[hh]So.com was launched in 2012 by the Chinese mobile software company Qihoo 360. It is the second largest search engine in China with a 30% share of the Chinese search market by the end of 2015.

Exhibit VI Baidu's Stock Price Chart

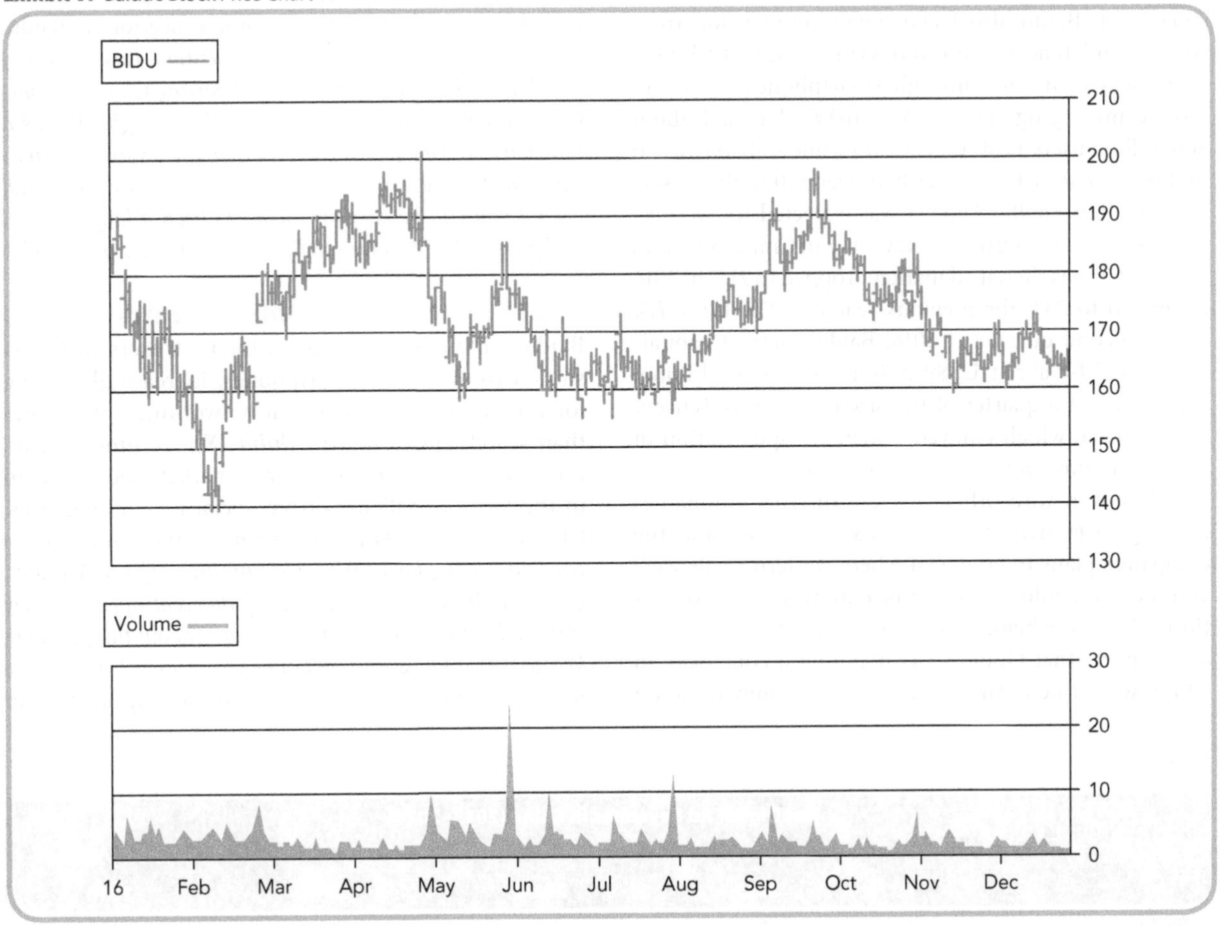

BIDU

210
200
190
180
170
160
150
140
130

Volume

30
20
10
0

16 Feb Mar Apr May Jun Jul Aug Sep Oct Nov Dec

Source: http://bigcharts.marketwatch.com

Exhibit VII China Search Engine Market Share

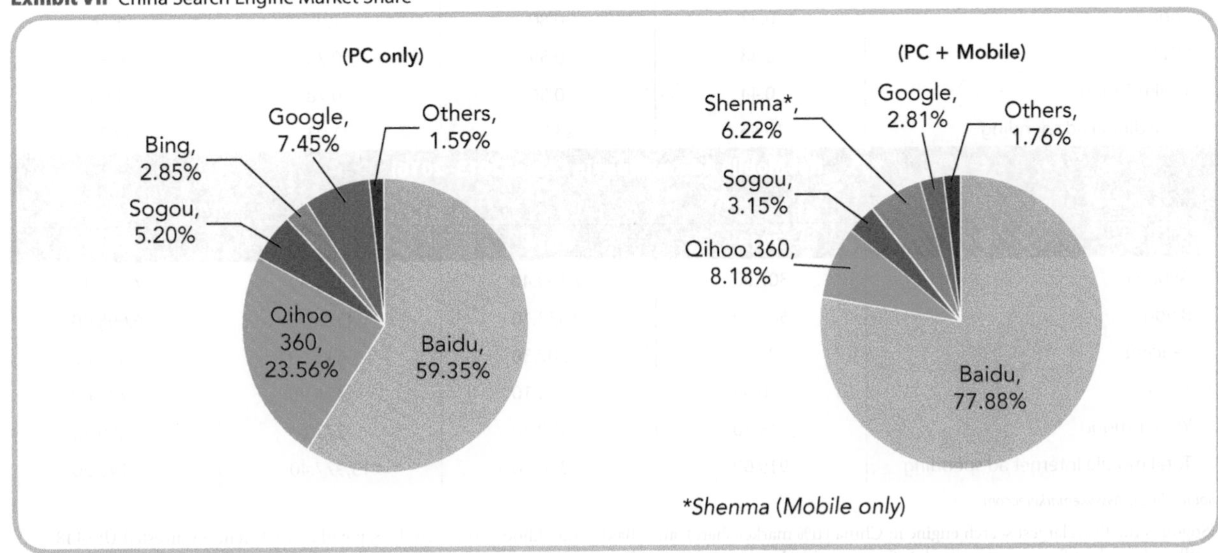

**Data as of August 2016.*
Adapted from https://statcounter.com/

Sogou.com,[ii] who were steadily growing their user base since 2014. Baidu also faced tough competition from Alibaba and Tencent who were vying to attract Chinese customers primarily through smartphones. Tencent's mobile messaging service Weixin/WeChat had about 800 million users as of August 2016 while Alibaba owned mobile browser UC Browser had over 500 million users globally. Reportedly, Alibaba was expected to overtake Baidu in Mobile Internet Ad Revenues in China as Baidu's share in China's digital ad market dropped to 21% in 2016 compared to 28% the previous year ***(see Exhibit VIII).*** In the second quarter of 2016, Baidu's market capitalization fell by about US$9 billion to US$55.7 billion, leaving it just a quarter of the size of its rivals Tencent and Alibaba, which enjoyed a market capitalization of US$ 227 billion and US$207 billion respectively.

Moreover, with other Chinese Internet companies rushing to launch their own search engines and the company's plans to go global where western rivals were entrenched, Baidu was set to face more serious competition than ever before, said some analysts. There were also reports that Google was planning a comeback in China with a new Android app store. Commenting on the threat from American Internet companies, Kaiser Kuo, Director of international communications at Baidu, said, "*We would welcome more competition. It's even fair to say that in the years immediately following Google's departure, we got a little slack, put on a little weight. It was a little too easy. Google is a great company. They invested in us early on. They're now talking about coming back. That said, it's not going to be easy for them. It's been a long absence, and people's habits have solidified around other products.*"[23]

Rapid Shift Toward Mobile Internet Usage

Baidu was under pressure as Internet users in China shifted from PCs to smartphones, increasingly opting for mobile devices and social networking apps rather than search engines ***(see Exhibit IX).*** Commenting on how relevant the broader search market would remain in the face of challenges from social networking apps, CEO Li said, "*We face a new problem. Will search still be relevant? Going forward people can directly go to WeChat, go to Facebook. . . . go to a lot of different apps. Do they still need search? And we need to worry about this problem. We need to address this kind of new consumer behavior, we need to keep innovating, we need to come up with better*

Exhibit VIII

Net Digital Ad Revenues in China (2013–2016)				
				In billions of US Dollars
	2013	**2014**	**2015**	**2016**
Baidu	4.56	6.85	9.43	12.63
Alibaba	4.75	5.87	7.59	9.61
Tencent	0.70	1.10	1.61	2.31
Sohu	0.57	0.80	1.06	1.26
SINA	0.48	0.59	0.70	0.81
Youku Tudou	0.44	0.56	0.78	1.05
Total digital ad spending	16.46	23.87	31.03	39.72
Net Mobile Ad Revenues in China (2013–2016)				
				In millions of US Dollars
	2013	**2014**	**2015**	**2016**
Alibaba	307.50	2,193.40	4,750.30	7,348.10
Baidu	501.80	2,533.10	4525.10	6,695.00
Tencent	83.50	307.30	513.60	992.80
Sohu	0.00	265.10	474.90	729.60
Youku Tudou	13.10	180.20	271.80	390.10
Total mobile Internet ad spending	919.60	7,356.50	13,977.40	22,140.20

Source: https://www.emarketer.com

[ii]Sogou is the third largest search engine in China (11% market share), after Baidu and Qihoo 360 search. In September 2013, Tencent invested US$448 million in cash in Sogou and merged its Soso search-related businesses and certain other assets with Sogou in order to reinforce and strengthen Sogou as a leader in the large and fast-growing China market for search and Internet services, particularly for the mobile platform.

Exhibit IX Mobile Search Engine Users and Penetration in China (2010–2015)

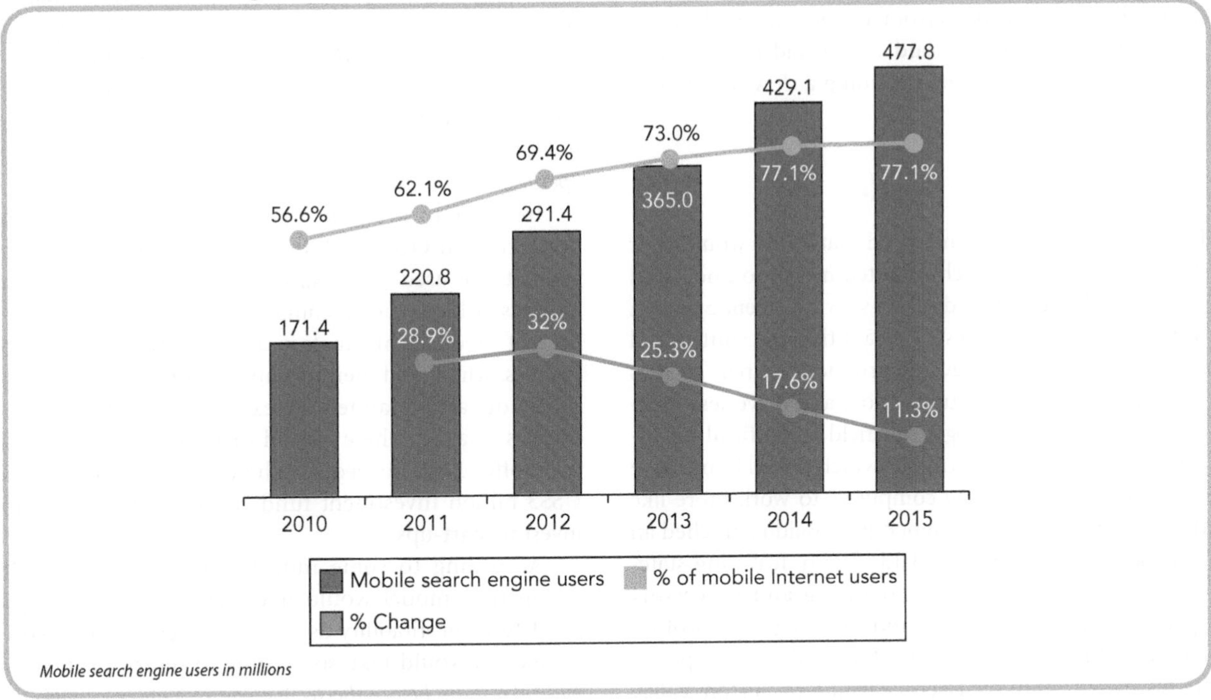

Adapted from China Internet Network Information Center (CNNIC),33rd Statistical Report on Internet Development in China , July 26, 2016.

solutions for our users,"[24] Li said. The rapid shift toward mobile usage in China contributed to a slowdown in annual revenue growth rates. During Q1 2015, Baidu's revenue per online marketing customer fell by 9.8% on flat growth in the customer base.

Baidu's mobile search monthly active users (MAUs) were 667 million in the month of June 2016, an increase of 6% year-over-year. In Q1 2016, mobile revenue represented 60% of total revenues, compared to 50% for the corresponding period in 2015.[25] Though the monthly active users for Baidu's mobile search rose rapidly from 540 million in Q4 2014 to 600 million in Q1 2015, Baidu was feeling margin pressure as monetization rates on mobile searches were low compared to desktop, and slowed top-line growth for Baidu. Some analysts felt that Baidu's mobile search business was at risk considering the rate at which it was losing market share to search engines Qihoo 360 and Shenma.[jj] *"So, with nearly $6.5 billion in 12-month revenue, the majority of which comes from search, and expected revenue growth of 54% and 40% over the next two years, respectively, expectations are high, and Baidu is yet to prove to investors that it can maintain market share. Therefore, Baidu's future doesn't look nearly as promising as its past, and investors might be best suited by avoiding the temptation of investing in the so-called Chinese Google,"*[26] said Brain Nichols, an analyst at Motley Fool.

Lack of Profitability in Non-core Divisions

Baidu's investment in sectors outside its dominant desktop search business weighed heavily on its profitability. The company's operating margin fell to 15.3% at the end of September 2016 compared to 17.6% in 2015. Baidu's heavy spending to buy market share in the O2O space had raised concerns among some investors about whether the search giant had what it took to successfully differentiate itself from competitors. *"I think the decision to launch O2O and video content is on the right track, but their applications and video content are not competitive enough compared with other rivals in the market making them less attractive to users,"*[27] said Ricky Lai, an analyst with Hong Kong-based investment holding company Guotai Junan International Holdings. CEO Li said he did not expect Baidu to improve its earnings in the short term because of its heavy spending on the O2O services business. Moreover, in July 2016, he withdrew his proposed

[jj]Shenma is a mobile search engine jointly launched by Chinese mobile Internet company UCWeb and Alibaba in 2014.

US$2.8 billion bid to buy Baidu's entire 80.5% stake in iQiyi following objections from a major shareholder.

In addition, analysts said Baidu had to overcome some additional challenges including a slowing Chinese economy.

A New Business Model

In May 2016, CEO Li announced that Baidu would shift its business from a search-oriented model to one based on Artificial Intelligence due to a slowing revenue growth in its core search business. He said that the shift would allow the company to develop products in areas such as voice search, automatic translation, and driverless vehicles. Baidu was exploring a sub-field of artificial intelligence known as deep learning[kk] which aimed to improve search results by training computers to work more like the human brain. In September 2016, Baidu launched an artificial system called the Baidu Brain, featuring state-of-the-art technology for recognizing and processing speech, images, and words and building user profiles based on big data analysis. In 2014, Baidu had opened its research facility on Deep Learning in Silicon Valley and appointed Artificial Intelligence (AI) researcher Andrew Ng as Chief Scientist of Baidu. Ng was to lead Baidu Research, with labs in Beijing and Silicon Valley. Reportedly in 2015 Baidu had stepped up its investment in research and development by 46% to US$1.6 billion compared to 2014. It had set up a US$200 million venture capital unit to invest in Artificial Intelligence projects. In August 2016, Baidu unveiled an augmented reality platform called DuSee that would allow mobile users in China to test out smartphone augmented reality on their mobile devices. The company planned to integrate the technology directly into its flagship Mobile Baidu search app.

As part of its focus on Artificial Intelligence, in September 2016, Baidu partnered with Nvidia Corporation[ll] to develop a computing platform for self-driving cars. Baidu began testing the cars in the US and planned to launch a practical model in the market by 2018. It had already tested its autonomous vehicle in Beijing in December 2015. Experts felt that Baidu would have a competitive advantage over other Chinese automakers that tested their Artificial Intelligence in the US due to its local knowledge of road conditions in China. However, some analysts felt that it might take some time for Baidu to scale up. According to Cao He, an analyst with Minzu Securities in Beijing, *"There is a long way ahead for Baidu and other companies trying to mass produce and sell autonomous driving cars. Given the wide diversity of road conditions from one place to another, it is unlikely for any company to come up with a sizable industry operation within five years."*[28]

In order to promote Artificial Intelligence-driven healthcare, in October 2016, Baidu launched Melody, a chatbot that used Artificial Intelligence to connect with patients, ask questions, compare responses with a database of medical information and suggest diagnoses to doctors, who could then recommend the treatment.

Baidu also planned to expand into other areas such as finance, where Li said that Baidu could potentially offer loans to people. The company had set up a US$3 billion investment fund called Baidu Capital to invest in start-ups.

According to some industry observers, the shift in business model would likely affect the company's short-term profitability as the investments in non-core businesses would take some time to return profits. *"It will take years before the technology is mature enough for monetization. So far, there is still a lack of visibility on the prospects for these initiatives, and the search business should continue to remain the sole pillar for the company in the next few years,"*[29] said Alex Yao, an analyst at JPMorgan Chase & Co.[mm]

Can Baidu Bounce Back?

China, with about 710 million Internet users as of June 2016, was the world's fastest-growing online market. As of September 2016, Baidu continued to dominate the Chinese search engine market with a market share of 54.3% followed by Qihoo 360 (29.24%) and Sogou 14.71%. In the third quarter ended September 2016, Baidu's revenues were RMB, 18.253 billion (US$2.737 billion), a 0.7% decrease from the corresponding period in 2015. Net income was RMB 3.102 billion (US$465.2 million), a 9.2% increase compared to the corresponding period of the previous year. Revenue from online marketing services decreased by 6.7% year on year and 2.6% quarter on quarter due to a slump in the number of active online marketing customers.

CEO Li said it would take some time before the revenue and profits of Baidu, which had endured a

[kk]Deep learning is a field related to artificial intelligence that aims to leverage computing tasks by imitating the way the human brain works.
[ll]Nvidia Corporation is a US-based visual computing technology company.
[mm]JPMorgan Chase & Co is a US-based global financial services company.

number of setbacks in 2016, started returning to their normal pace of growth. He said the negative impact of tightened Internet advertising laws would continue in the fourth quarter of 2016 with revenue predicted to be down up to 2.2% quarter on quarter. However, some analysts feared that in the meantime Baidu's rivals might catch up and develop technologies and services that might blunt the company's competitive edge. *"You can get past the regulatory hurdles but then people have to make a decision on whether the advertising revenue growth by that point is going to be spread among a lot more players. It's hard to draw a direct line between artificial intelligence and revenue growth outside of search,"*[30] remarked Kirk Boodry, an analyst at research firm New Street Research.

Going forward, CEO Li planned to invest heavily in Baidu's two core growth segments—Transaction Services and Artificial Intelligence. He said that despite the lack of profitability resulting from high investment, the O2O business would be a good driver of growth in revenue in the future due to a positive trend in the Chinese e-commerce industry. He said that even though Baidu's growth could continue to slip in the short term, the company was poised for solid long-term growth considering the massive growth potential in the Chinese Internet market and its competitiveness in the market. According to Li, *"Baidu will rise to new heights, as long as we maintain the trust and loyalty of our users and continue to be at the forefront of innovation. This may mean doing the hard things, but the right things, for which there is no compromise."*[31]

NOTES

1. "Baidu's (BIDU) CEO Robin Li on Q2 2016 Results - Earnings Call Transcript," http://seekingalpha.com, July 29, 2016.
2. Rick Munarriz, "Baidu Will Bounce Back," www.fool.com, June 28, 2016.
3. "Baidu Grabs Search Engine Market," www.china.org, February 2, 2004.
4. "Baidu.com, China's Market Share Search Engine Leader," www.ruggedelegantliving.com, July 12, 2005.
5. "Baidu Grabs Search Engine Market," www.china.org, February 2, 2004.
6. "Google Sells Baidu Stake to Focus on Its Own China Site," www.articles.latimes.com, June 23, 2006.
7. "Baidu.com, Inc." www.ipo.nasdaq.com, July 20, 2005.
8. "Baidu Shares More than Quadruple in Debut," www.chinadaily.com, August 6, 2005.
9. "For Us, Buy Us," www.thebusinessofamericaisbusiness.biz, December 3, 2006.
10. "For Us, Buy Us," www.thebusinessofamericaisbusiness.biz, December 3, 2006.
11. Jonathan Watts, "The Man Behind China's Answer to Google: Accused by Critics of Piracy and Censorship," www.guardian.co.uk, December 8, 2005.
12. Kai Pan, "Google Left China = Baidu Gained = Chinese Netizens Lose," http://chinadivide.com, June 6, 2010.
13. Michele Chandler, "Baidu Takes on Alibaba In 'Land Grab' For China's O2O," www.investors.com, October 26, 2015.
14. "Is Baidu Reaching Saturation?" http://seekingalpha.com, October 17, 2016.
15. Michele Chandler, "Baidu Takes on Alibaba in 'Land Grab' For China's O2O," www.investors.com, October 26, 2015.
16. "Baidu Reveals Strategy Behind Overseas Expansion," www.chinadaily.com.cn, December 17, 2015.
17. Neelima Mahajan, "Growth Engine: China's Search Giant Baidu," http://knowledge.ckgsb.edu.cn, March 12, 2013.
18. Arjun Kharpal, "Baidu—the Google of China—Eyes Expansion to US, Europe: CEO," www.cnbc.com, July 1, 2016.
19. Neelima Mahajan, "Growth Engine: China's Search Giant Baidu," http://knowledge.ckgsb.edu.cn, March 12, 2013.
20. C. Custer, "Baidu's Problem Goes Way Deeper Than a Dead College Student," www.techinasia.com, May 3, 2016.
21. Bien Prez, "After a Crisis-Filled Second Quarter, Online Search Giant Baidu Looks to Better Days Ahead," www.scmp.com, July 28, 2016.
22. "Market Share and Broader Chinese Economy Risks Will Impact Baidu," www.forbes.com, September 8, 2015.
23. "Baidu is More Than Just Google of China," www.pressreader.com, December 26, 2015.
24. Arjun Kharpal, "Baidu—the Google of China—Eyes Expansion to US, Europe: CEO," www.cnbc.com, July 1, 2016.
25. "Baidu Mobile Search Users Reached 663 Mn in March 2016," www.chinainternetwatch.com,,April 29, 2016.
26. Brian Nichols, "3 Big Reasons Baidu's Success Won't Last," www.fool.com, September 15, 2014.
27. Gillian Wong and Tess Stynes, "Investment in Offline Services Hits Baidu Profits," www.wsj.com, July 27, 2015.
28. "Baidu Enters the Global Race for Driverless Car Domination, www.bloomberg.com, January 25, 2016.
29. "Baidu's Vision of Future: Robot Taxis, Chinese Home Gadgets,"www.bloomberg.com, September 1, 2016.
30. David Ramli, "Baidu Delivers More Bad News to Investors as China Curbs Ads," www.bloomberg.com, July 29, 2016.
31. "Baidu's (BIDU) CEO Robin Li on Q2 2016 Results—Earnings Call Transcript," http://seekingalpha.com, July 29, 2016.

CASE 3

Future of the Autonomous Automobile: A Strategy for BMW

By Olaf J. Groth, Ph.D., Eleonora Ferrero and Aleksey Malyshev

Norbert Riedheim, the head of BMW's Future Car group, which is situated between BMW's global strategy, marketing and research and development (R&D) units, has just been informed that three automakers have received California permits to test an on-road autonomous automobile: Google testing on a Toyota car, Volkswagen's Audi, and Mercedes-Benz. BMW did not apply, because the company was in the process of developing a relationship with Baidu, the Chinese Google-like Internet company, to start testing in Shanghai and Beijing. At the same time, Apple announced its electric-autonomous iCar concept. However, BMW has been making significant investments in the space of autonomous driving and reconfirmed its intentions to lead in this space during its recent shareholder meetings.

Reviewing BMW's innovation legacy, the state of the autonomous auto ecosystem, and a range of critical uncertainties, Riedheim thinks about potential alternative futures for the evolution of the space. His reflections are driven by a need to present a strategy to the Board of BMW during an upcoming high stakes meeting. What kind of business should BMW aim to be over the next 10 to 15 years? What are its aspirations? What strategy should the company pursue and why?

Introduction[1]

Norbert Riedheim, the head of BMW's Future Car group in its global research and development (R&D) division, has just been informed that three automakers have received California permits to test an on-road autonomous automobile: Google testing on a Toyota car, Volkswagen's Audi, and Mercedes-Benz. BMW did not apply for the permit because the company was in the process of developing a relationship with Baidu, the Chinese Google-like Internet company, to start testing similar automobiles in Shanghai and Beijing. Given the rapidly changing scenarios, he wonders what position BMW should aspire to, and what their strategy should be.

Riedheim has been in Silicon Valley and knows all those companies well, and enjoys friendly relations with management and even selective partnerships with Google. He knows that in the era of "co-opetition" new technologies and new alliances can change the chessboard of innovation very quickly. In order for the company to remain relevant for the next 20 years, he and his colleagues need to be vigilant and stay on top of the latest developments in the ecosystem of autonomous driving. BMW is focused and committed to developing autonomous vehicles, as evidenced by CEO Harald Krueger revealing at a BMW's recent shareholder meeting that the company is gearing up to launch its first autonomous vehicle by 2021: "*. . . the BMW iNEXT, our new innovation driver, with autonomous driving, digital connectivity, intelligent lightweight design, a totally new interior and ultimately bringing the next generation of electro-mobility to the road.*"[1]

Riedheim is excited by this bold vision. He has been at the company for a long time in different positions. Having signed on with the automaker right after his graduate studies in engineering, he spent 3 years as an assistant to the general manager of a factory producing the 3-series sedan, followed by shorter stints in supply chain, marketing and finally product management for the company's i3-series, the company's first foray into electric mobility. Having witnessed the engineering and marketing prowess of his employer, he is confident that BMW will master the autonomous challenge as well. Yet, Riedheim knows that the evolution of the autonomous automobile is still in its very beginning stages. How will

[1]Some names of certain persons and programs are being used for narrative purposes. They are either fictitious or have been altered. Narrative statements on the part of these persons do not necessarily represent the official views or opinions of the companies mentioned in this case.

Professor Olaf Groth of Hult International Business School, with assistance from Eleonora Ferrero and Aleksey Malyshev (both Hult MBAs, 2014), developed this fictitious case based on discussions with various company officials and from published materials. It is not meant as an endorsement or critique of any particular company, nor intended to be a source of primary data.

Acknowledgement [1] The authors wish to thank the helpful people of Quid.com for making their technology available for the illustrations which appear in Figures 2 and 3 in this case and for their tireless counsel on its use and value.

this new world evolve and how will BMW evolve its position in it? What will he say about BMW's emerging strategy in his upcoming briefing with an important BMW board member?

He goes back to his desk, and reviews the facts once more.

A Brief History of BMW

The automaker got its start as a manufacturer of aircraft engines in Munich, Germany, in March 1916 and turned into a motorcycle and automobile company in 1928.[2] Since then, BMW has manufactured motorcycles and cars. It is most well known for its high-quality cars in the upper segment of the market. After WWII the company had to restore its manufacture and reputation. The first car that started a new era for BMW was the 501 model, a famous classic today that quickly established the company as a producer of high-quality, technically advanced cars. Most prominent among its superior engineering capabilities are its engines, which many experts attribute to its early legacy in aero-turbines ("turbine" still being the nickname of its 6-cylinder car engines). In 1973 the factory in Munich started building the BMW 2002 turbo engine. This was the same year that the first oil crisis hit the western world, which had become dependent on cheap gas. Sales of gas-guzzling volume-produced performance cars slumped and BMW started to develop a strong skillset in more fuel-efficient turbo-diesel engines.

In 1990 the Bavarians, leveraging their competency in making high-agility, precision steering, introduced a new kind of rear axle that allows the rear wheels to turn a few degrees in the same direction as the front wheel. This improved car stability in turns at high speed, as well as the fun of the driving experience by a BMW driver, which is central to BMW's value proposition. Since then, few other manufacturers have managed to match this active handling experience, which today is a hallmark of the BMW brand.

In 2001 the company built another competency, this time pioneering cutting edge electronics: a new kind of "head unit" (the control and entertainment console that sits in the center of a dashboard). It was called "iDrive" and it allowed operating the unit easily with a joystick-like knob giving tactile feedback to the driver, without having to take his or her eyes off the road. iDrive had been developed in collaboration with BMW's Technology Office in Palo Alto, at the heart of Silicon Valley. After an initial period of drivers' adjustment to the new technology and user interface, the iDrive and various iDrive-like derivatives quickly became a common feature in luxury and performance automobiles of many brands.

Finally, on January 8th 2014 during the Consumer Electronic Show in Las Vegas, BMW demonstrated its first fully automated car prototypes based on its regular car models.[3] The car uses 360 degree radar technology, as well as a set of other sensors including cameras and ultrasound to accelerate, steer, and brake without driver intervention. The company also demonstrated another feature called "Emergency Stop Assistant," which will pull the vehicle to the side of the road, stop, and activate an emergency call in case the driver experiences an unexpected health condition, such as fainting, a heart attack or a stroke.[4] These advancements demonstrated the ability of BMW to stay on top of the new technology.

A litany of prizes and awards recognized BMW's strengths:

- **Brand reputation:** BMW is acknowledged worldwide as a successful carmaker. In 2012, Forbes elected BMW as the most reputable business in the world, and in 2016 it became the second most valuable brand in the automotive industry, with a market value of $26.4 billion.[5]
- **Handling, engines and traction motors:** BMW was able to become a market leader in the production of engines, which led the company to win several 'engine of the year' awards, in an industry where technology is a top priority and competition is fierce.
- **Information technology integration:** BMW was able to integrate technology innovation in its vehicles, winning international prizes such as the Berthold Leibinger Innovation award in 2014 for its laser-light technology and the Autoblog's 2014 Technology of the Year award for the whole technology suite working together on the BMW i8.[6]
- **Environmentally friendly vehicles:** BMW researched dual fuel engines, hydrogen-driven cars, and hybrid electric cars. Furthermore, 80% of its automobiles are made from recycled and recyclable materials.[7] The Brand won the World Green Car of the Year Award in 2015 at the New York International Auto Show[8] and at the 2014 Los Angeles Auto Show, BMW was presented with the Green Car of the Year Award from the Green Car Journal for the BMWi3.[9]

The Ecosystem of Autonomous Driving Today

The idea of cars driving themselves has existed for a few decades, since the early days of Tsukuba Lab in Japan in 1977 and the European EUREKA Prometheus project in 1987. But only recently, with the advances in computer technology, has it become a reality. The 2004, 2005, and 2007 Urban Challenges conducted by the Defense Advanced Research Projects Agency (DARPA) in the U.S. yielded significant advances, with cars eventually completing a 132-mile course successfully as exemplified by the winner of the 2005 DARAP Urban Challenge: Stanford University's VW Touareg "Stanley."

The domain of autonomous driving promises stunning prospects as well as some key uncertainties. It is at the intersection of large opportunity and the uncertainty of a number of future trends that could affect the domain to take a turn in one direction or another. According to Navigant Research, annual sales of autonomous vehicles could reach nearly 95 million by 2035.[10] Morgan Stanley analysts also believe that self-driving cars will change the auto industry.[11]

At the core of the self-driving car is state-of-the-art microprocessors, i.e., computer chips called Central Processing Units (CPU) or Graphical Processing Units (GPU). GPUs are CPUs that have special capabilities related to processing imagery or graphics. Two major players in the microprocessor technology market are working on the hardware for self-driving cars—Intel,[12] maker of CPUs and NVIDIA, maker of GPUs. Recently, through cooperation with these Silicon Valley stars, car manufacturers globally have obtained processing technology that powers critical components to allow them to build self-driving cars. Several companies and research centers[13] are working on an even more powerful type of processor—Quantum Computers that will be able to handle massive computational tasks in parallel—a quality essential for the artificial intelligence needed for autonomous driving. With Google recently joining the effort,[14] the prospect of creating one (quantum computer?) becomes more realistic.

There are different levels of self-driving, which means 'autonomous automobile' can mean different things to different people. For BMW to craft a more nuanced strategy, the company will need to draw the distinction between the different modes of the car's autonomous assistance for the driver:

Self-parking: A car with this feature can park itself without driver intervention. This is primarily a convenience feature for most drivers, but can also aid drivers that are physically impaired. It can help avoiding fender-bender accidents that may increase car insurance costs.

Lane control: Helps the driver to steer though curving highway roads. This is mainly a security feature that helps drivers to avoid potentially dangerous accidents like the car driving into oncoming traffic or veering off the road.

Speed control in heavy traffic: This feature goes a bit further by allowing the driver to let the car navigation system accelerate and slow down the vehicle when the car moves in a traffic jam. This adds the driver some relief to an otherwise tiring journey through tough traffic conditions.

Fully automated car: The highest level of automation is achieved when the car can drive itself in any conditions, including driving through crossroads and crosswalks with or through traffic lights, making turns, changing lanes, keeping distance with other vehicles, and responding to any kind of emergency situations. In this case the driver inputs the destination into the navigation system and allows it to drive. This feature has been widely discussed as the future of mobility. Most drivers would spend their time being entertained, being social, or being productive in their cars.

Fully Automated Cars: The Competitive Landscape

While BMW[15] and Audi[16] have already presented prototypes of fully automated cars, other car manufacturers are developing and testing partial autonomy approaches. Toyota/Lexus are working on the concept of assisted driving. Tesla recently announced that it is already installing navigation hardware on its cars,[17] although its system is not intended to take full control either, but rather provide assistance for the driver to improve safety. GM first invested $500M in ride-hailing company Lyft and then the two companies announced plans to test a fleet of autonomous Chevrolet Bolt electric taxis on the road within a year.[18]

Other players are more skeptical: Volvo's head of R&D, Peter Mertens, has been very direct in saying that the prospect of a driver reading a newspaper or answering e-mails while driving "is a very, very long term vision."[19] The carmaker is concentrated on safety instead, such as object avoidance and more traditional protection such as material strength. Yet, in a surprising twist, that same year, (which year?) Uber's Founder and Co-CEO Travis Kalanick, started to hire dozens of autonomous auto experts at leading technical institutions, and it was

Figure 1 Select Carmaker Competitors Positioning for Autonomous Driving

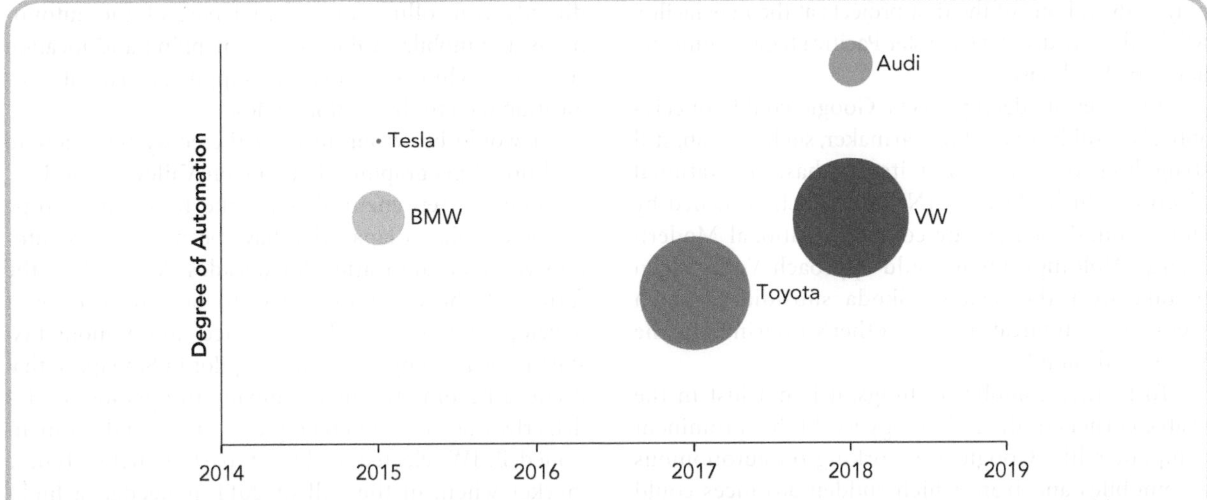

The chart above represents projected year of availability of Autonomous Automobiles for some car manufacturers. The size of the bubbles corresponds to the total car production by the company for the year 2013. The X axis shows the year in which car makers are expected to go to market with their versions of autonomous cars. The Y axis shows the degree of autonomy, as described above.

Volvo with its well-established reputation of making some of the safest automobiles on the road, that heeded the call to partner.[20]

Along similar lines, Ford engineer Torsten Wey opined that he does not believe cars will ever be fully autonomous: "I doubt we will ever get there," he said.[21] According to Wey there are situations when the car's autopilot is not intelligent enough to make decisions. The human driver does not only consider behavior of his own car, but also takes into account behaviors of others. Experienced drivers can intuitively predict what other cars on the road will do and act accordingly, augmenting the measurable data of the moment with their own experience. For instance, when a driver sees a car in front of them slow down to turn into a restaurant parking lot, the driver can judge that the car will likely not stop right there in the middle of the lane, based on subtle contextual clues and a lifetime of learning. A computerized system, however, does not yet have that intuition and will not acquire it for a long time. Yet earlier, Ford tripled its autonomous vehicle development fleet and accelerated its on-road software and sensor testing.[22]

Clearly, automakers are in an uncomfortable dance of cautioning expectations yet forging ahead full steam. But this diversity of signals, views and approaches between car makers is only the beginning of a complex picture: as a seasoned, technology-savvy strategist, Norbert Riedheim knows that competition may not only come from established players, but also from new entrants into a given market: BMW needs to anticipate.

One of these new entrants is Internet giant Google, which demonstrated its self-driving car in the summer of 2014. The technological program at the heart of the Google car is called Google Chauffeur.[23] It is an example of a truly driverless car that can move itself in a targeted, pre-programmed fashion from point A to point B using advanced sensors that collect and interpret data from the environment. This is enabled by multiple Google technologies, including its Maps navigation technology. Google uses a Toyota-brand vehicle for testing its autonomous driving system, but it is not in a formal joint venture with the firm and could still choose any other automaker as a partner.[24] Being cash-rich, the company could also develop its own car, as has been successfully demonstrated by Tesla.

Alternatively, much like Tesla, Google could cooperate with an established carmaker (in Tesla's case it was a design collaboration with Lotus in the UK). Along those lines, the company announced its new self-driving technology development center in Novi, Michigan, in May 2016 and one of the first projects at the new facility will be the self-driving Chrysler Pacifica hybrid minivan, developed in-house.[25]

But given its deep pockets, Google could conceivably also still buy an ailing carmaker, such as Saab, still struggling to recover after its purchase by National Electric Vehicles Sweden (NEVS), which is owned by Hong Kong-based energy company National Modern Energy Holdings. Or it could approach Volkswagen to take over the Seat or Skoda subsidiary, which seem to be duplicating each other's offerings in the VW brands family.

To further complicate things, it is not just in the visible corners of the technology world that prominent companies like Google are working on autonomous automobiles and from which sudden advances could emerge. In start-ups, universities, and R&D centers around the world, leading technologists are working on pre-commercial solutions. In early 2013 there were multiple reports about companies and individuals who were working on an affordable self-driving feature. One of them is Professor Paul Newman from Oxford University who works on self-driving technology that utilizes cheap sensors.[26] Also, Intel awarded the top prize in its Gordon E. Moore competition[27] to a Romanian teenager for using artificial intelligence to create a viable model for a low-cost, self-driving car. One company took it a step further and designed a commercial self-driving accessory that can be installed on selected models of compatible cars with sensors mounted on the rooftop. It is a startup called Cruise,[28] which emerged from a Silicon Valley incubator, Y-Combinator, and started accepting pre-orders for it assisted driving system in mid-2014. In March 2016, Cruise was acquired by GM, which appears to be interested in integrating the system into the design of its own cars.

Another critical element of autonomous driving—mapping and location services—is also flourishing globally, especially in Europe. Nokia Corporation's former mapping business, HERE—based in Berlin—provides an open platform for cloud-based maps. HERE is not only the main alternative to Google Maps, but also the market leader in built-in car navigation systems. According to Nokia's website,[29] four out of five cars in North America and Europe feature HERE integrated in-dash navigation. Not surprisingly, in August 2015 BMW, Audi, and Daimler announced their acquisition of HERE.[30] These 3 automobile companies will be directly controlling an essential part of the autonomous automobiles' value chain—mapping and location services—while securing the supply of critical geolocation data in their automobiles.

It would be wrong to limit the ecosystem view to traditional geographies, like Silicon Valley in the U.S., or other entrepreneurial hubs like Berlin in Europe and R&D labs in Japan that have been strong in automotive or IT innovation for decades. A look into the future of the automobile has to take into account developments in Asia. For instance, autonomous taxi startup nuTonomy announced a pilot in Singapore that it could become the first company to operate Level-4 driverless taxis commercially in a city.[31] And, as mentioned, BMW selected Baidu as its partner in the Chinese market when, in the Fall of 2014, it needed a high-resolution GPS system to start testing in Shanghai and Beijing, two of the most demanding, densely populated, and vast automotive markets in the world. And now Baidu claims it is developing its own automated car, but unlike Google, it works on driver assistance and is not a fully self-driving car.

The Chinese market is already the largest and the fastest growing in the world, with 18 million cars sold in 2013,[32] a compound annual growth rate (CAGR) between 2005 and 2012 of 18.1%, and an expected 6.3% average year-over-year growth through 2020 making it a tremendously important market for BMW.

Luckily, BMW made an early, courageous decision to enter the Chinese market, benefiting from the excellent relationships held by a former BMW board member and former government executive in charge of the company's government relations. The effort bore fruit: in 2013 BMW sold 390,713 cars in China, up 20% from a year earlier. This meant that China had officially overtaken the U.S. (375,782 cars sold) as the group's biggest market and had outpaced the overall company's market growth of 13.9 percent.[33]

As Riedheim leans back in his sleek BMW carbon fiber chair, he wonders how this ecosystem might evolve and how should BMW position itself within it? What are some plausible, alternative futures? Having studied disruptive innovation and strategy throughout the years, Riedheim knows that big bets often don't pay off because too many variables in a market forecast change. So, understanding these alternative futures first will help him to craft a strategy that is robust against different market states.

Figure 2 Investments and Resources as Represented by Patent Growth in Key Technology Spaces Related to Autonomous Automobiles (Graphic Developed Through Quid.com)

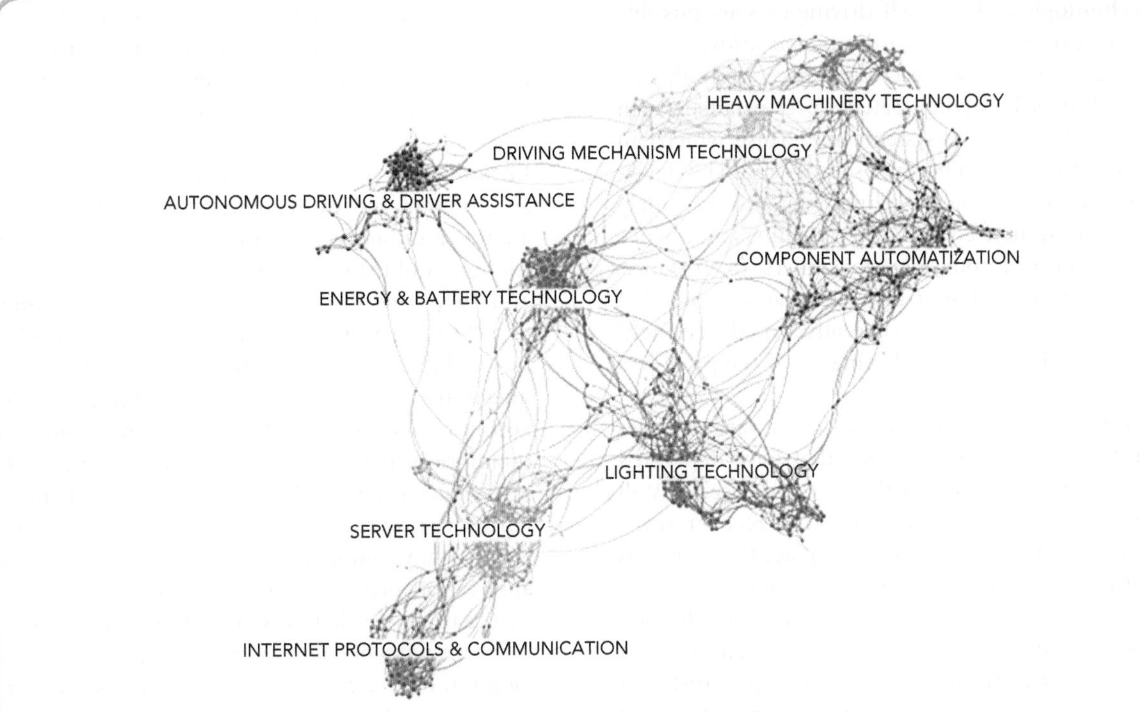

This image shows the vast expanse of the technology ecosystem that contributes intellectual property and capabilities to the domain of autonomous automobiles. The volume of innovation is substantial and hints at the commercial promise that innovators see in this area. In the last five years the following patents have been registered: 208 for Component Automatization, 168 for Lighting Technology, 119 for Server Technology, 118 for Driving Mechanism Technology, 101 for Energy and Battery Technology, 94 for Heavy Machinery Technology, 87 for Internet Protocols & Communication, and finally 81 for Autonomous Driving & Driver Assistance. Please see the Appendix for a list of the Most Frequent All Original Patent Assignees and Locations of Origin.

Exploring the Future

Through his work with design consultancies over the years, Riedheim has learned that this exploration first requires a clear view of all the uncertainties that could combine to pivot the market and ecosystem in one direction or another.

Key Uncertainties

Many uncertainties related to self-driving automobiles will prompt both business executives and policy makers to take action of one kind or another. In this complex ecosystem issues emerge in six different areas:

- **Social:** Who will use self-driving cars? Autonomous vehicles can be used to transport people who cannot drive, either because they are elderly, too young, physically or visually impaired. A car that today is driven by a family member can become an independent transportation vehicle for all family members, even those under 18 and without a driver's permit. However, it is not clear if, or how, this technology might be adopted by the consumer majority. What will be their aspirations, concerns, anxieties, and potential mistakes? Additionally, the permissible behaviors allowed in the car itself will depend on whether the vehicle is fully self-driving. For instance, driver-passengers could be able to spend their time in the car messaging, reading, or working. Drinking alcohol might also be permissible, since the fully autonomous car will not require any intervention by the passenger . . . or will it? What if systems fail and driver-passengers are required to become active drivers?

- **Technological:** Today self-driving cars are possible because of the existing hardware and software technology. However, as described, there are both cars with fully self-driving features pre-installed (such as Google's car), and systems like Cruise, which can allow other cars to become self-driving. The development cost of these technologies differs widely and will influence pricing to consumers and hence the adoption response by consumers: for instance, a survey by JD Power and Associates found that only 20% of Americans currently would 'definitely' or 'probably' buy a self-driving car if the price was only $30.000.[34]
- **Economic:** Firstly, there are of course various crises in Asia, the U.S. and Europe that have depressed consumer spending over the past two decades. Will the global and regional economies recover sufficiently to enable consumers to replace their vehicles with new, unproven autonomous ones, or would they resort to buying pre-owned vehicles that are cheaper and use more established technologies? Secondly, self-driving vehicles will impact different market players. Insurance companies might change their business models based on a lower rate of accidents. Driverless vehicles may allow some companies to save money on drivers (such as taxi or bus companies). Also at the national level, research from The University of Texas[35] estimated that if just 10% of vehicles were self-driving, a country such as the U.S. could save about $37 billion a year on healthcare and environmental costs. For the same reason, the U.K. government has announced its commitment to spend £10 million on a test-bed for self-driving cars.[36] Finally, the cost and purchasing power in different regions will weigh into the market economics in different ways, since self-driving cars will change the current production process and countries will facilitate autonomous automobile adoption among consumers in different ways and along different timelines.
- **Environmental:** Pollution regulations will change, considering the new emissions generated by self-driving cars, which may be lower than the emissions generated by cars today. This assumption is based on two main factors: first, autonomous vehicles will be able to optimize their consumption by themselves based on road conditions as well as acceleration and breaking behavior, and second, electric cars and smart charging infrastructure may at some point converge on autonomous automobiles, such that gasoline could become obsolete.
- **Legal:** Self-driving cars have to be explicitly legal and encouraged by regulators, not just be tolerated as a dubious "gray area." Bad or lagging legislation could slow down the investment required and therefore the development of the technology. Furthermore, authorities have to develop new liability frameworks to answer the following questions: who has what kind of influence over autonomous cars "misbehaving" and who will therefore bear the legal and financial responsibility? Would it be the driver, the software or the IT hardware provider, the data processing companies, the telecom companies linking cars wirelessly, the application providers for different functionalities that may have little to do to with driving but could interfere with behavior in the car, the car manufacturer, or the company responsible for the car's maintenance?
- **Ethical:** Two main aspects represent key uncertainties in this area. The first issue concerns privacy: what information will be collected by autonomous automobiles, and who has access to it? The second point regards safety. How can autonomous cars be prevented from being hacked, getting virus-infected, and being used for remote criminal activities such as terrorist attack or drug delivery? How does society address computer-savvy minors hacking into cars and sending them on remote joy rides? Will physically or visually impaired passengers be at the mercy of malfunctioning autonomous driving intelligence?

To get more information about these and many other uncertainties and assumptions, both governments and private companies have started to experiment. In the U.S., California, Nevada, and Florida allow companies to use self-driving cars on the road for testing purposes.[37] Meanwhile, BMW has tested its self-driving car in Europe, and recently also got permission from the Chinese government to test its cars in Shanghai and Beijing.

Figure 3 Map of "Hot Topics" Related to Autonomous Driving that Gained Public Attention on the Internet (Graphic Developed Through Quid.com)[2]

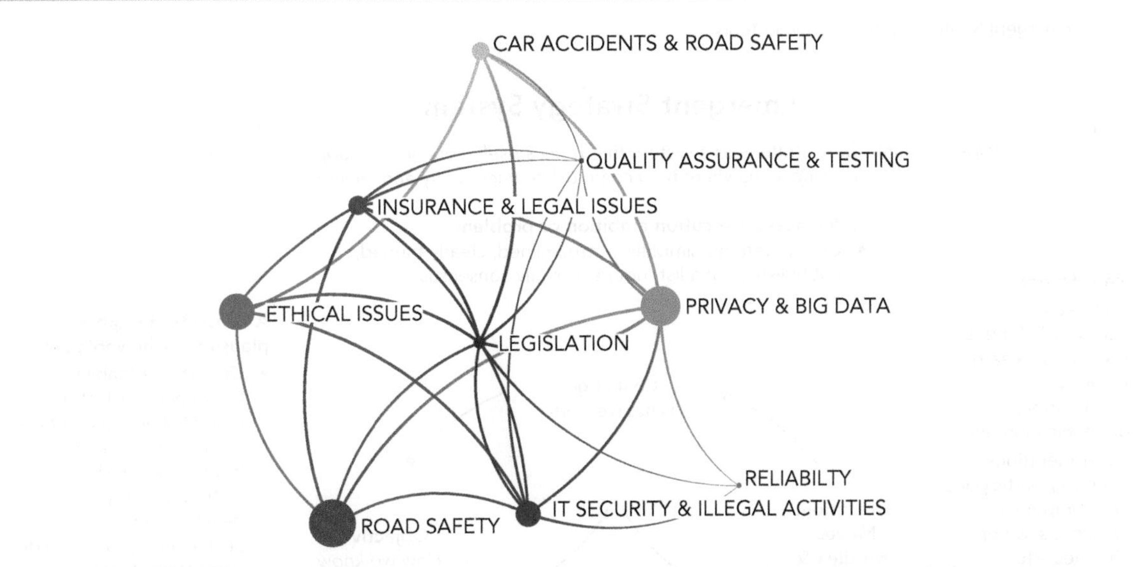

This graphic shows some of the key uncertainties from a public perspective, as articulated through news and other coverage on the Internet. It demonstrates that many of the issue areas are interconnected, supporting the point that the autonomous car is a complex system of systems with 2nd and 3rd order effects that could be undesirable and are on the minds of consumers and legislators, i.e., potential buyers, for that reason.

But Riedheim knows time is critical: the Board will feel that BMW has to make the strategic investment, partnering, and positioning decisions now, even absent perfect information, if they are to be at the forefront. Questions he'll need to be ready to answer:

1. **Strategic challenge/aspiration:** Given the changing scenario, what kind of business should BMW aim to be over the next 10 to 15 years? What are its aspirations?
2. **Objectives:** What are the key metrics that would indicate BMW met the challenge and achieved its goal?
3. **Opportunity:** What is the size of the opportunity for BMW?
4. **Competitive advantages:** Given BMW's current competencies, (e.g., internal capabilities, market positions), which ones will be hard to replicate in the emerging automobile industry ecosystem? (carmakers, Internet companies, technology startups, R&D labs, governments, insurance companies, suppliers, etc.)? Which ones does it still need to build and develop, and why?
5. **Moves:** What concrete immediate actions should BMW take now to build external positions and internal capabilities? What types of hurdles or failures are possible and should be accepted as part of the entrepreneurial path? What kind of learning milestones should the company set for itself?

As Riedheim sits down to start work on these questions, he knows the burden on him is considerable: the future of this iconic company is at stake.

[2]The authors wish to thank the helpful people of Quid.com for making their technology available for this case and for their tireless counsel on its use and value. DO YOU NEED THIS HERE SINCE YOU HAVE AT THE START? WOULD ELIMINATE.

Exhibits

Exhibit 1 Emergent Strategy System (ESS) and Tools

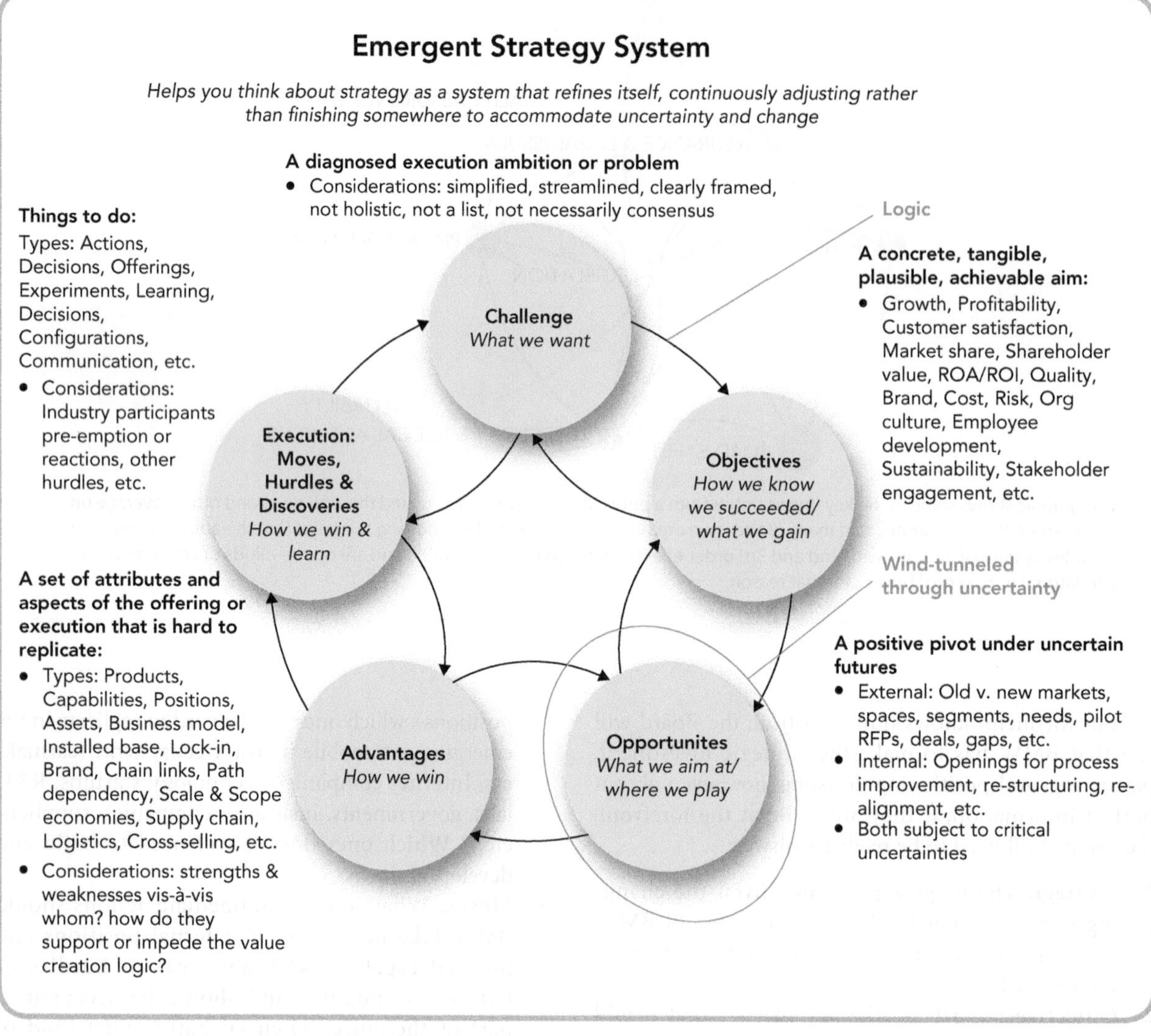

Exhibit 1 (cont.) Emergent Strategy System (ESS) and Tools

Tools and Frameworks for the ESS

Analysis can be conducted and insights can be gained with these concepts and frameworks, amongst others... But quality output is the priority over framework use.

Challenge
What we want

Challenge definition - always identify the highest order challenge first, then "unpack" it or break it down:
1. A meaningful, unmet business aspiration
2. An observed, business-critical, high-impact problem

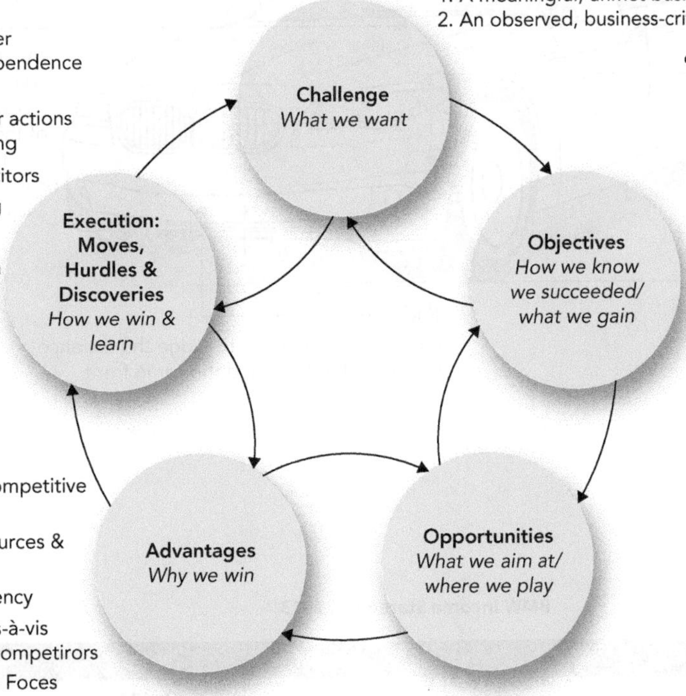

Objectives
How we know we succeeded/ what we gain

- Tangible goal posts that, e.g. value created, products created/sold, costs to be reduced, revenue attained, profit made, market share held, customer satisfaction scores received, geographies or parts-of-populations covered, strategic optionality built, etc.

Opportunities
What we aim at/ where we play

- Markets with network effects
- Market future evolution (STEEPLE uncertainties and scenarios)
- Futurized 5+ Forces
- Market concentration
- Value chain segments
- Fit & feasibility/attractiveness
- Desirable total addressable market funnel
- Futurized market segmentation
- Buyer profiles
- Futurized or relational SWOT

Advantages
Why we win

- Sustainable competitive advantage
- Strategic resources & capabilities
- Core competency
- Positioning vis-à-vis customers & competirors
- Futurized Five Foces
- Defensibility of platforms and value chain positions
- Strategic agility

Execution: Moves, Hurdles & Discoveries
How we win & learn

- Vertical v. horizontal v. diagonal integration in value chains & grids
- Campaigns for competition under strategic interdependence (CSI)
- Blue Ocean - four actions and value mapping
- Low-cost competitors
- Downturn pricing
- Strategic agility
- Frugal innovation
- Open innovation (not discussed)
- Business model innovation (not discussed)

Exhibit 2 BMW Autonomous Car[38]

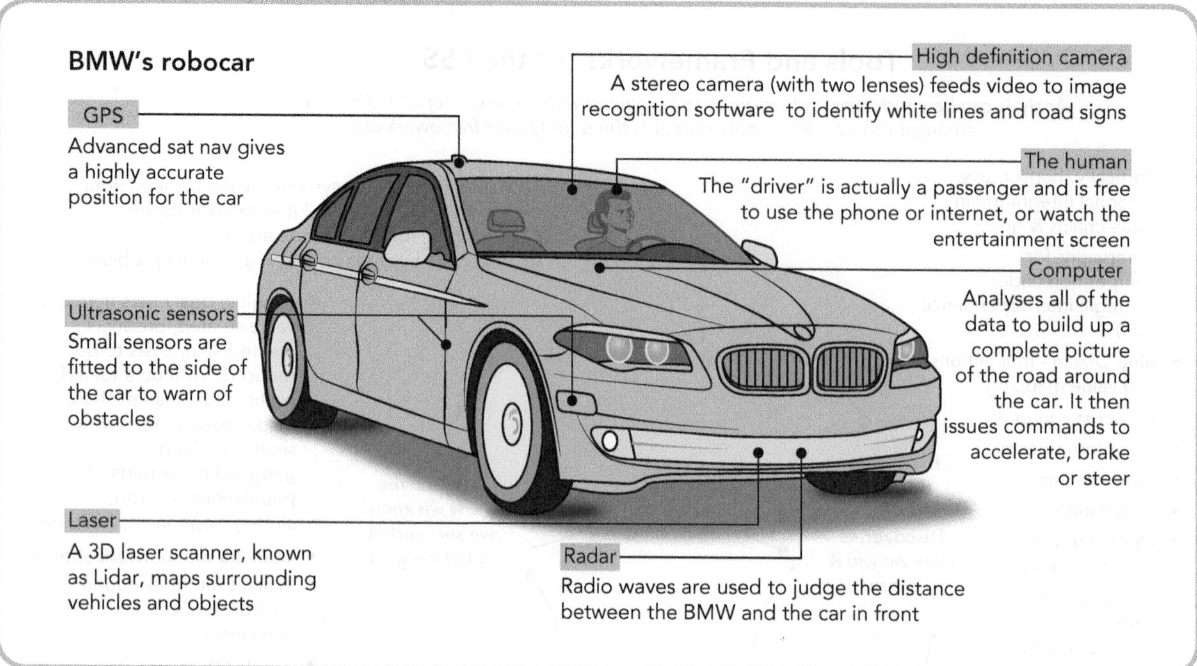

Exhibit 3 Financial Data

BMW Income Statement 2013[39]

In € million	Notes	2013	2012
Revenues	14	**60,474**	58805
Cost of sales		**−47,067**	−46,252
Gross profit		**13,407**	**12,553**
Selling expenses		**−3,528**	−3,684
Administration expenses		**−2,141**	−1,701
Research and development expenses		**−4,362**	−3,573
Other operating income and expenses	15– 16–	**542**	703
Result on investments	17–	**373**	598
Financial result	18–	**−328**	−99
Profit from ordinary activities		**3,963**	**4,797**
Income taxes	19–	**−1,629**	−1,635
Other taxes		**−45**	−31
Net Profit		**2,289**	**3,131**
Transfer to revenue reserves	20–	**−582**	−1,491
Unappropriated profit available for distribution		**1,707**	**1,640**

Exhibit 3 (cont.) Financial Data

BMW in Figures 2013[40]

		2013	2012	Change in %
Revenues	€ million	**60,474**	58,805	2.8
Export ratio	%	**81.5**	79.6	
Production				
Automobiles[1]	units	**2,006,366**	1,861,826	7.8
Motorcycles	units	**110,127**	113,811	3.2
Sales volume				
Automobiles[1]	units	**1,995,903**	1,868,158	6.8
Motorcyles	units	**110,039**	110,857	0.7
Capital expenditure	€ million	**3,203**	2,776	15.4
Depreciation, amortisation and impairment losses	€ million	**1,732**	1,613	7.4
Workforce at end of year		**77,110**	74,571	3.4
Tangible, intangible and investment losses	€ million	**12,833**[2]	11,078	15.8
Current assets, prepayments and surplus of pension and similar plan assets over liabilities	€ million	**20,932**	20,887	0.2
Subscribed capital	€ million	**656**	656	–
Reserves	€ million	**8,166**	7,568	7.9
Equity	€ million	**10,529**	9,864	6.7
as % of tangible, intangible and investment assets	%	**82.0**	89.0	
Balance sheet total	€ million	**33,765**	31,965	5.6
Cost of materials	€ million	**43,402**	42,178	2.9
Personnel costs	€ million	**6,419**	6,030	6.5
Taxes	€ million	**1,674**	1,666	0.5
Net profit	€ million	**2,289**	3,131	26.9
Dividend	€ million	**1,707**[3]	1,640	4.1
per share of common stock with a per value of € 1 each	€	**2.60**[3]	2.50	
per share of preferred stock with a per value of € 1 each	€	**2.62**[3]	2.52	

[1]Including supplies of series parts to BMW Brilliance Automotive Ltd., Shenyang.

[2]Including transfer of non-current assets in conjunction with merger of BMW Peugeot Citroën Electrification GmbH, Munich.

[3]Proposed by the Board of Management.

BMW Research and Development 2013[41]

'Research and development expenditure for the year rose by 21.3 % to € 4,792 million, mostly for projects aimed at securing the Group's future business (2012: € 3,952 million). The research and development ratio was 6.3 %, 1.2 percentage points higher than in the previous year (2012: 5.1 %).

The ratio of capitalised development costs to total research and development costs for the period (capitalisation ratio) was 36.4 % (2012: 27.6 %). Amortisation of capitalised development costs totalled € 1,069 million (2012: € 1,130 million). Further information on research and development expenditure is provided in the section Results of Operations, Financial Position and Net Assets and in note 10 to the Group Financial Statements.

Total research and development expenditure, comprising research costs, development costs not recognised as assets on the one hand and capitalised development costs excluding the scheduled amortisation thereof on the other, was as follows:'

in € million	2013	2012
Research and development expenses	4,117	3,993
Amortisation	–1,069	–1,130
New expenditure for capitalized development costs	1,744	1,089
Total research and development expenditure	4,792	3,952

Exhibit 4 Google Car

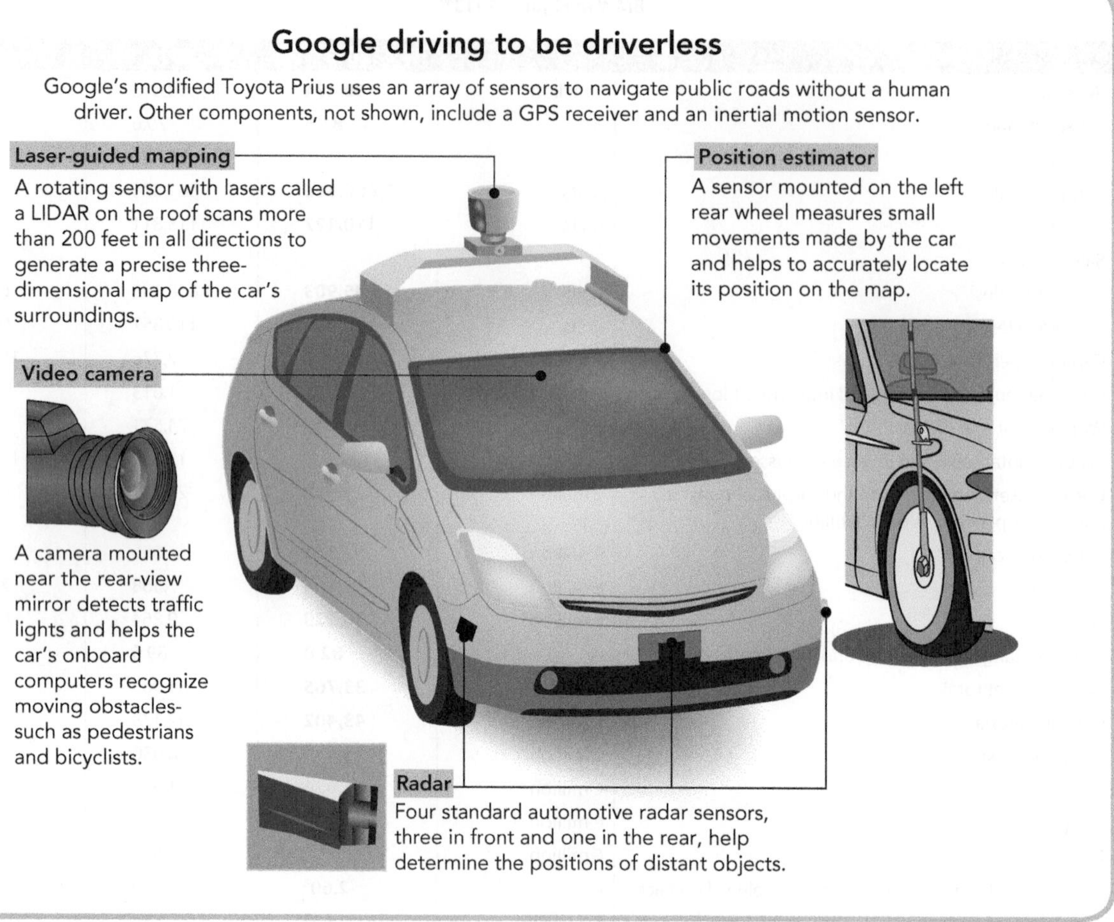

Source: The New York Times

Exhibit 5 Patents by Most Frequent All Original Assignees & Most Frequent Filing Location

Most Frequent Original Company Assignee

- Google Inc
- Gm Global Technology Operations Inc
- Gen Motors Global Operation Technology
- Daimler Ag
- Hyundai Motor Co Ltd
- Electronics & Telecom Res Inst
- Valeo Schalter & Sensoren Gmbh
- Siemens Ag
- Bosch Gmbh Robert

Most Frequent Original Filling Location

United States of America
World Intellectual Property Organization Germany
China Republic of Korea Japan
European Patent Office United Kingdom
Taiwan

NOTES

1. Abhimanyu Ghoshal, *BMW will launch its first self-driving car in 2021,* The Next Web Retrieved from http://thenextweb.com/gadgets/2016/05/13/bmw-will-launch-first-self-driving-car-2021/
2. Rory Buckeridge, *Audi promises driveless cars by 2016*, Techradar, November 18th 3014, Retrieved from http://www.techradar.com/news/car-tech/audi-promises-driv%20erless-cars-by-2016-1273437
3. Rory Buckeridge, *Driverless cars within two years? Not a chance, says Volvo top bod,* Techradar, December 6th 2014, Retrieved from http://www.techradar.com/us/news/car-tech/driverless-cars-within-two-years-not-a-chance-says-volvo-top-bod-1275805
4. James Mills, *Ford says fully autonomous cars may never be possible*, The Sunday Times, July 25th 2014, Retrieved from http://www.driving.co.uk/news/exclusive-ford-says-fully-autonomous-cars-may-never-be-po
5. Statista.com, *Most Valuable automotive brands worldwide by* Retrieved from http://www.statista.com/statistics/267830/brand-values-of-the-top-10-most-valuable-car-brands/
6. Autoblog, *BMW i8 named Autobolg's 2014 Tecnology of the Year,* November 19th 2014, Retrieved from http://www.autoblog.com/2014/11/19/bmw-i8-named-autoblogs-2014-technology-of-the-year/
7. BMW.com, Retrieved from http://www.bmw.com/com/en/insights/corporation/bmwi/sustainability.html
8. World Car Awards, *BMW i8 wins 2015 world green car award,* 2017 Press Release World Car Awards, Retrieved from http://www.wcoty.com/web/media_release.asp?release=100&
9. Sebastian Blanco, *BMW i3 wins 2015 Green Car of the Year award,* AutoBlog, November 20th 2014, Retrieved from http://www.autoblog.com/2014/11/20/bmw-i3-wins-2015-green-car-of-the-year-award/
10. Paul Eisenstein, *Nissan ramps up push into self-driving vehicles*, CNBC, Retrieved from http://www.cnbc.com/id/101846396
11. Morgan Stanley, *Autonomous Cars: the Future is Now*, January 23rd 2015, Retrieved from http://www.morganstanley.com/public/11152013.html
12. Intel, Technology and Computing Requirements for Self-Driving Cars, Intel Corporation 2014, Retrieved from http://www.intel.com/content/dam/www/public/us/en/documents/white-papers/automotive-autonomous-driving-vision-paper.pdf
13. Two innovative companies include Rigetti http://www.rigetti.com/ and Dwavesys http://www.dwavesys.com/
14. Stephen McBride, *Google to build quantum computer*, ITP.net, September 3rd 2014, Retrieved from http://www.itp.net/599671-google-to-build-quantum-computer
15. Dave Lee, *CES 2014: BMW shows off 'drifting' self-drive cars*, BBC News, January 8th 2014, Retrieved from http://www.bbc.com/news/technology-25653253
16. Bruce Upbin, *Let's go for a ride with Audi's self-driving car,* Forbes, January 8th 2014, Retrieved from http://www.forbes.com/sites/bruceupbin/2014/01/08/lets-go-for-a-ride-in-traffic-with-audis-self-driving-car-video/
17. The Tesla Motors Team, *Dual Motor Model S and Autopilot*, October 10th 2014,Retrieved from http://www.teslamotors.com/blog/dual-motor-model-s-and-autopilot
18. Andrew Hawkins, *GM is investing $500M in Lyft*, The Verge, January 4th 2016 Retrieved from http://www.theverge.com/2016/1/4/10706250/gm-lyft-driverless-cars-ride-sharing-investment
19. Rory Buckeridge, *Driverless cars in two years?,* T3, December 5th 2014, Retrieved from, http://www.t3.com/news/driverless-cars-in-two-years-bulls-t-says-volvo-man-as-he-launches-car-into-a-ditch
20. Max Chafkin. *Uber's Self-Driving Fleet Arrives in Pittsburg Next Month.* Bloomberg Features. August 18th, 2016. Retrieved from http://www.bloomberg.com/news/features/2016-08-18/uber-s-first-self-driving-fleet-arrives-in-pittsburgh-this-month-is06r7on
21. James Mills *Exclusive: Ford Says Fully Autonomous Cars May Never Be Possible,* The Sunday Times, July 25th 2014, Retrieved from http://www.driving.co.uk/news/exclusive-ford-says-fully-autonomous-cars-may-never-be-possible/
22. *Ford Tripling Autonomous Vehicle Development Fleet, Accelerating On-Road Testing of Software and Sensors.* Ford Motor Company Media Center. January 5, 2016. Retrieved at https://media.ford.com/content/fordmedia/fna/us/en/news/2016/01/05/ford-tripling-autonomous-vehicle-development-fleet--accelerating.html
23. Google Self-Driving Cars Project, Retrieved from https://www.google.com/selfdrivingcar/
24. Peter Valdes-Dapena, Toyota reveals self-driving car, CNN Money, January 7th 2013, Retrieved from http://money.cnn.com/2013/01/04/autos/toyota-self-driving-cars/
25. Google Self-Driving Cars Project, Retrieved from https://plus.google.com/+SelfDrivingCar/posts/cwvk4uan3bM
26. Richard Alleyne, *British researches on the road to an affordable self-driving car,* The Telegraph February 15th 2013, Retrieved from http://www.telegraph.co.uk/motoring/news/9871743/British-researchers-on-the-road-to-an-affordable-self-driving-car.html
27. Sid Perkins, *Teens take home science gold at Intel ISEF,* Science News, May 20th 2013, Retrieved from https://www.sciencenews.org/blog/scene/teens-take-home-science-gold-intel-isef
28. Y Combinator, *For $10,000, your car can drive itself,* Blog Y Combinator, June 24th 2014 Retrieved from http://blog.ycombinator.com/for-10-dollars-000-your-car-can-drive-itself-cruise-yc-w14
29. James Etheridge, *25% more carspowered by HERE in 2014,* HERE Website, Retrieved from http://360.here.com/2014/07/24/25-cars-powered-by-here-2014/
30. Sarwant Singh, *HERE Acquisition by the Germans: Open innovation on the cards,* Forbes, August 5th 2015, Retrieved from http://www.forbes.com/sites/sarwantsingh/2015/08/05/here-acquisition-by-the-germans-opens-innovation-on-the-cards/#a0b10744210d
31. Robert Hackett, *Singapore is getting driverless Taxi Cabs,* Fortune, April 5th 2016, Retrieved from http://fortune.com/2016/04/05/singapore-driverless-car-taxi-nutonomy/
32. Statista.com, *Cars sales in China from 2008 to 2016,* Retrieved from http://www.statista.com/statistics/233743/vehicle-sales-in-china/
33. Samuel Shen, Kazunori Takada, Matt Driskill, *China edges out U.S. as BMW's biggest market on 2013 sales,* UK Reuters, January 10th 2014, Retrieved from http://uk.reuters.com/article/2014/01/10/uk-bmw-china-idUKBREA090AI20140110
34. Jeff Youngs, *2013 U.S Automotive Emerging Technologies Study Results,* J.D. Power, April 26th 2013, Retrieved from http://autos.jdpower.com/content/study-auto/f85EfAp/2013-u-s-automotive-emerging-technologies-study-results.htm
35. Brad Plumer, *Here's what it would take for self-driving cars to catch on,* The Washington Post, October 23rd 2013, Retrieved from http://www.washingtonpost.com/blogs/wonkblog/wp/2013/10/23/heres-what-it-would-take-for-self-driving-cars-to-catch-on/
36. Stian Westlake *Self-driving cars: a10M punt that could transform the UK,* Nesta, December 4th 2013, Retrieved from http://www.nesta.org.uk/blog/self-driving-cars-ps10m-punt-could-transform-uk?gclid=CNvtwlq_xcECFfHKtAodXhwAgA
37. Maggie Clark, *States take the wheel on driverless cars,* USA TODAT, July 29th 2013, Retrieved from http://www.usatoday.com/story/news/nation/2013/07/29/states-driverless-cars/2595613/
38. Brad Plumer, *Here's what it would take for self-driving cars to catch on,* The Washington Post, October 23rd 2013, Retrieved from http://www.washingtonpost.com/blogs/wonkblog/wp/2013/10/23/heres-what-it-would-take-for-self-driving-cars-to-catch-on/
39. BMW, *Annual Report 2013,* Retrieved from https://www.bmwgroup.com/content/dam/bmw-group-websites/bmwgroup_com/ir/downloads/en/2013/report2013.pdf
40. BMW, *Annual Report 2013,* Retrieved from https://www.bmwgroup.com/content/dam/bmw-group-websites/bmwgroup_com/ir/downloads/en/2013/report2013.pdf
41. BMW, *Annual Report 2013,* Retrieved from https://www.bmwgroup.com/content/dam/bmw-group-websites/bmwgroup_com/ir/downloads/en/2013/report2013.pdf

CASE 4

An Examination of the Long-term Healthcare Industry in the USA

David Thornblad Ph.D.
Zachary Sumner

According to the most recent National Population Projections provided by the United States Census, the following two demographic trends are expected to occur:

1. From 2015 to 2060, the percentage of people aged 65 and older will grow from 14.88% to 23.55% of the population. It is the only age group that will grow as a percentage of the population. (Exhibit 1)
2. From 2015 to 2060, life expectancy for men will increase from 77.1 to 84 years of age and from 81.7 to 87.1 for women. (Exhibit 2)

These trends suggest that there will be increased demand for services that cater to a large demographic of aging people who will live longer than previous generations. As people age, the demand for healthcare increases. One study found that people aged 65 to 74 spend about 3 times more on healthcare-related expenses than 35-to 44-year-olds; those 75 and older spend over 5 times as much (Reinhardt, 2003). Consequently, the size of the long-term healthcare industry has been estimated to be between $210.9 and $317.1 billion dollars (Harris-Kojetin L, 2016), and the healthcare and social assistance industry is expected to be the largest employing sector during the next decade (Bureau of Labor Statistics, 2015). Seeing an opportunity to fulfill this need, a host of firms have rushed to take advantage of these changing demographics.

Health-related Services for An Aging Population

A general term for the services these firms provide is 'long-term' and 'post-acute' healthcare. Post-acute encompasses an array of healthcare services *after* an injury, illness, or disability. It is estimated that 35% of patients need follow-up care after they are discharged from the hospital (Genesis Healthcare, 2016, p. 3). Some of the common services that are provided are:

- *Home Healthcare:* These services allow patients to remain at home and still receive any medical support they require. Healthcare providers come to the patient's home to take vital signs (blood pressure, temperature), make sure the patient is eating and drinking, and taking their medication (Medicare, 2016). It is generally less expensive than a hospital or skilled nursing facility.
- *Rehabilitation Services:* These services can be provided in many settings (hospitals, skilled nursing centers, at home) and seek to restore or improve a patient's independence after an injury.
- *Skilled Nursing Facilities:* These facilities provide skilled nurses on a twenty-four hour basis to patients

Exhibit 1 Percent Distribution of the Projected Population by Sex and Selected Age Groups for the United States: 2015 to 2060

	2015	2020	2025	2030	2035	2040	2045	2050	2055	2060
Under 18 years	22.91%	22.16%	21.60%	21.22%	20.91%	20.56%	20.26%	20.06%	19.90%	19.75%
18 to 64 years	62.20%	60.97%	59.42%	58.16%	57.69%	57.78%	57.98%	57.85%	57.40%	56.70%
65 years and over	14.88%	16.87%	18.98%	20.62%	21.39%	21.66%	21.75%	22.09%	22.70%	23.55%

(U.S. Census Bureau, 2014a)

Exhibit 2 Projected Life Expectancy at Birth: 2015 to 2060

	2015	2020	2030	2040	2050	2060
Both sexes	79.4	80.2	81.7	83.0	84.4	85.6
Male	77.1	78.0	79.6	81.2	82.7	84.0
Female	81.7	82.4	83.7	84.8	86.0	87.1

(U.S. Census Bureau, 2014b)

that do not require more advanced services that a hospital can provide.

- *Assisted/Senior Living Facilities:* These facilities provide simpler services to elderly patients who do not need twenty-four hour care. These facilities offer meals, medication management, hygiene support, and dressing and transportation services.
- *Hospice Care:* Hospice facilities are for terminally ill patients, allowing them to finish their life in as much comfort as possible. Hospice patients do not receive treatments to attempt to cure an illness, but they do provide bereavement services to families and loved ones.

As may be deduced from the types of services listed above, the majority of patients for post-acute firms are elderly. This is because as people age normally simple injuries, such as injuries due to falling down, can have profound health impacts. Further, elderly people tend to have weakened immune systems and can have difficulty fighting illnesses (American Accreditation HealthCare Commission, 2014; Centers for Disease Control and Prevention, 2016).

Industry Participants

Three major firms that focus on healthcare for the elderly are Genesis Healthcare, National HealthCare Corporation, and The Ensign Group. Each firm has a slightly different strategy as to how to service the needs of the aging population.

Genesis Healthcare offers inpatient services through a network of skilled nursing and assisted/senior living facilities. Additionally, they supply rehabilitation and respiratory therapy to more than 1,700 locations in 45 states as well as the District of Columbia. Their assisted/senior living facilities are usually located in urban or suburban areas. In terms of strategy, the firm states that it seeks a higher profit margin than some of its competitors. Genesis believes that the most important factors that influence its performance are its reputation, the cost and quality of services, responsiveness to patient/resident needs as well as the ability to provide support in other areas such as third-party reimbursement, information management and patient recordkeeping. The firm also suggests that some competitors may not adhere to the Anti-Kickback Statute that prohibits payments for referrals, which allows these competitors to attract more patients (Genesis Healthcare, 2016, p. 31). Kickbacks to obtain patients may allow competitors to compete at lower profit margins due to economies of scale.

National Healthcare Corp (NHC) was founded in 1971 and its primary business services include skilled nursing facilities in association with assistant living and independent living facilities for seniors. At the end of 2015, NHC operated 74 skilled nursing facilities in nine states with over 9,400 beds. The firm has over 13,000 employees and NHC offers tuition reimbursement to employees in order to recruit, retain, and maintain a qualified workforce. The company faces competition in every market in which they have a presence and state that no firm has a monopoly with the exception of some smaller rural markets. NHC attracts patients through referrals from hospitals, doctors, as well as church groups and community service organizations. Their annual report notes that the patient's families often play a vital role in selecting a nursing home for their loved ones. Therefore, NHC believes their competitive advantages are their reputation and the physical appearance of their facilities in order to encourage family members to take their loved ones to a NHC facility (National Healthcare Corporation, 2016).

The Ensign Group was started in 1999 with the vision of establishing the standard of excellence in skilled nursing care. During the 2001 recession Ensign acquired multiple facilities that offered skilled nursing, personalized rehabilitation, and technologically advanced medical care services to a wide variety of clientele. With a focus on acquiring underperforming medical facilities and turning them around, Ensign has been adding facilities across the United States (Ensign Group, 2016). Ensign Group follows a differentiation strategy by maximizing the value they can provide to clients and charging them appropriately. The company provides state of the art facilities, in-home therapeutic services to patients who are unable to leave their homes, and tailored care—the focus is on providing quality care for patients that do not mind paying for such services and facilities, even if Medicare does pay for part of it. The company has faced criticism and lawsuits, alleging that they filed false claims with Medicare and that they would provide rehabilitative services that the patient did not need, culminating in a $48 million dollar lawsuit settlement in 2013 (Justice, 2013).

One strategic concern shared by all firms in the industry is that while demand for their services will be growing due to an aging population, it is fairly easy to enter the industry (Genesis Healthcare, 2016, p. 31). A 2016 report, in association with the U.S. Centers for Disease Control and Prevention, on the long-term healthcare industry found that there were approximately 67,000 regulated providers servicing 9 million people in the country (Harris-Kojetin L, 2016).

Sources of Revenue

Firms in this industry receive the majority of their revenue from government sources, particularly Medicare and Medicaid. However, these revenue sources only cover certain services that these firms provide, therefore it is important to understand the types of Medicare and Medicaid.

Medicare is provided by the federal government to people 65 or older as well as the disabled. In general, there are three types, or parts, of Medicare that are important for patients to understand.

- Part A—Covers inpatient stays at hospitals, skilled nursing facilities, nursing home care, hospice, and home health services.
- Part B—Covers services and supplies needed to treat chronic conditions, as well as preventive care like flu shots. It can also cover obtaining a second opinion from a doctor, as well as laboratory tests and ambulance services. Patients pay a monthly fee for this coverage.
- Part C—Medicare Advantage Plans, sometimes called "Part C" is supplemental insurance offered by private companies approved by Medicare to cover expenses not covered by Parts A and B.
- Part D—Provides prescription drug coverage through private insurance companies that have contracts with the government.

Medicaid is provided by state governments, with matching funds from the federal government, to patients or families with low incomes or little resources. Elderly patients can receive Medicaid in additional to Medicare, but patients only become eligible for Medicaid once they have exhausted their other assets.

Medicare and Medicaid are the main sources of income in the senior and post-acute healthcare industry. As shown on Exhibit 3, in 2015 Genesis Healthcare, Ensign Group, and National Healthcare received an average 32.93% of revenues from Medicare and 37.63% of revenues from Medicaid. This totals to 70.57% of revenues coming from government-related sources. Complicating the issue for the industry is that Medicare and Medicaid have been steadily lowering reimbursement rates for taking care of patients, or increasing reimbursements by lower rates than expected (Genesis Healthcare, 2016). Given the importance of Medicare and Medicaid, government sources of revenue are uncertain in the long term.

Affordable Care Act

President Obama signed the Affordable Care Act into law on March 23, 2010. The law aimed to transform the practices of doctors and hospitals to lower cost while driving better health outcomes for patients. To do so, United States citizens were mandated to have health insurance. This requirement sought to lower healthcare insurance costs since there was a larger pool of consumers which lowered overall financial risk for insurance companies. It also required that insurance companies could not deny people coverage for pre-existing conditions. A year later, the Congressional Budget office estimated that the Affordable Care Act would "significantly decrease Medicare outlays relative to what they would have been under prior law" (Elmendorf, 2011, p. 44). The major components of the legislation are as follows:

- All individuals were required to obtain healthcare insurance through some entity, which may include their employer's healthcare plan, Medicare, Medicaid, or another public insurance plan. Individuals who did not do so were subject to a penalty.
- A minimum healthcare insurance coverage was established.

Exhibit 3 Sources of Revenue for Major Firms (Percentage of Total Revenue)

	Genesis			Ensign			National Healthcare			Average		
Year ended December 31	2015	2014	2013	2015	2014	2013	2015	2014	2013	2015	2014	2013
Medicare	26	27	28	32.8	34.9	35.8	40	39	40	32.93	33.63	34.60
Medicaid	53	53	52	34.9	35.5	36.4	25	26	25	37.63	38.17	37.80
3rd party Insurance / Managed Care	11	10	9	15.4	14.2	13.1	11	11	10	12.47	11.73	10.70
Private assets and other	10	10	11	16.9	15.4	14.7	24	24	25	16.97	16.47	16.90

(Ensign Group, 2016; Genesis Healthcare, 2016; National Healthcare Corporation, 2016)

- Insurance companies could not deny coverage to people with pre-existing conditions, which companies could do before the law took effect.
- The government established healthcare exchanges where individuals could purchase healthcare coverage.
- Dependents, generally children, could stay on their parent's healthcare insurance until their 26th birthday.

While the legislation is highly controversial, it could be argued to have both positive and negative results for hospitals as well as the long term and post-acute healthcare industry. On the positive side, when more individuals have insurance, there are more patients who can pay for the services these firms provide. However, if people have insurance, they may go to a doctor for preventative care. Such care may prevent devastating illnesses, which would lower the amount of patients who need post-acute healthcare services.

When President Trump took office, he and the republican-controlled congress worked to repeal or replace Obamacare immediately. Some of the arguments to repeal or replace include:

- The cost individuals pay for insurance each year is increasing.
- Insurance companies are pulling out of regions that are not profitable enough for them; likely due to a low and decreasing % of young and healthy people buying insurance.
- The cost the government pays to subsidize low-income individuals, so that they can afford insurance, is increasing.

These concerns suggest that the long-term financial feasibility of Obamacare may not be sustainable by the federal government, though this contention is highly debated. Congress was unable to pass repeal or replace legislation within the first six months of the Trump presidency.

Future of Medicare and Medicaid

As noted at the beginning of the case, people aged 65 and older will become the largest population demographic in the United States (Exhibit 1) and people are living longer than ever (Exhibit 2). Given that the United States government is paying for the majority of hospital treatments as well as post-acute treatments for this demographic, it is important to understand the stability of Medicare and Medicaid as revenue sources to the industry.

As shown in Exhibit 4, the United States Congressional Budget Office estimates that from 2015 to 2025, federal government expenses paid to Medicare will increase 20%, and Medicare, as well as expenses related to the Affordable Care Act, will increase 14%, while tax revenues will only increase 3%. Additionally, Social Security is paid to individuals over the age of 65 and expenses associated with it will increase 16%. When examining the rate of change from 2015 to 2060 (the year in which the demographic changes on page 1 refer), Medicare expenses will increase 123%, Medicaid and Affordable Care Act expenses will increase 55%, and Social Security expenses will increase 24%. However, it is estimated that tax revenues will increase only 20%, which may be because the typical tax paying demographic, age 18–64, will become an increasingly smaller percentage of the population (Exhibit 1). This suggests that in the long term, the government may not be able to maintain Medicare, Medicaid, and Social Security without additional tax increases.

Exhibit 4 Estimated Percentage of GPD of Tax Revenues and Cost of Social Programs

Fiscal Year	Tax Revenues	Social Security	Medicare	Medicaid, CHIP, and Exchange Subsidies
2015	17.7	4.9	3.0	2.2
2020	18.1	5.2	3.1	2.4
2025	18.3	5.7	3.6	2.5
2030	18.6	6.1	4.2	2.6
2035	19.0	6.3	4.7	2.7
2040	19.4	6.2	5.1	2.9
2045	19.9	6.0	5.5	3.0
2050	20.3	5.9	5.9	3.2
2055	20.8	5.9	6.3	3.3
2060	21.2	6.1	6.7	3.4
Percent Change from 2015				
Fiscal Year	**Tax Revenues**	**Social Security**	**Medicare**	**Medicaid, CHIP, and Exchange Subsidies**
2025	3%	16%	20%	14%
2060	20%	24%	123%	55%

(U.S. Congressional Budget Office, 2015)

Future of the Healthcare Industry

Given the increasing costs of healthcare for an aging population, the current healthcare industry model may not be sustainable in the long term. What options do individuals, firms, and the government have to deal with this issue?

REFERENCES

American Accreditation HealthCare Commission. (2014). Aging changes in immunity. Medical Encyclopedia. Retrieved 4/22/2016, from https://www.nlm.nih.gov/medlineplus/ency/article/004008.htm

Bureau of Labor Statistics. (2015). Employment Projections: 2014–24 Summary.

Centers for Disease Control and Prevention. (2016). Important Facts about Falls. Retrieved 4/22/2016, from http://www.cdc.gov/homeandrecreationalsafety/falls/adultfalls.html

Elmendorf, Douglas. (2011). CBO's 2011 Long-Term Budget Outlook (pp. 44): Congressional Budget Office.

Ensign Group, Inc. (2016). 2015 10-K Annual Filling.

Genesis Healthcare, Inc. (2016). 2015 10-K Annual Filling.

Harris-Kojetin L, Sengupta M, Park-Lee E, et al. (2016). Long-term care providers and services users in the United States: Data from the National Study of Long-Term Care Providers, 2013–2014 *Vital Health Stat* (Vol. 38).

Justice, United States Department of. (2013). Nursing Home Operator to Pay $48 Million to Resolve Allegations That Six California Facilities Billed for Unnecessary Therapy. from https://www.justice.gov/opa/pr/nursing-home-operator-pay-48-million-resolve-allegations-six-california-facilities-billed

Medicare. (2016). What's home healthcare & what should I expect? Retrieved 4/22/2016, 2016, from https://www.medicare.gov/what-medicare-covers/home-health-care/home-health-care-what-is-it-what-to-expect.html

National Healthcare Corporation. (2016). 2015 10-K Annual Filling.

Reinhardt, Uwe E. (2003). Does The Aging Of The Population Really Drive The Demand For Healthcare? *Health Affairs, 22*(6), 27–39. doi: 10.1377/hlthaff.22.6.27

U.S. Census Bureau, Population Division. (2014a). Table 6. Percent Distribution of the Projected Population by Sex and Selected Age Groups for the United States: 2015 to 2060. Retrieved 4/22/2016, from http://www.census.gov/population/projections/data/national/2014/summarytables.html

U.S. Census Bureau, Population Division. (2014b). Table 17. Projected Life Expectancy at Birth by Sex, Race, and Hispanic Origin for the United States: 2015 to 2060 (NP2014-T17). Retrieved 4/22/2016, from http://www.census.gov/population/projections/data/national/2014/summarytables.html

U.S. Congressional Budget Office. (2015). Long-Term Budget Projections–June 2015. Retrieved 4/22/2016, from https://www.cbo.gov/about/products/budget_economic_data

CASE 5

CrossFit at the Crossroads

"I'm not trying to grow a business . . . I'm doing the right things for the right people for the right reasons"

-Greg Glassman, Owner of CrossFit, Inc. [3]

It's a pleasant July morning in Carson, California, in 2016 as Greg Glassman, the founder of CrossFit, Inc. makes his way across the Stubhub Center turf and sits down on one of the black Rogue plyoboxes that line the back perimeter of the stadium. He gazes out past the ongoing rows of boxes, connected rigs, and zigzag sprint course to see the sun starting to rise over the grandstand canopy. Just 15 hours earlier those grandstands were filled with thousands of passionate screaming fans cheering on the final contestants of the 2016 Reebok CrossFit Games. A slight grin appears across his face as he lets out a faint but subtle chuckle to himself, almost as if he can't believe that he has built the fitness industry's fastest-growing brand.

The tenth consecutive CrossFit Games, the largest CrossFit sporting event in the world, was now over and Glassman started to reflect back on how quickly his creation has risen in just a few decades. In 1995, he was a personal trainer looking for a place to train his loyal clientele after being kicked out of yet another commercial gym because management did not approve of his unorthodox training methods, and now, he is a multi-millionaire who owns one the largest brands in the fitness industry. That unorthodox training method, well, it is now one of the most popular fitness workouts in the world and is arguably becoming one of the fastest growing sports of all time. Everything has happened so fast, he thought to himself while watching the cleanup crew start to tear down the event setup, we barely even have a concrete business plan, he jokes but deep down inside he knows that it is true. CrossFit has evolved so rapidly that Glassman and his relatively small but fiercely loyal employees have been forced to make important company decisions on the go. Evident by CrossFit's unprecedented growth, those decisions have more often than not been correct but with little time to reflect on the company's aim and future, how could he be fully confident in the direction his company was heading and what does the future hold for a fitness company operating in an ever changing, potentially fad-like industry?

As Glassman got up to leave the stadium to catch the quick flight back to the Silicon Valley in the company jet, he decided he was going to disrupt his normal routine and take a few days off to think. His plan is to use this time to genuinely reflect on where his company has come and how the business has reached elite status as one of the largest fitness brands in the world. What can CrossFit, Inc. do to improve, what new trends can they capitalize on, where is the future of the company and sport going, and how can they avoid that dark irrelevant fate where so many fitness startup companies eventually end up?

History of Crossfit

Greg Glassman

Greg Glassman, born on July 22, 1956 to a rocket scientist father and a stay at home mother, was raised in the Los Angeles, CA suburb of Woodland Hills. Around the age of one, Glassman was diagnosed with Polio, a disease that affects the nerves in a person's spine and affects muscle movement. Growing up though, Glassman did not let this disease define who he was as he turned to sports such as gymnastics, cycling, and weightlifting to counteract his inability to participate in contact sports. His aptitude on the pull up bar along with having powerful upper body strength led him to excel at the rings in gymnastics, but a freak injury on a routine dismount in high school left him with a permanent limp and unable to compete. Glassman subsequently turned to coaching, a decision that would eventually define who he is and create a legacy most people only dream of.

Glassman refers to himself as a "rabid libertarian," [1] a term defined as "an advocate of the doctrine of free-will." [2] In high school, Glassman habitually read and studied the theories of Milton Friedman, an American economist who wrote such books as 'Capitalism and Freedom' and the 50th anniversary edition rewrite

This case was written by Andrew Callaghan and Dr. Charles B. Shrader of Iowa State University, July 2016. It is intended to be used as a basis for classroom discussion rather than as a demonstration of either effective or ineffective management of a situation. The case reflects the views of the authors and not the exact thoughts and opinions of CrossFit, Inc. management. Part of the information in this case is derived from the authors' personal experiences with the case company. Some of the opening and closing managerial situations included in the case are fictional and are for illustrative purposes only.

of F.A. Hayek's 'The Road to Serfdom.' It's here where Glassman's management theories would form the basis of his future business model, or lack there-of. At age 18, Glassman took a job as a gymnastics coach at the YWCA in Pasadena, CA. Little did he know at the time, this being his first real coaching gig, that it would eventually be his calling in life. He attended college but never graduated, stating "I went to a half dozen institutions, but I was just there for the girls." [3] His passion was fitness training and throughout the late 1970s and '80s he worked as a personal trainer. His commitment, knowledge, and extremely brash personality attracted people to enlist his services in the Silicon Valley area, but it was also his unique and unconventional methods toward fitness that allowed him to lure in not only the computer tech leaders and local service workers but also celebrities and professional athletes alike.

Results are what ultimately define success and Glassman knew how to attain them, but his methods were unusual and his workouts were seen as in your face and bordering on intimidating. So intimidating to the average gym goer in fact that he had been kicked out of seven or more commercial gyms as a result. Glassman's attitude toward fitness can be described as confident and assertive with firm beliefs, but that confidence can also be interpreted as defiant and arrogant. In a *60 Minutes* episode, when asked if he doesn't like to be told what to do, Glassman responded with a chuckle and said "Oh, I don't mind being told what to do . . . I just won't do it." [4] But that is who Greg Glassman is and that defiance is why he now owns 100% of the fastest growing fitness program and emerging sport in the world, CrossFit.

The Beginning

In the late 1980s and early '90s, Glassman tinkered with his workouts and found success with his clients by combining High Intensity Training (HIT) with heavy fundamental movements and sprints. His workouts were loud, intense, and demanding but also successful and his client base started to expand. In 1995, after being asked to leave what would be his last commercial gym, Glassman decided to open his own training facility in Santa Cruz, CA. CrossFit (at the time Cross-Fit) was born. Glassman had a goal in mind to establish a fitness program that would not only motivate participants to exercise but also to constantly work toward achieving a high level of fitness. [5] At the time, Glassman was still training clients solo, but after he started to become overbooked he soon realized that he could train multiple people together and still provide a safe environment as well as the required attention to each participant to be effective. With that he would also be able to increase his profits by charging a reduced rate to each member but add more members to each session. [6] Glassman found that his clients enjoyed the idea of group fitness, and after he was hired to train the Santa Cruz Police Department, the idea of "The CrossFit Community" was formed.

In 2000, CrossFit, Inc. was legally established by Glassman and his (now ex) wife Lauren. When prompted by his oft-traveling clients to build a website and post workouts of the day (WOD), so that they could train on the road, Crossfit.com was created. In 2002, the first CrossFit affiliate was started in Seattle, WA (CrossFit North) by former Navy Seal Dave Werner and partners Robb Wolf and Nick Nibler. In the same year, the *CrossFit Journal* was published in which Glassman wrote three seminal articles explaining CrossFit's principles and theories, titled "What is Fitness?", "Foundations," and "The Garage Gym."

Crossfit Philosophy

What is Fitness? (According to CrossFit, Inc.)

One of CrossFit's first newsletter articles [7] set out to explain the company philosophy by questioning previously proposed definitions of what it meant to be truly fit. The article challenged the notions of Merriam-Webster, Outside Magazine ("Fittest Man on Earth"), and the industry leading National Strength and Conditioning Association (NSCA), by concluding that their definitions were either too broad or too narrow. The CrossFit article concluded that previous attempts to define fitness were inadequate. Glassman, however, defined fitness through a meaningful and measurable way as "increased work capacity across broad time and modal domains," [8] where broad time means "length of duration of effort" and modal domains "variety of activity." [9] In the *What is Fitness?* article, Glassman defines three standards/models that they use for evaluating and guiding fitness. Together they outline CrossFit's view of fitness as 1) ten general physical skills widely defined by physiologists, 2) performance of athletic tasks, and 3) energy systems that drive all human action (Exhibit 1). CrossFit's aim is not to specialize in one certain task of fitness but to be a "jack of all trades." The article states, "Our specialty is not specializing. Combat, survival, many sports and life reward this kind of fitness, and on average punish the specialist."

Exhibit 1 CrossFit's 3 Standard Principles

1) 10 recognized General Physical Skills:
   - If your goal is optimum physical competence, then all general physical skills must be considered:
   1) **Cardiovascular endurance/Respiratory endurance** – The ability of body systems to gather, process, and deliver oxygen
   2) **Stamina** – The ability of body systems to process, deliver, store, and utilize energy
   3) **Strength** – The ability of a muscular unit or combination of muscular units to apply force
   4) **Flexibility** – The ability to maximize the range of motion at a given joint
   5) **Power** – The ability of a muscular unit or combination of muscular units to apply maximum force in minimum time
   6) **Speed** – The ability to minimize the time cycle of a repeated movement
   7) **Coordination** – The ability to combine several distinct movement patterns into a singular distinct movement
   8) **Agility** – The ability to minimize transition time from one movement pattern to another
   9) **Balance** – The ability to control the placement of the body's center of gravity in relation to its support base
   10) **Accuracy** – The ability to control movement in a given direction or at a given intensity

2) The essence of this view is that fitness is about performing well at any and every task imaginable. Picture a hopper loaded with an infinite number of physical challenges where no selective mechanism is operative, and being asked to perform feats randomly drawn from the hopper. This model suggests that your fitness can be measured by your capacity to perform well at these tasks in relation to other individuals.

   The implication here is that fitness requires an ability to perform well at all tasks, even unfamiliar tasks, tasks combined in infinitely varying combinations. In practice this encourages the athlete to disinvest in any set notions of sets, rest periods, reps, exercises, order of exercises, routines, periodization, etc. Nature frequently provides largely unforeseeable challenges; train for that by striving to keep the training stimulus broad and constantly varied.

3) Three metabolic pathways that provide the energy for all human action
   1) Phosphagen Pathway – Dominates the highest powered activities (10 seconds or less)
   2) Glycolytic Pathway – Dominates moderate powered activities (up to several minutes)
   3) Oxidative Pathway – Dominates low-powered activities (excess of several minutes)

Total Fitness = The fitness that CrossFit promotes and develops requires competency and training in each of these three pathways or engines.

Source: Glassman, Greg. "What is Fitness?" *The CrossFit Journal* (October 2002): 1–4. Web.

Foundations

The *Foundations* article presented CrossFit's approach to generalized comprehensive fitness and away from the traditional workouts of isolation movements and extended aerobic sessions that the majority of the population participates in. [10] CrossFit works with "compound (functional) movements and shorter high intensity cardiovascular sessions" because they believe that the two theories combined are "radically more effective at eliciting nearly any desired fitness result" than any other form of fitness. The CrossFit workout can be universal as the movements and weights can be scaled to fit any participant, or "athlete," as CrossFit's members are called. Outsiders are often amazed that CrossFit athletes range from professional athletes and military special ops to the elderly and handicapped and everyone in-between. In the "60 Minutes" episode, when Glassman was asked if he would have a 75-year-old doing deadlifts his answer is simply, "Uh huh, yeah, to say no is to say that if you drop your pen on the ground, you're not going to pick it up. It's a deadlift, it's picking something up off the ground. It does not require a physician's 'Ok.' If your physician doesn't think you should deadlift, you need to get a new doctor."

The Garage Gym

Glassman also strongly believed that the equipment in a typical gym was useless. In simple terms he believed a gym should resemble a barn or garage. It should be open and uncluttered, and the equipment should require the use of muscle in the most natural fitness sense. CrossFit boxes were basic and austere. Modern gyms had fancy weight machines focused on isolation work. CrossFit, on the other hand, tried to develop overall fitness and conditioning as a philosophy. The whole thing was oriented toward a natural and more primitive approach to basic conditioning.

Glassman is such a firm believer in his methodology that he strongly believes that between diet and exercise, CrossFit can even be a solution to chronic diseases. The Centers for Disease Control and Prevention (CDC) has identified lack of exercise, poor nutrition, tobacco use, and high alcohol intake as health risks that contribute toward many of the illnesses and early deaths related to chronic diseases. Glassman advocates that CrossFit targets two of those four conditions which are normally prescribed with prescription drugs (high blood pressure) or steroids (low muscle mass), "the problem is being inactive and poor nutrition. It's a lifestyle issue." [1]

The CrossFit Journal, or newsletter, became an important means for the company to disseminate Glassman's philosophy. Newsletters were published on a monthly basis and included articles dealing with box operations, fitness training, and lifestyle. For example, the August 2014 CrossFit Journal contained a story about how affiliate owners compensate coaches and trainers. The story offered ideas on how to go beyond simple financial incentives to motivate coaches and trainers. Motivational ideas included: equal pay for both affiliate owners and trainers, enhanced education and certification programs for trainers, specialty programs for members, and building long-term relationships with trainers. Examples and success stories from CrossFit centers in California, New England, and New Zealand were shared. The goal of the newsletter was to offer affiliate owners and trainers alike ideas on how to make each box more capable in terms of enhancing fitness and changing lives. [48]

Workout Methodology and Structure

CrossFit workouts are based on constantly varied functional movements (real-life movements) that incorporate a mix of aspects from gymnastics, weightlifting, and cardio all while being performed at relatively high intensity (Exhibit 2—list of exercises). The workouts are typically performed in a gym, or "garage gym" because of the rough appearance and similarities to at-home stripped down style gyms, that the CrossFit community refers to as a "box" and which includes an array of weights, racks, boxes, bands, and balls but is void of commercial style machines (Exhibit 3—list of equipment). The workouts are roughly 60 minutes in length and typically include four phases: Warm-up/Stretch, Skill Development Segment (SDS), WOD, and an Individual or Group Stretch (Exhibit 4). The SDS focuses on Olympic type lifts or calisthenics (bodyweight movements), and the WOD generally contain a combination

Exhibit 2 List of CrossFit Exercises

Weightlifting	Gymnastics	Cardio/ Calisthenics
Deadlifts	Bar Muscle Up	Air Squats
Front & Back Squats	Rings Muscle Up	Box Jumps
Power Clean	Dips	Jump Rope
Hang Clean	Strict Pull Up	Rowing
Sumo Deadlift High Pull	Kipping Pull Up	Wall Ball
Snatch		Sprints
Overhead Squat		Jogging
Push Jerk		Jumping Jacks
Push Press		Sit Ups
Shoulder Press		Push Ups
Thruster		
Tire Flip		

Exhibit 3 List of Equipment

Weightlifting	Gymnastics	Cardio/ Calisthenics
Squat Racks/Rig System	Pull-up Stations/ Rigs	Medicine Balls
Bumper Plates	Rings	Bands
Barbells	Ropes	PVC Pipes
Dumbbells	Hand Chalk	Ab Mats
Kettlebells		Rowers
Sand bags		Boxes
Dip Belts		Hurdles
Steel Plates		Jump Ropes
Large Tires		Foam Rollers
Push Sleds		

Exhibit 4 Daily Workout Example

Metcon (Time)
5 Rounds for time
3 Power Cleans 165/115 (male/female)
6 Box Jumps 30"/24" (male/female)
9 Toes 2 Bar
*8-min time cap

Rest 3 minutes then

Metcon (Time)
10,9,8,7,6,5,4,3,2,1
Shoulder to Overhead 135/95
Pull-ups
*13-minute time cap

Rest 4 minutes then

Metcon (Time)
3,6,9,12,15
Deadlifts 225/155
Burpees
*12-minute time cap
*ADD UP TOTAL TIME & RECORD

of all movements performed in high-intensity bouts that can last anywhere from 4 to 24 minutes long depending on that day's goals. The workouts are designed to arouse an athlete's competitive nature not only within themselves but also with the other competitors. Times and repetitions are recorded on either large whiteboards or computer systems, which then rank the athlete's performances.

The CrossFit philosophy that workouts should be repeatable and measurable is the basis for self-improvement. The "Benchmark Workouts" were originally named after "girls," so that the athletes could easily identify the unified workout, and have grown to include Hero WOD in honor of fallen military, law enforcement, and firefighters (Exhibit 5). The intent of the Benchmark workouts is for athletes to perform them periodically, say

Exhibit 5 "Girl" WODs

"Amanda"	"Diane"	"Jackie"	"Nicole"
9-7-5	Deadlift 225 lbs	1000 meter row	Run 400 meters
Muscle Up	Handstand push-ups	Thruster 45 lbs (50 reps)	Max rep Pull-ups
Squat Snatch (135/95)	21-15-9 reps, for time	Pull-ups (30 reps)	As many rounds as possible in 20 minutes
"Angie"	**"Elizabeth"**	**"Karen"**	**"Cindy"**
100 Pull-ups	Clean 135 lbs	Wall-ball 150 shots	5 Pull-ups
100 Push-ups	Ring Dips	(men 20#-10' – women 14#-9')	10 Push-ups
100 Sit-ups	21-15-9 reps, for time	For time	15 Squats
100 Squats			As many rounds as possible in 20 min
"Annie"	**"Eva"**	**"Kelly"**	**"Helen"**
Double-unders	Run 800 meters	Run 400 meters	400 meter run
Sit-ups	2 pood KB swing, 30 reps	30 box jump, 24 inch box	1.5 pood Kettlebell swing × 21
50-40-30-20 and 10 rep rounds; for time	30 pullups	30 Wall ball shots, 20 pound ball	Pull-ups 12 reps
			3 rounds for time
"Barbara"	**"Fran"**	**"Linda"**	**"Nancy"**
20 Pull-ups	21-15-9 reps, for time	Deadlift 1 1/2 BW	400 meter run
30 Push-ups	Thruster 95 lbs	Bench BW	Overhead squat 95 lbs × 15
40 Sit-ups	Pull-ups	Clean 3/4 BW	5 rounds for time
50 Squats		10/9/8/7/6/5/4/3/2/1 rep	5 rounds for time
"Chelsea"	**"Grace"**	**"Lynne"**	
5 Pull-ups	Clean and Jerk 135 lbs	Bodyweight bench press	
10 Push-ups	30 reps for time	pullups	
15 Squats		5 rounds for max reps. .	
Each min on the min for 30 min			
"Christine"	**"Isabel"**	**"Mary"**	
3 rounds for time	Snatch 135 pounds	5 Handstand push-ups	
500 m row	30 reps for time	10 1-legged squats	
12 Body Weight Dead Lift		15 Pull-ups	
21 Box Jumps		As many rounds as possible in 20 min	

continued

Exhibit 5 (cont.) "HERO" WODs

JT	Michael	Badger	Nate
21-15-9 reps, for time	3 rounds for time	3 rounds for time	As many rounds as possible in 20 min
Handstand push-ups	Run 800 meters	95 pound Squat clean, 30 reps	22 Muscle-ups
Ring dips	50 Back Ext	30 Pull-ups	4 Handstand Push-ups
Push-ups	50 Sit-ups	Run 800 meters	8 2-Pood Kettlebell swings
Daniel	**Murph**	**Josh**	**Jason**
50 Pull-ups	For Time	For time	100 Squats
400 meter run	1 mile Run	95 pound Overhead squat, 21 reps	5 Muscle-ups
95 pound Thruster, 21 reps	100 Pull-ups	42 Pull-ups	75 Squats
800 meter run	200 Push-ups	95 pound Overhead squat, 15 reps	10 Muscle-ups
95 pound Thruster, 21 reps	300 Squats	30 Pull-ups	50 Squats
400 meter run	1 mile Run	95 pound Overhead squat, 9 reps	15 Muscle-ups 25 Squats
50 Pull-ups		18 Pull-ups	20 Muscle-ups

*For a Complete List log onto https://crossfitiota.com/bench-marks/hero-wods/

a few times per year, and compare scores to track their overall fitness progress. Glassman presented his theory in the September 2003 *CrossFit Journal* article in which he introduced the "girls": "only by repeating workouts can we confidently measure our progress." [11]

The CrossFit Diet

Greg Glassman's regular response when asked about what CrossFit can do for a person is that it can deliver you to your "genetic potential." "Look at her! That's what nature would have carved from her a million years ago" was Glassman's reaction after seeing one of his well-toned athletes working out, but it is not just the workout that CrossFitters are encouraged to practice. [4] They are also urged to follow one of a few specific diets that, based on personal goals, will provide CrossFit members with increased energy, optimized health and will reduce the risk of chronic diseases. The seemingly most widely used diet is the Paleo Diet which is based on every day, modern type foods that "mimic the food groups of human's pre-agricultural, hunter-gatherer ancestors." [12] In Glassman's *World Class Fitness in 100 Words* [7] statement, he provides some CrossFit diet advice: "eat meat and vegetables, nuts and seeds, some fruit, little starch and no sugar. Keep intake to levels that will support exercise but not body fat." The Paleo Diet generally fits these criteria as its directions suggest people consume high protein, lower carbs, high fiber, and moderate fat intake (Exhibit 6—Paleo Diet food options). While a few of CrossFit's top athletes have confessed about not following a strict diet to a 'T' [13], it's made quite obvious that following one of the suggested diet options while participating in CrossFit is recommended and will positively affect the athlete no matter if they are beginners or top flight competitors.

Some CrossFit diet followers have become celebrities and authors in their own right. A good example is Christmas Abbott, author of the Badass Body Diet. [46] This diet combines healthy eating guidelines with high-intensity workout plans for individual body types. Following this plan, athletes at all levels can set personal goals for developing toned cores and reducing body fat. Ms. Abbott also has infused an element of fun into each workout—noting that people tend to stay with a workout plan longer if the workout is enjoyable.

Business

CrossFit, Inc. is 100% privately owned by Greg Glassman—an ownership situation that totally fits his style. In 2012, CrossFit began business as a 50/50 partnership between Glassman and his ex-wife. At that time, because of a contentious situation, Glassman's ex-wife's share was almost sold to Anthos Capital, an investment firm looking to invest in one of America's fastest growing brands. In the 11th hour though, Glassman was able

Exhibit 6 Paleo Diet Foods

Do's:					
Meats	**Seafood**	**Veggies**	**Oils/Fats**	**Nuts**	**Fruits**
Poultry	Shrimp	Asparagus	Coconut Oil	Almonds	Apples
Pork	Lobster	Avocado	Olive Oil	Cashews	Berries
Pork Chops	Clams	Brussel Sprouts	Macadamia Oil	Hazelnuts	Peaches
Steak	Salmon	Carrots	Avocado Oil	Pecans	Plums
Veal	Tuna	Spinach	Grass-fed Butter	Sunflower Seeds	Mango
Bacon	Shark	Celery			Grapes
Ground Beef	Tilapia	Broccoli			Lemon
Venison	Trout	Peppers			Lime
Buffalo	Walleye	Cabbage			Oranges
Bison	Crab	Zucchini			Bananas
Jerky	Scallops				
	Oyster				
Don't's:					
Dairy	**Grains**	**Legumes**	**Snacks**		
Cheese	Cereal	Beans	Pretzels		
Non-fat Creamer	Pasta	Peas	Chips		
Butter	Bread	Peanuts	Cookies		
Milk	English Muffin	Peanut Butter	Pastries		
Yogurt/Pudding	Sandwiches	TOFU	Hot Dogs		
	Crackers	Mesquite	Fries		
	Oatmeal	Miso	Artificial Sweeteners		
	Corn	Soybeans	Pop/Soda		
	Pancakes		Fruit Juices		
	Hash Browns		Energy Drinks		
	Beer				

*These are an option list/not exact. Please see source for more information.

Source: http://ultimatepaleoguide.com/paleo-diet-food-list/

to secure a matching loan through Summit Partners (Boston) for $16,093,000 and put a halt to the potential sale. [14] With Glassman in full control, he could operate the company autonomously, without input from outside corporate investors.

CrossFit, Inc. does not have to answer to shareholders or a board of directors. The headquarters, which handles the business operations, is located in Washington, D.C. and the Media Office, the lifeblood of CrossFit's day-to-day technology operations, is based out of Silicon Valley. CrossFit's model resembles its owner's libertarian beliefs, as the growth of the company has come directly from its affiliation program that permits individuals to own and operate their own box while using the CrossFit name and allows them to run their business with independence and autonomy.

Affiliation

CrossFit-affiliated boxes started in 2002 with the CrossFit North opening and have spread like wildfire throughout the world. To open a box, essentially all one has to do is fill out an application, pay $3,000 per year, attend a 2-day seminar detailing the business and the workout methodology, and pass a test to become a Level 1 instructor ($1000). When confronted about the seemingly easy nature of this process, CrossFit's fearless leader's response was:

"Amazing huh?... Here's how it used to be: all you had to do was have the money. . . and you don't even have to take a test. That's where every other chain came from, someone just launched 'em." [4]

CrossFit box owners have the freedom to manage their box in their best interests so that they can cater to the local demographic. To Glassman, his main concern is not about what hours the affiliate owners are operating, the location in which they choose to open their business, or the music that is played; his only concern is that they follow CrossFit's physiology and methodology. [1] Each affiliate is locked into their original annual fee in case the fee is ever raised. In fact, there are affiliates, who got in early, that still pay only $500 per year.

CrossFit, Inc. created CrossFit RRG (Risk Retention Group), which is a captive stock insurance company that allows American affiliates to purchase specific CrossFit general liability and professional liability policies designed to cover the unusual risks boxes are susceptible to. [15] CF-RRG is a form of self-insurance where the affiliate owners purchase stock and become shareholders (1-time fee of $1,000). Box owners who buy into the group are involved in the underwriting, risk management, claims administration, and financial committees. [16] Boxes earning less than $125,000 per year pay a yearly premium of $1,185 with boxes that earn greater than $125,000 per year paying an extra $8.70 per $1,000 of gross revenue earned. Affiliations are urged to purchase insurance from CF-RRG rather than an outside vendor because CrossFit endures unique circumstances that most liability policies may not thoroughly cover. Owning this specialized policy, box owners are eliminating the possibility of omissions and will have the most comprehensive coverage available. International CrossFit boxes are insured through somewhat similar companies such as the *CrossFit International Insurance Programme*, which is run through Lloyd's of London and covers box owners in the UK. [17]

Growth

Glassman admits that when he started CrossFit he did not have a business plan, that his goal was simply "being committed not to screw it up," and that he has stuck by that plan ever since. [18] The numbers, though, would suggest otherwise. In 2016, a little over a decade and a half since CrossFit, Inc. was formed, Glassman's corporation has become one of the fastest growing fitness companies of all time. With roughly 13,000 gyms in 142 different countries, CrossFit, Inc. rakes in close to $100 million and the CrossFit brand's estimated ecosystem is approximately in the $4 billion range (2016). [18] The scary part? The company is still growing. "I don't know how you compete against me" said Glassman in an interview with CNBC.

CrossFit, Inc. brings in most of its profits from two main sources: 1) affiliates and 2) CrossFit Training Certification courses. But even with CrossFit's rapidly growing business it is hard to look anywhere else but the core concepts that have brought them to this point: technology and having a loyal group dynamic culture that has adopted CrossFit as more than a workout but a way of life. CrossFit is a technology company. It started with Glassman posting workouts, journal articles, and an easy-to-use blog onto www.crossfit.com. Since then, the company's success has followed the growth of the Internet. One ten-minute browsing session on their website and you can find CrossFit's mission, workout methodology, limitless instructional videos, workouts of the day, nutritional ideas, gym locations, and much, much more, all for FREE. Yes, for *free*! When asked about the financial implications of giving away free content and how that makes sense in today's capitalistic economy, Glassman replied "it didn't until we did it, the more video we give away, the more money we make." [4] The *all exposure is good exposure* philosophy has assembled one of the largest viral communities in the world and when combined with their devout and enthusiastic allegiance toward the brand, largely explains why CrossFit, Inc. has been able to grow at the record-breaking pace it has.

The Community

CrossFit is much more than just a fitness regimen—it has evolved into a distinctive community within itself where its followers are amazingly loyal and dedicated. For many, CrossFit has become a way of life. CrossFit affiliates have been extraordinarily successful in creating an atmosphere where its members feel a sense of belonging which motivates them to come back day after day and push themselves harder, whether that's to beat the person next to them or just to improve from their previous scores. The CrossFit Community members have taken a leading role in marketing the

CrossFit brand. They have created an almost obsessive-like adoration for CrossFit to the point where they actively promote the sport through any outlet possible. It has prompted outsiders to joke that "the first rule of CrossFit is that you never stop talking about CrossFit," parodying a line from the Brad Pitt movie, Fight Club. [19] Whether box members are viewed as loyal, fanatic, annoying, or crazy one thing for certain is that their dedication to spreading the brand, whether intentionally or unintentionally, has been an exceptionally lucrative model for CrossFit, Inc.

Glassman insists that he has not recruited one person to CrossFit. To him CrossFit has an open door policy and anyone who wants to join is welcomed to do so. [4] Through tremendous leadership and coaching, CrossFit has been able to provide an atmosphere where its members seek to live their lives in a state of optimal health and fitness in a time where health and fitness are becoming less of a priority. [5] The members work out together multiple times per week often creating a team-like bond. This type of interaction, uniting by a common goal or interest, is similar to the family-like atmosphere most sports or military teams have. The CrossFit Community is also able to attract members through their group volunteer and charitable.

American sociologist Ray Oldenburg introduced the idea of a "Third Place" for healthy human existence. [20] He believed that humans must live in a balance of three realms: 1) Home/Family Life, 2) Work Life—where people spend most of their time, and 3) a Third Place—inclusively sociable places. Third Places are described as "anchors" of community life and facilitate & foster broader, more creative social interaction. One of the main characteristics of Third Places is that they act as a "leveler," which means they place no importance on an individual's status in society and allows for a sense of commonality between members. They are highly accessible places, where friendships develop that fill the human need for "intimacy and affiliation." In what used to be the traditional Third Place, church, studies have shown that the new generation of millennials have been leaving the religious life behind, [21] thus creating a void in many people's lives. The CrossFit Community, through its affiliates, have been able to provide that Third Place for many of its members. The box offers its athletes a place where they can build those social relationships and have a sense of "place." In turn, its members adopt the CrossFit lifestyle as one of their main identities and that which becomes a part of who they are. This could explain why they "always talk about CrossFit" or post CrossFit related content to social media outlets. CrossFit, in a (smaller) sense, is as much a part of many of its members' lives as say their families, therefore creating that automatic impulse to constantly want to talk or interact with other about their CrossFit lives, the same as they would about their children or significant others.

In a 2014 CrossFit demographic study, the data did illustrate that the millennial generation had the highest level of participants but not by as much as many would think. They only comprised 40% of participants while the 35–44 age group consisted of 20% with the under 18's covering 18%. [22] Along with the age demographic they found that CrossFit is evenly split 50/50 between female and male participants thus attesting to the fact that the CrossFit workout is feasible at any age, male or female.

Technology and Social Media

The shift toward social media outlets becoming a primary form of contact in today's society has vastly affected the field of communication, marketing work and advertising. Gone are the days where the majority of adults actually dial someone's number up and speak to them over the phone as social media has increased the ability and frequency in which people can "checkup" on one another in a much less personal way. In a 2014 social media study, it was found that 52% of online adults now use at least two forms of social media sites and the numbers showed that usage of young adults (18–29 y/o) on Instagram, just one form of social media, was around 53%. [23] The CrossFit Community is no stranger to this as the basis of their growth can be attributed to increased action on the Internet and social media sites from its members.

When CrossFit, Inc. launched its first blog system, which allowed box owners to communicate not only with headquarters, the media team, and other affiliates at the click of a mouse but also with their own clientele, they created an easy medium where information could be shared at a faster pace and to a larger audience. Just because Glassman himself has not recruited anyone over social media that does not mean his loyal followers have not. The Internet communication concept has spread to more common and interactive uses of social media (YouTube, Facebook, Twitter, Instagram, etc.) now within specific box communities as a way to mass market their new and exciting fitness program with outsiders. Since the mid-2000s box owners and community members have hit the social media world running and are no strangers to posting pictures, videos, or workout statuses from their experiences or the CrossFit world. Social media is an incredibly accessible and cost-effective way to reach a wide audience in little time, and the more community members post the more CrossFit's ecosystem grows. It's a multiplier effect that spreads the CrossFit brand like wildfire. A 2012 study on Internet usage found that 23% of U.S. Internet users under the age of 35 said they would buy a brand because of a friend's social endorsement, such as a "like" on Facebook. [24] This is a growing trend in the capitalistic technological world we live in, and for businesses looking to grow it is almost a must that they use social media as a marketing outlet.

Although many of the CrossFit customers who actively post personal information on social media understand the logic or intent of spreading "the word" about CrossFit, often times they are also engaging in a form of self-promotion. As adults, people start to have fewer tangible goals they can point to and share as a source of pride. Their high school accolades have lost social value and their current work accomplishments usually do not translate well to social media. CrossFit fills that void and allows members to take pride in their accomplishments, whether it is losing weight, hitting a new personal record, or even simply proving that they have gotten off the couch and are participating in an intense workout. [25] A 2014 sociological study [26] on "trophies of surplus enjoyment" (photo's, merchandise, trinkets, etc.) found that people hunt for trophies at events they attend not just for their fandom and remembrance but also as envy-inducing commodities they can share on social media so that others can acknowledge them through "likes," "favorites," and "retweets." This is often what CrossFit community members are doing when posting photos and videos to social media. The pictures or videos of them participating in CrossFit act as "acquired trophies" so that others can socially recognize their efforts and potentially elevate their "status" in the viewer's eyes.

The CrossFit Community's indulgence in social media, evidenced by the rapid success of CrossFit as a sport and a brand, further proves that their presence in the technological and social media world has been a surefire benefit. The CrossFit Community as a whole understands the value of social media, and whether their intentions are of the conscious or unconscious nature, they use this medium to pique the interest of outsiders about as well as anybody.

The CrossFit Games

From the very first journal article introducing CrossFit to a larger scale, Greg Glassman has challenged the idea of who is the "fittest on earth." The CrossFit philosophy of defining fitness through meaningful and measurable ways opened up a door for competition to exist. Enter, The CrossFit Games, which have been held annually since 2007 and continue to grow at record numbers each year. The games are a physically and mentally demanding competition held over a few days where competitors are blind to the certain events until right before they participate. At the end, the overall winners are awarded the title "Fittest on Earth."

The first games in 2007, held on CrossFit Games Director Dave Castro's parents' land in California, consisted of first-come participation with the winner receiving a $500 prize. Popularity grew with The Games as the company grew and in 2011 The CrossFit Games hit a banner year as CrossFit, Inc. signed Reebok to a 10-year title sponsorship as well as having the games broadcasted through ESPN3 (online). [27] With the rising number of participants yearly, CrossFit adopted an online qualification format that included three stages. Stage 1, known as 'The Open,' occurs in March when contestants submit weekly scores online from recently released competition workouts from crossfit.com. The scores are validated through affiliates, or video is uploaded proving participants score times. The top qualifiers from pre-determined regions will participate in Stage 2, regional events, held throughout the world in order to qualify for Stage 3, The CrossFit Games. In 2011, online participation totaled 26,000 submissions and has grown exponentially as 2016 online submissions totaled 308,000 people, a CrossFit Games record. [28]

With Reebok and ESPN on board, The CrossFit Games are now considered a top flight fitness competition and are broadcast worldwide live on ESPN. The winners in 2016 will receive $275,000 and the total prize pool, paid from the Reebok contract, is $2,200,000 and will rise annually throughout the length of the contract (Exhibit 7). Even though The CrossFit Games are not a large profit source for CrossFit, Inc. the magnitude of what The Games brings to the company is immeasurable. The exposure of the competition alone is one of the driving forces in making CrossFit the number one fitness enterprise on the planet and looking at the yearly increase in participants, prize money and attendance, The Games momentum does not appear to be slowing down.

Exhibit 7 The CrossFit Games History Data

Year	Participant Data # of Participants	
2007	60 (no open)	Games
2008	300 (cap - no open)	Games
2009	146 (post regionals)	Games
2010	86 (post regionals)	Games
2011	26,000+	Open
2012	69,240	Open
2013	138,000+	Open
2014	209,000+	Open
2015	273,000+	Open
2016	308,000+	Open

Year	Participant Data (Open) Winner	Total Prize Purse	Sponsor
2007	$500	$1,000	
2008	$1,500	$3,000	
2009	$5,000	$10,000	
2010	$25,000	$50,000	Progenex
2011	$250,000	$1,000,000	Reebok
2012	$250,000	?	Reebok
2013	$275,000	?	Reebok
2014	$275,000	$1,750,000	Reebok
2015	$275,000	$2,000,000	Reebok
2016	$275,000	$2,200,000	Reebok
2017	?	$2,400,000	Reebok
2018	?	$2,600,000	Reebok
2019	?	$2,800,000	Reebok
2020	?	$3,000,000	Reebok

*Spaces with '?' mean we were unable to find accurate numbers.

Sources: http://www.everylastrep.com/fitness-for-beginners/look-crossfit-games-history
http://games.crossfit.com/content/history

Industry Competition

At the beginning of 2016 there were numerous fitness centers competing in a growing national and global market. Primary activities for this industry included operating health clubs, gyms, aerobic and exercise centers, and other fitness-related facilities. The industry was fragmented with many companies that were growing and combining across regional and product lines. Demand for fitness and recreation centers continued to increase thereby causing the number of people employed in the industry to increase. By 2015 there were almost 33,000 fitness centers in the United States. The industry employed approximately 568,000 people that same year. [29] In 2016, the overall industry had grown to $27.1 billion in revenue and $2.8 billion in profits. Membership fees were the single largest revenue component and member retention was the key to a center's profitability. Fitness centers competed on brand recognition, customer service, price, and services offered. [47]

Even though competition was great, industry entry barriers were considered to be low. It was possible to lease equipment and buildings and both equipment and buildings had long life spans. Many start-ups were able to use second hand or previously used equipment. Wages were low. There were not many regulations other than zoning and building permit processes at the local levels. Access to capital for start-ups was readily available in most instances. The only real entry barrier was the brand loyalty and recognition built up by established gyms and fitness centers. Fitness center memberships were on the rise. However, in the future, it was expected that entry barriers would rise due to the possibility that corporate wellness programs would create strong demand for large-scale memberships, thereby creating barriers for newer companies. [47]

Yet even with all this activity in the business of fitness there was evidence that additional growth was possible. A 2016 study of nine countries by Censuswide, a global consultancy, found that the average person spent only 0.7% of their life exercising—or stated differently, out of an average person's 25,915 days on earth, they tend to spend only 180 days exercising. [30] However, the number of adults aged 20 to 64 spending leisure times exercising and on sports was increasing. Plus, the number of employers viewing exercise as an important component of employee health was also on the rise. Therefore, in the minds of many these findings established the need for increased emphasis on global fitness. The view of industry experts was that there was plenty of room for growth for both large companies and niche players (See Exhibit 8 for possible fitness niches). The industry was expected to grow, in terms of industry value added (IVA- a measure of the industry's contribution to the economy overall) by approximately 3% from 2016 to 2021. [47]

CrossFit competed in this industry with a unique value proposition that was more a philosophy of fitness than a business model. It appealed strongly to the largest market segment—consumers aged 34 years and younger. [47] Still, other companies thrived in the industry as well. Among the industry leaders were Anytime Fitness, Arcadia Fitness, Gold's Gym, GoodLife Fitness, LA Fitness, Planet Fitness, 24 Hour Fitness and Zumba. LA Fitness and Planet Fitness were publicly traded companies while most other competitors were private or closely held firms. Each company sought large-scale expansion while at the same time targeting particular segments for growth.

Anytime Fitness. As the name implies, Anytime Fitness operates fitness centers that are open for workouts twenty-four hours a day 365 days a year. Anytime Fitness, with more than 3 million members, was one of the fastest-growing and most progressive fitness businesses in the world. It received notoriety as one of *Entrepreneur Magazine's* top 10 fastest-growing franchises across all industries in 2015. From its first center in 2002 it grew into all fifty states and twenty countries with 38 wholly owned and approximately 3,000 franchised centers worldwide in 2016. For example, they opened a fitness center in Rome in 2016. The co-founder Chuck Runyon, used private equity and franchising to finance the company's rapid growth. Also to facilitate growth, in 2016 it moved into a new building and expanded to 300 employees at its headquarters in Woodbury, Minnesota. Runyon expected to continue growing the company at a rate of approximately 400 franchisees annually toward of goal of 4,500 centers by 2020. Starting a franchise cost between \$100,000 and 500,000 plus a \$30–37,500 franchise fee. Anytime required franchise owners to pay a \$549 monthly royalty. In 2017, the parent company of Anytime Fitness, Self Esteem Brands, was diversifying into salons and other fitness-related businesses. [31]

Arcadia and GoodLife. With more than 365 operating fitness centers, GoodLife Fitness was the largest fitness company in Canada. Members could join for around

Exhibit 8 Top 20 Worldwide Fitness Trends for 2017

1. Wearable technology
2. Body weight training
3. High-intensity interval training
4. Educated, certified, and experienced fitness professionals
5. Strength training
6. Group training
7. Exercise is medicine
8. Yoga
9. Personal training
10. Exercise and weight loss
11. Fitness programs for older adults
12. Functional fitness
13. Outdoor activities
14. Group personal training
15. Wellness coaching
16. Worksite health promotion
17. Smartphone exercise apps
18. Outcomes measurements
19. Circuit training
20. Flexibility and mobility rollers

Source: Worldwide Survey of Fitness Trends for 2017 by Walter R. Thompson, PhD., ACSM's Health & Fitness Journal, November/December 2016

$50 a month and specific classes were available for an additional fee. TRX suspension training classes were the most popular starting at $199 for six weeks. These classes kept members involved through a progressive training structure—each new class building upon what members learned in previous classes. Many GoodLife centers were oriented toward women's fitness. GoodLife provided individual trainers as well as individualized workout sessions for class members in order to mesh with member work schedules. Another Canadian fitness company, Arcadia, specialized in fitness programs for women taught by women that emphasized the use of gravity and body weight as resistance. Arcadia and GoodLife occupied some of the same competitive space in a growing market. The Canadian fitness industry generated over $2 billion in revenue and was growing at an annual rate of over two per cent. Approximately five million Canadian citizens were members of fitness clubs in 2012. [32,33]

LA Fitness. This company began in 1984 in Covina, in Southern California. It mission is to provide lifelong good health benefits to an increasingly diverse membership base. The business model was to tailor each individual fitness center to the specific needs of the community into which the company expanded. LA Fitness viewed its competence as being able to understand and meet the distinctive needs of the metropolitan communities in which they operated. They offered workouts and programs to people of all ages and fitness levels. The company strove to be family-friendly. Growth goals for LA Fitness centered on the idea of making fitness more available to larger segments of the community. It offered access to free weights, weight machines, and cardio to members. [34]

Planet Fitness. Planet Fitness was also a large and fast-growing competitor in this industry. In 2015, it maintained over 1,100 spacious and clean facilities (most of these were franchises) in 47 states with a large selection of Planet-Fitness branded equipment. Their slogan is: 'We're not a gym. We're Planet Fitness.' Typical centers were 20,000 square feet filled with purple and yellow cardio and weight-training equipment of all types. Memberships were inexpensive relative to other centers and Planet Fitness offered unlimited fitness instruction to all members. Their goal was to appeal to a broad market by creating a welcoming and non-intimidating, 'judgment-free,' fitness environment for anyone. Company revenue for 2015 was $1.5 billion and it had aggressive plans that included growing equipment sales, expanding franchise royalties, driving revenue growth, and growing into a broad range of markets. Planet Fitness planned to increase the number of stores in the United States to over 4,000 and to grow into Canada in the near future. [35]

Gold's Gym. Gold's Gym considered itself the original fitness company. Founded by Joe Gold in Venice, California in 1965 it gained notoriety in the documentary movie *Pumping Iron* starring two young weight-lifting sensations Arnold Schwarzenegger and Lou Ferrigno. Gold's had over 3 million members in 22 countries and 38 states in 2016. It offered weight-training primarily but also cycling, martial arts, muscle endurance, Yoga, and Zumba. However, it was strength training that set Gold's apart from other centers. The company claimed to be able to enhance the strength of members, with the additional claim that with physical strength came strength to excel at other aspects of life. Gold's Gym was privately held. [36]

24 Hour Fitness. 24 Hour Fitness competed in a market space similar to Anytime Fitness and Planet Fitness. 24 Hour operated 400 centers for four million members in seventeen states. The company had run successfully for over thirty years offering convenience to its members. It had accessible, affordable, convenient places for people of all fitness levels and abilities. Its business model was oriented toward allowing each individual to seek out his or her own fitness goals and pursue them on their own terms. [37]

Zumba. Zumba began operations in 2001. By 2016 it had grown to almost 200,000 centers or locations worldwide. The basic idea of Zumba fitness was to burn calories through dance-related aerobic routines. Zumba centers or classes were found in churches, hospitals, schools, and universities. Almost any room large enough with a good sound system would suffice as a Zumba center. The company also aggressively sold Zumba workouts on CD. The main goal was to provide a non-threatening atmosphere where participants could dance and have fun. Zumba tended to appeal to mothers because they could work out at home. Company executive also claimed that people tended to stay with Zumba longer than other competitors because it was fun. Zumba sold itself as being 'fitnesstainment.' [38]

Criticism

The growth of CrossFit is undeniable and the future of the company and sport is still as bright as ever, but CrossFit like most fitness industry startups is facing a certain degree of criticism and skepticism. Throughout the first decade and a half, CrossFit has faced an array of naysayers who criticize CrossFit's methods, techniques, safety measures, and legitimacy. The following are a few of CrossFit's most common criticisms:

Cult. One of the most widely mentioned criticisms of the CrossFit industry is that it is a "cult." Doubters of CrossFit feel that the family-oriented atmosphere that CrossFit revolves around resembles that of a cult-like following. Typical arguments insist that CrossFit brainwashes its members with their workout effectiveness, paying large membership fees (generally around $100/month), to being led by a 'leader' who dictates how they should act, to being elitists who only socialize with other CrossFit members.

Injury/Safety. Outsiders have often claimed that the CrossFit workout can be unsafe for its participants. The intensity and competitive nature can lead to too much heavy lifting and improper form all the way through the rep sets opening up opportunities for injury. The most commonly mentioned injury/disease used against CrossFit is rhabdomyolysis. Shortened in the CrossFit world to "rhabdo," this is caused by the death of muscle fibers and the release of their contents into the blood stream. [29] Rhabdo results from overexertion, which leads to the body's muscles breaking down and potentially causing kidney failure. Although it can be deadly, it is usually a treatable disease.

Legitimacy. Many proponents of CrossFit argue that the workout methods do not produce realistic results—that the libertarian methods of allowing box owners to create their own workouts within an entire methodology opens up the risk for unqualified coaches to piece together workouts that are not safe and do not translate into results. [30] High Intensity Interval Training (HIIT) is widely considered one of the best forms of exercise to burn fat, and CrossFit is no stranger to utilizing this method. But many feel CrossFit fails at this in their mix of intensity versus volume. Some contend that CrossFit uses HIIT as a fitness test and not necessarily for the best results. For example, a widely used HIIT method is TABATA (named for Japanese Scientist Dr. Izumi Tabata), which uses eight rounds of one exercise (bike, sprints, etc.) that includes 20 seconds of all-out work and 10 seconds of rest. CrossFit has a workout called 'TABATA THIS' in which athletes complete rows, air squats, pull ups, push ups, and sit ups . . . for 40 intervals! Critics say that this far exceeds the accepted mix and exposes participants to a decrease in intensity because of the large volume as well as a breakdown in technique, which both can lead to less effective and more dangerous results. [31]

Saturating the Market. While most of CrossFit's criticism comes from outside the community, there are affiliate owners who have concerns regarding the rapid pace at which CrossFit has grown. One box owner who has seen the rise of CrossFit through increased usage of social media pointed out that "growth doesn't equate to quality." He wonders if the rapid growth is just inflating a trend or if CrossFit will become a permanent fitness fixture. [32]

While many business owners are reluctant to respond to public criticism for fear that it will damage their reputation, CrossFit, Inc. and their legion of followers are the exact opposite. CrossFit has a team of employees who patrol the Internet looking to defend the brand with an iron fist against anyone and everyone who tries to deface it. Glassman has an entire team of lawyers dedicated only to defending the brand name as well as its trademark from people around the world who attempt to use the CrossFit name without paying for it. When asked why, Glassman explains, "if you don't defend it, you won't have a brand for long. We are in shark-infested waters and I've got shark-repellant attorneys." [4]

What Next?

After a few days of relaxation, reflection, and thought, Glassman came to the confirmation that he was content as to where CrossFit was, both the brand and the workout. He understood that he is one of the fortunate ones to break through the "fad" stage in the fitness industry and is truly on the verge of creating not just a revolutionary workout but an entirely new sport, and he did it his way. With that thought though, he knows that there are future decisions that must be made to allow the brand to continue to grow and some of those decisions could conflict with CrossFit's current culture, values, and philosophies.

Sticking to CrossFit's roots as a technology leveraging fitness company, he thought about the future, how they can continue to stay on the cutting edge of technology and what avenues would be beneficial to continue to grow the CrossFit brand. Now that CrossFit, Inc. is in a place of financial stability, he also kicked around the idea of starting to get involved in large outside advertising to increase the brand's recognition and reach, such as stadium naming rights and national television advertising. Would the opportunity to increase his brand awareness through mainstream advertising, a path that CrossFit typically has not followed, help or hurt the loyalty aspect of his devout followers, and what would the impact be at the local affiliate network?

The sport of CrossFit is undoubtedly growing. The Reebok CrossFit Games are increasing each year in participants, attendance, and revenue. His firm belief that CrossFit athletes are the "fittest on earth" due to their well-rounded abilities is something that he would adamantly defend anywhere. With the Rio 2016 Olympic games approaching, he cannot help but dream about CrossFit being an event in future Olympics. The exposure of CrossFit, at the largest stage of worldwide competition, has the capability to solidify CrossFit as a major sporting event, not to mention the potential financial impact. The ability for CrossFit's dedicated athletes to have the opportunity to compete for their countries would be incredible, Glassman thought. But, for this ever to happen, he knows that drastic changes would have to take place. First off, in addition to the International Olympic Committee (IOC), an international governing body would be needed to oversee the sport [33], undoubtedly limiting his power as CrossFit's sole decision maker. Policies and regulations would be altered and CrossFit staples such as the random nature of events that the CrossFit Games are known for, amongst others, would most likely change. Is this something that he, personally, is willing to do to grow the sport? Can the sport of CrossFit survive and grow on its own? What would the impact be at the national and local levels with the radical changes that would likely occur?

Glassman's thoughts then reverted to CrossFit, Inc.'s affiliate business model and how current trends could impact the company's growth. How could they address some of the criticism surrounding CrossFit and how would potential remedies impact the company financially? For example, should CrossFit, Inc. mandate continuing education for coaches and do they charge for this, or do they go in the opposite direction and invest in their coaches, in an attempt to increase the competency at each affiliate? Lastly, his attention turned to how he should handle the issue of large corporate CrossFit gyms, such as Boston's Reebok CrossFit Back Bay, who operate full-service, state-of-the-art boxes. [34] Since the beginning, the "Garage Gym," a stripped down, rather unsightly facility with only the essential equipment needed for a hard-core workout, has been the standard. Allowing corporate companies to open "globo-gym" type facilities with full service amenities such as locker rooms and all hours' access could change the landscape of CrossFit affiliations as they currently exist. Even if these facilities stay true to CrossFit's roots (equipment, loud music, etc.), what would the effects be on the local affiliates' ability to survive? Would there be a 'Walmart-Effect' [35] and if so, should they increase the corporate-sized gyms' yearly fee to offset the loss of small affiliates? Would this be detrimental to the CrossFit philosophy or would it further legitimize CrossFit as a high end fitness option?

As Glassman sat at his desk wondering how these opportunities and potential changes would affect the CrossFit world, he leaned back in his chair and scanned the room looking at all of the pictures, posters, and plaques hanging on his wall. Each one represented something different but all of them contributed to the growth of CrossFit in their own way. Then he noticed one in particular. It was a small 8 × 10 frame, somewhat lost among the other flashy pieces, but it carried more meaning than anything up there. It was a photo of him and the officers from the Santa Cruz Police Department, the original CrossFit group. He realizes that changes are inevitable, but the photo reminds him that CrossFit grew from the dedication, commitment, and loyalty of its community. Moving forward he would like his decisions to remain true to those roots and his libertarian approach, because that is the essence of his success.

Exhibit 9 Eight Things You Probably Didn't Know about Crossfit

1. **You don't have to be young or in great shape to try CrossFit** (CrossFit is for beginners, experienced athletes, the fit, and the un-fit)
2. **CrossFit works out your mind as well as your body** (a common reason for gym cancellation has to do with mindset of the member—CrossFit defeats this by training the mind to work through soreness and fatigue)
3. **CrossFit has a strong connection to law enforcement and military officials** (CrossFit is popular with police and military specialized teams across the country)
4. **CrossFit commemorated a set of workouts to fallen soldiers** (common in boxes around the world—these workouts are named in honor of fallen soldiers who were CrossFit followers)
5. **CrossFit gyms have exclusive owners** (in order to open up your own CrossFit 'box' you need more than cash—you will need to write an essay, complete an application, pay a yearly fee, and complete instructor training courses; this enhances the quality of gyms across the board)
6. **CrossFit offers a 'Kids' program** (parents can bring their kids to a growing number of the gyms)
7. **CrossFit has a Paleo Diet kitchen on premises** (for member convenience—works like a subscription service at many of the boxes)
8. **CrossFit is 60% female** (there are about 6 million CrossFit women members)

Source: http://www.interesticle.com/fitness-and-health/8-things-you-probably-didnt-know-about-crossfit

Exhibit 10 CrossFit, Inc. Growth Contributors

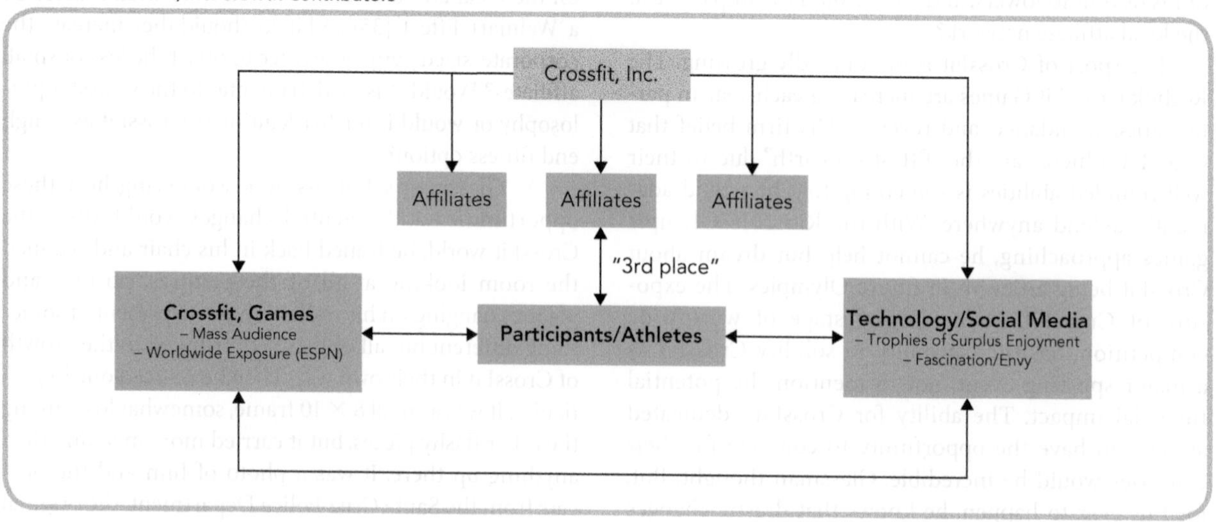

Exhibit 11 Worldwide CrossFit Box Locations Map

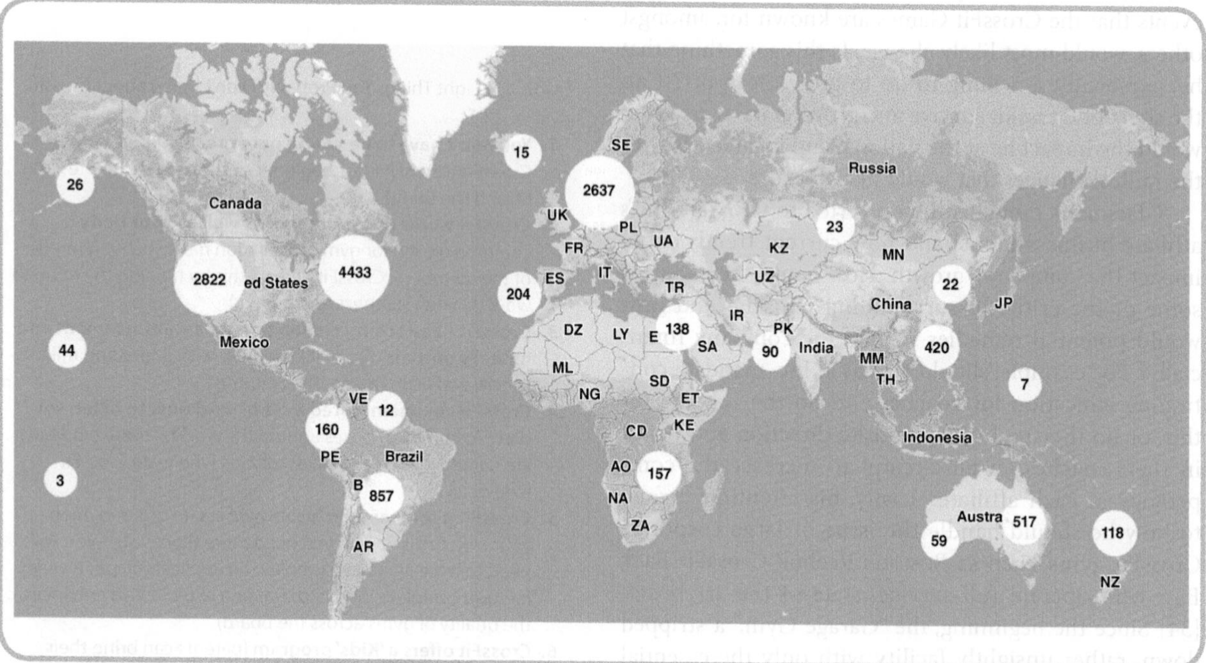

Source: https://map.crossfit.com/

NOTES

1. Wang, Christine. "How a Health Nut Created the World's Biggest Fitness Trend." *CNBC.* (5 Apr. 2016). Web. 12 April 2016.
2. "Libertarian." *Merriam-webster.com.* Merriam-Webster. Web. 4 April 2016.
3. Bowles, Nellie. "Exclusive: On the Warpath with CrossFit's Greg Glassman." *Maxim.* Maxim Media Inc., (8 Sept. 2015). Web. 10 Apr. 2016.
4. Alfonsi, Sharyn. "King of CrossFit." *CBSNews.* CBS Interactive, (10 May 2015). Web. 14 Apr. 2016.
5. Kuhn, Steven. "The Culture of CrossFit: A Lifestyle Prescription for Optimal Health and Fitness." *ISU ReD: Research and eData.* (8 Sept. 2013): 1–15. Web. 10 Apr. 2015.
6. "Origins of CrossFit" *The Box Mag.* Cruz Bay Publishing Inc., (9 Oct. 2012) Web. 14 Apr. 2016.
7. Glassman, Greg. "What is Fitness?" *The CrossFit Journal* (October 2002): 1,2,4. Web. 10 Apr. 2016.
8. "What is CrossFit?" *www.crossfit.com.* Web. 15 Apr. 2016. https://www.crossfit.com/what-is-crossfit
9. "What Do You Mean by Broad Time and Modal Domains?" *www.vigilantecrossfit.com.* Web. 20 Apr. 2016. http://www.vigilantecrossfit.com/what-do-you-mean-by-broad-time-and-modal-domains.html
10. Glassman, Greg. "Foundations" *The CrossFit Journal* (Apr. 2002). Web. 10 Apr. 2016.
11. Glassman, Greg. "Benchmark Workouts" *The CrossFit Journal* (Sept. 2003). Web. 10 Apr. 2016.
12. "The Paleo Diet Premise" *www.thepaleodiet.com.* Web. 16 Apr. 2016. http://thepaleodiet.com/the-paleo-diet-premise/
13. Lieberman, Bari. "Extreme Athletes and Their Extreme Diets" *www.refinery29.com.* (15 Aug. 2014) Web. 16 Apr. 2016—"Apparently, crisp pork belly isn't just a favorite of the casual CrossFitter; the elite athletes love it, too. Four-time winner Rich Froning told me that he averages about a pound or two of bacon per week. He shared his "bacon explosion" recipe with Project Mayhem; it involves woven bacon layers, sausage, and BBQ sauce."
14. Ufford, Matt. "CrossFit Wins Court Case, Avoids Corporate Takeover" *www.sbnation.com.* (15 Nov. 2012) Web. 15 Apr. 2016.
15. https://www.crossfitrrg.com/what-is-rrg
16. Burger, Russell; Darsh, Lisbeth; Pitts, Lynne. "The CrossFit Risk Retention Group Insurance by and for the CrossFit Community" *The CrossFit Journal.* (31 Mar. 2009). Web. 10 Apr. 2016.
17. http://www.crossfitiip.com/index.php
18. Ozanion, Mike. "How CrossFit Became A $4 Billion Brand" *www.Forbes.com.* Forbes Magazine. (25 Feb 2015). Web. 12 Apr. 2016.
19. Professional Physical Therapy and Training. "The First Rule of CrossFit is Never Stop Talking about CrossFit" *www.professionalptandtraining.com.* Web. 24 Apr. 2016 contributions. The emphasis of self-sacrifice and the actions of helping and honoring others that affiliates engage in is an appealing feature that can attract new members who want to be a part of something that has a deeper meaning.
20. Oldenburg, Ray. *The Great Good Place.* New York: Paragon House, 1989. Print.
21. Burke, Daniel. "Millennials Leaving Church in Droves, Study Says" *www.cnn.com.* Cable News Network. (14 May 2015). Web. 22 Apr. 2016.
22. "Latest CrossFit Market Research Data" *www.rallyfitness.com.* (28 Nov. 2014). Web. 21 Apr. 2016. https://rallyfitness.com/blogs/news/16063884-latest-crossfit-market-research-data
23. Duggan, Maeve; et al. "Social Media Update 2014" *Pew Research Center Internet Science Tech RSS.* (9 Jan. 2015). Web. 16 Apr. 2016.
24. "The Ripple Effect of Following a Brand on Social Media" *www.emarketer.com.* (10 July 2012). Web. 24 Apr. 2016 http://www.emarketer.com/Article/Ripple-Effect-of-Following-Brand-on-Social-Media/1009177
25. "Why CrossFit Dominates Social Media" *www.remedypr.com.* Remedy Communications. Web. 21 Apr. 2016.
26. Krier, D., and Swart, W.J. "Trophies of Surplus Enjoyment" *Critical Sociology* 42.3 (2014): 371–92. Web. 16 Apr. 2016.
27. http://games.crossfit.com/content/history
28. Tabata Times. "How Fast Are The CrossFit Games Growing? The Numbers Tell the Story." *www.tabatatimes.com.* (Nov. 2013). Web. 16 Apr. 2016.
29. (Source:http://www.startribune.com/at-the-new-headquarters-of-anytime-fitness-there-s-room-to-work-play-and-grow/375487341/).
30. (Source:http://finance.yahoo.com/news/reebok-survey-humans-spend-less-130600235.html;_ylt=AwrC0wxxrSxXzVEAkNqTmYlQ;_ylu=X3oDMTBzcDJ2Y28yBGNvbG8DYmYxBHBvcwMxMwR2dGlkAwRzZWMDc2M-)
31. (Source:http://www.franchisetimes.com/January-2016/20-to-Watch-Whats-trending-in-2016/, and http://www.startribune.com/at-the-new-headquarters-of-anytime-fitness-there-s-room-to-work-play-and-grow/375487341/, and http://www.anytimefitnessfranchise.com/)
32. (Source: Arcadia Fitness London by Jaclyn Caims, 2013, Richard Ivey School of Business case version 2014-04-23.
33. (Source: http://www.goodlifefitness.com/memberships/default.aspx)
34. Source: https://www.lafitness.com/Pages/about.aspx)
35. (Source: http://investor.planetfitness.com/investors/about-planet-fitness/default.aspx)
36. (Source: http://www.goldsgym.com/why-golds-gym/about-golds/)
37. (Source: http://www.24hourfitness.com/company/about_us/)
38. (source:http://finance.yahoo.com/news/popular-exercise-class-took-over-162700512.html;_ylt=AwrC0wxxrSxXzVEAidqTmYlQ;_ylu=X3oDMTBya2hmZ3R1BGNvbG8DYmYxBHBvcwM2BHZ0aWQDBHNlYwNzYw--)
39. http://www.webmd.com/a-to-z-guides/rhabdomyolysis-symptoms-causes-treatments
40. Fitjerk. "How CrossFit Forges Elite Failure" *www.revealthesteel.com.* (20 June 2012). Web. 25 Apr. 2016. http://revealthesteel.com/how-crossfit-forges-elite-failure/
41. Sulaver, Rob. "Metcon: The Greatest Weight-loss Exercise in the History of Gravity" *www.schwarzenegger.com.* (9 Apr. 2013). Web. 5 Apr. 2016.
42. "The CrossFit Revolution Empowered by Social Media" *www.sporttechie.com.* (12 Apr. 2012). Web. 18 Apr. 2016. http://www.sporttechie.com/2012/04/12/the-crossfit-revolution-empowered-by-social-media-109/
43. http://www.olympic.org/
44. http://reebokcrossfitbackbay.com/
45. http://www.investopedia.com/terms/w/walmart-effect.asp
46. (Source: http://www.popsugar.com/fitness/How-Get-Rid-Belly-Cellulite-37477876)
47. IBISWorld Industry Report 71394 Gym, Health & Fitness Clubs in the US, Sarah Turk, January 2016.
48. The CrossFit Journal, by Emily Beers, August 2014.

CASE 6

New Business Models for Heise Medien: Heading for the Digital Transformation

I am not one of those who believe that print is no longer a business model for the long term.

Dr. Alfons Schräder, CEO of Heise Medien GmbH & Co. KG (October 2014)

For years, practically all newspaper and magazine publishers in Germany, but also across the world, have tried to influence the transformation of the media in a way profitable to themselves. "Transformation of the media" was understood to mean the change in the media landscape brought by the availability of broadband Internet and the pressure on the media from online offerings that are mostly free. And for Heise Medien GmbH & Co. KG (called *Heise Zeitschriften Verlag GmbH* before 1 April 2015), that was one of the really current issues. The company is, among other things, publisher of the magazine *c't* and operator of the platform *heise online*. The publishing house was broadly positioned, online as well as in print media. The company possessed powerful brands, and highly qualified, experienced journalists. In recent years it has taken risks by branching out into new areas of business within the industry—and with real success.

But Ansgar Heise and Dr. Alfons Schräder, both managers of Heise Medien, were not satisfied. They had found many good answers to the current challenges, and were well positioned on the market. But Heise and Schräder wanted more. Out of all these solutions, they wanted to come up with a business model for Heise Medien overall that could better illustrate both the online and print business.

The Heise Media Group

The Founding Years

The company history of *Heise Mediengruppe* dates back to the year 1949, when editor Heinz Heise founded this publishing house in Hannover. As Germany was growing and emerging, Heise recognized very early that the country's telephone service would continue to develop quickly. The decision to publish telephone books proved to be spot-on. The offering was later supplemented by loose-leaf legal documentation and government-agency handbooks. Five years after the founder's son Christian Heise took over the helm, *Heise Verlag* joined another trend in Germany: the increasing spread of computers of all kinds. In 1977 the electronics magazine *Elrad* was published, and this was the publisher's first magazine. In 1983 the computer magazine that is still the leader today on the German-speaking market, *c't*, arose out of a supplement to Elrad. Further successful publications were the magazine *iX*, which targets a professional audience, and *Technology Review*. But even the original publishing entity is developing further. First, the company developed additional telephone-book markets by opening new offices in the early 1990s. Then in 1992, the company bought the publishing group *Hinstorff Verlag* in Rostock, thus expanding its offerings to include picture books, nonfiction, fiction, audiobooks, children's books, and calendars.

The Internet Age

After the computer magazine *iX* started the first online news in 1994, the editors of *c't* developed it within a very short time into *heise online*, one of the best-known online news brands. Alongside that, the first phonebook directories were available on the Internet shortly after. With www.dastelefonbuch.de and www.dasoertliche.de, *Heise Mediengruppe* was running two powerful platforms in Germany. At the turn of the millennium, the company employed a staff of about 500, and with Ansgar Heise the third generation of the family moved into top management, making clear that even after attaining that size, the company and its culture were still characterized by tradition and a sense of being a family business. The group's attitude toward new technologies remains open and aggressive. Heise Mediengruppe is one of the first companies to make online telephone books available on mobile

This case was written by **Prof. Dr. Frank Bau, Helene Blumer, and Artem Matveev** all at University of applied sciences HTW Chur, Switzerland. It is intended to be used as a basis for class discussion rather than to illustrate either effective or ineffective handling of a business situation.

We gratefully acknowledge the cooperation and support from the Heise Medien GmbH & Co. KG, Germany.

Contact: frank.bau@htwchur.ch

devices such as smartphones and tablets. Along with that are business-to-business services covering multimedia advertising, Internet presence, and search-engine marketing.

Even in the age of the Internet, the magazine *c't* is the most subscribed-to IT magazine in Europe, and thereby the flagship for the business area that was meanwhile spun off as *Heise Zeitschriften Verlag* (Heise Magazine Publishing). The team of 70 experts and the *c't* test lab are important ingredients in the magazine publisher's recipe for success. On this basis, special issues and spinoffs are born, such as *c't Digitale Fotografie, Mac & i* and *MAKE* (formerly c't *Hardware Hacks)*. Many of the products of *Heise Mediengruppe*, in particular those of *Heise Zeitschriften Verlag* [Heise Magazine Publishing], are available online as e-papers and through associated apps.

Heise Zeitschriften Verlag / Heise Medien

In addition to the publishing unit for directory media and telephone books (*Heise RegioConcept*), *Heise Medien* with its flagships *c't* and *Heise Online* makes up a second important part of the media group. The publishing house is a unique success story, particularly with its print magazine *c't* and the IT news website *heise online*. The goal was always to develop the publishing house into the leading media entity in the subject area of IT and technology.

In addition, the company has consistently added new sub-brands (online these were heise netze, heise security, heise open, heise developer, heise resale, heise autos, and *TechStage/BestBoyz*. In the print/online mix they were *heise foto /c't Digitalfotografie, Mac & i*, and *c't Hacks/Make*). And there were indeed some that didn't work out, products (like *heise resale*) that didn't function strategically as had been hoped. In addition, the brands' different personalities and communications channels were developed through conferences, conventions, and online through *Heise Business Services* (a platform for lead generation with a white paper database, webcasts, and webinars). Also, *heise Preisvergleich* ("heise price comparison") was incorporated by *Geizhals.at* as a white-label solution on *heise online*.

Supporting this great portfolio of sub-brands and activities, General Manager Alfons Schräder sees the clear strategy of his publishing house in this way:

that we continue not to lose sight of the existing business [the print-media business], and that we work on its further evolution.[1]

And we do continue to believe very much in print. We know, of course, that the future of print will be very different from its past. But I am not one of those who believe that print is no longer a business model for the long term.[2]

Strategy in Action

Implementation of the publishing house's strategy led to many new formats, online as well as in print media. In the years 1994 to 1996, the platform www.heise.de established itself as one of the most important German-language news platforms in the IT field.[3] In 2014, 19 formats were bundled on the platform (Appendix 2). While the publishing house mobilized *c't, iX*, and *Telepolis* as its strong and established brands, there were also newer brands like *Mac & i, c't Hacks*, or *Preisvergleich. c't Hacks* took in the young, very active, and ambitious so-called "maker scene." For chief editor of *c't* Johannes Endres, one of the pioneers of *c't Hacks*, the maker scene was incredibly important to the development of future target groups. These were target groups that, as the name suggests, simply wanted to make things, conceive their own technical devices, and build them.

It's about people that get into technology for fun and as a hobby. . . . [The target group] extends from school kids tinkering with certain things, to amateur radio operators, traditional and now older gentlemen, that in this way we can also bring in.[4]

Preisvergleich was further strengthened in 2014 when *Heise Medien* took over a controlling share of the price-comparison platform *geizhals*. Since 2005, Heise and the Vienna-based operating company of *geizhals.de* became linked through capital investments. In 2014 Heise took a majority share in *Preisvergleich Internet Services AG* in Vienna.

A further acquisition was the blog *BestBoyZ* in March. *BestBoyZ* focuses on the smartphone and tablet industry and was fully integrated into the offerings of *Heise Online's* platform *techstage.de*. Heise thus brought about 60,000 *Youtube* subscribers and potentially over 22,000 *Facebook* fans to their offerings.[5] *Techstage.de* was one of the platforms that fulfilled Schräder's desire to reach new target markets.

In print as well as online, new formats arose in the area of photography. *c't Digitale Fotografie* was a thematic offshoot of *c't* and was quickly developed further into a separate magazine. The online offerings followed and subsequently created an interesting stage for strategic experiments. What was particularly new about this was the fact that it involved non-free content that was developed on this platform. So in print there was the magazine *c't Digitale Fotografie*, and then there was the online *Heise Foto Club*, which offered flexible paid memberships.

For Dr. Schräder, *c't Digitale Fotografie* was the successful example for his basic strategy to grow and evolve starting out of his print-media business, and to survive in a publishing entity where the rules were no longer the old ones.

But if they build unique and good content—it just has to really be good—then I'm convinced we will still have print products even in twenty or thirty years. . . . [those] will be niche products. They are much more expensive. You can see that here with our c't, which, for example, at the moment costs €4.20. And something like c't Digitalfotografie, which has fewer pages, costs €9.90. But it still sells 30,000 copies of every issue. You just see, there is a shift.

The advertising business has gone down significantly, and circulation has gone down, while the price for an issue has gone up. That's why today we have, for example, a mix of about 70% sales revenue and only 30% advertising revenue. And earlier that was 50/50.[6]

So Alfons Schräder was firmly convinced that purely Internet-based business models were not sustainable in the long term, and only the right mix could deliver success.

techstage.de

A further result of the strategy that Schräder pursued was *techstage.de*, a format that was above all supposed to appeal to younger target groups that *c't* couldn't reach any more. *techstage.de* was an offering for users with different habits of information use who need a different depth of information compared to, for example, the typical subscriber of *c't*. One of the striking features of *techstage.de* was tech duels, where two online editors duelled on current issues in the information and communications technology industry in a funny and casual video dialogue. The offerings were not created by the *c't* journalists, but by staff acquired or assigned specifically for techstage.de. The content was completely free, so later it had to earn money through display, affiliate systems, and later more from transaction-based business. The business was difficult to assess. There were tech duels that reached over a hundred thousand visitors, but also some that brought a mere 5000 clicks, and thus hardly could have been profitable. Business Development Manager Fabien Röhlinger had difficulty naming precise figures, but as he saw it,

An online contribution, regardless of whether it's news or a video, has to bring about 20,000 visits in order to be profitable through display and transaction-based sales.[7]

The Magazine-Publishing Industry in Upheaval

In recent years, we can observe a variety of changes on the German magazine market. Circulation is sinking slowly, but steadily. On the one hand there are an array of causes that manifest themselves in declining sales, while on the other hand a variety of operators are busy bracing themselves against this decline. Even in the 1970s, a dark future was forecast for magazines as a format, since they are the easiest to do without and the easiest to be replaced by other media. But there's life in the old dog yet: Today the variety of magazines in layout, price, and content is enormous and as many magazines as ever are on display at kiosks.[8] Certainly, magazine publishers have to work with significantly lower turnover in printed media: Revenue of €5 billion for magazines with German *audiences in 2011 will fall to about €3.6 to €3.8 billion in 2015. Circulation* revenue could fall from €2.6 billion to €2.4 or €2.5 billion, and advertising sales could sink from €1.4 billion to €1.2 or €1.3 billion.[9]

For a long time the strategy of market penetration dominated among magazines, and this could be carried out well for so long because the publishers, thanks to clear positioning, worked different segments. But at the beginning of the 1990s, competition changed decisively on the magazine market: The markets were saturated. In order to continue growing on the German market, new titles must be launched. Demand from advertisers for ever more unique target groups led to increasing numbers of titles with correspondingly specific orientation. The huge expansion in computer use, private as well as professional, gives the segment of computers and communications a much higher-than-average growth rate.[10]

The Main Drivers of Change

The publishing industry faces a variety of changes. People speak of the age of the Internet, of omnipresent media offerings and the miniaturization of communication technologies, of an individualization of society that takes us from collective to compartmentalized entertainment offerings, of a demographic shift, of a population that is constantly changing. The effects of these developments are vast. From 2002 to 2008, retail sales of consumer magazines shrank by about 14%, while subscriptions had to accept a decline of about 7%. The observed trend toward lower circulation and at the same time a greater number of titles can be explained by society's increasing differentiation, where it gets compartmentalized into ever smaller arenas.[11] This opens up opportunities for success in niche products, for example the magazine *Landlust*, while the big, wide-reaching concepts are like interchangeable titles in oversaturated segments and could in the future reach a point of crisis.[12] Demographic changes lead to more elderly, and some very elderly, residents of Germany reading magazines, and fewer younger ones doing so. So the established magazines could last comfortably into the near future, since the demographic majority of their readers may be much older but they are still reading the magazines that they are accustomed to.[13] We could summarize that the transformation in the magazine industry results from three challenges: demographic change, individualization and fragmentation of target groups, and the development of new media formats with the Internet.

The Digital Revolution

If we look at the technological drivers of the transformation, then we see that in addition to the Internet, the convergence of technologies and media are also having an effect—previously separate information and communication technologies (for example, Internet TV) are merging and are driving new innovations in products and services. Highly successful business models established over the course of decades, and above all focused on printed media, are thus clearly in question. Freely available online offerings come into direct competition with the classic printed magazine, causing the readership and above all the advertising market to shrink. Magazine companies are reacting to this partly by setting up their own online editorial teams. But magazine content cannot be transferred one-to-one, since this would lead to a case of self-cannibalization, where information that has been prepared professionally at great expense is given away for free.[14] Some publishing houses are currently trying out payment models. For example, *Welt* and *Bild*, as well as *Süddeutsche Zeitung* want to introduce some paid content by the end of 2014.[15] Whether the concept of paywalls works, or just drives the readership to the competition, remains to be seen.

Now that print and digital media have coexisted for years, and after a decade of growing media diversity, we can now see the first losers: In 2012, *Frankfurter Rundschau* announced bankruptcy, *Financial Times Deutschland* was shutting down, *Süddeutsche Zeitung* was preparing big cuts,[16] and *Springer-Verlag* was intending to focus more on digital services and sold several traditional publications: *Bild der Frau, Hörzu* und *Hamburger Abendblatt*.[17]

And IT publishers are faring no differently than other publishers. So far, no one has found a sure formula for mastering the digital revolution. Even here, the free mentality is seen as the main cause of the decline in print media. The question arises of how to monetize digital content, since financing the business with only the classic advertising revenue is no longer possible. One possibility is lead generation. Aside from high-value IT reporting, IT publishers are increasingly offering both offline and online events that bring producers together with interested people, for example, the webinars and events from Heise.

What's clear is that not all print publications will survive the digital transformation. And anyone who doesn't take into account the changes in media usage with apps, tablet editions, e-papers, or videos will have a hard time making headway in the future marketplace.[18]

Current Developments in Print and Online

Business Models

For *Heise Medien*, the issue of business model and strategic orientation were among the most important in the 2010s. On one hand, there was still the subscriber- and ad-based business with print magazines. But at the same time, there were inevitably offers online that accompanied and supplemented them. For years, publishers around the world had difficulty determining a dominant system. Finally, *Springer Verlag* with *Bild plus* and the *New York Times* brought attention to themselves with paid offerings, without providing any convincing or lasting solutions. One of the basic questions seemed to be whether to erect a paywall. And beyond that, were many further options for generating sales online.

For Johannes Endres, editor-in-chief of *c't* and *heise online*, the question of business model is important. In his view, there is paid content in publishing, the most exclusive published content should allow for display of advertising space that one can sell to customers. The distinction between online and print is, for Endres, just a question of the channel, not of the business model. Likewise, in variations of subscription, paid content on demand, paywalls, and so on he sees only as variations of payment systems or price structure. That would be a component of the business model, but not of its core.

A substantial portion of the revenue generated through *heise.de* is once again so-called transaction-based revenue. This has been generated when the advertising customer's website is reached through the media provider's website. If the magazine *c't*, for example, publishes on its website a printer test conducted with its own resources, then it's very likely that someone reading the test summary will click on a link placed there that leads to a webpage where the devices of the test's winner are available. The exclusivity of content in the possession of *heise.de* confers strong competitive advantages. This was certainly of great importance when working together with price portals such as *geizhals.at* or even the energy-industry comparison portal *verivox.de*. Transaction-based revenue has contributed between 7% and 12% of total sales revenue for *heise.de* (Appendix 3).

The Future of Print and Online

Print media itself has come under increasing pressure every year since the development of the Internet, and the end of the print era has been declared repeatedly. But actually neither daily newspapers nor journals have disappeared from our everyday life, even though circulation has been falling. A study by the *Verband Deutscher Zeitschriftenverleger (VDZ)* [Association of German Magazine Publishers] and the business consulting group *KPMG*[19] recommended that publishers continue to rely on print as well as online publishing. Forty-four percent of the publishers participating in the study's survey rated developing their subscription business, for example, as very important again. But at the same time, new products and distribution channels needed to be continually developed through trial and error. This was how the publishing industry's concept of the "Landlust" effect came into being, whereby a supposedly obscure niche aims for a seemingly unreachable level of circulation. The *Landlust* magazine reached circulation of over one million in 2015, higher than *Der Spiegel* (882,000 issues), *Stern* (753,000 issues) and *Focus* (516,000).[20] That proved that the old print formats could be successful despite the threat from the Internet.

The online realm, which appeared so superior and powerful, was on the other hand not so easy to manage profitably. "The royal road for paid content is not yet found, concludes Markus Kreher, Head of Media at *KPMG*.[21] In the study carried out by *KPMG* and *VDZ* titled *Erlösstrategien 2015* [Revenue Strategies 2015], payment and price models were addressed most of all as the approach to solving the problem.[22] One of the big problems was the user. "Users online are indeed pretty asocial," says Röhlinger bitingly of the circumstance that many very technically savvy users have been gradually taking away website providers' basis of existence, by using ad blockers and other tools. So paywalls and premium plans are on the agenda of all publishers.

Competitors

In the kitchenette of the editors of *c't* and *heise online*, nicely mounted magazine racks hold some of the most important German language computer and IT magazines, among them publications like *Chip, Computerbild, Computerwoche, Macwelt, PC Magazin,* and many others. And that was only a small selection of their direct competitors. The media portal www.fachzeitungen.de listed over 200 magazine titles in the category *Internet and Computer*.[23] Among them, of course, were also very specialized journals with negligible circulation. But the rack in Johannes Endres' kitchenette covered the most important of the magazines from the *statista* list of the twenty highest-circulation publications in IT and telecommunications (Appendix 1). What looked like a lot of competition, Johannes Endres addressed in a relaxed way:

For c't, there isn't really a competing product. And we don't really read the other magazines. Of course, we take a look inside to see what they're offering. But c't doesn't really have any competition of its own, as arrogant and ignorant as that may sound.[24]

That's because for Endres, the founders of *c't* in the 1980s couldn't buy the IT magazine they wanted on the German-speaking market. And so they made one for themselves according to their own ideas and wishes. And in that way the pioneers of that time met the needs of many thousands of other IT specialists and enthusiasts who wanted to get deep into what at the time was still new material. And even up to today, no other print magazine on the market has been able to match the quality of the content that Heise has itself produced. None of the competitors' magazines could, for example, match the tests carried out in their own laboratories and written by their own technical journalists. Nevertheless, Johannes Endres didn't ignore the fact that the needs of readers and IT users could also change, and that other magazines with less substantiated content also eventually found a readership. And then there were also online offerings from magazines, or even pure online offerings such as *Golem.de* that were not backed up by any magazine publisher, but as far as Fabien Röhlinger and Johannes Endres were concerned came closest to the quality of *c't*. Dr. Alfons Schräder, General Manager of *Heise Medien*, saw two main competitors.

We have two rivals that have different characteristics. One is IDG *and the other is* Chip Burda, *in other words* CHIP Communications GmbH. *The two of them operate very differently and their competitiveness keeps diminishing over time.*[25]

While *IDG* in Schräder's perception had already practically left the print media business, and then had backtracked somewhat convincingly, *Chip* has focused heavily on the online market and in doing so has even posted good results. *Chip* has aimed more at the consumer area and has been substantially stronger in gaming than *Heise Zeitschriften Verlag*.

Out of the great range of online services and print offerings, a few brands have stood out: *Chip, Heise Online / c't, PC-Welt, Computerbild* and *golem.de*, the latter with online offerings only. In several of these competing offers, Endres naturally saw significant competition. In the print segment, most of all those subscription-based magazines serving the target group of IT professionals and very ambitious private users, *c't* was clearly the top dog for him.

CHIP Communications GmbH

With a guaranteed paid circulation of 193,000 issues, the magazine *CHIP* was the third-biggest computer magazine in Germany in 2015, after *Computerbild* and *c't*.[26] *CHIP* had existed since 1978 and belonged to *Hubert Burda Media*, one of the biggest German publishing groups, which was also active internationally. *CHIP* was one of the 82 magazines of *Burda Verlag* in Germany, but the group's only IT magazine. In addition to the main issue that appeared monthly, *CHIP Foto Video Digital*, there were also *CHIP* special issues like *CHIP Test & Kauf*. Tests and buyers guides, as well as the download directory, were core pieces of the *CHIP.de* magazine's online presence. *CHIP* represented itself as a testing authority, technical advisor, and trend barometer.[27]

Computer Bild Digital GmbH

COMPUTER BILD Digital GmbH was a subsidiary of *Axel Springer AG* in Hamburg. The online and print brands were *Computerbild* and *computerbild.de*. In the media data, *Computerbild* defined its target group as technical multipliers with buying power who enjoy consuming. With *computerbild.de* the company generated over 13 million so-called unique users, over 46 million visits, and over 240 million page impressions.[28] In the print realm, *COMPUTER BILD Digital GmbH* designated 3.43 million readers and advertised to them as a reliable advisor using tests, courses, and reports.[29] Meanwhile the biweekly magazine clearly put a high value on easy and understandable explanations of deep knowledge in PC, telecommunications, Internet, and entertainment electronics.

IDG Communications GmbH

This US company was present on the German-speaking market in print as well as online, in particular with the title *PC-Welt*. Since 1974, its Munich-based German subsidiary *IDG Communications Media AG* has been present on the German market and is a significant competitor with up to 20 print and online formats for the target groups, IT and financial decision-makers, consumer and small business, and also gamers.[30]

Compared to competitors like *Heise, Computerbildgolem.de*, and *Chip, IDG* differentiated itself particularly through expanded marketing services and an event area with workshops and seminars, as well as large events.[31] The three most important print formats of *IDG* in Germany were *Computerwoche* with a circulation of around 12,500 in 2014 (including e-papers), *PC-Welt* with about 104,000 issues, and *Gamestar*[32] at 69,000.

golem.de

With the tagline "IT news for professionals," the online service of Berlin's *Klaß & Ihlenfeld Verlag* positioned itself clearly in the segment of the *Heise* flagship *c't*. The parent company of *Klaß & Ihlenfeld Verlags* is *Computec Media AG* from Fürth. The guiding principle[33] of *golem.de* is strongly congruent with the self-concept of *c't* for *Heise Medien. golem.de* sees itself as a group of technically inspired enthusiasts with high journalistic standards who want to offer high-value information to early adopters—those who understand technology early and want to use it. The vision that the company has set for itself is no less than "[to] become the only contact point in the German-speaking region that a reader interested in technology needs in order to be comprehensively and thoroughly informed."[34]

The Future of Heise Medien

What might the future bring? In the following points, Dr. Alfons Schräder summarized what for him are the most important drivers of the transformation that he wants to approach proactively:

- The revenue mix is changing.
- Media brands are developing multidimensional spheres of business (print, online, congresses, conferences, webinars, apps, video tutorials, paid content, and more).
- Readers are prepared to pay for digital content (especially for apps and their use, but also retail sales, clubs, etc.).

- Online business survives from a mix of display, real-time advertising (RTA), transactions, solutions, and lead generation.
- Along with those, new revenue sources are developing for publishers such as corporate publishing, solutions, services, market research, etc.

How would all of that fit into one business model? And how would such a model look, which conforms to Schräder's strategy, and at the same time leads to a clear positioning on the market while remaining open enough to react flexibly to future technological developments while meeting new market needs?

Appendix

Appendix 1 German Magazine Market by Circulation Numbers[35,36]

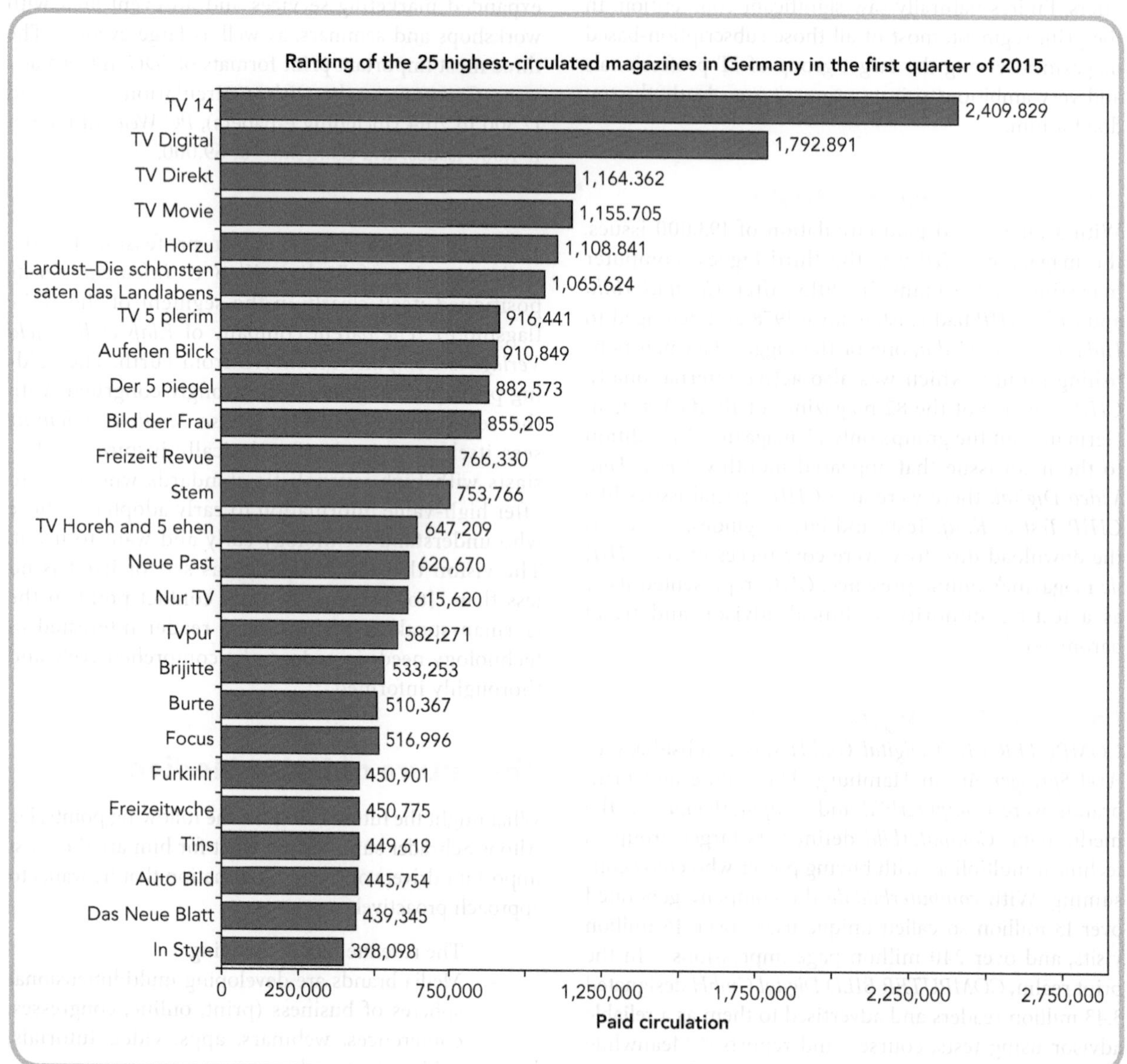

Appendix 1 (cont.) German Magazine Market in Numbers

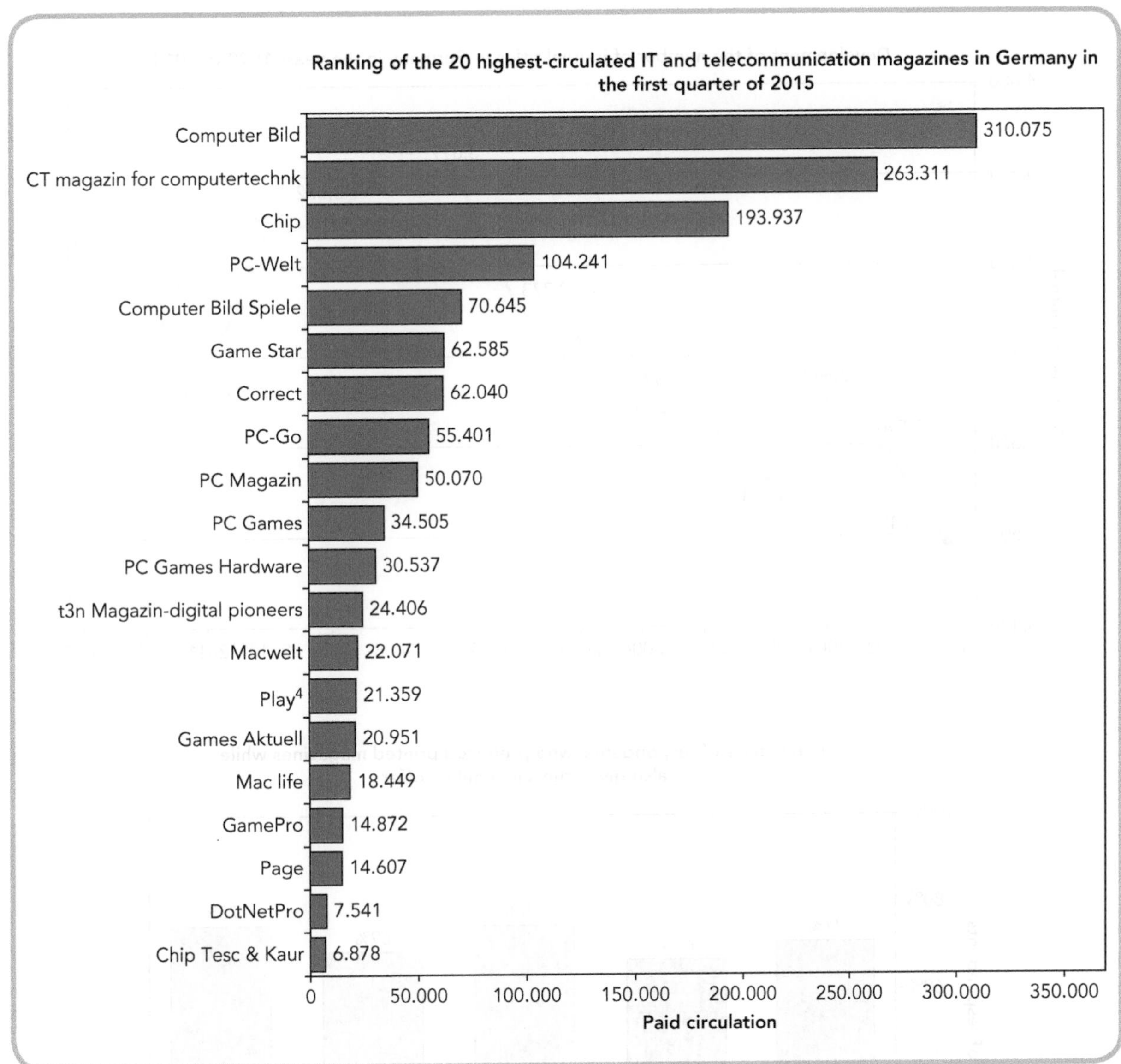

continued

Appendix 1 (cont.) German Magazine Market in Numbers

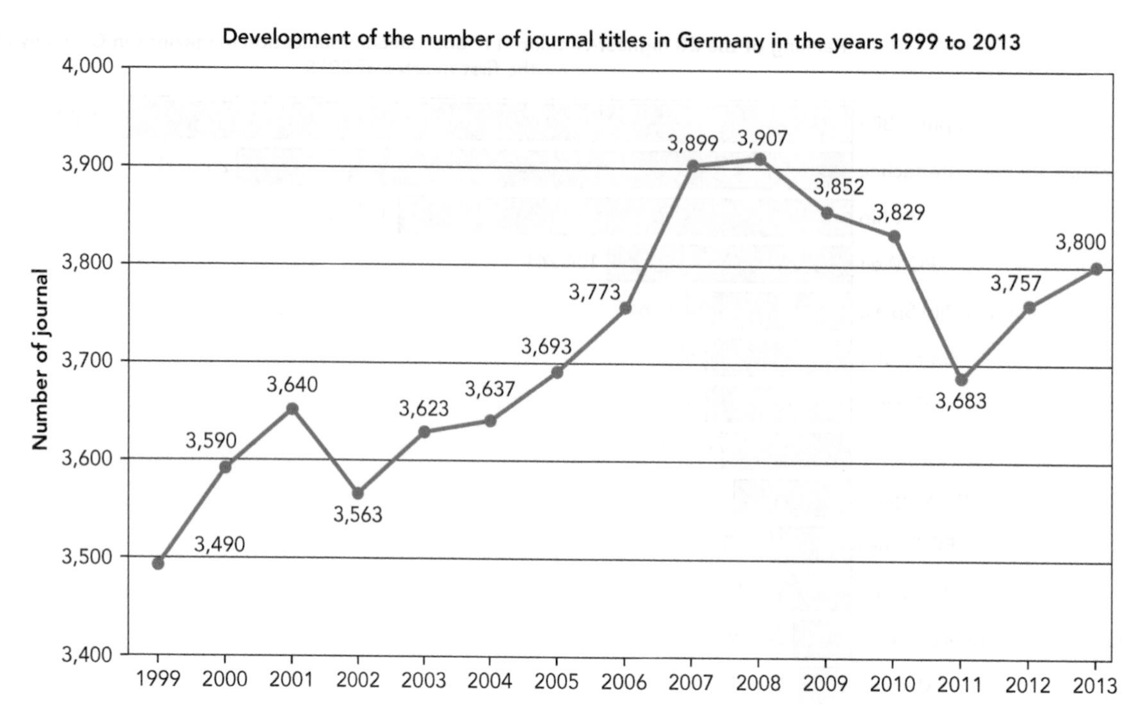

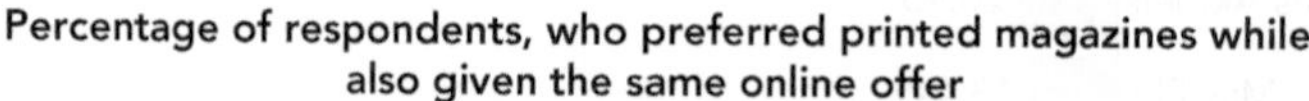

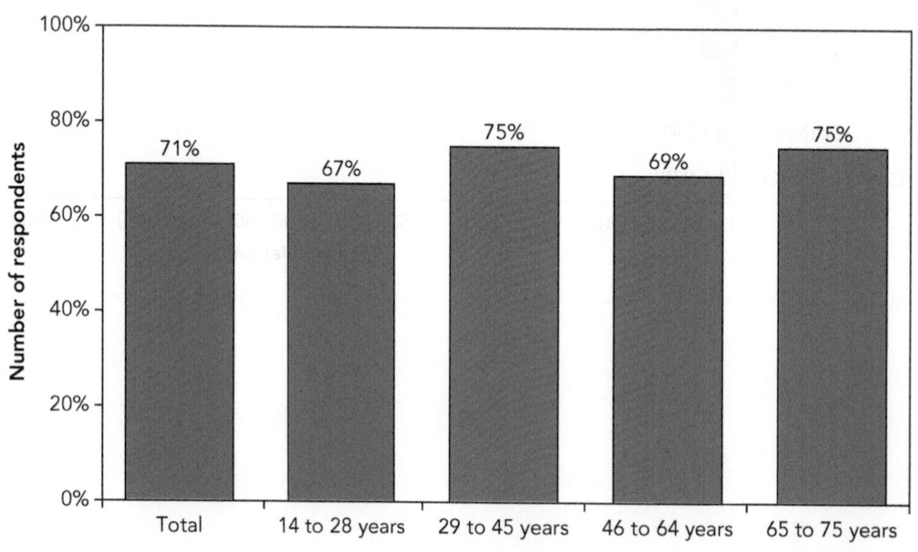

Appendix 1 (cont.) German Magazine Market in Numbers

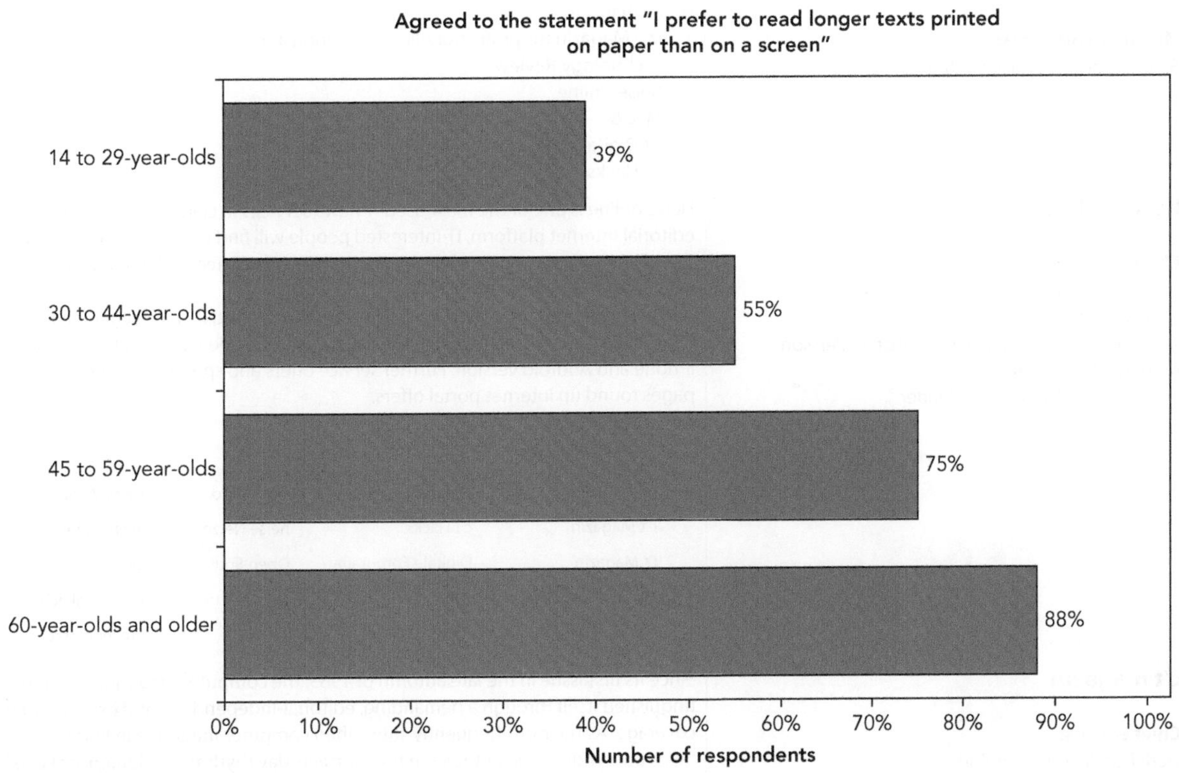

Agreed to the statement "I prefer to read longer texts printed on paper than on a screen"

	Number of respondents
14 to 29-year-olds	39%
30 to 44-year-olds	55%
45 to 59-year-olds	75%
60-year-olds and older	88%

0% 10% 20% 30% 40% 50% 60% 70% 80% 90% 100%

Number of respondents

Appendix 2 Company Structure

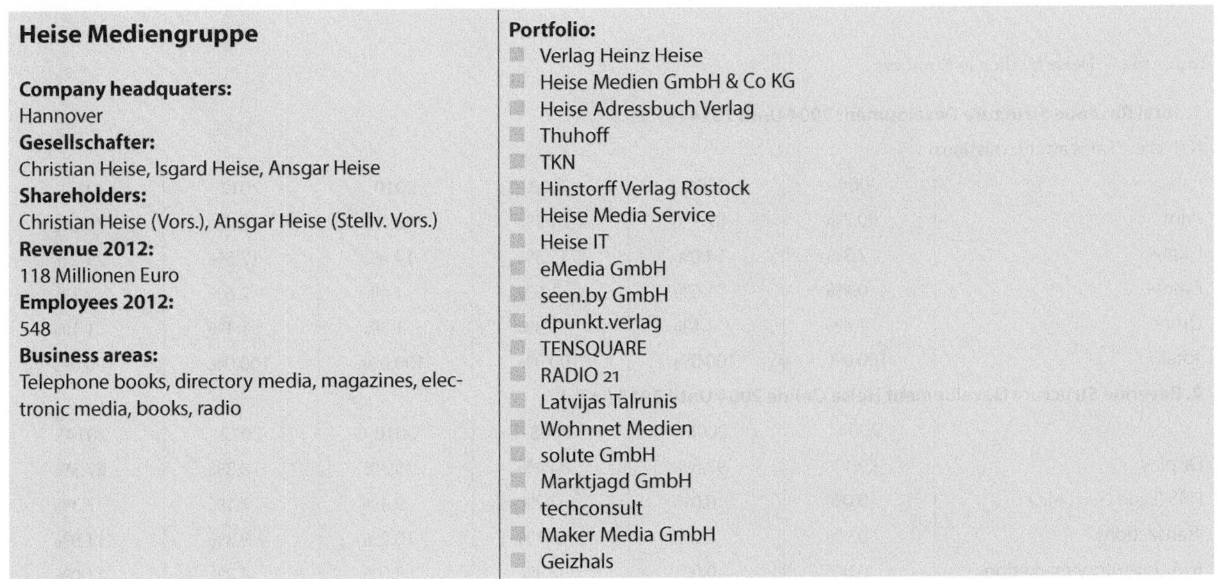

Heise Mediengruppe

Company headquaters:
Hannover
Gesellschafter:
Christian Heise, Isgard Heise, Ansgar Heise
Shareholders:
Christian Heise (Vors.), Ansgar Heise (Stellv. Vors.)
Revenue 2012:
118 Millionen Euro
Employees 2012:
548
Business areas:
Telephone books, directory media, magazines, electronic media, books, radio

Portfolio:
- Verlag Heinz Heise
- Heise Medien GmbH & Co KG
- Heise Adressbuch Verlag
- Thuhoff
- TKN
- Hinstorff Verlag Rostock
- Heise Media Service
- Heise IT
- eMedia GmbH
- seen.by GmbH
- dpunkt.verlag
- TENSQUARE
- RADIO 21
- Latvijas Talrunis
- Wohnnet Medien
- solute GmbH
- Marktjagd GmbH
- techconsult
- Maker Media GmbH
- Geizhals

continued

Appendix 2 (cont.) Company Structure

Heise Medien **Managing directors:** Ansgar Heise, Dr. Alfons Schräder	**Products:** ▪ *c't* magazin ▪ iX - Magazin für professionelle Informationstechnik ▪ Technology Review ▪ heise online ▪ Mac & i ▪ *c't* Digitale Fotografie ▪ *c't* Hacks
heise online **Chief editor:** Johannes Endres **Publishers:** Christian Heise, Ansgar Heise, Christian Persson **Managing directors:** Ansgar Heise, Dr. Alfons Schräder	Heise online is one of the most used IT news services in Germany. In the cross-editorial Internet platform, IT-interested people will find daily information from the editorial departments of the magazine titles c't, iX, Technology Review, as well as the online magazine Telepolis. At the heise-shop, the majority of the publications of c't, iX and Technology Review are available for a paid download. A free heise.de app is available as an iPhone and Android version. Further service offers and specialized thematic pages round up Internet portal offers. **Heise Download** **techstage.de** heise online · Telepolis · heise Foto · heise Video c't Magazin · c't Hacks · heise Netze · TechStage iX Magazin · Digitale Fotografie · Open Source · Download Technology Review · heise Autos · heise Security · Preisvergleich Mac & i · heise Developer · Stellenmarkt
c't magazin **Chief editors:** Detlef Grell, Johannes Endres **Publishers:** Christian Heise, Ansgar Heise, Christian Persson **Managing directors:** Ansgar Heise, Dr. Alfons Schräder	Since its first issue in the late autumn of 1983, the computer magazine *c't* has distinguished itself through a demanding, editorial-independent, and expert-based coverage. As the most frequently subscribed computer magazine in Europe, *c't* takes up a wide range of topics in the fourteen-day rhythm. In addition, *c't* keeps its readers daily informed through the cross-editorial Internet portal heise online.

Appendix 3 Heise Medien in Numbers

1. Total Revenue Structure Development 2004 Until 2014 (in %)

Net sales (Sales after remissions)

	2004	2006	2008	2010	2012	2014
Print	90.7%	82.9%	81.7%	82.6%	78.7%	75.0%
Digital	7.3%	14.0%	15.5%	14.6%	17.5%	21.2%
Events	0.4%	1.6%	1.6%	1.4%	2.6%	2.7%
Other	1.6%	1.4%	1.3%	1.3%	1.1%	1.1%
Total	100.0%	100.0%	100.0%	100.0%	100.0%	100.0%

2. Revenue Structure Development Heise Online 2004 Until 2014 (in %)

	2004	2006	2008	2010	2012	2014
Display	99.1%	97.8%	84.4%	75.3%	76.3%	67.3%
HBS (Lead Gen., etc.)	0.0%	0.0%	2.2%	9.4%	7.1%	7.3%
Transactions	0.9%	2.2%	6.7%	10.2%	9.3%	11.9%
RTA/ Inventory marketing	0.0%	0.0%	2.3%	3.5%	4.2%	11.0%
External marketing	0.0%	0.0%	4.4%	1.7%	3.0%	2.4%
Total	100.0%	100.0%	100.0%	100.0%	100.0%	100.0%

Appendix 3 (cont.) Heise Medien in Numbers

3. Cost Structure Development 2004 Until 2014

Change of costs in % 2004 and 2014

Costs: For example: Production costs Print (print / paper), external editing, sales costs / logistics, conference costs

For example: Infrastructure, marketing, external programming / IT services, AfA

Person cost: e.g. In addition to editorial, sales, sales, central functions also internal developers for digital products and IT department.

	Sum from 2004			Sum from 2014				
	Individual cost	Overhead cost	Staff costs	Individual cost	Overhead Cost	Staff costs	Total: sum from 2004	Total: sum from 2014
Print	97.40%	71.62%	72.48%	83.88%	47.82%	59.35%	86.31%	67.58%
Digi	2.19%	8.53%	8.33%	12.09%	22.90%	23.00%	4.92%	18.42%
Events	0.00%	0.00%	0.00%	2.43%	1.59%	1.71%	0.00%	1.99%
Other	0.41%	19.85%	19.19%	1.60%	27.69%	15.94%	8.77%	12.02%
Total result	100%	100%	100%	100%	100%	100%	100%	100%

Development of Personnel Costs

Year	Print	Digi	Events	Other	Total result
2004	100%	100%		100%	100%
2006	104%	190%	100%	106%	112%
2008	110%	289%	712%	114%	129%
2010	111%	302%	228%	98%	126%
2012	122%	370%	388%	127%	145%
2014	122%	410%	601%	123%	148%

Development of Individual Costs

Year	Print	Digi	Events	Other	Total result
2004	100%	100%		100%	100%
2006	95%	351%	100%	94%	100%
2008	92%	514%	197%	89%	102%
2010	76%	422%	486%	172%	85%
2012	76%	502%	2382%	171%	87%
2014	69%	443%	2442%	310%	80%

Development of Total Costs

Year	Print	Digi	Events	Other	Total result
2004	100%	100%		100%	100%
2006	97%	247%	100%	131%	128%
2008	103%	303%	69%	153%	138%
2010	85%	264%	67%	149%	121%
2012	87%	291%	19%	181%	125%
2014	86%	346%	18%	180%	129%

continued

Appendix 3 (cont.) Heise Medien in Numbers

4. Subscription to the last Delivered Edition of the Year

Only paid subscriptions

	2004 Year total		...	2014 Year total		
	All subscriptions	Print subscriptions		All subscriptions	Print subscriptions	Digitale subscriptions
all Profit-Center	287'012	287'012		301'797	296'838	4'959
c't Magazin	237'915	237'915		224'870	220'982	3'888
DigiFoto	0	0		12'024	12'019	5
Mac & i	0	0		12'520	12'122	398
Hardware Hacks	0	0		8'106	8'106	0
iX	37'464	37'464		31'955	31'287	668
TR	11'633	11'633		12'322	12'322	0

Appendix 4 General Market Data[37,38,39]

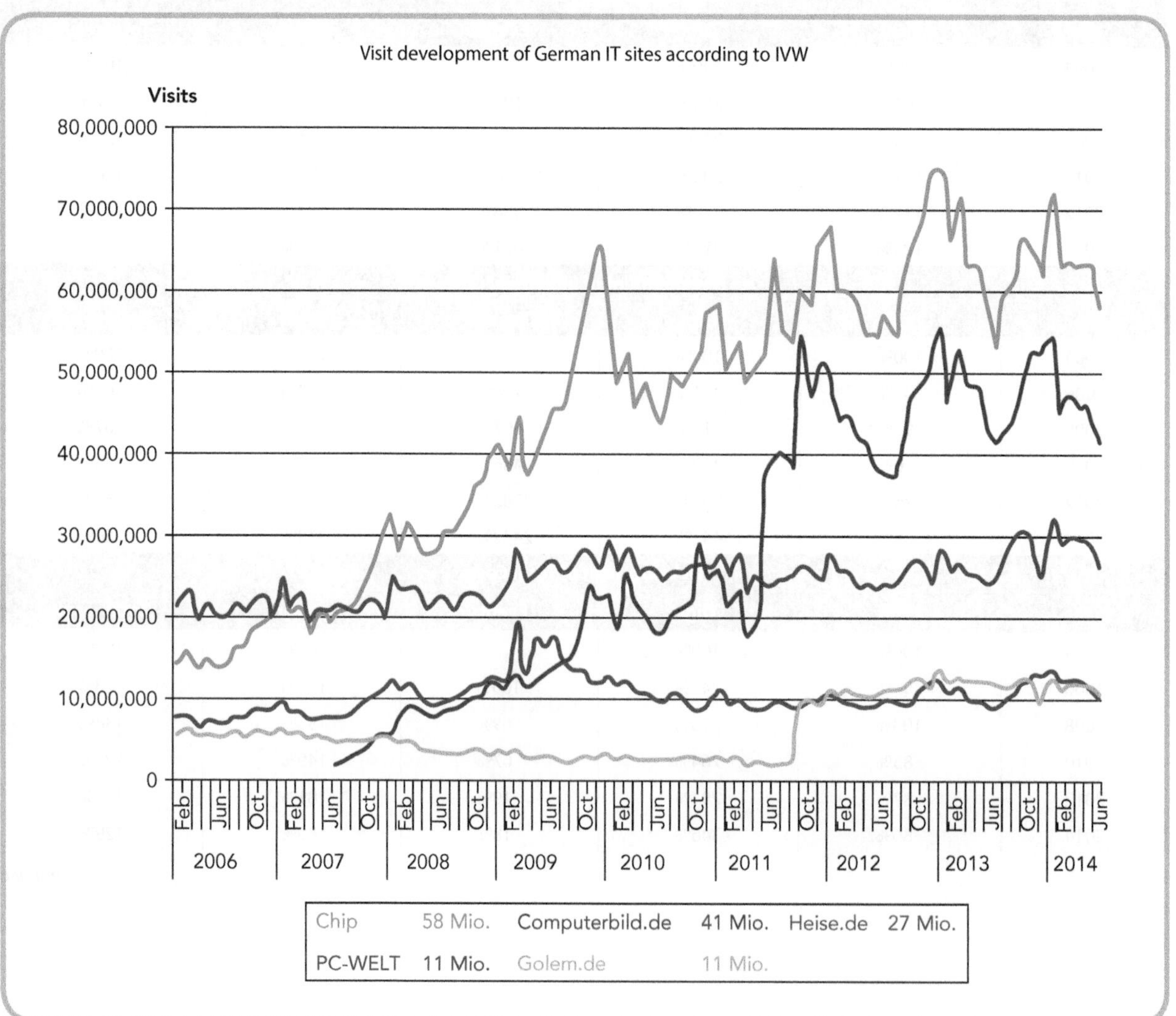

Appendix 4 (cont.) General Market Data

Online PIs:
Juni 2014: 31,65 Mio. (Quelle: IVW)
Online Visits:
Juni 2014: 9,69 Mio. (Quelle: IVW)
Unique User:
1,33 Mio. (Quelle: AGOF internet facts 2014-05)

Magazines in the IT / Telecom segment with the highest sales circulation in the 1st quarter of 2013.

Magazine	Paid circulation 1/2013	Change to 1/2012 (in %)
Computer bild (Axel Springer)	494.009	−9.6
C't magazin for computertechnik (Heise Zeitschriften verlag)	290.071	−4.8
Chip (Chip communication)	226.626	−10.1
PC-Welt (IDG magazine media)	208.603	−13.9
Computer bild spiele (Axel springer)	144.294	−12.9

Data from 1 to 5 are displayed from a total of 5

Appendix 5 Glossary

Search Engine Marketing

Search Engine Marketing (SEM): Design of measures for improved searchability on search engine results pages.

Search Engine Advertising (SEA): Search engine advertising means to place paid ads on search engine results pages (for example, through the Google Adwords system).

Search Engine Optimization (SEO): Search engine optimization refers to measures that aim to improve the position of a web presence in the free organic search results of a search engine.

Google Adwords

Google Adwords is a system that allows customers to book keywords in an auction or fixed-price process. If the booked terms are accessed and clicked on by users of the Google search engine, the customer will be liable for payment.

Affiliate marketing

In affiliate marketing, the marketing operator uses a variety of affiliates to market their service or product. The advantage is the distribution of the marketing effort on several partners, which are paid for success only. There are different remuneration forms:

Pay per Lead: for the generation of a customer contact (for example, entry in a newsletter distribution list or ordering a catalog)

Pay per Click: for each click on a link or banner displayed on the website or in the email of the affiliate.

Pay per Sale: a fixed amount or a percentage interest in the selling price is paid for each sale, which is effected through the advertising campaign of the affiliate.

One of the most famous affiliate networks is Amazon. Hundreds of thousands of websites link directly to the website of Amazon in order to buy the desired title directly. Once the sale takes place, Amazon pays a sales commission to the partner (affiliate).

Transaction-based business model

In a transaction-based business model, for example, a market service is offered in the function of a broker, which incurs charges or commissions in the event of the closure of a transaction. Typical examples of this are Ebay or websites of tourism brokers, such as Expedia or Billigfluege.de. The difference to affiliate marketing is that only the re-linking of the users is not payable, but actually a transaction has to be made.

Advertising-based business model

Advertising-based business models attempt to generate as many visits to the website as possible with services or content on a web page, and to permanently ensure that the website becomes a coveted advertising space (display). This means that companies pay money to allow their advertising to appear on the website. The use of the website and the services offered there is generally free of charge for the Internet user. This business model is often used, for example, by price comparison pages or free news services.

Paid Content

The basic model Paid Content tries to attract ready-to-pay users with the most attractive and exclusive content possible on the operated media (online and offline). Online would thus charge a usage fee for certain contents, offline a magazine or a newspaper subscription would be sold and thus sales generated.

REFERENCES

Dierks, S. (2009): Quo vadis Zeitschriften? Änderung der Medienlandschaft und Auswirkungen auf den Pressekäufer. Wiesbaden: VS Verlag für Sozialwissenschaften.

Hamann, G. (2012, November 29): Im Sturm: Wie guter Journalismus überleben wird – und was wir heute über morgen wissen. *Zeit Online*. Abgerufen am 24.12.2014 unter http://www.zeit.de/2012/48/Medien-Zeitung-Journalismus/komplettansicht

Hauser, J. (2012, November 11): Medien im Wandel: Wie Zeitschriftenverlage digital mit der Werbeindustrie mehr verdienen könnten. *Frankfurter Allgemeine*. Abgerufen am 24.12.2014 unter http://blogs.faz.net/medienwirtschaft/2012/11/08/weniger-einnahmen-mit-gedruckten-zeitschriften-wie-verlage-digital-mit-der-werbeindustrie-mehr-verdienen-koennten-88/

Heckel, C., & Rußmann, H. (2009): Demografischer Wandel und seine Bedeutung für Zeitschriften. In S. Dierks (Hrsg.), *Quo vadis Zeitschriften? Änderung der Medienlandschaft und Auswirkungen auf den Pressekäufer* (S. 137-148). Wiesbaden: VS Verlag für Sozialwissenschaften.

IDG Communication Media AG (2013): IDG Deutschland Gesamtportfolio. Abgerufen unter http://www.idg.de/portal/unternehmen/idg-deutschland-427 am 21.01.2015.

Novak, D. (2009): Gesellschaft und Medien im Wandel. In S. Dierks (Hrsg.), *Quo vadis Zeitschriften? Änderung der Medienlandschaft und Auswirkungen auf den Pressekäufer* (S. 99-112). Wiesbaden: VS Verlag für Sozialwissenschaften.

PR-COM (2014, September 18): Nachgefragt: Wie sieht die digitale Zukunft der IT-Medien aus? Abgerufen am 24.12.2014 unter http://www.pr-com.de/de/nachgefragt-sieht-digitale-zukunft-it-medien

Riepl, W. (1972): Das Nachrichtenwesen des Altertums: mit besonderer Rücksicht auf die Römer. Hildesheim: Olms.

Schulz, S., Steinmetz, V., & Teevs, C. (2013, July 25): Ausverkauf der Print-Sparte: Springer kappt seine Wurzeln. Abgerufen am 24.12.2014 unter http://www.spiegel.de/wirtschaft/unternehmen/axel-springer-verlag-verkauft-printprodukte-analyse-der-strategie-a-913107.html

Tschörtner, A., & Schenk, M. (2009): Profil des deutschen Publikumszeitschriftenmarktes – eine Analyse der Entwicklungsbedingungen. In S. Dierks (Hrsg.), *Quo vadis Zeitschriften? Änderung der Medienlandschaft und Auswirkungen auf den Pressekäufer* (S. 19–44). Wiesbaden: VS Verlag für Sozialwissenschaften.

Clasen, N. (2013): Der digitale Tsunami – Das Innovators Dilemma der traditionellen Medienunternehmen. Abgerufen am 21.10.2015 unter: http://onlinejournalismusblog.com/2013/10/13/warum-medien-online-kaum-geld-verdienen/

NOTES

1. Interview mit Dr. Alfons Schräder, October 2014.
2. Interview mit Dr. Alfons Schräder, October 2014.
3. Image brochure from Heise Medien Gruppe (2012).
4. Interview with Johannes Endres, August 2014.
5. http://www.heise-medien.de/presse/Heise-Zeitschriften-Verlag-kauft-Blog-2133245.html. Accessed on 28-Nov-2014.
6. Interview with Johannes Endres, August 2014.
7. Interview with Fabien Röhlinger, August 2014.
8. Compare Tschörtner and Schenk, 2009, p. 19
9. Compare Hauser, 2012
10. Compare Tschörtner and Schenk, 2009, pp. 20–23
11. Compare Novak, 2009, p. 101
12. Compare Tschörtner & Schenk, 2009, pp. 22–30
13. Compare Heckel and Rußmann, 2009, pp. 137–140
14. Compare Tünte, Helbig, Peters, and Große-Kreul, 2010
15. Compare PR-COM, 2014
16. Compare Hamann, 2012
17. Compare Schultz, Steinmetz, and Teevs, 2013
18. Compare PR-COM, 2014
19. Compare Priller/Pauker (2013)
20. http://de.statista.com/statistik/daten/studie/36716/umfrage/die-groessten-zeitschriften-nach-auflage/
21. Compare Priller/Pauker (2013), p. 72
22. Compare Priller/Pauker (2013)
23. http://www.fachzeitungen.de/seite/p/kat/katid/27
24. Interview with Johannes Endres, August 2014.
25. Interview with Dr. Alfons Schräder, October 2014.
26. http://de.statista.com/statistik/daten/studie/375894/umfrage/it-und-telekommunikationszeitschriften-mit-den-hoechsten-auflagen/
27. http://www.chip-media.de/chip-print/chip/titelportraet.html
28. Computer Bild Digital GmbH (2014): fact sheet. Accessed at http://www.axelspringer-mediapilot.de/artikel/computerbild.de-Aktuelles-computerbild.de_1131771.html.
29. Computer Bild Digital GmbH (2015): fact sheet. Accessed at http://www.axelspringer-mediapilot.de/portrait/COMPUTER-BILD-COMPUTER-BILD_670594.html.
30. http:// http://www.idg.de/portal/unternehmen/idg-deutschland-427
31. IDG (2013).
32. http://www.idg.de/portal/print/idg-zeitschriften-461
33. www.golem.de/sonstiges/leitbild.html.
34. www.golem.de/sonstiges/leitbild.html.
35. http://de.statista.com/statistik/daten/studie/36716/umfrage/die-groessten-zeitschriften-nach-auflage/
36. http://de.statista.com/statistik/daten/studie/375894/umfrage/it-und-telekommunikationszeitschriften-mit-den-hoechsten-auflagen/
37. http://www.chip.de/cxo/3017439/CHIP_Online_Mediadaten.pdf
38. http://www.iqm.de/medien/online/golemde/media/aktuelle-themen-32/
39. http://de.statista.com/statistik/daten/studie/156296/umfrage/auflagen-von-zeitschriften-im-segment-it-telekommunikation/

CASE 7

IVEY | Publishing

Illinois Tool Works: Retooling for Continued Growth and Profitability[1]

In June 2016, Illinois Tool Works (ITW) was at a critical juncture in its evolution. The company had identified a number of lofty goals in its 2015 annual report to be achieved by the end of 2017. ITW expected to reach above 200 basis points in organic growth above the market (assumed at 3 per cent), a 23 per cent operating margin, a 20 per cent after-tax return on invested capital, 100 per cent free cash flow as a percentage of net income, and 12 to 14 per cent shareholder returns.[2] At the beginning of the year, riding on a successful 2015, these targets had seemed eminently achievable, based on ITW's performance up to 2012 (see Exhibit 1) and more recent performance (see Exhibit 2). However, in 2016, the U.S. and world economies seemed to face a variety of challenges, including political uncertainty in the United States and Europe because of a presidential election and the United Kingdom's vote to exit from the European Union, as well as continued weaknesses in emerging markets and volatile currencies, among other factors.

Since taking over as chief executive officer (CEO) in 2012 after the untimely death of his predecessor David Speer, E. Scott Santi had implemented a number of divestments and consolidated the 800 small divisions he had inherited into 84 larger divisions, reducing the complexity of the company and improving its prospects for organic (rather than acquisitions-driven) growth, albeit with an accompanying reduction in revenues.[3] Results had been encouraging. However, Santi's strategy was dependent on achieving continued organic growth and undertaking bigger acquisitions, each posing its own set of challenges. Continued organic growth would depend on environmental developments, and ITW had already

Exhibit 1 Illinois Tool Works' Ten-Year Summary of Key Performance

	2012	2011	2010	2009	2008	2007	2006	2005	2004	2003
Operating revenues ($ million)	17,924	17,787	15,416	13,573	16,544	15,550	13,254	12,029	10,836	9,201
Operating income ($ million)	2,847	2,731	2,254	1,383	2,410	2,535	2,286	2,021	1,808	1,407
Operating income margin (%)	15.9	15.4	14.6	10.2	14.6	16.3	17.2	16.8	16.7	15.3
Net income ($ million)	2,870	2,071	1,503	973	1,519	1,870	1,718	1,495	1,339	1,024
Return on average invested capital (%)	15	16.8	14.6	10.6	15.4	17.4	17.5	16.9	15.9	12.9
Number of acquisitions	23	28	24	20	50	52	53	22	24	28
Cash paid for acquisitions ($ million)	723	1,308	497	281	1,547	813	1,379	627	588	204
Total debt ($ million)	5,048	3,990	2,868	3,075	3,682	2,299	1,418	1,211	1,125	976
Total-debt-to-total-capitalization ratio	32.3	28.5	23.1	26.1	32.4	19.7	13.6	13.8	12.8	11

Note: All currency amounts are in US$.

Source: ITW, "Differentiated Business Model Differentiated Performance: 2015 Annual Report," Illinois Tool Works, March 23, 2016, accessed November 29, 2016, http://investor.itw.com/~/media/Files/I/ITW-IR/documents/online-proxy-voting/2015-itw-annualreport.pdf.

Professor Nitin Pangarkar wrote this case solely to provide material for class discussion. The author does not intend to illustrate either effective or ineffective handling of a managerial situation. The author may have disguised certain names and other identifying information to protect confidentiality.

Exhibit 2 Illinois Tool Works' Recent Results (in US$ Millions)

	2015		2014		2013	
	Revenues	Operating Profits	Revenues	Operating Profits	Revenues	Operating Profits
Automotive	2,529	613	2,590	600	2,396	490
Test and measurement and electronics	1,969	322	2,204	340	2,176	321
Food equipment	2,096	498	2,177	453	2,047	385
Polymers and fluids	1,712	335	1,927	357	1,993	335
Welding	1,650	415	1,850	479	1,837	464
Construction products	1,587	316	1,707	289	1,717	238
Specialty products	1,885	439	2,055	440	2,007	408
Intersegment revenue	−23	−71	−26	−70	−38	−127
Total	13,405	2,867	14,484	2,888	14,135	2,514

Source: ITW, "Differentiated Business Model Differentiated Performance: 2015 Annual Report," Illinois Tool Works, March 23, 2016, accessed November 29, 2016, http://investor.itw.com/~/media/Files/I/ITW-IR/documents/online-proxy-voting/2015-itw-annualreport.pdf.

been adversely affected by the struggles of its customers in the oil and gas sectors. Large acquisitions, such as the US$470 million[4] purchase of Engineered Fasteners and Components in early 2016, also posed higher implementation risks, which would likely result in significant performance issues if the strategy failed to meet its goals.[5] Santi's strategy had yielded excellent results over the past few years, but there was considerable uncertainty about achieving future goals.

History

In 1912, Frank W. England, Paul B. Goddard, Oscar T. Hogg, and Carl G. Olson formed ITW, a company that manufactured and sold metal-cutting tools. Supported by Chicago financier Byron L. Smith, the company quickly expanded to include products such as truck transmissions and pumps, which were in demand because of America's involvement in World War I. Before the end of the decade, three other companies were formed—the DeVilbiss Company, the Hobart Brothers Company, and Signode—which would later become parts of ITW.

The company continued to develop new engineered products, as well as grow its portfolio of products through acquisitions. Its engineering excellence earned the company representation on the War Production Board in World War II. In 1940, Harold B. Smith, the company's CEO at the time, implemented the strategy of decentralization, which was still a key ITW organizational strategy in 2016.

Soon after its 50th anniversary, the company was listed on the New York Stock Exchange. During the 1960s, ITW further strengthened its position in the construction, industrial, and packaging markets, as well as expanding into international markets, which continued through the 1980s. Signode had by this time become a large multinational manufacturer of metal and plastic strapping, stretch film, industrial tape, application equipment, and related products. Its merger with ITW doubled the company's size. In 1996, Jim Farrell became chairman of ITW and refined the company's strategy towards numerous smaller acquisitions.[6]

The ITW Business Model

By its own accounts, the ITW business model was composed of three elements: the 80/20 management process, customer-back innovation, and a decentralized entrepreneurial culture.[7]

The 80/20 management process implied focusing on the most rewarding areas such as the most profitable customers. The simplicity of this principle enabled ITW to concentrate its efforts, resources, and investments on key customers and products that were best positioned for profitable organic growth.

One concrete example of implementation of the 80/20 principle was provided in the manufacturing of nails for wood-framed houses. ITW's analysis revealed that four types of nails accounted for 80 per cent of the volume and more than 20 other types of nails accounted for 20 per cent of the volume. To distinguish the products based on their salience, ITW started making the high-volume nails in different manufacturing cells from the other nails. Over time, ITW moved the high-volume nails to separate plants from the low-volume nails. Speer, the executive vice-president at the time, summarized the benefits of this approach as follows: "If you keep them together, you end up compromising on both. If you separate them, you optimize both."[8]

ITW's customer-back innovation placed an emphasis on solving customer problems. ITW had a strong intellectual property portfolio. Of its 16,000 granted and pending patents, 1,900 had been applied for in 2015 alone. ITW also took pride in applying technology expertise to solve customers' problems. For example, after realizing that smaller, fuel-efficient automobile engines generated higher levels of noise and vibration, ITW developed the WaveShear Isolation Springs to dampen noise and vibration.[9]

Another example of customer-back innovation, the "click and collect food equipment" initiative, offered customers who ordered perishable groceries online temperature-controlled lockers placed at strategic locations (proximate to customers) with the convenience of a flexible pick-up service, rather than having to wait for delivery.[10]

ITW promoted a decentralized-entrepreneurial culture. The company believed that its employees understood its business model, strategy, and core values, which allowed ITW to empower its business teams to make decisions and customize their approach to specific customers and end markets. In other words, ITW employees thought and acted like entrepreneurs and delivered results.

Products

ITW competed in seven broad product areas: automotive original equipment manufacturer,[11] food equipment, test measurement and electronics, welding equipment, power and fluids, construction products, and specialty products (see Exhibit 3). In 2015, each of the seven product groups accounted for revenue ranging from US$1.6 billion to US$2.5 billion across various geographical areas (see Exhibit 4).

Exhibit 3 Illinois Tool Works' Product Portfolio

Automotive OEM	Under this vertical, ITW designed and manufactured fasteners, interior and exterior components, and powertrain and braking systems for OEMs and their top-tier suppliers.
Food equipment	Under this vertical, ITW offered products in ware wash, cooking, refrigeration, and integrated services to institutional, industrial, restaurant, and retail customers around the world.
Test measurement and electronics	ITW's test and measurement business provided specialized test and measurement products to a diverse set of customers operating in highly regulated, demanding environments. ITW's electronics business provided manufacturing and maintenance, repair, and operations solutions that served the semiconductor, industrial, life sciences, and automotive industries, among others.
Welding equipment	This ITW division offered value-added equipment and specialty consumables for a variety of industrial and infrastructure applications.
Power and fluids	Under this vertical, ITW offered specialized adhesives, lubricants, and additives for global wind energy, automotive aftermarket, aerospace, construction, industrial, and automotive customers.
Construction products	ITW's construction products group was a supplier of engineered fastening systems and related consumables and software. These products were uniquely specified for a variety of materials, including wood, concrete, steel, and engineered lumber for the residential, commercial, and renovation markets.
Specialty products	ITW's specialty products segment was composed of diverse businesses who met the needs of large customers with specific solution requirements. Specialty products businesses included consumer packaging products such as zippers on re-sealable bags and multi-packaging carriers (six-pack rings); software and equipment for warehouse automation; single-use products for the medical industry; aircraft ground support equipment; and, coating and metalizing businesses for the branding and security markets.

Note: OEM = original equipment manufacturer.

Source: ITW, "Differentiated Business Model Differentiated Performance: 2015 Annual Report," Illinois Tool Works, March 23, 2016, accessed November 29, 2016, http://investor.itw.com/~/media/Files/I/ITW-IR/documents/online-proxy-voting/2015-itw-annualreport.pdf.

Exhibit 4 Illinois Tool Works' Portfolio and Performance

	2015 Total Revenues by Geography	2015 Operating Margin (%)	Patent Portfolio (Granted and Pending)	Key Brands	Remarks
Automotive	US$2.5 billion North America: 47% EMEA: 34% APAC: 19%	24.2	2,755	Deltar, ITW Shakeproof ITW Drawform	Organic revenue CAGR of 8% since 2012
Test measurement and electronics	US$2.0 billion North America: 42% EMEA: 28% APAC: 30%	16.3	1,753	*Test and measurement:* Buehler, Instron, Brooks Instrument, Avery Weigh-Tronix, Wilson *Electronics:* Kester, Vitronics Soltec, Speedline, SIMCO-ION, Despatch Industries, Texwipe, Stockvis Tapes, Loma Systems, Magnaflux	Revenue CAGR of 14% since 2005
Food equipment	US$2.1 billion North America: 55% EMEA: 36% APAC: 9%	23.7	1,178	Baxter, Foster, Hobart, Stero, Traulsen, Vesta, Vulcan, Bonnet, MBM, Elro	Operating margin improvement of 660 basis points since 2012
Polymers and fluids	US$1.7 billion North America: 55% EMEA: 23% APAC: 22%	19.6	602	Black Magic, DensitD, Devcon, ITW Wind Group, Permatex, Plexus rainx, Wynn's	Operating margin improvement of 380 basis points since 2012
Welding	US$1.6 billion North America: 76% EMEA: 11% APAC: 13%	25.2	3,012	Miller, Hobart, Tregaskiss, Bernard	Revenue CAGR of 8% since 1993
Construction products	US$1.6 billion North America: 41% EMEA: 30% APAC: 29%	19.9	3,325	Alpine, ITW Buildex, Paslode, Ramset, Red Head, Spit, Reid	Operating margin improvement of 830 basis points since 2012
Specialty products	US$1.9 billion North America: 58% EMEA: 27% APAC: 15%	23.3	3,927	Filtertek, Hartness, Hi-Cone, Meurer, Zip-Pak	Operating margin improvement of 380 basis points since 2012

Note: EMEA = Europe, the Middle East, and Africa; APAC = Asia Pacific; CAGR = compound annual growth rate

Source: "Business Segments," Illinois Tool Works, accessed on June 22, 2016, www.itw.com/business-segments/; ITW, "Differentiated Business Model Differentiated Performance: 2015 Annual Report," Illinois Tool Works, March 23, 2016, accessed November 29, 2016, http://investor.itw.com/~/media/Files/I/ITW-IR/documents/online-proxy-voting/2015-itw-annualreport.pdf.

Decentralization[12]

Decentralization had been a key pillar of ITW's strategy since 1940. Until 2012, when Santi took over as CEO, the company practiced an extreme form of decentralization by acquiring small companies in most cases, and at other times, creating hundreds of small units from bigger companies that had either grown internally or had been acquired (e.g., Signode). Jim Farrell, an ITW CEO who had accelerated the implementation of the decentralization strategy, explained its advantage: "We're competitive in the marketplace. So run your consolidated model. It seems to me my costs are lower than yours with my decentralized model."[13] ITW's acquisitions followed by the implementation of a decentralization strategy were referred to by *Forbes* magazine as a form of "conquer and divide."[14] The extreme practice of decentralization was also pursued with vigour under Farrell's successor Speer, who once aimed to have 1,000 small divisions under the ITW umbrella.

Under the extreme decentralization strategy, ITW would typically consider splitting a business unit when the revenues reached the $50 million range. The resulting small size of the divisions would reduce the possibility of achieving economies of scale, but ITW found that it would enable the small divisions to be more focused and competitive. ITW's former vice-chairman Frank Ptak explained the concept as follows:

We love competing against a big company, because their management teams don't have the same feel that our people have. It's not that we're smarter. It's that our people are only concentrating on one small part of the market. They are like entrepreneurs—it's not an exaggeration. The basic advantage is you have people down in the trenches who really understand the business because they are specifically dedicated to it.[15]

Extreme decentralization had another important ramification. It enhanced career opportunities for ITW's employees, and high-performing employees could have the opportunity to be in charge of a business at a young age. In fact, ITW pitched these entrepreneurial opportunities to attract high-quality employees.

Believing in the benefits from the decentralized strategy, ITW consciously deemphasized synergies. Its headquarters hosted only tax, audit, and associated financial functions; investor relations; a skeleton human resource department staff; and a research and development group that supported the individual businesses with application development.[16] This strategy allowed each senior executive at the headquarters to handle multiple businesses. For example, in 2007, 50 executives at the headquarters level were in charge of 750 units in the United States and in 48 foreign countries.[17]

The corporate management didn't specify financial targets for divisions, preferring to have targets percolate from the bottom up. The top management, however, required each division to continuously show improvement, especially in terms of margins. As Farrell once stated, "We expect all of our businesses to move up their margins each year, whether they are a 5 per cent- or a 35 per cent-margin business. Incentive compensation strongly reinforces the earnings emphasis, with 50 per cent of bonus opportunity directly tied to them."[18]

The dramatic performance enhancement from the extreme decentralization strategy was evident, especially in terms of growth. Between 1965 and 1972, as a part of ITW's Fastex division, ITW's Deltar business grew to achieve sales of $2 million (see Exhibit 5). After separation from Fastex in 1972, Deltar grew rapidly and was divided many times. Whenever opportunities arose, it also added new divisions, especially between 1995 and 1999, when its insert-moulded business grew revenues from $40 million to $135 million by adding five divisions. By 1999, the original Deltar business had been divided into 26 different units and had revenues of $300 million.[19]

Exhibit 5 An illustration of Illinois Tool Works' Decentralization Strategy

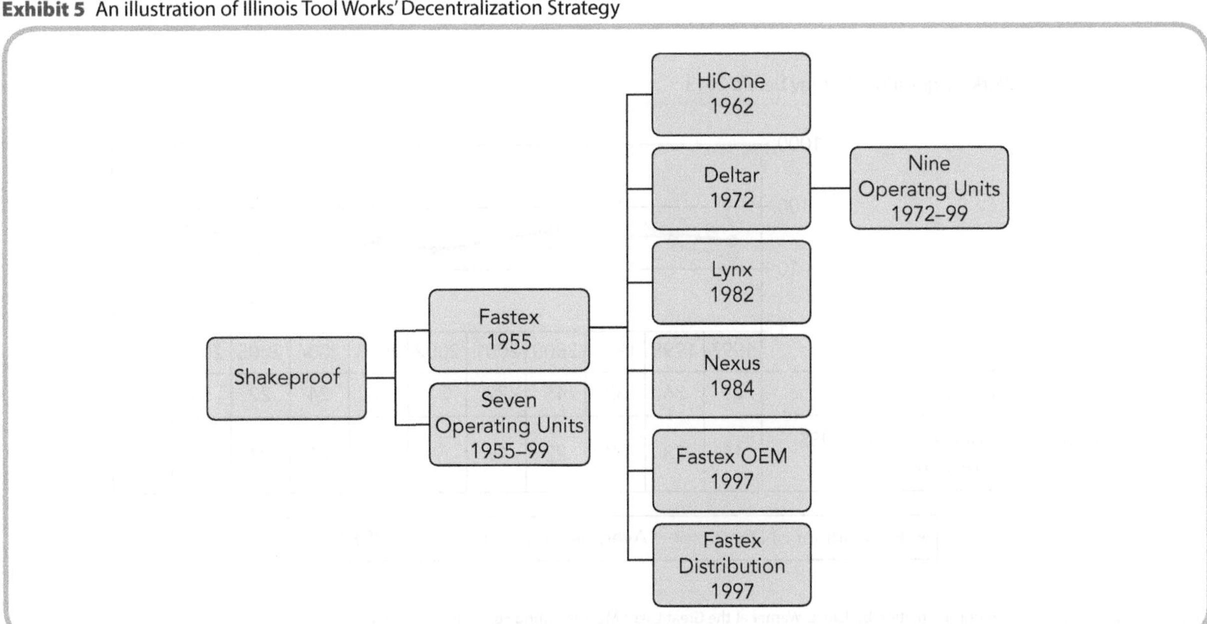

Source: Company files. PowerPoint presentation by Jane L. Warner at the Great Lakes Manufacturing Forum in June 2008.

Acquisitions

ITW had always undertaken acquisitions. However, under CEOs Farrell and Speer, ITW implemented a strategy of undertaking up to 30–50 acquisitions per year, in some years. ITW typically focused on targets valued under $100 million that were available at less than 1.1 times the book value (see Exhibits 1 and 6).[20] Speaking about ITW's preference for small acquisitions over large acquisitions, former CFO Jon Kinney once said, "When you acquire just one large business, all the assumptions you made about it and what ITW can do with it had better be correct. You're putting all your eggs in one basket."[21] In rare cases, ITW made large acquisitions and divided the large acquired company into many small pieces, as in the case of Signode, which was acquired for $800 million in 1986 and then divided into 50 companies.[22]

ITW's acquisitions strategy was based on a number of rules of thumb. It sought targets that filled gaps in its capabilities, such as complementary product expertise or relationships with important customers. The acquisitions were also typically initiated by middle managers, rather than flowing down from the top, which ensured that implementation issues would be taken into account before the acquisition, instead of afterwards. Recognizing that a typical middle manager would likely lack the necessary skills to find or undertake acquisitions, former CEO Speer implemented two-day acquisition workshops for business unit managers.[23] ITW also tried to minimize the negative impact on the morale of target employees post-acquisition by retaining the identity of the target company. It would only stipulate that target companies attempt to integrate at a broad level (e.g., by using a company-wide accounting package), and seek simplicity and operational excellence through deploying the 80/20 principle. Finally, ITW was careful not to use acquisitions for novel situations, such as entering new countries. It developed its own knowledge-base about a country by establishing owned-operations before embarking on acquisitions. In 2005, out of ITW's 21 businesses in China, only one had been through an acquisition, and that one was converted from a joint venture. At the same time, only two of its 11 businesses in India had started out as joint ventures and were subsequently converted into wholly-owned subsidiaries.[24]

In general, the acquired companies' employees and management seemed to appreciate the benefits of ITW's approach. For example, in 2005, ITW acquired Permatex; the next year, Permatex's marketing director Tony Battaglia commented on the acquisition:

They are very decentralized though, so we operate independently. However, ITW does train all of its companies to operate efficiently by using 80/20 simplification processes. That has helped us to focus better on customers and products. Financially, it has allowed us to step up our market research, category management, and website investments. . . . Permatex is an ideal platform to bring on additional aftermarket acquisitions in the future.[25]

Exhibit 6 Illinois Tool Works' acquisition strategy before 2013

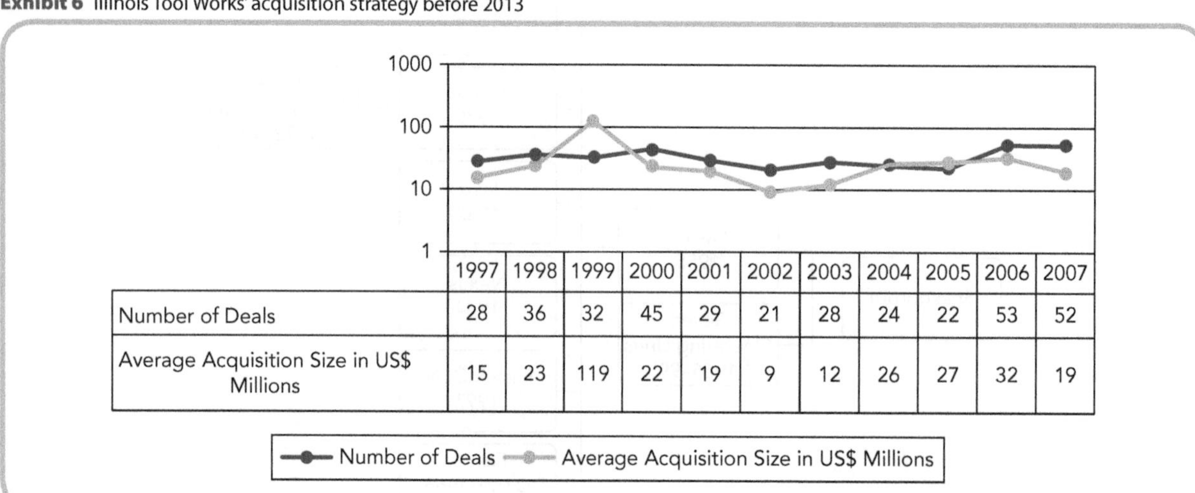

	1997	1998	1999	2000	2001	2002	2003	2004	2005	2006	2007
Number of Deals	28	36	32	45	29	21	28	24	22	53	52
Average Acquisition Size in US$ Millions	15	23	119	22	19	9	12	26	27	32	19

Source: Company files. PowerPoint presentation by Jane L. Warner at the Great Lakes Manufacturing Forum in June 2008.

ITW's Acquisition of Precor: An Illustration of Its Acquisition Strategy and Approach to Operational Excellence

ITW's acquisition of Precor served as an excellent example of the transformation it brought about in acquired companies. Since its inception in 1983, Precor had gained a reputation as an innovative and leading manufacturer of exercise equipment in the United States and internationally. Despite its innovation and market-leading revenues, Precor exhibited poor performance with regard to a variety of metrics at the time of its acquisition by ITW. Its on-time shipments stood at a dismal 42 per cent. It had a rather unwieldy supply chain, consisting of as many as 3,000 suppliers, with most suppliers accounting for small volumes, and its employee turnover was high.

ITW implemented a number of its usual policies at Precor: the 80/20 rule, product line simplification, rationalization of manufacturing plants and suppliers, and workflow simplification. Within three years, the new strategy had produced spectacular results. The percentage of on-time deliveries improved from 42 to 91, headcount was reduced from 952 to 456, and the number of plants was reduced from seven to five without negatively affecting production. Inventory levels went down by 40 per cent and warranty claims by 57 per cent, resulting in savings of millions of dollars. After bringing about a dramatic improvement in Precor's financial results, ITW sold Precor in 2002 for €180 million[26] to Amer Sports, based in Helsinki, Finland.[27]

Organization and Human Resources Policies

ITW implemented a number of organizational and human resources policies that were aligned with its broader enterprise-level strategy, as well as other functional-level policies.

Throughout its history, ITW had emphasized continuity and stability in terms of its leadership. When Santi assumed the role of CEO, he was only the sixth CEO in the company's 100-year history, implying an average tenure of more than a decade. Many of the CEOs had also previously worked in ITW for a long time, and thus were steeped in the ITW culture and tradition. For example, Santi had spent his entire working career at ITW. Since 1995, ITW had also adopted a tradition that each incoming CEO be presented with a crystal frog wearing a golden crown and bearing the name of prior CEOs, signalling to the incoming CEO that the counsel of previous CEOs was always available.

ITW's culture was informal and relationship-driven, as described by Santi: "It's a lot of conversations. It's not a lot of memos. It's not a lot of PowerPoints, but it's a lot of belly-to-belly conversations and creating that alignment, engagement, and enthusiasm that turns this culture loose."[28] Echoing similar thoughts, former CEO Farrell had once said:

> *I want to see your eyes; I want to see if you're getting it. If you're not, I haven't communicated very well. And I clearly can't do that via e-mail. In our organization, we rely so much on trusting our people to do the right things that trying to talk to them electronically would diminish that personal communication and compromise our business success.*[29]

Many other executives described ITW's culture as highly egalitarian and down-to-earth. ITW's headquarters were described by an article in the *Crain's Chicago Business* as "a cluster of nondescript low-rise buildings, [where] there is no executive cafeteria and the only reserved parking spaces are for the food and mail trucks." Former ITW vice-chairman Ptak once remarked: "You realized that there was a part of business and a part of making money that wasn't so draconian. That you could be nice."[30]

Retooling ITW's Strategy

In January 2012, ITW reached an agreement with activist investor Relational Investors (Relational), which had acquired a small stake in ITW. According to the agreement, Relational's principal and co-founder David Batchelder would join the ITW board of directors.[31] Relational had suggested a strategy makeover for ITW consisting of centralizing its operations and divestment of a number of its small divisions. Many analysts agreed with Relational's suggestions primarily because ITW's strategy of small acquisitions and extreme decentralization had resulted in lagging returns versus peers since the onset of the global recession in 2007.[32] After assuming the role of CEO in November 2012, Santi moved quickly to implement a new strategy based on divestment of small divisions that sold commoditized products, or that were likely to grow slowly.

Taking Stock in 2016

By the end of 2015, ITW had made considerable progress in implementing its new strategy (see Exhibit 7).

Exhibit 7 Results Obtained from Implementation of Strategic Realignment

Performance metric	2012	2015	Remarks
Operating margin	15.9%	21.4%	Improvement of 550 basis points
After-tax ROIC	14.5%	20.4%	Improvement of 590 basis points
Earnings per share	3.21	5.13	CAGR of 17%

Note: ROIC = return on invested capital; CAGR = compound annual growth rate.

Source: ITW, "Differentiated Business Model Differentiated Performance: 2015 Annual Report," Illinois Tool Works, March 23, 2016, accessed November 29, 2016, http://investor.itw.com/~/media/Files/I/ITW-IR/documents/online-proxy-voting/2015-itw-annualreport.pdf.

Its 2015 annual report noted progress in terms of the following aspects:

- **Portfolio aligned with organic growth focus:** After more than 30 divestitures undertaken since the beginning of 2013, ITW's portfolio spread over seven core areas was balanced across end markets and geographies, highly profitable, and resilient to economic shocks.
- **Scaling up of operating structure:** This initiative, carried out since early 2013, had reduced (more accurately, reduced and consolidated) the number of ITW divisions from more than 800 to 84. The new ITW was simpler (smaller number of divisions) and more focused.
- **Ready to grow:** In 2015, 60 per cent of ITW's businesses achieved ready-to-grow status and 45 per cent grew organic revenue at an average of 6 per cent, despite a challenging external economic environment. The company expected to have 85 per cent or more of businesses in ready-to-grow status by the end of 2016.

The Road Ahead

While ITW and Santi had much to be proud of with regard to a long history of accomplishments and recent success in reorienting its strategy, respectively, many challenges remained.

Santi's and ITW's biggest challenge was related to achieving continued growth after abandoning its strategies of numerous small acquisitions and extreme decentralization. The challenge came in two forms. First, ITW would have to generate a good portion of its future growth in revenues and profits organically rather than through acquisitions. Although the portfolio had been streamlined over the past three years, a period over which investors had tolerated negative revenue growth, and it had resulted in better margins, future organic growth seemed critical. This was especially important because it would be difficult to continuously improve margins through cost cutting and operational improvements. Secondly, ITW had changed its acquisition strategy from numerous small acquisitions to "needle-moving" large acquisitions. Targets in larger acquisitions were less likely to be under the radar of other potential acquirers, and hence, less likely to be undervalued. Unlike small companies, which ITW had historically acquired, the opportunities to implement operations improvements strategies were also likely to be limited for larger targets because many companies in the latter category would already have efficient operations in place.

Going forward, ITW also had to make important choices about resource allocation across product groups, based on their past performance and future prospects. In summary, Santi and ITW had to make appropriate decisions for continued superior performance.

NOTES

1. This case has been written on the basis of published sources only. Consequently, the interpretation and perspectives presented in the case are not necessarily those of Illinois Tool Works or any of its employees.
2. ITW, "Differentiated Business Model Differentiated Performance: 2015 Annual Report," Illinois Tool Works, March 23, 2016, accessed November 29, 2016, http://investor.itw.com/~/media/Files/I/ITW-IR/documents/online-proxy-voting/2015-itw-annualreport.pdf.
3. Joe Cahill, "How CEO Santi Is Changing ITW," PN: Crain's Chicago Business, April 23, 2014, www.plasticsnews.com/article/20140423/NEWS/140429947/how-ceo-santi-is-changing-itw.
4. All currency amounts are in US$ unless otherwise specified.
5. "ITW to Acquire ZF EF&C," Fastener + Fixing Magazine, January 28, 2016, accessed on November 3, 2016, www.fastenerandfixing.com/news/itw-to-acquire-zf-ef-c.
6. Information on the historical development of ITW is taken from "About ITW: Our History," Illinois Tool Works, accessed

November 3, 2016, www.itw.com/about-itw/our-history.
7. Information in this section is taken from "About ITW: How We Work," Illinois Tool Works, accessed November 3, 2016, www.itw.com/about-itw/how-we-work/; ITW, "Differentiated Business Model," op. cit.
8. Tim Stevens, "Breaking up Is Profitable to Do: A Paragon of Decentralization, Illinois Tool Works Turns a Raft of Small Business Units into Big Dollars at the Bottom Line," *Industry Week*, December 21, 2004, accessed November 3, 2016, www.industryweek.com/companies-amp-executives/breaking-profitable-do.
9. ITW, "Differentiated Business Model," op. cit.
10. Ibid.
11. Original equipment manufacturer means that ITW's products would not be incorporated into other manufacturers' products before being sold to the end user.
12. The discussion in this section draws from Nitin Pangarkar, *High Performance Companies: Successful Strategies from the World's Top Achievers* (Singapore: John Wiley & Sons (Asia) Pte. Ltd., 2012).
13. Patricia O'Connell, "The Rules of James Farrell's Game: Illinois Tool Works' CEO Explains How He Has Handled More Than 200 Acquisitions since 1995. In His Case, Unorthodox Methods Pay Dividends," Bloomberg, August 6, 2001, accessed October 14, 2016, www.bloomberg.com/news/articles/2001-08-05/the-rules-of-james-farrells-game.
14. Mark Tatge "Conquer and Divide," *Forbes*, April 16, 2001, accessed October 14, 2016, www.forbes.com/forbes/2001/0416/080.html.
15. Stevens, op. cit.
16. Ibid.
17. Christopher C. Williams, "The Sharpest Tool in the Shed: Illinois Tool Works Will Weather Downturns in Housing and Autos and Continue to Build upon Worldwide Economic Growth," *Barron's: U.S. Edition*, July 9, 2007, accessed November 29, 2016, www.barrons.com/articles/SB118377500631659893.
18. Stevens, op. cit.
19. The nine operating units noted in Jane L. Warner's presentation at the Great Lakes Manufacturing Forum in June 2008 were broken up further into more units; Stevens, op. cit.
20. Ilan Brat, "Turning Managers into Takeover Artists: How Conglomerate ITW Mints New Deal Makers to Fuel its Expansion," *The Wall Street Journal*, April 6, 2007, accessed November 29, 2016, www.wsj.com/articles/SB117582097241361698.
21. Stevens, op. cit.
22. Ibid.
23. Brat, op. cit.
24. "ITW's Formula for Innovation," Bloomberg, October 19, 2005, accessed November 29, 2016, www.bloomberg.com/bw/stories/2005-10-18/itws-formula-for-innovation.
25. aftermarketNews Staff, "Executive Interview with Tony Battaglia, Director of Marketing for Permatex," AMN: aftermarketNews, October 16, 2006, accessed October 14, 2016, www.aftermarketnews.com/executive-interview-with-tony-battaglia-director-of-marketing-for-permatex/.
26. € = European euro; US$1 = €0.90 on June 1, 2016.
27. Drew Desilver, "Fitness Company Bulks up: After Landing a Couple of Key Acquisitions, Woodinville-based Precor is Setting its Sights on Further Integrating Electronics and Entertainment with Exercise," *The Seattle Times*, March 9, 2006, accessed on October 14, 2016, http://connect.precor.com/pdf/fit_bulk_ENGLISH.pdf.
28. Meribah Knight, "The Tool Man Planning a Makeover of Century-old ITW," Crain's Chicago Business, March 23, 2013, accessed October 14, 2016, www.chicagobusiness.com/article/20130323/ISSUE01/303239975/the-tool-man-planning-a-makeover-for-century-old-itw.
29. Stevens, op. cit.
30. Meribah Knight, op. cit.
31. Bob Tita, "Illinois Tool Works Reaches Agreement with Activist Shareholder," *The Wall Street Journal*, blog, January 13, 2012, accessed October 14, 2016, http://blogs.wsj.com/deals/2012/01/13/illinois-tool-works-reaches-agreement-with-activist-shareholder/.
32. Kate MacArthur, "Activist Investor Puts ITW on Notice to Overhaul Business Strategy," Crain's Chicago Business, January 21, 2012, accessed June 23, 2016, www.chicagobusiness.com/article/20120121/ISSUE01/301219975/activist-investor-puts-itw-on-notice-to-overhaul-business-strategy.

CASE 8

UltraRope: Crafting a Go-to-market Strategy for Kone's Innovative 'UltraRope' Hoisting Cable

Developing new and useful elevator concepts for our customers is a significant task here. We aim to keep our elevators one step above the competition, all year.

- Petteri Valjus, Senior Expert, Hoisting Mechanics, Technology, Kone, Finland

"The best products don't always win," said Petteri Valjus—a senior technology expert at Kone Corporation, one of the global leaders in the elevator and escalator industry. "It takes more than that, and that's why the UltraRope is a winner." Valjus was musing over a few go-to-market strategies with his colleague, Raimo Pelto-Huikko, at the company headquarters in Espoo, Finland, and although it was a cold dark day in December 2014, the mood inside was optimistic.

The UltraRope was a technological breakthrough announced by Kone in June 2013. It was a new hoisting cable made of carbon fibre that doubled elevator travel distances to heights of more than a kilometre and weighed 90% less than conventional steel ropes. "It also has an exceptionally long lifespan, twice that of steel rope," said Pelto-Huikko, Kone's design specialist and UltraRope patent holder with the honorific nickname, *Mr. Carbon Fibre.*

With a small budget, Pelto-Huikko initiated the research phase in 2004. The project gained speed, and by 2006 Valjus was brought on for his expertise in hoisting mechanics. In 2010 the UltraRope prototype began rigorous testing at Kone's Tytyri facility in Finland, the world's deepest elevator testing site, descending 300 metres underground, where it underwent a punishing stress regiment. Shortly after the UltraRope launch, Kone won the elevator contract for the kilometre-high Kingdom Tower in Jeddah, Saudi Arabia, expected to be completed by 2018.

Valjus and Pelto-Huikko saw extraordinary potential for the premium priced UltraRope. The global elevator equipment market was anticipated to grow 6% annually through 2017.[1] Most of this growth was concentrated in Asia Pacific. Demand from China, which accounted for half of sales generated, was decreasing. Any slack could potentially be offset by strong growth projected in high-income areas of Brazil, India and the Middle East. There were even opportunities in the more mature markets of North America, Europe and Japan.

Installation was just one aspect of equipment demand. Modernisation of older elevator systems was another major driver, and elevator servicing, such as inspection, maintenance, upkeep and part replacement was yet another dimension. Kone operated along all points of the lifecycle.

By October 2014, Kone had completed its first UltraRope contract where it upgraded the Kone elevator systems at the iconic Marina Bay Sands in Singapore. But high profile contracts like those in Saudi Arabia and Singapore were only a first step; Valjus and Pelto-Huikko had grander aspirations. What would it take for Kone to succeed in driving UltraRope adoption and drive greater market penetration of Kone products and services worldwide?

The Elevator Industry

Vertical transportation, as it is known in the industry, was delineated along three axes: installation, maintenance and modernisation. In the 1960s, US firms dominated the global elevator industry, but by the 1990s the sector took on greater multinational characteristics. The industry was dominated by four firms that controlled 65% of the global elevator and escalator market: Otis, part of America's United Technologies (often considered a pioneer in the industry), Kone of Finland; ThyssenKrupp of Germany and Schindler of Switzerland.[2] These brands were closely followed by their Japanese counterparts Fujitec Elevator Company, Mitsubishi Elevator Company, Toshiba, Hitachi, and Hyundai of Korea for the remaining market.

This case was written by Professor Kirsti Lindberg-Repo, Dr Saumya Sindhwani and Christopher Dula at the Singapore Management University. The case was prepared solely to provide material for class discussion. The authors do not intend to illustrate either effective or ineffective handling of a managerial situation. The authors may have disguised certain names and other identifying information to protect confidentiality.

Otis was the largest of these companies, but had lost market share between 2010 and 2013. Its decline was mostly due to being underpriced by competitors with cheaper manufacturing costs, and by small local maintenance companies with closer proximity to clients offering cheaper rates. Not wanting to compete on cost, Otis decided to start focusing more on high-end premium products and services, with special emphasis given to maintenance response times. In this regard, some companies were actively exploring sensor technologies along with the 'Internet of Things' to bring maintenance into the 21st century.

Installation

Most elevators systems on the market consisted of pre-engineered elevators. Such systems had a standardised layout and were designed to use mass produced stock components and fit within standard shaft dimensions of most buildings. Pre-engineered elevator systems were quicker and easier to install than custom-made systems. Economies of scale in production meant that cost savings could be passed on to customers, with maintenance costs being cheaper due to the standardisation of the product.

Custom-designed elevators were considerably more expensive and were developed for buildings with special needs, such as hospitals, industrial complexes and ultra-high-rise buildings. However, all building projects were unique—and each building had to be evaluated on an individual basis to determine what kind of elevator system was most suitable for that building's needs.

Large elevator manufacturers and third party experts consulted building owners and developers on identifying what systems were most suitable. Factors like tenant profiles, height, local regulations and building code all came under consideration. For example, a single tenant office building would have very different needs compared to a mixed-use residential and commercial building. Elevator speed, maintenance elevators, express elevators, sky lobbies, relay logic controllers, comfort and safety features were just a few options that had to be decided on. Valjus said,

The equipment used matters a lot. Rope weight, for instance, makes up 65% to 70% of an elevator's moving mass. The payload is less than 10%.

Maintenance

The industry experienced high margins and the vast majority of these margins came from maintenance services. After all, people detested getting stuck in lifts, and so customers would pay US$2,000 to US$5,000 a year to keep each machine running smoothly.[3] These margins were between 25% and 35%, compared with 10% for new equipment.[4]

Revenue from maintenance was far more stable than that from installations. For example, in 2013, 11 million machines were in operation globally, and many needed little more than a cursory check every few months.[5] This provided an easy yet lucrative market for maintenance services. Installations, however, were more subject to the whim of macroeconomic fluctuations. In fact, Kone and its peers made more than half their profits from services that were often secured by maintenance contracts at the time of installation. This created high barriers to entry as a newcomer would need to establish a strong network of technicians prior to commencing operations. However, price competition on the part of incumbents was negligible.

Thousands of small independent companies made up a substantial segment of the industry, involved in maintenance services. Maintenance service companies were often founded by former employees of the leading elevator manufacturing companies who were attracted by the stable demand and high profitability of maintenance contracts. However, the industry was experiencing greater consolidation as larger manufacturing companies like Kone bought out more and more of the smaller maintenance companies throughout the 2000s. Newer sophisticated elevator control systems also relied on proprietary maintenance devices. By 2010, 60% to 80% of contracts for newly installed elevators were awarded to large manufacturing companies.

Maintenance contracts were highly variable, ranging anywhere from full service maintenance, monitoring and upkeep, to individual parts servicing, to just periodic inspection and lubrication. Strict safety regulation and insurance policies required building owners to have some kind of maintenance contract and/or regime in place. Moreover, building owners were ultimately held responsible for user safety; liability was not typically transferred by maintenance contracts. For this reason, it was important that building owners and developers carefully evaluate manufacturing and maintenance companies as reputation was important.

Modernisation

Most buildings had a usable lifespan of at least 60 years. Elevator systems could easily last upwards of 30 years, even 50 years, if properly maintained. Yet most systems were upgraded every 10-15 years. Upgrades could be relatively simple, such as changing the interior look of the elevator cab and replacing aging parts, to something more drastic, like replacing the entire system. A complete modernisation overhaul was more labour intensive than an installation for a new building. Kone's biggest contract to date was the Washington D.C. metro modernisation project.

There were several reasons for modernising. One was the changing environmental regulations around the world, which called for greater energy efficiency and created demand for more efficient elevator drive systems. Also, improvements in technology, such as better automation, could lower maintenance costs and optimise elevator dispatch. For example, as buildings aged, servicing costs became more important in terms of a building's operational expenses. Additionally, renovation work and changing tenant profiles could place different kinds of demands on a building's vertical transportation. The elevator experience was considered to be one of the biggest determinants of tenant satisfaction; and even something as simple as remodelling the [elevator] cab interior could go a long way towards changing perceptions and improving a building's reputation.

Trends

An estimated 70 million people in the world—more than twice the entire population of Australia—moved into cities every year.[6] This, among other factors, caused global demand for new elevators to increase exponentially, from 300,000 units a decade ago to nearly 700,000 in 2013. China, where two thirds of new elevator units were installed, accounted for much of this rise.[7]

Kone was cautious about the company's position in China. Schindler, for example, was relocating manufacturing capabilities to China and hiring locals for top management, which would help save on costs and improve business relationships. It was also bringing new factories on line in India. After China, Schindler planned to target Mongolia, Kazakhstan, the Baltic states bordering Russia and Africa. The company was hoping that within the next few years, it would overtake Kone as the second largest elevator equipment company in the world.

The key megatrends impacting the growth of the elevator industry included:

- Urbanisation, which was the single most important megatrend impacting the global elevator and escalator industry, and was expected to drive demand for years to come. The concentration of people in urban areas increased the importance of having smooth and efficient means of moving people from one place to another, or at least up and down.
- An aging population that created major changes in the global demographic structure. The growing number of elderly individuals had increased the importance of accessibility in buildings and urban infrastructure.
- Safety was an important concern worldwide, and national and international safety codes and standards played a key role in determining upgrades and modernisation of elevators and escalators.
- The environment was also a major concern, especially since buildings accounted for approximately 32 per cent of total final energy consumption in 2013.[8] Elevators and escalators could account for 2-10 percent of the energy consumption of an individual building.

Kone

Kone Corporation was a global provider of elevator and escalator equipment as well as a provider of maintenance and modernisation solutions. Headquartered in Espoo, Finland, the company employed over 47,000 people with operations in the Americas, Europe, the Middle East and Africa (EMEA) and Asia Pacific as of 2014 (refer to **Exhibit 1** for Kone's Life Cycle Services).

Exhibit 1 Life Cycle Services

KONE supports its customers every step of the way, for the lifespan of their building: from planning and design through installation and maintenance to modernization

- *Expert design and planning services: KONE supports customers throughout the planning phase to ensure the proposed People Flow® solutions deliver maximum benefit.*
- *Efficient and safe installation services: KONE's proven, cost effective installation processes follow strict quality and safety guidelines. They are designed to ensure all equipment meets and even exceeds customer expectations.*
- *Professional maintenance services: KONE offers a wide range of maintenance and monitoring solutions that maximise safety and reliability while minimising downtime and costs. These include smart preventive services, expert advice and rapid response.*
- *Comprehensive modernisation services: KONE's flexible modernisation offering gives customers full control over the upgrade of their elevators, escalators, auto walks and automated building doors. KONE's modernisation services help customers determine when and how to upgrade equipment to ensure a lifetime of optimal operation and to maximize customers' return on investment.*

Source: Kone, reprinted with permission

Exhibit 2 Kone Milestones

1987:	V3F frequency converter launched, improving energy efficiency of KONE hoisting machines.
1991:	KONE became the first company to utilise regenerative drives in its elevators.
1993:	The energy-efficient planetary gear for escalators is introduced.
1996:	The first machine-room-less elevator, KONE MonoSpace®, was launched, providing up to 70% energy savings compared to conventional technology.
2004:	The KONE EcoMod™ solution was launched, enabling modernisation of escalators without removing the truss, saving construction time and materials.
2005:	KONE MonoSpace was the first elevator to include LED lighting as a standard feature.
2006:	KONE unveiled the solar-powered elevator concept.
2007:	The KONE Innotrack™ autowalk was launched—the first autowalk to feature an energy-efficient gearless drive.
2009:	High-performance regenerative drives for the full range of KONE elevators launched.
2009:	New efficient gear outside step band drive launched for KONE escalators and autowalks.
2009:	KONE MiniSpace™ elevator awarded A-class energy certification (VDI standard 4707).
2010:	Kone energy-efficient sliding door solution launched.
2010:	The KONE MonoSpace elevator received an A-class energy certification based on the VDI guideline in measurements performed by the independent parties.
2011:	KONE's elevators in five net-zero energy buildings in Europe and in North America
2011:	KONE MonoSpace® 700 and KONE Double Deck received an A-class energy certification
2012:	KONE launched completely renewed and more energy efficient KONE EcoDisc® hoisting machine for the KONE elevators.

Source: Kone, Company Website, "About Us", Key milestones, http://marine.kone.com/about-us/environment/solutions/key-milestones/, accessed April 2015.

Founded in 1910 as a small electrical repair shop, the company would eventually boast a long history of innovation, strategic acquisitions and commercial success (refer to **Exhibit 2** for key milestones).

In 1918, Kone began manufacturing and installing its own elevators, and in 1957 expanded internationally into Sweden. For the next forty years the company experienced significant organic growth through global sales in products and services. From 2000 to 2015, Kone engaged in aggressive acquisition-based expansion, and by the end of fiscal year 2013, the company had recorded more than US$1.2 billion in operating profit (refer to **Exhibit 3 & 4** for key financial statements and Kone's locations).

The development of Kone's experience in high-rise buildings began in the mid-1970s when it bought the European subsidiaries of American Westinghouse, doubling its business volume and gaining skyscraper expertise, which up to that point it had lacked. Another milestone was Kone's acquisition of Australia's EPL in 1990. This acquisition marked a significant point of learning for Kone, as it began to understand the elements involved in a comfortable high-rise elevator ride.

In the mid-1990s, Kone made a breakthrough with the introduction of the world's first elevator that did not require a machine room, the Kone MonoSpace. These types of innovation did not come without recognition. In 2012, Kone was included on the *Forbes* list of the 100 most innovative companies in the world for the second year running. Kone also received the coveted "World Architecture News (WAN) Product of the Year Award" in 2012 for the new Kone MonoSpace 500 elevator. WAN, which had an audience of 220,000 architects worldwide, selected the Product of the Year to celebrate and promote the best in architectural products and materials.

Beyond elevators, the company's product portfolio included auto-walks, escalators, automatic doors, real-time monitoring and access control systems, which provided improvements to maintenance and safety. In addition, Kone also provided its own branded maintenance and service agreements to residential buildings, office buildings, public transportation and airports, hotels, retail centres, special buildings and medical facilities. Its customers were primarily builders, building owners, facility managers and developers.

A substantial number of its products and services were marketed under the 'Kone' brand, which followed the mantra of *Dedicated People Flow*. Its solutions aimed to provide a smooth flow of people at locations as diverse as the Marina Bay Sands

Exhibit 3 Consolidated Financial Statements (in USD millions)[9]

	Jan 1-Dec 31, 2013	Jan 1-Dec 31, 2012
Consolidated statement of income		
Sales	8,426.44	7,629.32
Operating income	1,158.84	961.93
Income before taxes	1,167.47	977.61
Net income	866.76	742.66
	31-Dec-13	31-Dec-12
Consolidated statement of financial position		
Total non-current assets	2,355.96	2,354.38
Total current assets	4,138.71	3,885.52
Total assets	6,494.67	6,239.91
Total equity	2,096.22	2,228.83
Total current liabilities	3,910.69	3,478.46
Consolidated statement of cash flows		
Cash flow from operations before financing items and taxes	1,474.50	1,301.54
Cash flow from operating activities	1,242.71	1,145.10
Cash flow from investing activities	−180.98	−267.65
Cash flow after investing activities	1,061.60	877.46
Cash flow from financing activities	−941.51	−859.34
Change in cash and cash equivalents	120.09	120.09

Order received		Jan 1-Dec 31, 2013
	2011	5,427
	2012	6,680
	2013	7,476
Order book		Jan 1-Dec 31, 2013
	2011	5,285
	2012	6,138
	2013	6,791

Sales by business	Jan 1-Dec 31, 2013
New equipment	54%
Modernisation	14%
Maintenance	32%
Sales by area	Jan 1-Dec 31, 2013
Europe, Middle East, and Africa	46%
Americas	16%
Asia-Pacific	38%
Personnel by area	Jan 1-Dec 31, 2013
Europe, Middle East, and Africa	47%
Americas	13%
Asia-Pacific	40%

Source: Kone, 2013 Financial Statements

Exhibit 4 Kone Locations

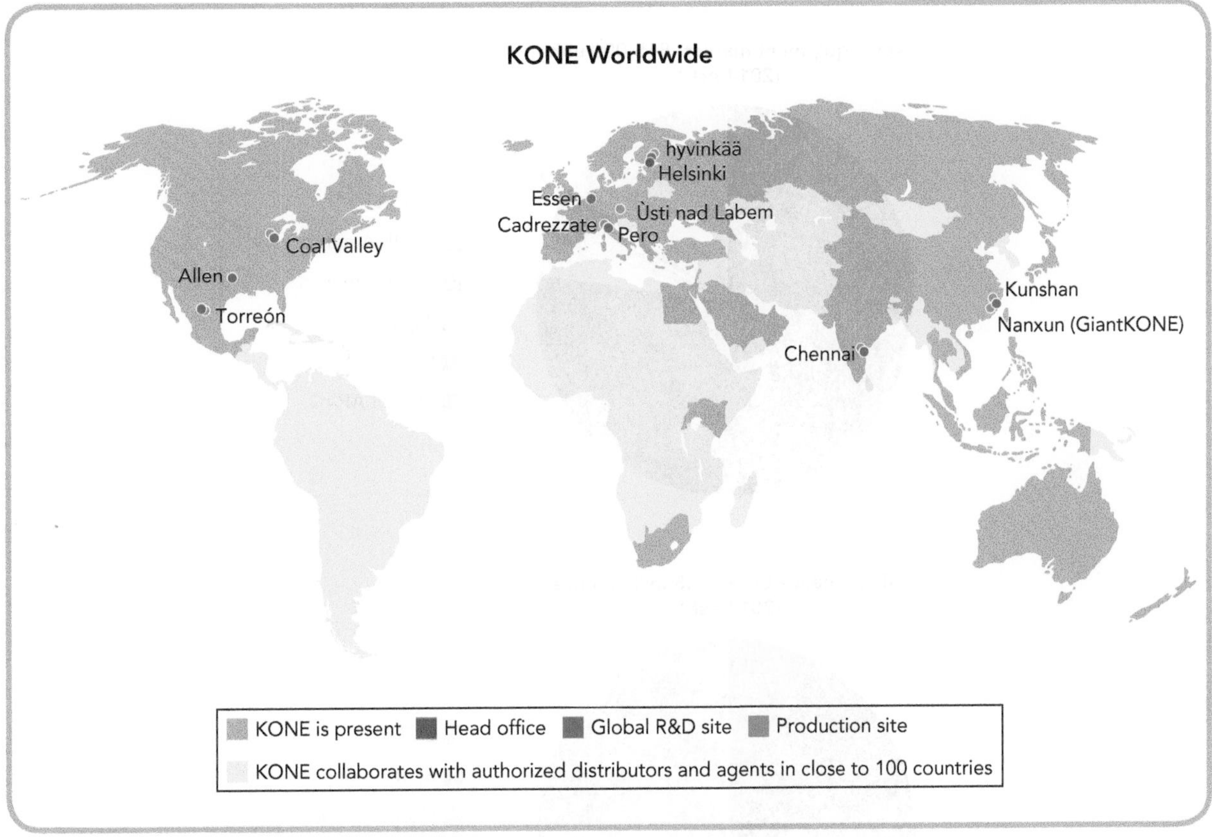

Source: Kone, reprinted with permission

integrated resorts in Singapore, The Shard in London, Europe's tallest building, and the Trump International Hotel and Tower in Chicago. Matti Alahuhta, CEO and president of the Kone Corporation between 2005 and 2014, added,

Our aim is to deliver the people flow experience. Passion for innovation is an integral part of our culture.

Market performance

In the elevator market, customers typically weighed three factors: installation costs, maintenance costs and return on investment.

Elevator demand was disparate across industry sectors and geography. The trend towards rising levels of urbanisation and greater population densities were pushing up property values in emerging markets, which incentivised the development of new residential and commercial high-rises. New orders for elevator systems and equipment were highest in Asia Pacific (refer to **Exhibit 5** for growth driver and market size).

In a Q42014 Earnings Call, the successor CEO and President of Kone to Alahuhta, Henrik Ehrnrooth, said,

We're looking at significant growth driven by China, Singapore and Australia. New equipment makes up 55% of our sales—40% of these sales originate in Asia Pacific, with about 30% coming from China—this is better than the overall 10% growth rate for elevator demand in China. To put all this growth in perspective, back in 2005 Asia Pacific represented just 12% of our new equipment sales. For 2014 we'll deliver 154,000 elevators worldwide. Last year was 130,000 and the year before was 124,000.[10]

Price competition for new equipment and installation in China was tight, but stable. Within China, there were significant differences between cities and provinces, with certain cities already experiencing excess capacity and weak demand as the government implemented more

Exhibit 5 Elevator Market and Growth Drivers

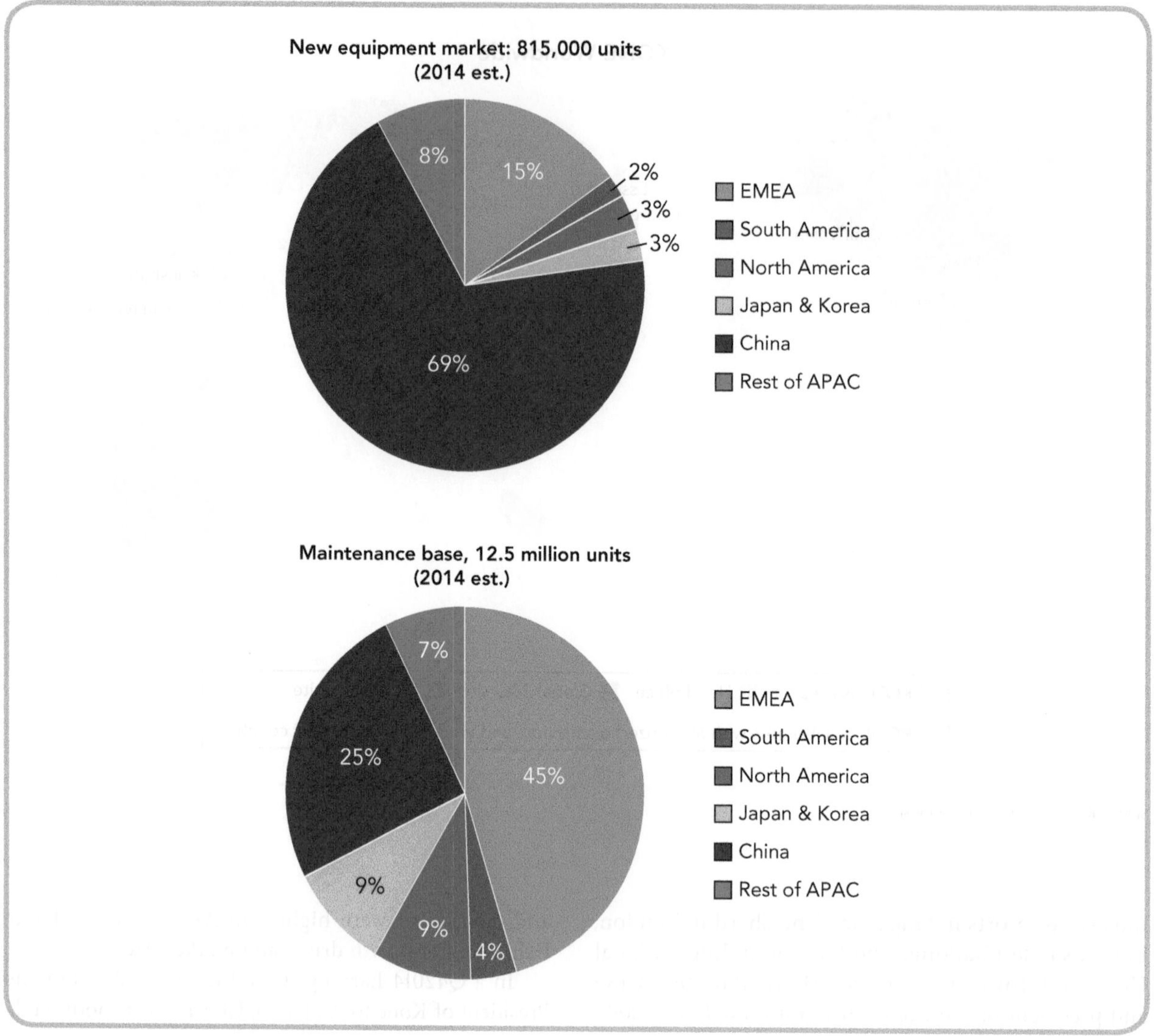

Source: Evli, "Kone: Machinery/ Finland", April 27, 2015. Spot Comment.

cooling measures in 2013 to rein in overheating property markets.

In 2014, Kone expected growth to remain stable in Asia Pacific over the next few years, though new equipment growth rates would start declining as the market matured. India was promising, though there was significant exchange rate risk and difficulty securing finance. There were strong developments in parts of the Middle East and Africa that were experiencing a boom in high-rise construction. However, growth in new equipment sales was declining across Europe, the Americas and the Middle East. Indeed, skyscraper construction was highly correlated with boom and bust cycles.

The modernisation and maintenance sectors were performing relatively well in North America following an ongoing, albeit slow economic recovery from the 2007/08 Financial Crisis. Australia was the biggest modernisation market in Asia Pacific, and Europe continued to lag but had considerable potential given the age of its infrastructure and large market size.

Modernisation was a cyclical business and constituted about 13% of Kone's global sales. Overall, sales from the company's modernisation business slightly declined in 2014. Maintenance made up 32% of Kone's global sales. And even though price competition was intense, margin remained healthy and growth was stable. For Kone, modernisation and maintenance presented excellent growth opportunities—having an average of 6% annual sales growth in the past few years leading up to 2014. Nonetheless, competition was fiercest in these sectors.

The UltraRope

Throughout the past century, Kone had made systematic and long-term investments into research and development capabilities. As Kone strived to perfect customer service, it also explored using technologies traditionally linked to other industries. Kone tracked customer needs and monitored market developments and changes in trends while also seeking ways to improve working methods.

Nurturing innovation

Raimo Pelto-Huikko was the man responsible for making the first prototype of the carbon fibre rope, having built it with his own hands. Coupled with the knowledge of high rise elevators that Valjus had brought to the table and his instinctive faith in carbon-fibre, a material he had been speculating about since the 1980s, Pelto-Huikko had set out to put the new technology into play.

The thought process of Valjus and Pelto-Huikko was characterised by creative freedom. This was part of Kone's work culture as the senior management of the firm had often stated, "generally, it all starts with development." They nurtured this idea by recognising that one of Kone's most significant tasks was to, "develop new and useful elevator concepts for [their] customers". Kone aimed to keep their elevators one step above the competition, all year round, and that attitude was apparent in the amount of leeway they provided to their employees. When company goals were aligned with the employee's thought processes and mentality, innovative disruptions seemed to emerge entirely by themselves.

In 2004, Pelto-Huikko began the research phase. Kone's leadership allocated a small budget and the permission to start. This home hobby slowly started gaining momentum and at one point established great potential, to the point that in 2006, Valjus gathered together the research group with the objective of taking these innovative ideas forward. The prospect of using carbon fibre had a lot of potential.

According to Pelto-Huikko, Kone provided support for the idea of investigating carbon-fibre as a hoisting material from the very beginning,

We intended to begin the research phase [in 2004]. Kone's leadership allocated a small budget and the permission to start. It all began with small steps forward.

In this case, the action of allocating some sort of budget as well as permission to begin research was the first move in the direction of disruptive innovation. Pelto-Huikko continued by noting that one question they had was "whether to walk down the path of finding subcontractors or to begin a cooperative research effort?"

In order to encourage in-house development, Kone's management formed a group in 2006, with the objective of creating innovation and progress for the project. This action was seen a necessary method for the firm's leadership to further enhance the innovative environment at the company.

Carbon fibre

Carbon fibre was invented in the late 1950s and early 1960s. However, when the Cold War ended, it was no longer needed for military production and an oversupply led to a fall in prices. This was when sports companies began using the product to exploit its strength. Carbon fibre was both stronger and lighter than steel. In particular, the material had great tensile strength, meaning it was hard to break when being pulled apart. That strength came from the chemical bonds between carbon atoms, the same sort that gave strength to diamonds. Carbon fibre had already changed the way the world made cars, rockets and planes. It was even a key aspect of modern prosthetics and medical technology. Kone's biggest rival, Otis, had also been looking at carbon fibre for use; however, the bulk of their research was in the area of strengthening steel cables.

Strength testing

By mid-2007, the UltraRope was born, after which Kone began putting the rope through rigorous testing beginning with lab testing conditions, and then, by 2010, full scale testing at Tytyri in 2010. Tytyri was the world's highest elevator testing shaft, situated in Lohja, Finland, embedded partly underground in a limestone mine. The facility was opened in 1998, and for the first time anywhere in the world, elevators destined for buildings over 200 metres tall could be tested before installation. Tytyri reached down to 333 metres below ground; the mine provided an ideal testing environment for high-rise elevators. The conditions at Tytyri were extreme: elevators had to endure dripping water, near-freezing temperatures and high humidity, meaning they were tested to withstand just about any condition a building might face. Additionally, various simulations allowed testing for a range of factors, including how the human body withstood different speeds and changes in pressure during the ride. As of 2013, the highest comfortable speed for people to travel in an elevator was ten metres per second. At Tytyri, speeds of up to 17 meters per second could be tested.[11]

Physical properties like tensile strength, bending lifetime, material aging, and the effect of extreme temperature and humidity were just some of the parameters that were measured and tested for UltraRope. After the rope passed these rigorous tests, the product was considered fit enough for a commercial launch.

With all the rigorous testing complete, the final UltraRope looked much like a flat piece of black liquorice. Instead of steel wires, Kone's hoisting line comprised four fibre tapes sealed in transparent plastic about three centimetres wide and three millimetres thick. It was more like a belt than a rope and looked like a school ruler covered with plastic tape. Made of a carbon fibre core surrounded by a unique high-friction coating, the new rope weighed only about 10-20 percent of a similar strength conventional steel rope. Put simply, the new technology enabled massive cuts in the deadweight that moved up and down every time someone hopped into a high-rise elevator. Less deadweight meant less energy consumption and operating cost. For example at 800 metres, the moving mass of a steel cable lifts about 108,600 kilograms. At the same height the UltraRope had a moving mass of 13,900 kilograms. For further comparison, a steel cable lift at 100 metres had a moving mass of 13,000 kilograms. Such weight reduction provided a 40 percent energy saving.[12]

Weighing options

Having already undergone a number of development steps both in real and simulated conditions, UltraRope had the potential to be a disruptive product in the elevator industry. Kone attributed the product to an innovative work culture and long-term investment in research and development. In this way, Kone believed that instead of incremental innovations in existing hoisting technology, the company could disrupt existing hoisting technologies and business models.

Towards the end of 2014 the UltraRope was receiving great press; it had just won the Kingdom Tower contract and had already been installed in Tower 3 of the Marina Bay Sands Hotel, a prominent feature on Singapore's skyline. The Economist had even hailed it has a technological breakthrough, bringing the world closer to realising a science fiction reality. Valjus, however, knew it would take a lot more than that to leverage the UltraRope as a key market share driver.

He believed that the greatest growth potential lay in modernisation and lucrative maintenance contracts. And in this respect, he was optimistic about Kone's Preferred Maintenance Partner programme, which had begun about a year earlier in 2013 when the company started investing a lot more into developing their sales setup, competencies and management. But Valjus realised it would be a slog,

In the past few years, Kone has had a slightly negative competition balance—which is the balance between the numbers of units we win versus the ones we lose to the market. Thankfully we're starting to make some gains in terms of maintenance contract conversions.

But loyalty programmes were nothing new to the industry. And the other players, like Otis, also had excellent services and equipment technologies. Active equipment monitoring to improve maintenance services, design consulting, and various technologies to improve elevator efficiency were essentially standard practice. Valjus and Pelto-Huikko believed the UltraRope was key to setting Kone apart from the competition. However, innovation was just one aspect of success. A winning *go-to-market* strategy was another.

NOTES

1. Freedonia. "World Elevators Market", December 2013, www.reportbuyer.com, accessed April 2015.
2. The Economist, "Top floor, please", March 16, 2013, http://www.economist.com/news/business/21573568-things-are-looking-up-liftmakers-top-floor-please, accessed May 2015.
3. Ibid.
4. Ibid.
5. Ibid.
6. Ibid.
7. Ibid.
8. "FAQs: Energy efficiency", International Energy Agency, 2014, http://www.iea.org/aboutus/faqs/energyefficiency/, accessed May 2015.
9. US$1 = 0.82262 euros as at 31 Dec 2014.
10. Kone, Q4 2014 Earnings Call—Final Fair Disclosure Wire (Quarterly Earnings Reports), Transcripts 01/29/2015.
11. "Tytyri—the world's highest elevator test shaft", http://mediacentre.kallaway.co.uk/pdf/KONEs-elevator-test-laboratoryTytyri-final.pdf, accessed May 2015.
12. Ibid.

CASE 9

SMU SINGAPORE MANAGEMENT UNIVERSITY

MatchMove: Business Model Evolution

It was January 2014, and Shailash Naik, CEO of MatchMove Global Pte Ltd was rather pleased to have closed 2013 with yet another feather in the cap for his company. MatchMove, an online entertainment service provider, had just been ranked 25th out of the 500 fastest-growing technology companies in the 2013 Deloitte Technology Fast 500 Asia Pacific rankings, a yearly publication that was well regarded in the technology and gaming industry.

When MatchMove was founded in early 2009, Naik and his COO, Leow Hsueh Huah (HH), had been in a rush to carry out their vision for the company. From their time working with a videogame company in the US, they had talked to various companies with large Internet audiences, and had identified a gap in the Asian market for a company-specific platform that incorporated casual gaming, social networking and e-commerce capabilities. MatchMove wanted to be this platform. Finally, in late 2009, MatchMove signed up its first large client, global technology company Yahoo!, to provide such services for Yahoo! Southeast Asia. This early deal enabled MatchMove to build a depth of capability on its cloud-based platform. The company also contracted with game developers to create its own store of quality games that it could offer to its clients.

In essence, MatchMove was set up to provide a service as a B2B game/entertainment platform. Its key value proposition was to become an intermediary, and more, between game companies with "high (gaming) content" profiles, but which traditionally had low web traffic. In addition, it was targeting companies like Yahoo! and Microsoft that had large consumer portals and high traffic–but were perhaps lacking in certain types of content, and hence losing users to websites like Facebook and iTunes which served as communities of social networks and also possessed platforms for gaming. By having a large or dedicated social networking community and strong content profile, these companies could keep users on their websites for longer, which translated into greater revenue generation. Aside from creating a closed e-commerce system to accept payments for services on its clients' websites, MatchMove envisioned creating an open payments portal for all users for multiple merchants. It just did not have a concrete idea of what that strategy would look like yet.

By 2012, MatchMove had revamped its back-end system to meet the demands of a growing number of clients. The company had also ventured into various other opportunities, such as gamification, which were related to its core business. However, Naik wanted to accomplish even more. He was eager to create the next technological disruption to existing commerce, finance and other sectors, and capture new opportunities coming up in the market. Naik's mantra was to "fail fast", and to take risks. He saw far greater potential in the product that was beyond its initial value proposition, and just needed to decide where to take it from its current position, and what business model would best accomplish those goals.

Changes in the Gaming Industry

In 2012, the global video games market, worth US$66.3 billion, was estimated to grow at a compound annual growth rate of 6.7% to reach US$86.1 billion in 2016 (refer to **Exhibit 1** for the Video Game Market Revenues Worldwide, by Segment, 2012–2016).[1] Although the segment that dominated this category was traditional video console gaming, the share of this type of gaming was falling, with social games and smartphone/tablet games on the ascent.[2] This represented a significant technological disruption that conventional publishers and studios were unprepared for, and unskilled to handle. Coupled with this trend was the falling cost of mobile and social game development, which opened the door to many new and often inexperienced, but creative, developers. This lowered the risk of developing new games, and enabled faster game distribution through established social networking channels—thus leading to expedited profits and attracting more attention from investors into the industry.[3]

This case was written by Professor Ted Tschang and Adina Wong at the Singapore Management University. The case was prepared solely to provide material for class discussion. The authors do not intend to illustrate either effective or ineffective handling of a managerial situation. The authors may have disguised certain names and other identifying information to protect confidentiality.

Exhibit 1 The Video Game Market Revenues Worldwide, by Segment

Video Game Market Revenues Worldwide, by Segment, 2012–2016 (billions, % of total and CAGR)						
	2012	**2013**	**2014**	**2015**	**2016**	**CAGR**
TV/console	36.70%	36.10%	34.80%	33.50%	32.40%	3.50%
Massive multiplayer online game	19.80%	21.20%	21.90%	22.30%	22.70%	10.40%
Smartphone	10.60%	12.10%	13.60%	15.00%	16.20%	18.80%
Social/casual	10.20%	9.40%	8.60%	7.90%	7.30%	−1.70%
PC/Mac	9.80%	8.60%	7.50%	6.60%	5.80%	−6.40%
Handhelds	9.80%	7.30%	6.10%	5.10%	3.90%	−15.00%
Tablet	3.20%	5.30%	7.50%	9.60%	11.60%	47.60%
Total revenues	$66.30	$70.40	$75.20	$80.50	$86.10	6.70%

Note: Video game revenues by Region in 2013 (in US$ billions)—Asia-Pacific (25.1%), North America (22.8%), EMEA (19.5%), Latin America (3%).

Source: Newzoo BV, "2013 Global Games Market Report," June 6, 2013, via eMarketer (accessed 15 June 2014).

Social and casual gaming was a big part of the trend. In a report on online social gaming by Datamonitor, digital online games were defined as those that "utilizes a player's social graph to provide an enhanced game experience, facilitates and encourages communication about the game outside of the game, and has a minimal barrier to entry (one click away)."[4]

The rising popularity of social-networking sites such as Facebook (as well as online casual game websites like Popcap) had established the foundation for consumers to experience and consume this new genre of games, and to have new, more social, gaming experiences, thereby illustrating the increased importance of social games.

Besides, social games, other than being a new revenue stream for social-networking sites (in addition to advertising), also attracted users to register and to remain on social-networking sites for a longer period of time.[5] Well-known social media games included Farmville (developed by Zynga) on Facebook, and Angry Birds on the iPhone smartphone.[6] Social games typically earned revenues through a 'freemium' model, where players were given free access to the basic features of a game, but had to pay to access more features and higher levels in the game.[7] Unlike the players of traditional console games—who were typically younger males with dedicated leisure time to play a game—players of the more casual social games had a different profile, being mostly older, and female.[8]

Gaming in Asia

In the beginning of 2013, Asia was the region with the largest number of video gamers online at 477 million (39%), and also the largest revenue share globally at US$25.1 billion (36%).[9] PriceWaterhouseCoopers's 2011 *Global Entertainment and Media Outlook 2010–2014* recognised that although earlier low-tech phones had prevented the 'monetisation' of social media games, this would now change with the introduction of 3G wireless mobile infrastructure and widespread uptake of smartphones in the region,

The growth of smartphones is driving social gaming in Asia. Mobile now provides an environment that allows games to be developed to the standard of regular console and online games, and this has already led to an explosion in casual gaming. [In 2011], the region is already home to more wireless phone subscribers than the rest of the world combined, and currently accounts for 63 per cent of global wireless gaming spend.[10]

However, the report also recognised challenges to the online gaming business in the region,

The partnership between game developers, platform owners, and brands is important, and ideally should be a natural process by now. However, in the real world this is not happening as there are constraints and limitations to how branded content can be integrated into the production of games. Each Asian market, from Japan to China, from Korea to the Philippines, has a lively social gaming scene, but with specific characteristics and different tastes that need to be catered to.[11]

Gestating an Idea

Cryptologic

It was in this environment that Naik made his foray into the Asian online gaming industry and built up his company to capitalise on what he saw was a huge but untapped market potential. Naik had begun his career in technology, working as a project manager to deliver Oracle and SAP technology solutions to multinational companies that were clients of PricewaterhouseCoopers and Ernst & Young consulting services. From there, he started to understand business needs from a technology perspective, and how business worked at the back-end to drive front-end processes. His next move was in a strategy and operations role as Managing Director, Strategy and Operations, Asia Pacific for Cisco Systems, a US-based multinational technology firm.

In 2007, a US-based, NASDAQ-listed gaming company, Cryptologic, had approached Naik to be their CEO. Cryptologic was trying to move into this new "space" even as they maintained an existing organisational structure and business model—one that was based on publishing games and built up through acquisitions of studios. Cryptologic's plan was to be a business-to-consumer (B2C) company for online gamers, providing a platform for users to play game content that it owned exclusively. In this role, Naik went around Asia acquiring gaming studios and platforms to build up Cryptologic's proprietary online gaming platform. He acquired five studios for the company and started to understand the online gaming business in more depth. He understood that the challenge facing game developers was 'high content, low traffic', or being able to attract enough players to play their games. Typically, a player's awareness of a game spread via word-of-mouth, but also through paid marketing campaigns.

From B2C to B2B

In working for Cryptologic, Naik and HH, his CFO at Cryptologic, became keenly aware of a few converging trends and started to explore options that could capitalise on these opportunities, after realising that the Cryptologic organisation structure (which focused on the end consumer), could not accommodate their interest in creating a new business model and value proposition for other businesses as clients.

Naik and his team had conducted business dialogues and carried out market research for six months. Based on concurrent conversations with search engine companies, as well as telecommunications companies that had high user traffic on their websites, Naik came to an interesting observation,

The problem was that users were now changing their style [manner of playing games]. Instead of going to a website and consuming news and games and meeting their friends individually, they now wanted it all in one space—and were all converging on spaces like Facebook and so on. Meanwhile, the big brands and the telcos were saying—hang on, these are our users, and we'd better offer them something else we'll lose them.

At the same time, Naik and HH recognised that there was another trend in the market. A common practice was for game developers to launch their games on social networking platforms such as Facebook, where Facebook would share revenues earned from game players with the game developer. However, over time, the margin that Facebook was taking from this revenue stream became higher and higher, with less revenue coming back to the game developer. Major game developers such as Zynga then started to use Facebook more as a source, and not the ultimate destination for users. Where previously Facebook would host Zynga's games, now Facebook users who wanted to play a Zynga game would be redirected to a Zynga website to play the game there. This was pushing the game developers to create their own gaming platforms—but with correspondingly weaker "traffic" than the larger portals and social media giants.

With this combination of insights, Naik started developing the concept of a business-to-business (B2B) business model of his own, to work with large multinationals to help them solve their problem of 'high traffic, low content'. He had further conversations with companies such as Yahoo! and Microsoft, which were keen to attract more users to their websites and keep them there for a longer time, earning additional revenues through casual games and online purchases on their sites.

Naik confessed that he had conceived a grand plan from the beginning,

These large multinational companies all had the following pain points—How do I keep users on my website? How do I get quality content? And how do I do all this without additional headcount? We discovered this while investing in the smaller companies and so decided to combine this into a new service combining the whole package—social gaming, social networking and e-commerce. We had a core vision about all three as a package, because we knew that if we didn't do so, we wouldn't be able to get scale. And only once we get scale, would the business be sustainable. The whole world thought we were crazy.

Naik also realised that unless they were able to offer all three arms to a client, it would be easy for a big client to say "I can do the games, or one of the other pieces, myself."

Naik and HH then put together a presentation to show their potential clients how their business model was well thought out and would address all the pain points. This all-in-one value proposition approach turned out to be of great value to their clients—all of whom immediately asked, "how do I sign up?"-giving Naik and his team the confidence that there was indeed a market opportunity there.

In 2009, in the midst of the global financial crisis, Naik and HH left their well-paying jobs with Cryptologic to start a company of their own.[12] They had done all their due diligence, and the timing was too compelling for this new business model.

MatchMove

MatchMove is to online entertainment and e-commerce what software providers SAP and Oracle are to enterprise software.

—Shailesh Naik, CEO, MatchMove Pte Ltd[13]

In February 2009, MatchMove Pte Ltd was incorporated in Singapore, with Naik as the CEO, and HH as the COO. "Finding people to work for us was the hardest in the beginning", Naik said. "Not everyone wants to work for start-ups. It was hard to get Singaporeans to apply for our job openings, so we had to head-hunt for people in China."[14] Eventually they overcame this problem and by June 2013, MatchMove had 46 employees in Singapore, Indonesia, the Philippines, Vietnam, China and the US.[15]

The MatchMove Proposition

MatchMove helps online businesses increase revenue, user engagement and loyalty through the strategic use of its sophisticated games, social networking and site gamification and e-payments platform.

—MatchMove website[16]

MatchMove would provide an entertainment platform as a service to clients, and would offer a selection of games and apps which their clients could host on their own portals for their own customers. They would become a 'curator' of sorts, choosing and testing the best games from various game developers, and also providing the technology platform. In Naik's words, it would provide "infrastructure for companies that are keen to offer games on their sites but do not want to do it on their own".[17] The closed social network platform allowed users to perform actions such as to click 'like' on content and comment on one another's activities on the portal. Building its library of Internet- and subsequently mobile-enabled games, MatchMove targeted the telecommunications, media and technology (TMT) segment. Naik said,

We initially targeted the big Western multinationals, knowing that their management in Asia would probably be frustrated with the lack of local products, and at the same time see the opportunity slipping away.

Many of these were Asian offices of US multinationals, which lacked the resources to customise the US-based content from their US headquarters in a way that was appealing to Asian users. Naik was very clear from the beginning on how MatchMove should position itself,

*We don't acquire [game] content generation [capabilities]. We've always invested in distribution and the platform. So we want to be like a B2B iTunes, where games can come from anywhere. So it's this ecosystem where we want to be the platform, and we will integrate payments with the platform. We will be the central cog in the wheel that brings everyone together. We will invest in infrastructure, support, and platform, because that's what really captures the value (refer to **Exhibit 2** for a concept diagram of MatchMove's business).*

In short, MatchMove aimed to offer content management (games), transaction management (e-commerce), and the technology platform as a one-stop package to customers in Asia.

Naik and his team realised that there were fundamental differences between games in the US and in Asia. For instance, Western games were heavily invested in character intellectual property like *Batman* or *Superman*, whereas Asian games tended to be a variation of popular fictional or historical content, like the 'Monkey King' myth or the 'Three Kingdoms' novel. Asian characters, even villains, could look cute. They recognised that their value proposition had to focus on the Asian games market, with Asian-made games for the Asian arms of Web portals and other sites, for their Asian clients. There would of course be crossover games (games that crossed over cultures) later, but addressing the regional consumer taste was at the core of their differentiated offering.

Exhibit 2 Concept Diagram of Matchmove's Business

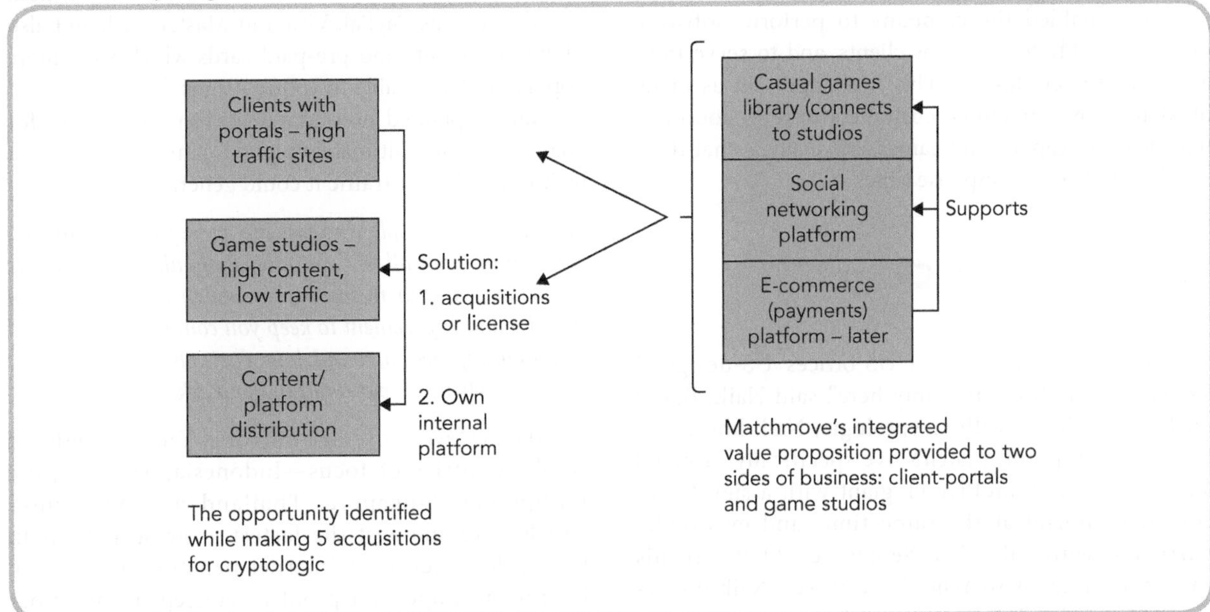

Source: Author's concept diagram

Naik recalled how ground-breaking this business model and its value proposition was to the industry, or for that matter, in all the industry verticals that their business model spanned,

In 2009, Digital Capital (a private equity investor in the digital entertainment space), named MatchMove twice in a report together with Facebook, Uniclip, Trimedia, and Popcap. This put us on the global map. People were viewing the industry in those days as verticals—developers, publishers, portals, aggregators . . . We came in saying that we are disrupting the business model—we are working right across all these verticals . . . we've got the whole suite.

MatchMove was essentially operating a two-sided market business model–servicing the game developers on the one hand, and the portals and other Web companies on the other. Game developers would benefit by working with MatchMove as they could gain information on the volume of customers accessing their games, and MatchMove provided transparency on payments due to them. MatchMove looked for more and bigger clients for developers to distribute games to, and sought to create a two-way cycle where building trust with more of the popular game developers enabled them to attract larger clients as well. Whilst Apple's iTunes store took 30% of margins from games, MatchMove was willing to take as low as a five percent margin from game developers that it had an exclusive relationship with.

The Remaining Pieces of the Puzzle

By September 2009, the private equity market had started recovering from the post-financial crisis doldrums, and amidst the flurry of deals being sealed in the industry, MatchMove managed to raise US$1.6 million (S$2 million)[18] of funds from Singapore-based private equity firm Vickers Venture Partners to kick-start their first project with Yahoo! Southeast Asia.[19] As of June 2013, the company had managed to raise an additional US$5.5 million (SGD$7 million) of funding from private equity firms in the US, Europe and China. Ultimately, MatchMove had to seek other potential investors and game developers in order to secure funding. This was a time-consuming back-and-forth process that required a lot of trust building.

From the start, MatchMove had decided to put its platform entirely in the 'Cloud'[20]. This made it easy for the company to update all its clients with new software and services.[21] Importantly, the cloud-based platform enabled the company to perform software updates quickly for overseas clients, and to serve their gamer customers faster.[22] This was important as many of MatchMove's potential customers were in countries outside of Singapore, and games, especially at that time, required fast server response times.

Getting the First Client

Yahoo!

Yahoo! Asia was using their US offices' US-designed games, and "failing miserably here", said Naik. Based on his experience with Cryptologic, Naik knew this to be a weak point. MatchMove specifically targeted Yahoo!-Asia and another IT giant with a significant consumer portal at the same time, and eventually partnered with Yahoo! in September 2009.[23] In his earlier meetings with Yahoo! executives, Naik understood that Yahoo! Asia, being at its core an Internet search portal, had no resources to curate a stable of Asian-specific games on its website. Yahoo! had earlier acquired a game company to develop games exclusively for its website, but their games had become increasingly obsolete as they could not keep up with evolving technologies such as Flash, and upcoming content trends such as social gaming.

Naik gave Yahoo! a proposed solution to their problems. MatchMove would be responsible for the technology transition of existing and new games to new technology platforms. It would also make it possible for Yahoo! to avoid paying the upfront costs for new game development; instead MatchMove handled the payments to the game developers on their end. They achieved this by standardising the terms offered to all game developers who worked with them. By handling the negotiations and accounting on behalf of Yahoo! for the hundreds of different game developers that were on the Yahoo! Platform, MatchMove acted as a consolidator and complemented Yahoo! in areas that Yahoo! did not have the bandwidth to accomplish.

In this way, MatchMove could work out a consistent revenue sharing scheme with game developers and publishers. The deal made a total of 143 titles available for purchase on Yahoo!'s online store, making Yahoo! one of the top sites in Southeast Asia offering the most popular casual game titles.[24] Additionally, a payment gateway provided on the platform enabled MatchMove's clients to collect payments from their end users via payment services such as PayPal, Visa and MasterCard, and also Mobile payments and pre-paid cards which were more popular and accessible to young Asians.[25]

Naik explained how MatchMove tested games for quality, although ultimately a 'good' game was measured by how much user traffic it could generate,

We have a few people who test the game from end to end, running through all the episodes. It should not be totally predictable, and there should be enough of an element of surprise and engagement to keep you coming back . . . good workmanship, design, sound, lots of episodes . . . The real test though is when you put it out in the market.

MatchMove's coverage mirrored Yahoo! Southeast Asia's countries of focus—Indonesia, Malaysia, the Philippines, Singapore, Thailand and Vietnam—which were amongst the fastest growing nations in the world in terms of Internet penetration.[26] Yahoo! became an important proof of concept to build out MatchMove's sophisticated product architecture. The 'Yahoo!-grade' project involved building a multiple-country, multi-language and even multi-currency platform that included standards of performance and customer service that made it easier to acquire a future customer base.

Pricing for MatchMove's platform was on a subscription basis, and customers paid between US$7,921 (SGD$10,000) to US$39,605 (SGD$50,000) per month to use it, saving themselves millions of dollars in having to build up the capability on their own.[27]

Building In Speed and Flexibility

After a few months spent building up its customer base, Naik decided to be more focused on MatchMove's strengths, and the competition never really got a foothold,

We had competitors at two places when we first arrived—Yahoo! and Starhub were talking to two other companies (one European and the other a US billion dollar concern)—which did not offer the whole package. And they said they would offer this in three months, but we said that we would do it in two weeks, then two days, then five minutes.

Starhub[28] told us during final talks why they were choosing us even though we weren't established, we weren't known—we didn't even have a company. They said—'you're offering me local games . . . (and) a faster time to market'.

Once we identified those two factors as key selection criteria for B2B customers, we worked harder and faster on improving our capabilities in those areas. We had to build the e-commerce function as a necessary aspect to get the flow of money for their customers to pay. If you were a customer on Yahoo! Asia, which was in six countries, you had the option to pay for games on a local website through a local payment provider.

AppKungfu's Origins

The realisation that speed and scalability (across clients) were their competitive advantages eventually led Naik and HH to revamp MatchMove's platform.

When we went in to design our overall ecosystem, we made sure that our deployment got faster and faster. My architects and product designers were constantly looking to improve our speed to market . . . so competitors could never catch up in the key areas where we believed our clients told us we had a competitive advantage. So when our competitors needed three months to deploy a solution, we were able to do it in weeks. From there, we started to improve the technology to be able to deploy a large scale solution in just days. Global competitors from the US and Europe stopped competing with us and pulled out whenever they heard we were in the running. We had started to accelerate away from the competition by focusing on our key differentiators...not as we saw them, but as our clients saw them.

By late 2010, MatchMove had so much demand for its services that Naik knew that its platform would not be scalable. For every project MatchMove took on, they had to have engineers' onsite at the client's office to integrate MatchMove's backend system with the clients—and each integration project took six to eight weeks. The decision was thus made to revamp MatchMove's platform, to make it modular and enable clients to self-service to set up their websites, which also changed the range of customers that MatchMove targeted. Naik explained,

Once we saw the emerging pipeline, we thought here was an opportunity to scale this big time. And so we stepped back to revamp the whole platform, and renamed it AppKungfu–offering it to just anyone who wanted it, not just our target enterprise customers. You could be a young girl in Taiwan who was selling t-shirts online, and now wanted to add games and social networking. We already had the core technology, and we wanted to offer a 'freemium' model, so anyone who wanted to use it at a basic level could do so. In 2010 we started to rewrite, and in 2011, we had a product that could be used both 'B2C' and 'B2B'.

In the beginning of 2012, MatchMove unveiled AppKungfu, which was a patent-pending system of application programming interfaces (API).[29] Customers could 'self-service' and choose to enhance their websites with social networking features such as sharing and achievements tracking.[30] As Nate Wang, VP of Marketing at MatchMove described,

Imagine playing with Lego blocks. You no longer have to take the entire castle. You can now take the right tower and add it to your own castle. If that's not enough, you can break it down into the individual bricks and customise it any way you like.[31]

With this new API-based platform, 'what would normally take two years [to implement] is often done in less than two weeks'.[32] The result of the AppKungfu platform was that it enabled standard websites to be converted, sometimes within mere hours, to a full Internet and mobile experience.[33]

AppKungfu also incorporated new and powerful features for MatchMove's customers. The use of APIs allowed customers to collected data on users' activities and preferences on their websites, so that they could target customers and cross-sell relevant products with this information.[34]

In line with the 'freemium' business model, MatchMove made the basic platform free for customers on a self-service basis. Customers paid a monthly subscription fee for licencing and value-added services such as single-sign on capability, and intellectual property rights. Naik described the change that AppKungfu brought to MatchMove's way of doing business,

At that point, we were not limited anymore, and could start targeting geographically rather than sector wise . . . we added French, Spanish, Arabic [language versions of the platform] and so on . . . Over time, we made more and more self-service . . . if a customer was really big and serious, we would give them more customised attention.

On the developer side, starting with ten game developers and 300 game titles when they first started working with Yahoo!, MatchMove's stable of games grew to 50 developers and 3000 titles about a year later. This was largely because of its API-based platform that made it easier for software developers to integrate into the MatchMove platform from anywhere in the world.

Further Moves

The Move into Gamification

In 2012, MatchMove developed the opportunity in what Naik called an 'adjacent space'—gamification. As the MatchMove website explained to potential corporate clients,

Gamification ensures that users fall in love with performing the actions that you want.[35]

Gamification was part of the next wave of technology-related trends gaining popularity in the market after casual games and social networking. In essence, 'gamification' was the application of the mechanics of games to non-game scenarios, to make an activity more fun and engaging.[36] An example was getting high scores on a leaderboard for sales numbers achieved. MatchMove saw a way to link this to the clients already using their platform for gaming and social networking, and apply gamification to internal enterprise issues like corporate employee training and increasing employee commitment through participation in games. Naik shared how MatchMove developed this new revenue stream,

Gamification was at that time a new term. So we looked at it and realised that actually, we know how to do this stuff. It required the underlying social networking platform, so we had two engineers work on it for three months, and we came up with the gamification product. We created a prototype, pushed it out to a few customers. They loved it . . . Almost all our clients are going onto it.

In addition, MatchMove also provided monitoring and implementation tools through AppKungfu that enabled companies to perform the back end analytics and evaluate if gamification had promoted the desired improvement in internal metrics, such as productivity or reduced absenteeism.

Failing Fast

MatchMove also experimented with projects that did not succeed as well. Up until 2012, it had at least three to four failures. For instance, it attempted to go into branded hardware, but the supplier failed to deliver because the Android[37] boom in the 2010's took up all the suppliers' production capacity. In 2010, the company tried to launch a kid-friendly Internet browser with a Korean partner, a project that did not take off because of language difficulties. Naik noted, "We fail fast. If a project does not gain traction in three months and lift-off in six, we move on".

However, Naik was also selective about the new ventures that the company took on, as with its growing reputation, MatchMove received an increasing number of offers for partnerships. He explained,

The core seeds were the same, but we continued to grow each one. Gamification was just an extension; it was highly opportunistic. How the business model evolves is that we look at what's in front of us, what's nearby, what's around the corner–and then try to determine whether it fits in with our grand plan of entertainment, social networks, and e-commerce. . . . Rarely have we said 'this is really cool, sooner or later people will catch on, let's just throw it out there.' Whenever we are after something, we always go and talk to potential channel partners, customers. . . .

It was for the same reason that MatchMove said 'no' to American Idol, FOX and other clients which approached them for television-related ventures that integrated video streaming and new technologies onto their websites. Those were perceived to be a poor fit with MatchMove's core value proposition.

The Next Move

By the time MatchMove found its way into 25th place in the Deloitte Technology Fast 500 Asia Pacific rankings, the company had become one of the fastest growing technology firms in South-East Asia and had a three-year revenue growth rate of 902 percent, with revenue for the 2012 financial year at just under US$8 million (SGD$10 million).[38] Naik took stock of the company's progress so far,

We have 150 enterprise customers across the world; they in turn have about 300 million users. We have hundreds of social APIs. We offered content and social plug-ins and e-commerce. We offer "your own branded social entertainment site [set up] in one week, across multiple devices, across nine languages." We now have hundreds of payment providers across many countries.

So far, MatchMove had been building its business as a full service games service provider that included a financial services component. Naik knew that he wanted this offering to be stretched to incorporate other services for adjacent markets with similar purposes, but was yet unclear on the direction. However, Naik's research had revealed e-commerce to be the next big opportunity. He explained,

In Asia 80% of transactions are cash-based. Only 20% goes through cards. This is the whale we were looking

Exhibit 3 Data on Payment Types used for Online Purchases in Asia and other Regions

Noncash Transactions Worldwide, by Region, 2011 & 2012 (billions, % change and CAGR)				
	2011	2012 (1)	CAGR	% change
North America	124	130	3.70%	4.80%
Europe (2)	82	85	4.30%	3.50%
Latin America (3)	29	34	15.80%	14.60%
Mature Asia-Pacific (4)	30	33	11.00%	8.70%
CEMEA (5)	21	27	26.30%	25.50%
Emerging Asia (6)	20	25	19.70%	24.40%

Note: (1) forecast; (2) includes Eurozone; (3) includes Brazil, Mexico and other; (4) includes Australia, Japan, Singapore and South Korea; (5) includes Russia and Poland; (6) includes China, Hong Kong, India and other.

Source: Capgemini and Royal Bank of Scotland (RBS), "World Payments Report 2013," Sep 16, 2013, via eMarketer, (accessed 11 January 2012).

Payment Method Share of Ecommerce Transactions in Select Countries in Asia-Pacific, 2012 (% of total)						
	Card	Bank Transfers*	Ewallets	Mobile	Direct Debits	Other**
South Korea	73.80%	4.50%	2.10%	1.50%	0.30%	17.80%
Japan	56.00%	3.50%	6.60%	0.30%	0.90%	32.70%
Australia	53.40%	22.50%	20.00%	0.70%	1.30%	2.10%
Indonesia	26.00%	39.00%	2.70%	0.10%	1.20%	31.00%
Philippines	24.60%	20.10%	13.90%	7.50%	2.30%	31.60%
Thailand	24.50%	30.00%	4.80%	1.40%	0.80%	38.50%
India	24.00%	29.30%	1.50%	4.00%	3.70%	37.50%
China	15.00%	20.40%	44.30%	1.90%	na	18.40%
Vietnam	8.60%	56.10%	8.60%	0.30%	1.20%	25.20%

Note: read as 53.4% of ecommerce transactions in Australia were by credit card; *includes real-time and offline bank transfers; **includes local card schemes, pre-pay cards or vouchers, post-pay methods requiring payment at an affiliated outlet or store, e-invoices and digital currency

Source: WorldPay, "Your Global Guide to Alternative Payments" in collaboration with First Annapolis Consulting, Jan 17, 2014, via eMarketer, (accessed 15 June 2014).

for (refer to ***Exhibit 3*** *for data on payment values and types used for online purchases in Asia and other regions). We always had the vision that one day we were going to offer an e-commerce (payment) capability that would work not only on our customer (enterprise) side, but be an open wallet. The basic criteria was to allow anyone in Asia to shop online anywhere. That's what the vision was.*

By January 2014, MatchMove had already built up the seeds of its next business model evolution. It had developed a robust and complete API-based platform for both B2B and B2C that hosted games and social networking capabilities, which could be extended to gamification. The rollout of its platform in the region had also enabled it to build an e-commerce platform where it could help its clients collect payments in local currencies domestically in ten countries in Asia, scaling beyond the six countries it had started with when Yahoo! Southeast Asia had on-boarded as their first client.

Naik thought that with the depth of the e-commerce payment capability that MatchMove had, it could do more than just service its existing stable of customers. He envisioned an open network that could tap on the current trend of the 'unbanked' and 'uncarded'. Could he do this alone, or should he look for a partner? How would this idea work, in reality? He knew that MatchMove would need to evolve its business model to tap on this next big opportunity.

NOTES

1. Newzoo BV, 2013 Global Games Market Report, June 6, 2013, via eMarketer, accessed June 2014.
2. Ibid.
3. Eric Savitz and Kushal Saha, "Mobile/Social Trends Driving Video Game Sector M&A", Forbes.com, July 11, 2011, via Business Source Complete, accessed June 2014.
4. Ibid.
5. Datamonitor, "Online Social Gaming Case Study: A Viable CPG Marketing Opportunity?", Datamonitor, January 2011, via EBSCOHost, accessed June 2014.
6. Ibid.
7. Eric Savitz and Kushal Saha, "Mobile/Social Trends Driving Video Game Sector M&A", Forbes.com, July 11, 2011, via Business Source Complete, accessed June 2014.
8. Demographically, a study in 2012 found the majority of social gamers to be at least 30 years old, with more than 50% married and more than 70% female. Social games, which were closely linked to social networking, were also played for the purpose of competing with people that the player knew. These games were normally played when the player had small windows of time available, such as when travelling on the bus or train, in the office for a quick break, or when the baby was napping. eMarketer, "The 2013 Entertainment", *Media & Advertising Market Research Handbook*, January 2013, via eMarketer, accessed June 2014.
9. Newzoo BV, 2013 Global Games Market Report, June 6, 2013, via eMarketer, accessed June 2014.
10. Michael O'Neill, "Social takes gaming to a new level", PricewaterhouseCoopers LLP's Global Entertainment and Media Outlook: 2010–2014, April 2011, via Business Source Complete, accessed June 2014.
11. Ibid.
12. Yuen-C Tham, "MatchMove Games", Singapore Press Holdings Limited, May 26, 2010, via Factiva, accessed April 2014.
13. Aaron Tan, "SME Tech; They do the hard work for you in just weeks", Singapore Press Holdings Limited, June 12, 2013, via Factiva, accessed April 2014.
14. Ibid.
15. Ibid.
16. MatchMove, "MatchMove Expands Social Media Capabilities", November 14, 2011, http://www.MatchMove.com/corporate/MatchMove-expands-social-media-capabilities/, accessed April 2014.
17. Yuen-C Tham, "MatchMove Games", Singapore Press Holdings Limited, May 26, 2010, via Factiva, accessed April 2014.
18. SG$1 = US$0.79209, on 1 June 2013, www.oanda.com, accessed 13 June 2014.
19. Gabriel Chen,–Private equity sector here turning the corner, September 24, 2009, "Singapore Press Holdings Limited", via Factiva, accessed April 2014.
20. Cloud computing was the practice of using a network of remote servers hosted on the Internet to store, manage, and process data, rather than a local server or a personal computer. The only alternative to storing data on the Cloud was to have regional Internet data centres (IDCs), which were far too expensive for MatchMove to maintain as they were just starting out. https://www.google.com.sg/?gfe_rd=cr&ei=ELOaU82lN6eM8Qfkg4C4Ag&gws_rd=ssl#q=define+cloud+computing, accessed June 2014.
21. Aaron Tan,–SME Tech; They do the hard work for you in just weeks, "Singapore Press Holdings Limited", June 12, 2013, via Factiva, accessed April 2014.
22. Interestingly, as a result of the decision to host its software on the Cloud to be more responsive to gamers, MatchMove had to turn down funding from Singapore's Infocomm Development Authority (IDA), which would have provided government funded server-based solutions. It was a tough decision for MatchMove to make, because to them, at that time, it was a lot of money. However, the IDA was only focused on the usage of Singapore-based IDCs.
23. MatchMove, "Yahoo! Signs Strategic Partnership with MatchMove Games to Offer Consumers Hundreds of Popular Casual Game Titles", September 17, 2009, http://www.MatchMove.com/corporate/!-signs-strategic-partnership-with-MatchMove-games/, accessed April 2014.
24. MatchMove, "MatchMove Games Opens Online Store", December 10, 2009, http://www.MatchMove.com/corporate/MatchMove-games-opens-online-store/, accessed April 2014.
25. Aaron Tan, "SME Tech; They do the hard work for you in just weeks", Singapore Press Holdings Limited, June 12, 2013, via Factiva, accessed April 2014.
26. MatchMove, "Yahoo! Signs Strategic Partnership with MatchMove Games to Offer Consumers Hundreds of Popular Casual Game Titles", September 17, 2009, http://www.MatchMove.com/corporate/Yahoo-signs-strategic-partnership-with-MatchMove-games/, accessed April 2014.
27. Aaron Tan, "SME Tech; They do the hard work for you in just weeks", Singapore Press Holdings Limited, June 12, 2013, via Factiva, accessed April 2014.
28. Starhub was a fully integrated info-communications company providing a wide range of services for TV, mobile, internet and other platforms in Singapore.
29. An Application Programming Interface referred to a language and message format used by an application program to communicate with the operating system or some other control program such as a database management system (DBMS) or communications protocol. APIs were implemented by writing function calls in the program, which provided the linkage to the required subroutine for execution. Thus, an API implied that a driver or program module was available in the computer to perform the operation or that software must be linked into the existing program to perform the tasks. Refer http://www.pcmag.com/encyclopedia/term/37856/api, accessed June 2014.
30. Aaron Tan, "SME Tech; They do the hard work for you in just weeks", Singapore Press Holdings Limited, June 12, 2013, via Factiva, accessed April 2014.
31. MatchMove, "MatchMove Expands Social Media Capabilities", November 14, 2011, http://www.MatchMove.com/corporate/MatchMove-expands-social-media-capabilities/, accessed April 2014.
32. MatchMove, "Deloitte Honors MatchMove as the Fastest-Growing Tech Company in Southeast Asia", December 13, 2013, http://www.MatchMove.com/corporate/deloitte-honors-MatchMove-as-the-fastest-growing-tech-company-in-southeast-asia/, accessed April 2014.
33. Game developers could similarly use the APIs to integrate their games onto MatchMove's platform, to be in turn made available to MatchMove's customer websites and their millions of users. Refer "AppKungfu,–What is AppKungfu", http://www.appkungfu.net/overview/what-is-appkungfu, accessed April 2014.
34. While games were the primary type of content available, the platform could easily

power and socialise music and other forms of digital entertainment. Refer MatchMove, "MatchMove Launches Patent-Pending Social Networking and Gamification Product", August 13, 2014, http://www.MatchMove.com/corporate/MatchMove-launches-patent-pending-social-networking-and-gamification-product/, accessed April 2014.

35. MatchMove, "Gamification", http://www.MatchMove.com/corporate/gamification/, accessed April 2014.
36. The Oxford Dictionary, "Gamification", http://www.oxforddictionaries.com/definition/english/gamification, accessed April 2014.
37. Android referred to an operating system for smartphones, tablets and laptops from the Google-sponsored Open Handset Alliance. Android was a Linux OS, and Android apps were programmed in Java. www.pcmag.com/encyclopedia/term/58426/android, accessed June 2014.
38. Jacqueline Cheok,–Two start-ups based here are fastest-growing firms in SE Asia, "Business Times Singapore", Dec 23, 2013, via Factiva, accessed April 2014.

CASE 10

The Movie Exhibition Industry: 2018 and Beyond

Steve Gove,
University of Vermont

The scene: On a cold, dark, nearly deserted location a solitary figure, the last of his kind, stands sentinel. In this remote place, little has changed while elsewhere the world is transforming. The philosophical question: Are the systems, structures, and heroes of the past still relevant or are they obsolete? The action: An epic battle, which (spoiler alert!) not all will survive. Is this the plot to *The Last Jedi*, 2017's most successful motion picture? Certainly, but the situation is also analogous to that facing movie exhibitors—movie theaters—in 2018. A timeline of the industry matches the plot twists of even the most gripping sci-fi fantasy adventure (**Exhibit 1**). Consider the facts:

- As shown in **Exhibit 2**, 2017's $11.1 billion in domestic box office receipts[1] was near historical highs, but down 2.5 percent from 2016's record-setting year. Domestic box office revenue records were set in five of the prior ten years, but declined in the other five.
- At first glance, the 1.236 billion tickets sold domestically is impressive. However, attendance declined nearly 6 percent from 2016 and the long-term trend in attendance is negative; each year fewer people go to the movies. 2017's attendance is the lowest since 1992 and is down 21 percent from the most recent peak in 2002.
- The trend in per capita admissions is negative. In 2017, the average number of films seen per person was 3.7; in 2006, it was 4.7.[2] Both are well down from 1946's peak 4 billion tickets sold when the typical person attended 28 movies a year.
- In recent years ticket price increases have exceeded inflation indicating some recent pricing power. At $8.97, the average ticket price has risen 30 percent since 2007 (**Exhibit 3**). Recent price increases, however, occur at the same time as attendance has declined, raising concerns that prices now exceed the value provided to a greater number of potential viewers.
- The demographic trends in exhibitors' core domestic market are changing. Studios target an audience of 12–24 year olds. While this demographic group will increase 15% by 2035, the fastest growing segment of the population is those 60 and older. This population segment will grow 36 percent by 2035. Unfortunately, at 2.5 visits per year, this audience currently attends the movies the least (**Exhibit 4**).
- Movies are more widely available than ever, creating new substitutes for where, when, and how they are viewed.
- The industry's major initiative to lower costs and draw audiences fizzled out: investments of $2.6 billion since 2005 in digital projection (**Exhibit 5**) have not reduced costs or yielded parity compared with home theaters. Audience interest in 3D movies, available with digitization, appears limited. 3D ticket sales peaked in 2010 at 17 percent of tickets and have declined steadily to just 11 percent in 2017 (**Exhibits 2 & 6**).
- Exhibitors have little control over their largest cost: rental fees for motion pictures. Costs are high due to a small number of suppliers with high bargaining power due to highly differentiated content (**Exhibits 7, 10, & 12**).
- The industry is increasingly bifurcated between two markets, domestic (clear signs of maturity such as a declining number of screens domestically, increasing threat of substitution, difficulty innovating, and signs of consolidation) and international (growth, rapidly expanding theater counts, rising attendance, and increasing revenues) (**Exhibits 1, 8, & 9**).

Much like the Jedi in the *Star Wars* saga, movie exhibitors are engaged in an epic struggle. Exhibitors, much like the Jedi, have held a seemingly unquestionable place within society. Exhibitors have long held a position as ***the*** local face of the entertainment industry in communities. Are movie theaters still relevant?

Exhibit 1 Top 25 Motion Pictures Based on 2017 Domestic Box Office

							Domestic		International			Global			
Movie	2016 Dom. Gross	Dom. Rank	Studio	Genre	MPAA Rating	Prod. Budget (mil.)	Domestic Box Office to Budget Ratio	% Opening Weekend	Gross (mil.)	Rank	Intl. Box Office to Budget Ratio	Gross (mil.)	Rank	% Gross Outside U.S.	Global Box Office to Budget Ratio
Star Wars: The Last Jedi	$620	1	BV	S-F Fan	PG-13	$200	3.6	35%	$524	9	2.6	$1,334	1	74%	2.6
Beauty and the Beast (2017)	$504	2	BV	Fan	PG	$160	7.9	35%	$760	3	4.7	$1,264	2	60%	4.7
Wonder Woman	$413	3	WB	Act/Adv	PG-13	$149	5.5	25%	$406	13	2.7	$821	9	49%	2.7
Jumanji: Welcome to the Jungle	$405	4	Sony	Act	PG-13	$90	10.7	14%	$557	6	6.2	$962	5	58%	6.2
Guardians of the Galaxy Vol. 2	$390	5	BV	Act/Adv	PG-13	$200	4.3	38%	$474	11	2.4	$864	7	55%	2.4
Spider-Man: Homecoming	$334	6	Sony	Act/Adv	PG-13	$175	5.0	35%	$546	7	3.1	$880	6	62%	3.1
It	$327	7	WB (NL)	Horr	R	$35	20.0	38%	$373	16	10.7	$700	12	53%	10.7
Thor: Ragnarok	$315	8	BV	Act/Adv	PG-13	$180	4.7	39%	$539	8	3.0	$854	8	63%	3.0
Despicable Me 3	$265	9	Univ.	Anim	PG	$80	12.9	37%	$770	2	9.6	$1,035	4	74%	9.6
Justice League	$229	10	WB	Act/Adv	PG-13	$165	4.0	41%	$429	12	2.6	$658	13	65%	2.6
Logan	$226	11	Fox	Act/Adv	R	$97	6.4	39%	$393	15	4.0	$619	14	63%	4.0
The Fate of the Furious	$226	12	Univ.	Act	PG-13	$250	4.9	44%	$1,010	1	4.0	$1,236	3	82%	4.0
Coco	$210	13	BV	Anim	PG	$100	8.1	24%	$597	5	6.0	$807	10	74%	6.0
Dunkirk	$188	14	WB	War	PG-13	$100	5.3	27%	$337	19	3.4	$527	18	64%	3.4
Get Out	$176	15	Univ.	Horr	R	$5	56.7	19%	$79	25	17.6	$255	25	31%	17.6
The LEGO Batman Movie	$176	16	WB	Anim	PG	$80	3.9	30%	$136	24	1.7	$312	22	44%	1.7
The Boss Baby	$175	17	Fox	Anim	PG	$75	7.0	29%	$353	17	4.7	$528	17	67%	4.7
The Greatest Showman	$174	18	Fox	Mus	PG	$84	5.2	8%	$259	20	3.1	$433	20	60%	3.1
Pirates of the Caribbean: Dead Men Tell No Tales	$173	19	BV	Adv	PG-13	$230	3.5	45%	$622	4	2.7	$795	11	78%	2.7
Kong: Skull Island	$168	20	WB	Act/Adv	PG-13	$185	3.1	36%	$399	14	2.2	$567	16	70%	2.2
Cars 3	$153	21	BV	Anim	G	$100	3.8	35%	$231	21	2.3	$384	21	60%	2.3
War for the Planet of the Apes	$147	22	Fox	S-F Act	PG-13	$150	3.3	38%	$344	18	2.3	$491	19	70%	2.3
Split	$138	23	Univ.	Horr Thrl	PG-13	$9	30.9	29%	$140	23	15.6	$278	24	50%	15.6
Wonder	$132	24	LG	Drama	PG	$70	4.3	21%	$168	22	2.4	$301	23	56%	2.4
Transformers: The Last Knight	$130	25	Para	Sci-Fi Act	PG-13	$217	2.8	34%	$475	10	2.2	$605	15	79%	2.2
Total for Top 25	$6,394					$3,186			$10,921			$15,509			
Average for Top 25	$256					$127	9.1	32%	$437		4.9	$700		62%	4.9

Notes: Data from Boxofficemojo.com, MPAA, other sources and author estimates and calculations.
2017 Gross is total domestic gross for all films originally released in 2017. Domestic, international, and total gross encompasses entire theatrical release.
Studios: BV = Disney/Buena Vista/Pixar; Fox = 20th Century Fox, LG = Lionsgate, NL = New Line, Para = Paramount, Sony = Sony, Univ = Universal, WB = Warner Bros.,
Genres as follows: Act = Action, Adv = Adventure, Anim = Animation, Com = Comedy, Drama = Drama, Fant = Fantasy, Horr = Horror, Musc—Musical, S-F = Science Fiction
Some production budgets estimated.
Domestic = U.S. and Canada; International = Outside U.S. and Canada; Global = all locations
B:P Ratio = Total box office (domestic, international, and global) to Production Budget.
% O.W. = percentage of total domestic box office from the opening weekend.
Internal rank and global rank are based on international and global gross among the domestic top 25 motion pictures only.

Exhibit 2 Domestic Box Office Receipts & Ticket Sales, 1980–2017

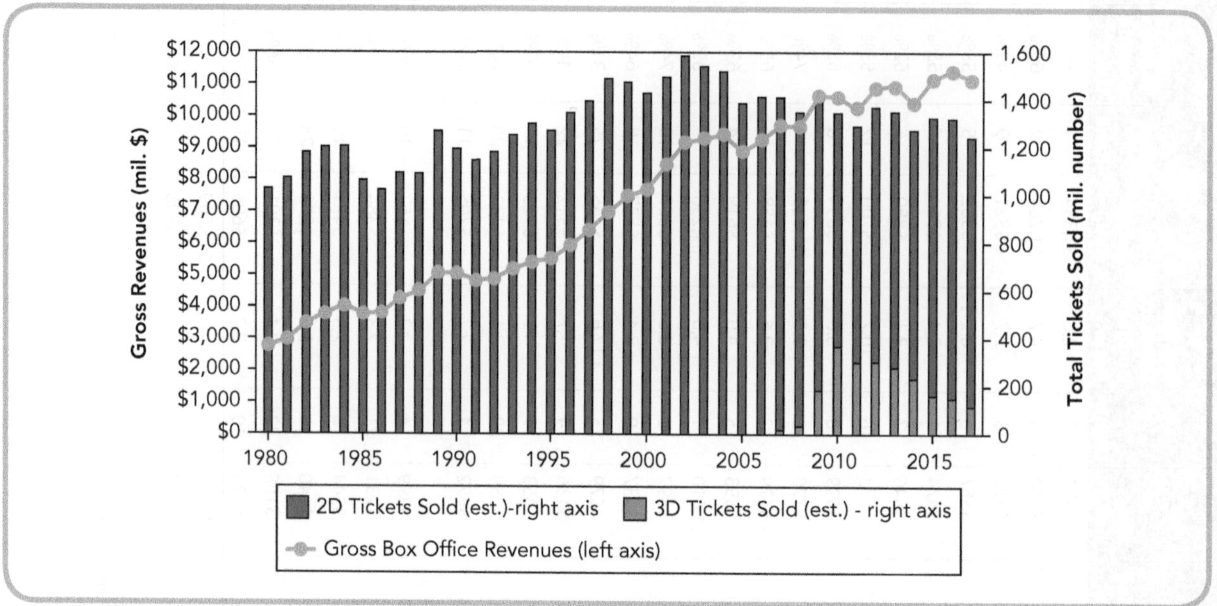

Data Source: Boxofficemojo.com, MPAA Theatrical Statistics & Theatrical and Home Entertainment Market Environment (THEME) Reports, and author estimates. Some years of 3D ticket volume estimated based on reported 3D revenues with ticket prices estimated as 30% premium over 2D.

Exhibit 3 Ticket Prices versus Inflation—1987–2017

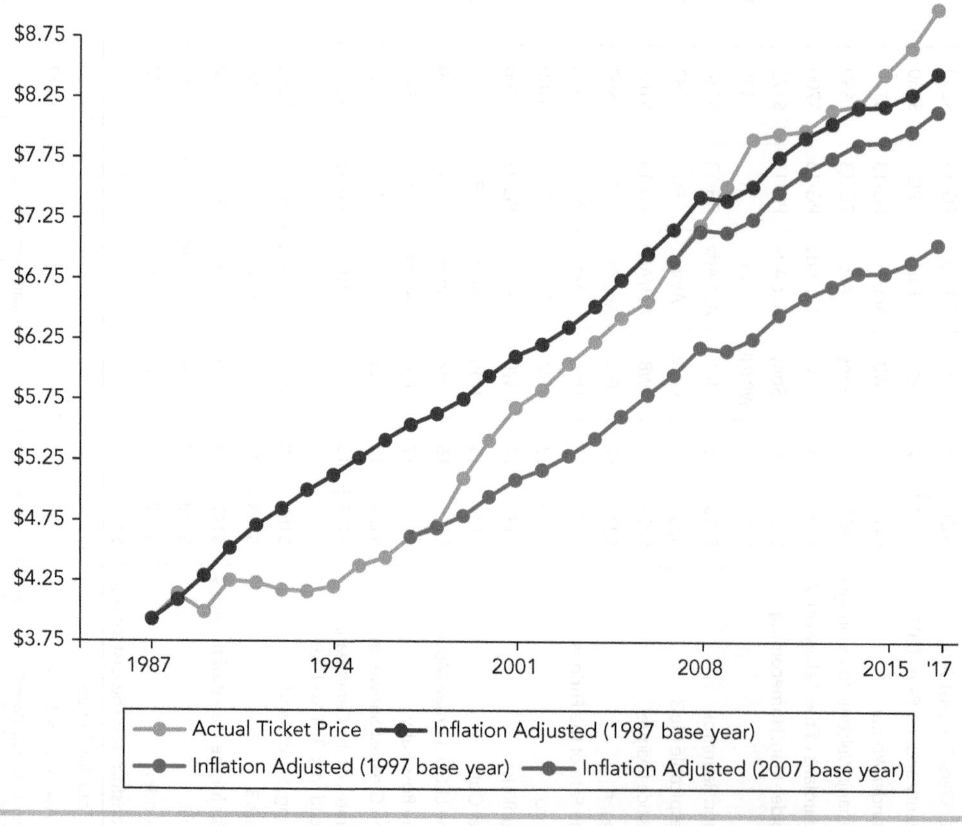

Notes: Inflation adjustments based on CPI values reported by Minneapolis Federal Reserve Bank, URL: https://www.minneapolisfed.org/community/financial-and-economic-education/cpi-calculator-information/consumer-price-index-and-inflation-rates-1913

Exhibit 4 U.S. Demographic & Admission Trends

	2017 Admissions			2018 Population		Est. 2035 Population		Change 2017–2035		Expected Impact of Change			
Age Segment	% of Tickets Purchased (2017)	Admissions Per Capita (2017)	% of Frequent Movie Goers[1]	# (mil.)	%	# (mil.)	%	# (mil.)	%	# Increase per Existing Screen (based on 40,246 screens)	New Annual Admissions per Screen (based on 2017 per capita rate)	Additional Admissions per Screen per Weekend	% of New Admissions
2 to 11 yrs	10%	2.9	8%	44.7	14%	50.0	13%	5.3	12%	131.6	381.8	7.3	9%
12 to 17 yrs	11%	4.9	13%	26.6	8%	30.6	8%	4.0	15%	99.5	487.7	9.4	11%
18 to 24 yrs	12%	4.7	12%	30.5	9%	35.7	9%	5.2	17%	130.2	612.0	11.8	14%
25 to 39 yrs	26%	4.4	26%	67.9	21%	73.3	19%	5.5	8%	136.5	600.8	11.6	14%
40 to 49 yrs	13%	3.6	15%	41.3	13%	48.7	13%	7.3	18%	182.2	655.8	12.6	15%
50 to 59 yrs	12%	3.0	13%	43.3	13%	43.8	12%	0.5	1%	12.3	36.8	0.7	1%
60 yrs+	16%	2.5	14%	71.7	22%	97.3	26%	25.6	36%	637.1	1,592.7	30.6	36%
	100%	U.S. Avg. in 2017 = 3.7	100%	326.0	100%	379.5	100%	53.5	15%	1,329.4	4,467.6	84.0	14%

Notes: Source: Data: U.S. Census (2014), https://www.census.gov/population/projections/data/national/2014/summarytables.html, author estimates, and MPAA Theatrical Statistics & Theatrical and Home Entertainment Market Environment (THEME) Reports.

[1] Frequent moviegoer defined by MPAA as one who attends the cinema at least once per month

[2] Based on 2017's 40,246 screens, actual # (not in mil.).

[3] Based on 2017 per capita admission rates by age group.

Exhibit 5 U.S. Theaters Screens 2000–2017

			Analog Screens			Digital Screens - Non-3D				Digital Screens - 3D					
Year	Total Screens	Change from Prior Year	#	Change from Prior Year	As % of Total Screens	#	Change from Prior Year	As % of Total Screen	Est. Digital Invest. ($ mil.)	#	Change from Prior Year	As % of Total Screens	As % of Digital Screens	Est. 3D Invest. ($ mil.)	Total Digital Investment ($ mil.)
2000	37,396		37,396		100.0%										
2001	36,764	−1.7%	36,764	−1.7%	100.0%										
2002	35,280	−4.0%	35,280	−4.0%	100.0%										
2003	36,146	2.5%	36,146	2.5%	100.0%										
2004	36,594	1.2%	36,594	1.2%	100.0%										
2005	38,852	6.2%	38,862	6.2%	100.0%	200		0.5%	$10						$10
2006	38,415	−1.1%	36,412	−6.3%	94.8%	2,003	901.5%	5.2%	$90						$90
2007	38,974	1.5%	34,342	−5.7%	88.1%	3,646	82.0%	9.4%	$82	986		2.5%	21.3%	$74	$156
2008	38,843	−0.3%	33,319	−3.0%	85.8%	4,088	12.1%	10.5%	$22	1,427	44.7%	3.7%	25.9%	$33	$55
2009	39,233	1.0%	31,815	−4.5%	81.1%	4,149	1.5%	10.6%	$3	3,269	129.1%	8.3%	44.1%	$138	$141
2010	39,547	0.8%	23,773	−25.3%	60.1%	7,937	91.3%	20.1%	$189	7,837	139.7%	19.8%	49.7%	$343	$532
2011	39,641	0.2%	14,020	−41.0%	35.4%	12,620	59.0%	31.8%	$234	13,001	65.9%	32.8%	50.7%	$387	$621
2012	42,803	8.0%	6,426	−54.2%	15.0%	21,643	71.5%	50.6%	$451	14,734	13.3%	34.4%	40.5%	$130	$581
2013	42,184	−1.4%	2,990	−53.5%	7.1%	24,042	11.1%	57.0%	$120	15,782	7.1%	37.4%	39.6%	$79	$199
2014	43,265	2.6%	1,747	−41.6%	4.0%	25,372	5.5%	58.6%	$67	16,146	2.3%	37.3%	38.9%	$27	$94
2015	43,661	0.9%	1,109	−36.5%	2.5%	26,111	2.9%	59.8%	$37	16,441	1.8%	37.7%	38.6%	$22	$59
2016	43,531	−0.3%	872	−21.4%	2.0%	25,914	−0.8%	59.5%	$0	16,745	1.8%	38.5%	39.3%	$23	$23
2017	43,036	−1.1%	0	−100.0%	0.0%	26,238	1.3%	61.0%	$16	16.978	1.4%	39.5%	39.3%	$17	**$34**
									$1,322					**$1,273**	**$2,595**

Notes: Based on author estimates and MPAA Theatrical Statistics & Theatrical and Home Entertainment Market Environment (THEME) Report on # screens. Estimated investments (cumulative) based on estimated cost of digital screen ($50,000 per installation) and digital 3D ($75,000 per installation).

Exhibit 6 Domestic 3D—Screens, Revenues, & Releases

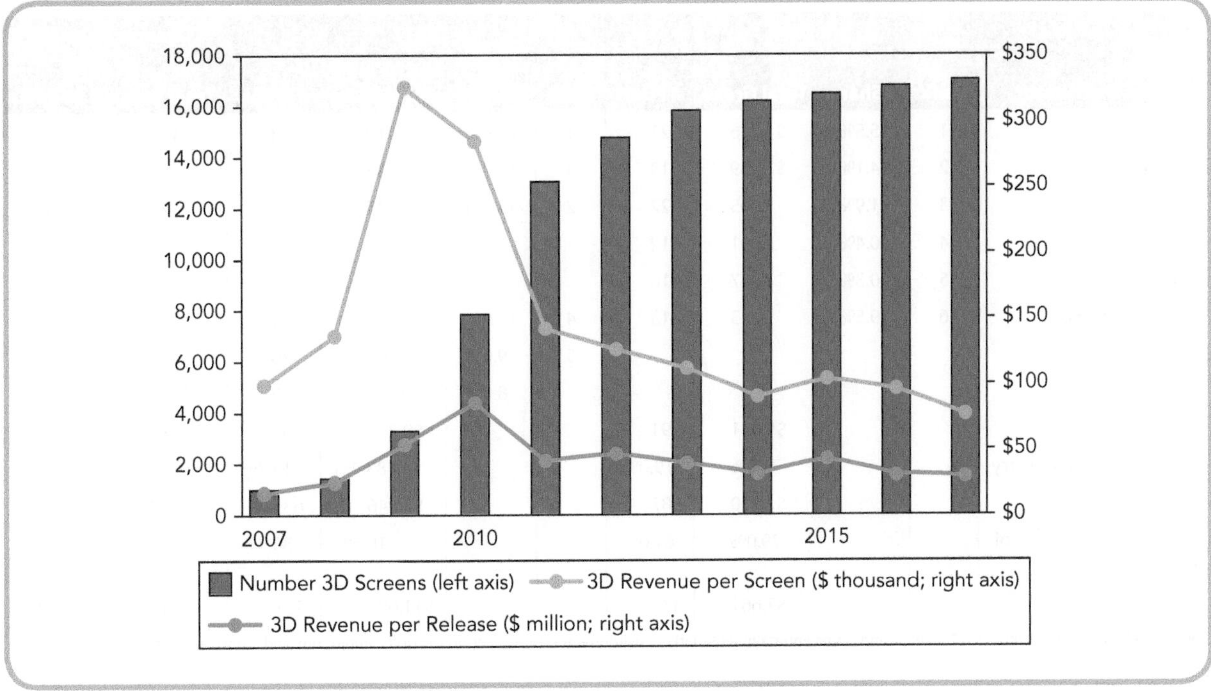

Notes: Data from MPAA Theatrical Statistics & Theatrical and Home Entertainment Market Environment (THEME) Reports, NATO, boxofficemojo, and author estimates.

Will they survive? Might movie theaters go the way of the Jedi and cease to exist? Might your local movie theater be *The Last Exhibitor*?

The Motion Picture Value Chain

The structure of the motion picture value chain has changed little since the 1920s. It consists of three stages: studio production, distribution, and exhibition—the theaters that show the films.

Studio Production

The studios produce the industry's life force: motion picture content. Studios are highly concentrated with the top six responsible for a minority of films, but the majority of domestic[3] film revenues (see **Exhibit 7**). Even within the top studios, concentration is increasing due to fewer films with larger budgets and global appeal. In 2017, the top six studios produced 101 major motion pictures (14 percent of films). Yet these films constitute 83 percent of all domestic box office receipts, up from 71 percent for the top six in 2000. Studios collectively released 738 films in 2017, an average of 14 per week. The math for exhibitors is this: Two are by Hollywood's major studios. Show those films or the audience will not attend. The combination of high studio concentration and highly differentiated content gives the studios considerable negotiating and pricing power over exhibitors.

The financial risk for studios is significant as production costs are considerable (**Exhibit 1**). Studios invested $3 billion for what became 2017's highest grossing 25 films ($127 million per film; range: $5 million to $250 million). Risks continue to increase as production budgets have skyrocketed. In 1980, the production budget for the highest grossing films averaged just $11 million. In the 1990s, films turned to special effects and costs reached $102 million (up 827 percent). Today, special effects alone can top $100 million for a major production. These investments, however, are no guarantee for success; a proven formula remains elusive. Many "sure things" flop at the box office while others surprise.

Large hauls at the box office are a poor indication of wise production decisions; profitability is the ratio of box office receipts to production cost. While Hollywood has long made assessing profitability nearly impossible, at a box office, gross to production cost ratio of 2.0 a film has generally covered its costs. *The Last Jedi's* $1.3 billion global box office covered its estimated $200 million cost of production 2.6 times (a success), but not a smash. Meanwhile a

Exhibit 7 Top 6 Studios / Distributors 2017

	2000				2017				% Change 2000–2017	
Studio / Distributor	**Rank**	**$ Share**	**Total Gross**	**# Films**	**Rank**	**$ Share**	**Total Gross**	**# Films**	**Total Gross**	**# Films**
Buena Vista	1	15.5%	$1,176	21	1	21.8%	$2,410	8	105%	−62%
Universal	2	14.1%	$1,069	13	3	13.8%	$1,529	14	111%	8%
Warner Bros.	3	11.9%	$905	22	2	18.4%	$2,035	20	125%	−9%
Paramount	4	10.4%	$791	12						
Dreamworks SKG	5	10.3%	$777	10						
20th Century Fox	6	9.5%	$723	13	4	12.0%	$1,326	14	24%	8%
Sony / Columbia					5	9.6%	$1,060	26	55%	−10%
Lionsgate					6	8.0%	$885	19	2574%	6%
Total for top 6			$5,441	91			$9,245	101	70%	11%
Top 6 as % of industry			71.0%	19.0%			83.4%	13.7%	17%	
All other studios			$2,220	387			$1,846	637	−17%	65%
All other studios as % of industry			29.0%	81.0%			16.6%	86.3%		
Industry Total			$7,661	478			$11,091	738	45%	54%

Source: MPAA Theatrical Statistics & Theatrical and Home Entertainment Market Environment (THEME) Reports, boxofficemojo.com, and author estimates.

largely unknown horror film, *Get Out*, produced for just $5 million, was an enormous critical and financial success. By the end of its theatrical run, the picture had grossed $176 million domestically, yielding a 56.7 ratio of box office receipts to production cost. The level of investments and risk results in studios putting return on their investment ahead of all other parties, including exhibitors.

Studios focus on 12–24 year olds, consistently the largest audience for movies. At just 17 percent of the U.S. population, this group purchases 23 percent of all tickets (per capital attendance of 4.8 movies per year). More narrowly, 10 percent of the population are "frequent" moviegoers, those who attend more than one movie per month, and are responsible for half of all ticket sales. 35 percent of these frequent moviegoers are 12–24 year olds.[4] Studios target this audience with PG and PG-13 fare including 20 of 2017's top 25 releases. However, more demographic trends are more favorable in other segments (**Exhibit 4**). While the U.S. population will increase 15 percent by 2035, this core audience will grow 16%, just 229 people per current theater screen or 21 additional attendees per screen on the typical weekend. The largest growth—in both percentage and number of individuals—is among 60+ year olds. This market currently has the lowest admissions per capita, just 2.5 annually, but represents a potentially lucrative market increasing by 25.6 million, up 36 percent. At current per capita attendance levels, the increased population in this segment adds more than 30 potential viewers per screen per weekend. Attracting this audience is largely outside of the control of the exhibitors, dependent instead on whether the studios produce films attractive to them.

Domestic exhibitors were once the sole distribution channel for films. This has changed dramatically. Within the top 25 domestic films, 62 percent of all box office revenue was from outside the domestic market. Over 73 percent of total global box office revenues are derived outside of the domestic market (**Exhibit 8**). Studios view this as their primary opportunity for growth, as both ticket sales and dollar volume are rising rapidly. From 2000 to 2017, domestic receipts grew at a compounded annual rate of under 3 percent while international grew at nearly 9 percent. Based on attendance, both India's 2.02 billion and China's 1.26 billion admissions in 2015 exceeded that of the U.S. Unlike the domestic market, attendance in these markets is increasing each year. The studios are also changing their perspective on ticket prices in large population markets. In India, for example, attendees pay an average of just $0.78. In China, it is $5.10.[5]

Exhibit 8 Domestic versus International Box Office Receipts 2000–2017

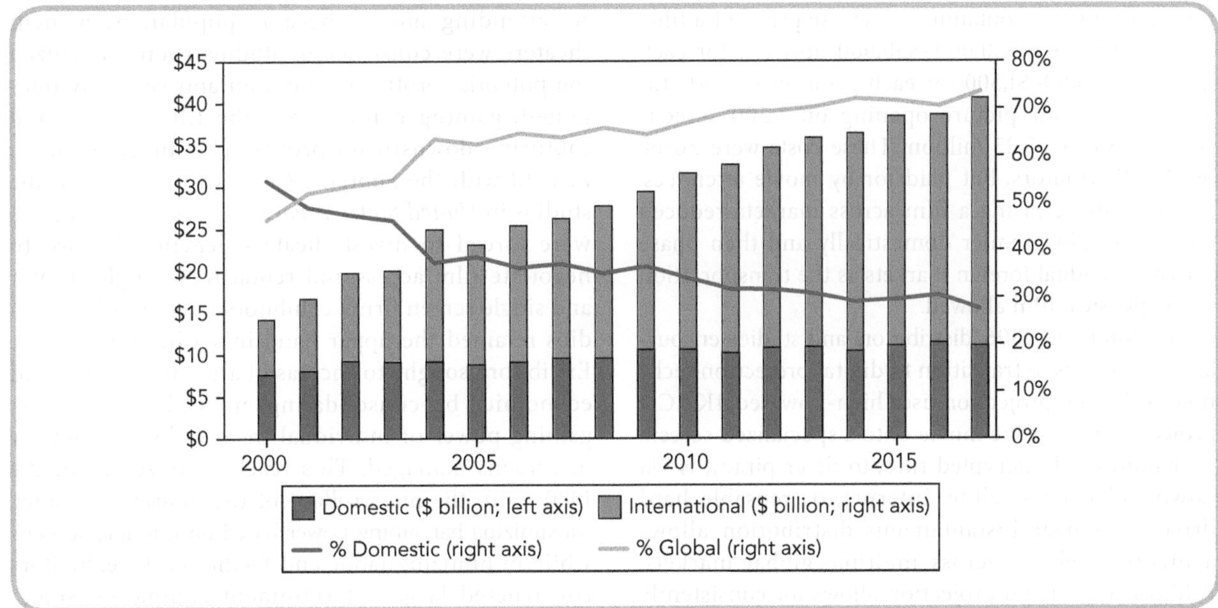

This has led studios to internationalize their content. While horror films like *Get Out* and dramas like *Wonder* require smaller production budgets than science fiction, action, and adventure films, they are riskier in international markets. The subtle nuances of a drama are easily lost across cultures and the appeal of horror films culturally dependent. Animated films targeting children, such as *Coco* and *Cars 3,* and action-packed franchise films with known characters, little dialogue, made in 3D, and laden with special effects, such as *The Fate of the Furious,* have the greatest potential for cross-cultural appeal. Yet, these films carry two risks: lack of appeal to the 60+ demographic segment in the U.S. and larger budgets. Action-packed franchise films target the 12–24-year-old segment of the population, but are the least desirable domestically among the fastest growing segment of the domestic market, those 60+. Costs are also higher, increasing the risk if a movie bombs. Among the top 10 highest internationally grossing U.S. studio-produced films in 2017, the average production budget was $158 million—one quarter higher than the average for the top 25—and only two animated films, *Despicable Me 3* and *Jumanji: Welcome to the Jungle,* had production under $100 million.

As studios shift their focus to the international market, they are increasingly less dependent on the domestic market, further increasing their bargaining power over exhibitors. The internationalization of the motion picture industry is starkly different for studios and exhibitors: Studios are seeking to increase revenues through product licensing, DVD and digital sales, and international expansion; domestic exhibitors remain wholly reliant on charging an unchanging core market of viewers to see movies.

Distribution

Distributors are the intermediaries between the studios and exhibitors. Distribution entails all steps following a film's artistic completion including marketing, logistics, and administration. Distributors negotiate a percentage of box office receipts for distribution services or purchase rights to films and profit directly from box office receipts. Distributors select and market films to exhibitors' booking agents, handle collections, audit reported attendance, and perform other administrative tasks. There are over 300 distributors, but the majority of work is done by a few majors, commonly a division of a studio. The production of 2017's *It*, an adaptation of Stephen King's book, was led by New Line Cinema with four other production companies credited. Warner Brothers released and distributed the film, both domestically and across international markets.

Until 2005, the distribution of motion pictures entailed the physical shipment of large reels of 35 mm film, a process largely unchanged since the 1940s.

Each theater would receive a shipment of heavy physical canisters containing a "release print" of a film. These prints cost $20,000–$30,000 up-front for each film plus $1,000–$1,500 for each print. Print costs for a modern major picture opening on 3,500 screens come to $3.50–$5.25 million. These costs were borne by the distributors, but paid for by movie attendees. Sequentially releasing a film across markets reduced costs. It would premier domestically and then phase across individual foreign markets as the transportation of the physical film allowed.

Beginning in 2006, distributors and studios encouraged exhibitors to transition to digital projection technology. Digital projection uses high-powered 4K LCD projectors to cast the movie onto a specialized screen. Distribution of encrypted files, to deter piracy, is via download from satellite, Internet, or reusable hard drive. This near instantaneous distribution allows a picture's release across multiple global markets. Additionally, digital projection allows for consistently high-quality images, as there is no physical wear to the film, and enables the exhibition of "alternative content"—including sports, concerts, performance, and other events created and distributed outside of the motion picture studio value chain. This re-projecting of the domestic industry replaced film projection with digital. At the end of 2017, virtually 100 percent of commercial U.S. screens utilize digital projection, up from just five percent in 2006 (**Exhibit 5**). Each digital projection system serves a single screen and costs $50,000 to $75,000 including the projector, computers and hardware, and a specialized screen. This equates to a capital cumulative investment of approximately $2.6 billion in the U.S. alone. Virtual print fees, rebates from distributors on each film distributed digitally, partially funded the conversion. These fees, as much as 17 percent of rental costs, expired in 2013. Despite the cost savings of digital distribution, film rental rates, which include the cost of distribution, have averaged 50–55 percent of box office revenue for several decades. This suggests that the studios, not the exhibitors, benefit from the reduced cost of distribution.

Exhibition

Exhibitors—the local movie theater—provide a location where audiences can view a motion picture. The basic business model of exhibitors—using movies as the draw and selling concessions to make a profit—has changed little since the time of touring motion picture shows that would set up in town halls and churches. As attending movies became popular, permanent theaters were constructed. Studios soon recognized the potential profit in exhibition and vertically integrated, gaining control over the films shown and capturing downstream profits. This practice ended in 1948 with the Supreme Court's ruling against the studios in *United States v. Paramount Pictures*. Studios were forced to divest theaters, leaving the two to negotiate film access and rental fees. Single theater and single screen firms' exhibitors fared poorly as studios retained the upper hand in setting rental rates. Exhibitors sought to increase bargaining power and economies by consolidating, multiplying the bargaining power of individual theaters by the number of screens managed. This reached its zenith in the 1980s with the mass rollout of the multiplex concept. Maximizing bargaining power based on multiple screens while minimizing labor and facility costs, exhibitors constructed large entertainment complexes, sometimes with dozens of screens. Most of the original local single screen theaters closed, unable to compete on cost or viewing experience.

Today, the 10 largest exhibitor "circuits" operate 32 percent of theaters, controlling a disproportionate 54 percent of screens (**Exhibit 9**). In many industries, this high concentration of industry outlets would provide the firms with significant buying power. Larger circuits benefit from some power as larger circuits can negotiate slightly better prices on some concession supplies and access revenues from national advertisers. However, movie content is highly differentiated; theaters are not. An exhibitor trying to drive too hard of a bargain may miss showing a film on opening weekend. Thus, the true power rests with the studios and distributors.

At the top of the circuits are the four largest all national chains: AMC, Regal, and Cinemark serving the U.S., and Cineplex serving Canada. These chains operate large multiplexes, averaging 12 screens per location. These firms operate under one third of all U.S. and Canadian theater locations, but 54 percent of screens. The next tier of circuits consists of regional operators (Marcus, Harkins, Southern, B&B, National Amusements, and Malco). The regional operators control another 4.7 percent of theaters and 7.5 percent of screens. The remaining circuits, 63 percent of all theaters operating 38 percent of screens, range from smaller chains operating several miniplexes consisting of 2–7 screens down to single theater, single screen locations.

Exhibit 9 Leading Domestic Circuits 2017

		U.S. & Canada					Non-U.S. & Canada			Global		
Circuit & Headquarters Location	U.S. Theater Brands (Locations)	# Theaters	% of U.S. Theaters	# Screens	% of U.S. Screens	Avg. Screens per Theater	# Theaters	# Screens	% of Non-U.S. Screens	# Theaters	Screens	% Global Screens
AMC Theatres[*] Kansas City, KS	AMC & Carmike (national)	656	12.2%	8,218	20.4%	12.5	862	7,087	4.3%	1,802	15,380	9.0%
Regal Entertainment Group[**] Knoxville, TN	Regal, United Artists & Edwards (national)	566	10.5%	7,379	18.3%	13.0	3	23	0.0%	561	7,402	4.3%
Cinemark[***] Plano, TX	Cinemark & Century (national)	339	6.3%	4,561	11.3%	13.5	194	1,398	0.8%	533	5,959	3.5%
Cineplex Entertainment Toronto, ON Canada	Cineplex Cinemas, VIP, Galaxy & Silver City (Canada)	165	3.1%	1,683	4.2%	10.2	0	0	0.0%	165	1,683	1.0%
Marcus Theatres Milwaukee, WI	Marcus (WI, IL, IA, MN, MO, NE, ND & OH)	68	1.3%	885	2.2%	13.0	0	0	0.0%	68	885	0.5%
Harkins Theatres Scottsdale, AZ	Harkins (AZ, CA, CO, OK, & TX)	33	0.6%	501	1.2%	15.2	0	0	0.0%	33	501	0.3%
Southern Theatres New Orleans, LA	The Grand Theaters, AmStar Cinemas & Movie Tavern (LA, MS, NC, TX & FL)	44	0.8%	499	1.2%	11.3	0	0	0.0%	44	499	0.3%
National Amusements Norwood, MA	Showcase, Cinema de Lux, Multiplex, SuperLux and UCI (MA, NY, RI, CT, NJ & OH)	29	0.5%	392	1.0%	13.5	40	558	0.3%	69	950	0.6%
B&B Theatres Liberty, MO	B&B Theaters (MO, KS, OK, FL, TX, AR & MS)	47	0.9%	377	0.9%	8.0	0	0	0.0%	47	377	0.2%
Malco Theatres Inc. Memphis, TN	Malco & local names (TN, MS, AR, LA, MO, KY)	34	0.6%	353	0.9%	10.4	0	0	0.0%	34	353	0.2%
Total for top four		1,726	32.0%	21,841	54.3%	12.7	1,059	8,508	5.1%	3,061	30,424	17.7%
Total for # 5-10		255	4.7%	3,007	7.5%	11.8	40	558	0.3%	295	3,565	2.1%
Total for top 10		1,981	36.7%	24,848	61.7%	12.5	1,099	9,066	5.4%	3,356	33,989	19.8%
All others		3,417	63.3%	15,398	38.3%	4.5		157,291	94.6%		137,766	80.2%
Industry total		5,398	100.0%	40,246	100.0%	7.5		166,357	100.0%		171,755	100.0%

Notes: # Domestic (US & Canadian) theaters and screens based on 2017 NATO data & 2017 MPAA 2017 Theatrical statistics; 171,755 global screens is per MPAA Theatrical and Home Entertainment Market Environment (THEME) Report, author estimates for international theaters and screens for some firms.

[*]Under AMC: Odeon (Europe (U.K., Spain, Italy & Germany: 242 theaters /2,243 screens), Nordic (Scandinavia 68/473). Same common parent control of: Hoyts (Australia: 52/424), Wanda (China: 447/3,947).

[**]Guam, Saipan & American Samoa.

[***]Brazil (81 theaters / 608 screens), Colombia (35/193), Argentina (21/184), Central America (includes Honduras, El Salvador, Nicaragua, Costa Rica, Panama, and Guatemala, 16/120), Chile (18/126), Peru (13/93), Ecuador (7/45), Bolivia (1/13), Paraguay (1/10), and Curacao (1/6).

The Business of Exhibition

Exhibitors have three revenue sources: box office receipts, concessions, and advertising (see **Exhibits 10 & 12**). They have low discretion: their ability to influence revenues and expenses is limited. Exhibitor operating margins average a slim 10 percent; net income may fluctuate wildly based on the tax benefits of prior losses.

Box Office Revenues

Ticket sales constitute almost two-thirds of exhibition business revenues. The return, however, is quite small due to the power of the studios. Among the largest exhibitors, film rental fees average 54 percent of box office receipts. These costs are typically higher for smaller circuits. The bases for rental rates are: the size of the circuit and both the duration and seat commitment. While attendees may gripe about the average ticket price of $8.97, most do not realize that $4.85 (55 percent) goes to the studio. The exhibitor may not break even unless concessions are purchased.

The portion of box office revenues retained by the theater increases each week. On opening weekend, an exhibitor may pay the distributor 80–90 percent of the box office gross in rental fees, retaining only 10–20 percent. In subsequent weeks, the exhibitor's portion increases to as much as 80–90 percent. For truly event films, studios have considerable power and can capture a higher percentage of the box office. For *The Last Jedi*, the standard exhibition contract stipulated a rental rate of about 65 percent of the ticket price and required exhibitors to show the film on their largest screens for 4 weeks, or the rate increased to 70 percent.[6]

While non-opening weekends offer exhibitors larger margins, the studios focus on attracting audiences on opening weekend with well-funded publicity campaigns.

Exhibit 10 Typical Revenue & Expenses per Screen at an 8-Screen Theater

REVENUES	Annual	%	Avg. Weekend
Box Office Revenue	$275,477	63%	$5,298
Concessions	$146,491	33%	$2,817
Advertising	$18,426	4%	$354
Total Revenues ($13.34 per admission)	$440,394	100%	$8,469
EXPENSES			
Fixed			
Facility	$66,059	15%	$1,270
Labor	$39,635	9%	$762
Utilities	$48,443	11%	$932
Other SG&A	$79,271	18%	$1,524
Total Fixed Costs	$233,409	53%	$4,489
Variable			
Film Rental	$148,758	54%	$2,861
Concession Supplies	$20,509	14%	$394
Total Variable Costs	$169,266	36%	$3,255
Total Expenses	$402,675	89%	$7,744
OPERATING INCOME	$37,719	8.6%	$725

Notes:
Box Office Revenue: 1,236,000,000 attendees in 2017 / 40,246 screens = 30,711 attendees annually per screen X $8.97 per ticket = $275,477 annual box office revenue per screen. Data reported in Exhibits 2 and 9.
Concessions Revenue: 30,711 attendees annually per screen X $4.77/admission (avg. concessions sales per admission from Exhibit 12 (AMC, Regal & Cinemark) = $146,491
Advertising Revenue: $750 million in 2017 (exhibit 11) / 1,236,000,000 attendees in 2017 = $0.60 / admission X 30,711 attendees annually per screen = $18,426 annually.
Fixed Expenses: Author estimates based on analysis of select large exhibitor SEC filings, MPAA and NATO data; scaled to a single screen within an 8-theater multiplex; values may deviate from industry average and any individual firm.
Variable Expenses: Film rental: 54% of Box Office Admission Revenue based on average for AMC, Regal & Cinemark in the domestic market.
Concession Supplies: 14% Percentage of Concession Revenue
Average weekend calculated as Annual / 52

Focusing on getting audiences to the theater on the opening weekend results in lower marketing expenses for each film, keeps the film pipeline flowing with releases, and avoids competition between films for a common audience (e.g., two R-rated comedies opening the same weekend). Among 2017's top 10 releases, an average of 32 percent of total domestic revenues were on the opening weekend. Two 2017 films, *The Fate of the Furious* and *Pirates of the Caribbean: Dead Men Tell No Tales*, received more than 40 percent of their total domestic box office revenue in the opening weekend. While these films draw audiences, they are less lucrative than films staying in the theater for multiple weeks. Exhibitors can actually keep more of the box office receipts from films such as *The Greatest Showman*, with just 9 percent of total revenue in the opening weekend, and *Jumanji: Welcome to the Jungle* and *Get Out*, which each had less than 20 percent of revenues on the opening weekend.

Such films are, however, the exception. A weak opening weekend typically results in a short run in theaters as attendance declines when studio-funded marketing campaigns shift toward the next film. In industry terminology, the "multiple" (the percentage coming after opening weekend) has been declining steadily, falling 25 percent since 2002.[7] This limits an exhibitor's potential to save on film rental costs by skipping opening weekend. A theater will typically lose attendees as audiences seek another theater if one does not show a film on opening weekend.

Concessions

A frequent moviegoer lament is high concession prices. At an average of $4.77 per admission, concessions constitute one-third of exhibitor revenues. Direct costs of under 15 percent make concessions the primary source of exhibitor profit. Three factors drive concession profits: attendance, pricing, and material costs. The most important is attendance: more attendees yields more concession sales. Sales influence price. The $5.00 and $9.00 price points for the large soda and popcorn are not accidental, but the result of considerable market research and profit maximization calculations. The inputs are largely commodities. Volume purchases reduce costs. Large circuits negotiate better prices on everything from popcorn and soda pop to cups and napkins.

Once consisting of only boxed candy, popcorn, and soft drinks purchased at the counter in the lobby, concessions now include a variety of food, drink, and location options. Concession options such as hamburgers, salads, hot appetizers, and alcoholic beverage sales increase average concession sales per patron. They must, however, be considered in conjunction with higher costs for kitchen facilities, labor, and food ingredients. A $15 burger has a lower gross margin percentage than a $9 tub of popcorn due to higher food costs, but may not the same profit in dollars. Patrons may skip one $5 soda for several rounds of $8 beer, wine, or bar sales.

Exhibitors have placed increased attention on concessions due to dual appeal: audiences are attracted to the new experience of dining at the theater while exhibitors benefit from the sale of higher dollar concessions. Exhibitors are aggressively pursuing this revenue stream through a variety of means including enhanced counter service, in-lobby and in-theater ordering, and waiter service. The profitability of these approaches requires careful evaluation to ensure profitability is increased.

Advertising

The low margins derived from ticket sales cause exhibitors to focus on other sources of revenue. The highest margin, therefore the most attractive, is advertising, including pre-show and lobby advertising and previews. Advertising revenues have increased from $186 million in 2002 to $751 million in 2017 (**Exhibit 11**).[8] More importantly, the time devoted to ads in each showing has increased. The number of previews has also increased from just three or four, ten years ago to six or seven, currently. This includes the two typically provided to the studio as part of the film rental agreement.[9] Though advertising constitutes just five percent of exhibitor revenues, it is highly profitable and growing. Instead of paying for short films' top show prior to the feature, exhibitors show ads, which they are paid to show. Advertising revenues for exhibitors averaged $18,652 per screen in 2017, $0.61 per admission, up 15 percent in just five years.[10] Yet audiences express dislike for advertising at the theater and, if dissatisfaction increases, may opt to view movies at home. Balancing the lucrative revenues from ads with audience tolerance is an ongoing struggle for exhibitors.

The Major Exhibitor Circuits

Four exhibitor "circuits" dominate the domestic market, collectively controlling 34 percent of domestic theaters but a disproportionate 55 percent of screens. The four circuits serve different geographic areas and operate with different business-level strategies (see **Exhibit 9**).[11] AMC is the largest domestic exhibitor with 8,218 screens in 656 theaters. Domestically, the circuit uses the AMC and Loews chains to concentrate on urban areas near large population centers such as those in California,

Exhibit 11 Exhibitor Advertising Revenue (Total & Per Admission)

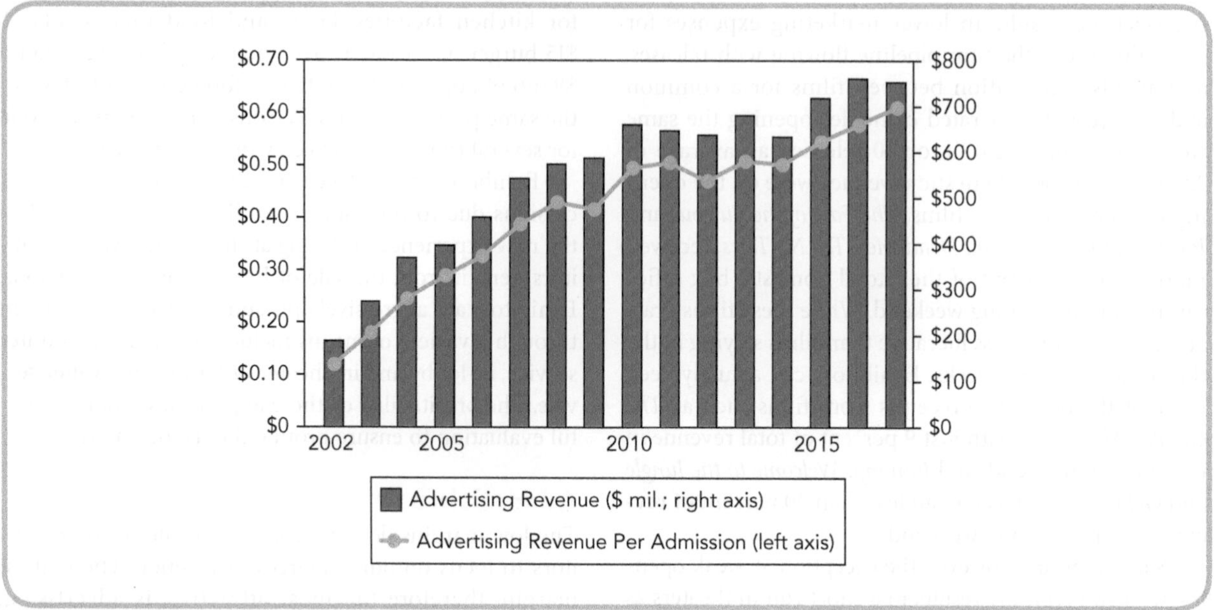

Sources: Author calculations based on data from Cinema Advertising Council, 2017, MPAA Theatrical Statistics & Theatrical and Home Entertainment Market Environment (THEME) Report, boxofficemojo.com

Florida, and Texas with megaplex theaters averaging 12.5 screens. By offering 3-D, IMAX, and other premium viewing experiences, AMC's ticket prices are consistently near the top of the market. Concession sales per attendee is also the highest among the majors at $5.06 per patron (see **Exhibit 12**).

AMC's operations became much more diverse in 2016 when it acquired the former #4 domestic circuit, Carmike Theaters. Carmike focused on small to mid-sized markets, targeting populations of less than 100,000 that have few alternative entertainment options. They served this market with no-frills locations averaging 10 screens per theater. At $1 below the industry average, the ticket price reflects the low cost. Concessions sales per patron were the lowest in the industry. Carmike's locations have been rebranded as AMC and AMC Classic locations. The acquisition of Carmike made AMC the largest domestic theater chain with control over 20 percent of domestic screens. Combining the companies was expected to reduce costs by $35 million annually.[12]

Dalian Wanda Group, a Chinese conglomerate with commercial real estate and cultural holdings, acquired AMC in 2012 for a reported $2.6 billion.[13] To many observers, the acquisition signaled the start of an expected wave of consolidation and globalization in the movie exhibition industry. At the time of the acquisition, Wanda operated some 150 theaters in China as well as significant studio production facilities. The acquisition resulted in Wanda becoming both the single largest and the most geographically diverse exhibitor globally. Since the acquisition of AMC, Wanda has continued its acquisition approach to expansion by purchasing the European Odeon circuit and Australia's Hoyts. In 2017, Wanda/AMC announced the acquisition of Nordic, another European-based circuit with operations in Scandinavia. Once finalized, Wanda/AMC will be the world's largest theater circuit with more than 15,000 screens across more than 1,800 theaters. The scale and reach of the company is unprecedented: one company controlling nearly 10 percent of global screens across all of the major viewing markets. This scale could result in greater leverage negotiating rental rates.

Unlike AMC, Regal, the second largest domestic chain, operates nearly exclusively in the U.S. with its namesake Regal as well as United Artists and Edwards Theaters. The firm operates 7,379 screens across 566 theaters. Regal focuses on midsize markets using multi- and megaplexes with 13 screens per location, with an average ticket price of $10.20 and average concession sales of $4.72 per admission. Cinemark, the #3 domestic circuit by size, operates 339 domestic locations with 4,559 screens under the Cinemark and Century brands. Cinemark serves smaller markets, operating as the sole theater in 90 percent of its markets. Its average ticket price is $7.78. Cinemark was the first domestic circuit to expand beyond the domestic market and currently

Exhibit 12 Select 2017 AMC, Cinemark & Regal Financials

	AMC*	Cinemark**	Regal***
Theater and Attendance Information			
Screens (U.S. only)	8,224	4,559	7,322
Theaters (U.S. only)	649	339	560
Screens per Theater (U.S. only)	12.7	13.4	13.1
Total US Attendance (in thousands)	240,974	174,400	196,900
Avg. Ticket Price	$9.67	$7.78	$10.20
Avg. Concessions	$5.06	$4.53	$4.72
Avg. Ad Revenue per admittance	$0.72	$0.43	$1.14
Avg. Revenue per admittance	$15.45	$12.74	$16.06
Avg. Attendance per screen	29,301	38,254	26,892
Avg. Admission revenue per screen	$283,344	$297,616	$274,294
Income Statement ($ mil.)			
Revenues			
Admissions	$2,330.90	$1,356.90	$2,008.10
Concessions	$1,220.10	$790.10	$930.20
Other Income	$172.50	$75.10	$224.70
Total Revenues	$3,723.50	$2,222.10	$3,163.00
Admissions as % of Revenues	62.60%	61.06%	63.49%
Concessions as % of Revenues	32.77%	35.56%	29.41%
Other as % of Revenues	4.63%	3.38%	7.10%
Expenses			
Film rental and advertising	$1,224.70	$756.40	$1,067.80
Concessions	$176.60	$112.80	$123.80
Building, wages, utilities & other operating costs	$2,285.50	$1,030.70	$1,699.70
Total Cost of Operation	$3,686.80	$1,899.90	$2,891.30
Operating Income	$36.70	$322.20	$271.70
Operating Income per admission	$0.15	$1.85	$1.38
Operating Income as % total revenue	0.99%	14.50%	8.59%
Film rental and advertising as % of admission revenues	52.54%	55.74%	53.17%
Concessions costs as % of concession revenues	14.47%	14.28%	13.31%
Buildings, wages, utilities & other costs as % of Total Revenues	61.38%	46.38%	53.74%
Net Income ($ in mil.)	($530.70)	$197.50	$112.30
Net profit margin	−14.25%	8.89%	3.55%
Net profit per admission***	($2.20)	$1.13	$0.81

Notes:

Data source: SEC filings & author estimates.

* AMCs financial performance is for U,S, operating segment only. Net income includes $230.3 in corporate borrowing and $187.9 in losses of non-consolidated entities.

** Cinemark's Theater and Attendance Information and operating data is for domestic operations only. Operating income, total cost of operations, and net income estimated based on consolidated operations.

*** Cinemark's Net income per admission calculated using global admissions and consolidated income.

operates 1,398 screens in 194 theaters across 15 Central and South American countries. Canadian-based Cineplex Entertainment is the fourth largest domestic.[14] The result of several mergers and acquisitions, the circuit operates 165 theaters with 1,683 screens across Canada.

Major circuits compete based on geographic locations, not direct competition. The differentiators operate in higher cost locations near shopping and restaurants, within or in front of the mall. The cost leaders position theaters in less trafficked locations with lower rent such as in a strip mall or behind the shopping mall. Beyond location, there are more differences within each exhibitor's offerings than across circuits. The industry has a history of new offerings, including air conditioning, digital projection, and stadium seating among many others, being tested by a circuit in individual theaters, then being implemented in all of their theaters or within a select set. Once introduced, competitors quickly adopt innovations as well as each one trying to lure customers to the theater and, to a lesser extent, away from competing theaters within a market. The result is that most theaters are indistinguishable from one another: A ticket booth, a lobby, snack bar, and multiple theaters each containing a projector, screen, sound system, and rows of seats. The same movies—produced, developed, and released by one of the major studios—shown with nearly the same start times. Audiences pay, within a dollar or two within a local market, nearly the same price for admission in the low price versus differentiated theater.

Despite the apparent homogeneity and cooptation, these innovations keep the movie exhibition industry relevant. What keeps customers returning to the theater? What attracts the audience?

Attracting the Audience

A recent CBS News poll indicates the movie theater is currently the *least* likely place for a viewer to watch a movie, well behind television and computer screens.[15] It is therefore important for exhibitors to understand why people choose to watch a movie in the theater as opposed to engaging one of a myriad of other viewing options. Traditionally, the draw of the theater may have been far more important than what film was showing. Moviegoers describe attending the theater as an experience, with the appeal owing to[16]:

- watching the giant theater screen
- hearing a theatrical sound system
- the opportunity to be out of the house
- not having to wait to see a particular movie
- the theater as a location option for a date

The ability of theaters to provide experiences beyond what audiences can achieve at home is diminishing. Of the reasons why people go to the movies, the place aspects (i.e., the theater as a place to be out of house and as a place for a date) seem the most immune to substitution. While "third spaces," places outside of the home where people can gather, meet, talk and linger, have become more common, theaters offer a unique opportunity for people to simultaneously be together while not talking. Few teenagers want a movie and popcorn with their date at home with mom and dad.

The overall "experience" offered by theaters falls short for many. Marketing research firm, Mintel, reports the reasons for *not* attending the theater more frequently are largely the result of the declining experience. This is due to the overall cost, at home viewing options, interruptions such as cell phones in the theater, rude patrons, the overall hassle, and ads prior to the show.[17] The *Wall Street Journal* reported on the movie-going experience quite negatively, noting interruptions ranging from the intrusion of soundtracks in adjacent theaters to cell phones, out-of-order ticket kiosks, and a seemingly endless parade of preshow ads.[18]

The time allocated to pre-show ads has even inspired criticism by industry insiders. Toby Emmerich, New Line Cinema's head of production, faced a not-so-common choice: to attend opening night in a theater or in a private screening room at actor Jim Carrey's home. Because he generally enjoys the experience of watching a film among a large audience, he chose the theater. However, after sitting through 15 minutes of ads, he lamented to his wife that perhaps they should have attended the private screening after all.[19]

The Home Viewing Substitution

Rapid improvements and cost reductions in home viewing technology and the widespread availability of timely and inexpensive content are making home viewing a viable substitute to theater exhibition. The unique value proposition offered by movie theaters' large screens, the audio quality of a theatrical sound system, and avoiding the long wait for viewing the movie are fading.

Home Viewing Substitution: Screen & Sound

Televisions have historically been small, expensive appliances with poor sound quality, faring poorly in comparison to the big screen and sound system offered by the local theater. This has changed dramatically in the last decade as televisions have become larger, offer better picture and sound quality, and are cheaper. The average television is increasingly a large, high definition model coupled with inexpensive yet impressive audio system.

Compared to home equipment options of the past, even modest in-home technology increasingly represents a viable visual substitute to the big screen at the theater.

In 1997, the average TV set was a 23". This increased to 32" in 2010 and to 39" in 2014.[20] In 2018, the purchase of sets 55" and larger is common. Sharp, a leading TV manufacturer, predicts the *average* screen will exceed 60" in the very near future.[21] The increase in size has been possible due to increases in resolution, owing to a U.S. Federal Communication Commission mandate that all broadcasters convert to digital broadcasting by 2009. This led to a transition from the then-standard 480 horizontal lines of resolution to the high definition (HD) standard with 1080 lines of resolution.[22] As of 2017, more than 83 percent of U.S. households have at least one HD television, most 32" or larger, allowing for very high-quality visual images.

HD televisions have been available since 2000, but initially were cost prohibitive. Wholesale prices for televisions fell 65 percent from the late 1990s to 2007[23] as manufacturing economies from the production of LCD screens emerged. In 2005, the average 32" HDTV set retailed for $1,566. By 2009, five years following mass adoption, the average price declined by 76 percent to $511. By 2016, the ten-year mark, the average price had fallen 84 percent to under $250.

Bundled home theater systems include 65" 3D capable TV, surround sound audio, and Blu-ray player offering a movie experience that rivals many theaters, all for under $1,000. According to Mike Gabriel, Sharp's head of marketing and communications, the high-tech home theater that once seemed just the privilege of the wealthy has now become a staple among most average American homes.[24] Overall, home TVs are becoming larger and offer high-quality images that reduce the differentiated appeal of the "giant" screen offered by exhibitors.

If the size and resolution of today's home television screens are a problem for exhibitors, the next generation may be catastrophic, and the next-next generation apocalyptic. The next wave of televisions—"Ultra" HD (UHD) or 4K—is shifting from early adopters to mainstream purchasers. A 4K set has four times the resolution of a 1080 set. Despite an average sale price of $1,250 in 2018, sales of UHD TVs are the fastest growing category and constitute the majority of sets larger than 60".

Of course, electronics companies are already working on the next-next thing: 8K televisions.[25] The higher resolution will be most noticeable in very large TV sets, those 85" and up. To appreciate the differences in picture quality, especially at large screen size, it is helpful to think in terms of image size, such as from a digital camera. Each frame in a standard 1080 broadcast is equivalent to a 2-megapixel image. Like a digital photo, there are limits on enlargement before the eye can identify individual pixels. This can become noticeable in 50" 1080 TVs when viewed closely. A 4K TV has 4000 horizontal lines, comparable to an 8-megapixel image. In the next-next generation of televisions, 8K, each frame is the equivalent of a 32-megapixel image.[26] This allows for viewing on very large screens, those above 120", without any noticeable pixilation. The first commercially available 8K television (native 8K content is not yet available) is a 98" set by LG. The initial price? $55,000.[27] Potential purchasers should keep in mind that TV set prices drop dramatically. If 8K follows the price trend of LCD TV, look for that 98" LG 8K set to be well below $5,000 in just a few years.

How large and how high a resolution a television must be to substitute for a theater screen is subjective. For many, a laptop screen is sufficient; for others, only the true wall-size screen offered by the local exhibitor will do. What is clear, the unique value provided by home television and sound systems is rapidly eroding the unique value proposition offered by exhibitors. The most common projection standard in theaters, the one exhibitors just invested $2.6 billion in during the conversion to digital, is 4K. The history of technology updates to compete on visual quality is as old as the exhibition business itself. To maintain an advantage in the visual experience provided at the theater, exhibitors must consider the next generation of 8K and 16K projectors or lose the visual quality advantage to home viewing.

Home Viewing Substitution: Content & Timing

Even the best home theater offers little value without content. Unfortunately, for exhibitors, home content is flourishing and goes well beyond movies. Consumer spending on home entertainment content including disk purchases, digital downloads, and streaming subscriptions totaled $47.8 billion in 2017.[28] All companies serving this market—studios, exhibitors, rental and on-demand companies, networks, and streaming firms—are fighting to keep and grow their revenue stream.

Studios maximize profits by releasing motion pictures in a series of "windows" under which the sooner a motion picture is viewed following the theatrical release the costlier it is to see it. It begins with theatrical release, generating $4.85 per admission for the studio. The next window is consumer purchase of the motion picture: DVD or digital sales. Studios receive $12 to $15 per copy purchased. The purchaser is increasingly, to the detriment of exhibitors, a consumer who opted not to see the movie in a theater.[29] Studios once relied on DVD sales to fuel profits, but physical DVD sales declined from $13.7 billion in 2006 to $5.5 billion in 2016 (decline of 60 percent).[30] Digital sales are on the rise, but 2016s $2 billion total sales suggests consumers are opting to stream or subscribe instead of purchasing movies. Sales revenues in 2016 were only half of what they were at their peak.[31] To spur sales and capitalize on marketing expenditures from the theatrical release, studios have reduced the time between theatrical release and DVD availability. The window to DVD release has declined from 23.7 weeks in 2000 to 14.4 weeks in 2017. Movies are available for purchase, as digital files or as DVDs, approximately one week sooner every two years (see **Exhibit 13**).

Digital video on demand (VOD) is the first in a series of rental options. VOD is provided by cable companies, iTunes, Amazon, and others exceeded $2 billion in 2017. VOD generates approximately $3.50 for the studio per purchase.[32] Releasing a motion picture shortly after it exits theaters; while it is still in the theater; even at the time of theatrical opening—"simultaneous release"—are all options. While premium VOD would have a negative impact on exhibitors, its potential revenue for studios—as much as $59.99 per purchase—is attractive. Exhibitors have previously banded together against premium VOD by threatening to boycott films by studios. Some studios, notably Disney, appear committed to the current theatrical release model.[33]

Physical rental, once the only rental option, is in rapid decline. Studios net approximately $1.25 per DVD sold to a physical rental company.[34] The dominant physical rental was store-based firms, such as Blockbuster Video, but is now a kiosk-based model, dominated by RedBox. From 2015 to 2016, the physical rental market declined by 19 percent to $2.5 billion.[35] RedBox, the industry leader, reported a same-location rental decline of 4.9 percent in 2015 despite rentals costing as little as $1.25 per night.[36]

Streaming is the fastest growing portion of the rental market and among the most cost effective for viewers. Streaming includes Netflix, Amazon Prime Video, Hulu, HBONow, and others. License rates to streaming services vary considerably based on the popularity of the movie; some estimates put the average studio net below $0.50 per viewing, among the least profitable channels for the studio.[37] The growth of streaming sufficiently cannibalized DVD and digital sales to the point that studios imposed a 28-day delay from DVD sales to the availability of streaming. Exhibitors voiced strong encouragement when several studios expressed a desire

Exhibit 13 DVD Announcement & Release Windows (in weeks)

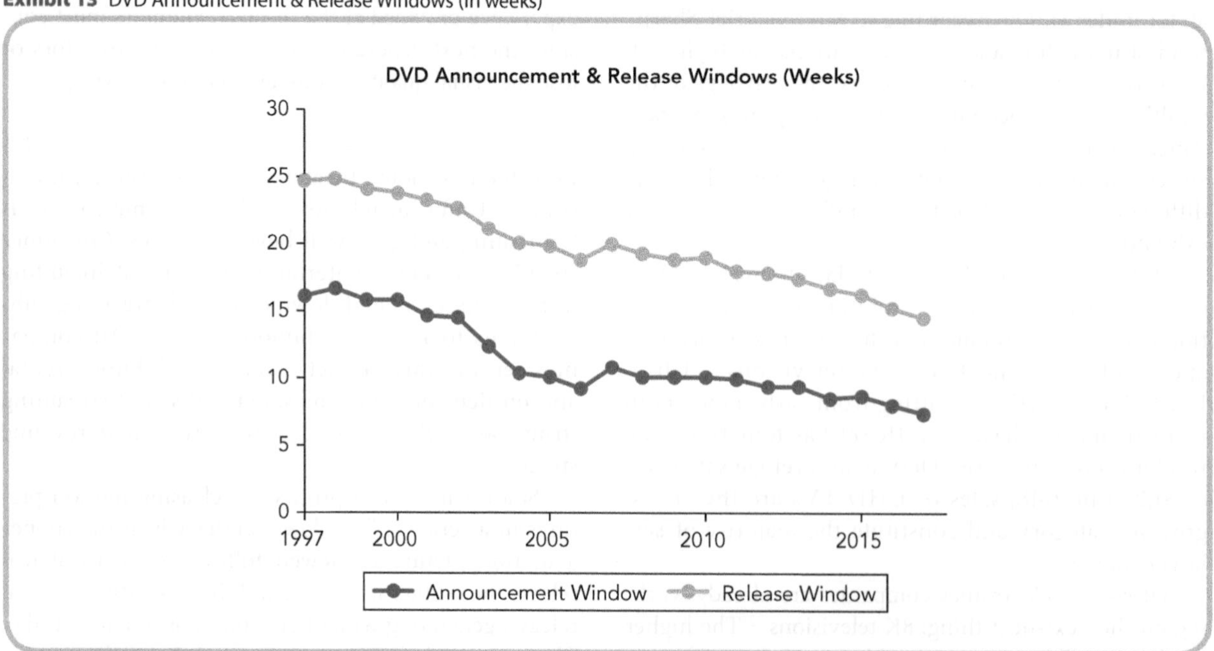

Data source: National Association of Theater Owners (NATO) press releases on Average video release window and Average video announcement.
URL: http://www.natoonline.org/data/windows/

for a 56-day delay to increase DVD sales. Both Netflix and Amazon offer SD as well as HD formats and are beginning to offer content in the 4K format. The most distant from the theatrical release, and providing the least revenue to studios, is a showing on a subscription movie channel (e.g., HBO, Showtime, and Cinemax), a subscription cable television channel (e.g., TNT, FX, and AMC), or a major over-air broadcast network (e.g., ABC, CBS, NBC, and Fox).

Beyond the growth in opportunities to see motion pictures outside of their theaters, exhibitors face reduced attendance due to interest in non-film content. Movies are no longer the sole draw for audiences. Content beyond movies increasingly is a substitute to exhibitors. Motion pictures have been *the* outlet for Hollywood's best talent. This changed in 1999 with the premier of HBO's *The Sopranos*. The series ran for six years, winning multiple awards including those for writing, acting, and directing. The series cemented a shift in artistic attention to the small screen. Many writers had a realization: Unlike a movie, which requires characters and story to evolve over 120 minutes, in a television format they could evolve over several seasons, each consisting of 10, 20, even 30 or more hours on screen. Other series emerged including *Mad Men* and *Breaking Bad*. The production of today's *The Walking Dead* and *House of Cards* has roots in the success of *The Sopranos*.

The time viewing streaming content is time not spent at the theater. The average American spends 2.8 hours daily watching television.[38] Scaled differently, the time typically spent at the theater each *year* is equal to about *two days* of television viewing. For exhibitors, the time someone spends binge watching the last season of a show or just hanging out to 'Netflix and chill' presents a lost revenue opportunity.

Overall, the availability of quality content and the visual and audio experience available in the home are rapidly converging, some would argue, surpassing offerings available at the theater. Paul Dergarabedian, president of Hollywood.com's box-office division, labels it a "cultural shift" in how people view entertainment.[39] People are more interested in content than ever before. Unfortunately, for movie exhibitors, there is more competition than ever in both the content worth viewing and ways to do so.

Recent Exhibitor Initiatives

With attending a movie costing nearly $20 a person including admission, a drink, and a snack versus the alternative of the sunk cost of an existing Netflix subscription, how can exhibitors compete? In what areas should exhibitors be making their investments to continue to offer a unique theater-going experience? Exhibitors have historically been innovators. Exhibitors were among the first commercial adopters of air conditioning, which perhaps drew in as many customers as a refuge from summer heat as for entertainment. Advances in projection systems, screens, and sound systems all improved the experience. Others innovations increase experience quality while also lowering costs. The ubiquitous stadium-style seating was once an experience differentiator, but was equally beneficial as it reduced the square footage needed per seat. This reduced the size and cost of facilities. Exhibitors continue to pursue a number of strategic initiatives aimed at increasing attendance, increasing the viewer's willingness to pay, and lowering costs.

At no time in the movie exhibition industry's existence have the stakes seemed so high. Attendance is declining. The wait needed to see a movie outside of the theater has never been shorter. Content other than motion pictures is increasingly popular. Impressive screens and sound systems are common in homes. Cell phones, ads, and sticky floors mar the overall experience at the theater. What will it take to bring audiences back to the theater?

Market researcher, Mintel, reports that 80 to 90 percent of theaters goers would pay a premium of $1 to $2 each for a wide range of options to make the experience either decrease the negatives of the current theater-going experience or to make it more luxurious.[40] Improved video and sound quality, improvements to seating (including luxurious materials such as leather, sofa-style seating, footrests, long with more legroom), the ability to choose and reserve a seat location in advance, immersive viewing experiences such as 4D, higher end food and drink options, the ability to order from your seat in the theater, and adult-only screens are among those desired. Exhibitors and their suppliers are developing, testing, and rolling out a range of options addressing these. Some are for individual screens, others for all screens within a theater complex. Theaters will invest in those strategic initiatives to draw audiences and produce revenue in excess of costs.

Projection Innovations

The conversion to digital projection and rollout of 3D are not the end of projection innovations. Some directors are opting to increase image quality through the number of frames per second (fps) of film from the long established standard of 24 to 48 and higher. Screeners of Ang Lee's *Billy Lynn's Long Halftime Walk* shown with 4K 3D laser projection at 120 frames per second used described the visual experience in terms like "impeccably bright" and "stunning detail and clarity."[41] Commercially, the film fared poorly in wide release, due in part to a lack of theaters equipped with the required projection equipment. Thus, there exists something of a catch-22: Some attendees will pay a premium for enhanced visual quality, but it requires both exhibitors and film producers to commit to making the investments needed. To date, few of either have.

Most large circuits offer some form of extra-large screens.[42] Traditionally located only in specially constructed dome-shaped theaters in science museums, the original IMAX format utilized film that was 10 times the size of that used in standard 35mm projectors. IMAX now operates more than 600 screens. These circuit-based IMAX digital screens are far smaller than the original IMAX screens, but can be much larger than the typical theater screen. Located within Regal and AMC theater complexes, the screens are often independent, and booked and operated by IMAX. Action films, usually in 3D, are a staple. To capture more of this differentiated revenue, several circuits have begun creating their own super-size screens and formats. IMAX is typically a $3 to $7 premium per ticket. Revenues for IMAX Corporation grew approximately 30 percent from 2013 to 2017.[43]

Audio systems are being improved. In the 1980s, theaters impressed viewers with 7.1 sound systems—two rear channels (left and right), two channels mid screen, two near the screen, one under the screen, and a subwoofer channel for bass. Such systems have long been available for homes. To keep theater sound as a differentiator, Dolby® Laboratories has created Atmos™, a full surround system with up to 64 individual channels for speakers in a theater, including multiple ceiling speakers that can truly immerse the audience in sound.[44] While exhibitors may benefit, Dolby has licensed a home version that emulates the experience in home theaters.

Alternative Content / Event Cinema

Exhibitors' transition to digital projection served as an enabling technology for alternative content, also called event cinema, a broad term encompassing virtually any content that is not a motion picture. This includes live concerts and theater, standup comedy, sporting events, television series premiers and finales, even virtual art gallery tours. Event cinema is the fastest growing segment at the box office, increasing from $112 million worldwide in 2010[45] to $277 million in 2014, and expected to reach $1 billion—about five percent of the box office—by 2019.[46] Ticket prices average $12.33 per event. Event cinema content can be singular events, such as recent concerts, or series attracting repeat visits, such as *Metropolitan Opera Live* shown in 2,000 venues in 70 countries across six continents.[47] The 2017–2018 season features 10 live events on Saturday afternoons with encore rebroadcasts on Wednesdays.

Distribution is performed by entities such as Digital Cinema Distribution Coalition (DCDC), a consortium of major circuits that owns and operates its own satellite network for distribution. A number of firms have emerged to provide content such as Fathom Events, which distributes a variety of music, sports, television, and other alternative content. Fathom's clients include more than 875 theaters. Fathom events have sold more than 18 million tickets.[48] Having an intermediary for a distributor is essential for exhibitors as the cost of pursuing and licensing content is prohibitive for individual exhibitors. The cross-exhibitor cooperation also affords marketing opportunities not economically available to an individual exhibitor.

Alternative content is a supplement to motion picture content. It is best during off-peak movie attendance times such as Monday through Thursday when as little as five percent of theater seats are occupied.[49] Bud Mayo, former CEO of the Digiplex Digital Cinema Destinations theater chain prior to an acquisition by Carmike, described the approach: "What happens with those [alternative content] performances is that single events will out gross certainly the lowest-grossing movie playing that theater that day. The relationship has averaged more than 10 times the lowest-grossing movie for the entire day."[50] In marginal dollar terms, alternative content can be a boon on otherwise slow nights. A Wednesday showing of Broadway's *West Side Story* at a Digitech theater had an average ticket price of $12.50 and grossed $2,425. In comparison, screens showing films that night grossed just $56 to $73 each. The alternative content also brought in nearly 200 additional customers who may purchase concessions.[51]

The success of events rests heavily on having a built-in fan base or the ability to market individual events. Dan Diamond, VP of Fathom Events, reports that their most successful event came as a surprise: the November 25, 2013 showing of *Dr. Who: The Day of the Doctor* in celebration of the 50th anniversary of *Dr. Who*, the popular BBC series. The box office gross was the largest on a per-screen basis for the day, raking in over $17,000 per location.[52] The challenge for exhibitors, accustomed to studio marketing campaigns promoting each week's box office release, is the development of capabilities in marketing single night events to niche audiences at low cost.

Luxury Theaters

Several chains and new entrants are trying to lure attendees with the promise of a luxury experience. Established players like AMC and Regal are reseating screens and entire theaters with premium seats. Smaller theater chain iPic, with 17 locations across the U.S., offers perhaps the most luxurious theater available outside of a private screening room, complete with reclining leather chairs, pillows, and blankets. Lobbies resemble stylish high-end hotels and feature a cocktail lounge and full in-theater restaurant service. Complete with a membership program, the theaters operate more like social clubs than traditional theaters. Ticket purchases, $16–$27 per seat without food, are made not at a ticket booth but rather with a concierge.[53]

Another chain, Cinépolis, is a subsidiary of Mexican theater company Cinépoli. Cinépolis began with one location in San Diego in 2011 and has since expanded to 20 locations through development and acquisition.[54] Offerings differ by location, ranging from standard theaters with leather rocking seats to full service at-your-seat dining with bar service. Tickets for luxury screens average nearly $20. The company offers something for everyone: Some showings are restricted to those 21 and older while other theaters feature Cinépolis Junior with a children's in-theater playground available for use for 20 minutes before a movie starts.[55]

Immersion Experiences: 4D & Beyond

The first wave of immersive experiences was 3D technology. Ten years ago, 3D was to be the next great projection technology and revenue producer, but its appeal has waned. 3D's share of domestic ticket sales peaked in 2010 at 7 percent of tickets and has since been in a steady decline to 11 percent of tickets sold in 2017. It remains a draw in international markets.

The second wave of immersive experiences draws the viewer further into the action by combining 3D, off-screen special effects, and motion seating synchronized to the on-screen action into a "4D" experience.[56] Some theaters add additional immersive elements by introducing scents into the theater, using off-screen light effects, and even water sprayers to bring the action of the movie off the screen and into theater. An encounter with a dinosaur on a dark and stormy night is seen on the screen, heard through the sound system, and felt through a shaking seat. The encounter is even more real when water sprays and strobe lights flash. The whole experience can become a drink spilling experience. Liability waivers, minimum age requirements, and cautions are all standard. Wary of repeating the less-than-expected results of 3D, 4D is being touted as occupying a niche within the broader theater experience. The 4D experience typically comes at a surcharge of $8–$12 over standard tickets.

The third wave of immersion will merge movies with video games. Exhibitors, producers, and equipment companies are working on interaction elements ranging from simple interactions such as shooting on-screen targets with lasers to more complex bullet screens where you can text your thoughts about scenes and the movie and they are projected onto the screen in real time.[57] All are seeking to provide a more immersive and interactive experience than passive sitting and movie watching. Some industry observers anticipate that immersion technologies will include feedback systems and story forks where the actions and choices of the audience lead to plot twists and different story outcomes with each viewing. Eventually, the line between what constitutes a movie versus a video game may blur.

Concession Initiatives

Expanding beyond the standard concession stand offers exhibitors opportunities to capture new revenue streams. Three main formats for concessions have emerged.

Expanded In-Lobby. Many theaters have expanded the concession counter beyond candy, popcorn, and soda. This expanded in-lobby dining causes many theater lobbies to resemble mall food courts. In- and off-lobby restaurants operated or licensed by the exhibitor allow for pre-theater dining. Taking a page from restaurants where a primary profit center is often the bar, some theaters now configure the lobby around a bar, with expanded and upscale fare, beer, and alcohol service.

In-Theater Dining. Many theaters have adopted in-theater dining with orders placed from one's seat in the theater and delivered by waiters. Chunky's Cinema and Pub, with four New England locations, locates theaters in lower cost underutilized former retail locations. The format combines burger, salad, and sandwich options with beverages, including beer. The format is flat theater with banquet style tables. The seating is unique: Lincoln Town Car seats on castors that allow for easy cleaning. Alamo Drafthouse Cinemas takes a similar approach using a stadium-seating configuration. A single bar-style table in front of each row of seats serves as a table for customer's orders. In comparison to traditional theaters, these formats see significant increases in food and beverage sales.

Upscale Within Theater Dining. Several circuits are targeting the high end of the dining market, focusing on the experience of the theater with luxurious settings and upscale food. In addition to their standard theaters, AMC has developed Dine-In Theaters with two theater configurations. Their Fork & Screen theaters are much like the Alamo Drafthouse Cinema with enhanced stadium theater seats and in-theater wait service on an expanded menu. Their Cinema Suite theaters make the experience more intimate. Customers, 21 and older, purchase tickets for specific seats in smaller theaters equipped with reclining lounge chairs, complete with footrests, and order at their seat using a computerized system.

Advertising Initiatives

Exhibitors are keen to expand highly profitable advertising, but do so in ways that do not diminish the theater experience. On- and off-screen advertisements generate revenue. Off-screen advertising such as promotional videos, lobby events, and sponsored concession promotions are nine percent of revenues. The majority, 91 percent, comes from on-screen ads for upcoming releases, companies, and products that play before the feature presentation.

Both exhibitors and advertisers seek ways to make on-screen ads more palatable to audiences. Many ads are in 3D with production quality rivaling a studio release. Theaters are also incorporating innovative technologies such as crowd gaming into ads where the movement or sound of the audience controls on-screen actions. In 2015, audiences in 100 Screenvision-equipped theaters selected the driving experience and virtually drove an XC90 as part of Volvo's re-launch of the vehicle. Attendees selected the scene, steered the car, and controlled the vehicle's speed by waving.[58] The equipment required? A wireless video camera above the screen, a Web-enabled laptop containing the game linked to the developer's website, and inexpensive motion-sensing technology all linked to the theater's digital projector.

Advertisers are keen on increasing the engagement of movie audiences to increase the return on ads.[59] From onscreen QR codes to Bluetooth devices that drop advertiser websites directly into the browser on attendees' phones, interactive is the next step in theater advertising. Making ads enjoyable and useful rather than loathed may create an opportunity to increase this small but high-margin component of exhibitor revenues. Given all of these advertising initiatives, exhibitors may eventually draw from the pages of free software: The ability to pay a premium for an ad-free experience.

Seating

Movie theaters are among the minority of entertainment venues selling tickets without a commitment to the purchaser's viewing experience. Sports and concertgoers, for example, always know where they will be seating in relation to a performance. Movie theaters have long been the province of a first-come, first-select seating model. However, all of the major exhibition chains have incorporated elements of reserved seating—purchasing a ticket tied to a specific seat during a specific showing—into their theaters. These take a variety of forms, ranging from theaters consisting entirely of reserved seat screens, to specific screens consisting exclusively of reserved seats, to screens with mixed open and reserved options. For the exhibitor, reserved seating requires a reservation and seat selection system and the ability to enforce seating and reconcile disputes, but comes with additional revenues. Reserved seating is frequently a service surcharge, not part of the ticket price, of $1 to $3 per seat. Reserved seating is currently one aspect of luxury formats with prices in the $15 range—about double the industry average—but moving into economy theaters too.

Dynamic Pricing

The technology needed for reserved seating is a gateway to dynamic pricing systems. Matinee, youth, and senior discounts are the primary pricing tiers. Most non-movie events have multiple pricing levels based on seating, show time, and weekday versus weekend. Movie theaters have limited flexibility due to the contract restrictions. "Dynamic pricing," which incorporates demand into pricing models, is the next generation of ticket pricing.[60] The simplest models involved surcharges for big-budget blockbuster films in their first few days of release. Odeon & UCI, two European chains purchased by AMC, already price using this approach.[61]

A more advanced approach is to adjust prices for each movie, day of the week, show time, and even seat location based on demand tracked in real-time.[62] This could mean radical changes including lower ticker prices for off time and poorly attended movies and increased prices for prime seats at peak times and opening weekend. For the theater, dynamic pricing offers the opportunity to fill otherwise unsold seats and to move showings between screens based on demand. Australian chain Cineplex offers dynamic pricing, but studios are cautious. Disney, for example, has set and required payment of a minimum average ticket price for some films.[63] For customers, dynamic pricing offers the opportunity to reduce the cost of attending the theater. Do you not want to spend more than $5 to see a particular movie? Apps are on their way to find locations and show times matching your criteria.

Beyond Content

Many smaller exhibitors are seeking increased profitability beyond movies by reimagining their theaters as multi-entertainment venues. By adding activities such as game rooms, bowling, even laser tag, and at-table trivia, a theater becomes a one-stop location for family-friendly entertainment. Frank Theaters, for example, combines movies, bowling, and games for the whole family with dining in its locations, making it possible to spend an entertaining evening at the theater without ever seeing a movie.

Is Yours the Last Theater?

The existence of the Jedi approached folklore status in 2017s *The Last Jedi*. Many have heard of them, but sightings are rare. Might the local movie theater soon be as rare as the Jedi? While theaters experiment with a variety of initiatives to draw viewers, the clock is ticking. Prior initiatives, most recently 3D, have failed to live up to their potential as a durable and enduring way to attract audiences.

NOTES

1. Ticket sales and box office data from: www.boxofficemojo.com, MPAA Theatrical Statistics & THEME reports, UNESCO data, and other sources. Analysis by author.
2. MPAA 2017 THEME Report and U.S. census data.
3. North American Theater Owner Association (NATO), MPAA, and other industry groups collectively define the "domestic" market as including both the U.S. and Canadian markets.
4. MPAA Theatrical Statistics (2016 and earlier) and MPAA 2017 Theatrical and Home Entertainment Market Environment (THEME) report.
5. UNESCO. UNESCO Feature Films Dataset. Accessed July 13, 2017, http://data.uis.unesco.org/#.
6. Schwartzel, E. (2017, Nov 1, 2017). Disney Lays Down the Law for Theaters on 'Star Wars: The Last Jedi'. *Wall Street Journal*. Retrieved 2017/11/01, from https://www.wsj.com/articles/disney-lays-down-the-law-for-theaters-on-star-wars-the-last-jedi-1509528603?mg5prod/accounts-wsj
7. Fritz, B., & Kaufman, A. "Solid start, fast fade for movies," *LA Times*, December 30, 2011, latimes.com/entertainment/news/movies/la-fi-ct-box-office-wrap-20111230,0,2205189.story.
8. Based on several press releases form the Cinema Advertising Council including: Council, C. A. (2018). Cinema advertising closes out 2017 with revenue topping $750 million for the second year running. NEW YORK AND LAS VEGAS: Cinema Advertising Council and Cinema Advertising Council. "Cinema advertising closes out record year with revenue topping $750 million for the first time." Last modified March 29, 2017, http://docs.wixstatic.com/ugd/eeeab3_ce921557d97d4e8986b21825c45bcf40.pdf.
9. Fritz, B. "Movie Theaters, Studios in Tiff Over Trailer Lengths." *Wall Street Journal*, January 27, 2014.
10. Author calculations based on Cinema Advertising Council. (2016) data, SEC filings, NATO press releases, and author estimates.
11. Data on the firms, theaters and screens, location, etc. from web sites and SEC filings.
12. Lang, B. "AMC Acquires Carmike Cinemas for $1.1 Billion, Making It World's Largest Theater Chain." *Variety*. Last modified March 3, 2016, http://variety.com/2016/film/news/amc-acquires-carmike-cinemas-for-1-1-billion-making-it-worlds-largest-theater-chain-1201722224/.
13. Kung, M., & Back, A. "Chinese conglomerate buys AMC movie chain in U.S." *Wall Street Journal*, May 21, 2012, 2.
14. Cineplex Entertainment. Cinemark 2016 Form 10-K. Accessed March 2017, http://irfiles.cineplex.com/reportsandfilings/home/AIF_2017_03_27_final.pdf.
15. Survey: How do you watch movies? CBS News, Produced by CBS Sunday Morning, March 8, 2017.
16. Mintel Report, Movie Theaters - US - February 2008 - Reasons to go to Movies over Watching a DVD
17. Mintel Report, Movie Theaters - US - February 2008 - Reasons Why Attendance is not Higher
18. Kelly, K., Orwall, B. and Sanders, P. "The Multiplex Under Siege," *Wall Street Journal*, December 24, 2005, P1.
19. Incident reported in Patrick Goldstein, "Now playing: A glut of ads," *Los Angeles Times*, July 12, 2005 in print edition E-1; Accessed December 5, 2008, http://articles.latimes.com/2005/jul/12/entertainment/et-goldstein12.
20. HIS Markit. "LCD TV Shipment Forecast Revised Upward on Strong Consumer Demand for Larger Sizes," DisplaySearch Reports IHS. Last modified December 31, 2014, http://news.ihsmarkit.com/press-release/design-supply-chain-media/lcd-tv-shipment-forecast-revised-upward-strong-consumer-dema.
21. "Average TV size up to 60-inch by 2015 says Sharp," *TechDigest*. Accessed December 11, 2008, http://www.techdigest.tv/2008/01/average_tv_size.html.
22. DuBravac, 2007
23. Ibid.
24. Price data on later years based on author analysis of retail LCD pricing of 32" sets on BestBuy.com, Amazon.com, and other sites. Early pricing data reported in *CNN Money* (Producer), 2010. *CNN Holiday Money*, 2010, "32-Inch LCD TV Average Prices." *CNN Holiday Money*. Accessed 2010, http://money.cnn.com/2010/11/24/technology/lcd_tv_deals/#.
25. Moynihan, T. "8K TVs Are Coming to Market, and Your Eyeballs Aren't Ready." *Wired*. Last modified January 7, 2016, https://www.wired.com/2016/01/8k-tvs-coming-to-market/.
26. Ibid.
27. Wong, R. "This $55,000 98-inch 8K TV is actually 'cheap'." Last modified September 3, 2016, http://mashable.com/2016/09/03/cheap-8k-tvs-are-coming-chinese-brands/#JzDkNbymamqT.
28. Motion Picture Association of America (2017). 2017 THEME Report: Theatrical and Home Entertainment Market Environment (THEME). MPAA.org.
29. Jannarone, J. "As Studios Fight Back, Will Coinstar Box Itself Into a Corner?" *Wall Street Journal*, February 6, 2012, p. C6.
30. Kung, M. "Movie Magic to Leave Home For?," *Wall Street Journal*, May 10, 2012, pp. D1–D2. and Shepard, K. "Streaming video outpaces DVD sales for first time in 2016: Report," *The Washington Times*. Last

modified January 6, 2017, http://www.washingtontimes.com/news/2017/jan/6/netflix-other-streaming-video-services-outpace-dvd/.

31. Digital Home Entertainment Group. "DEG report: U.S. Consumer spending by format 2016 year end." Accessed April 2017, http://degonline.org/wp-content/uploads/2017/01/2016-Q4-DEG-Home-Entertainment-Spending_Rev-3.0_01.04.17_-External_-Distribution_Final.pdf.
32. Jannarone, J. "As Studios Fight Back, Will Coinstar Box Itself Into a Corner?" *Wall Street Journal*, February 6, 2012, p. C6.
33. McNary, D. "Disney's Bob Iger Shuns Early Home Movie Releases." *Variety*. Last modified May 9, 2017, http://variety.com/2017/film/news/disneys-early-home-movie-releases-1202421565/.
34. Jannarone, J. "As Studios Fight Back, Will Coinstar Box Itself Into a Corner?" *Wall Street Journal*, February 6, 2012, p. C6.
35. Digital Home Entertainment Group. "DEG report: U.S. Consumer spending by format 2016 year end." Accessed April 2017, http://degonline.org/wp-content/uploads/2017/01/2016-Q4-DEG-Home-Entertainment-Spending_Rev-3.0_01.04.17_-External_-Distribution_Final.pdf.
36. Outerwall Inc. "Outerwall, Inc. (Redbox) SEC Form 10-K Filing." Accessed July 2017, sec.edgar.gov.
37. Jannarone, J. "As Studios Fight Back, Will Coinstar Box Itself Into a Corner?" *Wall Street Journal*, February 6, 2012, p. C6.
38. U.S. Bureau of Labor Statistics. "American Time Use Survey Summary (USDL-16-1250)." Last modified June 27, 2017, https://www.bls.gov/news.release/atus.nr0.htm.
39. Verrier, R. "U.S. theater owners get lump of coal at box office," *LA Times*. Last modified December 30, 2011, latimes.com/entertainment/news/movies/la-fi-ct-theaters-20111230,0,7228622.story.
40. Mintel report. Movie Theaters - US - November 2014.
41. Bishop, B. "Ang Lee's new film shows the peril and incredible promise of high-frame rate movies." Last modified April 17, 2016, https://www.theverge.com/2016/4/17/11446020/ang-lee-billy-lynns-long-halftime-walk-hfr-nab.
42. Dodes, R. "IMAX Strikes Back," *Wall Street Journal*. Last modified April 19, 2012, http://online.wsj.com/article/SB10001424052702304299304577347940832511540.html?KEYWORDS5IMAX+strikes+back.
43. IMAX 2017 10-K Filing, Accessed via www.sec.gov June 8, 2018.
44. Dolby Laboratories. "Dolby Atmos Cinema Sound," Accessed July 2017, https://www.dolby.com/us/en/index.html.
45. Sony. "Alternative Content for Theatres" *Sony Digital Cinema 4K*, 2011, 1.
46. Ross, J. "Making the Case for Event Cinema." Last modified January 21, 2016, http://www.eventcinemaassociation.org/assets/eca-0000-asset-doc-making-the-case-for-event-cinema—jonathan-ross.pdf
47. Metropolitan Opera. "Metropolitan Opera: Our Story." Accessed July 2017, http://www.metopera.org/About/The-Met/.
48. Fathom Events. "Fathom Events: Who We Are." Accessed July 2017, http://corporate.fathomevents.com/.
49. Cinedigm. "Investor Presentation: Jefferies 2012 Global Technology, Media & Telecom Conference." Last modified May 2012, http://files.shareholder.com/downloads/AIXD/2302444840x0x567367/4a213e2c-11ae-4cdc-8dd1-970919ac80ac/CIDM%20IR%20deck%20050712%20Short.pdf.
50. Ellingson, A. "Who's stressed about digital cinema? Not Digiplex's Bud Mayo." *The Business Journal—LA*, October 15, 2012.
51. Ibid.
52. Storm, A. "Alternative content takes center stage: lessons in success from those who've made it work." *Film Journal International*, May 2014.
53. iPic company website (www.ipictheaters.com) and iPic Theaters "iPic Theaters: Become an iPic Member." Accessed July 2017, https://www.ipictheaters.com/#/createaccount/trial.
54. Cineapolis website (www.cinepolisusa.com/locations) and Winfrey, G. "Why Luxury Theater Chain Cinépolis is Buying Up Movie Houses All Across the U.S." *IndieWire*. Last modified July 22, 2016, http://www.indiewire.com/2016/07/luxury-theater-chain-cinepolis-expanding-us-cinemas-1201707606/.
55. Holmes, A. "A Movie Theater Built a Playground In Front Of The Screen, and People are Pissed," *Cinemablend*. Accessed July 2017, http://www.cinemablend.com/news/1632940/a-movie-theater-built-a-playground-in-front-of-the-screen-and-people-are-pissed.
56. Kung, M. " Movie Magic to Leave Home For?," *Wall Street Journal*, May 10, 2012, pp. D1–D2.
57. O'Connor, S. "Chinese cinemas post text messages on-screen during movies." *TechDigest*. Last modified August 21, 2014, http://www.techdigest.tv/2014/08/chinese-cinemas-post-text-messages-on-screen-during-movies.html.
58. Tadena, N. "Volvo Puts Moviegoers in Driver's Seat in New Interactive Ads," *Wall Street Journal*. Last modified August 15, 2015, https://blogs.wsj.com/cmo/2015/08/18/volvo-puts-moviegoers-in-drivers-seat-in-new-interactive-ads/.
59. Cooper, J. " Going to the Movies Could Be a Fully Interactive Experience by 2020," *Adweek*. Last modified January 7, 2016, http://www.adweek.com/brand-marketing/why-going-movies-will-be-fully-interactive-experience-2020-168896/.
60. Lazarus, D. " Movie tickets: Now how much would you pay?" *LA Times*, April 26, 2012.
61. Hughes, W., "AMC considers raising ticket prices on big-budget blockbusters," Last modified November 18, 2016, http://www.avclub.com/article/amc-considers-raising-ticket-prices-big-budget-blo-246162.
62. PRWeb (2018). B&B Theatres and Dealflicks Launch Dynamic Inventory of Full-Priced Movie Tickets and Deals.
63. Verhoeven, D., and Coate, B. "Coming soon to a cinema near you? Ticket prices shaped by demand." *The Conversation*. Last modified February 6, 2017, http://theconversation.com/coming-soon-to-a-cinema-near-you-ticket-prices-shaped-by-demand-72260.

CASE 11

Ivey | Publishing

Pacific Drilling: The Preferred Offshore Driller

From June 2014 to January 2015, the market price of oil fell from US$115[1] per barrel down to $49 per barrel.[2] As oil prices went down, so did the appetite of energy companies for offshore exploration. Further compounding the problems was the oversupply of rigs, due to drillers having overbuilt during the boom times. As of March 2015, there was no near-term recovery in sight for oil prices, which had major implications for Pacific Drilling, a growing offshore drilling company based in Texas. Founded in 2006, Pacific Drilling owned and operated a fleet of eight high-specification drillships operating in ultra-deepwater drilling environments in depths up to 3.7 kilometres (km) and offered the most advanced drilling technology available. As of 2015, the company had nearly 1,600 employees and had generated more than $1 billion in annual revenue (see Exhibits 1, 2, and 3).

With growing competition from rivals—both emerging and more established companies—Pacific Drilling sought to expand its customer base. However, the close

Exhibit 1 Pacific Drilling Income Statements, 2012–2014

	Years Ended December 31		
(in thousands, except per share amounts)	**2014**	**2013**	**2012**
Revenues			
Contract drilling	$ 1,085,794	$ 745,574	$ 638,050
Cost and expenses			
Contract drilling	(459,617)	(337,277)	(331,495)
General and administrative	(57,662)	(48,614)	(45,386)
Depreciation	(199,337)	(149,465)	(127,698)
	(716,616)	(535,356)	(504,579)
Loss of hire insurance recovery	–	–	23,671
Operating income	369,178	210,218	157,142
Other income (expense)			
Costs on interest rate swap termination	–	(38,184)	–
Interest expense	(130,130)	(94,027)	(104,685)
Total interest expense	(130,130)	(132,211)	(104,685)
Costs on extinguishment of debt	–	(28,428)	–
Other income (expense)	(5,171)	(1,554)	3,245
Income before income taxes	233,877	48,025	55,702
Income tax expense	(45,620)	(22,523)	(21,713)
Net income	$ 188,257	$ 25,502	$ 33,989
Earnings / common share, basic	$ 0.87	$ 0.12	$ 0.16
Weighted average number of common shares, basic	217,223	216,964	216,901
Earnings / common share, diluted	$ 0.87	$ 0.12	$ 0.16
Weighted average number of common shares, diluted	217,376	217,421	216,903

Source: Company documents.

Haiyang Li, Frédéric Jacquemin, and Toby Li wrote this casesolely to provide material for class discussion. The authors do not intend to illustrate either effective or ineffective handling of a managerial situation. The authors may have disguised certain names and other identifying information to protect confidentiality.

Version: 2016-04-08

Exhibit 2 Pacific Drilling Balance Sheets, 2013–2014

(in thousands, except par value)	2014	2013
Cash and cash equivalents	$ 167,794	$ 204,123
Accounts receivable	231,027	206,078
Materials and supplies	95,660	65,709
Deferred financing costs, current	14,665	14,857
Deferred costs, current	25,199	48,202
Prepaid expenses and other current assets	17,056	13,889
Total current assets	551,401	552,858
Property and equipment, net	5,431,823	4,512,154
Deferred financing costs, current	45,978	53,300
Other assets	48,099	45,728
Total assets	6,077,301	5,164,040
Liabilities and shareholders' equity		
Accounts payable	$ 40,577	$ 54,235
Accrued expenses	45,963	66,026
Long-term debt, current	369,000	7,500
Accrued interest	24,534	21,984
Derivative liabilities, current	8,648	4,984
Deferred revenue, current	84,104	$ 96,658
Total current liabilities	572,826	251,387
Long-term debt, net of current maturities	2,781,242	2,423,337
Deferred revenue, current	108,812	88,465
Other long-term liabilities	35,549	927
Total long-term liabilities	2,925,603	2,512,729
Common shares, $0.01 par value per share, 5,000,000 shares authorized, 232,770 and 224,100 shares issued, and 215,784 and 217,035 shares outstanding as of December 31, 2015, and December 31, 2013, respectively	2,175	2,170
Additional paid-in capital	2,369,432	2,358,858
Treasury shares, at cost	(8,240)	–
Accumulated other comprehensive loss	(20,205)	(8,557)
Retained earnings	235,710	47,453
Total shareholders' equity	2,578,872	2,399,924
Total liabilities and shareholders' equity	6,077,301	5,164,040

Source: Company documents.

relationships that it had cultivated with its existing partners (which had helped its early stage growth) raised concerns that the driller had become too closely linked to them (in terms of culture, processes, and technology) to effectively translate its efficiency gains to new producer partners.

The company's chief executive officer (CEO), Christian J. Beckett, and his team received a range of opinions about what the company should do to weather the storm and emerge stronger. Investors also felt the pain from the company's stock price sliding from $11 per share in 2014 to less than $4 per share, as did

Exhibit 3 Pacific Drilling Cash Flow Statements, 2012–2014

(in thousands)	2014	2013	2012
Cash flow from operating activities:			
Net income	$ 188,257	$ 25,502	$ 33,989
Adjustments to reconcile net income to net cash provided by operating activities:			
Depreciation expense	199,337	149,465	127,698
Amortization of deferred revenue	(109,208)	(72,515)	(95,750)
Amortization of deferred costs	51,173	39,479	70,660
Amortization of deferred financing costs	10,416	10,106	13,926
Amortization of debt discount	817	445	–
Write-off of unamortized deferred financing costs	–	27,644	–
Costs on interest rate swap termination	–	38,184	–
Deferred income taxes	18,661	(3,119)	(3,766)
Share-based compensation expense	10,484	9,315	5,318
Changes in operating assets and liabilities:			
Accounts receivable	(24,949)	(53,779)	(89,721)
Materials and supplies	(29,951)	(16,083)	(6,640)
Prepaid expenses and other assets	(56,493)	(30,840)	(61,548)
Accounts payable and accrued expenses	20,865	12,301	33,865
Deferred revenue	117,001	94,482	156,967
Net cash provided by operating activities	396,410	230,587	184,998
Cash flow from investing activities:			
Capital expenditures	(1,136,205)	(876,142)	(449,951)
Decrease in restricted cash	–	172,184	204,784
Net cash used in investing activities	(1,136,205)	(703,958)	(245,167)
Cash flow from financing activities:			
Proceeds from shares issued under share-based compensation plan	95	–	–
Proceeds from long-term debt	760,000	1,656,250	797,415
Payments on long-term debt	(41,833)	(1,480,000)	(218,750)
Payments for costs on interest rate swap termination	–	(41,993)	–
Payments for financing costs	(7,569)	(62,684)	(19,853)
Purchases of treasury shares	(7,227)	–	–
Net cash provided by financing activities	703,466	71,573	558,812
Increase (decrease) in cash and cash equivalents	(36,329)	(401,798)	498,643
Cash and cash equivalents, beginning of period	204,123	605,921	107,278
Cash and cash equivalents, end of period	$ 167,794	$ 204,123	$ 605,921

Source: Company documents.

the stock price of all offshore drillers during that time (see Exhibit 4). As he considered the available options, Beckett faced another critical crossroad. The company had survived tough times before—in the early stages of the company's development, the team had successfully manoeuvred through the 2008 financial crisis as the credit markets collapsed. But as Beckett admitted, the current challenge was unique in many ways, and Pacific Drilling was a different company from earlier. However, it remained to be answered to what extent

Exhibit 4 High Correlation Between Offshore Drillers Stocks and Oil Price, December 2013 to 2014

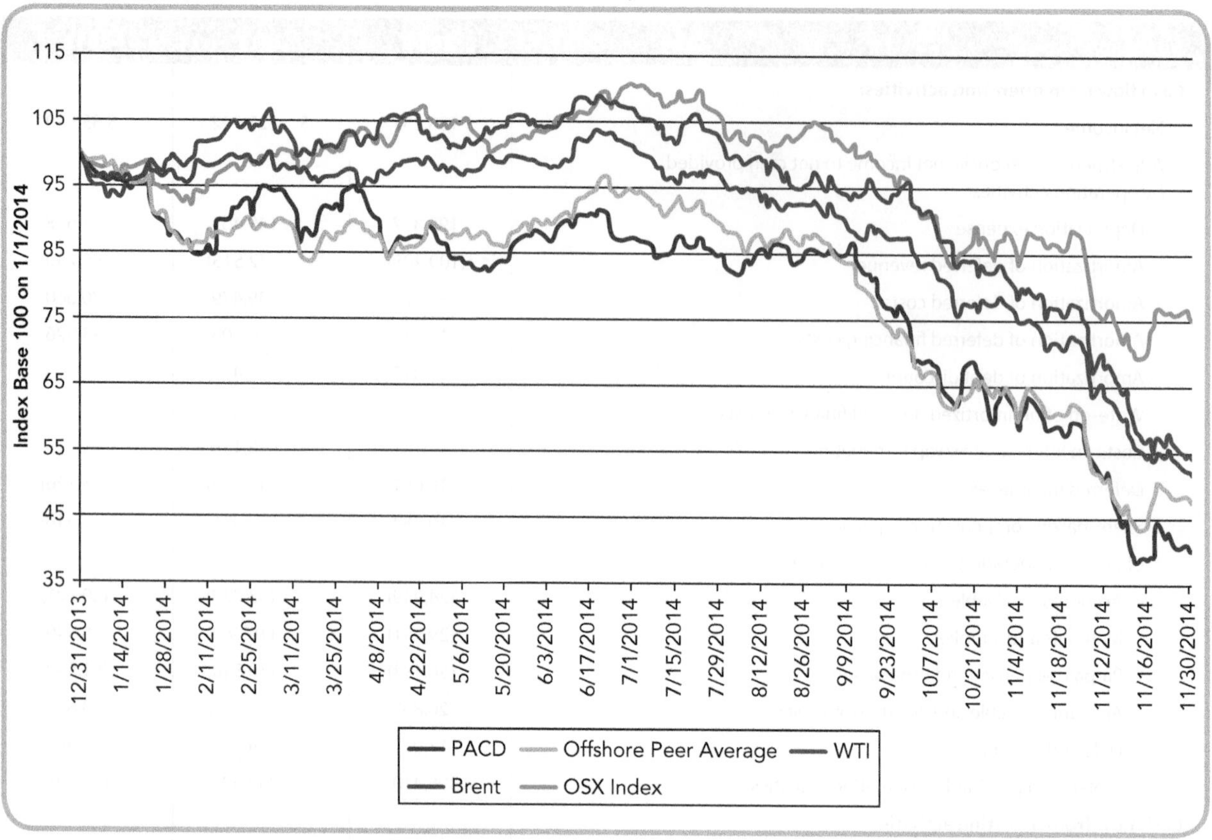

Note: PACD = Pacific Drilling; WTI = West Texas Intermediate; OSX = Oil Service Sector Index
Source: Organization of the Petroleum Exporting Countries; Yahoo finance; and company analysis.

Beckett and his team could rely on what they had successfully done in the past, and to what extent they would need to adapt.

The Offshore Drilling Industry

The offshore oil industry involved the exploration and production of oil and gas from underwater wells, often in locations off continental coasts but sometimes in inland seas and lakes. Offshore sites held greater promise than onshore sites for oil producers to develop their oil reserves, and achieve higher production rates, especially in less explored deepwater sites. For instance, in recent years, the greatest increases of any offshore drilling region had been the demand for ultra-deepwater rigs in the Golden Triangle of Oil, which consisted of the Gulf of Mexico and the waters off the coasts of South America and West Africa (see Exhibit 5). Over the past decade, deepwater discoveries had far outpaced those in shallow water.[3]

Developing a well usually involves two main players: the oil producer and the driller that physically drills the well in accordance with the producer's specifications. A small number of oil companies owned a few offshore rigs and conducted drilling in-house. Most companies, however, outsourced the work to drilling contractors. Some producers, known as independent producers, focused solely on the upstream, or early stage, activities of exploration and production (e.g., Anadarko). Others were integrated multinational corporations (e.g., BP, ExxonMobil, Chevron, and Shell) and state-owned companies (e.g., Brazil's Petrobras and Saudi Arabia's Aramco) that also performed downstream or later stage activities, such as refining and marketing of the extracted oil and gas.

Oil exploration began with geological and seismological research on a potential well. Next was the purchase or lease of the promising ocean terrain, almost always from governments. Once sufficient due diligence was completed and the rights to explore the site were secured, producers typically contracted with drillers

Exhibit 5 The Golden Triangle of Oil That Drove Ultra-Deepwater (UDW) Demand Growth 2009–2014

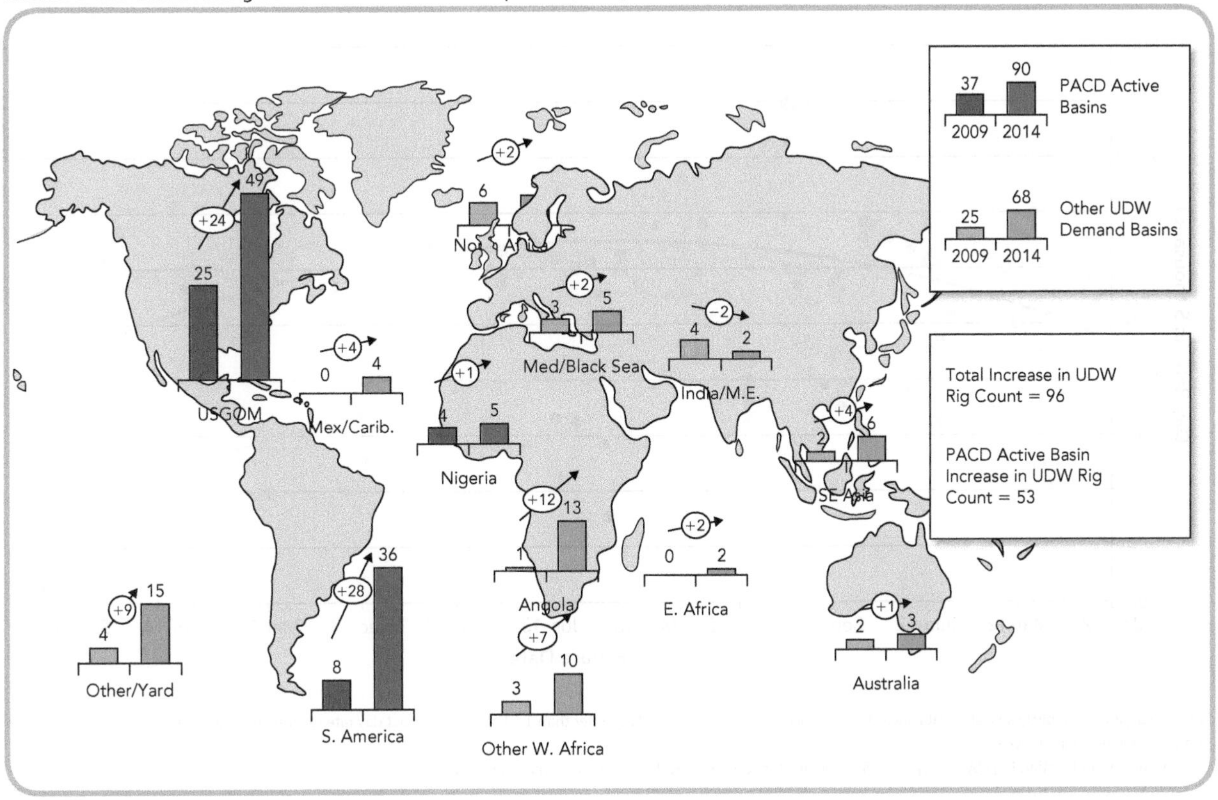

Note: PACD = Pacific Drilling; USGOM = U.S. Gulf of Mexico; Mex. = Mexico; Carib. = the Caribbean; Med = the Mediterranean; M.E. = Middle East

Source: "Ultra-Deepwater Demand Growth," ODS-Petrodata, Inc., accessed April 12, 2015; Company analysis.

to drill exploratory wells. If the results were encouraging, drilling began on development wells in the area for eventual oil extraction. How quickly drilling, and then extraction, could be accomplished depended on the supporting infrastructure (e.g., pipelines connecting to processing facilities) around the drilling site, weather conditions, and geological characteristics. Another factor was productivity, which was a function of the drilling technology used and the working experience of the producer-drilling teams.

Offshore drilling typically used three types of rigs: jack-ups, semi-submersibles, and drillships. *Jack-ups* were used in shallow water (up to approximately 0.12 kms of water), and their operating deck was supported by multiple legs that extended down to the ocean floor. *Semi-submersibles* (semis) could operate in water depths of up to 3 kms. They floated on submerged pontoons with an operating deck that was well above the water's surface. *Drillships* could operate in water depths of up to 3.6 kms. They looked like large, ocean-going freighters with a drilling derrick mounted in the centre of the ship. They offered greater mobility and deck space than semis and were therefore often preferred in remote locations. Their larger size also allowed them to provide greater operational efficiency through enhancements such as dual derricks[4] and additional drilling equipment.

Drillers competed to lease their rigs to producers. The drillers were usually paid based on day rates,[5] which varied widely across rig types. Deepwater oil reserves were much more difficult to tap and required more advanced equipment and expertise than some other locations. As a result, day rates for semis and drillships could be three to five times higher than jack-up rates. Day rates also varied in relation to market conditions and could be further differentiated by the quality and efficiency of the drilling rigs and services, which were often the result of technological and processing innovations that could ultimately provide lower total drilling costs for the producer (see Exhibit 6). Day rates were usually locked-in through negotiated contracts, with the duration of the contracts and the lead time decided on

Exhibit 6 Day Rate Trends for Floating Rigs by Rig Quality (2012–2014)

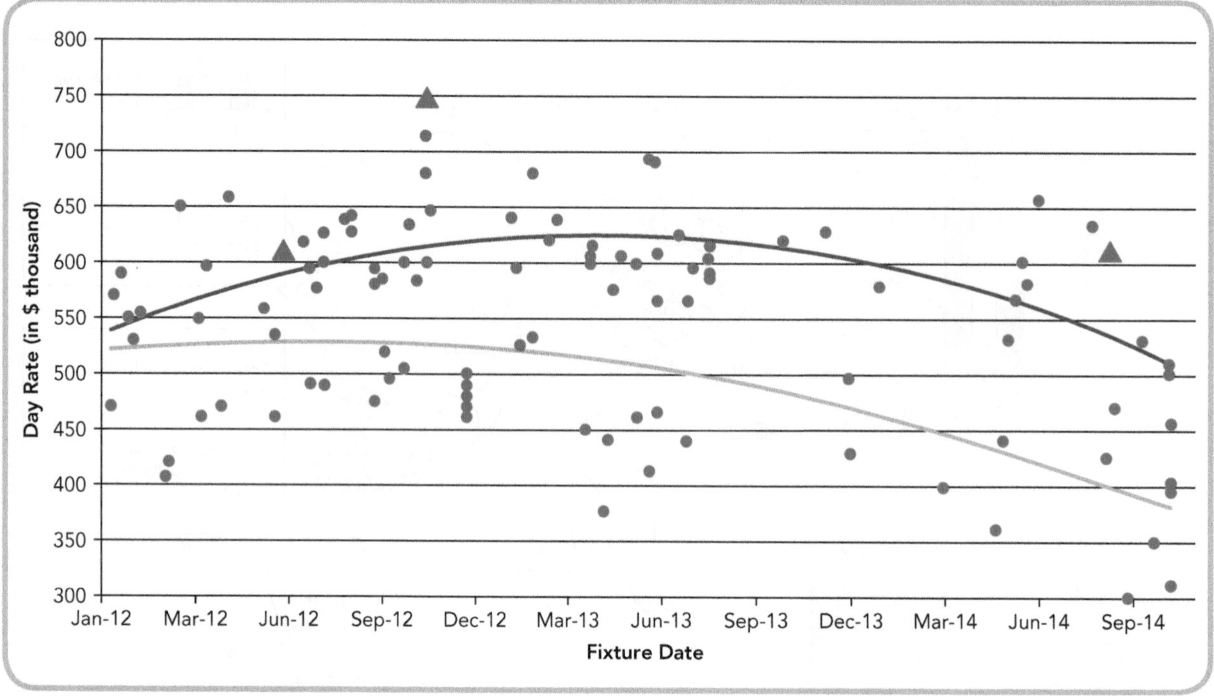

Note: Analysis uses publicly available data; includes rigs with water depth capability greater than 1.5 kms and contract day rate revenue from mutual contracts greater than one year.

Source: "Trends for Floating Rigs by Rig Type," ODS-Petrodata, Inc., accessed April 12, 2015; Company analysis.

prior to the start of the contract. However, day rates also fluctuated with market conditions.

Many factors could affect a producer's choice of driller. For example, national oil companies often held public tenders and chose drillers based on the rig's suitability and the day rate. International oil companies had been known to be much more reliant on existing relationships.[6] Because relocating rigs was costly and time-consuming,[7] producers seeking to develop wells in a certain region were more likely to contract a driller that already had the required type of rig ready in the area. In certain geographic locations, government regulation and local content criteria could be barriers to entry, thereby playing a significant role in the selection of a drilling contractor.

Rigs that were not leased out were usually "stacked" (i.e., idle), or taken out of service, by the driller to minimize operating costs. A "hot-stacked" rig remained fully crewed, standing by, ready for work if a contract could be obtained, and the downtime was used for maintenance and repairs; a "warm-stacked" rig retained some of the crew and underwent a reduced level of maintenance and repairs; and a "cold-stacked" rig was completely vacated and its doors welded shut.[8]

The offshore drilling industry rose and fell with oil prices (see Exhibit 4). The early 1970s witnessed a spike in oil prices due to actions by the Organization of the Petroleum Exporting Countries (OPEC) that increased the supply of offshore rigs as drillers rushed to meet the increase in drilling demand. The industry later suffered an overcapacity of rigs when prices came back down during the mid-1970s.[9] Such cycles continued with the oil price spike in 1979, its collapse in early 1986, and its recovery in 1987. Oil prices remained depressed during the 1990s until 1998, due to the economic slowdown in Asia, then started climbing in the early 2000s, which pushed utilization rates, and thereby day rates, to historical highs. The financial crisis that started in 2008 caused utilization rates and day rates to decline sharply again, as oil prices fell below $40 per barrel from their peak of $140 per barrel a year earlier.[10]

Players in the offshore drilling industry included both diversified drillers (e.g., Transocean, Seadrill, Ensco, Noble, Diamond, Rowan, and Atwood) and niche drillers (e.g., Ocean Rig). Larger, diversified drillers had fleets that included rigs of various types and typically had a broader geographic presence (see Exhibit 7).

Exhibit 7 Profiles of Pacific Drilling's competitors

Transocean	Transocean operated the largest fleet in the offshore drilling industry with 85 rigs (15 jack-ups, 39 semi-submersibles, and 31 drillships) with an average age of 17 years. The company's market capitalization was approximately $6.8 billion, which was the second largest in the industry. It had an operational presence in the waters of the United States, Norway, the United Kingdom, West Africa, Brazil, South East Asia, and Australia. Over the past five years, the company had delivered operating margins of about 22 per cent, which was below the industry average. The company's strategy was to upgrade its fleet and divest its non-core assets.
Seadrill	Seadrill operated 57 rigs (25 jack-ups, 15 semi-submersibles, and 17 drillships). With an average age of 3.4 years. It was one of the youngest fleets in the industry. The company's market capitalization was $5.9 billion. Over the past five years, the company had also had the second-highest operating margins in the industry at about 40 per cent. It had an operational presence in the waters of the United States, Mexico, Norway, Brazil, West Africa, the Middle East, and Asia Pacific. Its strategy was to maintain its technology advantage by continuing to invest heavily in fleet renewal and growth.
Ensco	Ensco operated 74 rigs (46 jack-ups, 18 semi-submersibles, and 10 drillships) with an average age of 19.6 years. The company's market capitalization of $7.1 billion was the largest in the industry, and it generated average operating margins of 40 percent over the previous five years. It had an operational presence in the waters of the United States, Brazil, the Mediterranean, the Middle East, Africa, Europe, and Asia Pacific. Its strategy was to update its fleet, invest in employee training, and maintain its diverse geographic presence.
Noble	Noble operated 39 rigs (19 jack-ups, 11 semi-submersibles, and nine drillships) with an average age of 15.8 years, which made it the second oldest fleet in the industry. The company's market capitalization was $4.4 billion. It had a diverse operational presence with rigs operating in the waters of the United States, Brazil, Mexico, the United Kingdom, the Middle East, Africa, and Australia. The company performed just below the industry average, delivering operating margins of around 27 per cent over the previous five years. Its strategy was to update its fleet, invest in employee training, and maintain its diverse geographic presence.
Diamond	Diamond operated 41 rigs (six jack-ups, 30 semi-submersibles, and five drillships) with an average age of 30.4 years, which made it the oldest fleet in the industry. The company's market capitalization was $5.3 billion. Over the previous five years, the company delivered operating margins of about 31 per cent, which was in line with the industry average. The company had a very low level of debt relative to its size and in comparison to its peers. At the same time, its older rigs enabled the company to be very competitive on rig pricing. The company strategy was to maintain its attractive pricing and its financial strength.
Rowan	Rowan operated 34 rigs (30 jack-ups and four drillships) with an average age of 16.4 years. The company's market capitalization was $2.9 billion. It operated rigs in the waters of the United States, Saudi Arabia, the United Kingdom, Norway, and Malaysia. The company generated average operating margins of about 23 per cent over the previous five years. The company's strategy focus was to maintain its diverse geographic presence, be more cost-effective, and execute better.
Atwood	Atwood operated 14 rigs (five jack-ups, five semi-submersibles, and four drillships) with an average age of 9.6 years. The company's market capitalization was $1.9 billion. It had an international presence, with rigs in the waters of the United States, Australia, Equatorial Guinea, and Thailand. The company achieved the highest operating margins in the industry over the previous five years at about 44 per cent. Its strategy was to continue growing while maintaining its operational efficiency.
Ocean Rig	Ocean Rig operated 13 rigs and focused on drilling in deeper waters (two semi-submersibles and 11 drillships) with an average age of 3.3 years. The company's market capitalization was $1.2 billion. It had a rig presence in the waters of Brazil, Angola, Norway, and Ireland. Its operating margins were at the industry average of approximately 30 per cent. The company's strategic focus was to grow its fleet of high-specification drilling rigs and to broaden its geographic reach.

Source: "Oil Drillers," ODS-Petrodata, accessed April 12, 2015; Yahoo finance; company analysis.

Chris Beckett: CEO and the First Employee

With the initial purchase of a drillship under construction, Pacific Drilling was founded in 2006 as a subsidiary of Tanker Pacific, one of the largest tanker fleet owners in the world. After ordering a second rig in 2007, the company transferred its rigs to a joint venture with 50–50 ownership with Transocean. In 2008, Pacific Drilling expanded its activities beyond the joint venture to include four ultra-deepwater drillships, which had been constructed in South Korea at Samsung Heavy Industries, one of the three largest shipyards in the world. At the same time, Beckett was approached by Idan Ofer, an Israeli tycoon and the principal of Tanker Pacific. Ofer asked Beckett to be the company's first employee and to lead the development of Pacific Drilling as CEO. Beckett, a 2002 MBA graduate from Rice University in Texas, had previously been the head of corporate planning at Transocean, a strategy consultant at McKinsey, and the U.S. land seismic manager at Schlumberger.

Exhibit 8 Fleet Composition by Rig Capability and Type

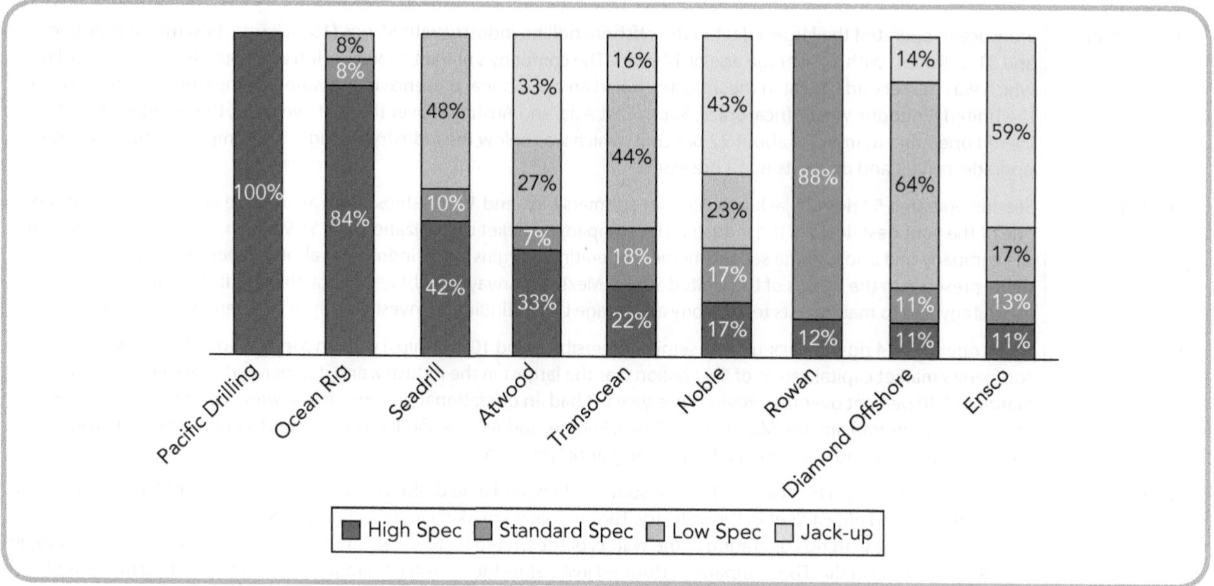

Source: Company documents; "Fleet Composition by Rig Capability," ODS-Petrodata, Inc., accessed April 12, 2015.

As the CEO of a start-up, Beckett challenged the industry's conventional wisdom:

Back to 2004 and 2005, the industry was coming out of the downturn. . . . There was a belief in most of the established drillers that they would sit on what they had, and they would own the market. They would have a strong market position. There was an absolutely strong belief that nobody from outside could enter the industry. No clients would take the risk to work with a new driller without any proven record. Also, no lenders would take the risk to build several-hundred-million-dollar assets with a new player.

Despite huge challenges and personal risks, Beckett believed that the offshore drilling industry was changing and provided great opportunity for a start-up such as Pacific Drilling, which focused on premier technology and ultra-deepwater drilling. In particular, he noted:

When we started Pacific Drilling, it was with the view that the assets that were being designed, built, and delivered into the market around 2005 and 2006 onwards were, for the first time in the industry, explicitly supposed to outcompete those of the previous generation by being more efficient: by reducing the time to drill a well. A lot of the incumbents missed that as a fundamental change, and they believed that if they didn't build rigs then nobody would build rigs and that they could continue with the technology that they had and control the market. What happens in most industries is that somebody comes in from the outside and delivers the technology to the market place and supersedes them by using disruptive technology.

In November 2014, Beckett won the Ernst & Young (EY) Entrepreneur of the Year National Award in the Energy, Cleantech, and Natural Resources category for his leadership in growing the start-up company into a highly respected niche player in the offshore drilling market. "Chris Beckett is the definition of a high-growth entrepreneur," said Mike Kacsmar, EY Entrepreneur of the Year Americas program director. "He's grown a world-class team based on that entrepreneurial spirit, and he encouraged his employees to make an impact by identifying novel approaches and seeing those ideas through to implementation."[11]

Firm Strategy

Beckett strongly believed that the new generation of rigs would be fundamentally more efficient than the existing generation. Over time, the previous generation would become obsolete. Therefore, his vision of Pacific Drilling was that of a preferred, high-specification, floating-rig drilling contractor. The strategy was to use its consistent fleet of ultra-deepwater drillships, which were built by the top-of-the-class shipyard Samsung Heavy

Exhibit 9 Number of Floating Rigs in Global Fleet by Delivery Year (1971–2014)

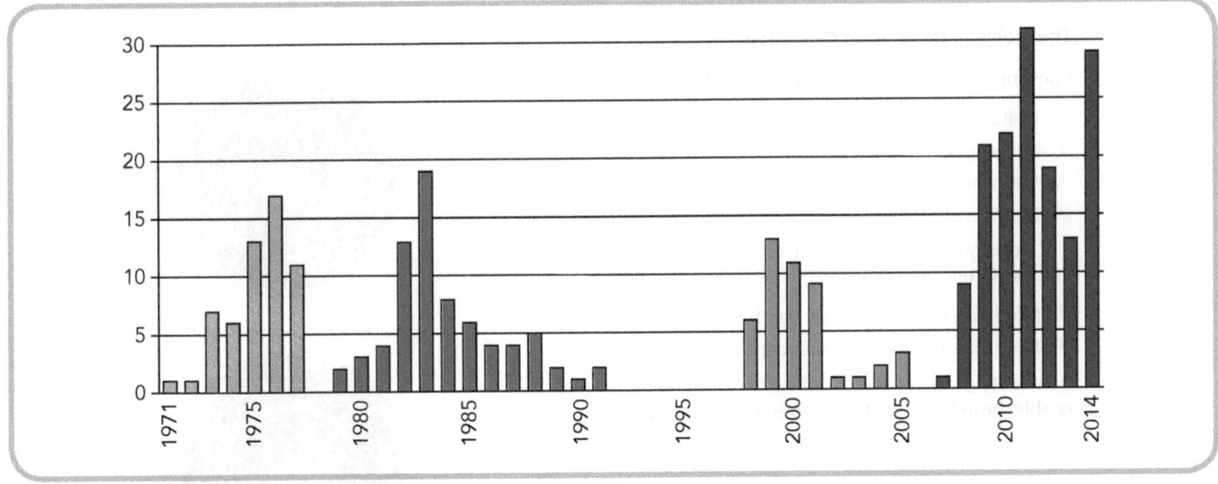

Source: Company documents; "Floating Rigs by Delivery Year," ODS-Petrodata, Inc., accessed April 12, 2015.

Industries, outfitted with the newest drilling packages by National Oilwell Varco, and managed by a highly experienced team to provide differentiated drilling services for its customers. This focus gave Pacific Drilling a strong competitive advantage over companies such as Transocean, which was more diversified and less focused (see Exhibits 8 and 9). Beckett explained his vision of the company:

The benefit that we had and that we foresaw for Pacific Drilling was to be focused on one asset class and not allow ourselves to be dragged into other asset classes. We could therefore optimize our maintenance systems, procurement, operating programs, and safety programs to deliver the best results with this one asset class.

In 2008, Beckett and his team prepared a thorough technical and safety-drilling manual, but the industry did not seem ready for what Pacific Drilling was offering. One potential client that Beckett pursued requested that the company rework its manual and prepare a new proposal. Saddled with debt and yet to book its first customer, Pacific Drilling considered the prospect of a compromise by revising the manual to align with the standard industry practices. However, Beckett and his team knew that the compromise would mean losing what they believed to be the company's key differentiator. So they instead held firm and asked the customer to reconsider.

That potential client was Chevron, the first and ultimately most supportive customer throughout Pacific Drilling's growth, eventually contracting more than half of the company's drillships. As Chevron officials later admitted, the original manual that had been proposed was among the best they had ever seen. Beckett reflected on that challenging but rewarding situation:

So we were able to build a relationship with Chevron based on relationships we had in previous companies. They knew the people they were dealing with, and they could get comfortable that those people would be committed to delivering the product and service quality. They could look at who the financial backers were and where we were building rigs, and all the associated pieces came to a comfort factor that we would do what we planned to do.

The collaboration with Chevron also yielded access to a technological innovation: dual-gradient drilling (DGD), a process that enabled an oil company to access reservoirs that had previously been considered "undrillable." Unlike conventional drilling that used only one drilling fluid, DGD employed two different fluids in the wellbore—one in the drilling riser, with below-average density, and the other below the wellhead, with above-average density. Using DGD allowed the driller to overcome narrow pore pressure fracture gradient margins and to drill larger and deeper holes using fewer casing strings. It also helped the driller to better manage downhole pressure as the drill bit moved through various types of geologies such as sand, shale, and tar (see Exhibit 10).

DGD was technologically proven in the late 1990s; however, it had not yet been deployed on a commercial rig. While Chevron expected DGD to reduce the total

Exhibit 10 Dual-Gradient Drilling

The Problem: Deep Water Challenges

Conventional drilling methods have potential challenges:

- Well control / lost circulation
- Challenging cement jobs
- Mechanical challenges with tight tolerance tools
- Restrictive completions

The industry is drilling even more difficult wells. We now routinely drill nearly "un-drillable" wells:

- More than 9,000-metre well depth
- More than 1,800-metre water depth

New floating rigs capable of drilling to 12,000-metre well depth enable the industry to attempt even more deep water projects.

Conventional Casing Program

Deepwater Casing Program

The Solution: Dual Gradient Drilling

With DGD, we literally replace the mud in the drilling riser with a seawater-density fluid and use a denser mud below the mudline to achieve the same bottom hole pressure.

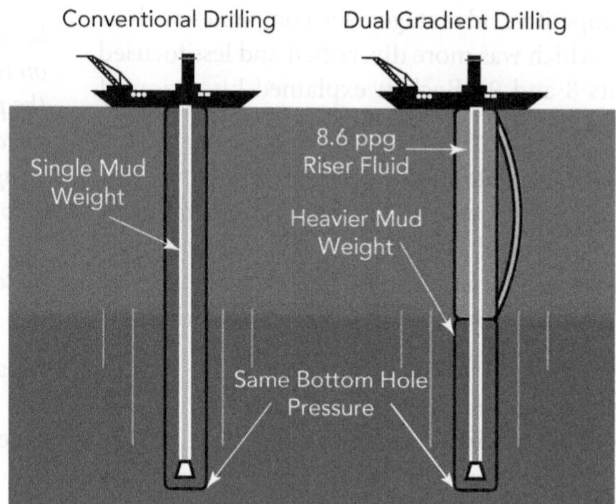

Note: DGD = dual gradient drilling; ppg = pore pressure gradient

Source: Chevron, Dale Straub Presentation at the International Association of Drilling Contractors' Dual Gradient Drilling seminar, Madrid, Spain (April 7, 2014).

cost to drill a well, the company had not yet worked with a drilling contractor to fully implement the technology. Pacific Drilling management was aware of the potential for DGD and embraced the possibilities to work with Chevron on developing processes and procedures. It took about six months before Chevron was comfortable that Pacific Drilling was the right partner to commercialize DGD, leading to Pacific Drilling's first drilling contract.

Pacific Drilling's close relationship with Chevron was among the few relative constants in an often volatile and unpredictable market. Chevron had contracted four drillships with Pacific Drilling to date for operations in the Gulf of Mexico and Nigeria. The justification was simple: Pacific Drilling rigs were equipped with the capabilities that Chevron desired, and collaboration among the companies' employees, both onshore and offshore, had become seamless.

After Chevron had signed the first contract, opportunities from other producers emerged for Pacific Drilling. Chevron's willingness to repeatedly work with the new company was an endorsement of the substantial value that Pacific Drilling could deliver to its customers. With a more established reputation, Pacific Drilling was able to broaden its customer base to include Total (one drillship in Nigeria) and Petrobras (one drillship in Brazil). By the end of 2014, the company had signed $2.7 billion in contracts (see Exhibit 11).

Working with Chevron to implement DGD also helped Pacific Drilling improve and refine its operating and management systems. Implementation of DGD technology demanded that Pacific Drilling work closely with Chevron on the development of operating procedures and employee training. At the time, Pacific Drilling operated two drillships that were DGD-capable (i.e., the Pacific Santa Ana and Pacific Sharav). Frédéric Jacquemin, the director of the DGD program at Pacific Drilling at the time, noted that "with DGD, integrating a new technology is not only about equipment but it is also about defining new processes and training people."

Although the full deployment of DGD technology was still a work in progress, Pacific Drilling's close collaboration with Chevron led to a corporate emphasis on process innovations and technological leadership. Pacific Drilling continued to invest in technological innovation in an effort to keep its fleet as up-to-date as possible. For example, its newest rigs were equipped with automated drilling systems that reduced the number of personnel on the drilling floor, substantially improving drilling speed while also reducing safety risks. The company also equipped its rigs with a higher than usual amount of drilling mud storage and processing capability, which allowed the rig to move more quickly through the drilling process and also to be more self-sufficient: a particular advantage in remote operating locations, where the cost of support vessels was high.

Pacific Drilling implemented SAP software on all of its drillships to better monitor daily rig operations and respond in real time to unforeseen problems. Traditionally, workers on a rig monitored their tasks using pen and paper and provided hard-copy reports to their supervisors. The SAP software helped to continually update information across functions during the drilling process, improving operational efficiency. The company reduced the amount of downtime (non-operating time due to malfunctions) and ultimately improved safety, both of which increased profitability and benefit to customers.

Pacific Drilling developed its own company management system using the highest standards (see Exhibit 12). The company had the advantage of being able to implement this system from the beginning, whereas most of its peers had to adapt management systems to their legacy corporate practices. The company also emphasized consistency in its processes and procedures. For example, the company went through an exhaustive exercise to develop

Exhibit 11 Pacific Drilling Growth Profile

	First Quarter of 2011	Fourth Quarter of 2014
Number of rigs	4	8
Number of operating rigs	0	6
Number of drilling contracts	2	6
Contract backlog (in $ billions)	$1.5	$2.7
Number of employees	Approximately 500	Approximately 1,600
Market capitalization (in $ billions)	$2.1	$1.0

Source: Company documents.

Exhibit 12 Pacific Drilling Management System (Ms)

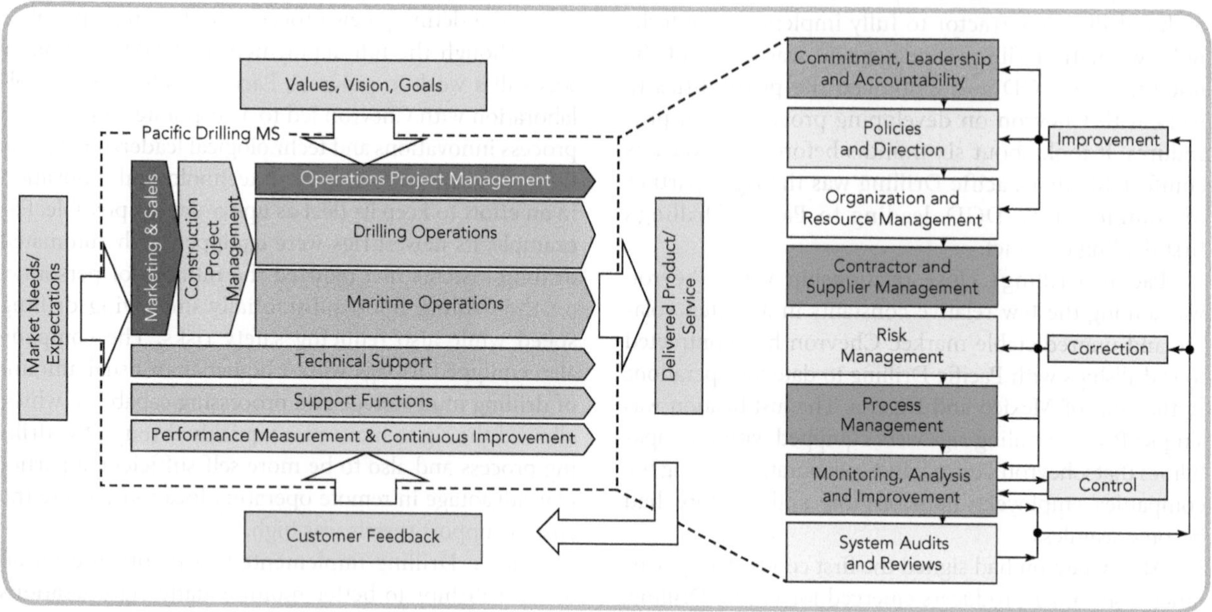

Source: Company documents.

a standardized framework for making operations and maintenance decisions related to a key piece of equipment on its rigs. When Pacific Drilling showed the framework to its clients, it was told that no other driller had made this type of effort to better manage the equipment.

Firm Culture and Organizational Structure

Pacific Drilling had set clearly defined values that provided a framework for corporate decision-making and employee behaviour. The company's core principles were cleverly embodied using the mnemonic of its name PACIFIC (see Exhibit 13).

To build the company's legitimacy and credibility, Beckett recruited highly experienced experts with proven track records from a variety of professional backgrounds. In doing so, he aimed to find the best solutions and processes for the start-up company. Beckett also knew that in this industry, talent and connections were key. To attract star employees, he offered promotions from their current positions, as well as the opportunity of a lifetime—helping to build a new company. Beckett also promised less organizational hierarchy, and he kept his word by creating a leaner, flatter company.

Pacific Drilling's organizational structure provided advantages through shorter communications paths, ease of collaboration, and efficient decision-making (see Exhibit 14). For example, the marketing of rigs was traditionally done by a dedicated marketing team, which then handed over the contract to the operations department to run the rigs. However, the company encouraged

Exhibit 13 Pacific Drilling Company Values

Proactive:	Continually refining its approach to anticipate stakeholder needs
Accountable:	Taking responsibility for actions and performance as individuals and as a company
Customer oriented:	Striving to exceed customer expectations
Integrity:	Acting honestly and fairly in all they do
Financially responsible:	Maximizing long-term value creation for shareholders
Innovative:	Seeking creative solutions in every aspect of its business
Community focused:	Ensuring a sustainable and positive impact on the communities where they work

Source: Company documents.

Exhibit 14 Pacific Drilling Organizational Chart after Reorganization in February 2015

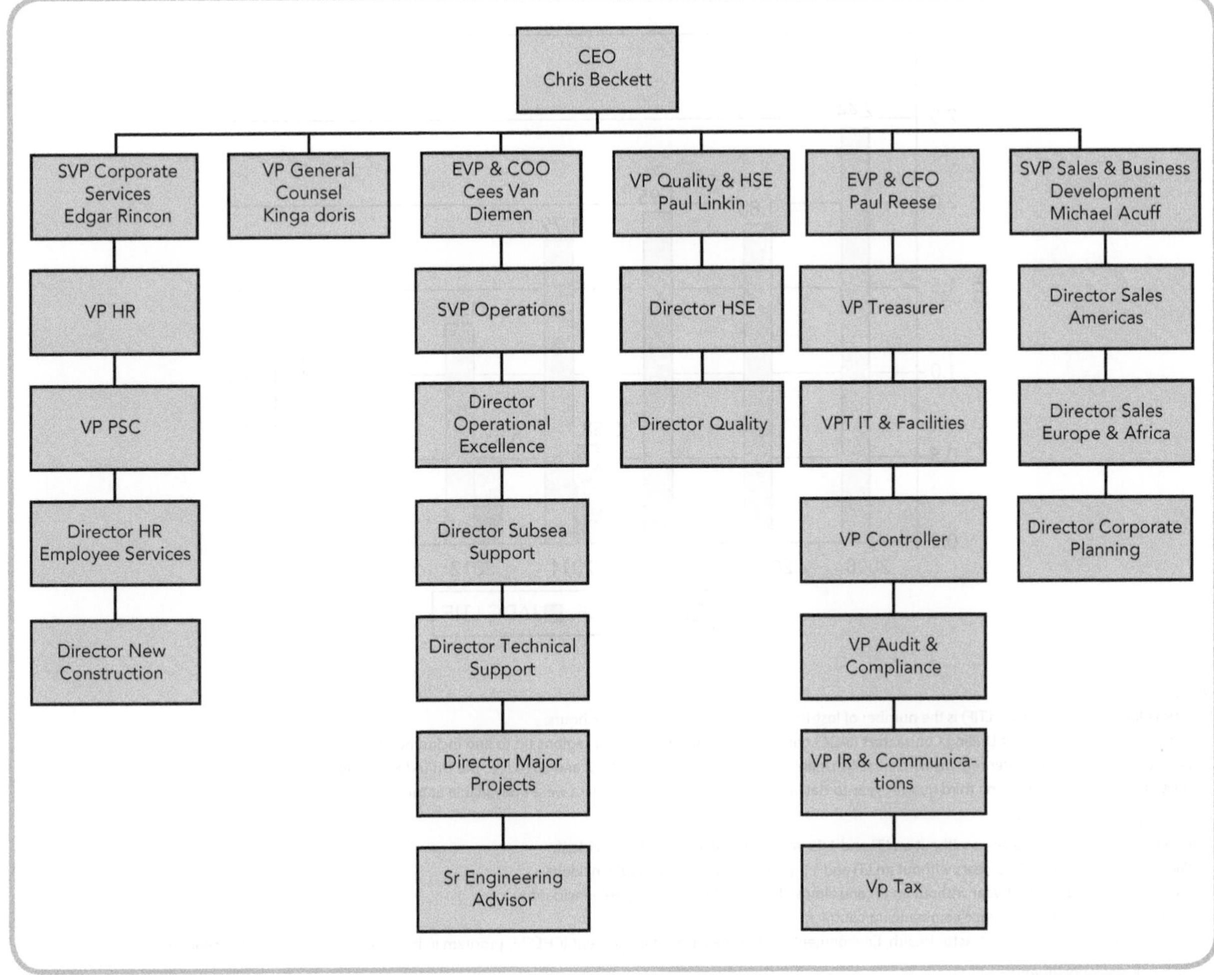

Note: CEO = chief executive officer; SVP = senior vice-president; VP = vice-president; EVP = executive vice-president; COO = chief operating officer; HSE = health, safety, and environment; CFO = chief financial officer; HR = human resources; PSC = procurement and supply chain; IT = information technology; IR = investor relations; Sr = senior.

Source: Company documents.

its marketing and operations teams to work together with the client from the first stage of negotiation until the end of the drilling campaign, which resulted in greater consistency between what the marketing team promised and what was actually done, increasing the company's credibility and building stronger relationships with the client.

Beckett also recognized that the company needed a culture of entrepreneurship and accountability.[12] Employees were empowered to make suggestions and take ownership of processes and projects. Pacific Drilling focused on hiring employees who fit with the company's culture. Every potential employee was interviewed by three established employees. Through this process, the company selected recruits who were dedicated to performing above the average and who had enthusiasm for building a unique company. These qualities were reflected in a commitment the company made to its employees: "Pacific Drilling is committed to be the employer of choice in the offshore drilling industry and provide the tools and resources to enable its people to deliver consistently exceptional performance."

Given the inherently dangerous nature of the industry, Beckett and his management team consciously strived to develop a culture of safety, even at the expense of stopping drilling operations. The company implemented the Stop Work Obligation, which dictated that it was the responsibility and duty of any individual to stop any work that the employee felt had an unacceptable level of risk or other concern. This directive went beyond the traditional Stop Work Authority that was an industry

Exhibit 15 Pacific Drilling's Safety Performance as of The End of 2014

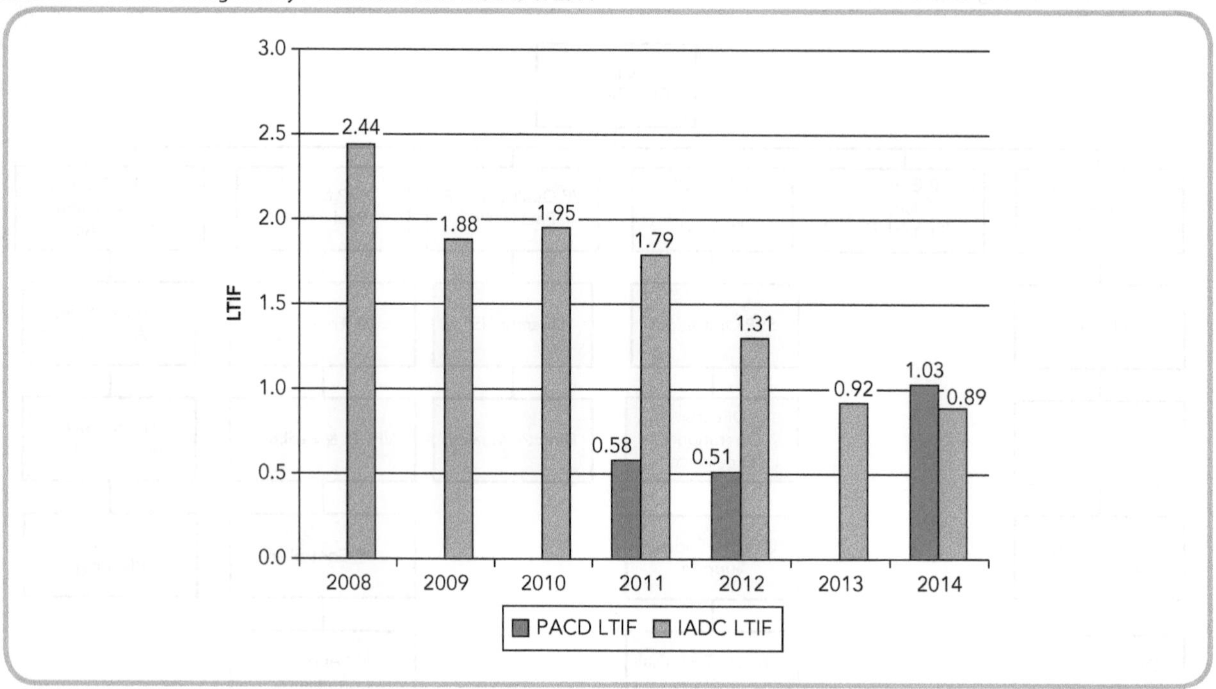

Notes:

Lost Time Incidents Frequency (LTIF) is the number of lost-time incidents per million work hours.

- International Association of Drilling Contractors (IADC) data include all land and water regions up to and including 2012.
- IADC data only include water regions where Pacific Drilling (PACD) was working in 2013 and 2014 (i.e., the United States, Africa, and South America).
- IADC data for 2014 is up to the third quarter year-to-date information only. Full 2014 data were unavailable at the time of writing.

Key 2014 safety achievements:

- Pacific Bora achieved 3.75 years without an LTI and 1.75 years without a recordable incident.
- Pacific Scirocco achieved 3.5 years without an LTI and 1.5 years without a recordable incident.
- Pacific Khamsin achieved 1 year without an LTI and almost 1 year without a recordable incident.
- Pacific Sharav had zero LTIs since commencing contract.
- "A" rating on the Chevron Contractor Health, Environment, and Safety (HES) Management (CHESM) program in both deepwater and the Nigerian business units.

Source: Company documents.

practice and gave employees the right to stop work but didn't require them to do so.

In an industry where producers valued drillers' reputation for safety, Pacific Drilling had achieved multiple years without any lost-time incidents on several rigs. Its safety performance had been recognized with an "A" rating on the Chevron Contractor Health, Environment, and Safety Management program in the Gulf of Mexico and in Nigeria. Pacific Drilling was also the first drilling contractor to certify its safety and environmental management systems with the Center for Offshore Safety (see Exhibit 15).

Challenges

Growth and Customer Base Challenges

Beckett and his team had planned to expand the company's fleet from the current eight drillships to 12. The need to contract out these ships pushed the company to broaden its customer base beyond relying on Chevron. In this industry, producers had usually been more likely to contract drillers with whom they had worked with before, in part because of the efficiency gained from a prior working relationship.

As Pacific Drilling sought to broaden its customer base, there was some concern that the company was tied too closely to Chevron. The technology, processes, and culture that Pacific Drilling had developed were significantly influenced by the company's close collaboration with Chevron. There was a concern that efficiency would be lost, even if only temporarily, when changing to a different drilling partnership. Evidence had shown that a given producer demonstrated productivity gains in a partnership with one driller, resulting from having acquired "relationship-specific" capabilities over the time that the two companies had worked together. However, these gains often did not translate to the same level of productivity gains in partnerships with new drillers,[13] which seemed to explain Chevron's preference to continue to contract Pacific Drilling. Chevron's support was fundamental in Pacific Drilling's success as a new entrant, but its ability to grow as a more mature company was likely to be constrained by that very same factor.

Technology Challenges

The technology advantage that Pacific Drilling had over competitors for deepwater drillships was also being challenged as other drillers upgraded their floater fleets. Competitors' rigs scheduled for delivery in 2016 and 2017 would have incremental technological advantages over Pacific Drilling's first rig.

Market Challenges

The price of oil had been tumbling since mid-2014, while North American shale oil production had grown rapidly and global energy demand had been weakening. For offshore drillers, existing contracts that had been nearing completion had been less likely to be extended. For available rigs, competition among drillers became intense as day rates were pushed down.

Over the previous decade, the number of offshore rigs worldwide had increased from approximately 670 to 950. Although the offshore floating rig count increased from approximately 200 to 350 from 2004 to late 2014, average utilization rates also increased over the same time period, from around 77 per cent to 86 per cent. Historically, newer rigs competed down in their day rates, causing older rigs to be stacked, either permanently or until the market recovered. Recently, though, the industry seemed to have undergone a fundamental shift. Once demand began collapsing in 2014, there was an overcapacity of deepwater rigs, and drillers struggled to find new contracts for their available rigs. The current industry downturn and significant rig oversupply led to deepwater drillships and semis being cold-stacked for the first time in history (see Exhibit 16).

Pacific Drilling's immediate issue was to secure a contract on two of its drillships, Pacific Meltem and

Exhibit 16 Floating Rig Utilization after 1985 by Build Cycle

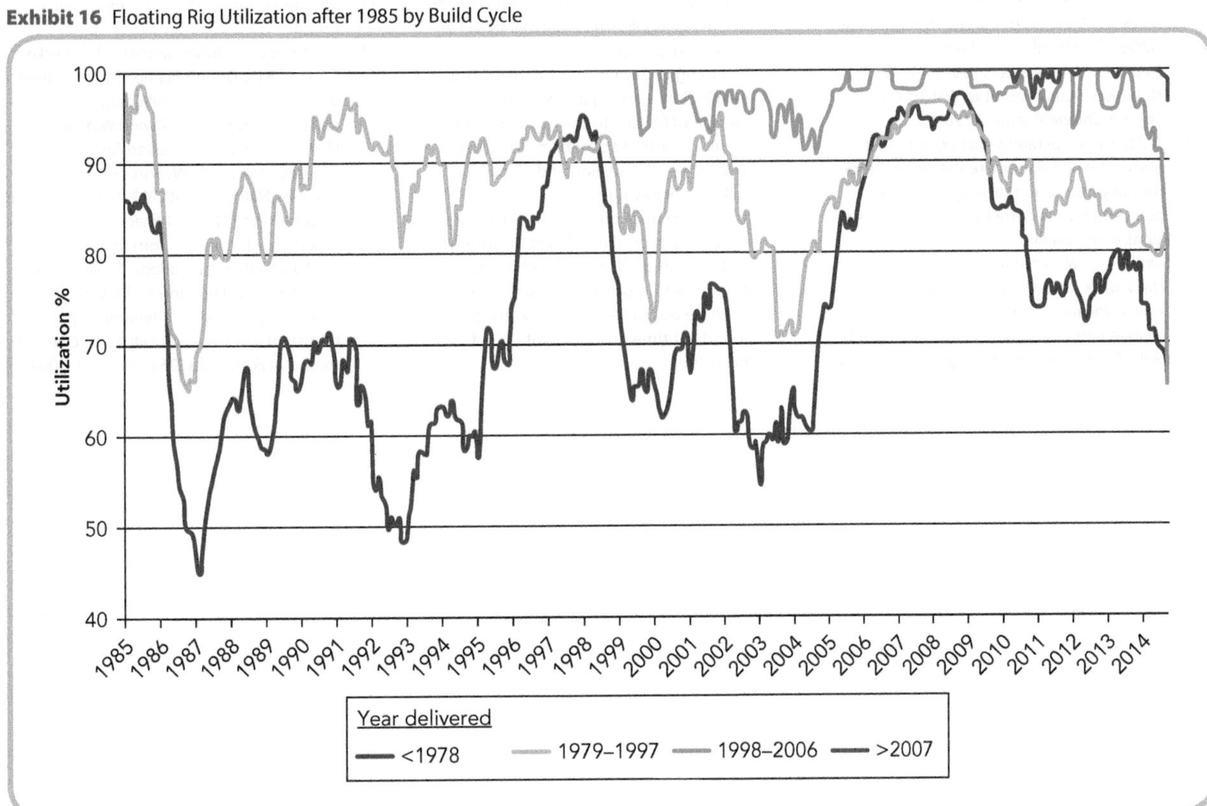

Source: Company documents.

Pacific Mistral, that had been sitting idle. Because modern drillships had rarely been cold-stacked, keeping the crew on board was costly. The company was also concerned about two additional drillships: Pacific Khamsin, which would come off contract in late 2015, and Pacific Zonda, scheduled for delivery from the shipyard in late 2015.

Strategic Choices

Pacific Drilling had come to a critical juncture, and important decisions had to be made. As a more mature company, Pacific Drilling had been confronting a different competitive landscape. During the past year, very few new contracts had been awarded in the industry. Some of the company's peers were willing to bid significantly below market rates to win the few new jobs available. Looking forward, Pacific Drilling had a significant number of high-specification floating rigs available to be contracted. Although there had been weak demand for very high-specification rigs, there had also been relatively limited supply, which supported the company's contracting prospects.

Overcoming challenges had been nothing new for Beckett. Yet, with the challenging market environment and other constraints, Beckett made the following statement in a letter to employees: "Despite the weakening market, we expect further growth in 2015, but we must continue to execute well on our growth plans and secure new contracts to deliver on this expectation."

NOTES

1. All currency amounts are in US$ unless otherwise specified.
2. Brad Plumer, "Why Oil Prices Keep Falling—And Throwing the World into Turmoil," Vox Media Inc., updated January 23, 2015, accessed April 12, 2015, www.vox.com/2014/12/16/7401705/oil-prices-falling.
3. Deutsche Bank Markets Research, "What Is New? Key Stats & Event to Watch," *Oilfield Services Chronicle*, June 23, 2014.
4. A derrick is a pyramid-shaped structure above the rig floor where the crown block, monkey board, and racking board are supported. Dual derricks have two drilling units on one hull.
5. Drillers usually charge oil producers on a daily work rate, which varies depending on the location, the type of rig, and the market conditions. For example, by March 2015, Pacific Drilling's average day rate was $558,000 and Diamond Offshore's rate was $450,000.
6. Ramon Casadesus-Masanell, Kenneth Corts, and Joseph McElroy, *The Offshore Drilling Industry in 2011* (Boston, MA: Harvard Business School, 2011). Available from Ivey Publishing, product no. 711543.
7. According to Casadesus-Masanell, Corts, and McElroy, moving a jack-up rig from the Gulf of Mexico to the North Sea took about a month, and mobilization alone cost between $2 million and $5 million, exclusive of day rates.
8. As a cost-reduction step, a cold-stacked rig is often stored in a harbour, shipyard, or designated offshore area because its contracting prospects look bleak. It will be out of service for extended periods of time and may not be actively marketed.
9. Robert B. Barsky and Lutz Kilian, "Oil and the Macroeconomy Since the 1970s," *Journal of Economic Perspectives* 18, no. 4 (Fall, 2004): 115–134.
10. Casadesus-Masanell, Corts, and McElroy, op. cit.
11. Ernst & Young Global Limited, "Chris Beckett, CEO of Pacific Drilling, Named EY Entrepreneur of the Year™ 2014 National Energy, Cleantech and Natural Resources Award Winner," November 15, 2014, accessed April 12, 2015, www.ey.com/US/en/Newsroom/News-releases/News-EY-US-EOY-2014-Chris-Beckett-Pacific-Drilling-National-Energy-AwardWinner.
12. Based on information from the company's Media and Public Relations department.
13. Ryan Kellogg, "Learning by Drilling: Interfirm Learning and Relationship Persistence in the Texas Oilpatch," *Quarterly Journal of Economics* 126 (2011): 1961–2004.

CASE 12

Pfizer

January 2017

"When Ian Read, an accountant and company lifer, took over as Pfizer's chief executive in December 2010, the drug firm was facing the impending patent expiration of Lipitor, the best-selling drug ever made, and the utter failure of one of the most lavishly funded research laboratories on the planet to develop much of anything. The stock was suffering, and Read's predecessor–Jeffrey Kindler, a bearlike lawyer hired from McDonald's–had just spent $68 billion to buy rival drug maker Wyeth in a Hail Mary strategy shift. Now Read had to make it work."[1]

Company and Industry Background

Pfizer was established in 1849 in Brooklyn, New York, by cousins Charles Pfizer and Charles Erhart with a loan of $2,500 from Pfizer's father.[2] Today, 167 years later, Pfizer Inc. has international revenues of $49 billion, which makes it the second-largest pharmaceutical manufacturer in the world.[3] Despite Pfizer's success, the company has faced many challenges over the last few decades. The pharmaceutical industry is heavily influenced by legal, political, and technological forces, and all indications are that the industry will continue to experience dramatic changes.

Since the passing of the Food and Drug Act in 1906, the Food and Drug Administration (FDA) has had regulatory authority over drugs in the United States. The scope of its initial authority was limited and in 1938 President Roosevelt signed the Food, Drug and Cosmetic Act (FD&C) into law, which significantly expanded federal oversight of drug manufacturing and marketing.[4] In addition to granting the FDA authority to mandate pre-market review of drugs, the FD&C also allowed the FDA to regulate drug labeling and advertising. Then, in 1992, Congress passed the Prescription Drug User Fee Act, which enables the FDA to collect fees from drug manufacturers to aid in funding the pre-market review process for new drug approvals.[5] The effect of these reforms was significant increases in the time and cost for drug manufacturers to bring new drugs to market.

In 2006, a study estimated the cost of bringing a new drug to market was between $802 million and $2 billion, depending on the type of drug being developed and the number of drugs being developed simultaneously.[6] The study found that approximately 60% of the total cost of drugs was related to pre-market clinical trials required by the FDA. As inflation, increased regulation, and other factors have affected the pharmaceutical industry, a 2012 study indicated that the cost per drug for the largest manufacturers has increased to over $5.5 billion.[7] For Pfizer, the total Research & Development (R&D) cost for each drug that received FDA approval was $7.7 billion between 1997 and 2011.[8] The steep rise in development costs has forced many large drug manufacturers—including Pfizer—to cut R&D budgets in an attempt to control rising costs.[9]

The reduction in R&D funding in reaction to expanding costs has led to stifled innovation and revealed a crisis looming ahead for many large drug manufacturers in the industry. Not only have many drug companies' blockbuster drugs gone off patent in recent years, but the reductions in R&D spending have resulted in drug pipelines that have failed to produce anything of significant value.[10] The number of new drugs approved by the FDA per billion dollars of R&D expenditures has halved every nine years since 1950.[11] The rapid increase in the cost of drug development and the reduction in the approval frequency of blockbuster-level drugs has led many industry experts to largely consider the current, fully integrated business model of large pharmaceutical companies to be unsustainable.[12]

Business and Strategies

Like most large pharmaceutical manufacturers, Pfizer pursues a "blockbuster" business model that is heavily reliant on its R&D pipeline to consistently develop and launch high volume drugs—drugs with expected annual revenues of $1 billion or greater.[13] In 2012, Pfizer began

Written by Jeffrey S. Harrison, Ryan McGowan, Kevin O'Neill, Lauren Shotwell, and Joshua Torres at the Robins School of Business, University of Richmond.

Exhibit 1 Pfizer Business Segment Comparisons

Business Segment Financials
Innovative vs Established Segments

	2015		2014		2013	
	Innovative	Established	Innovative	Established	Innovative	Established
Revenues	$26,758	$21,587	$24,005	$25,149	$23,602	$27,619
Cost of Sales	3,650	4,486	3,848	4,570	3,675	4,732
% of revenue	13.60%	20.80%	16.00%	18.20%	15.60%	17.10%
Selling, informational, and administrative expenses	6,807	3,572	6,162	3,903	5,520	4,714
R&D Expenses	3,030	758	2,549	657	2,154	737
Amortization of intangible assets	94	36	69	85	58	100
Restructuring charges and certain acquisition-related costs	–	–	–	–	6	–
Other (income)/deductions—net	(1.087)	(150)	(1.096)	(265)	(576)	(216)
Income from continuing operations before provision for taxes on income	$14,264	$12,885	$12,472	$16,199	$12,765	$17,552

Source: 2015 Pfizer Annual Report.

restructuring its operations into a new commercial operating model. Pfizer divested its infant nutrition business for $11.9 billion and spun-off its animal health unit, Zoetis. Additionally, Pfizer restructured its operations into two primary business segments: Innovative Products and Established Products. Pfizer's Innovative Products business is further divided into the Global Innovative Pharma (GIP) and Global Vaccines, Oncology, and Consumer Healthcare (VOC) businesses.[14] Ian Read commented regarding the restructuring: "This represents the next steps in Pfizer's journey to further revitalize our innovative core. Our new commercial model will provide each business with an enhanced ability to respond to market dynamics, greater visibility and focus, and distinctive capabilities."[15] Exhibit 1 contains some useful financial comparisons between Pfizer's Innovative Products and its Established Products.

Innovative Products Business

Global Innovative Pharma (GIP) Business. This business focuses on developing, registering and commercializing novel, value-creating medicines that improve patients' lives. Therapeutic areas include inflammation, cardiovascular/metabolic, neuroscience and pain, rare diseases and women's/men's health, and include leading brands, such as Xeljanz®, Eliquis®, and Lyrica®. GIP has a robust pipeline of medicines in inflammation, cardiovascular/metabolic disease, pain, and rare diseases.[16]

Global Vaccines, Oncology, and Consumer Healthcare Business. This segment consists of three businesses with the following key elements: (1) poised for high, organic growth; (2) distinct specialization and operating models in science, talent, and market approach; and (3) structured to ideally position Pfizer to be a market leader on a global basis.[17] Consumer products include Advil®, Centrum®, Robitussin®, Nexium®, and ChapStick®.

Established Products Business

Global Established Pharma (GEP) Business. This area consists of three primary product segments: (1) Peri-LOE products which are losing or approaching a losing position in market exclusivity; (2) legacy established products in developed markets that have lost market exclusivity and those with growth opportunities; and (3) emerging market products with growth opportunities such as organic initiatives, partnerships, product enhancements, sterile injectables, and biosimilars.[18] Examples of established products include Celebrex®, EpiPen®, Zoloft®, and Lypitor®.

Pricing Strategy

Pfizer's and other large drug companies' revenue growth has been largely dependent on raising the price of older drugs, particularly those nearing patent expirations. Approximately 34% of Pfizer's revenue growth over the past three years has come from increasing prices on existing drugs.[19] Over this period, Pfizer has increased the price of Viagra by 57%, of Lyrica by 51%, and of Premarin by 41%. A 2013 study by the AARP found that the price of Lipitor rose by 9.3% in the year preceding patent expiration, and by 17.5% in 2011, the year of expiration.[20] Pfizer is not alone in these practices. AbbVie and Bristol-Myers Squibb have both been reported as generating a very significant amount of their revenue growth from price increases. Drug pricing scandals and increased media and societal attention on drug pricing in general makes Pfizer's reliance on pricing strategy to drive top-line revenue growth unsustainable. This is evident in the drug industry's flat net pricing in 2015.[21]

Growth Strategy

Pfizer has become one of the largest pharmaceutical companies in the world primarily as a result of aggressive mergers and acquisitions (M&A). Pfizer's acquisitions have been focused on two main strategies: expanding its capabilities and acquiring brands with strong revenues. Many of Pfizer's acquisitions have provided new capabilities for the organization, such as biologics with the acquisition of Warner-Lambert in 2000 and biosimilar drugs with the acquisition of Hospira in 2015. Additionally, Pfizer acquired the rights to the best-selling drug Lipitor in its 2000 acquisition of Warner-Lambert and the rights to Celebrex and Bextra in its 2003 acquisition of Pharmacia Corporation. From Pfizer's press releases and company history, a brief timeline of Pfizer's major acquisitions (and divestitures) is outlined below[22]:

2000: Pfizer acquires Warner-Lambert for $90 billion for their biologics and consumer products portfolio, along with the rights to Lipitor.

2003: Pfizer acquires Pharmacia Corporation for $60 billion and acquires the rights to Celebrex, Bextra, Detrol, and Xalatan.

2005: Pfizer acquires Vicuron Pharmaceuticals for $1.9 billion for their antibiotic research and development.

2006: Pfizer sells its consumer products division to Johnson & Johnson for $16.6 billion.

2007: Pfizer acquires Coley Pharmaceutical for $164 million for their portfolio of biotechnology, cancer, and vaccine drugs.

2009: Pfizer acquires Wyeth for $68 billion for their portfolio of biotech drugs.

2010: Pfizer acquires King Pharmaceuticals for $3.6 billion and acquires the rights to EpiPen.

2015: Pfizer Acquires Hospira for $16 billion for their biosimilar and injectable drugs portfolio, as well as infusion technologies.[23]

2016: Pfizer acquires Anacor Pharmaceuticals for $5.1 billion for their topical anti-inflammatory drugs and acquires the rights to Crisaborole.[24]

2016: Pfizer acquires Medivation for $14 billion for its prostate cancer drug Xtandi.[25]

Pfizer has attempted unsuccessfully to acquire a foreign drug company and relocate its headquarters overseas. CEO Ian Read has said numerous times that the company faces a competitive disadvantage with foreign rivals that have significantly lower tax bills.[26] These sorts of deals are called corporate inversions—transactions undergone by a U.S. company that moves its tax residence to a foreign country in order to reduce U.S. taxes.[27] In 2014, Pfizer attempted a merger with rival AstraZeneca, which faced fierce opposition from lawmakers on either side. In the end, Pfizer walked away from the $118 billion deal after rejection by AstraZeneca's board.[28]

In 2016 Pfizer entered into an agreement to merge with Allergan. The $160 billion deal would have created the largest pharmaceutical company in the world and would have allowed Pfizer to relocate its headquarters to Allergan's home country of Ireland in order to take advantage of their lower corporate tax rate.[29] However, on April 4, 2016, the U.S. Department of Treasury took measures to limit corporate inversions.[30] Previously, a company realized tax benefits for inversions only when the foreign company would contribute 20% or greater of the combined company's assets. The new ruling disregards the last three years of U.S. acquisitions by the foreign entity when determining the foreign company's relative size under the combined entity. The new rule was the predominant factor that caused Pfizer to pay $150 million to walk away the Allergan deal.[31] Pfizer would not have realized the full tax benefit of the inversion because Allergan's relative size would have fallen below the 20% threshold under the new tax rules.

Innovation Strategy

Pfizer has a long history of investing in R&D for the development of blockbuster drugs. However, many industry experts believe the age of blockbuster drugs has come to an end and that new blockbusters will be rare.[32] They argue that the opportunities for revolutionary drugs have been mostly exploited, with very few areas of medicine in which breakthrough drugs can have a huge impact. In light of industry trends, Pfizer has shifted its strategy of maintaining an industry-leading drug pipeline from in-house development to being more reliant on strategic partnerships and mergers and acquisitions.

To support its interest in strategic partnerships, in 2004 Pfizer founded Pfizer Venture Investments (PVI). Its goal is to identify and invest in strategic areas and businesses at the leading edge of healthcare science and technologies. PVI started with a $50 million annual budget and was Pfizer's way of staying ahead of industry trends and investing in companies which are developing compounds and technologies that will enhance Pfizer's drug pipeline and help drive the future of the pharmaceutical industry.[33] In January 2016, Pfizer announced that it would be expanding its investment strategy to include investments in early-stage scientific innovations in immuno-oncology, gene therapy, and other cutting-edge fields. Pfizer invested nearly $46 million in four companies in these fields: BioAtla, NextCure Inc., Cortexyme Inc., and 4D Molecular Therapists, Inc. Pfizer's strategic partnership with these and other firms provides a world-class resource in start-up organizations to accelerate the pace of scientific innovation and to help develop their pipeline of drugs.[34]

Inside Pfizer

Management Team

CEO, Ian C. Read. Ian C. Read was elected CEO of Pfizer in December of 2010 and Chairman of the Board in 2011, taking over from Jeffrey Kindler. Read has spent his entire career at Pfizer, starting as an operational auditor. Read's B.S. in chemical engineering and accounting experience set the groundwork for a successful career in pharmaceuticals. Some of his previous roles included CFO of Pfizer Mexico, Country Manager of Pfizer Brazil, President of Pfizer's International Pharmaceuticals Group, Executive Vice President of Europe, and Corporate Vice President. Read also serves on the boards of Pharmaceutical Research Manufacturers of America (PhRMA), which represents the leading innovative biopharmaceutical research companies.[35]

Executive VP Strategy Portfolio and Commercial Operations, Laurie J. Olso. Laurie Oslo oversees long-term strategy, execution of commercial objectives, and advises portfolio functions for R&D investment strategies. She started working for Pfizer in 1987 in Marketing Research. As an economics graduate from the State University of New York at Stony Brook and with a MBA from Hofstra University, her experiences span across domestic and global leadership positions in marketing, commercial development, strategy, analytics corporate responsibility, and operations. Her most recent role was Senior Vice President of Portfolio Management and Analytics, and within that role she was part of the task force that "redesigned Pfizer's R&D organization to strengthen its pipeline and improve efficiency."[36]

Executive VP Chief Development Officer, Rod MacKenzie, PhD. Rod MacKenzie received his PhD from Imperial College, London, after getting his chemistry degree from the University of Glasgow. As the co-inventor of Darifenacin, which was sold in 2003 due to regulatory issues, MacKenzie held various positions within Pfizer before assuming his current position.[37] His role oversees "the development and advancement of Pfizer's pipeline of medicines in several therapeutic areas." He serves on the Portfolio Strategy and Investment Committee and sits on the Board of Directors for ViiV Healthcare.[38]

Executive VP Business Operations and CFO, Frank D'Amelio. Frank D'Amelio joined the company in September 2007 and oversees finance, business development, and business operations. He has been ranked as a top CFO for various years by Institutional Investor magazine. He has led the organization in many mergers, spin-offs, and sales, such as: Pfizer and Wyeth merger, sale of their nutrition business, and the spin-off of Zoetis. His experience comes from his many leadership roles at Alcatel-Lucent, including Senior Executive Vice President of Integration and Chief Administrative Officer, and his experience as COO of Lucent Technologies. Frank earned his MBA in Finance from St. John's University and his bachelor's degree in Accounting from St. Peter's College. Representing Pfizer, he currently serves on the Board of Directors for many organizations. They include, Humana, Inc., Zoetis, Inc., the Independent College Fund of New Jersey, and the Gillen-Brewer School. [39]

Major Shareholders

Pfizer is a publicly traded company with approximately 6.2 billion shares outstanding at December 31, 2015.[40] According to Yahoo Finance, among Pfizer's primary shareholders are institutional investment companies Vanguard Group, Inc., BlackRock Institutional Trust Company, and JPMorgan Chase & Co., who own 6.32%, 4.95%, and 1.89% of total outstanding shares, respectively. Additionally, Pfizer's only major non-institutional shareholders are all executive-level leadership within the organization.

Human Resources

Human resource efforts are led by Charles H. Hill III, who has been the Executive Vice President of Worldwide

Human Resources since December 2010. Prior to that assignment, Hill was Senior Vice President of Human Resources for the Worldwide Biopharmaceuticals Businesses from 2008 through December 2010. On December 31, 2015, Pfizer employed approximately 97,900 employees across the globe.[41]

In 2007, Pfizer Global Manufacturing, a global manufacturing site in the U.K., was recognized for their Explorer training program. The Explorer program was a year long and covered team dynamics that included purpose, leadership, motivation, meetings, and the environment, among other topics. For each of the four training segments, there were pre-workshop activities, two-day workshops, post-workshop assignments, and a follow-up workshop.[42]

Pfizer also uses traditional techniques to develop their personnel. Employees are expected to collaborate with their direct leaders to create individual development plans. They have also implemented a tool called Mentor Match. It is designed to allow employees to volunteer as a mentor or search for mentors with certain characteristics. Managers are encouraged to give frequent and in-depth performance appraisals in lieu of the standard annual review process. Pfizer also uses short-and medium-term job rotations or projects to help further the development of their employees.[43]

Organizational Culture

Upon taking charge of Pfizer in 2010, Read soon discovered that many of the processes in place at Pfizer were broken. The process for FDA drug applications was so bad that the FDA sometimes refused to even review submitted applications. Read demanded answers, and the only answer he received was that everyone knew the application didn't meet the required quality standards, but nobody was willing to speak out about it. Read's response was to hand every employee a gold coin with the words "Straight Talk" on one side and "OWNIT!" on the other side. It was Read's way of empowering his employees to speak up to their boss when they believe they are wrong, but above all, to create accountability.[44] Since then, OWNIT! has become ingrained in Pfizer's culture.[45]

Mission, Purpose, and Values[46]

Pfizer's mission is: "To be the premier, innovative biopharmaceutical company."

Pfizer's purpose is: "Innovate to bring therapies to patients that significantly improve their lives."

Pfizer's core values are: "Customer focus; Community; Respect for people; Performance; Collaboration; Leadership; Integrity; Quality; Innovation."

Operations & Supply Chain

Each of the Innovative Products and Established Products businesses is led by a single manager responsible for both commercial productivity and research and development activities that meet proof-of-concept requirements. The Innovative Products Business is tasked with development and commercialization of new medicines and vaccines. The Established Products Business focuses on branded generic medicines and legacy brands that have lost or will lose market exclusivity in the short term. Both businesses have geographic footprints that span developed and emerging markets.[47]

Pfizer has a truly global supply chain network with 64 internal manufacturing facilities, over 200 supply chain partners, and 134 logistics centers in 2015. Pfizer claims to have over 850 major product groups. Due to the high demands for traceability, Pfizer employs a serialization program across its supply chain. Pfizer also uses their Highly Orchestrated Supply Network (HOSuN) to connect inventory, transportation, logistics and its associated security, compliance, environmental health and safety, and other functions into a truly integrated system. They also use HoSuN for business continuity risk assessment and resolution.[48]

Manufacturing pharmaceuticals can be extremely complex. For example, the vaccine known as Prevenar 13 was produced for the one-billionth-time in 2015. According to Pfizer, manufacturing Prevenar 13 includes the participation of 1700 employees, 678 quality tests, 400 different raw materials, and 580 steps in manufacturing, over 2 years.[49]

Pfizer earned 56% of its 2015 revenue from operations outside the United States, which represented \$27.1 billion. Japan is the second largest market, behind the United States.[50]

Marketing and Distribution

Pfizer promotes its products within the global biopharmaceutical business to healthcare providers and patients. Pfizer's marketing organization is responsible for educating a wealth of stakeholders regarding product approved uses, benefits, and risks. Pfizer employs a direct-to-consumer advertising campaign in the U.S.; this provides similar information and suggests that interested customers have discussions with their doctor. Pfizer's "Global Consumer Healthcare business uses its own sales and marketing organizations to promote its products and occasionally uses distributors in smaller markets." Television, digital, print, and in-store media are all used to advertise to consumers.[51]

In the U.S., all products must be approved by the FDA prior to any marketing campaigns. The FDA oversight includes "regulations that govern the testing, manufacturing, safety, efficacy, labeling and storage of our products, record keeping, advertising, and promotion."[52] There are also several federal and state laws that were enacted to prevent fraud and abuse, including false claim and anti-kickback laws. Pfizer encounters "similar regulatory and legislative issues in most other countries."[53]

Pfizer has been criticized in the past regarding some of its foreign marketing practices. In August 2012, the U.S. Securities and Exchange Commission fined Pfizer $45 million dollars for violating the US Foreign Corrupt Practices Act. In order to secure regulatory approval, sales, and increased prescriptions, several subsidiaries of Pfizer had been bribing foreign officials. The bribes had been concealed under marketing and promotion expenses in the accounting records. Pfizer reported the violations voluntarily in 2004 and subsequently implemented anti-corruption training.[54]

From a distribution perspective, prescription pharmaceutical products primarily are sold primarily to wholesalers. In 2015, the "top three biopharmaceutical wholesalers accounted for approximately 34% of our total revenues (and 74% of total U.S. revenues)."[55] Pfizer also does some direct shipments to retailers, hospitals, pharmacies, and clinics. For its vaccines, Pfizer "primarily sell[s] directly to individual provider offices, the Centers for Disease Control and Prevention and wholesalers."[56]

Financial Condition

Over the past five years, Pfizer's revenues have been steadily decreasing, reducing net income to a five-year low of $6.96 billion. A decrease in revenue from continuing operations is the primary cause of the decrease in revenues. The spin-off of Zoetis had a compounding effect on both the decrease in revenues and cost of sales post 2013. Current assets were steady over the past three years; however, there was a recent dip in short-term investments. Goodwill is increasing, reflecting the premiums paid for acquisitions in recent years. Pfizer's short-term borrowing has increased almost twofold in the past five years. Overall, Pfizer's balance sheet has been fairly steady the past two years, but Pfizer's total liabilities are slightly higher and its total equity slightly lower in 2015 compared to 2014. Both of these years are lower compared to pre-Zoetis spin-off levels.[57] Exhibits 2 and 3 contain detailed Pfizer financial information.

Exhibit 2 Pfizer Income Statements

Consolidated Statements of Income—USD ($) Shares in Millions, $ in Millions	2015	2014	2013	2012	2011
Income Statement [Abstract]					
Revenues	$ 48,851	$ 49,605	$ 51,584	$ 58,986	$ 65,259
Costs and expenses:					
Cost of sales	9,648	9,577	9,586	11,334	14,076
Selling, informational, and administrative expenses	14,809	14,097	14,355	16,616	18,832
Research and development expenses	7,690	8,393	6,678	7,870	9,074
Amortization of intangible assets	3,728	4,039	4,599	5,175	5,544
Restructuring charges and certain acquisition-related costs	1,152	250	1,182	1,880	2,930
Other (income)/deductions—net	2,860	1,009	(532)	4,031	2,499
Income from continuing operations before provision for taxes on income	8,965	12,240	15,716	12,080	12,304
Provision for taxes on income	1,990	3,120	4,306	2,562	3,909
Income from continuing operations	6,975	9,119	11,410	9,518	8,395
Discontinued operations:					
Income from discontinued operations—net of tax	17	(6)	308	297	350
Gain/(loss) on disposal of discontinued operations—net of tax	(6)	55	10,354	4,783	1,304
Discontinued operations—net of tax	11	48	10,662	5,080	1,654
Net income before allocation to noncontrolling interests	6,986	9,168	22,072	14,598	10,049
Less: Net income attributable to noncontrolling interests	26	32	69	28	40
Net income attributable to Pfizer Inc.	$ 6,960	$9,135	$ 22,003	$ 14,570	$ 10,009

Source: Pfizer Annual Reports.

Exhibit 3 Pfizer Balance Sheets

Consolidated Balance Sheets—USD ($) $ in Millions	2015	2014	2013	2012	2011
Assets					
Cash and cash equivalents	$ 3,641	$ 3,343	$ 2,183	$ 10,081	$ 3,182
Short-term investments	19,649	32,779	30,225	22,318	23,270
Trade accounts receivable, less allowance for doubtful accounts	8,176	8,401	9,357	10,675	13,058
Inventories	7,513	5,663	6,166	6,076	6,610
Current tax assets	2,662	2,566	4,624	6,170	9,380
Other current assets	2,163	2,843	3,613	3,567	5,317
Assets of discontinued operations and other assets held for sale	–	–	76	5,944	–
Total current assets	43,804	55,595	56,244	64,831	60,817
Long-term investments	15,999	17,518	16,406	14,149	9,814
Property, plant and equipment, less accumulated depreciation	13,766	11,762	12,397	13,213	15,921
Identifiable intangible assets, less accumulated amortization	40,356	35,166	39,385	45,146	51,184
Goodwill	48,242	42,069	42,519	43,661	44,569
Noncurrent deferred tax assets and other noncurrent tax assets	1,794	1,944	1,554	1,565	5,697
Other noncurrent assets	3,499	3,513	3,596	3,233	–
Total assets	$167,460	$167,566	$172,101	$185,798	$188,002
Liabilities and Equity					
Short-term borrowings, including current portion of long-term debt	$10,160	$5,141	$6,027	$6,424	$4,016
Trade accounts payable	3,620	3,210	3,234	2,921	3,678
Dividends payable	1,852	1,711	1,663	1,733	1,796
Income taxes payable	418	531	678	979	1,009
Accrued compensation and related items	2,359	1,841	1,792	1,875	2,120
Other current liabilities	10,990	9,153	9,951	13,812	15,066
Liabilities of discontinued operations	–	–	21	1,442	1,224
Total current liabilities	29,399	21,587	23,366	29,186	28,909
Long-term debt	28,818	31,541	30,462	31,036	34,926
Pension benefit obligations, net	6,310	7,885	4,635	7,782	6,355
Postretirement benefit obligations, net	1,809	2,379	2,668	3,491	3,344
Noncurrent deferred tax liabilities	26,877	23,317	25,590	21,193	18,861
Other taxes payable	3,992	4,353	3,993	6,581	6,886
Other noncurrent liabilities	5,257	4,883	4,767	4,851	6,100
Total liabilities	102,463	95,944	95,481	104,120	105,381
Commitments and contingencies					
Preferred stock, no par value, at stated value	$ 26	$ 29	$ 33	$ 39	$ 45
Common stock	459	455	453	448	445
Additional paid-in capital	81,016	78,977	77,283	72,608	71,423

continued

Exhibit 3 (cont.) Pfizer Balance Sheets

Consolidated Balance Sheets—USD ($) $ in Millions	2015	2014	2013	2012	2011
Employee benefit trusts	–	–	–	–	(3)
Treasury stock, shares at cost	(79,252)	(73,021)	(67,923)	(40,122)	(31,801)
Retained earnings	71,993	72,176	69,732	54,240	46,210
Accumulated other comprehensive loss	(9,522)	(7,316)	(3,271)	(5,953)	(4,129)
Total Pfizer Inc. shareholders' equity	64,720	71,301	76,307	81,260	82,190
Equity attributable to noncontrolling interests	278	321	313	418	431
Total equity	64,998	71,622	76,620	81,678	82.621
Total liabilities and equity	$ 167,460	$167,566	$ 172,101	$ 185,798	$188,002

Source: Pfizer Annual Reports.

Competitive Landscape

Major Competitors

The pharmaceutical industry invests heavily in research and clinical trials and relies on obtaining FDA approval and patent protection for its products to ensure prolonged profits while the next "miracle" drug is under research. There are high payoffs when a drug is successfully brought to market; but there also great costs, in the form of massive time and monetary investments for failures, if it is not. Among Pfizer's largest competitors are Merck, Novartis, Bristol-Myers, and Johnson & Johnson.[58] Exhibit 4 contains some comparative financial ratios for these competitors.

Merck & Co. (MRK). Merck & Co. was founded in 1891 and had $39.5B in 2015 revenues, making it one of the largest pharmaceuticals companies in the world today. The cholesterol-lowering drug branded Zetia, which is Merck's 2nd largest revenue generator, is a direct competitor to Pfizer's drug Lipitor (patent expired in 2011). Zetia is selling at a rate of nearly $3 billion a year, whereas Lipitor is generating $1.86B.[59]

Major Acquisitions[60]:

1993: Merck acquired Medco Containment Services, Inc. ($6B)
2009: Schering-Plough merged with Merck & Co. ($41B merger)
2014: Merck acquired Cubist Pharmaceuticals ($8.4B)

Novartis AG (NVS). Founded in 1996 in Switzerland, Novartis AG is the pharmaceutical industry's world leader in sales, generating $50.4B in 2015 revenues. Novartis has several oncology products in the pipeline that will directly compete with Pfizer pharmaceuticals. Currently its best sellers are prescription treatments for cancer, multiple sclerosis, and macular degeneration.[61]

Major Acquisitions[62]:

1999: Formed by merger with Ciba-Geigy and Sandoz Laboratories
2005: Acquired Hexal and Eon Labs ($8.29B)
2006: Acquired Chiron Corp. ($5.1B)
2010: Acquired Alcon ($39.3B)
2012: Acquired Fougera Pharmaceuticals ($1.5B)

Bristol-Myers Squibb (BMY). Bristol-Myers Squibb was founded in New York in 1887 and had $18.8B in 2015 revenues. They produce the market-leading antipsychotic drug, Abilify, which is widely used for treating schizophrenia. Bristol-Myers Squibb, like the majority of pharmaceuticals companies, derives the bulk of its profits from a limited number of expensive specialty drugs or much wider market spread of cheaper drugs.[63]

Major Acquisitions[64]:

2009: Acquired Medarex
2010: Acquired ZymoGenetics
2015: Acquired Flexus Biosciences ($1.25B) and Cardioxyl ($2B)
2016: Acquired Padlock Therapeutics ($600M) & Cormorant Pharmaceuticals ($520M)

Johnson & Johnson (JNJ). Founded in 1886, Johnson & Johnson is an American multinational medical devices, pharmaceutical (40% by revenues) and consumer packaged goods manufacturer. Besides over-the-counter products for self-treatment and at-home medication, Johnson & Johnson produces high-priced

Exhibit 4 Comparative Financial Ratios

	Pfizer	Merck	Novartis	Bristol-Myers Squibb	Johnson & Johnson
Research over Revenue %	15.74	16.97	17.73	35.79	12.91
Revenue INR Mil	48,851	39,498	50,387	16,560	70,074
Gross Margin %	80.3	62.2	65.5	76.4	69.3
Operating Income INR Mil	11,824	6,928	8,977	1,890	18,065
Operating Margin %	24.2	17.5	17.8	11.4	25.8
Net Income INR Mil	6,960	4,442	17,783	1,565	15,409
Earnings Per Share INR	1.11	1.56	7.29	0.93	5.48
Dividends INR	1.12	1.81	2.67	1.49	2.95
Payout Ratio % *	82.7	48.4	77.7	139.6	55.6
Shares Mil	6,257	2,841	2,403	1,679	2,813
Book Value Per Share * INR	10.82	16.39	32.31	9.08	25.86
Operating Cash Flow INR Mil	14,512	12,421	11,897	1,832	19,279
Cap Spending INR Mil	−1,496	−1,283	−3,505	−820	−3,463
Free Cash Flow INR Mil	13,016	11,138	8,392	1,012	15,816
Free Cash Flow Per Share * INR	2.22	1.65	3.97	0.64	5.3
Working Capital INR Mil	14,405	10,561	-863	2,398	32,463
Tax Rate %	22.2	17.44	13.6	21.47	19.73
Net Margin %	14.25	11.25	35.29	9.45	21.99
Asset Turnover (Average)	0.29	0.39	0.39	0.51	0.53
Return on Assets %	4.13	4.44	13.84	4.78	11.65
Financial Leverage (Average)	2.59	2.28	1.71	2.23	1.88
Return on Equity %	10.24	9.52	24.06	10.75	21.87
Return on Invested Capital %	7.11	6.74	19.28	7.83	17.55
Interest Coverage	8.48	9.04	13.16	12.29	35.78

Source: Morningstar.com

specialty drugs used in the treatment of autoimmune diseases, prostate cancer, and HIV/AIDS.[65]

Major Acquisitions[66]:

2006: Acquired consumer healthcare business of Pfizer ($16.6B)
2013: Acquired Aragon Pharma ($1B)
2014: Alios BioPharma, Inc ($1.75B)

External Environment

The pharmaceutical industry is heavily influenced by legal, political, and technological forces. Societal views on issues such as drug pricing and tax evasion have created demand for increased government regulation.

Regulation

In the U.S., pharmaceutical companies are under the regulation granted to the Food and Drug Administration. The FDA has primarily provided oversight over pharmaceutical product quality through two actions: reviewing drug applications and inspecting factories for compliance with good manufacturing practices. In an effort to reduce recognized shortcomings, such as high levels of product recalls, shortages of critical drugs, and limited inspection efforts, the FDA created an Office of Pharmaceutical Quality (OPQ) in January 2015. The OPQ was created to enhance oversight of drug quality for all pharmaceuticals.[67] Its mission is to assure supply of quality drugs to the American market, use enhanced science and risk-based methods, leverage quantitative and expert assessments for product oversight, encourage development and adoption of new technologies, and "provide seamless integration of review inspection, surveillance, policy, and research across the product life cycle."[68]

FDA oversight impacts several areas of the value chain. For example, the FDA increased the importance of audit trails of information in manufacturing when 21 CFR part 11 came into effect. The update requires anyone designing, manufacturing, or testing pharmaceuticals to follow the guidelines. This encouraged manufacturers to keep better electronic records to include timestamps, validation, and signatures. 21 CFR part 11 was built unto the National Drug Code (NDC), which was passed in 2007. The NDC required manufacturers to use a serialized code on the product to improve traceability throughout the supply chain post-manufacturer.[69]

Affordable Care Act

In 2014, the Internal Revenue Service issued final regulations for the Branded Prescription Drug Fee (BPD), an annual non-tax deductible fee imposed on branded prescription drug manufacturers, which was included in the Patient Protection and Affordable Care Act (ACA). The new legislation requires government-funded drug programs to report yearly prescription drug sales data to the Department of Treasury. The reporting programs include: Medicare, Medicaid, TRICARE, and the Department of Veterans Affairs. The branded prescription drug fee is allocated to manufacturers based on their relative percentage of total reported prescription drug sales.[70] The total 2014 BPD fee, according to the IRS fee schedule, was $3 billion—Pfizer's portion was approximately $220 million, which was paid in 2015.[71]

The ACA also amended the Public Health Service (PHS) Act to expedite FDA approval of biosimilars—drugs that are generic versions of FDA-approved biologic products. A manufacturer must show clinical evidence that a new product is "highly similar" in effectiveness to an FDA-approved reference biologic. Once the FDA receives the trial data for a biosimilar, the ACA allows the FDA to pursue a fast-track approval process. Prior to 2010, no biosimilar products had been approved by the FDA.[72] As of August 2016, three biosimilar products had been approved.[73]

Drug Pricing Concerns

Public outrage over increasing drug prices came to a head recently, with many scandals receiving national headline attention. One such incident occurred when Turing Pharmaceuticals raised the price of Daraprim—a drug used predominantly by AIDS patients and pregnant women—from $13.50 to $750 per pill, over a 5,000% increase.[74] Another such incident involved Mylan, the company that manufacturers the injector EpiPen, which contains a drug used to treat life-threatening allergy attacks (a drug Pfizer manufacturers). Mylan increased the price of EpiPen from $265 to over $600 in less than three years.[75] Many believe the increase was in response to a settlement agreement in 2012 under which Mylan agreed to allow a generic competitor to enter the market in 2015.

The rising cost of healthcare in the United States is a growing concern among voters, and societal pressures are seeing health care reform and regulation on drug prices reaching political platforms and ballots across the country. Political lobbyists on both sides are spending millions of dollars to influence the outcome of such initiatives. One such initiative, Proposition 61 in California, would limit the amount that state agencies pay for prescription drugs to that of the U.S. Department of Veterans Affairs, which normally receives a 20 to 25% discount on its prescription drug prices. Pfizer donated more than $9.4 million to political action groups in opposition to Prop 61, and in total pharmaceutical companies contributed $109 million (Merck & Co. $9.4 million and Johnson & Johnson $9.3 million).[76]

Looking Forward

Ian Read has been at Pfizer's helm for the past six years. With the patent expiration for Lipitor behind him, the best-selling drug in history is no longer contributing as much to Pfizer's bottom line. Is the firm still capable of delivering a sustainable pipeline of profitable drugs, or are major changes to strategy and operations necessary? And is Pfizer's opportunity for significant inversions over with the failed takeover attempts of both AstraZeneca and Allergan? To add to these issues, drug pricing scandals and healthcare reform have created an environment of active political reform. How can Pfizer navigate the upcoming challenges that growing societal discontent with "big pharma" and the rising cost of healthcare present? Do these threats also provide opportunities? How can Pfizer best be positioned for growth and profitability in this challenging business environment?

NOTES

1. Herper, M. 2015. Innovation's Accountant. *Forbes*, November 2: 58.
2. Pfizer. 2015. Pfizer Inc: Exploring Our History 1849–1899. Pfizer.com
3. Pfizer Inc. 2015. *2015 Financial Report*. New York, NY: Pfizer Inc.
4. FDA. Significant Dates in U.S. Food and Drug Law History. http://www.fda.gov/AboutFDA/WhatWeDo/History/Milestones/ucm128305.htm
5. Ibid.
6. Adams, Christopher and Brantner, Van V. 2006. Estimating the Cost of New Drug Development: Is it Really $802 Million? *Health Affairs*, 25(2): 420–428.
7. Harper, M. 2013. The Cost of Creating a New Drug Now $5 Billion, Pushing Big Pharma to Change. *Forbes (Online)*. August 11. http://www.forbes.com/sites/matthewherper/2013/08/11/ how-the-staggering-cost-of-inventing-new-drugs-is-shaping-the-future-of-medicine/#2fe419416bfc, Accessed October 20, 2016.
8. Herper, M. 2015. Innovation's Accountant. *Forbes*, November 2: 58–62.
9. Rockoff, Jonathan D. 2010. Pfizer Plans to Cut Research Spending By Up To $3B. *Wall Street Journal (Online)*. February 4. http://www.wsj.com/articles/SB10001424052748704259304575042863590302630, Accessed October 15, 2016.
10. Cohen, Jeff, Gangi, William, Lineen, Jason, and Manard, Alice. 2005. *Strategic Alternatives in the Pharmaceutical Industry*. Unpublished Research Paper from the Center for Biotechnology Management, Kellogg School of Management. Northwestern University, IL.
11. Blanckley, Alex, Boldon, Helen, Scannell, Jack W., and Warrington, Brian. 2012. Diagnosing the Decline in Pharmaceutical R&D. *Nature Reviews Drug Discovery*. March, Vol. 11: 191–200.
12. Jackie, Hunter and Stephens, Susie. 2010. Is Open Innovation the Way Forward for Big Pharma? *Nature Reviews Drug Discovery*. February, Vol 9: 87–88.
13. Gilbert, Jim, Henske, Preston and Sigh, Anshish. 2003. Rebuilding Big Pharma's Business Model. *The Business & Medicine Report*, 21(10).
14. Pfizer to reorganize business units. *New York Business Journal (Online)*. July 29, 2013. http://www.bizjournals.com/newyork/news/2013/07/29/pfizer-to-reorganize-business-units.html
15. Armstrong, Drew. Pfizer Splits Up Operations Ahead of Possible Breakup. *Bloomberg (Online)*. http://www.bloomberg.com/news/articles/2013-07-29/pfizer-to-split-internal-operations-ahead-of-possible-breakup. Accessed November 4, 2016.
16. Pfizer. 2014. *Annual Review 2014*. New York, NY: Pfizer, Inc.
17. Ibid.
18. Ibid.
19. Herper, M. 2015. Innovation's Accountant. *Forbes*, November 2: 58–62.
20. Keister, Kim. 2013. Does a Top Drugmaker's Playbook Stifle Competition? *AARP (Online)*. http://blog.aarp.org/2013/06/17/how-pfizer-protected-lipitor-profits-as-patent-expired-pay-for-delay/, Accessed October 2016.
21. Herper, M. 2015. Innovation's Accountant. *Forbes*, November 2: 58–62.
22. Pfizer. 2015. Pfizer Inc: Exploring Our History 2000–Present. Pfizer.com
23. Pfizer. 2015. Pfizer to Acquire Hospira. *News & Media. Press Releases*. New York, NY: Pfizer, Inc.
24. Pfizer. 2016. Pfizer to Acquire Anacor. *News & Media. Press Releases*. New York, NY: Pfizer, Inc.
25. Pfizer. 2016. Pfizer to Acquire Medivation. *News & Media. Press Releases*. New York, NY: Pfizer, Inc.
26. Herper, M. 2015. Innovation's Accountant. *Forbes*, November 2: 58–62.
27. U.S. Department of the Treasury. 2016. Treasury Announces Additional Action to Curb Inversions, Addresses Earnings Stripping. *Treasury.gov. Press Center. Press Releases*. April 4.
28. AstraZeneca. 2014. Statement Regarding Pfizer Withdrawal. *Media Centre. Press Releases*. London, United Kingdom: AstraZeneca plc.
29. McCoy, Kevin. 2015. Pfizer and Allergan merge in $160B tax inversion deal. *USA Today (Online)* November 23. http://www.usatoday.com/story/money/2015/11/23/pfizer-allergan-merger/76248478/, Accessed October 20, 2016.
30. U.S. Department of the Treasury. 2016. Treasury Announces Additional Action to Curb Inversions, Addresses Earnings Stripping. *Treasury.gov. Press Center. Press Releases*. April 4.
31. McCoy, Kevin. 2015. Pfizer and Allergan merge in $160B tax inversion deal. *USA Today (Online)* November 23. http://www.usatoday.com/story/money/2015/11/23/pfizer-allergan-merger/76248478/, Accessed October 20, 2016.
32. Carroll, Stuart. 2009. Goodbye blockbuster medicines; hello new pharmaceutical business models. *The Pharmaceutical Journal (Online)*. http://www.pharmaceutical-journal.com/opinion/comment/goodbye-blockbuster-medicines-hello-new-pharmaceutical-business-models/10966185.fullarticle, Accessed November 10, 2016.
33. Pfizer. 2015. Pfizer Inc: Venture Investments. Pfizer.com
34. Pfizer. 2016. Pfizer Expands R&D Equity Investment Strategy to Access Early-Stage Scientific Innovations. *News & Media. Press Releases*. New York, NY: Pfizer, Inc.
35. Pfizer. 2016. Proxy Statement for 2016 Annual Meeting of Shareholders. 2015 Finanical Report. *SEC 2016 From DEF 14A*. New York, NY: Pfizer Inc.
36. Pfizer. 2015. Pfizer Inc: Leadership and Structure. Meet Executive Leaders. Pfizer.com
37. Langley, Allison. 2003. Pfizer to Sell Drug to Rival to Soothe Regulators. *New York Times (Online)*. March 19. http://www.nytimes.com/2003/03/19/business/pfizer-to-sell-drug-to-rival-to-soothe-regulators.html, Accessed October 2016.
38. Pfizer. 2015. Pfizer Inc: Leadership and Structure. Meet Executive Leaders. Pfizer.com.
39. Ibid.
40. Pfizer Inc. 2015. *2015 Financial Report*. New York, NY: Pfizer Inc.
41. Pfizer Inc. 2015. *2015 Financial Report*. New York, NY: Pfizer Inc.
42. Pfizer Global manufacturing finds the formula for success. 2007. *Human Resources Management International Digest*, 15(1), 8–10.
43. Pfizer. 2015. Pfizer Inc: Working at Pfizer. Career Growth and Colleague Development. Pfizer.com
44. Herper, M. 2015. Innovation's Accountant. *Forbes*, November 2: 58–62.
45. Stallard, Michael. 2015. Pfizer's Straight Talk on Culture. *Helping Leaders Create Cultures that Connect (Online)*. September 16. http://www.michaelleestallard.com/pfizers-straight-talk-on-culture, Accessed Oct 10, 2016.
46. Pfizer. 2015. Pfizer Inc: About Us. Mission, Vision and Purpose. Pfizer.com
47. Pfizer Inc. 2015. *2015 Financial Report*. New York, NY: Pfizer Inc.
48. Pfizer. 2015. *Annual Review 2015*. New York, NY: Pfizer, Inc
49. Ibid.
50. Pfizer Inc. 2015. *2015 Financial Report*. New York, NY: Pfizer Inc.
51. Pfizer Inc. 2015. *2015 Financial Report*. New York, NY: Pfizer Inc.
52. Ibid.
53. Ibid.
54. Big pharma placed in malpractice spotlight. 2012. *Pharmaceutical Technology Europe*, 24(9), 8.
55. Pfizer Inc. 2015. *2015 Financial Report*. New York, NY: Pfizer Inc.
56. Ibid.
57. Ibid.
58. Ibid.
59. Merck & Co. 2015. *2015 Annual Report*. Whitestation, NJ: Merck & Co. Inc.

60. Vij, Ravi. 2016. Pharma industry Merger and Acquisition Analysis 1995 to 2015. *Revenues and Profits (Online)*. http://revenuesandprofits.com/pharma-industry-merger-and-acquisition-analysis-1995-2015/, Accessed October 20, 2016.
61. Novartis. 2015. *2015 Annual Report*. Basel, Switzerland: Novartis International AG.
62. Vij, Ravi. 2016. Pharma industry Merger and Acquisition Analysis 1995 to 2015. *Revenues and Profits (Online)*. http://revenuesandprofits.com/pharma-industry-merger-and-acquisition-analysis-1995-2015/, Accessed October 20, 2016.
63. Bristol-Myers Squibb. *2015 Annual Report*. New York, NY: Bristol-Myers Squibb Co.
64. Vij, Ravi. 2016. Pharma industry Merger and Acquisition Analysis 1995 to 2015. *Revenues and Profits (Online)*. http://revenuesandprofits.com/pharma-industry-merger-and-acquisition-analysis-1995-2015/, Accessed October 20, 2016.
65. Johnson & Johnson. *2015 Annual Report*. New Brunswick, NJ: Johnson & Johnson Inc.
66. Vij, Ravi. 2016. Pharma industry Merger and Acquisition Analysis 1995 to 2015. *Revenues and Profits (Online)*. http://revenuesandprofits.com/pharma-industry-merger-and-acquisition-analysis-1995-2015/, Accessed October 20, 2016.
67. FDA. *FDA Pharmaceutical Quality Oversight. One Quality Voice. http://www.fda.gov/downloads/AboutFDA/CentersOffices/OfficeofMedicalProductsandTobacco/CDER/UCM442666.pdf*
68. Yu, Lawrence X., and Janet Woodcock. FDA Pharmaceutical Quality Oversight. *International Journal of Pharmaceuticals*, 491(1-2): 2–7.
69. European Automation. 2014. How FDA regulations are shaping the pharmaceutical manufacturing sector. *PACE*. http://newman.richmond.edu:2048/login?url=http://search.proquest.com.newman.richmond.edu:2048/docview/1628839996?accountid=14731
70. IRS. Annual Fee on Branded prescription Drug Manufacturers and Importers. https://www.irs.gov/businesses/corporations/annual-fee-on-branded-prescription-drug-manufacturers-and-importers
71. Pfizer Inc. 2015. *2015 Financial Report*. New York, NY: Pfizer Inc.
72. PwC. 2015. *2015 Health Research Institute Annual Report*. London, United Kingdom: PricewaterhouseCoopers.
73. Hawana, Joanne and Kuyers, Sarah Beth S. 2016. Biosimilar FDA Approvals on the Horizon As More States Enact Substitution Laws. *Healthlawpolicymatters.com*. August 31. https://www.healthlawpolicymatters.com/2016/08/30/biosimilar-fda-approvals-on-the-horizon/, Accessed November 5, 2016.
74. Why the drug price scandal won't be enough to keep down prices. 2016. *Fortune (Online)*. http://fortune.com/2015/10/26/drug-prices-daraprim-turing-scandal/, Accessed November 4, 2016.
75. Tuttle, Brad. 2016. Why the EpiPen Price Scandal Sums Up Everything We Hate About Big Business & Politics. *Yahoo Finance (Online)*. September 21. http://finance.yahoo.com/news/why-epipen-price-scandal-sums-162803743.html, Accessed Nov. 4, 2016.
76. Rowan, Harriett Blair. 2016. Drug Companies spend $109 million to blaock vote to lower drug prices. *MarketWatch (Online)*. November 6. http://www.marketwatch.com/story/drug-companies-spend-109-million-to-block-vote-to-lower-drug-prices-2016-11-06, Accessed November 10, 2016.

CASE 13

Publix Supermarkets, Inc.

January 2018

Shortly after being named as CEO in 2016, the Publix Board of Directors authorized Todd Jones to move forward with opening ten new stores in the highly competitive Richmond, Virginia market.[1] The company's expansions out of its home market of Florida have paid off handsomely so far, with Publix now a close number 3 in market share in Georgia and gaining on its competition in Tennessee.[2] Stressing service and a unique store experience, Jones believed Publix would remind Richmond shoppers of the now-shuttered, service-oriented Ukrop's Super Markets and allow the company to quickly gain market share at the expense of its grocery nemeses, Walmart and Kroger. However, Richmond also marked the first time Publix would face Wegmans, a grocer with a similar background and focus on service, as well as a new European arrival, Lidl.[3] Would the expansion work?

Company Background

George Jenkins opened the first Publix supermarket in Winter Haven, Florida, on September 6, 1930, in the midst of the Great Depression.[4] The story of Publix's inception has become corporate lore, an anecdote to explain the company's devotion to its employees. As the story goes, Jenkins was a successful manager at a Piggly Wiggly in Winter Haven. However, when Piggly Wiggly's new corporate owner refused an audience with Jenkins, who had driven eight hours to see him, Jenkins left in disgust, and resolved to start a rival store upon his return to Florida.[5]

Jenkins' single small grocery store has grown dramatically in the decades since. By the end of 2016, revenue surpassed $34 billion and Publix operated 1,136 supermarkets located primarily in the southeastern United States, with this number reaching 1,161 by November of 2017 (a store breakdown appears at Exhibit 1).[6] In addition to its stores, the company maintains nine distribution centers (seven of which are in Florida) and eleven manufacturing plants (nine in Florida, two in Georgia) producing dairy goods, fresh foods, and bakery items.[7] Eighty-five percent of revenue is derived from traditional grocery sales, which includes dairy, produce, meat, and seafood, with the remaining 15% coming from health and beauty care, general merchandise, pharmacy, floral, and other products and services. Publix offers customers nationally recognized brands as well as private labels and relies on its own distribution centers for the majority of its product offerings.[8]

One of Publix's greatest strengths is its customer service—it has ranked number one among supermarkets on the American Consumer Satisfaction Index for 14 straight years.[9] The company's longstanding motto captures this focus: "Where Shopping is a Pleasure." Publix, as an employee-owned company, also boasts strong employee satisfaction, as it has been one of Fortune's 100 Best Companies to Work for in America for 19 straight years.[10] Publix is also identified as one of the most socially responsible companies in America, ranking second overall (right behind Wegman's) and second among Millennials (just behind Tesla Motors) in a recent Harris poll.[11]

Business and Strategies

Publix operates in the highly competitive retail food industry. Its 1,136 supermarkets are located in the southeast and mid-Atlantic regions of the country—Florida, Georgia, Alabama, South Carolina, North Carolina, Tennessee, and, as of 2017, Virginia.

Operational Strategy

The company's core strategies focus on customer service, product quality, shopping environment, competitive pricing, and convenient locations. Publix believes its focus on these areas has been critical to the company's success. Further, management believes continued focus in these areas is the key to differentiation, sustained market share, and financial growth in an increasingly competitive industry.[12]

Customer Service. Publix is renowned for its "relentless focus on pleasing customers."[13] Jenkins, the

Exhibit 1 Store Locations

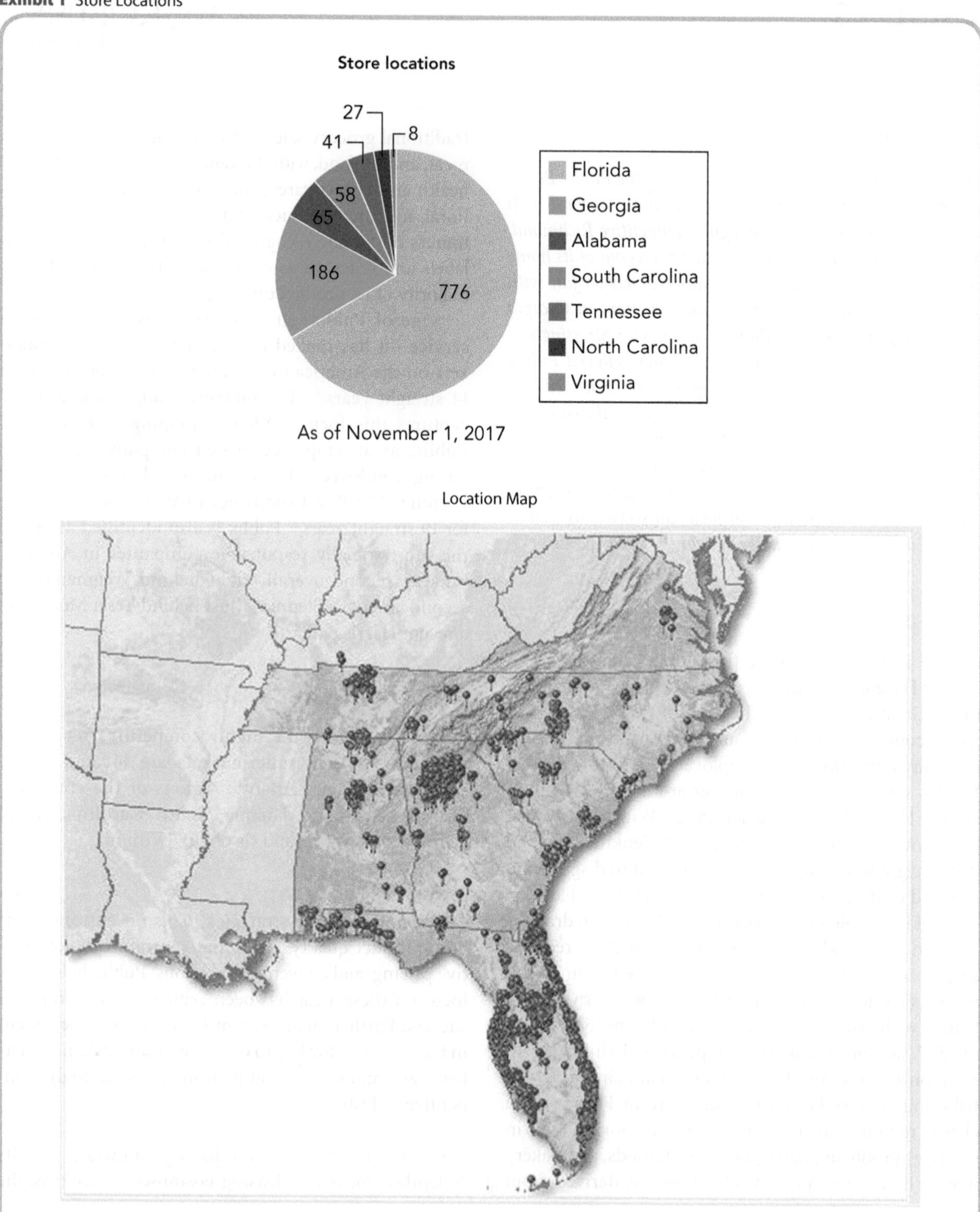

*Source: Publix Super Markets, Inc. Locations. http://store.publix.com/publix, Accessed November 22, 2017.

company's founder, called on each Publix employee to "make each customer's day a little bit better because they met you."[14] That mantra continues to shape the behavior of Publix employees even today. Employees practice Publix's 10-foot and 10-second rules, speaking to and smiling at everyone with 10 feet and greeting customers within the first 10 seconds of their arrival in a department.[15] And, instead of giving customers aisle numbers to find an item, Publix employees are trained to get the item for the customer. To ensure shoppers move quickly through checkout, Publix implemented a "two-customer-per-line goal" enforced by the company's proprietary, predictive staffing software.[16] While a visit to almost any other grocer means carrying out your own groceries, at Publix "[w]e pride ourselves on our outstanding customer service. That service includes taking your groceries to your vehicle."[17] However, the additional customer service offered by Publix leads to high operating costs relative to industry peers.[18] Contrary to industry norms, Publix doesn't have a loyalty program. The company has stated repeatedly that it eschews loyalty programs because "every customer deserves the best we have to offer."[19]

Product Quality. As part of its efforts to please its customers, Publix places considerable emphasis on product quality. Like many of its competitors, Publix offers a number of private-label products, with the company utilizing three different house brands. Its "Publix" brand is its basic offering, with "Publix Greenwise" focused on organic and natural offerings and its "Publix Premium" for higher price point products.[20]

Shopping Environment. Publix also focuses on the cleanliness and appearance of its stores, constantly refreshing stores with 156 supermarkets remodeled in 2016 alone.[21] This is a continuation of the company's recent strategy of renovating over 10% of its stores annually, with 154 remodels completed in 2015 and 138 in 2014.[22] As Publix completes these projects, it is also prioritizing convenience and sustainability. Beyond the Publix bakery and deli, renovated stores feature a pharmacy, a floral department and, appearing in at least 20 locations in 2017, a Starbucks cafe.[23] Outside of the store, Publix is reminding customers of its commitment to the environment by offering curbside recycling and charging stations for electric vehicles.[24]

Competitive Pricing. Publix freely acknowledges that it focuses on service over price.[25] However, it does not ignore price, and when compared against some of its rivals, its prices are actually lower. Publix also offers a number of savings opportunities, such as digital coupons, and is well known for its Buy One-Get One (BOGO) promotions.[26] The company is seen as substituting a combination of digital coupons and BOGO promotions for the loyalty programs used by many large rivals such as Kroger.[27]

Convenient Locations. Publix supermarkets are often located in strip shopping centers where Publix is the anchor tenant. On occasion, Publix will enter into joint ventures with real estate developers in the development of these shopping centers. Publix owns the land and real estate at 274 of its 1,136 locations. The company owns the building while leasing the land at 57 locations. The remaining supermarkets are leased, with renewals scheduled within 20 years. Publix supermarkets range in size from 28,000 to 61,000 square feet, allowing the company to operate in more locations than some of its competitors.[28]

Growth Strategy. Organic growth is rare in the grocery industry. Oftentimes organic growth does not result in success due to already saturated markets with established local brands as well as a void in accessible, quality real estate.[29] Nonetheless, Publix enjoyed considerable success through a deliberate strategy of organic growth, first in its home Florida market and then northward through the Southeast. The company is now expanding into its seventh state, Virginia, in 2017.

Innovation Strategy. Although some observers critique Publix for focusing too much on continued expansion of its brick and mortar footprint, Publix is not ignoring the trends in online grocery purchasing and grocery delivery.[30] Even though an earlier attempt at grocery delivery (Publix Direct) failed in 2003, in 2016 Publix began testing a grocery delivery service through Instacart. Today, Publix offers grocery delivery through Instacart in as little as two hours to customers who live in areas surrounding more than half its stores. By 2020, the company plans to offer Instacart services from all of its stores.[31] Beyond helping time-starved customers with grocery delivery, Publix is expanding its Online Easy Ordering (OEO) service. Now, over 200 bakery and deli items such as custom cakes can be ordered through the Publix website and picked up at a local store.[32]

Publix has also made significant investments in the meal-kit and meal takeaway space. Its "Aprons" product line includes recipes with shopping information tailored to the store, cooking classes offered in the store in several locations, and now pre-made meal kits available in several Publix locations in Florida.[33] Unlike some competitive offerings, Publix tailors its meal kit offerings to different levels of cooking experience, with simple reheat options for more complicated preparations.[34]

Inside Publix

Key Executives

CEO, Randall Todd Jones, Sr. Todd Jones was named CEO when Ed Crenshaw stepped down after 8 years leading Publix. Jones has worked at Publix for 36 years, starting his career as a store clerk. He worked in a number of positions within the company on his way to the CEO role, most recently serving as President of Publix since 2008.[35] Although Jones is the first non-family member to lead Publix, he is seen as extremely knowledgeable and is well-respected within the company.[36]

Chairman, William E. Crenshaw. Ed Crenshaw is the grandson of Publix's founder, George Jenkins. Crenshaw has worked for Publix for 42 years and served as the CEO from 2008 to 2016. Upon stepping down as CEO, Crenshaw transitioned to the Chairman for the Publix board of directors.[37] Like Jones, Crenshaw's career with the company began as a clerk, and he worked his way through the company en route to the corner office. Crenshaw spent a portion of his executive career with the company outside of Florida, leading Publix's entrance into the Georgia market during the 1990s.[38]

Executive Vice President and Chief Financial Officer, David R. Phillips. Similarly to Jones and Crenshaw, David Phillips is a career Publix employee, starting as an internal auditor with the company in 1984. Phillips has held a number of financial roles within Publix, including controller and treasurer, before being promoted to CFO in 1999. With the elevation of Todd Jones to CEO, the Publix board gave additional responsibilities to Phillips and promoted him to executive vice president.[39]

Senior Vice President, Alison M. Smith. Alison Smith joined Publix in 1995 in a part-time role, before rising through the senior human resources ranks with stints as director of employment and staffing beginning in 1999 and director of organizational development in 2004. She has a PhD in industrial/organizational psychology, and was recently promoted by Jones to provide strategic oversight of human resources, customer care & social media, and media & community relations.[40]

Vice President, Omnichannel and Application Development, Erik Katenkamp. Erik Katenkamp joined Publix in 1995 from the aerospace industry. With a background in industrial engineering, Katenkamp has served in a number of IT-related roles at Publix, including IT business manager, director of application delivery, and vice president of information systems.[41] Katenkamp's position was newly created by the company in August of 2017, as Publix took steps toward strengthening its digital offerings and more thoroughly integrating them within its shopping experience.[42] Omnichannel is a multichannel approach to retailing that helps a consumer experience a seamless shopping experience, whether shopping online or from a traditional store.

Vice President of Real Estate Assets, William Rayburn. Woody Rayburn started with Publix in 1993 as a business analyst. He transitioned to an asset manager role in 2000, becoming director of real estate assets in 2003. In 2017, Jones elevated Rayburn to a vice president position,[43] reflecting both confidence in Rayburn and the fact that the company's real estate activities have grown tremendously, with the total amount of real property owned by the company having tripled over the last decade.[44]

Employee Owned

With over 180,000 employees, Publix is the nation's largest employee-owned company.[45] Company stock is made available only to current employees and the company's Board of Directors. The employee stock ownership plan (ESOP) contains provisions prohibiting any transfer for value without the owner first offering the common stock to the company. Market price of the company's common stock is determined by its Board of Directors, who derive the value based on competitor's financials and how they relate to Publix, as well as comparing competitors' common stock price.

As of February 2017, there were 179,000 unique holders of record of Publix common stock.[46] Over time, the ESOP has proven astoundingly successful, with over a fifteen percent average annual return since its inception in 1974.[47] In addition to a great benefit for employees, research states that employee ownership can boost corporate profits by as much as 4%.[48] Some observers have noted that Publix's ESOP ownership structure, and its people-first management style, may be its greatest strength.[49]

Beyond its positive effects on employee engagement and retention, the ESOP structure has also served as an effective deterrent to employees unionizing and potentially threatening the Publix mission. The company's feelings on unions are overtly addressed in its employee handbook—"owners don't need unions."[50]

Human Resources

One of Publix's top corporate strategic priorities is investing in its employees, or associates, as they are referred to within the organization. In addition to being an ESOP where employees have the exclusive option to invest in the company they work for, each Publix associate is surveyed annually for feedback on leadership, business tools, compensation packages, and policies.[51] Associates are encouraged to take advantage of educational programs to help achieve the company's business objectives as well as enhance one's skills and knowledge. Dedication, commonly referred to in the company as "bleeding green," is also rewarded with compensation increases as well as options for growth within the organization. All staffers who have put in 1,000 work hours per year receive an additional 8.5% of their total pay in the form of Publix stock.

Publix promotes from within and each store displays an advancement chart that highlights how each associate can become a manager. Associates are encouraged to rotate to various business segments within the organization, including but not limited to real estate, grocery, and distribution. [52] With the focus Publix places on its associates, it has received national attention regularly as a top performer in many metrics, the most recent of which are shown in Exhibit 2. Perhaps the most telling of all, Publix's annual employee turnover rate is 5%. Its industry peers can experience turnover as high as 65%.[53]

Exhibit 2 2016 Awards and Recognitions

- Fortune's 100 Best Workplaces for Millennials
- Fortune and the Great Place to Work Institute's 15 Best Workplaces in Retail
- Fortune's Most Important Private Companies
- Fortune's 100 Best Companies to Work For in America for 19 consecutive years
- Fortune's Most Admired Companies for 23 consecutive years
- J.D. Power & Associates — highest-ranking pharmacy in overall satisfaction in the supermarket segment eight of the last 10 years
- Glassdoor's Candidates' Choice Awards: 50 Best Places to Interview

*Source: Publix Super Markets, Inc. Company Overview: Awards and Achievements. http://corporate.publix.com/about-publix/company-overview/awards-achievements, Accessed November 22, 2017.

Organizational Culture

Publix has embraced a stakeholder theory approach to management. Its corporate structure elevates its "associates" (employees) to the position of owner and shareholder. Its mission statement and business strategies put the customer front and center. The company's charitable arm, Publix Charities, gives back to local communities. And, its sustainability efforts like annual greenhouse gas inventories, smart irrigation systems, curbside recycling, and charging stations for electric vehicles are becoming commonplace at Publix locations.[54]

With all things—operations, working conditions, productivity, products, service, etc.—Publix applies a Continuous Quality Improvement (CQI) philosophy. The methodologies used to accomplish CQI goals are: Work Improvement Now (WIN), which creates an expectation for employees to immediately improve their own processes; and Quality Improvement Process (QIP), which sets the same expectation but at the department and company level.[55]

The Publix culture doesn't just encourage feedback and continuous improvement. Each employee is said to have a responsibility, as an owner of the company, to improve the way stores are run each day. An open-door policy and an annual staff survey (Associate Voice Survey) are just two of the strategies employed by Publix to facilitate feedback and continuous improvement.[56]

Mission, Purpose, and Values

The Publix mission, "to be the premier quality food retailer in the world," is supported by the company's commitment to be:

- Passionately focused on customer value;
- Intolerant of waste;
- Dedicated to the dignity, value, and employment security of associates;
- Devoted to the highest standards of stewardship for stockholders; and
- Involved as responsible citizens in (its) communities.[57]

Operations & Supply Chain

At the end of 2016, Publix operated 53.4 million square feet of supermarket space in its 1,136 supermarkets.[58] Approximately 74% of the total cost of products purchased at Publix are supplied and delivered by its nine owned and operated distribution centers and 11 manufacturing plants.[59] Due to this infrastructure, Publix is not dependent on a single supplier. However, with seven of its nine distribution centers located in Florida, it is currently stretching the range of its supply chain operations.

Any further geographic expansion would require additional distribution centers or a revisit of the company's operations and supply chain strategy.[60]

Marketing

Publix employs its own marketing team of around 100 associates representing 50 different positions.[61] When Publix enters a new state, its message does not represent anything groundbreaking, but simply attempts to relay its culture to its new market. In 2015, when Publix expanded into North Carolina, a spokesperson stated, "[o]ur message remains consistent in connecting on an emotional level with our customer and our potential customers, but sharing our culture becomes more important. In newer markets, we highlight our Publix Guarantee more and promote that we don't have a loyalty program—that every customer deserves the best we have to offer."[62] The Publix Guarantee states "We will never knowingly disappoint you." The marketing team at Publix focuses on geographical areas of operation where Publix is expanding its television, radio, and social media advertising. As of November 2017, Publix's Facebook site had nearly 2.8 million followers.[63]

Financial Condition

Over the past five years, Publix's revenue has grown from $27.7 billion in 2012 to $34.3 billion in 2016, representing a compound annual growth rate of 4.35%. Over the same time period, net income has increase from $1.55 billion to $2.03 billion, representing a compound annual growth rate of 5.48%. Thus, not only are sales increasing, due to in-store year-over-year growth as well as store count increases, but net income is increasing at a faster rate. COGS, gross margin, and SG&A as a percent of sales have remained fairly constant in the last three years. Publix issued 4 quarterly dividend payments in 2016 totaling $0.8675 per share. Publix has always carried extremely low amounts of debt with its debt-to-equity ratio as low as 30% in 2016.[64] Liquidity is not a concern to Publix with an improving year-over-year current ratio landing at 1.56 in 2016. Publix's income statement and balance sheet for the past five years can be found in Exhibits 3 and 4.

Exhibit 3 Publix Super Markets, Inc. Income Statement

Income Statement USD ($) in Millions					
	2012	**2013**	**2014**	**2015**	**2016**
Revenue	$27,707	$29,148	$30,802	$32,619	$34,274
Cost of revenue	19,911	20,937	22,233	23,460	24,734
Gross profit	7,796	8,210	8,570	9,159	9,540
Operating expenses					
Sales, General, and administrative	5,631	5,890	6,169	6,481	6,788
Other operating expenses					
Total operating expenses	5,631	5,890	6,169	6,481	6,788
Operating income	2,165	2,320	2,401	2,678	2,752
Other income (expense)	137	146	169	191	189
Income before income taxes	2,303	2,466	2,570	2,869	2,940
Provision for income taxes	750	812	835	904	915
Net income	**$1,552**	**$1,654**	**$1,735**	**$1,965**	**$2,026**
Earnings per share					
Basic	1.98	2.12	2.23	2.54	2.63
Diluted	1.98	2.12	2.23	2.54	2.63
Weighted average shares outstanding					
Basic	783	780	779	774	769
Diluted	783	780	779	774	769
EBITDA	**$2,796**	**$2,821**	**$2,914**	**$3,260**	**$3,376**

Source: Company Annual Reports; Morningstar.

Exhibit 4 Publix Super Markets, Inc. Balance Sheet

Consolidated Balance Sheet USD ($) in Millions	2012	2013	2014	2015	2016
Assets					
Current Assets					
Cash and cash equivalents	$337	$302	$407	$352	$438
Short-term investments	797	830	999	1,377	1,592
Total cash	1,135	1,131	1,407	1,729	2,030
Receivables	519	540	549	724	715
Inventories	1,409	1,507	1,598	1,741	1,722
Deferred income taxes	58	56	71	51	77
Prepaid expenses		26	109	70	50
Other current assets	28				
Total current assets	3,149	3,260	3,734	4,314	4,596
Non-current Assets					
Land	689	716	936	1,158	1,416
Fixtures and equipment	4,588	3,759	4,102	4,303	4,582
Other properties	3,703	3,944	4,629	5,252	5,984
Property and equipment, at cost	8,979	8,419	9,667	10,712	11,982
Accumulated Depreciation	4,289	3,614	3,944	4,325	4,695
Property, plant and equipment, net	4,691	4,805	5,723	6,387	7,287
Equity and other investments	4,236	5,162	5,232	5,226	5,147
Other long-term assets	203	320	395	431	434
Total non-current assets	9,129	10,286	11,350	12,045	12,868
Total Assets	**$12,278**	**$13,547**	**$15,083**	**$16,359**	**$17,464**
Liabilities					
Current liabilities					
Short-term debt	5	38	25	57	114
Accounts payable	1,307	1,383	1,538	1,676	1,610
Deferred income taxes					
Taxes payable		20	13	10	13
Accrued liabilities	909	938	1,122	1,161	1,207
Other current liabilities					
Total current liabilities	2,221	2,379	2,698	2,903	2,944
Non-current liabilities					
Long-term debt	153	125	193	180	137
Deferred taxes liabilities	327	357	389	425	474
Accrued liabilities					
Pensions and other benefits	117	103	107	102	103
Minority interest	47	51	42	37	24
Other long-term liabilities	331	316	353	319	310
Total non-current liabilities	975	951	1,083	1,062	1,047
Total liabilities	3,196	3,329	3,781	3,965	3,991

continued

Exhibit 4 (cont.) Publix Super Markets, Inc. Balance Sheet

Consolidated Balance Sheet USD ($) in Millions	2012	2013	2014	2015	2016
Stockholders' equity					
Common stock	776	777	774	770	763
Other Equity	(2,273)				
Additional paid-in capital	1,627	1,899	2,201	2,556	2,850
Retained earnings	6,641	7,454	8,218	9,041	9,837
Accumulated other comprehensive income	2,311	87	109	26	23
Total stockholders' equity	9,082	10,217	11,303	12,394	13,473
Total liabilities and stockholders' equity	**$12,278**	**$13,547**	**$15,083**	**$16,359**	**$17,464**

Source: Company Annual Reports; Morningstar.

Publix financial performance compares favorably with its peers. Publix prices its products slightly higher than Kroger, but lower than Whole Foods, indicated by the COGS and Gross Margin percent of sales metrics. Impressively, Publix's net income is approximately equal to that of Kroger even though its revenue is only 31% of its larger rival. The company's operating margin is the envy of its peer group, with it exceeding that of Kroger by almost 2.5 times, and nearly doubling that of Walmart. Key comparison data appears in Exhibit 5.

The Industry

Publix operates as a traditional grocery store, garnering the third-largest market share of any grocer (excluding Walmart) in the United States.[65] Historically, the industry contained a number of smaller companies, but recent years have seen consolidation and bankruptcies in the face of increasing competitive pressure.[66] Since the economy rebounded consumers with higher disposable income moved back to purchasing premium, organic and all natural food brands, which helped to drive up overall industry revenue.[67] As one observer noted, the "grocery business isn't what it used to be" as a convergence of market forces bear down on traditional grocers like Publix.[68] An increasing number of competitors now chase the grocery dollar, and changes in how consumers shop and consume food loom large over the company.

Major Competitors in the Richmond Market

Kroger. Founded in 1883, Kroger is the largest grocery store chain in the United States[69] and the third-largest retailer in the world.[70] Kroger operates behind its namesake brand as well as over 20 regional brands in 35 states. Kroger generated over $115 billion in revenue in 2016, as it came off of its first full year of owning Harris Teeter, a regional brand operating in the Carolinas.[71] Historically a strong financial performer, Kroger has disappointed recently, with its stock down over 40% for 2017.[72] While it has curtailed its expenditures on new stores,[73] Kroger is investing aggressively in technological improvements, with the company operating its own data analytics unit and spending heavily on tools such as an infrared system allowing it to monitor checkout wait times and deploy additional clerks automatically in response.[74] Kroger also recently launched its "ClickList" service in a number of markets, where a customer can order groceries online and pick them up, curbside, at the store.[75]

Kroger is also the market leader in leveraging loyalty card data—over 97% of purchases are made by shoppers holding a loyalty card.[76] Kroger uses this data to construct target offers, often by mailing coupons to specific customers. The company reports achieving redemption rates of up to 65% with some of these offers, compared to an industry average of roughly 5%.[77] In addition to customer loyalty, Kroger also packs its newer stores with additional services, such as banking, a florist, or a Starbucks counter, which research data indicates helps the company fend off new market entrants and may decrease overall sales losses by up to 8%.[78]

Food Lion. Based in Salisbury, North Carolina, Food Lion operates over 1,000 grocery stores in 10 Southeastern and Mid-Atlantic states. They have over 63,000 employees and serve about 10 million customers per week.

Exhibit 5 Key Ratio Comparisons

	Publix			Walmart			Kroger			Whole Foods		
	2014	2015	2016	2015	2016	2017	2015	2016	2017	2015	2016	2017
Financials (USD) ($ in millions)												
Revenue	$30,802	$32,619	$34,274	$485,651	$482,130	$485,873	$108,465	$109,830	$115,337	$15,389	$15,724	$16,030
Gross Margin %	27.8	28.1	27.8	24.8	25.1	25.6	21.2	22.2	22.4	35.2	34.4	33.7
Operating Income	2,401	2,678	2,752	27,147	24,105	22,764	3,137	3,576	3,436	861	857	459
Operating Margin %	7.8	8.2	8	5.6	5	4.7	2.9	3.3	3	5.6	5.5	2.9
Net Income	1,735	1,965	2,026	16,363	14,694	13,643	1,728	2,039	1,975	536	507	245
Margins % of Sales												
COGS	72.18	71.92	72.17	75.17	74.87	74.35	78.84	77.84	77.60	64.81	65.59	66.33
Gross Margin	27.82	28.08	27.83	24.83	25.13	25.65	21.16	22.16	22.40	35.19	34.41	33.67
SG&A	20.03	19.87	19.81	19.24	20.13	20.96	16.47	17.00	17.39	29.60	28.96	29.83
Operating Margin	7.79	8.21	8.03	5.59	5.00	4.69	2.89	3.26	2.98	5.59	5.45	2.86
Net Int Inc & Other	0.55	0.59	0.55	(0.48)	(0.51)	(0.47)	(0.45)	(0.44)	(0.45)	0.11	(0.19)	(0.26)
EBT Margin	8.34	8.80	8.58	5.11	4.49	4.22	2.44	2.82	2.53	5.71	5.26	2.60
Profitability Ratios												
Return on Assets %	12.12	12.5	11.98	8.01	7.29	6.85	5.78	6.33	5.57	9.33	8.39	3.76
Financial Leverage (Average)	1.33	1.32	1.3	2.5	2.48	2.56	5.64	4.97	5.45	1.52	1.97	1.95
Return on Equity %	16.13	16.58	15.66	20.76	18.15	17.23	32.01	33.34	28.98	14.14	14.5	7.36
Return on Invested Capital %	15.85	16.27	15.37	14.14	13.08	12.51	12.14	13.11	11.64	13.91	13.52	6.69
Interest Coverage				11.08	9.49	9.66	6.43	7.42	6.58		21.17	9.51
Revenue %												
Year over Year	5.68	5.90	5.07	1.96	(0.73)	0.78	10.26	1.26	5.01	8.42	2.18	1.95
3-Year Average	4.26	5.59	5.55	2.81	0.91	0.67	6.27	4.32	5.45	9.57	6.77	4.14
5-Year Average	4.67	5.19	4.75	3.54	2.71	1.68	7.17	5.97	5.00	11.31	9.24	6.50
Net Income %												
Year over Year	4.92	13.24	3.09	2.13	(10.20)	(7.15)	13.76	18.00	(3.14)	(7.43)	(5.41)	(51.68)
3-Year Average	5.17	8.18	6.99	1.39	(4.74)	(5.22)	42.12	10.85	9.14	4.81	(2.74)	(24.92)
5-Year Average	8.36	7.99	6.31	2.68	(2.16)	(2.77)	89.88	12.81	26.82	16.87	8.15	(12.05)
Efficiency Ratios												
Payables Period	23.98	25	24.24	37.9	38.88	40.37	21.2	23.01	23.54	10.44	10.65	11.64
Receivables Turnover	56.54	51.24	47.64	72.19	77.75	84.8	91.07	73.22	68.19	73.99	68.37	66.24
Inventory Turnover	14.32	14.06	14.29	8.11	8.06	8.26	15.08	14.42	14.06	21.2	20.28	21.52

The company has been operating since 1957, and its name was originally Food Town. In 1974 Food Lion was acquired by the Belgium-based Delhaize Group, which subsequently merged with Koninklijke Ahold, based in the Netherlands. Food Lion now operates as a part of Ahold Delhaize, which operates in 11 countries through 6,556 stores.

Food Lion's slogan is "Count on me" and they offer a double money back guarantee if their food is not fresh. Like Kroger, they have a loyalty card program. They have about 28,000 products in each store, including approximately 7,000 store brands.[79] Food Lion bases its marketing messages on low price and high quality, but in reality their prices are not particularly low nor is their quality higher than other stores. Their service quality is not higher than average either, and many of their stores are outdated. Basically, there is very little that differentiates Food Lion from other supermarkets in the areas where it operates, although there is a certain segment of customers that are loyal to the company based on family tradition—that is, they grew up with their families shopping at Food Lion.

Walmart. No retailer can ignore Walmart. In 2016, Walmart generated over $486 billion in revenue,[80] making it the largest retailer in the world.[81] Walmart operates over 4,600 stores across the United States,[82] and its low-price model is in stark contrast to Publix.[83] Although historically Publix has made a 40% higher profit on groceries than Walmart,[84] in all but its home market of Florida, Walmart continues to command a higher market share of grocery shoppers.[85] Walmart leverages its enormous scale to exert pricing power over its suppliers, passing the resulting savings onto consumers.[86]

While Walmart may have been the original disrupter to the grocery marketplace, Walmart executives acknowledge that "[t]here's never been a more disruptive time in the history of retail."[87] Like Kroger, Walmart is not standing still; it has pursued a number of acquisitions in the online space (including acquiring the online marketplace jet.com) to bolster its digital presence.[88] Walmart also recently entered into a partnership with Google, where visitors to Google's online shopping portal can make purchases from Walmart.[89] As with Kroger's ClickList, Walmart shoppers can now make grocery purchases online and pick them up at hundreds of its locations.[90] Leveraging its large store footprint, and infamous logistics prowess, Walmart now offers "pickup discounts" to online shoppers who are willing to pick up items at a nearby Walmart store.[91] To further its growth in urban areas, Walmart also continues to invest in its Neighborhood Market stores, which are much smaller than its traditional Supercenter format, with the company having now opened over 735 locations around the country.[92] To date, however, Publix has successfully survived "the Goliath-like Walmart assault" on its home market in Florida.[93]

Aldi/Lidl. Aldi began shortly after World War II in Germany, near the city of Essen. Offering just 250 basic grocery items, the company swiftly established itself as a leader in the German grocery market.[94] Today, where Walmart may carry 120,000 different items in one of its Supercenters, Aldi stocks between 1,300 and 1,600.[95] This dramatically reduces complexity, and costs, allowing Aldi to undercut Walmart by 17% on a basket of 30 typical household items.[96] Aldi has operated in the United States since the 1970s, quietly building up a network of 1,600 stores in 35 states, but recently announced it would build another 900 stores over the next five years.[97] This follows its decision to invest over $1.6 billion in renovating its existing stores.[98]

Lidl, founded several decades later in 1973, also pursues a similarly ruthlessly efficient approach to the grocery business as its German compatriot.[99] When it entered the U.K. market in 1994, Lidl upended its grocery sector.[100] Today, Lidl commands 5.2% of the British market (and growing).[101] Lidl opened its first U.S. stores in Virginia, North Carolina, and South Carolina, and promises its prices in the United States will be up to 50% lower than its competitors (excluding Aldi).[102]

Although cutthroat competitors in their home market of Germany and in the U.K., Aldi and Lidl have at least one thing in common—they ignore the Internet "almost entirely."[103] Both see online sales as self-cannibalizing, moving from a proven, high-profit channel (physical stores) to an unproven, less-profitable channel (online). U.K. observers estimate that its traditional grocers (such as Tesco and Sainsbury's) make less than a fifth of their already-slim typical margin on online sales.[104] Indeed, Morgan Stanley estimates that for a traditional retailer, every percentage-point increase in its e-commerce sales equates to a half a point contraction in the retailer's margins.[105]

The companies also share a fervor for private-label goods, shunning well-known brands in favor of their own products. The typical Aldi or Lidl store contains up to 90% private-label goods.[106] By limiting stocks of name brand items, the German rivals can extract even greater supplier concessions than the notoriously aggressive Walmart.[107] Nevertheless, they put significant efforts into quality. Aldi in particular has been successful in positioning itself as offering high-quality, value-priced private-label products.[108]

Whole Foods. If Aldi and Lidl form one bracket of the brick and mortar grocery market, Whole Foods forms the other. Derisively referred to as "Whole Paycheck" for its pricing structure,[109] Whole Foods nonetheless grew rapidly from its founding in Texas in 1980.[110] It built a strong following as a purveyor of natural and organic foods, developing a cachet among affluent urbanites willing to pay for these offerings and a unique shopping experience.[111] Whole Foods stores contain well-trained staff and offer a number of services, including prepared meals, wine bars, and other similar amenities. However, like the low-price German chains, Whole Foods developed a robust private label brand (365 Everyday Value) which consumers identified as offering high quality.[112]

Nonetheless, recently Whole Foods found itself under pressure from Walmart, Kroger, and others such as Publix. Kroger in particular began aggressively expanding its organic offerings, with the large chain selling more organic and natural products ($16 billion)[113] than Whole Foods total sales in 2016.[114] With Whole Foods weakened, in a move seen as upending the U.S. grocery market, Amazon stepped in and acquired the chain in 2017.[115] Amazon immediately moved to lower prices on a number of Whole Foods items, and made available through its powerful website Whole Foods' 365 Everyday Value products.[116] Whole Foods locations provide Amazon an existing supply chain and over 450 brick and mortar locations where it can sell Amazon products as well as provide for pickup of online grocery orders.[117] Amazon gives Whole Foods the strength of a $140 billion/year retailer with a CEO in pursuit of fully integrating Amazon into the lives of its customers.[118]

Wegman's. Any discussion of Publix almost inevitably involves a comparison to Wegman's, the Northeastern powerhouse based near Rochester, New York. Like Publix, Wegman's is a member of Fortune's Great Places to Work Legends, having been named to the list for 20 years in a row.[119] It is privately held, focused on service and pays its employees far above the industry standard for grocers.[120] And the two are alike in another key aspect—they are both on the march, expanding their geographic reach and colliding in the Virginia market.[121] Unlike Publix, however, Wegman's relies upon a much smaller number of stores, with its typical store size of 120,000 square feet nearly doubling that of the largest Publix.[122] Only opening 3–4 new stores per year,[123] Wegman's average per-store sales of almost $90 million is three times the average per-store sales of Publix.[124]

External Environment/Trends

Too Many Stores? In addition to a number of strong competitors in the marketplace, broader market trends are buffeting the grocery market. Less than half of grocery shoppers now do their food shopping at one primary supermarket.[125] In 2016, convenience stores sold $73 billion of prepared foods, beverages and other food services, up 72% from 2010.[126] Two-thirds of sales at dollar stores (Dollar General, Family Dollar, and others) are food, beverages, and other consumables.[127] Grocery shoppers are also visiting alternatives like farmer's markets, and buying fewer items per trip.[128] Given this selection of alternative brick and mortar locations for grocery purchases, little surprise that Barclays now says that 38 of the top 50 grocery markets in the United States are too saturated by food retail on a per capita basis.[129] With numerous large competitors, Richmond may be one of these over-saturated markets.

To Cook or Not to Cook? Unfortunately for traditional grocers, many consumers today do not cook at home. Millennials, the largest consumer demographic group, spend 42% of their monthly food budget on food prepared outside the home.[130] Grocery spending by Millennials is $1,000 less per year (adjusted for inflation) than their parents spent in 1990.[131] Older consumers, who no longer have a need to prepare a large family meal, are following Millennials in seeking out prepared foods.[132] Online prepared meal kits, available from companies such as Blue Apron and Plated, have been enjoying robust growth, with some 24% of Millennials having subscribed to a meal kit service at some point and growth estimated at over 25% per year over the next five years.[133] Albertsons, the large privately held grocery chain based in Idaho, recently announced a deal to purchase Plated, and Amazon has launched its own kit service and plans to make available Whole Foods-branded kits as part of its acquisition of the organic grocer.[134]

Omnichannel/Online. Online grocery sales have grown 10.1% over the last five years and are expected to grow at a rate of 6.7% over the next five, with total sales predicted to reach $13.5 billion in 2017.[135]

Amazon's move to acquire Whole Foods is not the only digital impact on traditional grocers. While the potential for Amazon to disrupt the market is seen as high (almost anyone that sells groceries saw its stock fall on the date Amazon announced the deal, with Kroger leading the path downward at a 9.2% clip),[136] potentially just as disruptive is the integration of online ordering and mobile apps into grocery shopping. Kroger's in-house analytics team is building a mobile application that will populate a shopping list, together with locations in the store, from a user's recipe.[137] Both Walmart (through its Sam's Club division) and Kroger are piloting mobile applications that allow shoppers to scan items as they move through the store, paying through the app as they exit.[138] And, as noted above, both are growing the number of locations that provide curbside pickup of online orders, a potentially savvy move as market research suggests that 76% of online shoppers have an interest in picking up grocery items bought online.[139]

In addition to online sales picked up at traditional stores, a number of online platforms and delivery services exist. Peapod, owned by the Dutch grocery giant Ahold Delhaize, counts 350,000 customers in 23 major metropolitan markets.[140] Instacart, an online grocery delivery service, has recently agreed to partnerships with Kroger, Costco, and several smaller regional chains.[141] Shipt, another last-mile online provider, announced plans to be in over 100 markets by the end of the year, concentrating in the south and Midwest, delivering for companies such as Costco and Meijer.[142]

U.S. Economy. By December 2017, the economy had rebounded from the Great Recession and the stock markets were hitting all-time highs weekly. Real per capita disposable personal income (measured in constant 2009 dollars) had increased from $36,235 in January 2013 to $39,368 in May of 2017.[143] The United States was experiencing sustained economic growth it had not seen in years and the country's gross domestic product had increased by an average of 2.1% over the past eight years, marking the third-longest economic expansion in U.S. history.[144] While many economists and financial analysts were optimistic about the direction of the economy, an increasing number were becoming concerned that such continued growth was unsustainable. More and more analysts were beginning to question economic fundamentals, and with stocks trading at a multiple of earnings only previously seen in 1929 and 2000, some feel a market correction is looming.[145]

Healthiness/Better-For-You. The success of Whole Foods, and the growing importance of organics and natural goods to other grocery chains highlight shifting consumer preference toward grocery items seen as more healthful (Kroger reports that 14% of its total sales in 2016 were for its "Simple Truth" line of organic and natural products).[146] Health-oriented markets like Whole Foods, Trader Joe's, Earth Fare and Sprouts Farmers Market have made inroads into the Florida grocery market, largely at the expense of Publix.[147] Survey data suggests customers continue to demand a greater variety of all-natural and organic products, with 82% of households purchasing organic products in 2016.[148] Organic products expanded 8.4% in 2016 alone.[149] Perhaps more importantly, with consumers willing to pay a premium for such products, they have (at least prior to Amazon's recent price cuts at Whole Foods) delivered consistently higher margins for retailers.[150]

Looking Forward

Publix continues to enjoy growth in sales, a healthy gross margin and strong financial returns. The company is confident that its steady northward geographic expansion will continue supporting long-term growth for Publix. However, the highly competitive situation the company now faces in Richmond Virginia may be indicative of things to come. Wegmans, Lidl and Aldi very recently entered this market, and Kroger, Walmart, Food Lion and Whole Foods already have a significant presence. The continued expansion of Aldi and Lidl will put considerable price pressure on everyone in the Southeastern grocery market. So the over-saturation Publix is facing in Richmond is, in a sense, a good test case for what the company is likely to experience from now on in many or most of its markets.

Faced with these sorts of challenges, can the company's labor-intensive, service-first, real estate heavy model continue to support growth in the future? Will customers migrate towards costs savings wherever they may be found, whether at a brick-and-mortar competitor or online? Will Publix's partnership strategy with Instacart allow it to meet the online challenge? Does the company need to increase investment in its Aprons meal kit and prepared foods or should it focus more on expanding higher margin private label products and organic offerings? Should Publix abandon its long-standing aversion to a loyalty program? Basically, how can Publix position itself for continued growth when faced with this challenging business environment?

NOTES

1. Griffin, J. 2016. Publix to Grow with Purchase of 10 Virginia Stores. *Tampa Bay Times*, July 15: Local 4.
2. Griffin, J. 2016. Publix Takes on New Turf. *Tampa Bay Times*, February 14: Business 1.
3. Trigaux, R. 2016. Publix Faces Tough Foe in Wegman's. *Tampa Bay Times*, July 19: Local 4.
4. Publix Super Markets, Inc. 2017. Publix Corporate History. http://corporate.publix.com/about-publix/culture/history, Accessed November 19, 2017.
5. Watters, Pat. 1980. *Fifty Years of Pleasure: The Illustrated History of Publix Super Markets, Inc.* Lakeland, Florida: Publix Super Markets, Inc.
6. Publix Super Markets, Inc. 2017. Publix Facts & Figures. http://corporate.publix.com/about-publix/company-overview/facts-figures, Accessed November 19, 2017.
7. *Ibid.*
8. Publix Super Markets, Inc., 2017. *Form 10-K.* Lakeland, Florida: Publix Super Markets, Inc.: 1.
9. *The Economist*. 2007. Business: The opposite of Walmart; Publix. 383(8527): 71.
10. Publix Super Markets, Inc. 2017. Publix Awards & Achievements. http://corporate.publix.com/about-publix/company-overview/awards-achievements, Accessed November 19, 2017.
11. Harris Poll, 2017. Wegmans, Publix Super Markets, Amazon, Tesla And USAA Draw Top Social Responsibility Scores In Harris Poll. http://www.theharrispoll.com/business/Top-Social-Responsibility-Scores.html, Accessed November 22, 2017.
12. Publix Super Markets, Inc., 2017. *Form 10-K.* Lakeland, Florida: Publix Super Markets, Inc.: 2–3.
13. Tkaczyk, C. 2016. My Five Days of 'Bleeding Green.' *Fortune*, March 15, Vol. 173: 4, 167.
14. *Ibid.*
15. Publix Super Markets, Inc. 2017. *Your Associate Handbook.* Lakeland, Florida: Publix Super Markets, Inc.: 1–3.
16. Solomon, B. 2013. The Walmart Slayer: How Publix's People-First Culture Is Winning The Grocer War. *Fortune*, August 12: 1.
17. Publix Super Markets, Inc., 2017. Customer Service FAQ:What is your policy on carryout service. http://www.publix.com/faq/customer-service, Accessed November 23, 2017.
18. Publix Super Markets, Inc., 2017. *Form 10-K.* Lakeland, Florida: Publix Super Markets, Inc.: 2–3.
19. Springer, J. 2015. The Power of Pleasure at Publix. *Supermarket News*. January 5.
20. Publix Super Markets, Inc., 2017. Publix Brands. http://www.publix.com/savings/publix-brands, Accessed November 23, 2017.
21. Publix Super Markets, Inc., 2017. *2016 Annual Report*. Lakeland, Florida: Publix Super Markets, Inc.: 2.
22. Publix Super Markets, Inc., 2016. *Form 10-K.* Lakeland, Florida: Publix Super Markets, Inc.: 11.
23. Publix Super Markets, Inc., 2017. *2016 Annual Report*. Lakeland, Florida: Publix Super Markets, Inc.: 3.
24. Publix Super Markets, Inc., 2017. Sustainability. http://sustainability.publix.com/, Accessed November 26, 2017.
25. Ostrowski, J. 2017. Publix service lauded; price gripes persist. *Palm Beach Post*, September 3: Accent & Arts 1D.
26. *Ibid.*
27. Springer, J. 2015. The Power of Pleasure at Publix. *Supermarket News*. January 5.
28. Publix Super Markets, Inc., 2017. *Form 10-K.* Lakeland, Florida: Publix Super Markets, Inc.: 4.
29. Springer, J. 2015. The Power of Pleasure at Publix. *Supermarket News*. January 5.
30. Griffin, J. 2017. Challenge for Publix: Stay Ahead. *Tampa Bay Times*, January 22: Business 1.
31. Bouffard, K. 2017. Pubix to offer delivery from all stores in 4 years. *Sarasota Herald-Tribune*, June 8. http://www.heraldtribune.com/news/20170608/publix-to-offer-deliveries-from-all-stores-in-4-years, Accessed November 23, 2017.
32. Publix Super Markets, Inc., 2017. *2016 Annual Report*. Lakeland, Florida: Publix Super Markets, Inc.: 3.
33. Publix Super Markets, Inc. 2017. Publix Aprons. http://www.publix.com/recipes-planning, Accessed November 24, 2017.
34. Griffin, J. 2017. Publix's Prep Work. *Tampa Bay Times*, May 14:Business B1.
35. Arnold, K. 2016. Publix CEO brings energy to new role. *Orlando Sentinel*, January 23: A1.
36. *Ibid.*
37. Valverde, M. 2016. Publix CEO retiring after 42 years of service. *Sun-Sentinel*, April 28: Business D1.
38. *Ibid.*
39. Publix Super Markets, Inc., 2017. Publix Names Executive Vice President, Senior Vice President of Retail Operations and Two New Vice Presidents. http://corporate.publix.com/about-publix/newsroom/news-releases/publix-announces-promotion-of-four-company-leaders, Accessed November 19, 2017.
40. Publix Super Markets, Inc., 2017. Publix Announces Officer Promotions. http://corporate.publix.com/about-publix/newsroom/news-releases/publix-announces-officer-promotions, Accessed November 19, 2017.
41. Publix Super Markets, Inc., 2017. Publix Announces Vice President of Omnichannel and Application Development. http://corporate.publix.com/about-publix/newsroom/news-releases/publix-announces-vice-president-of-omnichannel-and-application-development, Accessed November 19, 2017.
42. Troy, M. 2017. Publix accelerates omnichannel efforts. *Retail Leader*, August 15. https://retailleader.com/publix-accelerates-omnichannel-efforts, Accessed November 19, 2017.
43. Publix Super Markets, Inc., 2017. Publix Announces Officer Promotions. http://corporate.publix.com/about-publix/newsroom/news-releases/publix-announces-officer-promotions, Accessed November 19, 2017.
44. Acosta, G. 2017. Publix prepares to win with real estate. *Retail Leader*, August 22. https://retailleader.com/publix-prepares-win-real-estate, Accessed November 19, 2017.
45. Simons, J. 2016. Employee Ownership Can Boost Corporate Profits; Companies that reward workers with stakes in the business have an edge over those that don't, shows a global study. *Wall Street Journal (Online)*, September 6. https://www.wsj.com/articles/employee-ownership-can-boost-corporate-profits-1473177179, Accessed November 19, 2017.
46. *Ibid.*
47. Tkaczyk, C. 2016. My Five Days of 'Bleeding Green.' *Fortune*, March 15, Vol. 173: 4, 168.
48. *Ibid.*
49. Solomon, B. 2013. The Walmart Slayer: How Publix's People-First Culture Is Winning The Grocer War. *Fortune*, August 12: 1.
50. Publix Super Markets, Inc. 2017. *Your Associate Handbook.* Lakeland, Florida: Publix Super Markets, Inc.: 1–2.
51. Publix Super Markets, Inc. 2017. Why Publix: Benefits. http://corporate.publix.com/careers/why-publix/benefits, Accessed November 22, 2017.
52. Solomon, B. 2013. The Walmart Slayer: How Publix's People-First Culture Is Winning The Grocer War. *Fortune*, August 12: 1.
53. Tkaczyk, C. 2016. My Five Days of 'Bleeding Green.' *Fortune*, March 15, Vol. 173: 4, 168.
54. Publix Super Markets, Inc., 2017. Sustainability. http://sustainability.publix.com/, Accessed November 26, 2017.
55. Publix Super Markets, Inc. 2017. *Your Associate Handbook.* Lakeland, Florida: Publix Super Markets, Inc.: 1–2.
56. Publix Super Markets, Inc. 2017. *Your Associate Handbook.* Lakeland, Florida: Publix Super Markets, Inc.: 1-7-8.
57. Publix Super Markets, Inc. 2017. Company Overview: Mission Statement & Guarantee. http://corporate.publix.com/about-publix/company-overview/mission-statement-guarantee, Accessed November 22, 2017.
58. Publix Super Markets, Inc., 2017. *Form 10-K.* Lakeland, Florida: Publix Super Markets, Inc.: 5.

59. Publix Super Markets, Inc., 2017. *Form 10-K.* Lakeland, Florida: Publix Super Markets, Inc.: 1.
60. Kritzer, A. 2016. Publix Sets Its Sights on Northern Virginia, metro DC area. *Tampa Bay Business Journal.* May 24. https://www.bizjournals.com/tampabay/blog/morning-edition/2016/03/publix-set-its-sights-on-northern-virginiametro-d.html, Accessed November 22, 2017.
61. Publix Super Markets, Inc. 2017. Departments—Marketing. http://corporate.publix.com/careers/support-areas/corporate/departments/marketing, Accessed November 27, 2017.
62. Springer, J. 2015. The Power of Pleasure at Publix. *Supermarket News.* January 5.
63. Publix Super Markets, Inc. 2017. Facebook landing page. https://www.facebook.com/publix/. Accessed November 22, 2017.
64. Publix Super Markets, Inc., 2017. *Form 10-K.* Lakeland, Florida: Publix Super Markets, Inc.: 4.
65. Guattery, M. 2017. *IBISWorld Industry Report 44511: Supermarkets & Grocery Stores in the U.S.*, 25. Retrieved October 24, 2017 from IBISWorld database.
66. Haddon, H. & Risso, L. 2017. Business News: Regional Grocery Stores Feel Squeeze Amid Upheaval. *Wall Street Journal*, August 14: B3.
67. Guarttery, M. 2017. *IBISWorld Industry Report 44511: Supermarkets & Grocery Stores in the U.S.*, 5. Retrieved October 24, 2017 from IBISWorld database.
68. Levishon, B. 2017. Kroger's Competition Problem. *Barron's*, June 12: M5.
69. Guarttery, M. 2017. *IBISWorld Industry Report 44511: Supermarkets & Grocery Stores in the U.S.*, 25. Retrieved October 24, 2017 from IBISWorld database.
70. Haddon, H. 2017. Business News: Kroger Braces for Amazon—grocer needs to show it can defend its turf against online power; results due on Friday. *Wall Street Journal*, September 5: B3.
71. Guarttery, M. 2017. *IBISWorld Industry Report 44511: Supermarkets & Grocery Stores in the U.S.*, 25. Retrieved October 24, 2017, from IBISWorld database.
72. Grant, C. 2017. Investors are Right to Worry About the Future of Kroger. *Wall Street Journal*, September 9: B12.
73. Haddon, H. 2017. Grocers Hit by Glut of Retail Space—industry is vulnerable to store closures after rapid growth amid shift in shopping habits. *Wall Street Journal*, August 1: B1.
74. Haddon, H. 2017. The Future of Food (A Special Report)—Grocers Imagine the Store of the Future: Straight from Kroger labs: customized ads, smart shelves, sensors that deploy cashiers. *Wall Street Journal*, October 16, 2017: R8.
75. Low, E. 2017. Amazon Takes Root; E-commerce leader's growth could get another big boost from its push into groceries. *Investor's Business Daily*, July 25, 2016: A1.
76. *The Economist.* 2017. Forsake all others; Loyalty schemes—If you want loyalty, get big data. 424(9057): 62.
77. Haddon, H. 2017. The Future of Food (A Special Report)—Grocers Imagine the Store of the Future: Straight from Kroger labs: customized ads, smart shelves, sensors that deploy cashiers. *Wall Street Journal*, October 16, 2017: R8.
78. Obeng, E., Luchs, R, Inman, J & Hulland, J. 2016. Survival of the Fittest: How Competitive Service Overlap and Retail format Impact Incumbents' Vulnerability to New Entrants. *Journal of Retailing*, 92(4) 383–396.
79. About Us—Food Lion, https://www.foodlion.com/about-us/, Accessed March 14, 2018.
80. Bhattarai, A. 2017. Walmart rallies employees, gears up to take on Amazon. *Washington Post*, June 1: A11.
81. Haddon, H. 2017. Business News: Kroger Braces for Amazon—grocer needs to show it can defend its turf against online power; results due on Friday. *Wall Street Journal*, September 5: B3.
82. Bhattarai, A. 2017. Walmart rallies employees, gears up to take on Amazon. *Washington Post*, June 1: A11.
83. *The Economist.* 2007. Business: The opposite of Walmart; Publix. 383(8527): 71.
84. *Ibid.*
85. Griffin, J. 2016. Publix Takes on New Turf. *Tampa Bay Times*, February 14: Business 1.
86. Guarttery, M. 2017. *IBISWorld Industry Report 44511: Supermarkets & Grocery Stores in the U.S.*, 30. Retrieved October 24, 2017 from IBISWorld database.
87. Bhattarai, A. 2017. Walmart rallies employees, gears up to take on Amazon. *Washington Post*, June 1: A11.
88. *Ibid.*
89. Wakabayasi, D. & Corkery, M. 2017. Walmart And Google Partner, Eyes On Amazon. *The New York Times*, August 23: B1.
90. *Ibid.*
91. Halzack, S. 2017. Walmart's new lure: 'Pickup discounts.' *Washington Post*, April 12: A11.
92. Guarttery, M. 2017. *IBISWorld Industry Report 44511: Supermarkets & Grocery Stores in the U.S.*, 31. Retrieved October 24, 2017 from IBISWorld database.
93. Griffin, J. 2016. Grocery Growth in Florida No Threat to Publix. *Tampa Bay Times*, May 1: Business 1.
94. Turner, Z. 2017. Aldi Bets Limited Choice Will Lure U.S. Shoppers—Private German grocer tries to upend market with manic eye on costs. *Wall Street Journal*, September 22: A1.
95. *Ibid.*
96. *Ibid.*
97. *The Economist.* 2017. A Lidl late? America's grocery market. 423(9045): 67.
98. Turner, Z. 2017. Aldi Bets Limited Choice Will Lure U.S. Shoppers—Private German grocer tries to upend market with manic eye on costs. *Wall Street Journal*, September 22: A1.
99. *The Economist.* 2017. The broccoli heresy; Discount grocers. 425(9064): 62.
100. Nassauer, S. & Haddon, H. 2017. German Grocer Enters Walmart's Turff—Discounter Lidl brings market-winning ways to U.S. at fraught time for food retailers. *Wall Street Journal*, May 17: B1.
101. *The Economist.* 2017. The broccoli heresy; Discount grocers. 425(9064): 62.
102. *The Economist.* 2017. A Lidl late? America's grocery market. 423(9045): 67.
103. *The Economist.* 2017. The broccoli heresy; Discount grocers. 425(9064): 62.
104. *Ibid.*
105. *The Economist.* 2017. Sorry, we're closed; American retailing. 423(9040): 68.
106. *The Economist.* 2017. A Lidl late? America's grocery market. 423(9045): 67.
107. Turner, Z. 2017. Aldi Bets Limited Choice Will Lure U.S. Shoppers—Private German grocer tries to upend market with manic eye on costs. *Wall Street Journal*, September 22: A1.
108. *Ibid.*
109. Ostrowski, J. 2017. Publix Service Lauded, price gripes persist; Consumer Reports readers give the chain almost identical reviews. *Palm Beach Post*, September 3, 2017: Accent & Arts1D.
110. Gasparro, A. & Haddon, H. 2017. Amazon's Whole Foods Takeover: How a Pioneer Lost Its Way—Whole Foods set the pace with healthier fare, but its prices and rivals caught up with it. *Wall Street Journal*, June 17: A5.
111. *Ibid.*
112. Guarttery, M. 2017. *IBISWorld Industry Report 44511: Supermarkets & Grocery Stores in the U.S.*, 30. Retrieved October 24, 2017 from IBISWorld database.
113. Haddon, H. 2017. Business News: Kroger Braces for Amazon—grocer needs to show it can defend its turf against online power; results due on Friday. *Wall Street Journal*, September 5: B3.
114. Guarttery, M. 2017. *IBISWorld Industry Report 44511: Supermarkets & Grocery Stores in the U.S.*, 30. Retrieved October 24, 2017 from IBISWorld database.
115. *The Economist.* 2017. Whole hog; Amazon buys Whole Foods. 423(9046): 61.
116. Stevens, L. & Haddon, H. 2017. Amazon Clobbers Grocers With Whole Foods Salvo. *Wall Street Journal*, August 25: A1.
117. *Ibid.*
118. Cusumano, M. 2017. Technology and Strategy Management—Amazon and Whole Foods: Follow the Strategy (and the Money). *Communications of the ACM.* 60(10) 24–26.
119. Wegmans Food Markets, Inc. 2017. Company Overview. https://www.wegmans.com/about-us/company-overview.html, Accessed November 23, 2017.
120. Boyle, M. & Kratz, E. 2005. The Wegmans Way. *Fortune*, January 24, Vol. 151: 2.

121. Trigaux, R. 2016. Publix Faces Tough Foe in Wegman's. *Tampa Bay Times*, July 19: Local 4.
122. Bhattari, A. 2017. Wegmans plans to open store at Fannie Mae site. *Washington Post*, May 23:Metro B5.
123. *Ibid.*
124. Wegmans Food Markets, Inc. 2017. Company Overview. https://www.wegmans.com/about-us/company-overview.html, Accessed November 23, 2017.
125. Haddon, H. 2017. The Future of Food (A Special Report)—Grocers Imagine the Store of the Future: Straight from Kroger labs: customized ads, smart shelves, sensors that deploy cashiers. *Wall Street Journal*, October 16, 2017: R8.
126. Haddon, H. 2017. Grocers Hit by Glut of Retail Space—industry is vulnerable to store closures after rapid growth amid shift in shopping habits. *Wall Street Journal*, August 1: B1.
127. *Ibid.*
128. Giammona, C. 2017. Why the Retail Crises Could be Coming to American Groceries. *Bloomberg*. May 4. https://www.bloomberg.com/news/articles/2017-05-04/why-the-retail-crisis-could-be-coming-to-americangroceries. Accessed October 29, 2017.
129. *Ibid.*
130. *Ibid.*
131. Haddon, H. 2016. Millennials Vex Grocers—Key age group spends less at supermarkets, explores alternatives, such as online services. *Wall Street Journal*, October 31: B5.
132. *Ibid.*
133. Haddon, H. 2017. Business News: Albertsons to Buy Plated Meal Service—Deal marks first purchase of its kind by a national chain of supermarkets. *Wall Street Journal*, September 21: B5.
134. *Ibid.*
135. Alvarez, A. 2017. *IBISWorld Industry Report OD5085: Online Grocery Sales in the U.S.*, 3. Retrieved November 13, 2017 from IBISWorld database.
136. Eule, A. & Bary, A. 2017. Amazon and Whole Foods: Grocery Apocalypse? *Barron's*, June 19: 17.
137. Haddon, H. 2017. The Future of Food (A Special Report)—Grocers Imagine the Store of the Future: Straight from Kroger labs: customized ads, smart shelves, sensors that deploy cashiers. *Wall Street Journal*, October 16, 2017: R8.
138. *Ibid.*
139. Smith, D. 2016. *Mintel: Grocery Retailing US November 2016*, 4. Retrieved October 24, 2017 from Mintel database.
140. Alvarez, A. 2017. *IBISWorld Industry Report OD5085: Online Grocery Sales in the U.S.*, 21. Retrieved November 13, 2017, from IBISWorld database.
141. Brown, L. 2017. Schnucks expanding delivery as Instacart enters St. Louis. *St. Louis Post-Dispatch*, January 29: Business E1.
142. Haddon, H. 2017. Business News: Fresh Pressure on Grocery Delivery—Amazon's deal for Whole Foods adds new element to burgeoning market. *Wall Street Journal*, June 30: B5.
143. **Federal Reserve Economic Data**. Real Disposable Personal Income: Per Capita. Federal Reserve Bank of St. Louis. https://fred.stlouisfed.org/series/A229RX0, Accessed November 19, 2017.
144. Epstein, G. 2017. Can the Expansion Last Into 2020? *Barron's*, June 26: 33.
145. Strauss, L. 2017. The Dow Notches a Strong September. *Barron's*, October 2: M3–M5.
146. Haddon, H. 2017. Business News: Kroger Braces for Amazon—grocer needs to show it can defend its turf against online power; results due on Friday. *Wall Street Journal*, September 5: B3.
147. Griffin, J. 2017. Challenge for Publix: Stay Ahead. *Tampa Bay Times*, January 22: Business 1.
148. Guarttery, M. 2017. *IBISWorld Industry Report 44511: Supermarkets & Grocery Stores in the U.S.*, 6–7. Retrieved October 24, 2017, from IBISWorld database.
149. *Ibid.*
150. *Ibid.*

CASE 14

Driving Innovation and Growth at Starbucks: From Howard Schultz to Kevin Johnson

In 2017, Seattle-based global coffee chain Starbucks Corporation was named the third most admired company in the world and the number one company worldwide in the food service industry by *Fortune*.[a] The magazine also ranked Starbucks as number one in the areas of innovation, people management, use of corporate assets, social responsibility, quality of management, financial soundness, long-term investment, and quality of products and services. Since inception, Starbucks had innovated in its business model. Starbucks' passion to innovate manifested in the way the company sourced its coffee beans, developed new beverages, created unique store concepts, and achieved digital breakthroughs.

Starbucks showed positive signs of changes and achieved remarkable growth under the leadership of Howard Schultz, who became its CEO in 1987. Schultz, over his two stints as CEO (1987 to 2000 and 2008 to 2017),[b] used innovation as an integral part of the Starbucks corporate DNA for the company both to differentiate itself in the coffee industry and to grow its bottom line. "*Industry-leading innovation is driving our core business and creating further separation from competitors all around the world,*[1] said Schultz.

However, with the departure of Schultz in 2017, it was a big challenge for the new CEO, Kevin Johnson to carry forward Starbucks' mission and address the challenges emerging within the company. One of the most pressing challenges before him was to solve the congestion problem caused by the coffee chain's mobile platform. The introduction of the mobile ordering system with its seamless and personalized experience to customers posed both opportunities and threats for Starbucks. Moreover, analysts were concerned about the coffee chain's ambitious plan to have more than 12,000 new stores by 2021 as they feared that the bottlenecks created by the new technology might affect the company's sales and put its store expansion plan in jeopardy.

About Starbucks

Starbucks, an American food and beverage company, was founded in 1971 by three partners, Gordon Bowker, Jerry Baldwin, and Zev Siegl, to sell premium coffee beans and specialty coffee equipment. Schultz, who was later to become CEO of Starbucks, first visited a Starbucks store in 1981 and became intrigued with the Starbucks operation. A year later, he joined the company as manager of retail sales and marketing. Fascinated by the passionate coffee culture of Italy, he suggested to the founders that they create such an espresso bar atmosphere in the US. But, when they turned down his proposal, Schultz decided to leave the company and start his own coffee bar—II Giornale—in Seattle. In 1987, he purchased Starbucks with the support of local investors and he rebranded his II Giornale coffee outlets as Starbucks Corporation.

In the new millennium, Starbucks stores offered hot and cold beverages, whole bean and ground coffees, ready-to-drink beverages, full-leaf teas, and various food products such as pastries, snacks, hot and cold sandwiches, and packaged food items as well as beverage-making equipment like mugs and tumblers. Since the company went public in 1992, Starbucks proved to be one of the most successful examples of a mid-sized, reasonably-priced business in the public market that performed exceptionally well for its shareholders. During Schultz's initial tenure as CEO (1987–2000), the company noticed a more than tenfold rise in the stock price between the launch of its IPO in 1992 and his resignation in 2000[2] in order to concentrate on the company's global strategy. In the early part of the year 2007, Starbucks got into some trouble, largely attributed to its aggressive store expansion plan over the previous decade which, according to Schultz, had led to the "watering down" of its brand.[3] After the return of Schultz as CEO in 2008, Starbucks achieved a turnaround and witnessed a strong period of company expansion and investor enthusiasm,

[a]Headquartered in New York City, Fortune is a multinational business magazine, published and owned by Time Inc.
[b]Schultz was succeeded by Orin Smith who was CEO from 2000 to 2005. Jim Donald was the CEO from 2005 to 2008.

This case was written by **Benudhar Sahu**, (IBS Hyderabad) under the direction of **Trilochan Tripathy**, (XLRI Jamsedpur) and **Debapratim Purkayastha** (IBS Hyderabad). It was compiled from published sources, and is intended to be used as a basis for class discussion rather than to illustrate either effective or ineffective handling of a management situation.

Exhibit 1 Starbucks' IPO Valuation (2008–2016)

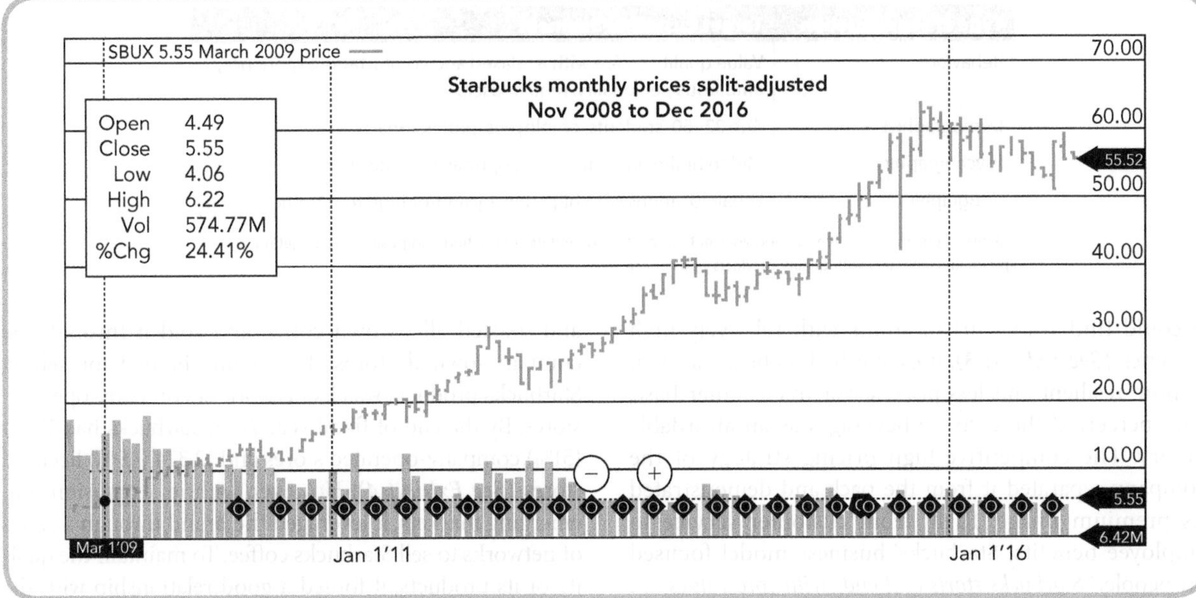

Source: www.seekingalpha.com/article/4034092-starbucks-buy-coffee-sell-stock

moving the IPO valuation from under US$4.00 per share, split-adjusted to over US$60 in 2016 ***(See Exhibit 1)***.

After his second successful run as CEO, Schultz stepped down as CEO of the company in early 2017. Johnson, who was serving as president and chief operating officer of Starbucks and was a seven-year member in the company's board, succeeded Schultz. As of April 2017, the company operated more than 24,000 retail stores in 70 countries worldwide.[4] For the fiscal year 2016, Starbucks had earned net revenue of US$21.32 billion, up from US$19.16 billion in 2015, and its revenue almost doubled from US$10.7 billion to US$21.32 billion between 2010 and 2016 ***(See Exhibit 2)***.

Starbucks' Business Model

Starbucks' business model was set in motion in 1987 when Schultz set up Starbucks Corporation. The coffee chain leveraged its resources to create competitive capabilities and core competencies to formulate its business model. Unlike other American restaurant chains, Starbucks had accepted the standard retail business model from the very beginning of its business operation, where the retail locations of the company generated the majority of its net revenue.

Starbucks had segmented its market by geography and demography by locating its stores in areas where

Exhibit 2 Starbucks' Key Financials

Particulars	As and for the Fiscal Year Ended Data						
	2016	2015	2014	2013	2012	2011	2010
Starbucks Net Sales or Revenues	21.32	19.16	16.45	14.89	13.3	11.7	10.71
Cost of Goods Sold (COGS)	8.51	7.79	6.86	6.38	5.81	4.95	4.46
Starbucks Gross Profit	12.8	11.38	9.59	8.51	7.49	6.75	6.25
Research & Development Expense	–	–	–	–	–	–	–
Selling General & Admin Expense	7.65	6.88	5.8	8.21	4.94	4.5	4.32
Starbucks Net Income (Profit/Loss)	2.82	2.76	2.07	0.0083	1.38	1.25	0.9456
Starbucks Earnings Per Share Basic Net	1.90	1.82	1.36	1.13	0.90	0.81	0.62
Starbucks Earnings Per Share Diluted Net	1.90	1.82	1.36	1.13	0.90	0.81	0.62

*Note: Fiscal year is October-September. All values in USD billions except per share data.

Adapted from http://amigobulls.com/stocks/SBUX/income-statement/annual

Exhibit 3 Market Segmentation of Starbucks

Type of Segmentation	Target Customer Segment
Behavior	Value quality coffee with a relaxed and comfortable experience, ambitious personality, regular users
Demographics	Age 22–60, students, employees, professionals
Psychographic	Mid to higher income, young optimistic mindset
Geographic	Urban locations with high density and/or high foot traffic

Adapted from www.research-methodology.net/starbucks-segmentation-targeting-and-positioning-targeting-premium-customers-with-quality-products-and-service/

it could find young urban adults with relatively high incomes ***(See Exhibit 3)***. It established its business with a more resilient and less price-sensitive customer base, who perceived these coffee beverages as an affordable luxury. The competitive high pricing strategy of the company separated it from the pack and demonstrated its premium image. Right from customer service to employee benefits, Starbucks' business model focused on people. "*Starbucks starts and ends with core values . . . [and] the core values emanate from and around relationships with people*,"[5] said Anne McGonigle, the company's vice president for special projects. In addition to serving great quality coffee, Starbucks delivered an amazing experience to its customers through its reliable and friendly service and rich in-store experience. The Starbucks mission to "*inspire and nurture the human spirit—one person, one cup and one neighbourhood at a time*"[6] directly correlated with the experience that a customer had in each store.

The coffee chain had an extensive product line strategy, creating a variety of products beyond simply the coffee beans. Schultz called its business model "vertical integration to the extreme,"[7] as the company purchased and roasted all its own coffee and sold it through the company-owned stores. The main channel for selling Starbucks products was its network of company-operated stores. By the end of fiscal year 2016, Starbucks had 12,711 (51%) company-operated stores and 12,374 (49%) licensed stores (***See Exhibit 4***). However, with its expansion into emerging markets, it leveraged the brand through a series of networks to sell Starbucks coffee. To maintain the quality of its products, it forged a good relationship with the suppliers and called them partners of the company.

Starbucks adopted an aggressive branding strategy to position itself as a powerful brand in the global coffee chain. Analysts pointed out that Starbucks positioned its brand in the coffee market as a good customer experience brand with attractive store design, unique environment, elegant taste, and high-quality coffee beans. The Starbucks brand leveraged itself without advertising. The company had always portrayed itself as a high-quality product and believed in word-of-mouth to win over customers. The overall business model of Starbucks was sensitive to the cultural differences of the international market. The company customized its products and services according to the taste and preferences of customers.

Exhibit 4 Starbucks' Company-operated and Licensed Store Status (Fiscal Year 2016)

Store Operation	Americas	% of Total Americas Stores	CAP	% of Total CAP Stores	EMEA	% of Total EMEA Stores	All Other Segments	% of Total All other Segments Stores	Total	% of Total Stores
Company-operated stores	9,019	58%	2,811	44%	523	20%	358	91%	12,711	51%
Licensed stores	6,588	42%	3,632	56%	2,119	80%	35	9%	12,374	49%
Total	15,607	100%	6,443	100%	2,642	100%	393	100%	25,085	100%

Adapted from https://s21.q4cdn.com/369030626/files/doc_financials/2016/Annual/FY16-Annual-Report-on-Form-10-K.pdf

Schultz: The Architect of Innovation

Schultz steered Starbucks to become a strong performing global coffee chain. When he again took charge as Starbucks' CEO in 2008, he found that the company's rapid expansion had distracted it from making its stores an inviting place with innovative products. One of the key priorities of his seven-point transformation agenda to revive the company was to "*create innovative growth platforms worthy of our coffee*."[8] In order to innovate and recreate the experience of the Italian coffee bar culture at Starbucks stores, Schultz brought in changes in the in-store design and ensured that the stores evolved into relevant customer destinations. He invested heavily in staff training programs, making the training fun and innovative. Schultz worked out strategies to attract, motivate, and reward store employees in a manner that would create a favorable work culture and would result in the high performance of the company.

Schultz proved the power of a different kind of business model which "balances profit with social responsibility."[9] He desperately realized the need to get back to the core and make the changes necessary to evoke the company's heritage, tradition, and passion for the Starbucks experience. Schultz wanted to be different, so he created an enduring, special experience for his customers who walked into the coffee store. He believed that one of the ways in which Starbucks could win over the expectations of the consumers was by creating the kind of innovation that was customer-facing. Schultz established the idea of the 'third place' experience. He offered his customers options and the luxury of customization of products in the stores.

Schultz continued to experiment with new ideas, products, different store formats, alternative partnership arrangements, and various in-store music mixes. He learned from each of these experiments, and suitably adapted them to the Starbucks stores. Schultz pioneered the introduction of many digital initiatives and directed much innovation at Starbucks related to health and wellness products.

In 2017, Schultz stepped down as CEO but would remain involved with Starbucks as executive chairman, focusing on innovation and social impact activities, among other things. The move was aimed at refreshing the Starbucks brand, which was facing increasing competition from specialty roasters as well as from mass coffee purveyors who were introducing more high-end drinks.

Starbucks' Business Model Innovation

Innovation was at the heart of Starbucks' business model. During the economic recession of the late 2000s, Starbucks managed to survive and even thrive in business by modifying its operational policies and systems to address new regulations and other developments. Instead of introducing a new business model during the company's sluggish period of growth, Starbucks incorporated new innovation to the brand by following its own organizational strategy. According to Robert Teagle, Starbucks' EMEA[c] IT director, "*It's all about innovation—managing innovation and how it relates to us in the retail world. Really thinking about how we at Starbucks think about innovation, how we think about it internally, how we think about it in terms of our customers, bringing innovation to everything we do. Whether that's a product, or whether it's in the technology, we try to bring innovation to the fore*."[10]

Starbucks, one of the founding members of the International Foodservice Manufacturers Association's (IFMA[d]) Center of Innovation Excellence,[e] was a world-recognized leader in the industry in terms of exploiting information technology and technological developments. By utilizing its immense potential in product innovation and location strategy and its marketing ability, Starbucks positioned itself in the market as a highly reputed premier coffee brand. According to Jim Donald, former CEO of Starbucks (2005–2008), "*Starbucks has become an enduring, global brand by continually raising the bar and finding ways to innovate throughout all areas of the business*."[11]

Product Innovation

Innovation of new product ideas was the prime focus of the company's competitive strategy, enabling it to charge a premium price. It was committed to delivering the highest quality products through continuous innovation. To match the changing consumer tastes and preferences, the firm kept its menu always fresh by constantly offering something new, including seasonally available beverages, drive-thru accessibility, and channel development. Besides products, the packaging innovation of the company represented selling high-quality "ready brew" coffee[12] in individual serving sizes. The coffee chain partnered with a number of organizations for product innovation, which also demonstrated its social commitment objectives.

To meet the growing demand for high-quality coffee globally, Starbucks used digital technology to ensure that its

[c]EMEA stands for Europe, Middle East, and Africa. It is commonly used in business as a way to locate an office or convey service coverage for a particular business.
[d]Established in 1952, the IFMA provides its members with the insights and best practices required to drive increased market share and operational excellence.
[e]The Center of Innovation Excellence provides IFMA members and their customers with a deeper understanding of new product success that are unique to food service industry.

supply chain operated at maximum efficiency at all times. In 2015, Starbucks achieved a milestone when it demonstrated that 99% of the Starbucks Coffee supply chain was verified as ethically sourced.[13] Starbucks considered its supply chain strategy an integral part of its sustainability strategy.

Location Strategy

Starbucks was able to identify the most attractive store location in an area through its real estate team and this worked to its advantage. The coffee chain adjusted its business model to make the store more of a destination and leveraged technology to drive continuous traffic to the stores. In contrast to the conventional "redo the store layout" strategy,[14] Starbucks adopted a technology-oriented strategy to design its stores. This strategy encouraged the employees to think freely about the company and contribute significantly in terms of new ideas and concepts to improve the store formats. The opening of new concept stores, such as the Reserve Roastery and Tasting Room stores, offered a highly customized and elevated experience to the company's targeted wealthy customers and coffee connoisseurs. "*Our stores are where our users enjoy our products and on average they spend 3–5 minutes if they are just grabbing a coffee or about half an hour if they are having it in store. It is a short period of time and our innovations have to be focused on making their experience a better one,*"[15] Teagle said.

Starbucks redefined a highly competitive coffee business environment by adding music, free Wi-Fi service, wireless charging facility, relaxed seating, and luxurious interiors within the stores. In addition, Starbucks Digital Network provided free access to news and entertainment from sources like *The Wall Street Journal, USA Today,* ESPN,[f] and Nick Jr.[g] To track customer preferences and machine performance, the company fitted many of its stores with high-spec Clover coffee machines, which used a cloud-based server known as Clover Net.

The Starbucks Experience

After the 2007–08 crisis, Starbucks had to rebuild its customer relationship to show the world that it cared for quality and consistency. The customer-centered business model compelled the company to think on entirely new levels—"new-to-company" and even "new-to-world" products, services, and technologies.[16] The coffee giant learned the skill of keeping its current and future customers happy through innovations that differentiated it from the mass-market. Starbucks' customer base positioning enabled the company to offer customer service that often exceeded their expectations. According to Micah Solomon, a contributor to *Forbes*, "*Starbucks spends a lot of time measuring and improving how well they match their customers' speed expectations—delivering a custom (truly from scratch) beverage in a matter of minutes. They don't let the need for speed suck the life out of the Starbucks experience.*"[17] Customer satisfaction being a key component of Starbucks' strategy, the company treated each customer specially, so that they felt that they were in a special place.

Starbucks not only altered traditional coffee houses into a pleasant experience, but also transitioned coffee into a social platform that appealed to customers seeking a premium experience. It created an aspirational brand with highly loyal and delighted customers who repeatedly came to the stores for their unique experience. In addition to coffee, Starbucks offered a most suitable environment for relaxing and socializing with friends. At Starbucks, customers shared a common passion for creating the ultimate coffee experience, which motivated the company to improve its products, services, and technologies through innovation. Unlike other coffee chains, Starbucks' value proposition focused on offering customers a Starbucks Experience, a 'third place' experience away from work and home, where people could spend quality time with friends or alone enjoying quality coffee, beverages, and fresh food ***(See Exhibit 5)***.

Consumers valued Starbucks' products and services as they saved money with additional purchases through frequent spender benefits. The company launched Starbucks card in 2001 to allow consumers to purchase the gift cards for friends.

Employee Motivation

To ensure quality customer service and maximum customer satisfaction, Starbucks put the emphasis on recruiting and training the best talent in the industry. This added great value to its brand reputation. Starbucks recognized the employee's contribution to building the successful business model and called them partners by offering them stock options in the company. Starbucks' approach

Exhibit 5 Structure of Core Value Propositions of Five Franchise Chains

Company	Core Value Proposition
Dunkin' Brands	Coffee and donuts
Krispy Crème	Donuts, coffee, and ice cream
McDonald's	Hamburgers, salads, and coffee
Panera Bread	Fresh bread sandwiches, salads, and coffee
Starbucks	Third place and coffee

Adapted from www.forbes.com/sites/panosmourdoukoutas/2013/11/05/dunkin-brands-panera-bread-and-starbucks-three-winning-business-models/#590699b9200d

[f]ESPN is the US-based leading global cable and satellite sports entertainment channel, owned by ESPN Inc.

[g]Nick Jr. is an American digital cable and satellite television channel, aiming at young children aged under 7 years.

to food and beverage development seemed to be a cross-functional and collaborative process, wherein hundreds of partners throughout the company participated to guide product innovation. The employees led the success of new products and technology innovations and even 'breakthroughs' in the company.[18] Starbucks partnered with Arizona State University[h] (ASU) to expand its innovative tuition-reimbursement program that offered a chance to its employees to pursue their personal and professional career.

Digital Technology

Starbucks introduced technological innovation, a significant part of the strategy to promote its stores. The coffee chain was more cautious about adding and remodelling stores because it saw digital as a growth avenue. During Starbucks' fourth quarter earnings conference call in 2015, Schultz said, "*The technology innovations we are introducing are further strengthening our brand, improving our efficiency and in-store execution, increasing our profitability, enabling us to further extend our lead over competitors, and, most importantly, enabling us to deliver an elevated Starbucks experience to our customers.*"[19] In addition to the R&D facility at the corporate headquarters, Starbucks had Centers of Innovation Excellence (CIE) around the world to deliver locally relevant products and help customers enjoy the Starbucks experience everywhere.

Starbucks created and leveraged an innovative marketing strategy to expand its outreach, which in turn led to higher revenue, profit, and total shareholder return. It used social media for marketing and social commerce. The social media strategy of the company revolved around its website and six additional social platforms—Twitter Inc.,[i] Facebook, Inc.,[j] Pinterest,[k] Google Plus,[l] YouTube,[m] and My Starbucks Idea. The company linked its social media strategy objectives with technology channels like mobile apps to appeal to the online community. One of the company's new tactics of launching food trucks allowed on-the-go customers to grab a quick coffee in an accessible way. Speaking to *Marketing Magazine*[n] on the company's plan to become a leader in the digital space, Schultz said, "*Social media is a natural extension of our brand because we want to do things that are unexpected and to speak to all sorts of people who are engaged in social media.*"[20]

Starbucks took advantage of its crowd sourcing platform, **My Starbucks Idea,** to innovate and improve its products in the social media. The platform encouraged customers to exchange ideas with each other and help the company understand their needs and concerns. By giving customers an opportunity to view the brand and by responding to it, it was able to reignite the brand trust. Another social media initiative that allowed customers to personalize the company's offerings was **My Starbucks Signature**. The process required customers to get themselves involved in developing and naming their own signature drink on a well-designed website, and share the new flavor with the community.

As a mobile disruptor, Starbucks embraced mobile apps for the promotion of its brand and sales of products earlier than the competition. Introduced in 2009, the Starbucks mobile app developed from a basic mobile payment app into an integral part of Starbucks' digital ecosystem. The mobile and digital technologies enabled Starbucks to extend its reach and deepen its emotional connection with customers across the world. The company incentivized customers who used the mobile app to buy and pay. As a pioneer in mass market technology, Starbucks made it easy to order online to eliminate delays from lines and directly connect with a barista. "*We have to keep pushing innovation inside and outside of our stores, and we have to be as relevant for our customers on their phone, as we are inside the Starbucks experience,*"[21] said Schultz.

The mobile and digital strategies of Starbucks revolved around its loyalty program. The coffee chain diligently crafted its loyalty program over the years and considered it as the best in the coffee shop industry. In an earnings conference call, Schultz said the growth of the company's loyalty program "*continues to be our most important business driver as new members contribute not only short-term increases in revenue and profit, but also to long-term loyalty for years to come.*"[22]

Starbucks gained customer attention through the launching of innovative reward programs and game changing concepts, a key to drive growth. The coffee chain designed reward programs to encourage the use of mobile ordering, which led to enticing rewards. Starbucks customers learned about the improvements and expansions made by the company through the leading-edge digital initiatives, including the loyalty program, **My Starbucks Rewards**. The program enabled customers to keep track of rewards and stars in real time and pay for their purchases with their phones. Starbucks partnered

[h]ASU is a leader in employing innovative educational technology to deliver tailored academic support.
[i]Twitter is the US-based social network company, allowing users to post and interact with messages.
[j]Founded in 2004, Facebook is an American for-profit corporation and a popular free social media website.
[k]Headquartered in San Francisco, Pinterest is a web and mobile application start-up that help people to discover and save creative ideas on the World Wide Web.
[l]Google Plus is a social networking service that is owned and operated by Google.
[m]Started in 2005, YouTube is an American video-sharing website.
[n]Launched in 2002, Marketing magazine is a leading source of advertising, marketing, and media intelligence in Asia.

with *The New York Times* to avail of the top news and a selection of articles via the Starbucks mobile app for the My Starbucks Rewards loyalty members. "*We see a future in which the Starbucks retail experience seamlessly extends to the mobile devices our millions of customers carry with them every day*,"[23] said Schultz, in a press release.

To increase customers' loyalty, Starbucks introduced two free new apps for customers—the **MyStarbucks** app and the **Starbucks Card Mobile.** While the MyStarbucks app enabled customers to search stores, browse the menu, and explore Starbucks coffee, the Starbucks Card Mobile app allowed them to register themselves, balance check, and refill Starbucks gift cards. Speaking on the Starbucks Card Mobile app, Stephen Gillett, senior vice president of digital ventures at Starbucks, said, "*We're really venturing into new waters in terms of mobile payment.*"[24]

Starbucks unveiled an innovative conversation ordering system called '**My Starbucks Barista**' for the Starbucks Mobile app. It used Artificial Intelligence (AI) and the voice computing system to allow users to place their orders via voice command or a messaging interface. Starbucks expected this to enhance customer loyalty and engagement and further extend the accessibility of its app.

Starbucks' digital ecosystem achieved a turning point in 2015 with the introduction of its mobile ordering system known as '**Mobile Order & Pay**' (MOP). Integrated into the Starbucks Mobile App and My Starbucks Rewards loyalty program, the MOP initiative allowed customers to place their orders ahead on the app, bypass the line entirely, and pick up their order later from the chosen location. The mobile ordering technology transformed Starbucks from a coffee shop to digital shop. The MOP experience delivered on all the three key customer expectations—ease, simplicity, and speed. It benefited Starbucks by opening up an additional revenue avenue and helped in getting the information it needed to continuously satisfy customers.

The popularity of MOP extended Starbucks' leadership position in mobile commerce and customer loyalty. The digital efforts of the coffee chain generated stunning returns and its technology partnerships reinforced the passion among customers to venture into Starbucks' locations. By December 2016, Starbucks became a global market leader in mobile payments with 12 million Starbucks Rewards members (up 18% YoY), and 8 million mobile-paying customers, with one out of three using MOP.[25] In the early part of 2017, the mobile payments technology accounted for over 20% of the total transactions at Starbucks,[26] a percentage higher than that of others in the food and beverage industry. "*Of all the new traffic-driving initiatives for the company, Mobile Order & Pay is at the top of that list and we are confident that it will be game-changing for our customers and our business*,"[27] said Adam Brotman, Starbucks chief digital officer.

Challenges

Despite Starbucks' longstanding efforts at spreading innovations throughout the business model, the coffee chain became a victim of its own innovation, industry experts observed. After taking charge as CEO of the company, Johnson faced a tough time as Starbucks posted its slowest comparable-sales growth in the US since the global recession. Launching of food had long been a challenge for Starbucks and the coffee chain had overhauled its food menu several times to keep up the growing demand of customers. Johnson unveiled a new lunchtime menu called Mercato, and its success would likely determine whether Starbucks was able to achieve its goal of doubling food sales in the years to come. On the customer front, Johnson would likely face the challenge of maintaining Starbucks' ecosystem and customer retention. Industry experts felt that as Johnson innovated and the company evolved, he would have to maintain the focus on the customer that had made the brand so powerful. However, one of the key issues that Johnson faced was the mobile payment system that dragged down customer traffic. Johnson admitted that "*The tremendous success of mobile order and pay has also created a new operational challenge in our highest volume stores that has been building for several quarters—significant congestion at the handoff plane*."[28]

The launch of MOP no doubt reduced long lines at the cash register, but it caused some problems in the service. It led to congestion at the checkout point due to many advance orders and discouraged customers, who sometimes left the counter without ordering. Although Starbucks endorsed mobile technology as a potential operational efficiency booster, the company ended up missing its selling expectations when customers walked out of the stores. Starbucks called it a challenging environment for the company which lowered its revenue forecast from a double digit increase to within an 8% and 10% increase for fiscal year 2017.[29] Further, the coffee chain reported that its transactions had dropped 2% in the first quarter of fiscal year 2017,[30] in large part due to the problems caused by mobile ordering. It seemed to be the coffee chain's most urgent challenge, especially when the company was focusing on its e-commerce, the potential source of business growth. Further, Starbucks faced the biggest challenge of declining foot traffic in its stores as consumers shifted more to the e-commerce platform. With the coffee chain's stores packed with mobile orders, service slowed down drastically, alienating customers. Observers expected that

Johnson would have to find a solution to jam-packed Starbucks stores that might actually be costing the company sales.

The Road Ahead

Looking forward, Starbucks devised a massive growth plan, supported by its business model innovation. According to the coffee chain's projections, approximately 12,000 new stores would be added globally, taking the total to 37,000 stores by 2021.[31] On the premium front, Starbucks considered its Roastery stores an impressive success of its business model innovation. It had plans to globalize the Roastery experience and build more high-end Roastery experiences at its Starbucks stores, adding Starbucks Reserve "experience bars" to about 20% of its locations by 2021.[32] In December 2016, Starbucks launched a five-year plan including an ambitious multi-year strategy to elevate the entire Starbucks brand and customer experience globally and extend Starbucks' leadership around coffee, retail, and mobile. The coffee chain planned to capture the enormous global growth opportunities ahead through the power of its brand, the strength in its business, and its world-class talent management.

Despite its potential growth plan, analysts felt that Starbucks' mobile ordering system could raise some concerns and growth could continue to decelerate in the future if Johnson failed to find a fast fix. Johnson was optimistic about the future of the company. "*We both embrace innovation—Howard through the lens of an entrepreneur and a merchant, me through the lens of the technologist. We both care about growing a company and certainly his life's work has created this beautiful company called Starbucks and the opportunity for me to take that and stay true to the mission, the values, and the core business as we scale it will be a great opportunity that I look forward to*,"[33] he said. According to some analysts, it remained to be seen whether Johnson would be able to continue the digital drive at Starbucks unabated to attract customers and maintain the company's leadership position in the food service industry going forward.

NOTES

1. "Starbucks Presents its Five-Year Plan for Strong Global Growth," www.news.starbucks.com, December 7, 2016.
2. "Why did Howard Schultz Leave Starbucks, only to Return Eight Years Later? (SBUX)," www.investopedia.com, March 30, 2015.
3. Andrew Ward, "Why Schultz has Caused a Stir at Starbucks," www.ft.com, February 26, 2007.
4. Lindsey Reinmuth and Hailey Lynch, "Does Long-Term Caffeine Consumption Protect Your Brain?," www.healthyagaingproject.org, February 11, 2017.
5. Ranjay Gulati, Sarah Huffman, and Gary L. Neilson, "The Barista Principle—Starbucks and the Rise of Relational Capital," www.strategy-business.com, July 17, 2002.
6. "Starbucks—Business-Level Strategy Essay," www.bartleby.com, January 12, 2014.
7. Ken Favaro, "Vertical Integration 2.0: An Old strategy Makes a Comeback," www.strategy-business.com, May 6, 2015.
8. "Starbucks' Quest for Healthy Growth: An Interview with Howard Schultz," www.mckinsey.com, March, 2011.
9. Tony Schwartz, "Why I Appreciate Starbucks," www.hbr.org, April 4, 2011.
10. Derek du Preez, "A Coffee Catch up with Starbucks EMEA IT Director Robert Teagle," www.diginomica.com, August 22, 2014.
11. "Starbucks New Innovation myStarbucks Starbucks card Mobile Application," www.scribd.com.
12. Darrel Suderman, "Coffee Innovation from Starbucks," www.fastcasual.com, October 18, 2010.
13. "Year in Review 2015: Starbucks Innovations," www.news.starbucks.com, December 26, 2015.
14. Shezray Husain, Feroz Khan and Waqas Mirza, "Brewing Innovation," www.businesstoday.in, September 28, 2014.
15. Archana Venkatraman, "Starbucks Uses Cloud to Manage Innovation and Disruptive Technologies," www.computerweekly.com, October 10, 2014.
16. "What's Brewing within Starbucks' Innovation Division," www.stage-gate.com.
17. Micah Solomon, "Slow down like Starbucks: Great Customer Service Is Fast, But Never Rushed," www.forbes.com, November 1, 2014.
18. "What's Brewing at Starbucks' Innovation Division," www.ifmaworld.com, October 26, 2012.
19. Larry Dignan, "Starbucks' Digital Transformation: The Takeaways Every Enterprise Needs to Know," www.zdnet.com, November 1, 2015.
20. Nicola Watts, "5 Shots of Innovation from Starbucks," www.ogilvydo.com, November 12, 2015.
21. "11 Updates to Starbuck's Creative Ideas and Innovation," www.digitalsparkmarketing.com.
22. Rebecca Harris, "Why Starbucks Is Winning At Loyalty," www.marketingmag.ca, July 28, 2015.
23. "Starbucks Creates First-of-its-Kind Digital News Experience with The New York Times," www.news.starbucks.com, July 21, 2015.
24. Caroline McCarthy, "Future of Mobile Commerce, in a Skinny Vanilla Latte?," www.cnet.com, September 23, 2009.
25. Elena Mesropyan, "Starbucks: The Unlikely Winner in Mobile Payments," www.letstalkpayments.com, December 14, 2016.
26. Simon, "Starbucks Is Leading the Pack in Mobile Payments," www.thisisglance.com, February 28, 2017.
27. "Starbucks Details Five-Year Plan to Accelerate Profitable Growth," www.news.starbucks.com, December 4, 2014.
28. "Starbucks to Dedicate New store to Mobile Orders," www.mobilepaymentstoday.com, March 31, 2017.
29. Craig Adeyanju, "Starbucks: A Victim of its Own Innovation? (SBUX)," www.investopedia.com, January 27, 2017.
30. Kate Taylor, "A Key Innovation at Starbucks and Chipotle is Turning into a Major Problem," www.businessinsider.in, March 5, 2017.
31. "Starbucks Presents its Five-Year Plan for Strong Global Growth," www.news.starbucks.com, December 7, 2016.
32. Chelsea Stone, "Starbucks Is Expanding Its High-End Reserve brand," www.glamour.com, December 7, 2016.
33. Julia La Roche, "Starbucks' Schultz and Johnson Tell Us About the Challenges Facing the Company," https://finance.yahoo.com, March 23, 2017.

CASE 15

Sturm, Ruger & Co. and the U.S. Firearms Industry

January 2018

Christopher J. Killoy was named President and Chief Executive Officer of Sturm, Ruger & Company in May of 2017. He was tasked with establishing direction as firearm demand continued to slow following a record breaking increase in gun sales.[1] The significant spike in 2016, a presidential election year, was at least partly the result of consumer fears that a Hillary Clinton presidency would result in stronger gun regulation.[2]

Bad news and regulatory threats tend to serve as positive influences for the highly volatile U.S. gun and ammunition manufacturing industry.[3] Calls for increased gun control measures drive Americans to purchase weapons based on concerns that the federal government might further limit Second Amendment rights.[4] In addition, terrorism and high-profile mass shootings also tend to increase gun purchases, as Americans remain concerned with their personal safety, as well as the looming potential for new regulations that could ultimately restrict their personal freedoms.[5]

Given that Ruger operates in an industry characterized by random and significant swings, how can Killoy develop a strategy that will help the company both navigate and thrive in this volatile environment?

Bill Ruger: A Man with a Passion

Bill Ruger, co-founder of Sturm, Ruger & Company, Inc., had a passion for firearms that was ignited when his father gave him his first rifle on his twelfth birthday. In high school, Ruger joined the rifle team and spent much of his free time reading books on firearms and disassembling guns, just so he could learn more about how they operated. At age 22, he dropped out of college with two years remaining and accepted an offer from the United States Government to be a machine gun designer. The salary was not enough to support his family, so he left after only months on the job.

With World War II on the horizon, the U.S. Army was looking to replace its machine gun. Consequently, it published specific requirements which Ruger himself used to build a prototype. When he could not find a manufacturer that was willing to produce his design, he decided to join Auto-Ordnance Corporation, a firearms manufacturer with multiple government contracts. During Ruger's four years with the company, he learned valuable mass production manufacturing techniques and realized the importance of product innovation for stimulating demand and gaining a competitive advantage over competitors.

In 1946, Ruger left Auto-Ordnance to start The Ruger Corporation—a venture through which he hoped to accomplish three things: (1) supply parts to the firearms industry; (2) develop a hardware tool line; and (3) produce an automatic pistol. Unfortunately, this venture did not go as planned. A short three years later, the company went bankrupt. Through this failure, Ruger learned a valuable lesson that shaped the future of Sturm, Ruger & Company: when you borrow money, it is much easier to fail than if you have no debt at all.

In 1949, Ruger met firearms enthusiast Alexander Sturm, a Yale graduate from an affluent family. Together, they founded Sturm, Ruger & Company, Inc. to manufacture the automatic pistol that Ruger had intended to produce in his failed company. The company was seeded with a $50,000 investment that came from Sturm, and with Ruger's new "no borrowing" policy, the company has no long-term debt to this day.

In 1951, Sturm died of hepatitis, so Ruger went on to run the company by himself. Ruger was known for his high level of integrity and frugal mentality. Rather than splurging on fancy offices, he would pay out dividends to his shareholders because he believed that they had better uses for the cash than he had. Ruger was extremely motivated by his passion for firearms, and that passion transformed the company from its humble beginnings in 1949 to generating over $200 million in sales by the time Ruger retired in 2000.[6]

Written by Eryn Berquist, Julian Cha, Jeffrey S. Harrison, Kelsey Heady, Lindsay Kennedy, Will MacIlwaine, Bikram Saini, Natalie Schmidt, and Jason Werts at the Robins School of Business, University of Richmond.

Company Overview

Today, Sturm, Ruger & Company ("Ruger") is principally engaged in the design, manufacture, and sale of firearms to domestic customers. Since 1990, Ruger has been publicly traded on the New York Stock Exchange under the stock ticker RGR. The company operates with two distinct business segments: Firearms and Investment Castings. The Firearms segment offers products in three industry product categories: rifles, pistols, and revolvers. There are several available models within each product category, each of which varies based on caliber, finish, barrel length, and other features. Under the Investment Casting segment, the company manufactures and sells investment castings made from steel alloys and metal injection molding parts for internal use in the firearms segment, with minimal sales to outside customers. In 2016, investment castings represented merely 1% of total sales. The majority of Ruger sales are domestic, with exports accounting for only 3%. As of 2017, Ruger employed approximately 2,110 full-time employees. In addition to the full-time employees, Ruger employed roughly 320 temporary employees to supplement its workforce.[7]

Vision

From its start in 1949, Ruger has lived up to its motto of being an "arms maker for responsible citizens"[8] and has strived to achieve its vision:

"Sturm, Ruger & Co., Inc. is one of the nation's leading manufacturers of rugged, reliable firearms for the commercial sporting market. The only full-line manufacturer of American-made firearms, Ruger offers consumers over 400 variations of more than 30 product lines. For more than 60 years, Ruger has been a model of corporate and community responsibility."[9]

Consistent with its emphasis on community responsibility, many advertisements focus on the importance of being a safe gun owner, while safety messages are posted on the Ruger website. Ruger believes in and invests in educational programs emphasizing safe gun ownership and gun use, knowing that this education has the potential to save lives.[10] The company has dedicated materials and other resources to the promotion of gun safety to all gun owners, including through youth programs. Each Ruger gun is designed with safety in mind by incorporating both internal and external safety measures. Recently, Ruger partnered with Project HomeSafe to deliver gun safety materials and cable locks to inner city gun owners who may not otherwise have access to the needed gun safety materials.[11] However, these types of programs are sometimes met with skepticism. As Ruger has stated in its Ruger Red Book—Firearms Ownership in America—Our Responsibility for the Future:

"Firearms safety education can and has demonstrably reduced needless accidents with firearms, particularly among younger persons. Yet, any suggestion of such a widespread educational program is immediately met with the response that it is actually 'promoting guns.' If we took this attitude toward sex and drug education programs, we would be accused of being naïve and immature."[12]

Management

Ruger has a very seasoned and talented top management team. Ruger's CEO, Christopher Killoy, was previously the President and Chief Operating Officer of Ruger, and has been employed by Ruger in some capacity since 2006. Killoy was also involved in the gun and ammunition manufacturing field before joining Ruger, as the Vice President of Sales and Marketing at Smith & Wesson. Killoy offers experience to Ruger, both as a seasoned veteran in the gun and ammunition manufacturing business, and through his membership on the Board of Directors of the Sporting Arms and Ammunition Manufacturing Institute and the International Hunter Education Association Foundation. Killoy served in the United States Army Armor division.

Mark Lang has served as Ruger's Group Vice President since February 18, 2008. He arrived with considerable business experience, having previously served as the President of the Custom Products Division for Mueller Industries, as well as a manufacturing executive with Thomas & Betts, Black & Decker, and General Electric.

Thomas Dineen has a longstanding history with the company, joining Ruger in 1997 as a Manager of Corporate Accounting. He worked as an Assistant Controller from 2001 to 2003 before being promoted to Treasurer and CFO in 2003. Dineen was promoted to Vice President and CFO on May 24, 2006.

Thomas Sullivan was hired as the Vice President of Newport and Mayodan Operations and Pine Tree Castings on August 14, 2006, after previously serving as the Manufacturing Executive at IMI Norgren, Rexnord, and TRW Automotive. Sullivan brings extensive knowledge of supply chain operations, manufacturing, and product development to Ruger. He has demonstrated a continued dedication to education as a student and teacher of the Toyota Production System for the last fifteen years.

Kevin Reid started with Ruger in July 2001 as Assistant General Counsel. From there he was promoted to Director of Marketing in June of 2007. As the Director of Marketing, Reid not only oversaw daily marketing activities, but he also successfully led two highly anticipated product launches. On April 23, 2008 the Board of Directors elected Reid to serve in his current position of Vice President and General Counsel. Reid served in the United States Marine Corps from 1980–1984.

Shawn Leska has a longstanding history with Ruger, starting with the company in 1989 as an Accounting Office Assistant. He climbed the ranks of the organization and was promoted to Director of Sales in November of 2011. As Director of Sales he worked through several new product launches and was involved in sales programs and corporate initiatives. In his twenty-nine years with Ruger, Leska has developed strong industry relationships.[13]

Background information for the Ruger Board of Directors is included in Exhibit 1.

Exhibit 1 Sturm, Ruger & Co., Inc. Board of Directors

***C. Michael Jacobi**, Chairman*—Mr. Jacobi has served on the Board since June of 2006. He is President of Stable House 1, LLC, a private company that specializes in real estate development. Jacobi is a Certified Public Accountant and brings considerable audit experience to the Board of Directors.

***John A. Cosentino, Jr.**, Vice Chairman*—Mr. Casentino is a founding partner of the Ironwood Manufacturing Fund and has served on the Board since August 2005. He has considerable experience as a manufacturing executive and leading several private investments.

Michael O. Fifer—Mr. Fifer served as the CEO from September, 2006 to May, 2017 and has been an active member of the Board since 2006. He possesses considerable industry experience from his tenure. Fifer earned a BS in Physics from the United States Naval Academy, an MBA from Harvard Business School, and served as a submarine officer in the United States Navy.

Sandra S. Froman—Ms. Froman has been an active member of the National Rifle Association since 1992. She served as Vice President from 1998 to 2005 and as President of the NRA from 2005 to 2007. Ms. Froman has a BS in Economics from Stanford University and a JD from Harvard Law School. She currently practices as a private civil attorney for her own firm.

Terrence G. O'Connor—Mr. O'Connor joined the Board with considerable financial and audit experience. He currently serves on the Nominating and Corporate Governance Committee and helps drive strategy for Ruger as a member of the Risk Oversight Committee. He received a Mechanical Engineering degree from the Imperial College in London.

Amir P. Rosenthal—Mr. Rosenthal has been on the Board since 2010. He was Chief Financial Officer of Performance Sports Group, LTD. for seven years and is a current Director at Ruger.

Ronald C. Whitaker—Mr. Whitaker has served on the Board since 2006. He retired from Hyco International after serving as the organization's CEO from 2003 to 2011.

Phillip C. Widman—Mr. Widman is a current director at Ruger and has served on the Board since January of 2010. His experience includes years of financial roles, CFO of Philip Service Corporation, and work as an independent consultant.

Source: Sturm, Ruger & Company, Inc. Board of directors & corporate officers. http://ruger.com/corporate/BOD.html. Accessed November 30, 2017

Operations

Sturm, Ruger & Co. is headquartered in Southport, Connecticut, and maintains manufacturing facilities in Newport (New Hampshire), Prescott (Arizona), Mayodan (North Carolina), and Earth City, Missouri. The Newport facility is the largest, at 350,000 square feet, and is the only facility that manufactures both firearms and castings. The Prescott and Mayodan facilities sit at 230,000 and 220,000 square feet respectively and manufacture only firearms. Finally, the Earth City facility is the smallest, with only 35,000 square feet, and manufactures only castings.[14]

Historically speaking, new product introductions do not tend to cannibalize demand for existing products in this industry. Often, with the launch of a new product, the demand for mature products tends to grow as well. As a result, machines are not freed up and additional manufacturing space is ultimately required.[15] Consequently, with the surge in sales from 2013 to 2016, several manufacturers, including Ruger, tried to increase their facilities and production capabilities to account for the industry growth. Once President Trump took office, facility expansion efforts stopped.[16]

Ruger is very strategic about its manufacturing facility locations. For a city to qualify as a potential location candidate, it must contain abundant electrical supply, good transportation, a good workforce in the community, numerous available engineers with strong manufacturing skills, and a building with space for future expansion. If these requirements are all fulfilled, Ruger then evaluates the city's crime and drug-use rates because all employees are required to pass a federal background check.[17]

Gun manufacture is similar to the manufacture of other metal products with moving parts that require precision machining and assembly.[18] A typical gun contains between 50 and 100 parts. The precision parts are made from raw steel shapes using expensive computer-controlled machining stations.[19] Third parties supply Ruger with various raw materials for its firearms and castings. These materials include things such as fabricated steel components, walnut, birch, beech, maple, and laminated lumber for rifle stocks, wax, ceramic material, metal alloys, various synthetic products, and other component parts. Given the limited supply of these raw materials in the marketplace, the purchase prices tend to fluctuate based on a number of market factors.[20] Parts are assembled and finished by hand (sometimes with elaborate metal etching or other design work), and weapons are individually test-fired.[21]

Research and Development

Innovation and new products drive demand for Ruger firearms. Bill Ruger was a big proponent of innovation and made it a priority for his company. While he was CEO, he made guns that he wanted to shoot, overseeing every design detail. In 1981, he stated, "If I really personally like it, then I can be fairly sure and positive that there will be a lot of other people who feel the same way."[22] To this day, the company remains focused on R&D efforts, hiring the best engineers and dedicating 141 employees toward R&D efforts.[23] In 2016, 2015, and 2014, the Company spent approximately $8.7 million, $8.5 million, and $10.0 million, respectively, on research and development activities related to new products and to the improvement of existing products. About 30% of firearm sales are driven by new products, defined as those products having been in the market for less than two years.[24]

Marketing

Ruger is known for providing high-quality products at low prices. In the early years of the company's history, Bill Ruger recognized that the company did not have the kind of brand name that some of its competitors had, so Ruger was forced to figure out a way to produce high-quality firearms at a lower cost. That is when he implemented the precision investment casting technique, which allowed for the production of castings out of the highest strength alloys available at a reasonable cost. As a result of this technique, Ruger had the highest margins in the industry, which helped keep prices low.[25] The company still prices a number of its products modestly, such as its SR1911 Lightweight Commander Style Pistol and its LCP II, which in turn offers consumers more value at a better price.[26]

Ruger's products have excellent reputations, exemplified by the fact that the company has been given the Firearms Manufacturer of the Year award by the National Association of Sporting Goods Wholesalers for eleven straight years.[27] The company supports this reputation by advertising through a number of channels, including magazines, online advertising, and trade shows.[28] Ruger also uses promotional marketing tactics to create special relationships with its dealers. One example of this is the "Rapid Retail Rewards Program," also known as the "4R Program." This program awards points to dealers who sell Ruger guns. Those points can then be redeemed for free Ruger firearms. Thus, the program helps keep dealers satisfied while also increasing sales and gaining more exposure for Ruger products.[29]

Ruger firearms are primarily sold through a network of federally licensed, independent wholesale distributors who purchase the products directly from Ruger and then resell them to federally licensed, independent retail firearms dealers. Each distributor carries the entire line of firearms manufactured by Ruger for the commercial market. Currently, 18 distributors service the domestic commercial market, with an additional 23 distributors servicing the domestic law enforcement market, and 41 distributors servicing the export market. In 2016, Ruger's 4 largest distributors accounted for 65% of total sales: Davidson's (19%); Lipsey's (17%); Jerry's/Ellett Brothers (15%); and Sports South (14%).[30]

Civilians purchase firearms through gun stores, sporting goods stores, individual sellers, and some large retail stores. Ruger's website is also an important avenue through which customers can familiarize themselves with guns, although regulations restrict how individuals can purchase firearms online. An individual can buy a gun online from a federal firearms license holder. The license holder then ships the gun to a licensed dealer, and the consumer has to go directly to the dealer for a background check before picking up the gun.[31]

Ruger performs a semi-monthly review of the estimated sell-through from the independent distributors to retailers, as well as of the inventory levels in its warehouses and in the warehouses of its independent distributors. These reviews allow the company to better plan production levels and appropriately manage inventory levels. Computer systems are used for the extensive documentation required to track each individual gun.[32] Ruger aims to turn its inventory six to eight times per year. Despite a tough second quarter in 2017, Ruger was still able to turn inventory five and a half times.[33]

Human Resources

Ruger's training programs for employees vary depending on the type of employment. In 2011, the company implemented the Ruger Code of Ethics, which provides the Board, management, and employees with the necessary tools needed to comply with industry standards.[34] Additionally, the Code helps create a workplace that promotes accountability among its employees and ensures that Ruger is holding itself accountable to its customers.[35] The company's employees participate in a profit sharing plan and bonuses are awarded to employees based on the company's financial success.[36] The company actively recruits individuals via the employment page on its website and continuously posts new openings available in each of the company's facilities.[37]

Financial Condition

Over the last five years, overall revenue for Ruger has been choppy.[38] For example, revenue decreased in 2015 to $551 million dollars, followed by a subsequent increase to $664 million dollars in 2016.[39] Total current assets have been steadily increasing over the past five years, while total current liabilities have remained relatively constant.[40] Ruger's cash and short-term investments have experienced a major increase in the last three years, increasing from a little less than $9 million in 2014 to $87 million in 2016.[41] Ruger's Q3 2017 financial results indicate that the company is not meeting Wall Street expectations for its earnings per share and sales.[42] Ruger's operating profit margin in 2016 was 20.4%.[43] Exhibits 2 and 3 contain detailed financial information.

Exhibit 2 Sturm, Ruger & Company Income Statements

Consolidated Statements of Income and Comprehensive Income *(In thousands, except per share data)*			
Year ended December 31,	**2016**	**2015**	**2014**
Net firearms sales	$658,433	$544,850	$542,267
Net castings sales	5,895	6,244	2,207
Total net sales	664,328	551,094	544,474
Cost of products sold	444,774	378,934	375,300
Gross profit	219,554	172,160	169,174
Operating Expenses:			
Selling	56,146	49,864	44,550
General and administrative	29,004	27,864	28,899
Defined benefit pension plans settlement charge	–	–	40,999
Other operating income, net	(5)	(113)	(1,612)
Total operating expenses	85,145	77,615	112,836
Operating income	134,409	94,545	56,338
Other income:			
Royalty income	1,142	1,084	468
Interest income	14	5	2
Interest expense	(186)	(156)	(152)
Other income (expense), net	542	622	584
Total other income, net	1,512	1,555	902
Income before income taxes	135,921	96,100	57,240
Income taxes	48,449	33,974	18,612
Net income and comprehensive income	$87,472	$62,126	$ 38,628
Basic Earnings Per Share	$4.62	$3.32	$1.99
Diluted Earnings Per Share	$4.59	$3.21	$1.95
Cash Dividends Per Share	$1.73	$1.10	$1.62

Source: Sturm, Ruger & Company, Inc. 2016. ***Form 10-K.*** Southport, CT: Sturm, Ruger & Company, Inc: 52.

Exhibit 3 Sturm, Ruger & Company Balance Sheets

Consolidated Balance Sheets *(Dollars in thousands, except per share data)*		
December 31,	**2016**	**2015**
Assets		
Current Assets		
Cash and cash equivalents	$ 87,126	$ 69,225
Trade receivables, net	69,442	71,721
Gross inventories	99,417	81,278
Less LIFO reserve	(42,542)	(42,061)
Less excess and obsolescence reserve	(2,340)	(2,118)
Net inventories	54,535	37,099
Deferred income taxes	8,859	8,219
Prepaid expenses and other current assets	3,660	3,008
Total Current Assets	223,622	189,272
Property, Plant, and Equipment	331,639	308,597
Less allowances for depreciation	(227,398)	(204,777)
Net property, plant and equipment	104,241	103,820
Other assets	27,541	22,791
Total Assets	$355,404	$315,883
Liabilities and Stockholders' Equity		
Current Liabilities		
Trade accounts payable and accrued expenses	$ 48,493	$ 42,991
Product liability	1,733	642
Employee compensation and benefits	25,467	28,298
Workers' compensation	5,200	5,100
Income taxes payable	–	4,962
Total Current Liabilities	80,893	81,993
Product liability	86	102
Deferred income taxes	8,525	6,050
Contingent liabilities (Note 17)	–	–
Stockholders' Equity		
Common stock, non-voting, par value $1:		
Authorized shares – 50,000; none issued		
Common stock, par value $1:		
Authorized shares – 40,000,000		
2016 – 24,034,201 issued,		
18,688,511 outstanding		
2015 – 23,775,766 issued,		
18,713,419 outstanding	24,034	23,776
Additional paid-in capital	27,211	29,591
Retained earnings	293,400	239,098
Less: Treasury stock—at cost		
2016 – 5,345,690 shares		
2015 – 5,062,347 shares	(78,745)	(64,727)
Total Stockholders' Equity	265,900	227,738
Total Liabilities and Stockholders' Equity	$355,404	$315,883

Source: Sturm, Ruger & Company, Inc. 2016. ***Form 10-K.*** Southport, CT: Sturm, Ruger & Company, Inc: 50–51.

The U.S. Gun and Ammunition Industry

The U.S. gun and ammunition manufacturing industry has over $13 billion in annual revenues (see Exhibit 4 for other industry facts). Approximately half of that revenue is generated by the top seven domestic manufacturers, which include American Outdoor Brands, Colt, National Presto, Remington Outdoor, Vista Outdoor, Sig Sauer, and Ruger. Products include ammunition and firearms such as shotguns, rifles, revolvers, pistols, and machine guns. Demand is driven mostly by hunters, gun enthusiasts, and weapon upgrades by law enforcement.[44] Profitability is closely linked to marketing efforts made by individual companies.[45] The industry is costly to compete in due to high initial investment costs, considerable research and development costs, and high machine operation costs. Large companies benefit from purchasing economies when they acquire materials from suppliers.[46] However, small companies can effectively compete by producing premium-priced, high-quality, or decorative guns.[47] The three major market segments within the guns and ammunition manufacturing industry include civilians and law enforcement, the military, and exports.[48]

Growth in the U.S. gun industry was stagnant from 2012 to 2017. Even so, some analysts expect the industry to grow 3.5% annually from 2017 to 2022. Defense spending and increased legislation are predicted to have a major impact on the growth of the industry over the next five years.[49] However, there is so much volatility in the industry that trends are hard to predict (See Exhibit 5).

Close Rival American Outdoor Brands Corporation

In many ways, American Outdoor Brands Corporation (AOBC—FY Sales of $903 M) is Ruger's closest rival. It is a domestic gun manufacturer that sells nearly the same number of firearms as Ruger, has a similar balance in sales between handguns and long guns, and many of its weapons compete head-to-head through the same retailer channels. AOBC grew from a single firearms operating division founded in 1852 under the widely known Smith & Wesson brand to multiple operating divisions and consumer brands today. AOBC now serves as the holding company for the historic Smith & Wesson Corp., Battenfeld Technologies, Inc., and Crimson Trace Corporation, which represent firearms, manufacturing services, accessories, and electro-optics divisions. AOBC operates in two business segments: (1) Firearms (which includes the Firearms and Manufacturing Services divisions) and (2) Outdoor Products & Accessories (which includes Accessories and Electro-Optics divisions).[50] The firearms division, which accounted for roughly 95% of revenues for FY 2017, produces and sells handguns (pistols and revolvers) and long guns (rifles).[51] AOBC has added to its growth through several acquisitions in the past few years, including $211.1 million in acquisitions in 2016/2017.[52] Annual revenue increased by 25–30% each year from 2015 to 2017, and net income grew from $49.6 million in 2015 to $127.8 million in 2017.[53]

AOBC's mission is: "To leverage our employees' capabilities and experiences to design, produce, and market high-quality, innovative firearms, accessories, and outdoor products that meet the needs and desires of our consumers and professional customers while delivering a healthy financial performance." The company's vision is: "To be the leading provider of quality products for the shooting, hunting, and rugged outdoor enthusiast."

Like Ruger, AOBC has a strong emphasis on innovation. The company releases new products every few years with new features and technology. This keeps consumers excited for new opportunities to enhance their firearms collections. Following the successful launch of

Exhibit 4 Economic Impact of the Sporting Arms and Ammunition Industry in the United States

Tax Impact	Business Taxes	Excise Taxes
Federal Taxes	$3,843,285,200	$838,059,600
State Taxes	$2,695,451,100	
Total Taxes	$6,538,736,300	$838,059,600

	Direct	Supplier	Induced	Total
Jobs (FTE)	141,500	66,614	93,009	301,123
Wages	$5,847,837,400	$4,522,015,700	$4,813,571,600	$15,183,424,700
Economic Impact	$20,223,132,100	$15,525,775,600	$15,502,536,200	$51,251,443,900

Source: The Firearm Industry Trade Association, Firearms and ammunition industry economic impact report, https://www.nssf.org/government-relations/impact/, Accessed November 30, 2017.

Exhibit 5 External Influences on Gun Sales

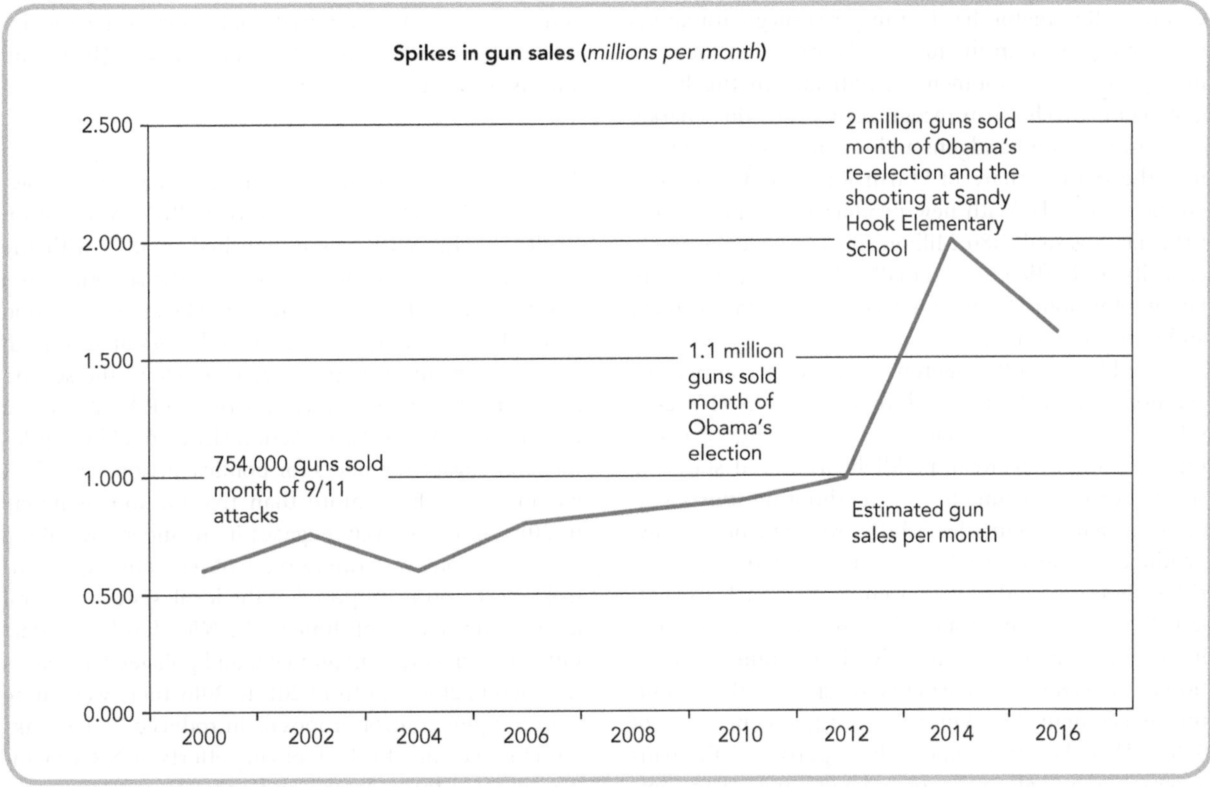

Source: Aisch, G. 2016. What happens after calls for new gun restrictions? Sales go up. ***The New York Times (Online).*** June 13. https://www.nytimes.com/interactive/2015/12/10/us/gun-sales-terrorism-obama-restrictions.html. Accessed November 30, 2017.

the M&P Shield pistol in 2012, AOBC launched the M&P 2.0 Pistol in 2017. This new product has an upgraded trigger, grip and frame from the popular M&P Pistol used by many law enforcement agencies today.[54] Their two main production plants in Springfield, Massachusetts and Houlton, Maine have sometimes become strained during high demand periods, leading to huge backlogs.[55] In May of 2014, then Smith and Wesson acquired Tri Town Precision Plastics, a previous supplier of polymer molding and prototyping for their products.[56] Once acquired, the new operating name became Deep River Plastics, LLC. The acquisition helped ease capacity problems by significantly shortening the time it took the company to get materials from Tri Town and provided an additional 150,000 square foot production facility to be used to increase production capacity.

In the U.S., five prominent arms distributors account for most of AOBC's sales. The company also sells firearms directly to law enforcement agencies. In addition, a significant portion of its firearms are sold overseas, mainly through commercial distributors.[57] In 2017, AOBC announced that it had decided to streamline and standardize its distribution process. The company plans to create a Logistics and Customer Service Division that will operate from a new 500,000 square foot distribution center in Missouri. The center will be equipped with latest technology, which will help to improve their operating efficiency by serving as a central distribution center.[58]

Other Significant Competitors

Remington Outdoor Company (2016 Sales of $865 M), founded in 1816, is the oldest firearms manufacturer in the US. The firm is well known for manufacturing rifles and shotguns, as well as ammunition. Remington is the market leader in long guns with a 15.8% market share in the domestic rifle market in 2014.[59] While the firm was not active in the handgun market for most of its existence, it entered this segment in 2010 with the R1 1911. The company believes this is an area of opportunity, as the handgun market continues to grow. Finally, Remington is a major player in the ammunition market, with three major brands under the firm's umbrella. Remington has two major strategic initiatives to sustain growth in the future. The first is to focus on new product development, specifically in the handgun segment. The firm recognizes the growing market opportunity with handguns and is committed to cutting into the market share of Sturm Ruger and American Outdoor Brands. With new product development, the firm has invested $180 Million to increase operational capacity and efficiency.[60] Finally, Remington hopes to tap into the domestic and international law enforcement and military defense markets.

In addition to Remington, a few other competitors are noteworthy. Vista Outdoor Operations (FY 2017 sales of $2.5 B) has outdoor sports (i.e., outdoor cooking equipment, eyewear, paddleboards) and shooting sports business segments.[61] Vista's shooting sports segment, which accounts for a little over half of its sales, produces firearms such as centerfire rifles, rimfire rifles, shotguns, and range systems.[62] Vista sells to civilians, law enforcement agencies, the government, and international markets.[63] Its Federal Premium ammunition brand is number one in market share in the ammunition segment. Sig Sauer, Inc. (est. recent sales of $305 M) makes and imports handguns and firearms accessories, and also sells apparel and knives. The company is the largest member of a worldwide business group of firearms manufacturers.[64]

Also, smaller competitor Colt Defense (est. recent sales of $54 M) is an American firearms manufacturer that designs, develops, and manufactures handguns, long guns, and other firearms for international military, law enforcement, and individual domestic consumers.[65] In addition, National Presto Industries (2016 sales of $342 M) is primarily a housewares and electrical appliance company. However, in 2001, the company purchased AMTEC, which allowed it to enter the defense segment. This segment "manufactures precision mechanical and electromechanical assemblies for the U.S. Government and prime contractors."[66] In addition, numerous companies compete in the U.S. with very inexpensive firearms. For example, Cobra Enterprises, based in Utah, and Hi-Point Firearms (Strassell's Machine, Inc.) manufacture handguns that can sell for less than $200.

No discussion of gun industry competition would be complete without mentioning international competitors that sell their products in the U.S. Glock is chief among these competitors in the handgun segment. Glock, Inc., based in Smyrna, Georgia, operates as a subsidiary of GLOCK Ges.m.b.H of Austria. The company has been very successful in the law enforcement and military segments in the U.S., and sells its products commercially. Other international companies with significant gun sales in the U.S. include Beretta (Italy) and Taurus International (Brazil).

The National Rifle Association

The U.S. gun and ammunition industry has a very powerful political ally in the National Rifle Association ("NRA"). The NRA was established in 1875 with the purpose to "promote and encourage rifle shooting on a scientific basis." It has since grown to be an organization focused on training, education, and marksmanship. In 1975, recognizing the great need to defend the second amendment through political action, NRA established the Institute of Legislative Action (ILA) to lobby legislators and engage members for political action. The NRA has grown to have more than five million members in 2017, and it actively engages its members by calling them to action every time a piece of restrictive "gun control" legislation is proposed at the local, state, or federal level.[67] Since its establishment, the NRA has had a great influence on American gun laws and policies. CBS News reported in 2016 that from 2011 to 2016, there were more than 100 gun control proposals introduced by lawmakers. However, due to the lobbying efforts of NRA members, none of those passed, and only a few were brought to the house and senate floor.[68] In addition, when a gun tragedy occurs, the NRA quickly releases a statement in an effort to promote pro-firearm interests.[69]

The NRA is very active during presidential campaigns, contributing to the campaigns of candidates that support expanded gun rights and targeting those who threaten to control or regulate guns.[70] In the 2016 election, the group threw its support behind President Donald Trump, and against Democratic opponent Hillary Clinton.[71] Nevertheless, its political power is greater at the state level than the federal level. It uses a "grading system" to grade each politician on their willingness to support NRA causes, and the NRA uses those "grades" to help determine the best candidate to represent the Republican party in state elections.[72]

Any firm in the industry that chooses to cross the NRA does so at its own peril. Smith & Wesson (now AOBC) learned this the hard way. Starting in 1998, cities and counties around the USA, fueled by the momentum of earlier legal suits against cigarette makers, filed suits against gun makers. Smith & Wesson was hit with lawsuits by over 28 cities, suing it for damages caused by gun violence. In response to these suits, Ed Schultz, Smith & Wesson's CEO at that time, met with the Clinton Administration, and settled on an agreement that would further regulate and control the way it manufactures firearms. As part of the agreement, Smith & Wesson agreed, amongst other things, to include a second hidden serial number on its firearms to offset the tendency for criminals to scratch out the number, to include a small lock in each gun that would prevent the trigger from being pulled, and to develop a "smart-gun technology" by 2003 that would allow handguns to be fired only by authorized users. The NRA did not like the new agreement, and sought to mobilize its members to boycott Smith & Wesson products. That same year, Smith & Wesson suffered a decrease in sales by 40%, causing it to lay off 15% of its workforce, and subsequently replacing its CEO. By 2001 things were so bad at Smith & Wesson that it was sold by its parent company, Tomkins PLC, for a mere $15 million.[73] The company then sought to, and was successful in, regaining a prominent position in the U.S. gun industry. They did so, in part, by publicly rejecting the terms of the Clinton gun safety agreement and coming up with a new line of high-capacity pistols and an assault-style rifle, the first of its kind for the company. These new products became best sellers, and the Bush administration also helped by awarding Smith & Wesson with several new federal contracts.[74]

Social and Political Forces

The gun industry in the U.S. is subject to state and federal regulations. Most federal regulations are implemented through the Bureau of Alcohol, Tobacco, Firearms, and Explosives (ATF). All manufacturers, dealers, and retailers must have a federal license in order to participate in the industry. Prospective buyers are subject to point-of-sale background checks, and those with criminal records or any other disqualifying factors are restricted from making a purchase. Some state and municipal governments have gun laws that are stricter than federal laws. Such laws may prohibit entire classes of firearms, ammunition, or ammunition magazines from being sold in the respective governing area. Gun manufacturers are also subject to state and federal laws and regulations regarding the use, storage, and disposal of hazardous materials.[75]

In today's political climate, there is a lot of talk about gun violence, gun control, and individual rights. The NRA has done well informing Americans of their Second Amendment right to bear arms. The media has done a terrific job of highlighting recent gun violence, mass shootings, and terrorist attacks to motivate Americans in two different ways. Some view these stories and desire personal protection, and are subsequently motivated to purchase a gun. Others view the same story and call for a lock-down on gun purchasing and stricter gun regulations. The media has continuously highlighted these types of stories, resulting in many Americans believing that gun violence has escalated in the U.S. In fact, gun violence dropped significantly from the 1990s to the early 2000s and has remained more or less stable since 2005.[76] On the other hand, it is still a serious problem. Data from the U.S. Centers for Disease Control and Prevention (CDC) show that on an average day, 93 Americans are killed with firearms.[77]

Two very significant pieces of legislation have influenced the U.S. gun industry. In September 1994, a Federal Assault Weapons Ban (AWB) went into effect, which prohibited the manufacture, transfer, and possession of certain assault weapons and all large capacity magazines (LCMs), but the law expired in 2004.[78] Since then, assault-style weapons and LCMs are common characteristics of guns discussed in policy debates because they are disproportionately used in mass shootings.[79] For instance, the suspect in the mass shooting at a movie theater in Aurora, Colorado, used an assault rifle with a 100-round magazine. Similar weapons were used in the mass shootings at Virginia Tech University and Fort Hood, Texas. The deadliest mass shooting by an individual in U.S. history occurred in October 2017 when the shooter used a bump-fire stock to make a semiautomatic weapon perform like a machine gun. The shooting prompted support in the U.S. Congress for legislation that would ban bump fire stocks and the National Rifle Association (NRA) supported these regulations.[80] In November 2017, Massachusetts became the first state to ban the sale, possession, or use of such devices.[81]

In October 2005, Congress passed the Protection of Lawful Commerce in Arms Act (PLCAA), which was put in place to protect firearm manufacturers from being held liable when crimes have been committed with their products.[82] The firearms industry has successfully defended numerous civil action lawsuits from gun violence victims due to this federal law. For instance, in October 2016, a Connecticut superior court judge dismissed a lawsuit filed by the families of victims of the 2012 Sandy Hook Elementary School shooting against a firearm company. However, in November 2017, families of victims appealed to the Connecticut Supreme Court, which will now decide if the families' claims can proceed. This case will be a test of the federal law, which protects firearms manufacturers from liability claims.[83] If this law is repealed or changed, then arms manufacturers may have to allocate substantial financial resources to fight and settle such claims.[84]

Moving Forward

Killoy and Ruger face significant challenges and uncertainty. Gun violence has the potential to restrict possession of guns in the U.S.; however, consumer fears of firearm bans and stricter gun control measures actually lead many consumers to purchase firearms.[85] Competition is fierce from domestic manufacturers and imports, and cheap gun manufacturers are cutting into the market share of the high-quality manufacturers. The balance of power between the typically anti-regulation Republicans and pro-regulation Democrats could change with any national election.

How can Ruger continue to compete well against its rivals, both domestic and foreign? Should the company diversify to hedge its risks? If so, into what business or businesses, and how should it enter? Should Ruger take a serious look at international expansion? If the company makes changes that will require significant resources, is it time to consider some long-term debt? Or perhaps the company should just wait a while before making changes to see what happens with regulation.

NOTES

1. Seeking Alpha. 2017. Vista Outdoor—A value play. *Seeking Alpha (Online)*. November 5. https://seekingalpha.com/article/4120735-vista-outdoor-value-play?page=1. Accessed November 30, 2017.
2. Stroebe, W. 2017. The impact of the Orlando mass shooting on fear of victimization and gun-purchasing intentions: Not what one might expect. *PLoS One (Online)*. August 11. https://doaj.org/article/e4e8d631d829456980957f3f3ced8816. Accessed November 30, 2017: 5.
3. Baldwin, G. 2016. A trader's guide to the firearms sector. *Modern Trader (Online)*. March. https://search.proquest.com/docview/1765138228?pq-origsite=summon&accountid=14731&selectids=10000008,1006323: 17.
4. *Ibid.*
5. *Ibid.*
6. Skonieczny, M. 2010. Sturm, Ruger & Co.: The Apple Inc. of the firearms industry. *Seeking Alpha (Online)*. October 7. https://seekingalpha.com/article/228895-sturm-ruger-and-company-the-apple-inc-of-the-firearms-industry. Accessed November 30, 2017.
7. Sturm, Ruger & Company, Inc. 2016. *Form 10-K*. Southport, CT: Sturm, Ruger & Company, Inc.
8. Sturm, Ruger & Company, Inc. Firearms ownership in America—Our responsibility for the future. Southport, CT: *Sturm, Ruger & Company, Inc. (Online)*. http://www.ruger.com/pdf/redBook.pdf: 2.
9. Sturm, Ruger & Company, Inc. Firearms ownership in America—Our responsibility for the future. Southport, CT: *Sturm, Ruger & Company, Inc. (Online)*. http://www.ruger.com/pdf/redBook.pdf: 2.
10. *Ibid.*
11. Sturm, Ruger & Company, Inc. Firearms safety for responsible citizens. Southport, CT: *Sturm, Ruger & Company, Inc. (Online)*. http://www.ruger.com/pdf/blueBook.pdf. Accessed November 30, 2017: 13.
12. *Ibid*, 8.
13. Sturm, Ruger & Company, Inc. Board of directors & corporate officers. http://ruger.com/corporate/BOD.html. Accessed November 30, 2017.
14. Sturm, Ruger & Company, Inc. 2016. *Form 10-K*. Southport, CT: Sturm, Ruger & Company, Inc: 15.
15. Craver, R. 2013. Transcript offers insight into Ruger's strategy. *Winston Salem Journal (Online)*. July 14. http://www.journalnow.com/business/business_news/local/transcript-offers-insight-into-ruger-s-strategy/article_92aab68c-eb69-11e2-aef8-001a4bcf6878.html. Accessed November 26, 2017.
16. Sturm, Ruger & Co. 2017. *Form 8-K*. Southport, CT: Sturm, Ruger & Co. November 1: 9.
17. *Ibid.*
18. Hoover's. 2017. Gun & ammunition manufacturing: First research custom report. *Hoover's Inc. (Online)*. November 20. http://subscriber.hoovers.com.newman.richmond.edu:2048/H/industry360/overview.html?industryId=1200. Accessed November 30, 2017.
19. Hoover's. 2017. Gun & ammunition manufacturing: First research custom report. *Hoover's Inc. (Online)*. November 20. http://subscriber.hoovers.com.newman.richmond.edu:2048/H/industry360/overview.html?industryId=1200. Accessed November 30, 2017.
20. Sturm, Ruger & Company, Inc. 2016. *Form 10-K*. Southport, CT: Sturm, Ruger & Company, Inc: 13.
21. Hoover's. 2017. Gun & ammunition manufacturing: First research custom report. *Hoover's Inc. (Online)*. November 20. http://subscriber.hoovers.com.newman.richmond.edu:2048/H/industry360/overview.html?industryId=1200. Accessed November 30, 2017.
22. Skonieczny, M. 2010. Sturm, Ruger & Co.: The Apple Inc. of the firearms industry. *Seeking Alpha (Online)*. October 7. https://seekingalpha.com/article/228895-sturm-ruger-and-company-the-apple-inc-of-the-firearms-industry. Accessed November 30, 2017.
23. Sturm, Ruger & Company, Inc. 2016. *Form 10-K*. Southport, CT: Sturm, Ruger & Company, Inc: 8.
24. Sturm, Ruger & Company, Inc. 2017. *Form 8-K*. Southport, CT:, Sturm, Ruger & Company, Inc. October 31: 3.
25. Skonieczny, M. 2010. Sturm, Ruger & Co.: The Apple Inc. of the firearms industry. *Seeking Alpha (Online)*. October 7. https://seekingalpha.com/article/228895-sturm-ruger-and-company-the-apple-inc-of-the-firearms-industry.
26. Strategic Defence Intelligence. 2016. Sturm, Ruger, & Company, Inc. *Strategic Defense Intelligence (Online)*. December 20. https://search.proquest.com/docview/1850338596?pq-origsite=summon&accountid=14731. Accessed November 30, 2017: 31–32.
27. Sturm, Ruger & Co. 2017. *Form 8-K*. Southport, CT: Sturm, Ruger & Co. November 1: 4.
28. Sturm, Ruger & Company, Inc. 2017. Sturm, Ruger & Company, Inc. announces executive appointments. June 1. http://www.ruger.com/news/2017-06-01.html. Accessed November 30, 2017.
29. Autry, J. 2012. Ruger's rapid retail rewards program returns. *Shooting Industry (Online)*. September. http://fmgpublications.ipaperus.com/FMGPublications/ShootingIndustry/Sep2012/?page=24. Accessed November 30, 2017: 24.
30. Sturm, Ruger & Company, Inc. 2016. *Form 10-K*. Southport, CT: Sturm, Ruger & Company, Inc:

31. Plumer, B. 2013. Just how easy is it to buy a gun over the internet? *Wahington Post (Online)*. August 5. https://www.washingtonpost.com/news/wonk/wp/2013/08/05/is-it-really-so-easy-to-buy-a-gun-over-the-internet/?utm_term=.b39c5abe0ede. Accessed November 30, 2017.
32. Seeking Alpha. 2017. Q3 2017 earnings results. https://seekingalpha.com/article/4119201-sturm-ruger-and-company-inc-rgr-ceo-chris-killoy-q3-2017-results-earnings-call-transcript?page=. Accessed November 28, 2017.
33. Sturm, Ruger & Co. 2017. *Form 8-K*. Southport, CT: Sturm, Ruger & Co. August 3.
34. Sturm, Ruger & Company, Inc. 2011. Code of business conduct and ethics. *Sturm, Ruger & Company, Inc. (Online)*. http://ruger.com/corporate/PDF/CGD-Code_of_Ethics.pdf. Accessed November 30, 2017.
35. *Ibid.*
36. Sturm, Ruger & Company, Inc. 2013. Exciting employment opportunities at Ruger. March 6. http://www.ruger.com/news/2013-03-06a.html. Accessed on November 30, 2017.
37. Sturm, Ruger & Company, Inc. Employment. http://www.ruger.com/footer/employment.html. Accessed on November 30, 2017.
38. Sturm, Ruger & Company, Inc. 2016. *Form 10-K*. Southport, CT: Sturm, Ruger & Company, Inc: 52.
39. *Ibid.*
40. *Ibid*, 50.
41. *Ibid.*
42. Maks, F. 2017. Ruger's weak results foreshadow American outdoor brands losses? *Seeking Alpha (Online)*. November 3. https://seekingalpha.com/article/4120446-rugers-weak-results-foreshadow-american-outdoor-brands-losses. Accessed on November 30, 2017.
43. CFRA. 2017. Sturm, Ruger & Company, Inc. *CFRA Equity Research Quantitative Stock Report (Online)* November 24. Accessed November 30.
44. Longo, D. 2017. Guns & ammunition manufacturing in the US. *IBISWorld Industry Report (Online)*. June. http://clients1.ibisworld.com/reports/us/industry/default.aspx?entid=662. Accessed November 30, 2017.
45. Hoover's. 2017. Gun & ammunition manufacturing: First research custom report. *Hoover's Inc. (Online)*. November 20. http://subscriber.hoovers.com.newman.richmond.edu:2048/H/industry360/overview.html?industryId=1200. Accessed November 30, 2017.
46. Longo, D. 2017. Guns & ammunition manufacturing in the US. *IBISWorld Industry Report (Online)*. June. http://clients1.ibisworld.com/reports/us/industry/default.aspx?entid=662. Accessed November 30, 2017: 24–25.
47. Hoover's. 2017. Gun & ammunition manufacturing: First research custom report. *Hoover's Inc. (Online)*. November 20. http://subscriber.hoovers.com.newman.richmond.edu:2048/H/industry360/overview.html?industryId=1200. Accessed November 30, 2017.
48. Longo, D. 2017. Guns & ammunition manufacturing in the US. *IBISWorld Industry Report (Online)*. June. http://clients1.ibisworld.com/reports/us/industry/default.aspx?entid=662. Accessed November 30, 2017: 16.
49. *Ibid.*
50. Smith & Wesson Holding Corporation. 2016. Smith & Wesson Holding Corporation Schedules Meeting of Stokeholders: Holding Corporation to be Renamed American Outdoor Brands Corporation. PR Newswire. Springfield, MA: Smith & Wesson Holding Corporation.
51. Statistica, 2017. Net Sales for American Outdoor Brands Corporation for fiscal year 2017, by product (in million U.S. dollars). https://www.statista.com/statistics/253913/net-sales-of-smithundwesson-by-product/
52. Ibid.
53. American Outdoor Brands Corporation. 2017. *American Outdoor Brands Corporation: 2017 Annual Report*. Springfield, MA: American Outdoor Brands Corporation.
54. Smith & Wesson, 2017. *History of Smith & Wesson (Online)*. http://www.smith-wesson.com/company/history. Accessed November 27, 2017.
55. *MarketLine*. 2014. Company Profile: Smith and Wesson Corporation. May 7: 6.
56. Ibid.
57. Smith and Wesson. 2014. *Smith & Wesson Holding Corporation: 2016 Annual Report*. Springfield, MA:Smith and Wesson Holding Corporation.
58. American Outdoor Brands Corporation. 2017. *American Outdoor Brands Corporation: 2017 Annual Report*. Springfield, MA: American Outdoor Brands Corporation.
59. Remington Outdoor Company, Inc. *Form 10-K*. Madison, North Carolina: Remington Outdoor Company, Inc.
60. Ibid.
61. Vista Outdoor Inc. 2016. *2016 annual report to stockholders*. Farmington, UT: Vista Outdoor Inc.: 1.
62. *Ibid*, 6.
63. *Ibid.*
64. Sig Sauer, The history of Sig Sauer, https://www.sigsauer.com/company/history/, Accessed November 30, 2017.
65. Colt Defense, LLC. 2013. *Form 10-K*. Colt Defense, LLC. December 31: 4.
66. National Presto Industries, Inc. 2017. *Form 10-K*. Eau Claire, Wisconsin: National Presto Industries, Inc.: 0, F-17.
67. National Rifle Association. 2017. A Brief History of the NRA. *NRA (Online)*. https://home.nra.org/about-the-nra/ Accessed November 27, 2017.
68. Shabad, R. 2016. *Why More Than 100 Gun Control Proposals in Congress Since 2011 Has Failed*. TV News Story. CBS News. June 20.
69. Hickey, W. 2013. This is How the Gun Industry Funnels Tens of Millions of Dollars to the NRA. *Business Insider (Online)*. Jan 16. http://www.businessinsider.com/gun-industry-funds-nra-2013-1. Accessed November 27, 2017.
70. Lee, C. G. 2012 . *Guns in American Society: An Encyclopedia of History, Politics, Culture, and the Law*. California: ABC-CLIO.
71. Reinhard, B and Ballhaus R. 2016. NRA Shows Support for Donald Trump. *Wall Street Journal*, Accessed November 27
72. Gross, T., & Spies, M. 2017. *NRA-Backed Gun Laws Have Found Success in State Legislatures Across the U.S.* Radio Interview. National Public Radio. October 5: Fresh Air Segment.
73. Dao, J. 2000. Under Legal Siege, Gun Maker Agrees To Accept Curbs. *The New York Times*. March 18: A2; Frontline PBS. 2015. *How the NRA Made an Example of Smith & Wesson*. TV Show Segment. PBS Channel; Donn, J. 2000. Battered By Reaction to Deal, Smith & Wesson Announces Layoffs. *The Associated Press*. October 19; Donn, J. 2000. Battered By Reaction to Deal, Smith & Wesson Announces Layoffs. *The Associated Press*. October 19; Wayne, L., & Butterfield, F. 2000. Gun Makers See Betrayal in Decision by Smith & Wesson. *The New York Times*. March 18; O'Conell, V., & Barrett, P. M. 2002. Smith & Wesson Retools Image as Lawsuits Falter. *The Wall Street Journal*. October 16.
74. Rudolf, J. 2012. Smith & Wesson Broke Clinton-Era Gun Safety Pledge to Boost Profits. *HuffPost (Online)*. https://www.huffingtonpost.com/2012/12/21/smith-wesson-clinton-bush-nra_n_2348503.html. Accessed November 30, 2017.
75. Hoover's. 2017. Gun & ammunition manufacturing: First research custom report. *Hoover's Inc. (Online)*. November 20. http://subscriber.hoovers.com.newman.richmond.edu:2048/H/industry360/overview.html?industryId=1200. Accessed November 30, 2017.
76. Krogstad, J. 2015. Gun homicides steady after decline in 90's: Suicide rate edges up. October 21. http://www.pewresearch.org/fact-tank/2015/10/21/gun-homicides-steady-after-decline-in-90s-suicide-rate-edges-up/. Accessed November 30, 2017.
77. "Fatal Injury Reports," Injury Prevention & Control: Data & Statistics (WISQARS), https://webappa.cdc.gov/sasweb/ncipc/mortrate.html. Accessed November 30, 2017;

78. Chu, V. S. 2013. *Federal Assault Weapon Ban- Legal issues (Online)* https://fas.org/sgp/crs/misc/R42957, Accessed November 24, 2017.
79. Fallman, M. & Aronsen, G. A 2017. *Killing machines: Half of mass shooters used high capacity magazines (Online)* http://www.motherjones.org, Accessed November 24, 2017.
80. Smith, M. J. 2017. N.R. A. supports new rules on Bump stock devices. *The New York Times.* October 5.
81. Del. V. L. 2017. *Massachusetts Bans Bump Stocks since Vegas Massacre. CNN (Online).* November 6. http://www.cnn.com/2017/11/06/us/massachusetts-bump-stock-ban/index.html. Accessed November 24, 2017.
82. Congressional record. 2005. *Protection of Lawful Commerce in Arms Act.* Public law 109–92—OCT. 26, 2005.
83. Bellon,T. 2017. Newtown Families Seek to Hold Gun Maker Accountable in Connecticut Court. *US News.* November 14.
84. American Outdoor Brands Corporation. 2017. *American Outdoor Brands Corporation: 2017 Annual Report.* Springfield, MA: American Outdoor Brands Corporation.
85. Longo, D. 2017. Guns & ammunition manufacturing in the US. *IBISWorld Industry Report (Online).* June. http://clients1.ibisworld.com/reports/us/industry/default.aspx?entid=662. Accessed November 30, 2017: 5.

CASE 16

The trivago Way—Growing Without Growing Up?

HHL Leipzig Graduate School of Management is a university-level institution and ranks among the leading international business schools. The goal of the oldest business school in German-speaking Europe is to educate effective, responsible, and entrepreneurially-minded leaders. HHL stands out for its excellent teaching, its clear research focus, its effective knowledge transfer into practice as well as its outstanding student services. According to the *Financial Times*, HHL ranks first in Germany and fifth globally for its entrepreneurship focus within the M.Sc. and EMBA programs. HHL is accredited by AACSB International. www.hhl.de

On the night of December 16, 2016, Rolf Schrömgens, trivago's CEO and managing director, gazed over the New York City skyline. Only a few hours previously, he and his co-founders had rung the stock market opening bell at NASDAQ and, thereby, realized the largest IPO of a German company in NASDAQ history.

A feeling of disbelief washed over him as he considered the incredible journey the team had taken. What had started only a decade earlier as a small, online-travel community had become the world's leading hotel meta-search engine. Each month, it linked 120 million travelers with 1.3 million hotels in 190 countries. In 2013, trivago had signed a USD 632 million deal in which travel giant Expedia acquired 61.6% of trivago's shares. Since then, the firm had continued to grow rapidly. Only two weeks prior to the IPO, trivago had released its figures for yet another record year. From 2015 to 2016, its revenue had again increased by more than 50% to EUR 754 million. Moreover, in 2016, the firm hired employee number 1,200 and the fast-paced recruitment continued.

Now, in the silence of his hotel room, Rolf's mind turned to the question that had often preoccupied him in recent months: Would trivago be able to remain the entrepreneurial, driven company he had built and loved?

He thought back to the days prior to trivago's emergence. He and his co-founders had worked for large corporations that were focused on high efficiency but functioned on the basis of bureaucratic processes and rigid routines. As such, these corporations were not open to change or innovation, and Rolf and his associates felt they were not desirable places to work. Consequently, the goal of not "becoming corporate" became a core premise for building trivago. The task had been easy when trivago was still a small start-up, but its rapid growth made preserving the firm's entrepreneurial capacity an increasingly challenging task.

Business Model

In 2016, trivago's field of business could be described as hotel-related online marketing and distribution. The firm provided a two-sided, online meta-search platform that connected travelers seeking hotel accommodations with more than 200 booking sites and 1.3 million hotels. With 1.4 billion visits and 487 million qualified referrals[1] in 2016, trivago was the largest hotel meta-search platform in the world. What differentiated trivago's business model from that of online travel agents (OTAs) was its value proposition as an independent information provider. trivago did not sell hotel rooms. Instead, it organized large amounts of hotel-related information from multiple sources to offer the optimal basis for making a booking decision. Thus, trivago helped users convert their initial interest into a clear, specific booking intention, thereby fulfilling their personal needs.

Given the large number of hotels, even in smaller cities, finding the right place to stay could be time consuming and frustrating for travelers, who generally faced an overload of information. trivago supported accommodation seekers in this regard by providing real-time transparency regarding a large set of hotels, room availability, and prices (Exhibit 1). Moreover, it reduced the number of booking sites a user had to visit before booking. All of trivago's services were free for the traveler.

OTAs faced the challenge of winning customers. A duopoly of industry giants—Expedia, Inc. (e.g., Expedia .com, TripAdvisor, eLong, Hotels.com) and The Priceline

This case was written by Sabina Pielken, Philipp Veit, and Professor Dr. Stephan Stubner, HHL Leipzig Graduate School of Management. Sabina Pielken and Philipp Veit contributed equally to this project and should be considered co-first authors.

The case is intended to be used as the basis for class discussion rather than to illustrate either the effective or ineffective handling of a management situation. Information used in this case was compiled from public sources and through primary data collection. The latter was made possible through the generous co-operation of trivago N.V.

Exhibit 1 Traveler Value Added

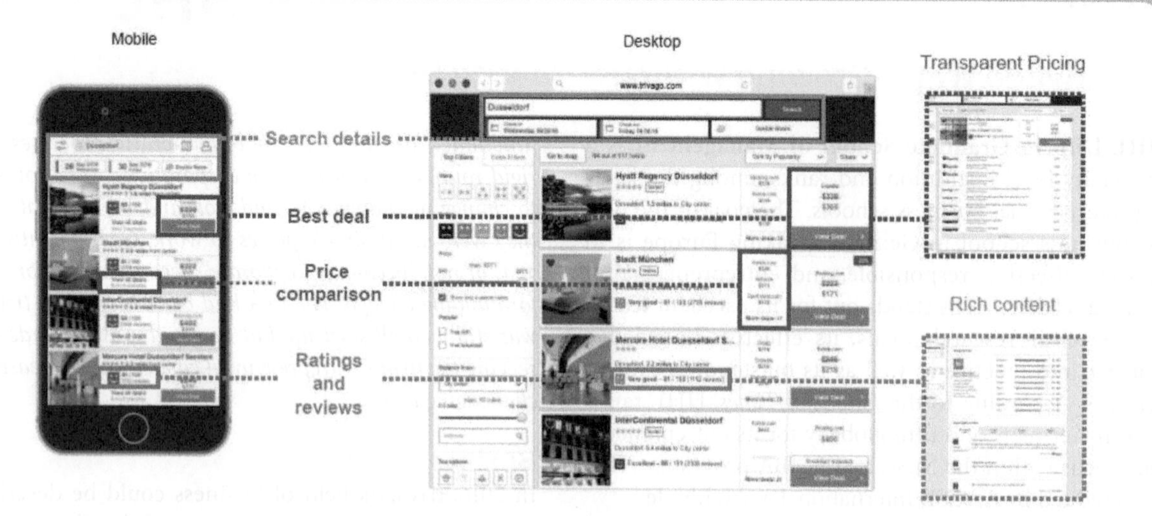

Travelers entered their desired location, room choice, date of stay, and individual preferences, such as hotel rating, family friendliness, and customer ranking. They then received a filtered and synthesized list of hotels from multiple sources ranked by price, popularity, or distance to city center. trivago further enriched this information through, for example, a distilled, easy-to-use rating review. After a hotel was selected, the accommodation seeker received an overview of all available booking providers and their corresponding prices. As such, trivago offered a one-stop method for researching hotels and initiating bookings.

Source: trivago earnings call, Q1 2017.

Group (e.g., Priceline.com, Booking.com, Agoda, Kayak) with their various sub-sites—dominated online distribution. For example, 75% of US online hotel bookings went through Expedia, Inc. in 2014, while 60% of online bookings of European hotels in 2015 went through The Priceline Group. The OTAs competed for direct bookings with each other, offline booking providers, and the hotel brands themselves (Exhibit 2). OTAs typically worked with hotels using a commission-based model and they received commissions of 15–30% of the room price.

Exhibit 2 Hotel Booking Channels—Market Shares (2015)

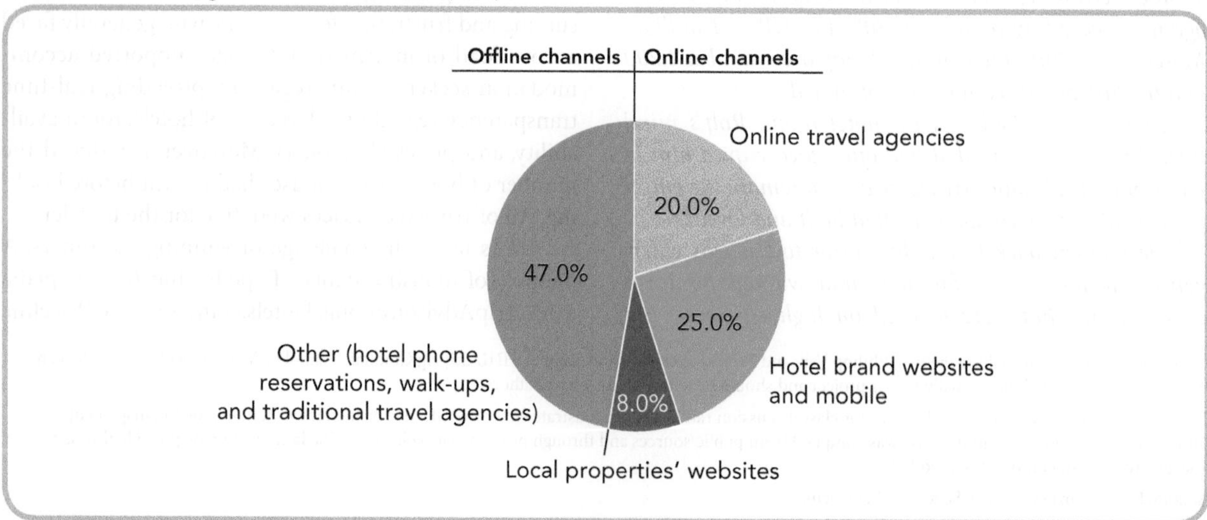

Source: Authors' illustration based on Skift (2016).

Exhibit 3 Online Advertisement Spending—The Priceline Group Versus Expedia, Inc. (USDbn)

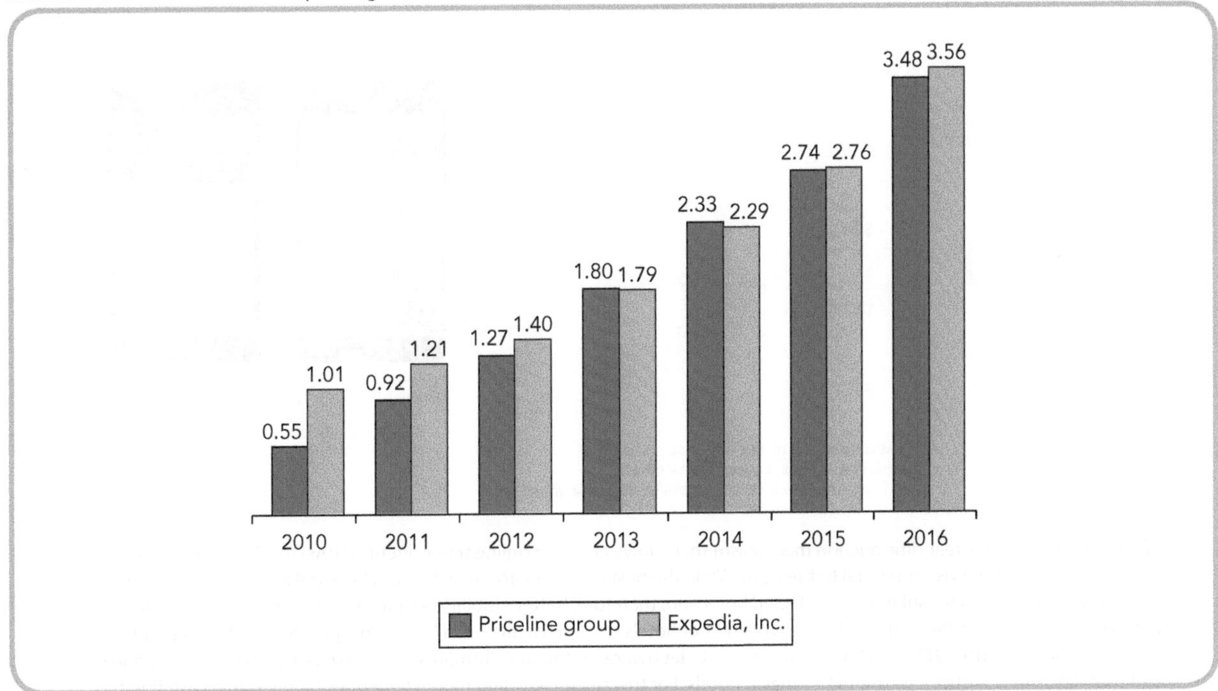

Note: Expedia, Inc. online advertisement spending estimated based on The Priceline Group's average online advertisement share multiplied by Expedia's total marketing expenditure.

Source: Online advertisement data for The Priceline Group as displayed by Statista (2017).

As the same hotel could be booked through various travel agents and platforms, OTAs invested heavily in marketing in order to be the premier access point for room distribution (Exhibit 3). trivago added value to OTAs by offering them direct customer access, as well as a performance-based measurable marketing and distribution channel (Exhibit 4). trivago monetized its business using a cost-per-click (CPC) bidding-platform (Exhibit 5) and a flat fee for managing premium features on hotel profiles.

Meta-Search Competition

trivago faced head-on competition in its own competitive environment. By 2016, hotel meta-search had

Exhibit 4 ROAS Comparison, trivago versus Online Travel Agent (OTA) (example)

A hotel in Berlin launched a marketing campaign on trivago that referred customers directly to the hotel's own booking engine. The following results were achieved, which can be compared to those of a traditional OTA-based business.

trivago		Online Travel Agent (OTA)	
Marketing budget	EUR 1,000/month	**Average OTA commission**	25% on net room price
Clicks	1,891	**Average net room price**	EUR 120/night
Bookings	71	**OTA commission**	EUR 30/night
Room nights	133	**Room nights**	133
Channel revenue	EUR 15,960	**Channel revenue**	EUR 15,960
ROAS	(EUR 15,960/EUR 1,000) = **1596%**	**ROAS**	EUR 15,960/(EUR 30*133) = **400%**

Source: Case authors based on hebsdigital (2013).

Exhibit 5 Overview of Monetization—CPC Bidding

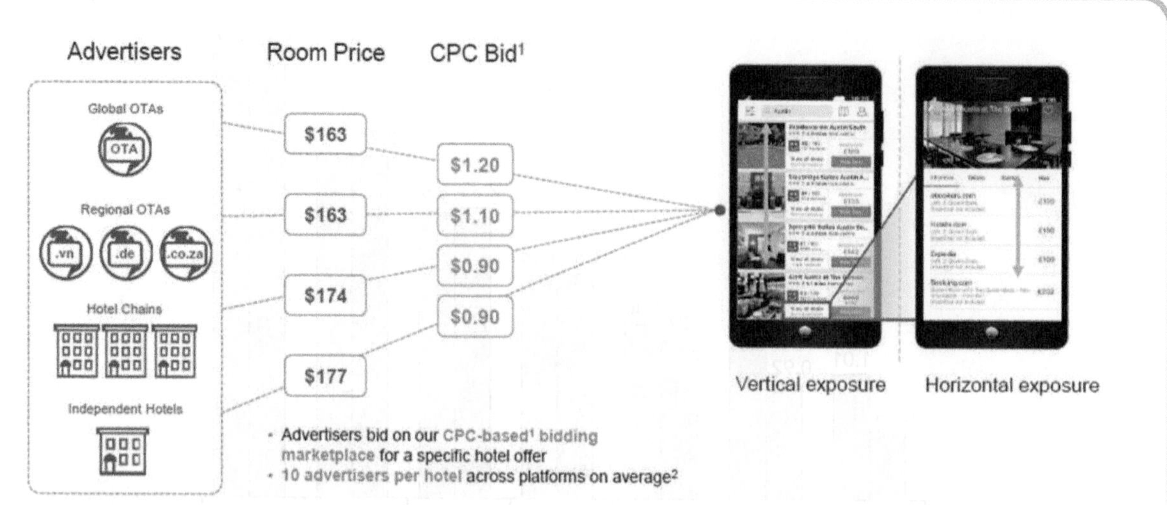

CPC bidding relies on a real-time auction mechanism that allows hotels or online travel agents (OTAs) to define a maximum pay-per-click price for a visitor referral to their site. While the best price for a room will always be listed at the top, the highest bid receives a higher page ranking for a selected hotel and, therefore, better visibility. Actual CPCs are determined by the competitive forces reflected in the willingness of OTAs or hotels to match a given bid based on a pre-defined budget and maximum bidding price. OTAs and hotels can choose to let trivago automatically manage their bids to increase convenience and usability. This is particularly useful for smaller hotels. For trivago, the bidding model generates highly stable cash flows—if a bidder drops out, sales are still guaranteed through another auction participant.

Source: trivago earnings call, Q1 2017.

become the starting point for 30% to 50% of hotel-related online searches and the area was still growing rapidly. Therefore, firms invested heavily in building brand recognition to capture market share. trivago and its major meta-search competitors, Kayak and TripAdvisor, engaged in a constant and fierce fight to serve as the "front gate" for the customer. One key driver of competition in these two-sided platform markets was found in cross-site network effects. In other words, the value generated for travelers increased with the number of hotels listed on a platform, as they therefore had more freedom of choice. On the other hand, an active presence on trivago became more attractive for hotels and OTAs, as more travelers could be reached. This influenced the share of marketing budgets committed to trivago. Consequently, for trivago and its competitors, the number of users was highly significant, as higher numbers resulted in increasing returns to scale and enhanced profitability given the sites' highly scalable infrastructure.

Thus, trivago developed in a fast-pace, competitive environment where it wanted to play the leading role. Rolf stated: "In two, three, or four years, one company in the market will dominate the top of the funnel. We want to be that player."

Starting Up: 2004–2009

The Initial Idea

In early 2004, Rolf provided the initial spark to what would become one of Germany's biggest start-up success stories of the early twenty-first century. He called Peter Vinnemeier and Stephan Stubner. These close friends had studied together and worked together as co-founders of ciao.com, a review-based evaluation platform for products and services from mobile phones to hotels. The three met for breakfast at Tresznjewski, a restaurant in the cultural heart of Munich. At that breakfast, Rolf pitched his business idea to his friends: creating a "digital Wikipedia for travel" in the form of a web-based, focused community for sharing travel experiences. The website would be monetized through a CPM[2] payment model for affiliate marketing banners, which could be placed next to the focal content ranging from personal travel guides and tips to travelogues, evaluations, and pictures. The idea was met with immediate approval, as Peter and Stephan were both strong believers in the power of user-generated content, a belief based on their experiences at ciao.com.

Rolf's proposal came during the golden era of online marketing. Advertisers were willing to pay a three-digit price per thousand advertising impressions (CPM) and many young firms were entering the online-marketing field in order to take advantage of the high returns. Driven by their entrepreneurial spirit, Rolf, Peter, and Stephan soon started working on the initial idea in a single-room office under a garage in Düsseldorf. Given their limited resources, they focused on bootstrapping their endeavor to build a great product that would enable them to at least pay the bills.

In June 2005, trivago GmbH was founded and the first beta version of trivago went live in Germany.

Team and Working Mode in the Early Years

In early 2006, Stephan left trivago and Malte Siewert, also a former fellow student, joined the firm as a co-founder. Moreover, a first business-angel funding round was completed, which also provided trivago with valuable contacts and expertise. Later that year, Rolf as CMO, Peter as CTO, and Malte as CFO started looking for employees to support them in their respective functions. Employees were usually hired as interns and were offered a permanent position after successfully completing an internship. By early 2007, the first interns had been permanently hired. At this early stage, everyone was still doing a bit of everything and the employees supported one another wherever possible.

Within a short period of time, the small trivago team managed to develop a passionate and dedicated working mode, which was highly result oriented and performance driven. All work pursued at trivago had to directly and measurably affect the business. The founders made important decisions together and although they did not always agree, each of them was committed to accepting the majority vote. In addition, decisions were based on analytics rather than on emotions. In order to pursue a project and allocate resources accordingly, the founders had to be convinced of sufficient "short-term" return potential. At the same time, early employees welcomed the positive relationships among each other and with the founders, who were always accessible and open to new ideas. The founders' unrestricted accessibility was underpinned by the fact that the door to their office was almost always open. Even though the founders expected their employees to work independently on their tasks and to equip themselves with the knowledge they needed, employees were encouraged to directly approach them whenever they needed support or assistance. The founders favored informal and constructive direct peer-to-peer-communication not only among themselves but also with and among their employees. As one of the first employees stated:

What made trivago special from the first day was the feeling of family. The founders wanted us to reach our objectives, but they also wanted us to enjoy working for trivago and being part of the team.

Finding Product-Market Fit

Success did not come easily. By the end of 2006, advertisers' satisfaction with their advertisements' performance on trivago's site was decreasing, as the advertisements generated too few direct bookings. The devil was in the details. For example, advertised hotels were often unrelated to the content on trivago's site. As advertisers were unable to find a solution, trivago developed a software algorithm to match hotel advertisements with site content. Moreover, as the different advertisements often featured the same hotels at different prices, trivago created a database that bundled the advertisements together, which allowed it to display different prices for the same product without showing double entries. This marked the birth of trivago's price-comparison feature. In addition to hotel advertisements, trivago experimented with a variety of other products (e.g., flights, holiday packages) and tried to license its software algorithm to generate additional revenue. Moreover, the company began to expand internationally. It was present in the United Kingdom, Spain, France, Sweden, Poland, and Italy by the end of 2007.

2008 was a groundbreaking year for trivago. An additional funding round, which aimed at supporting trivago's growth and internationalization, was completed. The funds backing trivago contributed additional industry expertise and network contacts. Nevertheless, trivago's revenue was declining, and the founders felt a need to reconsider their ambitions and search for ways of securing the company's liquidity. Despite the availability of funding, the founders insisted that the business needed to quickly pay for itself. In other words, subsisting on venture capital was not an option. Therefore, during a "legendary management offsite" meeting in 2008, Malte, Peter, and Rolf pondered the company's future. Rolf described the situation:

We had not yet understood that people were visiting our site for the price comparison, not because we were the "travel wiki" we aimed to be. That was when we realized we were doing too many things at the same time . . . software licensing, flights . . . We realized that if we continued like that, trivago would never amount to anything.

On the basis of the firm's strengths, the founders decided to limit their business operations to meta-search and price comparisons for hotels only. To manifest this focus, they formulated trivago's mission statement: "to be the traveler's first and independent source of information for finding the ideal hotel at the lowest rate." This mission statement was to guide all future business decisions. Three months later, trivago relaunched the entire website. Notably, by the end of 2008, the company had extended its market presence to Russia, Greece, and the Netherlands, and it had 19 employees. At the time, more than 2.5 million visitors per month were searching 225,000 hotels around the globe.

In conjunction with the mission statement's introduction, the founders intensively discussed brand-building opportunities. One important reason for doing so was to become more independent of Google and its dominant search-market position by increasing the ratio of branded traffic. The founders knew that trivago could only be travelers' primary and independent source of information if travelers considered trivago before any other source. For this purpose, trivago needed to be a recognized brand. At the time, TV spots were the medium of choice for reaching a broad audience. Convinced of the value of TV advertisement, trivago invested half of the capital it had previously collected from investors. The plan worked and trivago's advertising spots struck a chord with the German TV audience. The TV spots were a key driver of trivago's success, as reflected in the year-on-year revenue growth rate of nearly 400% from 2009 to 2010.

Growing Without Growing Up?: 2010–2016

Growth Numbers and Office Locations

In 2010, trivago took its TV presence international and aired TV campaigns in five European countries. That year, the meta-search engine could compare hotel prices from more than 100 websites. Every second person in Germany and Spain recognized the trivago brand. In fact, Spain became trivago's strongest market in 2011. Moreover, in 2011, trivago launched TV advertisements in the United States and Brazil.

The company's internationalization, marketing activities, and increasing product complexity fueled the need for more manpower. With 46 employees in 2010, trivago had already more than doubled its workforce from 2008 and, in 2011, the company welcomed employee number 100. The growing number of employees forced trivago to frequently change office locations, as capacity limits were quickly reached. Hence, in December 2011, after having changed office locations twice since its foundation, trivago moved for the third time. Its new office was located at "Bennigsen-Platz" in Düsseldorf. In terms of interior design, trivago favored open-space offices. The meeting rooms were individually designed and furnished, and often named after employees' hometowns. Relaxation areas, table-soccer games, and a climbing wall were introduced for recreation purposes, while complimentary drinks and healthy snacks were made available in trivago's shared office kitchens. In addition, gym classes were provided free of charge.

In 2012, 315 employees already called trivago their working home. External growth also remained strong and, by the end of 2012, trivago was present in 33 markets, 13 more than at the beginning of 2010. At that time, the period of significant organizational growth was topped off with Expedia, Inc. announcing that it would buy a 61.6% strategic stake in trivago, making the company the first German start-up worth more than one billion dollars. The Expedia deal did not affect trivago's appetite for growth. In the ensuing years, trivago expanded into 22 new countries across Europe, South America, Africa and Asia, adding 150 new partner websites and hotel chains to its price-comparison network. The increase in the number of hotels listed in its database from 700,000 in 2013 to more than 1 million in 2016 led to an increase in brokered hotel rooms to 1.4 billion. Even though trivago strongly insisted on a one-office policy, it opened up two innovation centers, one in Leipzig, Germany, and the other in Palma de Mallorca, Spain, in 2013. However, management insisted that new offices should only be opened if regulatory or entrepreneurial (e.g., innovations apart from the core product) interests justified it. Moreover, the new offices were kept as small as possible, as the Düsseldorf office was to always be "home" to at least 90% of trivago's employees. By 2014, trivago had become the world's leading hotel meta-search company. The trivago growth engine was further fueled by the skyrocketing employee numbers, which rose from 571 in 2013 to more than 1,200 in 2016.

The increasing number of employees soon started to challenge the "Benningsen-Platz" office's capacity. New office space was continuously added by spreading employees across multiple floors and, later, to surrounding buildings. During this time, however, the top management team was alarmed by the increasing physical distance among employees. The founders feared that it could lead to communication challenges, social detachment, and empire building, which could negatively affect day-to-day cooperation, trust building, and information exchange. Slower working and learning processes were the dreaded, potential consequences. Therefore, in early 2016, trivago announced that it had commissioned the construction of a trivago campus in Düsseldorf, where all employees would be reunited in 2018.

Workforce Characteristics

Members of trivago's workforce shared many characteristics from the beginning. For example, most of the employees were young, and they came from diverse cultural and educational backgrounds. The hiring of international talents was seen as particularly advantageous. As one employee outlined:

We always looked to recruit talented people from around the world who are still in the early stages of their careers and reflective. We need pragmatic people with an agile mindset and a willingness to continue learning.

The fact that these employees were willing to leave their home countries and move to Düsseldorf implied that they were adventurous, willing to take risks, and able to adapt to a new environment. Moreover, as many new employees were new to Düsseldorf without social contacts outside the firm, employees often quickly developed friendships, which contributed to trivago's team spirit. These features were all greatly appreciated in the entrepreneurial environment of trivago. In contrast, more experienced employees who had been socialized in corporations were often seen as difficult to integrate, as they were frequently already shaped by firm cultures that promoted rigidity, less openness to new ideas, and strong career aspirations.

Despite trivago's established practice of hiring young professionals who did not have extensive experience with other companies and the fact that the company generally wanted to promote internally, hiring some experienced personnel was unavoidable from a skills perspective. Certain external hires were seen as vital, as trivago's size required increasingly advanced management and leadership capabilities. Moreover, these professionals were expected to be able to bring in new managerial impulses for professionalizing the organization without making trivago "corporate" in its working style. In 2015, the top management team was expanded beyond the group of founders. Andrej Lehnert and Johannes Thomas were promoted from within trivago to become managing directors. Both had been with trivago since 2011. Moreover, Axel Hefer left the German online furniture retailer Home 24 AG, where he had served as COO and CFO, to join trivago in 2016. Like the three founders, Axel had studied at HHL Leipzig Graduate School of Management. Initially, Axel led the Country Development department, but he was soon promoted to the top management team.

By the end of 2016, the top management team's competencies were distributed as follows: Axel was CFO and the managing director for finance, legal and international; Andrej was the managing director for marketing and business intelligence; Johannes was the managing director for advertiser relations, business operations, and strategy; Malte was the managing director for trivago's marketplace-related business; Peter was the managing director for technology; and Rolf was CEO, and responsible for products, people, and culture.

Organizational Structure

In 2010, departments and teams began to evolve on an as-needed basis. While departments were expected to function with a high degree of freedom, an increasingly specialized range of tasks required more cross-team coordination. Compared to the early years in which each employee covered a broad range of issues, job profiles became particularized and, therefore, changed significantly. Hierarchies and clearer responsibilities began to emerge within each department and team. In terms of leadership structure, the chain at trivago was basically as follows: managing directors were responsible for department leads, department leads were responsible for their team leads, and team leads were responsible for their team members. Moreover, a basic matrix structure evolved in which country-development teams were supported by functional teams active in, for example, marketing, technology, finance, and HR.

However, the founders were wary of formal management and control structures, which they felt could limit subsidiarity and compromise decision speed across the organization. They feared that increasingly specialized tasks could lead to silo-based thinking, and that evolving hierarchical structures could give rise to status asymmetries in which individuals perceived discrimination in the supply of information and the degree of decision autonomy depending on their hierarchical status. To counter the emergence of such asymmetries, the founders tried to nurture an "absence of ego" mentality. They believed that such a mentality was vital for the success of a knowledge-driven business in which the accessibility and flow of information and data formed the basis of competitiveness. One step towards an "absence of ego" mentality was the founders' official announcement that trivago would remain a company without job titles. As one employee explained:

At trivago, it is important to respect others' knowledge and inspiration, not their titles. Decision processes should not be slowed down because an individual feels a need to get approval from various levels. Instead, the individual should be empowered to make his or her own decisions and work independently.

The official statement from top management seemed necessary, as employees had started to create titles on their own. One employee described this period: "It was a bit weird . . . We had interns calling themselves 'Senior Vice-President,' while their team leads did not have titles themselves." The employees' reaction to the abolishment of titles took the form of a series of questions: "If we do not have titles, how do I emphasize the expectations linked to my position?", "How am I supposed to lead?" and "How am I supposed to be led?"

To strike a balance between the title-free environment and the clear role expectations, a self-developed categorization pattern called "Responsibility Scope" was introduced in the early 2010s. This scope was expressed in a three-stage system: developers, executors, and supporters. Supporters were expected to be temporary, topic-specific project leaders whose work was guided by daily or multiple meetings during the week. Executors were to take on managerial responsibility for their own divisions, and their work focused on goals and their attainment. trivago considered the role expectations for supporters and executors as similarly to be found in other companies, while it viewed the developer role as more unique. Developers were expected to act as entrepreneurs within the company, resulting in small and fast "firms-within-the-firm" with the aim of keeping trivago adaptable. Rolf explained:

Developers are expected to be independent players inside the organization who think of the company as their own. They are granted entrepreneurial freedom, they are motivated, and they are led by inspiration and only sporadic meetings. Developers need to be self-reflective to such a point that they abandon their position if it is no longer meaningful to the company.

Company Values and Purpose

After surpassing 150 employees in 2012, trivago's management started to sense growing anonymity. It became increasingly difficult to remember everyone's name and personal communication became more complex. This development alarmed the founders, as it could dilute the highly cherished start-up spirit. In 2013, therefore, the company hired a dedicated employee to take over the function of "Strategy & Organization," which had formerly been handled by Rolf. The department's purpose was to ensure that trivago would not be driven by bureaucracy or politics. The newcomer's first task was to create a formalized description of the values inherent in trivago's culture. For this purpose, in-depth interviews were conducted with trivago employees, especially those hired in the early days. Furthermore, employees were asked to participate in a company survey and describe what trivago meant to them. The survey and interview results were aggregated and then discussed in an open meeting with interested developers. This enabled the identification and formulation of six core values: trust, authenticity, entrepreneurial passion, power of proof, unwavering focus, and fanatic learning (Exhibit 6). Employees who had been with trivago since the early days did not view these values as something new. Instead, the core-value list was a written representation of what had been always felt and lived at trivago. To stress the overall importance of trivago's values and foster their internalization, they were prominently communicated both within and outside the firm. In addition to displaying the values on office walls and on the website, the values were discussed with all employees holding leadership responsibility, as trivago believed that living the values was only possible if these employees served as role models in this regard.

In 2016, trivago introduced its purpose statement: "empower to get more out of life." This message was designed to emphasize the feeling that each trivago employee and the company as a whole should strive for and to clarify the company's purpose. When reflecting on the purpose statement, Rolf stated:

We put a lot of thought into the development of that statement. In essence, 'empower' means creating a basis from which an individual can be successful—a basis from which he or she can get more out of life. "To get more out of life" represents personal learning and growth. It is an individualistic, non-competitive approach that focuses on continuous personal development. This purpose also represents the founding team's motivation for establishing trivago—freedom and personal development.

Management Style and Planning

Instead of resting on their laurels after the Expedia deal in March 2013, the founders were still driven to continually improve trivago as a product and as a company. Every employee would soon know their mantra: "never great, never wise, never done." Expedia had contractually agreed

Exhibit 6 trivago's Core Values

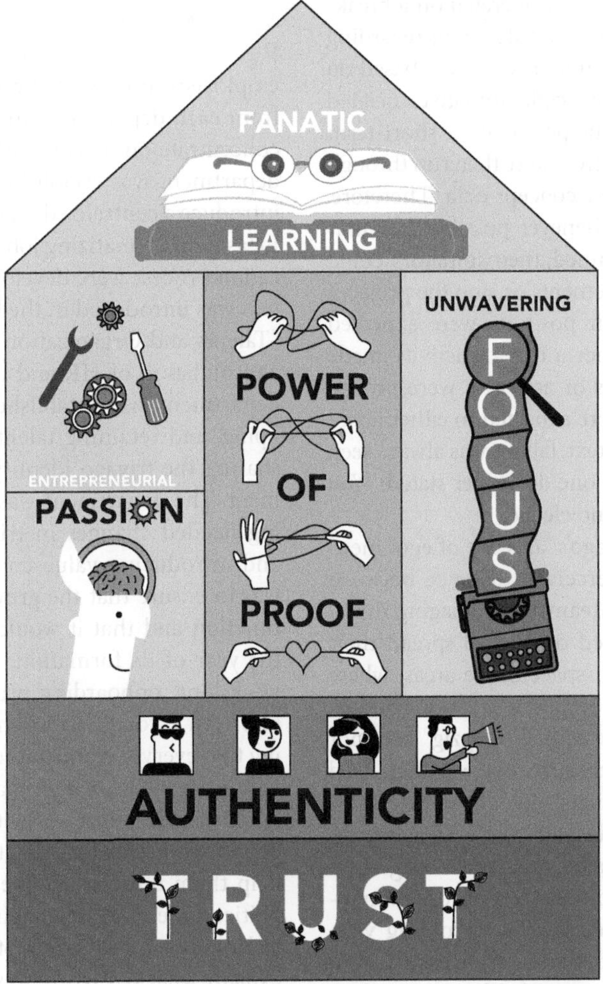

- Trust: We want to build an environment in which mutual trust can develop that gives employees the confidence to discuss matters openly and act freely.
- Authenticity: We aim to be authentic and appreciate constructive and straight feedback.
- Entrepreneurial passion: We believe that entrepreneurial passion drives us forward to continuously try out new and improved ways of thinking and doing.
- Power of proof: We believe that data, used correctly, can lead to empirical, proof-based decisionmaking across the organization.
- Focus: We focus our energy on our mission of being the traveler's first and independent source of information for finding the ideal hotel at the lowest rate. This mission drives where we spend our time and focus. We believe that multiple small, incremental improvements toward this goal add up to long-term success.
- Learning: We never stand still and choose to remain open minded and inquisitive. We try new ideas and continue to challenge received wisdom.

Source: Image—trivago (2017), text—trivago IPO prospectus (2016).

to a hands-off approach, which was an important requirement for the founders. Therefore, trivago continued to operate independently and its founders remained in place.

trivago continued to finance its expansion solely through its own profits, such that it operated on a break-even basis. As in the early trivago days, decisions regarding investments in new initiatives and growth were based on an analytical trial-and-error principle: initiatives needed to be analytically sound and the potential for short-term revenue had to be visible. Initiatives were then run through a test phase to obtain proof-of-concept data. Therefore, decisions were data-driven whenever possible. If initiatives did not work out as planned, their initiators could either make justifiable improvements or stop the projects. Employees, regardless of their position, were expected to constantly challenge whether a task or activity made sense. Whenever certain tasks or activities were proven to add no value, employees were expected to either adapt or terminate them. In this context, failure was always seen as an opportunity to learn. As one developer stated: "You need to be willing to pay for knowledge."

In 2015, to emphasize trivago's "absence of ego" mentality and to decrease the perceived distance between employees and the managing team, the managing directors moved out of their shared office and spread their work stations across the open-space office areas, where they could mingle with their respective teams. The former management office room, named "Leipzig" in honor of the place where the founders first met, was then used for weekly management meetings.

In 2015, trivago also introduced a yearly Management Workshop and a Strategy Summit. During the Management Workshop, managing directors developed the company's overall strategic priorities for the upcoming year. Those priorities were then presented and discussed in a subsequent Strategy Summit attended by the developers. Generally, these strategic priorities were expected to support trivago's mission as formulated in 2008 and to be compatible with trivago's core values. Moreover, based on a critical review of the previous year, they included ideas for adjustments necessary to achieve the mission. Finally, strategic priorities were to be viewed as guiding lights rather than fixed goals. Eventually, the tasks related to these strategic priorities were not delegated from top-down. Instead, the teams developed their own missions and strategic priorities based on the overall strategic guiding lights, trivago's mission statement, and trivago's values. As Rolf stated: "At trivago, we emphasize the need to convince, not command, people. Therefore, we do not enforce strategic initiatives from the top down." This need to convince instead of command was also reflected in how meetings were conducted. Employees were granted freedom to only attend meetings if they individually perceived them as value-adding.

Systems and Processes

Recruiting. The need to increase the number of employees amplified the recruitment efforts required from each department. In order to let each department concentrate on its core tasks, a Human Resources (HR) department was established in early 2010. HR began to introduce a centralized recruiting process that same year. Ideas for systematizing job advertisements and the application process were developed by HR in 2011, and a system was introduced in the following year. In 2014, a joint "Talents and Organization" (TO) team, the result of the consolidation of HR and the "Strategy & Organization" department, was established to focus recruiting, developing, and retaining talent, as well as the best ways of sharing the trivago identity in a rapid-growth environment. The department was also charged with anticipating needed changes in trivago's organizational design and introducing value-conforming measures. The aim was to ensure that the growing organization would still function and that it would not "become corporate." In the year of its formation, TO introduced a structured, week-long, onboarding process. On their first day, new hires ran through an extensive process aimed at ensuring that everyone understood the trivago values and why they were vital for the organization. The new hires also familiarized themselves with the challenges of different departments through practical case studies designed to help them understand the various roles and responsibilities. One of the managing directors took the time to welcome each new group of employees and to personally explain what trivago represented. TO also introduced a structured offboarding process aiming at understanding why employees left the company and where improvements could be made.

In 2014, more than 260 people were hired, while the number of applications exceeded 45,000. While trivago had no rigid recruitment criteria, cultural fit with the company was key, especially as the need for experienced hires with specialized functional expertise increased with continuing professionalization. As one developer stated:

If you are someone who needs clear direction—for this problem I go to "A" and for another problem I go to "B," you will not be happy here. Here at trivago, you always need to find new approaches and figure out who can help you yourself. Also, we do not have a hierarchy of communication—you can approach anyone who might be of help.

Therefore, the right traits, which were labelled as "trivago skills" (e.g., intrinsic motivation, positivity, trust in others) and "universal skills" (e.g., taking ownership, welcoming of change, determination) were viewed as crucial for trivago employees.

Performance Evaluations, Rewards, and Employee Development. Given the continued growth in employee numbers and departments, trivago introduced additional measures to reduce the risk of status asymmetries and strengthen the entrepreneurial core. In 2012, HR introduced a customized 360-degree feedback tool. Initially an Excel document, the tool developed over the years into a professional in-house peer-evaluation software that was constantly adapted. As of 2014, the "trivago 360" reflected the six trivago values and the universal skills, which served as the basis for evaluations of employees' individual job performance (Exhibit 7). Twice each year, every employee had to be provided with feedback by the person to whom he or she reported. The content of that feedback was based on input from the employee's direct peers.

Exhibit 7 360-degree Feedback Criteria

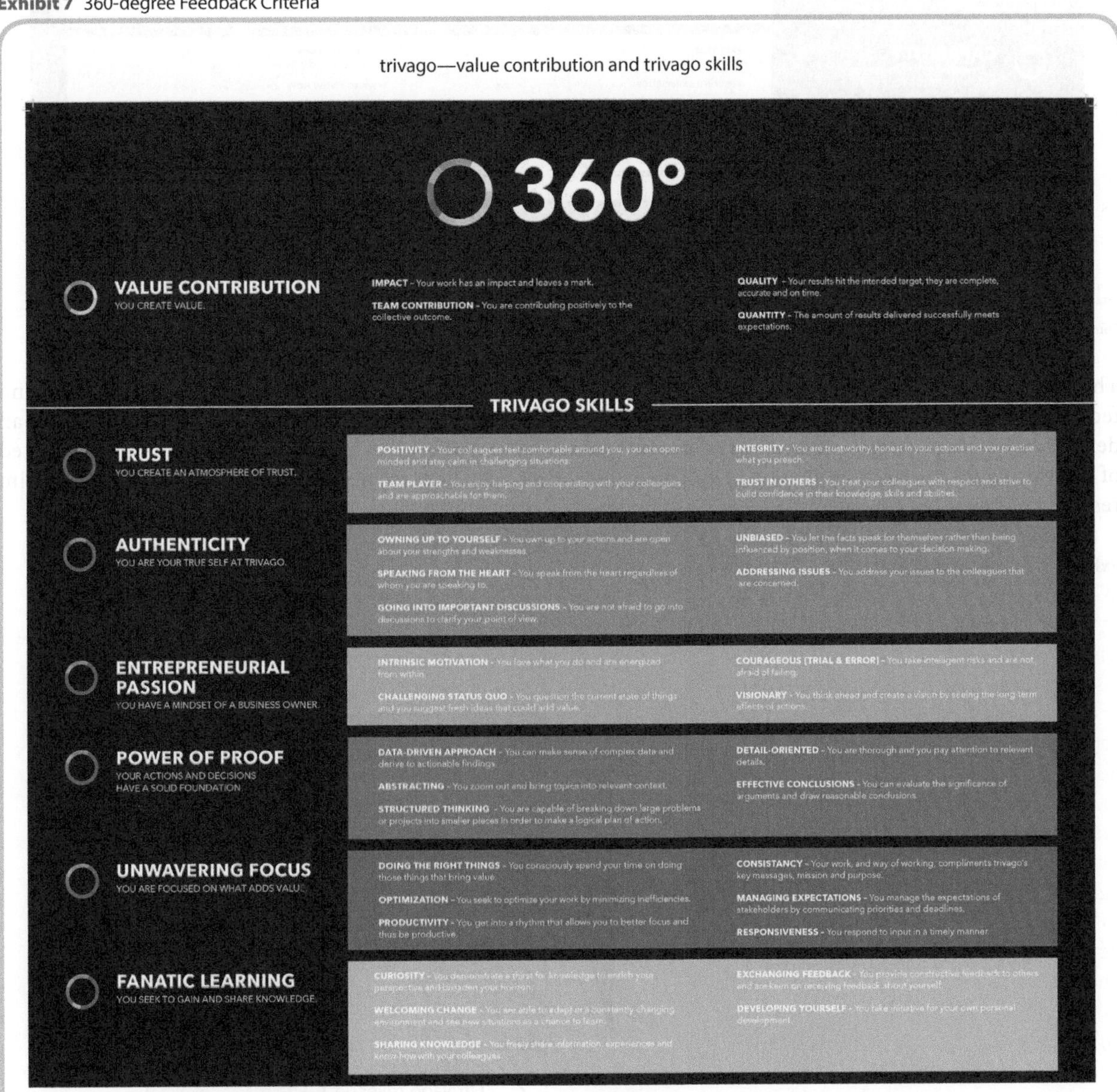

continued

Exhibit 7 360-degree Feedback Criteria (*continued*)

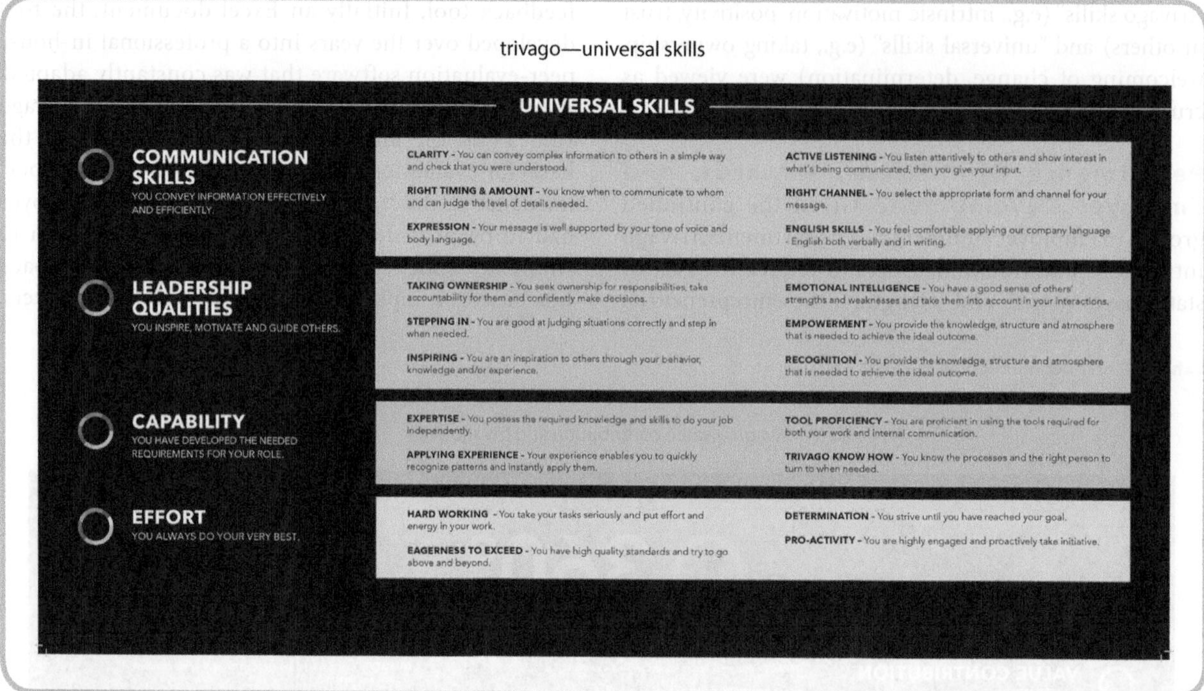

Source: trivago (2017); the original trivago 360-degree feedback poster has been graphically adapted for the sake of readability.

The aim in this regard was to enable a fair, unbiased feedback process and to reduce employees' dependence on the people to whom they reported. Instead of appearing as superiors, employees with leadership responsibility were encouraged to function as mentors.

Prior to the introduction of the "trivago 360" tool, no mandatory, standardized feedback mode existed. If an employee received feedback, it usually solely reflected the evaluation of the person responsible for him or her.

Exhibit 8 Online Hotel Market—KPIs, Size, and Potential

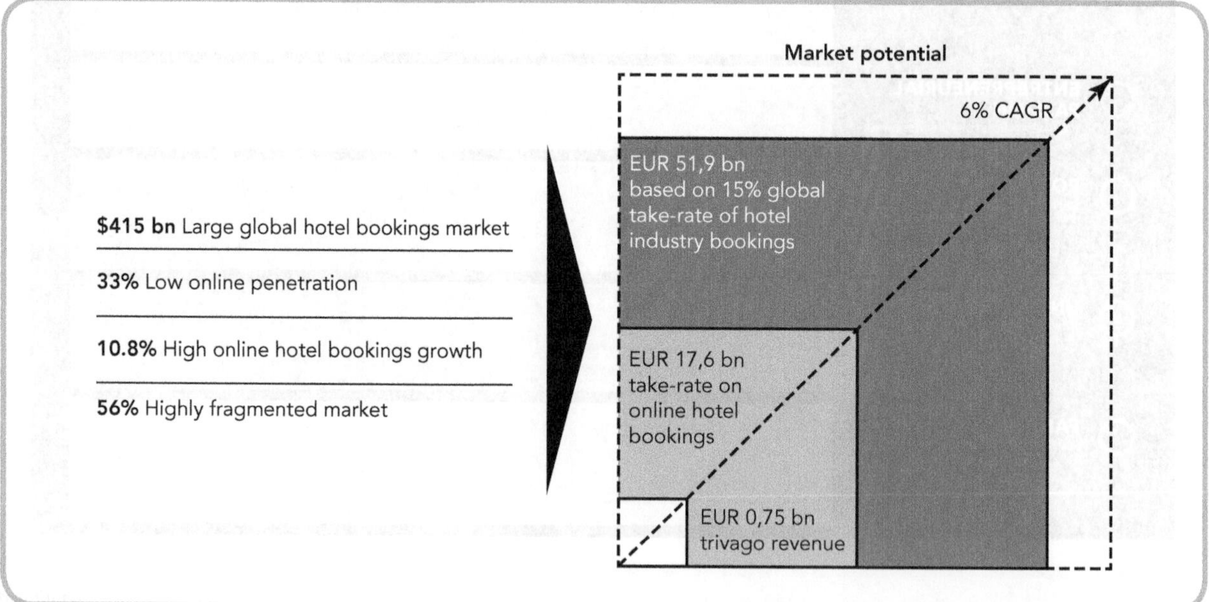

Source: trivago earnings call, Q1 2017.

Trivago established and openly communicated its philosophy of trust-based working hours and vacation days. The company's employees had neither a fixed number of working hours nor any limitations on the number of vacation days. This philosophy was mainly attributable to the founders' conviction that how much someone worked was not an appropriate measure of performance. As long as results were achieved on time and with the expected level of quality, the amount of time invested in a certain task did not matter.

To keep employees motivated and aligned, trivago further professionalized its incentives in 2015. One step was the introduction of a structured "Salary Review Process," which was intended to align compensation levels and remove differences among departments. The process itself was linked to the trivago values via the 360-degree feedback tool. The aim was to incentivize value-conforming behavior in order to foster the living of the trivago spirit and to move authority over compensation into the hands of the group. Furthermore, two types of ad-hoc bonuses were introduced in 2016. Executives with direct leadership responsibility could grant an instant bonus to reward exceptional efforts that went well beyond expectations. Such rewards were designed to support employees' intrinsic motivations and replace variable salary components, which were seen as extrinsic motivators. Extrinsic motivators, in turn, were not viewed as appropriate tools for motivating people in the long term. Moreover, each employee received a monthly bonus allowance with which to reward co-workers. As Rolf explained:

I believe that the era of managing systems based on extrinsically motivating people is over. The idea that people do not want to work is outdated. In a knowledge-worker environment, you cannot really control people anyway. Therefore, the only viable option is to make sure people are intrinsically motivated to achieve something.

In 2015, TO introduced a management-development training program in response to trivago's preference for internal promotion. With an average employee age of around 28 and the company rapidly growing, many executives with leadership responsibility had to quickly adapt to their new responsibilities. Although trivago viewed personal development as a "pull responsibility" (e.g., it would pay for self-selected seminars if the

Exhibit 9 Hotel Market Fragmentation—Hotel Chains versus Single Hotel Room Supply, 2014 (in '000)

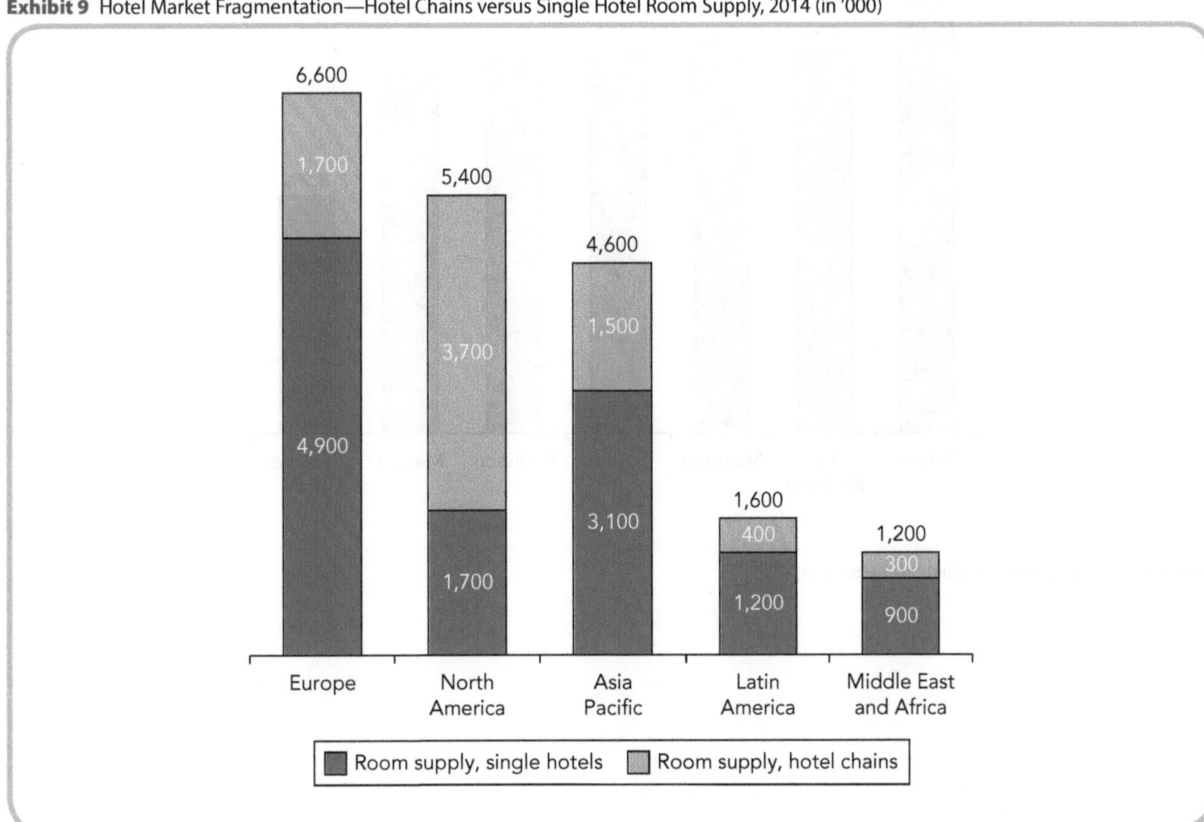

Source: Adapted from ESSEC, Graf (2016) based on STR Global (2014).

Exhibit 10 Price Premium, Branded Hotels, 2015

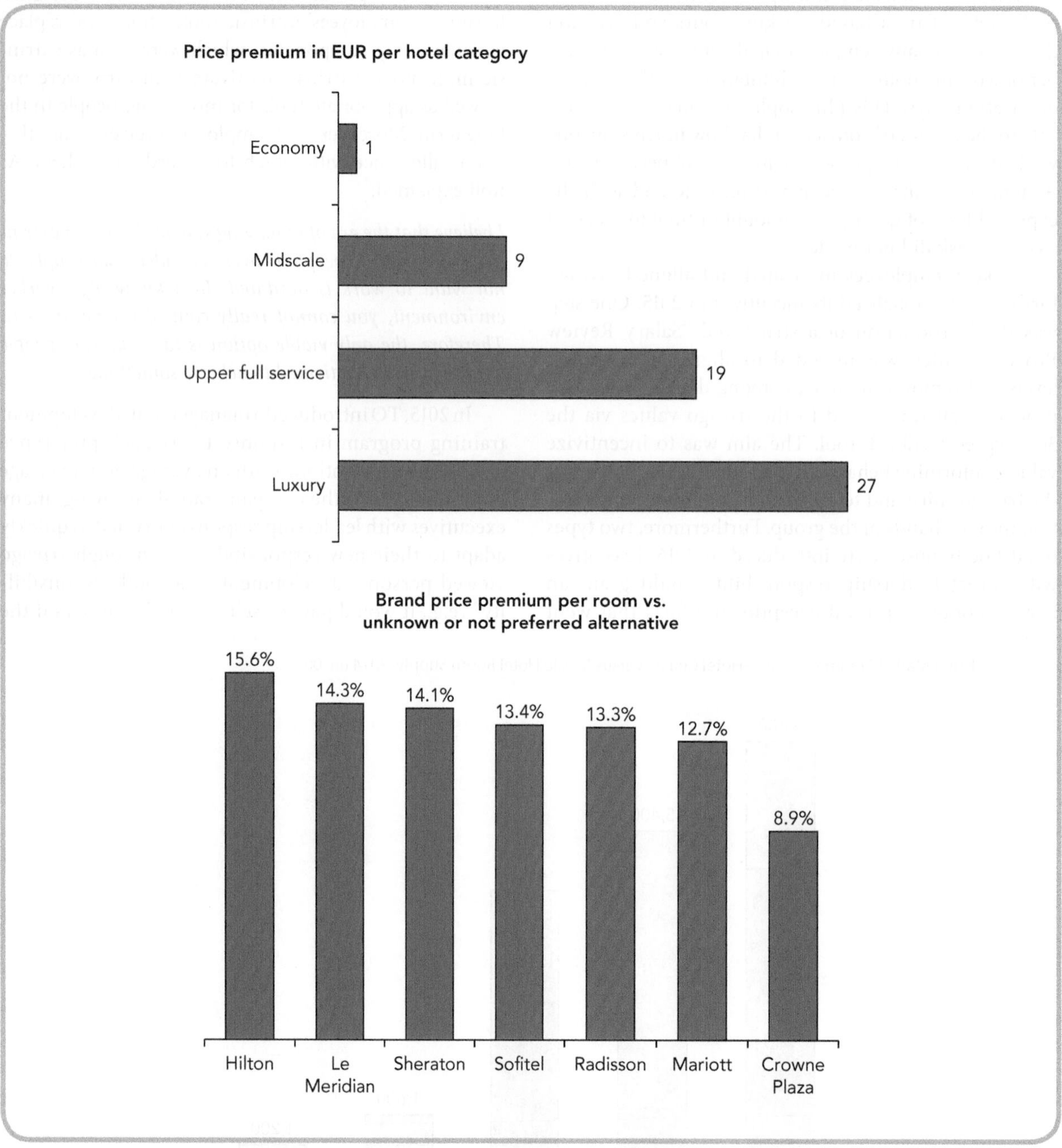

Source: Hotel News Now based on BDRC Continental (2015).

need was reasonably justified), the company offered its own "trivago Academy," which covered a variety of topics chosen to inspire employees and broaden their thinking. As one developer accentuated: "You can find the knowledge you need somewhere in the company, but we expect you to equip yourself with what you need!".

Communication. The increasing specialization and rising headcount affected decision speed. One developer responsible for multiple country teams discussed this issue:

One of the greatest issues I am fighting against is the fact that we are getting slow in all departments. That seems to come naturally with size . . . We can decide to do something, but when I ask about it later, nothing has happened because people are waiting for a meeting or someone is on vacation. Now there are too many people involved, which was never an issue in the past.

Similarly, communication flows started to slow. One department lead described this problem:

In the old days, I knew who was doing what and could just walk over there if I needed something . . . Today I sometimes do not even know where to go! This is why we need to continuously strive to also professionalize the way we keep our culture alive.

Exhibit 11 Hotel Room Distribution—Background Information

Demand for hotel rooms is often seasonal and price elastic. In most regions, guests stay an average of two nights. As a result, hoteliers face short sales cycles and intense pressure to distribute rooms. Effective room distribution is crucial, as stable occupancy rates have a significant leverage effect on profitability due to a high share of fixed costs for personnel and maintenance. In addition, distribution channels for hotel rooms consist of several disintegrated legacy technology platforms, such as pre-Internet central reservations systems (CRS), global distribution systems (GDS), telephone booking systems, and other offline sales platforms. Online channels consist of online travel agents (OTAs), the hotels' own booking engines, and meta-search sites. In general, channels differ in terms of technical complexity, margins, and average booking terms (e.g., last-minute versus well in advance), but can all contribute significant revenue? Therefore, hotels face pressure to simultaneously manage multiple channels using distinct IT systems.

Source: Case authors.

To keep direct communication flowing and avoid information silos, trivago implemented a set of communication and coordination tools. One was known as "trivago talk," a kind of an internal social-media application. It was introduced to allow for the sharing of company information and easier identification of peers. The tool was centered around work-related topics, such as announcements of new team members, discussions of technical issues, and invitations to joint leisure activities, such as soccer training. "trivago knowledge," a company

Exhibit 12 Planned Post-IPO Shareholder Structure, 2016—trivago N.V.

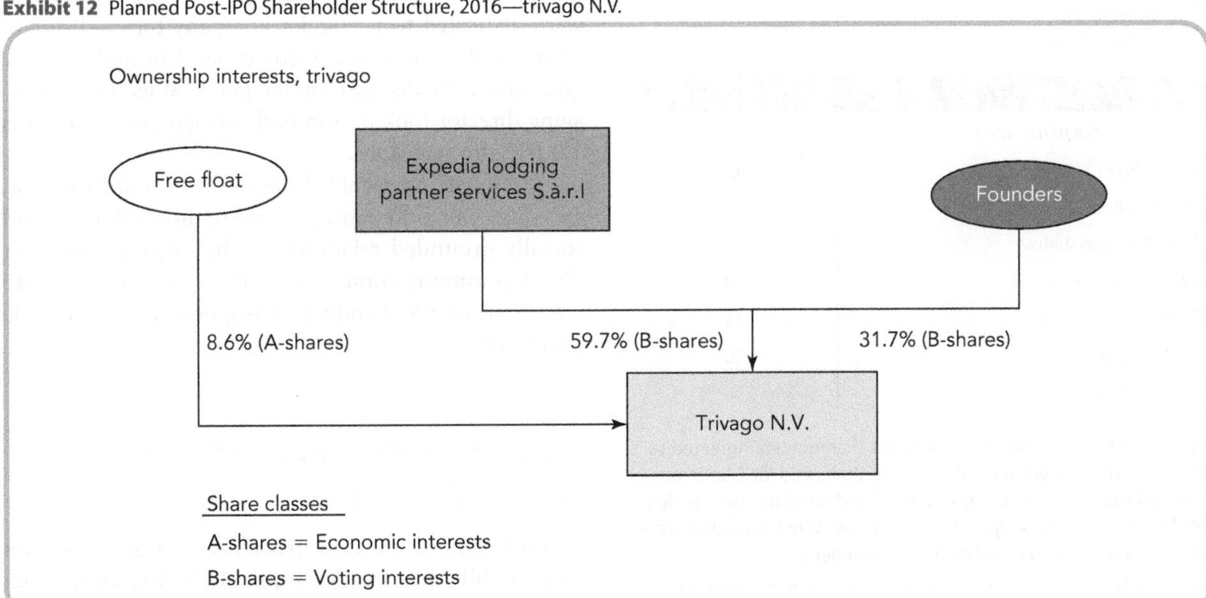

Source: trivago IPO prospectus (2016).

wiki, was developed to consolidate information on all departments, teams, and current and past projects and initiatives. "Slack," an instant messaging tool for teams, was introduced in 2015 to ensure day-to-day communication and increase communication efficiency. Finally, "trivago task" was introduced to allow for jobs to be assigned to service functions, such as requests for new mail accounts.

Given its awareness of the potential for silo thinking, inertia, and stereotyping in daily work routines, and its desire to strengthen the sense of community and transparent communication, trivago organized four events for the entire company on a yearly basis: a Christmas party (introduced in 2007), a trivago Update Meeting in the spring (introduced in 2008), a company trip (introduced in 2010), and a summer party (introduced in 2015). The Update Meeting began with the managing directors presenting the firm's strategic priorities for the year and ended with a party. The trivago trip was a four-day trip designed as a cross-departmental bonding tool. The trip focused on fun activities that were oriented toward connecting people across departments. Each team was also encouraged to regularly organize its own events, such as bowling or team dinners. For this purpose, an event budget of EUR 30 per team member was available monthly. Twice each year, this monthly budget was used for events at which participating members of all teams were mixed randomly.

Exhibit 13 Supervisory Board Members

The following people were members of trivago's Supervisory Board as of January 2017.

Name	Age
Supervisory Board members	
Mieke S. De Schepper	41
Peter M. Kern	49
Dara Khosrowshahi	47
Frédéric Mazzella	40
Mark D. Okerstrom	43
Niklas Östberg	36
David Schneider	34

Pursuant to the Amended and Restated Shareholders' Agreement, Mrs. De Schepper, Mr. Kern, Mr. Khosrowshahi, and Mr. Okerstrom were selected to serve as Supervisory Board members by Expedia. Mr. Mazzella, Mr. Östberg, and Mr. Schneider were selected to serve as Supervisory Board members by the founders.

Source: Table—trivago company website (2017), text—based on trivago IPO prospectus (2016).

In 2014, TO introduced a yearly company-wide survey that asked each staff member to identify company strengths and areas in need of improvement. The TO team was in continuous dialog with all departments in order to be close to the needs of employees and anticipate changing company needs. As one HR consultant outlined: "It is part of my job to have my ears on the ground, as our employees know what needs to be done." Many TO projects resulted from trivago's bottom-up approach to employee involvement and communication. As one TO team member stated:

We constantly need to ask ourselves and others whether a standardized tool or process is really the best way to solve a certain issue. When implementing projects, we must convince people, which requires continuous communication and explanations.

Whenever possible, new tools and suggestions for processes were tested in one or two departments. This was seen as important, as TO would only proceed with a company-wide rollout if the testing department fully backed the project and was willing to publicly support it based on the perceived benefits. Even then, TO typically produced tools that could still be declined by individual departments and teams. One developer said: "If I do not see the value in something that has been proposed, I just do not do it. Nobody has ever tried to argue with me about it."

Another opportunity for feedback and discussion initiated in 2015 and coordinated by TO were "trivago Fridays." These events were regular Q&A panels that were dedicated to particular company topics. Prior to each panel, all employees could hand in and vote for questions to be discussed at the panel. At least one managing director took part in each trivago Friday and was available for questions.

The focus on establishing outlets for information exchange not only aimed to strengthen informal and socially grounded relationships, but also to allow for direct communication and feedback across the entire organization, independent of responsibilities and role expectations.

trivago's IPO: Not the End but the Beginning

Toward the end of 2016, trivago announced its plan to go public and to do so quickly. When addressing potential investors, Rolf stated: "You will be investing in a company with an amazing culture with so much focus on learning that, regardless of what happens in the future, we will always be able to adapt." In this vein, trivago's CFO clarified the company's growth ambitions:

In our business, there is a trade-off between growth and profitability. However, from our perspective, it would not be a good idea to aggressively improve profitability while sacrificing growth. This is because our growth, as such, is more than a revenue figure.

On December 16, 2016, Rolf, Peter, Malte, and Axel rang the NASDAQ stock market opening bell. The room was filled with trivago employees, all of whom represented the group effort that had made trivago's success possible. At trivago, the IPO was seen not as the end but as the beginning of a new chapter in trivago's path to continued growth. For additional information see Exhibits 8–14.

When Rolf's mind again turned to the many people who made trivago the firm it had become, he felt a sense of renewed energy. He stopped pondering and focused on the challenge ahead—the need to "stay entrepreneurial" and avoid "becoming corporate" in order to secure future growth and success.

Exhibit 14 Shareholder's Agreement—Background Information

"The Amended and Restated Shareholders' Agreement contains certain provisions that could result in the departure of certain of our senior management. If the Founders, collectively, hold less than 15% of our outstanding Class A shares and Class B shares (calculated as if all securities convertible, exercisable or exchangeable for Class A shares or Class B shares had been converted, exercised or exchanged), they lose certain contractual rights to nominate members of our management board. In such case, our supervisory board may also request from the Founders, the resignation of members of the supervisory board who have been nominated by the Founders. In addition, the general meeting of shareholders, which is controlled by Expedia, has broad discretion to remove members of our management board with and without cause, irrespective of the Founders' holdings. If the general meeting of shareholders has reasonable cause, as defined in the Amended and Restated Shareholders' Agreement, for such removal, Expedia has the unilateral right, subject to certain exceptions, to purchase all of such members shares."

Source: trivago IPO prospectus (2016).

NOTES

1. Qualified referral: a unique visitor who clicks on at least one referral to a booking page. For example, if a single visitor clicks on multiple hotel offers in trivago's search results in a given day, they count as multiple referrals, but as only one qualified referral.
2. CPM: cost-per-mille ad-impressions. In banner marketing, one view equals one impression.

CASE 17

The Volkswagen Emissions Scandal

In October 2015, Mathias Müller became CEO of Volkswagen (VW), the 78-year-old economic jewel of Germany. His predecessor, Martin Winterkorn, who had led VW for eight years, had resigned suddenly in the midst of one of the biggest scandals to ever hit VW and the auto industry. In September, VW had admitted to United States regulators that it had deliberately installed "defeat devices" in many of its diesel cars, which enabled the cars to cheat on federal and state emissions tests, making them able to pass the tests and hit ambitious mileage and performance targets while actually emitting up to 40 times more hazardous gases into the atmosphere than legally allowed. The discovery had prompted the US Environmental Protection Agency (EPA) to halt final certification of VW's 2016 diesel models, and VW itself had halted sales of its 2015 models. As fallout from the defeat devices developed, VW posted its first quarterly loss in more than 15 years, and its stock plummeted. Winterkorn and several other top executives were replaced, and VW abandoned its goal of becoming the world's largest automaker. In addition to significant financial implications, VW was rapidly losing its prized reputation as a trustworthy company capable of outstanding engineering feats.

Volkswagen Background: The Power of German Engineering[1]

In 1937, VW was founded in Germany under the Nazi regime by the labor unions with the help of Ferdinand Porsche, the inventor of the Beetle (the people's car). Tasked with making a car that was affordable for all consumers, VW's flagship car, the compact and iconic Beetle, first rolled off the manufacturing floor in 1945, and by 1949, half of all passenger cars produced in West Germany were built by VW. The company began exporting cars in the late 1940s, and by 1955, the company had sold over one million Beetles worldwide. The Beetle would eventually surpass Ford's Model T as the highest-selling model ever built, reaching sales of more than 15 million by 1972. When sales of the Beetle began to decline in the late 1970s, VW branched into other models, including the Passat, Jetta, Golf, and Polo. The VW brand eventually folded into a broader public holding company, Volkswagen AG, which by 2014 owned 12 subsidiaries, including VW passenger cars, Audi, Porsche, and Bentley.

By 2014 (**Exhibit 1**), VW was one of the biggest firms in the world. It had factories in 31 countries, employed almost 600,000 people worldwide, and sold its cars around the world. In 2014, it sold 10.2 million vehicles, a 5% growth over 2013, and reached its goal of taking over the title of "world's largest auto manufacturer" from Toyota. Sales revenue in 2014 was EUR202 billion, with an operating profit of EUR12 billion (**Exhibit 2**).[2]

The shareholders of Volkswagen AG were largely made up of descendants of Porsche (50% ownership), but VW also had significant ownership from the German state of Lower Saxony (20% ownership) and Qatar's sovereign wealth fund (17% ownership), as well as independent shareholders who made up 10% ownership.[3] Per German corporate law, Volkswagen AG had a 20-member supervisory board responsible for corporate governance, rather than a board of directors. As required by law, 50% of the seats were allocated to VW's labor force (union representatives and employees that are elected representatives of the union), leaving the other 10 seats to be divvied up among the shareholders. As of 2015, only one of these seats was held by an outsider (Annika Falkengren, the CEO of a Swedish bank); the other nine were as follows: five to members of the Porsche and Piëch (relatives of the Porsche) families, two to Lower Saxony, and two to Qatar.[4]

At a time when Europe was continuing to recover from the global financial crisis, VW was one of the most significant engines in the German economy. In May 2015, it was listed by *Forbes* as the largest public company in Germany by revenue, surpassing its nearest competitor, Daimler, by almost USD100 billion.[5] It was also one of Germany's

This public-sourced case was prepared by Luann J. Lynch, Almand R. Coleman Professor of Business Administration, Cameron Cutro (MBA '16), and Elizabeth Bird (MBA '16). It was written as a basis for class discussion rather than to illustrate effective or ineffective handling of an administrative situation.

Exhibit 1 Timeline of Events

2007
Martin Winterkorn becomes CEO of VW and through his Strategy 2018 sets ambitious goals for vehicle sales.

2008
After canceling deal with BlueTec technology, VW announces new clean diesel technology called Lean NOx Trap and designed to meet regulations.

2009
VW's Jetta wins Green Car of the Year award.

2011
In reaction to growing public concern, the EPA announces plans to further regulate US emissions by offering "credits" to companies for using new technology, such as hybrid or electric cars, to improve the environmental effects of their fleets. Credits were not offered to diesel manufacturers.

2013
A nonprofit group, the ICCT, notices that diesel technology in United States appears to be cleaner—begins road testing of diesel vehicles.

2014
Researchers turn over the results of the study to the US EPA. The EPA opens investigation and questions VW about the findings. VW denies accusations of wrongdoing.

VW reaches its Strategy 2018 sales goal early, selling over 10 million vehicles and surpassing Toyota in sales volume, thereby becoming the world's largest automaker.

2015
The EPA and the state of California prepare for further testing and confirm that initial test findings are consistent.

September 18, 2015
VW publicly admits that it had installed defeat devices on nearly 500,000 diesel vehicles across 14 models sold in the United States since 2009.

September 23–25, 2015
Martin Winterkorn resigns as CEO, and Mathias Müller becomes new CEO.

Source: Created by author based on the order of events as portrayed in the case.

largest employers.[6] Wolfsburg, Germany, the town in Lower Saxony where VW was headquartered, owed its existence to the company: it was created out of farmland to be the original site for manufacturing the VW Beetle. By the mid-2000s, the company owned the town's professional soccer team, its major hotels, and even an automotive theme park that attracted millions of visitors per year.[7]

The company's stated values included "customer focus, superior performance, creating value, renewability, respect, responsibility, and sustainability."[8] These values were intended to guide decisions made by employees throughout the company and were accompanied by a 25-page Code of Conduct on which every employee was trained after joining VW. This Code of Conduct was written in 2009 and systematically rolled out to employees across the globe in 2010. It addressed topics such as management culture and collaboration, anticorruption, and fair competition, and it was intended to be a "guidepost that combines the essential basic principles of our activities and supports our employees in mastering the legal and ethical challenges in their daily work."[9] In addition, all VW employees received compliance training; 185,000 were trained on compliance in 2014.[10]

Throughout its history, VW had been widely admired for its innovation in design and engineering. It was one of the first companies to introduce the three-way catalytic converter, prompting it to boast on its website that it was a "pioneer of low-emission monitoring."[11] The company experienced its first brush with US emissions standards in the 1970s, however, when the EPA caught it installing defeat devices that would allow it to cheat on newly enacted emissions standards. At the time, it paid a USD120,000 fine.[12]

VW had also been known for its quirky advertising highlighting its unique products and top-notch engineering. The company made advertising history

Exhibit 2 Volkswagen Group Key Financials, Prescandal

	Vehicles Sold	Revenue (EUR millions)	Operating Profit (EUR millions)
2007	6,191,618	108,897	6,151
2008	6,271,724	113,808	6,333
2009	6,309,743	105,187	1,855
2010	7,278,440	126,875	7,141
2011	8,361,294	159,337	11,271
2012	9,344,559	192,676	11,498
2013	9,728,250	197,007	11,671
2014	10,217,003	202,458	12,697

Data source: Volkswagen AG annual reports.

with its "Think Small" campaign in the United States in the 1950s, which encouraged Americans to consider smaller vehicles like the Beetle. In recent years, it stressed its virtue through advertisements proclaiming "the power of German engineering," with commercials featuring engineers sprouting angel wings. At a time when most major US automakers were still struggling to recover from the global financial crisis and both Toyota and General Motors were reeling from major safety recalls, VW was perceived as reliable, successful, and innovative. In his 2014 annual letter to shareholders, CEO Martin Winterkorn wrote: "We stand for strength, reliability, and long-term success—even under less favorable conditions."[13]

"The power of German engineering" was more than just a marketing tagline for VW; it was a motto, a way of doing business, and a symbol of national pride. Germany had become a country that prided itself on its world-class engineering and precision manufacturing.[14] In part due to the country's engineering prowess, the automobile industry had become a powerhouse in Germany, and VW had become the leader in that industry. This dominance in manufacturing helped Germany weather the 2008 global financial crisis and kept unemployment low. Germany was able to boost employment and its economy largely through its ability to export products; automobiles made up a full one-fifth of this market. The strength of VW and much of the German economy depended on the growth of its engineering exports, making German engineering more than a just a point of national pride—it was an economic necessity.[15]

VW Leadership and Strategy 2018

Winterkorn, who took over as CEO in 2007, was focused on leading VW through its Strategy 2018, an ambitious plan to position the company as a global and environmental leader. The overarching goal of the strategy was to transform VW into the world's largest automaker. Said Winterkorn, "Our pursuit of innovation and perfection and our responsible approach will help to make us the world's largest automaker by 2018—both economically and ecologically." Strategy 2018 had four primary goals: (1) to sell 10 million+ vehicles per year (thus making VW the world's largest automaker); (2) to become the world leader in customer satisfaction and quality; (3) to achieve an 8% return on sales; and (4) to be the most attractive employer in the automotive industry.[16] Throughout Winterkorn's tenure, VW made steady progress on each of these goals.

Under the leadership of Winterkorn and his mentor, VW Chairman Ferdinand Piëch (a grandson of VW founder Porsche and himself VW CEO from 1993 until 2002), VW became a tightly controlled, highly centralized company. Its corporate culture was one of command-and-control, with leadership setting aggressive goals and senior executives involved in even relatively minor decisions.[17] The company gained a reputation for being hard-charging and brutally competitive, and former employees described an environment in which subordinates were fearful of ever admitting failure or contradicting their superiors.

Both Piëch and Winterkorn came from engineering backgrounds and kept a close eye on product development. Piëch, who recruited Winterkorn to Audi in 1981 and became his mentor for more than 25 years, would boast that he elicited superior performance by "terrifying his engineers."[18] It was well known that VW executives and engineers would be "shaking in their boots prior to presentations before Piëch, knowing that if he was displeased, they might be fired instantly."[19] By the time he became CEO in 2007, Winterkorn was considered "a cold, distant figure . . . known for obsessive attention to detail."[20] Unlike other contemporary auto industry CEOs who were experts in financial management and turnarounds, Winterkorn was considered a "classic car guy."[21] He was known for carrying a gauge with him at all times to measure flaws in vehicles as they came off the production line and for publicly disparaging subordinates. Said an industry analyst, "He doesn't like bad news. Before anyone reports to him, they make sure they have good news."[22]

Winterkorn was relentless in his pursuit of becoming the world's largest automaker. Speaking at the opening of VW's new factory in Chattanooga, Tennessee, in 2011, he promised that "by 2018, we want to take our group to the very top of the global car industry."[23] Although VW was growing, these promises were still considered ambitious, especially in the United States, a market that VW had previously neglected and where it held a reputation for selling expensive and undesirable cars.[24] In order to meet Winterkorn's goals, the US market would be a critical component to success. The company would need to sell 1 million vehicles (800,000 Volkswagens and 200,000 Audis) annually, tripling its 2007 sales.[25]

Achieving Ambitious Goals While Meeting Regulations[26]

In the mid-2000s, when Winterkorn began his tenure as CEO and announced VW's goal of becoming the world's largest automaker within the next decade, the auto industry in the United States and around the world was facing significant engineering challenges. Persistently high prices at the gas pump and toughening mileage standards put pressure on automakers to design more fuel-efficient vehicles, while growing concerns about climate change spurred increasingly stringent emissions regulations. In order to drive sales, automakers needed to find ways to optimize fuel efficiency and emissions while still designing the high-performing vehicles that Americans had become accustomed to driving. The market for hybrid-electric cars, notably Toyota's Prius, was growing rapidly.[27]

Rather than compete with Toyota and other automakers in the hybrid market, VW had opted for a strategy of diesel, viewing it as a huge growth opportunity within the US car market and a viable eco-friendly alternative. While diesel made up almost half of new car sales in Europe, it held just 5% of the US auto market in 2007,[28] and Winterkorn believed it was an opportune time to expand diesel sales in the United States. Diesel offered a cheaper, more powerful alternative to hybrid vehicles, promising high fuel efficiency without sacrificing powerful performance. But before it could market fuel-efficient diesel in the United States, VW had to overcome one major roadblock: diesel cars generated significantly more nitrogen oxide (NOx) than gasoline-powered engines, making it difficult for them to clear the stringent American emissions standards without sacrificing fuel efficiency or performance. In order to sell its cars in the US market, a critical part of the company's goal of becoming the world's largest car manufacturer, VW would have to engineer a way to strip its cars of these pollutants to meet US regulations (**Exhibit 3**).

In 2005, Wolfgang Bernhard, VW's head of brand, was in charge of designing the next-generation diesel engine for consumer cars that would provide both fuel efficiency and meet low US emission standards. Bernhard chose a strategy seen as controversial within the VW management team. Rather than develop an in-house solution, he instead adopted a competitor's technology, a Daimler invention called BlueTec. BlueTec used a substance called urea—essentially cat urine—to neutralize NOx. It required that VW install an extra pump and tank of urea in each vehicle, at a cost of EUR300 per vehicle. But just two years later, in 2007, boardroom battles within VW led to the appointment of Winterkorn as CEO, who promptly ousted Bernhard and cancelled the BlueTec deal. VW leadership stressed that BlueTec was too expensive, took up too much space in small cars, would hamper fuel efficiency, and that VW did not need to partner with an archrival to achieve its engineering goals.

Exhibit 3 Background on US Emissions Regulations[1]

The EPA both sets minimum standards for fuel efficiency for a company's fleet of vehicles and regulates emissions according to the Clean Air Act. The Clean Air Act, passed by the United States Congress in 1970, was designed to combat a number of air pollution problems threatening environmental safety and public health. As the country had grown more industrialized and urban, dense smog was visible in many of the nation's cities and prompted a public outcry for government action. The Clean Air Act required the EPA to "establish national ambient air quality standards for certain common and widespread pollutants based on the latest science."[2] One of the key provisions emphasized minimizing pollution from motor vehicles, focusing on emissions of carbon monoxide, volatile organic compounds, and NOx. Emissions standards were gradually tightened over time.

The Clean Air Act requires that the EPA certify that all motor vehicles sold in the United States meet federal emissions standards. Without this certification, a vehicle cannot be sold in the United States. For decades, tests on new models to be released in the United States have been conducted at indoor laboratories as opposed to performing actual driving tests on the road. The tests use dynamometers—essentially car treadmills—which simulate driving and measure the exhaust emissions of a stationary car. The tests are conducted in laboratories rather than on the road to achieve cost efficiency and ensure standardization of the test from vehicle to vehicle within a fleet.[3]

[1]Most of the information in this section is from the EPA's "Clean Air Act Overview," https://www.epa.gov/clean-air-act-overview; "Clean Air Act Text," https://www.epa.gov/clean-air-act-overview/clean-air-act-text; "Clean Air Act Requirements and History," https://www.epa.gov/clean-air-act-overview/clean-air-act-requirements-and-history; and "Progress Cleaning the Air and Improving People's Health," https://www.epa.gov/clean-air-act-overview/progress-cleaning-air-and-improving-peoples-health (all accessed Jan. 16, 2015); as well as http://www.bloomberg.com/news/articles/2015-10-21/how-could-volkswagen-s-top-engineers-not-have-known.

[2]https://www.epa.gov/clean-air-act-overview/clean-air-act-requirements-and-history.

[3]"EPA Should Do More Road Emissions Tests, Critics Say," *Automotive News*, September 29, 2015, http://www.autonews.com/article/20150929/OEM11/150929807/epa-should-do-more-road-emissions-tests-critics-say (accessed Jun. 20, 2016).

Source: Created by author.

VW engineers were suddenly on their own to find a way to meet stringent US emissions standards on diesel without sacrificing mileage or performance, and they needed to find it quickly. As it struggled to come up with a solution, the company was forced to delay for six months the release of the new diesel Jetta that was to be at the center of its new marketing push.

Whatever solution was devised, software was likely to be at the center of it. Modern cars contained approximately 100 million lines of software code that controlled everything from basic operations to media to safety. Software could also help a car control the amount of pollutants it emitted, by monitoring carbon monoxide and NOx emissions and then diverting pollutants to special systems that converted them into less harmful substances. Around the time that VW engineers were struggling to determine the right solution, auto industry–supplier Bosch gave VW diesel engine-management software for use during testing. This software could detect when a vehicle was in a testing environment and activated emissions-controlling devices. Bosch believed VW was only using this software during its internal testing, and sold the software to VW with the understanding that utilizing the software in publicly sold vehicles was illegal.[29]

Clean Diesel Sales Take Off

By 2008, it appeared that "the power of German engineering" had once again pulled through. VW announced the rollout of a new clean diesel technology called the Lean NOx Trap, which it claimed had solved the problem of delivering high fuel efficiency while still meeting emissions standards. The new technology garnered considerable attention for VW. Its 2009 clean diesel Jetta TDI won the Green Car of the Year award, beating out hybrids and electric vehicles. It hosted a multiweek "dieselution tour" to "change any outdated perceptions about diesel technology" and prove its environmental virtue.[30] Some of its vehicles were reportedly getting almost 60 mpg, which was unheard of for a nonelectric or hybrid car. At a conference on diesel emissions the same year, a VW executive boasted that "you don't have to sacrifice power to be environmentally conscious."[31] Clean diesel became the centerpiece of VW's US marketing strategy, and sales took off. Diesel sales grew by 20% in 2010, 26% in 2011, and 25% in 2012, though they began to taper off slightly in 2013 and 2014.[32] By 2014, VW's diesel cars accounted for 21% of the company's US sales.[33]

In 2011, VW's goal of selling 1 million vehicles in the United States was beginning to look achievable. US domestic companies struggled under the weight of economic crises and bailouts, and Toyota and Honda had yet to fully recover from the impact on production of the 2011 Japanese earthquake. By 2012, VW claimed 3% market share in the United States,[34] up from 2.5% in 2011 and 2.2% in 2010.[35] VW sales in the United States hit 440,000 in 2014, more than double 2009 sales.[36]

By 2014, VW was well on its way to achieving all four Strategy 2018 goals. Worldwide sales grew steadily at approximately 7.2% CAGR from 2007, when Winterkorn took over, to 2014.[37] Most notably, the company reached its sales goal in 2014, selling more than 10 million vehicles and surpassing Toyota in sales volume, thereby becoming the world's largest automaker four years ahead of the deadline it had set for itself (**Exhibit 4**).[38]

Exhibit 4 Worldwide Annual Car and Light Truck Sales by Manufacturer, 2005–2015

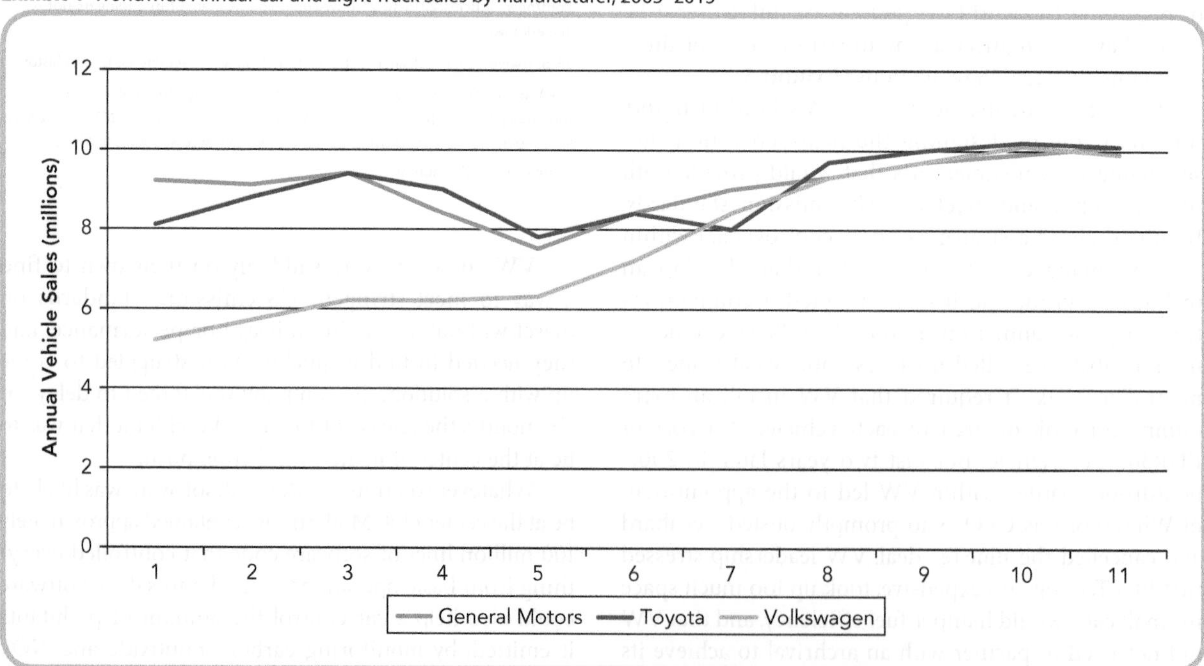

Data source: Created by author using data obtained from Bloomberg.

Sales were particularly strong for VW vehicles in China, growing 10% since 2013.[39] Yet sales in the United States were causing concern. US consumers' tastes had shifted toward midsized SUVs, an area in which VW had very few offerings. By 2014, VW held only 2.2% market share in the United States,[40] and VW sales dipped down to just around 370,000, far short of the 800,000 projected and just barely above the company's 2011 numbers.

While VW invested in its US diesel strategy, EPA officials in the Obama administration announced in 2011 a plan to require automakers to increase fleet-wide fuel efficiency from an average of 35.5 mpg to 54.5 mpg by 2025, while also further reducing emissions. To help car manufacturers offset the business implications of these ambitious new standards, companies were able to earn credits for utilizing groundbreaking technology that improved the environmental effects of their fleets, such as hybrids and electric cars. Credits could be used to lower the average fleet miles per gallon or emissions rating of the manufacturer that would otherwise be over the EPA limits. But credits were not offered to diesel manufacturers, as diesel technology was not viewed as the future of environmental car manufacturing. Automakers that had invested in diesel, such as VW and Mercedes-Benz, lobbied for diesel cars to be eligible to earn credits due to the technology's superior fuel efficiency. These firms had made the decision to invest in diesel on the basis that it was environmentally conscious, but the EPA argued that diesel traditionally emitted much higher levels of NOx than gasoline-powered vehicles, and therefore would not allow diesel cars to earn the credits. This left VW with a fleet that did not meet the EPA's new standards, and unlike its competitors, the company had no credit-earning hybrid cars.

Scandal Unfolds[41]

In 2013, a nonprofit group called the International Council on Clean Transportation (ICCT) noticed something strange: diesel technologies appeared cleaner in the United States than in Europe. The ICCT hoped to identify what made diesel technologies superior in the United States in order to improve emissions in Europe. The traditional in-lab emissions tests had not provided any clues to the engineering differences, which were producing lower-emission vehicles in the United States, so the researchers proposed on-road (as opposed to in-lab) testing of diesel cars in order to better understand these differences. They partnered with West Virginia University's Center for Alternative Fuels, Engines, and Emissions and California environmental regulators to perform tests on several types of diesel vehicles, starting with a BMW X5, a VW Jetta, and a VW Passat (all three selected by chance; they were models conveniently available to the researchers). The researchers compared in-lab and on-road emissions and mileage performance.

Almost immediately, the two VW vehicles stood out. They performed flawlessly in the lab, but once on the open road, their emissions were significantly higher, as shown in **Table 1**. What the researchers unexpectedly uncovered was that these differences were perhaps not the result of superior engineering, but rather the result of cars specifically designed to take advantage of testing environments.

In early 2014, the researchers turned over the surprising results of the study to the US EPA, which questioned VW about the findings. VW flatly denied any accusations of wrongdoing. The West Virginia University researcher who led the tests said VW "tried to poke holes in our study and its methods, saying we didn't know what we were doing."[42] The researchers eventually conducted an in-depth examination of VW's software, reviewing millions of lines of code for something to explain the strange discrepancy in emissions. They discovered an unusual set of instructions that was sent to emissions controls whenever the vehicle was only utilizing two of its four wheels (as it would during in-lab testing). In essence, the vehicle recognized whether it was in a test lab or on the road. The defeat device limited emissions in the lab (therefore hindering performance), but once out on the road, emissions returned to levels far above federal regulations and performance did not suffer.

Armed with this information, EPA officials threatened to withhold certification of VW and Audi's 2016

Table 1 Emissions Test Results.

	EPA Limit	2015 Jetta In-Lab Testing	2015 Jetta On-Road Testing
Emissions level (grams of NOx emitted per mile)	0.07	0.07	2.45 (~35 × higher than legal limit)

Data sources: Bloomberg Businessweek, http://www.bloomberg.com/news/articles/2015-10-21/how-could-volkswagen-s-top-engineers-not-have-known; EPA, https://www3.epa.gov/otaq/consumer/f99017.pdf.

diesel models, which forced VW's hand. On September 18, 2015—one week after being named the world's "most sustainable automaker"[43]—the company publicly admitted that it had installed defeat devices on nearly 500,000 diesel vehicles across 14 models sold in the United States since 2009, when the clean diesel technology launched (**Exhibit 5**). This number was later scaled up to 11 million vehicles worldwide. It was discovered that the vehicles were emitting up to 40 times the US legal limit of pollution into the atmosphere.[44]

VW officials apologized but vehemently denied widespread knowledge of the defeat devices within the company, blaming a few engineers for the error and claiming that senior management had no knowledge of wrongdoing. They claimed that the millions of lines of software code made it impossible for anyone to know every line, particularly upper management, meaning that engineers could have included the emissions-defeating protocol without management knowing.[45] Michael Horn, VW's CEO of American operations, testified before Congress in October 2015, stressing that the defeat devices were "not a corporate decision" and were instead the work of "a couple of software engineers."[46] As members of Congress expressed disbelief that VW's senior leadership did not know about the devices, Horn admitted, "I agree, that's very hard to believe."[47]

Despite denying any wrongdoing, CEO Martin Winterkorn resigned five days after the scandal became public, stating that "I am stunned that misconduct on such a scale was possible in the Volkswagen Group. As CEO I accept responsibility for the irregularities that have been found in the diesel engines . . . even though I am not aware of any wrong doing on my part." (See **Exhibit 6** for Winterkorn's full statement.)

Exhibit 5 US Models with Defeat Device

Affected 2.0-Liter Diesel Models:
- Jetta (2009–2015)
- Jetta Sportwagen (2009–2014)
- Beetle (2012–2015)
- Beetle Convertible (2012–2015)
- Audi A3 (2010–2015)
- Golf (2010–2015)
- Golf Sportwagen (2015)
- Passat (2012–2015)

Affected 3.0-Liter Diesel Models:
- Volkswagen Touareg (2014)
- Porsche Cayenne (2015)
- Audi A6 Quattro (2016)
- Audi A7 Quattro (2016)
- Audi A8 (2016)
- Audi A8L (2016)
- Audi Q5 (2016)

Data source: EPA, "Volkswagen Light Duty Diesel Vehicle Violations for Model Years 2009–2016," https://www.epa.gov/vw (accessed Feb. 28, 2016).

Exhibit 6 Postscandal Statement by Martin Winterkorn, September 23, 2015

"I am shocked by the events of the past few days. Above all, I am stunned that misconduct on such a scale was possible in the Volkswagen Group.

As CEO I accept responsibility for the irregularities that have been found in diesel engines and have therefore requested the Supervisory Board to agree on terminating my function as CEO of the Volkswagen Group. I am doing this in the interests of the company even though I am not aware of any wrong doing on my part.

Volkswagen needs a fresh start—also in terms of personnel. I am clearing the way for this fresh start with my resignation.

I have always been driven by my desire to serve this company, especially our customers and employees. Volkswagen has been, is, and will always be my life.

The process of clarification and transparency must continue. This is the only way to win back trust. I am convinced that the Volkswagen Group and its team will overcome this grave crisis."

Source: "Statement by Prof. Dr. Winterkorn," Volkswagen US Media Newsroom, September 23, 2015, http://media.vw.com/release/1070/ (accessed Jun. 20, 2016).

Fallout[48]

The fallout of the scandal was swift and far-reaching. Regulators across the United States and across the globe opened investigations. In the United States, the EPA stated that VW could face up to USD18 billion in fines—USD37,500 per car for each of the estimated 500,000 cars impacted.[49] The FBI opened a criminal probe, as did the attorneys general of all 50 states, and the Justice Department opened a civil lawsuit against the company over the deception. Outside of the United States, Germany and the European Union also opened criminal investigations, and German officials raided VW's headquarters days after the scandal came to light.[50]

The scandal had considerable immediate effects on VW's business. In the wake of VW's admission, the EPA withheld final certification on VW's 2016 diesel models, and VW voluntarily halted sales of its 2015 models still in inventory. As diesel vehicles composed approximately 20% of VW's US sales, this significantly affected VW's performance. In October, VW reported its first quarterly loss in 15 years. Furthermore, its market cap shrunk by one-third in the month after the scandal went public (**Exhibit** 7), and the company quickly abandoned its goal of remaining the world's largest automaker.[51] In addition to Winterkorn's resignation, at least nine senior managers were quickly suspended or put on leave, and Matthias Müller, formerly the Porsche brand chief, was appointed VW's new CEO.

VW's American operations and dealers were severely hurt by the scandal they claimed to have known nothing about. VW America said in a statement to American customers, "The recent TDI (Turbocharged Direct Injection) news is a disappointment to the entire VW of America family. We sincerely apologize, and we recognize this matter has jeopardized the strong relationship between our loyal owners and the brand."[52] The scandal had a considerable effect on independent VW dealers, who were crippled by the sudden drop in sales. VW paid dealers up to USD1,000 per car and wired cash to dealers to handle the crisis locally.[53] In November, American consumers who had purchased the vehicles that were affected received a goodwill package in the mail, which included USD1,000 and 24-hour roadside assistance and did not require the consumer to release VW of any liability.

The German economy expected to see a substantial change as a result of VW's actions. The German auto industry, led by VW, accounted for 20% of German exports and 3% of German GDP. One in seven jobs were directly or indirectly linked to the industry, and the country was steeling itself for potential job losses.[54] The city of Wolfsburg, Germany, where VW was headquartered, issued an immediate budget and hiring freeze and halted all infrastructure projects in anticipation of substantially reduced corporate taxes coming from its hometown company.[55] "While the German economy defied Greece, the euro crisis and the Chinese slowdown, it could now be facing the biggest downside risk in a long while," Carsten Brzeski, chief economist at Germany's ING-DiBa bank, wrote. "The irony of all of this is that the threat could now come from the inside, rather than from the outside."[56]

In June 2016, VW agreed to a $14.7 billion settlement in the emissions scandal. The settlement was estimated to provide $10 billion to fund buybacks of vehicles from approximately 475,000 vehicle owners and additional cash compensation of $2.7 billion was to assist in environmental clean-up and $2 billion to fund programs by the EPA and California that focused on cleaner vehicles. The company could still face additional civil penalties or charges in other countries, and the company and some of its executives could face criminal charges as well.[57]

Exhibit 7 VW Share Price around Scandal September 15–23, 2015

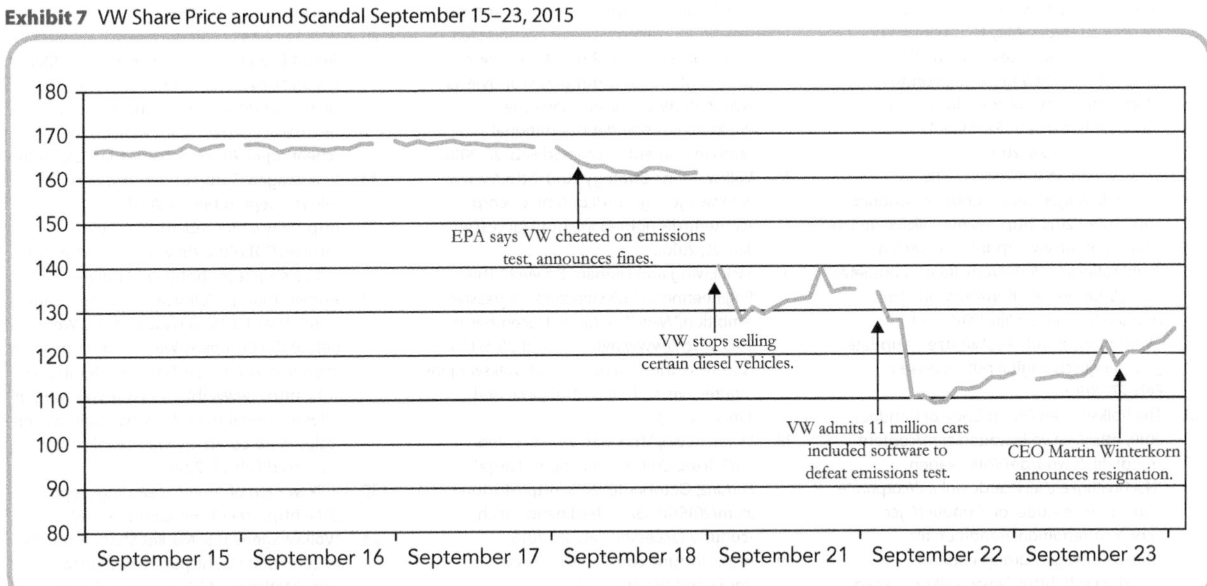

Data source: Created by author with stock price data from Bloomberg.
Source for announcements: *New York Times*.

NOTES

1. Most of the material in the first paragraph of this section comes from Tim Bowler, "Volkswagen: From the Third Reich to Emissions Scandal," BBC, October 2, 2015, http://www.bbc.com/news/business-34358783; and from Volkswagen's own company history and annual reports, available at http://www.volkswagenag.com/content/vwcorp/content/en/the_group/history.html and http://www.volkswagenag.com/content/vwcorp/info_center/en/publications/publications.acq.html/archive-on/icr-financial_publications!annual_reports/index.html (accessed Jan. 17, 2016).
2. EUR = euros.
3. Richard Milne, "Volkswagen: System Failure," *Financial Times*, November 4, 2015, http://www.ft.com/cms/s/2/47f233f0-816b-11e5-a01c-8650859a4767.html?siteedition=uk#axzz4BTTrG0FY (accessed Feb. 28, 2016).
4. Hans Dieter Pötsch, the company's former finance director who was close to the Porsche and Piëch families, became chairman of the supervisory board in 2015, replacing Ferdinand Piëch, who was the company's CEO from 1993 to 2002 and chairman of the supervisory board from 2002 to 2015.
5. Steve Schaefer and Andrea Murphy, " The World's Biggest Public Companies," *Forbes*, May 2015, http://www.forbes.com/global2000/ (accessed Feb. 27, 2016; USD = US dollars.
6. http://www.forbes.com/global2000/.
7. Joann Muller, "How Volkswagen Will Rule the World," *Forbes*, May 6, 2013, http://www.forbes.com/sites/joannmuller/2013/04/17/volkswagens-mission-to-dominate-global-auto-industry-gets-noticeably-harder/#52b13a501ab6 (accessed Feb. 28, 2016).
8. Volkswagen annual report, 2016.
9. The Volkswagen Group Code of Conduct, September 2015, http://www.volkswagenag.com/content/vwcorp/info_center/en/publications/2015/09/Verhaltensgrundsaetze_des_Volkswagen_Konzerns.bin.html/binarystorageitem/file/20150930_Verhaltensgrunds%C3%A4tze+-+update_coc_englisch_digital.pdf (accessed Feb. 27, 2016).
10. The Volkswagen Group Code of Conduct, 2010, http://en.volkswagen.com/content/medialib/vwd4/de/Volkswagen/Nachhaltigkeit/service/download/corporate_governance/Code_of_Conduct/_jcr_content/renditions/rendition.file/the-volkswagen-group-code-of-conduct.pdf; http://www.volkswagenag.com/content/vwcorp/info_center/en/publications/2015/09/Verhaltensgrundsaetze_des_Volkswagen_Konzerns.bin.html/binarystorageitem/file/20150930_Verhaltensgrunds%C3%A4tze+-+update_coc_englisch_digital.pdf. Although the two versions are similar, the earlier one contains signatures from VW CEO Martin Winterkorn and other top executives; the newer version, republished after the scandal, omits these signatures.
11. Danny Hakim, Aaron M. Kessler, and Jack Ewin, "As Volkswagen Pushed to Be No. 1, Ambitions Fueled a Scandal," *New York Times*, September 26, 2015, http://www.nytimes.com/2015/09/27/business/as-vw-pushed-to-be-no-1-ambitions-fueled-a-scandal.html?action=click&contentCollection=International%20Business®ion=Footer&module=WhatsNext&version=WhatsNext&contentID=WhatsNext&moduleDetail=undefined&pgtype=Multimedia&_r=1 (accessed Jan. 25,2016).
12. http://www.nytimes.com/2015/09/27/business/as-vw-pushed-to-be-no-1-ambitions-fueled-a-scandal.html?action=click&contentCollection=International%20Business®ion=Footer&module=WhatsNext&version=WhatsNext&contentID=WhatsNext&moduleDetail=undefined&pgtype=Multimedia&_r=1.
13. Volkswagen annual report, 2014.
14. Chiyo Robertson, "The Best Engineers Come from Germany," BBC News, September 18, 2013, http://www.bbc.com/news/business-24131534 (accessed Jan. 25, 2016).
15. Rick Noack, "For Germans, VW Scandal is a National Embarrassment," *Washington Post*, September 23, 2015, https://www.washingtonpost.com/news/worldviews/wp/2015/09/23/for-germans-the-volkswagen-scandal-is-a-national-embarrassment/ (accessed Feb. 27, 2016).
16. Volkswagen's Strategy 2018, http://www.volkswagenag.com/content/vwcorp/content/de/homepage.html (accessed Jan. 25, 2016).
17. Jack Ewing and Graham Bowley, "The Engineering of Volkswagen's Aggressive Ambition," *New York Times*, December 13, 2015, http://www.nytimes.com/2015/12/14/business/the-engineering-of-volkswagens-aggressive-ambition.html (accessed Jan. 25, 2016).
18. Doran Levin, "The Man who Created VW's Toxic Culture Still Looms Large," *Fortune*, October 16, 2015, http://fortune.com/2015/10/16/vw-ferdinand-piech-culture/ (accessed Feb. 23, 2016).
19. http://fortune.com/2015/10/16/vw-ferdinand-piech-culture/.
20. http://fortune.com/2015/10/16/vw-ferdinand-piech-culture/.
21. http://www.forbes.com/sites/joannmuller/2013/04/17/volkswagens-mission-to-dominate-global-auto-industry-gets-noticeably-harder/#52b13a501ab6.
22. http://www.forbes.com/sites/joannmuller/2013/04/17/volkswagens-mission-to-dominate-global-auto-industry-gets-noticeably-harder/#52b13a501ab6.
23. http://www.nytimes.com/2015/09/27/business/as-vw-pushed-to-be-no-1-ambitions-fueled-a-scandal.html.
24. http://www.forbes.com/sites/joannmuller/2013/04/17/volkswagens-mission-to-dominate-global-auto-industry-gets-noticeably-harder/#52b13a501ab6.
25. http://www.forbes.com/sites/joannmuller/2013/04/17/volkswagens-mission-to-dominate-global-auto-industry-gets-noticeably-harder/#52b13a501ab6.
26. Most of the information in this section is from Dune Lawrence, Benjamin Elgin, and Vernon Silver, "How Could Volkswagen's Top Engineers Not Have Known?," Bloomberg Businessweek, October 21, 2015, http://www.bloomberg.com/news/articles/2015-10-21/how-could-volkswagen-s-top-engineers-not-have-known- (accessed Jan. 25, 2016).
27. "U.S. HEV Sales by Model," US Department of Energy Alternative Fuels Data Center, January 2016, http://www.afdc.energy.gov/data/ (accessed Apr. 1, 2016).
28. William Boston, "Volkswagen Emissions Investigation Zeroes In on Two Engineers," *Wall Street Journal*, October 5, 2015, http://www.wsj.com/articles/vw-emissions-probe-zeroes-in-on-two-engineers-1444011602 (accessed Jan. 25, 2016).
29. Bob Sorokanich, "Report: Bosch Warned VW About Diesel Emissions Cheating in 2007," *Car and Driver*, September 28, 2015, http://blog.caranddriver.com/report-bosch-warned-vw-about-diesel-emissions-cheating-in-2007/ (accessed Jan. 25, 2016).
30. Volkswagen Group of America press release, September 26, 2007.
31. http://www.bloomberg.com/news/articles/2015-10-21/how-could-volkswagen-s-top-engineers-not-have-known-.
32. Angelo Young, "Volkswagen Diesel Scandal: Here's How Bad Volkswagen Sales Were Before the Company Was Caught Cheating," *International Business Times*, September 25, 2015, http://www.ibtimes.com/volkswagen-diesel-scandal-heres-how-bad-volkswagen-sales-were-company-was-caught-2114603 (accessed Feb. 27, 2016).
33. Volkswagen of America earnings report, 2014, http://media.vw.com/release/907/.
34. "Volkswagen's U.S. Market Share from 2012 to 2014," Statista, http://www.statista.com/statistics/343189/market-share-of-volkswagen-in-the-us/ (accessed Mar. 3, 2016).
35. "Volkswagen in the U.S.: An Evolving Growth Story," Volkswagen Group of

America presentation, January 10, 2012, http://www.volkswagenag.com/content/vwcorp/info_center/en/talks_and_presentations/2012/01/Global_Auto_Industry_Conference.bin.html/binarystorageitem/file/Volkswagen+in+the+US+-+An+Evolving+Growth+Story.pdf (accessed Mar. 3, 2016).
36. Neal E. Boudette, "How VW Veered Off Target," *Automotive News*, January 26, 2016, http://www.autonews.com/article/20150126/RETAIL01/301269949/how-vw-veered--off-target (accessed Feb. 28, 2016).
37. Bloomberg Intelligence, Automobiles Dashboard, Annual Unit Sales by Manufacturer (accessed Mar. 31, 2016).
38. http://www.nytimes.com/2015/09/27/business/as-vw-pushed-to-be-no-1-ambitions-fueled-a-scandal.html.
39. Henk Bekker, "2014 (Full Year) China and Worldwide German Luxury Car Sales," Best Selling Cars, January 9, 2015, http://www.best-selling-cars.com/china/2014-full-year-china-worldwide-german-luxury-car-sales/ (accessed Feb. 28, 2016).
40. http://www.statista.com/statistics/343189/market-share-of-volkswagen-in-the-us/.
41. http://www.bloomberg.com/news/articles/2015-10-21/how-could-volkswagen-s-top-engineers-not-have-known-; http://www.nytimes.com/2015/09/27/business/as-vw-pushed-to-be-no-1-ambitions-fueled-a-scandal.html.
42. http://www.nytimes.com/2015/09/27/business/as-vw-pushed-to-be-no-1-ambitions-fueled-a-scandal.html.
43. Richard Hardyment, "CSR after Volkswagen Scandal," TriplePundit, October 28, 2015, http://www.triplepundit.com/2015/10/csr-volkswagen-scandal/ (accessed Jun. 20, 2016).
44. Guilbert Gates, Jack Ewing, Karl Russell, and Derek Watkins, "Explaining Volkswagen's Emissions Scandal," *New York Times*, June 1, 2016, http://www.nytimes.com/interactive/2015/business/international/vw-diesel-emissions-scandal-explained.html?_r=0 (accessed Jun. 20, 2016).
45. Paul Kedrosky, "An Engineering Theory of the Volkswagen Scandal," *New Yorker*, October 16, 2015, http://www.newyorker.com/business/currency/an-engineering-theory-of-the-volkswagen-scandal (accessed Jan. 15, 2016).
46. "'It Was Installed For This Purpose,' VW's U.S. CEO Tells Congress About Defeat Device," NPR, October 8, 2015, http://www.npr.org/sections/thetwo-way/2015/10/08/446861855/volkswagen-u-s-ceo-faces-questions-on-capitol-hill (accessed Jan. 25, 2016).
47. http://www.npr.org/sections/thetwo-way/2015/10/08/446861855/volkswagen-u-s-ceo-faces-questions-on-capitol-hill.
48. Most of this section comes from http://www.nytimes.com/interactive/2015/business/international/vw-diesel-emissions-scandal-explained.html?_r=0.
49. Chris Isidore, "Volkswagen Could Be Hit with $18 Billion in U.S. Fines," CNN, January 4, 2016, http://money.cnn.com/2016/01/04/news/companies/volkswagen-emissions-cheating-suit-fine/ (accessed Jan. 25, 2016).
50. http://www.npr.org/sections/thetwo-way/2015/10/08/446861855/volkswagen-u-s-ceo-faces-questions-on-capitol-hill.
51. Clifford Atiyeh, "Everything You Need to Know About the VW Diesel-Emissions Scandal," *Car and Driver*, May 11, 2016, http://blog.caranddriver.com/everything-you-need-to-know-about-the-vw-diesel-emissions-scandal/ (accessed Jun. 20, 2016).
52. "We're Working to Make Things Right," Volkswagen website, www.vwdieselinfo.com (accessed Feb. 27, 2016).
53. http://www.npr.org/sections/thetwo-way/2015/10/08/446861855/volkswagen-u-s-ceo-faces-questions-on-capitol-hill.
54. Ruth Bender, "Town that VW Built Views Future with Caution," *Wall Street Journal*, October 2, 2016, http://www.wsj.com/articles/town-that-vw-built-views-future-with-caution-1443797584 (accessed Jan. 25, 2016).
55. http://www.wsj.com/articles/town-that-vw-built-views-future-with-caution-1443797584.
56. Jack Ewing, "Volkswagen CEO Martin Winterkorn Resigns amid Emissions Scandal," *New York Times*, September 23, 2016, http://www.nytimes.com/2015/09/24/business/international/volkswagen-chief-martin-winterkorn-resigns-amid-emissions-scandal.html (accessed Jan. 25, 2016).
57. Chris Isidore and David Goldman," Volkswagon Agrees to Record $14.7 Billion Settlement over Emissions Cheating," CNN Money, June 28, 2016, http://money.cnn.com/2016/06/28/news/companies/volkswagen-fine/ (accessed Jul. 15, 2016); David Shepardson and Joel Schectman, "VW Agrees to Buy Back Diesel Vehicles, Fund Clean Air Efforts," Reuters, June 28, 2016, http://www.reuters.com/article/us-volkswagen-emissions-settlement-idUSKCN0ZD2S5 (accessed Jul. 15, 2016); Jack Ewing and Hiroko Tabuchi, "VW's U.S. Diesel Settlement Clears Just One Financial Hurdle," *New York Times*, June 28, 2016, http://www.nytimes.com/2016/06/29/business/vw-diesel-emissions-us-settlement.html (accessed Jul. 15, 2016).

CASE 18

UNIVERSITY of VIRGINIA | DARDEN Business Publishing

The Wells Fargo Banking Scandal

We've been called, true or not, "the king of cross-sell."
—Wells Fargo CEO John Stumpf's 2010 letter to shareholders

On October 25, 2016, Timothy J. Sloan, the new CEO of Wells Fargo bank, addressed 1,200 of his employees in Charlotte, North Carolina, for the first time. "I want to apologize to all of you," Sloan began. "I want to say we're sorry for the pain you have experienced as team members as a result of our company's failures."[1]

Sloan, a 29-year veteran of Wells Fargo and previously its COO and president, had been named to the company's top position two weeks earlier, when then-CEO John Stumpf resigned amid fallout from the banking scandal for which Sloan apologized. In September, Wells Fargo had agreed to a $185 million settlement with the Consumer Financial Protection Bureau (CFPB) and two other regulatory bodies, admitting it had opened unauthorized accounts for millions of its consumers.

At the heart of the scandal were the company's community banking sales practices, which focused relentlessly on cross-selling multiple products to existing customers. Bank employees alleged that the pressure to sell products was so great that they were effectively forced to engage in illegal behavior to meet performance goals. During a five-year period, 5,300 bank employees were fired for improper sales behavior. When the CFPB settlement came to light, public outrage over the behavior of a bank many believed to be one of the few remaining good guys led to the resignation of Stumpf and other top executives, a dramatic drop in share price, and the loss of Wells Fargo's prized place as "the world's most valuable bank."

"My primary objective," said Sloan to his employees, "is to restore trust in Wells Fargo—restore pride in our company and mission. That may seem like a long way off today, but I promise you we will.

I think it all begins with understanding where things broke down, and where we failed—as a culture, a company, and as leaders."[2]

Wells Fargo Background[3]

Wells Fargo was founded in 1852 in San Francisco by Henry Wells and William Fargo and initially offered financial services as well as express delivery services necessary to meet the needs of customers flocking to the West during the California gold rush. Its famed delivery network—epitomized by its ubiquitous stagecoaches—allowed it to grow into a national brand by the early 20th century, even as its commercial banking focused primarily on Northern California until the 1980s. A series of mergers and acquisitions—most a takeover by Norwest bank of Minneapolis in 1998—helped Wells Fargo become one of nation's largest commercial banks by the beginning of 21st century. In addition to serving individuals and small businesses through commercial banking, Wells Fargo also had practices in wholesale banking, investment banking, wealth management, insurance brokering, loan servicing, and more.

John Stumpf became Wells Fargo's CEO in 2007 and its chairman in 2010. One of 11 children of rural Minnesota dairy farmers, Stumpf often cited his humble upbringing and hard-working, Midwestern values when he explained the way he approached management and leadership. "Even though we were very poor financially, we learned the value of plural pronouns—us, we, and ours," he told *Forbes* in 2012. "There wasn't a lot of time for I, me, and my."[4] He got his start in financial services as a repo man, joined Norwest Bank in 1982, and worked his way up through the community bank. After Norwest's 1998 merger with Wells Fargo, Stumpf led Wells Fargo's community banking division and was named company president in 2005, eventually succeeding Richard Kovacevich as CEO and chairman.[5]

Wells Fargo emerged from the 2008–2009 global financial crisis in a considerably better position than many others banks.[6] It benefited from a low cost of funds, diversity of revenue sources, and a refusal to sell some of the most complex synthetic investment vehicles

This case was prepared by was prepared by Luann J. Lynch, Almand R. Coleman Professor of Business and Cameron Cutro (MBA '16). It was written as a basis for class discussion rather than to illustrate effective or ineffective handling of an administrative situation.

and no-documentation loans that opened other banks up to considerable risk. While it lost market share in the mortgage business from 2003–2007, that setback was viewed as a sign of virtue when other banks collapsed. However, Wells Fargo did not emerge from the crisis unscathed: in 2012, Wells Fargo reached a $175 million settlement agreement with the Department of Justice over claims of discriminatory lending practices targeting African American and Hispanic homeowners during the housing boom.[7] It also paid $6.5 million to the SEC to settle charges related to the sale of risky mortgage-backed securities.[8]

Given its relative strength during the crisis, Wells Fargo agreed in 2008 to acquire Wachovia, which at the time was the fourth-largest bank holding company in the country and dominated East Coast banking, for $12.5 billion. Wachovia was forced into sale by the United States government during the 2008 banking crisis because of the substantial losses it had experienced from its loan business, the failure of similar banks, and fear that Wachovia would not be able to meet its depositors' requests for funds. In his 2008 letter to shareholders, CEO Stumpf wrote: "Our merger . . . has created the United States' premier coast-to-coast community banking presence, the most extensive distribution system of any financial services company across North America."[9] Effectively merging two banking giants was viewed as an enormous challenge, as it required creating a combined network of 11,000 branches, 12,000 ATMs, 70 million customers, and over 200,000 employees.[10]

After the Wachovia purchase, Wells Fargo got a vote of confidence from one of America's most respected investors, Warren Buffett. A longtime investor in Wells Fargo, Buffett's Berkshire Hathaway increased its ownership of the company steadily from 2009–2013, saying he believed in Wells Fargo's business model and management.[11] "You can't take away Wells Fargo's customer base," Buffett told *Fortune* shortly after the investment. "It grows quarter by quarter. And what you make money off of is customers . . . and not doing anything dumb. And that's what they do."[12] By 2015, Berkshire Hathaway owned approximately 9.5% of Wells Fargo shares.[13]

Wells Fargo enjoyed a sterling public reputation compared to other banks. Based in San Francisco, away from the major New York banks, Wells Fargo was "one of the most respected financial institutions in the country, viewed as a kindly, exceedingly well-run neighborhood-oriented bank with only modest aspirations for the rough-and-tumble world of Wall Street investment banking."[14] It was regularly ranked on *Barron's* "world's most respected companies" list, attaining a rank of seven in 2015.[15]

By 2015, Wells Fargo enjoyed a reputation as the "world's most valuable bank."[16] It ranked first in market value among all U.S. banks by year-end, ranked third in terms of assets, and earned $22.9 billion in profits from $86.1 billion of revenue (up 2% from 2014). It proudly stated in its annual reports that "we serve one in three households in the United States." Wells Fargo stressed that the key to its success was its ability to manage risk at every level. "We think everyone here is a risk manager," Stumpf told the *San Francisco Chronicle* in 2015. "Whether it's your official title or not, everything we do is part of that."[17]

In annual reports and elsewhere, Wells Fargo stressed the importance of its approximately 265,000 employees (known as "team members"). "We have always believed that our team members are our most valuable resource, and we want them to be with us for the long term," Stumpf wrote in his 2015 letter to shareholders.[18] Wells Fargo boasted of hiring one of the most diverse workforces in corporate America, with more women and minority employees than any other bank.

Since the 1990s, Wells Fargo's mission had been consistent: "to satisfy our customers' financial needs and help them succeed financially."[19] The bank believed this consistent mission and focus was key to continued growth, and it had six key priorities to achieving this: Putting Customers First, Growing Revenue, Managing Expenses, Living our Vision and Values, Connecting with Communities and Stakeholders, and Managing Risk. Wells Fargo leadership also maintained an explicit and consistent set of core values it believed set it apart and helped the bank succeed: People as a Competitive Advantage, Ethics, What's Right for Customers, Diversity & Inclusion, and Leadership. The company provided all employees with a 37-page book, *Vision and Values*, which included a letter from the CEO, explaining the bank's priorities, values, and culture in detail, and also outlined the importance of ethical behavior while ensuring the bank was financially successful.[20]

In speeches and annual reports, CEO Stumpf frequently referenced the bank's values as key to its success. His 2011 annual report to shareholders lauded Wells Fargo's 270,000 employees, who were "guided by our values and what we stand for: honoring and supporting our people, striving for the highest ethical standards, doing what's right for our customers, learning from diversity, and calling on everyone to be leaders."[21]

The Community Banking Division and Cross-Selling[22]

At the heart of Wells Fargo's success was its community banking division, whose purpose was to provide a wide range of financial solutions (such as checking and savings accounts, loans, and credit cards) to households and small businesses. In 2015, it consisted of almost 6,000 local bank branches across the United States. The division was responsible for 57% of Wells Fargo's annual revenue.[23] In addition, it was the public face of Wells Fargo, as the branches symbolized the bank's fundamental connection to Main Street.

Community banking was led since 2007 by Carrie Tolstedt, a 27-year veteran of Wells Fargo who had previously served as a regional manager and vice president of regional banking.[24] A Nebraska native, Tolstedt was known for her tireless work ethic and obsessive attention to detail.[25]

The division was vast and organized in a broad hierarchical structure. Tolstedt managed three regional bank executives, who were responsible for 54 regional presidents. The regional presidents managed 120 area managers, who in turn oversaw 600 district managers in charge of 5,700 branch managers.[26] Beneath these branch managers were the approximately 100,000 branch bankers and tellers responsible for selling and servicing financial products for individuals and small businesses.

The primary strategy of Wells Fargo's community banking was a practice known as "cross-selling," or generating more business from existing customers by selling them additional products. For example, customers who opened checking accounts would be encouraged to open savings accounts, credit cards, or mortgages at the same bank. A common practice across financial services companies (and many other industries), cross-selling is viewed as a key strategy to win market share in an increasingly commoditized market and retain customers over the long term.

While all banks emphasized cross-selling, Wells Fargo was unique in both the importance it placed on the strategy and its remarkable success at it. Cross-selling became a key component of Wells Fargo strategy around the time it merged with Norwest bank in 1998. Norwest CEO Kovacevich saw cross-selling as a major competitive advantage and wanted Norwest to be "the Wal-Mart of financial services, supplying 100% of customers' industry average needs."[27] Norwest was able to sell an average of four products per customer compared to an industry average of two.[28] In the years following the merger, Wells Fargo continually emphasized the importance of cross-selling in its annual reports:

Our primary strategy . . . is to increase the number of products our customers utilize and to offer them all of the financial products that fulfill their needs. Our cross-sell strategy...[facilitates] growth in both strong and weak economic cycles, as we can grow by number of products our current customers have with us, gain new customers in our extended markets, and increase market share in many businesses."[29]

"We've been called, true or not, the 'king' of cross-sell,'" wrote Stumpf in his 2010 letter to shareholders:

To succeed at it, you have to do a thousand things right. It requires long-term persistence, significant investment in systems and training, proper team member incentives and recognition, taking the time to understand your customers' financial objectives, then offering them products and solutions to satisfy their needs so they can succeed financially . . . The bad news is it's hard to do. The good news is it's hard to do, because once you build it, it's a competitive advantage that can't be copied.[30]

Wells Fargo was the only major bank to explicitly report on its cross-selling results in its annual reports and securities filings.[31] Wells Fargo began regularly reporting on the average number of products per customer in annual reports around 1998, as it was one of several strategic initiatives for the firm. Around 2001, Wells Fargo began referring to its cross-selling strategy as "Going for Gr-Eight!," a reference to its goal of averaging eight products per customer, which it estimated was approximately half the financial-services products an average individual needed during a lifetime.

Wells Fargo enjoyed considerable success with its cross-selling strategy. The average number of products per customer grew from 3.2 in 1998, when Norwest acquired Wells Fargo, to 6.11 in 2015 (**Table 1**).[32] By comparison, the national average was 2.71.[33] Wells Fargo "is the master at this," an independent bank consultant told the *Los Angeles Times* in 2013. "No other bank can touch them."[34]

Wells Fargo's strength at cross-selling was seen as crucial to the success of its Wachovia acquisition. Buying Wachovia's assets would provide a significantly larger geography for Wells Fargo's community banking, and its cross-selling ability, combined with Wachovia's famed customer service, was seen as a highly promising feature of the merger.[35]

The bank consistently emphasized that cross-selling and the long-term customer growth and retention it led

Table 1 Average Number of Products Per Retail Banking Customer at Wells Fargo, 1998–2015.

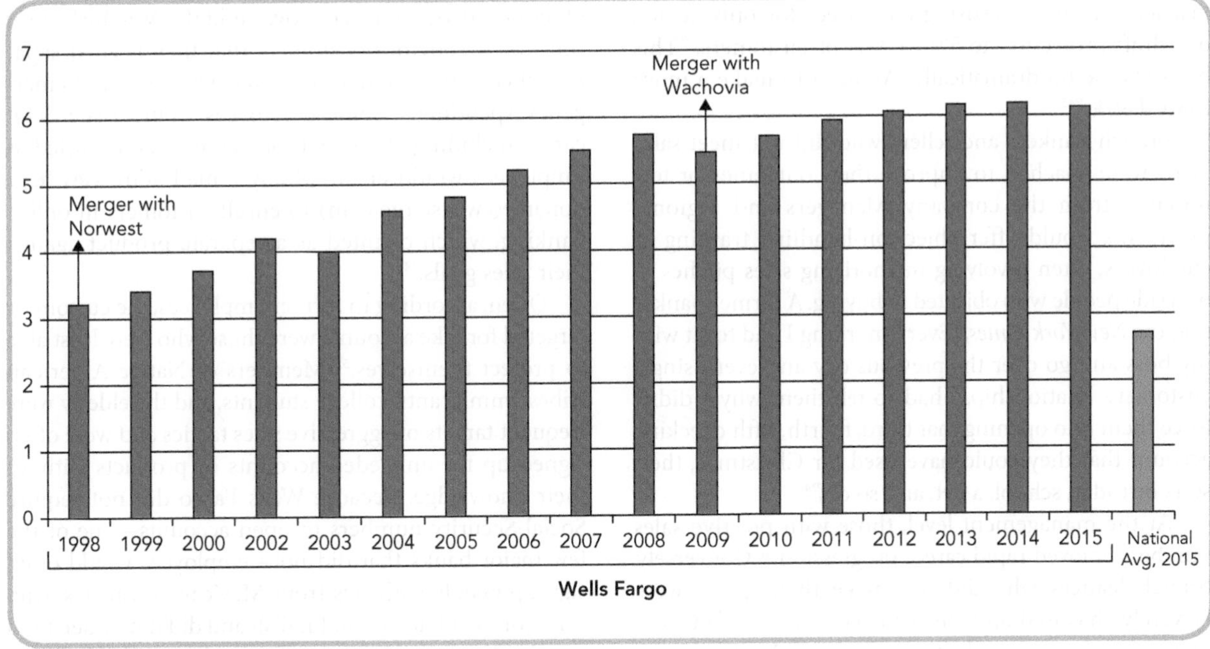

Data sources: Wells Fargo annual reports; Wall Street Journal.

to depended on the strength of relationships between its branch employees and its customers. Successful cross-selling was essentially a proxy for "earning deep and long-lasting relationships" with customers, which required "not only knowing our customers, but also understanding how they defined financial success."[36] In this way, the firm viewed cross-selling as a logical extension of its mission to satisfy its customers' financial needs. "Earning lifelong relationships, one customer at a time, is fundamental to achieving our vision," wrote Stumpf in 2015.

In order to make progress toward its ambitious goal of eight products per customer, Wells Fargo's community banking division relied on the salesmanship of its branch bankers and tellers. Throughout the division, managers focused on hiring and developing staff who could engage with customers, understand their needs, and sell them products to meet those needs. They also developed incentive programs that encouraged bank personnel to sell. Personal bankers, who earned approximately $14 to $19 per hour, relied on sales incentive payments for 15% to 20% of their compensation, while tellers, who earned approximately $11 to $13 per hour, derived about 3% of their pay from sales and service incentives.[37] District management had specific sales goals they had to meet to earn bonuses, and cross-selling metrics was one factor considered in determining the annual bonus for Division President Carrie Tolstedt.

Sales metrics were regularly reported from individual branches up through the management hierarchy of the division. Community banking head Tolstedt stressed sales volume and number of products per customer and "unrelentingly focused on numbers showing growth," according to former employees.[38] Branch personnel were assigned ambitious sales targets, and progress was tracked in a daily "Motivator Report" sent to managers and discussed regularly in conference calls.[39] According to allegations in recent lawsuits, the measurement of progress against sales targets was relentless. "Daily sales for each branch, and each employee, were reported and discussed by Wells Fargo's district managers four times a day, at 11:00 a.m., 1:00 p.m., 3:00 p.m., and 5:00 p.m."[40]

Former employees have described, in lawsuits and news articles, examples of the importance managers placed on employee sales' numbers. One area president told employees to "do whatever it takes" to sell.[41] Personal bankers had daily and hourly sales goals.[42] At some branches, employees could not go home until their sales quotas for the day were met.[43] "The branch managers were always asking, 'how many solutions did you sell today? They wanted three to four a day," reported one former employee to the *New York Times*.[44] A 2011 e-mail obtained by the *Los Angeles Times* shows a California district manager chastising employees for only selling overdraft protection to 5% to 38% of customers. "This has to come up dramatically. We need to make a move toward 80%."[45]

Branch bankers and tellers who did not meet sales goals were coached to improve their outcomes or terminated from the company. Managers and regional presidents would offer objection-handling training to employees, often involving memorizing sales pitches to override people who objected to buying. A former banker told the *New York Times*, "Every morning I had to sit with my boss and go over the previous day and every single customer's relationship. I had to tell them why I didn't force them into opening that third, fourth, fifth checking account that they could have used for Christmas, their son's birthday, school, a pet, and so on."[46]

At the management level, those with positive sales numbers enjoyed rapid career progression.[47] Conversely, branch leaders who did not make their quota were "severely chastised and embarrassed in front of 60-plus managers in your area by the community banking president."[48]

It was well-known that Wells Fargo aggressively sold products to customers and that customers were often frustrated by being constantly asked to buy more. A 2015 study of the 10 largest banks, conducted by management consulting firm cg42, revealed a frustration among Wells Fargo customers with the bank trying to get them to sign up for products they didn't need or want. This frustration was expressed by 43% of Wells Fargo customers, compared to an average of 24% for the remaining nine banks. This frustration was also expressed by Wells Fargo customers more than customers of others banks in the cg42's 2011 and 2013 studies.[49]

Employees Resort to Cheating[50]

Beginning 2013, reports in the press and allegations in lawsuits suggested that some Wells Fargo employees had resorted to questionable behavior in order to meet their sales goals. Employees would open additional accounts—checking accounts, online banking accounts, credit cards, and more—for existing customers without their knowledge or authorization.

A former banker told the *Los Angeles Times* in 2013 that employees at his Los Angeles branch would open accounts and credit cards for customers without their knowledge, blaming it on a computer glitch if customers complained.[51] Employees would encourage customers to bundle products and then "incorrectly inform customers that certain products are available only in packages with other products."[52] One employee told the *New York Times* she would convince customers that they needed separate checking accounts for travel, groceries, and emergency spending.[53] Some employees would issue debit cards, including PINs, without consumer knowledge. Employees would create phony e-mail addresses (e.g., noname@wellsfargo.com) to enroll customers in online banking, which counted as a separate product against their sales goals.[54]

Often, according to former employees, the customers targeted for fake accounts were those who were least able to protect themselves.[55] Members of Native American tribes, immigrants, college students, and the elderly were frequent targets of aggressive sales tactics and were often signed up for unneeded accounts or products without their knowledge. Because Wells Fargo did not require Social Security numbers to open accounts—one of the few major banks that did not—employees would often sign up people with IDs from Mexican consulates, who sometimes did not speak English and did not understand what products they were signing up for. "Bankers wanted the quickest, easiest sale—the low-hanging fruit,"—said one former employee in San Jose. The majority of cases of phony accounts happened in clusters in Southern California, Arizona, and Florida, though examples were cited across the country.[56]

These allegations prompted federal and state regulators to investigate. In September 2016, after an extensive investigation, the CFPB reported: "Wells Fargo employees secretly opened unauthorized accounts to hit sales targets and receive bonuses . . . The bank had compensation incentive programs for its employees that encouraged them to sign up existing clients for deposit accounts, credit cards, debit cards, and online banking." Analysis done by Wells Fargo and reported by the CFPB concluded that employees opened more than 1.5 million deposit accounts and over 500,000 credit card accounts that may not have been authorized by consumers. Some consumers were then charged fees to maintain the accounts.[57]

Several employees who witnessed unethical behavior or undue pressure from management reported it to supervisors or through the company's ethics hotline. Some employees even wrote to Stumpf directly.[58] A number of these employees have since claimed they were terminated shortly after making whistle-blower calls. One banker in Pennsylvania was terminated for tardiness days after e-mailing human resources to report that management had instructed him to open phony accounts.[59] Another in California was terminated for "not meeting expectations" three days after calling into the ethics hotline to report colleagues opening unauthorized accounts.[60]

Wells Fargo Responds to Allegations of Fraud[61]

I do want to make it very clear that there was no orchestrated effort . . . by the company. We never directed nor wanted our employees . . . to provide products and services to customers they did not want or need.

—Wells Fargo CEO John Stumpf's testimony to U.S. Senate Committee on Banking, Housing, and Urban Affairs, September 2016

Wells Fargo was aware of employees opening unauthorized accounts several years before the 2016 CFPB report made the scandal public. According to testimony provided by Stumpf to the U.S. Senate Banking Committee, Wells Fargo realized it had a problem as early as 2011 and began taking steps to "detect and deter unethical conduct."

In 2011, Wells Fargo piloted a Quality-of-Sale Report Card in California, which used data analytics to monitor sales patterns to identify potentially unethical behavior. It monitored the number of inactive or unfunded accounts and set limits on the percentage of accounts that were unused. However, one former manager noted that the limits—no more than 45% of debit cards were inactive, and no more than 27.5% of new accounts were unfunded—were so high that they did little to spur reform.[62] This report card was scaled nationwide in 2012 and in 2013 became part of the incentive compensation program.

Wells Fargo also began reducing the number of sales that employees needed for incentive bonuses. From 2012 to 2015, the number of sales required to make incentive bonuses dropped by 30%. Wells Fargo also reduced the emphasis on sales goals in performance evaluations.

Wells Fargo expanded the ethics training materials provided to managers in order to make clear what was right and what was wrong. It explicitly told employees at ethics workshops not to create fake accounts for clients.[63]

The bank also began terminating employees who it believed had practiced unethical behavior in order to record sales. Between 2011 and 2016, the bank terminated approximately 5,300 employees. Most of those terminated were branch tellers and bankers, but about 10% were managers. One area president was also terminated.[64]

Yet despite these efforts, the unethical sales practices persisted, which some employees blamed on the continued existence of ambitious sales goals. "They warned us about this type of behavior and said 'You must report it,' but the reality was that people had to meet their goals. They needed a paycheck." said one former personal banker.[65] Managers talked constantly about strategies for increasing sales, and leadership publicly lauded those with the highest sales figures.[66]

When reporters and investigators asked how these unethical practices could have occurred, Wells Fargo leadership consistently pointed to the individual actions of employees and defended its choice to terminate these employees. "I'm unaware of any overbearing sales culture," then-CFO Timothy Sloan said in an interview with the *Los Angeles Times* in 2013. In his Senate testimony, Stumpf stressed that the 5,300 who were terminated made up only 1% of the retail banking workforce in a given year. In any given year, 1,000 out of 100,000 employees "didn't get it right. But I have to say, the vast majority did do it right . . . every day."[67] "The 1% that did it wrong, who we fired, terminated, in no way reflects our culture nor reflects the great work the other vast majority of the people do," said a Wells Fargo spokesman. "That's a false narrative."[68]

In 2015, Wells Fargo hired third-party auditors from PricewaterhouseCoopers to determine how many customers could have been impacted by the fraudulent sales practices. It was this investigation that determined, as the CFPB later reported, that approximately 1.5 million deposit accounts (2% of all deposit accounts) could have been unauthorized, resulting in approximately $2.2 million in fees for consumers. Likewise, 565,000 credit cards—about 6% of all those issued—had not been activated, had no activity, and were assumed to be unauthorized. These cards resulted in $400,000 in fees for consumers. All consumers were reimbursed for the fees.

Two months before the CFPB publicly announced its settlement with Wells Fargo, the bank announced the retirement of Community Bank President Tolstedt, effective January 1, 2017. In announcing her retirement, Stumpf praised her as a "one of our most valuable Wells Fargo leaders, a standard bearer of our culture, a champion for our customers."[69] Tolstedt, who earned $27 million in her last three years with the bank, was expected to retire with approximately $125 million in stock and options.

Fallout

Because of the severity of these violations, Wells Fargo is paying the largest penalty the CFPB has ever imposed. Today's action should serve notice to the entire industry that financial incentive programs, if not monitored carefully, carry serious risks that can have serious legal consequences.

—CFPB Director Richard Cordray

On September 8, 2016, the CFPB announced that it and two other regulators had agreed to a $185 million settlement with Wells Fargo over the fraudulent sales practices employed by its branch workforce over the course of several years. This was the largest penalty the CFPB, founded in 2011, had ever imposed, but was relatively minor compared to other government settlements with banks in recent years over discriminatory mortgage lending and questionable securities practices, including fines imposed upon Wells Fargo.[70]

In the days following the announcement, outrage spread and congressional hearings were planned, and Wells Fargo saw its share price begin to fall. Shares dropped 13% in the month after the scandal went public, and Wells Fargo lost its place as the country's most valuable bank by market capitalization.[71] Warren Buffett repeated his commitment to the company, but stated "Wells Fargo . . . designed a system that produced bad behavior . . . The big mistake was they didn't do something about it."[72]

The day of the announcement, Wells Fargo stated that "we regret and take responsibility for any instances where customers may have received a product that they did not request."[73] It announced that it would be overhauling its performance-incentive program and removing product sales goals starting January 1. After considerable uproar from the media, the bank changed course and announced on September 29 that sales quotas would be eliminated as of October 1.[74]

CEO John Stumpf initially rejected calls to resign, stating that "the best thing I could do right now is lead this company, and lead this company forward."[75] His subsequent testimony in front of the U.S. Senate Banking Committee and House Financial Services Committee created a furor among lawmakers, including Senator Elizabeth Warren who stated "Your definition of accountability is to push blame to low-level employees . . . it's gutless leadership."[76]

On September 29, independent members of Wells Fargo's Board of Directors announced that Stumpf would be forfeiting his unvested equity—worth approximately $41 million—and would not receive a bonus in 2016. Two weeks later, on October 12, Stumpf announced his resignation from the bank effective immediately, stating: "While I have been deeply committed and focused on managing the Company through this period, I have decided it is best for the Company that I step aside."[77] Former CFO Tim Sloan was named CEO effective immediately. The company also split the role of CEO and chairman, effective December 1.[78]

Community Banking President Tolstedt, who had planned to retire at the end of the year, left the company shortly after the scandal broke. She received none of the planned severance or 2016 bonus and also forfeited unvested equity.

Wells Fargo began an internal investigation into the rumors of retaliation against whistle-blowers, announcing in January 2017 that it had found evidence that some employees may have been terminated for reporting questionable sales behavior to the ethics hotline.[79]

Wells Fargo also went to work to rebuild its image, running commercials, taking out full-page advertisements in most major newspapers, and setting up a special commitment website stating ways in which the company was working to "make things right" and "build a better Wells Fargo," including changing leadership and introducing an employee performance plan based on customer service.[80]

It remained to be seen what the impact of the scandal would be on customer retention and growth. An October 2016 survey by consulting group cg42 found that 30% of Wells Fargo's retail customers were exploring banking alternatives and projected that the bank would lose $99 billion in deposits over the next 12 to 18 months. Similarly, the number of consumers interested in doing business with Wells Fargo had plummeted.[81]

Moving Forward[82]

As Tim Sloan addressed his employees in October 2016, he acknowledged some of the underlying problems that had led to the scandal: product and sales goals that resulted in questionable behavior, a failure of management to respond adequately to unethical practices, warning signs that could have been heeded sooner. "It's also important to note there are no quick fixes to our challenges," he said. "My pledge to you is that we will keep these lessons, and others we discover, part of our ongoing conversation, so we may learn from our mistakes."

Sloan closed by stressing Wells Fargo's mission:

We want to satisfy our customers' financial needs and help them succeed financially. This is why Wells Fargo exists. If our customers don't succeed, we don't. The mission remains worthwhile because of the pride and satisfaction it gives us, and because of the opportunity it offers us to deliver value to customers, investors, and communities. This is our legacy and our future, and it's worth fighting for.

NOTES

1. Prepared remarks from Wells Fargo CEO Tim Sloan, October 25, 2016, https://stories.wf.com/companywide-address-ceo-tim-sloan/ (accessed Jan. 14, 2017).
2. Prepared remarks from Wells Fargo CEO Tim Sloan, October 25, 2016.
3. Primary source for this section: "Wells Fargo History," https://www.wellsfargohistory.com/history/ (accessed Jan. 14, 2017).
4. Matt Schifrin and Halah Touryalai, "The Bank that Works," *Forbes*, January 25, 2012, http://www.forbes.com/forbes/2012/0213/feature-john-stumpf-wells-fargo-bank-that-works.html (accessed Jan. 29, 2017).
5. "Executive Profile: John G. Stumpf," *Bloomberg*, http://www.bloomberg.com/research/stocks/private/person.asp?personId=292951&privcapId=4504437 (accessed Jan. 29, 2017).
6. Adam Lashinsky, "Riders on the Storm," *Fortune*, April 20, 2009, http://archive.fortune.com/2009/04/19/news/companies/lashinsky_wells.fortune/index.htm (accessed Dec. 14, 2016).
7. "Justice Department Reaches Settlement with Wells Fargo Resulting in More Than $175 Million in Relief for Homeowners to Resolve Fair Lending Claims," Department of Justice press release, July 12, 2012, https://www.justice.gov/opa/pr/justice-department-reaches-settlement-wells-fargo-resulting-more-175-million-relief (accessed Jan. 29, 2017).
8. Sarah Lynch, "Wells Fargo to Pay More Than $6.5 Million to Settle SEC Charges," *Reuters*, August 14, 2012, http://www.reuters.com/article/us-sec-wells-fargo-idUSBRE87D0P720120814 (accessed Jan. 29, 2017).
9. Wells Fargo annual report, 2008.
10. http://archive.fortune.com/2009/04/19/news/companies/lashinsky_wells.fortune/index.htm.
11. GuruFocus, "Why Warren Buffett Keeps Buying Wells Fargo," *Forbes*, January 4, 2013, https://www.forbes.com/sites/gurufocus/2013/01/04/why-warren-buffett-keeps-buying-wells-fargo/#600439312ced (accessed Mar. 5, 2017).
12. Adam Lashinsky, "Warren Buffett on Wells Fargo," April 24, 2009, http://archive.fortune.com/2009/04/19/news/companies/lashinsky_buffett.fortune/index.htm?postversion=2009042006 (accessed Jan. 14, 2017).
13. Yahoo! Finance, Wells Fargo & Company profile, https://finance.yahoo.com/quote/WFC/holders?p=WFC (accessed Jan. 29, 2017).
14. William Cohan, "Wells Fargo Scandal May be Sign of a Poisonous Culture," *New York Times*, September 16, 2016, https://www.nytimes.com/2016/09/17/business/dealbook/wells-fargo-scandal-may-be-sign-of-a-poisonous-culture.html?_r=0 (accessed Dec. 13, 2016).
15. Vito Racanelli, "Apple Tops *Barron's* List of Respected Companies," *Barron's*, June 27, 2015, http://www.barrons.com/articles/apple-tops-barrons-list-of-respected-companies-1435372737 (accessed Jan. 29, 2017).
16. Most of the information in this paragraph comes from the Wells Fargo annual report, 2015.
17. Thomas Lee, "For Wells Fargo CEO John Stumpf, Social Issues a Minefield," *San Francisco Chronicle*, November 6, 2015, http://www.sfchronicle.com/business/article/For-Wells-Fargo-CEO-John-Stumpf-social-issues-a-6616329.php (accessed Dec. 15, 2016).
18. Wells Fargo annual report, 2015.
19. Sources for this entire paragraph are Wells Fargo annual reports and the 2015 edition of *The Vision & Values of Wells Fargo*, https://www08.wellsfargomedia.com/pdf/invest_relations/VisionandValues04.pdf.
20. https://www08.wellsfargomedia.com/pdf/invest_relations/VisionandValues04.pdf.
21. Wells Fargo annual report, 2011.
22. Primary sources for this entire section include: E. Scott Reckard, "Wells Fargo's Pressure-Cooker Sales Culture Comes at a Cost," *Los Angeles Times*, December 21, 2013, http://www.latimes.com/business/la-fi-wells-fargo-sale-pressure-20131222-story.html (accessed Jan. 14, 2017); and Laura Keller, Dakin Campbell, and Kartikay Mehrotra, "Wells Fargo's Stars Thrived While 5,000 Workers Got Fired," *Bloomberg*, November 3, 2016, https://www.bloomberg.com/news/articles/2016-11-03/wells-fargo-s-stars-climbed-while-abuses-flourished-beneath-them (accessed Apr. 21, 2016).
23. Wells Fargo annual report, 2015.
24. "Carrie L. Tolstedt," profile on MarketsWiki, http://www.marketswiki.com/wiki/Carrie_L._Tolstedt (accessed Jan. 29, 2017).
25. Emily Glazer, "Carrie Tolstedt: in the Eye of the Wells Fargo Storm," *Wall Street Journal*, September 29, 2016, http://www.wsj.com/articles/carrie-tolstedt-in-the-eye-of-the-wells-fargo-storm-1474326652 (accessed Jan. 29, 2017).
26. https://www.bloomberg.com/news/articles/2016-11-03/wells-fargo-s-stars-climbed-while-abuses-flourished-beneath-them.
27. Bethany McLean, "Is This Guy the Best Banker in America?," *Fortune*, July 6, 1998, http://archive.fortune.com/magazines/fortune/fortune_archive/1998/07/06/244842/index.htm (accessed Jan. 29, 2017).
28. http://archive.fortune.com/magazines/fortune/fortune_archive/1998/07/06/244842/index.htm.
29. Wells Fargo annual report, 2011.
30. Wells Fargo annual report, 2010.
31. Emily Glazer, "At Wells Fargo, How Far Did Bank's Sales Culture Go?," *Wall Street Journal*, November 30, 2015, http://www.wsj.com/articles/at-wells-fargo-how-far-did-banks-sales-culture-go-1448879643 (accessed Dec. 14, 2016).
32. Wells Fargo annual reports, 1998–2015.
33. Rachel Louise Ensign, "What the Wells Fargo Cross-Selling Mess Means for Banks," *Wall Street Journal*, September 15, 2016, http://www.wsj.com/articles/what-the-wells-fargo-cross-selling-mess-means-for-banks-1473965166 (accessed Jan. 14, 2017).
34. http://www.latimes.com/business/la-fi-wells-fargo-sale-pressure-20131222-story.html.
35. http://archive.fortune.com/2009/04/19/news/companies/lashinsky_wells.fortune/index.htm.
36. Wells Fargo annual report, 2015.
37. Salary information from PayScale, "Average Hourly Rate for Wells Fargo Bank Employees," updated January 19, 2017, http://www.payscale.com/research/US/Employer=Wells_Fargo_Bank/Hourly_Rate

(accessed Mar. 5, 2017); bonus information from http://www.latimes.com/business/la-fi-wells-fargo-sale-pressure-20131222-story.html.

38. https://www.bloomberg.com/news/articles/2016-11-03/wells-fargo-s-stars-climbed-while-abuses-flourished-beneath-them.
39. https://www.bloomberg.com/news/articles/2016-11-03/wells-fargo-s-stars-climbed-while-abuses-flourished-beneath-them.
40. Athena Cao, "Lawsuit Alleges Exactly How Wells Fargo Pushed Employees to Abuse Customers," *TIME*, September 29, 2016, http://time.com/money/4510482/wells-fargo-fake-accounts-class-action-lawsuit/ (accessed Dec. 15, 2016).
41. Kartikay Mehrotra, "Wells Fargo Ex-Manager's Suit Puts Scandal Blame Higher Up Chain," *Bloomberg*, December 8, 2016, https://www.bloomberg.com/news/articles/2016-12-08/wells-fargo-ex-managers-suit-puts-scandal-blame-higher-up-chain (accessed Jan. 14, 2017).
42. http://www.wsj.com/articles/what-the-wells-fargo-crossselling-mess-means-for-banks-1473965166.
43. http://www.latimes.com/business/la-fi-wells-fargo-sale-pressure-20131222-story.html.
44. Michael Corkery and Stacy Cowley, "Wells Fargo Warned Workers Against Sham Accounts, but 'They Needed a Paycheck,'" *New York Times*, September 16, 2016, https://www.nytimes.com/2016/09/17/business/dealbook/wells-fargo-warned-workers-against-fake-accounts-but-they-needed-a-paycheck.html?action=click&contentCollection=DealBook&module=RelatedCoverage®ion=EndOfArticle&pgtype=article (accessed Dec. 15, 2016).
45. http://www.latimes.com/business/la-fi-wells-fargo-sale-pressure-20131222-story.html.
46. Both examples in this paragraph from Stacy Cowley, "Voices from Wells Fargo: 'I Thought I was Having a Heart Attack,'" *New York Times*, October 20, 2016, https://www.nytimes.com/2016/10/21/business/dealbook/voices-from-wells-fargo-i-thought-i-was-having-a-heart-attack.html?rref=collection%2Ftimestopic%2FWells%20Fargo%20%26%20Company&action=click&contentCollection=business®ion=stream&module=stream_unit&version=latest&contentPlacement=2&pgtype=collection&_r=0 (accessed Dec. 14, 2016).
47. https://www.bloomberg.com/news/articles/2016-11-03/wells-fargo-s-stars-climbed-while-abuses-flourished-beneath-them.
48. http://www.latimes.com/business/la-fi-wells-fargo-sale-pressure-20131222-story.html.
49. C. Cumming, "Wells Fargo Customers Join Cross-Selling Backlash," December 2, 2015, http://www.financial-planning.com/news/wells-fargo-customers-join-cross-selling-backlash (accessed Feb. 1, 2017).
50. Primary sources for this entire section include: http://www.latimes.com/business/la-fi-wells-fargo-sale-pressure-20131222-story.html; CFPB report, *New York Times* 'heart attack'(?).
51. http://www.latimes.com/business/la-fi-wells-fargo-sale-pressure-20131222-story.html.
52. http://time.com/money/4510482/wells-fargo-fake-accounts-class-action-lawsuit/.
53. Stacy Cowley, "'Lions Hunting Zebras': Ex-Wells Fargo Bankers Describe Abuses," *New York Times*, October 20, 2016, https://www.nytimes.com/2016/10/21/business/dealbook/lions-hunting-zebras-ex-wells-fargo-bankers-describe-abuses.html?action=click&contentCollection=DealBook&module=RelatedCoverage®ion=EndOfArticle&pgtype=article (accessed Dec. 14, 2016).
54. Emily Glazer and Christina Rexrode, "Wells Fargo CEO Defends Bank Culture, Lays Blame with Bad Employees," *Wall Street Journal*, September 13, 2016, http://www.wsj.com/articles/wells-fargo-ceo-defends-bank-culture-lays-blame-with-bad-employees-1473784452 (accessed Jan. 14, 2017).
55. https://www.nytimes.com/2016/10/21/business/dealbook/lions-hunting-zebras-ex-wells-fargo-bankers-describe-abuses.html?action=click&contentCollection=DealBook&module=RelatedCoverage®ion=EndOfArticle&pgtype=article.
56. https://www.bloomberg.com/news/articles/2016-11-03/wells-fargo-s-stars-climbed-while-abuses-flourished-beneath-them.
57. Consumer Financial Protection Bureau press release, "Consumer Financial Protection Bureau Fines Wells Fargo $100 Million for Widespread Illegal Practice of Secretly Opening Unauthorized Accounts," September 8, 2016, http://www.consumerfinance.gov/about-us/newsroom/consumer-financial-protection-bureau-fines-wells-fargo-100-million-widespread-illegal-practice-secretly-opening-unauthorized-accounts/ (accessed Jan. 15, 2017).
58. Stacy Cowley, "At Wells Fargo, Complaints about Fraudulent Accounts Since 2005," *New York Times*, October 11, 2016, https://www.nytimes.com/2016/10/12/business/dealbook/at-wells-fargo-complaints-about-fraudulent-accounts-since-2005.html?action=click&contentCollection=DealBook&module=RelatedCoverage®ion=EndOfArticle&pgtype=article (accessed Jan. 14, 2017).
59. Matt Egan, "Wells Fargo Admits to Signs of Worker Retaliation," *CNNMoney*, January 23, 2017, http://money.cnn.com/2017/01/23/investing/wells-fargo-retaliation-ethics-line/index.html (accessed Jan. 29, 2017).
60. Stacy Cowley, "Wells Fargo Workers Claim Retaliation for Playing by the Rules," *New York Times*, September 26, 2016, http://www.nytimes.com/2016/09/27/business/dealbook/wells-fargo-workers-claim-retaliation-for-playing-by-the-rules.html (accessed Jan. 14, 2017).
61. Primary source for content in this section is John Stumpf's prepared testimony to the U.S. Senate Banking Committee on September 20, 2016, http://www.banking.senate.gov/public/index.cfm/2016/9/an-examination-of-wells-fargo-s-unauthorized-accounts-and-the-regulatory-response (accessed Jan. 29, 2017); and John Stumpf's prepared testimony to the U.S. House of Representatives Committee on Financial Services on September 29, 2016, http://financialservices.house.gov/uploadedfiles/hhrg-114-ba00-wstate-jstumpf-20160929.pdf (accessed Jan. 29, 2017).
62. Dan Freed and E. Scott Reckard, "Wells Fargo Faces Costly Overhaul of Bankrupt Sales Culture," *Reuters*, October 12, 2016, http://www.reuters.com/article/us-wells-fargo-accounts-profits-analysis-idUSKCN12C0E3 (accessed Jan. 15, 2017).
63. https://www.nytimes.com/2016/09/17/business/dealbook/wells-fargo-warned-workers-against-fake-accounts-but-they-needed-a-paycheck.html?action=click&contentCollection=DealBook&module=RelatedCoverage®ion=EndOfArticle&pgtype=article.
64. https://www.google.com/?gws_rd=ssl#q=++Kartikay+Mehrotra,+%E2%80%9CWells+Fargo+Ex-Manager%E2%80%99s+Suit+Puts+Scandal+Blame+Higher+Up+Chain.%E2%80%9D&spf=136.
65. https://www.nytimes.com/2016/09/17/business/dealbook/wells-fargo-warned-workers-against-fake-accounts-but-they-needed-a-paycheck.html?action=click&contentCollection=DealBook&module=RelatedCoverage®ion=EndOfArticle&pgtype=article.
66. https://www.bloomberg.com/news/articles/2016-11-03/wells-fargo-s-stars-climbed-while-abuses-flourished-beneath-them.
67. https://www.nytimes.com/2016/09/17/business/dealbook/wells-fargo-scandal-may-be-sign-of-a-poisonous-culture.html?_r=0.
68. http://www.wsj.com/articles/wells-fargo-ceo-defends-bank-culture-lays-blame-with-bad-employees-1473784452.
69. Wells Fargo press release, "Wells Fargo's Carrie Tolstedt to Retire at Year's End; Mary Mack to Succeed Her as Head of Community Banking Effective July 31," July 12, 2016, https://www.wellsfargo.com/about/press/2016/tolstedt-to-retire_0712/ (accessed Jan. 14, 2017).
70. Stephen Grocer, "A List of the Biggest Bank Settlements," *Wall Street Journal*, June 23, 2014, http://blogs.wsj.com/moneybeat

/2014/06/23/a-list-of-the-biggest-bank -settlements/ (accessed Mar. 5, 2017).

71. https://finance.yahoo.com/quote/WFC /holders?p=WFC.
72. Matt Egan, "Warren Buffett Hasn't Sold a Single Share of Wells Fargo Following Scandal," *CNNMoney*, November 11, 2016, http://money.cnn.com/2016/11/11/investing /warren-buffett-wells-fargo-scandal/ (accessed Jan. 29, 2017).
73. Wells Fargo press release, "Wells Fargo Issues Statement on Agreements Related to Sales Practices," September 8, 2016, https:// www.wellsfargo.com/about/press/2016 /sales-practices-agreements_0908.content (accessed Jan. 14, 2017).
74. Wells Fargo press release, "Wells Fargo Chairman and CEO John Stumpf Provides an Update on Actions to Address Wrongful Sales Practices in the Company's Retail Bank," September 29, 2016, https://www .wellsfargo.com/about/press/2016/chairman -ceo-update-on-wrongful-sales-practices _0929.content (accessed Jan. 14, 2017).
75. Abigail Stevenson, "Wells Fargo CEO John Stumpf Says He Will Not Resign," *CNBC*, September 14, 2016, http://www.cnbc.com /2016/09/13/wells-fargo-ceo-john-stumpf -says-he-will-not-resign.html (accessed Mar. 5, 2017).
76. U.S. Senate Banking Committee hearing, "An Examination of Wells Fargo's Unauthorized Accounts and the Regulatory Response," September 20, 2016, http://www .banking.senate.gov/public/index.cfm /hearings?ID=B80F9B81-4331-4F95-91BC -718288EC9DA0 (accessed Mar. 5, 2017).
77. Wells Fargo press release, "Wells Fargo Chairman, CEO John Stumpf Retires; Board of Directors Elects Tim Sloan CEO, Director; Appoints Lead Director Stephen Sanger Chairman, Director Elizabeth Duke Vice Chair," October 12, 2016, https://www .wellsfargo.com/about/press/2016/ceo -john-stumpf-retires_1012.content (accessed Jan. 15, 2017).
78. Wells Fargo press release, "Wells Fargo Amends By-Laws to Require Separation of Chairman and CEO Roles," Dec. 1, 2016, https://www.wellsfargo.com/about /press/2016/separation-chairman-ceo -roles_1201.content (accessed Jan. 15, 2017).
79. http://money.cnn.com/2016/11/11/investing /warren-buffett-wells-fargo-scandal/.
80. Wells Fargo website, "We're Building a Better Wells Fargo," https://www .wellsfargo.com/commitment/ (accessed Jan. 15, 2017).
81. Matt Egan, "Wells Fargo's Reputation is Tanking Survey Finds," October 24, 2016, *CNNMoney*, http://money.cnn.com /2016/10/24/investing/wells-fargo-fake -accounts-angry-customers/ (accessed Apr. 24, 2017).
82. Prepared remarks from Wells Fargo CEO Tim Sloan, October 25, 2016.

CASE 19

ZF Friedrichshafen's Acquisition of TRW Automotive: Making the Deal

Introduction

The case study "*ZF Friedrichshafen's Acquisition of TRW Automotive*" describes the German automotive supplier ZF Friedrichshafen AG's strategic takeover of the USA-based automotive supplier TRW Automotive Holdings Corp. As both companies were already among the largest car manufacturing suppliers in the world before the deal, this acquisition was one of the largest transactions both within the industry and in the stock market year 2015 in general. Also, the acquisition indicates the tremendous structural change within an industry that is mainly driven by market consolidation and a focus on innovation, with the concept of "autonomous driving" at its core.

The objective of this case study is to illustrate the dynamics of a megamerger by using ZF's acquisition of TRW Automotive as an example. In order to illustrate the time sequence of processes in a transaction of this size and the complex structure of the parties involved, the texts are arranged chronologically as in a play, and together they take the form of a sequence of acts. In order to indicate the history of the company's origins appropriately, the texts reflect the opinion and knowledge of the public at particular points in time. In addition, we try to

Main Actors (as they appeared in the acquisition process)

Companies		
ZF	Dr. Stefan Sommer	Chief Executive Officer
	Dr. Konstantin Sauer	Member of the Board of Management: Corp. Finance, IT, M&A
	Juergen Holeksa	Member of the Board of Management: Corp. HR and IR, Corp. Governance, Service Companies, Region Asia Pacific
	Dr. Franz Kleiner	Member of the Board of Management: Region North America
	Dr. Holger Klein	Chief Integration Management Officer
	Prof. Dr. Giorgio Behr	ZF's Chairman of the Supervisory Board
TRW	John C. Plant	Chairman of the Board, President, and CEO
	Patrick Olney	Executive Vice President and COO
	Peter J. Lake	Executive Vice President Sales & Business Development
	Joe Cantie	Executive Vice President and CFO
	Neil Marchuk	Executive Vice President, HR
	Robin Walker-Lee	General Counsel and Secretary
	Mark Stewart	Executive Vice President
	Luke Van Dongen	Vice President: Quality and Operations Effectiveness
	Jerome Dorlack	Vice President: Materials Management, Logistics, Value Analysis & Engineering and Supplier Development
	Aine Denari	Chief Integration Management Officer
Employer and Employee Representation		
	Achim Dietrich-Stephan	Employee Representative

This case was written by Henning Düsterhoff, Günter Müller-Stewens (University of St. Gallen), Kathrin Pfeifle, and Max Ringlstetter (University of Eichstätt-Ingolstadt). It is intended to be used as the basis for class discussions rather than to illustrate either the effective or the ineffective handling of a management situation. The case was compiled from published sources and internal company data.

This case is part of the University of St. Gallen case collection at the Case Centre: http://www.thecasecentre.org/educators/ordering/whatsavailable/collections/stgallen

create a simulation-like atmosphere by inviting students to connect more closely with the events depicted.

Our information sources include press articles and the websites of the companies involved, as well as internal materials from ZF TRW and interviews with key actors within ZF.

I. Understanding the Context of the Deal

Background: The Deal

Looking back, it is not that easy to remember which of the two events went off like the bigger bomb: the call that came in mid-September 2014 or the fact that the automotive supplier ZF Friedrichshafen AG signed a deal to buy its USA-based competitor TRW (a company similar in size) the very same day, as the man told you over the phone: "ZF signed a merger agreement in the amount of USD 12.4 bn on 15 September 2014, with the local board. A 16% premium was paid on the market price of TRW. The price was equivalent to a multiple roughly 7.5 times EBITDA. This is one of the largest transactions both within the industry and in the stock market year 2015 in general," he added. The caller further stated that his boss, Dr. Stefan Sommer, Chief Executive Officer of ZF, had described the rationale behind the acquisition as follows: "As one of the world's leading suppliers, we aim to offer the automotive industry complete system solutions for the megatrends of the future."[1]

"This opportunity, as compelling as it sounds, does not come without risks," the man went on. "Both companies are looking back on a long history in their industry where TRW is listed on the stock exchange, and ZF Friedrichshafen AG is in the hands of two foundations. The shareholders are the Zeppelin Foundation (93.8%) and the Dr. Juergen and Irmgard Ulderup Foundation (6.2% of shares). Next year, in 2015, ZF will celebrate 100 years of existence. TRW is 14 years older." The man continued: "When comparing both enterprises with each other (see Figure 1), you can identify a number of challenges and risks with regard to the transaction: A company approximately the same size as the buyer needs to be integrated. In addition, different cultures and nationalities have to be combined in a new joint one. Furthermore, both companies are quite complementary regarding locations, business areas, and customer groups, which results in low levels of cost synergies but promising growth opportunities." (cf. Appendix 1). You asked yourself why this partner of a top-tier consulting company was telling you all this over the phone.

Background: The Competitive Situation in the Global Automotive Industry

After the call, it took you a while to grasp what had just happened. Dr. Holger Klein, a former partner at the McKinsey office where you worked as an analyst during your gap year, recalled your performance and your name and even asked whether you would have time to meet him at the FEZ (Forschungs- und Entwicklungszentrum[3]) at ZF's headquarters in Friedrichshafen the following day. That left you with very little time to prepare and research the topic! On your way to Friedrichshafen the next morning, you found some more time to prepare and review your findings:

In 2014, the total size of the global automotive supplier market came to EUR 620 bn, a 20% rise since 2010.[4] Since the bottom of the financial crisis in 2009, automotive suppliers had seen strong growth, mainly due to growing vehicle production volumes in the main markets.

Most recently, 2014 was a record year for automotive suppliers with a global EBIT margin of 7.5%[5]: On average, automotive suppliers have outperformed their customers in terms of profitability, although the sector still has room for improvement, compared with other industries (cf. Appendices 2 and 3). However, performances vary and depend on four key factors: (1) region, (2) company size, (3) product focus, and (4) business model.[6]

1. **Region**: After-crisis development showed that some regions outperformed others to a certain extent. Especially suppliers from the NAFTA[1] region were able to improve their performance significantly. By contrast, Europe-based suppliers were just recently impacted by their weak home market, as 2013 showed lower sales than 2012. However, their great advantage is their leading technology positions in many different segments, as well as their favorable customer mix. In the meantime, Asian companies are leading the market in terms of sales, but they also face decreasing margin levels as growing competition puts them under pressure.
2. **Company size**: The expression "*size matters*" holds true in the automotive supplier industry. Economies of scale are an important driver in an industry where larger companies have continuously become more profitable. Large multinational suppliers profit from globalization, while upper-end midsize companies (EUR 2.5–10 bn in revenue) seem to be "*stuck in the middle,*" as their performance is below average. This development indicates that size is an important

[1]NAFTA = North American Free Trade Agreement

Figure 1 Comparison between ZF and TRW[2]

	ZF	TRW Automotive
Name	ZF Friedrichshafen AG	TRW Automotive, Inc.
Type	Stock corporation (AG)	Stock corporation (Inc.)
Traded as	Non-listed	Listed on NYSE: TRW
Ownership	Zeppelin Foundation	Free float
Predecessors	ZF Friedrichshafen AG	TRW Inc.
Founded	1915	1904
Industries	Automotive industry (car and CV), rail transport, marine engineering, aviation	Automotive industry
Headquarters	Friedrichshafen, Baden-Wuerttemberg, Germany	Livonia, Michigan, USA
Number of locations	121 facilities in 27 countries	185 facilities in 24 countries
Area served	Worldwide	Worldwide
Divisions	(1) Car Powertrain Technology (2) Car Chassis Technology (3) Commercial Vehicle Technology (4) Industrial Technology	(1) Automotive Components (2) Chassis Systems (3) Electronics (4) Occupant Safety Systems
Employees	72.463	66.100
CEO	Stefan Sommer (CEO)	John Plant (Chairman & CEO)
Sales	EUR 18.415 m (2014) EUR 16.800 m (2013) EUR 15.500 m (2012)	USD 17.539 m (FY 2014) USD 17.435 m (FY 2013) USD 16.444 m (FY 2012)
EBIT ZF/ Operating income TRW	EUR 1.098 m (2014) EUR 807 m (2013) EUR 643 m (2012)	USD 501 m (FY 2014) USD 1.227 m (FY 2013) USD 1.085 m (FY 2012)
Investments in R&D	EUR 891 m (2014) EUR 836 m (2013) EUR 770 m (2012)	USD 694 m (FY 2014) USD 735 m (FY 2013) USD 623 m (FY 2012)
Total assets	– EUR 826 m (2011)	USD 10.900 m (FY 2012) –
Total equity	–	USD 7.300 m (FY 2012)
Website	www.zf.com	www.trw.com

success factor and that suppliers should aim to leverage scale on the cost side in order to gain a competitive position in the future.

3. **Product focus**: Some types of products lead to higher profitability than others. While tire suppliers could benefit from strong aftermarket business in recent years, powertrain margins, which are still on a high level, are under pressure because of intensified competition. Exterior suppliers come third in the profitability ranking. Finally, while electronics suppliers are becoming increasingly important in the market, their profitability in terms of EBIT margin is below the automotive supplier industry average (5.5% vs. 7.2%). As a result, players may want to take measures into consideration that would help them become industry leaders in the near future.

Figure 2 The Historical Development of ZF and TRW

A Brief Historical Overview: ZF Friedrichshafen AG	
1915	Luftschiffbau Zeppelin creates Zahnradfabrik Friedrichshafen GmbH (ZF) for the development and manufacturing of special gears for airships and other aircraft. The Zeppelin foundation controls the company.
1921	Firm is converted from a limited private company (GmbH) to a stock corporation (AG).
1932	The company begins producing automotive steering systems.
1947	Complete responsibility for the Zeppelin foundation is transferred to the city of Friedrichshafen. Three years later, 90% of ZF's ownership is assigned to the Zeppelin-Stiftung foundation.
1992	The company changes its name from Zahnradfabrik Friedrichshafen AG to ZF Friedrichshafen AG.
2000	ZF and Sauer form ZF Graziano Materials Handling Components GmbH, a joint venture to combine forklift transmission operations.
2001	Acquisition of Mannesmann Sachs AG. Division is renamed ZF Sachs AG.
2008	Joint venture with ArvinMeritor to reduce noncore operations within the company.
2014	ZF Friedrichshafen AG makes an EBIT of EUR 891 m on sales of EUR 18.4 bn.

A Brief Historical Overview: TRW Automotive Holdings Corp.	
1901	The Cleveland Cap Screw Company is founded.
1926	Company is renamed Thompson Products, after its general manager Charles Thompson.
1953	Simon Ramo and Dean Wooldridge found The Ramo-Wooldridge Corporation.
1958	TRW (Thompson Ramo Wooldridge) is founded when Thompson Products merges with Ramo-Wooldridge.
2002	Aerospace company Northrop Grumman acquires competitor TRW and sells TRW's automotive division to private equity firm Blackstone Group.
2004	TRW goes public. The main shareholders are Blackstone (56.7%), Northrop Grumman (17.2%), and TRW management (1.7%).
2014	TRW makes an operating income of USD 501 m on sales of USD 17.5 bn.

4. **Business model**: Different business models performed differently. In particular, product innovators clearly outpaced process specialists in terms of profitability. Car manufacturers show a strong demand for innovative products as they feature a higher differentiation potential and thus a higher willingness to pay. High entry barriers and high consolidation are key characteristics of innovation-driven segments. The latter is caused by steadily rising costs for R&D, making it difficult for smaller companies to cope with the strong pressure for innovations. As a result of this high level of innovation pressure, alliance and cooperation in the product innovation sector are regarded as particularly important.

Along with operational performance, many suppliers have improved their liquidity and financing situation significantly and find themselves today in a more stable position than in 2007, before the crisis. Financial resources provide the companies with the opportunity to react to upcoming challenges for the industry.

In fact, the automotive supplier industry is facing a period of constant change. According to a Roland Berger study, industry dynamics are characterized by a continued shift of end-customer demand to Asia, increasing M&A activities by emerging market investors, technological innovations in the field of driver assistance and connectivity, and finally also the volatility of currency and capital markets, which has a significant impact on world trade.

However, according to a report by McKinsey, even though there are several scenarios (see Figure 3) and a game-changing disruption is on the rise, there is still no

Figure 3 Overview of the High-disruption vs. the Low-disruption Scenario

Overview of the High-Disruption vs. Low-Disruption Scenario	High	Low
Diverse mobility		
City policies discouraging private vehicles	Intensified	Steady
New, on-demand business models	Prevalent	Limited
Model shift away from car ownership to shared mobility	Significant	Limited
Autonomous driving		
Regulatory challenges are overcome	Fast	Gradual
Development of safe and reliable technical solutions	Comprehensive	Incomplete
Consumer acceptance and willingness to pay	Enthusiastic	Limited
Electrification		
Battery prices continue to decline	Rapid	Protracted
Regulator-driven emission restrictions	Intensified	Gradual
Consumer demand for electrified powertrains	Widespread	Restrained
Connectivity		
Uptake of car connectivity globally	Vast majority	Partial
Consumers regularly using paid content	Mainstream	Limited

(Source: McKinsey&Company 2016, p. 4)

integrated perspective on how the automotive industry will look in 10–15 years as a result of these trends.[7] Roughly two years ago, ZF started to analyze and revise its long-term corporate strategy, as Mr. Juergen Holeksa, member of the board at ZF, stated: "*In this process, we realized that there are three global technology-driven megatrends in particular that we should pay attention to: semi- or fully autonomous driving, safety, and fuel efficiency.*"[8]

Questions to Help Understand the Context of the Deal

As a consultant to the deal parties and after considering your findings, ask the following questions: What are the industry characteristics, and how is ZF prepared to face these and any other future challenges?

I.1 *Industry characteristics:*
What are the challenges and dynamics in the automotive industry?

I.2 *ZF's strategy and new positioning:*
What is the rationale for the ZF TRW deal?

I.3 *Alternatives to the acquisition of TRW:*
Identify and evaluate alternatives that ZF could have undertaken to meet the objectives of the defined strategy.

II. Fundamental Decisions in M&A Processes

Arriving in Friedrichshafen, a rather small town located right next to Lake Constance on the border with Switzerland and blessed with a wonderful lakeside view and about 60,000 inhabitants, you cannot help but smile: This town welcomes—and in a way even owns—a company that has more than double as many employees around the world as this town's number of inhabitants.

Dr. Klein, a former partner at McKinsey and at present the Chief Integration Management Officer at ZF, welcomes you to his office. After some small talk about general developments in the automotive sector and a few more challenging questions on ZFs positioning (which you were prepared for), he describes the acquisition process from the first rumors in the summer until the deal was signed a couple of days ago, in September 2014.

10 July 2014

Rumors of ZF Friedrichshafen AG's Imminent Acquisition of TRW

It was a wake-up call for the whole industry when rumors started to spread that ZF Friedrichshafen AG is about to make an imminent takeover bid to TRW Automotive Holdings Corp. As both companies are among the largest car manufacturing suppliers in the world, this deal would be one of the largest transactions ever in the industry. Furthermore, the acquisition would mark the beginning of a tremendous structural change within the industry that would mainly be driven by market consolidation and a focus on innovation.

To some extent, insiders were not surprised by the rumors. It was not long before that Stefan Sommer, ZF's CEO, had announced the company's ambitions to *invest heavily in technology for autonomous driving*, a field in which TRW had pushed for market leadership over time.

Based in Livonia, Michigan, in the USA, *TRW Automotive* develops and produces (among others) video and radar technology that enables semi-automatic driving. TRW is the market leader in the field of security systems and a pioneer in car dynamics, assistance systems, as well as electronics and software systems. The company recently reported sales of about EUR 17.5 bn, making it almost as large as ZF. Continuously increasing investments in R&D are a key issue for TRW and drive it into M&A negotiations. Without more capital from the outside, the company would not be able to maintain its high level of innovation.

ZF Friedrichshafen AG is the world's largest independent gear drive manufacturer. In 2014, for the first time, it was ranked among the top ten global suppliers. The company had just recently announced its aim to increase revenues from around EUR 17 bn to more than EUR 40 bn by 2025. That means more than doubling its sales in about 10 years—an ambitious goal. To reach this goal, external growth through increased M&A activities would appear to be indispensable, as it is rather unlikely to achieve such growth organically. In addition to strategic objectives, macroeconomic factors provide favorable conditions, as a historically low level of interest rates boosts M&A activities around the world. The time seems right for a megamerger and for ZF to fulfill its strategy by acquiring a strong competitor (cf. Appendices 4 and 5).

"On July 10, 2014, certain media outlets reported that TRW had received a preliminary acquisition proposal from ZF. Later that day, TRW issued a press release confirming that it had received a preliminary, non-binding proposal to acquire TRW and that TRW was evaluating the proposal as well as other strategic alternatives to enhance stockholder value. In its press release, TRW also indicated that it had retained Goldman Sachs as its financial advisor. Later that same day, ZF publicly confirmed that it was in the preliminary stages of discussing a possible acquisition of TRW. The closing price of TRW's common stock on July 10, 2014 was $98.91, up $7.51 from the closing price of TRW's common stock on July 9, 2014, the trading day before the media reports and the TRW and ZF public statements."[9]

Initial reports state that ZF values the target at around USD 11–12 bn, while the company's market price is around USD 11 bn. The media welcomes the news and reports favorably on the transaction, expecting ZF to enhance its market power and to demonstrate market leadership.

30 July 2014

First Valuation Indicates Progress in Negotiations

Unofficial statements report ZF was about to pay roughly USD 105 per share for the target, which would produce a price of nearly USD 12 bn. This valuation equals an EBITDA multiple of 7.5, based on TRW's figures expected for 2014.[10] Thus, the deal would become one of the most expensive transactions ever seen in the car manufacturing supplier industry. The value of TRW shares falls by 2.6% to USD 101.89.

15 September 2014

ZF and TRW Sign a Merger Agreement for ZF's Acquisition of TRW

Barely two months after the first rumors in the industry, the deal is set up, and a final offer is announced. The board of TRW, a Delaware company, unanimously accepts ZF's offer to acquire all shares in the company for USD 105.6 per share, totaling USD 12.4 bn. ZF's offer of USD 105.6 per share in cash represents a premium of 1.7% to TRW's closing price of USD 103.85 on Friday, 12 September. Including debts taken over with the acquisition, the deal has a total volume of USD 13.5 bn.

"Following the meeting of the TRW Board on September 15, 2014, prior to the opening of trading of TRW's common stock on the NYSE, the parties executed the merger agreement and finalized the other documentation related to the proposed transaction and ZF executed its credit agreement (and related ancillary agreements) providing for its committed debt financing. Each of TRW and ZF also issued press releases announcing the transaction."[11] The final "*yes*" is subject to TRW shareholder approval, which is expected by November.

In order *to finance the acquisition*, ZF is planning on issuing bonds within six months after the closing. In the meantime, a bank consortium that includes Citigroup and Deutsche Bank provides the company with credit lines. In addition, ZF holds EUR 1.9 bn in cash. However, the company does not state whether it wants to make use of its reserves for the acquisition. According to management, the high leverage will be reduced by increasing growth over the next few years.

If approved, ZF would become, together with Bosch, the third-largest car manufacturing supplier, right after Continental and Denso, a Japanese supplier. Faced with the upcoming stronger competition, Bosch CEO Volkmar Denner states: "*We generally approve of increasing competition and do not see any issues here.*" From a strategic point of view, both parties complement each other quite well, since TRW is mainly active in the mass market, while ZF focuses on premium segments. Both companies share the competitive advantage of technology leadership.

Taking precautions against antitrust concerns, ZF sold its steering systems division (ZFLS), which used to be a joint venture with Bosch. In so doing, it avoids any issues with antitrust law that might result from the continued cooperation with ZFLS and its employees, which became essential for a successful closing with TRW. The deal was announced the same day the TRW offer was published. ZF CEO Sommer stated that the divestment was a severe cut, as the products of the joint venture were of good quality and ZFLS accounted for 13,000 employees and a turnover of EUR 4.1 bn.[12] In preparation for the merger, *TRW also sold its linkage and suspension business* to Tokyo conglomerate THK Co. Ltd. The divestiture, with annual sales of about USD 550 m, was subject to customary conditions, including regulatory approvals. TRW Chairman and CEO John C. Plant stated that "*in addition to resolving the company's overlap position relating to TRW's pending acquisition by ZF Friedrichshafen AG (...) this agreement represents a great outcome for both TRW and the business*," as the pairing with THK will further strengthen the linkage and suspension's business position as an industry leader.

"Further divestments are expected," Dr. Klein tells you. The following questions are important to the analysis.

Questions on Fundamental Decisions in M&A Processes

Suppose it is September 2014, and you are assigned to provide decision-making support for strategic processes and decisions after the merger agreement was signed but before the approval of TRW shareholders in an Extraordinary General Meeting (EGM; This special meeting will take place in Atlanta, Georgia, on November 19, 2014 at 10:00 a.m., Eastern Time). There is a lot to decide on…

II.1 *Acquisition procedure:*
Which aspects need to be considered in an acquisition process—and when? Draw a rough timeline.

a. *Due diligence*: In principle, which options are open to you regarding the due diligence process? Which of these options would you select in the case of ZF TRW? Is the Board of Directors allowed to give access to internal documents? What are possible consequences? Explain your decision.

b. *Share price development*: How would you interpret the share price development of TRW in Appendix 6? Give a brief explanation.

c. *Financing*: Which options are open to you regarding the financing of the deal? Decide for one of these options and explain your choice.

II.2 *Legal topics:*

a. *Antitrust:* Transatlantic M&A's often require that antitrust clearances be obtained in several jurisdictions before the deal may proceed. In the case of ZF TRW, what could ZF have to deal with after signing the merger agreement? Think about possible antitrust topics and give reasons for your answer.

b. *Clearance—pre-closing guidelines*: What is typical for the phase between signing and closing? Think about the pre-closing guidelines generally required by antitrust law. What is allowed, and what is not?

II.3 *Type of integration:*
Which type of integration would you decide on? Explain your decision.

Appendix

Appendix 1 Complementary Product Portfolio of ZF and TRW

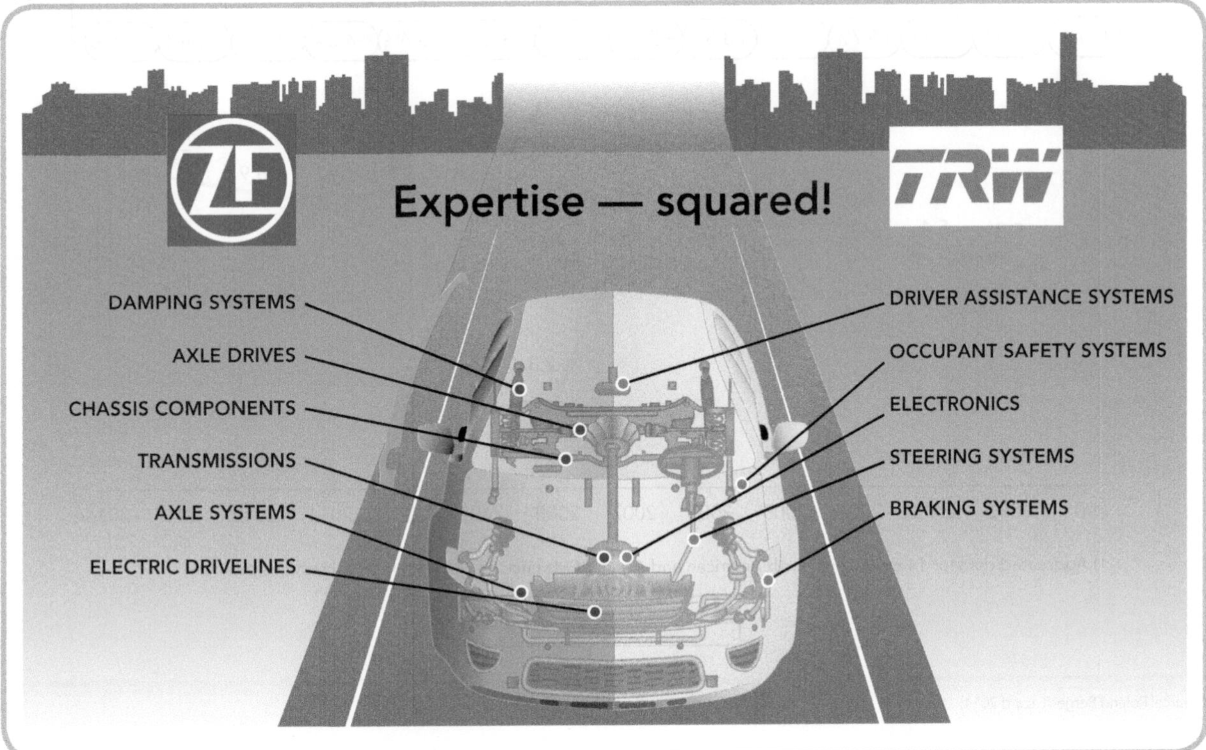

(Source: ZF Friedrichshafen AG, internal)

Appendix 2 Key Supplier Performance Indicators, 2005–2014e

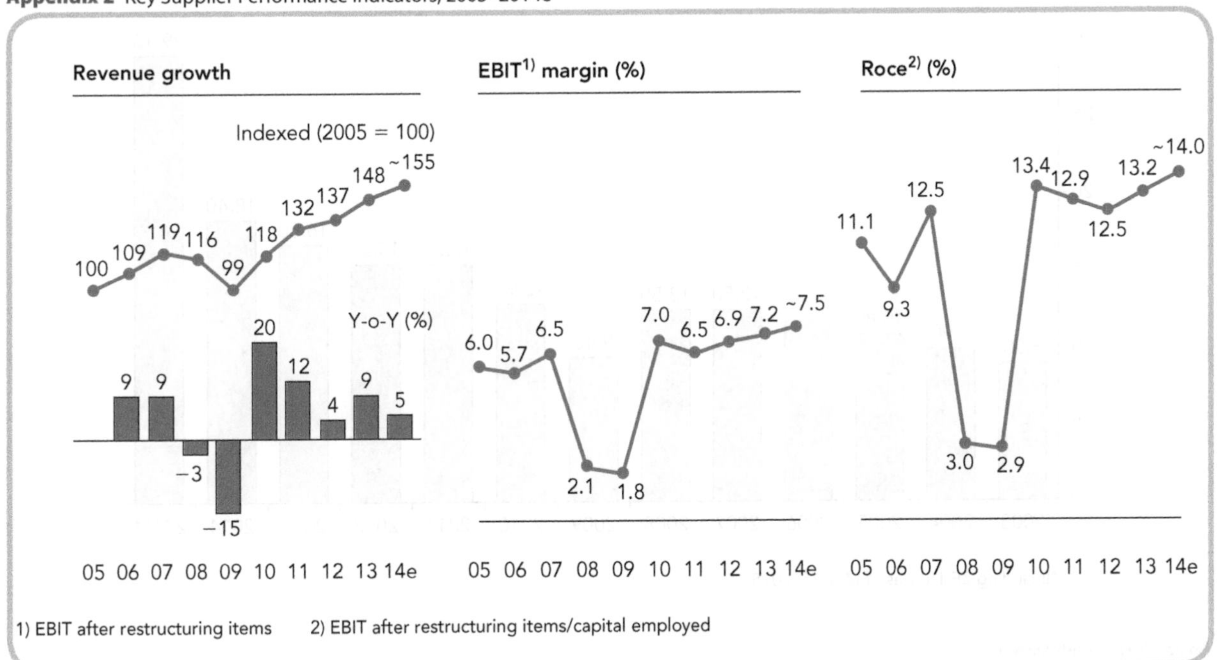

(Source: Roland Berger/Lazard 2014)

Appendix 3 OEM and Supplier Profitability (EBIT Margin), 2001–2014e [%]

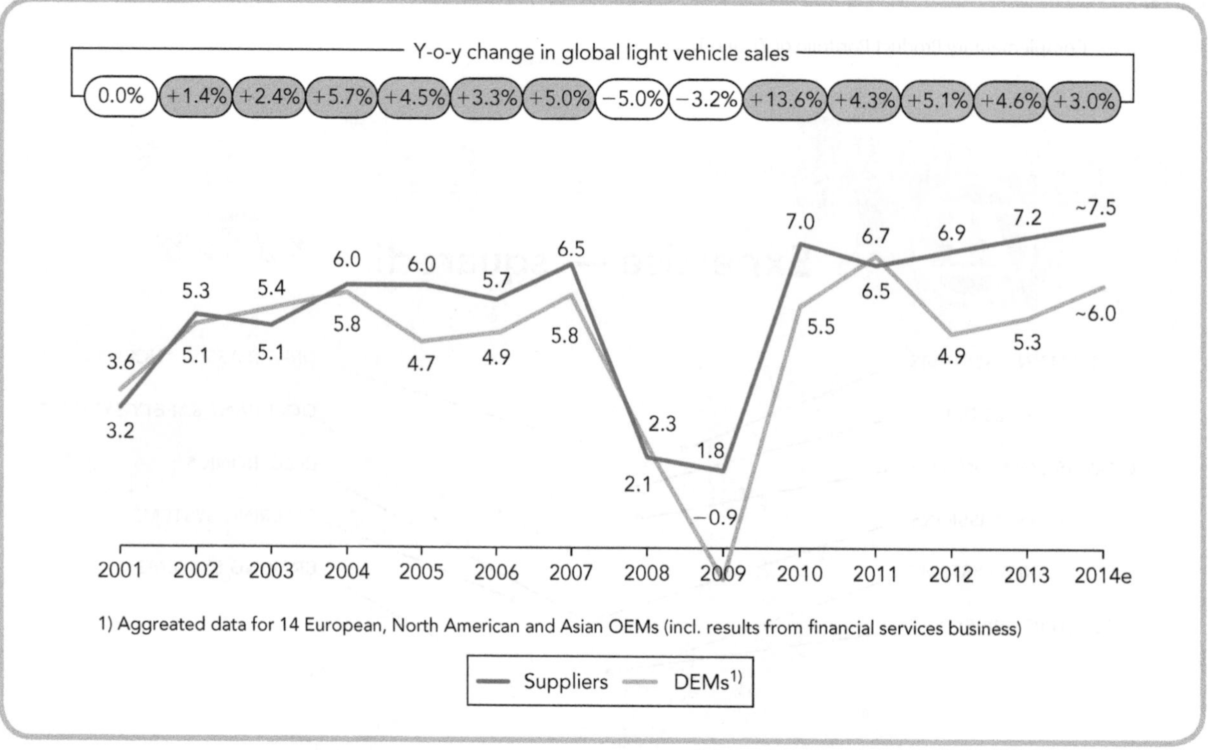

(Source: Roland Berger/Lazard 2014)

Appendix 4 ZF Revenue in Bn EUR, 2003–2015

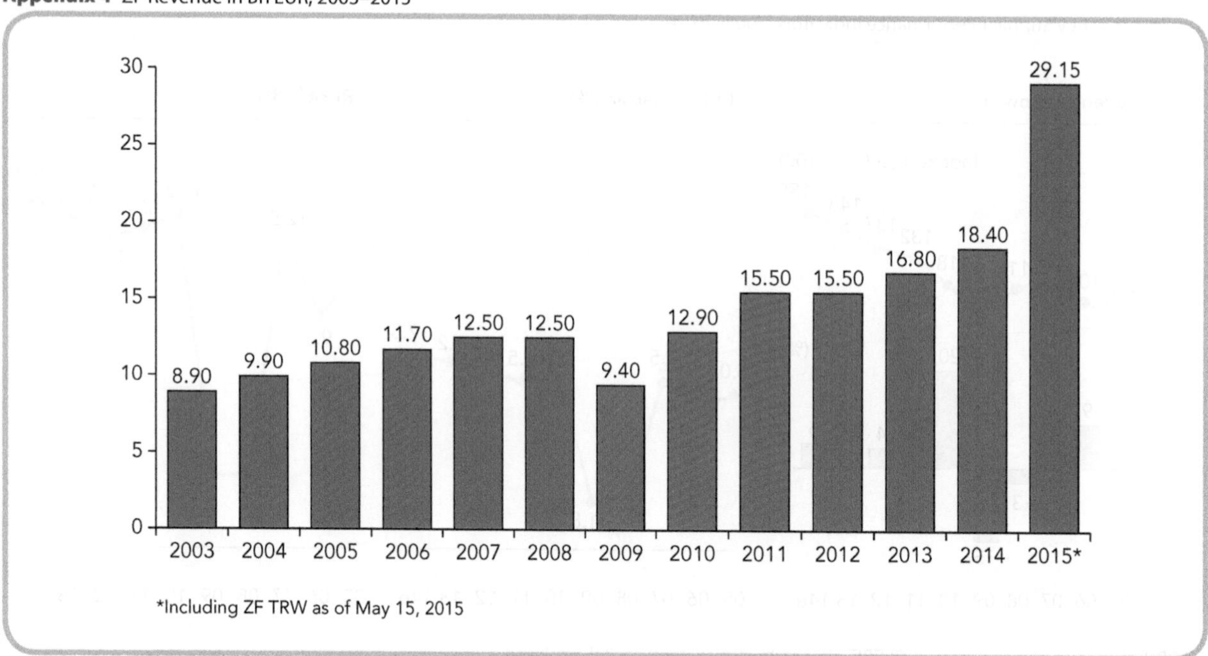

(Source: ZF Friedrichshafen AG)

Appendix 5 TRW Revenue in Bn USD, 2003–2014

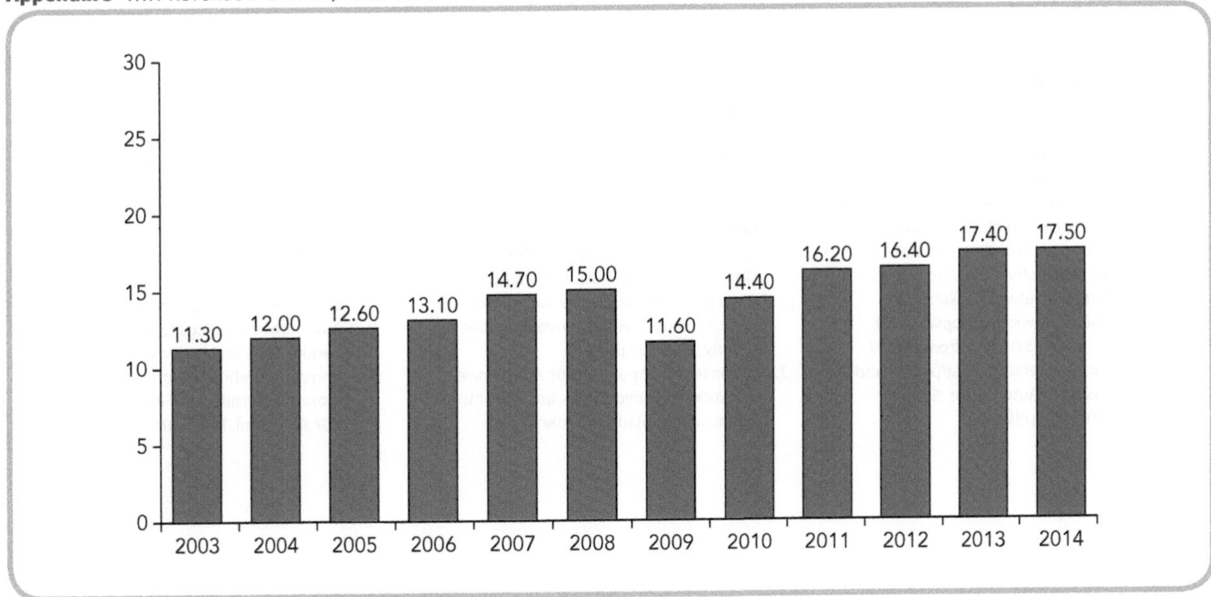

Appendix 6 ZF TRW Automotive Holdings Corp. (NYSE: TRW)

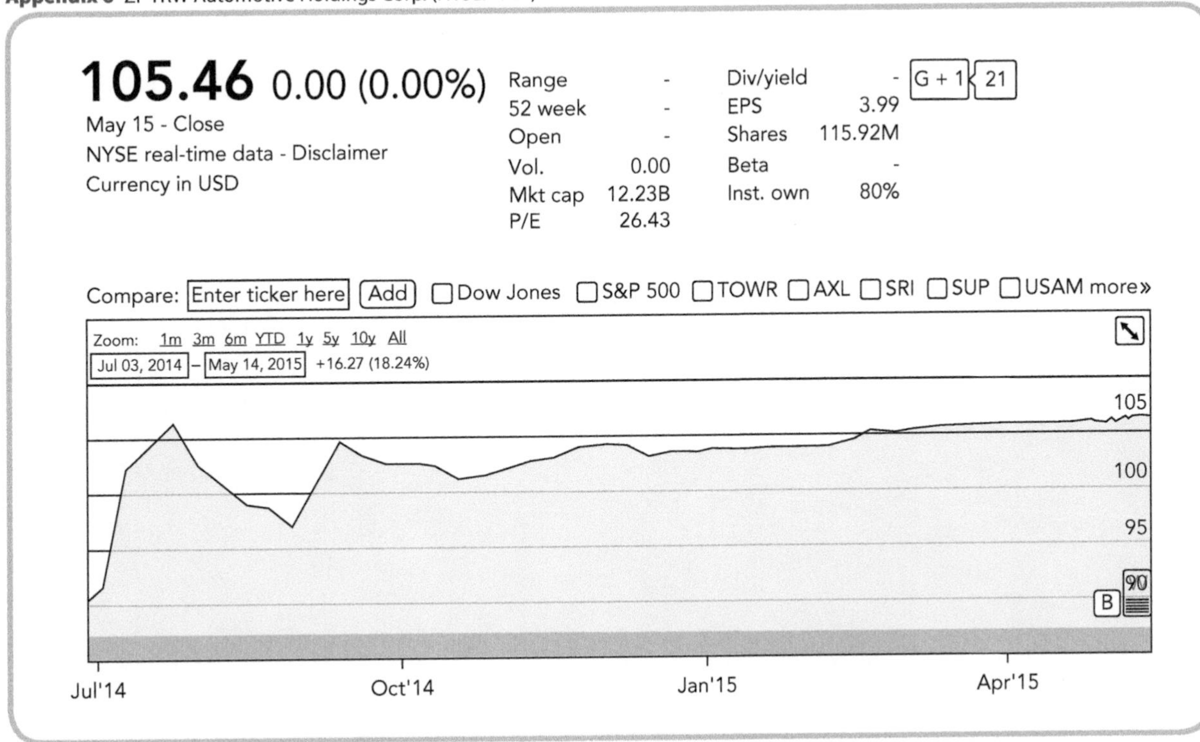

NOTES

1. ZF Presseinformation: *Going Forward Together: Prospects for the new ZF*. 01.07.2015.
2. Until the completion of the acquisition of TRW, ZF and TRW were legally independent companies with separate financial statements – ZF reported according to IFRS, and, until the closing of the acquisition, TRW reported according to US-GAAP.
3. Center for Research and Development.
4. Roland Berger Strategy Consultants (2014): *Global Automotive Supplier Study*. Downloaded on 15.04.2015, from http://www.rolandberger.de/media/pdf/Roland_Berger_Global_Automotive_Supplier_Study_20141209.pdf
5. Roland Berger Strategy Consultants (2014): *Global Automotive Supplier Study*. Downloaded on 15.04.2015, from http://www.rolandberger.de/media/pdf/Roland_Berger_Global_Automotive_Supplier_Study_20141209.pdf
6. Roland Berger Strategy Consultants (2014): *Global Automotive Supplier Study*. Downloaded on 15.04.2015 from http://www.rolandberger.de/media/pdf/Roland_Berger_Global_Automotive_Supplier_Study_20141209.pdf
7. McKinsey&Company (2016): *Automotive Revolution–perspective towards 2030*. In: Advanced Industries, January 2016.
8. Zeitschrift Führung + Organisation (zfo): *Herausforderungen und Risiken einer Grossakquisition*. Juni 2015 (6), S. 400–404.
9. United States Securities and Exchange Commision (SEC): *Schedule 14A* by TRW Automotive Holdings Corp., S.35.
10. Reuters: *Insider – ZF und TRW kommen in Übernahmeverhandlungen voran*. 30.09.2014.
11. United States Securities and Exchange Commision (SEC): *Schedule 14A* by TRW Automotive Holdings Corp.
12. Handelsblatt online: www.handelsblatt.com/unternehmen/industrie/zulieferer-bosch-uebernimmt-zf-lenksysteme/10701612.html, 14.09.2014

CASE 20

The Rise and Fall of ZO Rooms[1]

Founded in 2014, ZO Rooms had entered the budget hotel space in India with lofty ambitions. Its seven founders who had formed Zostel Hospitality Pvt. Ltd., India's first backpacking hotel chain the previous year with the motto "Changing the way India travels,"[2] were confident and optimistic. They believed that despite entering a year later than OYO rooms, the pioneer in the space, ZO's lean and scalable business model would lead to explosive growth. Their confidence was indeed borne out over the next year, as the company signed up hundreds of hotels and thousands of rooms under its banner. ZO had also raised as much as $47 million from globally reputed investors such as Tiger Global and Orios Venture Partners ($15 million in July 2015 and $32 million in September 2015), suggesting a high degree of confidence in the prospects of the sector as well as ZO's business model.[3]

By late 2015 however, a perfect storm had hit the online budget hotel aggregation (OBA) sector in general and ZO in particular. The company (and its close peers) had been blocked from listing its hotels on their websites by online travel agents (OTAs) such as Yatra.com (an aggregator similar to Expedia.com); several competitors with similar (or slightly different) business models had jumped into the fray increasing the level of competition and putting pressure on prices (see Exhibit 1); and the company was finding it difficult to raise further capital to finance its ambitious expansion. Buffeted by these adverse events, ZO agreed to be acquired by OYO, its bigger and better-funded rival, in an arrangement under which ZO's shareholders would get a small stake in the combined company. Clearly, something had gone very wrong for this early-mover (though not first mover) in the rapidly growing segment.

History

Seven co-founders, all recent graduates of leading educational institutes in India, established Zostel Hospitality Pvt. Ltd. in August 2013 with their own savings but were also able to raise funding from angel investors such as Bangalore-based Presha Paragash.[4] The founders believed that unbranded budget hotels in India offered an uncertain experience to their customers including wrong images, fake reviews, uncertain booking statuses, poor amenities, and unhygienic ambiance. Their vision was "to clean this space and provide a suave, tech-savvy option of accommodation to today's youth."[5]

Industry Economics

The travel and tourism industry in India had witnessed strong growth especially since the year 2000, concurrently with growth in the general economy. The emergence of a large middle class that had higher disposable income and appetite for travel was a key driver for this growth.[6] According to Vikas Saxena, CEO of messaging company Nimbuzz and an investor in Wudstay, an OBA, the size of the Indian travel market was as much as US$70 billion.[7] According to a report by HVS and The World Travel and Tourism Council, the travel industry in India was expected to reach 1,747 million travelers by 2021, which would require 188,500 additional hotel rooms.[8]

Exhibit 1 Characteristics of ZO Rooms and a Few Key Rivals

Aggregator	Founded	Cities	Hotels	Funded	Funded by
OYO	2013	149	4000+	$125 million	SoftBank, Sequoia Capital, Lightspeed Venture
ZO	2014	54	800+	$ 47 million	Tiger Global and Orios Venture
StayZilla	2010	4,000+ locations	30,000+ properties	$ 20 million	IAN, Matrix, Nexus
Treebo	2015	8	24	$ 6 million	Matrix Partners
Fab Hotels	2015	29	200+	$ 5 million	Accel Partners
Wudstay	2015	2	40	$ 3 million	Mangrove Capital

Source: Shweta Saxena, "Challenges in Room Aggregation Business in India', December 9, 2015, http://www.exploringstartups.com/challenges-in-room-aggregation-business-in-india/, accessed on August 16, 2017.

Mid-range and budget hotels accounted for a significant proportion of the Indian lodging market with some estimates placing the size of the budget hotel business at US$20 billion in 2015.[9] A room in a budget hotel would be priced anywhere between INR 1000 and INR 2500 per night (approximately US$15 to US$35), depending on the location and amenities.[1] Mid-range hotels would generally be priced below INR 5,000 per night. According to Paavan Nanda, a co-founder of Zostel and ZO, there was a gap in demand versus supply for budget rooms. He estimated the supply of budget rooms in 2015 at two million, mostly from non-chain hotels. These figures were similar to consulting firms HVS' estimates of 1.8 million unbranded rooms and 112,000 branded rooms.[10] Another source estimated that India was short of 150,000 budget hotel rooms in 2015.[11] Nanda further estimated that while the demand for budget rooms was growing at 35 percent, the supply was only growing at 15 percent and hence the demand–supply gap would widen over time.[12]

The strong expected growth of budget hotels could be attributed to a couple of reasons: first, the purchasing power of leisure travelers (and even some business travelers) was limited and they could rarely afford luxury (or even mid-range) hotels; second, unlike the luxury and mid-range hotel segments which focused on very large cities such as Mumbai, Delhi and Bangalore (called Tier I cities), budget hotels could be found in more diverse locations including smaller cities (also called Tier II and III cities), industrial towns, pilgrim destinations and leisure destinations, implying greater market potential; third, building budget hotels was attractive for hotel owners, primarily because they could be built faster and more cost-effectively, an important criterion in a country where access to capital was not easy.[13]

The budget hotels industry had many different types of players. Other than large chains (e.g., domestically-owned chains such as Ginger Hotels by the Tata group, a large conglomerate), the majority of hotels suffered from lack of awareness among target customers (lack of discovery) and, as a consequence, unsold inventory. These issues could be directly attributed to two factors: lack of marketing and/or technological skills, and resistance to the adoption of latest (and cost-effective) technological tools such as online marketing through own websites or apps, and inventory and property management software. The latter was partly attributable to the unfamiliarity with how technology might help but also because of resource (specifically funds) scarcity. In fact, even many chains which typically owned less than 50 hotels,[14] didn't have sufficient knowledge and clarity on the essential requirements and demands of the tech-savvy budget traveler, an increasingly important segment. In this regard, a comment by Pranav Maheshwari, a co-founder of Vista Rooms, another OBA, was instructive: "Most hoteliers don't understand how to digitally enable their business. They struggle with online bookings, automated check in and checkout never mind the situation around managing reviews. We talk with our partners on a constant basis and believe we can make a difference."[15]

The lack of technological sophistication of a typical budget hotel player had created opportunities for new entrants to innovate with their superior technological skills and asset light models. These included OBAs that had entered recently such as OYO Rooms and ZO Rooms, as well as the more established OTAs who marketed a broader range services including airline tickets, hotel rooms and rental cars on behalf of the owners. The OBAs' business models varied but they generally involved many of the following: raising venture capital; developing a website and a smartphone app; signing up hotels as partners (with or without prepayment for inventory and on a partial or full inventory basis); getting the hotel owners to provide a standardized offering (including renovations of physical facilities as needed); and aggressively trying to market the rooms on behalf of the hoteliers mostly through online channels and sometimes through significant price discounts. Both the OBAs and OTAs could offer consumers tremendous choices compared to standalone hotels or even chains, a key advantage of the aggregation strategy. For instance, in August 2015, Yatra.com, a leading OTA, claimed that it had the biggest selection of budget properties with more than 40,000 three-star and below properties on its books.[16]

ZO's Business Model

ZO's primary focus was on two segments: leisure travelers and corporate travelers on a budget who were likely to choose a reliable brand of budget hotels that was available in every locality within a city.[17] There were several cornerstones of ZO's strategy.

1. Like other OBAs (and OTAs), ZO did not own any of the hotels but approached the hotel owners to brand their inventory (typically partial inventory) as ZO Rooms. The hotel owner had to make changes,

1. The exchange rate for 2015 varied between 63.24 and 66.41 INR to one US dollar. Source: http://www.xe.com/currencycharts/?from=USD&to=INR&view=5Y, accessed on August 16, 2017.

at its own costs, in the room (e.g., renovations) according to ZO's standard, with ZO acting as a consultant to the owner. Dharamveer Chouhan, a co-founder of ZO's parent company Zostel, said that ZO had a thorough checklist before it took a hotel on board. "We have an Audit app which has a 200-point checklist on which each hotel is tested—parameters like size of the hotel, linen quality, staff qualification. Once the hotel goes through the audit and the report is generated, we evaluate on which points the hotel needs to work on. Our back-end team helps the hotel owner with the costing of how much they have to invest in the property to become a ZO Rooms partner."[18]

2. Hotel owners who signed up with ZO could expect improved occupancy since the hotel would be featured on ZO's website. Unlike OTAs (or marketplaces), where the hotel owners could list on multiple platforms, ZO required exclusivity from the owners. Chouhan further clarified the differences between OTAs and ZO: "Unlike a marketplace approach where the hotel once listed remains as is, we work with our hotel partners. We contribute marketing, technology, analysis of data and ensure that the hospitality service is of top-notch standard. A marketplace will never be able to invest in the technological solution when it comes to hospitality partners. Getting hotels online and ensuring online booking is a straightforward mechanism."[19] ZO also installed tablets at the hotel reception, which helped it manage inventory and also facilitate a quick check-in. In fact, it claimed to be the first chain of hotels to install mobile tablets at the properties' reception areas. The technology helped ZO to manage live inventory (through tracking of available inventory) and ensured a one-touch check-in.[20]
3. ZO had a dedicated revenue maximization team that took cues from existing occupancy levels and historic data trends to come up with dynamic pricing, including last minute deals. According to Nanda, ZO worked on achieving high occupancy levels, exceeding 85%, versus the 50 to 55% achieved by many unbranded hotels.[21]
4. ZO charged hotels under its banner around 15% of sales that were generated through ZO's platform, similar to the percentage charged by OTAs. The company believed that despite paying these charges the partner hotels were better off because of the help it offered them in a variety of areas. In contrast to some of its competitors, ZO's business model did not include pre-buying inventory from the hotel owners and then selling it at discounted rates, which was identified a key cause of cash burn by one of the participants in the industry.[22] Nanda said: "We like to keep it sustainable and capital-efficient."[23]
5. ZO's top management believed that it was hyper-local and hence improved accessibility of budget accommodation for customers. In every city served by ZO, there would be multiple affiliated hotels spread throughout the city. ZO's app geo-detected a customer's location and booked a customer into the nearest room available with a single touch.[24]
6. Partnerships were another key element of the business model, though this aspect of the strategy was somewhat under-developed because of the young age of the company. In May 2015, after building a presence in thirteen cities, ZO formed a partnership with Uber and food delivery startup Foodpanda, to provide a seamless experience for travelers to travel, eat, and stay.[25] The alliance would provide free Uber rides, 50% off coupons on Foodpanda orders and cashback, after checking into any of the 150+ listed properties on the ZO platform at the time.[26] Additionally, the company also offered promotions with a narrower scope, such as cashback when a customer paid with Olamoney (Ola was India's leading online transportation network company).
7. The company also offered cash back to first-time users in addition to location-specific promotions (e.g., on hotels in Goa) as well as time-specific promotions (e.g., around the time of major festivals).
8. Rapid expansion within and across categories was another key aspect of strategy. ZO had rapidly expanded the number of hotels and the number of rooms under its platform (discussed under the next heading, Performance). Additionally, in September 2015, ZO launched ZO Prime, a premium offering in the category of three-star hotels across India, which would help customers with all the amenities and luxuries as per three-star standards. ZO Rooms launched this offering with 500 ZO Prime rooms across large cities such as Mumbai and Delhi. The price of ZO Prime started at INR 2,000 which included a number of services to its customers including complimentary Wi-Fi, breakfast, and air-conditioned rooms, among others. At the time, ZO also planned to launch other premium offerings like ZO-Apartments, ZO-Homes, and ZO-Star.[27]

ZO's Performance

The initial customer response to ZO's launch was quite encouraging. Its asset-light model enabled quick scaling up and by April 2015, the four-month-old ZO had signed up 100 hotels across 10 cities and was signing up new hotel partners at the rate of two hotels a day. The company's co-founder noted that ZO had "experienced a very welcoming response across online as well as offline channels" and was renting 15,000 room nights a month. He expected this number to go up post the company's launch on social media and its mobile app. He also noted that ZO had signed up with more than 20 multinational companies to be their accommodation partner. The company planned to have more than 1000 hotels across 50 cities in India on its platform by the end of the calendar year.[28]

By August 2015, ZO had scaled its presence up to 600 hotels and 6,000 rooms priced between INR 1,000 and INR 3,000 across 35 cities. The rapid scaling up was useful in building buzz and awareness among customers as well as for signing more hotel partners. According to the company, it was renting 4,000 room nights a day, across the country at an average rate of INR 1,800 for a room night.[29]

By October 2015, ZO could boast of having 11,000 rooms across 1000 hotels and 50 cities on its platform. Despite this impressive growth, it lagged the market leader OYO which had 30,000 rooms across 3,000 properties and 135 destinations.[30]

In November 2015, ZO had 300 employees, with 3-member teams to handle each of the cities.[31] The company claimed that it was running a very lean model and its competitors employed twice as many staff per city served.

Customer opinions about ZO's offering remained variable. On the Google Playstore, the app which had between 10,000 and 500,000 downloads, earned a rating of 3.8/5.0. Some customers had noted positive comments especially about the money saved by booking through ZO's platform, but some customers reported that it was difficult to use the app (unable to open, not detecting network, crashing) while some other customers accused the company of listing hotels falsely on its site, cancelling bookings at the last minute and not having as a good policy as close competitors about cancellations and refunds.[32] On the company's Facebook page also, some unhappy customers had noted negative comments about the company.[33]

The company's claims of not discounting rooms also seemed to be inaccurate, possibly because its competitors (at least some of whom were buying inventory from hotel owners and thus sunk costs) were aggressively offering discounts. On its Facebook page, ZO offered steep discounts, sometimes offering rooms for as little as INR 99 (albeit with terms and conditions). It offered discounts of as much as 50% even in popular tourist destinations like Goa. [34]

The Perfect Storm for ZO and other OBAs

In April 2015, the Delhi High Court granted a stay order to OYO Rooms against ZO Rooms, ordering the latter to stop using confidential information and software of OYO. In its lawsuit, OYO had alleged that the new room booking platform implemented by ZO was copied from OYO.[35] To support its claim, OYO submitted emails and CCTV footage in which ex-employees of OYO stole proprietary software from the company, and left to join Zostel.[36] ZO's co-founder Nanda vehemently denied any wrongdoing: "No illegality has been committed by us. We are in possession of the material that would demonstrate how a false and fabricated story has been created by OYO only out of business rivalry, just to kill any competition."[37]

The competition was also getting more intense. According to one estimate (startup data-tracker Tracxn), by November 2015, there were over 180 startups in the online travel and destination discovery space, among which 40 had raised around $300 million of funding.[38] The number of OBAs itself was estimated at around 30, with the pioneer and frontrunner OYO enjoying the benefits of a large capital base (including a $100 million round of capital raising in August 2015) and the backing of Softbank, the well-known Japanese venture capital firm.[39]

As the upstart OBAs such as ZO and OYO chipped away at their market share for hotel bookings, OTAs such as Goibibo, Yatra, and MakeMyTrip saw few benefits in providing a distribution channel to the OBAs. Rajesh Magow, CEO of MakeMyTrip, said that the new competitors had a very similar business model as their own, and that it didn't make long-term strategic sense to let them grow (see Exhibit 2).[40] Blockage by the OTAs would affect the OBAs adversely—for ZO Rooms, 10% of the business was contributed by the OTAs and for OYO, the percentage was between 10 and 15%.[41] Nanda put on a brave face about the OTAs' aggressive move and said: "There will be a small dip in bookings, but our growth from our app and other

Exhibit 2 OTA's Launch of Budget Brands to Compete with OBAs

OTA	Year of starting	Own budget hotel brand	Number of cities	Number of rooms	Financing
MakeMyTrip	2000	Value + (2015)	35	1,000	IPO/Stock (went public in 2010)
Yatra	2006	TG Rooms and Stays (2015)	60	1,000	Funding received-$105 million
Goibibo	2009	GoStays (2015)	99	1,384	Subsidiary of Ibibo Group

Source: Shweta Saxena, "Challenges in Room Aggregation Business in India', December 9, 2015, http://www.exploringstartups.com/challenges-in-room-aggregation-business-in-india/, accessed on August 16, 2017.

associations will more than make up for it. This transition is not a shock for us. Our growth is mostly driven by our app and website."[42]

By November 2015, the OTAs had scaled up their aggressive response by venturing into the budget accommodation space themselves to exploit the growth opportunity. Goibibo launched GoStays and Yatra launched its TG Rooms, TG Stays in over 60 cities to cater to budget travelers providing both hotel & guest house options.[43] Yatra also launched Homestay to enhance its accommodation marketplace. MakeMyTrip too had launched Value+43.[44] Generally, hotels provided a good return on investment if high occupancy levels could be achieved and since the OTAs were extremely strong in distribution (of hotel rooms as well as other services) with strong awareness among customers, they were confident of profitable entry into the budget hotel segment.[45] Many OTAs also enjoyed the backing of multinational firms (e.g., the South African media conglomerate Naspers had invested in Goibibo; and Norwest Venture Partners, a unit of Wells Fargo Bank in the United States of America, had invested in Yatra) and deeper pockets than the OBAs.

Despite the more intense competition some observers such as Mr Amit Taneja of Cleartrip.com believed that there was enough room in the market for both OBAs and OTAs to co-exist.[46] On the other hand, Live Mint, the online portal of a leading business newspaper in India, was more skeptical. It noted that while the market potential was large and demand for budget rooms exceeded supply, the OBA business was an unproven business with an unclear revenue potential that was witnessing intensified competition.[47]

By December 2015, *The Economic Times* reported that ZO and its parent Zostel Hospitality were cash strapped and were struggling to convince investors to put in additional money, partly because some of the optimism about the budget hotel space in India had been tempered.[48] Unconfirmed reports of the ZO and OYO merger were already making the rounds by this time.

Acquisition of ZO by OYO

In December 2015 SoftBank, which had earlier (August 2015) taken part in a $100 million round of funding in OYO Rooms, announced that OYO would acquire ZO Rooms for an unspecified deal value.[49] The deal closing was said to have happened after extensive negotiations, lasting a few months. The deal was made in such a way that it would allow OYO to selectively take on and integrate ZO's assets (such as part of its team and technology) and contracts.[50] The founders of Zostel Hospitality Pvt. Ltd. reportedly got an equity stake of approximately 2.5% stake in the combined company while the investors in ZO, including Tiger Global Management LLC, Orios Venture Partners, and angel investors would receive approximately 4–5% of the combined company.[51] *The Economic Times* noted that ZO had not been able to keep up with OYO's fundraising. An anonymous analyst commented that the deal suggested that cash (or access to it) was the differentiator between survivors in the space and others.[52]

Earlier, while reporting on the acquisition, *The Economic Times* had reported that after the acquisition, ZO's parent (Zostel Hospitality) was expected to wind up and might be unable to pay all its creditors such as vendors and advertising and branding firms.

Commenting on the acquisition, Rohit Bhatiani, director, Deloitte Touche Tohmatsu India LLP, a consulting firm, said: "This was a much needed consolidation in the hyper competitive space of budget hotel accommodation. But the bigger challenge will be to see how the company is going to set up a proper mechanism to provide consistency of service and the whole diligence process of getting properties on board."[53]

ZO's distress and subsequent acquisition held many lessons for technology startups in India in general, and rival OBAs in particular. But, what were these lessons? ZO's business model seemed to burn less cash than some other OBAs who prepaid for inventory from the partner hotels, and hence less susceptible to running out of cash. Clearly, there were other factors at work. Was ZO's expansion at breakneck speed the issue? As Harish HV, a consultant at Grant Thornton, had said after the merger announcement: "The trick is if someone can find the right way to stay profitable, grow and maintain consistent customer experience."[54] Had ZO delivered on either of the elements of the trick mentioned by Mr Harish? Was that a key reason for ZO's downfall? Or had ZO deviated too much from some of its original strategies such as less discounting because of the intensity of competition. Had ZO diluted its focus by trying out too many strategies such as the launch of ZO Prime before consolidating its position in the OBA sector? Or was it simply the access to funds and ZO was caught in the wrong place, at the wrong time with VCs becoming cautious about the sector? Was the difference between OYO and ZO simply the size of the funding they had received?

NOTES

1. This case was written by Professor Nitin Pangarkar and Ayush Singhal, an undergraduate engineering student at the Indian Institute of Technology, Kharagpur, India. The case is intended to be used as a teaching tool and does not illustrate either effective or ineffective handling of a managerial situation.
2. Indo-Asian News Service, "Zostel: Make your trip affordable with India's first backpackers'hostel," *The Indian Express*, May 27, 2015, accessed August 15, 2017, http://indianexpress.com/article/good-news/zostel-make-your-trip-affordable-with-indias-first-backpackers-hostel/.
3. "Zo-Room," Crunchbase, accessed August 15, 2017, shttps://www.crunchbase.com/organization/zo-rooms#/entity.
4. Harsimran Julka, "Startup Wars: Oyo Rooms vs Zostel case gets murkier in Courts," Economics Times, April 27, 2015, accessed August 15, 2017, http://tech.economictimes.indiatimes.com/news/startups/startup-wars-oyo-rooms-vs-zostel-case-gets-murkier-in-courts/47063307.
5. Indo-Asian News Service, "Zostel: Make your trip affordable with India's first backpackers'hostel," *The Indian Express*, May 27, 2015, accessed August 15, 2017, http://indianexpress.com/article/good-news/zostel-make-your-trip-affordable-with-indias-first-backpackers-hostel/
6. According to Vilas Pawar, CEO of Choice Hotels, India, quoted in Neha Pradhan, "Success story of budget hotels: A balancing act," April 7, 2014, accessed August 15, 2017, http://www.hospitalitybizindia.com/detailNews.aspx?aid=19154&sid=5
7. Tausif Alam, "Wudstay shows the way to a sustainable business model in the budget hotel segment," Your Story, January 5, 2016, accessed August 15, 2017, https://yourstory.com/2016/01/wudstay-business-model/.
8. "India likely to have around 1,747 million travellers by 2021: Report," *Times of India*, March 25, 2012, accessed August 15, 2017, https://timesofindia.indiatimes.com/business/india-business/India-likely-to-have-around-1747-million-travellers-by-2021-Report/articleshow/12403909.cms
9. According to Prafulla Mathur, founder of Wudstay, a budget hotel aggregator startup. Quoted in Tausif Alam, "Wudstay shows the way to a sustainable model in the budget hotel segment," January 05, 2016, accessed August 15, 2017, https://yourstory.com/2016/01/wudstay-business-model/
10. Paloma Ganguly, "College dropout at 17, millionaire at 22, Ritesh Agarwal says he is in no hurry," Tech in Asia, June 7, 2016, accessed August 15, 2017, https://www.techinasia.com/ritesh-agarwal-oyo-millionaire-in-no-hurry
11. Jai Vardhan,"Zostel founders dive into the low-budget hotel space with ZO Rooms," Your Story, April 16, 2015, accessed August 15, 2017, https://yourstory.com/2015/04/zo-rooms/
12. Sangeetha Chengappa, "ZO Rooms on expansion mode," The Hindu, August 16, 2015, accessed August 15, 2017, http://www.thehindubusinessline.com/companies/zo-rooms-on-expansion-mode/article7547017.ece
13. According to Vilas Pawar, CEO of Choice Hotels, India, quoted in Neha Pradhan, "Success story of budget hotels: A balancing act," April 7, 2014, accessed August 15, 2017, http://www.hospitalitybizindia.com/detailNews.aspx?aid=19154&sid=5
14. According to data from ibibo.com, an OTA, most chains would fall in this category. accessed August 15, 2017, https://www.goibibo.com/hotels/chain/
15. Martin Cowen, "India sets the standard for branded budget hotels,"Tnooz, August 30, 2015, accessed August 15, 2017, https://www.tnooz.com/articles/India-branded-accommodation-StayVista-OYO-ZO-Stayzilla-Treebo-Yatra/.
16. Martin Cowen, "India sets the standard for branded budget hotels,"Tnooz, August 30, 2015, accessed August 15, 2017, https://www.tnooz.com/articles/India-branded-accommodation-StayVista-OYO-ZO-Stayzilla-Treebo-Yatra/
17. Jai Vardhan,"Zostel founders dive into the low-budget hotel space with ZO Rooms,"Your Story, April 16, 2015, accessed August 15, 2017, https://yourstory.com/2015/04/zo-rooms/
18. Saumya Tewari, "Make room for branded online hotel chains," October 09, 2015, accessed August 15, 2017, http://www.afaqs.com/news/story/45908_Make-room-for-branded-online-hotel-chains
19. Saumya Tewari, "Make room for branded online hotel chains," October 09, 2015, accessed August 15, 2017, http://www.afaqs.com/news/story/45908_Make-room-for-branded-online-hotel-chains
20. Beckett, "ZO Rooms – Get wallet balance up to 800rs instantly + refer to get up to 5000rs," Article Blog, accessed August 15, 2017, https://www.earticleblog.com/zo-rooms-get-wallet-balance-up-to-800rs-instantly-refer-to-get-up-to-5000rs-limited-time-offer.html
21. Jai Vardhan,"Zostel founders dive into the low-budget hotel space with ZO Rooms," Your Story, April 16, 2015, accessed August 15, 2017, https://yourstory.com/2015/04/zo-rooms/
22. Tausif Alam, "Wudstay shows the way to a sustainable business model in the budget hotel segment," Your Story, January 05, 2016, accessed August 15, 2017, https://yourstory.com/2016/01/wudstay-business-model/.
23. Jai Vardhan,"Zostel founders dive into the low-budget hotel space with ZO Rooms," Your Story, April 16, 2015, accessed August 15, 2017, https://yourstory.com/2015/04/zo-rooms/
24. Jai Vardhan,"Zostel founders dive into the low-budget hotel space with ZO Rooms,"Your Story, April 16, 2015, accessed

August 15, 2017, https://yourstory.com/2015/04/zo-rooms/

25. Evelyn Fok, "Uber, Foodpanda & ZO Rooms tie-up to offer free rides, discounts & cashbacks," EtTech, May 6, 2015, accessed August 15, 2017, http://tech.economictimes.indiatimes.com/news/mobile/uber-foodpanda-zo-rooms-tie-up/47167037
26. "An Uber, Foodpanda, ZO Rooms tie-up just made your travel experience more convenient," First Post, May 16, 2015, accessed August 15, 2017, http://www.firstpost.com/business/uber-foodpanda-zo-rooms-tie-just-made-travel-experience-easier-2230256.html
27. "ZO Rooms launches 3-star segment services in metros," *The Economics Times*, September 19, 2015, accessed August 15, 2017, http://economictimes.indiatimes.com/industry/services/hotels-/-restaurants/zo-rooms-launches-3-star-segment-services-in-metros/articleshow/49154516.cms
28. Jai Vardhan,"Zostel founders dive into the low-budget hotel space with ZO Rooms," Your Story, April 16, 2015, accessed August 15, 2017, https://yourstory.com/2015/04/zo-rooms/
29. Sangeetha Chengappa, "ZO Rooms on expansion mode," The Hindu, August 16, 2015, accessed August 15, 2017, http://www.thehindubusinessline.com/companies/zo-rooms-on-expansion-mode/article7547017.ece
30. Aditi Shrivastava, "Online travel agencies like MakeMyTrip, Goibibo, Yatra blocked OYO & ZO Rooms from their websites," The Economics Times, October 28, 2015, accessed August 15, 2017, http://economictimes.indiatimes.com/small-biz/startups/online-travel-agencies-like-makemytrip-goibibo-yatra-blocked-oyo-zo-rooms-from-their-websites/articleshow/49559966.cms
31. Sangeetha Chengappa, "ZO Rooms on expansion mode," The Hindu, August 16, 2015, accessed August 15, 2017, http://www.thehindubusinessline.com/companies/zo-rooms-on-expansion-mode/article7547017.ece
32. "Google Play Store," accessed August 15, 2017, https://play.google.com/store/apps/details?id=com.app.zorooms
33. Facebook page, "ZO Rooms," accessed August 15, 2017, https://www.facebook.com/zorooms/
34. Facebook page, "ZO Rooms," accessed August 15, 2017, https://www.facebook.com/zorooms/
35. Harsimran Julka, "Startup Wars: Oyo Rooms vs Zostel case gets murkier in Courts," *The Economics Times*, April 27, 2015, accessed August 15, 2017, http://tech.economictimes.indiatimes.com/news/startups/startup-wars-oyo-rooms-vs-zostel-case-gets-murkier-in-courts/47063307.
36. Shashidhar KJ, "It's official, OYO Rooms acquires rival ZO Rooms," Medianama, February 11, 2016, accessed August 15, 2017, https://www.medianama.com/2016/02/223-oyo-rooms-zo-rooms-acquisiton/.
37. Harsimran Julka, "Startup Wars: Oyo Rooms vs Zostel case gets murkier in Courts," Economics Times, April 27, 2015, accessed August 15, 2017, http://tech.economictimes.indiatimes.com/news/startups/startup-wars-oyo-rooms-vs-zostel-case-gets-murkier-in-courts/47063307.
38. Gadget 360 , "MakeMyTrip Launches Value+ Chain; Blocks Oyo Rooms and ZO Rooms," November 13, 2015, accessed August 15, 2017,http://gadgets.ndtv.com/internet/news/makemytrip-launches-value-chain-blocks-oyo-rooms-zo-rooms-764672
39. Priyanaka Sahay, "Oyo Rooms has acquired ZO Rooms: SoftBank," Livemint, February 11, 2016, accessed August 15, 2017, http://www.livemint.com/Companies/xuiwyocuFosCu6l1T6DfuJ/Oyo-Rooms-has-acquired-Zo-Rooms-says-SoftBank.html
40. Gadget 360 , "MakeMyTrip Launches Value+ Chain; Blocks Oyo Rooms and ZO Rooms," November 13, 2015, accessed August 15, 2017,http://gadgets.ndtv.com/internet/news/makemytrip-launches-value-chain-blocks-oyo-rooms-zo-rooms-764672
41. Aditi Shrivastava, "Online travel agencies like MakeMyTrip, Goibibo, Yatra blocked OYO & ZO Rooms from their websites," The Economics Times, October 28, 2015, accessed August 15, 2017, http://economictimes.indiatimes.com/small-biz/startups/online-travel-agencies-like-makemytrip-goibibo-yatra-blocked-oyo-zo-rooms-from-their-websites/articleshow/49559966.cms
42. Aditi Shrivastava, "Online travel agencies like MakeMyTrip, Goibibo, Yatra blocked OYO & ZO Rooms from their websites," *The Economics Times*, October 28, 2015, accessed August 15, 2017, http://economictimes.indiatimes.com/small-biz/startups/online-travel-agencies-like-makemytrip-goibibo-yatra-blocked-oyo-zo-rooms-from-their-websites/articleshow/49559966.cms
43. Pooja Sareen, "The Oyo-ZO Rooms Acquisition Deal Is Falling Apart," Inc42, December 18, 2015, accessed August 15, 2017, https://inc42.com/buzz/oyo-zo-rooms-acquisition-deal-falling-apart/#.WZLYplUjHIU
44. Shrutika Verma and Mihir Dalal, "India:Oyo Rooms looks to buy struggling rival ZO Rooms," Deal Street Asia, Decemeber 3, 2015, accessed August 15, 2017, https://www.dealstreetasia.com/stories/india-oyo-rooms-looks-to-buy-struggling-rival-zo-rooms-21981/
45. Divya Sathyanarayanan, "How online travel firms like Yatra and Cleartrip are enteringing into the budget accommodation space," August 27, 2015, accessed August 15, 2017, http://economictimes.indiatimes.com/industry/services/hotels-/-restaurants/how-online-travel-firms-like-yatra-and-cleartrip-are-enteringing-into-the-budget-accommodation-space/articleshow/48690068.cms
46. Shweta Saxena, "Challenges in Room Aggregation Business in India," Exploring Start-ups, December 9, 2015, accessed August 15, 2017, http://www.exploringstartups.com/challenges-in-room-aggregation-business-in-india/
47. Priyanaka Sahay, "Oyo Rooms has acquired ZO Rooms: SoftBank," Livemint, February 11, 2016, accessed August 15, 2017, http://www.livemint.com/Companies/xuiwyocuFosCu6l1T6DfuJ/Oyo-Rooms-has-acquired-Zo-Rooms-says-SoftBank.html
48. Aditi Shrivastava and Madhav Chanchani, "Oyo Rooms to acquire Zo Rooms in an all-stock deal," The Economics Times, December 17, 2015, accessed August 15, 2017, http://economictimes.indiatimes.com/small-biz/startups/oyo-rooms-to-acquire-zo-rooms-in-an-all-stock-deal/articleshow/50210682.cms?intenttarget=no
49. Priyanaka Sahay, "Oyo Rooms has acquired ZO Rooms: SoftBank," Livemint, February 11, 2016, accessed August 15, 2017, http://www.livemint.com/Companies/xuiwyocuFosCu6l1T6DfuJ/Oyo-Rooms-has-acquired-Zo-Rooms-says-SoftBank.html
50. Varnana Choudhary, "Softbank Confirms Zo Room's Acquisition By Oyo," I am wire, November 2, 2016, accessed August 15, 2017, http://www.iamwire.com/2016/02/oyo-rooms-acquires-zo-rooms/131940
51. Priyanaka Sahay, "Oyo Rooms has acquired ZO Rooms: SoftBank," Livemint, February 11, 2016, accessed August 15, 2017, http://www.livemint.com/Companies/xuiwyocuFosCu6l1T6DfuJ/Oyo-Rooms-has-acquired-Zo-Rooms-says-SoftBank.html
52. Aditi Shrivastava and Madhav Chanchani, "Oyo Rooms to acquire ZO Rooms in an all-stock deal," *The Economics Times*, December 17, 2015, accessed August 15, 2017, http://economictimes.indiatimes.com/small-biz/startups/oyo-rooms-to-acquire-zo-rooms-in-an-all-stock-deal/articleshow/50210682.cms?intenttarget=no
53. Priyanaka Sahay, "Oyo Rooms has acquired ZO Rooms: SoftBank," Livemint, February 11, 2016, accessed August 15, 2017, http://www.livemint.com/Companies/xuiwyocuFosCu6l1T6DfuJ/Oyo-Rooms-has-acquired-Zo-Rooms-says-SoftBank.html
54. Patanjali Pahwa,"OYO-Zo merger leaves competition underwhelmed," Business Standards, February 11, 2016, accessed August 15, 2017, http://www.business-standard.com/article/companies/oyo-zo-merger-leaves-competition-underwhelmed-116021100424_1.html

NAME INDEX

D

E

F

G

H

Q

T

U

V

W

X

Y

Z

COMPANY INDEX

SUBJECT INDEX

Note: Page numbers followed by f or t represent figures or tables respectively.

G

H

I